Spain

THIS EDITION WRITTEN AND RESEARCHED BY

Isab... ...lsalska, ... Sainsbury,

15 355 356 X

Contents

PICOS DE EUROPA P494

PARK GÜELL P260

Contents

BARCELONA P232

PAELLA P44

Contents

SPECIAL FEATURES

Welcome to Spain

Passionate, sophisticated and devoted to living the good life, Spain is both a stereotype come to life and a country more diverse than you ever imagined.

An Epic Land

Spain's diverse landscapes stir the soul. The Pyrenees and the Picos de Europa are as beautiful as any mountain range on the continent, while the snowcapped Sierra Nevada rises up improbably from the sun-baked plains of Andalucía; these are hiking destinations of the highest order. The wildly beautiful cliffs of Spain's Atlantic northwest are offset by the charming coves of the Mediterranean. And everywhere you go, villages of timeless beauty perch on hilltops, huddle in valleys and cling to coastal outcrops as tiny but resilient outposts of old Spain.

A Culinary Feast

Food and wine are national obsessions in Spain, and with good reason. The touchstones of Spanish cooking are deceptively simple: incalculable variety, traditional recipes handed down through the generations, and an innate willingness to experiment and see what comes out of the kitchen laboratory. You may experience the best meal ever via tapas in an earthy bar where everyone's shouting, or via a meal prepared by a celebrity chef in the refined surrounds of a Michelin-starred restaurant. Either way, the breadth of gastronomic experience that awaits you is breathtaking.

Art Imitates Life

Poignantly windswept Roman ruins, cathedrals of rare power and incomparable jewels of Islamic architecture speak of a country where the great civilisations of history have risen, fallen and left behind their indelible mark. More recently, what other country could produce such rebellious and relentlessly creative spirits as Salvador Dalí, Pablo Picasso and Antoni Gaudí and place them front and centre in public life? Here, grand monuments to the past coexist alongside architectural creations of such daring that it becomes clear Spain's future will be every bit as original as its past.

Fiestas & Flamenco

For all the talk of Spain's history, this is a country that lives very much in the present and there's a reason 'fiesta' is one of the best-known words in the Spanish language – life itself is a fiesta here and everyone seems to be invited. Perhaps you'll sense it along a crowded, postmidnight street when all the world has come out to play. Or maybe that moment will come when a flamenco performer touches something deep in your soul. Whenever it happens, you'll find yourself nodding in recognition: *this* is Spain.

Why I Love Spain

By Anthony Ham, Writer

The life that courses relentlessly through the streets here always produces in me a feeling that this is a place where anything can happen. Here, the passions of Spain's people are the fabric of daily life; this is a country with music in its soul, a love of fine food and wild landscapes, and a special talent for celebrating all the good things in life.

For more about our writers, see page 864

Above: Park Güell (p260), Barcelona

Spain

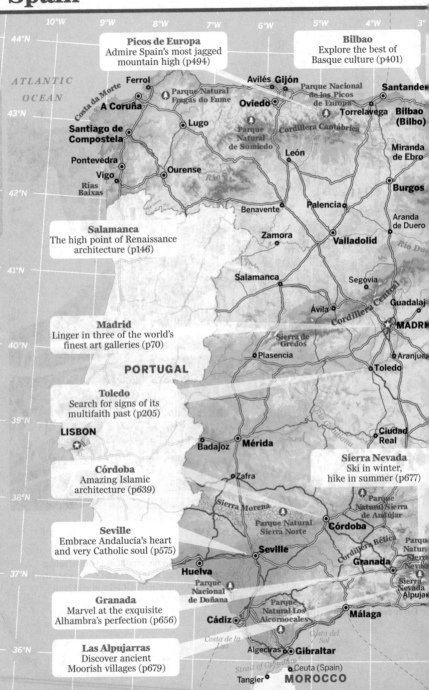

Picos de Europa
Admire Spain's most jagged mountain high (p494)

Bilbao
Explore the best of Basque culture (p401)

Salamanca
The high point of Renaissance architecture (p146)

Madrid
Linger in three of the world's finest art galleries (p70)

Toledo
Search for signs of its multifaith past (p205)

Córdoba
Amazing Islamic architecture (p639)

Seville
Embrace Andalucía's heart and very Catholic soul (p575)

Sierra Nevada
Ski in winter, hike in summer (p677)

Granada
Marvel at the exquisite Alhambra's perfection (p656)

Las Alpujarras
Discover ancient Moorish villages (p679)

ATLANTIC OCEAN

PORTUGAL

MOROCCO

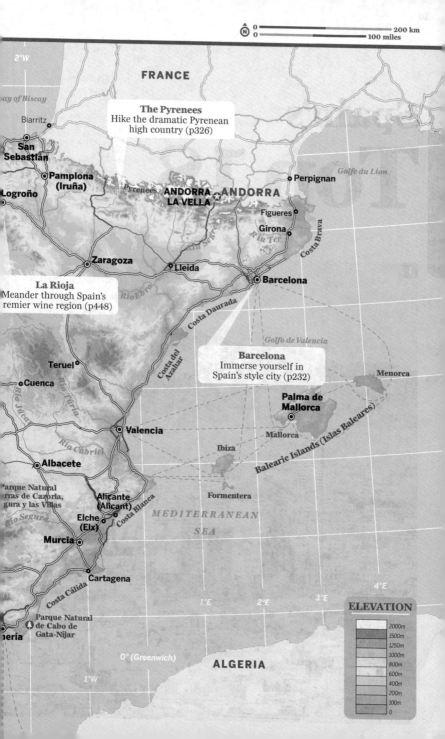

N 0 ⌢
0 ————————————— 200 km
————————————— 100 miles

2°W

FRANCE

The Pyrenees
Hike the dramatic Pyrenean
high country (p326)

ay of Biscay

Biarritz

Golfe du Lion

San
Sebastián

Pamplona
(Iruña)

Perpignan

Logroño

Pyrenees

ANDORRA ANDORRA
LA VELLA

Figueres

Girona

Rio Segre

Riu Ter

Costa Brava

Zaragoza

Lleida

Barcelona

Rio Ebro

La Rioja
Meander through Spain's
remier wine region (p448)

Costa Daurada

Golfo de Valencia

Teruel

Costa del Azahar

Barcelona
Immerse yourself in
Spain's style city (p232)

Menorca

Cuenca

Rio Turia

Palma de
Mallorca

Balearic Islands (Islas Baleares)

Valencia

Mallorca

Rio Cabriel

Ibiza

Albacete

arque Natural
rras de Cazorla,
gura y las Villas

Alicante
(Alacant)

Formentera

Rio Segura

Elche
(Elx)

Costa Blanca

MEDITERRANEAN

Murcia

SEA

Cartagena

Costa Cálida

4°E

1°E

2°E

3°E

ELEVATION

Parque Natural
de Cabo de
Gata-Níjar

ería

0° (Greenwich)

ALGERIA

1°W

	2000m
	1500m
	1250m
	1000m
	800m
	600m
	400m
	200m
	100m
	0

Spain's
Top 18

Barcelona

1 Home to cutting-edge architecture, world-class dining and pulsating nightlife, Barcelona (p232) has long been one of Europe's most alluring destinations. Days spent wandering the cobblestone lanes of the Gothic quarter, basking on Mediterranean beaches or marvelling at Gaudí masterpieces across the city. By night, Barcelona is a whirl of vintage cocktail bars, gilded music halls, innovative eateries and dance-loving clubs, with the party extending well into the night. There are also colourful markets, hallowed arenas (such as Camp Nou where FC Barcelona plays), and a calendar packed with traditional Catalan festivals.

Pintxos in San Sebastián

2 Chefs here have turned bar snacks into an art form. Sometimes called 'high cuisine in miniature', *pintxos* (Basque tapas) are piles of flavour often mounted on a slice of baguette. As you step into any bar in central San Sebastián (p417), the choice lined up along the counter will leave you gasping. In short, this is Spain's most memorable eating experience. Although the atmosphere is always casual, the serious business of experimenting with taste combinations (a Basque trademark) ensures that it just keeps getting better.
Sea urchin *pintxos*

The Alhambra

3 The palace complex of Granada's Alhambra (p657) is close to architectural perfection. It is perhaps the most refined example of Islamic art anywhere in the world, not to mention the most enduring symbol of 800 years of Moorish rule in what was known as Al-Andalus. From afar, the Alhambra's red fortress towers dominate the Granada skyline, set against a backdrop of the Sierra Nevada's snow-capped peaks. Up close, the Alhambra's perfectly proportioned Generalife gardens complement the exquisite detail of the Palacio Nazaríes. Put simply, this is Spain's most beautiful monument.

La Sagrada Família

4 The Modernista brain-child of Antoni Gaudí, La Sagrada Família (p251) remains a work in progress more than 80 years after its creator's death. Fanciful and profound, inspired by nature and barely restrained by a Gothic style, Barcelona's quirky temple soars skyward with an almost playful majesty. The improbable angles and departures from architectural convention will have you shaking your head in disbelief, but the detail of the decorative flourishes on the Passion Facade, Nativity Facade and elsewhere are worth studying for hours.

Flamenco

5 The soundtrack to Europe's most passionate country, flamenco (p806) has the power to lift you out of the doldrums and stir your soul. It's as if by sharing in the pain of innumerable generations of dispossessed misfits you open a door to a secret world of musical ghosts and ancient spirits. On the other side of the coin, flamenco culture can also be surprisingly jolly, jokey and tongue-in-cheek. There's only one real proviso: you have to hear it live, preferably in its Seville-Jerez-Cádiz heartland, although anywhere in Andalucía should do.

Flamenco dancers at Seville's Feria de Abril (p29)

MATTES RENÁ/GETTY IMAGES ©

Madrid Nightlife

6 Madrid is not the only European city with nightlife, but few can match its intensity and street clamour (p116). As Ernest Hemingway said, 'Nobody goes to bed in Madrid until they have killed the night'. There are wall-to-wall bars, small clubs, live venues, cocktail bars and megaclubs beloved by A-list celebrities all across the city, with unimaginable variety to suit all tastes. But it's in the *barrios* (districts) of Huertas, Malasaña, Chueca and La Latina that you'll really understand what we're talking about.

Renaissance Salamanca

7 Luminous when floodlit, the elegant central square of Salamanca (p146), the Plaza Mayor, is possibly the most attractive in all of Spain. It is just one of many highlights in a city whose architectural splendour has few peers in the country. Salamanca is home to one of Europe's oldest and most prestigious universities, so student revelry also lights up the nights. It's this combination of grandeur and energy that makes so many people call Salamanca their favourite city in Spain.

Semana Santa

8 Return to Spain's medieval Christian roots in the country's dramatic Easter celebrations. Religious fraternities parade elaborate *pasos* (figures) of Christ and the Virgin Mary through the streets to the emotive acclaim of the populace; the most prestigious procession is the *madrugada* (early hours) of Good Friday. Seen for the first time, it's an utterly compelling fusion of pageantry, solemnity and deep religious faith. The most extraordinary processions are in Castilla y León, Castilla La Mancha and Andalucía, but if you choose one, make it Sevilla (p592).

Sierra Nevada & Las Alpujarras

9 Dominated by the Mulhacén (3479m), mainland Spain's highest peak, the Sierra Nevada (p677) makes a stunning backdrop to Granada. Skiing in winter and hiking in summer can be mixed with exploration of the fascinating villages of Las Alpujarras, arguably Andalucía's most engaging collection of *pueblos blancos* (white towns). The hamlets of Las Alpujarras resemble North Africa, oasis-like and set amid woodlands and the deep ravines for which the region is renowned.

Pradollano (p677) in Parque Nacional Sierra Nevada

ANTONIO LUIS/GETTY IMAGES ©

Hiking in the Pyrenees

10 Spain is a walker's destination of exceptional variety, but we reckon the Pyrenees in Navarra (p441), Aragón and Catalonia offer the most special hiking country. Aragón's Parque Nacional de Ordesa y Monte Perdido is one of the high points (pun intended) of the Pyrenees, while its glories are mirrored across the provincial frontier of Parque Nacional d'Aigüestortes i Estany de Sant Maurici in Catalonia. It's tough but rewarding terrain, a world of great rock walls and glacial cirques, accompanied by elusive but soulful Pyrenean wildlife.

Madrid's Golden Art Triangle

11 Madrid is one of the fine-arts capitals of the world, with an extraordinary collection of galleries concentrated in a patch of city-centre real estate (p87). The Museo del Prado, housing works by Goya, Velázquez, El Greco and masters from across Europe, is the showpiece, but within a short stroll are the Centro de Arte Reina Sofía, showcasing Picasso's Guernica, plus works by Dalí and Miró, and the Museo Thyssen-Bornemisza, which carries all the big names.
Centro de Arte Reina Sofía (p92)

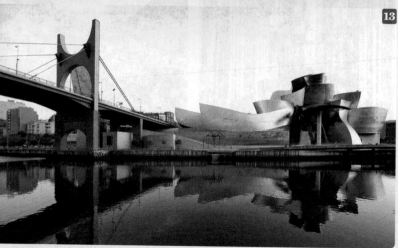

Córdoba's Mezquita

12 A church that became a mosque before reverting back to a church, Córdoba's Mezquita (p641) charts the evolution of Western and Islamic architecture over a 1000-year trajectory. Its most innovative features include some early horseshoe arches, an intricate mihrab, and a 'forest' of 856 columns, many of them recycled from Roman ruins. The sheer scale of the Mezquita reflects Córdoba's power as the most cultured city in 10th-century Europe. It was inspiration for even greater buildings to come, notably in Seville and Granada.

Bilbao

13 It only took one building, a shimmering titanium fish called the Museo Guggenheim Bilbao (p401) from a byword for industrial decay into a major European art centre. But while it's this iconic building that draws the visitors, it's the hard-working soul of this city that ends up captivating. And there's plenty to entrance: riverside promenades, clanky funicular railways, superb pintxos bars, an iconic football team, a clutch of quality museums and, yes, a shimmering titanium fish.
Museo Guggenheim Bilbao (p401)

PETER UNGER/GETTY IMAGES ©

Seville

14 Nowhere is as quintessentially Spanish as Seville (p575), a city of capricious moods and soulful secrets, which has played a pivotal role in the evolution of flamenco, bullfighting, baroque art and Mudéjar architecture. Blessed with year-round sunshine and fuelled culturally by a never-ending schedule of ebullient festivals, everything seems more amorous here, a feeling not lost on legions of 19th-century aesthetes, who used the city as a setting in their romantic works of fiction. Head south to the home of Carmen and Don Juan and take up the story.

La Rioja Wine Country

15 La Rioja (p452) is the sort of place where you could spend weeks meandering along quiet roads in search of the finest drop. The mainstays in this region are bodegas offering wine tastings and picturesque villages that shelter excellent wine museums. The Frank Gehry–designed Hotel Marqués de Riscal, close to Elciego, has been likened to the Museo Guggenheim Bilbao in architectural scale and ambition, and has become the elite centre for wine tourism in the region.

Asturian Coast

16 According to one count, the emerald-green northern Spanish region of Asturias (p475) boasts more than 600 beaches. While the coolness of the Atlantic may be a drawback for those planning on catching some sun, the beauty of many of these frequently wild and unspoiled stretches is utterly breathtaking. Even better, the villages of the coast and hinterland are among the prettiest anywhere along the Spanish shoreline, and the food served in this part of the country is famous throughout Spain.
Cudillero (p487)

Cabo de Gata

17 For a cherished memory of what the Spanish coastline used to look like before megaresorts gatecrashed the Costa del Sol, come to Cabo de Gata (p722), a wild, rugged, golf-course-free zone where fishing boats still reel in the day's catch and bold cliffs clash with the azure Mediterranean. Considering it's one of the driest areas of Europe, the Cabo is abundant with feathered fauna and scrubby vegetation. It's also a protected area, so you can wave goodbye to your car; biking and hiking are the best means of transport.

Camino de Santiago

18 Every year, tens of thousands of pilgrims and walkers with all manner of motivations set out to walk across northern Spain. Their destination, Santiago de Compostela (p507), is a place of untold significance for Christians, but the appeal of this epic walk goes far beyond the religious. With numerous routes across the north, there is no finer way to experience the pleasures and caprices of Spain's natural world. Even completing one stage will leave you with a lifetime of impressions.

Walking sticks with the symbol of the Camino

Need to Know

For more information, see Survival Guide (p811)

Currency
Euro (€)

Language
Spanish (Castilian). Also Catalan, Basque and Galician.

Visas
Generally not required for stays of up to 90 days per 180 days (visas are not required at all for members of EU or Schengen countries). Some nationalities need a Schengen visa.

Money
ATMs widely available. Credit cards accepted in most hotels, restaurants and shops.

Mobile Phones
Local SIM cards are widely available and can be used in European and Australian mobile phones. Not compatible with many North American or Japanese systems.

Time
Central European Time (GMT/UTC plus one hour).

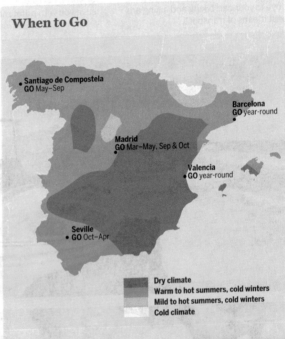

When to Go

Santiago de Compostela
GO May–Sep

Barcelona
GO year-round

Madrid
GO Mar–May, Sep & Oct

Valencia
GO year-round

Seville
GO Oct–Apr

Dry climate
Warm to hot summers, cold winters
Mild to hot summers, cold winters
Cold climate

High Season
(Jun–Aug, public holidays)

➡ Accommodation books out and prices increase by up to 50%.

➡ Low season in parts of inland Spain.

➡ Expect warm, dry and sunny weather; more humid in coastal areas.

Shoulder
(Mar–May, Sep & Oct)

➡ A good time to travel: mild, clear weather and fewer crowds.

➡ Local festivals can send prices soaring.

Low Season
(Nov–Feb)

➡ Cold in central Spain; rain in the north and northwest.

➡ Mild temperatures in Andalucía and the Mediterranean coast.

➡ This is high season in ski resorts.

➡ Many hotels are closed in beach areas but elsewhere prices plummet.

Useful Websites

Fiestas.net (www.fiestas.net) Festivals around the country.

Lonely Planet (www.lonelyplanet.com/spain) Destination information, hotel bookings, traveller forums and more.

Renfe (Red Nacional de los Ferrocarriles Españoles; www.renfe.com) Spain's rail network.

Tour Spain (www.tourspain.org) Culture, food and links to hotels and transport.

Turespaña (www.spain.info) Spanish tourist office's site.

Oh Hello, Spain (ohhellospain.blogspot.co.uk/) An English-language blog, aimed at young-ish travellers.

Important Numbers

Emergencies ☏112

English-speaking Spanish international operator ☏1008 (for calls within Europe) or ☏1005 (rest of the world)

International directory enquiries ☏11825 (calls to this number cost €2)

National directory enquiries ☏11818

Operator for calls within Spain ☏1009 (including for domestic reverse-charge (collect) calls)

Exchange Rates

Australia	A$1	€0.63
Canada	C$1	€0.64
Japan	¥100	€0.77
New Zealand	NZ$1	€0.60
UK	UK£1	€1.30
US	US$1	€0.90

For current exchange rates see www.xe.com.

Daily Costs

Budget: Less than €80

➡ Dorm bed: €20–30

➡ Double room in *hostal* (budget hotel): €55–65 (more in Madrid and Barcelona)

➡ Self-catering and lunch *menú del día* (daily set menu): €10–15

➡ Use museum and gallery 'free admission' afternoons

Midrange: €80-175

➡ Double room in midrange hotel: €65–140

➡ Lunch and/or dinner in local restaurant: €20–40

➡ Car rental: per day from €25

Top End: More than €175

➡ Double room in top-end hotel: €140 and up (€200 in Madrid and Barcelona)

➡ Fine dining for lunch and dinner: €150–250

➡ Double in *parador* (luxurious state-owned hotel): €120–200

Opening Hours

Standard opening hours are for high season only and tend to shorten outside that time.

Banks 8.30am–2pm Monday to Friday; some also open 4pm–7pm Thursday and 9am–1pm Saturday

Central post offices 8.30am–9.30pm Monday to Friday, 8.30am–2pm Saturday (most other branches 8.30am–8.30pm Monday to Friday, 9.30am–1pm Saturday)

Nightclubs Midnight or 1am to 5am or 6am

Restaurants Lunch 1pm–4pm, dinner 8.30pm–11pm or midnight

Shops 10am–2pm and 4.30pm–7.30pm or 5pm–8pm; big supermarkets and department stores generally open 10am–10pm Monday to Saturday

Arriving in Spain

Adolfo Suárez Madrid-Barajas Airport (Madrid; p826) The Metro (€4.50 to €5, 30 minutes to the centre) runs from 6.05am to 1.30am; the Exprés Aeropuerto bus (30 to 40 minutes, €5) runs 24 hours between the airport and Puerta de Atocha train station or Plaza de Cibeles. There are also private minibuses or taxis (€30).

El Prat Airport (Barcelona; p826) Buses cost €5.90 and run every five to 10 minutes from 6.10am to 1.05am; it's 30 to 40 minutes to the centre. Trains (€4.10, 25 to 30 minutes to the centre) run half-hourly from 5.42am to 11.38pm. Taxis cost €25 to €30 and reach the centre in 30 minutes.

Getting Around

Spain's public transport system is one of the best in Europe, with a fast and supermodern train system, extensive domestic air network, an impressive and well-maintained road network, and buses that connect villages in the country's remotest corners.

Train Extremely efficient rail network, from slow intercity regional trains to some of the fastest trains on the planet. More routes are added to the network every year.

Car Vast network of motorways radiating out from Madrid to all corners of the country, shadowed by smaller but often more picturesque minor roads.

Bus The workhorses of the Spanish roads, from slick express services to stop-everywhere village-to-village buses.

For much more on **getting around**, see p828

First Time Spain

For more information, see Survival Guide (p811)

Checklist

➡ With huge airfare differences, check *all* airlines before booking your flight.

➡ Check if you can use your phone in Spain and ask about roaming charges.

➡ Book your first night's accommodation to ensure an easy start to your trip.

➡ Check the calendar to work out which festivals to visit or avoid.

➡ Organise travel insurance.

What to Pack

➡ Passport and/or national ID card (EU citizens) and carry it on you.

➡ Spanish phrasebook – not everyone speaks English.

➡ Money belt, and padlock for your suitcase/backpack.

➡ Headphones for bus or train journeys and Skype calls.

➡ Two-pin continental Europe travel plug.

➡ Earplugs for noisy Spanish nights.

➡ Renfe (train) app and a hiking one downloaded to your phone.

Top Tips for Your Trip

➡ To blend in with the locals (and avoid going hungry), adjust your body clock on arrival. In no time at all you'll be eating lunch at 2.30pm and dinner at 9pm.

➡ A few words of Spanish can go a long way. English is widely (but not universally) spoken.

➡ Spain is a food-obsessed country – linger over your meals and always ask for the local speciality.

➡ Unless you're in a hurry, avoid motorways and take scenic roads.

What to Wear

Spain has come a long way since the 1950s when visiting tourists were fined and escorted from Spanish beaches by police for wearing bikinis. Just about anything goes now, and you'll rarely feel uncomfortable because of what you're wearing. Northern Spain and much of the interior can be bitterly cold in winter – come prepared with plenty of warm clothing. You should also carry some form of wet-weather gear if you're in the northwest. Spaniards are generally quite fashion-conscious and well-dressed – in the cities in particular, they rarely dip below smart casual.

Sleeping

Accommodation in Spain can be outrageously good value by European standards. Reserving a room is always recommended in high season.

Paradors State-run hotels often in stunning historic buildings; can be surprisingly well-priced, especially in low season.

Hotels Everything from boutique to family-run with an equally wide range of rates.

Hostales Small, simpler yet comfortable hotel-style places, often with private bathrooms.

Casas rurales Rural homes with usually rustic, simple rooms that be reserved individually or as a block.

Camping and youth hostels For the budget-minded traveller. Quality varies but they're great places to meet people.

Money

The most convenient way to bring your money is in the form of a debit or credit card, with some extra cash in case of an emergency.

Many credit and debit cards can be used for withdrawing money from *cajeros automáticos* (ATMs) that display the relevant symbols such as Visa, MasterCard, Cirrus etc. There is usually a charge (around 1.5% to 2%) on ATM cash withdrawals abroad.

Bargaining

Haggling over prices is accepted in some markets, and shops *may* offer a small discount if you're spending a lot of money. Otherwise expect to pay the stated price.

Tipping

Tipping is almost always optional.

Restaurants Many Spaniards leave small change, others up to 5%, which is considered generous.

Taxis Optional, but most locals round up to the nearest euro.

Bars It's rare to leave a tip in bars (even if the bartender gives you your change on a small dish).

Etiquette

Greetings Spaniards almost always greet friends and strangers alike with a kiss on each cheek, although two males only do this if they're close friends. It is customary to say 'Hola,

Language

English is quite widely spoken, especially in larger cities and popular tourist areas, less so in rural villages and among older Spaniards. Learning a little Spanish (Castilian, or *castellano*) before you come will, however, greatly increase your appreciation of the country, not least through your ability to converse with locals. Many restaurants (but by no means all) now have English-language menus, but some museums have labels only in Spanish. See the Language chapter (p834) for more information.

1 What time does it open/close?
¿A qué hora abren/cierran? a ke o·ra ab·ren/thye·ran

The Spanish tend to observe the siesta (midday break), so opening times may surprise you.

2 Are these complimentary?
¿Son gratis? son gra·tees

Tapas (bar snacks) are available pretty much around the clock at Spanish bars. You'll find they're free in some places.

3 When is admission free?
¿Cuándo es la entrada gratuita?
kwan·do es la en·tra·da gra·twee·ta

Many museums and galleries in Spain have admission-free times, so check before buying tickets.

4 Where can we go (salsa) dancing?
¿Dónde podemos ir a bailar (salsa)?
don·de po·de·mos eer a bai·lar (sal·sa)

Flamenco may be the authentic viewing experience in Spain, but to actively enjoy the music you'll want to do some dancing.

5 How do you say this in (Catalan/Galician/Basque)?
¿Cómo se dice ésto en (catalán/gallego/euskera)?
ko·mo se dee·the es·to en (ka·ta·lan/ga·lye·go/e·oos·ke·ra)

Spain has four official languages, and people in these regions will appreciate it if you try to use their local language.

buenos días' or 'Hola, buenas tardes' (in the afternoon or evening) when meeting someone or when entering a shop or bar, and 'Hasta luego' when leaving.

Eating and drinking Spanish waiters won't expect you to thank them every time they bring you something, but they may expect you to keep your cutlery between courses in more casual bars and restaurants.

Visiting churches It is considered disrespectful to visit churches for the purposes of tourism during Mass and other worship services.

Escalators Always stand on the right to let people pass.

What's New

Fast-Train Expansion

Spain's fast-train network just got bigger, cutting travel time significantly from Madrid to numerous regional towns, among them León, Palencia, Zamora and Salamanca, while Galicia also just got a whole lot closer. (www.renfe.com)

Goya in Zaragoza

Zaragoza's already fabulous Museo Ibercaja Canón Aznar (p365) has received a facelift, a new name (Museo Goya - Colección Ibercaja) and 39 new works, including some Goyas.

Wolf-Watching

The Sierra de la Culebra offers Europe's best wolf-watching and it has the freshly minted Centro de Lobo Ibérico de Castilla y León (p173) and the Festival Territorio Lobo (p174) to prove it. There's also the new Casa y Cercado del Lobo (p476) in Belmonte de Miranda, Asturias.

Caminito del Rey

This lofty, vertigo-inducing walkway, halfway up the sheer El Chorro gorge north of Málaga (p695), reopened in March 2015 after a €4-million renovation. It's one of Spain's most spectacular paths.

Market Food

Madrid and Barcelona long ago recognised the value of converting their fresh-food markets into fashionable foodie hang-outs, but the trend is only now spreading into smaller towns, most enjoyably in Mérida (p569) and Vejer (p633).

Game of Thrones

Game of Thrones has fallen in love with Spain. Filming locations for seasons Five and Six included Peñíscola (p750), Girona (p312), Seville's Alcázar (p582) and Granada's Alhambra (p657).

Oviedo Openings

Oviedo is staking a claim for the cultural capital of the north. The city's Museo de Bellas Artes de Asturias (p476) just got a whole lot bigger, while the exquisite pre-Romanesque Camara Santa in the Catedral de San Salvador (p476) has finally reopened.

The Real Altamira

For the first time since 2002, the Unesco World Heritage–listed Cueva de Altamira (p470) is offering guided visits into the real cave (not the replica that most visitors see) for a select, and very lucky few.

Cool City Makeovers

If you're too cool for Barcelona, consider these: Gijón (p480) has gone for a London-style bohemian cafe scene, arty Málaga (p684) has spruced up its port district along with new museums, while Cáceres (p549) is an increasingly sophisticated foodie destination.

Galician Trails

The spectacular new hiking trails along Galicia's coastline are brilliant, especially the Camiño Natural da Ruta do Cantábrico (Ribadeo to O Vicedo) and the Ruta do Solpor de Europa (Muxía to Praia de Nemiña).

A New Parador

It's not often that a new *parador* (luxurious, state-owned hotel) is born, which is why we're so excited about the luxury conversion of the picturesque Castillo de Monterrei in Verin (p547) in southeastern Galicia. Even if you don't stay, come for a visit.

For more recommendations and reviews, see lonelyplanet.com/Spain

If You Like...

Incredible Art

Spain's artistic tradition is one of Europe's richest and most original, from local masters to Europe's finest, who flourished under Spanish royal patronage. The result? Art galleries of astonishing depth.

Museo del Prado Quite simply one of the world's best galleries. (p87)

Centro de Arte Reina Sofia Picasso's *Guernica*, Dalí and Miró. (p92)

Museo Thyssen-Bornemisza Works by seemingly every European master. (p93)

Museo Picasso Málaga More than 200 works by Picasso, Málaga's favourite son. (p685)

Museu Picasso Unrivalled collection from Picasso's early years. (p249)

Museu Nacional d'Art de Catalunya Epic collection that includes some extraordinary Romanesque frescos. (p265)

Teatre-Museu Dalí As weird and wonderful as Salvador Dalí himself. (p322)

Museo Guggenheim Bilbao Showpiece architecture and world-class contemporary art. (p401)

Islamic Architecture

Almost eight centuries of Muslim empires bequeathed to Spain Europe's finest accumulation of Islamic architecture, especially in the former Moorish heartland of Al-Andalus (Andalucía), which encompassed Granada, Córdoba and Seville.

Alhambra An extraordinary monument to the extravagance of Al-Andalus, breathtaking in scope and exquisite in its detail. (p657)

Mezquita Perfection wrought in stone in Córdoba's one-time great mosque, one of Al-Andalus' finest architectural moments. (p641)

Alcázar Exquisite detail amid a perfectly proportioned whole in Seville. (p582)

Giralda The former minaret represents a high point in Seville's Islamic skyline. (p575)

Aljafería A rare Moorish jewel in the north. (p365)

Alcazaba Málaga's 11th-century palace-fortress. (p685)

Teruel A splendid, little-known collection of Mudéjar design, proof that Islam's influence outlasted Islamic rule. (p392)

Roman Ruins

Hispania was an important part of the ancient Roman Empire for almost five centuries and it left behind a legacy of fine sites scattered around the country.

Mérida The most extensive Roman remains in the country. (p565)

Segovia An astonishing Roman aqueduct bisects the city. (p158)

Lugo Spain's finest preserved Roman walls encircle this Galician city. (p544)

Itálica Iberia's oldest Roman town with a fine amphitheatre, close to Seville. (p602)

Baelo Claudia Intact Roman town with views of Africa on Andalucía's far southern coast. (p634)

Zaragoza A fine theatre, beautifully restored forum, baths and a former river port. (p364)

Villa Romana La Olmeda Spain's best-preserved Roman villa laid with exquisite mosaic floors. (p178)

Torre de Hércules In A Coruña, this 1st-century-AD lighthouse sits on what was then the furthest tip of the civilised world. (p519)

Beaches

Despite Spain's summer popularity, the country's surfeit of coastal riches means that an unspoiled beach experience remains a possibility. You just need to know where to look.

Cabo de Gata A wildly beautiful reminder of the Andalucían coast as it once was. (p722)

Costa de la Luz Unbroken stretches of sand along a beautiful coast from Tarifa to Cádiz. (p632)

Playa de la Concha One of the most beautiful city beaches anywhere in the world. (p417)

Costa Brava Rugged coast with windswept cliffs, pristine hidden coves and wide sandy beaches. (p303)

Rías Baixas Dramatic long ocean inlets and islands strung with many a fine sandy strand. (p526)

Staying Out Late

From sophisticated cocktail bars to beachside *chiringuitos* (bars), from dance-until-dawn nightclubs to outdoor *terrazas* (bars with outdoor tables), Spanish nightlife is diverse, relentless and utterly intoxicating.

Madrid Bars, nightclubs, live-music venues and nights that roll effortlessly into one another. (p116)

Valencia Barrio del Carmen and Russafa nights are famous throughout Spain, with a roaring soundtrack in the city's oldest quarter. (p744)

Barcelona Glamorous and gritty nightspots for an international crowd. (p285)

Top: Cabo de Gata (p722)
Bottom: Port Olímpic, Barcelona (p249)

Zaragoza The heartbeat of Aragón with fabulous tapas bars and drinking bars that don't crank up until well after midnight. (p369)

Seville Long, hot nights and the essence of Andalucia's passion come to life. (p597)

Sitges Gay-driven, but hetero-friendly, Sitges is coastal Catalonia's party town. (p352)

Spanish Food

Spain obsesses about food with an eating public as eager to try something new as they are wary lest their chefs stray too far from one of Europe's richest culinary traditions.

Pintxos in San Sebastián
Spain's culinary capital, with more Michelin stars than Paris and the country's best *pintxos* (Basque tapas). (p423)

Paella in Valencia The birthplace of paella and still the place for the most authentic version – think chicken, beans and rabbit. (p741)

Catalan cooking in Barcelona Home city for Catalonia's legendary cooking fuelled by Spain's finest food markets. (p277)

Tapas in La Latina, Madrid
Rising above Madrid's modest home-grown cuisine, this inner-city *barrio* (district) showcases the best tapas from around Spain. (p109)

Seafood in Galicia The dark arts of boiling an octopus and the Atlantic's sea creatures (goose barnacles, anyone?) are pure culinary pleasure. (p533)

Roasted meats in the interior
Cochinillo asado (roast suckling pig) and *cordero asado lechal* (roast spring lamb) are fabulous staples. (p161)

Wine Tasting

In many parts of the country you won't find anything *but* wines from Spain. La Rioja is the king of Spanish wine regions, but there's so much more to be discovered.

La Rioja wine region Bodegas, wine museums and vineyards to the horizon – this is Spanish wine's heartland. (p448)

Ribera del Duero Spain's favourite wine region in waiting, with bodegas all along the valley. (p192)

Penedès wine country The *cavas* (sparkling wines) that are Spain's favourite Christmas drink. (p353)

El Puerto de Santa María The sherry capital of the world, with numerous bodegas open for visits and tastings. (p617)

Somontano One of Spain's most underrated wine regions, with dozens of vineyards open to the public. (p390)

Galicia Up-and-coming region with fruity white *albariño*, a revival of native grape varieties. (p526)

Asturias Spain's cider capital where's it's poured expertly, straight from the barrel. (p475)

Hiking

Spanish landscapes are continental in variety and include some of Europe's premier hiking destinations, from the Pyrenees in the north to the quiet valleys of Andalucía in the south.

Parque Nacional de Ordesa y Monte Perdido Pyrenean high country at its most spectacular. (p380)

Camino de Santiago One of the world's most famous walks, which can last a couple of days or weeks. (p507)

Picos de Europa Jagged peaks and steep trails inland from the Bay of Biscay. (p494)

Parc Nacional d'Aigüestortes i Estany de Sant Maurici
Romanesque churches and rampart-like ridge lines in the Catalan Pyrenees. (p339)

Sierra Nevada Wildlife and stunning views in the shadow of mainland Spain's highest mountain. (p677)

Sierra de Grazalema White villages and precipitous mountains in Andalucía. (p628)

PLAN YOUR TRIP IF YOU LIKE...

Month by Month

January

In January ski resorts in the Pyrenees in the northeast and the Sierra Nevada, close to Granada in the south, are in full swing. Snow in Catalonia is usually better in the second half of the month. School holidays run until around 8 January, so book ahead.

☆ Three Kings

El Día de los Reyes Magos (Three Kings' Day), or simply Reyes, on 6 January, is the highlight of a Spanish kid's calendar. The evening before, three local politicians dress up as the three wise men and lead a sweet-distributing frenzy (Cabalgata de Reyes) through most towns.

February

This is often the coldest month in Spain, with temperatures close to freezing, especially in the north and inland regions. If you're heading to Carnaval, accommodation is at a premium in Cádiz, Sitges and Ciudad Rodrigo.

☆ Carnaval

Riotously fun, Carnaval ends on the Tuesday 47 days before Easter Sunday, and involves fancy-dress parades and festivities. It's wildest in Cádiz (p613), Sitges (p351), Badajoz (p573) and Ciudad Rodrigo (p153). Other curious celebrations are held at Vilanova i la Geltrú and Solsona.

☆ Fiesta Medieval

In one of Spain's coldest corners, Teruel's inhabitants don their medieval finery and step back to the Middle Ages with markets, food stalls and a re-enactment of a local lovers' legend during the Fiesta Medieval; 2017 marks the 800th anniversary of the legend so expect even more merriment than usual. (p394)

March

With the arrival of spring, Spain shakes off its winter blues (such as they are), the weather starts to warm up ever so slightly and Spaniards start dreaming of a summer by the beach.

☆ Festival de Jerez

One of Spain's most important flamenco festivals takes place in the genre's heartland in late February or early March. (p624)

☆ Las Fallas de San José

The extraordinary festival of Las Fallas consists of several days of all-night dancing and drinking, first-class fireworks and processions from 15 to 19 March. Its principal stage is Valencia city, and the festivities culminate in the ritual burning of effigies in the streets. (p739)

April

Spain has a real spring in its step, with wildflowers in full bloom, Easter celebrations and school holidays. It requires some advance planning (book ahead), but it's a great time to be here.

☆ Semana Santa (Holy Week)

Easter (the dates change each year) entails parades of *pasos* (holy figures), hooded penitents and huge crowds. It's extravagantly celebrated in Seville (p592), as well as Málaga (p688), Ávila (p145), Cuenca (p225), Lorca (p773) and Zamora (p172).

☆ Moros y Cristianos (Moors & Christians)

Colourful parades and mock battles between Christian and Muslim 'armies' in Alcoy, near Alicante, make Moros y Cristianos one of the most spectacular of many such festivities staged in Valencia and Alicante provinces in late April. Other versions are held elsewhere at other times. (p762)

☆ Feria de Abril (April Fair)

This weeklong party, held in Seville in the second half of April, is the biggest of Andalucía's fairs. *Sevillanos* dress up in their traditional finery, ride around on horseback and in elaborate horse-drawn carriages and dance late into the night. (p591)

☆ Romería de la Virgen

On the last Sunday in April, hundreds of thousands of people make a mass pilgrimage to the Santuario de la Virgen de la Cabeza near Andújar, in Jaén province. A small statue of the Virgin is paraded about, exciting great passion. (p718)

May

A glorious time to be in Spain, May sees the countryside carpeted with spring wildflowers and the weather can feel like summer is just around the corner.

☆ Feria del Caballo (Horse Fair)

A colourful equestrian fair in Andalucía's horse capital, Jerez de la Frontera, the Feria del Caballo is one of Andalucía's most festive and extravagant fiestas. It features parades, horse shows, bullfights and plenty of music and dance. (p624)

◉ Córdoba's Courtyards Open Up

Scores of beautiful private courtyards in Córdoba are opened to the public for the Fiesta de los Patios de Córdoba. It's a rare chance to see an otherwise-hidden side of Córdoba, strewn with flowers and freshly painted. (p646)

☆ Fiesta de San Isidro

Madrid's major fiesta celebrates the city's patron saint with bullfights, parades, concerts and more. Locals dress up in traditional costumes, and some of the events, such as the bullfighting season, last for a month. (p102)

☆ WOMAD

Cáceres hosts the annual WOMAD, a fabulous festival dedicated to world music and drawing top-notch musicians from across the globe to perform in the city's medieval squares. (p552)

June

By June, the north is shaking off its winter chill and the Camino de Santiago's trails are becoming crowded. In the south, it's warming up as the coastal resorts ready themselves for the summer onslaught.

☆ Romería del Rocío

Focused on Pentecost weekend (the seventh after Easter), this festive pilgrimage is made by up to one million people to the shrine of the Virgin in El Rocío. This is Andalucía's Catholic tradition at its most curious and compelling. (p607)

☆ Feast of Corpus Cristi

On the Thursday in the ninth week after Easter (sometimes May, sometimes June), religious processions and celebrations take place in Toledo (p211) and other cities. The strangest celebration is the baby-jumping tradition of Castrillo de Murcia (p191).

☆ Electronica Festival

Performers and spectators come from all over the world for Sónar, Barcelona's two-day celebration of electronic music, which is said to be Europe's biggest festival of its kind. Dates vary each year. (p272)

☽ Wine Battle

Haro, one of the premier wine towns of La Rioja, enjoys the Batalla del Vino on 29 June. Participants squirt wine all over the place in one of Spain's messiest playfights, pausing only to drink the good stuff. (p452)

☆ Primavera Sound

One of Spain's biggest music festivals, Primavera Sound – in Barcelona over three days in late May or early June – lures a host of international DJs and musicians. (p272)

July

Temperatures in Andalucía and much of the interior can be fiercely hot, but July is a great time to be at the beach and is one of the best months for hiking in the Pyrenees.

☆ Festival de la Guitarra de Córdoba

Córdoba's contribution to Spain's impressive calendar of musical events, this fine international guitar festival ranges from flamenco and classical to rock, blues and beyond. Headline performances take place in the city's theatres and Plaza de Toros. (p646)

☆ Running of the Bulls

The Fiesta de San Fermín is the weeklong nonstop festival and party in Pamplona with the daily *encierro* (running of the bulls) as its centrepiece. The antibullfighting event, the Running of the Nudes, takes place two days earlier. (p438)

☆ Fiestas del Apóstol Santiago

The Día de Santiago (25 July) marks the day of Spain's national saint (St James) and is spectacularly celebrated in Santiago de

Compostela. With so many pilgrims around, it's the city's most festive two weeks of the year. (p511)

☆ Festival Internacional de Benicàssim

Spain is awash with outdoor concert festivals attracting big-name acts from around the country and abroad, especially in summer. This one, in the Valencian town of Benicàssim, remains one of the original and best. (p749)

August

Spaniards from all over the country join Europeans in converging on the coastal resorts of the Mediterranean. Although the weather can be unpredictable, Spain's northwestern Atlantic coast offers a more nuanced summer experience.

☆ Festival Internacional de Teatro Clásico

The peerless Roman theatre and amphitheatre in Mérida, Extremadura, become the stage for the classics of ancient Greece and Rome, and the occasional newbie such as Will Shakespeare. Performances are held most nights during July and August. (p568)

☆ Galician Wines

The fabulous wines of Galicia are the reason for the Fiesta del Albariño in Cambados on the first weekend of August. Expect five days of music, fireworks and intensive consumption of

Galicia's favourite fruity white wine. (p528)

☆ Natural Cider Festival

Gijón's Fiesta de la Sidra Natural gives expression to the Asturian obsession with cider and includes an annual world-record attempt for the number of people simultaneously pouring cider in one place. It also involves musical concerts. (p480)

☆ Galician Octopus

Galicia's passion for octopus boils over at the Festa do Pulpo de O Carballiño on the second Sunday in August. Tens of thousands of people converge on the small town of Carballiño to eat as much of the stuff as they can. (p541)

☆ La Tomatina

Buñol's massive tomatothrowing festival, held in late August, must be one of the messiest get-togethers in the country. Thousands of people launch about 100 tonnes of tomatoes at one another in just an hour or so! (p748)

September

This is the month when Spain returns to work after a seemingly endless summer. Numerous festivals take advantage of the fact that weather generally remains warm until late September at least.

☆ Bienal de Flamenco

There are flamenco festivals all over Spain through-

out the year, but this is the most prestigious of them all. Held in Seville in even-numbered years (and Málaga every other year), it draws the biggest names in the genre. (p592)

🍷 La Rioja's Grape Harvest

Logroño celebrates the feast day of St Matthew (Fiesta de San Mateo) and the year's grape harvest. There are grape-crushing ceremonies and endless opportunities to sample the fruit of the vine in liquid form. (p449)

🎆 Barcelona's Big Party

Barcelona's co-patron saint is celebrated with fervour in the massive four-day Festes de la Mercè in September. The city stages special exhibitions, free concerts and street performers galore. (p272)

☆ San Sebastián Film Festival

It may not be Cannes, but San Sebastián's annual two-week celebration of film is one of the most prestigious dates on Europe's film-festival circuit. It's held in the second half of the month and has been gathering plaudits since 1957. (p421)

🎆 Romans & Carthaginians

In the second half of the month, locals dress up to re-enact ancient battles during the festival of Carthagineses y Romanos in Cartagena. It's among the more original mock battles staged around Spain to honour the distant past. (p771)

Top: Catedral de Santiago de Compostela (p507)
Bottom: La Tomatina (p748), Buñol

October

Autumn can be a lovely time to be in Spain, with generally mild temperatures throughout the country, although the winter chill can start to bite in central and northern parts of the country.

Fiestas del Pilar

In Zaragoza on 12 October, the faithful mix with hedonists to celebrate this festival dedicated to Our Lady of the Pillar; the pillar in question is in the cathedral, but much of the fun happens in the bars nearby. (p368)

Fiesta de Santa Teresa

The patron saint of Ávila is honoured with 10 days of processions, concerts and fireworks around her feast day. Huddled behind medieval walls, the festival brings to life the powerful cult of personality surrounding Ávila's most famous daughter. (p145)

November

A quiet time on the festival calendar, November is cool throughout the country. Depending on the year, the ski season usually begins in this month in the Pyrenees and Sierra Nevada.

December

The weather turns cold, but Navidad (Christmas) is on its way. There are Christmas markets, *turrón* (nougat) in abundance, an extra long weekend at the beginning of the month and a festive period that lasts until early January.

Navidad

On Navidad, the main get-together is on the night of 24 December (Noche Buena) with much feasting and merriment. Although Spanish families now celebrate both Christmas Day (when Papa Noel brings presents) and Three Kings on 6 January, the latter was traditionally the main present-giving occasion.

Noche Vieja

The night of 31 December was traditionally a family affair, with a family dinner before the young folk head out after midnight. At midnight on Noche Vieja, all eyes turn to the television as the 12 chimes are broadcast live from Madrid's Puerta del Sol and Spaniards young and old try to eat a grape for every chime of the clock as they ring out.

Christmas Markets

Although not quite in the same league as the Christmas markets further north in Europe, Spain does have its share of Christmas markets. Watch out for the traditional *belén*, the large-scale nativity that appears in some shop windows and public squares. Most markets are given over to garish wigs, masks, sweets and tacky modern souvenirs. The biggest markets are in Madrid, Barcelona, Zaragoza, Seville and Granada.

Itineraries

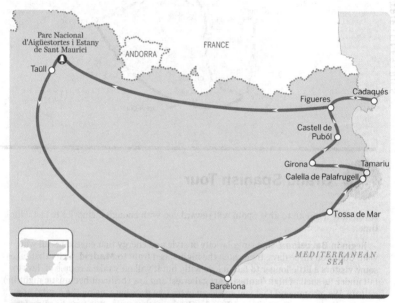

 Barcelona & Around

Spend a lifetime in Barcelona and it may not be enough, filled as it is with so many intensely wonderful experiences. But drag yourself away, and you'll soon discover that the wider Catalonia region is a brilliant place to explore.

You'll need a minimum of two days in **Barcelona** to soak up Gaudí, taste the city's culinary excellence and wander its old town. When you can tear yourself away, rent a car and head north along the Mediterranean shoreline, passing through **Tossa de Mar** and its castle-backed bay, then **Calella de Palafrugell** and **Tamariu**, two beautifully sited coastal villages, before heading inland to pass the night in wonderful **Girona**. The next day is all about Salvador Dalí, from his fantasy castle **Castell de Puból** to his extraordinary theatre-museum in **Figueres**, and then his one-time home, the lovely seaside village of **Cadaqués**. The next morning leave the Mediterranean behind and drive west in the shadow of the Pyrenees – a long day in the saddle, but a day with one jaw-dropping vista after another. Your reward is a couple of nights based in **Taüll**, gateway to the utterly magnificent **Parc Nacional d'Aigüestortes i Estany de Sant Maurici**. A loop south via Lleida then east will have you back in Barcelona by midafternoon on your final day.

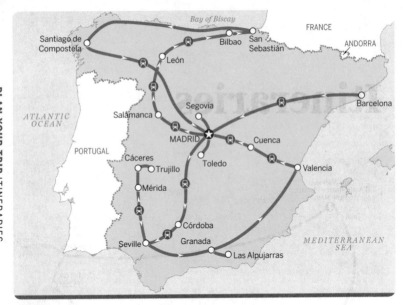

Grand Spanish Tour

1 MONTH

If you have a month to give, Spain will reward you with enough memories to last a lifetime.

Begin in **Barcelona**, that singular city of style and energy that captivates all who visit. Count on three days, then catch the high-speed train to **Madrid**, a city that takes some visitors a little longer to fall in love with, but it will only take a couple of days to fall under its spell of high (fantastic art galleries) and low (brilliant hedonistic nightlife) culture. We recommend that you spend an extra two days here, using the capital as a base for day trips to **Segovia** and **Toledo**. Catch another train, this time heading for **Salamanca**, that platteresque jewel of Castilla y León. After a night in Salamanca, travel north by train to **León** to stay overnight and see the extraordinary stained-glass windows of its cathedral, and then continue on to **Bilbao**, home of the Museo Guggenheim Bilbao and so much that is good about Basque culture. Spend a night here, followed by another couple in splendid **San Sebastián**. A couple of days' drive along the Cantabrian, Asturian and Galician coasts will take you along Spain's most dramatic shoreline en route to **Santiago de Compostela**, where a couple of nights is a minimum to soak up this sacred city. Wherever you travel in the north, from San Sebastián to Santiago, make food a centrepiece of your visit.

Catch the train back to Madrid, then take a high-speed train to **Córdoba** (two nights) and **Seville** (two nights). While you're in the area, detour north by bus or train to the Roman ruins of **Mérida** (one night), the fabulous old city of **Cáceres** (one night) and medieval **Trujillo** (one night). Return to Seville and make immediately for **Granada** (two nights). Add an extra couple of nights and a rental car and you can visit the lovely villages of **Las Alpujarras**. Keep the car (or catch the train) and travel from Granada to **Valencia** to spend a couple of days enjoying its architecture, paella and irresistible energy. You've just enough time to catch the high-speed train to cliff-top **Cuenca** (one night) on your way back to Madrid at journey's end.

2 WEEKS Castile & Aragón

The Spanish interior may not fit the stereotype of sun, sand and sangría, but we love it all the more for that. This route takes in lesser-known cities and stunning villages that lie beyond well-trodden tourist trails.

From **Madrid**, head to some of the loveliest towns of the heartland: **Segovia**, with its Disney-esque castle, walled **Ávila** and vibrant **Salamanca** will occupy four days of your time with short train rides connecting the three. Trains also connect you to the towns of **León** and **Burgos**, home to two of Spain's most extraordinary churches. An extra night in Burgos allows you to take a day trip to the medieval villages of **Covarrubias** and **Santo Domingo de Silos**, where you might catch a service of Gregorian chants. Make for **Zaragoza**, one of Spain's most vibrant cities, with a wealth of monuments and great tapas – two days is a must. Rent a car and head for the hills where **Sos del Rey Católico** perches like a Tuscan hill town. Drive south to overnight in dramatic **Daroca**, encircled by mountains and ruined city walls, then on to **Teruel**, with its Mudéjar gems. Finish your journey in **Albarracín**, a spectacular village, with medieval architecture as extraordinary as its setting.

10 DAYS Northern Spain

Spain's Mediterranean Coast may get the crowds, but the country's northern coastline from San Sebastián to Santiago is one of the most spectacular in Europe.

There is no finer introduction to the north of the country than **San Sebastián**, with its dramatic setting and fabulous food. Two nights is a minimum. Less than three hours west by train, **Bilbao** is best known as the home of the Museo Guggenheim Bilbao and warrants at least a night, preferably two. To make the most of the rest of the coast, you'll need a car. Cantabria's cobblestone medieval **Santillana del Mar**, the rock art at **Altamira** and the village of **Ribadesella** will fill one day, with another taken up by the valleys of the **Picos de Europa**. After a third night in irresistible **Oviedo**, tackle Galicia's coastline, one of Spain's natural wonders, punctuated with secluded fishing villages and stunning cliffs. As you make your way around the coast for a further two nights, don't miss **Cabo Ortegal**, dynamic **A Coruña** and the **Costa da Morte**. For the last two nights, linger in **Santiago de Compostela**, a thoroughly Galician city, a place of pilgrims, fine regional cuisine and a cathedral of rare power.

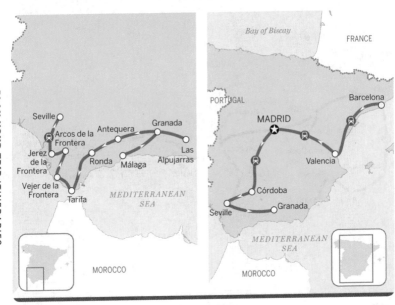

10 DAYS Andalucían Adventure

There's more to Andalucía than the monument-rich cities, although these are not to be missed. This route takes you through three iconic cities and some of the region's most beautiful villages.

Begin in **Málaga**, which has enough attractions to keep you occupied for one very full day – don't miss the Picasso Museum. No Andalucian itinerary is complete without at least a few nights in peerless **Granada** with its astonishing Alhambra, gilded Capilla Real and medieval Muslim quarter of Albayzín. Rent a car and make for the valleys of **Las Alpujarras** with their other-worldly scenery and North African–style villages; stay overnight. If you've kept the car, head west for three days along quiet back roads to some of Andalucia's most spectacular villages and towns: Mudéjar **Antequera**, spectacular **Ronda**, **Tarifa** with its bohemian air, beguiling **Vejer de la Frontera**, and **Arcos de la Frontera**, one of Andalucía's most glorious *pueblos blancos* (white villages). With three days left, leave the car and spend a night in **Jerez de la Frontera**, allowing time to visit its sherry bodegas, then catch a train north to flamenco-rich **Seville**, which is, for many, the essence of Andalucía.

2 WEEKS Essential Spain

If you want to understand why many visitors fall in love with Spain and never want to leave, look no further than its vibrant, passionate, extraordinarily beautiful cities. This itinerary takes you through the best Spain has to offer.

So many Spanish trails begin in **Barcelona**, one of the coolest places on earth. Explore the architecture and food, before catching the train to **Valencia** for another dose of nightlife and the wonders of the Ciudad de las Artes y las Ciencias. This is the home of paella; if you only try Spain's signature dish once, make it here. A fast train whisks you to mighty **Madrid** for the irresistible street energy, pretty plazas and one of the richest concentrations of art museums on the planet. Another fast train takes you deep into Andalucía, with **Córdoba** your entry point. The highlight is the 7th-century Mezquita, which captures the essence of Spain's formerly Islamic south. From Córdoba it's a short hop to fabulous **Seville**. But we've saved the best til last: **Granada**, once capital of Muslim Al-Andalus, boasts the extraordinary Alhambra, its alter ego the Albayzín, and a food scene that embraces Spanish culinary culture in all its variety.

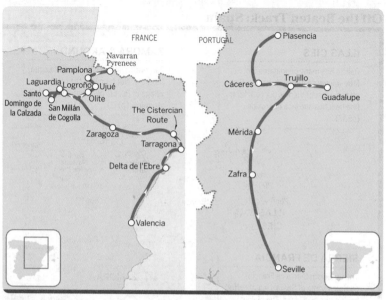

 ## Mediterranean to Mountains

2 WEEKS

This journey takes you from the shores of the Mediterranean to the deep valleys of the Pyrenees. You'll need a car to cover this in two weeks. Your reward is a chance to visit some of northwestern Spain's lesser-known jewels.

Begin in **Valencia**, that most appealing of Mediterranean cities, then drive north-west, pausing in the flamingo-rich **Delta de l'Ebre** en route to **Tarragona**, one of Catalonia's most underrated destinations, with its fabulous Roman ruins. From Tarragona, head inland along the **Cistercian Route**, then cut through Aragón to vibrant, historic **Zaragoza**. After a couple of days in the Aragonese capital, pause overnight in the engaging provincial capital of **Logroño**. Continue west through the fine monastery towns of **Santo Domingo de la Calzada** and **San Millán de Cogolla** and then on into La Rioja, Spain's premier wine-producing region – **Laguardia** is a wonderful base. Head out into the eastern reaches of Navarra, for the beguiling fortress towns of **Olite** and **Ujué**, then on to pretty **Pamplona**. From here, climb into the **Navarran Pyrenees**, at their most beautiful in the Valle del Baztán and Valle del Roncal.

 ## Extreme West

10 DAYS

Extremadura is one of Spain's least known corners, which is all the more reason to visit.

Begin with a night in Extremadura's north, in **Plasencia**, which is jammed with notable buildings, churches and convents. From Plasencia, catch the bus or train to **Cáceres**, whose Ciudad Monumental is one of the finest surviving medieval cores in any Spanish city. After two nights here, regular buses take an hour to nearby **Trujillo**, a smaller but equally enchanting relic of the Middle Ages. Spend two nights here: one to explore the warren of cobbled lanes, and another to rent a car for a day trip to the charming hill town and pilgrims' destination of **Guadalupe**. From Trujillo it's just over an hour by bus south to **Mérida**, but the journey spans the centuries: Mérida boasts some of Spain's most impressive Roman ruins, and you'll need at least two nights here to take it all in. Further south again by bus across the dry plains lies whitewashed **Zafra**, a precursor to Andalucía in spirit, architecture and geography. After a night in Zafra, all roads lead to magical **Seville**, one of Andalucía's (and Spain's) most captivating cities.

Off the Beaten Track: Spain

ILLAS CÍES

Galicia has many candidates for little-known secrets but the Illas Cíes, off the coast of Vigo, is our pick for its fine beaches and lack of crowds. (p537)

ZAMORA & AROUND

Zamora is a little-visited Romanesque treasure. Not far away, the medieval village of Puebla de Sanabria is stunning. (p171)

SIERRA DE FRANCIA

The timeworn Sierra de Francia contains some of Spain's least-visited back-country villages. The pick is probably La Alberca but San Martín del Castañar is utterly beguiling. (p155)

WESTERN EXTREMADURA

Western Extremadura is the land time forgot, from the quiet valleys of the Sierra de Gata and Las Hurdes to remote Alcántara (p555) with its fine Roman bridge.

CÁDIZ

Cádiz is all about narrow white-washed streets where the seafood and wine flow freely in summer. The nearby beaches are some of Spain's best. (p610)

BAEZA & ÚBEDA

These twin towns (p709 and p711) in the north of Andalucía are two of Spain's finest Renaissance gems. Better still, they're lightly touristed.

Map labels:

Bay of Biscay

Costa da Morte
Ferrol
Avilés
Gijón
Santander

A Coruña
Oviedo
Parque Nacional de los Picos de Europa
Torrelavega

ATLANTIC OCEAN
Santiago de Compostela
Lugo
Parque Natural de Somiedo
Cordillera Cantábrica
León

Pontevedra
Ourense
Río Sil
Burgos

ILLAS CÍES
Vigo
Benavente
Palencia
Aranda de Duero

Valladolid
Río Duero

ZAMORA
Salamanca
Segovia

SIERRA DE FRANCIA
Ávila
Guadalajara

Cordillera Central
MADRID

PORTUGAL
Plasencia
Aranjuez
Toledo

WESTERN EXTREMADURA
Río Tajo

LISBON
Badajoz
Mérida
Ciudad Real

Río Guadiana

Zafra
Parque Natural Sierra de Andújar
ÚBEDA

Parque Natural Sierra Norte
Córdoba
BAEZA

Huelva
Seville
Cordillera Bética

Parque Nacional de Doñana
Granada
Parque Natural Sierra Nevada

CÁDIZ
Parque Natural Los Alcornocales
Málaga

Costa de la Luz
Costa del Sol

Algeciras
Gibraltar

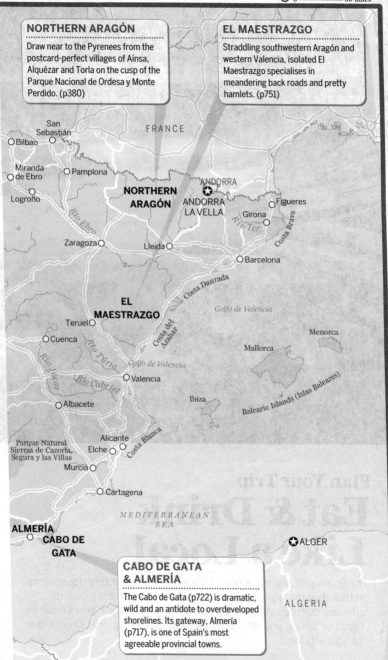

NORTHERN ARAGÓN

Draw near to the Pyrenees from the postcard-perfect villages of Aínsa, Alquézar and Torla on the cusp of the Parque Nacional de Ordesa y Monte Perdido. (p380)

EL MAESTRAZGO

Straddling southwestern Aragón and western Valencia, isolated El Maestrazgo specialises in meandering back roads and pretty hamlets. (p751)

CABO DE GATA & ALMERÍA

The Cabo de Gata (p722) is dramatic, wild and an antidote to overdeveloped shorelines. Its gateway, Almería (p717), is one of Spain's most agreeable provincial towns.

Calçots, a winter speciality

Plan Your Trip
Eat & Drink
Like a Local

For Spaniards, eating is one of life's more pleasurable obsessions. In this chapter, we'll help you make the most of this fabulous culinary culture, whether it's demystifying the dark art of ordering tapas or taking you on a journey through the regional specialities of Spanish food.

The Year in Food

Southern Spain's relatively balmy climate ensures that, unusually for Europe, fruit and vegetables can be grown year-round.

Winter (Dec–Feb)

Across inland Spain, winter is the time for fortifying stews (such as *cocido* or *fabada*) and roasted meats, especially *cochinillo* (suckling pig) and *cordero* (spring lamb).

Winter to Spring (Nov–Apr)

Catalans salivate over *calçots*, those large spring onions that are eaten with your hands and a bib, and *romesco* (a rich red-peppers-and-ground-almond sauce). This is *pulpo* (boiled octopus) season in Galicia.

Summer (Jun–Aug)

The cold soups *gazpacho* and *salmorejo* (specialities of Andalucía) only appear in summer. Rice dishes by the Mediterranean are another key ingredient of the Spanish summer.

Autumn (Sep–Nov)

La Rioja's grape harvest gets underway in September. The Fiesta de San Mateo in Logroño (21 September) gets it all happening.

Food Experiences

Food & Wine Festivals

Feria del Queso (p556) An orgy of cheese tasting and serious competition in Trujillo in late April or early May.

Feira do Viño do Ribeiro (p542) Ribadavia in Galicia's south hosts one of the region's biggest wine festivals in early July.

Fiesta del Albariño (p528) Five days of music, fireworks and intensive consumption of Galicia's favourite fruity white wine in the first week of August.

Festa do Pulpo de O Carballiño (p541) Carballiño in Galicia sees 70,000 people cram in for a mass octopus-eating binge on the second Sunday of August.

Batalla del Vino (p452) Every 29 June in Haro in La Rioja they have a really messy wine fight.

Fiesta de la Sidra Natural (p480) This August fiesta in Gijón includes an annual world-record attempt on the number of people simultaneously pouring cider.

Fiesta de San Mateo (p449) In Logroño, La Rioja's September grape harvest is celebrated with grape-crushing ceremonies and tastings.

Meals of a Lifetime

Arzak (p424) This San Sebastián restaurant is the home kitchen of Spain's most revered father-daughter team.

Martín Berasategui Restaurant (p424) One of Spain's most respected celebrity chefs. Also in San Sebastián.

El Celler de Can Roca (p316) This Girona eatery represents everything that's good about innovative Catalan cuisine.

Sergi Arola Gastro (p116) Catalan master chef who has taken Madrid by storm.

Tickets (p285) Barcelona restaurant from the stable of Spain's most decorated chef.

La Terraza del Casino (☑91 532 12 75; www.casinodemadrid.es; Calle de Alcalá 15; mains €35-45, lunch set menu €69; ◷1-4pm & 9pm-midnight Mon-Sat) In Madrid, this is one of the country's temples to laboratory-led innovations.

Quique Dacosta (p755) Molecular gastronomy brought to the Mediterranean. In Denia.

DiverXo (p116) Madrid's only three-Michelín-starred eatery.

Cheap Treats

Tapas or pintxos Possibly the world's most ingenious form of snacking. Madrid's La Latina *barrio* (district), Zaragoza's El Tubo and most Andalucían cities offer rich pickings, but a *pintxo* (Basque tapas) crawl in San Sebastián's Parte Vieja is one of life's most memorable gastronomic experiences.

Chocolate con churros These deep-fried doughnut strips dipped in thick hot chocolate are a Spanish favourite for breakfast, afternoon tea or at dawn on your way home from a night out.

Madrid's Chocolatería de San Ginés (p116) is the most famous purveyor.

Bocadillos Rolls filled with *jamón* (cured ham) or other cured meats, cheese or (in Madrid) deep-fried calamari.

Pa amb tomaquet Bread rubbed with tomato, olive oil and garlic – a staple in Catalonia and elsewhere.

Cooking Courses

Alambique (p102) Cooking classes in Madrid covering Spanish and international themes.

Cooking Club (p102) Respected program of classes across a range of cooking styles. In Madrid.

Apunto (Map p104; 91 702 10 41; www.apuntolibreria.com; Calle de Hortaleza 64; per person from €40; Chueca) Excellent range of cooking styles in Madrid.

Catacurian (97 782 53 41; www.catacurian.com) English-language wine and cooking classes in the Priorat region with Catalan chef Alicia Juanpere and her American partner.

Espai Boisa (p271) Excellent three-hour courses with a focus on local ingredients and recipes, and plenty of time to taste what you cook. In Barcelona.

L'Atelier (958 857 501; http://www.ivu.org/atelier/index-eng; Calle Alberca 21; cooking classes per person per day €50) Award-winning vegetarian chef Jean-Claude Juston runs vegetarian cooking courses in Andalucía's Las Alpujarras.

La Janda (p633) In Vejer de la Frontera, cooking is combined with Spanish classes.

Dare to Try

Oreja Pig's ear, cooked on the grill. It's a little like eating gristly bacon.

Callos Tripe cooked in a sauce of tomato, paprika, garlic and herbs. It's a speciality of Madrid.

Rabo de toro Bull's tail, or oxtail stew. It's a particular delicacy during bullfighting season in Madrid and Andalucía, when the tail comes straight from the bullring...

Percebes Goose barnacles from Galicia. The first person to try them sure was one adventurous individual, but we're glad they did.

Garrotxa Formidable Catalan cheese that almost lives up to its name.

Caracoles Snails. Much loved in Catalonia, Mallorca and Aragón.

Morcilla Blood sausage. It's blended with rice in Burgos, with onion in Asturias.

Criadillas Bull's testicles. Eaten in Andalucía.

Botillo Spanish version of haggis from Castilla y León's Bierzo region.

Local Specialities

Food

Spaniards love to travel in their own country, and given the riches on offer, they especially love to do so in pursuit of the perfect meal. Tell a Spaniard that you're on your way to a particular place and they're sure to start salivating at the mere thought of the local speciality, and they'll surely have a favourite restaurant at which to enjoy it.

Basque Country & Catalonia

The confluence of sea and mountains has bequeathed to the Basque Country an extraordinary culinary richness – seafood and steaks are the pillars upon which Basque cuisine were traditionally built. San Sebastián, in particular, showcases the region's diversity of culinary experiences and it was from the kitchens of San Sebastián that *nueva cocina vasca* (Basque nouvelle cuisine) emerged, announcing Spain's arrival as a culinary superpower.

Catalonia blends traditional Catalan flavours with an openness to influences from the rest of Europe. All manner of seafood, paella, rice and pasta dishes, as well as Pyrenean game dishes, are regulars on Catalan menus. Sauces are more prevalent here than elsewhere in Spain.

Inland Spain

The best *jamón ibérico* comes from Extremadura, Salamanca and Teruel, while *cordero asado lechal* (roast spring lamb) and *cochinillo asado* (roast suckling pig) are winter mainstays. Of the hearty stews, the king is *cocido,* a hotpot or stew with a noodle broth, carrots, cabbage, chickpeas, chicken, *morcilla* (blood sausage), beef and lard. *Migas* (breadcrumbs, often cooked with chorizo and served with grapes) are also regulars.

Cheeses, too, are specialities, from Extremadura's *Torta del Casar* (a creamy, spreadable cheese) to Castilla-La Mancha's *queso manchego* (a hard sheep's cheese).

JAMÓN: A PRIMER

There's no more iconic presence on the Spanish table than cured ham from the high plateau, and *jamónes* hanging from the ceiling is one of Spain's most enduring images.

The Origins of Jamón

The recipe for cured meats such as *jamón* is most often attributed to a noble Roman, Cato the Elder, who changed the course of Spanish culinary history with his tome *De Re Rustica*.

Types of Jamón

Spanish *jamón* is, unlike Italian prosciutto, a bold, deep red and well marbled with buttery fat. At its best, it smells like meat, the forest and the field.

Like wines and olive oil, Spanish *jamón* is subject to a strict series of classifications. *Jamón serrano* refers to *jamón* made from white-coated pigs introduced to Spain in the 1950s. Once salted and semidried by the cold, dry winds of the Spanish sierra, most now go through a similar process of curing and drying in a climate-controlled shed for around a year. *Jamón serrano* accounts for about 90% of cured ham in Spain.

Jamón ibérico – more expensive and generally regarded as the elite of Spanish hams – comes from a black-coated pig indigenous to the Iberian Peninsula and a descendant of the wild boar. Gastronomically, its star appeal is its ability to infiltrate fat into the muscle tissue, thus producing an especially well-marbled meat. If the pig gains at least 50% of its body weight during the acorn-eating season, it can be classified as *jamón ibérico de bellota*, the most sought-after designation for *jamón*.

Jamón Regions

There's something about sampling *jamón* close to its source, and these are the most famous *jamón*-producing villages:

Guijuelo (Castilla y León) (p156) South of Salamanca.

Monesterio (Extremadura) (p572) South of Zafra; also has Spain's best *jamón* museum.

Montánchez (Extremadura) Southwest of Cáceres.

Jabugo (Andalucía) Northwest of Sevilla.

Teruel (Aragón) (p392) Southern Aragón. Check out www.jamondeteruel.com.

Eating Jamón

The best-quality *jamón* is most commonly eaten as a starter or a *ración* (large tapa); on menus it's usually called a *tabla de jamón ibérico* (or *ibérico de bellota*). Cutting it is an art form and it should be sliced so wafer-thin as to be almost transparent. Spaniards almost always eat it with bread.

Cheaper types of *jamón* appear in a *bocadillo de jamón* (roll filled with *jamón*) or in small pieces in everything from *salmorejo cordobés* (a cold tomato-based soup from Córdoba) to *huevos rotos* (eggs and potatoes).

Another local version in Aragón is *las delicias de Teruel* (*jamón* served with toasted bread and fresh tomato).

Galicia & the Northwest

Galicia is known for its bewildering array of seafood, and the star is *pulpo á feira* (spicy boiled octopus, called *pulpo gallego* or spelled *pulpo á galega* in the local Galician language), a dish whose constituent elements (octopus, oil, paprika and garlic) are so simple yet whose execution is devilishly difficult. Neighbouring Asturias and Cantabria produce Spain's best *anchoas* (anchovies).

In the high mountains of Asturias and Cantabria, the cuisine is as driven by mountain pasture as it is by the daily comings and goings of fishing fleets. Cheeses are particularly sought after, with special fame reserved for the untreated cow's-milk cheese *queso de Cabrales. Asturianos* (Asturians) are also passionate about their *fabada asturiana* (a stew made with pork, blood sausage and white beans) and *sidra* (cider) straight from the barrel.

Valencia & Murcia

There's so much more to the cuisine of this region than oranges and paella, but these signature products capture the essence of the Mediterranean table. You can get a paella just about anywhere in Spain, but to get one cooked as it should be cooked, look no further than the restaurants in

THE PERFECT PAELLA

There's something life-affirming about a proper Spanish paella, cheerily yellow like the sun and bursting with intriguing morsels. It seems to promise warm days and fine company. But there's more to this most Valencian of dishes than meets the eye. Here we give you the insider scoop.

Origins

Originally domesticated in China some 10,000 years ago, rice was brought to Spain by the Moors in the 8th century AD. The low-lying wetlands of the Valencian coast were perfect for its cultivation but it was viewed with suspicion by the Catholic re-conquerors, due to outbreaks of malaria in rice-growing regions.

Secrets of the Rice

Traditional Valencian paellas can have almost any ingredients, varying by region and season. The base always includes short-grain rice, garlic, olive oil and saffron. The best rice is bomba, which opens accordion-like when cooked, allowing for maximum absorption while remaining firm. Paella should be cooked in a large shallow pan to enable maximum contact with flavour. And for the final touch of authenticity, the grains on the bottom (and only those) should have a crunchy, savoury crust known as the *socarrat*.

Fiesta Rices

Paella competitions are a common feature of fiestas in Valencia. Judges look for taste, colour, perfectly done rice, distribution of ingredients and quality of *socarrat*. Also common are giant paellas, made in huge pans. Jesus feeding the 5000 was nothing compared to some of these monsters – the largest fed 110,000 people out of a pan 21m wide and weighing 23 tons.

Tips on Ordering

Rice dishes are traditional in Catalonia, Valencia and Andalucía, so that's where they are best eaten. Check out the clientele first. No locals? Walk on by.

Restaurants should take 20 minutes or more to prepare a rice dish – beware if they don't – so expect to wait. You can pre-order so it's ready sooner. Though rice dishes are usually for a minimum of two, some places will do one for a solo diner if asked.

Paella has all the liquid evaporated, *meloso* rice dishes are wet, and *caldoso* rice dishes come with liquid.

Try This at Home

➡ Brown the meat or seafood with olive oil in the pan over high heat, brown the garlic, then add vegetables – more equals more flavour – and fry lightly on lower heat.

➡ When meat and vegetables are cooked, add the rice, spread out thinly across the pan. Add water or stock, about three parts liquid to one part rice. It's better to err on the side of less liquid so as not to overcook the rice.

➡ Rice cooks in about 15 minutes; the first nine on high heat, then the last few low.

➡ Add saffron and/or colouring towards the end and garnish.

Vineyard in La Rioja (p448)

Valencia's waterfront Las Arenas district or La Albufera.

Murcia's culinary fame brings us back to the oranges. The littoral is known simply as 'La Huerta' ('the garden'). Since Moorish times, this has been one of Spain's most prolific areas for growing fruit and vegetables.

Andalucía

Seafood is a consistent presence the length of the Andalucían coast. Andalucíans are famous above all for their *pescaito frito* (fried fish). A particular speciality of Cádiz, fried fish Andalucían-style means that just about anything that emerges from the sea is rolled in chickpea and wheat flour, shaken to remove the surplus, then deep-fried ever so briefly in olive oil, just long enough to form a light, golden crust that seals the essential goodness of the fish or seafood within.

In a region where summers can be fierce, there's no better way to keep cool than with a *gazpacho andaluz* (Andalucían gazpacho), a cold soup with many manifestations. The base is almost always tomato, cucumber, vinegar and olive oil.

Wines

All of Spain's autonomous communities, with the exceptions of Asturias and Cantabria, are home to recognised wine-growing areas.

La Rioja, in the north, is Spain's best-known wine-producing region. The principal grape of Rioja is the *tempranillo*, widely believed to be a mutant form of the pinot noir. Its wine is smooth and fruity, seldom as dry as its supposed French counterpart. Look for the 'DOC Rioja' classification on the label and you'll find a good wine.

Not far behind are the wine-producing regions of Ribera del Duero in Castilla y León, Navarra, the Somontano wines of Aragón, and the Valdepeñas region of southern Castilla-La Mancha, which is famous for its quantities rather than quality, but is generally well priced and remains popular.

For white wines, the Ribeiro wines of Galicia are well regarded. Also from the area is one of Spain's most charming whites – *albariño*. This crisp, dry and refreshing drop is unusual, designated as it is by grape rather than region.

The Penedès region in Catalonia produces whites and sparkling wine such as *cava*, the traditional champagne-like toasting drink of choice for Spaniards at Christmas.

Wine Classification

Spanish wine is subject to a complicated system of classification. If an area meets certain strict standards for a given period, covering all aspects of planting, cultivating and ageing, it receives Denominación de Origen (DO; Denomination of Origin) status. There are currently over 60 DO-recognised wine-producing areas in Spain.

An outstanding wine region gets the much-coveted Denominación de Origen Calificada (DOC), a controversial classification that some in the industry argue should apply only to specific wines, rather than every wine from within a particular region. At present, the only DOC wines come from La Rioja in northern Spain and the small Priorat area in Catalonia.

The best wines are often marked with the designation '*crianza*' (aged for one year in oak barrels), '*reserva*' (aged for two years, at least one of which is in oak barrels) and '*gran reserva*' (two years in oak and three in the bottle).

Sherry

Sherry, the unique wine of Andalucía, is Spain's national dram and is found in almost every bar, *tasca* (tapas bar) and restaurant in the land. Dry sherry, called *fino*, begins as a fairly ordinary white wine of the palomino grape, but it's 'fortified' with grape brandy. This stops fermentation and gives the wine taste and smell constituents that enable it to age into something sublime. It's taken as an *aperitivo* (aperitif) or as a table wine with seafood. *Amontillado* and *oloroso* are sweeter sherries, good for after dinner. *Manzanilla* is grown only in Sanlúcar de Barrameda near the coast in southwestern Andalucía and develops a slightly salty taste that's very appetising. It's possible to visit bodegas (wineries) in Sanlúcar, as well as in Jerez de la Frontera and El Puerto de Santa María.

How to Eat & Drink

Having joined Spaniards around the table for years, we've come to understand what eating Spanish-style is all about. If we could distil the essence of how to make food a highlight of your trip into a few simple rules, they would be these: always ask for the local speciality; never be shy about looking around to see what others have ordered before choosing; always ask the waiter for their recommendations; and, wherever possible, make your meal a centrepiece of your day.

When to Eat

Breakfast

Desayuno (breakfast) Spanish-style is generally a no-nonsense affair taken at a bar midmorning or on the way to work. A *café con leche* (half coffee and half milk) with a *bollo* (pastry) or croissant is the typical

---

ORDERING TAPAS

Unless you speak Spanish, ordering tapas can seem one of the dark arts of Spanish etiquette. Fear not – it's not as difficult as it appears.

In the Basque Country, Zaragoza and many bars in Madrid, Barcelona and elsewhere, it couldn't be easier. With tapas varieties lined up along the bar, you either take a small plate and help yourself or point to the morsel you want. If you do this, it's customary to keep track of what you eat (by holding on to the toothpicks, for example) and then tell the bar staff how many you've had when it's time to pay. Otherwise, many places have a list of tapas, either on a menu or posted up behind the bar. If you can't choose, ask for '*la especialidad de la casa*' (the house speciality) and it's hard to go wrong.

Another way of eating tapas is to order *raciones* (literally 'rations'; large tapas servings) or *media raciones* (half-rations; smaller tapas servings). Remember, however, that after a couple of *raciones* you'll be full. In some bars you'll also get a small (free) tapa when you buy a drink.

Above: Tapas

Right: Typical Spanish *desayuno* (breakfast) of *café con leche* and *bollo* (pastry)

SCISETTI ALFIO/SHUTTERSTOCK ©

Tortilla de patatas

breakfast. Another common breakfast order is a *tostada,* which is simply buttered toast.

In hotels, breakfast can begin as early as 6.30am and may continue until 10am (usually later on weekends).

Lunch

Lunch (*comida* or *almuerzo*) is the main meal of the day. During the working week few Spaniards have time to go home for lunch, so most people end up eating in restaurants, and all-inclusive three-course meals (*menús del día*) are as close as they can come to eating home-style food without breaking the bank. On weekends or in summer, Spaniards are not averse to lingering for hours over a meal with friends and family.

Lunch rarely begins before 2pm (restaurant kitchens usually open from 1.30pm until 4pm).

Dinner

Dinner (*cena*) is usually a lighter meal, although that may differ on weekends. Going out for a drink and some tapas is a popular way of eating dinner in many cities.

It does vary from region to region, but most restaurants open from 8.30pm to midnight, later on weekends.

Vegetarians & Vegans

Such is their love for meat, fish and seafood, many Spaniards, especially the older generation, don't really understand vegetarianism. As a result, dedicated vegetarian restaurants are still pretty thin on the ground outside the major cities.

That said, while vegetarians – especially vegans – can have a hard time, and while some cooked vegetable dishes can contain

> ### PRICE INDICATORS
>
> In our reviews, restaurants are grouped according to price range (€ to €€€). The order within each of those ranges follows the author's preference. The following price brackets refer to a standard main dish:
>
> **€** less than €10
>
> **€€** from €10 to €20
>
> **€€€** more than €20

ham, the eating habits of Spaniards are changing; an ever-growing selection of vegetarian restaurants is springing up around the country. Barcelona and Madrid, in particular, have plenty of vegetarian restaurants to choose from.

Otherwise, salads are a Spanish staple and often are a meal in themselves. You'll also come across the odd vegetarian paella, as well as dishes such as *verduras a la plancha* (grilled vegetables); *garbanzos con espinacas* (chickpeas and spinach); and potato dishes, such as *patatas bravas* (potato chunks bathed in a slightly spicy tomato sauce) and *tortilla de patatas* (potato and onion omelette). The prevalence of legumes ensures that *lentejas* (lentils) and *judías* (beans) are also easy to track down, while *pan* (bread), *quesos* (cheeses), *alcachofas* (artichokes) and *aceitunas* (olives) are always easy to find. *Tascas* (tapas bars) usually offer more vegetarian choices than sit-down restaurants.

If vegetarians feel like a rarity among Spaniards, vegans will feel as if they've come from another planet. To make sure that you're not misunderstood, ask if dishes contain *huevos* (eggs) or *productos lácteos* (dairy).

Where to Eat

asador Restaurant specialising in roasted meats.

bar de copas Gets going around midnight and serves hard drinks.

casa de comidas Basic restaurant serving well-priced home cooking.

cervecería The focus is on *cerveza* (beer) on tap.

horno de asador Restaurant with a wood-burning roasting oven.

marisquería Bar or restaurant specialising in seafood.

restaurante Restaurant.

taberna Usually a rustic place serving tapas and raciones (large tapas).

tasca Tapas bar.

THE TRAVELLERS' FRIEND – MENÚ DEL DÍA

One great way to cap prices at lunchtime on weekdays is to order the *menú del día*, a full three-course set menu, water, bread and wine. These meals are priced from around €10, although €12 and up is increasingly the norm. You'll be given a menu with a choice of five or six starters, the same number of mains and a handful of desserts – you choose one from each category; it's possible to order two starters, but not two mains.

---

terraza Open-air bar, for warm-weather tippling and tapas.

vinoteca Wine bars where you can order by the glass.

Menu Decoder

a la parilla grilled

asado roasted or baked

bebidas drinks

carne meat

carta menu

casera homemade

ensalada salad

entrada entrée or starter

entremeses hors d'oeuvres

frito fried

menú usually refers to a set menu

menú de degustación tasting menu

pescado fish

plato combinado main-and-three-veg dish

postre dessert

raciones large-/full-plate-size serving of tapas

sopa soup

Spain's Foodie Highlights

GALICIA

It's all about the seafood – the daily Atlantic catch includes the country's widest variety of sea creatures. (p522)

SEGOVIA

Inland Spain's passion for the pig and roasted meats reaches its high point with sublime *cochinillo asado* – roast suckling pig. (p161)

MADRID

Rises above its unexciting local cuisine with fabulous variety from every Spanish region, and the world's oldest restaurant. (p109)

MONESTERIO

One of Spain's finest sources of *jamón ibérico*, with a museum dedicated to *jamón*, in Extremadura's deep south. (p572)

SEVILLE

Classic Andalucian tapas country, with a focus on tile-walled bars, abundant olives and all manner of tapas without too many elaborations. (p593)

JEREZ DE LA FRONTERA

Spiritual home of Spain's sherry obsession, with plenty of bodegas and ample bars in which to sample the local *fino*. (p625)

Bay of Biscay

ATLANTIC OCEAN

Costa da Morte

Ferrol

GALICIA

Santander

Oviedo

Parque Nacional de los Picos de Europa

Santiago de Compostela

Lugo

Parque Natural de Somiedo

Cordillera Cantábrica

Pontevedra

Ourense

León

Burgos

Benavente

Palencia

Aranda de Duero

Zamora

Salamanca

SEGOVIA

Ávila

Guadalajara

Cordillera Central

MADRID

Plasencia

Toledo

Ciudad Real

LISBON

PORTUGAL

Badajoz

Mérida

Zafra

MONESTERIO

Parque Natural Sierra de Andújar

Parque Natural Sierra Norte

Córdoba

Úbeda

SEVILLE

Cordillera Bética

Huelva

Parque Nacional de Doñana

Granada

Parque Natural Sierra Nevada

JEREZ DE LA FRONTERA

Parque Natural Los Alcornocales

Málaga

Costa de la Luz

Costa del Sol

Gibraltar

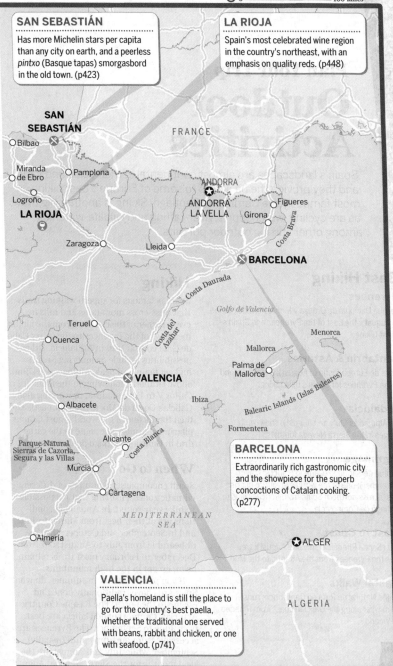

0 ——— 200 km
0 ——— 100 miles

SAN SEBASTIÁN

Has more Michelin stars per capita than any city on earth, and a peerless *pintxo* (Basque tapas) smorgasbord in the old town. (p423)

LA RIOJA

Spain's most celebrated wine region in the country's northeast, with an emphasis on quality reds. (p448)

BARCELONA

Extraordinarily rich gastronomic city and the showpiece for the superb concoctions of Catalan cooking. (p277)

VALENCIA

Paella's homeland is still the place to go for the country's best paella, whether the traditional one served with beans, rabbit and chicken, or one with seafood. (p741)

FRANCE

SAN SEBASTIÁN
Bilbao
Miranda de Ebro
Pamplona
Logroño
LA RIOJA
Zaragoza
Lleida
ANDORRA
ANDORRA LA VELLA
Figueres
Girona
Costa Brava
BARCELONA

Costa Daurada
Golfo de Valencia
Teruel
Cuenca
Costa del Azahar
Menorca
Mallorca
Palma de Mallorca
Balearic Islands (Islas Baleares)
VALENCIA
Albacete
Ibiza
Formentera
Parque Natural Sierras de Cazorla, Segura y las Villas
Alicante
Costa Blanca
Murcia
Cartagena
MEDITERRANEAN SEA
Almería
ALGER

ALGERIA

Plan Your Trip
Outdoor Activities

Spain's landscapes are almost continental in their scale and variety, and they provide the backdrop to some of Europe's best hiking, most famously the Camino de Santiago. Skiing is another big draw, as are cycling, water sports, river-rafting and wildlife-watching, among other stirring outdoor pursuits.

Best Hiking

Pyrenees
Parque Nacional de Ordesa y Monte Perdido (June to August): the best of the Pyrenees and Spain's finest hiking.

Cantabria & Asturias
Picos de Europa (June to August): a close second to the Pyrenees for Spain's best hiking.

Andalucía
Las Alpujarras (July and August): snow-white villages in the Sierra Nevada foothills.

Pilgrimage
Camino de Santiago (Camino Francés; May to September): one of the world's favourite pilgrimages, across northern Spain from Roncesvalles to Santiago de Compostela.

Coast to Coast
GR11 (Senda Pirenáica; July and August): traverses the Pyrenees from the Atlantic to the Med.

Coastal Walks
Camiño Natural da Ruta do Cantábrico: runs 133km west along the Galician coast from Ribadeo to O Vicedo.

Hiking

Spain is famous for superb walking trails that criss-cross mountains and hills in every corner of the country, from the alpine meadows of the Pyrenees to the sultry Cabo de Gata coastal trail in Andalucía. Other possibilities include conquering Spain's highest mainland peak, Mulhacén (3479m), above Granada; following in the footsteps of Carlos V in Extremadura; or walking along Galicia's Costa da Morte (Death Coast). And then there's one of the world's most famous pilgrimage trails – the route to the cathedral in Galicia's Santiago de Compostela.

When to Go

Spain encompasses a number of different climatic zones, ensuring that it's possible to hike year-round. In Andalucía conditions are at their best from March to June and in September and October; they're unbearable from July to August, but from December to February most trails remain open, except in the high mountains.

If you prefer to walk in summer, do what Spaniards have traditionally done and escape to the north. The Basque Country, Asturias, Cantabria and Galicia are best from June to September. The Pyrenees are accessible from mid-June until (usually) September, while July and August are the ideal months for the Sierra Nevada. August

Parque Natural de Somiedo (p491)

is the busiest month on the trails, so if you plan to head to popular national parks and stay in *refugios* (pilgrim hostels), book ahead.

Conversely, hiking anywhere in the Pyrenees can be splendid in September and into early October – the summer crowds have gone, there's (usually) still enough sunshine to go with the lovely autumn colours and there's plenty of room in the *refugios*.

Hiking Destinations
Pyrenees

The Pyrenees, separating Spain from France, are Spain's premier walking destination. The range is utterly beautiful: prim and pretty on the lower slopes, wild and bleak at higher elevations, and relatively unspoilt compared to some European ranges. The Pyrenees contain two outstanding national parks: Aigüestortes i Estany de Sant Maurici (p339) and Ordesa y Monte Perdido (p380).

The spectacular GR11 (Senda Pirenáica) traverses the range, connecting the Atlantic (at Hondarribia in the Basque Country) with the Mediterranean (at Cap de Creus

in Catalonia). Walking the whole 35- to 50-day route is an unforgettable challenge, but there are also magnificent day hikes in the national parks and elsewhere.

Picos de Europa

Breathtaking and accessible limestone ranges with distinctive craggy peaks (usually hot rock-climbing destinations too) are the hallmark of Spain's first national park, the Picos de Europa (www.picosdeeuropa. com), which straddles the Cantabria, Asturias and León provinces and is fast gaining a reputation as the place to walk in Spain.

A new hiking itinerary known as El Anillo de Picos links together the Picos' most important *refugios* in several neat loops. Visit www.elanillodepicos.com for further details.

Elsewhere in Spain

To walk in mountain villages, the classic spot is Las Alpujarras (p679), near the Parque Nacional Sierra Nevada in Andalucía. The Sierra de Cazorla (p714), Sierra de Grazalema (p629) and Sierra de Aracena (p608) are also outstanding. The long-distance GR7 trail traverses these three

ROCK CLIMBING

Spain offers plenty of opportunities to see the mountains and gorges from a more vertical perspective. For an overview of Spanish rock climbing, check out the Spain information on the websites of Rockfax (www.rock-fax.com) and Climb Europe (www.climb-europe.com). Both include details on the best climbs in the country. Rockfax also publishes various climbing guidebooks covering Spain.

regions – you can walk all or just part of the route, depending on your time and inclination.

Great coastal walking abounds, even in heavily visited areas such as the south coast (try Andalucía's Cabo de Gata; p722).

In Galicia, the Camiño Natural da Ruta do Cantábrico, inaugurated in 2015, is an excellent walking and biking trail running 133km west along the Galician coast from Ribadeo (p525) to O Vicedo, west of Viveiro. It's well signposted and there are information boards at places of interest en route. It passes the famous Praia As Catedrais, among other places. Other excellent Galician routes include the Ruta do Solpor de Europa (from Muxía (p515) to the Praia de Nemiña via beautiful beaches, spectacular capes and quaint hamlets) and the Ruta del Litoral (Camariñas to Camelle).

Another fine coastal path is the Camí de Ronda, the coastal path that runs all the way up the Costa Brava (p303) and is really rather special in places.

Information

Region-specific walking (and climbing) guides are published by Cicerone Press (www.cicerone.co.uk).

Madrid's La Tienda Verde (p819) and Librería Desnivel (p819) both sell maps (the best Spanish ones are *Prames* and *Adrados*) and guides.

Camino de Santiago

The door is open to all, to sick and healthy, not only to Catholics but also to pagans, Jews, heretics and vagabonds.

This is how a 13th-century Latin poem described the Camino. Eight hundred years later these words still ring true. The Camino de Santiago (Way of St James) originated as a medieval pilgrimage and, for more than 1000 years, people have taken up the Camino's age-old symbols – the scallop shell and staff – and set off on the adventure of a lifetime to the tomb of St James the Apostle, in Santiago de Compostela, in the Iberian Peninsula's far northwest.

Today the most popular of the several *caminos* (paths) to Santiago de Compostela is the Camino Francés, which spans 783km of Spain's north from Roncesvalles, on the border with France, to Santiago de Compostela in Galicia, and attracts walkers of all backgrounds and ages, from countries across the world. And no wonder: its list of assets (culture, history, nature) is impressive, as are its accolades. Not only is it Council of Europe's first Cultural Itinerary and a Unesco World Heritage site but, for pilgrims, it's a pilgrimage equal to visiting Jerusalem, and by finishing it you're guaranteed a healthy chunk of time off purgatory.

To feel, absorb, smell and taste northern Spain's diversity, for a great physical challenge, for a unique perspective on rural and urban communities, and to meet intriguing travel companions, this is an incomparable walk. *'The door is open to all'* ...so step on in.

History

In the 9th century a remarkable event occurred in the poor Iberian hinterlands: following a shining star, Pelayo, a religious hermit, unearthed the tomb of the apostle James the Greater (or, in Spanish, Santiago). The news was confirmed by the local bishop, the Asturian king and later the pope. Its impact is hard to truly imagine today, but it was instant and indelible: first a trickle, then a flood of Christian Europeans began to journey towards the setting sun in search of salvation.

Compostela became the most important destination for Christians after Rome and Jerusalem. Its popularity increased with an 11th-century papal decree granting it Holy Year status: pilgrims could receive a plenary indulgence – a full remission of your lifetime's sins – during a Holy Year. These occur when Santiago's feast day (25 July) falls on a Sunday: the next one isn't until 2021.

The 11th and 12th centuries marked the heyday of the pilgrimage. The Reformation

Camino Francés

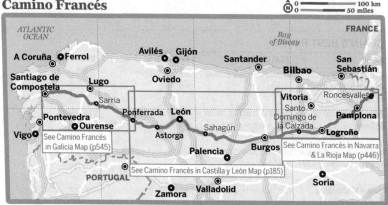

was devastating for Catholic pilgrimages, and by the 19th century, the Camino had nearly died out. In its startling late 20th-century reanimation, which continues today, it's most popular as a personal and spiritual journey of discovery, rather than one necessarily motivated by religion.

Routes

Although in Spain there are many *caminos* (paths) to Santiago, by far the most popular is, and was, the Camino Francés, which originated in France, crossed the Pyrenees at Roncesvalles and then headed west for 783km across the regions of Navarra, La Rioja, Castilla y León and Galicia. Waymarked with cheerful yellow arrows and scallop shells, the 'trail' is a mishmash of rural lanes, paved secondary roads and footpaths all strung together. Starting at Roncesvalles, the Camino takes roughly two weeks to cycle or five weeks to walk.

But this is by no means the only route, and the summer crowds along the Camino Francés have prompted some to look at alternative routes: in 2005, nearly 85% of walkers took the Camino Francés; by 2015 this had fallen to 65% and four alternative routes were added to the Camino de Santiago's Unesco World Heritage listing in 2015. Increasingly popular routes include:

Camino de la Costa/Camino del Norte From Irún along the coasts of the Basque Country, Cantabria and Asturias, then across Galicia to Santiago.

Camino Vasco-Riojano An alternative start to the Camino Francés, beginning in Irún.

Camino Primitivo Links the Camino del Norte (from Villavicosa, close to Oviedo) with Melide along the main Camino Francés.

Camino Lebaniego From either Santander or San Vicente Barquera to Liébana in Cantabria; not actually a Camino de Santiago but part of the Unesco listing nonetheless.

Camino Portugués North to Santiago through Portugal.

Vía de la Plata From Andalucía north through Extremadura, Castilla y León and on to Galicia.

A very popular alternative is to walk only the last 100km (the minimum distance allowed) from Sarria in Galicia in order to earn a Compostela certificate of completion from the Catedral de Santiago de Compostela.

PILGRIM HOSTELS

There are around 300 *refugios* (pilgrim hostels) along the Camino, owned by parishes, 'friends of the Camino' associations, private individuals, town halls and regional governments. While in the early days these places were run on donations and provided little more than hot water and a bed, today's pilgrims are charged €5 to €10 and expect showers, kitchens and washing machines. Some things haven't changed though – the *refugios* still operate on a first-come, first-served basis and are intended for those doing the Camino solely under their own steam.

SPAIN'S BEST PARKS

PARK	FEATURES	ACTIVITIES	BEST TIME TO VISIT
Parc Nacional d'Aigüestortes i Estany de Sant Maurici (p339)	beautiful Pyrenees lake region	walking, wildlife-watching	Jun-Sep
Parque Nacional de Doñana (p605)	bird and mammal haven in Guadalquivir delta	4WD tours, walking, wildlife-watching, horse riding	year-round
Parque Nacional de los Picos de Europa (p494)	beautiful mountain refuge for chamois, and a few wolves and bears	walking, rock climbing	May-Jul & Sep
Parque Nacional de Monfragüe (p564)	spectacular birds of prey	birdwatching	Mar-Oct
Parque Nacional de Ordesa y Monte Perdido (p380)	spectacular section of the Pyrenees, with chamois, raptors and varied vegetation	walking, rock climbing	mid-Jun–Jul & mid-Aug–Sep
Parques Nacional and Natural Sierra Nevada (p677)	mainland Spain's highest mountain range, with ibexes, 60 types of endemic plants and the beautiful Alpujarras valleys on its southern slopes	walking, rock climbing, mountain biking, skiing, horse riding	year-round, depending on activity
Parque Natural de Cabo de Gata-Níjar (p722)	sandy beaches, volcanic cliffs, flamingo colony and semidesert vegetation	swimming, birdwatching, walking, horse riding, diving, snorkelling	year-round
Parque Natural de las Sierras de Cazorla, Segura y Las Villas (p715)	abundant wildlife, 2300 plant species and beautiful mountain scenery	walking, driving, mountain biking, wildlife-watching, 4WD tours	Apr-Oct
Parque Natural de Somiedo (p491)	dramatic section of Cordillera Cantábrica	walking	Jul-Sep
Parc Natural de la Zona Volcànica de la Garrotxa (p328)	beautiful wooded region with 30 volcanic cones	walking	Apr-Oct
Parc Natural del Cadí-Moixeró	steep pre-Pyrenees range	rock climbing, walking	Jun-Sep
Parque Natural Sierra de Aracena y Picos de Aroche	rolling, lightly wooded hill country, stone villages	hiking	year-round
Parque Natural Sierra de Grazalema (p628)	lovely, green, mountainous area with rich bird life	walking, caving, canyoning, birdwatching, paragliding, rock climbing	Sep-Jun
Parque Natural Sierra de Gredos	beautiful mountain region, home to Spain's biggest ibex population	walking, rock climbing, mountain biking	Mar-May & Sep-Nov

Another possibility is to continue on beyond Santiago to the dramatic 'Lands End' outpost of Fisterra (Finisterre), an extra 88km, or Muxia (a further 30km), which is considered sacred by pilgrims as it was here that the Virgin appeared (in a stone boat) before Santiago.

Information

For more information about the Credencial (like a passport for the Camino, in which pilgrims accumulate stamps at various points along the route) and the Compostela certificate, visit the website of the cathedral's Centro Internacional de Acollida aos Peregrinos (http://peregrinossantiago.es).

If you're in Santiago, the new premises of the Museo das Peregrinacións e de Santiago (p511), almost alongside the cathedral, provide fascinating insights into the phenomenon of Santiago (man and city) down the centuries.

There are a number of excellent Camino websites:

Caminolinks (www.santiago-compostela.net/caminos) Complete, annotated guide to many Camino websites.

Mundicamino (www.mundicamino.com) Excellent, thorough descriptions and maps.

Camino de Santiago (www.caminodesantiago.me) Contains a huge selection of news groups, where you can get all of your questions answered.

When to Walk

People walk and cycle the Camino year-round. In May and June the wildflowers are glorious and the endless fields of cereals turn from green to toasty gold, making the landscapes a huge draw. July and August bring crowds of summer holidaymakers and scorching heat, especially through Castilla y León. September is less crowded and the weather is generally pleasant. From November to May there are fewer people on the road as the season can bring snow, rain and bitter winds. Santiago's feast day, 25 July, is a popular time to converge on the city.

National & Natural Parks

Much of Spain's most spectacular and ecologically important terrain – about 40,000 sq km or 8% of the entire country, if you

> ## VÍAS VERDES
> Spain has a growing network of Vías Verdes (literally 'Green Ways', but equivalent to the 'rail trail' system in other countries), an outstanding system of decommissioned railway tracks that have been converted into bicycle (or hiking) trails. They're usually terrific cycling routes with their gentle gradients, many pass through scenic countryside and there are many bikes for rent at various points along the routes. There are more than 2000km of these trails spread across (at last count) 102 routes all across the country, and they range from 1.2km to 84.4km in length. Check out www.viasverdes.com for more information.

include national hunting reserves – is under some kind of official protection. Nearly all of these areas are at least partly open to walkers, naturalists and other outdoor enthusiasts, but degrees of conservation and access vary.

The *parques nacionales* (national parks) are areas of exceptional importance and are the country's most strictly controlled protected areas. Spain has 15 national parks: 10 on the mainland, four in the Canary Islands and one in the Balearic Islands. The hundreds of other protected areas fall into at least 16 classifications and range in size from 100-sq-metre rocks off the Balearics to Andalucía's 2099-sq-km Parque Natural de Cazorla. For more information, visit www.magrama.gob.es/es/red-parques-nacionales/.

Canyoning

For exhilarating descents into steep-walled canyons by any means possible (but in the care of professional guides), look no further than Alquézar (p384) in Aragón, one of Europe's prime locations for this popular sport. Alquézar's numerous activities operators can also arrange rock climbing and rafting in the surrounding Sierra de Guara.

Canyoning is also possible in Cangas de Onís (p496) in the Picos de Europa

Cycling

Spain has a splendid variety of cycling possibilities, from gentle family rides to challenging two-week expeditions. If you avoid the cities (where cycling can be nerve-racking), Spain is also a cycle-friendly country, with drivers accustomed to sharing the roads with platoons of Lycra-clad cyclists. The excellent network of secondary roads, usually with comfortable shoulders to ride on, is ideal for road touring.

Cycling Destinations

Every Spanish region has both off-road (called BTT in Spanish, from *bici todo terreno*, meaning 'mountain bike') and touring trails and routes. Mountain bikers can head to just about any sierra (mountain range) and use the extensive *pistas forestales* (forestry tracks).

Galicia has set up several Centros BTT in rural areas with bikes and helmets for rent, and signposted routes in the local areas, including one in the very scenic Ribeira Sacra area. For more information, check www.turgalicia.es/centrosbtt.

One highly recommended and challenging off-road excursion takes you across the snowy Sierra Nevada. Classic long-haul touring routes include the Camino de Santiago, the Ruta de la Plata and the 600km Camino del Cid, which follows in the footsteps of Spain's epic hero, El Cid, from Burgos to Valencia. Guides in Spanish exist for all of these, available at bookshops and online.

Information

Bike Spain (p102) in Madrid is one of the better cycling tour operators.

Most of the cycling guidebooks in publication are in Spanish:

➡ *España en bici*, by Paco Tortosa and María del Mar Fornés. A good overview guide, but quite hard to find.

➡ *Cycle Touring in Spain: Eight Detailed Routes*, by Harry Dowdell. A helpful planning tool; also practical once you're in Spain.

➡ *The Trailrider Guide – Spain: Single Track Mountain Biking in Spain*, by Nathan James and Linsey Stroud. Another good resource.

Skiing & Snowboarding

For winter powder, Spain's skiers (including the royal family) head to the Pyrenees of Aragón and Catalonia. Outside the peak periods (the beginning of December, 20 December to 6 January, Carnaval and Semana Santa), Spain's top resorts are relatively quiet, cheap and warm in comparison with their counterparts in the Alps.

The season runs from December to April, though January and February are generally the best, most reliable times for snow. However, in recent years snowfall has been a bit unpredictable.

Skiing & Snowboarding Destinations

In Aragón, two popular resorts are Formigal (p375) and Candanchú (p375). Just above the town of Jaca, Candanchú has some 42km of runs with 51 pistes (as well as 35km of cross-country track). In Catalonia, Spain's first resort, La Molina (p336), is still going strong and is ideal for families and beginners. Considered by many to have the Pyrenees' best snow, the 72-piste resort of Baqueira-Beret (p343) boasts 30 modern lifts and 104km of downhill runs for all levels.

Spain's other major resort is Europe's southernmost: the Sierra Nevada (p677), outside Granada. The 80km of runs here are at their prime in March, and the slopes are particularly suited for families and novice-to-intermediate skiers.

Information

If you don't want to bring your own gear, Spanish ski resorts have equipment hire, as well as ski schools. Lift tickets cost between €35 and €55 per day for adults, and €25 and €35 for children; equipment hire costs from around €20 per day. If you're planning ahead, Spanish travel agencies frequently advertise affordable single- or multiday packages with lodging included.

Scuba Diving & Snorkelling

There's more to Spain than what you see on the surface – literally! Delve under the ocean waves anywhere along the country's almost 5000km of shoreline and a whole new Spain opens up, crowded with marine life and including features such as wrecks, sheer walls and long cavern swim-throughs. The numerous Mediterranean dive centres cater to an English-speaking market and offer single- and multiday trips, equipment rental and certification courses. Their Atlantic counterparts (in San Sebastián, Santander and A Coruña) deal mostly in Spanish, but if that's not an obstacle for you, the colder waters of the Atlantic will offer a completely different, and very rewarding, underwater experience.

A good starting point is the reefs along the Costa Brava, especially around the Illes Medes (p317) marine reserve, off L'Estartit (near Girona).

Southern Spain's best diving and snorkelling is around Cabo de Gata (p722) in Andalucía, followed by Cabo de Palos in Murcia. On the Costa del Sol (p692), operators launch to such places as La Herradura Wall, the *Motril* wreck and the Cavern of Cerro Gordo.

Paco Nadal's book *Buceo en España* provides information province by province, with descriptions of ocean floors, dive centres and equipment rental.

Surfing

The opportunity to get into the waves is a major attraction for beginners and experts alike along many of Spain's coastal regions. The north coast of Spain has, debatably, the best surf in mainland Europe.

The main surfing region is the north coast, where numerous high-class spots can be found, but Atlantic Andalucía gets decent winter swells. Despite the flow of vans loaded down with surfboards along the north coast in the summer, it's actually autumn through to spring that's the prime time for a decent swell, with October probably the best month overall. The variety of waves along the north coast is impressive: there are numerous open, swell-exposed beach breaks for the summer months, and some seriously heavy reefs and points that only really come to life during the colder, stormier months.

Surfing Destinations

The most famous wave in Spain is the legendary river-mouth left at Mundaka (p415). On a good day, there's no doubt that it's one of the best waves in the world. However, it's not very consistent, and when it's on, it's always very busy and very ugly.

Heading east, good waves can be found throughout the Basque Country. Going west, into neighbouring regions of Cantabria and Asturias, you'll also find a superb range of well-charted surf beaches, such as Rodiles in Asturias and Liencres in Cantabria; Playa de Somo in Santander is another good spot.

Galicia's beaches are an increasingly popular surfing destination. Even so, if you're looking for solitude, some isolated beaches along Galicia's beautiful Costa da Morte (p514) remain empty even in summer. In the Rías Altas, Praia de Pantín (p523), close to Cedeira, has a popular right-hander and in late August or early September it hosts the Pantín Classic, a qualifying event in the World Surf League. There are also some summer surf schools in the area.

In southwest Andalucía there are a number of powerful, winter beach breaks, particularly between Tarifa and Cádiz; El Palmar is the best, while weekdays off Conil de la Frontera (located northwest of Cabo de Trafalgar) can be sublimely lonely.

Information

In summer a shortie wetsuit (or, in the Basque Country, just board shorts) is sufficient along all coasts except Galicia, which picks up the icy Canaries current – you'll need a light full suit here.

Surf shops abound in the popular surfing areas and usually offer board and wetsuit hire. If you're a beginner joining a surf school, ask the instructor to explain the rules and to keep you away from the more experienced surfers.

There are a number of excellent surf guidebooks to Spain:

➡ Lonely Planet author Stuart Butler's English-language *Big Blue Surf Guide: Spain*.

➡ José Pellón's Spanish-language *Guía del Surf en España*.

➡ Low Pressure's superb *Stormrider Guide: Europe – the Continent*.

Windsurfing & Kitesurfing

The best sailing conditions are to be found around Tarifa (p700), which has such strong and consistent winds that it's said that the town's once-high suicide rate was due to the wind turning people mad. Whether or not this is true, one thing is without doubt: Tarifa's 10km of white, sandy beaches and perfect year-round conditions have made this small town the windsurfing capital of Europe. The town is crammed with windsurfing and kite-surfing shops, windsurfing schools and a huge contingent of passing surfers. However, the same wind that attracts so many devotees also makes it a less than ideal place to learn the art.

If you can't make it as far south as Tarifa, then the lesser-known Empuriabrava in Catalonia also has great conditions, especially from March to July. If you're looking for waves, try Spain's northwest coast, where Galicia can have fantastic conditions.

Information

An excellent guidebook to windsurfing and kitesurfing spots across Spain and the rest of Europe is Stoked Publications' *The Kite and Windsurfing Guide: Europe*.

The Spanish-language website www.windsurfesp.com gives very thorough descriptions of spots, conditions and schools all over Spain.

Kayaking, Canoeing & Rafting

Opportunities abound in Spain for taking off in search of white-water fun along its 1800 rivers and streams. As most rivers are dammed for electric power at some point along their flow, there are many reservoirs with excellent low-level kayaking and canoeing, where you can also hire equipment.

In general, May and June are best for kayaking, rafting, canoeing and hydrospeeding (water tobogganing). Top white-water rivers include Catalonia's turbulent Noguera Pallaresa, Aragón's Gállego

---

HANG-GLIDING & PARAGLIDING

If you want to take to the skies either *ala delta* (hang-gliding) or *parapente* (paragliding), there are a number of specialised clubs and adventure-tour companies here. The Real Federación Aeronáutica España (www.rfae.es) gives information on recognised schools and lists clubs and events.

---

and Ésera, Cantabria's Carasa and Galicia's Miño.

Zamora Natural (p173), which is known for its wolf-watching excursions, also does kayaking trips to the spectacular Parque Natural Arribes del Duero (north of Ciudad Rodrigo) and rafting at the Parque Natural Lago de Sanabria (northeast of Puebla de Sanabria). But the real highlight of its calendar is its eight- or nine-day kayaking descent of the Río Duero (or Río Douro on the Portuguese side of the border), from close to Zamora down to Oporto in Portugal, on the shores of the Atlantic. You camp by the river bank along the way and departures can take place between June and October, depending on demand. It costs a bargain €680 per person. It has a separate website dedicated to the expedition: www.douroexpediciones.com.

For fun and competition, the crazy 22km, en masse Descenso Internacional del Sella (p484) canoe race is a blast, running from Arriondas in Asturias to coastal Ribadesella. It's held on the first weekend in August.

Information

Patrick Santal's *White Water Pyrenees* thoroughly covers 85 rivers in France and Spain for kayakers, canoeists and rafters.

Stand-Up Paddling

Stand-up paddling (SUP) is finally catching on in Spain. You'll find it happening anywhere there are water sports around the Spanish coast, but it's a particular trend in Santander, Cantabria, where most surf schools now run SUP outings, courses and there's even SUP yoga not far away...

Plan Your Trip

Travel with Children

Spain is a family-friendly destination with excellent transport and accommodation infrastructure, food to satisfy even the fussiest of eaters, and an extraordinary range of attractions that appeal to both adults and children. Visiting as a family does require some careful planning, but no more than for visiting any other European country.

Children's Highlights

Spain has a surfeit of castles, horse shows, fiestas and ferias, interactive museums, flamenco shows and even the Semana Santa (Holy Week) processions, to name just a few highlights for kids.

Beaches

Spain's beaches, especially those along the Mediterranean coast, are custom-made for children: many (particularly along the Costa Brava) are sheltered from the open ocean by protective coves, while most others are characterised by waveless waters that quietly lap the shore. Yes, some can get a little overcrowded in the height of summer, but there are still plenty of tranquil stretches of sand if you choose carefully.

➡ **Playa de la Concha, San Sebastián** (p417) This is Spain's most easily accessible city beach.

➡ **Aiguablava & Fornells** (p310) Sheltered, beautiful Costa Brava coves.

➡ **Zahara de los Atunes** (p307) Cádiz-province beach with pristine sand.

Best Regions for Kids

Mediterranean Spain

Spain's coastline may be a summer-holiday cliché, but it's a fabulous place for a family holiday. From Catalonia in the north to Andalucía in the south, most beaches have gentle waters and numerous child-friendly attractions and activities (from water parks to water sports for older kids).

Barcelona

Theme parks, a wax museum, a chocolate museum, all manner of other museums with interactive exhibits, beaches, gardens... Barcelona is one of Spain's most child-friendly cities – even its architecture seems to have sprung from a child's imagination.

Inland Spain

Spain's interior may not be the first place you think of for a family holiday, but its concentrations of castles, tiny villages and fascinating, easily negotiated cities make it worth considering.

MAICA/GETTY IMAGES ©

Children at Park Güell (p260)

Architecture of the Imagination

Many museums have started to incorporate an interactive element into what were once staid and static exhibits. Numerous major sights (such as the Alhambra and most art galleries) also have guidebooks aimed specifically at children. And then there's live flamenco, something that every child should see once in their lives.

➡ **Alcázar, Segovia** (p159) The inspiration for Sleeping Beauty's castle.

➡ **Park Güell** (p260) and **Casa Batlló** (p256) Gaudí's weird-and-wonderful Barcelona creations.

➡ **Castillo de Loarre, Aragón** (p389) The stereotypically turreted castle.

➡ **Casas Colgadas, Cuenca** (p223) Houses that hang out over the cliff.

➡ **Estadio Santiago Bernabéu** (p124) and **Camp Nou** (p292) Football, football, football...

➡ **Museo Guggenheim Bilbao** (p401) Watch them gaze in wonder.

Theme Parks & Horse Shows

Spain has seen an explosion of Disneyfied theme parks in recent years. Parks range from places that re-create the era of the dinosaurs or the Wild West to more traditional parks with rides and animals.

➡ **Dinópolis, Teruel** (p394) This is a cross between Jurassic Park and a funfair.

➡ **PortAventura** (p357) Fine amusement park close to Tarragona.

➡ **Terra Mítica, Benidorm** (p757) Where the spirit of Disneyland meets the Med.

➡ **Oasys Mini Hollywood, Almería** (p721) Wild West movie sets in the deserts.

➡ **Zoo Aquarium de Madrid** (p95) Probably Spain's best zoo.

➡ **Parc d'Atraccions, Barcelona** (p265) Great rides and a puppet museum.

➡ **Real Escuela Andaluza del Arte Ecuestre** (p623) Andalucían horse shows in all their finery.

Planning

For general advice on travel with young ones, see Lonely Planet's *Travel with Children* or visit www.travelwithyourkids.com and www.familytravelnetwork.com.

When to Go

If you're heading for the beach, summer (especially July and August) is the obvious choice – but it's also when Spaniards undertake a mass pilgrimage to the coast, so book well ahead. It's also a good time to travel to the mountains (the Pyrenees, Sierra Nevada). The interior can be unbearably hot during the summer months, however – Seville and Córdoba regularly experience daytime temperatures of almost 50ºC.

Our favourite time for visiting Spain is in spring and autumn, particularly May, June, September and October. In all but the latter month, you might be lucky and get weather warm enough for the beach, but temperatures in these months are generally mild and the weather often fine.

Winter can be bitterly cold in much of Spain – fine if you come prepared and even better if you're heading for the snow.

What to Bring

Although you might want to bring a small supply of items that you're used to (this is particularly true for baby products) in case of emergency (or a Sunday when most pharmacies and supermarkets are closed), Spain is likely to have everything you need.

➡ Baby formula in powder or liquid form, as well as sterilising solutions such as Milton, can be bought at *farmacias* (pharmacies).

➡ Disposable *panales* (nappies, or diapers) are widely available at supermarkets and *farmacias*.

➡ Fresh cow's milk is sold in cartons and plastic bottles in supermarkets in big cities, but can be hard to find in small towns, where UHT is often the only option.

Accommodation

Most hotels (but rarely budget establishments) have cots for small children, although most only have a handful, so reserve one when booking your room. If you're asking for a cot, it can be a good idea to ask for a larger room as many Spanish hotel or *hostal* (budget hotel) rooms can be on the small side, making for very cramped conditions. Cots sometimes cost extra, while other hotels offer them for free.

In top-end hotels you can sometimes arrange for child care, and in some places child-minding agencies cater to temporary visitors. Some top-end hotels – particularly resorts – but also some *paradores* (luxurious state-owned hotels) – have play areas or children's playgrounds, and many also have swimming pools.

Eating Out with Children

Food and children are two of the great loves for Spaniards, and Spanish fare is rarely spicy so kids tend to like it.

Children are usually welcome, whether in a sit-down restaurant or in a chaotically busy bar. Indeed, it's rare that you'll be made to feel uncomfortable as your children run amok, though the more formal the place, the more uncomfortable you're likely to feel. In summer the abundance of outdoor terraces with tables is ideal for families; take care, though, as it can be easy to lose sight of wandering kids amid the scrum of people.

You cannot rely on restaurants having *tronas* (high chairs), although many do these days. Those that do, however, rarely have more than one (a handful at most), so make the request when making your reservation or as soon as you arrive.

Very few restaurants (or other public facilities) have nappy-changing facilities.

A small but growing number of restaurants offer a *menú infantil* (children's menu), which usually includes a main course (hamburger, chicken nuggets, pasta and the like), a drink and an ice cream or milkshake for dessert.

One challenge can be adapting to Spanish eating hours – when kids get hungry between meals it's sometimes possible to zip into the nearest *tasca* (tapas bar) and get them a snack, and there are also sweet shops scattered around most towns. That said, we recommend carrying emergency supplies from a supermarket for those times when there's simply nothing open.

Transport

Spain's transport infrastructure is world-class, and high-speed AVE trains render irrelevant the distances between many major cities. Apart from anything else, most kids love the idea that they're travelling at nearly 300km/h.

Discounts are available for children (usually under 12) on public transport. Those under four generally go free.

You can hire car seats (usually for an additional cost) for infants and children from most car-hire firms, but you should always book them in advance. This is especially true during busy travel periods, such as Spanish school holidays, Navidad (Christmas) and Semana Santa.

It's extremely rare that taxis have child seats – unless you're carrying a portable version from home, you're expected to sit the child on your lap, with the seatbelt around you both.

Regions at a Glance

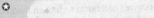

Madrid

Galleries
Nightlife
Food

Art's Golden Mile

Madrid is one of the world's premier cities for public art, with the Museo del Prado, the Centro de Arte Reina Sofía and the Museo Thyssen-Bornemisza all within easy walking distance of each other. And they're just the start.

Killing the Night

Nightclubs that don't really get busy until 3am. Sophisticated cocktail bars where you mingle with A-list celebrities while sipping your mojito. A dynamic live-music scene that begins with flamenco before moving on to jazz and every other genre imaginable.

Tapas & Traditional Food

Traditional Madrid food is nothing to get excited about, but the world's oldest restaurant and the best in Spanish cooking make for memorable eating experiences. The neighbourhood of La Latina has one of the country's finest concentrations of tapas bars.

p70

Castilla y León

Medieval Towns
Villages
Food

City as Art

Rich in history, cathedrals and other grand public monuments, the splendid towns of old Castile can be difficult to choose between. But if we have to choose, it would be plateresque Salamanca, fairy-tale Segovia and gorgeous León.

Quiet Pueblos

The villages of Castilla y León feel like Spain before mass tourism and the modern world arrived on Iberian shores, from the Sierra de Francia in the far southwest to medieval hamlets such as Pedraza de la Sierra, Covarrubias, Puebla de Sanabria and Calatañazor.

Hearty Inland Fare

Roasted and grilled meats are specialities in the Spanish interior, so much so that Spaniards travel here from all over the country for a winter meal. *Jamón* (cured ham) and other cured meats from Guijuelo are another regional passion.

p141

Toledo & Castilla-La Mancha

History
Literature
Villages & Castles

City of Three Faiths

In the Middle Ages, Toledo was one of the most cosmopolitan cities in Spain, as shown by some fine landmarks from that era – a poignant mosque, fine Jewish sites and a cathedral of real power adorned with works by El Greco, Zurbarán and Velázquez.

Tilting at Windmills

The Don Quixote trail through Castilla-La Mancha offers the rare opportunity to follow the terrain trod by one of literature's most eccentric figures. Windmills and sweeping plains evoke Cervantes' novel to such an extent that you can almost hear Sancho Panza's patter.

Beautiful Villages

Amid the often-empty horizons of La Mancha, pretty villages can seem like oases. Almagro and Sigüenza are our favourites, while the castles close to Toledo – this was a long-time frontier between Moorish and Christian Spain – are simply magnificent.

p203

Barcelona

Architecture
Food
Art & History

Modernista Masterpieces

From Gaudí's unfinished masterpiece – the wondrous Sagrada Família – to Domènech i Montaner's celestial Palau de la Música Catalana, Catalan visionaries have made Barcelona one of Europe's great Modernista centres, a showcase for the imaginative, surreal and captivating.

Culinary Gems

Barcelona's artistry doesn't end at the drawing board. Feasting on seafood overlooking the Mediterranean, munching on tapas at the magnificent Boqueria market, indulging in celebrated Michelin-starred restaurants – it's all part of the Barcelona experience.

Artistry of the Past

A vibrant settlement of ancient Rome, Barcelona has over 2000 years of history hidden in its lanes. The Gothic centre has 14th-century churches and medieval mansions that hold more recent treasures, from a Picasso collection to pre-Columbian masterpieces.

p232

Catalonia

Food
Beaches
Hiking

The Catalan Kitchen

Vying with the Basque Country for Spain's highest per-capita ratio of celebrity chefs, Catalonia is something of a pilgrimage for gastronomes. Here, even in the smallest family establishments, cooks fuse ingredients from land and sea, always keeping faith with rich culinary traditions even as they head off in innovative new directions.

The Catalan Coast

The picturesque coastlines known as the Costa Brava and Costa Daurada are studded with pretty-as-a-postcard villages and beaches that are generally less crowded than those further south. And not far away, signposts to Salvador Dalí and the Romans make for fine day trips.

Spain's High Country

Northern Catalonia means the Pyrenees, where shapely peaks and quiet valleys offer some of the best hiking anywhere in the country.

p301

Aragón

Mountains
Villages
History

Head for the Hills

Perhaps the prettiest corner of the Pyrenees, northern Aragón combines the drama of steepling summits with the quiet pleasures of deep valleys and endless hiking trails. The Parque Nacional de Ordesa y Monte Perdido ranks among Spain's most picturesque national parks.

Stone Villages

Aragón has numerous finalists in the competition for Spain's most beautiful village, among them Aínsa, Sos del Rey Católico and Albarracín. Many sit in the Pyrenean foothills against a backdrop of snowcapped mountains.

Romans, Moors & Christians

Centred on one of Spain's most important historical kingdoms, Aragón is strewn with landmarks from the great civilisations of ancient and medieval times. Zaragoza in particular spans the millenniums with grace and fervour, and Teruel is an often-missed Mudéjar jewel.

p362

Bilbao, the Basque Country & La Rioja

Food
Wine
Villages

Spain's Culinary Capital

To understand the buzz surrounding Spanish food, head for San Sebastián, which is at once *pintxos* (Basque tapas) heaven and home to outrageously talented chefs. Challenging San Sebastián are Logroño, Vitoria and Pamplona.

The Finest Drop

La Rioja is to wine what the Basque Country is to food. Wine museums, wine tastings and vineyards stretching to the horizon make this Spain's most accessible wine region. And, of course, it accompanies every meal here.

Villages

There are stunning villages to be found throughout the Basque Country and La Rioja, but those in the Pyrenean foothills and high valleys of Navarra are a match for anything the rest of Spain has to offer.

p399

Cantabria & Asturias

Coastal Scenery
Mountains
Food

The Scenic Coast

Wild rocky walls encircle a beautiful sandy cove at Playa del Silencio, just one of hundreds of beaches tucked away along the rugged, emerald-green Asturian coastline, behind which rise gorgeous villages and marvellous mountainscapes.

Picos de Europa

The jagged Picos de Europa have some of the most stunning hiking country in Spain. Vertiginous precipices stretch down into the dramatic Garganta del Cares gorge, while the El Naranjo de Bulnes peak beckons from beyond high mountain passes.

Cheese & Cider

Knocking back cider is Asturias' favourite pastime, particularly along Oviedo's *el bulevar de la sidra,* while the tangy Cabrales cheese from the foothills of the Picos de Europa is one of Spain's best.

p457

Santiago de Compostela & Galicia

Coastal Scenery
Food
History

The Wildest Coast

Galicia's windswept coast is one of Europe's most dramatic and stunningly beautiful. On the Rías Altas, cliffs plunge from enormous heights into roiling Atlantic waters, interspersed with picturesque fishing villages and isolated sandy beaches.

Fruits of the Sea

Galicia has some of the world's best seafood, and fine meat from its rich pastures too. Head to Santiago de Compostela's bustling market, the Mercado de Abastos, for the best of both – and the chance to enjoy them at restaurants on the spot.

A Sacred Past

In few places are long-gone centuries as alive as they are in Santiago de Compostela. Its magnificent cathedral, churches, streets and plazas represent 1300 uninterrupted years as the goal of that great pilgrimage route, the Camino de Santiago.

p505

Extremadura

Medieval Towns
Roman Ruins
Food

Medieval Film Sets

Spain may be replete with wonderfully preserved old towns that date back to the Middle Ages, but Cáceres and Trujillo are up there with the best. Meandering along their cobblestoned lanes is a journey back into an epic past.

Roman Mérida

Spain's most beautiful Roman theatre, its longest Roman-era bridge, a breathtaking museum and a slew of other ruined glories – welcome to Emerita Augusta, now known as Mérida and Spain's finest Roman site. The fabulous bridge at Alcántara also merits a visit.

Ham & Cheese

Some of Spain's finest *jamón* comes from Extremadura, most notably from around Monesterio, which has Spain's best *jamón* museum. The Torta del Casar cheese from just north of Cáceres is another culinary star.

p548

Seville & Andalucía's Hill Towns

Music
History
Food & Wine

Cradle of Flamenco

The towns and cities of western Andalucía pretty much invented modern flamenco. Look no further than the *bulerías* of Jerez, the *alegrías* of Cádiz and the *soleares* of Seville – all of them performed with passion in local *tablaos* (choreographed flamenco shows) and *peñas* (flamenco clubs).

White Towns

They're all here, the famous white towns, with their hilltop castles, geranium flower boxes and somnolent churches. Arcos, Jimena, Grazalema, Vejer...the ancient sentinels on a once-volatile frontier that divided two great civilisations.

Fish & Sherry

Where the Atlantic meets the Mediterranean you're bound to find good fish, which the Andalucians traditionally deep-fry in olive oil to create *pescaíto frito*. Then there's the sherry made from grapes that grow near the coast – a perfect pairing.

p574

Granada & South Coast Andalucía

Architecture
Beaches
Walks

Glorious Granada

A celebrated Nasrid palace-fortress, a hilltop Moorish quarter, opulent *cármenes* (large mansions with walled gardens), and a baroque-Renaissance cathedral – the city of Granada is a magnificent collection of just about every architectural style known to European building.

Southern Beaches

The south coast's beaches are an industry, bagging more tourist euros than the rest of the region put together. Choose according to your budget and hipster-rating between Estepona, Marbella, Torremolinos, Málaga, Nerja and Almuñécar.

Wild Areas

Walk the dry, craggy coastline of Cabo de Gata, hitch onto the GR7 long-distance footpath in Las Alpujarras or get lost looking for wildlife on the trails in the highlands east of Cazorla. Andalucía has its untamed side, if you know where to look.

p653

Valencia & Murcia

Fiestas
Food
Beaches

Bulls, Fire & Knights in Armour

The biggest and noisiest party is Valencia's Las Fallas in March. But almost every *pueblo* (village) has its fiesta, usually with fireworks and often with bulls. Lorca's Semana Santa (Holy Week) festivities rival those of Andalucía.

Simmering Rice

Paella first simmered over an open fire in Valencia. Rice dishes are everywhere, supplemented by fish and seafood from the Mediterranean and the freshest of vegetables grown along the fertile coastal strip down into Murcia.

Strands & Rocky Coves

From small bays to vast beaches stretching over kilometres, from tiny rocky coves to the sandy sweeps of Denia, Benidorm and Murcia's Costa Cálida (Hot Coast), there's always room to stretch out your towel.

p727

On the Road

Madrid

POP 48.15 MILLION

Best Places to Eat

➡ Restaurante Sobrino De Botín (p110)

➡ DiverXo (p116)

➡ Platea (p113)

➡ Bazaar (p114)

➡ Mercado de San Miguel (p109)

Best Places to Sleep

➡ Hostal Central Palace Madrid (p103)

➡ Posada del León de Oro (p106)

➡ Hotel Silken Puerta América (p109)

➡ Praktik Metropol (p107)

➡ Hotel Orfila (p109)

Why Go?

Madrid is a miracle of human energy and peculiarly Spanish passions, a beguiling place with a simple message: this city knows how to live. It's true Madrid doesn't have the immediate cachet of Paris, the monumental history of Rome or the reputation for cool of that other city up the road. But it's a city whose contradictory impulses are legion, the perfect expression of Europe's most passionate country writ large. This city has transformed itself into one of Spain's premier style centres and its calling cards are many: astonishing art galleries, relentless nightlife, an exceptional live-music scene, a feast of fine restaurants and tapas bars, and a population that's mastered the art of the good life. It's not that other cities don't have these things: it's just that Madrid has all of them in bucketloads.

When to Go
Madrid

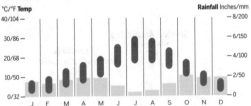

Jan–Feb Winter can be cold but glorious in Madrid when the weather's fine.

Mar–Apr Warmer spring weather brings *madrileños* (residents of Madrid) out into the city's *terrazas*.

Sep Madrid shakes off its summer torpor with (usually) lovely autumn weather.

History

When Iberia's Christians began the Reconquista (c 722) – the centuries-long campaign by Christian forces to reclaim the peninsula – the Muslims of Al-Andalus constructed a chain of fortified positions through the heart of Iberia. One of these was built by Mohammed I, emir of Córdoba, in 854, on the site of what would become Madrid. The name they gave to the new settlement was Mayrit (or Magerit), which comes from the Arabic word *majira*, meaning 'water channel'.

A Worthy Capital?

Madrid's strategic location in the centre of the peninsula saw the city change hands repeatedly, but it was not until 1309 that the travelling Cortes (royal court and parliament) sat in Madrid for the first time. Despite the growing royal attention, medieval Madrid remained dirt poor and small-scale: 'In Madrid there is nothing except what you bring with you,' observed one 15th-century writer. It simply bore no comparison with other major Spanish, let alone European, cities.

By the time Felipe II ascended the Spanish throne in 1556, Madrid was surrounded by walls that boasted 130 towers and six stone gates, but these fortifications were largely built of mud and designed more to impress than provide any meaningful defence of the city. Madrid was nonetheless chosen by Felipe II as the capital of Spain in 1561.

Madrid took centuries to grow into its new role and despite a handful of elegant churches, the imposing Alcázar and a smattering of noble residences, the city consisted of, for the most part, precarious white-washed houses. The monumental Paseo del Prado, which now provides Madrid with so much of its grandeur, was a small creek.

During the 17th century, Spain's golden age, Madrid began to take on the aspect of a capital and was home to 175,000 people, making it the fifth-largest city in Europe (after London, Paris, Constantinople and Naples).

Carlos III (r 1759–88) gave Madrid and Spain a period of comparatively commonsense government. After he cleaned up the city, completed the Palacio Real, inaugurated the Real Jardín Botánico and carried out numerous other public works, he became known as the best 'mayor' Madrid had ever had.

Madrileños (residents of Madrid) didn't take kindly to Napoleon's invasion and subsequent occupation of Spain in 1805 and, on 2 May 1808, they attacked French troops around the Palacio Real and what is now Plaza del Dos de Mayo. The ill-fated rebellion was quickly put down by Murat, Napoleon's brother-in-law and the most powerful of his military leaders.

Wars, Franco & Terrorism

Turmoil continued to stalk the Spanish capital. The upheaval of the 19th-century Carlist Wars was followed by a two-and-a-half-year siege of Madrid by Franco's Nationalist forces from 1936 to 1939, during which the city was shelled regularly from Casa de Campo and Gran Vía became known as 'Howitzer Alley'.

After Franco's death in 1975 and the country's subsequent transition to democracy, Madrid became an icon for the new Spain as the city's young people unleashed a flood of pent-up energy. This took its most colourful form in the years of *la movida*, the endless party that swept up the city in a frenzy of creativity and open-minded freedom that has in some ways yet to abate.

On 11 March 2004, just three days before the country was due to vote in national elections, Madrid was rocked by 10 bombs on four rush-hour commuter trains heading into the capital's Atocha station. The bombs had been planted by terrorists with links to al-Qaeda, reportedly because of Spain's then support for the American-led war in Iraq. When the dust cleared, 191 people had died and 1755 were wounded, many seriously. Madrid was in shock and, for 24 hours at least, this most clamorous of cities fell silent. Then, 36 hours after the attacks, more than three million *madrileños* streamed onto the streets to protest against the bombings, making it the largest demonstration in the city's history. Although deeply traumatised, Madrid's mass act of defiance and pride began the process of healing. Visit Madrid today and you'll find a city that has resolutely returned to normal.

In the years since, Madrid has come agonisingly close in the race to host the Summer Olympics, coming third behind London and Paris in the race for 2012, second behind Rio for 2016 before falling into the also-rans for the 2020 games. And, of course, Madrid was the scene of one of the

Madrid Highlights

❶ Museo del Prado
(p87) Watching the masterpieces of Velázquez and Goya leap off the canvas at the world-famous gallery.

❷ El Rastro
(p80) Searching for treasure in this massive Sunday flea market, then joining the crowds in Parque del Buen Retiro.

❸ Plaza de Santa Ana (p83) Soaking up the buzz with a *caña* (small beer) or glass of Spanish wine on this gorgeous square.

❹ La Latina (p110) Going on a tapas crawl in the medieval *barrio* (district) of La Latina.

❺ Chocolatería de San Ginés (p116) Ordering *chocolate con churros* (deep fried doughnut strips dipped in hot chocolate) close to dawn.

❻ Estadio Santiago Bernabéu (p124) Making a sporting pilgrimage to see the stars of Real Madrid play.

❼ Teatro Joy Eslava (p117) Dancing the night away and sampling the city's world-famous nightlife.

❽ Café de la Iberia (p138) Feasting on roast lamb in utterly charming Chinchón.

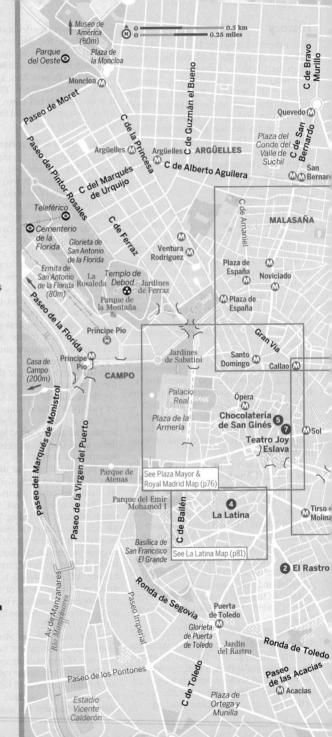

biggest celebrations in modern Spanish history when the Spanish World Cup–winning football team returned home in July 2010. These celebrations were almost matched two years later when Spain won the 2012 European Football Championships, again bringing much-needed cheer to a city affected deeply by Spain's severe economic downturn.

⊙ Sights

Madrid has three of the finest art galleries in the world: if ever there existed a golden mile of fine art, it would have to be the combined charms of the Museo del Prado, the Centro de Arte Reina Sofía and the Museo Thyssen-Bornemisza. Beyond the museums' walls, the combination of stately architecture and feel-good living is nowhere easier to access than in the beautiful plazas, where *terrazas* (cafes with outdoor tables) provide a front-row seat for Madrid's fine cityscape and endlessly energetic street life. Throw in some outstanding city parks (the Parque del Buen Retiro, in particular) and areas like Chueca, Malasaña and Salamanca, which each have their own identity, and you'll wonder why you decided to spend so little time here.

MADRID IN...

One Day
Begin in the **Plaza Mayor** (p75) with its architectural beauty, fine *terrazas* (terrazas) and endlessly fascinating passing Madrid parade. Wander down Calle Mayor, passing the delightful **Plaza de la Villa** (p77) en route, and head for the **Palacio Real** (p75). By then you'll be ready for a coffee (or something stronger) and there's no finer place to rest than in the **Plaza de Oriente** (p75). Double back up towards the **Plaza de la Puerta del Sol** (p83) then lose yourself in the Huertas area around **Plaza de Santa Ana** (p83), the ideal place for a long, liquid lunch. Stroll down the hill to the incomparable **Museo del Prado** (p87), one of Europe's best art galleries. In anticipation of a long night ahead, catch your breath in the **Parque del Buen Retiro** (p94). As the sun nears the horizon, climb to Madrid's best views at the **Mirador de Madrid** (p95) or **Círculo de Bellas Artes** (p87), before heading up along **Gran Vía** (p86) and into Chueca for Madrid's famously noisy and eclectic nightlife.

Three Days
Three days is a minimum for getting a real taste of Madrid. Spend a morning each on days two and three at **Centro de Arte Reina Sofía** (p92) and **Museo Thyssen-Bornemisza** (p93). Otherwise, pause in **Plaza de la Cibeles** (p95) to admire some of the best architecture in Madrid as you work your way north to the **Gran Café de Gijón** (p120), one of Madrid's grand old cafes. A quick metro ride across town takes you to the astonishing Goya frescoes in the **Ermita de San Antonio de la Florida** (p100). While you're in the area, consider a chicken-and-cider meal at **Casa Mingo** (p115). On another day, head for La Latina and the great restaurants and tapas bars along **Calle de la Cava Baja** (p112), or some cod tapas at **Casa Revuelta** (p112). If it's a Sunday, precede these outings with a wander through **El Rastro** (p80), one of the best flea markets in Europe.

One Week
If you're in town for a week, begin day four with some shopping. **Calle de Serrano** has just about everything for the designer-conscious, while **Calle de Fuencarral** (casual streetwear) or **Calle de Augusto Figueroa** (shoes) could also occupy an hour or two. Check out the bullring at **Plaza de Toros** (p97), and **Estadio Santiago Bernabéu** (p124), home to Real Madrid. Other possibilities that will deepen your Madrid experience include wandering through medieval and multicultural **Lavapiés** (p80) or seeing a live **flamenco performance** (p121). Day trips could include **Toledo** (p205) and **Segovia** (p158). Of the numerous royal residences in the Madrid vicinity, the most impressive is **San Lorenzo de El Escorial** (p136), but **Chinchón** (p138) is an enchanted alternative with ramshackle village charm written all over its colonnaded Plaza Mayor.

◉ Plaza Mayor & Royal Madrid

Downtown Madrid is where the story of Madrid began. As the seat of royal power, this is where the splendour of imperial Spain was at its most ostentatious and where Spain's overarching Catholicism was at its most devout – think expansive palaces, elaborate private mansions, ancient churches and imposing convents amid the clamour of modern Madrid.

★ Plaza Mayor   SQUARE

(Map p76; Ⓜ Sol) Madrid's grand central square, a rare but expansive opening in the tightly packed streets of central Madrid, is one of the prettiest open spaces in Spain, a winning combination of imposing architecture, picaresque historical tales and vibrant street life coursing across its cobblestones. At once beautiful in its own right and a reference point for so many Madrid days, it also hosts the city's main tourist office, a Christmas market in December and arches leading to laneways leading out into the labyrinth.

Ah, the history the plaza has seen! Designed in 1619 by Juan Gómez de Mora and built in typical Herrerian style, of which the slate spires are the most obvious expression, its first public ceremony was suitably auspicious – the beatification of San Isidro Labrador (St Isidro the Farm Labourer), Madrid's patron saint. Thereafter it was as if all that was controversial about Spain took place in this square. Bullfights, often in celebration of royal weddings or births, with royalty watching on from the balconies and up to 50,000 people crammed into the plaza, were a recurring theme until 1878. Far more notorious were the *autos-da-fé* (the ritual condemnations of heretics during the Spanish Inquisition), followed by executions – burnings at the stake and deaths by garrotte on the north side of the square, hangings to the south. These continued until 1790 when a fire largely destroyed the square, which was subsequently reproduced under the supervision of Juan de Villanueva, who lent his name to the building that now houses the Museo del Prado (p87). These days, the plaza is an epicentre of Madrid life.

The grandeur of the plaza is due in large part to the warm colours of the uniformly ochre apartments, with 237 wrought-iron balconies offset by the exquisite frescoes of the 17th-century Real Casa de la Panadería (Royal Bakery). The present frescoes date to just 1992 and are the work of artist Carlos Franco, who chose images from the signs of the zodiac and gods (eg Cybele) to provide a stunning backdrop for the plaza. The frescoes were inaugurated to coincide with Madrid's 1992 spell as European Capital of Culture.

★ Palacio Real   PALACE

(Map p76; ☎ 91 454 88 00; www.patrimonio nacional.es; Calle de Bailén; adult/concession €11/6, guide/audioguide €4/4, EU citizens free last two hours Mon-Thu; ⊙ 10am-8pm Apr-Sep, 10am-6pm Oct-Mar; Ⓜ Ópera) Spain's lavish Palacio Real is a jewel box of a palace, although it's used only occasionally for royal ceremonies; the royal family moved to the modest Palacio de la Zarzuela years ago.

When the *alcázar* burned down on Christmas Day 1734, Felipe V, the first of the Bourbon kings, decided to build a palace that would dwarf all its European counterparts. Felipe died before the palace was finished, which is perhaps why the Italianate baroque colossus has a mere 2800 rooms, just one-quarter of the original plan.

The official tour (self-guided tours are also possible and follow the same route) leads through 50 of the palace rooms, which hold a good selection of Goyas, 215 absurdly ornate clocks, and five Stradivarius violins still used for concerts and balls. The main stairway is a grand statement of imperial power, leading to the Halberdiers' rooms and to the sumptuous Salón del Trono (Throne Room), with its crimson-velvet wall coverings and Tiepolo ceiling. Shortly after, you reach the Salón de Gasparini, with its exquisite stucco ceiling and walls resplendent with embroidered silks.

Outside the main palace, visit the Farmacia Real (Royal Pharmacy) at the southern end of the patio known as the Plaza de la Armería (or Plaza de Armas). Westwards across the plaza is the Armería Real (Royal Armoury), a shiny collection of weapons and armour, mostly dating from the 16th and 17th centuries.

Plaza de Oriente   SQUARE

(Map p76; Plaza de Oriente; Ⓜ Ópera) A royal palace that once had aspirations to be the Spanish Versailles. Sophisticated cafes watched over by apartments that cost the equivalent of a royal salary. The Teatro Real (p122), Madrid's opera house and one of Spain's temples to high culture. Some of the

MADRID SIGHTS

Plaza Mayor & Royal Madrid

Templo de Debod (400m);
Teleférico (950m)

45

C de Isabel la Católica

C del Fomento

C de Leganitos

Cuesta de San Vicente

Jardines
de Sabatini

23

C de Bailén

Plaza de
la Marina
Española

C de Torija

42

37

C de la Bola

C Guillermo
Rolland

C de la Encarnación

34

Cuesta de Santo Domingo

Casa de Campo (900m);
Ermita de San Antonio
de la Florida (1km)

8

19

Plaza de la
Encarnación

C de San Quintín

26

C de Campomanes

Campo
del
Moro

Jardines
Cabo Naval

C Pavia

C de Arrieta

28

Palacio
Real

16 17

C de Felipe V

46

Plaza de
Isabel II

Ópera

3

C de Carlos III

24

36

Plaza
de la
Armería

Jardines de
Lepanto

C Lepanto

C de Vergara

C de la Amnistía

C de Escalinata

Palacio Real

1

C de Requena

C de Noblejas

Plaza de
Ramales

Plaza
Santiago

C Lazo

35

C del Factor

C de
San Nicolás

C de la Cruzada

50

21

C de Santiago

7

Plaza del
Biombo

C de Biombo

12

C del
Duque

20

32

5   6

Plaza
del Conde
de Miranda

14

15

C del Sacramento

Travesía del Sacramento

4

C del Cordón

51

44

C de la Pasa

C de Bailén

13

C del Rollo

C del Codo

C de San Justo

Parque
del Emir
Mohamed I

18

Plaza
de la Cruz
Verde

C de la Villa

C Conde

Plaza
del
Cordón

finest sunset views in Madrid... Welcome to Plaza de Oriente, a living, breathing monument to imperial Madrid.

At the centre of the plaza, which the palace overlooks, is an equestrian **statue of Felipe IV** (Map p76). Designed by Velázquez, it's the perfect place to take it all in, with marvellous views wherever you look. If you're wondering how a heavy bronze statue of a rider and his horse rearing up can actually maintain that stance, the answer is simple: the hind legs are sol-

The adjacent Jardines Cabo Naval, a great place to watch the sunset, adds to the sense of a sophisticated oasis of green in the heart of Madrid.

Campo del Moro
GARDENS

(Map p76; 91 454 88 00; www.patrimonio nacional.es; Paseo de la Virgen del Puerto; 10am-8pm Apr-Sep, 10am-6pm Oct-Mar; Príncipe Pío) These gardens beneath the Palacio Real were designed to mimic the gardens surrounding the palace at Versailles; nowhere is this more in evidence than along the east–west Pradera, a lush lawn with the Palacio Real as its backdrop. The gardens' centrepiece, which stands halfway along the Pradera, is the elegant Fuente de las Conchas (Fountain of the Shells), designed by Ventura Rodríguez, the Goya of Madrid's 18th-century architecture scene. The only entrance is from Paseo de la Virgen del Puerto.

Catedral de Nuestra Señora de la Almudena
CATHEDRAL

(Map p76; 91 542 22 00; www.museocatedral. archimadrid.es; Calle de Bailén; cathedral & crypt by donation, museum adult/child €6/4; 9am-8.30pm Mon-Sat, for Mass Sun, museum 10am-2.30pm Mon-Sat; Ópera) Paris has Notre Dame and Rome has St Peter's Basilica. In fact, almost every European city of stature has its signature cathedral, a stand-out monument to a glorious Christian past. Not Madrid. Although the exterior of the Catedral de Nuestra Señora de la Almudena sits in harmony with the adjacent Palacio Real, Madrid's cathedral is cavernous and largely charmless within; its colourful, modern ceilings do little to make up for the lack of old-world gravitas that so distinguishes great cathedrals.

Muralla Árabe
LANDMARK

(Map p76; Cuesta de la Vega; Ópera) Behind the cathedral apse and down Cuesta de la Vega is a short stretch of the original 'Arab Wall', the city wall built by Madrid's early-medieval Muslim rulers. Some of it dates as far back as the 9th century, when the initial Muslim fort was raised. Other sections date from the 12th and 13th centuries, by which time the city had been taken by the Christians.

Plaza de la Villa & Around
SQUARE

(Ópera) There are grander plazas in Madrid, but this intimate little square is one of Madrid's prettiest. Enclosed on three sides by wonderfully preserved examples of

id, while the front ones are hollow. That idea was Galileo Galilei's. Nearby are some 20 marble statues, mostly of ancient monarchs. Local legend has it that these ageing royals get down off their pedestals at night to stretch their legs.

Plaza Mayor & Royal Madrid

17th-century Madrid-style baroque architecture *(barroco madrileño)*, it was the permanent seat of Madrid's city government from the Middle Ages until recent years when Madrid's city council relocated to the grand Palacio de Comunicaciones on Plaza de la Cibeles.

The 17th-century Casa de la Villa (Map p76; Ópera) (Old Town Hall), on the western side of the square, is a typical Habsburg edifice with Herrerian slate-tiled spires. First planned as a prison in 1644 by Juan Gómez de Mora, who also designed the Convento de la Encarnación, its granite and brick facade is a study in sobriety. The final touches to the Casa de la Villa were made in 1693, although Juan de Villanueva, of Museo del Prado fame, made some alterations a century later. The Salón del Pleno (council chambers) were restored in the 1890s and again in 1986; the decoration is sumptuous neoclassical with late-17th-century ceiling frescoes. Ask at the Centro de Turismo de Madrid (p134) about guided tours to the Casa de la Villa. Look for the ceramic copy of Pedro Teixeira's landmark 1656 map of Madrid just outside the chambers.

On the opposite side of the square, the 15th-century Casa de los Lujanes (Map p76; Ópera) is more Gothic in conception with a clear Mudéjar (a Moorish architectural style) influence. The brickwork tower was 'home' to the imprisoned French monarch François I and his sons after their capture during the Battle of Pavia (1525). As the star prisoner was paraded down Calle Mayor, locals are said to have been more impressed by the splendidly attired Frenchman than they were by his more drab captor, the Spanish Habsburg emperor Carlos I. The tower's wooden door is a wonderful original.

Closed to the public at the time of writing, the Casa de Cisneros, built in 1537 by the nephew of Cardinal Cisneros, a key adviser to Queen Isabel, is plateresque in inspiration, although it was much restored and altered at the beginning of the 20th century. The main door and window above it are what remains of the Renaissance-era building. It's now home to the Salón de Tapices (Tapestries Hall), adorned with exquisite 15th-century Flemish tapestries.

The section of Calle Mayor that runs past the plaza witnessed one of the most dramatic moments in the history of early 20th-century Madrid. On 31 May 1906, on the wedding day of King Alfonso XIII and Britain's Victoria Eugenia, Catalan anarchist Mateu Morral threw a bomb concealed in a bouquet of flowers at the royal couple. Several bystanders died, but the monarch and his new wife survived, save for her blood-spattered dress. During the Spanish Civil War, Madrid's republican government briefly renamed the street Calle Mateu Morral.

Just down the hill from the plaza are the 18th-century baroque remakes of the Iglesia del Sacramento (Map p76; ☑91 547 36 24; Calle del Sacramento 11; MÓpera), the central church of the Spanish army, and the Palacio del Duque de Uceda (Map p76; Calle Mayor 79; MÓpera), which is now used as a military headquarters (the Capitanía General), but is a classic of the Madrid baroque architectural style and was designed by Juan Gómez de Mora in 1608.

Convento de las Descalzas Reales   CONVENT
(Convent of the Barefoot Royals; Map p76; www.patrimonionacional.es; Plaza de las Descalzas 3; €6, incl Convento de la Encarnación €8, EU citizens free Wed & Thu afternoon; ⊙10am-2pm & 4-6.30pm Tue-Sat, 10am-3pm Sun; MÓpera, Sol) The grim plateresque walls of the Convento de las Descalzas Reales offer no hint that behind the facade lies a sumptuous stronghold of the faith. The compulsory guided tour (in Spanish) leads you up a gaudily frescoed Renaissance stairway to the upper level of the cloister. The vault was painted by Claudio Coello, one of the most important artists of the Madrid School of the 17th century and whose works adorn San Lorenzo de El Escorial (p136).

Convento de la Encarnación   CONVENT
(Map p76; www.patrimonionacional.es; Plaza de la Encarnación 1; €6, incl Convento de las Descalzas Reales €8, EU citizens free Wed & Thu afternoon; ⊙10am-2pm & 4-6.30pm Tue-Sat, 10am-3pm Sun; MÓpera) Founded by Empress Margarita de

Austria, this 17th-century mansion built in the Madrid baroque style (a pleasing amalgam of brick, exposed stone and wrought iron) is still inhabited by nuns of the Augustine order. The large art collection dates mostly from the 17th century, and among the many gold and silver reliquaries is one that contains the blood of San Pantaleón, which purportedly liquefies each year on 27 July. The convent also sits on a pretty plaza close to the Palacio Real.

Iglesia de San Ginés   CHURCH
(Map p76; Calle del Arenal 13; ⊙8.45am-1pm & 6-9pm Mon-Sat, 9.45am-2pm & 6-9pm Sun; MSol, Ópera) Due north of Plaza Mayor, San Ginés is one of Madrid's oldest churches: it has been here in one form or another since at least the 14th century. What you see today was built in 1645 but largely reconstructed after a fire in 1824. The church houses some fine paintings, including El Greco's *Expulsion of the Moneychangers from the Temple* (1614), which is beautifully displayed; the glass is just 6mm from the canvas to avoid reflections.

Iglesia de San Nicolás
de los Servitas   CHURCH
(Map p76; ☑91 548 83 14; Plaza de San Nicolás 6; ⊙8am-1.30pm & 5.30-8.30pm Mon, 8-9.30am & 6.30-8.30pm Tue-Sat, 9.30am-2pm & 6.30-9pm Sun & holidays; MÓpera) Tucked away up the hill from Calle Mayor, this intimate little church is Madrid's oldest surviving building of worship; it is believed to have been built on the site of Muslim Mayrit's second

---

ⓘ MADRID CARD

If you intend to do some intensive sightseeing and travelling on public transport, consider the Madrid Card (1/2/3/5 days adult €47/60/67/77, child aged 6-12 €34/42/44/47; www.madridcard.com). It includes entry to over 50 museums in and around Madrid (including the Museo del Prado, Museo Thyssen-Bornemisza, Centro de Arte Reina Sofía, Estadio Santiago Bernabéu and Palacio Real), walking tours and discounts in a number of restaurants, shops and bars as well as for car rental. The Madrid Card can be bought online (slightly cheaper), at the Centro de Turismo de Madrid (p134) or at any of the sales outlets listed on the website.

mosque. The most striking feature is the restored 12th-century Mudéjar bell tower, although much of the remainder dates in part from the 15th century. The vaulting is late Gothic while the fine timber ceiling, which survived a fire in 1936, dates from about the same period.

◎ La Latina & Lavapiés

La Latina combines some of the best things about Madrid: the Spanish capital's best selection of tapas bars and a medieval streetscape studded with elegant churches. The *barrio's* (district's) heartland is centred on the area between (and very much including) Calle de la Cava Baja and the beautiful Plaza de la Paja.

Lavapiés, on the other hand, is a world away from the sophistication of modern Madrid. This is at once one of the city's oldest and most traditional *barrios* and home to more immigrants than any other central-Madrid *barrio*. It's quirky, alternative and a melting pot all in one. It's not without its problems, and the *barrio* has a reputation both for antiglamour cool and as a no-go zone, depending on your perspective.

★ **Basílica de San Francisco El Grande**   CHURCH
(Map p81; Plaza de San Francisco 1; adult/concession €3/2; ⊙mass 8-10.30am Mon-Sat, museum 10.30am-12.30pm & 4-6pm Tue-Sun Sep-Jun, 10.30am-12.30pm & 5-7pm Tue-Sun Jul & Aug; Ⓜ La Latina, Puerta de Toledo) Lording it over the southwestern corner of La Latina, this imposing and recently restored baroque basilica is one of Madrid's grandest old churches. Its extravagantly frescoed dome is, by some estimates, the largest in Spain and the fourth largest in the world, with a height of 56m and diameter of 33m.

Legend has it that St Francis of Assisi built a chapel on this site in 1217. The current version was designed by Francesco Sabatini, who also designed the Puerta de Alcalá (p94) and finished off the Palacio Real. He designed the church with an unusual floor plan: the nave is circular and surrounded by chapels guarded by imposing marble statues of the 12 apostles; 12 prophets, rendered in wood, sit above them at the base of the dome. Each of the chapels is adorned with frescoes and decorated according to a different historical style, but most people rush to the neo-plateresque Capilla de San Bernardino, where the central fresco was painted by Goya in the early stages of his career. Unusually, Goya has painted himself into the scene (he's the one in the yellow shirt on the right).

A series of corridors behind the high altar (accessible only as part of the guided visit) is lined with works of art from the 17th to 19th centuries; highlights include a painting by Francisco Zurbarán, and another by Francisco Pacheco, the father-in-law and teacher of Velázquez. In the sacristy, watch out for the fine Renaissance *sillería* (the sculpted walnut seats where the church's superiors would meet).

A word about the opening hours: although entry is free during morning Mass times, there is no access to the museum and the lights in the Capilla de San Bernardino won't be on to illuminate the Goya. At all other times, visit is by Spanish-language guided tour (included in the admission price). Just to confuse matters, you may face a similar problem if you're here on a Friday afternoon or any time Saturday if there's a wedding taking place.

★ **El Rastro**   MARKET
(Calle de la Ribera de los Curtidores; ⊙8am-3pm Sun; Ⓜ La Latina) A Sunday morning at El Rastro is a Madrid institution. You could easily spend an entire morning inching your way down the hill and the maze of streets that host El Rastro flea market every Sunday morning. Cheap clothes, luggage, old flamenco records, even older photos of Madrid, faux designer purses, grungy T-shirts, household goods and electronics are the main fare. For every 10 pieces of junk, there's a real gem (a lost masterpiece, an Underwood typewriter) waiting to be found.

The crowded Sunday flea market was, back in the 17th and 18th centuries, largely a meat market (*rastro* means 'stain', in reference to the trail of blood left behind by animals dragged down the hill). The road leading through the market, Calle de la Ribera de los Curtidores, translates as 'Tanners' Alley' and further evokes this sense of a slaughterhouse past. On Sunday mornings this is the place to be, with all of Madrid (in all its diversity) here in search of a bargain.

A word of warning: pickpockets love El Rastro as much as everyone else, so keep a tight hold on your belongings and don't keep valuables in easy-to-reach pockets.

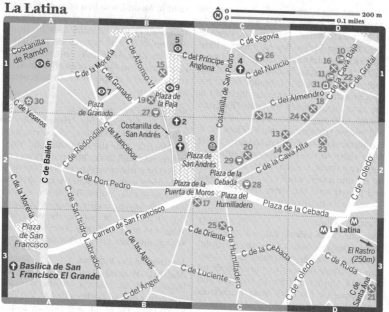

La Latina

Iglesia de San Andrés   CHURCH

(Map p81; Plaza de San Andrés 1; ⊙8am-1pm & 6-8pm Mon-Sat, 8am-1pm Sun; ⊠La Latina) This proud church is more imposing than beautiful and what you see today is the result of restoration work completed after the church was gutted during the civil war. Stern, dark columns with gold-leaf capitals against the rear wall lead your eyes up into the dome – all rose, yellow and green, and rich with sculpted floral fantasies and cherubs poking out of every nook and cranny.

Museo de San Isidro
MUSEUM

(Museo de los Orígenes; Map p81; ☑91 366 74 15; www.madrid.es; Plaza de San Andrés 2; ◷9.30am-8pm Tue-Sun Sep-Jul, 9.30am-2.30pm Tue-Fri & 9.30am-8pm Sat & Sun Aug; Ⓜ La Latina) FREE This engaging museum occupies the spot where San Isidro Labrador ended his days around 1172. A particular highlight is the large model based on Pedro Teixeira's famous 1656 map of Madrid. Of great historical interest (though not much to look at) is the 'miraculous well', where the saint called forth water to slake his master's thirst. In another miracle, the son of the saint's master fell into a well, whereupon Isidro prayed and prayed until the water rose and lifted his master's son to safety.

Plaza de la Paja
SQUARE

(Map p81; Ⓜ La Latina) Around the back of the Iglesia de San Andrés, the delightful Plaza de la Paja (Straw Square) slopes down into the tangle of lanes that once made up Madrid's Muslim quarter. In the 12th and 13th centuries, the city's main market occupied the square. At the top of the square is the Capilla del Obispo, while down the bottom (north side) of Plaza de la Paja, the walled 18th-century Jardín del Príncipe Anglona (Map p81; Plaza de la Paja; ◷10am-10pm Apr-Oct, 10am-6.30pm Nov-Mar; Ⓜ La Latina) is a peaceful garden.

Capilla del Obispo
CHURCH

(Map p81; ☑91 559 28 74; reservascapilla delobispo@archimadrid.es; Plaza de la Paja; €2; ◷10am-12.30pm Tue, 4-5.30pm Thu; Ⓜ La Latina) The Capilla del Obispo is a hugely important site on the historical map of Madrid. It was here that San Isidro Labrador, patron

---

GOYA IN MADRID

Madrid has the best collection of Goyas on earth. Here's where to find them:

Museo del Prado (p87)

Real Academia de Bellas Artes de San Fernando (p83)

Ermita de San Antonio de la Florida (p100)

Museo Lázaro Galdiano (p97)

Basílica de San Francisco El Grande (p80)

Museo Thyssen-Bornemisza (p93)

---

saint of Madrid, was first buried. When the saint's body was discovered there in the late 13th century, two centuries after his death, decomposition had not yet set in. Thus it was that King Alfonso XI ordered the construction in San Andrés of an ark to hold his remains and a chapel in which to venerate his memory.

Viaduct & Calle de Segovia
HISTORIC SITE

(Map p76; Ⓜ Ópera) High above Calle de Segovia, Madrid's viaduct, which connects La Morería with the cathedral and royal palace, was built in the 19th century and replaced by a newer version in 1942; the plastic barriers were erected in the late 1990s to prevent suicide jumps. Before the viaduct was built, anyone wanting to cross from one side of the road or river to the other was obliged to make their way down to Calle de Segovia and back up the other side.

Jardines de Las Vistillas
GARDENS

(Map p81; Ⓜ Ópera) West across Calle de Bailén from La Morería are the terrazas (open-air cafes) of Jardines de Las Vistillas, which offer one of the best vantage points in Madrid for a drink, with views towards the Sierra de Guadarrama. During the civil war, Las Vistillas was heavily bombarded by nationalist troops from the Casa de Campo, and they in turn were shelled from a republican bunker here.

La Morería
HISTORIC SITE

(Map p81; Ⓜ La Latina) The area stretching northwest from the Iglesia de San Andrés to the viaduct was the heart of the morería (Moorish Quarter). Strain the imagination a little and the maze of winding and hilly lanes even now retains a whiff of the North African medina. This is where the Muslim population of Mayrit was concentrated in the wake of the 11th-century Christian takeover of the town.

Iglesia de San Pedro El Viejo
CHURCH

(Map p81; ☑91 365 12 84; Costanilla de San Pedro; Ⓜ La Latina) This fine old church is one of the few remaining windows on post-Muslim Madrid, most notably its clearly Mudéjar (a Moorish architectural style) brick bell tower, which dates from the 14th century. The church is generally closed to the public, but it's arguably more impressive from the outside; the Renaissance doorway has stood since 1525. If you can peek inside, the nave dates from the 15th century, although

DON'T MISS

BARRIO DE LAS LETRAS

The area that unfurls down the hill east of Plaza de Santa Ana is referred to as the Barrio de las Letras (District of Letters), because of the writers who lived here during Spain's golden age of the 16th and 17th centuries. Miguel de Cervantes Saavedra (1547–1616), the author of *Don Quijote*, spent much of his adult life in Madrid and lived and died at **Calle de Cervantes 2** (Map p84; Ⓜ Antón Martín); a plaque (dating from 1834) sits above the door. Sadly, the original building was torn down in the early 19th century. When Cervantes died his body was interred around the corner at the **Convento de las Trinitarias** (Map p84; Calle de Lope de Vega 16; Ⓜ Antón Martín), which is marked by another plaque. Still home to cloistered nuns, the convent is closed to the public. A commemorative Mass is held for him here every year on the anniversary of his death, 23 April. Another literary landmark is the **Casa de Lope de Vega** (Map p84; ☎ 91 429 92 16; casamuseolopedevega.org; Calle de Cervantes 11; ⊙ guided tours every 30min 10am–6pm Tue–Sun; Ⓜ Antón Martín) **FREE**, the former home of Lope de Vega (1562–1635), Spain's premier playwright. It's now a museum containing memorabilia from Lope de Vega's life and work.

the interior largely owes its appearance to 17th-century renovations.

👁 Sol, Santa Ana & Huertas

The Plaza de la Puerta del Sol is Madrid's beating heart and the sum total of all Madrid's personalities, with fabulous shopping, eating and entertainment options. If nearby Huertas is known for anything, it's for nightlife that never seems to abate once the sun goes down. Such fame is well deserved, but there's so much more to Huertas than immediately meets the eye. Enjoy the height of sophisticated European cafe culture in the superb Plaza de Santa Ana, then go down the hill through Barrio de las Letras to the Centro de Arte Reina Sofía, one of the finest contemporary art galleries in Europe.

★ Plaza de Santa Ana   SQUARE

(Map p84; Plaza de Santa Ana; Ⓜ Sevilla, Sol, Antón Martín) Plaza de Santa Ana is a delightful confluence of elegant architecture and irresistible energy. It presides over the upper reaches of the Barrio de las Letras and this literary personality makes its presence felt with the statues of the 17th-century writer Calderón de la Barca and Federíco García Lorca, and in the Teatro Español (p124) (formerly the Teatro del Príncipe) at the plaza's eastern end. Apart from anything else, the plaza is the starting point for many a long Huertas night.

Situated in the heart of Huertas, the plaza was laid out in 1810 during the controversial reign of Joseph Bonaparte, giving breathing space to what had hitherto been one of Madrid's most claustrophobic *barrios*. The plaza quickly became a focal point for intellectual life, and the cafes surrounding the plaza thronged with writers, poets and artists engaging in endless *tertulias* (literary and philosophical discussions).

★ Real Academia de Bellas Artes de San Fernando   MUSEUM

(Map p84; ☎ 91 524 08 64; www.realacademia bellasartessanfernando.com; Calle de Alcalá 13; adult/child €6/free, Wed free; ⊙ 10am–3pm Tue–Sun Sep–Jul; Ⓜ Sol, Sevilla) Madrid's 'other' art gallery, the Real Academia de Bellas Artes has for centuries played a pivotal role in the artistic life of the city. As the royal fine arts academy, it has nurtured local talent, thereby complementing the royal penchant for drawing the great international artists of the day into their realm. The pantheon of former alumni reads like a who's who of Spanish art, and the collection that now hangs on the academy's walls is a suitably rich one.

Plaza de la Puerta del Sol   SQUARE

(Map p84; Ⓜ Sol) The official centre point of Spain is a gracious, crowded hemisphere of elegant facades. It is, above all, a crossroads: people here are forever heading somewhere else, on foot, by metro (three lines cross here) or by bus (many lines terminate and start nearby). Hard as it is to believe now, in Madrid's earliest days, the Puerta del Sol (Gate of the Sun) was the eastern gate of the city.

The main building on the square houses the regional government of the Comunidad de Madrid. The **Casa de Correos**, as it is

Sol, Santa Ana & Huertas

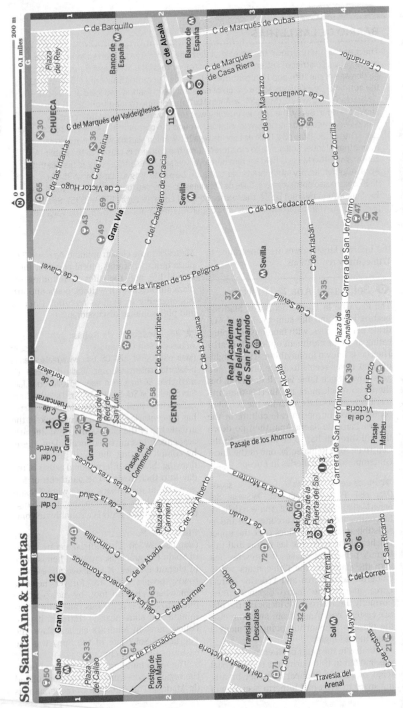

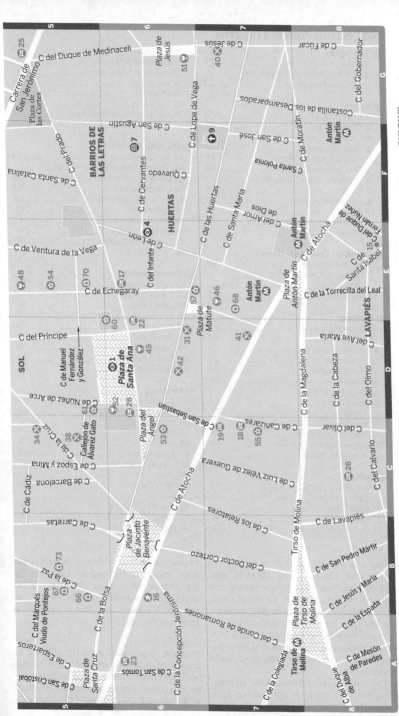

Sol, Santa Ana & Huertas

called, was built as the city's main post office in 1768. The clock was added in 1856 and on New Year's Eve people throng the square to wait impatiently for the clock to strike midnight, and at each gong swallow a grape – not as easy as it sounds! On the footpath outside the Casa de Correos is a plaque marking Spain's Kilometre Zero, the point from which Spain's network of roads is measured.

The semicircular junction owes its present appearance in part to the Bourbon king Carlos III (r 1759–88), whose equestrian statue (complete with his unmistakable nose) stands in the middle. Look out for the statue of a bear (Map p84; M Sol) nuzzling a *madroño* (strawberry tree) at the plaza's eastern end; this is the official symbol of the city.

Gran Vía　　　　　　　　　　　STREET
(Map p84; M Gran Vía, Callao) It's difficult to imagine Madrid without Gran Vía, the grand boulevard lined with towering belle-époque facades that climbs up through the centre of Madrid from Plaza de España then down to

Calle de Alcalá. But it has only existed since 1910, when it was bulldozed through what was then a labyrinth of old streets. Fourteen streets disappeared off the map, as did 311 houses, including one where Goya had once lived.

Plans for the boulevard were first announced in 1862 and so interminable were the delays that a famous *zarzuela* (satirical musical comedy), *La Gran Vía,* first performed in 1886, was penned to mock the city authorities. It may have destroyed whole *barrios*, but Gran Vía is still considered one of the most successful examples of urban planning in central Madrid since the late 19th century.

One eye-catching building, the **Edificio Carrión** (Map p76; cnr Gran Vía & Calle de Jacometrezo; M Callao) was Madrid's first pre-WWI tower-block apartment hotel. Also dominating the skyline about one-third of the way along Gran Vía is the 1920s-era **Telefónica building** (Map p84; Gran Vía; M Gran Vía), which was for years the highest building in the city. During the civil war, when Madrid was besieged by Franco's forces and the boulevard became known as 'Howitzer Alley' due to the artillery shells that rained down upon it, the Telefónica building was a favoured target.

Among the more interesting buildings is the stunning, French-designed **Edificio Metrópolis** (Map p84; Gran Vía; M Banco de España), built in 1905, which marks the southern end of Gran Vía. The winged victory statue atop its dome was added in 1975 and is best seen from Calle de Alcalá or Plaza de la Cibeles. A little up the boulevard is the **Edificio Grassy** (Map p84; Gran Vía 1; M Banco de España), with the Rolex sign and built in 1916. With its circular 'temple' as a crown, and profusion of arcs and slender columns, it's one of the most elegant buildings along Gran Vía.

Otherwise Gran Vía is home to around twice as many businesses (over 1050 at last count) as homes (nearly 600); over 13,000 people work along the street; and up to 55,000 vehicles pass through every day (including almost 185 buses an hour during peak periods). There are over 40 hotels on Gran Vía, but sadly just three of the 15 cinemas for which Gran Vía was famous remain.

Círculo de Bellas Artes   ARTS CENTRE, VIEWPOINT
(La Azotea; Map p84; ☑ 91 360 54 00; www.circulo bellasartes.com; Calle de Alcalá 42; admission to centre/roof terrace €1/4; ☺ roof terrace 9am-2am Mon-Thu, 9am-2.30am Fri, 11am-2.30am Sat & Sun; M Banco de España) For some of Madrid's best views, take the lift to the 7th floor of the 'Fine Arts Circle'. You can almost reach out and touch the glorious dome of the Edificio Metrópolis and otherwise take in Madrid in all its finery, including the distant mountains. Two bars, lounge music and places to recline add to the experience. Downstairs, the centre has exhibitions, concerts, short films and book readings. There's also a fine belle-époque cafe (p118) on the ground floor.

◉ El Retiro & the Art Museums

If you've just come down the hill from Huertas, you'll feel like you've left behind a madhouse for an oasis of greenery, fresh air and high culture. The Museo del Prado and the Museo Thyssen-Bornemisza are among the richest galleries of fine art in the world, and other museums lurk in the quietly elegant streets just behind the Prado. Rising up the hill to the east are the stately gardens of the glorious Parque del Buen Retiro.

★ **Museo del Prado**   MUSEUM
(Map p88; www.museodelprado.es; Paseo del Prado; adult/child €14/free, free 6-8pm Mon-Sat & 5-7pm Sun, audioguides €3.50, admission plus official guidebook €23; ☺ 10am-8pm Mon-Sat, 10am-7pm Sun; M Banco de España) Welcome to one of the world's premier art galleries. The more than 7000 paintings held in the Museo del Prado's collection (although only around 1500 are currently on display) are like a window onto the historical vagaries of the Spanish soul, at once grand and imperious in the royal paintings of Velázquez, darkly tumultuous in *Las pinturas negras* (The Black Paintings) of Goya, and outward looking with sophisticated works of art from all across Europe.

Spend as long as you can at the Prado or, better still, plan to make a couple of visits because it can be a little overwhelming if you try to absorb it all at once.

Entrance to the Prado is via the eastern **Puerta de los Jerónimos** (Map p88), with tickets on sale beneath the northern **Puerta de Goya** (Puerta de Goya; Map p88). Once inside, pick up the free plan from the ticket office or information desk just inside the entrance – it lists the locations of 50 of the Prado's most famous works and gives room numbers for all major artists.

El Retiro & the Art Museums

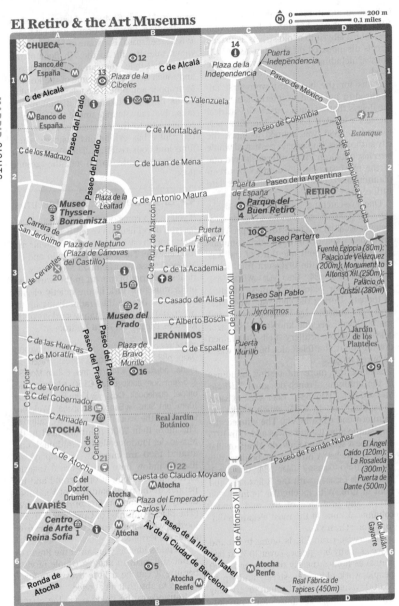

➡ Edificio Villanueva

Edificio Villanueva, the western wing of the Prado, was completed in 1785, as the neoclassical Palacio de Villanueva. Originally conceived as a house of science, it later served, somewhat ignominiously, as a cav-alry barracks for Napoleon's troops during their occupation of Madrid between 1808 and 1813. In 1814 King Fernando VII decided to use the palace as a museum, although his purpose was more about finding a way of storing the hundreds of royal paintings

El Retiro & the Art Museums

gathering dust than any high-minded civic ideals – this was an era where art was a royal preserve. Five years later the Museo del Prado opened with 311 Spanish paintings on display.

➡ Goya

Francisco José de Goya y Lucientes (Goya) is found on all three floors of the Prado, but we recommend starting at the southern end of the ground or lower level. In Room 65, Goya's *El dos de mayo* and *El tres de mayo* rank among Madrid's most emblematic paintings; they bring to life the 1808 anti-French revolt and subsequent execution of insurgents in Madrid. Alongside, in Rooms 67 and 68, are some of his darkest and most disturbing works, *Las pinturas negras;* they are so called in part because of the dark browns and black that dominate, but more for the distorted animalesque appearance of their characters.

There are more Goyas on the 1st floor in Rooms 34 to 37. Among them are two more of Goya's best-known and most intriguing oils: *La maja vestida* and *La maja desnuda*. These portraits, in Room 37, of an unknown woman, commonly believed to be the Duquesa de Alba (who may have been Goya's lover), are identical save for the lack of clothing in the latter. There are further Goyas on the top floor.

➡ Velázquez

Diego Rodríguez de Silva y Velázquez (Velázquez) is another of the grand masters of Spanish art who brings so much distinction to the Prado. Of all his works, *Las meninas* (Room 12) is what most people come to see. Completed in 1656, it is more properly known as *La família de Felipe IV* (The Family of Felipe IV). The rooms surrounding *Las meninas* contain more fine works by Velázquez: watch in particular for his paintings of various members of royalty who seem to spring off the canvas – Felipe II, Felipe IV, Margarita de Austria (a younger version of whom features in *Las meninas*), El Príncipe Baltasar Carlos and Isabel de Francia – on horseback.

➡ Spanish & Other European Masters

Having experienced the essence of the Prado, you're now free to select from the astonishingly diverse works that remain. If Spanish painters have piqued your curiosity, Bartolomé Esteban Murillo, José de Ribera and the stark figures of Francisco de Zurbarán should be on your itinerary. The vivid, almost-surreal works by the 16th-century master and adopted Spaniard El Greco, whose figures are characteristically slender and tortured, are also perfectly executed.

Another alternative is the Prado's outstanding collection of Flemish art. The fulsome figures and bulbous cherubs of Peter Paul Rubens (1577–1640) provide a playful antidote to the darkness of many of the other Flemish artists. His signature works are *Las tres gracias* (The Three Graces) and *Adoración de los reyes magos*. Other fine works in the vicinity include *The Triumph of Death* by Pieter Bruegel, Rembrandt's

Museo del Prado

PLAN OF ATTACK

Begin on the 1st floor with **Las meninas** ❶ by Velázquez. Although it alone is worth the entry price, it's a fine introduction to the 17th-century golden age of Spanish art; nearby are more of Velázquez' royal paintings and works by Zurbarán and Murillo. While on the 1st floor, seek out Goya's **La maja vestida and La maja desnuda** ❷, with more of Goya's early works in neighbouring rooms. Downstairs at the southern end of the Prado, Goya's anger is evident in the searing **El dos de mayo and El tres de mayo** ❸, and the torment of Goya's later years finds expression in the adjacent rooms with his **Las pinturas negras** ❹ (the Black Paintings). Also on the lower floor, Hieronymus Bosch's weird and wonderful **The Garden of Earthly Delights** ❺ is one of the Prado's signature masterpieces. Returning to the 1st floor, El Greco's **Adoration of the Shepherds** ❻, is an extraordinary work, as is Peter Paul Rubens' **Las tres gracias** ❼ which forms the centrepiece of the Prado's gathering of Flemish masters. (Note: this painting may be moved to the 2nd floor.) A detour to the 2nd floor takes in some lesser-known Goyas, but finish in the **Edificio Jerónimos** ❽ with a visit to the cloisters and the outstanding bookshop.

ALSO VISIT:

Nearby are Museo Thyssen-Bornemisza and Centro de Arte Reina Sofía. They form an extraordinary trio of galleries.

Las meninas (Velázquez)

This masterpiece depicts Velázquez and the Infanta Margarita. According to some experts, the images of the king and queen appear in mirrors behind Velázquez.

IMAGNO/GETTY IMAGES ©

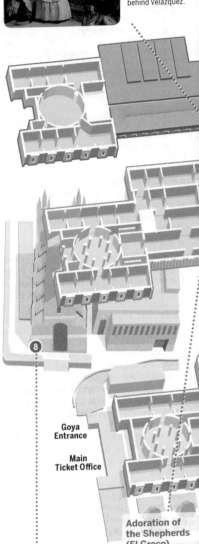

Goya Entrance

Main Ticket Office

Edificio Jerónimos

Opened in 2007, this state-of-the-art extension has rotating exhibitions of Prado masterpieces held in storage for decades for lack of wall space, and stunning 2nd-floor granite cloisters that date back to 1672.

Adoration of the Shepherds (El Greco)

There's an ecstatic quality to this intense painting. El Greco's distorted rendering of bodily forms came to characterise much of his later work.

Las tres gracias (Rubens)

A late Rubens masterpiece, *The Three Graces* is a classical and masterly expression of Rubens' preoccupation with sensuality, here portraying Aglaia, Euphrosyne and Thalia, the daughters of Zeus.

La maja vestida & La maja desnuda (Goya)

These enigmatic works scandalised early 19th-century Madrid society, fuelling the rumour mill as to the woman's identity and drawing the ire of the Spanish Inquisition.

Edificio Villanueva

El dos de mayo & El tres de mayo (Goya)

Few paintings evoke a city's sense of self quite like Goya's portrayal of Madrid's valiant but ultimately unsuccessful uprising against French rule in 1808.

Las pinturas negras (Goya)

Las pinturas negras are Goya's darkest works. *Saturno devorando a su hijo* evokes a writhing mass of tortured humanity, while *La romería de San Isidro* and *El aquelarre* are profoundly unsettling.

Information Counter & Audioguides

Gift Shop

Cafeteria

ónimos Entrance (Main Entrance)

Murillo Entrance

Velázquez Entrance

The Garden of Earthly Delights (Bosch)

A fantastical painting in triptych form, this overwhelming work depicts the Garden of Eden and what the Prado describes as 'the lugubrious precincts of Hell' in exquisitely bizarre detail.

Artemisa, and those by Anton Van Dyck. And on no account miss the weird and wonderful *The Garden of Earthly Delights* (Room 56A) by Hieronymus Bosch (c 1450–1516). No one has yet been able to provide a definitive explanation for this hallucinatory work, although many have tried.

And then there are the paintings by Dürer, Rafael, Tiziano (Titian), Tintoretto, Sorolla, Gainsborough, Fra Angelico, Tiepolo...

➡ **Edificio Jerónimos**

In contrast to the original Edificio Villanueva, the eastern wing (Edificio Jerónimos) is part of the Prado's stunning modern extension, which opened in 2007. Dedicated to temporary exhibitions (usually to display Prado masterpieces held in storage for decades for lack of wall space), and home to the excellent bookshop and cafe, its main attraction is the 2nd-floor cloisters. Built in 1672 with local granite, the cloisters were until recently attached to the adjacent Iglesia de San Jerónimo El Real, but were in a parlous state. As part of their controversial incorporation into the Prado, they were painstakingly dismantled, restored and reassembled.

⭐ **Centro de Arte Reina Sofía**   MUSEUM
(Map p88; 📞 91 774 10 00; www.museoreinasofia. es; Calle de Santa Isabel 52; adult/concession €8/ free, 1.30-7pm Sun, 7-9pm Mon & Wed-Sat free; ⊙ 10am-9pm Mon & Wed-Sat, 10am-7pm Sun; Ⓜ Atocha) Home to Picasso's *Guernica,* arguably Spain's single-most famous artwork, the Centro de Arte Reina Sofía is Madrid's premier collection of contemporary art. In addition to plenty of paintings by Picasso, other major drawcards are works by Salvador Dalí (1904–1989) and Joan Miró (1893–1983). The collection principally spans the 20th century up to the 1980s. The occasional non-Spaniard artist makes an appearance (including Francis Bacon's *Lying Figure;* 1966), but most of the collection is strictly peninsular.

The permanent collection is displayed on the 2nd and 4th floors of the main wing of the museum, the Edificio Sabatini. *Guernica's* location never changes – you'll find it in Room 206 on the 2nd floor. Beyond that, the location of specific paintings can be a little confusing. The museum follows a theme-based approach, which ensures that you'll find works by Picasso or Miró, for example, spread across the two floors. The only solution if you're looking for something specific is to pick up the latest copy of the *Planos*

de Museo (Museum Floorplans) from the information desk just outside the main entrance; it lists the rooms in which each artist appears (although not individual paintings).

In addition to Picasso's *Guernica,* which is worth the admission fee on its own, don't neglect the artist's preparatory sketches in the rooms surrounding Room 206; they offer an intriguing insight into the development of this seminal work. If Picasso's cubist style has captured your imagination, the work of the Madrid-born Juan Gris (1887–1927) or Georges Braque (1882–1963) may appeal.

The work of Joan Miró is defined by often delightfully bright primary colours, but watch out also for a handful of his equally odd sculptures. Since his paintings became a symbol of the Barcelona Olympics in 1992, his work has begun to receive the international acclaim it so richly deserves – the museum is a fine place to get a representative sample of his innovative work.

The Reina Sofía is also home to 20 or so canvases by Salvador Dalí, of which the most famous is perhaps the surrealist extravaganza that is *El gran masturbador* (1929). Among his other works is a strange bust of a certain *Joelle,* which Dalí created with his friend Man Ray (1890–1976). Another well-known surrealist painter, Max Ernst (1891–1976), is also worth tracking down.

If you can tear yourself away from the big names, the Reina Sofía offers a terrific opportunity to learn more about sometimes lesser-known 20th-century Spanish artists. Among these are Miquel Barceló (b 1957); *madrileño* artist José Gutiérrez Solana (1886–1945); the renowned Basque painter Ignazio Zuloaga (1870–1945); Benjamín Palencia (1894–1980), whose paintings capture the turbulence of Spain in the 1930s; Barcelona painter Antoni Tàpies (1923–2012); pop artist Eduardo Arroyo (b 1937); and abstract painters such as Eusebio Sempere (1923–85) and members of the Equipo 57 group (founded in 1957 by a group of Spanish artists in exile in Paris), such as Pablo Palazuelo (1916–2007). Better known as a poet and playwright, Federico García Lorca (1898–1936) is represented by a number of his sketches.

Of the sculptors, watch in particular for Pablo Gargallo (1881–1934), whose work in bronze includes a bust of Picasso, and the renowned Basque sculptors Jorge Oteiza (1908–2003) and Eduardo Chillida (1924–2002).

★Museo Thyssen-Bornemisza MUSEUM
(Map p88; ☑902 760511; www.museothyssen.
org; Paseo del Prado 8; adult/child €10/free, Mon
free; ⊗10am-7pm Tue-Sun, noon-4pm Mon; Ⓜ Banco de España) The Thyssen is one of the most
extraordinary private collections of predominantly European art in the world. Where the
Prado or Reina Sofía enable you to study the
body of work of a particular artist in depth,
the Thyssen is the place to immerse yourself
in a breathtaking breadth of artistic styles.
Most of the big names are here, sometimes
with just a single painting, but the Thyssen's
gift to Madrid and the art-loving public is to
have them all under one roof.

Begin on the top floor and work your way
down.

➡ Second Floor
The 2nd floor, which is home to medieval
art, includes some real gems hidden among
the mostly 13th- and 14th-century and predominantly Italian, German and Flemish
religious paintings and triptychs. Unless
you've got a specialist's eye, pause in Room
5, where you'll find one work by Italy's Piero
della Francesca (1410–92) and the instantly
recognisable *Portrait of King Henry VIII*
by Holbein the Younger (1497–1543), before
continuing on to Room 10 for the evocative
1586 *Massacre of the Innocents* by Lucas
Van Valckenberch. Room 11 is dedicated to
El Greco (with three pieces) and his Vene-
tian contemporaries Tintoretto and Titian,
while Caravaggio and the Spaniard José de
Ribera dominate Room 12. A single painting
each by Murillo and Zurbarán add further
Spanish flavour in the two rooms that follow, while the exceptionally rendered views
of Venice by Canaletto (1697–1768) should on
no account be missed.

Best of all on this floor is the extension
(Rooms A to H) built to house the collection
of Carmen Thyssen-Bornemisza. Room C
houses paintings by Canaletto, Constable
and Van Gogh, while the stunning Room H
includes works by Monet, Sisley, Renoir, Pissarro and Degas.

Before heading downstairs, a detour to
Rooms 19 through 21 will satisfy those devoted to 17th-century Dutch and Flemish
masters, such as Anton van Dyck, Jan Brue-
ghel the Elder, Rubens and Rembrandt (one
painting).

➡ First Floor
If all that sounds impressive, the 1st floor
is where the Thyssen really shines. There's
a Gainsborough in Room 28 and a Goya in

Room 31 but, if you've been skimming the
surface of this overwhelming collection,
Room 32 is the place to linger over each and
every painting. The astonishing texture of
Van Gogh's *Les Vessenots* is a masterpiece,
but the same could be said for *Woman
in Riding Habit* by Manet, *The Thaw at
Véthueil* by Monet, Renoir's *Woman with
a Parasol in a Garden* and Pissarro's quintessentially Parisian *Rue Saint-Honoré
in the Afternoon*. Room 33 is also something special, with Cézanne, Gauguin,
Toulouse-Lautrec and Degas, while the big
names continue in Room 34 (Picasso, Matisse and Modigliani) and 35 (Edvard Munch
and Egon Schiele).

In the 1st floor's extension (Rooms I to
P), the names speak for themselves. Room
K has works by Monet, Pissaro, Sorolla and
Sisley, while Room L is the domain of Gau-
guin (including his iconic *Mata Mua*), Degas
and Toulouse-Lautrec. Rooms M (Munch),
N (Kandinsky), O (Matisse and Georges
Braque) and P (Picasso, Matisse, Edward
Hopper and Juan Gris) round out an outra-
geously rich journey through the masters.
On your way to the stairs there's Edward
Hopper's *Hotel Room*.

➡ Ground Floor
On the ground floor, the foray into the
20th century that you began in the 1st-floor

extension takes over with a fine spread of paintings from cubism through to pop art.

In Room 41 you'll see a nice mix of the big three of cubism, Picasso, Georges Braque and Madrid's own Juan Gris, along with several other contemporaries. Kandinsky is the main drawcard in Room 43, while there's an early Salvador Dalí alongside Max Ernst and Paul Klee in Room 44. Picasso appears again in Room 45, another one of the gallery's standout rooms; its treasures include works by Marc Chagall and Dalí's hallucinatory *Dream Caused by the Flight of a Bee Around a Pomegranate, One Second Before Waking Up*.

Room 46 is similarly rich, with Joan Miró's *Catalan Peasant with a Guitar*, the splattered craziness of Jackson Pollock's *Brown and Silver I*, and the deceptively simple but strangely pleasing *Green on Maroon* by Mark Rothko taking centre stage. In Rooms 47 and 48 the Thyssen builds to a stirring climax, with Francis Bacon, Roy Lichtenstein, Henry Moore and Lucian Freud, Sigmund's Berlin-born grandson, all represented.

★ Parque del Buen Retiro   GARDENS

(Map p88; ⊗ 6am-midnight May-Sep, to 11pm Oct-Apr; Ⓜ Retiro, Príncipe de Vergara, Ibiza, Atocha) The glorious gardens of El Retiro are as beautiful as any you'll find in a European city. Littered with marble monuments, landscaped lawns, the occasional elegant building (the Palacio de Cristal is especially worth seeking out) and abundant greenery, it's quiet and contemplative during the week but comes to life on weekends. Put simply, this is one of our favourite places in Madrid.

Laid out in the 17th century by Felipe IV as the preserve of kings, queens and their intimates, the park was opened to the public in 1868 and ever since, whenever the weather's fine and on weekends in particular, *madrileños* from all across the city gather here to stroll, read the Sunday papers in the shade, take a boat ride or nurse a cool drink at the numerous outdoor *terrazas*.

The focal point for so much of El Retiro's life is the artificial lake (*estanque*), which is watched over by the massive ornamental structure of the Monument to Alfonso XII on the east side, complete with marble lions; as sunset approaches on a Sunday afternoon in summer, the crowd grows, bongos sound out across the park and people start to dance. Row boats (Map p88; per boat per 45min

weekdays/weekends €5.80/7.50; ⊗ 10am-8.30pm Apr-Sep, to 5.45pm Oct-Mar) can be rented from the lake's northern shore – an iconic Madrid experience. On the southern end of the lake, the odd structure decorated with sphinxes is the Fuente Egipcia (Egyptian Fountain): legend has it that an enormous fortune buried in the park by Felipe IV in the mid-18th century rests here. Hidden among the trees south of the lake is the Palacio de Cristal (🗹 91 574 66 14; www.museoreinasofia.es; ⊗ 10am-10pm Apr-Sep, 10am-6pm Oct-Mar; Ⓜ Retiro), a magnificent metal-and-glass structure that is arguably El Retiro's most beautiful architectural monument. It was built in 1887 as a winter garden for exotic flowers and is now used for temporary exhibitions organised by the Centro de Arte Reina Sofía. Just north of here, the 1883 Palacio de Velázquez (www.museoreinasofia.es; ⊗ 10am-10pm May-Sep, 10am-6pm Oct-Apr) is also used for temporary exhibitions.

At the southern end of the park, near La Rosaleda (Rose Garden) (Rose Garden) with its more than 4000 roses, is a statue of El Ángel Caído. Strangely, it sits 666m above sea level... In the same vein, the Puerta de Dante, in the extreme southeastern corner of the park, is watched over by a carved mural of Dante's Inferno. Occupying much of the southwestern corner of the park is the Jardín de los Planteles (Map p88), one of the least visited sections of El Retiro, where quiet pathways lead beneath an overarching canopy of trees. West of here is the moving Bosque del Recuerdo (Memorial Forest; Map p88), an understated memorial to the 191 victims of the 11 March 2004 train bombings. For each victim stands an olive or cypress tree. To the north, just inside the Puerta de Felipe IV, stands what is thought to be Madrid's oldest tree (Map p88), a Mexican conifer (*ahuehuete*) planted in 1633.

In the northeastern corner of the park is the Ermita de San Isidro (Map p98), a small country chapel noteworthy as one of the few, albeit modest, examples of Romanesque architecture in Madrid. When it was built, Madrid was a small village more than 2km away.

Puerta de Alcalá   MONUMENT

(Map p88; Plaza de la Independencia; Ⓜ Retiro) This imposing triumphal gate was once the main entrance to the city (its name derives from the fact that the road that passed under it led to Alcalá de Henares) and was surrounded by the city's walls. It was here that

CASA DE CAMPO

Sometimes called the 'lungs of Madrid', the 17-sq-km stand of greenery that is Casa de Campo (M Batán) stretches west of the Río Manzanares. There are prettier and more central parks in Madrid but its scope is such that there are plenty of reasons to visit. And visit the *madrileños* do, nearly half a million of them every weekend, celebrating the fact that the short-lived Republican government of the 1930s opened the park to the public (it was previously the exclusive domain of royalty).

For city-bound *madrileños* with neither the time nor the inclination to go further afield, it has become the closest they get to nature, despite the fact that cyclists, walkers and picnickers overwhelm the byways and trails that criss-cross the park. There are tennis courts and a swimming pool, as well as the Zoo Aquarium de Madrid (☑902 345014; www.zoomadrid.com; Casa de Campo; adult/child €22.95/18.60, €19.95/16.90 if purchased online; ⊙10.30am-10pm Sun-Thu, 10.30am-midnight Fri & Sat Jul & Aug, shorter hours Sep-Jun; ☒37 from Intercambiador de Príncipe Pío, M Casa de Campo) and the Parque de Atracciones (☑91 463 29 00; www.parquedeatracciones.es; Casa de Campo; adult/child €31.90/24.90; ⊙noon-midnight Jul & Aug, shorter hours Sep-Jun; ☒37 from Intercambiador de Príncipe Pío, M Batán). The Teleférico (☑91 541 11 18; www.teleferico.com; cnr Paseo del Pintor Rosales & Calle de Marqués de Urquijo; one-way/return €4.20/5.90; ⊙noon-9pm May-Aug, reduced hours Sep-Apr; M Argüelles) also takes you here with good views en route. At Casa de Campo's southern end, restaurants specialise in wedding receptions, ensuring plenty of bridal parties roaming the grounds in search of an unoccupied patch of greenery where they can take photos. Also in the park, the Andalucian-style ranch known as Batán is used to house the bulls destined to do bloody battle in the Fiestas de San Isidro Labrador.

Although it's largely for the better, something has definitely been lost from the days before 2003 when unspoken intrigues surrounded the small artificial lake, where several lakeside *terrazas* and eateries were frequented by an odd combination of day trippers, working girls and clients. By night, prostitutes jockeyed for position while punters kept their places around the lakeside *chiringuitos* (open-air bars or kiosks) as though nothing out of the ordinary was happening. The traffic in the middle of the night here was akin to rush hour in the city centre. The police shut this scene down and, thankfully, there are no more louche traffic jams, at least on weekends.

the city authorities controlled access to the capital and levied customs duties.

Plaza de la Cibeles
SQUARE

(Map p88; M Banco de España) Of all the grand roundabouts that punctuate the Paseo del Prado, Plaza de la Cibeles most evokes the splendour of imperial Madrid. The jewel in the crown is the astonishing Palacio de Comunicaciones. Other landmark buildings around the plaza's perimeter include the Palacio de Linares and Casa de América (☑91 595 48 00; www.casamerica.es; Plaza de la Cibeles 2; adult/child/student & senior €8/free/5; ⊙guided tours 11am, noon & 1pm Sat & Sun Sep-Jul, shorter hrs Aug, ticket office 10am-3pm & 4-8pm Mon-Fri, 11am-1pm Sat & Sun), the Palacio Buenavista (1769) and the national Banco de España (1891). The spectacular fountain of the goddess Cybele at the centre of the plaza is one of Madrid's most beautiful.

Mirador de Madrid
VIEWPOINT

(Map p88; www.centrocentro.org; 8th fl, Palacio de Comunicaciones, Plaza de la Cibeles; adult/child €2/0.50; ⊙10.30am-1.30pm & 4-7pm Tue-Sun; M Banco de España) The views from the summit of the Palacio de Comunicaciones are arguably Madrid's best, sweeping west down over the Plaza de la Cibeles, up the hill towards the sublime Edificio Metrópolis and out to the mountains. But the views are splendid whichever way you look. Take the lift up to the 6th floor, from where the gates are opened every half-hour. From there you can either take another lift or climb the stairs up to the 8th floor.

Iglesia de San Jerónimo El Real
CHURCH

(Map p88; ☑91 420 35 78; Calle de Ruiz de Alarcón; ⊙10am-1pm & 5-8.30pm Mon-Sat Oct-Jun, hours vary Jul-Sep; M Atocha, Banco de España) Tucked away behind the Museo del Prado, this chapel was traditionally favoured

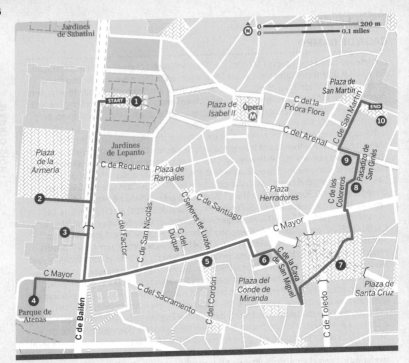

City Walk
Old Madrid

START PLAZA DE ORIENTE
END CONVENTO DE LAS
DESCALZAS REALES
LENGTH 2KM; TWO HOURS

Stroll past the architecture of imperial Madrid and into the heart of the modern city – two very different cities that often overlap.

Begin in **1** **Plaza de Oriente** (p75), a splendid arc of greenery and graceful architecture which could be Madrid's most agreeable plaza. You'll find yourself surrounded by gardens, the Palacio Real and the Teatro Real, and peopled by an ever-changing cast of *madrileños* at play. Overlooking the plaza, the **2** **Palacio Real** (p75) was Spain's seat of royal power for centuries. Almost next door is the **3** **Catedral de Nuestra Señora de la Almudena** (p77); it may lack the old-world gravitas of other Spanish cathedrals, but it's a beautiful part of the skyline.

From the cathedral, drop down to the **4** **Muralla Árabe** (p77), then climb gently up Calle Mayor, pausing to admire the last remaining ruins of Madrid's first

cathedral, Santa María de la Almudena, then on to **5** **Plaza de la Villa** (p77), a cosy square surrounded on three sides by some of the best examples of Madrid baroque architecture. A little further up the hill and just off Calle Mayor, the **6** **Mercado de San Miguel** (p109), one of Madrid's oldest markets, has become one of the coolest places to eat and mingle with locals in downtown Madrid.

Head down the hill along Cava de San Miguel, then climb up through the Arco de Cuchilleros to the **7** **Plaza Mayor** (p75), one of Spain's grandest and most beautiful plazas. Down a narrow lane north of the plaza, **8** **Chocolatería de San Ginés** (p116) is justifiably famous for its *chocolate con churros*, the ideal Madrid indulgence at any hour of the day. Almost next door, along pedestrianised Calle del Arenal, there's the pleasing **9** **Iglesia de San Ginés** (p79), one of the longest-standing relics of Christian Madrid.

A short climb to the north, the **10** **Convento de las Descalzas Reales** (p79) is an austere convent with an extraordinarily rich interior. In the heart of downtown Madrid, it's a great place to finish up.

by the Spanish royal family, and King Juan Carlos I was crowned here in 1975 upon the death of Franco. The sometimes-sober, sometimes-splendid mock-Isabelline interior is actually a 19th-century reconstruction that took its cues from the Iglesia de San Juan de los Reyes in Toledo; the original was largely destroyed during the Peninsular War. What remained of the former cloisters has been incorporated into the Museo del Prado.

Real Jardín Botánico   GARDENS
(Royal Botanical Garden; Map p88; ✎91 420 04 38; www.rjb.csic.es; Plaza de Bravo Murillo 2; adult/child €3/free; ⊙10am-9pm May-Aug, 10am-8pm Apr & Sep, 10am-7pm Mar & Oct, 10am-6pm Nov-Feb; ⓜAtocha) Although not as expansive or as popular as the Parque del Buen Retiro, Madrid's botanical gardens are another leafy oasis in the centre of town. With some 30,000 species crammed into a relatively small 8-hectare area, it's more a place to wander at leisure than laze under a tree, although there are benches dotted throughout the gardens where you can sit.

Caixa Forum   MUSEUM, ARCHITECTURE
(Map p88; ✎91 330 73 00; https://obrasocialla caixa.org/en/cultura/caixaforum-madrid/que-hacemos; Paseo del Prado 36; admission free, exhibitions from €4; ⊙10am-8pm; ⓜAtocha) This extraordinary structure is one of Madrid's most eye-catching landmarks. Seeming to hover above the ground, this brick edifice is topped by an intriguing summit of rusted iron. On an adjacent wall is the *jardín colgante* (hanging garden), a lush (if thinning) vertical wall of greenery almost four storeys high. Inside there are four floors of exhibition and performance space awash in stainless steel and with soaring ceilings. The exhibitions here are always worth checking out and include photography, contemporary painting and multimedia shows.

Antigua Estación de Atocha NOTABLE BUILDING
(Map p88; Plaza del Emperador Carlos V; ⓜA-tocha Renfe) In 1992 the northwestern wing of the Antigua Estación de Atocha (Old Atocha Train Station) was given a stunning overhaul. The structure of this grand iron-and-glass relic from the 19th century was preserved, while its interior was artfully converted into a light-filled tropical garden with more than 500 plant species. The project was the work of architect Rafael Moneo, and his landmark achievement was to create a thoroughly modern space that resonates

with the stately European train stations of another age.

Real Fábrica de Tapices   LANDMARK
(✎91 434 05 50; www.realfabricadetapices.com; Calle de Fuenterrabía 2; adult/child €4/3; ⊙10am-2pm Mon-Fri Sep-Jul, guided tours every half-hour; ⓜAtocha Renfe, Menéndez Pelayo) If a wealthy Madrid nobleman wanted to impress, he came here to the Real Fábrica de Tapices (Royal Tapestry Workshop), where royalty commissioned the pieces that adorned their palaces and private residences. The Spanish government, Spanish royal family and the Vatican were the biggest patrons of the tapestry business: Spain alone is said to have collected four million tapestries. With such an exclusive clientele, it was a lucrative business and remains so, 300 years after the factory was founded.

⊙ Salamanca

The *barrio* of Salamanca is Madrid's most exclusive quarter, defined by grand and restrained elegance. This is a place to put on your finest clothes and be seen (especially along Calle de Serrano or Calle de José Ortega y Gasset); to stroll into shops with an affected air and resist asking the prices; or to promenade between the fine museums and parks that make you wonder whether you've arrived at the height of civilisation.

★**Museo Lázaro Galdiano**   MUSEUM
(✎91 561 60 84; www.flg.es; Calle de Serrano 122; adult/concession/child €6/3/free, last hour free; ⊙10am-4.30pm Mon & Wed-Sat, 10am-3pm Sun; ⓜGregorio Marañón) This imposing early 20th-century Italianate stone mansion, set discreetly back from the street, belonged to Don José Lázaro Galdiano (1862–1947), a successful businessman and passionate patron of the arts. His astonishing private collection, which he bequeathed to the city upon his death, includes 13,000 works of art and objets d'art, a quarter of which are on show at any time.

★**Plaza de Toros & Museo Taurino** STADIUM
(✎91 356 22 00; www.las-ventas.com; Calle de Alcalá 237; ⊙10am-5.30pm; ⓜVentas) **FREE** East of central Madrid, the Plaza de Toros Monumental de Las Ventas (Las Ventas) is the most important and prestigious bullring in the world. A visit here (especially as part of a guided tour, which must be booked through Las Ventas Tour (✎687 739032; www.lasventastour.com; adult/child

Salamanca

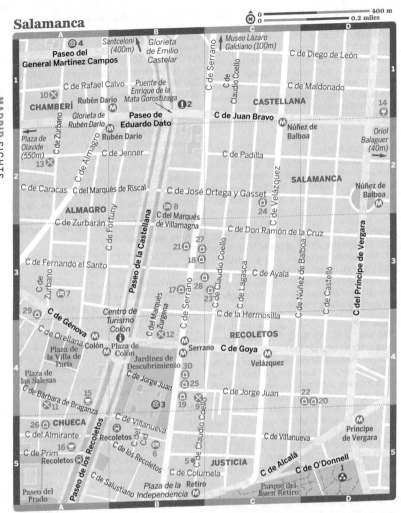

0   400 m
0   0.2 miles

MADRID SIGHTS

€14/8; ⊙10am-5.30pm, days of bullfight 10am-1.30pm) in advance) is a good way to gain an insight into this very Spanish tradition. There's also the fine **Museo Taurino** (⊘91 725 18 57; www.las-ventas.com; Calle de Alcalá 237) **FREE**, and the architecture will be of interest even to those with no interest in *la corridas* (bullfights).

Museo Arqueológico Nacional MUSEUM
(Map p98; http://man.mcu.es; Calle de Serrano 13; €3, free 2-8pm Sat & 9.30am-noon Sun; ⊙9.30am-8pm Tue-Sat, 9.30am-3pm Sun; Ⓜ Serrano) Reopened after a massive overhaul

of the building, the showpiece National Archaeology Museum contains a sweeping accumulation of artefacts behind its towering facade. Daringly redesigned within, the museum ranges across Spain's ancient history and the large collection includes stunning mosaics taken from Roman villas across Spain, intricate Muslim-era and Mudéjar handiwork, sculpted figures such as the *Dama de Ibiza* and *Dama de Elche,* examples of Romanesque and Gothic architectural styles and a partial copy of the prehistoric cave paintings of Altamira (Cantabria).

Salamanca

MADRID SIGHTS

Museo al Aire Libre　SCULPTURE
(Map p98; Paseo de la Castellana; ⊙24hr; ⓂRubén Darío) FREE This fascinating open-air collection of 17 abstract sculptures includes works by the renowned Basque artist Eduardo Chillida, the Catalan master Joan Miró, as well as Eusebio Sempere and Alberto Sánchez, one of Spain's foremost sculptors of the 20th century. The sculptures are beneath the overpass where Paseo de Eduardo Dato crosses Paseo de la Castellana, but somehow the hint of traffic grime and pigeon shit only adds to the appeal. All but one are on the eastern side of Paseo de la Castellana.

◉ Malasaña & Chueca

The inner-city *barrios* of Malasaña and Chueca are where Madrid gets up close and personal. Yes, there are rewarding museums and examples of landmark architecture sprinkled throughout. But these *barrios* are more about doing than seeing; more about experiencing life as it's lived by *madrileños* than ticking off a list of wonderful, if more static, attractions. Malasaña and Chueca are neighbourhoods with attitude and personality, where Madrid's famed nightlife, shopping and eating thrive. Malasaña is streetwise and down to earth, while Chueca, as Madrid's centre of gay culture, is more stylish and flamboyant.

Museo de Historia　MUSEUM
(Map p104; ☑91 701 16 86; www.madrid.es/museodehistoria; Calle de Fuencarral 78; ⊙11am-2pm & 4-7pm Tue-Fri, 10am-2pm & 4-7pm Sat & Sun; ⓂTribunal) FREE The fine Museo de Historia (formerly the Museo Municipal) has an elaborate and restored baroque entrance, raised in 1721 by Pedro de Ribera. Behind this facade, the collection is dominated by paintings and other memorabilia charting the historical evolution of Madrid. The highlights are Goya's *Allegory of the City of Madrid* (on the 1st floor), the caricatures lampooning Napoleon and the early 19th-century French occupation of Madrid (1st floor), and the expansive model of Madrid as it was in 1830 (basement).

Sociedad General de Autores y Editores　ARCHITECTURE
(General Society of Authors & Editors; Map p104; Calle de Fernando VI 4; ⓂAlonso Martínez) This swirling, melting wedding cake of a building is as close as Madrid comes to the work of Antoni Gaudí, which so illuminates Barcelona. It's a joyously self-indulgent ode to Modernisme and is virtually one of a kind in Madrid. Casual visitors are actively discouraged, although what you see from the street is impressive enough. The only exceptions are on the first Monday of October, International Architecture Day, when its interior staircase alone is reason enough to come.

Museo del Romanticismo MUSEUM
(Map p104; ☑91 448 10 45; museoromanticismo.
mcu.es; Calle de San Mateo 13; adult/child/student
€3/free/1.50, Sat after 2.30pm free; ⊘9.30am-
8.30pm Tue-Sat & 10am-3pm Sun May-Oct, 9.30am-
6.30pm Tue-Sat & 10am-3pm Sun Nov-Apr; ⓂTri-
bunal) This intriguing museum is devoted
to the Romantic period of the 19th century.
It houses a minor treasure trove of mostly
19th-century paintings, furniture, porcelain,
books, photos and other bits and bobs from
a bygone age and offers an insight into what
upper-class houses were like in the 19th century. The best-known work in the collection
is Goya's *San Gregorio Magno, Papa*.

**Antiguo Cuartel
del Conde Duque** NOTABLE BUILDING
(Map p104; Calle del Conde Duque 9; ⓂPlaza
de España, Ventura Rodríguez, San Bernardo) This
grand former barracks dominates Conde
Duque on the western fringe of Malasaña
with its imposing facade stretching 228m
down the hill. Built in 1717 under the auspic-
es of architect Pedro de Ribera, its highlight
is the extravagant 18th-century doorway, a
masterpiece of the baroque churrigueresque
style. These days it's home to a cultural
centre, which hosts government archives,
libraries, the Hemeroteca Municipal (Spain's
biggest collection of newspapers and magazines), temporary exhibitions and, when
it reopens, the Museo Municipal de Arte
Contemporáneo.

⊙ Parque del Oeste & Northern Madrid

This area wraps around central Madrid to
the north and west and contains some fabulous sights, and outstanding (if fairly widely
spread) places to eat, drink and watch live
music. But it's here perhaps more than anywhere else in Madrid that you get a sense
of the city as the *madrileños* experience it,
away from the tourist crowds. One *barrio* in
particular captures this sense of a city as locals live it. Immediately north of Chueca and
Malasaña, Chamberí has quiet, tree-lined
streets and one of the city's most underrated
squares, the Plaza de Olavide. It's not that
Chamberí has many sights to see – it's more
about soaking up the essence of Madrid with
scarcely a tourist in sight.

★**Ermita de San Antonio
de la Florida** GALLERY
(☑91 542 07 22; www.sanantoniodelaflorida.es;
Glorieta de San Antonio de la Florida 5; ⊘10am-
8pm Tue-Sun, hours vary Jul & Aug; ⓂPríncipe
Pío) **FREE** The frescoed ceilings of the Ermita de San Antonio de la Florida are one
of Madrid's most surprising secrets. It's been
recently restored and is also known as the
Panteón de Goya. The southern of the two
small chapels is one of the few places to see
Goya's work in its original setting, as painted by the master in 1798 on the request of
Carlos IV. Simply breathtaking.

The frescoes on the dome depict the
miracle of St Anthony, who is calling on a
young man to rise from the grave and ab-
solve his father, unjustly accused of his murder. Around them swarms a typical Madrid
crowd.

The painter is buried in front of the altar. His remains (minus the mysteriously
missing head) were transferred in 1919
from Bordeaux, France, where he died in
self-imposed exile in 1828.

★**Templo de Debod** RUIN
(www.madrid.es; Paseo del Pintor Rosales; ⊘10am-
2pm & 6-8pm Tue-Fri, 9.30am-8pm Sat & Sun
Apr-Sep, 9.45am-1.45pm & 4.15-6.15pm Tue-Fri
& 9.30am-8pm Sat & Sun Oct-Mar; ⓂVentura
Rodríguez) **FREE** Yes, that *is* an Egyptian temple in downtown Madrid. The temple was
saved from the rising waters of Lake Nasser
in southern Egypt when Egyptian president
Gamal Abdel Nasser built the Aswan High
Dam. After 1968 it was sent block by block
to Spain as a gesture of thanks to Spanish
archaeologists in the Unesco team that
worked to save the monuments that would
otherwise have disappeared forever.

Plaza de Olavide PLAZA
(ⓂBilbao, Iglesia, Quevedo) Plaza de Olavide
hasn't always had its current form. From

LOCAL KNOWLEDGE

PEDRO ALMODÓVAR'S MADRID LOCATIONS
....

Plaza Mayor (p75) *La Flor de mi
secreto*

El Rastro (p80) *Laberinto de
pasiones*

Villa Rosa (p123) *Tacones lejanos*

Café del Circulo de Bellas Artes
(p118) *Kika*

Viaduct (p82) *Matador*

1934 the entire plaza was occupied by a covered, octagonal market. In November 1974, the market was demolished in a spectacular controlled explosion, opening up the plaza as one of Madrid's most agreeable public spaces. To see the plaza's history told in pictures, step into Bar Méntrida at No 3 for a drink and admire the photos on the wall.

Museo Sorolla   GALLERY
(Map p98; ☑91 310 15 84; http://museosorolla.mcu.es; Paseo del General Martínez Campos 37; adult/child €3/free, Sun & 2-8pm Sat free; ⏱9.30am-8pm Tue-Sat, 10am-3pm Sun; MIglesia, Gregorio Marañón) The Valencian artist Joaquín Sorolla immortalised the clear Mediterranean light of the Valencian coast. His Madrid house, a quiet mansion surrounded by lush gardens that he designed himself, was inspired by what he had seen in Andalucía and now contains the most complete collection of the artist's works.

Parque del Oeste   GARDENS
(Avenida del Arco de la Victoria; MMoncloa) Sloping down the hill behind the Moncloa metro station, Parque del Oeste (Park of the West) is quite beautiful, with plenty of shady corners where you can recline under a tree in the heat of the day and enjoy fine views out to the west towards Casa de Campo. It has been a *madrileño* favourite ever since its creation in 1906.

Museo de América   MUSEUM
(☑91 549 26 41; www.mecd.gob.es/museodeamerica; Avenida de los Reyes Católicos 6; adult/concession €3/1.50, free Sun; ⏱9.30am-3pm Tue, Wed, Fri & Sat, 9.30am-7pm Thu, 10am-3pm Sun; MMoncloa) Empire may have become a dirty word but it defined how Spain saw itself for centuries. Spanish vessels crossed the Atlantic to the Spanish colonies in Latin America, carrying adventurers one way and gold and other looted artefacts from indigenous cultures on the return journey. These latter pieces – at once the heritage of another continent and a fascinating insight into imperial Spain – are the subject of this excellent museum.

🏃 Activities

Hammam al-Andalus   SPA
(Map p84; ☑91 429 90 20; http://madrid.hammamalandalus.com; Calle de Atocha 14; treatments €30-73; ⏱10am-midnight; MSol) Housed in the excavated cellars of old Madrid, this imitation of a traditional Arab bath offers massages and aromatherapy beneath graceful arches, accompanied by the sound of trickling water. Prices are cheapest from 10am to 4pm Monday to Friday; reservations are required.

Lab Room Spa   SPA
(Map p98; ☑91 431 21 98; www.thelabroom.com; Calle de Claudio Coello 13; ⏱11am-8.30pm Mon-Fri, 11am-8pm Sat; MRetiro) An exclusive spa and beauty parlour whose past clients include Penélope Cruz, Jennifer Lopez, Gwyneth Paltrow and Gael García Bernal, the Lab Room is close to the ultimate in pampering for both men and women. It offers a range of make-up sessions, massages and facial and body treatments; prices can be surprising reasonable.

👣 Tours

Visitas Guiadas Oficiales   TOUR
(Official Guided Tours; Map p76; ☑902 221424; www.esmadrid.com/programa-visitas-guiadas-oficiales; Plaza Mayor 27; per person €17-21; MSol) Over 40 highly recommended walking, cycling and roller-blade tours conducted in Spanish and English. Organised by the Centro de Turismo de Madrid. Stop by the office and pick up its *M – Visitas Guiadas/ Guided Tours* catalogue.

Spanish Tapas Madrid   TOUR
(☑672 301231; www.spanishtapasmadrid.com; per person from €40) Local boy Luis Ortega takes you through some iconic Madrid tapas bars, as well as offering tours that take in old Madrid, flamenco and the Prado.

Adventurous Appetites   WALKING TOUR
(☑639 331073; www.adventurousappetites.com; 4hr tours €50; ⏱8pm-midnight Mon-Sat) English-language tapas tours through central Madrid. Prices include the first drink but exclude food.

Insider's Madrid   WALKING TOUR
(☑91 447 38 66; www.insidersmadrid.com; tours from €70) An impressive range of tailor-made tours, including walking, shopping, fashion, fine arts, tapas, flamenco and bullfighting tours.

Wellington Society   WALKING TOUR
(☑609 143203; www.wellsoc.org; tours €65-90) A handful of quirky historical tours laced with anecdotes and led by the inimitable Stephen Drake-Jones. Membership costs €65 and includes a day or evening walking tour.

Bike Spain

BICYCLE TOUR

(Map p76; ☎91 559 06 53; www.bikespain. info; Calle del Codo; bike rental half-/full day from €12/18, tours from €35; ☺10am-2pm & 4-7pm Mon-Fri Apr-Oct, 10am-2pm & 3-6pm Mon-Fri Nov-Mar; ⓂÓpera) Bicycle hire plus English-language guided city tours by bicycle, by day or (Friday) night, as well as longer expeditions.

Urban Movil

TOUR

(Map p76; ☎687 535443, 91 542 77 71; www. urbanmovil.com; Plaza Santiago 2; 1/2hr Segway tours €40/65; ☺10am-8pm; ⓂÓpera) Segway tours around Madrid; prices include 10 minutes' worth of training before you set out. It also organises bike tours.

🎓 Courses

Flamenco

Academia Amor de Dios

DANCE COURSE

(Centro de Arte Flamenco y Danza Española; Map p84; ☎91 360 04 34; www.amordedios.com; 1st fl, Calle de Santa Isabel 5; ⓂAntón Martín) This is the best-known course for flamenco dancing (and probably the hardest to get into). Although it's more for budding professionals (as the list of past graduates attests to) than casual visitors, it does have the odd Spanish-language 'cursillo' (little course) that runs for a day or more. It's on the top floor of the Mercado de Antón Martín.

Fundación
Conservatorio Casa Patas

DANCE COURSE

(Map p84; www.conservatorioflamenco.org; Calle de Cañizares 10; one-hour class from €17, per month €40-75, joining fee €3; ⓂAntón Martín, Tirso de Molina) There's every conceivable type of flamenco instruction here, including dance, guitar, singing and much more. It's upstairs from the Casa Patas flamenco venue.

Cooking

Alambique

COOKING COURSE

(Map p76; ☎91 547 42 20; www.alambique.com; Plaza de la Encarnación 2; per person from €45; ⓂÓpera, Santo Domingo) Most classes here last from 2½ to 3½ hours and cover a range of cuisines. Most are conducted in Spanish, but some are in English and French.

Kitchen Club

COOKING COURSE

(Map p104; ☎91 522 62 63; www.kitchenclub.es; Calle de Ballesta 8; ⓂGran Vía, Callao) Kitchen Club spans the globe with a range of courses just off the back of Gran Vía in the city centre. After each course there's time to eat what you've cooked.

Cooking Club

COOKING COURSE

(☎91 323 29 58; www.club-cooking.com; Calle de Veza 33; per person from €51; ⓂValdeacederas) This regular, respected program of classes encompasses a vast range of cooking styles.

Language

Universidad Complutense

LANGUAGE COURSE

(☎91 394 53 25; http://pendientedemigracion. ucm.es/info/cextran/Index; Secretaria de los Cursos para Extranjeros, Facultadole Filologia (Edificio A) Universidad Complutense; ⓂCuidad Universitaria) A range of language and cultural courses throughout the year. An intensive semester course of 120 contact hours costs €1100, while month-long courses (48 hours) start from €442.

🎉 Festivals & Events

January & February

Arco

ART

(Feria Internacional de Arte Contemporánea; www. ifema.es) One of Europe's biggest celebrations of contemporary art, Arco draws galleries and exhibitors from all over the world to the Parque Ferial Juan Carlos I exhibition centre near Barajas airport. It's held mid-February.

May & June

Fiesta de la
Comunidad de Madrid

CULTURAL

On 2 May 1808 Napoleon's troops put down an uprising in Madrid, and commemoration of the day has become an opportunity for much festivity. The day is celebrated with particular energy in the bars of Malasaña.

Fiesta de San Isidro

CULTURAL

(www.esmadrid.com) Around 15 May Madrid's patron saint is honoured with a week of nonstop processions, parties and bullfights. Free concerts are held throughout the city, and this week marks the start of the city's bullfighting season.

Suma Flamenca

FLAMENCO

(www.madrid.org/sumaflamenca) A soul-filled flamenco festival that draws some of the biggest names in the genre to the Teatros del Canal in June.

Día del Orgullo de Gays,
Lesbianas y Transexuales

GAY PRIDE

(www.orgullogay.org) The colourful Gay Pride Parade, on the last Saturday in June, sets out from the Puerta de Alcalá in the early evening, and winds its way around the city in an explosion of music and energy, ending up at the Puerta del Sol.

July & August

Veranos de la Villa SUMMER FESTIVAL
(www.veranosdelavilla.com) Madrid's town hall stages a series of cultural events, shows and exhibitions throughout July and August, known as Summers in the City.

🛏 Sleeping

Madrid has high-quality accommodation at prices that haven't been seen in the centre of other European capitals in decades. Five-star temples to good taste and a handful of buzzing hostels bookend a fabulous collection of midrange hotels; most of the mid-rangers are creative originals, blending high levels of comfort with an often-quirky sense of style.

🛏 Plaza Mayor & Royal Madrid

Hostal Madrid HOSTAL, APARTMENT €
(Map p84; ☑91 522 00 60; www.hostal-madrid. info; Calle de Esparteros 6; s €35-62, d €45-78, d apt €45-150; ❉ 🛜; Ⓜ Sol) The 24 rooms at this well-run *hostal* have been wonderfully renovated with exposed brickwork, brand-new bathrooms and a look that puts many three-star hotels to shame. They also have terrific apartments (some recently renovated, others ageing in varying stages of gracefulness and ranging in size from 33 sq metres to 200 sq metres). The apartments have a separate website – www.apartamentos mayorcentro.com.

Los Amigos Sol
Backpackers' Hostel HOSTEL €
(Map p76; ☑91 559 24 72; www.losamigoshostel. com; 4th fl, Calle de Arenal 26; dm incl breakfast €28-33; @🛜; Ⓜ Ópera, Sol) If you arrive in Madrid keen for company, this could be the place for you – lots of students stay here, the staff are savvy (and speak English) and there are bright dorm-style rooms (with free lockers) that sleep from two to four people. There's also a kitchen for guests. A steady stream of repeat visitors is the best recommendation we can give.

★ Hostal Central
Palace Madrid HOSTAL, HOTEL €€
(Map p76; ☑91 548 20 18; http://centralpalace madrid.com; Plaza de Oriente 2; d without/with view €99/119; ❉ 🛜; Ⓜ Ópera) Now here's something special. The views alone here would

be reason enough to come and definitely worth paying extra for – rooms with balcony look out over the Palacio Real and Plaza de Oriente. But the rooms themselves are lovely and light filled, with tasteful, subtle faux-antique furnishings, comfortable beds, light wood floors and plenty of space.

ApartoSuites
Jardines de Sabatini APARTMENT €€
(Map p76; ☑91 198 32 90; www.jardinesde sabatini.com; Cuesta de San Vicente 16; studio without/with views from €85/110, ste without/with views from €125/150; ❉ 🛜; Ⓜ Plaza de España, Príncipe Pío) Modern, spacious studios and suites are only half the story at this terrific property just down the hill from Plaza de España. Definitely pay extra for a room with a view and the studios with a balcony and uninterrupted views over the lovely Jardines de Sabatini to the Palacio Real – simply brilliant. The Campo del Moro is just across the road.

Mario Room Mate BOUTIQUE HOTEL €€
(Map p76; ☑91 548 85 48; www.room-matehotels .com; Calle de Campomanes 4; s €80-125, d €100-175; ❉ 🛜; Ⓜ Ópera) Entering this swanky boutique hotel is like crossing the threshold of Madrid's latest nightclub, with staff dressed all in black, black walls and swirls of red lighting in the lobby. Rooms can be small, but have high ceilings, simple furniture and light tones contrasting smoothly with muted colours and dark surfaces. Some rooms are pristine white; others have splashes of colour with zany murals.

Hotel Meninas BOUTIQUE HOTEL €€
(Map p76; ☑91 541 28 05; www.hotelmeninas. com; Calle de Campomanes 7; s/d from €75/95; ❉ 🛜; Ⓜ Ópera) This is a classy, cool choice. The colour scheme is blacks, whites and greys, with dark-wood floors and splashes of fuchsia and lime green. Flat-screen TVs in every room, modern bathroom fittings, and even a laptop in some rooms, round out the clean lines and latest innovations. Past guests include Viggo Mortensen and Natalie Portman. Some rooms are on the small side.

🛏 La Latina & Lavapiés

Hostal Horizonte HOSTEL €
(Map p84; ☑91 369 09 96; www.hostalhorizonte. com; 2nd fl, Calle de Atocha 28; s/d €44/60, without bathroom €32/48; 🛜; Ⓜ Antón Martín) Billing itself as a hostel run by travellers for

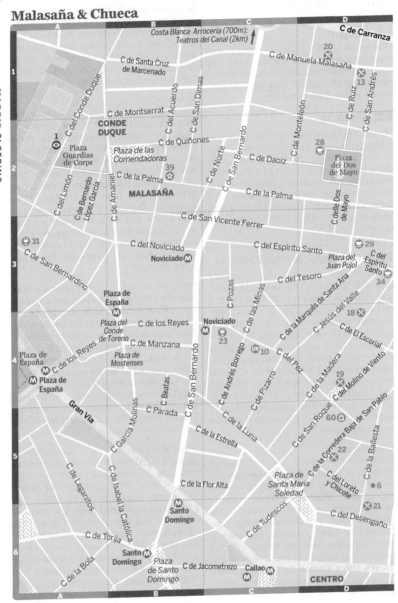

travellers, Hostal Horizonte is a well-run place. The rooms have far more character than your average hostel, with high ceilings, deliberately old-world furnishings and modern bathrooms. The King Alfonso XII room is especially well presented.

Cat's Hostel   HOSTEL €
(Map p84; ☎ 91 369 28 07; www.catshostel.com; Calle de Cañizares 6; dm €17-29; ❋ @ ☎; Ⓜ Antón Martín) Forming part of a 17th-century palace, the internal courtyard here is one of Madrid's finest – lavish Andalucian tilework,

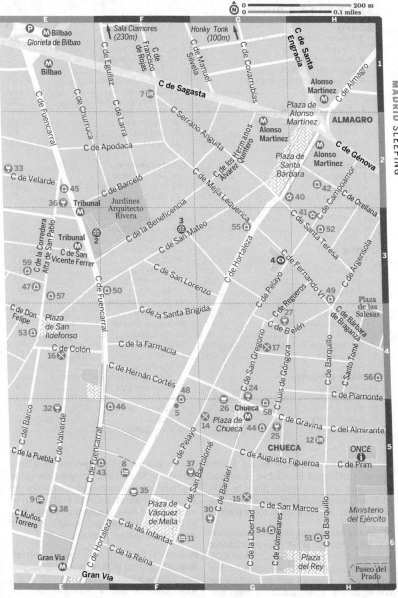

a fountain, a spectacular glass ceiling and stunning Islamic decoration, surrounded on four sides by an open balcony. There's a supercool basement bar with free internet and fiestas, often with live music. The rooms are functional.

Mad Hostel HOSTEL €

(Map p84; ☑91 506 48 40; www.madhostel. com; Calle de la Cabeza 24; dm €20-24; ✺@☎; ⓜ Antón Martín) From the people who brought you Cat's Hostel, Mad Hostel is similarly filled with life. The 1st-floor courtyard – with

Malasaña & Chueca

retractable roof – recreates an old Madrid *corrala* (traditional internal or communal patio) and is a wonderful place to chill, while the four- to eight-bed rooms are small-ish but clean. There's a small, rooftop gym.

★ **Posada del León de Oro**   BOUTIQUE HOTEL **€€**
(Map p81; ☎ 91 119 14 94; www.posadadelleon deoro.com; Calle de la Cava Baja 12; r from €105; ✳🖥; M La Latina) This rehabilitated inn has muted colour schemes and generally large rooms. There's a *corrala* in its core, and thoroughly modern rooms (some on the small side) along one of Madrid's best-loved streets. The downstairs bar is terrific.

Artrip   BOUTIQUE HOTEL **€€**
(☎ 91 539 32 82; www.artriphotel.com; Calle de Valencia 11; d/ste from €100/120; ✳🖥; M Lavapiés)

For an alternative but supremely comfortable take on Madrid life, Artrip is close to the big-three art museums and surrounded by plenty of private art galleries in the heart of multicultural Lavapiés. Rooms are dazzling white offset by strong splashes of colour and artful use of wooden beams.

Posada del Dragón   BOUTIQUE HOTEL **€€**
(Map p81; ☎ 91 119 14 24; www.posadadeldragon. com; Calle de la Cava Baja 14; r from €80; ✳🖥; M La Latina) At last, a boutique hotel in the heart of La Latina. This restored 19th-century inn sits on one of our favourite Madrid streets, and rooms either look out over the street or over the pretty internal patio. Some of the rooms are on the small side, but they've extremely comfortable beds, and bold, brassy colour schemes and designer

everything. There's a terrific bar-restaurant downstairs.

🛏 Sol, Santa Ana & Huertas

Madrid City Rooms
B&B €

(Map p84; ☎91 360 44 44; www.madridcity rooms.com; 2nd fl, Calle de la Cruz 6; s/d from €39/54; ❋🛜; ⓜSol) Don't let the exterior fool you because within, the simple yet colourful rooms, all with balconies and double-glazing, make for an excellent downtown budget bolt-hole. The friendly service, too, is a plus and the overall look is a touch more polished than your average *hostal*.

Hostal Luis XV
HOSTAL €

(Map p84; ☎91 522 10 21; www.hrluisxv.net; 8th fl, Calle de la Montera 47; s/d/tr from €44/58/74; ❋🛜; ⓜGran Vía) Everything here – especially the spacious rooms and the attention to detail – makes this family-run place feel pricier than it is. You'll find it hard to tear yourself away from the balconies outside every exterior room, from where the views are superb (especially from the triple in room 820) and you're so high up that noise is rarely a problem.

★Praktik Metropol
BOUTIQUE HOTEL €€

(Map p84; ☎91 521 29 35; www.hotelpraktik metropol.com; Calle de la Montera 47; s/d from €89/99; ❋🛜; ⓜGran Vía) You'd be hard-pressed to find better value anywhere in Europe than here in this recently overhauled hotel. The rooms have a fresh, contemporary look with white wood furnishings, and some (especially the corner rooms) have brilliant views down to Gran Vía and out over the city.

★Hotel Alicia
BOUTIQUE HOTEL €€

(Map p84; ☎91 389 60 95; www.room-mate hoteles.com; Calle del Prado 2; d €100-175, ste from €200; ❋🛜; ⓜSol, Sevilla, Antón Martín) One of the landmark properties of the designer Room Mate chain of hotels, Hotel Alicia overlooks Plaza de Santa Ana with beautiful, spacious rooms. The style (the work of designer Pascua Ortega) is a touch more muted than in other Room Mate hotels, but the supermodern look remains intact, the downstairs bar is oh-so-cool, and the service is young and switched on.

Catalonia Las Cortes
HOTEL €€

(Map p84; ☎91 389 60 51; www.hoteles-catalonia. es; Calle del Prado 6; s/d from €150/180; ❋🛜; ⓜAntón Martín) Occupying an 18th-century

palace and renovated in a style faithful to the era, this elegant hotel is a terrific choice right in the heart of Huertas. It's something of an oasis surrounded by the nonstop energy of the streets in this *barrio* (district), and the service is discreet and attentive. It gets plenty of return visitors, which is just about the best recommendation we can give.

Hotel Plaza Mayor
HOTEL €€

(Map p84; ☎91 360 06 06; www.h-plazamayor. com; Calle de Atocha 2; s/d from €37/47; ❋🛜; ⓜSol, Tirso de Molina) We love this place. Sitting just across from the Plaza Mayor, here you'll find stylish decor, helpful staff and charming original elements of this 150-year-old building. The rooms are attractive, some with a light colour scheme and wrought-iron furniture. The pricier attic rooms boast dark wood and designer lamps, and have lovely little terraces with wonderful rooftop views of central Madrid.

Hotel Urban
LUXURY HOTEL €€€

(Map p84; ☎91 787 77 70; www.derbyhotels. com; Carrera de San Jerónimo 34; r from €225; ❋🛜🏊; ⓜSevilla) This towering glass edifice is the epitome of art-inspired designer cool. It boasts original artworks from Africa and Asia; dark-wood floors and dark walls are offset by plenty of light; and the dazzling bathrooms have wonderful designer fittings – the washbasins are sublime. The rooftop swimming pool is one of Madrid's best and the gorgeous terrace is heaven on a candlelit summer's evening.

Me Meliá Reina Victoria
LUXURY HOTEL €€€

(Map p84; ☎91 701 60 00; www.memadrid. com; Plaza de Santa Ana 14; r from €175; ❋🛜; ⓜSol, Antón Martín) Once the landmark Gran Victoria Hotel, the Madrid home of many a famous bullfighter, this audacious new hotel is a landmark of a different kind. Overlooking the western end of Plaza de Santa Ana, this luxury hotel is decked out in minimalist white with curves and comfort in all the right places.

🛏 El Retiro & the Art Museums

★Lapepa Chic B&B
B&B €

(Map p84; ☎648 474742; www.lapepa-bnb.com; 7th fl, Plaza de las Cortes 4; s/d from €63/69; ❋🛜; ⓜBanco de España) A short step off the Paseo del Prado and on a floor with an art nouveau interior, this fine little B&B has lovely rooms with a contemporary, clean-lined look so different from the dour *hostal* furnishings you'll find elsewhere – modern art or even a bedhead lined with flamenco shoes gives this place personality in bucketloads.

Hotel Mora
HOTEL €€

(Map p88; ☑91 420 15 69; www.hotelmora. com; Paseo del Prado 32; s/d from €67/86; ❋ ⸛; Ⓜ Atocha) Alongside the landmark Caixa Forum, close to the main museums and a short (uphill) walk from the city centre, this simple, friendly hotel is a conveniently located and extremely well-priced option. Rooms are a little sparse and the furnishings a tad tired, but they're spacious and clean, and some look out across the Paseo del Prado.

★ Hotel Ritz
LUXURY HOTEL €€€

(Map p88; ☑91 701 67 67; www.ritzmadrid.com; Plaza de la Lealtad 5; d from €325, ste €850-5000; ❋ ⸛; Ⓜ Banco de España) The grand old lady of Madrid, the Hotel Ritz is the height of exclusivity. One of the most lavish buildings in the city, it has classic style and impeccable service that is second to none. Unsurprisingly it's the favoured hotel of presidents, kings and celebrities. The public areas are palatial and awash with antiques, while rooms are extravagantly large, opulent and supremely comfortable.

🛏 Salamanca

Hotel Jardín de Recoletos
HOTEL €€

(Map p98; ☑91 781 16 40; www.recoletos-hotel. com; Calle de Gil de Santivanes 6; d/tr from €185/212; ❋ ⸛; Ⓜ Retiro, Serrano) Attractive rooms are a given here, although decor varies from a more classic, understated look to wall-length modern photos and abundant use of wood. The overall feel is that of a downtown oasis, sheltered from the worst of Madrid's notorious noise and with a lovely terrace and garden area. The location is within walking distance of just about anywhere downtown.

Villa Magna
HOTEL €€€

(Map p98; ☑91 587 12 34; www.villamagna.es; Paseo de la Castellana 22; d €300-380, ste from €460; Ⓟ ❋ ⸛; Ⓜ Rubén Dario) This is a very Salamanca address, infused as it is with elegance and impeccable service. The look is brighter than you might imagine with the use of Empire chairs, Bauhaus ideas and even Chinese screens. The rooms are studiously classic in look with supremely comfortable furnishings and plenty of space. No expense has been spared in the rooftop suites.

🛏 Malasaña & Chueca

★ Hostal Main Street Madrid
HOSTAL €

(Map p76; ☑91 548 18 78; www.mainstreet madrid.com; 5th fl, Gran Vía 50; r from €61; ❋ ⸛; Ⓜ Callao, Santo Domingo) Excellent service is what travellers rave about here, but the rooms – modern and cool in soothing greys – are also some of the best *hostal* rooms you'll find anywhere in central Madrid. It's an excellent package and not surprisingly they're often full, so book well in advance.

Hostal América
HOSTAL €

(Map p104; ☑91 522 64 48; www.hostalamerica. net; 5th fl, Calle de Hortaleza 19; s/d €45/55; ❋ ⸛; Ⓜ Gran Vía) Run by a lovely mother-and-son team, the América has superclean, spacious and IKEA-dominated rooms. As most rooms face onto the usual interior 'patio' of the building, you should get a good night's sleep despite the busy area. For the rest of the time, there's a roof terrace – quite a luxury for a *hostal* in downtown Madrid – with tables, chairs and a coffee machine.

Hostal La Zona
HOSTAL €

(Map p104; ☑91 521 99 04; www.hostallazona. com; 1st fl, Calle de Valverde 7; s incl breakfast €38-58, d incl breakfast €50-70; ❋ ⸛; Ⓜ Gran Vía) Catering primarily to a gay clientele, the stylish Hostal La Zona has exposed brickwork, subtle colour shades and wooden pillars. We like a place where a sleep-in is encouraged – breakfast is served from 9am to noon, which is exactly the understanding Madrid's nightlife merits. Arnaldo and Vincent are friendly hosts.

Albergue Juvenil
HOSTEL €

(Map p104; ☑91 593 96 88; www.ajmadrid.es; Calle de Mejía Lequerica 21; dm incl breakfast €19-23; ❋ @ ⸛; Ⓜ Bilbao, Alonso Martínez) If you're looking for dormitory-style accommodation, you'd need a good reason to stay anywhere other than here while you're in Madrid. The Albergue has spotless rooms, no dorm houses more than six beds (each has its own bathroom), and facilities include a pool table, a gymnasium, wheelchair access, free internet, laundry and a TV/DVD room with a choice of movies.

★ Only You Hotel
BOUTIQUE HOTEL €€

(Map p104; ☑91 005 22 22; www.onlyyouhotels. com; Calle de Barquillo 21; d €158-260; ❋ @ ⸛; Ⓜ Chueca) This stunning new boutique hotel makes perfect use of a 19th-century Chueca mansion. The look is classy and contemporary and is the latest project by respected interior designer Lázaro Rosa-Violán. Nice touches include all-day à la carte breakfasts and a portable router that you can carry out into the city to stay connected.

Hotel Óscar
BOUTIQUE HOTEL €€

(Map p104; 📞 91 701 11 73; www.room-matehoteles. com; Plaza de Vázquez de Mella 12; d €90-225, ste €150-280; ❄️ 🛜; M Gran Vía) Hotel Óscar belongs to the highly original Room Mate chain of hotels, and the designer rooms ooze style and sophistication. Some have floor-to-ceiling murals, the lighting is always funky, and the colour scheme has splashes of pinks, lime greens, oranges or more-minimalist black and white.

Hotel Abalú
BOUTIQUE HOTEL €€

(Map p104; 📞 91 531 47 44; www.hotelabalu.com; Calle del Pez 19; d/ste from €75/119; ❄️ 🛜; M Noviciado) Malasaña's very own boutique hotel is starting to age and the word on the street is that it's not what it was. Even so, it's located on cool Calle del Pez and each room (some on the small side) has its own design drawn from the imagination of designer Luis Delgado, from retro chintz to Zen, baroque and pure white.

🛏️ Parque del Oeste & Northern Madrid

⭐ Innside Madrid Luchana
HOTEL €€

(📞 91 292 29 40; www.melia.com; Calle de Luchana 22; d €119-179, ste from €221; ❄️ 🛜; M Bilbao) Classy, contemporary rooms in an early-20th-century, neoclassical palace close to Plaza de Olavide in Chamberí make for a pleasant alternative to staying downtown. The wrap-around Innside Loft with views has abundant light and a modern four-poster bed.

⭐ Hotel Silken Puerta América
LUXURY HOTEL €€

(📞 91 744 54 00; www.hoteles-silken.com; Av de América 41; d/ste from €125/250; 🅿️ ❄️ 🛜; M Cartagena) Given the location of their hotel (halfway between the city and the airport) the owners knew they had to do something special – to build a self-contained world so innovative and luxurious that you'd never want to leave. Their idea? Give 22 of architecture's most creative names (eg Zaha Hadid, Norman Foster, Ron Arad, David Chipperfield, Jean Nouvel) a floor each to design.

⭐ Hotel Orfila
HOTEL €€€

(Map p98; 📞 91 702 77 70; www.hotelorfila.com; Calle de Orfila 6; r from €222; 🅿️ ❄️ 🛜; M Alonso Martínez) One of Madrid's best hotels, Hotel Orfila has all the luxuries of any five-star hotel – supremely comfortable rooms, for a start – but it's the personal service that elevates it into the upper echelon; regular guests get bathrobes embroidered with their own initials. An old-world elegance dominates the decor, and the quiet location and sheltered garden make it the perfect retreat at day's end.

🍴 Eating

Madrid has transformed itself into one of Europe's culinary capitals, not least because the city has long been a magnet for people (and cuisines) from all over Spain. Travel from one Spanish village to the next and you'll quickly learn that each has its own speciality; travel to Madrid and you'll find them all.

🍴 Plaza Mayor & Royal Madrid

⭐ Mercado de San Miguel
TAPAS €€

(Map p76; www.mercadodesanmiguel.es; Plaza de San Miguel; tapas from €1; ⏱️ 10am-midnight Sun-Wed, 10am-2am Thu-Sat; M Sol) One of Madrid's oldest and most beautiful markets, the Mercado de San Miguel has undergone a stunning major renovation. Within the early 20th-century glass walls, the market

---

LOCAL KNOWLEDGE

WHAT'S COOKING IN MADRID?

➡ *Cocido a la madrileña* (Madrid meat and-chickpea hotpot) at **Taberna La Bola** (p110), **Lhardy** (p113) or **Malacatín** (p111)

➡ *Cordero o cochinillo asado* (roast lamb or suckling pig) at **Restaurante Sobrino de Botín** (p110)

➡ *Sopa de ajo* (garlic soup) **Posada de la Villa** (p111)

➡ *Callos a la madrileña* (Madrid-style tripe) at **Taberna La Bola** (p110)

➡ *Huevos rotos* (potatoes cooked with eggs and jamón) at **Casa Lucio** (p111) or **Almendro 13** (Map p81; 📞 91 365 42 52; Calle del Almendro 13; mains €7-15; ⏱️ 1-4pm & 7.30pm-midnight Sun-Thu, 1-5pm & 8pm-1am Fri & Sat; M La Latina)

has become an inviting space strewn with tables. You can order tapas and sometimes more substantial plates at most of the counter-bars, and everything here (from caviar to chocolate) is as tempting as the market is alive.

Gourmet Experience
FOOD COURT €€

(Map p84; 9th fl, Plaza del Callao 2; mains €8-20; ⊘10am-10pm; Ⓜ Callao) Ride the elevator up to the 9th floor of the El Corte Inglés department store for one of downtown Madrid's best eating experiences. The views here are fabulous, especially those that look down over Plaza del Callao and down Gran Vía, but the food is also excellent, with everything from top-notch tapas to gourmet hamburgers.

Casa María
SPANISH €€

(Map p76; ✆91 559 10 07; www.casamariaplaza mayor.com; Plaza Mayor 23; tapas from €2.90, 4/6 tapas €11/16, mains €9-18; ⊘noon-11pm; Ⓜ Sol) A rare exception to the generally pricey and mediocre options that surround Plaza Mayor, Casa María combines professional service and a menu that effortlessly spans the modern and traditional. There's something for most tastes, with carefully chosen tapas, lunchtime stews and dishes such as sticky rice with lobster.

Taberna La Bola
MADRILEÑO €€

(Map p76; ✆91 547 69 30; www.labola.es; Calle de la Bola 5; mains €16-24; ⊘1.30-4.30pm & 8.30-11pm Mon-Sat, 1.30-4.30pm Sun, closed Aug; Ⓜ Santo Domingo) Taberna La Bola (going strong since 1870 and run by the sixth generation of the Verdasco family) is a much-loved bastion of traditional Madrid cuisine. If you're going to try *cocido a la madrileña* (meat-and-chickpea stew; €21) while in Madrid, this is a good place to do so. It's busy and noisy and very Madrid.

★ Restaurante Sobrino de Botín
CASTILIAN €€€

(Map p76; ✆91 366 42 17; www.botin.es; Calle de los Cuchilleros 17; mains €19-27; ⊘1-4pm & 8pm-midnight; Ⓜ La Latina, Sol) It's not every day that you can eat in the oldest restaurant in the world (the *Guinness Book of Records* has recognised it as the oldest – established in 1725). The secret of its staying power is fine *cochinillo asado* (roast suckling pig; €25) and *cordero asado* (roast lamb; €25) cooked in wood-fired ovens. Eating in the vaulted cellar is a treat.

✖ La Latina & Lavapiés

Bar Santurce
SPANISH €

(✆646 238303; www.barsanturce.com; Plaza General Vara del Rey 14; bocadillos from €2.50, raciones from €3.90; ⊘9am-3pm Tue-Sun; Ⓜ La Latina) This basic bar is famous for its *sardinas a la plancha* (sardines cooked on the grill) and *pimientos de padrón* (fiery green peppers). It's wildly popular on Sundays during El Rastro market when it can be difficult to even get near the bar. The *media ración* (half serve) of six sardines for €2 is Madrid's best bargain.

★ Taberna Matritum
MODERN SPANISH €€

(Map p81; ✆91 365 82 37; Calle de la Cava Alta 17; mains €12-22; ⊘1.30-4pm & 8.30pm-midnight Wed-Sun, 8.30pm-midnight Mon & Tue; Ⓜ La Latina) This little gem is reason enough to detour from the more popular Calle de la Cava Baja next door. The seasonal menu here encompasses terrific tapas, salads and generally creative cooking – try the *cocido* croquettes or the winter *calçots* (large spring onions) from Catalonia. The wine list runs into the hundreds and it's sophisticated without being pretentious. Highly recommended.

La Antoñita
MODERN SPANISH €€

(Map p81; ✆91 119 14 24; www.posadadeldragon. com; Calle de la Cava Baja 14; tapas from €5.90, mains from €13; ⊘2-11pm; Ⓜ La Latina) The restaurant of the stunning new hotel Posada del Dragón (p106), this fine place retains some features (exposed wooden beams, heavy stonework) of the original inn. There are tapas at the bar and a range of creative dishes ('fun market cooking' such as *secreto ibérico con guacamole* – pork fillet with guacamole – or the five types of marinated tomatoes) in the rear sit-down restaurant.

Lamiak
TAPAS €€

(Map p81; ✆91 365 52 12; Calle de la Cava Baja 42; raciones €5-11; ⊘1-4pm & 8pm-midnight Tue-Sat, 1-4pm Sun; Ⓜ La Latina) Another casual La Latina tapas bar, Lamiak is filled to the rafters on Sundays and busy at other times, thanks to its contemporary exhibitions, laid-back atmosphere, good wines and tapas dishes such as tomato with goat's cheese and caramelised onion, or red pepper stuffed with seafood.

Enotaberna del León de Oro
SPANISH €€

(Map p81; ✆91 119 14 94; www.posadadelleon deoro.com; Calle de la Cava Baja 12; tapas from

€3.50, mains €14-20; ⏱1-4pm & 8pm-midnight; Ⓜ La Latina) The stunning restoration work that brought to life the Posada del León de Oro (p106) also bequeathed to La Latina a fine new bar-restaurant. The emphasis is on matching carefully chosen wines with creative dishes (such as baby squid with potato emulsion and rocket pesto) in a casual atmosphere. There are also plenty of gins to choose from. It's a winning combination.

La Musa Latina
MODERN SPANISH €€

(Map p81; ☎91 354 02 55; www.grupolamusa.com/restaurante-lamusalatina; Costanilla de San Andrés 1; cold/hot tapas from €4/6, mains €4.50-12; ⏱10am-1am Mon-Wed, 10am-1.30am Thu, 10am-2am Fri & Sat, 10am-1am Sun; Ⓜ La Latina) Laid-back La Musa Latina has an ever-popular dining area and food that's designed to bring a smile to your face – the hanging kebabs have achieved something close to legendary status. The outdoor tables are lovely when the weather's warm, while the downstairs bar in the former wine cellar, complete with table tennis and table football, is also charming.

El Estragón
VEGETARIAN €€

(Map p81; ☎91 365 89 82; www.elestragonvegetariano.com; Plaza de la Paja 10; mains €8-15; ⏱11.30am-midnight; 🖊; Ⓜ La Latina) A delightful spot for crêpes, vegie burgers and other vegetarian specialities, El Estragón is undoubtedly one of Madrid's best vegetarian restaurants, although attentive vegans won't appreciate the use of butter. Apart from that, we're yet to hear a bad word about it, and the *menú del día* (daily set menu; from €9) is one of Madrid's best bargains.

Malacatín
MADRILEÑO €€

(Map p81; ☎91 365 52 41; www.malacatin.com; Calle de Ruda 5; mains €11-15; ⏱11am-5.30pm Mon-Sat & 8.15-11pm Thu & Fri, closed Aug; Ⓜ La Latina) If you want to see *madrileños* (people from Madrid) enjoying their favourite local food, this is one of the best places to do so. The clamour of conversation bounces off the tiled walls of the cramped dining area adorned with bullfighting memorabilia. The speciality is as much *cocido* as you can eat (€20).

The *degustación de cocido* (taste of *cocido*; €5) at the bar is a great way to try Madrid's favourite dish.

⭐ Casa Lucio
SPANISH €€€

(Map p81; ☎91 365 82 17, 91 365 32 52; www.casalucio.es; Calle de la Cava Baja 35; mains

LOCAL KNOWLEDGE

BOCADILLO DE CALAMARES

One of the lesser-known culinary specialities of Madrid is a *bocadillo de calamares* (a baguette-style roll filled to bursting with deep-fried calamari). You'll find them in many bars in the streets surrounding Plaza Mayor and neighbouring bars along Calle de los Botaneros, off Plaza Mayor's southeastern corner including La Campana (Map p76; ☎91 364 29 84; www.calamareslacampana.com; Calle de Botoneras 6; bocadillos €2.70; ⏱9am-11pm Sun-Thu, 9am-midnight Fri & Sat; Ⓜ Sol) or La Ideal (Map p76; ☎91 365 72 78; Calle de Botoneras 4; bocadillos €2.70; ⏱9am-11pm Sun-Thu, 9am-midnight Fri & Sat; Ⓜ Sol). At around €2.70, it's the perfect street snack.

€18-28; ⏱1-4pm & 8.30pm-midnight, closed Aug; Ⓜ La Latina) Lucio has been wowing *madrileños* with his light touch, quality ingredients and home-style local cooking since 1974 – think eggs (a Lucio speciality) and roasted meats in abundance. There's also *rabo de toro* (bull's tail) during the Fiestas de San Isidro Labrador and plenty of *rioja* (red wine) to wash away the mere thought of it.

The lunchtime *guisos del día* (stews of the day), including *cocido* on Wednesdays, are also popular. Casa Lucio draws an august, well-dressed crowd, which has included the former king of Spain, former US president Bill Clinton and Penélope Cruz.

Posada de la Villa
MADRILEÑO €€€

(Map p81; ☎91 366 18 80; www.posadadelavilla.com; Calle de la Cava Baja 9; mains €19-28; ⏱1-4pm & 8pm-midnight Mon-Sat, 1-4pm Sun, closed Aug; Ⓜ La Latina) This wonderfully restored 17th-century *posada* (inn) is something of a local landmark. The atmosphere is formal, the decoration sombre and traditional (heavy timber and brickwork), and the cuisine decidedly local – roast meats, *cocido*, *callos* (tripe) and *sopa de ajo* (garlic soup).

🍽 Sol, Santa Ana & Huertas

La Finca de Susana
SPANISH €

(Map p84; ☎91 369 35 57; www.grupandilana.com/es/restaurantes/la-finca-de-susana; Calle de Arlabán 4; mains €7-12; ⏱1-3.45pm & 8.30-11.30pm Sun-Wed, 1-3.45pm & 8.15pm-midnight Thu-Sat;

A TAPAS TOUR OF MADRID

La Latina & Lavapiés

Madrid's home of tapas is La Latina, especially along Calle de la Cava Baja and the surrounding streets. Almendro 13 (p109) is famous for quality rather than frilly elaborations, with cured meats, cheeses, tortillas and *huevos rotos* (literally 'broken eggs') the house specialities. Down on Calle de la Cava Baja, Taberna Txakolina (Map p81; ☎ 91 366 48 77; www.tabernatxakolinamadrid.com; Calle de la Cava Baja 26; tapas from €4; ☺ 8pm-midnight Tue, 1-4pm & 8pm-midnight Wed-Sat, 1-4pm Sun; Ⓜ La Latina) does Basque 'high cuisine in miniature'; wash it all down with a *txacoli*, a sharp Basque white. Casa Lucas (Map p81; ☎ 91 365 08 04; www.casalucas.es; Calle de la Cava Baja 30; tapas/raciónes from €5/12; ☺ 1-3.30pm & 8pm-midnight Thu-Tue, 1-3.30pm Wed; Ⓜ La Latina) and La Chata (Map p81; ☎ 91 366 14 58; Calle de la Cava Baja 24; mains €10-23, tapas from €3; ☺ 1-4pm & 8.30pm-midnight Thu-Mon, 8.30pm-midnight Tue & Wed; Ⓜ La Latina) are also hugely popular. Not far away, Juana La Loca (Map p81; ☎ 91 364 05 25; Plaza de la Puerta de Moros 4; tapas from €5, mains €8-19; ☺ noon-1am Tue-Sun, 8pm-1am Mon; Ⓜ La Latina) does a magnificent *tortilla de patatas* (potato and onion omelette), as does Txirimiri (Map p81; ☎ 91 364 11 96; www.txirimiri.es; Calle del Humilladero 6; tapas from €4; ☺ noon-4.30pm & 8.30pm-midnight Mon-Sat, closed Aug; Ⓜ La Latina).

Plaza Mayor, Sol & Huertas

For *bacalao* (cod), Casa Labra (Map p84; ☎ 91 532 14 05; www.casalabra.es; Calle de Tetuán 11; tapas from €1.25; ☺ 11.30am-3.30pm & 6-11pm; Ⓜ Sol) has been around since 1860 and was a favourite of the poet Federico García Lorca. However, many *madrileños* wouldn't eat *bacalao* anywhere except Casa Revuelta (Map p76; ☎ 91 366 33 32; Calle de Latoneros 3; tapas from €2.80; ☺ 10.30am-4pm & 7-11pm Tue-Sat, 10.30am-4pm Sun, closed Aug; Ⓜ Sol, La Latina), clinched by the fact that the owner painstakingly extracts every fish bone in the morning.

In Huertas, La Casa del Abuelo (Map p84; ☎ 902 027334; www.lacasadelabuelo.es; Calle de la Victoria 12; raciónes from €9.50; ☺ noon-midnight Sun-Thu, noon-1am Fri & Sat; Ⓜ Sol) is famous for *gambas a la plancha* (grilled prawns) or *gambas al ajillo* (prawns sizzling in garlic on little ceramic plates) and a *chato* (small glass) of the heavy, sweet El Abuelo red wine. For *patatas bravas* (fried potatoes lathered in a spicy tomato sauce), Las Bravas (Map p84; ☎ 91 522 85 81; www.lasbravas.com; Callejón de Álvarez Gato 3; raciónes €3.75-12; ☺ 12.30-4.30pm & 7.30pm-12.30am; Ⓜ Sol, Sevilla) is the place. Another good choice down the bottom of the Huertas hill is Los Gatos (p113) with eclectic decor and terrific canapés. Ramiro's Tapas Wine Bar (p113).

El Retiro, the Art Museums & Salamanca

Along the Paseo del Prado, there's only one choice for tapas and it's one of Madrid's best: Estado Puro (p113). In Salamanca, Biotza (p114) offers creative Basque *pintxos* (tapas) in stylish surrounds.

Chueca

Chueca is another stellar tapas barrio. Don't miss Bocaito (p115), a purveyor of Andalucian *jamón* (ham) and seafood. Bodega de La Ardosa (Map p104; ☎ 91 521 49 79; www.laardosa.es; Calle de Colón 13; tapas & raciónes €4-11; ☺ 8.30am-2am Mon-Fri, 12.45pm-2.30am Sat & Sun; Ⓜ Tribunal) is extremely popular for its *salmorejo* (cold, tomato-based soup), *croquetas, patatas bravas* and *tortilla de patatas,* while Casa Julio (p114) is widely touted as the home of Madrid's best *croquetas*. Other brilliant choices include Le Cabrera (p120) and Baco y Beto (p114).

Ⓜ Sevilla) It's difficult to find a better combination of price, quality cooking and classy atmosphere anywhere in Huertas. The softly lit dining area is bathed in greenery and the sometimes-innovative, sometimes-traditional food draws a hip young crowd. The duck con-

fit with plums, turnips and couscous is a fine choice. No reservations.

★ Vi Cool   MODERN SPANISH €€
(Map p84; ☎ 91 429 49 13; www.vi-cool.com; Calle de las Huertas 12; mains €8-19; ☺ 1.30-4.15pm

& 8.30pm-12.15am Tue-Sun; M Antón Martín) Catalan master chef Sergi Arola is one of the most restless and relentlessly creative culinary talents in the country. Aside from his showpiece Sergi Arola Gastro (p116), he has dabbled in numerous new restaurants around the capital and in Barcelona, and this is one of his most interesting yet.

It's a modern bar-style space with prices that enable the average mortal to sample his formidable gastronomic skill, dishes might include sardines marinated in oil from sun-dried tomatoes and fresh oregano, or fried prawns with curry and mint. There's another branch in Salamanca.

★ **Ramiro's Tapas Wine Bar**   TAPAS €€

(Map p84; ☑ 91 843 73 47; Calle de Atocha 51; tapas from €4.50, raciones from €10; ☉ 1-4.30pm & 8-11.30pm Mon-Sat, 1-4.30pm Sun; M Antón Martín) One of the best tapas bars to open in Madrid in recent years, this fine gastrobar offers up traditional tapas with subtle but original touches. Most of the cooking comes from Castilla y León but staff do exceptional things with cured meats, foie gras and prawns. Highly recommended.

★ **Casa Alberto**   TAPAS €€

(Map p84; ☑ 91 429 93 56; www.casaalberto. es; Calle de las Huertas 18; tapas €4-10, raciones €6.50-16, mains €14-21; ☉ restaurant 1.30-4pm & 8pm-midnight Tue-Sat, 1.30-4pm Sun, bar 12.30pm-1.30am Tue-Sat, 12.30-4pm Sun, closed Sun Jul & Aug; M Antón Martín) One of the most atmospheric old *tabernas* (taverns) of Madrid, Casa Alberto has been around since 1827 and occupies a building where Cervantes is said to have written one of his books. The secret to its staying power is vermouth on tap, excellent tapas at the bar and fine sit-down meals.

Casa Alberto's *rabo de toro* (bull's tail) is famous among aficionados, but the tavern is also known for its pig's trotters, snails, meatballs, croquettes and cod.

Los Gatos   TAPAS €€

(Map p84; ☑ 91 429 30 67; Calle de Jesús 2; tapas from €3.50; ☉ 11am-2am; M Antón Martín) Tapas you can point to without deciphering the menu and eclectic old-world decor (from bullfighting memorabilia to a fresco of skeletons at the bar) make this a popular choice down the bottom end of Huertas. The most popular orders are the *canapés* (tapas on toast), which, we have to say, are rather delicious.

★ **Lhardy**   SPANISH €€€

(Map p84; ☑ 91 521 33 85; www.lhardy.com; Carrera de San Jerónimo 8; mains €19-38; ☉ 1-3.30pm & 8.30-11pm Mon-Sat, 1-3.30pm Sun, closed Aug; M Sol, Sevilla) This Madrid landmark (since 1839) is an elegant treasure trove of takeaway gourmet tapas downstairs, while the six upstairs dining areas are the upmarket preserve of traditional Madrid dishes with an occasional hint of French influence. House specialities include *cocido a la madrileña* (meat-and-chickpea stew; €36), pheasant and wild duck in an orange perfume.

✘ El Retiro & the Art Museums

★ **Estado Puro**   TAPAS €€

(Map p88; ☑ 91 330 24 00; www.tapasenestado puro.com; Plaza Neptuno (Plaza de Cánovas del Castillo) 4; tapas €5-16, mains €13-22; ☉ noon-midnight Mon-Sat, noon-4pm Sun; M Banco de España, Atocha) This slick but casual tapas bar serves up fantastic tapas, such as the *tortilla española siglo XXI* (21st-century Spanish omelette, served in a glass...), lobster gazpacho and parmesan ice cream. The kitchen here is overseen by Paco Roncero, the head chef at **La Terraza del Casino** (p41) who learned his trade with master chef Ferran Adrià.

✘ Salamanca

★ **Platea**   SPANISH €€

(Map p98; ☑ 91 577 00 25; www.plateamadrid. com; Calle de Goya 5-7; ☉ 12.30pm-12.30am Sun-Wed, 12.30pm-2.30am Thu-Sat; M Serrano, Colón) Platea is one of the most exciting things to happen in Madrid's eating scene in years. The ornate Carlos III cinema opposite the Plaza de Colón has been artfully transformed into a dynamic culinary scene with more than a hint of burlesque. The chefs here boast six Michelin stars among them.

There are 12 restaurants (among them the outstanding Arriba), three gourmet food stores and cocktail bars.

Working with the original theatre-style layout, the developers have used the multi-level seating to array a series of restaurants that seem at once self-contained yet connected to the whole through the soaring open central space, with all of them in some way facing the stage area where cabaret-style or 1930s-era performances or live cooking shows provide a rather glamorous backdrop. It's where food court meets haute cuisine, a daring combination of lunch or dinner with

EL RINCÓN DE JEREZ

Out in the eastern reaches of Salamanca, the Andalucian bar El Rincón de Jerez (☏ 91 112 30 80; www.elnuevorincondejerez.es; Calle de Rufino Blanco 5; raciones €7-13; ⏲ 1-4.30pm & 7pm-midnight Tue-Sat, 1-4.30pm Sun Sep-Jul; Ⓜ Manuel Becerra) is utterly unlike anywhere else in Madrid. At 11pm from Tuesday to Saturday, they turn off the lights, light the candles and sing as one La Salve Rociera, a near-mythical song with deep roots in the flamenco and Catholic traditions of the south. It'll send chills down your spine.

floor show without the formality that usually infuses such places.

José Luis
SPANISH €€

(☏ 91 563 09 58; www.joseluis.es; Calle de Serrano 89; tapas from €5; ⏲ 8.30am-1am Mon-Fri, 9am-1am Sat, 12.30pm-1am Sun; Ⓜ Gregorio Marañón) With numerous branches around Madrid, José Luis is famous for its fidelity to traditional Spanish recipes. It wins many people's vote for Madrid's best tortilla de patatas (Spanish potato omelette), but it's also good for croquetas and ensaladilla rusa (Russian salad). This outpost along Calle de Serrano has a slightly stuffy, young-men-in-suits feel to it, which is, after all, very Salamanca.

Biotza
TAPAS, BASQUE €€

(Map p98; ☏ 91 781 03 13; Calle de Claudio Coello 27; cold/hot pintxos €2.80/3.40, raciones from €6, set menus from €18; ⏲ 1-5pm & 8pm-midnight Mon-Sat; Ⓜ Serrano) This breezy Basque tapas bar is one of the best places in Madrid to sample the creativity of bite-sized pintxos (Basque tapas) as only the Basques can make them. It's the perfect combination of San Sebastián–style tapas, Madrid-style pale-green/red-black decoration and unusual angular benches. The prices quickly add up, but it's highly recommended nonetheless.

There's also a more formal Basque restaurant out the back.

✕ Malasaña & Chueca

★ Casa Julio
SPANISH €

(Map p104; ☏ 91 522 72 74; Calle de la Madera 37; 6/12 croquetas €5/10; ⏲ 1-3.30pm & 6.30-11pm Mon-Sat Sep-Jul; Ⓜ Tribunal) A citywide poll for the best croquetas (croquettes) in Madrid would see half of those polled voting for Casa Julio and the remainder not doing so only because they haven't been yet. They're that good that celebrities and mere mortals from all over Madrid come here, along with the crusty old locals.

★ Bazaar
MODERN SPANISH €

(Map p104; ☏ 91 523 39 05; www.restaurantbazaar.com; Calle de la Libertad 21; mains €6.50-10; ⏲ 1.15-4pm & 8.30-11.30pm Sun-Wed, 1.15-4pm & 8.15pm-midnight Thu-Sat; Ⓜ Chueca) Bazaar's popularity among the well-heeled Chueca set shows no sign of abating. Its pristine white interior design, with theatre-style lighting and wall-length windows, may draw a crowd that looks like it's stepped out of the pages of ¡Hola! magazine, but the food is extremely well priced and innovative, and the atmosphere is casual.

Baco y Beto
TAPAS €

(Map p104; ☏ 91 522 84 41; Calle de Pelayo 24; tapas from €4; ⏲ 8pm-1am Mon-Fri, 2-4.30pm & 8.30pm-1am Sat; Ⓜ Chueca) Friends of ours in Madrid begged us not to include this place in our reviews and we must admit that we were tempted to keep this secret all to ourselves. Some of the tastiest tapas in Madrid are what you'll find here. The clientele is predominantly gay, and they, like our friends, can't have it all to themselves.

★ Albur
TAPAS €€

(Map p104; ☏ 91 594 27 33; www.restaurantealbur.com; Calle de Manuela Malasaña 15; mains €11-16; ⏲ 1-5pm & 8pm-12.30am Mon-Fri, 1pm-1am Sat & Sun; Ⓜ Bilbao) One of Malasaña's best deals, this place has a wildly popular tapas bar and a classy but casual restaurant out the back. The restaurant waiters never seem to lose their cool, and their extremely well-priced rice dishes are the stars of the show, although in truth you could order anything here and leave well satisfied.

Bon Vivant & Co
SEAFOOD €€

(Map p104; ☏ 91 704 82 86; www.bonvivantco.es; Calle de San Gregorio 8; mains €9-15; ⏲ 9am-1am Mon-Fri, 10am-2am Sat & Sun; Ⓜ Chueca) What a lovely little spot this is. Set on a tiny square, its wooden tables flooded with natural light through the big windows, Bon Vivant & Co is ideal for a casual meal, a quietly intimate encounter or simply an afternoon spent reading the papers. Food is simple but tasty – tapas, focaccias, salads, brunch...

Maricastaña

SPANISH €€

(Map p104; ☑ 91 082 71 42; www.maricastana madrid.com; Corredera Baja de San Pablo 12; mains €9-19; ⊙ 9am-2am Mon-Thu, 9am-2.30am Fri & Sat, 10am-2am Sun; Ⓜ Callao) This fabulous find sits in the increasingly cool corner of Malasaña that is flourishing just off the back of Gran Vía. The decor is quite lovely, all potted plants, creative lighting, iron pillars and rustic brickwork. The food is simple but excellent – try the pumpkin croquettes or the tuna pieces with bean shoots and strawberries.

La Mucca de Pez

TAPAS €€

(Map p104; ☑ 91 521 00 00; www.lamucca.es; Plaza Carlos Cambronero 4; mains €9-16; ⊙ 1pm-1am Mon-Fri, 1pm-2am Sat & Sun; Ⓜ Callao) The only problem with this place is that it's such an agreeable spot to spend an afternoon, it can be impossible to snaffle a table. An ample wine list complements the great salads, creative pizzas and a good mix of meat and seafood mains, while the atmosphere makes it all taste even better.

Bocaito

TAPAS €€

(Map p84; ☑ 91 532 12 19; www.bocaito.com; Calle de la Libertad 4-6; tapas €2-8, mains €10-29; ⊙ 1-4pm & 8.30pm-midnight Mon-Sat; Ⓜ Chueca, Sevilla) Film-maker Pedro Almodóvar once described this traditional bar and restaurant as 'the best antidepressant'. Forget about the sit-down restaurant (which is nonetheless well regarded) and jam into the bar, shoulder-to-shoulder with the casual crowd, order a few Andalucian *raciones* off the menu and slosh them down with some gritty red or a *caña* (small glass of beer).

La Paella de la Reina

MEDITERRANEAN €€

(Map p84; ☑ 91 531 18 85; www.lapaelladela reina.com; Calle de la Reina 39; mains €14-21; ⊙ 1-4pm & 7.30-11.30pm; Ⓜ Banco de España) Madrid is not renowned for its paella (Valencia is king in that regard), but Valencianos who can't make it home are known to frequent La Paella de la Reina. Like any decent paella restaurant, you need two people to make an order but, that requirement satisfied, you've plenty of choice. The typical Valencia paella is cooked with beans, chicken and rabbit.

La Musa

SPANISH, FUSION €€

(Map p104; ☑ 91 448 75 58; www.grupolamusa. com; Calle de Manuela Malasaña 18; cold/hot tapas from €4/6, mains €11-16; ⊙ 9am-midnight Mon-Wed, 9am-1am Fri, 1pm-2am Sat, 1pm-midnight Sun; Ⓜ San Bernardo) Snug, loud and un-pretentious, La Musa is all about designer decor, lounge music and memorably fun food. The menu is divided into three types of tapas – hot, cold and barbecue. Among the hot varieties is the fantastic *jabalí con ali-oli de miel y sobrasada* (wild boar with honey mayonnaise and *sobrasada* – a soft and spreadable mildly spicy sausage from Mallorca).

★ La Tasquita de Enfrente

MODERN SPANISH €€€

(Map p104; ☑ 91 532 54 49; www.latasquitade enfrente.com; Calle de la Ballesta 6; mains €17-32, set menus €45-69; ⊙ 1.30-4.30pm & 8.30pm-midnight Mon-Sat; Ⓜ Gran Vía) It's difficult to overstate how popular this place is among people in the know in Madrid's food scene. The seasonal menu prepared by chef Juanjo López never ceases to surprise while also combining simple Spanish staples to stunning effect. His *menú de degustación* (tasting menu; €50) or *menú de Juanjo* (€65) would be our choice if this is your first time. Reservations are essential.

✗ Parque del Oeste & Northern Madrid

Casa Mingo

ASTURIAN €

(☑ 91 547 79 18; www.casamingo.es; Paseo de la Florida 34; raciones €3-11; ⊙ 11am-midnight; Ⓜ Príncipe Pío) Opened in 1888, Casa Mingo is a well-known and vaguely cavernous Asturian cider house. It's kept simple here, focusing primarily on the signature dish of *pollo asado* (roast chicken, cut in quarters; €11) accompanied by a bottle of cider. Combine with a visit to the neighbouring Ermita de San Antonio de la Florida (p100).

★ Mama Campo

SPANISH €€

(☑ 91 447 41 38; www.mamacampo.es; Plaza de Olavide; mains €6-12; ⊙ 1.30-5.30pm & 8.30pm-1.30am Tue-Sat, 1.30-5.30pm Sun; Ⓜ Bilbao, Iglesia, Quevedo) There's a certain sameness to the bars that surround the Plaza de Olavide, but this new place changes everything. Positioning itself as an ecofriendly take on the Spanish *taberna* (tavern), it's gone for a winning white decor within and a fresh approach to Spanish staples, always with an emphasis on fresh, organic ingredients. It also has tables on the plaza, one of our favourites.

Costa Blanca Arrocería

SPANISH €€

(☑ 91 448 58 32; Calle de Bravo Murillo 3; mains €12-22; ⊙ 1.30-4pm Mon, 1.30-4pm & 8.30-11.30pm

Tue-Fri, 2-4pm & 8.30-11.30pm Sat & Sun; Ⓜ Quevedo) Even if you don't have plans to be in Chamberí, it's worth a trip across town to this casual bar-restaurant that offers outstanding rice dishes, including paella. The quality is high and prices are among the cheapest in town. Start with *almejas a la marinera* (baby clams) and follow it up with *paella de marisco* (seafood paella) for the full experience.

As always in such places, you'll need two people to make up an order.

Las Tortillas de Gabino SPANISH €€
(Map p98; ☎91 319 75 05; www.lastortillas degabino.com; Calle de Rafael Calvo 20; tortillas €9-15, mains €12-20; ⊘1.30-4pm & 9-11.30pm Mon-Sat; Ⓜ Iglesia) It's a brave Spanish chef that fiddles with the iconic *tortilla de patatas* (potato omelette), but the results here are delicious – such as tortilla with octopus, and with all manner of surprising combinations. This place also gets rave reviews for its *croquetas*. The service is excellent and the bright yet classy dining area adds to the sense of a most agreeable eating experience.

Reservations are highly recommended.

★ DiverXo MODERN SPANISH €€€
(☎915 70 07 66; http://diverxo.com; Calle de Padre Damián, 23; mains €70-90, set menus €95-200; ⊘2-3.30pm & 9-10.30pm Tue-Sat, closed three weeks in Aug; Ⓜ Cuzco) Madrid's only three-Michelin-starred restaurant, DiverXo in northern Madrid is one of Spain's most unusual culinary experiences. Chef David Muñoz is something of the enfant terrible of Spain's cooking scene. Still in his 30s, he favours what he has described as a 'brutal' approach to cooking – his team of chefs appear as you're mid bite to add surprising new ingredients.

The carefully choreographed experience centres around the short (2½-hour, seven-course) or long (four-hour, 11-course) menus, or the 'Wow' and 'Glutton Wow' menus, and is utterly unlike the more formal upmarket dining options elsewhere. The nondescript suburban setting and small premises (chefs sometimes end up putting the finishing touches to dishes in the hallway) only add to the whole street-smart atmosphere. Bookings up to six months in advance are required.

★ Santceloni CATALAN €€€
(☎91 210 88 40; www.restaurantesantceloni. com; Paseo de la Castellana 57; mains €44-71, set menus €150-180; ⊘2-4pm & 9-11pm Mon-Fri, 9-11pm Sat Sep-Jul; Ⓜ Gregorio Marañón) The Michelin-starred Santceloni is one of Madrid's best restaurants, with luxury decor, faultless service, fabulous wines and nouvelle cuisine from the kitchen of chef Óscar Velasco. Each dish is a work of art and the menu changes with the seasons, but we'd recommend one of the *menús gastronómicos* to really sample the breadth of surprising tastes.

★ Sergi Arola Gastro MODERN SPANISH €€€
(Map p98; ☎91 310 21 69; www.sergiarola.es; Calle de Zurbano 31; mains €49-58, set menus €49-195; ⊘2-3.30pm & 9-11.30pm Tue-Sat Sep-May; Ⓜ Alonso Martínez) Sergi Arola, a stellar Catalan celebrity chef who has adopted Madrid as his own, runs this highly personalised temple to all that's innovative in Spanish gastronomy. The menus change with the seasons but this is culinary indulgence at its finest, the sort of place where creativity, presentation and taste are everything. And oh, what tastes... Booking well in advance is necessary.

🍷 Drinking & Nightlife

Nights in the Spanish capital are the stuff of legend. They're invariably long and loud most nights of the week, rising to a deafening crescendo as the weekend nears. And what Ernest Hemingway wrote of the city in the 1930s remains true to this day: 'Nobody goes to bed in Madrid until they have killed the night.'

🍸 Plaza Mayor & Royal Madrid

★ The Sherry Corner WINE BAR
(Map p76; ☎681 007 700; www.sherry-corner. com; Stall 24, Mercado de San Miguel, Plaza de San Miguel; ⊘10am-9pm; Ⓜ Sol) The Sherry Corner, inside the Mercado de San Miguel, has found an excellent way to give a crash course in sherry. For €25, you get six small glasses of top-quality sherry to taste, each of which is matched to a different tapa. Guiding you through the process is an audioguide in eight languages (Spanish, English, German, French, Italian, Portuguese, Russian and Japanese).

★ Chocolatería de San Ginés CAFE
(Map p76; ☎91 365 65 46; www.chocolateria sangines.com; Pasadizo de San Ginés 5; ⊘24hr; Ⓜ Sol) One of the grand icons of the Madrid night, this *chocolate con churros* cafe sees a sprinkling of tourists throughout the

day, but locals pack it out in their search for sustenance on their way home from a nightclub somewhere close to dawn. Only in Madrid...

⭐ **Teatro Joy Eslava**   CLUB
(Joy Madrid; Map p76; ☑ 91 366 37 33; www.joy-eslava.com; Calle del Arenal 11; ⏰ 11.30pm-6am; Ⓜ Sol) The only things guaranteed at this grand old Madrid dance club (housed in a 19th-century theatre) are a crowd and the fact that it'll be open (it claims to have operated every single day for the past 29 years). The music and the crowd are a mixed bag, but queues are long and invariably include locals and tourists, and even the occasional *famoso* (celebrity).

Charada   CLUB
(Map p76; ☑ 663 230504; www.charada.es; Calle de la Bola 13; ⏰ midnight-6am Wed-Sun; Ⓜ Santo Domingo) Charada is a reliable regular on the Madrid clubbing scene. Its two rooms (one red, the other black) are New York chic with hardly a hint of the building's former existence as a brothel. The cocktails are original, and we especially like it when they turn their attention to electronica, but they also do disco and house. Admission is €12.

Anticafé   CAFE
(Map p76; Calle de la Unión 2; ⏰ 5pm-2am Tue-Sun; Ⓜ Ópera) Bohemian kitsch in the best sense is the prevailing theme here and it runs right through the decor, regular cultural events (poetry readings and concerts) and, of course, the clientele. As such, it won't be to everyone's taste, but we think that it adds some much-needed variety to the downtown drinking scene.

Café del Real   BAR
(Map p76; ☑ 91 547 21 24; Plaza de Isabel II 2; ⏰ 8am-1am Mon-Thu, 8am-2.30am Fri, 9am-2.30am Sat, 10am-11.30pm Sun; Ⓜ Ópera) A cafe and cocktail bar in equal parts, this intimate little place serves up creative coffees and a few cocktails to the soundtrack of chill-out music. The best seats are upstairs, where the low ceilings, wooden beams and leather chairs make for a great place to pass an afternoon with friends.

🍷 La Latina & Lavapiés

⭐ **Taberna Tempranillo**   WINE BAR
(Map p81; Calle de la Cava Baja 38; ⏰ 1-3.30pm & 8pm-midnight Tue-Sun, 8pm-midnight Mon; Ⓜ La

LA HORA DEL VERMUT

Sunday. One o'clock in the afternoon. A dark bar off Calle de la Cava Baja. In any civilised city the bar would be shut tight, but in Madrid the place is packed because it's *la hora del vermut* (vermouth hour), a long-standing tradition whereby friends and families head out for a quick aperitif before Sunday lunch. Sometimes referred to as *ir de Rastro* (going to the Rastro) because so many of the traditional vermouth bars are in and around El Rastro market, this Sunday tradition is deeply ingrained in *madrileño* culture. Some of the best bars for vermouth are along La Latina's Calle de la Cava Baja, while Casa Alberto (p113) is another legendary part of this fine tradition.

Latina) You could come here for the tapas, but we recommend Taberna Tempranillo primarily for its wines, of which it has a selection that puts numerous Spanish bars to shame; many wines are sold by the glass. It's not a late-night place, but it's always packed in the early evening and on Sundays after El Rastro.

⭐ **Delic**   BAR
(Map p81; ☑ 91 364 54 50; www.delic.es; Costanilla de San Andrés 14; ⏰ 11am-2am Sun & Tue-Thu, 11am-2.30am Fri & Sat; Ⓜ La Latina) We could go on for hours about this long-standing cafe-bar, but we'll reduce it to its most basic elements: nursing an exceptionally good mojito (€8) or three on a warm summer's evening at Delic's outdoor tables on one of Madrid's prettiest plazas is one of life's great pleasures. Bliss.

El Viajero   BAR
(Map p81; ☑ 91 366 90 64; www.elviajeromadrid.com; Plaza de la Cebada 11; ⏰ 5pm-2am Tue-Fri, noon-2.30am Sat, noon-midnight Sun; Ⓜ La Latina) The undoubted highlight of this landmark of La Latina nights is the rooftop *terraza*, which boasts fine views down onto the thronging streets. When the weather's warm, it's nigh on impossible to get a table. Our secret? Staff often close the *terraza* around 8pm to spruce it up a little before the evening rush; be ready to pounce when it reopens and thereafter guard your table with your life.

Gau&Café
CAFE

(www.gaucafe.com; 4th fl, Calle de Tribulete 14; ⊙11am-midnight Mon-Fri, 1.30pm-midnight Sat; M Lavapiés) Decoration that's light and airy, with pop-art posters of Audrey Hepburn and James Bond. A large terrace with views over the Lavapiés rooftops. A stunning backdrop of a ruined church atop which the cafe sits. With so much else going for it, it almost seems incidental that it also serves great teas, coffees and snacks (as well as meals).

Café del Nuncio
BAR

(Map p81; ☑91 366 08 53; Calle de Segovia 9; ⊙12.30pm-2.30am Sun-Thu, 12.30pm-3am Fri & Sat; M La Latina) Café de Nuncio straggles down a laneway to Calle de Segovia. You can drink on one of several cosy levels inside or, better still in summer, enjoy the outdoor seating that one local reviewer likened to a slice of Rome. By day it's an old-world cafe, but by night it's one of the best no-frills bars in the *barrio*.

🍷 Sol, Santa Ana & Huertas

★ La Venencia
BAR

(Map p84; ☑91 429 73 13; Calle de Echegaray 7; ⊙12.30-3.30pm & 7.30pm-1.30am; M Sol, Sevilla) La Venencia is a *barrio* classic, with fine sherry from Sanlúcar and *manzanilla* (chamomile-coloured sherry) from Jeréz poured straight from the dusty wooden barrels, accompanied by a small selection of tapas with an Andalucian bent. Otherwise, there's no music, no flashy decorations; it's all about you, your *fino* (sherry) and your friends. As one reviewer put it, it's 'a classic among classics'.

La Terraza del Urban
COCKTAIL BAR

(Map p84; ☑91 787 77 70; Carrera de San Jerónimo 34; ⊙noon-8pm Sun & Mon, noon-3am Tue-Sat mid-May–Sep; M Sevilla) A strong contender with The Roof and Splash Óscar (La Terraza de Arriba) (Map p104; Plaza de Vázquez de Mella 12; ⊙6.30pm-2.30am Wed & Thu, 4.30pm-2.30am Fri-Sun mid-May–mid-Sep; M Gran Vía) for the prize for best rooftop bar in Madrid, this indulgent terrace sits atop the five-star Urban Hotel and has five-star views with five-star prices. Worth every euro, but it's only open while the weather's warm, usually from sometime in May to latish September.

The Roof
COCKTAIL BAR

(Map p84; ☑91 701 60 20; www.memadrid. com; Plaza de Santa Ana 14; ⊙9pm-1.30am Mon-Thu, 8pm-3am Fri & Sat; M Antón Martín, Sol) High above the Plaza de Santa Ana, this sybaritic open-air (7th floor) cocktail bar has terrific views over Madrid's rooftops. The high admission price (€25) announces straight away that riff-raff are not welcome and it's a place for sophisticates, with chill-out areas strewn with cushions, funky DJs and a dress policy designed to sort out the classy from the wannabes.

Taberna La Dolores
BAR

(Map p84; ☑91 429 22 43; Plaza de Jesús 4; ⊙11am-1am; M Antón Martín) Old bottles and beer mugs line the shelves behind the bar at this Madrid institution (1908), known for its blue-and-white-tiled exterior and for a 30-something crowd that often includes the odd *famoso* (celebrity) or two. It claims to be 'the most famous bar in Madrid' – that's pushing it, but it's invariably full most nights of the week, so who are we to argue?

Café del Círculo de Bellas Artes
CAFE

(Map p84; ☑91 521 69 42; Calle de Alcalá 42; ⊙9am-1am Sun-Thu, to 3am Fri & Sat; M Sevilla) This wonderful belle époque cafe was designed by Antonio Palacios in 1919 and boasts chandeliers and the charm of a bygone era. Unless you're here between 1.30pm and 4.30pm or after 9pm (when dinners are served), you have to buy a token temporary club membership (€1) to drink here.

Cervecería Alemana
BAR

(Map p84; ☑91 429 70 33; www.cerveceria alemana.com; Plaza de Santa Ana 6; ⊙11am-12.30am Sun-Thu, to 2am Fri & Sat, closed Aug; M Antón Martín, Sol) If you've only got time to stop at one bar on Plaza de Santa Ana, let it be this classic *cervecería* (beer bar), renowned for its cold, frothy beers and a wider selection of Spanish beers than is the norm. It's fine inside, but snaffle a table outside in the plaza on a summer's evening and you won't be giving it up without a fight.

El Imperfecto
COCKTAIL BAR

(Map p84; Plaza de Matute 2; ⊙5pm-2.30am Mon-Thu, 3pm-2.30am Fri & Sat; M Antón Martín) Its name notwithstanding, the 'Imperfect One' is our ideal Huertas bar, with occasional live jazz and a drinks menu as long as a saxophone, ranging from cocktails (€7, or two mojitos for €10) and spirits to milkshakes, teas and creative coffees. Its pina colada is one of the best we've tasted and the atmosphere is agreeably buzzy yet chilled.

♀ El Retiro & the Art Museums

Kapital   CLUB
(Map p88; ☎91 420 29 06; www.grupo-kapital.com; Calle de Atocha 125; ⊙5.30-10.30pm & midnight-6am Fri & Sat, midnight-6am Thu & Sun; Ⓜ Atocha) One of the most famous mega-clubs in Madrid, this seven-storey venue has something for everyone: from cocktail bars and dance music to karaoke, salsa, hip hop and chilled spaces; there's even a 'Kissing Room'. Admission from €15.

♀ Salamanca

Geographic Club   BAR
(☎91 578 08 62; www.thegeographicclub.es; Calle de Alcalá 141; ⊙1pm-2am Sun-Thu, to 3am Fri & Sat; Ⓜ Goya) With its elaborate stained-glass windows, ethno-chic from all over the world and laid-back atmosphere, the Geographic Club is an excellent choice in Salamanca for an early-evening drink – try one of the 30-plus tropical cocktails. We like the table built around an old hot-air-balloon basket almost as much as the cavernlike pub downstairs.

Almonte   CLUB
(Map p98; ☎91 563 25 04; www.almontesalarociera.com; Calle de Juan Bravo 35; ⊙10pm-5am Sun-Fri, 10pm-6am Sat; Ⓜ Núñez de Balboa, Diego de León) If flamenco has captured your soul, but you're keen to do more than watch, head to Almonte. Live acts kick the night off, paying homage to the flamenco roots of Almonte in Andalucía's deep south. The young and the beautiful who come here have *sevillanas* (a flamenco dance style) in their soul and in their feet.

So head downstairs to see the best dancing. Dance if you dare.

♀ Malasaña & Chueca

★Museo Chicote   COCKTAIL BAR
(Map p84; ☎91 532 67 37; http://grupomercadodelareina.com/en/museo-chicote-en/; Gran Vía 12; ⊙5pm-3am Mon-Thu, to 3.30am Fri & Sat; Ⓜ Gran Vía) This place is a Madrid landmark, complete with its 1930s-era interior, and its founder is said to have invented more than 100 cocktails, which the likes of Hemingway, Ava Gardner, Grace Kelly, Sophia Loren and Frank Sinatra have all enjoyed at one time or another.

★Café Belén   BAR
(Map p104; ☎91 308 27 47; www.elcafebelen.com; Calle de Belén 5; ⊙3.30pm-3am Tue-Thu, 3.30pm-3.30am Fri, 1pm-3.30am Sat, 1-10pm Sun; Ⓜ Chueca) Café Belén is cool in all the right places – lounge and chill-out music, dim lighting, a great range of drinks (the mojitos are especially good) and a low-key crowd that's the height of casual sophistication. It's one of our preferred Chueca watering holes.

Ya'sta   CLUB
(Map p104; ☎91 521 88 33; www.yastaclub.net; Calle de Valverde 10; ⊙11.45pm-6am Wed-Sat; Ⓜ Gran Vía) Going strong since 1985 and the height of *la movida madrileña* (the Madrid scene), Ya'sta is a stalwart of the Malasaña night. Everything gets a run here, from techno, psychedelic trance and electronica to indie pop. Admission is €10; check their website for upcoming sessions.

1862 Dry Bar   COCKTAIL BAR
(Map p104; ☎609 531151; Calle del Pez 27; ⊙3.30pm-2am Mon-Thu, 3.30pm-2.30am Fri & Sat, 3.30-10.30pm Sun; Ⓜ Noviciado) Fab cocktails, muted early 20th-century decor and a refined air make this one of our favourite bars down Malasaña's southern end. Prices are reasonable, the cocktail list extensive and new cocktails appear every month.

Fábrica Maravillas   BAR, BREWERY
(Map p104; ☎915 21 87 53; http://fmaravillas.com; Calle de Valverde 29; ⊙6pm-midnight Mon-Fri, 12.30pm-midnight Sat & Sun; Ⓜ Tribunal, Gran Vía) Spain has taken its time in getting behind the worldwide trend of boutique or artisan beers, but it's finally starting to happen. The finest example of this in Madrid is Fábrica Maravillas, a microbrewery known for its 'Malasaña Ale'.

Morocco   CLUB
(Map p76; ☎91 531 51 67; www.morocco-madrid.com; Calle del Marqués de Leganés 7; €10; ⊙midnight-6am Fri & Sat; Ⓜ Santo Domingo, Noviciado) Owned by the zany Alaska, the standout musical personality of *la movida*, Morocco has decor that's so kitsch it's cool, and a mix of musical styles that never strays too far from 1980s Spanish and international tunes, with electronica another recurring theme. The bouncers have been known to show a bit of attitude, but then that kind of comes with the profession. Admission is €10.

Tupperware
BAR, CLUB

(Map p104; ☑91 446 42 04; www.tupperware club.com; Calle de la Corredera Alta de San Pablo 26; ⊙9pm-3am Mon-Wed, 8pm-3.30am Thu-Sat, 8pm-3am Sun; Ⓜ Tribunal) A Malasaña stalwart and prime candidate for the bar that best catches the enduring *rockero* (rocker) spirit of Malasaña, Tupperware draws a 30-something crowd, spins indie rock with a bit of soul and classics from the '60s and '70s, and generally revels in its kitsch (eyeballs stuck to the ceiling, and plastic TVs with action-figure dioramas lined up behind the bar).

By the way, locals pronounce it 'Tupperwarry'.

Antigua Casa Ángel Sierra
TAVERNA

(Map p104; ☑91 531 01 26; Calle de Gravina 11; ⊙noon-1am; Ⓜ Chueca) This historic old *taberna* is the antithesis of modern Chueca chic – it has hardly changed since it opened in 1917. As Spaniards like to say, the beer on tap is very 'well poured' here and it also has vermouth on tap. Fronting onto the vibrant Plaza de Chueca, it can get pretty lively on a weekend evening when it spills over onto the plaza.

Café de Mahón
CAFE

(Map p104; ☑91 532 47 56; Plaza del Dos de Mayo 4; ⊙noon-1.30am Mon-Thu, to 3am Fri-Sun; Ⓜ Bilbao) If we had to choose our favourite slice of Malasaña life, this engaging little cafe, with outdoor tables that watch out over Plaza del Dos de Mayo, would be a prime candidate. It's beloved by *famosos* as much as by the locals catching up for a quiet drink with friends.

Le Cabrera
COCKTAIL BAR

(Map p98; ☑91 319 94 57; www.lecabrera.com; Calle de Bárbara de Braganza 2; ⊙7pm-2am Sun, Wed & Thu, 7pm-2.30am Fri & Sat; Ⓜ Colón, Alonso Martínez) In the basement below the exciting tapas bar (tapas €3.50-22; ⊙8pm-midnight Wed, Thu & Sun, 8pm-2.30am Fri & Sat; Ⓜ Colón, Alonso Martínez) of the same name, this cocktail bar is every bit as appealing. The 60-plus different cocktail varieties are the work of Diego Cabrera, the long-standing barman of renowned master chef Sergi Arola.

Lolina Vintage Café
CAFE

(Map p104; ☑91 523 58 59; www.lolinacafe. com; Calle del Espíritu Santo 9; ⊙10am-12.30am Sun-Thu, 10am-2am Fri & Sat; Ⓜ Tribunal) Lolina Vintage Café seems to have captured the essence of the *barrio* in one small space, with its studied retro look (comfy old-style chairs and sofas, gilded mirrors and 1970s-era wallpaper). It's low-key, full from the first breakfast to closing time and they cater to every taste with salads and cocktails.

Café Manuela
CAFE

(Map p104; ☑91 531 70 37; Calle de San Vicente Ferrer 29; ⊙4pm-2am Sun-Thu, 4pm-2.30am Fri & Sat; Ⓜ Tribunal) Stumbling into this graciously restored throwback to the 1950s along one of Malasaña's grittier streets is akin to discovering hidden treasure. There's a luminous quality to it when you come in out of the night and, like so many Madrid cafes, it's a surprisingly multifaceted space, serving cocktails and delicious milkshakes, and offering board games atop the marble tables.

Bar Cock
COCKTAIL BAR

(Map p84; ☑91 532 28 26; www.barcock.com; Calle de la Reina 16; ⊙4pm-3am Mon-Fri, 7pm-3am Sat & Sun; Ⓜ Gran Vía) With a name like this, Bar Cock could go either way, but it's definitely cock as in 'rooster', so the atmosphere is elegant and classic rather than risqué. The decor evokes an old gentlemen's club, but it is beloved by A-list celebrities and A-list wannabes, and a refined 30-something crowd who come here for the lively atmosphere and great cocktails.

El Jardín Secreto
BAR

(Map p104; ☑91 541 80 23; www.eljardin secretomadrid; Calle del Conde Duque 2; ⊙5.30pm-12.30am Sun-Wed, 6.30pm-1.30am Thu, 6.30pm-2.30am Fri & Sat; Ⓜ Plaza de España) 'The Secret Garden' is intimate and romantic in a *barrio* that's one of Madrid's best-kept secrets. Lit by Spanish designer candles, draped in organza from India and serving up chocolates from the Caribbean, El Jardín Secreto ranks among our most favoured drinking corners in Conde Duque. They serve milkshakes, cocktails and everything in between.

Gran Café de Gijón
CAFE

(Map p98; ☑91 521 54 25; www.cafegijon. com; Paseo de los Recoletos 21; ⊙7am-1.30am; Ⓜ Chueca, Banco de España) This graceful old cafe has been serving coffee and meals since 1888 and has long been favoured by Madrid's literati for a drink or a meal – *all* of Spain's great 20th-century literary figures came here for coffee and *tertulias*. You'll find yourself among intellectuals, conservative Franco diehards and young *madrileños* looking for a quiet drink.

Café-Restaurante El Espejo   CAFE

(Map p98; ☑91 308 23 47; www.restaurante
elespejo.com; Paseo de los Recoletos 31;
⊙8am-midnight; ⋈Colón) Once a haunt of
writers and intellectuals, this architectural
gem blends Modernista and art deco styles
and its interior could well overwhelm you
with all the mirrors, chandeliers and bow-
tied service of another era. The atmosphere
is suitably quiet and refined, although our
favourite corner is the elegant glass pavilion
out on the Paseo de los Recoletos.

La Vía Láctea   BAR, CLUB

(Map p104; ☑91 446 75 81; Calle de Velarde 18;
⊙8pm-3am Sun-Thu, 8pm-3.30am Fri & Sat; ⋈Tri-
bunal) A living, breathing and delightfully
grungy relic of *la movida,* La Vía Láctea
remains a Malasaña favourite for a mixed,
informal crowd who seems to live for the
1980s. The music ranges across rock, pop,
garage, rockabilly and indie. There are
plenty of drinks to choose from and by late
Saturday night anything goes. Expect long
queues to get in on weekends.

ⓣ Parque del Oeste & Northern Madrid

Real Café Bernabéu   BAR

(☑91 458 36 67; www.realcafebernabeu.es; Gate
30, Estadio Santiago Bernabéu, Av de Concha
Espina; ⊙10am-2am; ⋈Santiago Bernabéu)
Overlooking one of the most famous football fields on earth, this trendy cocktail bar
will appeal to those who live and breathe
football or those who simply enjoy mixing
with the beautiful people. Views of the stadium are exceptional, although it closes
two hours before a game and doesn't reopen until an hour after. There's also a good
restaurant.

☆ Entertainment

Madrid has a happening live-music scene
that owes a lot to the city's role as the cultural capital of the Spanish-speaking world.
There's flamenco, world-class jazz and a host
of performers you may never have heard of
but who may just be Spain's next big thing.
For a dose of high culture, there's opera and
zarzuela (satirical musical comedy).

☆ Plaza Mayor & Royal Madrid

Café de Chinitas   FLAMENCO

(Map p76; ☑91 547 15 02; www.chinitas.com;
Calle de Torija 7; admission incl drink/meal €36/48;

> **ⓘ WHAT'S ON IN MADRID?**
>
> **EsMadrid Magazine** (www.esmadrid.
> com) Monthly tourist-office listings.
>
> **Guía del Ocio** (www.guiadelocio.com)
> Weekly magazine available for €1 at
> news kiosks.
>
> **In Madrid** (www.in-madrid.com) Free
> monthly English-language expat pub-
> lication.
>
> **Metropoli** (www.elmundo.es/metro
> poli) *El Mundo* newspaper's Friday sup-
> plement magazine.

⊙shows 8pm & 10.30pm Mon-Sat; ⋈Santo Domingo) One of the most distinguished *tablaos* (flamenco venues) in Madrid, drawing in
everyone from the Spanish royal family to
Bill Clinton, Café de Chinitas has an elegant
setting and top-notch performers. It may
attract loads of tourists, but flamenco aficionados also give it top marks. Reservations
are highly recommended.

Las Carboneras   FLAMENCO

(Map p76; ☑91 542 86 77; www.tablaolas
carboneras.com; Plaza del Conde de Miranda 1;
⊙shows 8.30pm & 10.30pm Mon-Thu, 8.30pm &
11pm Fri & Sat; ⋈Ópera, Sol, La Latina) Like most
of the *tablaos* around town, this place sees
far more tourists than locals, but the quality
is nonetheless excellent. It's not the place
for gritty, soul-moving spontaneity, but it's
still an excellent introduction and one of
the few places that flamenco aficionados
seem to have no complaints about. Admission including drink/tapas/meal costs
€34/66/71.

Las Tablas   FLAMENCO

(Map p76; ☑91 542 05 20; www.lastablas
madrid.com; Plaza de España 9; ⊙shows 8pm
& 10pm; ⋈Plaza de España) Las Tablas has a
reputation for quality flamenco and reasonable prices (admission including drink
is €27); it could just be the best choice in
town. Most nights you'll see a classic flamenco show, with plenty of throaty singing
and soul-baring dancing. Antonia Moya and
Marisol Navarro, leading lights in the flamenco world, are regular performers here.

Café Berlin   JAZZ

(Map p76; ☑91 521 57 52; http://berlincafe.
es; Calle de Jacometrezo 4; ⊙9pm-3am Tue-Thu,
9pm-5am Fri & Sat; ⋈Callao, Santo Domingo) El
Berlín has been something of a Madrid jazz

MADRID ENTERTAINMENT

GAY & LESBIAN MADRID

Madrid is one of Europe's most gay-friendly cities. The heartbeat of gay Madrid is the inner-city *barrio* of Chueca, where Madrid didn't just come out of the closet, but ripped the doors off in the process. But even here the crowd is almost always mixed gay/straight. The best time of all to be in town if you're gay or lesbian is around the last Saturday in June, for Madrid's gay and lesbian pride march, Día del Orgullo de Gays, Lesbianas y Transexuales (p102). An excellent place to stay is Hostal La Zona (p108).

Librería Berkana (Map p104; 91 522 55 99; www.libreriaberkana.com; Calle de Hortaleza 62; 10.30am-9pm Mon-Fri, 11.30am-9pm Sat, noon-2pm & 5-9pm Sun; Chueca) One of the most important gay and lesbian bookshops in Madrid, Librería Berkana stocks gay books, movies, magazines, music, clothing, and a host of free magazines for nightlife and other gay-focused activities in Madrid and around Spain.

Mamá Inés (Map p104; 91 523 23 33; www.mamaines.com; Calle de Hortaleza 22; 9am-1.30am Sun-Thu, 9am-2.30am Fri & Sat; Chueca) A gay meeting place, this cafe-bar is never sleazy and has a laid-back ambience by day and a romantic air by night. You can get breakfast, yummy pastries and the word on where that night's hot spot will be. There's a steady stream of people coming and going throughout the day and they turn the lights down low as evening turns into night.

Café Acuarela (Map p104; 91 522 21 43; www.cafeacuarela.es; Calle de Gravina 10; 11am-2am Sun-Thu, 11am-3am Fri & Sat; Chueca) A few steps up the hill from Plaza de Chueca and long a centrepiece of gay Madrid – a huge statue of a nude male angel guards the doorway – this is an agreeable, dimly lit salon decorated with, among other things, religious icons.

It's ideal for quiet conversation and catching the weekend buzz as people plan their forays into the more clamorous clubs in the vicinity.

Club 54 Studio (Map p104; www.studio54madrid.com; Calle de Barbieri 7; 11am-3.30am Wed-Sun; Chueca) Modelled on the famous New York club Studio 54, this nightclub draws a predominantly gay crowd, but its target market is more upmarket than many in the *barrio*. Unlike other Madrid nightclubs where paid dancers up on stage try to get things moving, here they let the punters set the pace.

Sala Bash/Ohm (Map p84; www.ohmclub.es; Plaza de Callao 4; €12; midnight-6am Fri; Callao) The DJs who get you waving your hands in the air like you just don't care have made this club, as have its sessions that go by the name of 'Ohm', arguably the number-one nightspot for Madrid's gay community. The music never strays far from techno-house. Admission is €12.

Why Not? (Map p104; 91 521 80 34; www.whynotmadrid.com; Calle de San Bartolomé 7; 10.30pm-6am; Chueca) Underground, narrow and packed with bodies, gay-friendly Why Not? is the sort of place where nothing's left to the imagination (the gay and straight crowd who come here are pretty amorous) and it's full nearly every night of the week. Pop and top-40 music are the standard here, and the dancing crowd is mixed and serious about having a good time.

Black & White (Map p104; 91 521 24 92; Calle de la Libertad 34; 10pm-6.30am; Chueca) People *still* talk about the opening party of Black & White way back in 1982, and ever since it's been a pioneer of Chueca's gay nights. This place is extravagantly gay with drag acts, male strippers and a refreshingly no-holds-barred approach to life.

stalwart since the 1950s, although a recent makeover has brought flamenco, R&B, soul, funk and fusion into the mix. The art-deco interior ads to the charm. Headline acts play at 11pm, although check the website as some can begin as early as 9pm (admission from €5 to €14).

Teatro Real OPERA
(Map p76; 902 24 48 48; www.teatro-real.com; Plaza de Oriente; Ópera) After spending over €100 million on a long rebuilding project, the Teatro Real is as technologically advanced as any venue in Europe, and is the city's grandest stage for elaborate operas,

ballets and classical music. The cheapest seats are so far away you'll need a telescope, although the sound quality is consistent throughout.

La Coquette Blues
LIVE MUSIC

(Map p76; ☑ 91 530 80 95; Calle de las Hileras 14; ⊙ 8pm-3am Tue-Thu, 8pm-3.30am Fri & Sat, 7pm-3am Sun; M Ópera) Madrid's best blues bar has been around since the 1980s and their 8pm Sunday jam session is legendary. Live acts perform Tuesday to Thursday at 10.30pm and the atmosphere is very cool at any time.

☆ La Latina & Lavapiés

★ Corral de la Morería
FLAMENCO

(Map p81; ☑ 91 365 84 46; www.corraldela moreria.com; Calle de la Morería 17; ⊙ 7pm-12.15am, shows 9pm & 10.55pm; M Ópera) This is one of the most prestigious flamenco stages in Madrid, with 50 years' experience as a leading venue and top performers most nights. The stage area has a rustic feel, and tables are pushed up close. Admission including drink costs from €39; set menus from €40.

★ Casa Patas
FLAMENCO

(Map p84; ☑ 91 369 04 96; www.casapatas.com; Calle de Cañizares 10; ⊙ shows 10.30pm Mon-Thu, 9pm & midnight Fri & Sat; M Antón Martín, Tirso de Molina) One of the top flamenco stages in Madrid, this *tablao* always offers flawless quality that serves as a good introduction to the art. It's not the friendliest place in town, especially if you're only here for the show, and you're likely to be crammed in a little, but no one complains about the standard of the performances (admission including drink €36).

Sala Juglar
LIVE MUSIC

(☑ 91 528 43 81; www.salajuglar.com; Calle de Lavapiés 37; ⊙ 9.30pm-3am Sun-Wed, to 3.30am Thu-Sat; M Lavapiés) One of the hottest spots in Lavapiés, this great venue hosts a largely bohemian crowd who come from all over the city for a fine roster leavened with flamenco (9pm Sunday), rock and fusion. Admission from €5 to €15. After the live acts leave the stage around midnight, it's DJ-spun tunes.

☆ Sol, Santa Ana & Huertas

★ Sala El Sol
LIVE MUSIC

(Map p84; ☑ 91 532 64 90; www.elsolmad.com; Calle de los Jardines 3; ⊙ midnight-5.30am Tue-Sat Jul-Sep; M Gran Vía) Madrid institutions don't come any more beloved than Sala El Sol. It opened in 1979, just in time for *la movida madrileña* (the Madrid scene), and quickly established itself as a leading stage for all the icons of the era, such as Nacha Pop and Alaska y los Pegamoides.

★ Villa Rosa
FLAMENCO

(Map p84; ☑ 91 521 36 89; www.tablaoflamenco villarosa.com; Plaza de Santa Ana 15; ⊙ 11pm-6am Mon-Sat, shows 8.30pm & 10.45pm Sun-Thu, 8.30pm, 10.45pm & 12.15am Fri & Sat; M Sol) Villa Rosa has been going strong since 1914 and has seen many manifestations – it made its name as a flamenco venue and has recently returned to its roots with well-priced shows and meals that won't break the bank. Admission (show and drink) costs from €32/17 per adult/child.

★ Teatro de la Zarzuela
THEATRE

(Map p84; ☑ 91 524 54 00; http://teatrodela zarzuela.mcu.es; Calle de Jovellanos 4; ⊙ box office noon-6pm Mon-Fri, 3-6pm Sat & Sun; M Banco de España, Sevilla) This theatre, built in 1856, is the premier place to see *zarzuela*. It also hosts a smattering of classical music and opera, as well as the cutting edge Compañía Nacional de Danza. Tickets range from €5 to €50.

★ Café Central
JAZZ

(Map p84; ☑ 91 369 41 43; www.cafecentral madrid.com; Plaza del Ángel 10; ⊙ 12.30pm-2.30am Sun-Thu, 12.30pm-3.30am Fri & Sat, performances 9pm; M Antón Martín, Sol) In 2011 the respected jazz magazine *Down Beat* included this art deco bar on the list of the world's best jazz clubs, the only place in Spain to earn the prestigious accolade (said by some to be the jazz equivalent of earning a Michelin star). With well over 9000 gigs under its belt, it rarely misses a beat. Admission costs from €12 to €18.

Costello Café & Niteclub
LIVE MUSIC

(Map p84; ☑ 91 522 18 15; www.costelloclub. com; Calle del Caballero de Gracia 10; ⊙ 8pm-3am Sun-Wed, 6pm-3.30am Thu-Sat; M Gran Vía) Very cool. Costello Café & Niteclub weds smooth-as-silk ambience to an innovative mix of pop, rock and fusion in Warholesque surrounds. There's live music (pop and rock, often of the indie variety) at 9.30pm every night except Sundays, with resident and visiting DJs keeping you on your feet until closing time from Thursday to Saturday. Admission costs €5 to €10.

Cardamomo
FLAMENCO

(Map p84; ☑91 805 10 38; www.cardamomo.es; Calle de Echegaray 15; ☺10pm-3.30am & live shows 8pm & 10pm Wed-Mon; Ⓜ Sol, Sevilla) One of the better flamenco stages in town, Cardamomo draws more tourists than aficionados, but the flamenco is top notch. The early show lasts just 50 minutes, the latter 90 minutes. Admission including a drink for early/late sessions costs €25/39.

Teatro Español
THEATRE

(Map p84; ☑91 360 14 84; www.teatroespanol. es; Calle del Príncipe 25; Ⓜ Sevilla, Sol, Antón Martín) This theatre, which fronts onto the Plaza de Santa Ana, has been here in one form or another since the 16th century and is still one of the best places to catch mainstream Spanish drama, from the works of Lope de Vega to more recent playwrights.

Populart
JAZZ

(Map p84; ☑91 429 84 07; www.populart. es; Calle de las Huertas 22; ☺6pm-2.30am Sun-Thu, to 3.30am Fri & Sat, concerts 10pm; Ⓜ Antón Martín, Sol) One of Madrid's classic jazz clubs, this place offers a low-key atmosphere and top-quality music, which is mostly jazz with occasional blues, swing and even flamenco thrown into the mix. Compay Segundo, Sonny Fortune and the Canal Street Jazz Band have all played here. Shows start at 10pm but, if you want a seat, get here early.

☆ Malasaña & Chueca

Thundercat
LIVE MUSIC

(Map p104; ☑654 511457; www.thundercatclub. com; Calle de Campoamor 11; ☺10pm-6am Thu-Sat; Ⓜ Alonso Martínez) They keep it simple at Thundercat – it's rock, as classic as they can find it, with live gigs beginning after midnight and rolling on through the night.

Café La Palma
LIVE MUSIC, DANCE

(Map p104; ☑91 522 50 31; www.cafelapalma. com; Calle de la Palma 62; ☺5pm-3am Sun, Wed & Thu, 5pm-3.30am Fri & Sat; Ⓜ Noviciado) It's amazing how much variety Café La Palma has packed into its labyrinth of rooms. Live shows featuring hot local bands are held at the back, while DJs mix it up at the front. Admission ranges from free to €12.

El Junco Jazz Club
JAZZ

(Map p104; ☑91 319 20 81; www.eljunco.com; Plaza de Santa Bárbara 10; ☺10.30pm-5.30am Tue-Thu & Sun, 9pm-6am Fri & Sat, concerts 11pm Tue-Sun; Ⓜ Alonso Martínez) El Junco has estab-lished itself on the Madrid nightlife scene by appealing as much to jazz aficionados as to clubbers. Its secret is high-quality live jazz gigs from Spain and around the world, followed by DJs spinning funk, soul, nu jazz, blues and innovative groove beats. There are also jam sessions at 11pm in jazz (Tuesday) and blues (Sunday).

Concerts cost from €6 to €9; free on Sunday. The emphasis is on music from the American South and the crowd is classy and casual.

☆ Parque del Oeste & Northern Madrid

★ Estadio Santiago Bernabéu
STADIUM

(☑tickets 902 324324, tours 91 398 43 00/70; www.realmadrid.com; Av de Concha Espina 1; tour adult/child €19/13; ☺tours 10am-7pm Mon-Sat, 10.30am-6.30pm Sun, except match days; Ⓜ Santiago Bernabéu) Football fans and budding Madridistas (Real Madrid supporters) will want to make a pilgrimage to the Estadio Santiago Bernabéu, a temple to all that is extravagant and successful in football. The self-guided tours take you up into the stands for a panoramic view of the stadium, then pass through the presidential box, press room, dressing rooms, players' tunnel and even onto the pitch itself. The tour ends in the extraordinary Exposición de Trofeos (trophy exhibit). Better still for atmosphere is attending a game alongside 80,000 delirious fans.

For bigger games, tickets are difficult to find unless you're willing to take the risk with scalpers. For less important matches, you shouldn't have too many problems. Tickets can be purchased online, by phone or in person from the ticket office at gate 42 on Av de Concha Espina; for the last option, turn up early in the week before a scheduled game (eg a Monday morning for a Sunday game).

The football season runs from September (or the last weekend in August) until May, with a two-week break just before Christmas until early in the New Year.

For tours of the stadium, buy your ticket at window 10 (next to gate 7).

Honky Tonk
LIVE MUSIC

(☑91 445 61 91; www.clubhonky.com; Calle de Covarrubias 24; ☺9.30pm-5am Sun-Thu, 9.30pm-6am Fri & Sat; Ⓜ Alonso Martínez) Despite the name, this is a great place to see blues or local rock, though many acts have a little country, jazz or R&B thrown into the mix too. It's a fun vibe in a smallish club that's been around since the heady 1980s. Admission varies from free to €5; it opens 365 days a year.

Sala Clamores   LIVE MUSIC
(⏰91 445 79 38; www.clamores.es; Calle de Alburquerque 14; ⏱6.30pm-2am Sun-Thu, 6.30pm-5.30am Fri & Sat; Ⓜ Bilbao) Clamores is a one-time classic jazz cafe that has morphed into one of the most diverse live music stages in Madrid. Jazz is still a staple, but flamenco, blues, world music, singer-songwriters, pop and rock all make regular appearances. Live shows can begin as early as 7pm on weekends but sometimes really only get going after 1am!

🔒 Shopping

Our favourite aspect of shopping in Madrid is the city's plethora of small boutiques and quirky shops. Often run by the same families for generations, they counter the over-commercialisation of mass-produced Spanish culture with everything from fashions to old-style ceramics to rope-soled espadrilles or gourmet Spanish food and wine.

🔒 Plaza Mayor & Royal Madrid

★ El Arco Artesanía   HANDICRAFTS
(Map p76; ⏰913 65 26 80; www.artesaniaelarco.com; Plaza Mayor 9; ⏱10am-9pm Mon-Sat, 10am-5pm Sun; Ⓜ Sol, La Latina) This original shop in the southwestern corner of Plaza Mayor sells an outstanding array of homemade designer souvenirs, from stone, ceramic and glass work to jewellery and home fittings. The papier mâché figures are gorgeous, but there's so much else here to turn your head.

★ Antigua Casa Talavera   CERAMICS
(Map p76; ⏰91 547 34 17; www.antiguacasatalavera.com; Calle de Isabel la Católica 2; ⏱10am-1.30pm & 5-8pm Mon-Fri, 10am-1.30pm Sat; Ⓜ Santo Domingo) The extraordinary tiled facade of this wonderful old shop conceals an Aladdin's cave of ceramics from all over Spain. This is not the mass-produced stuff aimed at a tourist market, but comes from the small family potters of Andalucía and Toledo, ranging from the decorative (tiles) to the useful (plates, jugs and other kitchen items). The old couple who run the place are delightful.

El Jardín del Convento   FOOD
(Map p76; ⏰91 541 22 99; www.eljardindelconvento.net; Calle del Cordón 1; ⏱11am-3pm & 5.30-9pm Tue-Sun; Ⓜ Ópera) In a quiet lane just south of Plaza de la Villa, this appealing little shop sells home-made sweets baked by nuns in abbeys, convents and monasteries all across Spain.

El Flamenco Vive   FLAMENCO
(Map p76; ⏰91 547 39 17; www.elflamencovive.es; Calle Conde de Lemos 7; ⏱10am-1.45pm & 5-9pm Mon-Fri, 10am-1.45pm & 5-9pm Sat & 1st Sun of month; Ⓜ Ópera) This temple to flamenco has it all, from guitars and songbooks to well-priced CDs, polka-dotted dancing costumes, shoes, colourful plastic jewellery and literature about flamenco. It's the sort of place that will appeal as much to curious first timers as to serious students of the art. It also organises classes in flamenco guitar.

Maty   FLAMENCO
(Map p84; ⏰91 531 32 91; www.maty.es; Calle del Maestro Victoria 2; ⏱10am-1.45pm & 4.30-8pm Mon-Fri, 10am-2pm & 4.30-8pm Sat & 1st Sun of month; Ⓜ Sol) Wandering around central Madrid, it's easy to imagine that flamenco outfits have been reduced to imitation dresses sold as souvenirs to tourists. That's why places like Maty matter. Here you'll find dresses, shoes and all the accessories that go with the genre, with sizes for children and adults. These are the real deal, with prices to match, but they make brilliant gifts.

Maty also does quality disguises for Carnaval.

Casa Hernanz   SHOES
(Map p76; ⏰91 366 54 50; www.alpargateriahernanz.com; Calle de Toledo 18; ⏱9am-1.30pm & 4.30-8pm Mon-Fri, 10am-2pm Sat; Ⓜ La Latina, Sol) Comfy, rope-soled *alpargatas* (espadrilles), Spain's traditional summer footwear, are worn by everyone from the king of Spain down, and you can buy your own pair at this humble workshop, which has been hand-making the shoes for five generations; you can even get them made to order. Prices range from €5 to €40 and queues form whenever the weather starts to warm up.

Fnac   DEPARTMENT STORE
(Map p84; ⏰91 595 61 00; www.fnac.es; Calle de Preciados 28; ⏱10am-9.30pm Mon-Sat, 11.30am-9.30pm Sun; Ⓜ Callao) This four-storey megastore has a terrific range of CDs, as well as DVDs, video games, electronic equipment and books (including English- and other

DANITA DELIMONT/GETTY IMAGES ©

1. Olive oil, Mercado de San Miguel (p109) **2.** Flamenco dancers
3. Mercado de San Miguel **4.** El Rastro flea market (p80)

PETER ADAMS/GETTY IMAGES ©

Locals' Madrid

More than most other Spanish cities, Madrid can take time to get under your skin, but once it does it rewards your patience a thousand times over. A little local knowledge is the key.

A Very Madrid Sunday

Madrileños (residents of Madrid) like nothing better than Sunday morning at El Rastro flea market (p80), followed by tapas and vermouth around 1pm along Calle de la Cava Baja (p112) in La Latina. Then it's across town to the Parque del Buen Retiro (p94) where, east of the lake, crowds gather, drums start to beat and people begin to dance as the sun nears the horizon.

Food Icons

In this food-obsessed city you'll find countless treasures that capture the city's culinary essence. The Mercado de San Miguel (p109) epitomises the irresistible buzz that goes with eating here. Nearby Casa Revuelta (p112) is not much to look at but it's similarly adored by locals.

Informal Flamenco

Madrid has many outstanding flamenco stages but most are pretty formal affairs. While upstairs at **Candela** (☏91 467 33 82; www.candelaflamenco.com; Calle del Olmo 3; €10; ☺10.30pm-late) fits this description, the downstairs bar is for true aficionados and it's a more spontaneous proposition. Sometimes it works, some-times it doesn't, but therein lies the magic of flamenco.

Barrio Life

North of the centre, the locals reclaim their city. Plaza de Olavide (p100) is the heart and soul of Chamberí and offers an authentic slice of local life. It's not that there's much to see here: instead, the agreeable hum of local life, watched from the outdoor tables that encircle the plaza, is a fascinating window on how locals experience Madrid.

foreign-language titles); there's a large children's section on the 4th floor.

🔒 La Latina & Lavapiés

⭐**Botería Julio Rodríguez** HANDICRAFTS

(☑91 365 66 29; www.boteriajuliorodriguez.es; Calle del Águila 12; ⊙9.30am-2pm & 4.30-8pm Mon-Fri, 10am-1.30pm Sat; Ⓜ La Latina) One of the last makers of traditional Spanish wineskins left in Madrid, Botería Julio Rodríguez is like a window on a fast-disappearing world. They make a great gift and, as you'd expect, they're in a different league from the cheap wineskins found in souvenir shops across downtown Madrid.

⭐**Helena Rohner** JEWELLERY

(Map p81; ☑91 365 79 06; www.helenarohner. com.es; Calle del Almendro 4; ⊙9am-8.30pm Mon-Fri, noon-2.30pm & 3.30-8pm Sat, noon-3pm Sun; Ⓜ La Latina, Tirso de Molina) One of Europe's most creative jewellery designers, Helena Rohner has a spacious boutique in La Latina. Working with silver, stone, porcelain, wood and Murano glass, she makes inventive pieces and her work is a regular feature of Paris fashion shows. In her own words, she seeks to recreate 'the magic of Florence, the vitality of London and the luminosity of Madrid'.

Aceitunas Jiménez FOOD

(☑91 365 46 23; Plaza del General Vara del Rey 14; ⊙10.30am-2.30pm & 3.30-8pm Mon-Thu, 10.30am-2.30pm Fri & Sat, 10.30am-3pm Sun; Ⓜ La Latina) An institution during a Sunday stroll in El Rastro, this tiny shop serves up pickled olives in plastic cups and in all manner of varieties, as well as aubergines, garlics and anything else they've decided to soak in lashings of oil and/or vinegar.

🔒 Sol, Santa Ana & Huertas

Justo Algaba GIFTS

(Map p84; ☑91 523 37 17; www.justoalgaba. com; Calle de la Paz 4; ⊙10am-2pm & 5-8pm Mon-Fri, 10am-2pm Sat; Ⓜ Sol) This is where Spain's *toreros* (bullfighters) come to have their *traje de luces* (suit of lights, the traditional glittering bullfighting suit) made in all its intricate excess.

Tienda Real Madrid SPORTS

(Map p84; ☑91 755 45 38; www.realmadrid. com; Gran Vía 31; ⊙10am-9pm Mon-Sat, 11am-9pm Sun; Ⓜ Gran Vía, Callao) The Real Madrid club shop sells replica shirts, posters, caps and just about everything else under the sun to which it could attach a club logo. In the centre of town there's a smaller branch (Tienda Real Madrid; Map p84; ☑915 21 79 50; www.realmadrid.com; Calle del Carmen 3; ⊙10am-9pm Mon-Sat, 11am-8pm Sun; Ⓜ Sol), and, in the city's north, the stadium branch (p133).

Santarrufina RELIGIOUS

(Map p84; ☑91 522 23 83; www.santarrufina. com; Calle de la Paz 4; ⊙10am-2pm & 4.30-8pm Mon-Fri, 10am-2pm Sat; Ⓜ Sol) This gilded outpost of Spanish Catholicism has to be seen to be believed. Churches, priests and monasteries are some of the patrons of this overwhelming three-storey shop full of everything from simple rosaries to imposing statues of saints and even a litter used to carry the Virgin in processions. Head downstairs for a peek at the extravagant chapel.

José Ramírez MUSIC

(Map p84; ☑91 531 42 29; www.guitarras ramirez.com; Calle de la Paz 8; ⊙10am-2pm & 4.30-8pm Mon-Fri, 10.30am-2pm Sat; Ⓜ Sol) José Ramírez is one of Spain's best guitar makers and his guitars have been strummed by a host of flamenco greats and international musicians (including the Beatles). Using Honduran cedar, Cameroonian ebony and Indian or Madagascan rosewood, among other materials, and based on traditions dating back over generations, this is craftsmanship of the highest order.

Casa de Diego ACCESSORIES

(Map p84; www.casadediego.com; Plaza de la Puerta del Sol 12; ⊙9.30am-8pm Mon-Sat; Ⓜ Sol) This classic shop has been around since 1858, making, selling and repairing Spanish fans, shawls, umbrellas and canes. Service is old style and occasionally grumpy, but the fans are works of antique art. There's another branch (Map p84; ☑91 531 02 23; Calle del los Mesoneros Romanos 4; ⊙9.30am-1.30pm & 4.45-8pm Mon-Sat; Ⓜ Callao, Sol) nearby.

María Cabello WINE

(Map p84; ☑91 429 60 88; Calle de Echegaray 19; ⊙9.30am-2.30pm & 5.30-9pm Mon-Fri, 10am-2.30pm & 6.30-9.30pm Sat; Ⓜ Sevilla, Antón Martín) All wine shops should be like this. This family-run corner shop really knows its wines and the interior has scarcely changed since 1913, with wooden shelves and even a faded ceiling fresco. There are fine wines in abundance (mostly Spanish, and a few foreign bottles), with some 500 labels on show or tucked away out the back.

🏠 El Retiro & the Art Museums

Cuesta de Claudio Moyano Bookstalls
BOOKS

(Map p88; Cuesta de Claudio Moyano; ⊘hours vary; Ⓜ Atocha) Madrid's answer to the booksellers that line the Seine in Paris, these secondhand bookstalls are an enduring Madrid landmark. Most titles are in Spanish, but there's a handful of offerings in other languages. Opening hours vary from stall to stall, and some of the stalls close at lunchtime.

🏠 Salamanca

⭐ Agatha Ruiz de la Prada
FASHION

(Map p98; 🖉 91 319 05 01; www.agatharuiz delaprada.com; Calle de Serrano 27; ⊘10am-8.30pm Mon-Sat; Ⓜ Serrano) This boutique has to be seen to be believed, with pinks, yellows and oranges everywhere you turn. It's fun and exuberant, but not just for kids. It also has serious and highly original fashion. Agatha Ruiz de la Prada is one of the enduring icons of *la movida*, Madrid's 1980s outpouring of creativity.

Bombonerías Santa
FOOD & DRINK

(Map p98; 🖉 91 576 76 25; www.bombonerias-santa.com; Calle de Serrano 56; ⊘10am-2pm & 5-8.30pm Mon, 10am-8.30pm Tue-Sat, shorter hours in Jul & Aug; Ⓜ Serrano) If your style is as refined as your palate, the exquisite chocolates in this tiny shop will satisfy. The packaging is every bit as pretty as the *bombones* (chocolates) within, but they're not cheap – count on paying around €60 per kilo of chocolate.

Cuarto de Juegos
TOYS

(Map p98; 🖉 91 435 00 99; www.cuartodejuegos. es; Calle de Jorge Juan 42; ⊘10am-8.30pm Mon-Fri, 10.30am-2pm & 5-8pm Sat; Ⓜ Velázquez, Príncipe de Vergara) We're not sure if it's an official rule, but batteries seem to be outlawed at this traditional toy shop, where all kinds of old-fashioned board games and puzzles are still sold. Yes, there's Ludo, Chinese checkers and backgammon, but there's so much more here and they're not just for kids.

Oriol Balaguer
FOOD

(www.oriolbalaguer.com; Calle de José Ortega y Gasset 44; ⊘9am-8pm Mon-Fri, 10am-8pm Sat, 10am-2.30pm Sun; Ⓜ Núñez de Balboa) Catalan pastry chef Oriol Balaguer has a formidable CV – he worked in the kitchens of Ferran Adrià in Catalonia and won the prize for the World's Best Dessert (the 'Seven Textures of Chocolate') in 2001. More recently, his croissants won the title of Spain's best in 2014.

Mantequería Bravo
FOOD & DRINK

(Map p98; www.bravo1931.com; Calle de Ayala 24; ⊘9.30am-2.30pm & 5.30-8.30pm Mon-Fri, 9.30am-2.30pm Sat; Ⓜ Serrano) Behind the attractive old facade lies a connoisseur's paradise, filled with local cheeses, sausages, wines and coffees. The products here are great for a gift, but everything's so good that you won't want to share. Not that long ago, Mantequería Bravo won the prize for Madrid's best gourmet food shop or delicatessen – it's as simple as that.

Lavinia
WINE

(Map p98; 🖉 91 650 33 92; www.lavinia.es; Calle de José Ortega y Gasset 16; ⊘10am-9pm Mon-Sat; Ⓜ Núñez de Balboa) 🍷 Although we love the intimacy of old-style Spanish wine shops, they can't match the selection of Spanish and international wines available at Lavinia, which has more than 4000 bottles to choose from. It also organises wine courses, tastings and excursions to nearby bodegas (wineries). The 1st-floor restaurant is a fine gastronomic space.

Gallery
CLOTHING, ACCESSORIES

(Map p98; 🖉 91 576 79 31; www.gallerymadrid. com; Calle de Jorge Juan 38; ⊘10.30am-8.30pm Mon-Sat; Ⓜ Príncipe de Vergara, Velázquez) This stunning showpiece of men's and women's fashions and accessories (shoes, bags, belts and the like) is the new Madrid in a nutshell – stylish, brand conscious and all about having the right look. There are creams and fragrances, as well as quirkier items such as designer crash helmets. With an interior designed by Tomas Alia, it's one of the city's coolest shops.

Camper
SHOES

(Map p98; 🖉 91 578 25 60; www.camper.com; Calle de Serrano 24; ⊘10am-9pm Mon-Sat, noon-8pm Sun; Ⓜ Serrano) Spanish fashion is not all haute couture, and this world-famous cool and quirky shoe brand from Mallorca offers bowling-shoe chic with colourful, fun designs that are all about quality coupled with comfort. There are other outlets throughout the city, including a Malasaña shop (Map p104; 🖉 91 531 23 47; Calle de Fuencarral 42;

⊙10am-8pm Mon-Sat; Ⓜ Gran Vía, Tribunal) –
check out the website for locations.

De Viaje
BOOKS
(Map p98; ☎91 577 98 99; www.deviaje.
com; Calle de Serrano 41; ⊙10am-8.30pm
Mon-Fri, 10.30am-2.30pm & 5-8pm Sat; Ⓜ Serrano) Whether you're after a guidebook, a
coffee-table tome or travel literature, De
Viaje, Madrid's largest travel bookshop,
probably has it. Covering every region of the
world, it has mostly Spanish titles, but plenty in English as well. Staff are helpful, there's
also a travel agency and they sell North Face,
Columbia and Helly Hansen clothing.

Manolo Blahnik
SHOES
(Map p98; ☎91 575 96 48; www.manoloblahnik.
com; Calle de Serrano 58; ⊙10am-2pm & 4-8pm
Mon-Sat; Ⓜ Serrano) Nothing to wear to the
Oscars? Do what many Hollywood celebrities do and head for Manolo Blahnik. The
showroom is exclusive and each shoe is displayed like a work of art.

Purificación García
FASHION
(Map p98; ☎91 435 80 13; www.purificacion
garcia.com; Calle de Serrano 28; ⊙10am-8.30pm
Mon-Sat; Ⓜ Serrano) Fashions may come and
go but Puri consistently manages to keep
ahead of the pack. Her signature style for
men and women is elegant and mature designs that are just as at home in the workplace as at a wedding.

🏠 Malasaña & Chueca

Malababa
ACCESSORIES, FASHION
(Map p104; ☎91 203 59 51; www.malababa.
com; Calle de Santa Teresa 5; ⊙10.30am-8.30pm
Mon-Thu, 10.30am-9pm Fri & Sat; Ⓜ Alonso
Martínez) This corner of Chueca is one of
Madrid's happiest hunting grounds for the
style-conscious shopper who favours individual boutiques with personality above
larger stores. One such place, Malababa
features classy Spanish-made accessories,
including jewellery, handbags, shoes, purses and belts, and they're all beautifully arranged in this light-filled store.

Casa Postal
ANTIQUES
(Map p104; ☎91 532 70 37; www.casapostal.
net; Calle de la Libertad 37; ⊙10am-2pm &
5-7.45pm Mon-Fri, 11am-2pm Sat; Ⓜ Chueca) Old
postcards, posters, books and other period
knick-knacks fill this treasure cave to the
rafters. It's a wonderful slice of old Madrid
in which to lose yourself.

Objetology
HOMEWARES
(Map p104; ☎91 531 55 31; http://objetology.
eu; Calle de Colmenares 7; ⊙4-8pm Mon-Thu;
Ⓜ Chueca, Banco de España) This is the sort of
shop that was once the preserve of Barcelona, but now sits very comfortably in Chueca's cool surrounds. The home furnishings
here – chairs, lamps, tables and a suite of
decorative homewares – have a mostly vintage, mid-20th-century look to them but
there are older and newer pieces as well.

Zoom Edition
ARTS
(Map p104; ☎91 083 71 89; www.zoomedition.
com; Calle del Pez 1; ⊙11am-2.30pm & 5-9pm Mon-
Sat; Ⓜ Callo, Noviciado) Stunning photographic
prints by mostly Spanish photographers, including a growing portfolio of Madrid images, catch the eye at this new little gallery. All
are framed or unframed and ready to ship
around the world. Prices start from around
€35 and the quality is excellent.

Curiosite
GIFTS
(Map p104; ☎91 287 21 77; www.curiosite.es;
Calle de la Corredera Alta de San Pablo 28; ⊙11am-
9pm Mon-Sat; Ⓜ Tribunal) Some of Madrid's
more original gifts are on offer in this quirky
shop that combines old favourites (eg Star
Wars Lego, voodoo dolls) and a sideways
glance at mundane household items. It's
fun and modern and retro all at once, which
makes it a perfect fit for Malasaña.

Nest
GIFTS
(Map p104; ☎91 523 10 61; www.nest-boutique.
com; Plaza de San Ildefonso 3; ⊙11am-2.30pm
& 4-8.30pm Mon-Fri, 11am-3pm & 4-8.30pm Sat;
Ⓜ Tribunal) Small offerings of lamps, Japanese dolls, wrapping paper, jewellery
and so much more fills this intimate little
British-run boutique. It's difficult to describe
the secret of its success, but it unmistakably
has what Spaniards call *encanto* (charm)
and is a welcome recent addition to Malasaña's shopping portfolio.

Retro City
CLOTHING
(Map p104; Calle de Corredera Alta de San Pablo
4; ⊙noon-2.30pm & 5.30-9pm Mon-Sat; Ⓜ Tribunal) Malasaña down to its Dr Martens,
Retro City lives for the colourful '70s and
'80s and proclaims its philosophy to be
all about 'vintage for the masses'. Whereas
other such stores in the *barrio* have gone
for an angry, thumb-your-nose-at-society
aesthetic, Retro City just looks back with
nostalgia.

Kling   FASHION
(Map p104; [☎]91 522 51 45; www.kling.es; Calle de la Ballesta 6; ⏰11am-9pm Mon-Sat; [Ⓜ]Gran Vía) Like a classy version of Zara but with just a hint of attitude, Kling is housed in a reconceived former sex club (prostitutes still scout for clients outside) and is one of Madrid's best-kept secrets. It's ideal for fashion-conscious women who can't afford Salamanca's prices.

MacChinine   CHILDREN
(Map p104; [☎]91 701 05 18; www.macchinine.es; Calle de Barquillo 7; ⏰10am-2pm & 4.30-8.30pm Mon-Sat; [Ⓜ]Banco de España) Collectors and children will love this small shop in equal measure, packed as it is with perfectly created replica model cars and wooden and metal figures. There are also games, toys without batteries and all manner of perfectly proportioned knick-knacks.

Cacao Sampaka   FOOD
(Map p104; [☎]91 319 58 40; www.cacaosampaka.com; Calle de Orellana 4; ⏰10am-9.30pm; [Ⓜ]Alonso Martínez) If you thought chocolate was about fruit 'n' nut, think again. This gourmet chocolate shop is a chocoholic's dream come true, with more combinations to go with humble cocoa than you ever imagined possible. They also have a cafe that's good for lunch.

Loewe   FASHION
(Map p84; [☎]91 522 68 15; www.loewe.com; Gran Vía 8; ⏰10am-8.30pm Mon-Sat, 11am-8pm Sun; [Ⓜ]Gran Vía) Born in 1846 in Madrid, Loewe is arguably Spain's signature line in high-end fashion and its landmark store on Gran Vía is one of the most famous and elegant stores in the capital. Classy handbags and accessories are the mainstays and prices can be jaw-droppingly high, but it's worth stopping by here, even if you don't plan to buy.

There's another branch in **Salamanca** (Map p98; [☎]91 426 35 88; Calle de Serrano 26 & 34; ⏰10am-8.30pm Mon-Sat; [Ⓜ]Serrano).

Salvador Bachiller   ACCESSORIES
(Map p104; [☎]91 523 30 37; www.salvadorbachiller.com; Calle de Gravina 11; ⏰10.30am-9.30pm Mon-Thu, 10.30am-11pm Fri & Sat, noon-9pm Sun; [Ⓜ]Chueca) This is a discounted outlet for stylish and high-quality leather bags, wallets, suitcases and other accessories. This is leather with a typically Spanish twist – the colours are dazzling in bright pinks, yellows and greens. Sound garish? You'll change your mind once you step inside.

Lomography   GIFTS
(Map p104; [☎]91 310 44 18; www.lomography.es; Calle de Argensola 1; ⏰11am-8.30pm Mon-Sat; [Ⓜ]Alonso Martínez, Chueca) Dedicated to the Lomo LC-A, a 1980s-era Russian Kompakt camera that has acquired cult status for its zany colours, fisheye lenses and anticool clunkiness, this eclectic shop sells the cameras (an original will set you back €295) and offbeat design items, from bags and mugs to retro memorabilia loved by adherents of 'lomography'. You can even develop your Lomo photos here.

Patrimonio Comunal Olivarero   FOOD
(Map p104; [☎]91 308 05 05; www.pco.es; Calle de Mejía Lequerica 1; ⏰10am-2pm & 5-8pm Mon-Fri, 10am-2pm Sat Sep-Jun, 9am-3pm Mon-Sat Jul; [Ⓜ]Alonso Martínez) For picking up some of the country's olive-oil varieties (Spain is the world's largest producer), Patrimonio Comunal Olivarero is perfect. With examples of the extra-virgin variety (and nothing else) from all over Spain, you could spend ages agonising over the choices. The staff know their oil and are happy to help out if you speak a little Spanish.

Lurdes Bergada   FASHION
(Map p98; [☎]91 531 99 58; www.lurdesbergada.es; Calle del Conde de Xiquena 8; ⏰10am-2.30pm & 4.30-8.30pm Mon-Sat; [Ⓜ]Chueca, Colón) Lurdes Bergada and Syngman Cucala, a mother-and-son designer team from Barcelona, offer classy and original men's and women's fashions using neutral colours and all-natural fibres. They've developed something of a cult following and it's difficult to leave without finding something that you just have to have. They have another branch in **Malasaña** (Map p104; www.lurdesbergada.es; Calle de Fuencarral 70; ⏰10.30am-8.30pm Mon-Sat; [Ⓜ]Tribunal).

Poncelet   FOOD
(Map p98; [☎]91 308 02 21; www.poncelet.es; Calle de Argensola 27; ⏰10.30am-8.30pm Mon-Sat; [Ⓜ]Alonso Martínez) For 80 Spanish and another 240 European cheese varieties, this fine cheese shop is the best of its kind in Madrid. The range is outstanding and the staff really know their cheese.

Reserva y Cata   WINE
(Map p104; [☎]91 319 04 01; www.reservaycata.com; Calle del Conde de Xiquena 13; ⏰11am-2.30pm & 5-9pm Mon-Fri, 11am-2.30pm Sat; [Ⓜ]Colón, Chueca) This old-style shop stocks an excellent range of local wines, and the

knowledgable staff can help you pick out a great one for your next dinner party or a gift for a friend back home. It specialises in quality Spanish wines that you just don't find in El Corte Inglés.

There's often a bottle open so you can try before you buy.

El Templo de Susu
CLOTHING, ACCESSORIES

(Map p104; ☑91 523 31 22; Calle del Espíritu Santo 1; ⊙10am-2.30pm & 5.30-9pm Mon-Sat; Ⓜ Tribunal) They won't appeal to everyone, but El Templo de Susu's secondhand clothes from the 1960s and 1970s have clearly found a market among Malasaña's too-cool-for-the-latest-fashions types. It's kind of like charity shop meets vintage, which is either truly awful or retro cool, depending on your perspective.

Divina Providencia
FASHION

(Map p104; ☑91 521 10 95; www.divinaprovidencia.com; Calle de Fuencarral 42; ⊙10am-2.30pm & 5-8pm Mon-Sat; Ⓜ Tribunal, Gran Vía) Divina Providencia has moved seamlessly from fresh new face on the Madrid fashion scene to almost mainstream stylishness, with fun clothes for women and strong retro and Asian influences.

Isolée
FOOD, FASHION

(Map p84; ☑902 876136; www.isolee.com; Calle de las Infantas 19; ⊙11am-9pm Mon-Sat; Ⓜ Gran Vía, Chueca) Multipurpose lifestyle stores were late in coming to Madrid, but they're now all the rage and there's none more stylish than Isolée. It sells a select range of everything from clothes (Andy Warhol to Adidas) and shoes to CDs and food. They have another branch in Salamanca (Map p98; ☑902 876 136; Calle de Claudio Coello 55; ⊙11am-8.30pm Mon-Fri, 11am-9pm Sat; Ⓜ Serrano).

Snapo
CLOTHING, ACCESSORIES

(Map p104; ☑91 017 16 72; www.snaposhoponline.com; Calle del Espíritu Santo 6; ⊙11am-2pm & 5-8.30pm Mon-Sat; Ⓜ Tribunal) Snapo is rebellious Malasaña to its core, thumbing its nose at the niceties of fashion respectability – hardly surprising given that one of its lines of clothing is called Fucking Bastardz Inc. It does jeans, caps and jackets, but its T-shirts are the Snapo trademark; there are even kids' T-shirts for *really* cool parents.

Down through the years, we've seen everything from a mocked-up cover of 'National Pornographic' to Pope John Paul II with fist raised and 'Vatican *666*' emblazoned across the front. Need we say more?

🅰 Parque del Oeste & Northern Madrid

El Dragón Lector
BOOKS, CHILDREN

(☑91 448 60 15; www.eldragonlector.com; Calle de Sagunto 20; ⊙10am-2pm & 5-8.30pm Mon-Fri, 10.30am-2pm & 5.30-8pm Sat; Ⓜ Iglesia) Tucked away in a quiet corner of Chamberí, this fab little bookstore for little people has mostly Spanish titles, but some English-language ones as well.

Papelería Salazar
BOOKS, STATIONERY

(☑91 446 18 48; www.papeleriasalazar.es; Calle de Luchana 7-9; ⊙9.30am-1.30pm & 4.30-8pm Mon-Fri, 9.30am-1.30pm Sat; Ⓜ Bilbao) Opened in 1905, Papelería Salazar is Madrid's oldest stationery store and is now run by the fourth generation of the Salazar family. It's a treasure trove that combines items of interest only to locals (old-style Spanish bookplates, First Communion invitations) with useful items like Faber-Castell pens and pencils, maps, notebooks and drawing supplies.

It's a priceless relic of the kind that is slowly disappearing in Madrid.

Relojería Santolaya
ANTIQUES

(☑91 447 25 64; www.relojeriasantolaya.com; Calle Murillo 8; ⊙10am-1pm & 5-8pm Mon-Fri; Ⓜ Quevedo, Iglesia, Bilbao) Founded in 1867, this timeless old clock repairer just off Plaza de Olavide is the official watch repairer to Spain's royalty and heritage properties. There's not much that's for sale here, but stop by the tiny shopfront/workshop to admire the dying art of timepiece repairs, with not a digital watch in sight.

Bazar Matey
GIFTS

(☑91 446 93 11; www.matey.com; Calle de la Santísima Trinidad 1; ⊙9.30am-1.30pm & 4.30-8pm Mon-Sat; Ⓜ Iglesia, Quevedo) A wonderful store, Bazar Matey caters for collectors of model trains, aeroplanes and cars, and all sorts of accessories. The items here are the real deal, with near-perfect models of everything from old Renfe trains to obscure international airlines. Prices can be sky high, but that doesn't deter the legions of collectors who stream in from all over Madrid on Saturdays.

The kids will love it too.

Calzados Cantero
SHOES

(91 447 07 35; Plaza de Olavide 12; 9.45am-2pm & 4.45-8.30pm Mon-Fri, 9.45am-2pm Sat; M Quevedo, Iglesia, Bilbao) A charming old-world shoe store, Calzados Cantero sells a wide range of shoes at rock-bottom prices. But it is most famous for its rope-soled *alpargatas* (espadrilles), which start from €7. This store is a *barrio* classic, the sort of store to which parents bring their children as their own parents did a generation before.

Tienda Real Madrid
SPORTS

(91 458 72 59; www.realmadrid.com; Gate 55, Estadio Santiago Bernabéu, Av de Concha Espina 1; 10am-9pm Mon-Sat, 11am-7.30pm Sun; M Santiago Bernabéu) The club shop of Real Madrid sells caps, replica shirts, posters and anything else to which it could attach a club logo. From the shop window, you can see down onto the stadium itself.

ⓘ Information

DANGERS & ANNOYANCES

Madrid is generally safe, but as in any large European city, keep an eye on your belongings and exercise common sense.

➡ El Rastro, around the Museo del Prado and the metro are favourite pickpocketing haunts, as are any areas where tourists congregate in large numbers.

➡ Avoid park areas (such as the Parque del Buen Retiro) after dark.

➡ As a general rule, avoid deserted streets (which are rare in Madrid).

➡ Keep a close eye on your taxi's meter and try to keep track of the route to make sure you're not being taken for a ride.

EMERGENCY

To report thefts or other crime-related matters, your best bet is the **Servicio de Atención al Turista Extranjero** (Foreign Tourist Assistance Service; 91 548 80 08, 91 548 85 37; www. esmadrid.com/informacion-turistica/sate; Calle de Leganitos 19; 9am-midnight; M Plaza de España, Santo Domingo), which is housed in the central police station or comisaría of the National Police. Here you'll find specially trained officers working alongside representatives from the Tourism Ministry. They can also assist in cancelling credit cards, as well as contacting your embassy or your family.

There's also a general number (902 102112; 24-hour English and Spanish, 8am to midnight other languages) for reporting crimes.

Ambulance	061
EU Standard Emergency Number	112
Fire Brigade (*Bomberos*)	080
Local Police (*Policía Municipal*)	092
Military Police (*Guardia Civil*) For traffic accidents.	062
Policía Nacional	091
Teléfono de la Víctima, hotline for victims of racial or sexual violence.	902 180995

INTERNET ACCESS

Most of Madrid's internet cafes have fallen by the wayside. You'll find plenty of small *locutorios* (small shops selling phonecards and cheap phone calls) all over the city and many have a few computers out the back, but we don't list these as they come and go with monotonous regularity. In the downtown area, your best option is the Ayuntamiento's **Centro de Turismo de Madrid** (p134) on Plaza Mayor, which offers free internet for up to 15 minutes; its quieter branch beneath Plaza de Colón also offers free access.

MEDICAL SERVICES

Hospital General Gregorio Marañón (91 586 80 00; www.hggm.es; Calle del Doctor Esquerdo 46; M Sáinz de Baranda, O'Donnell, Ibiza) One of the city's main (and more central) hospitals.

Farmacia Mayor (91 366 46 16; Calle Mayor 13; 24hr; M Sol) Open around the clock and couldn't be more central.

Farmacia Velázquez 70 (91 575 60 28; Calle de Velázquez 70; 24hr; M Velázquez) Pharmacy in the Salamanca neighbourhood.

Unidad Medica (Anglo American; 91 435 18 23; www.unidadmedica.com; Calle del Conde de Aranda 1; 9am-8pm Mon-Fri, 10am-1pm Sat; M Retiro) A private clinic with a wide range of specialisations and where all doctors speak Spanish and English, with some also speaking French and German. Each consultation costs around €125.

POST

Correos Main Office (Map p88; 91 523 06 94; Paseo del Prado 1; 8.30am-9.30pm Mon-Fri, 8.30am-2pm Sat; M Banco de España) Madrid's central post office.

TOURIST INFORMATION

Centro de Turismo Colón (Map p98; www. esmadrid.com; Plaza de Colón 1; ⊙9.30am-8.30pm; Ⓜ Colón) A small, subterranean tourist office, accessible via the underground stairs on the corner of Calle de Goya and the Paseo de la Castellana.

Centro de Turismo de Madrid (Map p76; ⌀ 010, 91 454 44 10; www.esmadrid.com; Plaza Mayor 27; ⊙9.30am-8.30pm; Ⓜ Sol) The Madrid government's Centro de Turismo is terrific. Housed in the Real Casa de la Panadería on the north side of the Plaza Mayor, it allows free access to its outstanding website and city database, and offers free downloads of the metro map to your mobile; staff are helpful.

Punto de Información Turística Adolfo Suárez Madrid-Barajas T2 (www.esmadrid. com; between Salas 5 & 6; ⊙9am-8pm)

Punto de Información Turística Adolfo Suárez Madrid-Barajas T4 (www.esmadrid. com; Salas 10 & 11; ⊙9am-8pm)

Punto de Información Turística CentroCentro (Map p88; www.esmadrid.com; Plaza de la Cibeles 1; ⊙10am-8pm Tue-Sun; Ⓜ Banco de España)

Punto de Información Turística de Cibeles (Map p88; www.esmadrid.com; Plaza de la Cibeles; ⊙9.30am-8.30pm; Ⓜ Banco de España)

Punto de Información Turística del Paseo del Arte (Map p88; www.esmadrid.com; cnr Calle de Santa Isabel & Plaza del Emperador Carlos V; ⊙9.30am-8.30pm; Ⓜ Atocha)

ⓘ Getting There & Away

AIR

Madrid's **Adolfo Suárez Madrid-Barajas Airport** (⌀ 902 404704; www.aena.es; Ⓜ Aeropuerto T1, T2 & T3, Aeropuerto T4) lies 15km northeast of the city, and it's Europe's sixth-busiest hub, with almost 50 million passengers passing through here every year. The airport has four terminals. Terminal 4 (T4) deals mainly with flights of Iberia (Spain's national airline) and its partners (eg British Airways, American Airlines and Vueling), while the remainder leave from the conjoined T1, T2 and (rarely) T3.

To match your airline with a terminal, visit the Adolfo Suárez Madrid-Barajas section of www. aena.es and click on 'Airlines'.

Although all airlines conduct check-in (facturación) at the airport's departure areas, some also allow check-in at the Nuevos Ministerios metro stop and transport interchange in Madrid itself – ask your airline.

There are car-rental services, ATMs, money-exchange bureaus, pharmacies, tourist offices, left-luggage offices, and parking services at T1, T2 and T4.

BUS

Estación Sur de Autobuses (⌀ 91 468 42 00; www.estaciondeautobuses.com; Calle de Méndez Álvaro 83; Ⓜ Méndez Álvaro), just south of the M30 ring road, is the city's principal bus station. It serves most destinations to the south and many in other parts of the country. Most bus companies have a ticket office here, even if their buses depart from elsewhere.

Northwest of the centre and connected to lines 1 and 3 of the Metro, the subterranean Intercambiador de Autobuses de Moncloa sends buses out to the surrounding villages and satellite suburbs that lie north and west of the city. Major bus companies include the following:

➡ **ALSA** (p829) One of the largest Spanish companies with many services throughout Spain. Most depart from Estación Sur with occasional services from T4 of Madrid's airport and other stations around town.

➡ **Avanzabus** (p827) Services to Extremadura (eg Cáceres).

CAR & MOTORCYCLE

Madrid is surrounded by two main ring roads, the outermost M40 and the inner M30; there are also two partial ring roads, the M45 and the more distant M50. The R5 and R3 are part of a series of toll roads built to ease traffic jams. The big-name car-rental agencies have offices all over Madrid and offices at the airport, and some have branches at Atocha and Chamartín train stations.

TRAIN

Madrid is served by two main train stations. The bigger of the two is **Puerta de Atocha** (www. renfe.es; Ⓜ Atocha Renfe), at the southern end of the city centre, while **Chamartín** (⌀ 902 432343; Ⓜ Chamartín) lies in the north of the city. The bulk of trains for Spanish destinations depart from Atocha, especially those going south. International services arrive at and leave from Chamartín. For bookings, contact **Renfe** (⌀ 902 243 402; www.renfe.com).

High-speed **Tren de Alta Velocidad Española** (AVE) services connect Madrid with Barcelona, Burgos, Cádiz, Córdoba, Cuenca, Huesca, León, Lerida, Málaga, Palencia, Salamanca, Santiago de Compostela, Seville, Valencia, Valladolid, Zamora and Zaragoza.

ⓘ Getting Around

Madrid has an excellent public transport network. The most convenient way of getting around is via the metro, whose 11 lines crisscross the city; no matter where you find yourself you're never far from a metro station. The bus network is equally extensive and operates under the same ticketing system, although the sheer number of routes (around 200!) makes it more difficult for first-time visitors to master. Taxis in Madrid are plentiful and relatively cheap by European standards.

TO/FROM THE AIRPORT

Bus

The **Exprés Aeropuerto** (Airport Express; bus 203; www.emtmadrid.es; €5, 40 minutes; ⊙24hr) runs between Puerta de Atocha train station and the airport. From 11.30pm until 6am, departures are from the Plaza de Cibeles, not the train station. Departures take place every 13 to 20 minutes from the station or at night-time every 35 minutes from Plaza de Cibeles.

Alternatively from T1, T2 and T3 take bus 200 to/from the Intercambiador de Avenida de América (transport interchange on Avenida de América). The same ticket prices apply as for the metro. The first departures from the airport are at 5.10am (T1, T2 and T3). The last service from the airport is 11.30pm; buses leave every 12 to 20 minutes.

There's also a free bus service connecting all four terminals.

Metro

The easiest way into town from the airport is line 8 of the metro to the Nuevos Ministerios transport interchange, which connects with lines 10 and 6 and the local overground *cercanías* (local trains serving suburbs and nearby towns). It operates from 6.05am to 1.30am. A single ticket costs €4.50 including the €3 airport supplement. If you're buying a 10-ride Metrobús ticket (€12.20), you'll need to top it up with the €3 supplement if you're travelling to/from the airport. The journey to Nuevos Ministerios takes around 15 minutes, around 25 minutes from T4.

Minibus

AeroCITY (☑91 747 75 70, 902 151654; www.aerocity.com; per person from €17.85, express service from €34 per minibus) is a private minibus service that takes you door-to-door between central Madrid and the airport (T1 in front of Arrivals Gate 2, T2 between gates 5 and 6, and T4 arrivals hall). It operates 24 hours and you can book by phone or online. You can reserve a seat or the entire minibus; the latter operates like a taxi.

Taxi

A taxi to the centre (around 30 minutes, depending on traffic; 35 to 40 minutes from T4) costs a fixed €30 for anywhere inside the M30 motorway (which includes all of downtown Madrid). There's a minimum €20, even if you're only going to an airport hotel.

BICYCLE

BiciMAD (☑010, 91 529 82 10; www.bicimad.com; 1/2hr €2/6; ⊙24hr) To rent one of Madrid's publicly available electric bikes as

❶ TICKETS

Unless you're only passing through en route elsewhere, you should buy a Metrobús ticket valid for 10 rides (bus and metro) for €12.20; single-journey tickets cost €1.50. Tickets can be purchased from machines in the metro stations, as well as most *estancos* (tobacconists) and newspaper kiosks. Metrobús tickets are not valid on *cercanías* services (local trains serving suburbs and nearby towns). Children under four travel free.

Monthly or season passes (*abonos*) only make sense if you're staying long term and use local transport frequently. You'll need to get a *carnet* (ID card) from metro stations or tobacconists – take a passport-sized photo and your passport.

An Abono Transporte Turístico (Tourist Ticket; per 1/2/7 days €8.40/14.20/35.40) is also possible.

The fine for being caught without a ticket on public transport is €50 – in addition to the price of the ticket, of course.

a *usario ocasional* from one of the stations, choose a free card covering a one-, three- or five-day period. To secure the card, you pay a €150 deposit with a credit card – this amount is then adjusted according to how much you've used the bikes at the expiration of your card.

Called BiciMAD, it had, at last count, 1560 bikes available from 123 stations around the capital. While the system of annual subscriptions (*abonos*; €15 to €25) will most likely appeal only to residents, it is also possible to rent for one or two hours. Rentals are for a maximum of two hours at a time, with penalties charged (€4 per hour) for any time you use the bikes beyond that.

BUS

Buses operated by Empresa Municipal de Transportes de Madrid travel along most city routes regularly between about 6.30am and 11.30pm. Twenty-six night-bus *búhos* (owls) routes operate from 11.45pm to 5.30am, with all routes originating in Plaza de la Cibeles.

Fares for day and night trips are the same as for the metro: €1.50 for a single trip, €12.20 for a 10-trip Metrobús ticket. Single-trip tickets can be purchased on board.

METRO & CERCANÍAS

Madrid's modern metro (www.metromadrid.es), Europe's second largest, is a fast, efficient and safe way to navigate Madrid, and generally easier than getting to grips with bus routes. There are 11 colour-coded lines in central Madrid, in addition to the modern southern suburban MetroSur system as well as lines heading east to the population centres of Pozuelo and Boadilla del Monte. Colour maps showing the metro system are available from any metro station or online. The metro operates from 6.05am to 1.30am.

The short-range *cercanías* regional trains operated by **Renfe** (☑ 902 320320; www.renfe. es/cercanias/madrid) are handy for making a quick, north–south hop between Chamartín and Atocha train stations (with stops at Nuevos Ministerios and Sol), or for the trip out to San Lorenzo de El Escorial.

TAXI

You can pick up a taxi at ranks throughout town or simply flag one down. Flag fall is €2.40 from 7am to 9pm daily, €2.90 from 9pm to 7am and all day Saturday and Sunday. You pay between €1.05 and €1.20 per kilometre depending on the time of day. Several supplementary charges, usually posted inside the taxi, apply; these include €5.50 to/from the airport (if you're not paying the fixed rate); €3 from taxi ranks at train and bus stations; €3 to/from the Parque Ferial Juan Carlos I; and €6.70 on New Year's Eve and Christmas Eve from 10pm to 6am. There's no charge for luggage.

Among the 24-hour taxi services are **Tele-Taxi** (☑ 91 371 21 31; www.tele-taxi.es) and **Radio-Teléfono Taxi** (☑ 91 547 82 00; www.radiotelefono-taxi.com).

A green light on the roof means the taxi is *libre* (available). Usually a sign to this effect is also placed in the lower passenger side of the windscreen.

Tipping taxi drivers is not common practice, although most travellers round fares up to the nearest euro or two.

AROUND MADRID

The Comunidad de Madrid may be small but there are plenty of rewarding excursions that allow you to escape the clamour of city life without straying too far. Imposing San Lorenzo de El Escorial and graceful Aranjuez guard the western and southern gateways to Madrid. Also to the south, the beguiling village of Chinchón is a must-see, while Alcalá de Henares is a stunning university town east of the capital. To the north, picturesque villages (and skiing opportunities) abound in Sierra de Guadarrama and Sierra del Pobre.

San Lorenzo de El Escorial

POP 18,191 / ELEV 1032M

The Unesco World Heritage–listed palace and monastery complex of San Lorenzo de El Escorial is an impressive place, rising up from the foothills of the mountains that shelter Madrid from the north and west. The one-time royal getaway is now a prim little town overflowing with quaint shops, restaurants and hotels catering primarily to throngs of weekending *madrileños*. The fresh, cool air here has been drawing city dwellers since the complex was first ordered to be built by Felipe II in the 16th century. Most visitors come on a day trip from Madrid.

History

After Felipe II's decisive victory in the Battle of St Quentin against the French on St Lawrence's Day, 10 August 1557, he ordered the construction of the complex in the saint's name above the hamlet of El Escorial. Several villages were razed to make way for the huge monastery, royal palace and mausoleum for Felipe's parents, Carlos I and Isabel. It all flourished under the watchful eye of the architect Juan de Herrera, a towering figure of the Spanish Renaissance.

The palace-monastery became an important intellectual centre, with a burgeoning library and art collection, and even a laboratory where scientists could dabble in alchemy. Felipe II died here on 13 September 1598. In 1854 the monks belonging to the Hieronymite order, who had occupied the monastery from the beginning, were obliged to leave during one of the 19th-century waves of confiscation of religious property by the Spanish state, only to be replaced 30 years later by Augustinians.

◉ Sights

★ **Real Monasterio de San Lorenzo** MONASTERY, PALACE
(☑ 91 890 78 18; www.patrimonionacional.es; adult/concession €10/5, guide/audioguide €4/4, EU citizens free last three hours Wed & Thu; ⊙ 10am-8pm Apr-Sep, 10am-6pm Oct-Mar, closed Mon) The main entrance to this majestic monastery and palace complex is to the west. Above the gateway a statue of St Lawrence stands watch, holding a symbolic gridiron, the instrument of his martyrdom (he was roasted alive on one). From here you'll first enter the

Patio de los Reyes (Patio of the Kings), which houses the statues of the six kings of Judah.

Directly ahead lies the sombre basilica. As you enter, look up at the unusual flat vaulting by the choir stalls. Once inside the church proper, turn left to view Benvenuto Cellini's white Carrara marble statue of Christ crucified (1576). The remainder of the ground floor contains various treasures, including some tapestries and an El Greco painting – impressive as it is, it's a far cry from El Greco's dream of decorating the whole complex. Then head downstairs to the northeastern corner of the complex.

You pass through the Museo de Arquitectura and the Museo de Pintura. The former tells (in Spanish) the story of how the complex was built, the latter contains a range of 16th- and 17th-century Italian, Spanish and Flemish art.

Head upstairs into a gallery around the eastern part of the complex known as the Palacio de Felipe II or Palacio de los Austrias. You'll then descend to the 17th-century Panteón de los Reyes (Crypt of the Kings), where almost all Spain's monarchs since Carlos I are interred. Backtracking a little, you'll find yourself in the Panteón de los Infantes (Crypt of the Princesses).

Stairs lead up from the Patio de los Evangelistas (Patio of the Gospels) to the Salas Capitulares (Chapter Houses) in the southeastern corner of the monastery. These bright, airy rooms, with richly frescoed ceilings, contain a minor treasure chest of works by El Greco, Titian, Tintoretto, José de Ribera and Hieronymus Bosch (known as El Bosco to Spaniards).

Just south of the monastery is the **Jardín de los Frailes** (Friars Garden; ⏲10am-7pm Apr-Sep, 10am-6pm Oct-Mar, closed Mon), which leads down to the town of El Escorial (and the train station), and contains the **Casita del Príncipe** (www.patrimonionacional.es; ⏲10am-8pm Apr-Sep, 10am-6pm Oct-Mar, closed Mon), a little neoclassical gem built in 1772 by Juan de Villanueva under Carlos III for his heir, Carlos IV.

Eating

La Cueva SPANISH €€€

(☎91 890 15 16; www.mesonlacueva.com; Calle de Floridablanca 24; mains €20-32; ⏲1-4pm & 9-11pm) Just a block back from the monastery complex, La Cueva has been around since 1768 and it shows in the heavy wooden beams and hearty, traditional Castilian cooking - roasted meats and steaks are the mainstays, with a few fish dishes.

Getting There & Away

Every 15 minutes (every 30 minutes on weekends) buses 661 and 664 run to El Escorial (€4.20, one hour) from platform 30 at the Intercambiador de Autobuses de Moncloa in Madrid.

San Lorenzo de El Escorial is 59km northwest of Madrid and it takes 40 minutes to drive there. Take the A6 highway to the M600, then follow the signs to El Escorial.

A few dozen **Renfe** (p136) C8 *cercanías* make the trip daily from Madrid's Atocha or Chamartín train station to El Escorial (€5.40, one hour).

Aranjuez

POP 58,168

Unesco World Heritage-listed Aranjuez was founded as a royal pleasure retreat, away from the riff-raff of Madrid, and it remains an easy day trip to escape the rigours of city life. The palace is opulent, but the fresh air and ample gardens are what really stand out.

Sights

Palacio Real PALACE

(☎91 891 07 40; www.patrimonionacional.es; palace adult/concession €9/4, guide/audioguide €6/4, EU citizens last 3hr Wed & Thu free, gardens free; ⏲palace 10am-8pm Apr-Sep, 10am-6pm Oct-Mar, gardens 8am-9.30pm mid-Jun–mid-Aug, reduced hours mid-Aug–mid-Jun) The Royal Palace started as one of Felipe II's modest summer palaces but took on a life of its own as a succession of royals, inspired by the palace at Versailles in France, lavished money upon it. By the 18th century its 300-plus rooms had turned the palace into a sprawling, gracefully symmetrical complex filled with a cornucopia of ornamentation. Of all the rulers who spent time here, Carlos III and Isabel II left the greatest mark.

The obligatory guided tour (in Spanish) provides insight into the palace's art and history. And a stroll in the lush gardens takes you through a mix of local and exotic species, the product of seeds brought back by Spanish botanists and explorers from Spanish colonies all over the world. Within their shady perimeter, which stretches a few kilometres from the palace, you'll find the **Casa de Marinos**, which contains the **Museo de Falúas**, a museum of royal pleasure boats from days gone by. The 18th-century neoclassical Casa de Labrador is also worth a visit. Further away, towards Chinchón, is the pleasant Jardín del Príncipe, an extension of the massive gardens.

Eating

Casa Pablete
TAPAS €

(Calle de Stuart 108; tapas from €2.80, mains €11-19; ☺1.30-4pm & 8.30-11.30pm) Going strong since 1946, this casual tapas bar has a loyal following far beyond Aranjuez. Its *croquetas* (croquettes) are a major drawcard, as is the stuffed squid and it's all about traditional cooking at its best without too many elaborations.

Casa José
SPANISH €€€

(☑91 891 14 88; www.casajose.es; Calle de Abastos 32; mains €14-29, set menu €75; ☺1.45-3.30pm & 9-11.30pm Tue-Sat, 1.45-3.30pm Sun Sep-Jul) The quietly elegant Casa José is packed on weekends with *madrileños* (people from Madrid) drawn by the beautifully prepared meats and local dishes with surprising innovations. It's pricey but worth every euro.

❶ Getting There & Away

Coming by car from Madrid, take the N-IV south to the M305, which leads to the city centre.

Bus 423 runs to Aranjuez from Madrid's Estación Sur de Autobuses every 15 minutes or so (€4.20, 45 minutes).

From Madrid's Atocha station, C3 *cercanías* trains leave every 15 or 20 minutes for Aranjuez (€3.35, 45 minutes).

Chinchón

POP 5436

Chinchón is just 45km from Madrid but worlds apart. Although it has grown beyond its village confines, visiting its antique heart is like stepping back into a charming, ramshackle past. It's worth an overnight stay to really soak it up, and lunch in one of the *méson*-style (tavern-style) restaurants around the plaza is another must.

◉ Sights

The heart of town is its unique, almost circular Plaza Mayor, which is lined with sagging, tiered balconies – it wins our vote as one of the most evocative *plazas mayores* in Spain. In summer the plaza is converted into a bullring, and it's also the stage for a popular Passion play shown at Easter.

Chinchón's historical monuments won't detain you long, but you should take a quick look at the 16th-century Iglesia de la Asunción, which rises above Plaza Mayor, and the late 16th-century Renaissance Castillo de los Condes, out of town to the south. The castle was abandoned in the 1700s and was last used as a liquor factory.

▣ Sleeping

Hostal Chinchón
HOSTAL €

(☑91 893 53 98; www.hostalchinchon.com; Calle Grande 16; d/tr €50/65; ✲ ☎ ☒) The public areas here are nicer than the smallish rooms, which are clean but worn around the edges. The highlight is the surprise rooftop pool overlooking Plaza Mayor.

Parador de Chinchón
LUXURY HOTEL €€

(☑91 894 08 36; www.parador.es; Avenida Generalísimo 1; d from €142; ✲ ☎) The former Convento de Agustinos (Augustine Convent), Parador Nacional is one of the town's most important historical buildings and can't be beaten for luxury. It's worth stopping by for a meal or coffee (and a peek around) even if you don't stay here.

✗ Eating

Chinchón is loaded with traditional-style restaurants dishing up *cordero asado* (roast lamb). But if you're after something a little lighter, there is nothing better than savouring a few tapas and drinks on sunny Plaza Mayor.

Café de la Iberia
SPANISH €€

(☑91 894 08 47; www.cafedelaiberia.com; Plaza Mayor 17; mains €13-22; ☺12.30-4.30pm & 8-10.30pm) This is definitely our favourite of the *mesones* (home-style restaurants) on the Plaza Mayor perimeter. It offers wonderful food, including succulent roast lamb, served by attentive staff in an atmospheric dining area set around a light-filled internal courtyard (where Goya is said to have visited), or, if you can get a table, out on the balcony.

Mesón Cuevas del Vino
SPANISH €€

(☑91 894 02 06; www.cuevasdelvino.com; Calle Benito Hortelano 13; mains €12-23; ☺noon-4.30pm & 8-11pm Mon & Wed-Fri, noon-midnight Sat, noon-8pm Sun) From the huge goatskins filled with wine and the barrels covered in famous signatures, to the atmospheric caves underground, this is sure to be a memorable eating experience with delicious home-style cooking.

ⓘ Getting There & Away

Bus 337 runs half-hourly from Madrid to Chinchón (€4.20, 55 minutes). Buses leave from Madrid's Avenida del Mediterráneo, 100m east of Plaza del Conde de Casal.

Sitting 45km southeast of Madrid, Chinchón is easy to reach by car. Take the N-IV motorway and exit onto the M404, which makes its way to Chinchón.

Alcalá De Henares

POP 198,750

East of Madrid, Alcalá de Henares is full of surprises with historical sandstone buildings seemingly at every turn. Throw in some sunny squares and a legendary university, and it's a terrific place to escape the capital for a few hours.

⦿ Sights

Museo Casa Natal de Miguel de Cervantes   MUSEUM
(☑91 889 96 54; www.museocasanataldecervantes.org; Calle Mayor 48; ⊙10am-6pm Tue-Sun) FREE The town is dear to Spaniards because it's the birthplace of literary figurehead Miguel de Cervantes Saavedra. The site believed by many to be Cervantes' birthplace is re-created in this illuminating museum, which lies along the beautiful, colonnaded Calle Mayor.

Universidad de Alcalá   UNIVERSITY
(☑91 883 43 84; www.uah.es; guided tours €4; ⊙9am-9pm) FREE Founded in 1486 by Cardinal Cisneros, this is one of the country's principal seats of learning. A guided tour gives a peek into the Mudéjar chapel and the magnificent Paraninfo auditorium, where the King and Queen of Spain give out the prestigious Premio Cervantes literary award every year.

✖ Eating

Baratería   TAPAS €€
(☑91 888 59 25; Calle de los Cerrajeros 18; mains €12-19; ⊙open noon-midnight Thu-Tue) A wine bar, tapas bar and restaurant all rolled into one, Baratería is a fine place to eat whatever your mood. Grilled meats are the star of the show, with the ribs with honey in particular a local favourite.

Hostería del Estudiante   CASTILIAN €€
(☑91 888 03 30; www.parador.es; Calle de los Colegios 3; set menus from €33; ⊙1.30-4pm & 8.30-11pm) Based in the *parador*, this charming restaurant has wonderful Castilian cooking and a classy ambience in a dining room decorated with artefacts from the city's illustrious history.

ⓘ Getting There & Away

Alcalá de Henares is just 35km east of Madrid, heading towards Zaragoza along the A2.

Buses depart every five to 15 minutes from Madrid's Intercambiador de Avenida de América (€3.60, one hour).

The C2 and C7 *cercanías* trains make the trip to Alcalá de Henares daily (€2.40, 50 minutes).

Sierra de Guadarrama

North of Madrid lies the Sierra de Guadarrama, a popular skiing destination and home to several charming towns. In **Manzanares El Real** you can explore the small 15th-century **Castillo de los Mendoza** (☑91 853 00 08; admission incl guided tour €4; ⊙10am-5pm Tue-Fri, 10am-7.30pm Sat & Sun), a storybook castle with round towers at its corners and a Gothic interior patio.

Cercedilla is a popular base for hikers and mountain bikers. There are several marked trails, the main one known as the **Cuerda Larga** or **Cuerda Castellana**. This is a forest track that takes in 55 peaks between the Puerto de Somosierra in the north and Puerto de la Cruz Verde in the southwest.

Small ski resorts, such as **Valdesquí** (☑902 886 446; www.valdesqui.es; Puerto de Cotos; lift tickets day/afternoon €40/24; ⊙9am-4pm) and **Navacerrada** (☑902 882328; www.puertonavacerrada.com; lift tickets day/afternoon €28-35; ⊙9.30am-5pm) welcome weekend skiers from the city.

ⓘ Information

Centro de Información Valle de la Fuenfría (☑91 852 22 13; Carretera de las Dehesas; ⊙10am-6pm) Information centre located 2km outside Cercedilla on the M614.

ⓘ Getting There & Away

By car from Madrid, take the A6 motorway to Cercedilla. Bus 724 runs to Manzanares El Real from Plaza de Castilla in Madrid (€4.20, 45 minutes).

From Madrid's Intercambiador de Autobuses de Moncloa, bus 691 heads to Navacerrada (€5.10, one hour) and bus 684 runs to Cercedilla (€5.10, one hour).

From Chamartín train station you can get to Puerto de Navacerrada on the C8B *cercanías* line (€5.40, 1¾ hours with train change in Cercedilla, four daily), and Cercedilla on the C2 *cercanías* line (€4, 1½ hours, 15 daily).

Buitrago & Sierra Pobre

The 'Poor Sierra' is a toned-down version of its more refined western neighbour, the Sierra de Guadarrama. Popular with hikers and others looking for nature without quite so many creature comforts or crowds, the sleepy Sierra Pobre has yet to develop the tourism industry of its neighbours. And that's just why we like it.

Sights & Activities

Head first to Buitrago, the largest town in the area, where you can stroll along part of the old city walls. You can also take a peek into the 15th-century Mudéjar and Romanesque Iglesia de Santa María del Castillo and into the small and unlikely Picasso Museum (☑ 91 868 00 56; www.madrid.org/museo picasso; Plaza Picasso 1; ⊙ 11am-1.45pm & 4-6pm Tue-Fri, 10am-2pm & 4-7pm Sat, 10am-2pm Sun) FREE, which contains a few works that the artist gave to his barber, Eugenio Arias, and

is one of those rural treasures one stumbles across in the strangest places in Spain.

Hamlets are scattered throughout the rest of the sierra; some, like Puebla de la Sierra and El Atazar, make for pretty walks and are the starting point for winding hill trails.

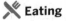 Eating

El Arco   NORTHERN SPANISH
(☑ 918 68 09 11; Calle Arco 6; mains €14-26; ⊙ 1-4pm Fri-Sun mid-Sep–mid-Jun, 1-4pm & 8.30-10.30pm Tue-Sat & 1-4pm Sun mid-Jun–mid-Sep) The best restaurant in the region, El Arco is located in Villavieja del Lozoya, close to Buitrago, and known for its fresh, creative cuisine based on local, seasonal ingredients and traditional northern Spanish dishes such as the classic Basque *bacalao al pil-pil* (salted cod and garlic in an olive-oil emulsion). The desserts and wine list also stand out.

ⓘ Information

Buitrago Tourist Office (☑ 91 868 16 15; Calle Tahona 19; ⊙ 9am-3pm Jul-Sep) For more information on Picasso Museum, visit the Buitrago tourist office.

ⓘ Getting There & Away

By car from Madrid, take the N-I highway to Buitrago.

Bus 191 leaves hourly from Madrid's Plaza de la Castilla to Buitrago (€5.10, 1½ hours).

Castilla y León

Best Places to Eat

➜ Restaurante El Fogón Sefardí (p161)

➜ Restaurante Cocinandos (p182)

➜ La Cocina de Toño (p151)

➜ El Huerto de Roque (p189)

➜ Alma de Ibérico (p157)

Best Places to Sleep

➜ Posada Real La Cartería (p175)

➜ Hostal de San Marcos (p181)

➜ Santa Cruz (p174)

➜ Microtel Placentinos (p150)

➜ Hotel Tres Coronas (p192)

Why Go?

If you're looking for a window on the Spanish soul, head to Castilla y León. This is Spain without the stereotypes: with vast plains, spectacular mountain peaks and evocative medieval towns and villages. Experience fabled cities like Salamanca, with its lively student population, and Segovia, famed for a fairy-tale fortress that inspired Disneyland's *Sleeping Beauty* castle. The multiturreted walls of Ávila have similar magical appeal, while the lofty cathedrals of León and Burgos are among Europe's most impressive. As with most of Spain, food here is an agreeable obsession, promising the country's best *jamón* (cured ham), roast lamb and suckling pig.

The region's story is equally told through its quiet back roads, half-timbered hamlets and isolated castles. From the scenic Sierra de Francia in the southwest to Covarrubias, Calatañazor and Medinaceli in the east, this is the hidden Spain most travellers never imagined still existed.

When to Go
Leon

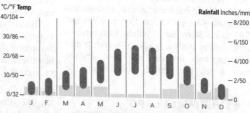

Mar & Apr Enjoy wild flowers in the countryside and soul-stirring Semana Santa processions.

Jun Get into holiday mode during annual fiesta time in Burgos, Soria and Segovia.

Sep Capture the youthful buzz of Salamanca as universities return to class.

Ávila

POP 58,935 / ELEV 1130M

Ávila's old city, surrounded by imposing city walls comprising eight monumental gates, 88 watchtowers and more than 2500 turrets, is one of the best-preserved medieval bastions in Spain. In winter, when an icy wind whistles in off the plains, the old city huddles behind the high stone walls as if seeking protection from the harsh Castilian climate. At night, when the walls are illuminated to magical effect, you'll wonder if you've stumbled into a fairy tale. It's a deeply religious city that for centuries has drawn pilgrims to the cult of Santa Teresa de Ávila, with its many churches, convents and high-walled palaces. As such, Ávila is the essence of Castilla and the epitome of old Spain.

◉ Sights

★ Murallas
WALLS

(www.muralladeavila.com; adult/child under 12yr €5/free; ☉10am-8pm Apr-Oct, to 6pm Nov-Mar; ☝) Ávila's splendid 12th-century walls stretch for 2.5km atop the remains of earlier Roman and Muslim battlements and rank among the world's best-preserved medieval defensive perimeters. Two sections of the walls can be climbed – a 300m stretch that can be accessed from just inside the Puerta del Alcázar, and a longer (1300m) stretch from Puerta de los Leales that runs the length of the old city's northern perimeter. The admission price includes a multilingual audioguide.

★ Catedral del Salvador
CATHEDRAL

(☎920 21 16 41; Plaza de la Catedral; admission incl audioguide €4; ☉10am-7pm Mon-Fri, 10am-8pm Sat, noon-6.30pm Sun) Ávila's 12th-century cathedral is both a house of worship and an ingenious fortress: its stout granite apse forms the central bulwark in the

ⓘ VISITÁVILA CARD

If you plan on seeing all of Ávila's major sights, it may be worth buying the Visitávila Card (per person €13), which is valid for 48 hours and covers entrance fees to the main sights around town.

historic city walls. The sombre, Gothic-style facade conceals a magnificent interior with an exquisite early-16th-century altar frieze showing the life of Jesus, plus Renaissance-era carved choir stalls and a museum with an El Greco painting and a splendid silver monstrance by Juan de Arfe. (Push the buttons to illuminate the altar and the choir stalls.)

Monasterio de Santo Tomás
MONASTERY, MUSEUM

(☎920220400; www.monasteriosantotomas.com; Plaza de Granada 1; €4; ☉10.30am-9pm Jul & Aug, 10.30am-2pm & 3.30-7.30pm Sep-Jun) Commissioned by the Reyes Católicos (Catholic Monarchs), Fernando and Isabel, and completed in 1492, this monastery is an exquisite example of Isabelline architecture, rich in historical resonance. Three interconnected cloisters lead to the church that contains the alabaster tomb of Don Juan, the monarchs' only son. There's also the impressive Museo Oriental (Oriental Museum), with 11 rooms of Far Eastern art, plus a more modest Museo de Historia Natural (Natural History Museum); both are included in the admission price.

Convento de Santa Teresa
CHURCH, MUSEUM

(☎920 21 10 30; www.teresadejesus.com; Plaza de la Santa; church & relic room free, museum €2; ☉9.30am-1.30pm & 3.30-9pm Tue-Sun) Built in 1636 around the room where the saint was born in 1515, this is the epicentre of the cult surrounding Teresa. There are three attractions in one here: the church, a relics room and a museum. Highlights include the gold-adorned chapel (built over the room where she was born), the baroque altar and the (albeit macabre) relic of the saint's ring finger, complete with ring. Apparently Franco kept it beside his bedside throughout his rule.

The elaborate chapel is lorded over by a baroque altar by Gregorio Fernández, which features a statue of the saint. There's also a basement museum dedicated to Santa Teresa, accessible from Calle Aizpuru.

Los Cuatro Postes
VIEWPOINT

Northwest of the city, on the road to Salamanca, Los Cuatro Postes provides the best views of Ávila's walls. It also marks the place where Santa Teresa and her brother were caught by their uncle as they tried to run away from home (they were hoping to achieve martyrdom at the hands of the Muslims). The best views are at night.

Castilla y León Highlights

1 **Salamanca** (p146) Lingering amid the city's architectural elegance and irresistible energy.

2 **León** (p178) Savouring the light in León's cathedral.

3 **Santo Domingo de Silos** (p191) Being transported to medieval times listening to Gregorian chants.

4 **Pedraza de la Sierra** (p163) Dining on *cordero asado* (roast lamb) in this gorgeous hilltop village.

5 **Medinaceli** (p201) Escaping city life in an historic village.

6 **Segovia** (p158) Finding yourself somewhere between ancient Rome and Disneyland.

7 **Sierra de la Culebra** (p173) Looking for wolves close to medieval Puebla de Sanabria.

8 **Sierra de Francia** (p155) Exploring beautiful villages that time forgot.

9 **Guijuelo** (p156) Going to the source to learn about – and taste – Spain's best *jamón*.

Ávila

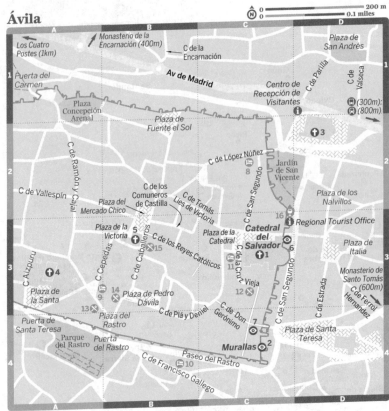

Ávila

◉ Top Sights
1 Catedral del Salvador	C3
2 Murallas	C4

◉ Sights
3 Basílica de San Vicente	D2
4 Convento de Santa Teresa	A3
5 Iglesia de San Juan Bautista	B3
6 Puerta de Los Leales	C3
7 Puerta del Alcázar	C4

🛏 Sleeping
8 Hostal Arco San Vicente	C2
9 Hotel El Rastro	A3
10 Hotel Las Leyendas	B4
11 Hotel Palacio Valderrábanos	C3

⊗ Eating
12 Hostería Las Cancelas	C3
13 Mesón del Rastro	A3
14 Posada de la Fruta	B3
15 Soul Kitchen	B3

🍷 Drinking & Nightlife
16 La Bodeguita de San Segundo	C3

Monasterio de la Encarnación MONASTERY (☎920 21 12 12; Calle de la Encarnación; church free, museum €2; ☉9.30am-1pm & 4-7pm Mon-Fri, 10am-1pm & 4-7pm Sat & Sun May-Sep, 9.30am-1.30pm & 3.30-6pm Mon-Fri, 10am-1pm & 4-6pm Sat & Sun Oct-Apr) North of the city walls, this unadorned Renaissance monastery is where Santa Teresa fully took on the monastic life and lived for 27 years. One of the three main rooms open to the public is where the saint is said to have had a vision of the baby Jesus. Also on display are relics, such as the piece of wood used by Teresa as a pillow (ouch!) and the chair upon which St John of the Cross made his confessions.

To reach here, head north from Plaza de Fuente el Sol, via Calle de la Encarnación, for approximately 500m.

Basílica de San Vicente CHURCH
(☑920 25 52 30; www.basilicasanvicente.es; Plaza de San Vicente; admission incl audioguide €2.30; ⊙10am-6.30pm Mon-Sat, 4-6pm Sun Apr-Oct, 10am-1.30pm & 4-6.30pm Mon-Sat, 4-6pm Sun Nov-Mar) This graceful church is a masterpiece of Romanesque simplicity: a series of largely Gothic modifications in sober granite contrasted with the warm sandstone of the Romanesque original. Work started in the 11th century, supposedly on the site where three martyrs – Vicente and his sisters, Sabina and Cristeta – were slaughtered by the Romans in the early 4th century. Their canopied cenotaph is an outstanding piece of Romanesque style, with nods to the Gothic.

Iglesia de San Juan Bautista CHURCH
(Plaza de la Victoria; ⊙Mass 10am & 7.30pm Mon-Sat, noon Sun) This quiet parish church dates from the 16th century and contains the font in which Santa Teresa was baptised on 4 April 1515. The church can be visited before and after Mass.

⚑ Festivals & Events

Semana Santa RELIGIOUS
(Holy Week; ⚑) Ávila is one of the best places in Castilla y León to watch the solemn processions of Easter. It all begins on Holy Thursday, though the most evocative event is the early morning (around 5am) Good Friday procession, which circles the city wall.

Fiesta de Santa Teresa CULTURAL
(⚑) This annual festival, held during the second week of October, honours the city's patron saint with processions, concerts and fireworks.

🛏 Sleeping

★ Hotel El Rastro HISTORIC HOTEL €
(☑920 35 22 25; www.elrastroavila.com; Calle Cepedas; s/d €35/55; ❄🤶) This atmospheric hotel occupies a former 16th-century palace with original stone, exposed brickwork and a natural, earth-toned colour scheme exuding a calm, understated elegance. Each room has a different form, but most have high ceilings and plenty of space. Note that the

owners also run a marginally cheaper *hostal* (budget hotel) of the same name around the corner.

Hostal Arco San Vicente HOSTAL €
(☑920 22 24 98; www.arcosanvicente.com; Calle de López Núñez 6; s €36-50, d €50-70; ❄🤶) This gleaming *hostal* has small, blue-carpeted rooms with pale paintwork and wrought-iron bedheads. Rooms on the 2nd floor have attic windows and air-con; some on the 1st floor look out at the Puerta de San Vicente. The corner room 109 is particularly spacious and attractive.

★ Hotel Palacio Valderrábanos HISTORIC HOTEL €€
(☑920 21 10 23; www.hotelpalaciovalderrabanos.com; Plaza de la Catedral 9; r €50-80) A stone's throw from the door of the cathedral, this distinguished, converted 14th-century palace has a quiet elegance about it, with high ceilings, polished floorboards and reassuring tones. Some rooms even look out at the cathedral.

Hotel Las Leyendas HISTORIC HOTEL €€
(☑920 35 20 42; www.lasleyendas.es; Calle de Francisco Gallego 3; s €40-57, d €52-80; ❄🤶) Occupying the house of 16th-century Ávila nobility, this intimate hotel overflows with period touches wedded to modern amenities. Some rooms have views out across the plains, others look onto an internal garden. The decor varies between original wooden beams, exposed brick and stonework, and more modern rooms with walls washed in muted earth tones. Breakfast is a little sparse.

🍴 Eating & Drinking

★ Soul Kitchen MODERN CASTILIAN €€
(☑920 21 34 83; www.soulkitchen.es; Calle de Caballeros 13; mains €10-20; ⊙10am-midnight Mon-Fri, 11am-2am Sat, 11am-midnight Sun) Opened in 2013, this restaurant has the kind of contemporary energy that can seem lacking in Ávila's more staid restaurants. The eclectic menu changes regularly and ranges from salads with dressings like chestnut and fig to hamburgers with cream of *setas* (oyster mushrooms). Lighter dishes include bruschetta with tasty toppings. Live music, poetry readings (and similar) take place in summer.

Mesón del Rastro CASTILIAN €€
(☑920 35 22 25; www.elrastroavila.com; Plaza del Rastro 1; mains €11-24; ⊙1-4pm & 9-11pm) The dark-wood-beamed interior announces

WHO WAS SANTA TERESA?

Teresa de Cepeda y Ahumada, probably the most important woman in the history of the Spanish Catholic Church, was born in Ávila on 28 March 1515, one of 10 children of a merchant family. Raised by Augustinian nuns after her mother's death, she joined the Carmelite order at age 20. After her early, undistinguished years as a nun, she was shaken by a vision of hell in 1560, which crystallised her true vocation: she would reform the Carmelites.

In stark contrast to the opulence of the church in 16th-century Spain, her reforms called for the church to return to its roots, taking on the suffering and simple lifestyle of Jesus Christ. The Carmelites demanded the strictest of piety and even employed flagellation to atone for their sins. Not surprisingly, all this proved extremely unpopular with the mainstream Catholic Church.

With the help of many supporters, Teresa founded convents all over Spain and her writings proved enormously popular. She died in 1582 and was canonised by Pope Gregory XV in 1622.

immediately that this is a bastion of robust Castilian cooking, which it has been since 1881. Expect delicious mainstays such as *judías del barco de Ávila* (white beans, often with chorizo in a thick sauce) and *cordero asado* (roast lamb), mercifully light salads and, regrettably, the occasional coach tour. The *menú degustacón*, priced for two people (€39), comes warmly recommended, but only if you're *really* hungry.

Hostería Las Cancelas CASTILIAN €€
(☑920 21 22 49; www.lascancelas.com; Calle de la Cruz Vieja 6; mains €16-24; ☺1-4pm & 7.30-11pm) This courtyard restaurant occupies a delightful interior patio dating back to the 15th century. Renowned for being a mainstay of Ávila cuisine (steaks, roast lamb or suckling pig), traditional meals are prepared with a salutary attention to detail. Reservations are recommended for weekends and most evenings.

Posada de la Fruta CASTILIAN, INTERNATIONAL €€
(www.posadadelafruta.com; Plaza de Pedro Dávila 8; raciones €4.50-13, bar mains €8-10, restaurant mains €13-20; ☺1-4pm & 7.30pm-midnight) Simple, tasty bar-style meals can be had in a light-filled, covered courtyard, while the traditional *comedor* (dining room) is typically all about hearty meat dishes offset by simple, fresh salads.

★**La Bodeguita de San Segundo** WINE BAR
(☑920 25 73 09; Calle de San Segundo 19; ☺11am-midnight Wed-Mon) Situated in the 16th-century Casa de la Misericordia, this superb wine bar is standing-room only most nights, though more tranquil in the quieter afternoon hours. Its wine list is renowned

throughout Spain, with over a thousand wines to choose from and tapas-sized creative servings of cheeses and cured meats as the perfect accompaniment.

❶ Information

Centro de Recepción de Visitantes (☑920 35 40 00, ext 370; www.avilaturismo.com; Avenida de Madrid 39; ☺9am-8pm Apr-Sep, to 5.15pm Oct-Mar) Municipal tourist office.

Regional Tourist Office (☑920 21 13 87; www.turismocastillayleon.com; Casa de las Carnicerías, Calle de San Segundo 17; ☺9.30am-2pm & 5-8pm Mon-Sat, 9.30am-5pm Sun Jul–mid-Sep, 9.30am-2pm & 4-7pm Mon-Sat, 9.30am-5pm Sun mid-Sep–Jul)

❶ Getting There & Away

Frequent services run from the **bus station** (☑920 25 65 05; Avenida de Madrid 2) to Segovia (€6.30, one hour), Salamanca (€7.10, 1½ hours, five daily) and Madrid (€9.90, 1½ hours); a couple of daily buses also head for the main towns in the Sierra de Gredos.

From Madrid the driving time is around one hour; the toll costs €9.35.

There are **Renfe** (☑902 240 202; www.renfe.es) services to Madrid (from €8.95, 1¼ to two hours), Salamanca (from €12, 1¼ hours) and León (from €26, from three hours, three daily).

Salamanca

POP 148,040

Whether floodlit by night or bathed in late afternoon light, there's something magical about Salamanca. This is a city of rare beauty, awash with golden sandstone overlaid with ochre-tinted Latin inscriptions – an extraordinary virtuosity of plateresque and Renaissance styles. The monumental highlights are many, with the exceptional Plaza Mayor (illuminated to stunning effect at night) an unforgettable highlight. But this is also Castilla's liveliest city, home to a massive Spanish and international student population that throngs the streets at night and provides the city with so much vitality.

⊙ Sights

★ Plaza Mayor   SQUARE
Built between 1729 and 1755, Salamanca's exceptional grand square is widely considered to be Spain's most beautiful central plaza. The square is particularly memorable at night when illuminated (until midnight) to magical effect. Designed by Alberto Churriguera, it's a remarkably harmonious and controlled baroque display. The medallions placed around the square bear the busts of famous figures.

Look for the controversial inclusion of Franco in the northeast corner – it's often either covered or vandalised. Bullfights were held here well into the 19th century; the last ceremonial *corrida* (bullfight) took place in 1992.

★ Universidad Civil   HISTORIC BUILDING
(☑923 29 44 00, ext 1150; Calle de los Libreros; adult/concession €10/5, audioguide €2; ⊙10am-6.30pm Mon-Sat, to 1.30pm Sun) Founded initially as the Estudio General in 1218, the university reached the peak of its renown in the 15th and 16th centuries. The visual feast of the entrance facade is a tapestry in sandstone, bursting with images of mythical heroes, religious scenes and coats of arms. It's dominated by busts of Fernando and Isabel. Behind the facade, the highlight of an otherwise-modest collection of rooms lies upstairs: the extraordinary university library, the oldest one in Europe.

★ Catedral Nueva   CATHEDRAL
(☑923 21 74 76; Plaza de Anaya; adult/child incl audioguide & admission to Catedral Vieja €4/3; ⊙10am-8pm Apr-Sep, 10am-5.15pm Oct-Mar) The tower of this late-Gothic cathedral lords over the city centre, its compelling churrigueresque (an ornate style of baroque architecture) dome visible from almost every angle. The interior is similarly impressive, with elaborate choir stalls, main chapel and retrochoir, much of it courtesy of the prolific José Churriguera. The ceilings are also exceptional, along with the Renaissance

doorways – particularly the Puerta del Nacimiento on the western face, which stands out as one of several miracles worked in the city's native sandstone.

★ Catedral Vieja   CATHEDRAL
(Plaza de Anaya; adult/child incl audioguide & admission to Catedral Nueva €4/3; ⊙10am-8pm Apr-Sep, 10am-5.15pm Oct-Mar) The Catedral Nueva's largely Romanesque predecessor, the Catedral Vieja is adorned with an exquisite 15th-century altarpiece, one of the finest outside Italy. Its 53 panels depict scenes from the lives of Christ and Mary and are topped by a haunting representation of the Final Judgment. The cloister was largely ruined in an earthquake in 1755, but the Capilla de Anaya houses an extravagant alabaster sepulchre and one of Europe's oldest organs, a Mudéjar work of art from the 16th century.

★ Convento de San Esteban   CONVENT
(☑923 21 50 00; Plaza del Concilio de Trento; adult/concession/child €3/2/free; ⊙10am-1.15pm & 4-7.15pm) Just down the hill from the cathedral, the lordly Dominican Convento de San Esteban's church has an extraordinary altar-like facade, with the stoning of San Esteban (St Stephen) as its central motif. Inside is a well-presented museum dedicated to the Dominicans, a splendid Gothic-Renaissance cloister and an elaborate church built in the form of a Latin cross and adorned by an overwhelming 17th-century altar by José Churriguera.

★ Museo de Art
Nouveau y Art Decó   MUSEUM
(Casa Lis; ☑923 12 14 25; www.museocasalis.org; Calle de Gibraltar; adult/under 12yr €4/free, Thu morning free; ⊙11am-2pm & 4-8pm Tue-Fri, 11am-8pm Sat & Sun Apr–mid-Oct plus Mon 11am-2pm &

> ### ⓘ SALAMANCA CARD
>
> The Salamanca Card (www.salamanca card.com; 24/48hr €22/25) covers most of the major sights in town (though not the Museo de Salamanca, Convento de las Dueñas or the Convento de las Úrsulas, nor the Universidad Civil audioguide), provides an MP3 audioguide to the city and entitles you to discounts in some restaurants, hotels and shops. Buy the card online or at the tourist office (p152).

Salamanca

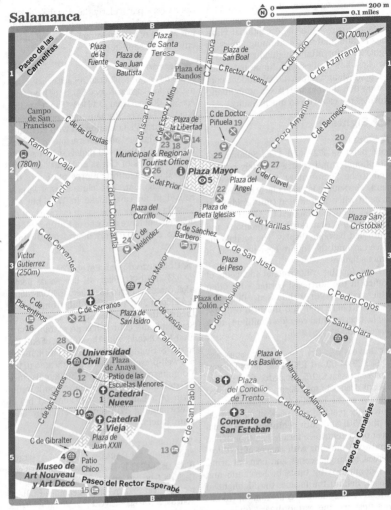

4-8pm Aug, 11am-2pm & 4-7pm Tue-Fri, 11am-8pm Sat & Sun mid-Oct–Mar; ⓕ) Utterly unlike any other Salamanca museum, this stunning collection of sculpture, paintings and art deco and art nouveau pieces inhabits a beautiful, light-filled Modernista (Catalan art nouveau) house. There's abundant stained glass and exhibits that include Lalique glass, toys by Steiff (inventor of the teddy bear), Limoges porcelain, Fabergé watches, fabulous bronze and marble figurines and a vast collection of 19th-century children's dolls (some strangely macabre), which kids will love. There's also a cafe and an excellent gift shop.

Real Clericía de San Marcos

CHURCH, TOWER

(San Marcos; ☎ 923 27 71 14, 923 27 71 00; Calle de la Compañia; San Marcos €3, Scala Coeli €3.75 (10am-2pm Tue free), combined ticket €6; ⓧ San Marcos 10.30am-12.45pm & 5-6.30pm Tue-Fri, 10am-1pm & 5-7.15pm Sat, 10.30am-1.30pm Sun, Scala Coeli 10am-5.15pm) Visits to this colossal baroque church and the attached Catholic university are via obligatory **guided tours** (in Spanish), which run every 45 minutes. You can also climb the **Scala Coeli** (tower) – some 166 steps, including the bell tower – to enjoy superb panoramic views.

Salamanca

Puerta de la Torre
VIEWPOINT

(Ieronimus; www.ieronimus.es; Plaza de Juan XXIII; €3.75; ☉10am-7.15pm) For fine views over Salamanca, head to the tower at the southwestern corner of the Catedral Nueva's facade. From here, stairs lead up through the tower, past labyrinthine but well-presented exhibitions of cathedral memorabilia, then – a real bonus – along the interior balconies of the sanctuaries of the Catedral Nueva and Catedral Vieja and out onto the exterior balconies.

Casa de las Conchas
HISTORIC BUILDING

(House of Shells; ☎923 26 93 17; Calle de la Compañía 2; ☉9am-9pm Mon-Fri, 9am-2pm & 4-7pm Sat & Sun) 𝐅𝐑𝐄𝐄 One of the city's most endearing buildings, Casa de las Conchas is named after the 300 scallop shells clinging to its facade. The house's original owner, Dr Rodrigo Maldonado de Talavera, was a doctor at the court of Isabel and a member of the Order of Santiago, whose symbol is the shell. It now houses the public library, entered via a charming colonnaded courtyard with a central fountain and intricate stone tracery.

Convento de Santa Clara
MUSEUM

(☎660 10 83 14; Calle Santa Clara 2; adult/senior/child €3/2/free; ☉9.30am-12.45pm & 4.25-6.10pm Mon-Fri, 9.30am-2.10pm Sat & Sun) This much-modified convent started life as a Romanesque structure and now houses a small museum. You can admire the beautiful frescos and climb up some stairs to inspect

the 14th- and 15th-century wooden Mudéjar ceiling at close quarters. You can visit only as part of a (Spanish-language) guided tour, which runs roughly every hour.

Convento de las Dueñas
CONVENT

(☎923 21 54 42; Gran Vía; €2; ☉10.30am-12.45pm & 4.30-5.30pm Mon-Sat) This Dominican convent is home to the city's most beautiful cloister, with some decidedly ghoulish carvings on the capitals.

🎓 Courses

University of Salamanca
LANGUAGE COURSE

(Cursos Internacionales, Universidad Civil; ☎923 29 44 18; www.cursosinternacionales.usal.es/en; Patio de las Escuelas Menores) Salamanca is one of the most popular places in Spain to study Spanish and the University of Salamanca is the most respected language school. Courses range from a three-hour daily course over two weeks (€425) to a 10-week course of five hours daily (€1975). Accommodation can be arranged.

🎏 Tours

Guided Tours
WALKING TOUR

(☎622 52 46 90; visitasplaza@hotmail.es; tour per person €8-10; ☉11am Mon-Thu, 11am & 8pm Fri, 10.30am, 11.30am, 4.30pm, 5pm & 8pm Sat, 10.30am Sun) Two-hour guided tours run from the tourist office on Plaza Mayor. Although there are variations, daytime tours take in the main monumental highlights of

CASTILLA Y LEÓN SALAMANCA

FROG-SPOTTING

Arguably a lot more interesting than trainspotting (and you don't have to wear an anorak and drink tea from a thermos flask), a compulsory task facing all visitors to Salamanca is to search out the frog sculpted into the facade of the Universidad Civil (p147). Once pointed out, it's easily enough seen, but the uninitiated can spend considerable time searching. Why bother? Well, they say that those who detect it without help can be assured of good luck and even marriage within a year; some hopeful students believe they'll be guaranteed to ace their examinations. If you believe all this, stop reading now – spoilers ahead.

If you need help, look at the busts of Fernando and Isabel. From there, turn your gaze to the largest column on the extreme right. Slightly above the level of the busts is a series of skulls, atop the leftmost of which sits our little amphibious friend (or what's left of his eroded self).

Salamanca, while the 8pm Friday and Saturday tour is all about local legends and curiosities. Buy your ticket in advance from the tourist office (p152).

🛏 Sleeping

Hostal Concejo   HOSTAL **€**
(☑ 923 21 47 37; www.hconcejo.com; Plaza de la Libertad 1; s €25-45, d €32-60; [P] [✳] [🛜]) A cut above the average *hostal,* the stylish Concejo has polished-wood floors, tasteful furnishings, light-filled rooms and a superb central location. Try to snag one of the corner rooms, such as number 104, which has a traditional, glassed-in balcony, complete with a table, chairs and people-watching views.

⭐**Salamanca Suite Studios**   APARTMENT **€€**
(☑ 923 27 24 65; www.salamancasuitestudios. com; Plaza de la Libertad 4; r €50-98; [✳] [🛜]) This excellent newish place has smart and contemporary modern suites and apartments with kitchens; some have Nespresso coffee machines, and all have bucketloads of style with their white-and-turquoise colour schemes. The location is lovely and central and the service is discreet but attentive.

⭐**Microtel Placentinos**   BOUTIQUE HOTEL **€€**
(☑ 923 28 15 31; www.microtelplacentinos.com; Calle de Placentinos 9; s/d incl breakfast Sun-Thu €57/73, Fri & Sat €88/100; [✳] [🛜]) One of Salamanca's most charming boutique hotels, Microtel Placentinos is tucked away on a quiet street and has rooms with exposed stone walls and wooden beams. The service is faultless, and the overall atmosphere one of intimacy and discretion. All rooms have a hydromassage shower or tub and there's an outside whirlpool spa (open summer only).

Rúa Hotel   HOTEL **€€**
(☑ 923 27 22 72; www.hotelrua.com; Calle de Sánchez Barbero 11; r from €55-95; [✳] [@] [🛜]) The former apartments here have been converted to seriously spacious rooms with sofas and fridges. Light-wood floors, rag-rolled walls and arty prints set the tone. You can't get more central than this.

Don Gregorio   BOUTIQUE HOTEL **€€€**
(☑ 923 21 70 15; www.hoteldongregorio.com; Calle de San Pablo 80; r/ste incl breakfast from €162/271; [P] [✳] [🛜]) A palatial hotel with part of the city's Roman wall flanking the garden. Rooms are decorated in soothing shades of cappuccino with crisp white linens and extravagant extras, including private saunas, espresso machines, complimentary minibar, king-size beds and vast hydromassage tubs. Sumptuous antiques and medieval tapestries adorn the public areas.

Hotel Rector   HOTEL **€€€**
(☑ 923 21 84 82; www.hotelrector.com; Paseo del Rector Esperabé 10; r from €150; [P] [✳] [🛜]) This luxurious hotel is an oasis of calm and luxury, and the antithesis of the cookie-cut homogeneity of the five-star chains. Expect vases of orchids, stained-glass windows, finely carved antiques and excellent service, as well as sumptuous, carpeted rooms. Bathrooms have Bulgari toiletries.

🍴 Eating

Mandala Café   MEDITERRANEAN **€**
(☑ 923 12 33 42; www.mandalasalamanca.com; Calle de Serranos 9-11; set menu €12.50; ⊘ 8am-11pm; [♿]) Come here with an appetite, as cool and casual Mandala offers a three-course set menu (unusually available for lunch *and* dinner) with dishes like black rice with sea-

food, and vegetable lasagne. There are also 18 flavours of hot chocolate, 45 types of milkshake, 56 juice combinations and more teas than we could count.

★ La Cocina de Toño
TAPAS €€

(📋923 26 39 77; www.lacocinadetoño.es; Calle Gran Via 20; tapas from €1.60, mains €7-22; ☺noon-4.30pm & 8-11.30pm Tue-Sat, noon-4.30pm Sun) This place owes its loyal following to its creative *pinchos* (tapas-like snacks) and half-servings of dishes such as escalope of foie gras with roast apple and passionfruit gelatin. The restaurant serves more traditional fare as befits the decor, but the bar is one of Salamanca's gastronomic stars. Slightly removed from the old city, it draws a predominantly Spanish crowd.

Zazu Bistro
ITALIAN €€

(www.restaurantezazu.com; Plaza de la Libertad 8; mains €11-17; ☺2-4pm & 8.30pm-midnight) Enjoy a romantic intimate ambience and Italian-inspired dishes like asparagus, mint and cheese risotto or farfalle with tomato, bacon, vodka and parmesan. The culinary surprises extend to desserts, like that delectable British standard, sticky toffee pudding. Every dish is executed to perfection. Snag a table by the window overlooking this tranquil square.

Igüazú Gastrobar
TAPAS €€

(📋923 21 27 21; www.igüazú-gastrobar.com; Calle de Toro 7; tapas from €1.50, raciones €6-15; ☺8am-midnight) This slick bar effortlessly segues from breakfast to all-day tapas with some terrific choices on the menu – try the Russian salad with red-pepper foam, for example. It's a good place to try *farinato*, a local pork sausage made with spices and, in

this case, quail egg, almonds and honey. The wine list is excellent and the atmosphere cool and classy.

Mesón Cervantes
CASTILIAN €€

(📋923 21 72 13; www.mesoncervantes.com; Plaza Mayor 15; mains €12-23, set menu €14.50; ☺10am-1.30am) Although there are outdoor tables on the square, the dark wooden beams and atmospheric buzz of the Spanish crowd on the 1st floor should be experienced at least once; if you snaffle a window table in the evening, you've hit the jackpot. The food's a mix of *platos combinados* (meat-and-three-veg dishes), salads and *raciones* (full-plate servings).

★ Victor Gutierrez
CONTEMPORARY SPANISH €€€

(📋923 26 29 73; www.restaurantevictorgutierrez.com; Calle de Empedrada 4; set menus €65-80; ☺1.30-4pm & 8.30-11.30pm Tue-Thu, 1.30-4pm & 9-11.30pm Fri & Sat, 2-4pm Sun; 📵) It may have moved premises but this is still the best table in town. Chef Victor Gutierrez has a Michelin star and his place has a justifiably exclusive vibe, with an emphasis on innovative dishes with plenty of colourful drizzle. The choice of what to order is largely made for you with some excellent set menus that change regularly. Reservations essential.

🍷 Drinking & Nightlife

Salamanca's large student population equals lively nights. Nightlife here starts very late, with many bars not filling until after midnight, when many cafe-bars morph into dance clubs. The so-called 'litre bars' on Plaza de San Juan Bautista are fun night-time hang-outs mainly for students (who clearly have better things to do than hit the books).

WHAT'S COOKING IN CASTILLA Y LEÓN?

Castilla y León's cuisine owes everything to climate. There's no better way to fortify yourself against the bitterly cold winters of the high plateau than with *cordero asado* (roast lamb), a speciality all over the province; or *cochinillo* (roast suckling pig), a particular speciality of Segovia that you can try at Casa Duque (p162). Other regional delights include *chuleton de Ávila* (T-bone steak, from Ávila) available at this city's traditional restaurants, such as Méson del Rastro (p145). Still on the meaty route, it's a fact that an estimated 60% of Spain's famous *jamón ibérico* (cured ham) comes from the Salamanca region, with the best coming from Guijuelo. Heading north, León is one of Spain's top cities *tapear* (to eat tapas) at great tapas bars like La Trébede (p181), which serves regional tasty bites like *pincho de morcilla* (blood sausage) free with your drink. Seeking more sophistication? This region is also home to an increasing number of exciting contemporary restaurants where traditional dishes are combined with innovative ingredients and expertise.

⭐ **Doctor Cocktail** COCKTAIL BAR
(☑ 923 26 31 51; Calle del Doctor Piñuela 5; ⓧ 4pm-late) Excellent cocktails, friendly bar staff and a cool crowd make for a fine mix just north of the Plaza Mayor. Apart from the creative list of cocktails, it has 32 different kinds of gin to choose from and above-average tonic to go with it.

⭐ **Tío Vivo** MUSIC BAR
(☑ 923 215 768; www.tiovivosalamanca.com; Calle del Clavel 3-5; ⓧ 3.30pm-late) Sip drinks by flickering candlelight to a background of '80s music, enjoying the whimsical decor of carousel horses and oddball antiquities. There's live music Tuesday to Thursday from midnight, sometimes with a €5 cover charge.

Café El Corrillo BAR
(☑ 923 27 19 17; www.cafecorrillo.com; Calle de Meléndez; ⓧ 8.30am-3am) Great for a beer and tapas at any time, with live music (especially jazz or singer-songwriters) on Sunday and Thursday nights from 10pm; concerts sometimes take place on other nights. The *terraza* (terrace) out back is perfect on a warm summer's evening.

Garamond CLUB
(☑ 923 26 88 98; www.garamondsalamanca.es; Calle del Prior 24; ⓧ 9pm-late) A stalwart of Salamanca nightlife with medieval-style decor. Garamond has music that's good to dance to without straying too far from the mainstream. No cover.

🛍 Shopping

⭐ **Mercatus** SOUVENIRS
(☑ 923 29 46 48; www.mercatus.usal.es; Calle de Cardenal Pla y Deniel; ⓧ 10am-8.15pm Mon-Sat, 10.15am-2pm Sun) The official shop of the University of Salamanca has a stunning range of stationery items, leather-bound books and other carefully selected reminders of your Salamanca visit.

La Galatea BOOKS
(☑ 689 41 87 89; www.lagalatea.es; Calle de los Libreros 28; ⓧ 10.30am-2pm & 5-8.30pm Tue-Sat) The first bookshop in decades to open along Salamanca's 'Street of the Booksellers' (there were once more than 50), this fine space combines a bargain table (with some books in English), some gorgeous Spanish-language rare antique books and a carefully chosen collection of LP records.

Convento de las Dueñas FOOD
(Gran Vía; ⓧ 10.30am-12.45pm & 4.30-5.30pm Mon-Sat) The time-honoured tradition of monks and nuns making sweets and selling them to a paying public is alive at this convent.

ℹ Information

Municipal & Regional Tourist Office (☑ 923 21 83 42; www.salamanca.es; Plaza Mayor 14; ⓧ 9am-2pm & 4.30-8pm Mon-Fri, 10am-8pm Sat, 10am-2pm Sun Easter–mid-Oct, 9am-2pm & 4-6.30pm Mon-Fri, 10am-6.30pm Sat, 10am-2pm Sun mid-Oct–Easter) The regional tourist office shares an office with the municipal office on Plaza Mayor. An audio city guide (www.audioguiasalamanca.es) is available with the appropriate app.

ℹ Getting There & Away

The bus and train stations are a 10- and 15-minute walk, respectively, from Plaza Mayor.

Buses include the following destinations: Madrid (regular/express €16/23, 2½ to three hours, hourly), Ávila (€7.10, 1½ hours, five daily), Segovia (€15, 2½ hours, four daily) and Valladolid (€8.60, 1½ hours, eight daily). There is a limited service to smaller towns with just one daily bus – except on Sunday – to La Alberca (€5.50, around 1½ hours), with stops in the villages of the Sierra de Francia, such as Mogarraz and San Martín del Castañar.

Regular trains depart to Madrid's Chamartín station (€24, 2½ hours), Ávila (€12, 1¼ hour) and Valladolid (from €10, 1½ hours).

ℹ Getting Around

Bus 4 runs past the bus station and around the old-city perimeter to Calle Gran Vía. From the train station, the best bet is bus 1, which heads into the centre along Calle de Azafranal.

Ciudad Rodrigo

POP 13,210

Close to the Portuguese border and away from well-travelled tourist routes, sleepy Ciudad Rodrigo is one of the prettier towns in western Castilla y León. It's an easy day trip from Salamanca, 80km away, but staying overnight within the sanctuary of its walls enables you to better appreciate the town's medieval charm.

👁 Sights

Murallas WALLS
FREE There are numerous stairs leading up onto the crumbling ramparts of the city walls that encircle the old town. You can

follow their length for about 2.2km around the town and enjoy fabulous views over the surrounding plains.

Museo del Orinal
MUSEUM

(Chamber Pot Museum; ☑952 38 20 87; www. museodelorinal.es; Plaza Herrasti; adult/child under 12yr €2/free; ☺11am-2pm & 4-7pm Mon-Sat, 11am-2pm Sun; ☑) Chamber pots, commodes, bed pans... Ciudad Rodrigo's Museo del Orinal may be located opposite the cathedral, but its theme is definitely more down to earth than otherworldly. This city is home to Spain's (possibly the world's) only museum dedicated to the not-so-humble chamber pot (or potty, as it is known in the UK). The private collection of former local resident José Maria del Arco, the collection comprises a staggering 1300 exhibits. Hailing from 27 countries, there are some truly historic pieces here.

Catedral de Santa María
CATHEDRAL

(Plaza de San Salvador 1; adult/concession €3/2.50, 4-6pm Sun free, tower €2; ☺church & museum 11am-2pm Mon-Fri, 11am-2pm & 4-6pm Sat, noon-2pm & 4-6pm Sun) This elegant, weathered sandstone cathedral, begun in 1165, towers over the historic centre. Of particular interest are the **Puerta de las Cadenas**, with splendid Gothic reliefs of Old Testament figures; the elegant **Pórtico del Perdón**; and inside, the exquisite, carved-oak choir stalls. You can also climb the **tower** at 1.15pm on Saturday and Sunday; the views are Ciudad Rodrigo's best. Opening hours were in a state of flux at the time of writing so check with the tourist office.

★Plaza Mayor
SQUARE

The long, sloping Plaza Mayor is a fine centrepiece for this beautiful town. At the top of the hill, the double-storey arches of the **Casa Consistorial** are stunning, but the plaza's prettiest building is the **Casa del Marqués de Cerralbo**, an early 16th-century town house with a wonderful facade. Sadly, cars are allowed to park around the perimeter, which diminishes the square's charm a bit.

Casa de los Vázquez
HISTORIC BUILDING

(Correos; Calle de San Juan 12; ☺8.30am-2.30pm Mon-Fri, 9.30am-1pm Sat) Even if you've nothing to post, the *correos* (post office) is worth stopping into to admire the magnificent *artesonado* (wooden Mudéjar ceiling), stained glass and medieval-style pictorial tiled friezes.

Palacio de los Ávila y Tiedra
HISTORIC BUILDING

(Plaza del Conde 3; ☺9am-7pm Mon-Sat) The 16th-century Palacio de los Ávila y Tiedra boasts one of the town's most engaging plateresque facades – it's the pick of a handful of fine examples that surround the Plaza del Conde. While most of the building is off limits, you can wander in to admire the pretty, compact courtyard surrounded by columns.

☞ Tours

Guided Tours
WALKING TOUR

(☑680 42 67 07; agotcir@gmail.com; day/night tours €6/7; ☺noon, 4.30pm & 8pm Sat, noon Sun) Run by the tourist office (p154), two-hour walking tours take in the main monuments of Ciudad Rodrigo. The 90-minute Saturday-night version is all about local legends.

✰ Festivals & Events

Carnaval
CARNIVAL

(www.carnavaldeltoro.es; ☑) Celebrated with great enthusiasm in February. In addition to the outlandish fancy dress, you can witness (or join in) an *encierro* (running of the bulls) and *capeas* (amateur bullfights).

🛏 Sleeping

★Parador Enrique II
HISTORIC HOTEL €€

(☑923 46 01 50; www.parador.es; Plaza del Castillo 1; r €125-145; P✳@🅿) Ciudad Rodrigo's premier address is a plushly renovated castle built into the town's western wall. Converted in 1931, it's the third-oldest *parador* in Spain. The views are good, the rooms brim with character and the restaurant is easily the best in town. The delightful terraced gardens out back overlook the Rio Agueda.

★Hospedería Audiencia Real
HISTORIC HOTEL €€

(☑923 49 84 98; www.audienciareal.com; Plaza Mayor 17; d €45-80; ✳🅿) Right on Plaza Mayor, this fine 16th-century inn has been beautifully reformed and retains a tangible historic feel with lovely exposed stone walls. Some rooms have wrought-iron furniture and several sport narrow balconies overlooking the square; the very best has a private, glassed-in alcove containing a table for two, ideal for reading the morning newspaper.

🍴 Eating

★Zascandil
TAPAS €

(☑665 63 58 84; Correo Viejo 5; pinchos €2.50, tostas €5.50-7; ☺1-4pm & 7.30-11pm) 🍴 A very fashionable spot with an art deco look to

WORTH A TRIP

ROAD TRIP: NORTH OF CIUDAD RODRIGO

One of the most dramatic landforms in Castilla y León, the Parque Natural Arribes del Duero is a little-known gem. This road trip takes you through some of the most picturesque country and villages.

The quiet SA324 north from Ciudad Rodrigo gives no hint of what lies ahead. At Castillo de Martín Viejo, 17km northwest of Ciudad Rodrigo, take the turn-off for Siega Verde (☑ 923 48 01 98; www.siegaverde.es; guided tour adult/concession €6/4; guided tours 11am, 12.30pm, 2pm & 3.30pm Sat, ☺ 11am & 12.30pm Sun), the Unesco World Heritage–listed archaeological site with 645 prehistoric rock carvings of animals and ancient symbols – it's one of the richest such collections in Europe. San Felices de los Gallegos, 40km north of Ciudad Rodrigo, has a pretty Plaza Mayor and a well-preserved castle. After Lumbrales, a further 10km to the north, the road (now the SA330) narrows and passes among stone walls and begins to buck and weave with the increasingly steep contours of the land. The Mirador del Cachón de Caneces (lookout) offers the first precipitous views. The road then drops down to the Puerto de la Molinero before climbing again to Saucelle (24km from Lumbrales) and then on to Vilvestre (31km), with pleasing views out towards the Río Duero and Portugal.

But it's at Aldeadávila, around 35km to the north, that you find the views that make this trip worthwhile. Before entering the village, turn left at the large purple sign. After 5.1km, a 2.5km walking track leads down to the Mirador El Picón de Felipe, with fabulous views down into the canyon. Returning to the road, it's a further 1km down to the Mirador del Fraile – the views of the impossibly deep canyon with plunging cliffs on both sides are utterly extraordinary. This is prime birdwatching territory, with numerous raptors nesting on the cliffs and griffon vultures wheeling high overhead on the thermals.

For an entirely different perspective, return to Aldeadávila, and at the eastern exit to the town follow the signs down to the lovely Playa del Rostro, from where 1½-hour boat journeys (☑ 627 63 73 49; www.corazondelasarribes.com; adult/child 3-9yr €16/8; ☺ noon & 6pm Aug, 6pm Mon-Fri, noon & 6pm Sat & Sun Jun & Jul, shorter hours rest of year; 🖬) follow the canyon to the base of the cliffs. There's also a solar catamaran (☑ 980 55 75 57; www.europarques.com; adult/child €16/8; ☺ noon & 5pm Aug, noon Mon-Fri, noon & 5pm Sat, Sun & public holidays Feb-Jul & Sep–mid-Dec, closed mid-Dec–Feb) that operates from the Portuguese side of the water.

Other options for exploring this area are the brilliant kayaking tours offered by Zamora Natural (p173) or birdwatching detours with Wild Wolf Experience (p173).

accompany the pretty-as-a-picture gastro tapas (such as sashimi and gourmet mini burgers). Organic vegies come from the owner's *huerta* (market garden) and eco-wines are served. There's live music in summer.

Mesón La Paloma　　　　TAPAS €€
(☑ 923 46 24 41; Calle de la Paloma 7; mains €8-20; ☺ 8am-11pm) One of those agreeable Spanish bars where you can have breakfast, graze on tapas or sit down for top-class meal. The grilled meats are a highlight, and it's a great place to try the local speciality, *farinato* (a rich, local pork sausage made with all manner of spices), in the form of a tapa.

Bar Restaurante Tamborino　　SPANISH €€
(☑ 923 46 00 22; Calle de Gigantes 8; mains €8-18; ☺ 1-4pm & 8.30-11pm) Spring lamb cooked in a wood-fired oven or rice with prawns and lobster – they may be radically different dishes but the specialities here are equally good.

ⓘ Information

Municipal Tourist Office (☑ 923 49 84 00; www.aytociudadrodrigo.es; Plaza Mayor 27; ☺ 10am-1.30pm & 4-7pm Sat & Sun Apr-Sep, shorter hours rest of year)

Regional Tourist Office (☑ 673 57 37 98; www.turismocastillayleon.com; Plaza de Amayuelas 5; ☺ 9am-2pm & 5-7pm Mon-Fri, 10am-2pm & 5-8pm Sat, 10am-2pm Sun)

ⓘ Getting There & Away

From the **bus station** (☑ 923 46 10 36; Campo de Toledo) there are up to 13 daily services (fewer on weekends) to Salamanca (€6.20, one hour). For the Sierra de Francia, you'll need to go via Salamanca.

Sierra de Francia

Hidden away in a remote corner of south-western Castilla y León and until recently secluded for centuries, this mountainous region with wooded hillsides and pretty stone-and-timber villages was once one of Spain's most godforsaken regions, but is today among Castilla y León's best-kept secrets. Quiet mountain roads connect villages that you could easily spend days exploring and where the pace of life remains relatively untouched by the modern world.

⊙ Sights

The main tourist centre of the Sierra de Francia is **La Alberca**. Having your own car enables you to immerse yourself in quiet villages such as **Mogarraz**, east of La Alberca, which has some of the most evocative old houses in the region. It's also famous for its *embutidos* (cured meats), as well as the more recent novelty of over 300 portraits of past and present residents, painted by local artist Florencio Maillo and on display outside the family homes. The history of this extraordinary project dates from the 1960s, when poverty was rife and many locals were seeking work, mainly in South America – they needed identity cards and it is these that inspired the portraits.

Miranda del Castañar, further east, is similarly intriguing, strung out along a narrow ridge. But **San Martín del Castañar** is the most enchanting, with half-timbered stone houses, flowers cascading from balconies, a bubbling stream and a small village bullring at the top of the town, next to the renovated castle with its historic cemetery (there is also an interpretation centre here). **Villanueva del Conde** is another lovely hamlet.

The main natural attraction of the region is the highest peak in the area, **Peña de Francia** (1732m). Topped by a monastery and reached by a sinuous 12km climb from close to La Alberca, it's a stunning place with views that extend east to the Sierra de Gredos, south into Extremadura and west towards Portugal.

⌖ Sleeping & Eating

Hostal Las Madras   HOSTAL **€**
(☑ 627 45 52 90; www.gruposierrarural.es; Plaza Juan José Hidalgo Acera 21, Villanueva del Conde; d from €39; ☎) An excellent budget-value *hostal* in the pretty little village of Villanueva del Conde; the rooms have exposed brick walls. The restaurant is similarly excellent.

Abadía de San Martín   HOTEL **€€**
(☑ 923 43 73 50; www.abadiadesanmartin.com; Calle Paipérez 24, San Martín del Castañar; d €65-75, ste €75-95; ☎) Lovely, contemporary rooms in a converted old home in one of the Sierra de Francia's loveliest villages, along with a well-regarded restaurant – what more could you ask for?

Hotel Spa Villa de Mogarraz   HOTEL **€€**
(www.hotelspamogarraz.com; Calle Miguel Ángel Maillo 54, Mogarraz; r €45-150; ✳☎) At the pedestrian entrance to gorgeous Mogarraz, this artfully converted spa-hotel has amply sized rooms, some with wooden beams, others with exposed stone walls. We especially like the views down the cobblestone main street from room 125. There's also a good restaurant.

ⓘ Information

There are no tourist offices in the Sierra de Francia. The tourist offices in Salamanca (p152) and Ciudad Rodrigo (p154) have limited information on the region.

ⓘ Getting There & Away

Roads lead into the Sierra de Francia from Ciudad Rodrigo (SA220), Salamanca (CL512 and SA210) and Béjar (SA220). The only public transport here is one or two buses a day from Salamanca.

The drive south into Extremadura through the dreamy Valle de las Batuecas is spectacular. Just beyond La Alberca, a sweeping panorama of cascading lower mountain ranges opens up before you. The road corkscrews down into the valley before passing through beautiful terrain that has been praised by poets and the writer/academic Miguel de Unamuno. Time your visit for spring when purple heather and brilliant yellow rapeseed blanket the hillsides.

ⓘ Getting Around

One daily bus from Salamanca passes through some Sierra de Francia villages from Monday to Saturday, but it's only of use to get to the region, rather than around it – you'll need your own wheels to properly explore the area.

TOURS SOUTH OF SALAMANCA

Olive Oil Tour (☑923 08 29 73; www.arribera.es; Camino de San Felices, Ahigal de los Aceiteros; per person €6) Olive oil is one of Spain's proudest culinary exports; this tour of an organic-olive-oil-producing farm north of Ciudad Rodrigo is a great foodie complement to the *jamón* (cured ham) tours available near Salamanca. Ring or email ahead to arrange your visit. It's close to the Portuguese border, so easily combined with a visit to the Parque Natural de Arribes de Duero.

Toro & Cerdo Tours (Faenas Camperas; ☑646 11 59 12; www.faenascamperas.com; Cabeza de Diego Gómez; adult/child Toro tour €30/15, Cerdo Ibérico tour €18/9) This company offers two excellent tours that explore two peculiarly Spanish obsessions: the *toro* (fighting bull) and the *cerdo ibérico* (Iberian pig, from which *jamón* is made). The tours take you to the village of Cabeza de Diego Gómez, west of Salamanca. You'll need your own wheels to get here – ask for directions at the tourist office (p152) in Salamanca.

La Alberca

POP 1125 / ELEV 1048M

La Alberca is one of the largest and most beautifully harmonious villages; a historic and harmonious huddle of narrow alleys flanked by gloriously ramshackle houses built of stone, wood beams and plaster. Look for the date they were built (typically the late 18th century) carved into the door lintels.

Numerous stores sell local products such as *jamón,* as well as baskets and the inevitable tackier souvenirs. The centre is the pretty-as-a-postcard **Plaza Mayor**; there's a market here on Saturday mornings.

Sleeping

★**Abadia de los Templarios** HOTEL €€
(☑923 42 31 07; www.abadiadelostemplarios.com; Ctra SA201 (Salamanca–La Alberca) Km 76; d/ste/villas from €115/135/110; P❈🖈🏊) Large rooms with wooden floors and wooden beams make this place an excellent choice. It's a large complex, close to the main entrance of town and on a pretty, leafy hillside, designed to recreate La Alberca's half-timbered architecture. There's also an on-site spa and swimming pool. Our only criticism is that it's often booked up by local tour groups.

★**Hotel Doña Teresa** HOTEL €€
(☑923 41 53 08; www.hoteldeteresa.com; Carretera Mogarraz; s/d from €60/90; P❈🖈) Lovely Doña Teresa is a perfect modern fit for the village's old-world charm. The large rooms combine character (wooden beams and exposed stone) with all the necessary mod cons; some open onto a garden. The

owners also run a spa 1.5km away, with various treatments available at reduced rates for guests.

Eating

Entrevinos SPANISH €€
(☑618 47 94 89; Plaza Mayor 3; mains €12-18; ☺1.30-4pm & 8.30-10.45pm) La Alberca's most creative kitchen holds fast to the town's meat-eating obsession, but does a few riffs along the way, such as the sirloin medallions cooked in a sauce of red wine, raspberries and caviar. A more contemporary look to the dining area and young owners are a nice alternative to the dark, wood-panelled restaurants with grumpy waiters elsewhere.

La Taberna CASTILIAN €€
(☑923 41 54 60; www.latabernadelaalberca.com; Plaza Mayor 5; mains €6-15; ☺1.30-4pm daily, plus 8pm-12.30am Fri & Sat; ☑🍴) Right on Plaza Mayor, with daily three-course menus plus gut-busting *parrilladas* (grills) of various meats (€12 per person) or – unusually – vegetables (€10). The upstairs dining room has views over the square.

ⓘ Getting There & Away

Buses travel between La Alberca and Salamanca (€5.50, around one to 1½ hours) twice daily on weekdays and once a day on weekends.

Guijuelo

POP 5780

Guijuelo may not be Castilla y León's prettiest town (in fact, it's rather ugly), but locals couldn't care a jot because this place is one of Spain's culinary superstars. Many experts agree that Spain's best *jamón* comes from Guijuelo and the surrounding area, and there are few better places in Spain to draw near to this very Spanish, rather delicious obsession.

◉ Sights

Museo de la Industria Chacinera   MUSEUM
(☑923 59 19 01; Calle de Teso de la Feria 9; adult/child €2/1; ◷10am-2pm Mon-Sat) Despite the rather functional name, this interactive museum is dedicated to *jamón* and nothing but. In the first room, videos demonstrate the production of *jamón* and the other *embutidos* (cured meats) for which Guijuelo is famous. The second room covers the special *cerdos ibéricos* (Iberian pigs) that form the centrepiece of this industry. The third and final room, which is not for the squeamish, is devoted to the ritual of *matanza* (the slaughter). Displays and videos are in Spanish only.

☞ Tours

A handful of Guijuelo *jamón* producers offer guided visits of their factories, which is an excellent way to immerse yourself in the local obsession. There are no fixed times, so you'll need to ring or email ahead to find out when they have groups leaving. The tourist office also has a list of those offering tours, and can help in arranging your visit, though we recommend enquiring in advance – if you wait until you're in town, you may find that there are no tours that day.

★**Alma de Ibérico**   FOOD TOUR
(☑923 58 09 44; www.almadeiberico.com; tour per person €20-30; ◷noon Sat, other times by appointment) This local *jamón* producer offers 45-minute factory tours, where you'll be surrounded by thousands of hanging hams and get to eat a *jamón*-dominated meal at the end. Most explanations are in Spanish, but it's still a sensory marvel even if you don't understand them. Email in advance or stop by its Guijuelo shop (p157) to arrange your tour – reservations are essential.

Simón Martín   FOOD TOUR
(☑923 58 01 29; www.simonmartin.es; tour per person €20-30; ◷by appointment) This respected Guijuelo *jamón* producer offers one-hour guided visits of its factory, initiating you into the world of producing, drying, salting and everything else that goes into making *jamón*. Ring or email ahead to arrange a time.

✖ Eating

Standout restaurants are few in Guijuelo, but that doesn't really matter when you can step into any bar in town, order a plate of *jamón* and know you've got the best.

★**Alma de Ibérico**   JAMÓN €
(☑923 58 09 44; Calle de Alfonso XIII 18; tapas from €2.95; ◷9.30am-7.30pm Mon-Fri, 11.30am-3.30pm Sat & Sun) Part shop, part *jamón*-tasting centre, part small bar, this fine place combines many impulses in one. We especially like it for the chance to sample a range of cured meats, or a *ración* of its best *jamón* with a glass of fine local wine.

El Pernil Ibérico   SPANISH €€
(☑923 58 14 02; Calle de Chinarral 6; mains €12-24; ◷9am-midnight) Spanish cooking – good and traditional – dominates here, alongside excellent *jamón* and a recommended *menu de degustación*.

🛍 Shopping

Sabor Guijuelo   FOOD
(☑923 58 12 87; Plaza Mayor 1; ◷10am-6.30pm) You could pick any of the shops around town selling *embutidos*, but this excellent little shop is just a stone's throw from the Plaza Mayor and the tourist office. Pick up one of its sliced, prepackaged *jamón ibérico de bellota en lonchas* (ham made from acorn-fed pigs) for around €10 and you'll quickly taste what all the fuss is about.

ℹ Information

Tourist Office (☑923 58 04 72; www.guijuelo.es; Plaza Mayor; ◷9am-3pm & 4-7pm Mon-Fri, 10am-2pm Sat) Signposted in the centre of town; it also has an office at the Museo de la Industria Chacinera (p157). Staff have lists of which local *jamón* producers offer visits, and they'll even help you set up a guided tour if you ask nicely.

ℹ Getting There & Away

Guijuelo lies just off the A66/E803, around 50km south of Salamanca, or 20km north of Béjar. A few buses each day pass through town each day towards Salamanca (€3.90 30 minutes) or Béjar (€2.25, 15 minutes).

Sierra de Béjar

Between the Sierra de Francia and the Sierra de Gredos, the Sierra de Béjar is home to delightful villages and rolling mountain scenery, normally snowcapped until well after Easter. It is an excellent region for outdoor activities, with signposted trails leading into the hills from numerous trailheads.

◉ Sights

The centre of the region is Béjar, with a partly walled, but somewhat neglected, old quarter straddling the western end of a high ridge. It's a dramatic sight if you're pulling into town from the A66.

Just east of the mountains is El Barco de Ávila, on the Río Tormes. It's lorded over by a proud, if ruined, castle.

The most scenic village in the region is tiny Candelario (population 970), a 5km detour from Béjar. Nudging against the steep foothills of the sierra, this charming village is dominated by mountain-stone-and-whitewash architecture clustered closely together to protect against the harsh winter climate; note the wooden half-doors at the entrance to many homes, which are typical of the town. It's a popular summer resort and a great base for hiking.

🛏 Sleeping & Eating

Casa de la Sal GUESTHOUSE €€
(☑923 41 30 51; www.casadelasal.com; Calle de la Fuente Perales 1, Candelario; r €69-90; ☎) Beautifully rustic and tastefully rough-hewn rooms with soothing pale colour schemes and attractive artworks make this friendly place an excellent Candelario base. The 'special' rooms have a sitting area.

Posada Puerta Grande GUESTHOUSE €€
(☑923 41 32 45; www.posadapuertagrande.com; Plaza del Humilladero 1, Candelario; r from €75; ☎) Exposed stone walls, wooden beams and tiled floors make for attractive rooms at the bottom of the hill that leads up into the old town. There's a restaurant and several other bar-restaurants nearby.

ℹ Information

Tourist Office (☑923 41 30 11; Calle de Manuel Fonseca 5, Candelario; ⊙10.30am-2.30pm & 5-7pm Sat, 10.30am-2.30pm Sun) Close to the entrance of the old town at the bottom of the hill. You might find the doors open from 5pm to 7pm, when the local library (with which the tourist office shares premises) is open.

ℹ Getting There & Away

Béjar lies along the route between Salamanca (€5.80, 45 minutes) and Plasencia (€7, one hour), with several buses a day pulling into town off the motorway. Occasional services run to Candelario from Salamanca.

THE CENTRAL PLATEAU

Segovia

POP 52,730 / ELEV 1002M

Unesco World Heritage–listed Segovia has always had a whiff of legend about it, not least in the myths that the city was founded by Hercules or by the son of Noah. It may also have something to do with the fact that nowhere else in Spain has such a stunning monument to Roman grandeur (the soaring aqueduct) surviving in the heart of a vibrant modern city. Or maybe it's because art really has imitated life Segovia-style – Walt Disney is said to have modelled Sleeping Beauty's castle in California's Disneyland on Segovia's Alcázar. Whatever it is, the effect is stunning: a magical city of warm terracotta and sandstone hues set amid the rolling hills of Castilla, against the backdrop of the Sierra de Guadarrama.

◉ Sights

⭐ **Acueducto** AQUEDUCT
Segovia's most recognisable symbol is El Acueducto (Roman Aqueduct), an 894m-long engineering wonder that looks like an enormous comb plunged into Segovia. First raised here by the Romans in the 1st century AD, the aqueduct was built with not a drop of mortar to hold the more than 20,000 uneven granite blocks together. It's made up of 163 arches and, at its highest point in Plaza del Azoguejo, rises 28m high.

The aqueduct was part of a complex system of aqueducts and underground canals that brought water from the mountains more than 15km away. Its pristine condition is due to a major restoration in the 1990s. For a different perspective, climb the stairs next to the aqueduct that begin behind the Centro de Recepción de Visitantes (p162).

⭐ **Catedral** CATHEDRAL
(☑921 46 22 05; Plaza Mayor; adult/concession €3/2, Sun morning free, tower tour €5; ⊙9.30am-6.30pm Apr-Sep, tower tour 10.30am, 9.30am-5.30pm Mon-Sat, 1.15-5.30pm Sun Oct-Mar, 12.30pm & 4pm year-round) Started in 1525 on the site of a former chapel, Segovia's cathedral is a powerful expression of Gothic

architecture that took almost 200 years to complete. The austere three-nave interior is anchored by an imposing choir stall and enlivened by 20-odd chapels, including the **Capilla del Cristo del Consuelo**, with its magnificent Romanesque doorway, and the **Capilla de la Piedad**, containing an important altarpiece by Juan de Juni. Join an hour-long guided tour to climb the tower for fabulous views.

★ **Alcázar** CASTLE
(☑ 921 46 07 59; www.alcazardesegovia.com; Plaza de la Reina Victoria Eugenia; adult/concession/child under 6yr €5/3/free, tower €2; ☺ 10am-6.30pm Oct-Mar, to 7.30pm Apr-Sep; ⊞) Rapunzel towers, turrets topped with slate witches' hats and a deep moat at its base make the Alcázar a prototype fairy-tale castle – so much so that its design inspired Walt Disney's vision of Sleeping Beauty's castle. Fortified since Roman days, the site takes its name from the Arabic *al-qasr* (fortress). It was rebuilt in the 13th and 14th centuries, but the whole lot burned down in 1862. What you see today is an evocative, over-the-top reconstruction of the original.

Plaza Mayor SQUARE
The Plaza Mayor is the nerve centre of old Segovia, lined by an assortment of buildings, arcades and cafes and with an open pavilion in its centre. It's also the site of the *catedral* and the regional tourist office (p162).

Museo Gastronómico MUSEUM
(☑ 921 46 01 47; www.museogastronomicode segovia.es; Calle de Daoiz 9; €3, with tasting €5; ☺ 10am-3pm Tue & 10am-8pm Wed-Mon Apr-Oct, 10am-3pm Tue & 10am-7pm Wed-Mon Nov-Mar) This engaging little private museum takes you through the wonderful world of Spanish foods, with a focus on those from the Segovia region. There are sections on local cheeses, wines, cured meats, *ponche segoviano* (see Sweet Treats, p162) and even a section on the local whisky, DYC. There are some good video displays (mostly in Spanish), though most sections of the museum have English summaries alongside the main text.

Monasterio de Santa María del Parral MONASTERY
(☑ 921 43 12 98; Calle Del Marqués de Villena; by donation; ☺ 11am & 5pm Wed-Sun) Ring the bell to see part of the cloister and church; the latter is a proud, flamboyant Gothic structure. The monks chant a Gregorian Mass at noon on Sundays, and at 1pm daily in summer.

ⓘ BEST VIEW OF TOWN

For *the* shot of Segovia for your computer wallpaper, head out of town due north (towards Cuéllar) for around 2km. The view of the city unfolds in all its movie-style magic, with the aqueduct taking a deserved star role.

Plaza de San Martín SQUARE
This is one of the most captivating small plazas in Segovia. The square is presided over by a statue of Juan Bravo; the 14th-century **Torreón de Lozoya** (☑ 921 46 24 61; Plaza de San Martín 5; ☺ 5-9pm Tue-Fri, noon-2pm & 5-9pm Sat & Sun) **FREE**, a tower that now houses exhibitions; and the **Iglesia de San Martín** (☺ before & after Mass), a Romanesque jewel with a Mudéjar tower and arched gallery.

Iglesia de Vera Cruz CHURCH
(☑ 921 43 14 75; Carretera de Zamarramala; €2; ☺ 10.30am-1.30pm & 4-7pm Tue-Sun Apr-Sep, 4-6pm Tue, 10.30am-1.30pm & 4-6pm Wed-Sun Oct-Mar) This 12-sided church is one of the best preserved of its kind in Europe. Built in the early 13th century by the Knights Templar and based on Jerusalem's Church of the Holy Sepulchre, it once housed a piece of the Vera Cruz (True Cross), which now rests in the nearby village church of Zamarramala (on view only at Easter). The curious two-storey chamber in the circular nave (the inner temple) is where the knights' secret rites took place.

⚔ Festivals & Events

Titirimundi International Puppet Festival THEATRE
(www.titirimundi.es; ⊞) A weeklong festival in mid-May that celebrates puppetry and puppet theatre with shows and street events throughout the city.

Fiestas de San Juan y San Pedro RELIGIOUS
(⊞) On San Juan's day (29 June), a pilgrimage takes place to a hermitage outside town. Throughout the six days of festivities, there are parades, concerts and bullfights.

⊨ Sleeping

Häb Urban Hostel HOSTAL €
(☑ 921 46 10 26; www.habhostel.com; Calle de Cervantes 16; r €50-82, f from €109; ⊞ ⊛ ☎) This bright new *hostal* – think doubles with private bathrooms rather than dorms with bunk beds, despite the name – is modern

Segovia

Map labels:

Carretera de Zamarramala
6
7
C del Marqués de Villena
Alameda del Parral
Río Eresma
C de San Marcos
Paseo de Santo Domingo de Guzmán
C del Pozo de la Nieve
Puerta de Santiago
Alcázar
2
Plaza de la Reina
Victoria Eugenia
C de Daoiz
8
14
Ronda de Don Juan II
Plaza de
San Esteban
C Judería Nueva
23
C de los Desamparados
C de Valdeláguila
C San Francisco
C de los Escuderos
17 21
C del Cronista Lecea
C Marqués del Arco
18
Río Clamores
10
3 Plaza Mayor
20
Cuesta de los Hoyas
Catedral
13 Regional Tourist Office
C Judería Vieja
22
4 C de Isabel la Católica
C de San Valentín
Cuesta de los Hoyas
Puente de Sancti Spíritu
Paseo de Ezequiel González
(280m)

---

and has a fine location just where the pedestrian street begins the climb up into the old town. Some rooms are on the small side, but the look is light and contemporary.

⭐**Hotel Palacio San Facundo** 　　　HISTORIC HOTEL **€€**
(☏921 46 30 61; www.hotelpalaciosanfacundo. com; Plaza San Facundo 4; s/d incl breakfast €90/120; ❋@🕾) Segovia's hotels are proving adept at fusing stylishly appointed modern rooms with centuries-old architecture. This place is one of the best, with an attractive columned courtyard, a warm colour scheme, chic room decor and a central location. The breakfast buffet is more generous than most.

⭐**Hospedería La Gran Casa Mudéjar** 　　　HISTORIC HOTEL **€€**
(☏921 46 62 50; www.lacasamudejar.com; Calle de Isabel la Católica 8; r €45-95; ❋@🕾) Spread over two buildings, this place has been magnificently renovated, blending genuine 15th-century Mudéjar carved wooden ceilings in some rooms with modern amenities. In the newer wing, top-floor rooms have fine mountain views out over the rooftops of

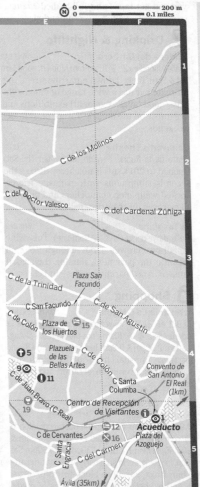

N 0 ___ 200 m
0 ___ 0.1 miles

Segovia

CASTILLA Y LEÓN SEGOVIA

✗ Eating

Segovianos (residents of Segovia) love their pigs to the point of obsession. Just about every restaurant boasts its *horno de asar* (roasts). The main speciality is *cochinillo asado* (roast suckling pig), but *judiones de la granja* (butter beans with pork chunks) also loom large.

Hotel Don Felipe
HISTORIC HOTEL €€

(☑ 921 46 60 95; www.hoteldonfelipe.es; Calle de Daoiz 7; s €50-65, d €60-103) This place gets rave reviews from travellers and it's not difficult to see why. Housed in a converted Segovia mansion and one of few hotels down the Álcazar end of the old town, the hotel has attractive rooms, some with fine views out over the rooftops. There's also a lovely garden out back.

Segovia's old Jewish quarter. Adding to the appeal is a small spa. The restaurant comes highly recommended.

★ Restaurante El Fogón Sefardí
JEWISH €€

(☑ 921 46 62 50; www.lacasamudejar.com; Calle de Isabel la Católica 8; tapas from €2.50, mains €14-25, set menus €18.50-24.50; ⊗ 1.30-4.30pm & 5.30-11.30pm) Located within the Hospedería La Gran Casa Mudéjar, this is one of the most original places in town. Sephardic Jewish cuisine is served either on the intimate patio

SWEET TREATS

If you are one of those people who scoffs all the marzipan off the Christmas cake, you will love Segovia's speciality: *ponche segoviano* (literally 'Segovian punch'). But it's far removed from that insipid, low-alcohol drink you used to consume as a spotty teenager – this is a rich, lemon-infused sponge cake coated with marzipan and topped with icing sugar in a distinctive criss-cross pattern. A good place to indulge in your *ponche* passion is the patisserie **Limón y Menta** (☑921 46 22 57; Calle de Isabel La Católica 2; cakes from €2.50; ☺9am-9.30pm Mon-Fri, to 8.30pm Sat & Sun), just off Plaza Mayor.

or in the splendid dining hall with original 15th-century Mudéjar flourishes. The theme in the bar is equally diverse. Stop here for a taste of the award-winning tapas. Reservations recommended.

★**Mesón José María**   CASTILIAN €€
(☑921 46 11 11; www.restaurantejosemaria.com; Calle del Cronista Lecea 11; mains €16-26; ☺restaurant 1-4pm & 8-11.30pm, bar 9am-1am Sun-Thu, 10am-2am Fri & Sat; ⊞) Offers fine bar tapas and five dining rooms serving exquisite *cochinillo asado* and other local specialities – most of which, including the suckling pig, are displayed in the window. The bar is standing-room only at lunchtime.

Cueva de San Esteban   SPANISH €€
(☑921 46 09 82; www.lacuevadesanesteban.com; Calle de Valdeláguila 15; mains €13.50-21; ☺1-11pm) All the usual Segovia dishes are here, but it's also a good place to try the *cocido* (meat and chickpea stew) that's so typical of inland Spain. On Thursday lunchtimes, the three-course *cocido completo* (€10) is Segovia's best bargain. Extensive wine lists are also a feature here.

★**Casa Duque**   SPANISH €€€
(☑921 46 24 87; www.restauranteduque.es; Calle de Cervantes 12; mains €19.50-24, set menus €36-39; ☺12.30-4.30pm & 8.30-11.30pm) *Cochinillo asado* has been served at this atmospheric *mesón* (tavern) since the 1890s. For the uninitiated, try the *menú de degustacion* (€37), which includes *cochinillo*. Downstairs is the informal *cueva* (cave), where

you can get tapas and full-bodied *cazuelas* (stews). Reservations recommended.

🍷 Drinking & Nightlife

Bodega del Barbero   WINE BAR
(Calle Alhóndiga 2; ☺10am-1am Mon-Fri, noon-1am Sat & Sun) Tucked down a narrow street, this intimate bar has a wide range of vino by the glass, good tapas, regular art exhibitions and live music on the outside terrace on summer weekends.

Canavan's Theatre   CLUB
(Plaza de la Rubia; ☺midnight-6.30am Thu-Sat) Opened in 2013, this is no cheesy disco – the decor is sumptuous with exquisite friezes, flocked wallpaper, chandeliers and an overall extravagant theatrical feel.

La Tasquina   WINE BAR
(Calle de Valdeláguila 3; ☺9pm-late) This wine bar draws crowds large enough to spill out onto the pavement, nursing their good wines, *cavas* (sparkling wines) and cheeses.

🛍 Shopping

Artesanía La Gárgola   ARTS & CRAFTS
(☑921 46 31 84; www.gargolart.com; Calle de la Judería Vieja 4; ☺10am-8pm Mon-Sat Jul & Aug, 11.30am-2.30pm & 5-8pm Tue-Sat Sep-Jun) Check out these unusual, high-quality handmade crafts and souvenirs in ceramic, wood and textile.

Montón de Trigo
Montón de Paja   ACCESSORIES, SOUVENIRS
(☑921 46 07 69; www.montondetrigomontonde paja.com; Plaza de la Merced 1; ☺11.30am-2pm & 3.30-7.30pm Mon-Fri, 11am-2.30pm & 4-7.30pm Sat & Sun, longer hours in summer) With handcrafted handbags, jewellery, block-prints of Segovia and a host of other artsy, locally made items, this shop is ideal for creative gifts.

ℹ Information

Centro de Recepción de Visitantes (☑921 46 67 20; www.turismodesegovia.com; Plaza del Azoguejo 1; ☺10am-8pm Mon-Sat, to 7pm Sun Apr-Sep, 10am-6.30pm Mon-Sat, to 5pm Sun Oct-Mar) Segovia's main tourist office runs at least two guided tours of the city's monumental core daily (€11 to €14 per person), usually departing at 10.30am and 4.30pm (although check as this schedule can change). Reserve ahead.

Regional Tourist Office (www.segoviaturismo. es; Plaza Mayor 10; ☺9.30am-2pm & 5-8pm Mon-Sat, 9.30am-5pm Sun Jul–mid-Sep, 9.30am-2pm & 4-7pm Mon-Sat, 9.30am-5pm Sun mid-Sep–Jul)

❶ Getting There & Away

The bus station is just off Paseo de Ezequiel González. **La Sepulvedana** (☑ 902 119699; www.lasepulvedana.es) buses run half-hourly to Segovia from Madrid's Paseo de la Florida bus stop (€7.95, 1½ hours). Buses also depart to Ávila (€6.30, one hour, eight daily) and Salamanca (€14.75, 2½ hours, four daily), among other destinations.

Of the two main roads down to the AP6, which links Madrid and Galicia, the N603 is the prettier.

There are a couple of services by train operated by **Renfe** (☑ 902 240 202; www.renfe.es): just three normal trains run daily from Madrid to Segovia (€8.25, two hours), leaving you at the main train station 2.5km from the aqueduct. The faster option is the high-speed Avant (€12.90, 28 minutes), which deposits you at the newer Segovia-Guiomar station, 5km from the aqueduct.

❶ Getting Around

Bus 9 does a circuit through the historic centre, bus 8 goes to Segovia train station and bus 11 goes to Segovia-Guiomar station. All services cost €1.20 and leave from just outside the aqueduct.

Around Segovia

Pedraza de la Sierra

POP 415

The captivating walled village of Pedraza de la Sierra, about 37km northeast of Segovia, is eerily quiet during the week; its considerable number of restaurants, bars and eclectic shops spring to life with the swarms of weekend visitors. It's a gorgeous place – one of the prettiest villages in this part of the country.

◉ Sights

Plaza Mayor   SQUARE
The evocative 14th-century Plaza Mayor is noteworthy for its ancient columned arcades.

Castillo de Pedraza   CASTLE
(☑ 607 66 16 18; www.elcastillodepedraza.es; Plaza del Castillo, Pedraza de la Sierra; €5; ⊙ 11am-2pm & 5-8pm Wed-Sun Apr-Sep, 11am-2pm & 4-7pm Oct-Mar) At the far end of town – go any further and you'll fall into the valley – stands the lonely Castillo de Pedraza, unusual for its intact outer wall. Begun in the 13th century, it sits atop far older fortifications.

★ Festivals & Events

Conciertos de las Velas   MUSIC
(☑ 921 50 99 60; admission free, concerts €49-79; ⊙ 1st & 2nd Sun in Jul) When Pedraza hosts the atmospheric Conciertos de las Velas, the electricity is shut down and live classical music is performed in a village lit only by candles. It's free to come here to see the town lit with candles – and is worth doing so – but the actual concerts cost extra.

🛏 Sleeping

El Hotel de la Villa   HOTEL €€
(☑ 921 50 86 51; www.elhoteldelavilla.com; Calle de Calzada 5; s/d from €75/100; ☏) An astonishing breadth of rooms at this

CASTILLA Y LEÓN AROUND SEGOVIA

DON'T MISS

A SPANISH VERSAILLES

The magnificent, elaborate baroque gardens of **La Granja de San Ildefonso** (www.patrimonionacional.es; Sierra de Guadarrama; gardens free, Palacio Real adult/child €9/free, fountains adult/child €4/2, EU citizens 3-6pm Oct-Mar & 5-8pm Apr-Sep free; ⊙ 10am-8pm Tue-Sun Apr-Sep, to 6pm Tue-Sun Oct-Mar; P ♿), famous for their 28 extravagant fountains depicting ancient myths, date from 1720, when French architects and gardeners, together with some Italian help, began laying out them out. There's also a maze. The 300-room **Palacio Real**, once a favoured summer residence for Spanish royalty and restored after a fire in 1918, is similarly impressive; it includes the colourful **Museo de Tapices** (Tapestry Museum).

The palace was built for the Bourbon King Felipe V, who chose this site in the western foothills of the Sierra de Guadarrama to recreate in miniature his version of Versailles, the palace of his French grandfather, Louis XIV. If you time your visit for Wednesday, Saturday or Sunday at 5.30pm you can see the **fountains** in action.

Up to a dozen daily buses to La Granja depart regularly from Segovia's bus station (€2.20, 20 minutes).

excellent place range from tiled floors, wooden beams and wrought-iron furnishings to frilly four-poster beds, floorboards and bright colours. Whichever one you choose, rest assured that the quality is high and the service excellent.

Hospedería de Santo Domingo INN €€
(☑921 50 99 71; www.hospederiadesantodomingo.com; Calle Matadero 3; s/d from €85/95; ✴🛜) This excellent *hospedería* (inn) has terrific rooms decked out in warm ochre and earth colours. Most have large terraces overlooking the low hills nearby, criss-crossed with drystone walls. Prices rise considerably on weekends.

🍴 Eating

El Soportal SPANISH €€
(☑921 50 98 26; www.restaurantesdepedraza.com; Plaza Mayor 3; mains €9.50-17, degustation menu €29; ⊙1-4pm & 9am-11.30pm Thu-Tue, 1-4pm Wed) Found behind the porticoes of a fine 16th-century Pedraza townhouse, El Soportal is one of Pedraza's most popular choices for *cordero asado*. Also popular is the bar, which stays open throughout the day (don't expect the restaurant to be open weeknights, despite official hours); a few small wooden tables sit out on the square. Bookings essential on weekends.

El Yantar de Pedraza SPANISH €€
(☑921 50 98 42; www.elyantardepedraza.com; Plaza Mayor; mains €12-23; ⊙1-4.30pm Wed-Sun) With arguably the loveliest setting in town overlooking Plaza Mayor from its upstairs balcony, El Yantar does near-perfect *cordero asado* and *cochinillo* and the repeat customers tell us all we need to know about the quality. Its set menus are excellent value, but other menu highlights include the light salads, the home-made *croquetas* (croquettes) and the local sheep's cheese.

La Olma de Pedraza SPANISH €€
(☑921 50 99 81; www.laolma.com; Plaza del Álamo 1; mains €12-22; ⊙1.30-4pm Sun-Thu, 1.30-4pm & 9-11pm Fri & Sat) On a small square just west of Plaza Mayor, this lovely place feels every bit like the rural bastion of traditional cooking that it is, but with warm service to match. Besides the usual, perfectly cooked roasted meats, try its *croquetas de setas* (wild mushroom croquettes); otherwise just let staff choose the dishes that play to their strengths.

ℹ Information

Tourist Office (☑921 50 86 66; www.pedraza.net; Calle Real 3; ⊙11am-2.30pm & 3-7.30pm Tue-Sun) Runs Spanish-language guided tours (per person €3) of the town at 12.30am and 5pm (except Mondays), if there are enough people.

ℹ Getting There & Away

Bus services to Pedraza are sporadic at best, with just a couple of weekly services from Segovia. Pedraza is just north of the N110.

WORTH A TRIP

CASTLES AROUND SEGOVIA

Coca Castle (☑617 57 35 54; www.castillodecoca.com; Coca; guided tours €2.70; ⊙tours 10.30am-1pm & 4.30-6pm Mon-Fri, 11am-1pm & 4-6pm Sat & Sun) A typically dusty, inward-looking Castilian village 50km northwest of Segovia, Coca is presided over by a stunning, all-brick 15th-century castle, a virtuoso piece of Gothic-Mudéjar architecture complete with a deep moat. It has been restored numerous times; serious damage was done to the castle during the French invasion in the early 19th century. You can wander along the ramparts for free, but to see the interior and climb to the top you'll need to join a tour.

Turégano (☑634 46 02 15; €2; ⊙11am-2pm & 4.30-7.30pm Wed-Sun Apr-Jun & Sep, 11am-2pm & 5-8pm Jul & Aug, 11am-2pm & 4-7pm Wed-Sun Oct, 11am-2pm & 4-6pm Wed-Sun Nov-Mar) Turégano, about 30km north of Segovia, is dominated by a unique 15th-century castle-church complex built by the then archbishop of Segovia, Juan Arias Dávila (who decided to make the town into a personal fortress). Both cutesy and formidable, the castle walls, with their sturdy ramparts and rounded turrets, are built around the facade of the Iglesia de San Miguel; ruined sections of the wall fan out across the surrounding countryside.

Valladolid

POP 306,830

Valladolid is a lively provincial Spanish city and a convenient gateway to northern Spain. An attractive place with a very Spanish character, the city's appeal is in its sprinkling of striking monuments, the fine Plaza Mayor and some excellent museums. By night, Valladolid comes alive as its large student population overflows from the city's boisterous bars.

History

Some of the great names of Spanish history – El Cid, Cervantes, Christopher Columbus and the merciless Inquisitor General Fray Tomás de Torquemada – were all connected with Valladolid. It was, for centuries, considered Spain's capital-in-waiting.

Fernando of Aragón and Isabel of Castilla (the Reyes Católicos, or Catholic Monarchs) married here discreetly in 1469. As Spain's greatest-ever ruling duo, they carried Valladolid to the height of its splendour. Its university was one of the most dynamic on the peninsula and Carlos I made Valladolid the seat of imperial government. Felipe II was born here in 1527 but, 34 years later, he chose to make Madrid the capital, forever casting the city into relative obscurity. As a minor consolation prize, Valladolid was named capital of Castilla y León and remains the seat of regional government.

⊙ Sights

★ **Museo Nacional de Escultura**   MUSEUM
(� 983 25 03 75; http://museoescultura.mcu. es; Calle de San Gregorio 2; adult/concession €3/1.50, Sun & 4-7.30pm Sat free; ⊙10am-2pm & 4-7.30pm Tue-Sat, 10am-2pm Sun) Spain's premier showcase of polychrome wood sculpture is housed in the former Colegio de San Gregorio (1496), a flamboyant Isabelline Gothic–style building where exhibition rooms line an exquisite, two-storey galleried courtyard. Works by Alonso de Berruguete, Juan de Juní and Gregorio Fernández are the star attractions. Don't miss Fernández' painfully lifelike sculpture of a dead Christ in Room 15 or the choir stalls in Room 8. And don't forget to look up – some of the ceilings are extraordinary.

★ **Casa-Museo de Colón**   MUSEUM
(⊡983 29 13 53; Calle de Colón; adult/child €2/ free, Wed adult €1; ⊙10am-2pm & 5-8.30pm

Tue-Sun; 🖭) The Casa-Museo de Colón is a superb museum spread over four floors. It has interactive exhibits, as well as wonderful old maps that take you on a journey through Christopher Columbus' (Cristóbal Colón in Spanish) trips to the Americas. The top floor describes Valladolid in the days of the great explorer (who died here in 1506).

★ **Plaza de San Pablo**   SQUARE
This open square is dominated by the exquisite **Iglesia de San Pablo**, which has one of northern Spain's most extraordinary church facades. Also here is the **Palacio de Pimentel** (⊙10am-2pm & 5-7pm Tue-Sat), the birthplace of Felipe II.

Catedral   CATHEDRAL
(⊡983 30 43 62; Calle Arribas 1; adult/concession €3/1.50; ⊙10am-1.30pm & 4.30-7pm Tue-Fri, 10am-2pm Sat & Sun, tours every 45min) Valladolid's 16th-century cathedral is not Castilla's finest, but it does have an extravagant altarpiece by Juan de Juní and a processional monstrance by Juan de Arfe in the attached **Museo Diocesano y Catedralicio** (Calle Arribas 1; adult/concession €3/1.50; ⊙10am-1.30pm & 4.30-7pm Tue-Fri, 10am-2pm Sat & Sun). Guided tours (adult/concession €5/4) of the cathedral and bell tower – views are fabulous – last 45 minutes; combined with a guided visit to the museum (adult/concession €8/6) it takes two hours. (You can visit the cathedral and museum on your own, but not the tower.)

Casa de Cervantes   MUSEUM
(⊡983 30 88 10; www.mecd.gob.es/museocasa cervantes; Calle del Rastro; adult/child under 12yr €3/free, Sun free; ⊙9.30am-3pm Tue-Sat, 10am-3pm Sun) Cervantes was briefly imprisoned in Valladolid; his house is happily preserved behind a quiet little garden. You can purchase a combined adult ticket that also admits you to the Museo Nacional de Escultura (p165) for €5.

Museo Patio Herreriano   GALLERY
(⊡983 36 29 08; www.museopatioherreriano.org; Calle de Jorge Guillén 6; adult/concession €3/2, Wed & Sun €1; ⊙11am-2pm & 5-8pm Tue-Fri, 11am-8pm Sat, 11am-3pm Sun) Dedicated to post-WWI Spanish art, this surprising museum contains works by Salvador Dalí, Joan Miró, Basque sculptor Eduardo Chillida, Jorge Oteiza, Antoni Tàpies and Esteban Vicente, all arrayed around the cloisters of a former monastery.

Valladolid

Valladolid (15km)

C San Quirce

Plaza de San Pablo

7

2 Museo Nacional de Escultura

3

10

Plaza Santa Brígida

Paseo de Isabel la Católica

C de Santo Domingo de Guzmán

C San Ignacio

18

C Angustias

C La Torrecilla

C León

C de Felipe II

Plaza de San Miguel

C Encarnación

C de Dr Cazalla

C de Jorge Guillén

9

C Antigua

C de San Benito

C Leopoldo

Plaza de los Arces

C Leopoldo

C del Conde Ansúrez

C de Rúa Oscura

C Sandoval

C de Macias Picavea

Plaza de la Rinconada

C de Correos

C Platerías

Plaza de Poniente

8

5

C de Campanas

C Peso

12

C de la Especería

C Cebadería

13

C Arribas

C San Lorenzo

20

Plaza Mayor

19

15

Plaza de Martí y Monsó

C de Correos

C Ferrari

C Regalado

C de Pedro Niño

16

C de la Pasión

17

C Constitución

C Duque de la Victoria

C Santuario

C Maria de Molina

C Montero Clavo

C Menéndez Pelayo

C Doctrinos

C Santa María

14

Plaza de España

C de Santiago

C Claudio Moyano

C Manteria

C Miguel Iscar

C del Rastro

Plaza de Madrid

Plaza de Zorrilla

4

C M Escobar

C Gamazo

C Dos de Mayo

Campo Grande

11

Hotel Meliá Recoletos (100m); (500m)

Hotel Gareus (50m)

Colegio de Santa Cruz HISTORIC BUILDING
(Calle Cardenal Mendoza; ⏰11am-2pm & 4.30-8pm Tue-Sat, 11am-2pm Sun) FREE Check out the lovely colonnaded patio and chapel (replete with a super-realistic Cristo de la Luz sculpture). Off the ground floor of the patio is Valladolid University's excellent permanent exhibition of terracotta artefacts from across Africa.

Valladolid

cation. Here you'll find king-size beds, plush, earth-colour furnishings and fabrics, polished parquet floors, dazzling marble bathrooms and space enough for a comfortable armchair. The entrance has a whiff of grandeur about it as well – which contributes to the surprise of the budget-bracket price.

Hostal París   HOSTAL €

(☑ 983 37 06 25; www.hostalparis.com; Calle de la Especería 2; s/d from €41/48; ❋ 🔊) One of the closest places to Plaza Mayor, Hostal París has clearly had the interior designers in. Washed in pale pastel colours with striking abstract art panels, good-size desks and flatscreen TVs, the rooms successfully combine comfort with a classy feel and budget prices.

★ Hotel Gareus   BOUTIQUE HOTEL €€

(☑ 983 21 43 33; www.hotelgareus.com; Calle de Colmenares 2; r from €68; ❋ 🔊) Polished floorboards, warm colours and creative lighting make these rooms some of the best in Valladolid. The service is similarly warm and welcoming and the place has a quiet sophistication. The location, just a 10-minute walk from the Plaza Mayor, is also excellent.

🛏 Sleeping

★ Hotel Mozart   HOTEL €

(☑ 983 29 77 77; www.hotelmozart.net; Calle Menéndez Pelayo 7; s/d €50/60; ❋ 🔊) This is an extremely well-priced hotel, given the quality of its refurbished rooms and the lo-

❶ VALLADOLID CARD

A terrific way to save your euros, the Valladolid Card (www.info.valladolid.es/turismo/servicios/valladolid-card; adult/child €7/5) allows free access to a number of museums – including the Museo Nacional de Escultura, Casa-Museo de Colón, Casa de Cervantes, Museo Patio Herreriano and the Catedral and its museum – plus free travel on the Bus Turístico de Valladolid (☑983 21 93 10; Acera de Recoletos; adult/child €7/5; ☺hourly 5-8pm Fri, noon-2pm & 5-8pm Sat & Sun Apr-Sep, hourly 5-7pm Fri, noon-2pm & 5-7pm Sat & Sun Oct-Mar) over a 24-hour period. The card can be purchased at either of the two tourist offices.

Hotel El Coloquio   HOTEL €€
(☑983 04 40 35; www.hotelelcoloquio.es; Plaza de la Universidad 11; r €74; P❈🛜) Attractive rooms with all manner of interesting angles dominate this four-star place that inhabits a reconstructed 19th-century building overlooking one of the quieter and prettier squares in downtown Valladolid. It's right next to the cathedral and service is excellent.

🍴 Eating

Valladolid is a great town to get into the tapas habit – you need look no further than the bars west of Plaza Mayor. Restaurants are also found in this region, and many of the tapas bars have more formal *comedores* (dining rooms) as well.

★ Martín Quiroga   CASTILIAN €€
(☑605 78 71 17; Calle San Ignacio 17; mains €15-19; ☺1.30-3.30pm & 8.30-11.30pm Mon-Sat) With just four tables and a waiting list of a month, you might imagine that this extraordinarily high-quality gastrobar would have prices to match. It doesn't. There is no menu – dishes depend on what's seasonally fresh and available from the market that day – but there's plenty of choice. Special diets are catered to with advance notice. Reservations essential.

Los Zagales de Abadía   CASTILIAN €€
(☑983 38 08 92; www.loszagales.com; Calle de la Pasión 13; mains €7-17, set menus €19.50-33; ☺1-4pm & 7-11pm Mon-Sat, 1-4pm Sun) The bar here is awash with hanging local produce, all represented in the prize-winning tapas displayed along the bar – this place has done well not just at local competitions but nationwide. To

see what all the fuss is about, try the Menú Maridaje: nine of their prize-winning tapas for €33. Servings are generous and the food excellent. Reservations recommended.

El Caballo de Troya   SPANISH €€
(Restaurante Santi; ☑983 33 93 55; www.restaurantesanti.es; Calle de Correos 1; restaurant mains €17.50-28.50, bar mains €8-22, set menu €25; ☺1.30-3.30pm & 9-11.30pm Mon-Sat, 2-4pm Sun) The 'Trojan Horse' is a Valladolid treat. The restaurant, set around a stunning, Renaissance-style courtyard, is as sophisticated in flavours as the dining room is classy in design – try the *solomillo con roquefort* (sirloin with Roquefort cheese). The *taberna* (tavern) downstairs also has brilliant *raciones*. Reservations are recommended for the restaurant, especially at weekends.

La Parrilla de San Lorenzo   CASTILIAN €€
(☑983 33 50 88; www.hotel-convento.com; Calle de Pedro Niño; mains €14-22; ☺2-4pm & 9pm-midnight Mon-Sat, 1.30-4.30pm Sun) Both a stand-up bar and a much-lauded restaurant in the evocative setting of a former 16th-century monastery, La Parilla de San Lorenzo specialises in upmarket Castilian cuisine (hearty stews, legumes and steaks). Check out the historic grill and giant domed oven, used specifically for roasting lamb and suckling pig. Reservations recommended.

🍸 Drinking & Nightlife

Café de la Comedia   COCKTAIL BAR
(☑983 34 00 80; Plaza de Martí y Monsó; ☺3.30pm-late) Decor here is suitably comedic, with Laurel and Hardy on the screen and Chaplin pics (and similar) decorating the walls. It's a reliable, popular choice that goes beyond fads and serves good cocktails and wines by the glass.

Be Bop   CLUB
(Plaza de Martí y Monsó; ☺3pm-late) One of an energetic strip of bars and clubs overlooking this pretty square, Be Bop styles itself as a G&T bar, with a good selection of local and international gins.

❶ Information

Tourist Office (☑983 33 08 93; www.info.valladolid.es; Plaza de Fuente Dorada; ☺11am-1.30pm & 5-7pm Tue-Sat, 11am-1.30pm Sun) Small municipal tourist office off Plaza Mayor.

Tourist Office (☑983 21 93 10; www.info.valladolid.es; Acera de Recoletos; ☺9.30am-2pm & 4-7pm Mon-Sat, 9.30am-3pm Sun)

ⓘ Getting There & Away

Ryanair (www.ryanair.com) and Vueling (www. vueling.com) have flights to Barcelona, while Hop! (www.hop.com) connects Valladolid with Paris-Orly.

More than a dozen daily high-speed AVE train services connect Valladolid with Madrid (€37, one hour); there are also slower services (2¾ hours) for €24.10. Other regular trains run to León (from €12.45, about two hours), Burgos (from €8.15, about 1½ hours) and Salamanca (from €10.45, 1½ hours).

ⓘ Getting Around

Valladolid's **airport** (www.aena.es/csee/ Satellite/Aeropuerto-Valladolid/es) is 10km northwest of the city centre. Linecar (www. linecar.es) has up to five daily bus services from Valladolid to the airport (one way/return €3/5). A taxi between the airport and the city centre costs €22/24 by day/night.

Local buses 2 and 10 pass the train and bus stations on their way to Plaza de España.

Around Valladolid

Medina de Rioseco

POP 4905

Medina de Rioseco is something of a faded jewel. This once-wealthy trading centre still has a tangible medieval feel, although, given the number of boarded-up frontages around Plaza Mayor, it's sadly much poorer these days. Head for Calle Mayor, with its colonnaded arcades held up by ancient wooden columns; market stalls set up here on Wednesday mornings.

◉ Sights

Iglesia de Santa María de Mediavilla   CHURCH
(Calle Santa María; guided tours in Spanish €2; ⊙11am-noon & 5-7pm Tue-Sun) This grandiose Isabelline Gothic work has three star-vaulted naves and the rightfully famous Capilla de los Benavente chapel. Anchored by an extravagant altarpiece by Juan de Juní and carved over eight years from 1543, it's sometimes referred to as the 'Sistine Chapel of Castilla' – it's certainly one of Spain's finest examples of Renaissance-era religious art.

Museo de San Francisco   CHURCH, MUSEUM
(☑983 70 00 20; www.museosanfrancisco.es; Paseo de San Francisco 1; adult/child €3/1; ⊙guided tours in Spanish 11am-1pm & 4-6pm Tue-Sun Mar, Apr & Oct, 11am-1pm & 5-7pm Tue-Sun May-Sep,

noon-1pm & 5-6pm Tue-Sat, noon-1pm Sun Nov-Feb) This 16th-century former convent has an extravagant *retablo* (altarpiece) by Fray Jacinto de Sierra, as well as a wide-ranging collection of sacred art.

Museo de Semana Santa   MUSEUM
(Calle de Lázaro Alonso; adult/concession/child €3.50/2.50/1; ⊙11am-2pm & 4-7pm Tue-Sun Apr-Sep, weekends only Oct-Mar) Medina de Rioseco is famous for its Easter processions, but if you can't be here during Holy Week, this museum provides an insight into the ceremonial passion of Easter here. Like its sister museum in Zamora (p172), it's dedicated to *pasos* (floats carried in Semana Santa processions) and an extensive range of other Easter artefacts.

🛏 Sleeping & Eating

Vittoria Colonna   HOTEL €
(☑983 72 50 87; www.hotelvittoriacolonna.es; Calle de San Juan 2B; s/d/ste €33/55/75; 🌣 ╗) This modern three-star hotel, with its raspberry-pink frontage, offers well-sized and well-appointed rooms a short walk from all of Medina de Rioseco's sights. Some rooms are nicer than others, but all have smart grey-and-white bathrooms.

Casa Manolo   CASTILIAN €€
(Calle Las Armas 4; mains €9-13; ⊙8am-midnight Fri-Wed) The best of a clutch of restaurants on this side street in the historic centre. The courtyard provides a pleasant setting for enjoying reliably good, hearty Castilian dishes.

Restaurante Pasos   CASTILIAN €€
(☑983 70 10 02; Calle de Lázaro Alonso 44; mains €14-22; ⊙11am-5pm & 8pm-midnight Tue-Sat, 2-10pm Sun) Come here for well-prepared typical Castilian fare that courts various flavours but stays firmly in the classical mould, with reliable dishes such as *chuletillas de lechazo* (lamb chops). Reservations recommended.

ⓘ Information

Tourist Office (☑983 72 03 19; www.medina derioseco.com; Paseo de San Francisco 1; ⊙10am-2pm & 4-6pm Tue-Sat, 10am-2pm Sun) Alongside the Museo de San Francisco.

ⓘ Getting There & Away

Up to eight daily buses run to León (€7.65, 1¼ hours); up to 10 go to Valladolid (€3.25, 30 minutes).

Tordesillas

POP 8975

Commanding a rise on the northern flank of Río Duero, this pretty little town has a historical significance that belies its size. Originally a Roman settlement, it later played a major role in world history in 1494, when Isabel and Fernando sat down here with Portugal to hammer out a treaty determining who got what in Latin America. Portugal got Brazil and much of the rest went to Spain.

◉ Sights

Museo del Tratado de Tordesillas MUSEUM
(⌨ 983 77 10 67; Calle de Casas del Tratado; ⊙ 10am-1.30pm & 5-7.30pm Tue-Sat, 10am-2pm Sun Apr-Sep, 10am-1.30pm & 4-6.30pm Tue-Sat, 10am-2pm Sun Oct-Mar) FREE Dedicated to the 1494 Treaty of Tordesillas, which divided the world into Spanish and Portuguese spheres of influence, the informative displays in this museum look at the world as it was before and after the treaty, with some fabulous old maps taking centre stage. There's also a multilingual video presentation.

Real Convento de Santa Clara CONVENT
(⌨ 983 77 00 71; www.patrimonionacional.es; Calle de Alonso Castillo Solorzano 21; adult/child €6/free, EU citizens & residents 4-6.30pm Wed & Thu free; ⊙ 10am-2pm & 4-6.30pm Tue-Sat, 10.30am-3pm Sun) Still home to a few Franciscan nuns living in near-total isolation, this Mudéjar-style convent dates from 1340, when it was begun as a palace for Alfonso XI. In 1494 the Treaty of Tordesillas was signed here. A 50-minute guided tour (in Spanish) takes in a wonderful Mudéjar patio left over from the palace, and the church with its stunning *techumbre* (roof). Other highlights include the Mudéjar door, Gothic arches, superb Arabic inscriptions and the Arab baths.

Plaza Mayor SQUARE
The heart of town is formed by the delightful porticoed and cobbled Plaza Mayor, its mustard-yellow paintwork offset by darkbrown woodwork and black grilles.

🍽 Sleeping & Eating

Hostal San Antolín HOSTAL €
(⌨ 983 79 67 71; www.hostalsanantolin.com; Calle San Antolín 8; s/d/tr €25/40/50; ❀ 🕾) Located near Plaza Mayor, the overall aesthetic is modern, with rooms painted in bright pastel tones. Its main focus is the attached restaurant (mains €12 to €19), with *raciones*

downstairs in the bar, a pretty flower-decked inner patio and an elegant menu.

Parador de Tordesillas LUXURY HOTEL €€
(⌨ 983 77 00 51; www.parador.es; Carretera de Salamanca 5; r €125; P ❀ 🕾 ☀) Tordesillas' most sophisticated hotel is the low-rise, ochre-toned *parador*, surrounded by pine trees and just outside town. Some rooms have four-poster beds, all are large and many look out onto the tranquil gardens. There's also a cafe and an excellent restaurant that showcases local specialities.

Don Pancho SPANISH €€
(⌨ 983 77 01 74; www.restaurantedonpancho. com; Plaza Mayor 10; mains €6-18; ⊙ 1-4pm & 8.30pm-midnight) Don Pancho, with its tiled bar and home cooking – including meats roasted in a wood-fire oven – is the best sit-down restaurant in the old town centre.

ⓘ Information

Tourist Office (⌨ 983 77 10 67; www.tordesil las.net; Calle de Casas del Tratado; ⊙ 10am-1.30pm & 5-7.30pm Tue-Sat, 10am-2pm Sun Apr-Sep, 10am-1.30pm & 4-6.30pm Tue-Sat, 10am-2pm Sun Oct-Mar)

ⓘ Getting There & Away

The **bus station** (⌨ 983 77 00 72; Avenida de Valladolid) is near Calle de Santa María. Regular buses depart for Valladolid (€2.30, 30 minutes) and Zamora (€5.15, one hour).

Toro

POP 9305

With a name that couldn't be more Spanish and a stirring history that overshadows its present, Toro is your archetypal Castilian town. It was here that Fernando and Isabel cemented their primacy in Christian Spain at the Battle of Toro in 1476. The town sits on a rise high above the north bank of the Río Duero and has a charming historic centre with half-timbered houses and Romanesque churches. In 2016, Toro hosted the prestigious 'Edades del Hombre' exhibition, a year-long showpiece of religious and sacred art from across Castilla y León.

◉ Sights

Colegiata Santa María La Mayor CHURCH
(Plaza de la Colegiata; church free, sacristy €2; ⊙ 10.30am-2pm & 5.30-7.30pm Tue-Sun Apr-Sep, 10.30am-2pm & 4.30-6.30pm Tue-Sun Oct-Mar) This 12th-century church rises above

the town and boasts the magnificent Romanesque-Gothic **Pórtico de la Majestad**. Treasures inside include the famous 15th-century painting *Virgen de la mosca* (Virgin of the Fly) in the sacristy; see if you can spot the fly on the virgin's robe. Entrance to the main sanctuary is free; an admission fee applies to the sacristy.

Monasterio Sancti Spiritus MONASTERY
(Calle del Canto 27; €4; ⊙ guided tours in Spanish 10.30am, 11.30am, 12.30pm, 4.30pm & 5.30pm) Southwest of the town centre, this monastery features a fine Renaissance cloister and the striking alabaster tomb of Beatriz de Portugal, wife of Juan I.

🛏 Sleeping

Zaravencia HOTEL **€**
(✆ 980 69 49 98; www.hotelzaravencia.com; Plaza Mayor 17; s/d incl breakfast €42/60; ❄ 🅿) Overlooking the lovely Plaza Mayor, this friendly place has a bar-restaurant downstairs and good-sized rooms, albeit with an anaemic decor of light-pine furniture and cream walls. Pay €10 more for a plaza view and balcony (it's worth it), although be aware that it can be noisy on weekends.

Hotel Juan II HOTEL **€€**
(✆ 980 69 03 00; www.hotelesentoro.es; Paseo del Espolón 1; s €60-70, d €62-85; 🅿 ❄ 🅿 🛆) Despite its modern red-brick exterior, the rooms here are charming, with warm terracotta-tiled floors, dark-wood furniture and large terraces. Request room 201 for its fabulous double-whammy vista of the Río Duero to one side and the Colegiata Santa María La Mayor to the other. The restaurant (mains €15 to €21), specialising in hearty meat dishes, is one of Toro's best.

🍴 Eating

La Esquina de Colas TAPAS **€**
(✆ 980 69 31 31; Plaza Mayor 24; tapas from €2.50; ⊙ 10am-4pm & 7.30pm-midnight Thu-Tue) Artfully conceived tapas lined up along the bar (try the marinated sardines) and a full list of toasts topped with all manner of tasty morsels make this Toro's best place for tapas.

Asador Castilla SPANISH **€€**
(✆ 980 69 02 11; Plaza Bollos de Hito; mains €13-22; ⊙ 1-4pm & 8.30pm-midnight Tue-Sun) Excellent service, roasted meats (the *cabrito*, roasted goat kid, is a particular speciality) and a pleasantly modern dining area

make this a good choice. It's barely 50m from Plaza Mayor.

ℹ Information

Tourist Office (✆ 980 69 47 47; www.turismo castillayleon.com; Plaza Mayor 6; ⊙ 10am-2pm & 4-7pm Tue-Sat, 10am-2pm Sun)

ℹ Getting There & Away

Regular buses operate to Valladolid (€4.90, one hour) and Zamora (€2.95, 30 minutes). There are two direct services to Salamanca (€5.70, 1½ hours) on weekdays.

Zamora

POP 64,425

First appearances can be deceiving: as with so many Spanish towns, your introduction to provincial Zamora is likely to be nondescript apartment blocks. But persevere, as the *casco historico* (old town) is hauntingly beautiful, with sumptuous medieval monuments that have earned Zamora the popular sobriquet 'Romanesque Museum'. It's a subdued encore to the monumental splendour of Salamanca and one of the best places to be during Semana Santa.

◉ Sights

Catedral CATHEDRAL
(✆ 980 53 19 33; Plaza de la Catedral; adult/child €4/free; ⊙ 10am-2pm & 5-8pm) Zamora's largely Romanesque cathedral features a square tower, an unusual, Byzantine-style dome surrounded by turrets, and the ornate **Puerta del Obispo**. The star attraction is the **Museo Catedralicio**, which features a collection of Flemish tapestries dating from the 15th century. Inside the 12th-century cathedral itself, the magnificent early-Renaissance choir stalls depict clerics, animals and a naughty encounter between a monk and a nun. Another major highlight is the **Capilla de San Ildefonso**, with its lovely Gothic frescos.

Castillo CASTLE
(Parque del Castillo; ⊙ 10am-2pm & 7-10pm Tue-Sun Apr-Sep, 10am-2pm & 4-6.30pm Tue-Sun Oct-Mar; 🅿) FREE This fine, aesthetically restored castle of 11th-century origin is filled with local sculptures; it is also possible to climb the tower and walk the ramparts. The surrounding park is a lovely place for a picnic.

Iglesia de San Juan de Puerta Nueva
CHURCH

(Plaza Mayor; ⏱10am-2pm & 5.30-8pm Tue-Sat, 10am-2pm Sun Apr-Sep, 10am-2pm & 4.30-7pm Tue-Sat, 10am-2pm Sun Oct-Mar) Iglesia de San Juan de Puerta Nueva provides a lovely Romanesque centrepiece for the central Plaza Mayor. Right outside, there's a fine statue of hooded Semana Santa penitents.

Iglesia de la Magdalena
CHURCH

(Rúa de los Francos; ⏱10am-2pm & 5.30-8pm Mon & Wed-Sat, 10am-2pm Sun Apr-Sep, 10am-2pm & 4.30-7pm Mon & Wed-Sat, 10am-2pm Sun Oct-Mar) The southern doorway of this church, set along the main thoroughfare through the old town, is considered the city's finest for its preponderance of floral motifs.

Iglesia de San Pedro y San Ildefonso
CHURCH

(Rúa de los Francos 39; ⏱10am-2pm & 5.30-8pm Tue-Sat, 10am-2pm Sun Apr-Sep, 10am-2pm & 4.30-7pm Tue-Sat, 10am-2pm Sun Oct-Mar) Besides its considerable Romanesque charm, the Iglesia de San Pedro y San Ildefonso has some Gothic touches.

Iglesia de Santa María La Nueva
CHURCH

(Calle de Carniceros; ⏱10am-2pm & 5.30-8pm Tue-Sat, 10am-2pm Sun Apr-Sep, 10am-2pm & 4.30-7pm Tue-Sat, 10am-2pm Sun Oct-Mar) This pretty church is actually a medieval replica of a 7th-century church destroyed by fire in 1158.

Museo de Semana Santa
MUSEUM

(☎980 53 22 95; www.semanasantadezamora.com; Plaza de Santa María La Nueva; adult/child €4/1.50; ⏱10am-2pm & 5-8pm Tue-Sat, 10am-2pm Sun) This museum will initiate you into the weird and wonderful rites of Easter, Spanish-style. It showcases the carved and painted *pasos* that are paraded around town during the colourful processions. The hooded models are eerily lifelike.

Museo Etnográfico
MUSEUM

(☎980 53 17 08; www.museo-etnografico.com; Plaza Viriato; adult/child €3/free; ⏱10am-2pm & 5-8pm Tue-Sun) This excellent museum is a window onto the cultural history of Castilla y León, with everything from artefacts from everyday life down through the ages to sections on local legends and fiestas. It also has a dynamic calendar of temporary exhibitions, workshops and performances. Admission is free Tuesday through Thursday from 7pm to 8pm and Sunday from 5pm to 8pm.

☆ Festivals & Events

Semana Santa
RELIGIOUS

(Holy Week) If you're in Spain during Holy Week (the week before Easter), make your way to Zamora, a town made famous for its elaborate celebrations. It's one of the most evocative places in the country to view the hooded processions. Watching the penitents weave their way through the historic streets, sometimes in near-total silence, is an experience you'll never forget.

🛏 Sleeping

★ Hostal Chiqui
HOSTAL €

(☎980 53 14 80; www.hostalchiqui.es; 2nd fl, Calle de Benavente 2; s/d from €30/40) This fine place is one of the best urban *hostales* in this part of Castilla y León, getting rave reviews and plenty of repeat visitors. Every room is different, but all are stylish and colourful, and the owners are switched on to what travellers need. All in all, it's outrageously good value.

NH Palacio del Duero
HOTEL €€

(☎980 50 82 62; www.nh-hotels.com; Plaza de la Horta 1; r from €75; P※@☎) In a superb position next to a lovely Romanesque church, the seemingly modern building has cleverly encompassed part of the former convent, as well as – somewhat bizarrely – a 1940s power station (the lofty brick chimney remains). As you'd expect from this excellent chain, the rooms here are plushly furnished and the service is attentive.

Parador Condes de Alba y Aliste
HISTORIC HOTEL €€€

(☎980 51 44 97; www.parador.es; Plaza Viriato 5; r €100-168; ※@☎❀) Set in a sumptuous 15th-century palace, this is modern luxury with myriad period touches (mostly in the public areas). There's a swimming pool and – unlike many *paradores* – it's right in the heart of town. On the downside, there is very limited parking available (just eight places). The restaurant (*menú del día* €35) is predictably *parador* quality.

🍴 Eating

La Rua
CASTILIAN €€

(☎980 53 40 24; Rúa de los Francos 21; mains €8.80-19; ⏱1-4pm Sun-Thu, 1-4pm & 8.30-11.30pm Fri & Sat) Devoted to down-home Zamora cooking, this central place is a good place to try *arroz a la zamorana* (rice with pork and ham), although you'll need two people ordering for staff to make it.

El Rincón de Antonio CASTILIAN €€€

(☑ 980 53 53 70; www.elrincondeantonio.com; Rúa de los Francos 6; tapas from €1.50, mains €20-24, set menus €32.50-55; ⊙ 1.30-4pm & 8.30-11.30pm Mon-Sat, 1.30-4.30pm Sun) A fine place offering tapas in the bar – there are 17 different cheese *raciones*, all from the Zamora area – as well as sit-down meals in a classy, softly lit dining area. There's a range of tasting menus in the restaurant, where dishes are classic with a contemporary twist. Reservations recommended.

❶ Information

Municipal Tourist Office (☑ 980 53 36 94; www.zamora-turismo.com; Plaza de Arias Gonzalo 6; ⊙ 10am-2pm & 5-8pm Mon-Sat, 10am-2pm Sun Apr-Sep, 10am-2pm & 4-7.30pm Mon-Sat, 10am-2pm Sun Oct-Mar)

Provincial Tourist Office (☑ 980 53 64 95; Plaza Viriato; ⊙ 10am-2pm & 4.30-8.30pm Mar-Oct, 10am-2pm & 4-7pm Nov-Feb) Information on the wider Zamora region.

Regional Tourist Office (☑ 980 53 18 45; www.turismocastillayleon.com; Avenida Príncipe de Asturias 1; ⊙ 10am-2pm & 4.30-8.30pm Mar-Oct, 10am-2pm & 4-7pm Nov-Feb)

❶ Getting There & Away

Bus services operate almost hourly to/from Salamanca (from €5.30, one hour, five to 13 daily), with less frequent departures on weekends. Other regular services include those to León (€9.75, 1½ hours), Valladolid (€7.65, 1½ hours) and Burgos (€16.80, 4½ hours).

The fast-train line has reached Zamora, cutting travel time to Madrid (from €15.30, 2¼ hours, four daily) considerably. Trains also head to Valladolid (€12.45, 1½ hours, one daily) and Puebla de Sanabria (from €9.25, 1¼ hours, four daily).

Around Zamora

Sierra de la Culebra

The Sierra de la Culebra, running along the Spanish–Portuguese border between Puebla de Sanabria and Zamora, consists of some lovely rolling hill country and pretty stone villages that rarely see foreign visitors. Best of all, this is the best place in Europe to see wolves in the wild.

WORTH A TRIP

ONE OF SPAIN'S OLDEST CHURCHES

The lonely San Pedro de la Nave (☑ 660 23 39 95, 696 29 24 00; Calle Larga, Campillo; €1.50; ⊙ 10.30am-1.30pm & 5-8pm Tue-Sun Apr-Sep, 10am-1.30pm & 4.30-6.30pm Fri & Sat, 10am-1.30pm Sun Oct-Mar), a 7th-century church about 24km northwest of Zamora, is a rare and outstanding example of Visigoth church architecture, with blended Celtic, Germanic and Byzantine elements. Of special note are the intricately sculpted capitals. The church was moved to its present site in Campillo in 1930, during the construction of the Esla reservoir, northwest of Zamora. To get there from Zamora, take the N122, then follow the signs to Campillo.

◉ Sights

Centro de Lobo Ibérico de Castilla y León MUSEUM, ZOO

(☑ 980 56 76 38; www.centrodellobo.es; Robledo; admission with/without guided tour €8/6; ⊙ 10.30am-2pm & 3.30-6pm Fri-Sun) This excellent interpretation centre devoted to the Iberian wolf opened in late 2015. Built in the form of a traditional, circular corral used by local farmers to protect their livestock from wolves, the centre has displays on legends surrounding wolves, their position in local culture and scientific studies of them. On the hill behind the main building, seven wolves inhabit three large enclosures, offering a good chance to take a photo if you missed seeing them in the wild.

ⵟ Activities

Wild Wolf Experience WILDLIFE-WATCHING

(☑ 636 03 14 72; www.wildwolfexperience.com) Englishman John Hallowell runs excellent wolf-watching (and birdwatching) excursions in the Sierra de la Culebra; he's a knowledgable guide and puts together packages that begin and end at Madrid or Oviedo airports. He can also combine it with bear-watching in Asturias.

Zamora Natural WILDLIFE-WATCHING

(☑ 655 82 18 99; www.zamoranatural.com; per person €50) If you're keen to catch a glimpse of a wolf or two in the Sierra de la Culebra, contact Zamora Natural, which runs year-round excursions, including a dawn and sunset spent at a lookout overlooking areas commonly frequented by wolves. Sightings are not guaranteed, though; chances range between 20% and 40%, with the best months from October through to May or June.

🎪 Festivals & Events

Festival Territorio Lobo   CULTURAL
(www.festivalterritoriolobo.com; Villardeciervos; �) early Aug or Sep) This fun festival features live music, great local food, presentations about the Iberian wolf and excursions into the sierra.

🛏 Sleeping

★ Santa Cruz   GUESTHOUSE €
(☑ 619 85 00 10; www.loscuerragos.com; Santa Cruz de los Cuérragos; r €50; P🐶) Now here's something a little bit special. Fernando and Carmen have been largely responsible for bringing this charming stone village back to life. Their lovely rural home is beautifully restored and decorated with exposed stone walls, polished floorboards, comfortable beds and a general warmth – it's the sort of place where you'll want to stay longer than you planned.

Hotel Remesal   HOTEL €
(☑ 980 65 49 11; www.hotelruralremesal.com; Calle de Mediodía 25, Villardeciervos; s/d €35/50; P🐶) This excellent three-star hotel in Villadeciervos has 10 pretty rooms, all with exposed stone walls and excellent heating. It's on the main road through town and makes a convenient base for exploring the sierra, with numerous wolf-watching locales relatively nearby.

🍴 Eating

La Enredadera   SPANISH €€
(☑ 980 59 31 21; Calle de Arriba 26, Ferreras de Arriba; mains €6.50-15, set lunch menu €12; ☉ 8.30am-10pm Thu-Tue) What a find! In the otherwise-nondescript village of Ferreras de Arriba, close to some of the best wolf-watching spots, La Enredadera looks for all the world like a cool urban cafe. The food is thoughtfully presented, the service is friendly and its specialities include *bacalao* (cod) or *carnes a la brasa* (grilled meats).

Hotel Remesal   SPANISH €€
(☑ 980 65 49 11; www.hotelruralremesal.com; Calle de Mediodía 25, Villardeciervos; mains €8-15, set lunch menu weekdays/weekends €10/12; ☉ 1-4pm

& 8.30-11pm) Pass through this hotel's workaday bar and into the light-filled restaurant, where staff serve up hearty meat dishes and a generous lunchtime *menú del día*.

ℹ Getting There & Away

The N631, which connects Zamora with Puebla de Sanabria, runs parallel to the Sierra de la Culebra, with numerous side roads climbing up into the hills. Villardeciervos is the largest village in the region. Robledo, home to the Centro de Lobo interpretation centre, lies at the northwestern end of the range and is accessible from Puebla de Sanabria.

Puebla de Sanabria

POP 1525

Close to the Portuguese border, this captivating village is a tangle of medieval alleyways that unfold around a 15th-century castle and trickle down the hill. This is one of Spain's loveliest hamlets and it's well worth stopping overnight: the quiet cobblestone lanes make it feel like you've stepped back centuries.

◉ Sights

Castillo   CASTLE
(adult/child under 12yr €3/free; ☉ 11am-2pm & 4-8pm Mon-Sat, 4-7pm Sun; P🚻) Crowning the village's high point and dominating its skyline for kilometres around, the castle has some interesting displays on local history, flora and fauna; a slide show about the culture and history of the village; and a camera obscura. Kids will love the chance to try on the pieces of armour. The views from the ramparts are also superb.

Plaza Mayor   SQUARE
At the top of the village, this striking town square is surrounded by some fine historical buildings. The 17th-century *ayuntamiento* (town hall) has a lovely arched facade and faces across the square to Iglesia de Nuestra Señora del Azogue (☉ noon-2pm & 4-6pm Fri, 11am-2pm & 4-7pm Sat & Sun), a pretty village church dating to the 12th century.

🛏 Sleeping

Hostal Carlos V   HOSTAL €
(☑ 980 62 06 18; www.hostalcarlosv.es; Avenida Braganza 6; r €50; 🌬🐶) The best budget deal here, the Carlos V has pleasant rooms, dazzling white bedding, extrafluffy towels, firm mattresses, rainforest shower heads and quality

toiletries. There's a good cafe-restaurant here as well. It's at the bottom of the hill at the entrance to the old town.

★ Posada Real La Cartería
HISTORIC HOTEL €€

(☎980 62 03 12; www.lacarteria.com; Calle Rúa 16; r from €93-155; ❉@☎) This stunning old inn is one of the best hotels in this part of the country. It blends modern comforts with all the old-world atmosphere of the village itself, featuring large, delightful rooms with exposed stone walls and wooden beams. The bathrooms have Jacuzzi tubs and there is even a small gym (as if walking around this hilly village wasn't exercise enough!).

La Hoja de Roble
HISTORIC HOTEL €€

(☎980 62 01 90; www.lahojaderoble.com; Calle Constanilla 13; s €45, d €55-85; ❉☎) Close to the bottom of the hill where you begin the climb up into the old town, this hotel is an outstanding choice. The building dates to the 17th century and the rooms have a real sense of history (exposed stone walls, original wooden beams) without ever being oppressive.There's also a wine bar and a good restaurant.

✗ Eating

★ Posada Real La Cartería
CASTILIAN €€

(☎980 62 03 12; www.lacarteria.com; Calle Rúa 16; mains €9-21; ⊘1-4pm & 9pm-midnight) The local obsession with wild mushrooms (*setas* and *boletus*) and *trucha* (trout) – caught in the river below the village – is alive and well.

La Posada de Puebla de Sanabria
CASTILIAN €€

(☎980 62 03 47; www.laposadadelavilla.com; Plaza Mayor 3; mains €10-14; ⊘1.30-4pm & 8.30-11pm Thu-Tue) This excellent restaurant right on Plaza Mayor has a white-tableclothed elegance and serves up local steaks and the wild mushrooms for which this region is famed. When the two are mixed, such as in the *tenera estofada con boletus*, a kind of hotpot of beef with wild mushrooms, the results are outstanding.

ⓘ Information

Tourist Office (☎980 62 07 34; www.turismo sanabria.es; ⊘1-2pm & 4-8pm Mon-Sat, 4-7pm Sun) Inside the castle. At the height of summer, it sometimes stays open as late as 10pm, but don't count on it.

ⓘ Getting There & Away

There are sporadic bus services to Puebla de Sanabria from Zamora (from €7.80, 1¼ hours).

Palencia
POP 81,180

Subdued Palencia boasts an immense Gothic cathedral, some pretty squares and a colonnaded main pedestrian street (Calle Mayor) flanked by shops and several other churches. It's a pretty town and one of the quieter provincial capitals. Most travellers visit the area on a day trip from nearby Valladolid.

⊙ Sights

Palencia is embellished with some real architectural gems, including the 19th-century Modernista **Mercado de Abastos** (Fresh Food Market) on Calle Colón, the eye-catching **Collegio Vallandrando** on Calle Mayor and the ornate neo-plateresque **Palacio Provincial** on Calle Burgos. Step into the lobby of the latter to admire the ceiling frieze of the city under attack by the Roman legions, dating from 1904 and painted by local artist Eugenio Oliva.

★ Catedral
CATHEDRAL

(☎979 70 13 47; www.catedraldepalencia.org; Calle Mayor Antigua 29; €5; ⊘10am-1.30pm & 4-7.30pm Mon-Fri, 10am-2pm & 4-5.30pm Sat, 4.30-8pm Sun Apr-Sep, 10am-1.30pm & 4-6pm Mon-Fri, 10am-1.30pm & 4-5.30pm Sat, 4-7pm Sun Oct-Mar) The sober exterior of this vast house of worship (one of the largest in Castilla) belies the extraordinary riches within – it's widely known as 'La Bella Desconocida' (Unknown Beauty). The **Puerta del Obispo** (Bishop's Door) is the highlight of the facade. Once inside, head for the **Capilla El Sagrario**: its ceiling-high altarpiece tells the story of Christ in dozens of exquisite panels. The stone screen behind the choir stalls is a masterpiece of bas-relief, attributed to Gil de Siloé.

Iglesia de San Miguel
CHURCH

(☎979 74 07 69; Calle de Mayor Antigua; ⊘9.30am-1.30pm & 6.30-7.30pm Mon-Sat, 9.30am-1.30pm & 6.30-8pm Sun) This church stands out for its tall Gothic tower with a castle-like turret. San Miguel's interior is unadorned and austerely beautiful. According to legend, El Cid was betrothed to his Doña Jimena here.

🍴 Sleeping & Eating

Hotel Colón 27   HOTEL €

(☑979 74 07 00; www.hotelcolon27.com; Calle de Colón 27; s €30-50, d €35-60; ❄️📶) This two-star place is decent downtown value, with comfortable, if drab, carpeted rooms sporting light-pine furniture, good firm mattresses, green-tiled bathrooms and small flat-screen TVs.

Eurostars Diana Palace   BUSINESS HOTEL €€

(☑979 01 80 50; www.eurostarsdianapalace.com; Avenida Santander 12; s/d incl breakfast €60/80; 🅿️❄️📶) A comfortable, albeit modern, block of a hotel within walking distance of the town centre.

★Restaurante Casa Lucio   CASTILIAN €€

(☑979 74 81 90; www.restaurantecasalucio.com; Calle de Don Sancho 2; mains €14.50-33; ⏱10am-midnight Mon-Sat, 10am-4pm Sun) This Palencia institution has recently combined an *asador* (restaurant specialising in roasted meats) with a slick new gastrobar. Gone is the air of tradition, replaced by a sense of creativity bursting out of the kitchen. It still does the Castilian speciality of *cordero asado* (€39 for two) – and exceptionally well – but it would be a shame to dine here and not try the creative tapas.

Gloria Bendita   CASTILIAN €€

(☑979 10 65 04; Calle la Puebla 8; mains €15-25; ⏱1.30-4pm & 8.30pm-midnight Mon-Sat, 1.30-4pm Sun; 📶) Ignore the drab surroundings of modern apartment blocks and seek out this, one of Palencia's new breed of elegant restaurants serving sophisticated Castilian cuisine with a modern twist. Meat and fish dishes are the emphasis here, with classics such as braised beef served with oyster mushrooms. There are just a handful of tables in an intimate space, so reservations are essential.

ⓘ Information

Patronato de Turismo (☑979 70 65 23; www.palenciaturismo.es; Calle Mayor 31; ⏱9.30am-2pm & 4-8pm Mon-Sat, 9.30am-5pm Sun Jul–mid-Sep, 9.30am-2pm & 4-7pm Mon-Sat, 9.30am-5pm Sun mid-Sep-Jul) Information about Palencia province and city, encompassing both the municipal and regional tourist offices.

ⓘ Getting There & Away

From the **bus station** (☑979 74 32 22; Carerra del Cementerio) there are regular services to Valladolid (€4.15, 45 minutes), Madrid (€17.45, 3½ hours) and Aguilar de Campóo (€7.65, 1½ hours).

The AVE fast train now connects Palencia to Madrid (€25.25, 1½ hours) and León (€15.50, 45 minutes). Other services include Burgos (from €6.20, 45 minutes) and Valladolid (from €4.25, 30 minutes).

Around Palencia

👁 Sights

Iglesia de Santa María La Blanca   CHURCH

(☑979 88 08 54; Villalcázar de Sirga; €1.50; ⏱10.30am-2pm & 4.30-7pm May–mid-Oct, noon-2pm & 5-6.30pm Sat & Sun mid-Oct–22 Dec & Feb–Apr) This extraordinary fortress-church, an important landmark along the Camino de Santiago, rises up from the Castilian plains between Frómista and Carrión de los Condes along the quiet P980. Begun in the 12th century and finished in the 14th, it spans both Romanesque and Gothic styles. Its soaring, elaborately carved portal is worth lingering over, while highlights inside include the royal tombs and an extravagant *retablo mayor* (altarpiece).

Iglesia de San Martín   CHURCH

(☑979 81 01 44; Frómista; adult/concession/child €1.50/1/free; ⏱9.30am-2pm & 4.30-8pm Apr-Sep, 10.30am-2pm & 3.30-6.30pm Oct-Mar) Dating from 1066 and restored in the early 20th century, this beautifully proportioned church is one of the loveliest Romanesque churches in rural Spain, adorned with a veritable menagerie of human and zoomorphic figures just below the eaves. The interior is a study in simplicity save for the column capitals, which are also richly decorated.

There are two buses daily from Palencia (€3.50, 30 minutes), but most people visit en route between Palencia and the north.

Basílica de San Juan   CHURCH

(☑628 72 08 85; Baños de Cerrato; €2, Wed free; ⏱10.30am-2pm & 4.50-8pm Tue-Sun Apr-Sep, 11am-2pm & 4-6pm Tue-Sun Oct-Mar) In Baños de Cerrato, close to the singularly unattractive rail junction of Venta de Baños, lies Spain's oldest church, the 7th-century Basílica de San Juan. Built by the Visigoths in 661 and modified many times since, its stone-and-terracotta facade exudes a pleasing, austere simplicity and features a 14th-century alabaster statue of St John the Baptist.

Montaña Palentina

These hills in the far north of Castilla y León offer a beautiful preview of the Cordillera Cantábrica, which divides Castilla from Spain's northern Atlantic regions. The scenery around here is some of the prettiest in the region, with barely remembered Romanesque churches and quieter-than-quiet back roads, where you're more likely to be slowed down by a tractor than annoyed by a tour bus.

Aguilar de Campóo

POP 7090

Aguilar de Campóo is a bustling town with some interesting monuments, but the main reason to come here is as a gateway for the stunning scenery and Romanesque churches of the Montaña Palentina, or to break up the journey between Palencia and Santander.

◉ Sights

Ermita de Santa Cecilia   CHURCH
(€1.50; ⊘ 11am-2pm & 5-8pm Tue-Sun Apr-Sep, 11am-2pm & 4-6pm Tue-Sun Oct-Mar) Overlooking the town and providing its picturesque backdrop is a 12th-century *castillo* (castle) and the graceful Romanesque Ermita de Santa Cecilia.

Monasterio de Santa María la Real   MONASTERY
(☑979 12 30 53; www.santamarialareal.org; Carretera de Cervera; €3, guided tour extra €2; ⊘ 10.30am-2pm & 4.30-7.30pm Jul-Sep, 4-8pm Tue-Fri, 10.30am-2pm & 4.30-7.30pm Sat & Sun Oct-Jun) Just outside town, on the highway to Cervera de Pisuerga, is the restored Romanesque Monasterio de Santa María la Real. Its 13th-century Gothic cloister with delicate capitals is glorious.

⌂ Sleeping & Eating

Posada Santa María La Real   HISTORIC HOTEL €€
(☑979 12 20 00; Carretera de Cervera; s/d from €60/70; P ❋ ☎) Inhabiting part of the Romanesque monastery of the same name, this charming *posada* (rural home) is the most atmospheric place to stay in the region. Some rooms have stone walls, while others are split-level; all are decked out in wood. The restaurant offers medieval-themed dinners and several set menus (from €15).

Hotel Restaurante Valentín   HOTEL €€
(☑979 12 21 25; www.hotelvalentin.com; Avenida Ronda 23; s €43-53, d €65-73; ☎) This sprawling, central hotel has little character but does boast large, comfortable rooms. There's a bustling and well-regarded restaurant on site.

ⓘ Information

Tourist Office (www.turismocastillayleon.com; Plaza de España 30; ⊘ 10am-1.45pm & 4-5.45pm Tue-Sat, 10am-1.45pm Sun)

ⓘ Getting There & Away

Buses bound for Burgos, Palencia and Santander depart at least once daily. Regular trains link Aguilar de Campóo with Palencia (from €7.60, 1½ hours), but the station is 4km from town.

WORTH A TRIP

THE ROMANESQUE CIRCUIT

There are no fewer than 55 Romanesque churches in the cool, hilly countryside surrounding Aguilar de Campóo; you could easily spend a day tracking them as you meander along quiet country trails.

At **Olleros de Pisuerga** there's a little church carved into rock; it's signposted as 'Ermita Rupestre'. Ask at Bar Feli on the main road through town for someone to open it up for you.

Further south, on a quiet back road, the Benedictine **Monasterio de Santa María de Mave** has an interesting 13th-century Romanesque church, the only part of the complex open to visitors; ask at the cafe next door for the key. It's off the main highway around 8km south of Aguilar de Campóo. Nearby, the **Monasterio de San Andrés de Arroyo** (www.sanandresdearroyo.es; guided tours €3; ⊘ 10am-12.30pm & 4-6pm) is an outstanding Romanesque gem – especially its cloister, which dates from the 13th century. Guided tours in Spanish run hourly.

WORTH A TRIP

IBERIA'S FINEST ROMAN VILLA

Okay, it's not Pompeii, but it is the most exciting and best preserved Roman villa on the Iberian Peninsula. Located seemingly in the middle of nowhere, the Villa Romana La Olmeda (www.villaromanalaolmeda.com; off CL615; adult/concession/child under 12yr €5/3/free, 3-6.30pm Tue free; ⊙10.30am-6.30pm Tue-Sun; P 🖮) is surrounded by fertile plains and hidden behind an incongruous, futuristic-looking building. Step inside, however, to be transported back to the 4th century AD – once the villa of a wealthy aristocrat and land owner, the property spans some 1000 sq metres and contains some of the finest mosaics to be discovered in a private Roman villa anywhere in Europe.

THE NORTHWEST

León

POP 129,550 / ELEV 837M

León is a wonderful city, combining stunning historical architecture with an irresistible energy. Its standout attraction is the cathedral, one of the most beautiful in Spain, but there's so much more to see and do here. By day you'll encounter a city with its roots firmly planted in the soil of northern Castilla, with its grand monuments, loyal Catholic heritage and a role as an important staging post along the Camino de Santiago. By night León is taken over by its large student population, who provide it with a deep-into-the-night soundtrack of revelry that floods the narrow streets and plazas of the picturesque old quarter, the Barrio Húmedo. It's a fabulous mix.

⊙ Sights

★ Catedral   CATHEDRAL
(⌨987 87 57 70; www.catedraldeleon.org; Plaza de Regia; adult/concession/under 12yr €5/4/free, combined ticket to the Claustro & Museo Catedralicio-Diocesano €8/6/free; ⊙9.30am-1.30pm & 4-8pm Mon-Fri, 9.30am-noon & 2-6pm Sat, 9.30-11am & 2-8pm Sun Jun-Sep, 9.30am-1.30pm & 4-7pm Mon-Sat, 9.30am-2pm Sun Oct-May) León's 13th-century cathedral, with its soaring towers, flying buttresses and breathtaking interior, is the city's spiritual heart.

Whether spotlit by night or bathed in glorious northern sunshine, the cathedral, arguably Spain's premier Gothic masterpiece, exudes a glorious, almost luminous quality. The show-stopping facade has a radiant rose window, three richly sculpted doorways and two muscular towers. The main entrance is lorded over by a scene of the Last Supper, while an extraordinary gallery of *vidrieras* (stained-glass windows) awaits you inside.

French in inspiration and mainly executed from the 13th to the 16th centuries, the windows' kaleidoscope of coloured light is breathtaking. There seems to be more glass than brick here – 128 windows with a surface of 1800 sq metres in all – but mere numbers cannot convey the ethereal quality of light permeating this cathedral.

Other treasures include a silver urn by Enrique de Arfe on the altar, containing the remains of San Froilán, León's patron saint. Also note the magnificent choir stalls.

Combine your time in the cathedral with a visit to the Claustro and Museo Catedralicio-Diocesano (Plaza de Regia; adult/concession/child under 12yr €5/4/free, combined ticket to the Catedral €8/6/free; ⊙9.30am-1.30pm & 4-8pm Mon-Fri, 9.30am-noon & 2-6pm Sat, 9.30-11am & 2-8pm Sun Jun-Sep, 9.30am-1.30pm & 4-7pm Mon-Sat, 9.30am-2pm Sun Oct-May), just around the corner. In the peaceful, light-filled *claustro* (cloisters), 15th-century frescos provide a perfect complement to the main sanctuary, while the museum has an impressive collection encompassing works by Juní and Gaspar Becerra, alongside a precious assemblage of early Romanesque carved statues of the Virgin Mary.

★ Museo de Arte Contemporáneo   ART
(Musac; ⌨987 09 00 00; www.musac.es; Avenida de los Reyes Leóneses 24; adult/concession/child €3/2/1, 5-9pm Sun & 7-8pm Tue-Thu free; ⊙10am-3pm & 5-8pm Tue-Fri, 11am-3pm & 5-9pm Sat & Sun) León's showpiece Museo de Arte Contemporáneo has been acclaimed for the 37 shades of coloured glass that adorn the facade; they were gleaned from the pixelisation of a fragment of one of the stained-glass windows in León's cathedral. Within the museum is one of Spain's most dynamic artistic spaces. The airy galleries mostly display temporary exhibitions of cutting-edge Spanish and international photography, video installations and other similar forms; it also has a growing permanent collection. Concerts are held here regularly.

★ **Panteón Real**   HISTORIC BUILDING

(Plaza de San Isidoro; €5, 4-6.30pm Thu €1; ⊙10am-1.30pm & 4-6.30pm Mon-Sat, 10am-2pm Sun) Attached to the Real Basílica de San Isidoro (p179), the stunning Panteón Real houses royal sarcophagi, which rest with quiet dignity beneath a canopy of some of the finest Romanesque frescos in Spain. Colourful motifs of biblical scenes drench the vaults and arches of this extraordinary hall, held aloft by marble columns with intricately carved capitals. The pantheon also houses a small museum where you can admire the shrine of San Isidoro, a mummified finger (!) of the saint and other treasures.

★ **Real Basílica de San Isidoro**   CHURCH

(☑987 87 61 61; Plaza de San Isidro; ⊙7.30am-11pm) Even older than León's cathedral, the Real Basílica de San Isidoro provides a stunning Romanesque counterpoint to the former's Gothic strains. Fernando I and Doña Sancha founded the church in 1063 to house the remains of the saint, as well as the remains of themselves and 21 other early Leónese and Castilian monarchs. Sadly, Napoleon's troops sacked San Isidoro in the early 19th century, but there's still plenty to catch the eye.

Convento de San Marcos   CONVENT

(Plaza de San Marcos; adult/concession/child under 12yr €5/4/free, combined ticket to the Cathedral €8/6/free) **FREE** You will have to check into the Hostal de San Marcos *parador* (p181) to appreciate most of this palatial former monastery, although the historic chapter house and magnificent cloister can be viewed by nonguests. The platersque exterior is also superb, sectioned off by slender columns and decorated with delicate medallions and friezes that date from 1513. It's particularly lovely when floodlit at night.

Casa de Botines   HISTORIC BUILDING

(Calle de Ruíz de Salazar) Antoni Gaudí's contribution to León's skyline is the castle-like, neo-Gothic Casa de Botines (1893) – though the zany architect of Barcelona fame seems to have been subdued by more sober León.

Plaza Mayor   SQUARE

At the northeastern end of the old town is the beautiful and time-worn 17th-century Plaza Mayor. Sealed off on three sides by porticoes, this sleepy plaza is home to a bustling produce market on Wednesday and Saturday. On the west side of the square is the late 17th-century, baroque old town hall.

Iglesia de Santa María del Mercado   CHURCH

(Plaza de Santa María del Camino; ⊙10am-1.30pm & 5-8pm Tue-Sun mid-Jun–mid-Sep, 11am-noon & 7-8pm Mon-Sat mid-Sep–mid-Jun) Down the hill, the careworn, stone Romanesque Iglesia de Santa María del Mercado looks out over a delightful square that feels like a cobblestone Castilian village square.

🎪 Festivals & Events

Semana Santa   RELIGIOUS

(Holy Week) León is an excellent place to see solemn Holy Week processions of hooded penitents, with the city's monuments as a stirring backdrop.

🛏 Sleeping

Hostal San Martín   HOSTAL €

(☑987 87 51 87; www.sanmartinhostales.es; 2nd fl, Plaza de Torres de Omaña 1; s/d €30/43, without bathroom €23/30; ☜) In a splendid central position occupying an 18th-century building, this is good old-fashioned budget value in the heart of town. The candy-coloured rooms are light and airy; all have small terraces. The spotless bathrooms have excellent water pressure and tubs, as well as showers, and there's a comfortable sitting area. The friendly owner can provide advice and a map.

★ **La Posada Regia**   HISTORIC HOTEL €€

(☑987 21 31 73; www.regialeon.com; Calle de Regidores 9-11; s incl breakfast €54-70, d €59-130; ✳☜) This place has the feel of a *casa rural*

ⓘ **LEÓN PASS**

Valid for 72 hours from the time of purchase, the Leon Pass (www.leonpass. es; per person €10) grants free entry to the Panteón Real (p179), Museo Sierra-Pambley (☑987 27 67 75; www. sierrapambley.org/museo; Plaza de la Regla 4; adult/concession €3/2; ⊙11am-2pm & 5-8pm Tue-Sun; ♿) and MUSAC (p178). Although it saves you only €1 off admission prices to these places, it does entitle you to discounts in some shops and a circuit on the cutesy tourist train (Plaza de San Marcelo; adult/child €4/3; ⊙10.45am-2pm & 5-9pm Jul & Aug, shorter hours rest of year) that leaves from Plaza de San Marcelo and does a circuit of the town.

León

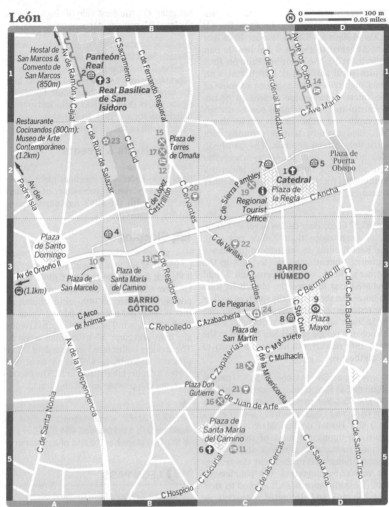

(village or farmstead accommodation) despite being in the city centre. The secret is a 14th-century building, magnificently restored (with wooden beams, exposed brick and understated antique furniture), with individually styled rooms and supremely comfortable beds and bathrooms. As with anywhere in the Barrio Húmedo, weekend nights can be noisy.

Hospedería Monástica Pax HOSTAL €€
(✆987 34 44 93; www.hospederiapax.com; Plaza de Santa María del Camino; r €54-79; ❄ 🖥) Overlooking one of the loveliest squares in León,

this excellent place inhabits a restored former monastery; the rooms are mostly spacious and stylishly appointed. Unless you're a really light sleeper, ask for a room overlooking the square.

Q!H BOUTIQUE HOTEL €€
(✆987 87 55 80; www.hotelqhcentroleon.com; Avenida de los Cubos 6; s €45-65, d €65-85; ❄🖥❄) Located within confessional distance of the cathedral, this boutique spa hotel occupies a historic 19th-century building that provides a suitable aesthetic canvas for the sharp modern design of the interi-

León

or. Rooms have cathedral views, a boldly accented colour scheme and steely-grey bathrooms. Prices increase with use of the spa and treatments.

★ **Hostal de San Marcos** HISTORIC HOTEL €€€
(☑987 23 73 00; www.parador.es; Plaza de San Marcos 7; d incl breakfast from €125; ❄@🛜) Despite the confusing *'hostal'* in the name, León's sumptuous *parador* is one of the finest hotels in Spain. With palatial rooms fit for royalty and filled with old-world luxury and decor, this is one of the Parador chain's flagship properties. As you'd expect, the service and attention to detail are faultless. It inhabits the landmark Convento de San Marcos (p179).

✗ Eating

La Trébede TAPAS €
(☑637 25 91 97; Plaza de Torres de Omaña; tapas from €2.50, raciones from €6.50; ⏰noon-4pm & 8pm-midnight Mon-Sat) As good for tapas (try the croquettes) as for first drinks (wines by the glass start at €1.50), La Trébede is always full. The decor is eclectic – deer's antlers, historic wirelesses and the scales of justice – and the sign outside declaring 350km to Santiago may just prompt you to abandon the Camino and stay a little longer.

El Picoteo de la Jouja TAPAS €
(Plaza de Torres de Omaña; tapas from €2.50) This intimate little bar has earned a loyal following for its concentration on traditional local tapas (try six for €13.50) and local wines, in-

cluding some from the nearby Bierzo region. The tapas include cured meats, snails and all manner of León specialities.

Restaurante Zuloaga CONTEMPORARY SPANISH €€
(☑987 23 78 14; www.restaurantezuloaga.com; Calle de Sierra Pambley 3; mains €16-26, menú del día €16; ⏰1-4pm & 8.30pm-midnight) Located in the vaults of an early 20th-century palace, this sophisticated place has a well-stocked cellar and a classy, adventurous menu. The *rodaballo a la parrilla con verduritas* (grilled turbot with vegetables) is particularly good.

Racimo de Oro TAPAS €€
(☑987 21 47 67; www.racimodeoro.com; Plaza de San Martín 8; raciones from €6.50, mains €11-20; ⏰1-5pm & 8pm-12.30am) A lovely brick-lined interior provides an appealing backdrop for this wildly popular tapas bar and restaurant, which is arguably the pick of the choices around Plaza de San Martín. The food is predominantly from Castilla y León's north, such as cured meats, strong cheeses and roasted red peppers.

La Mary MEDITERRANEAN €€
(☑987 04 34 47; www.lamaryrestaurant.com; Plaza Don Gutierre 5; mains €8-13, menú del día €10.95; ⏰1.30-4pm & 9-11.30pm Sun-Thu, 1.30-4pm & 9pm-midnight Fri & Sat) Opened in late 2013, the daily lunch menu here is excellent value. Dishes include Italian options like *caprese* salad (with real buffalo mozzarella), plus seafood with imaginative sides like broccoli purée; most of the Spanish rice dishes are

WORTH A TRIP

MONASTERIO DE SAN MIGUEL DE ESCALADA

Rising from Castilla's northern plains, the beautifully simple Monasterio de San Miguel de Escalada (by donation; ⊙10.15am-2pm & 4.30-8pm Tue-Sun) was built in the 9th century by refugee monks from Córdoba atop the remains of a Visigoth church dedicated to the Archangel Michael. Although little trace of the latter remains, the church is notable for its Islamic-inspired horseshoe arches, rarely seen so far north in Spain. The graceful exterior and its portico are balanced by the impressive marble columns within. The entrance dates from the 11th century.

To get here, take the N601 southeast of León. After about 14km, take the small LE213 to the east; the church is 16km after the turn-off.

for two only. The atmosphere is bright and contemporary and there are outside tables.

⭐ **Restaurante Cocinandos**   MODERN SPANISH €€€
(☑987 07 13 78; www.cocinandos.com; Calle de las Campanillas 1; set menu €42; ⊙1.45-3.30pm & 9.30-11pm Tue-Sat) The proud owner of León's only Michelin star, Cocinandos brings creative flair to the table with a menu that changes weekly with the seasons and market availability. The atmosphere is slightly formal so dress nicely and book in advance, but the young team puts diners at ease and the food is exceptional (in that zany new-Spanish-cuisine kind of way).

🍸 Drinking & Nightlife

⭐ **Camarote Madrid**   WINE BAR
(www.camarotemadrid.com; Calle de Cervantes 8; ⊙10am-4pm & 8pm-12.30am) With legs of ham displayed like some meaty Broadway chorus line, this popular bar is famed for its tapas – the little ceramic cup of *salmorejo* (a cold, tomato-based soup) is rightly famous. But the extensive wine list wins the day amid the buzz of a happy crowd swirling around the central bar.

Soho Vintage   COCKTAIL BAR
(☑626 47 25 25; Calle de Varillas 1; ⊙4pm-3.30am) Sultry lighting, Victoriana-themed decor with cabinets of dolls and model ships, and art deco prints (alongside some edgy contemporary artwork and photographs) equal a chic space for enjoying a pre- or post-dinner cocktail.

Delicatessen   BAR
(Calle de Juan de Arfe 10; ⊙10pm-4.30am) Just down the hill from Plaza de San Martín, this place is two bars in one. Head downstairs for indie rock or upstairs for the smarter, slick, electronica feel. The line between the

two often blurs and other tunes take over regardless of the genre – but it's always very cool and has been for years.

⭐ Entertainment

La Lola   LIVE MUSIC
(www.papaquijano.com; Calle de Ruiz de Salazar 22; ⊙9pm-5am Wed-Sat, live music from midnight) Come here to listen to Papa Quijano, a legendary Latino-rock crooner who has recorded several CDs and accrued quite a fan base. He has run this atmospheric bar since the 1970s. Dimly lit and with a back alcove encompassing part of the Roman wall, it won't be to everyone's taste but it's a fascinating place.

🛍 Shopping

⭐ **La Casa de los Quesos**   FOOD
(☑987 25 50 18; Calle de Plegarias 14; ⊙10am-2pm & 5-8.30pm Mon-Fri, 9.30am-2.30pm & 6-9pm Sat, 11.30am-2pm Sun) Cheese lovers will want to make a stop at this place that's been selling local cheeses since 1944 – you'll find every imaginable variety, with plenty of regional choices.

ℹ Information

Regional Tourist Office (☑987 23 70 82; www.turismocastillayleon.com; Plaza de la Regla 2; ⊙9.30am-2pm & 5-8pm Mon-Sat, 9.30am-5pm Sun)

ℹ Getting There & Around

The train and bus stations lie on the western bank of Río Bernesga, off the western end of Avenida de Ordoño II.

Bus services depart from the **bus station** (☑987 21 10 00; Paseo del Ingeniero Sáez de Miera) to Madrid (€22.95, 3½ hours, eight daily), Astorga (€3.60, one hour, 17 daily), Burgos (€5 to €15.50, two hours, three daily) and Valladolid (€10.20, two hours, nine daily).

Parking bays (€12 to €16 for 12 hours) can be found in the streets surrounding Plaza de Santo Domingo.

The AVE fast train network now reaches León, which has cut travel to time considerably to/from Valladolid (€19.50, 1¼ hours) and Madrid (€32.75, 2¼ hours), although there are cheaper and slower services. Other destinations include Burgos (from €9.85, two hours).

Astorga

POP 11,635 / ELEV 870M

Perched on a hilltop on the frontier between the bleak plains of northern Castilla and the mountains that rise up to the west towards Galicia, Astorga is a fascinating small town with a wealth of attractions out of proportion to its size. In addition to its fine cathedral, the city boasts a Gaudí-designed palace, a smattering of Roman ruins and a personality dominated by the Camino de Santiago. Most enjoyable of all, perhaps, is a museum dedicated to chocolate.

Sights

Palacio Episcopal   MUSEUM, ARCHITECTURE

(Museo de los Caminos; Calle de Los Sitios; €3, combined ticket with Museo Catedralicio €5; ⊙10am-2pm & 4-8pm Tue-Sat, 10am-2pm Sun Mar-Sep, 11am-2pm & 4-6pm Tue-Sat, 10am-2pm Sun Oct-Feb) Catalan architect Antoni Gaudí left his mark on Astorga in the fairy-tale turrets and frilly facade of the Palacio Episcopal. Built in the 19th century, it now houses the Museo de los Caminos (in the basement), an eclectic collection with Roman artefacts and coins; contemporary paintings (on the top floor); and medieval sculpture, Gothic tombs and silver crosses (on the ground and 1st floors). The highlight is the chapel, with its stunning murals and stained glass.

Catedral   CATHEDRAL

(Plaza de la Catedral; cathedral free, museum €3, combined ticket with Palacio Episcopal €5; ⊙9-10.30am Mon-Sat, 11am-1pm Sun) The cathedral's striking plateresque southern facade is created from caramel-coloured sandstone with elaborate sculptural detail. Work began in 1471 and continued over three centuries, resulting in a mix of styles. The mainly Gothic interior has soaring ceilings and a superb 16th-century altarpiece by Gaspar Becerra. The attached Museo Catedralicio (☑987 61 58 20; €3, combined ticket with Palacio Episcopal €5; ⊙10am-2pm & 4-8pm Tue-Sat, 10am-2pm Sun Mar-Sep, 11am-2pm & 4-6pm Tue-Sat, 10am-2pm

Sun Oct-Feb) features the usual religious art, documents and artefacts.

Museo del Chocolate   MUSEUM

(☑987 61 62 20; Avenida de la Estación 16; adult/child €2.50/free, combined ticket with Museo Romano €4; ⊙10.30am-2pm & 4.30-7pm Tue-Sat, 10.30am-2pm Sun; ⊡) Proof that Astorga does not exist solely for the virtuous souls of the Camino comes in the form of this quirky private museum. Chocolate ruled Astorga's local economy in the 18th and 19th centuries; this eclectic collection of old machinery, colourful advertising and lithographs inhabits a lovely old mansion within walking distance of the centre. Best of all, you get a free chocolate sample at the end.

Museo Romano   MUSEUM

(☑987 61 68 38; Plaza de San Bartolomé 2; adult/child €3/free, combined ticket with Museo del Chocolate €4; ⊙10.30am-2pm & 4.30-7pm Tue-Sun Jun-Sep, 10.30am-2pm & 4-6pm Tue-Sat, 10.30am-2pm Sun Oct-May; ⊡) Housed in the Roman *ergástula* (slave prison), the Museo Romano has a modest selection of artefacts and an enjoyable big-screen slide show on Roman Astorga.

Casa Romana   RUIN

(Calle de Padres Redentoristas) Remnants of a villa that once belonged to a wealthy Roman family survive under glass just down the hill from the Plaza de San Bartolomé. The highlight is the floor piece 'Mosaic of the Bear & the Birds', which once adorned one of the bedrooms.

Tours

Ruta Romana   WALKING TOUR

(☑987 61 69 37; rutaromana@ayuntamientode astorga.com; per person €4, combined ticket with Museo Romano €5; ⊙11am & 5pm Tue-Sat, 11am Sun) This 1¾-hour guided tour of Astorga's Roman remains (some of which are accessible only as part of this tour) is an excellent way to really get under the skin of the town's Roman past. The tours are conducted in Spanish only but most of the sites have English information panels.

Festivals & Events

Festividad de Santa Marta   RELIGIOUS

(⊡) The sacred and the profane mix seamlessly as Astorga celebrates its patron saint with fireworks and bullfights in the last week of August.

LAS MÉDULAS

The ancient Roman goldmines at Las Médulas, about 20km southwest of Ponferrada, once served as the main source of gold for the entire Roman Empire – the final tally came to a remarkable 3 million kg. It's stunningly beautiful, especially at sunset – one of the more bizarre landscapes you'll see in Spain. The best views are from the Mirador de Orellán, while there are some terrific walks from the village of Las Médulas.

Las Médulas' otherworldly aspect is not a natural phenomenon: an army of slaves honeycombed the area with canals and tunnels (some over 40km long), through which they pumped water to break up the rock and free it from the precious metal.

To get here take the N536 southwest of Ponferrada, then take signed turn-off in the village of Carucedo. On the outskirts of Carucedo, the road forks. The left fork leads to the pretty stone village of Orellán (2.8km on), which tumbles down into a valley, and then on to the car park for the Mirador de Orellán. From the car park it's a steep 750m climb up to the lookout, from where the views are breathtaking.

Returning to the fork, the right branch leads on to Las Médulas village (3km on). Park at the entrance to the village, then stop at at the Aula Arqueológico (☏ 987 42 28 48; www.ieb.org.es; €1.50; ☺ 10am-1.30pm & 4-8pm Apr-Sep, 10am-2pm Sat, 10am-1.30pm & 3.30-6pm Sun Oct-Mar), an interpretation centre with interesting displays on the history of the mines (admission €1.50); it also has information on the walks that weave among chestnut trees to the caves, quarries and bizarre formations left behind by the miners. If you're feeling fit, a 5.1km trail climbs to the Mirador de Orellán (one way/return 3/4½ hours) from here, but there are plenty of other shorter trails into the heart of Las Médulas. You can also enquire about horse riding in the area.

Las Médulas can get overwhelmed with visitors on weekends, but is much quieter during the week. Las Médulas village has a handful of restaurants and *casas rurales* in case you're tempted to linger.

🛏 Sleeping

Hotel Via de la Plata HOTEL €€
(☏ 987 61 90 00; www.hotelviadelaplata.es; Calle Padres Redentoristas 5; d/ste incl breakfast €80/100; ❄@🐾) Opened in 2012, this spa hotel occupies a handsome former monastery just off Plaza España. Guests receive a considerable discount for the spa treatments, which include the deliciously decadent-sounding *chocoterapia* (chocolate therapy). The rooms are slick and modern, with fashionable mushroom-brown and cream decor, tubular lights and full-size tubs, as well as showers.

Hotel Astur Plaza HOTEL €€
(☏ 987 61 89 00; www.hotelasturplaza.es; Plaza de España 2; s/d/ste from €55/75/110; ❄@🐾) Opt for one of the supremely comfortable rooms that face pretty Plaza de España – at weekends, however, you may want to forsake the view for a quieter room out the back. The suites have hydromassage tubs and there are three VIP rooms with 'super king-size' beds, but even the standard rooms here are good.

🍴 Eating

The local speciality is *cocido maragato,* a stew made of various meats, potatoes, chickpeas and a noodle soup. What makes it different to *cocido* elsewhere is that in Astorga they serve it in reverse: first the meats, then the vegetables, then the soup. Portions are huge, so one order usually feeds two, and it's really only considered a lunchtime dish (which is why most Astorga restaurants don't even bother opening in the evening). Bookings are essential on weekends.

Several pastry shops sell the traditional local *mantecadas,* a cake-like sweet peculiar to Astorga. One such place is Confitería Alonso (☏ 987 61 70 56; Calle de los Sitios 12; cakes from €2.50; ☺ 10am-2pm & 3.30-8.30pm Mon-Fri, 10am-2.30pm & 3.30-9pm Sat & Sun).

Restaurante Las Termas CASTILIAN €€
(☏ 987 60 22 12; www.restaurantelastermas.com; Calle de Santiago Postas 1; mains €9.50-20; ☺ 1-4pm Tue-Sun; 🌱) This lunchtime restaurant is run by Santiago (a popular name in these parts), who, apart from being a charming host, over-

sees a menu renowned for the quality of its *cocido maragato* (€21) and *ensalada maragata* (salad of chickpeas and cod).

Casa Maragata
SPANISH €€

(☑ 987 61 88 80; www.casamaragata.com; Calle de Húsar Tiburcio 2; cocido per person €21; ⊘1.30-4pm Wed-Mon) One of the better (and hence more popular) restaurants serving *cocido maragato*. In fact, it doesn't serve much else. There's another branch across town you can head to if this one's full.

Restaurante Serrano
CONTEMPORARY SPANISH €€

(☑ 987 61 78 66; www.restauranteserrano.es; Calle de la Portería 2; mains €14-22; ⊘12.30-4pm & 8-11.30pm Tue-Sun) The menu at upmarket Restaurante Serrano has a subtle gourmet flourish, with fresh summery starters, innovative meat and fish mains and plenty of tempting desserts with chocolate. It also serves *cocido maragato* and other local dishes. Reservations recommended.

ⓘ Information

Municipal Tourist Office (☑ 987 61 82 22; www.turismocastillayleon.com; Glorieta Eduardo de Castro 5; ⊘10am-2pm & 4-8pm) Helpful office opposite the Palacio Episcopal.

ⓘ Getting There & Away

Regular bus services connect Astorga with León (€3.60, one hour, 17 daily) and Madrid (from €26.90, 4½ hours, three daily). The train station is inconveniently a couple of kilometres north of town.

Sahagún

POP 2785 / ELEV 807M

A modest, albeit quietly picturesque town today, Sahagún was once home to one of Spain's more powerful abbeys and today remains an important way station for pilgrims en route to Santiago.

◉ Sights

Santuario de La Peregrina
CONVENT

(☑ 987 78 10 15; off Avenida Fernando de Castro; €3; ⊘11am-2pm & 6-8pm Tue-Sun Jul–mid-Sep, 11am-2pm & 4-6.30pm Wed-Sun, 4-6.30pm Tue mid-Sep–Jun) This 13th-century former convent has been stunningly restored, with glimpses of elaborate 13th-century frescos and 17th-century Mudéjar plasterwork (the latter is in the chapel to the right of the main nave). Contemporary artworks fill the spaces in between and a modern addition to the convent houses some excellent scale models of Sahagún's major monuments.

Iglesia de San Tirso
CHURCH

(Plaza de San Tirso; ⊘10am-2pm & 3-5.50pm Wed-Sat, 10am-2pm Sun) The early 12th-century Iglesia de San Tirso, at the western entrance to town, is an important stop on the Camino de Santiago. It's known for its pure Romanesque design and Mudéjar bell tower laced with rounded arches.

🛏 Sleeping & Eating

La Bastide du Chemin
HOSTAL €

(☑ 987 78 11 83; www.labastideduchemin.es; Calle Arco 66; s/d €28/40; 🐾) Opened in 2013, this small, cosy *hostal*, opposite the Albergue de

Camino Francés in Castilla y León

CAMINO DE SANTIAGO

Camino de Santiago Day Walk

The comparatively short stretch between Rabé de las Calzadas and Hontanas (18.8km, five hours) is best in springtime – this rolling *meseta* (plateau) walk brings solitude amid the wheat, allowing you to appreciate the region's uniquely lonely landscapes and villages.

Camino de Santiago: Burgos to León

Many pilgrims avoid this stretch of the Camino and take the bus, which is a pity as they are missing out on the subtle and ever-changing play of colours on the *meseta* (plateau). Contrary to popular opinion, it is not flat. Villages here are set low in long valleys, with occasional rivers, which rise up to the high barren plains.

There are large limestone rocks everywhere, and evocative sights, such as flocks of sheep led by solitary shepherds and isolated adobe villages. The path passes via Castrojeriz, with its castle dominating the town, while in better-known Frómista is the Iglesia de San Martín (p176), one of the jewels of early Spanish Romanesque architecture.

Between Carrión de los Condes and Calzadilla de la Cueza, the Camino coincides with a stretch of Roman road. Further on is Sahagún, which, despite appearances, was an immensely powerful and wealthy Benedictine centre by the 12th century; the Mudéjar-influenced brick Romanesque churches merit a visit.

Before reaching León, the Camino becomes monotonous, running through a long series of villages along paved, busy roads.

Peregrinos (Hostel for Pilgrims), has pleasant rustic rooms with beamed ceilings.

San Facundo　　　　　　　CASTILIAN €€
(Avenida de la Constitución 97-99; mains €14-25; ⊘noon-4pm & 8-11pm; 🛜👪) Part of the Hostal La Codorniz (📱987 78 02 76; www.hostal lacodorniz.com; Avenida de la Constitución 97; s/d €40/50; ❄🛜), this traditional restaurant, which has an impressive carved Mudéjar ceiling, specialises in succulent roasted meats.

ℹ️ Information

Tourist Office (📱987 78 21 17; www.sahagun. org; Calle del Arco 87; ⊘noon-2pm & 6-9pm Mon-Thu, 11am-2pm & 4-9pm Fri-Sun) Located within the Albergue de Peregrinos.

ℹ️ Getting There & Away

Trains run regularly throughout the day from León (from €5.45, 40 minutes) and Palencia (from €5.45, 35 minutes).

THE EAST

Burgos

POP 177,775 / ELEV 861M
The extraordinary Gothic cathedral of Burgos is one of Spain's glittering jewels of religious architecture – it looms large over the city and skyline. On the surface, conservative Burgos seems to embody all the stereotypes of a north-central Spanish town, with sombre grey-stone architecture, the fortifying cuisine of the high *meseta* (plateau) and a climate of extremes. But this is a city that rewards deeper exploration: below the surface lie good restaurants and, when the sun's shining, pretty streetscapes that extend far beyond the landmark cathedral. There's even a whiff of legend about the place: beneath the majestic spires of the cathedral lies the tomb of Burgos' favourite son, El Cid.

👁️ Sights

⭐ **Catedral**　　　　　　　CATHEDRAL
(📱947 20 47 12; www.catedraldeburgos.es; Plaza del Rey Fernando; adult/under 14yr incl audioguide €7/1.50, 4.30-6pm Tue free; ⊘10am-6pm) This Unesco World Heritage–listed cathedral, once a former modest Romanesque church, is a masterpiece. Work began on a grander scale in 1221; remarkably, within 40 years most of the French Gothic structure had been completed. You can enter from Plaza de Santa María for free for access to the Capilla del Santísimo Cristo, with its much-revered 13th-century crucifix, and the Capilla de Santa Tecla, with its extraordinary ceiling. However, we recommend that you visit the cathedral in its entirety.

The cathedral's twin towers went up in the 15th century; each represent 84m of richly decorated Gothic fantasy surrounded by a sea of similarly intricate spires. Probably the most impressive of the portals is the Puerta del Sarmental, the main entrance for visitors – although the honour could also go to the Puerta de la Coronería, on the northwestern side, which shows Christ surrounded by the evangelists.

Inside the main sanctuary, a host of other chapels showcase the diversity of the interior, from the light and airy Capilla de la Presentación to the Capilla de la Concepción, with its gilded, 15th-century altar, and the Capilla de Santa Ana, with its gorgeous *retablo*. The Capilla del Condestable, behind the main altar, bridges Gothic and plateresque styles; highlights here include three altars watched over by unusual star-shaped vaulting in the dome (it was closed for major restoration works at the time of writing). The sculptures facing the entrance to the chapel are 15th- and 16th-century masterpieces of stone carving, portraying the Passion, death, resurrection and ascension of Christ.

The main altar is a typically overwhelming piece of gold-encrusted extravagance, while directly beneath the star-vaulted central dome lies the tomb of El Cid. With so much else to catch the eye, it's easy to miss the sublime main dome, high above the main sanctuary – it's a masterpiece of the plateresque, with a few Gothic flourishes. Another highlight is Diego de Siloé's magnificent Escalera Dorada (Gilded Stairway) on the cathedral's northwestern flank.

Also worth a look is the peaceful cloister, with its sculpted medieval tombs. Off the cloister is the Capilla de Corpus Cristi, where, high on the northwestern wall, hangs what legend calls the coffin of El Cid, although doubts remain as to its origins. The adjoining Museo Catedralicio has a wealth of oil paintings, tapestries and ornate chalices, while the lower cloister covers the history of the cathedral's development, with a scale model to help you take it all in.

★ **Museo de la Evolución Humana** MUSEUM
(MEH; ☑902 02 42 46; www.museoevolucion humana.com; Paseo Sierra de Atapuerca; adult/concession/child €6/4/free, 4.30-8pm Wed, 7-8pm Tue & Thu free; ⊙10am-2.30pm & 4.30-8pm Tue-Fri, 10am-8pm Sat & Sun) This exceptional museum just across the river from the old quarter is a marvellously told story of hu-

man evolution. The basement exhibitions on Atapuerca (p192), an archaeological site north of Burgos where a 2007 discovery of Europe's oldest human fossil remains was made, are stunning; the displays on Charles Darwin and the extraordinary 'Human Evolution' section in the centre of the ground floor are simply outstanding. Even if you've no prior interest in the subject, don't miss it.

Museo del Retablo MUSEUM
(Altar Museum; Calle de Pozo Seco; incl church €2) Just west of the cathedral, in the Iglesia de San Esteban, the Museo del Retablo has a display of some 18 altars dating from the 15th to 18th centuries. Both were closed for restoration at the time of writing.

Cartuja de Miraflores MONASTERY
(☑947 25 25 86; ⊙10.15am-3pm & 4-6pm Mon-Sat, 11am-3pm & 4-6pm Sun) FREE Located in peaceful woodlands 4km east of the city centre, this monastery contains a trio of 15th-century masterworks by Gil de Siloé, the man responsible for so many of the more beautiful features in the Burgos cathedral. The walk to the monastery along Río Arlanzón takes about one hour. To get here, head north along Paseo de la Quinta (flanking the river), from where the monastery is clearly signposted.

Monasterio de las Huelgas MONASTERY
(☑947 20 16 30; www.monasteriodelashuelgas. org; €6, 4-5.30pm Wed & Thu free; ⊙10am-1pm & 4-5.30pm Tue-Sat, 10.30am-2pm Sun) A 30-minute walk west of the city centre on the southern river bank, this monastery was once among the most prominent in Spain. Founded in 1187 by Eleanor of Aquitaine, daughter of Henry II of England and wife of Alfonso VIII of Castilla, it's still home to 35 Cistercian nuns. Entry is via one-hour guided tour only – unhelpfully, they decide the timings of the tours only at the beginning of each session, so it's worth ringing ahead.

Arco de Santa María GATE
(☑947 28 88 68; ⊙11am-1.50pm & 5-9pm Tue-Sat, 11am-1.50pm Sun) The splendid Arco de Santa María was once the main gate to the old city and part of the 14th-century walls. It now hosts temporary exhibitions, but its real charm lies as a backdrop to the Puente de Santa María or Paseo de Espolón.

Castillo de Burgos CASTLE
(☑947 20 38 57; adult/child under 14yr €3.70/2.60; ⊙11am-2.30pm Sat & Sun; ⓓ) Crowning the leafy hilltop Parque de Castillo are the

Burgos

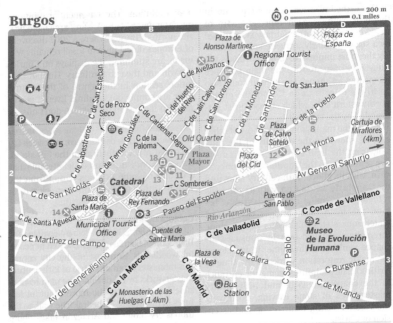

Burgos

massive fortifications of the rebuilt Castillo de Burgos. Dating from the 9th century, the castle has had a turbulent history, suffering a fire in 1736 and blown up by Napoleon's troops in 1813. There's a small museum covering the town's history; some of the original castle foundations are on view. Just south of the car park is a mirador (lookout) with great views of the cathedral and across the city.

🛏 Sleeping

★ Rimbombín
HOSTAL €

(☏ 947 26 12 00; www.rimbombin.com; Calle Sombrería 6; d/tr/apt from €39/59/70; ✴ ☏) Opened in 2013, this 'urban *hostal*' has an upbeat, contemporary feel – its slick white furnishings and decor are matched with light-pine beams and modular furniture. Three of the rooms have balconies overlooking the pedestrian street. Conveniently, it's in the heart of Burgos' compact tapas district. The apartment is excellent value for longer stays, with the same chic modern look and two bedrooms.

★ Hotel Norte y Londres
HISTORIC HOTEL €

(☏ 947 26 41 25; www.hotelnorteylondres.com; Plaza de Alonso Martínez 10; s €32-55, d €36-70; 🅿 @ ☏) Set in a former 16th-century palace and decorated with understated period charm, this fine, family-run hotel promises spacious rooms with antique furnishings and polished wooden floors. All rooms have pretty balconies; those on the 4th floor are more modern. The bathrooms are exceptionally large and the service friendly and efficient.

Hotel La Puebla
BOUTIQUE HOTEL €€

(☑ 947 20 00 11; www.hotellapuebla.com; Calle de la Puebla 20; s €39-95, d €49-95; ❄ @ ☎) This boutique hotel adds a touch of style to the Burgos hotel scene. The rooms aren't huge and most don't have views but they're softly lit, beautifully designed and supremely comfortable. Extra perks include bikes and a pillow menu; on the downside, some readers have complained about the level of street noise.

Hotel Meson del Cid
HISTORIC HOTEL €€

(☑ 947 20 87 15; www.mesondelcid.es; Plaza de Santa María 8; d/ste from €50/110; P ❄ ☎) Facing the cathedral, this hotel is in a centuries-old building. Rooms have Regency-style burgundy-and-cream fabrics, aptly combined with dark-wood furnishings and terracotta tiles. Several have stunning views of the cathedral (for a supplement of €10).

✖ Eating

Burgos is famous for its *queso* (cheese), *morcilla* (blood sausage) and *cordero asado*. There's a buzzing tapas scene close to the cathedral; other excellent choices can be found across the old quarter.

★ Cervecería Morito
TAPAS €

(☑ 947 26 75 55; Calle de Diego Porcelos 1; tapas from €3.40, raciones from €5.10; ☉ 12.30-3.30pm & 7-11.30pm) Cervecería Morito is the undisputed king of Burgos tapas bars and as such it's always crowded. A typical order is *alpargata* (lashings of cured ham with bread, tomato and olive oil) or the *revueltos Capricho de Burgos* (scrambled eggs served with potatoes, blood sausage, red peppers, baby eels and mushrooms) – the latter is a meal in itself.

★ El Huerto de Roque
CASTILIAN €€

(☑ 947 27 87 93; www.elhuertoderoque.com; Calle de Santa Águeda 10; mains €10.50-12.50, set menu €15; ☉ restaurant 1-4pm Tue-Sat, gastrobar 8pm-12.30am Thu, 8pm-1.30am Fri & Sat; ✐) ✆ Come here for an inexpensive lunch with plenty of choice. The emphasis is on the ecological, with a menu that changes with the seasons and according to what produce is fresh and good in the local market. The atmosphere throughout is boho-rustic, with original tiles, wooden furniture and edgy artwork.

The adjacent gastropub reflects a similar cuisine, tapas-style.

Mari Castaña
MODERN SPANISH €€

(☑ 947 20 61 55; www.maricastanaburgos.com; Paseo del Espolón 10; mains €8-18; ☉ 8.30am-11pm) This bright new place takes some tired old culinary concepts and freshens them up with great success. The *plato combinado*, that meat-and-three-veg warhorse, here retains the concept of a meal on one plate but is rethought with all fresh-market cooking. There's also breakfast, plates to share and some tempting set menus, including some that do wonderful things with mushrooms.

La Favorita
TAPAS €€

(☑ 947 20 59 49; www.lafavorita-taberna.com; Calle de Avellanos 8; tapas from €2.50; ☉ 10am-midnight Mon-Fri, noon-12.30am Sat & Sun) Away from the main Burgos tapas hub but still close to the cathedral, La Favorita has an appealing, barnlike interior of exposed brick and wooden beams. The emphasis is on local cured meats and cheeses (try the cheese platter for €12.90); wine by the glass starts at €2. The tapas menu includes beef sirloin with foie gras.

Casa Ojeda
CASTILIAN €€

(☑ 947 20 90 52; www.grupojeda.com; Calle de Vitoria 5; mains €15-25; ☉ 1-3pm & 8-11pm Mon-Sat, 1-4pm Sun) Dating from 1912, this Burgos institution, all sheathed in dark wood with stunning mullioned windows, is one of the best places in town to try *cordero asado* or *morcilla de Burgos*, but there are some surprising twists, such as the *solomillo* (sirloin) medallions with foie gras and essence of raspberry. The upstairs dining room has outstanding food and faultless service. Reservations recommended.

🍷 Drinking & Nightlife

There are two main hubs of nightlife. The first is along Calle de San Juan and Calle de la Puebla. For later nights on weekends, Calle del Huerto del Rey, northeast of the cathedral, has dozens of bars.

🔒 Shopping

Casa Quintanilla
FOOD

(☑ 947 20 25 35; www.casaquintanilla.es; Calle de la Paloma 22; ☉ 10am-2pm & 5-8.30pm Mon-Sat, 10am-2pm Sun) This is the pick of many stores around the town centre offering local produce that's ideal for a picnic or a gift for back home.

EL CID: THE HEROIC MERCENARY

Few names resonate through Spanish history quite like El Cid, the 11th-century soldier of fortune and adventurer whose story tells in microcosm the tumultuous years when Spain was divided into Muslim and Christian zones. That El Cid became a romantic, idealised figure of history, known for his unswerving loyalty and superhuman strength, owes much to the 1961 film starring Charlton Heston and Sophia Loren. Reality, though, presents a different picture.

El Cid (from the Arabic *sidi* for 'chief' or 'lord') was born Rodrígo Diaz in Vivar, a hamlet about 10km north of Burgos, in 1043. After the death of Ferdinand I, he dabbled in the murky world of royal succession, which led to his banishment from Castilla in 1076. With few scruples, El Cid offered his services to a host of rulers, both Christian and Muslim. With each battle, he became ever more powerful and wealthy.

It's not known whether he suddenly developed a loyalty to the Christian kings or smelled the wind and saw that Spain's future would be Christian. Either way, when he heard that the Muslim armies had taken Valencia and expelled all the Christians, El Cid marched on the city, recaptured it and became its ruler in 1094 after a devastating siege. At the height of his powers and reputation, the man also known as El Campeador (Champion) retired to spend the remainder of his days in Valencia, where he died in 1099. His remains were returned to Burgos, where he lies buried in the town's cathedral (p186).

Jorge Revilla JEWELLERY
(www.jorgerevilla.com; Calle de la Paloma 29; ⊘10am-2pm & 5-8pm Mon-Fri, 10am-2pm Sat) Local Burgos jewellery designer Jorge Revilla is becoming a global name for his exquisite and sophisticated silver pieces.

ℹ Information

Municipal Tourist Office (☏947 28 88 74; www.aytoburgos.es/turismo; Plaza de Santa María; ⊘9am-8pm daily Jun-Sep, 9.30am-2pm & 4-7pm Mon-Sat, 9.30am-5pm Sun Oct-May) Pick up its 24-hour, 48-hour and 72-hour guides to Burgos. These helpful itinerary suggestions can also be downloaded as PDFs from its website.

Regional Tourist Office (☏902 20 30 30; www.turismocastillayleon.com; Plaza de Alonso Martínez 7; ⊘9.30am-2pm & 4-7pm Mon-Sat, 9am-5pm Sun) Information about Burgos and the rest of Castilla y León.

ℹ Getting There & Away

Bus The **bus station** (☏947 26 55 65; Calle de Miranda 4) is south of the river, in the newer part of town. Regular buses run to Madrid (from €17, three hours, up to 20 daily), Bilbao (€9 to €13.40, two hours, eight daily) and León (€5 to €15.50, two hours, three daily).

Train The train station is a considerable hike northeast of the town centre; bus 2 (€1.20) connects the train station with Plaza de España. **Renfe** (☏947 20 91 31; www.renfe.com; Calle de la Moneda 21; ⊘9.30am-1.30pm & 5-8pm Mon-Fri), the national rail network, has

a convenient sales office in the centre of town. Destinations include Madrid (from €27.75, 2½ to 4½ hours, seven daily), Bilbao (from €13.75, three hours, four daily), León (from €12.30, two hours) and Salamanca (from €17.50, 2½ hours, three daily).

Around Burgos

The hinterland of Burgos is one of the loveliest areas for exploring quiet Castilian villages. Two stand out – Covarrubias and Santo Domingo de Silos – but this region's quiet back roads have plenty of hidden treasures and churches in the most unexpected places.

Covarrubias

POP 600 / ELEV 975M

A breath away from the Middle Ages, picturesque Covarrubias is one of Castilla y León's hidden gems. Spread out along the shady banks of the Río Arlanza, its distinctive, arcaded half-timbered houses overlook intimate cobblestone squares.

A good time to be here is for the Mercado de la Cereza (www.covarrubias.es), a medieval market and cherry festival held on the second weekend of July.

◉ Sights

★ **Colegiata de San Cosme y Damián** CHURCH
(€2.50; ⊘10.30am-2pm & 4-7pm Mon & Wed-Sat, 4.30-6pm Sun) This 15th-century Gothic

church has the evocative atmosphere of a mini cathedral. Home to Spain's oldest still-functioning church organ, it has a gloriously ostentatious altar, fronted by several Roman stone tombs, plus that of Fernán González, the 10th-century founder of Castilla. Don't miss the graceful cloisters and the *sacristia* (sacristy) with its vibrant 15th-century paintings by Van Eyck and tryptic *Adoracion de los Magis*. If there's no one in attendance (which is often), the cloisters and sacristy may be closed to visitors.

🛏 Sleeping & Eating

Hotel Rey Chindasvinto HOTEL €
(☑ 947 40 65 60; www.hotelreychindasvinto. com; Plaza del Rey Chindasvinto 5; s/d incl breakfast €38/51; ✳ ❄ 🛜) The best hotel in town, the Rey Chindasvinto has lovely, spacious rooms with wooden beams, exposed brickwork and a good restaurant. The owners are friendly but the service sometimes goes missing.

Casa Galín HOSTAL €
(☑ 947 40 65 52; www.casagalin.com; Plaza de Doña Urraca 4; s/d €25/40; 🛜) A cut above your average provincial *hostal*, Casa Galín has comfortable, rustic-style rooms in a traditional timbered building overlooking the main square. It's home to a popular restaurant for tapas, fish and roasted meats.

Restaurante de Galo CASTILIAN €€
(www.degalo.com; Calle Monseñor Vargas 10; mains €9-18; ⊙ 1.30-4pm Thu & Sun-Tue, 9-10.45pm Fri & Sat) This fine restaurant in the heart of Covarrubias is recommended for its robust traditional dishes, cooked in a wood-fired oven. You can sample the regional speciality of *cordero asado* (roast lamb). It also does a fine *olla podrida*, a medieval Castilian stew that includes red beans, ribs and blood sausage (it's much nicer than it sounds – terrific winter comfort food).

ℹ Information

Tourist Office (☑ 947 40 64 61; www.eco varrubias.com; Calle de Monseñor Vargas; ⊙ 10.30am-2pm Tue, 10.30am-2pm & 5-8pm Wed-Fri, 10.30am-3pm & 5.30-8pm Sat, 10.30am-3pm Sun) Located under the arches of the imposing northern gate, the tourist office runs guided tours at noon and 4.30pm most weekends. Also pick up its *Talleres Artesanos de Covarrubias* booklet which lists (and maps) seven art and craft workshops in the village.

ℹ Getting There & Away

Two buses travel between Burgos and Covarrubias on weekdays, and one runs on Saturday (€3.80, one hour).

Santo Domingo de Silos
POP 300

Nestled in the rolling hills south of Burgos, this tranquil, pretty, stone village has an unusual claim to fame: monks from its monastery made the British pop charts in the mid-1990s with recordings of Gregorian chants. The monastery is one of the most famous in central Spain, known for its stunning cloister. The surroundings and general sense of calm make this a fine place to spend a day or two.

◉ Sights

Abadia de Santo Domingo de Silos MONASTERY
(☑ 947 39 00 49; www.abadiadesilos.es; Calle de Santo Domingo 2; €3.50; ⊙ 10am-1pm & 4.30-6pm Tue-Sat, noon-1pm & 4-6pm Sun) The cloister and museum of this revered monastery is a treasure chest of some of Spain's most imaginative Romanesque art. The overall effect is spectacular, but the sculpted capitals are especially exquisite, with lions intermingled with floral and geometrical motifs. The guided tour covers the 17th-century **botica** (pharmacy) and a small **museum** containing religious artworks, Flemish tapestries and the odd medieval sarcophagus. Guided tours are in Spanish only; other visitors are usually allowed to wander more freely.

Basílica de San Sebastián CHURCH
(⊙ 6am-2pm & 4.30-10pm, vespers 6am, 7.30am, 9am, 1.45pm, 7pm & 9.30pm) Notable for its

---

ONLY IN SPAIN

Every year since 1620, the tiny village of Castrillo de Murcia (25km west of Burgos) has marked the feast of Corpus Cristi with the **Baby-Jumping Festival** (El Colacho; Castrillo de Murcia; ⊙ May or Jun). The village's babies are lined up on mattresses, then grown men leap over up to six supine (and somewhat bewildered) babies at a time. The ritual is thought to ward off the devil – but why jumping over babies? The villagers aren't telling. They do, however, assure us that no baby has been injured in the fiesta's recorded history.

pleasingly unadorned Romanesque sanctuary dominated by a multidomed ceiling, this is where you can hear the monks chant vespers six times a day. The church was granted the coveted status of basilica by papal decree in 2000.

🛏 Sleeping & Eating

Hotel Santo Domingo de Silos HOTEL, HOSTAL €
(📞 947 39 00 53; www.hotelsantodomingodesilos. com; Calle Santo Domingo 14; s €36-50, d €42-66, apt €70-115; 🅿 ❄ 🛜 🏊) This place combines a simple *hostal* with a three-star hotel with large, comfortable rooms (some with spa bathtubs) right opposite the monastery. It also has several nearby apartments, a swimming pool and underground parking. There's also a decent restaurant (mains €7 to €17) serving hearty but uninspiring food.

⭐ **Hotel Tres Coronas** HISTORIC HOTEL €€
(📞 947 39 00 47; www.hoteltrescoronasdesilos.com; Plaza Mayor 6; s incl breakfast €57-73, d incl breakfast €71-93; 🅿 ❄ 🛜) Set in a former 17th-century palace, this terrific hotel is brimming with character, with rooms of thick stone walls and old-world charm – including suits of armour and antique furnishings in the public spaces. The rooms at the front have lovely views over the square. The atmospheric restaurant, which specialises in meats roasted in a wood-fire oven, is the village's best.

ℹ Information

Tourist Office (📞 947 39 00 70; www.turismo-castillayleon.com; Calle de Cuatro Cantones 10; ⏰ 10am-1.30pm & 4-6pm Tue-Sun)

THE OLDEST EUROPEAN

The archeological site of Atapuerca (📞 902 02 42 46; www.atapuerca.org; guided tours in Spanish €6; ⏰ tours by appointment), around 15km west of Burgos, has long excited students of early human history. But archeologists made their greatest discovery here in July 2007 when they uncovered a jawbone and teeth of what is believed to be the oldest-known European: at 1.2 million years old it's some 500,000 years older than any other remains discovered in Western Europe. Unesco World Heritage–listed and still under excavation, the site is open only to visitors with advance reservations.

ℹ Getting There & Away

There is one daily bus (Monday to Saturday) from Burgos to Santo Domingo de Silos (€6.25, 1½ hours).

Ribera del Duero

The banks of the Río Duero are lined with poignant ruined castles amid pretty old towns such as El Burgo de Osma and Lerma, and cut through with two dramatic networks of canyons, the Cañón del Río Lobos and the Hoz del Duratón. Add to this the Ribera del Duero wine-producing region, one of Spain's most respected, and you could easily spend the best part of a week exploring the area.

Lerma

POP 2745 / ELEVATION 827M

If you're travelling between Burgos and Madrid and finding the passing scenery none too eye-catching, you'll find Lerma rising up from the roadside like a welcome apparition. An ancient settlement, Lerma hit the big time in the early 17th century, when Grand Duke Don Francisco de Rojas y Sandoval, a minister under Felipe II, launched an ambitious project to create another El Escorial. He failed, but the cobbled streets and delightful plazas of the historic quarter are an impressive legacy nonetheless.

👁 Sights

Pass through the Arco de la Cárcel (Prison Gate), off the main road to Burgos, climbing up the long Calle del General Mola to the massive Plaza Mayor, which is fronted by the oversized Palacio Ducal, now a *parador* notable for its courtyards and 210 balconies. To the right of the square is the Dominican nuns' Convento de San Blas, which can be visited as part of a guided tour (p193) via the tourist office.

A short distance northwest of Plaza Mayor, a pretty passageway and viewpoint, Mirador de los Arcos, opens up over Río Arlanza. Its arches connect with the 17th-century Convento de Santa Teresa.

Pasadizo de Duque de Lerma HISTORIC SITE
(€2) The Pasadizo de Duque de Lerma is a restored 17th-century subterranean passage that connects the Palacio Ducal with the Iglesia Colegial de San Pedro Apóstol. You can buy tickets at the tourist office (p193).

Plaza Mayor

SQUARE

Crowning the summit of the old town, the massive Plaza Mayor is fronted by the oversized **Palacio Ducal**, notable for its courtyards and 210 balconies. The square hosts a clothing and fresh food **market** on Wednesday mornings.

Activities

Guided Tours

WALKING TOUR

(per person €4, audioguides €3; ⊙ tours 10.30am, noon & 5pm Tue-Sun) Lerma's tourist office runs 1¼-hour guided tours of the town and most of its monuments. It also offers audioguides and an accompanying pamphlet and map that allow you to explore the town at your leisure.

Sleeping

Posada La Hacienda de Mi Señor

HISTORIC HOTEL €€

(⊉ 947 17 70 52; www.lahaciendademisenor. com; Calle El Barco 6; s/d incl breakfast €45/65; ✳@🕾) This charming, quirky place near the top of the town (it's a couple of blocks down the hill from the square) is your best midrange bet, with enormous rooms in a renovated, historic building. The candy-floss colour scheme will start to grate if you stay too long; request room 205 for a more muted paint palette.

★ Parador de Lerma

HISTORIC HOTEL €€€

(⊉ 947 17 71 10; www.parador.es; Plaza Mayor 1; r €90-165; P✳@🕾) Undoubtedly Lerma's most elegant place to stay, this *parador* occupies the renovated splendour of the old Palacio Ducal, but is devoid of the ostentatious decor (suits of armour etc) you find in some *paradors*. Even if you're not staying here, take a look at the graceful, cloistered inner patio. The rooms ooze luxury and character; the service is impeccable.

Eating

You're in the heart of Castilian wood-fired-oven territory here. Plaza Mayor is encircled by high-quality restaurants with *cordero asado* on the menu (€40 for two is a good price to pay).

Asador Casa Brigante

CASTILIAN €€

(⊉ 947 17 05 94; www.casabrigante.com; Plaza Mayor 5; mains €15-22, roast lamb for two €39; ⊙ 1.30-4pm) Our favourite *asador* in town is the outstanding Asador Casa Brigante – you won't taste better roast lamb anywhere. Ask

about its accommodation options nearby if you've eaten so much you're unable to move.

ⓘ Information

Tourist Office (⊉ 947 17 70 02; www.citlerma. com; Casa Consistorial; ⊙ 10am-1.45pm & 4-7pm Tue-Sun)

ⓘ Getting There & Away

There are eight daily buses from Burgos (€3.80, 30 minutes), with only four on Saturday or Sunday. Some buses coming from Aranda de Duero or Madrid also pass through – but most will leave you down the hill with a long climb to the top.

Peñafiel

POP 5430

Peñafiel is the gateway to the Ribera del Duero wine region, which makes it a wonderful base for getting to know the region's celebrated wines. Watched over by a fabulous castle and wine museum, and with one of the region's celebrated town squares, it even has a few charms of its own.

Sights

★ Castillo de Peñafiel

CASTLE

(Museo Provincial del Vino; ⊉ 983 88 11 99; castle adult/child €3.30/free, incl museum €6.60/ free; ⊙ 10.30am-2pm & 4-8pm Tue-Sun Apr-Sep, 10.30am-2pm & 4-6pm Tue-Sun Oct-Mar) Perched dramatically over Peñafiel, this castle houses the state-of-the-art **Museo Provincial del Vino**. A comprehensive story of the region's wines, this wonderful museum has interactive displays, dioramas and computer terminals. The rest of the castle, one of Spain's narrowest, can be visited on a (compulsory) 40-minute **guided tour**, which allows you to appreciate the castle's crenellated walls and towers (stretching over 200m, they're little more than 20m across). They were built and modified over 400 years, from the 10th century onward.

★ Plaza del Coso

SQUARE

Get your camera lens poised for one of Spain's most unusual town squares. This rectangular, sandy-floored 15th-century 'square' was one of the first to be laid out for this purpose – it's considered one of the most important forerunners of the *plazas mayores* across Spain. It's still used for bullfights on ceremonial occasions, and it's watched over by distinctive, half-timbered facades, as well as the grande dame of the castle up on the hill.

CASTILLA Y LÉON'S (DOC) WINE REGIONS

The wineries here are, overall, known for their robust reds, the perfect accompaniment to the traditional, hearty meat dishes. Increasingly, however, the region is producing good-quality white and *rosado* (rosé) wines.

Arlanza Known for its red *crianzas*, made from *tempranillo* grapes and produced by several bodegas, including the Señorío de Valdesneros.

Arribes One of the oldest wine regions, dating from Roman times; *Rufete* is the main grape variety here. Look for La Casita organic wines, including aromatic whites made from *malvasía* grapes.

Bierzo Best known for young red wines made with 70% *mencia* grape. Home of Spain's second most expensive red wine: La Faraona, produced by Bodega Descendientes de J Palacios.

Cigales Look for aromatic *rosados* made from *tempranillo* and *garnacha* grape varietals, which also form the basis of some robust red vintages.

Ribera del Duero The largest wine-producing region, covering some 9200 hectares. *Tempranillo*, cabernet sauvignon, malbec and merlot are the most popular grape varieties. Spain's celebrated Vega Sicilia comes from here, as well as the country's most expensive wine: Dominio de Pingus.

Rueda A region known for its dry aromatic white wines, made primarily from the *verdejo* grape variety.

Tierra de León The youngest Denominacíon de Origen (DO) region. Main grape varietals are *prieto picudo* and *mencía* for reds and *verdejo*, *albarín blanco* and *godello* for white wines, as well as rosés.

Tierra del Vino de Zamora Look for Bodegas Viñas del Cenit wines, including its namesake Cenit – produced from 100% *tempranillo* grapes and highly rated by *La Guía Peñín*, Spain's most famous wine guide.

Toro Produces heavy, *tempranillo*-based reds and famed for Bodega Namanthia's fruity and aromatic Termanthia, one of Spain's finest red wines.

Valles de Benavente Main grape varieties are *tempranillo*, *prieto picudo* and *mencía* for reds and *verdejo* and *malvasia* for white wines. Look for the light, sparkling Rosado de Aguja (rosé).

Convento de Las Claras WINERY
(☑ 983 88 01 50; www.bodegasconventodelasclaras. com; Carretera Pesquera de Duero, Km 1.5; tour & tasting €10; ☉ tours hourly 10am-1pm Mon-Fri, 12.30pm Sat, 11.30am Sun) Offers excellent wine tours and tasting, close to Peñafiel. It is particularly proud of its reds; the 2012 rosé deserves a special mention.

Legaris WINERY
(☑ 983 87 80 88; www.legaris.es; Curiel de Duero; tasting & tour €10; ☉ tours 11am, 1pm & 4.30pm Mon-Fri, 11.30am & 1pm Sat & Sun) Just five minutes from Peñafiel, this winery offers excellent tours and has a wine bar in a striking building. Well-regarded reds are its hallmark, with a remarkable system of 20 different types of carefully chosen barrels for ageing the wine.

Matarromera WINERY
(☑ 983 10 71 00; www.grupomatarromera.es; Valbuena de Duero; tasting & tour €10; ☉ 10am-2pm & 3-7pm Mon-Sat) One of the biggest of the Ribera del Duero wine producers, with a number of other wineries in the region. It produces excellent reds from the *tempranillo* grape that dominates in the Ribera de Duero region.

Protos WINERY
(☑ 983 87 80 11; www.bodegasprotos.com; Calle Bodegas Protos 24-28; tours €10; ☉ tours 10am, 11.30am, 1pm, 4.30pm & 6pm Mon-Fri, 10am, 11am, noon, 1pm, 4.30pm & 5.30pm Sat & Sun) This state-of-the-art winery in the shadow of the castle wall produces one of Ribera del Duero's better-known wines. It produces both reds and whites that are commonly found in shops and restaurants all across the country.

🛏 Sleeping

Hotel Convento Las Claras
HISTORIC HOTEL €€

(☎983 87 81 68; www.hotelconventolasclaras.com; Plaza de los Comuneros 1; s €80-105, d €95-130; P❄🛜🏊) This cool, classy hotel – a former convent – is an unexpected find in little Peñafiel, with rooms that are quietly elegant. There's also a full spa available, with thermal baths and treatments. On-site is an excellent restaurant with, as you'd expect, a carefully chosen wine list. Lighter meals are available in the cafeteria.

Hotel Castillo de Curiel
HISTORIC HOTEL €€

(☎983 88 04 01; www.castillodecuriel.com; Curiel de Duero; r from €100-125, ste €143; P🛜) Found just north of Peñafiel in the village of Curiel de Duero, this should be the hotel of choice for castle romantics. Occupying the oldest castle in the region (dating from the 9th century), the renovated hotel has lovely, antique-filled rooms, all with sweeping views. Another benefit is a well-regarded restaurant.

🍴 Eating

Asados Alonso
SPANISH €€

(☎983 88 08 34; Calle de Derecha al Coso 14; mains €14-18; ⏱1-4.30pm Thu-Sun) Staff keep it simple at this *asador* of long standing, with roast spring lamb cooked in a wood-fired oven and served with salad – many a visitor's idea of bliss.

La Casita de Peñafiel
SPANISH €€

(☎983 88 17 46; www.lacasitadepenafiel.com; Calle de Derecha al Coso 33; mains €9-15; ⏱9am-12.30am) A more informal option than the more celebrated *asadores*, La Casita de Peñafiel does a broad range of Spanish staples, including a few lesser-known dishes such as *codorniz escabechada* (pickled quail).

🛍 Shopping

Vinos Ojos Negros
WINE

(Plaza de San Miguel de Reoyo 1; ⏱9am-2pm & 5-8.30pm Mon-Fri, 9am-2.30pm & 4-8.30pm Sat) One of the better wine shops in town. It's not far from the river.

Ánagora
WINE

(☎983 88 18 57; Calle Derecha al Coso 31; ⏱10.30am-2pm & 5-8pm Mon, Tue, Thu & Fri, 11am-2pm & 5-8pm Sat, 11am-2pm Sun) An excellent wine shop in the heart of the old town.

ℹ Information

Tourist Office (Castillo de Peñafiel; ⏱11am-2.30pm & 5-8pm Sat & Sun Apr-Sep, 11.30am-2pm & 4.30-7pm Sat & Sun Oct-Mar) At the entrance to the castle high above the town.

Tourist Office (☎983 88 15 26; www.turismopenafiel.com; Plaza del Coso 31-32; ⏱10.30am-2.30pm & 5-8pm Tue-Sun Apr-Sep, 10.30am-2pm & 4.30-7pm Tue-Sun Oct-Mar) Runs guided tours (€3) at 1.30pm, Tuesday to Sunday. Also rents out bicycles (half-/full day €3/5).

ℹ Getting There & Away

Four or five buses a day run to Valladolid (€4.80, 45 minutes), 60km west of Peñafiel.

Sepúlveda
POP 1195 / ELEV 1313M

With its houses staggered along a ridge carved out by the gorge of Río Duratón, Sepúlveda is a favourite weekend escape for *madrileños* (Madrid residents) – especially for its famously good *cordero asado* and *cochinillo*. Wednesday is market day.

🛏 Sleeping

Hospedería de los Templarios
BOUTIQUE HOTEL €€

(☎921 54 00 89; www.hotelruralsepulveda.es; Plaza de España 19-20; r €70-90; 🛜) This aesthetically restored hotel has delightful rooms that are furnished with antiques but exude an ambience that is far from old-fashioned, with stylish bathrooms, warm washes of colour on the walls and some edgy artwork. Small terraces afford superb views.

Hotel Rural Vado del Duratón
HOTEL €€

(☎921 54 08 13; www.vadodelduraton.com; Calle de San Justo y Pastor 10; s €50-60, d €66-75; 🛜) Good if unspectacular rooms fill this four-star hotel not far from the centre of town. Rates are cheaper on weeknights.

OFF THE BEATEN TRACK

RELLO

Some 17km south of Berlanga de Duero, the hilltop stone village of Rello retains much of its medieval defensive wall and feels like the place time forgot. The views from the village's southern ledge are superb. There's at least one *casa rural* to stay in if you love peace and quiet.

Eating

Restaurante Figón Zute el Mayor   CASTILIAN €€

(☑921 54 01 65; www.figondetinin.com; Calle de Lope Tablada 6; mains €11-25; ☺1.30-4.30pm) A warmly recommended place, Figón Zute el Mayor is impossibly crowded on winter weekends, so be sure to reserve in advance.

Filka   CASTILIAN €€

(☑921 54 02 91; Plaza de España 4; main €16-22; ☺2-4pm & 8-11pm Wed-Mon) One of the few places in the centre that's open for dinner. If you're yearning for the local speciality *cordero asado* during the week, however, you need to let staff know (no need at weekends). Otherwise, the lamb chops are a sound meaty choice.

Information

Centro de Interpretación (☑921 54 05 86; www.miespacionatural.es; Calle del Conde de Sepúlveda 34; ☺10am-7pm; ♿) There is an excellent Centro de Interpretación in Sepúlveda that also has an informative permanent exhibi-tion about all aspects of the Parque Natural del Hoz del Duratón, including the flora and fauna. It's housed in part of the Iglesia de Santiago.

Getting There & Away

At least two buses link Sepúlveda daily with Madrid (€8, 2 hours).

Parque Natural del Cañón del Río Lobos

Some 15km north of El Burgo de Osma, this park promises forbidding rockscapes and a magnificent, deep-river canyon, as well as abundant vultures and other birds of prey. About 4km in from the road stands the Romanesque Ermita de San Bartolomé; drive to the car park and walk the final 1km. You can walk deeper into the park, but free camping is forbidden.

If you're driving through the park between El Burgo de Osma and San Leonardo de Yagüe, don't miss the wonderful views from the Mirador de La Galiana, which is sign-posted off the SO920. Otherwise, from the

---

DON'T MISS

CASTLES & SMALL CHURCHES

Castillo de Gormaz (Fortaleza Califal de Gormaz; Gormaz; ☺24hr) Some 14km south of El Burgo de Osma, one of Spain's most remarkable castles rises above the virtual ghost town of Gormaz (population 24). Built by the Muslims in the 10th century and reportedly the largest Muslim fortress in Europe, the castle was for centuries an important bastion along the frontier between Islamic armies and the Christian forces of the Reconquista. Most of its 21 towers remain and the walls stretch for over a kilometre.

Castillo de Berlanga de Duero (Berlanga de Duero; ☺10am-sunset Sat & Sun, guided tours 12.15pm, 1.15pm, 4.15pm & 6.15pm Sat, 12.15pm & 1.15pm Sun) Berlanga de Duero is lorded over by an extraordinary ruined castle made larger by the continuous ramparts at the base of its hill. The castle's oldest section dates from the 15th century, but most of the exterior was erected in the 16th century. The tourist office (☑975 34 34 33; www.berlangadeduero.es; Plaza Mayor 9, Berlanga de Duero; ☺10am-2pm & 4-8pm Sat & Sun), at the base of the castle next to the gate, runs free guided tours on weekends. If you want to visit from Monday to Friday, visit the town hall on Plaza Mayor to ask for the key.

Ermita de San Miguel de Gormaz (☑975 34 09 02; Gormaz; €1.50; ☺11am-2pm & 5-8pm Tue-Sun mid-Jul–mid-Sep, 11am-2pm & 4-7pm Sat & Sun rest of year) When Fernando seized the Castillo de Gormaz (p196) from its Islamic defenders in 1059, one of his first acts in the following year was to construct this small hermitage on the slopes below the castle. While it's not much to look at from the outside, its frescos inside the main sanctuary are stunning, and one of the region's best-kept secrets. The church is just beyond the village of Gormaz, on the road up to the castle.

Ermita de San Baudelio (€1; ☺10am-2pm & 4-8pm Apr-Sep, 10am-2pm & 4-6pm Oct-Mar) About 8km southeast of Berlanga de Duero stands the Ermita de San Baudelio, the simple exterior of which conceals a remarkable 11th-century Mozarabic interior. A great pillar in the centre of the only nave opens up at the top like a palm tree to create delicate horseshoe arches. It's one of rural Castilla's most surprising finds.

switchback road that climbs up the canyon, you'll have some fine views towards Ucero.

🛏 Sleeping

Camping Cañón del Río Lobos
CAMPGROUND €

(☑ 975 36 35 65; camping.riolobos@hotmail.com; sites per person/tent/car €5/5/6.25; ☺ Easter–mid-Sep; ☢) This highly regarded campground is near Ucero – if you're heading north along the switchback road that climbs up the canyon, you'll have some fine views back towards it.

Posada Los Templarios
GUESTHOUSE €€

(☑ 649 65 63 13; www.posadalostemplarios.com; Plaza de la Iglesia, Ucero; s €48-55, d €62-80, ste €92-102; ☢🅿) In Ucero, on the southern approach to the Parque Natural del Cañón del Río Lobos coming from El Burgo de Osma, is this fine old inn, which occupies a 17th-century home and has attractive rooms with exposed stone walls and a good restaurant.

ℹ Getting There & Away

There is no public transport to the park so you'll need your own wheels to get here. Access is via the SO920, which runs between El Burgo de Osma and San Leonardo de Yagüe.

El Burgo de Osma

POP 5155 / ELEV 943M

El Burgo de Osma is one of Castilla y León's most underrated medium-sized towns. Once important enough to host its own university, the town is still partially walled, has some elegant streetscapes and is dominated by a remarkable cathedral.

◉ Sights

Your initiation into the old town is likely to be along the broad Calle Mayor, its portico borne by an uneven phalanx of stone and wooden pillars. Not far along, it leads into Plaza Mayor, fronted by the 18th-century *ayuntamiento* and the sumptuous Hospital de San Agustín, which is where you'll find the tourist office.

If you exit El Burgo from near the cathedral on Plaza de San Pedro de Osma, take a left for the village of Osma, high above which stand the ruins of the 10th-century Castillo de Osma.

Catedral
CATHEDRAL

(☑ 975 34 03 19; Plaza de San Pedro de Osma; ☺ 10.30am-1pm & 4-7pm Tue-Sun) FREE Dating back to the 12th century, the cathedral's ar-chitecture evolved as a combination of the Gothic and, subsequently, baroque (notable in the weighty tower). The sanctuary is filled with art treasures, including a 16th-century main altarpiece and the Beato de Osma, a precious 11th-century codex (manuscript) displayed in the Capilla Mayor. Also of note are the light-flooded, circular Capilla de Palafox, a rare example of the neoclassical style in this region, and the beautiful cloister with original Romanesque traces.

🛏 Sleeping & Eating

Hotel Il Virrey
HOTEL €

(☑ 975 34 13 11; www.virreypalafox.com; Calle Mayor 2; r €50-60, ste €95-105; ☢🅿) This place has recently overhauled its decor. Now a curious mix of old Spanish charm and contemporary, public areas remain dominated by heavily gilded furniture, porcelain cherubs, dripping chandeliers and a sweeping staircase. Rates soar on weekends in February and March, when people flock here for the ritual slaughter (*matanza*) of pigs, after which diners indulge in all-you-can-eat feasts. Reservations essential.

Posada del Canónigo
HISTORIC HOTEL €€

(☑ 975 36 03 62; www.posadadelcanonigo.es; Plaza San Pedro de Osma 19; s/d incl breakfast €60/80; ☢🅿) The most imaginative choice here, with some rooms overlooking the cathedral from a handsome 16th-century building. Two comfortable sitting rooms offer a fireplace and library; the guest rooms are all different and overflowing with period charm, though it's rarely overdone (some are better than others). We like rooms 103 and 301, but ask to see a few if it's quiet.

Mesón Marcelino
SPANISH €€

(☑ 975 34 12 49; Calle Mayor 71; mains €12-32; ☺ 1-4.30pm & 8.30-11.30pm) A reliable choice along the main street, Mesón Marcelino feeds the passions of this unashamedly meat-loving town. It's all about *cordero* or *cochinillo asado* – roast lamb or suckling pig – with steaks and game meats as what passes for variety in El Burgo de Osma. Needless to say, the salads are an essential side order. It has a good tapas bar next door.

ℹ Information

Tourist Office (☑ 975 36 01 16; www.sorianite laimaginas.com; Plaza Mayor 9; ☺ 10am-2pm & 4-7pm Wed-Sun) Pick up a copy of its excellent *Tierra del Burgo* brochure to guide your steps around town.

WORTH A TRIP

UXAMA

Just outside El Burgo de Osma lie the ruins of Uxama (⊘24hr) **FREE**, with layers of history sprinkled lightly across the hills. Originally a Celto-Iberian settlement, it became an important Roman town after falling under Roman control in 99 BC; the town eventually fell to the Muslims in the 8th century. Low-lying remains of a former home and other fragments will make you wonder what else lies beneath the earth waiting to be excavated. Further into the site, the 9th-century Atalaya (watchtower) affords fabulous views over the surrounding countryside, especially northeast towards El Burgo de Osma and the Castillo de Osma.

A good dirt road runs through the site, which is signposted 3km west of El Burgo de Osma along the N122.

ⓘ Getting There & Away

Buses link El Burgo with Soria (€3.85, 50 minutes, two daily, one on Sunday) and Valladolid (€10.45, two hours, three daily).

Soria

POP 39,500 / ELEV 1055M

Small-town Soria is one of Spain's smaller provincial capitals. Set on the Río Duero in the heart of backwoods Castilian countryside, it's a great place to escape 'tourist Spain', with an appealing and compact old centre and a sprinkling of stunning monuments across the town and down by the river.

◉ Sights

★Monasterio de San Juan de Duero   RUIN
(⏐975 23 02 18; Camino Monte de las Ánimas; €1, Sat & Sun free; ⊘10am-2pm & 4-8pm Tue-Sat, 10am-2pm Sun May-Sep, 10am-2pm & 4-6pm Tue-Sat, 10am-2pm Oct-Apr) The most striking of Soria's sights, this wonderfully evocative and partially ruined cloister boasts exposed and gracefully interlaced arches, which artfully blend Mudéjar and Romanesque influences; no two capitals are the same. Inside the church, the carvings are worth a closer look for their intense iconography. It's located on the riverbank, down the hill from the historic centre.

★Ermita de San Saturio   HISTORIC BUILDING
(⏐975 18 07 03; Paseo de San Saturio; ⊘10.30am-2pm & 4.30-8.30pm Tue-Sat, 10.30am-2pm Sun May-Sep, 10.30am-2pm & 4.30-6.30pm Tue-Sat, 10.30am-2pm Sun Oct-Apr) **FREE** A lovely 2.3km riverside walk south from the Monasterio de San Juan de Duero will take you past the 13th-century church of the former Knights Templar, the Monasterio de San Polo (not open to the public) and on to the fascinating, baroque Ermita de San Saturio. This hermitage is one of Castilla y León's most beautifully sited structures, an octagonal structure that perches high on the riverbank and over the cave where Soria's patron saint spent much of his life.

Iglesia de Santo Domingo   CHURCH
(⏐975 21 12 39; Calle de Santo Tomé Hospicio; ⊘7am-9pm) Soria's most beautiful church is the Romanesque Iglesia de Santo Domingo. Its small but exquisitely sculpted portal is something special, particularly at sunset when its reddish stone seems to be aglow.

Plaza Mayor   SQUARE
The narrow streets of Soria's old town centre on Plaza Mayor. The plaza's appeal lies in its lack of uniformity, and in the attractive Renaissance-era ayuntamiento and the Iglesia de Santa María la Mayor, with its unadorned Romanesque facade and gilt-edged interior.

Palacio de
Los Condes Gomara   HISTORIC BUILDING
(Calle de Aguirre) A block north of the Plaza Mayor is the majestic, sandstone 16th-century Palacio de los Condes Gomara.

Museo Numantino   MUSEUM
(Paseo del Espolón 8; €1, Sat & Sun free; ⊘10am-2pm & 5-8pm Tue-Sat, 10am-2pm Sun Jul-Sep, 10am-2pm & 4-7pm Tue-Sat, 10am-2pm Sun Oct-Jun) Archaeology buffs with a passable knowledge of Spanish should enjoy this well-organised museum dedicated to finds from ancient sites across the province of Soria, in particular the Roman ruins of Numancia (p200). It has everything from mammoth bones to ceramics and jewellery, accompanied by detailed explanations of the historical developments in various major Celtiberian and Roman settlements.

Concatedral de San Pedro · CATHEDRAL

(☑975 22 58 91; Calle de San Agustín; cathedral free, cloister €2; ⊙cloister 11am-2pm & 4.30-7.30pm Tue-Sat, 11am-2pm Sun May-Sep, Mass times only Oct-Apr) Halfway up the hill towards the historic centre from the river, the Concatedral de San Pedro has a pleasing plat00esque facade. The 12th-century **cloister** is the most charming feature here: its delicate arches are divided by slender double pillars topped with capitals adorned with floral, human and animal motifs.

Festivals & Events

Fiestas de San Juan y
de la Madre de Dios · FIESTA

(www.sanjuaneando.com) Since the 13th century, the 12 *barrios* (districts) of Soria have celebrated this annual festival with considerable fervour. Held during the second half of June, the main festivities take place on Jueves (Thursday) La Saca, when each of the districts presents a bull to be fought the next day.

Sleeping

Hostería Solar de Tejada · BOUTIQUE HOTEL €

(☑975 23 00 54; www.hosteriasolardetejada.es; Calle de Claustrilla 1; s/d €50/55; ❄🐾) This handsome boutique hotel right along the historic quarter's pedestrianised zone has individually designed (albeit small) rooms with homey decor. Several have balconies overlooking the bustling pedestrian street.

Apolonia · BOUTIQUE HOTEL €€

(☑975 23 90 56; www.hotelapoloniasoria.com; Puertas de Pro 5; s/d incl breakfast from €55/62; ❄@🐾) Opened in mid-2013, this smart hotel has a contemporary urban feel with its charcoal, brown and cream colour scheme, abundance of glass, abstract artwork and, in four of the rooms, an interesting, if revealing, colour-lighting effect between the main room and the large walk-in shower – possibly best for romancing couples. The youthful management can arrange area excursions, such as truffle-hunting.

Hotel Soria Plaza Mayor · HOTEL €€

(☑975 24 08 64; www.hotelsoriaplazamayor.com; Plaza Mayor 10; s/d/ste from €56/64/85; ❄@) This hotel has terrific (if sometimes small) rooms, each with its own style of decor, overlooking either Plaza Mayor or a quiet side street. There are so many balconies that even some of the bathrooms have their own. The suites are very comfortable indeed.

Eating

Baluarte · CASTILIAN €€

(☑975 21 36 58; www.baluarte.info; Calle Caballeros 14; mains €12-24, menú degustación €46; ⊙1.30-4pm & 8.45-10.45pm Tue-Sat, 1.30-4pm Sun) Oscar Garcia is one of Spain's most exciting new chefs and this venture in Soria appropriately showcases his culinary talents. Dishes are based on classic Castilian ingredients but treated with just enough foam and drizzle to ensure that they're both exciting and satisfying without being too pretentious. Seasonal set menus are particularly worth watching for. Reservations essential.

Fogon del Salvador · CASTILIAN €€

(☑975 23 01 94; www.fogonsalvador.com; Plaza El Salvador 1; mains €13-22; ⊙1.30-4pm & 9pm-midnight; 🐾) A Soria culinary stalwart fronted by a popular bar, Fogon del Salvador has a wine list literally as long as your arm, and a fabulous wood-fired oven churning out succulent meat-based dishes such as *cabrito al ajillo* (goat with garlic), as well as a variety of steaks in all their glory.

Mesón Castellano · SPANISH €€

(☑975 21 30 45; www.mesoncastellanosoria.com; Plaza Mayor 2; mains €11-26; ⊙1.30-4pm & 9-11.30pm) With beamed ceilings, dangling flanks of ham, and the wall papered with proud photos of the local football team, this local institution serves some of the best tapas in town and delicious full meals in its *comedor*. The *cabrito asado* (roast goat kid) is a good order.

Information

Municipal Tourist Office (☑975 22 27 64; www.soria.es; Plaza Ramón y Cajal; ⊙10am-2pm & 4-7pm Tue-Sat, 10am-2pm Sun) Offers two-hour guided tours (€5) of the historic centre or the sights along the Río Duero on weekends, and more often in summer. Reserve in advance.

Regional Tourist Office (☑975 21 20 52; www.turismocastillayleon.com; Calle de Medinaceli 2; ⊙9.30am-2pm & 4-7pm Mon-Sat, 9.30am-5pm Sun) Information on both the town and the wider Castilla y León region.

Getting There & Away

From the **bus station** (☑975 22 51 60; Avenida de Valladolid), a 15-minute walk west of the city centre, there are regular services to Burgos (€11.50, 2½ hours), Madrid (€15.25, 2½ hours) and Valladolid (€14.90, three hours), as well as main provincial towns.

The **train station** (www.renfe.com; Carretera de Madrid) is 2.5km southwest of the city centre. Trains connect Soria with Madrid (€22.15, 2¾ hours, three daily), but there are few other direct services.

Around Soria

Calatañazor

POP 54 / ELEV 10771M

One of Castilla y León's most romantic tiny hilltop villages, Calatañazor is a charming detour. It's not visible from the highway (just 1km away) and has a crumbling medieval air. Pass through the town gate and climb the crooked, cobbled lanes, wandering through narrow streets lined by ochre stone-and-adobe houses topped with red-tiled roofs and conical chimneys. Scenes from the movie *Doctor Zhivago* were shot here.

◉ Sights

Towering above the village is the one-time Muslim fortress that gave Calatañazor its name (which comes from the Arabic Qala'at an-Nassur, literally 'The Vulture's Citadel'). Now in ruins, it has exceptional views from the walls and watchtowers, both down over the rooftops and north over a vast field called Valle de la Sangre (Valley of Blood). The name comes from an epic 1002 battle that saw the Muslim ruler Almanzor defeated.

There's also a church and a handful of artisan shops selling local products.

🛏 Sleeping & Eating

El Mirador de Almanzor GUESTHOUSE €
(☑975 18 36 42; www.elmiradordealmanzor.com; Calle Puerta Vieja 4; r €55-65; 🕾) This place at the upper end of the village, in a 15th-century, half-timbered home beneath the castle, is a fine Calatañazor choice. Rooms have exposed stone walls, wrought-iron furnishings and soft lighting.

Casa del Cura de Calatañazor GUESTHOUSE €€
(☑975 18 36 42; www.posadarealcasadelcura.com; Calle Real 25; r €65-75; 🕾) The most stylish rooms in Calatañazor are found here, around halfway up the hill on the main cobblestone thoroughfare through the village. Rooms have polished floorboards, chairs with zebra-skin upholstery and exposed wooden beams. The restaurant (mains from €13, *menu de degustación* €27) is also the best in the village.

ℹ Getting There & Away

There's no regular public transport to Calatañazor. If you're driving, the village lies around 1km north of the N122 – the well-signposted turn-off is about 29km west of Soria and about 27km northeast of El Burgo de Osma.

ROMAN SORIA

The area around Soria offers particularly rich pickings for those interested in the Roman presence on the Iberian Peninsula.

Villa Romana La Dehesa (Magna Mater; ☑626 99 25 49; www.villaromanaladehesa.es; Las Cuevas de Soria; €2, audioguide €2; ⊗11am-8pm Tue-Sat & 11am-2.30pm Sun Jul-Sep, shorter hours rest of year) This interpretation centre sits atop the site of an ancient Roman villa where stunning floor mosaics were found. The visit begins with a video presentation (in Spanish) of the villa's history, followed by a small museum of artefacts discovered at the site, before concluding with a walk along elevated walkways that overlook the remaining mosaics; the most spectacular mosaic now resides in Madrid's Museo Arqueológico (p98). The house, which was first unearthed in the 1930s, once covered 4000 sq metres.

Numancia's Roman Ruins (☑975 25 22 48; www.numanciasoria.es; Numancia; adult/concession/child under 13yr €5/3/free; ⊗10am-2pm & 4-8pm Tue-Sat, 10am-2pm Sun Jun-Sep, 10am-2pm & 4-7pm Tue-Sat, 10am-2pm Sun Mar-May & Oct, 10am-2pm & 4-6pm Tue-Sat, 10am-2pm Sun Nov-Feb) The mainly Roman ruins of Numancia, just outside the village of Garray (8km north of Soria), are all that remain of a city that proved one of the most resistant to Roman rule. Finally Scipio, who had crushed Carthage, starved the city into submission in 134 BC. Under Roman rule, Numancia was an important stop on the road from Caesaraugusta (Zaragoza) to Astúrica Augusta (Astorga).

Sierra de Urbión & Laguna Negra

The Sierra de Urbión, northwest of Soria, is home to the beautiful Laguna Negra (Black Lake), a small glacial lake resembling a black mirror at the base of brooding rock walls amid partially wooded hills.

Located 18km north of the village of Vinuesa, the lake is reached by a scenic, winding and sometimes bumpy road. It ends at a car park, where there's a small information office (⊙10am-2pm & 4-6.30pm Jun-Oct). It's a further 2km uphill to the lake, either on foot or via shuttle bus (return €1, departing half-hourly from 10am to 2pm and 4pm to 6.30pm June to October), which leaves you 300m short of the lake.

A steep trail leads from the lake up to the Laguna de Urbión in La Rioja or to the summit of the Pico de Urbión, above the village of Duruelo de la Sierra, and on to a series of other tiny glacial lakes.

Yanguas

POP 120

The tiny village of Yanguas, close to where Castilla y León climbs into La Rioja, is one of the loveliest villages of Soria's beautiful Tierras Altas (High Country). Yanguas is hemmed in by canyons and hills on all sides and its beautiful, stone-built architecture and cobblestone lanes, accessed beneath a medieval stone arch, are utterly charming.

🛏 Sleeping & Eating

Los Cerezos de Yanguas GUESTHOUSE €
(☑975 39 15 36; www.loscerezosdeyanguas.com; Paseo San Sebastián 6; s/d €48/56, 2-bedroom apt €127; 🅿️❄️🛜) Close to the entrance of town, this family-run *casa rural* occupies a typically stone-built Yanguas building. Rooms have an oldish style, with wooden bedheads and tiled or parquetry floors, but they're comfy enough. The home-cooked food is reason enough to stay here.

El Rimero de la Quintina GUESTHOUSE €
(☑625 48 58 74; www.elrimerodelaquintina.net; Calle de la Iglesia 4; r €55; ❄️🛜) At the top of the village just off Plaza de la Constitución, this fine *casa rural* has attractive rooms with wooden beams, tiled floors and pastel colours, not to mention a lovely garden out back.

ℹ Getting There & Away

There is no regular public transport to Yanguas, which is 47km northwest of Soria along the SO615.

South of Soria

Medinaceli

POP 770 / ELEV 1210M

One of Castilla y León's most beautiful *pueblos* (villages), Medinaceli lies draped along a high, windswept ridge just off the A2 motorway. Its mix of Roman ruins, cobblestone laneways and terrific places to stay and eat make an excellent base for exploring this beautiful corner of Castilla y León.

Far down the hill below the old town, modern Medinaceli, along a slip road just north of the A2 motorway, is the contemporary equivalent of a one-horse town.

◉ Sights

Arco Romano RUIN
Watching over the entrance to the town and visible on the approach, Medinaceli's 1st-century-AD Arco Romano (Roman triumphal arch) is one of the best preserved in Spain. It's also the only one in the country to boast three intact arches.

Plaza Mayor SQUARE
The partly colonnaded Plaza Mayor is a lovely centrepiece to the village. The oldest remaining building is the 16th-century Alhónidga, which is the only building on the square with two-storey colonnades.

Puerta Árabe GATE
Although modified down through the centuries, this gate on the west side of the village first served as one of four entrances to the settlement in Roman times and was an important gate during the era of Muslim occupation. It's a lovely corner, where narrow Medinaceli byways open out onto sweeping views of the rolling Castilian countryside.

Palacio Ducal PALACE
(☑975 32 64 98; Plaza Mayor; €2; ⊙10am-2pm & 4-7pm Thu-Mon) This largely 17th-century palace overlooks the Plaza Mayor, and hosts regular and high-quality exhibitions of contemporary art in rooms around the stunning two-storey Renaissance courtyard. In one of the rooms is a 2nd-century Roman mosaic and information panels on the mosaics that have been found around Medinaceli. The building's facade is the work of Juan Gómez de Mora, who designed Madrid's Plaza Mayor.

★ Festivals & Events

Festival Internacional de Música   MUSIC
(http://festivalmusicamedinaceli.blogspot.com.
es) On Saturdays and/or Sundays in July,
the Colegiata de Santa María (Plaza de
la Iglesia; by donation; ⊗11am-2pm & 4-8pm
Tue-Sun Jul & Aug, 11am-2pm & 4-6pm Sat & Sun
Sep-Nov & Easter-Jun, closed Dec-Easter) hosts
mostly classical concerts by international
performers.

Festival Ópera Medinaceli   MUSIC
(☑913 08 46 35) In the last week of July and
the first couple of weeks in August, Medinaceli's Palacio Ducal (p201) hosts fine op-
eratic performances.

⌂ Sleeping

★ **Medina Salim**   BOUTIQUE HOTEL €€
(☑975 32 69 74; www.hotelmedinasalim.com; Calle
Barranco 15; s/d incl breakfast €60/80; [P][❄][🛜])
A welcoming boutique hotel which sports
large, airy rooms with fridges and terraces
that overlook either the sweeping valley or
medieval cobblestones out front. Decor is
contemporary and light, with pale woodwork and excellent bathrooms. Perks include a small spa and a delightful breakfast
room that overlooks part of the original
Roman wall, where staff serve Medinaceli's
best breakfast.

La Ceramica   HOTEL €€
(☑975 32 63 81; www.laceramicacasarural.es; Calle
de Santa Isabel 2; s/d/tr incl breakfast €45/65/89,
d incl breakfast & dinner €83; ⊗Feb–mid-Dec; 🛜)
Located in the centre of the historic quarter,
the rooms here are intimate and comfortable, with a strong dose of rustic charm. The
attic room 22 is lovely, and the CR2 apartment, which sleeps four, feels just like home.
At certain times there is a two-night minimum stay.

✕ Eating

Asador de la Villa El Granero   CASTILIAN €€
(☑975 32 61 89; www.asadorelgranero.es; Calle
de Yedra 10; mains €13-20; ⊗1.30-4pm &
9-11pm May-Oct, shorter hours rest of year) This
well-signposted place, with a shop selling
local food products at the front, is thought
by many to be Medinaceli's best restaurant.
The *setas de campo* (wild mushrooms) are
something of a local speciality, thought unsurprisingly grilled and roasted meats dominate this bastion of hearty Castilian cooking.
Book ahead on summer weekends.

WORTH A TRIP

SANTA MARÍA DE LA HUERTA

Wonderful Cistercian monastery Santa
María de la Huerta (www.monasterio
huerta.org; €3; ⊗10am-1pm & 4-6pm
Mon-Sat, 10-11.15am & 4-6.30pm Sun) was
founded in 1162, expropriated in 1835,
then restored to the order in 1930; 20
Cistercians are now in residence. Before entering the monastery, note the
church's impressive 12th-century facade, with its magnificent rose window.
Inside the monastery, the Claustro de
los Caballeros is the more beautiful of
the two cloisters. Off it is the spare yet
gorgeous *refectorio* (dining hall); built
in the 13th century, it's notable for the
absence of columns to support its vault.

El Aljibe   SPANISH €€
(☑975 32 61 38; www.elaljibe.es; Calle Campo de
San Nicolás 11; mains €11-17; ⊗1-4pm & 9-11pm)
El Aljibe varies a little from the Medinaceli
norm with a bright, contemporary dining
area and occasional subtle twists on traditional dishes – we especially enjoyed the
secreto ibérico con miel y mostaza (Iberian
pork steak with honey and mustard). The
*potaje de garbanzos con bacalao y espin-
acas* (chickpea stew with cod and spinach)
is fantastic on a cold winter's day.

La Ceramica   SPANISH €€
(☑975 32 63 81; www.laceramicacasarural.es;
Calle de Santa Isabel 2; mains €9-18, set menus €15-24; ⊗1-3.30pm & 9-11pm, closed mid-
Dec–Jan) An intimate yet informal dining
experience, La Ceramics serves excellent
local specialities such as *migas del pastor*
(shepherd's breadcrumbs) or *ensalada de
codorniz* (quail salad), as well as the usual
meats.

ℹ Information

Tourist Office (☑975 32 63 47; www.medina
celi.es; Calle Campo de San Nicolás; ⊗10am-
2pm & 4-7pm Wed-Sun) Excellent tourist office
at the entrance to town, just around the corner
from the arch.

ℹ Getting There & Away

ALSA (www.alsa.es) runs up to four daily buses
to/from Soria (€5.54, 45 minutes) or Madrid
(€10.79, 1¾ hours) from the *ayuntamiento* in
the new town. There's no transport between the
old and new towns, and it's a steep hike.

Toledo & Castilla-La Mancha

Best Places to Eat

→ Figón del Huécar (p226)

→ Adolfo (p213)

→ Nöla (p230)

→ Calle Mayor (p229)

→ El Bodegón (p226)

Best Places to Sleep

→ La Casa del Rector (p221)

→ Antiguo Palacio de Atienza (p231)

→ La Vida de Antes (p218)

→ Hacienda del Cardenal (p211)

→ Casa Rural Tia Pilar de Almagro (p220)

Why Go?

The nation's third-largest region is also one of its quietest. Castilla-La Mancha not only has Spain's lowest population density, but it sees fewer tourists than any region outside Navarra. Located on a windswept but fertile plateau known as La Meseta, this is the land where Cervantes set the fictional journeys of Don Quijote. Reminders of the so-called 'ingenious gentleman of La Mancha' and his escapades resonate everywhere. With the tome under your arm, you can plan your own unhurried, hopefully less quixotic adventures amid old-fashioned windmills, Crusader-era castles, expansive vineyards and enough Quijote museums, statues and plazas to fill a small guidebook.

Elsewhere, the dramatic river gorges that slice sporadically through the Meseta have provided strategic sites for ancient cities. Toledo and Cuenca both offer spectacular history lessons amid winding narrow lanes, multifaith religious monuments and weighty art.

When to Go
Toledo

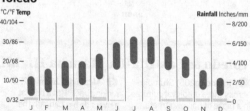

Mar & Apr See Cuenca's spine-tingling and atmospheric Semana Santa parades.

Apr & May Enjoy the countryside's colourful dazzle of wildflowers against a lush green landscape.

Sep & Oct Hike across Castilla-La Mancha's natural parks and picturesque villages.

Toledo & Castilla-La Mancha Highlights

1 Toledo (p205) Stumble across three medieval cultures in a maze of narrow streets.

2 Atienza (p230) Hiking into the hilltop-hugging medieval town of Atienza on a southern branch of the Camino de Santiago.

3 Consuegra (p215) Taking *the* Don Quijote shot of the windmills of Consuegra.

4 Alcalá del Júcar (p222) Kicking back with a beer at a riverside bar beneath the cascade of houses and a castle.

5 Museo de Arte Abstracto Español (p223) Visiting this recently upgraded museum in one of the extraordinary hanging houses of Cuenca.

6 Almagro (p220) Marvelling at the handsome plaza and historic theatre in this enticing town.

7 Oropesa (p215) **or Alarcón** (p228) Being king or queen of the castle, quite literally, by staying in a *parador*.

8 Sigüenza (p228) Checking out the chunky cathedral, hilltop castle and restaurants in the under-appreciated town of Sigüenza.

TOLEDO

POP 85,593 / ELEV 655M

In a world where religion continues to act as a divisive force, Toledo is a refreshing throwback. Dramatically sited atop a gorge overlooking the Río Tajo, it was known as the 'city of three cultures' in the Middle Ages, a place where – legend has it – Christian, Muslim and Jewish communities peacefully coexisted. Rediscovering the vestiges of this unique cultural synthesis remains modern Toledo's most compelling attraction. Horseshoe-arched mosques, Sephardic synagogues and one of Spain's finest Gothic cathedrals cram into its dense historical core. But the layers go much deeper. Further sleuthing will reveal Visigothic and Roman roots. Toledo's other forte is art, in particular the haunting canvases of El Greco, the influential, impossible-to-classify painter with whom the city is synonymous.

History

Already an important pre-Roman settlement, Toledo was eventually chosen as the capital of the post-Roman Visigothic kingdom. After being taken by the Moors in AD 711, the city rapidly grew to become the capital of an independent Arab *taifa* (small kingdom) and *the* centre of learning and arts in Spain.

Alfonso VI marched into Toledo in 1085 and, shortly thereafter, the Vatican recognised Toledo as a seat of the Spanish Church. Initially, Toledo's Christians, Jews and Muslims coexisted tolerably well. However, the eventual convert-or-get-out dictates issued to the Jews and Muslims stripped this multifaith city of the backbone of its social and economic life. Once Felipe II chose Madrid as his capital in the mid-16th century, Toledo went into decline, although its religious power within the Catholic Church remains undimmed.

Sights

★ **Catedral**   CATHEDRAL
(www.catedralprimada.es; Plaza del Ayuntamiento; adult/child €11/free; ⊙10am-6pm Mon-Sat, 2-6pm Sun) Toledo's illustrious main church ranks among the top 10 cathedrals in Spain. An impressive example of medieval Gothic architecture, its humongous interior is full of the classic characteristics of the style, rose windows, flying buttresses, ribbed vaults and pointed arches among them. Equally visitworthy is the art. The cathedral's sacristy is a veritable art gallery of old masters, with works by Velázquez, Goya and – of course – El Greco.

From the earliest days of the Visigothic occupation, the current site of the cathedral has been a centre of worship. During Muslim rule, it contained Toledo's central mosque, converted into a church in 1085, but ultimately destroyed 140 years later. Dating from the 1220s and essentially a Gothic structure, the cathedral was rebuilt from scratch in a melting pot of styles, including Mudéjar and Renaissance. The Visigothic influence continues today in the unique celebration of the Mozarabic Rite, a 6th-century liturgy that was allowed to endure after Cardinal Cisneros put its legitimacy to the test by burning missals in a fire of faith; they survived more or less intact. The rite is celebrated in the Capilla Mozarabe at 9am Monday to Saturday, and at 9.45am on Sundays.

The high altar sits in the extravagant Capilla Mayor, the masterpiece of which is the *retablo* (altarpiece), with painted wooden sculptures depicting scenes from the lives of Christ and the Virgin Mary; it's flanked by royal tombs. The oldest of the cathedral's magnificent stained-glass pieces is the rose window above the Puerta del Reloj. Behind the main altar lies a mesmerising piece of 18th-century churrigueresque (lavish baroque ornamentation), the Transparente, which is illuminated by a light well carved into the dome above.

In the centre of things, the coro (choir stall) is a feast of sculpture and carved

TOLEDO & CASTILLA-LA MANCHA TOLEDO

ⓘ PULSERA TURÍSTICA

The Pulsera Turística is a bracelet (€8) that gets you into six key Toledo sights (no time limit), all of which cost €2.50 on their own. Buy the bracelet at any of the sights covered, which are Monasterio San Juan de los Reyes (p207), Sinagoga de Santa María La Blanca (p210), Iglesia de Santo Tomé (p209), Iglesia del Salvador (Plaza del Salvador; €2.50; ⊙10am-6.45pm Sat-Thu, 10am-2.45 & 4-6.45pm Fri), Iglesia San Ildefonso (Iglesia de los Jesuitas; Plaza Juan de Mariana 1; admission €2.50; ⊙10am-6.45pm Apr-Sep, to 5.45pm Oct-Mar) and the Mezquita del Cristo de la Luz (p210).

wooden stalls. The 15th-century lower tier depicts the various stages of the conquest of Granada.

The tesoro, however, deals in treasure of the glittery kind. It's dominated by the extraordinary Custodia de Arfe: with 18kg of pure gold and 183kg of silver, this 16th-century processional monstrance bristles with some 260 statuettes. Its big day out is the Feast of Corpus Christi, when it is paraded around Toledo's streets.

Other noteworthy features include the sober cloister, off which is the 14th-century Capilla de San Blas, with Gothic tombs and stunning frescos; the gilded Capilla de Reyes Nuevos; and the sala capitular (chapter house), with its remarkable 500-year-old artesonado (wooden Mudéjar ceiling) and portraits of all the archbishops of Toledo.

The highlight of all, however, is the sacristía (sacristy), which contains a gallery with paintings by such masters as El Greco, Zurbarán, Caravaggio, Titian, Raphael and Velázquez. It can be difficult to appreciate the packed-together, poorly lit artworks, but it's a stunning assemblage in a small space. In an adjacent chamber, don't miss the spectacular Moorish standard captured in the Battle of Salado in 1340.

An extra €3 gets you entrance to the upper level of the cloister, and the bell tower, which offers wonderful views over the centre of historic Toledo.

★ Alcázar   FORTRESS, MUSEUM
(Museo del Ejército; Calle Alféreces Provisionales; adult/child €5/free, Sun free; ⊙10am-5pm Thu-Tue) At the highest point in the city looms the foreboding Alcázar. Rebuilt under Franco, it has been reopened as a vast military

EL GRECO IN TOLEDO

Of all Spain's old masters, El Greco is the most instantly recognizable. You don't need a degree in art history to be able to identify the talented Greek's distinctive religious canvases characterised by gaunt figures dressed in stark, vivid colours. Spread liberally around the museums and churches of Toledo, they practically jump out at you.

Born Doménikos Theotokópoulos in Crete in 1541, El Greco will always be intrinsically linked with Toledo, where he arrived as a bolshie 36-year-old in 1577. Never one to court popularity, the artist had already sparked controversy during a tempestuous apprenticeship in Italy where he had criticised the work of Michelangelo. His arrival in Spain proved to be equally thorny. Hindered by a thinly veiled arrogance and adhering to what were unconventional painting methods for the time (though 'revolutionary' by modern yardsticks), El Greco failed in his early attempts to ingratiate himself to the court of King Philip II. Gravitating instead to Toledo, he found an improbable artistic refuge where he worked to refine his style and establish his reputation.

Despite earning a degree of respectability during his lifetime, El Greco was largely ignored in the years following his death. Indeed, his prophetic work wasn't seriously reappraised until the early 20th century, when he was embraced by artists such as Picasso whose murky 'blue period' echoed the melancholy of some of El Greco's early compositions.

Outside Madrid's Museo del Prado, Toledo protects El Greco's greatest work. The Iglesia de Santo Tomé (p209) contains his magnum opus El entierro del Conde de Orgaz (The Burial of the Count of Orgaz), depicting the count's burial in 1322, with St Augustine and St Stephen descending from heaven to attend the funeral. Look out for El Greco himself and Cervantes among the guests. The nearby Museo del Greco also has a solid collection of El Greco's works.

One of the oldest convents in Toledo, the 11th-century Convento de Santo Domingo El Antiguo (🕿925 22 29 30; Plaza de Santo Domingo el Antiguo; admission €2.50; ⊙11am-1.30pm & 4-7pm Mon-Sat, 4-7pm Sun) includes some of El Greco's early commissions, other copies and signed contracts of the artist. Visible through a hole in the floor is the crypt and wooden coffin of the painter himself.

Other spots in Toledo where you can contemplate El Greco's works include the Museo de Santa Cruz, the sacristía (sacristy) in the Catedral (p205) and the Hospital de Tavera (Duque de Lerma 2; courtyard & chapel/full ticket €4/6; ⊙10am-2.30pm & 3-6.30pm Mon-Sat, 10am-2.30pm Sun).

museum. The usual displays of uniforms and medals are here, but the best part is the exhaustive historical section, with an in-depth overview of the nation's history in Spanish and English.

Abd ar-Rahman III raised an *al-qasr* (fortress) here in the 10th century, which was thereafter altered by the Christians. Alonso Covarrubias rebuilt it as a royal residence for Carlos I, but the court moved to Madrid and the fortress eventually became a military academy. The Alcázar was heavily damaged during the siege of the garrison by loyalist militias at the start of the civil war in 1936. The soldiers' dogged resistance, and the famous refusal of their commander, Moscardó, to give it up in exchange for his son's life, made the Alcázar a powerful nationalist symbol.

The exhibition is epic in scale and by the time you get to the end of the 19th century your feet will be begging for mercy, but like a well-run marathon, it's worth the physical (and mental) investment. The most macabre sight is the recreation of Moscardó's office wrecked with bullet holes; other highlights include the monumental central patio decorated with Habsburg coats of arms, and archaeological remains from Moorish times near the entrance.

★ Sinagoga
del Tránsito   SYNAGOGUE, MUSEUM
(☑925 22 36 65; http://museosefardi.mcu.es; Calle Samuel Leví; adult/child €3/1.50, after 2pm Sat & all day Sun free; ☉9.30am-7.30pm Tue-Sat Mar-Oct, 9.30am-6pm Tue-Sat Nov-Feb, 10am-3pm Sun year-round) This magnificent synagogue was built in 1355 by special permission from Pedro I. The synagogue now houses the Museo Sefardí. The vast main prayer hall has been expertly restored and the Mudéjar decoration and intricately carved pine ceiling are striking. Exhibits provide an insight into the history of Jewish culture in Spain, and include archaeological finds, a memorial garden, costumes and ceremonial artefacts.

Toledo's former *judería* (Jewish quarter) was once home to 10 synagogues and comprised some 10% of the walled city's area. After the expulsion of the Jews from Spain in 1492, the synagogue was variously used as a priory, hermitage and military barracks.

Museo de Santa Cruz   MUSEUM
(Calle de Cervantes 3; adult/child €5/free; ☉9.45am-6.15pm Mon-Sat, 10am-2.30pm Sun) It's

hard to imagine that this 16th-century building was once a hospital. If only modern hospitals were equipped with the kind of ornate plateresque portico that welcomes you to this beautiful arts and ceramics museum. The pièce de résistance is the huge ground-floor gallery laid out in the shape of a cross. The various art and sculpture exhibits are backed up by interesting explanatory boards that place all the pieces into historical context.

Sitting at one end, almost as if it were an altarpiece, is El Greco's *Sagrada Familia con Santa Ana*.

Equally salubrious is the cloister, which you must cross to access the extensive ceramics collection housed on the first floor.

Museo del Greco   MUSEUM, GALLERY
(☑925 22 44 05; http://museodelgreco.mcu.es; Paseo del Tránsito; adult/child €3/1.50, after 2pm Sat & all day Sun free; ☉9.30am-7.30pm Tue-Sat Mar-Oct, to 6pm Nov-Feb, 10am-3pm Sun) In the early 20th century, an aristocrat bought what he thought was El Greco's house and did a meritorious job of returning it to period style. He was wrong – El Greco never lived here – but the museum remains. As well as the house itself, with its lovely patio and informative details on the painter's life, there are excavated cellars from a Jewish-quarter palace and a good selection of paintings, including a Zurbarán, a set of the apostles by El Greco and works by his son and followers.

Mirador del Valle   VIEWPOINT
To get the ultimate photo of Toledo you need to cross the Río Tajo and climb the road on the other side to this strategic viewpoint. You can either walk up from the Puente Nuevo de Alcántara (there's pavement all the way), or catch the Trainvision from Plaza de Zocodover. The view is not dissimilar to the one depicted by El Greco in his famous landscape, *Vista de Toledo* (1596–1600).

Monasterio San Juan
de los Reyes   MONASTERY
(www.sanjuandelosreyes.org; Calle San Juan de los Reyes 2; €2.50; ☉10am-6.30pm Jun-Sep, 10am-5.30pm Oct-May) This imposing 15th-century Franciscan monastery and church was provocatively founded in the heart of the Jewish quarter by the Catholic monarchs Isabel and Fernando to demonstrate the supremacy of their faith. The rulers had planned to be buried here but eventually ended up in their prize conquest, Granada. The highlight is the amazing two-level cloister,

Toledo

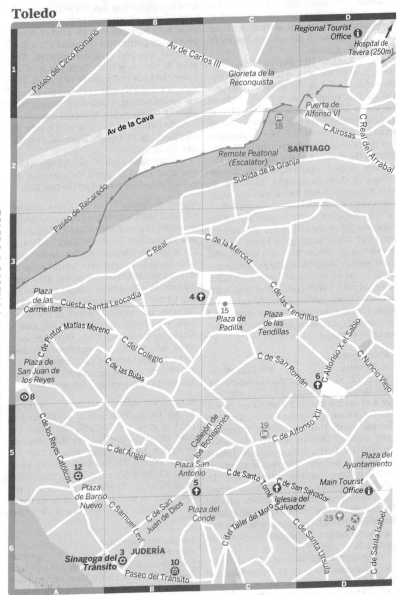

a harmonious fusion of late ('flamboyant') Gothic downstairs and Mudéjar architecture upstairs, with superb statuary, arches, vaulting, elaborate pinnacles and gargoyles surrounding a lush garden with orange trees and roses.

The adjacent church has a series of enormous coats of arms of the Catholic monarchs, who were never shy about self-publicising. Outside, note the chains dangling from the northeastern facade – they once belonged to

Map labels:

0   200 m
0   0.1 miles

(1.5km)
(150m)
Plaza del Solar
C de Azacanes
Puerta del Sol
C de Gerardo Lobo
Paseo del Miradero
Albergue San Servando (300m);
(600m)
Puente de Alcántara
Río Tajo
C del Cristo de la Luz
C Núñez de Arce
C de Recoletos
C de las Armas
7
28
C de la Sillería
Plaza San Agustín
Tourist Office
14
C de Santa Fe
9
C de los Alfileritos
23
Plaza de San Nicolás
C Nueva
Plaza de Zocodover
11
31
Arco de la Sangre
C de Cervantes
17
21
C de las Cadenas
C de Comercio
C de la Plata
Alféreces Provisionales
1
Alcázar
C Cordonerías
C Barrio Rey
Plaza de Magdalena
25
Alcázar
Puente Nuevo de Alcántara
C de la Sinagoga
26
C Juan Labrador
Cuesta de Carlos V
Mirador del Valle (1km);
La Ermita (1.2km);
Parador Conde de Orgaz (1.8km)
22
30
Plaza Mayor
C de General Moscardó
Catedral
2
C de Sixto Ramón Parro
13
C Pascuales
C del Cardenal Cisneros
16
20
C Locum
27
Plaza San Justo
Cuesta de San Justo
LA CANDELARIA
C de Ave María
Callejón de San Pedro
Plaza del Colegio de Infantes
Cuesta del Can
Río Tajo

Christian prisoners liberated from Muslim Granada.

Iglesia de Santo Tomé   CHURCH
(www.santotome.org; Plaza del Conde; €2.50; ⊙10am-6.45pm mid-Mar–mid-Oct, 10am-5.45pm mid-Oct–mid-Mar) Iglesia de Santo Tomé contains El Greco's most famous masterpiece *El entierro del conde de Orgaz* (The Burial of the Count of Orgaz), which is accessed by a separate entrance on Plaza del Conde. When the count was buried in 1322, Sts Augustine

Toledo

and Stephen supposedly descended from heaven to attend the funeral. El Greco's work depicts the event, complete with miracle guests including himself, his son and Cervantes.

Mezquita del Cristo de la Luz   MOSQUE
(Calle del Cristo de la Luz; €2.50; ⊙10am-2pm & 3.30-5.45pm Mon-Fri, 10am-5.45pm Sat & Sun) On the northern slopes of town you'll find a modest, yet beautiful, mosque (the only one remaining of ten that used to stand in Toledo) where architectural traces of medieval Muslim conquerors are still in evidence. Built around AD 1000, it suffered the usual fate of being converted into a church (hence the religious frescos), but the most of the original vaulting and arches survived.

Sinagoga de Santa María La Blanca   SYNAGOGUE
(Calle de los Reyes Católicos 4; €2.50; ⊙10am-6.45pm Jun-Sep, to 5.45pm Oct-May) The lesser of Toledo's two Mudéjar synagogues has five naves divided by rows of horseshoe and multifoil arches. Originally the upper arches opened onto the rooms where women worshipped; while the men were down below. You can admire the stucco work and ornate capitals gleaming after a recent restoration.

Activities

★ **Senda Ecológica**   WALKING
This remarkably varied walking path tracks the Río Tajo through a steep-sided gorge where you'll feel as if you've left the city far behind (although urban life reverberates only metres above you). It stretches between the Azarquiel and San Martín bridges and contains some relatively wild stretches where a wooden walkway has been stapled to the rockface.

Fly Toledo   ADVENTURE SPORTS
(📞693 46 48 45; www.flytoledo.com; Puente de San Martín 2; 1 jump €10; ⊙10.30am-6.30pm) Heavy museum legs sometimes need to relieve themselves and this bracing high-wire act that catapults vertigo-shunners across the Río Tajo gorge via the longest urban *tirolina* (zip-line) in Europe might just do the trick. The ride begins and ends close to the San Martín bridge on the western side of town.

Courses

Universidad de Castilla-La Mancha   LANGUAGE COURSE
(www.uclm.es/fundacion/esto; Plaza de Padilla) The University of Castilla-La Mancha runs an ESTO (Spanish in Toledo) program with various language courses. Visit its website for more details.

🎉 Festivals & Events

Corpus Christi
RELIGIOUS

This is one of the finest Corpus Christi celebrations in Spain, taking place on the Thursday 60 days after Easter Sunday. Several days of festivities reach a crescendo with a procession featuring the massive Custodia de Arfe.

Virgen del Sagrario
CULTURAL

Taking place on 15 August (Assumption Day), this is when you can drink of the cathedral's well water, believed to have miraculous qualities – the queues for a swig from an earthenware *botijo* (jug) can be equally astonishing. It's also the city's main fiesta, with plenty of partying guaranteed.

🛏️ Sleeping

Oasis Backpackers Hostel
HOSTEL €

(☎ 925 22 76 50; www.hostelsoasis.com; Calle Cadenas 5; dm/d €14/34; @ 🖥️) One of four Oasis hostels in Spain, this relatively new affair sparkles with what have become the chain's glowing hallmarks: laid-back but refreshingly well-organised service and an atmosphere that is fun without ever being loud or obnoxious. There are private rooms if you're not up for a dorm-share, and lots of free information on city attractions.

Hostal Alfonso XII
HOSTEL €

(☎ 925 25 25 09; www.hostal-alfonso12.com; Calle de Alfonso XII; s €32-55, d €42-55; ❋ 🖥️) In a great location in the *judería,* this quality *hostal* (budget hotel) occupies an 18th-century Toledo house, meaning there's twisty passages and stairs, and compact rooms in curious places. It's got plenty of charm.

Albergue San Servando
HOSTEL €

(☎ 925 22 45 58; www.reaj.com; Subida del Castillo; dm under/over 30 €14/17; ❋ @ 🖥️ 🏊) Occupying digs normally reserved for *paradores* (luxurious state-owned hotels) is this unusual youth hostel encased in a 14th-century castle built by the Knights Templar, no less. Dorms have either two single beds or two double bunks, and there's a cafeteria serving meals as well as a summer pool. If you're not an HI member, you'll need to buy a card here.

La Posada de Manolo
BOUTIQUE HOTEL €

(☎ 925 28 22 50; www.laposadademanolo.com; Calle de Sixto Ramón Parro 8; s/d from €44/55; ❋ 🖥️) This memorable hotel has themed each floor with furnishings and decor reflecting one of the three cultures of Toledo: Christian, Islamic and Jewish. There are stunning views of the old town and cathedral from the terrace.

⭐Hacienda del Cardenal
HISTORIC HOTEL €€

(☎ 925 22 49 00; www.hostaldelcardenal.com; Paseo de Recaredo 24; r incl breakfast €70-120; ❋ 🖥️) This wonderful 18th-century mansion has soft ochre-coloured walls, arches and columns. Some rooms are grand, while others are spartan, and all come with dark furniture, plush fabrics and parquet floors. Several rooms overlook the glorious terraced gardens.

Casa de los Mozárabes
APARTMENT €€

(☎ 925 21 17 01; www.casadelosmozarabes.com; Callejón de Menores 10; apt €90-155; ❋ 🖥️) Occupying a historical Toledo house on a quiet central lane, these excellent apartments have modern furnishings that combine

---

TOLEDO TOURS

Various companies offer guided (and usually themed) walking tours around the town. Themes include Three Cultures (Muslim, Christian and Jewish) and El Greco. There are also night tours based around local legends.

Rutas de Toledo (☎ 630 70 93 38; www.rutasdetoledo.es; Calle de Sixto Ramón Parro 9; per person €5-12) A good mix of standard tours (El Greco, Sefardi) with more creative night tours, including some with actors in traditional dress.

Toledo Tres Culturas (☎ 603 42 08 20; www.toledo3culturas.com; per person €10-15) A range of day and night tours lasting from 1½ to two hours.

Toledo City Tour (adult single/day €5.50/9, child €2.75/4.50) Open-top bus tour that circles the city with some fabulous panoramic views. Unusually, there's a hop-on, hop-off or single-trip option.

Toledo Cultura y Vino (www.toledoculturayvino.com; per person €12-20) Tours focused on El Greco and the city's Sefardi Jewish culture.

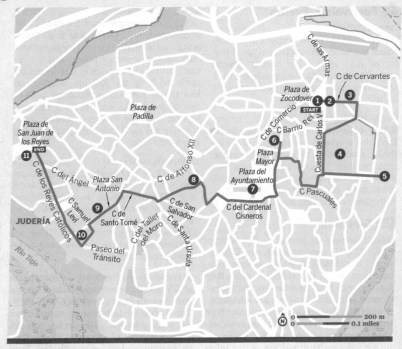

City Walk
A Stroll Through History

START PLAZA DE ZOCODOVER
END MONASTERIO SAN JUAN DE LOS REYES
LENGTH 2KM, 1½–2½ HOURS

Start off in central ❶ **Plaza de Zocodover**, for centuries the city's marketplace and scene for bullfights and Inquisition-led burnings at the stake, then pass through the ❷ **Arco de la Sangre** on the eastern side of the square to admire the facade of the ❸ **Museo de Santa Cruz** (p207). Up the hill to the south is Toledo's signature ❹ **Alcázar** (p206), beyond which (follow Cuesta de Carlos V along the west wall of the Alcázar and then turn left to walk down Calle de General Moscardó) there are some fine ❺ **views over the Río Tajo**. As the Alcázar's commanding position and sweeping views attest, Toledo was perfectly sited for medieval defences.

Follow the spires down the hill to the west, passing the remnants of a mosque, ❻ **Mezquita de las Tornerías**, before reaching the ❼ **Catedral** (p205), the spiritual home of Catholic Spain. Twist your way northwest to the ❽ **Centro Cultural San Marcos**. Housed in the 17th-century San Marcos church, its the original domed roof, complete with ceiling frescos, creates an evocative gallery space for temporary art exhibitions.

Down the hill you enter the heart of Toledo's old Jewish quarter. Admire the swords in the shops along ❾ **Calle de San Juan de Dios** and head past the ❿ **Sinagoga del Tránsito** (p207) to admire further cliff-top views over the river. The synagogue takes on a special poignancy if you continue along Calle de los Reyes Católicos to the splendid ⓫ **Monasterio San Juan de los Reyes** (p207). Spain's Catholic rulers hoped this church would represent the ultimate triumph of their religion over others. This is a fine spot to end your walk, but you could drop down from here to the riverside pathway that will take you on a half-circuit of the old town back to near your starting point (an additional 2km).

well with the exposed brick and original features of the building. There's a common lounge area with a pool table and a few weights.

Casa de Cisneros
BOUTIQUE HOTEL €€

(📞925 22 88 28; www.hospederiacasadecisneros. com; 12 Calle del Cardenal Cisneros; s/d €40/66; ❄️📶) Right by the cathedral, this lovely 16th-century house was once the home of the cardinal and Grand Inquisitor Cisneros (often known as Ximénes). It's a top choice, with cosy, seductive rooms with original wooden beams and walls, and voguish bathrooms. Archaeological works have revealed the remains of Roman baths and part of an 11th-century Moorish palace in the basement.

⭐Parador Conde de Orgaz
HOTEL €€€

(📞925 22 18 50; www.parador.es; Cerro del Emperador; r €105-207; 🅿️❄️📶🏊) High above the southern bank of Río Tajo, Toledo's low-rise *parador* has a classy interior and sublime-at-sunset city views. The *parador* is well signposted: turn right just after crossing the bridge northeast of the old centre. You'll need a car or be prepared to pay for a taxi.

🍴 Eating & Drinking

Alqahira Rincón de Oriente
MIDDLE EASTERN €

(📞925 67 32 60; Calle de la Ciudad 7B; dishes €8-10; 🕐12.30-4.30pm & 7.30-11.30pm Thu-Tue) Befitting the so-called 'city of three cultures', the Alqahira taps into Toledo's Moorish side. Its shadowy interior furnished with flowing drapes and silver teapots is reminiscent of one of Granada's famous *teterías* (teahouses), while its short, simple menu plugs tasty morsels of felafel and baklava. Service from the Egyptian-Moroccan staff is megacourteous and the atmosphere is suitably exotic.

There's no alcohol served.

Bar Ludena
SPANISH €

(Plaza de Magdalena 10; raciones €2-12; 🕐10.30am-4.30pm & 8-11.30pm) Despite its central location close to Toledo's main tourist thoroughfare, Ludena retains a wholesome local image courtesy of the flock of regulars who – despite tourist infiltration – still frequent it. Join them as they prop up the bar with a *caña* (beer) and a plate of the Toledano speciality, *carcamusa* (pork and vegetable stew).

> ## MARZIPAN
>
> Not a marzipan fan? Think again. You probably won't have tasted it so good anywhere else. Toledo is famed for this wonderful almond-based confectionery, which every shop seems to sell. The Santo Tomé marzipan brand is highly regarded and there are several outlets in town, including one on Plaza de Zocodover (p214). Even the local nuns get in on the marzipan act; most of the convents sell the sweets.

Alfileritos 24
MODERN SPANISH €€

(www.alfileritos24.com; Calle de los Alfileritos 24; mains €19-20, bar food €4.50-12; 🕐9.30am-midnight Sun-Thu, to 1am Fri & Sat) The 14th-century surroundings of columns, beams and barrel-vault ceilings are snazzily coupled with modern artwork and bright dining rooms in an atrium space spread over four floors. The menu demonstrates an innovative flourish in the kitchen, with dishes such as green rice with quail or loins of venison with baked-in-the-bag Reineta apple.

La Abadía
CASTILIAN, TAPAS €€

(www.abadiatoledo.com; Plaza de San Nicolás 3; raciónes €4-15; 🕐bar 8am-midnight, restaurant 1-4pm & 8.30pm-midnight) In a former 16th-century palace, this atmospheric bar and restaurant has arches, niches and coloured bottles lined up as decoration, spread throughout a warren of brick-and-stone-clad rooms. The menu includes lightweight dishes and tapas, but the 'Menú de Montes de Toledo' (€19) is a fabulous collection of tastes from the nearby mountains.

⭐Adolfo
MODERN EUROPEAN €€€

(📞925 22 73 21; Callejón Hombre de Palo 7; mains €25-28; 🕐1-4pm & 8pm-midnight Mon-Sat, 1-4pm Sun) Toledo doffs its hat to fine dining at this temple of good food and market freshness. Run by notable La Mancha–born chef Adolfo Muñoz, the restaurant has been around for over 25 years, and in that time has morphed into one of Spain's best gourmet establishments. The king of Spain – no less – has sung the praises of Adolfo's partridge.

Hostal del Cardenal
SPANISH €€€

(📞925 22 49 00; www.hostaldelcardenal.com; Paseo de Recaredo 24; mains €18-25; 🕐1-4pm & 8-11pm) This hotel restaurant enjoys one of Toledo's most magical locations for dining alfresco: it's tucked into a private garden entered via its own gate in the city walls. The food is classic Spanish, with roast meats – suckling pig and lamb are the best dishes on show here – to the fore. It's a bit touristy, but the location is unforgettable on a warm summer's night.

Casa Aurelio SPANISH €€€
(☑ 925 22 41 05; www.casa-aurelio.com; Calle de la Sinagoga 6; mains €18-22; ☺ 1-4.30pm & 8-11.30pm Tue-Sat, 1-4.30pm Mon) Purporting to be Toledo's oldest restaurant, Casa Aurelio has been around since 1953 and still ranks among the best of Toledo's traditional eateries. Game, fresh produce and time-honoured dishes are prepared with panache. There's another branch (Plaza del Ayuntamiento; mains €8-16; ☺ 9:30am-6pm Mon, Wed & Sun, 10:30am-6pm & 8pm-midnight Fri & Sat) near the cathedral.

★ **Libro Taberna**
El Internacional BAR, CAFE
(Ciudad 15; ☺ 8pm-1.30am Tue-Thu, noon-1.30am Fri & Sat, noon-4pm Sun) 🍴 If you think Toledo is more touristy than trendy, you clearly haven't dipped your hipster detector into the cool confines of El Internacional, a proud purveyor of slow food, spray-painted tables, rescued 1970s armchairs, and beards.

🛍 Shopping

Casa Cuatero FOOD, DRINK
(☑ 925 22 26 14; www.casacuartero.com; Calle Hombre de Palo 5; ☺ 10am-2pm & 5-8pm Mon-Fri, 10am-3pm & 4-8pm Sat) Just north of the cathedral, this fabulous food shop (here since 1920) sells marzipan, cured meats, wines, cheeses and all manner of local delicacies from around Castilla-La Mancha. It's ideal for gifts to take back home or to stock up for a picnic.

Santo Tomé FOOD
(☑ 925 22 11 68; www.mazapan.com; Plaza de Zocodover 7; ☺ 9am-10pm) Pick up some of Toledo's famed marzipan (almond-based confectionery) at this outlet of the highly regarded local brand.

🛈 Information

Main Tourist Office (☑ 925 25 40 30; www.toledo-turismo.com; Plaza Consistorio; ☺ 10am-6pm) Within sight of the cathedral. There's another office (☺ 10am-7pm) in Plaza de Zocodover and one at the train station (Estación de Renfe; ☺ 9.30am-3pm).

🛈 TAKE THE ESCALATOR

A remonte peatonal (series of escalators; ☺ 7am-11pm Mon-Fri, 8am-2am Sat, 8am-10pm Sun) starting near the Puerta de Alfonso VI and ending near the Monasterio de Santo Domingo El Antiguo, is a good way to avoid the steep uphill climb to reach the historic quarter of town.

Regional Tourist Office (☑ 925 22 08 43; Puerta de Bisagra; ☺ 10am-2pm & 3-7pm Mon-Fri, 10am-3pm & 4-6pm Sat, 10am-3pm Sun) North of the old town.

🛈 Getting There & Away

To get to most major destinations, you'll need to backtrack to Madrid.

From Toledo's **bus station** (Avenida de Castilla La Mancha), buses depart for Madrid's Plaza Elíptica roughly every half-hour (from €5.42, one hour to 1¾ hours); some direct, some via villages. There are also daily services to Cuenca (€14.20, 3¼ hours).

From the pretty **train station** (☑ 902 24 02 02; Paseo de la Rosa), high-speed Alta Velocidad Española (AVE) trains run every hour or so to Madrid (€12.90, 30 minutes).

🛈 Getting Around

Buses (€1.50) run between Plaza de Zocodover and the bus station (bus 5) and train station (buses 61 and 62).

The **Trainvision** (adult/child €4.40/1.50; ☺ 10am-8.30pm Sun-Fri, to 10pm Sat) trolleybus runs around the main monuments and up to the Mirador del Valle. It leaves from Plaza Zocodover every 30 minutes.

Driving in the old town is a nightmare. There are several underground car parks throughout the area. Zones blocked off by bollards can be accessed if you have a hotel reservation. At the base of the old town are several large free car parks.

THE WEST

Talavera de la Reina

POP 88,548

Talavera de la Reina, long famous worldwide for its eponymous ceramics, has a laid-back appeal. The finest example of its many tiled buildings is the Basílica de Nuestra

Señora del Prado (Jardines del Prado), sometimes dubbed the 'Sistine chapel of ceramics' for its intricate tilework: the church is gracefully adorned with the city's finest *azulejos* (tiles), many of them painted with religious themes.

Within the old city walls is **Museo Ruiz de Luna** (Pl de San Agustín; admission €3; ⊙9am-3pm Tue-Fri, 10am-2pm & 4-7pm Sat, 10am-2pm Sun), housing local ceramics dating from the 16th to 20th centuries in a handsome brick monastery. To buy contemporary ceramics, there's the **Cerámica San Agustín** (☑925 80 89 16; www.ceramicasanagustin.es; Puerta del Río 9; ⊙9am-2pm & 4-8.30pm Mon-Fri, 9am-2pm Sat) nearby, or you can check out the factories and shops along the road leading west to the A5 motorway.

❶ Information

Tourist Office (☑925 82 63 22; www.talavera.org/turismo; Ronda del Cañillo 22; ⊙9.30am-2pm & 5-7pm Mon-Fri, 10am-2pm Sat & Sun) Especially good on the local ceramics industry. It's located next to the old Roman bridge.

❶ Getting There & Away

The bus station is in the town centre. Regular buses between Madrid and Badajoz stop in Talavera de la Reina. Autocares Toletum (www.autocarestoletum.com) runs buses to Toledo (from €7.15, 1½ hours) roughly hourly.

Oropesa

POP 2818

The village of Oropesa, 34km west of Talavera de la Reina and enticingly visible south from the N5 motorway, is dominated by – and famous for – its turreted 14th-century **castle** (adult/child €3/1.50; ⊙10am-2pm & 4-6pm Tue-Sun) that looks north across the plains towards the Sierra de Gredos.

⌷ Sleeping

La Hostería de Oropesa　　　　HOTEL €
(☑925 43 08 75; Paseo Escolar 5; s/d incl breakfast €50/65; ℙ❄) La Hostería, just below Oropesa's castle, has pretty, individually decorated rooms with beamed ceilings and a popular restaurant with tables spilling out into a flower-festooned courtyard.

Parador　　　　HISTORIC HOTEL €€
(☑925 43 00 00; www.parador.es; Plaza Palacio 1; r €75-145; ℙ❄🛜) Attached to Oropesa's hilltop castle is a 14th-century palace housing Spain's second-oldest *parador*, which has managed to retain a heady historical feel without the 'overheritaging' that typifies many Spanish *paradores*. The rooms are large and luxurious, with heavy brocade curtains and antiques. Read Somerset Maugham's rave review of the place in the lobby and ask to see San Pedro de Alcántara's sleeping quarters, hidden in the bowels of this former palace.

❶ Getting There & Away

From Talavera de la Reina, buses (€3.60, 40 minutes) travel here three or four times daily.

THE SOUTH

Consuegra

POP 10,668

If you choose one place to go windmill-spotting in Castilla-La Mancha, make it Consuegra, where you can get that classic shot of nine *molinos de viento* (windmills) flanking Consuegra's 12th-century **castle** (adult/child €4/free; ⊙10am-1.30pm & 4.30-6.30pm Mon-Fri, 10.30am-1.30pm & 4.30-6.30pm Sat & Sun Jun-Sep, shorter hrs Oct-May).

Down in the town, it's worth tracking down the **Plaza Mayor**, with its pretty 1st-floor balconies.

WHAT'S COOKING IN CASTILLA-LA MANCHA?

➥ *Queso manchego* (La Mancha cheese) – most Castilla-La Mancha restaurants offer this as an entrée; **Villadiego** (☑926 21 07 14; www.quesosvilladiego.com; Carretera Poblete-Alarcos Km 2, Poblete; ⊙9am-2pm Mon-Fri) takes you to the source

➥ *Berenjenas de Almagro* (eggplants from Almagro) – Restaurante Abrasador (p221)

➥ *Perdiz a la toledana* (partridge stewed Toledo-style) – Casa Aurelio (p214)

➥ *Mazapan* (marzipan) – Santo Tomé (p214)

On the Trail of Don Quijote

Few literary landscapes have come to define an actual terrain quite like the La Mancha portrayed in Miguel de Cervantes' *El ingenioso hidalgo Don Quijote de la Mancha*, better known in Spain as *El Quijote*.

The Man from La Mancha

In a village in La Mancha whose name I cannot recall, there lived long ago a country gentleman...

Thus begins the novel and thus it was that the village where our picaresque hero began his journey had always remained a mystery. That was, at least, until 10 eminent Spanish academics marked the 400th anniversary of the book's publication in 1605 by carefully following the clues left by Cervantes.

Their conclusion? That **Villanueva de los Infantes** (Map p204; population 5581) in Castilla-La Mancha's far south was Don Quijote's starting point. These days, the town is otherwise most memorable for its ochre-hued Plaza Mayor, surrounded by wood-and-stone balconies and watched over by the 15th-century Iglesia de San Andrés. If you're staying overnight, look no further than **La Morada de Juan de Vargas** (☎926 36 17 69; www.lamoradadevargas.com; Calle Cervantes 3; d €69-75; ❄️🛜).

Staying for the Knight

There is little consensus as to where Don Quijote went next, and there are as many *rutas de Don Quijote* (Don Quijote routes) as there are La Mancha towns eager to claim an impeccable Cervantes

1. Windmills of Consuegra (p215)
2. Iglesia de San Andrés, Villanueva de los Infantes
3. Don Quijote statue, Plaza de España, Madrid

pedigree. In fact, few towns are actually mentioned by name in the book.

One that does appear is the now-unremarkable town of Puerto Lápice, southeast of Toledo. It was here that Don Quijote stayed in an inn that he mistook for a castle and, after keeping watch over it all night, convinced the innkeeper to knight him. El Toboso, northeast of Alcázar de San Juan, also appears in the book as the home of Dulcinea, the platonic love of Quijote. Nowadays you'll find in El Toboso the 16th-century **Casa-Museo de Dulcinea** (Calle Don Quijote 1; €3; ⊙10am-2pm & 4-7.30pm Tue-Sat, 10am-2pm Sun), as well as the obligatory Don Quijote statue and a library with more than 300 editions of the book in various languages.

Windmills

Don Quijote may have spent much of his quest tilting at windmills *(molinos de viento),* but nowhere is the exact location of these 'monstrous giants', against whom honourable battles must be fought, revealed. The finest windmills are arguably the nine of Consuegra (p215), strung out along a ridge line that rises from the pancake-flat plains, and clearly visible from far away. Mota del Cuervo, northeast of Alcázar de San Juan, also has some seven candidates, but Campo de Criptana (p218) is Consuegra's main rival. Only 10 of Campo de Criptana's original 32 windmills remain, but they sit dramatically above the town. Local legend also maintains that Cervantes was baptised in the town's Iglesia de Santa Maria.

WORTH A TRIP

CASTILLO DE BELMONTE

The Castillo de Belmonte (www.
castillodebelmonte.com; adult/child €8/4;
⊙10am-2pm & 4.30-8.30pm Tue-Sun Jun-
Sep, 10am-2pm & 3.30-6.30pm Oct–mid-
Feb, 10am-2pm & 4-7pm mid-Feb–May) is
how castles *should* look, with turrets,
largely intact walls and a commanding
position over the village. The castle
was once home to France's Empress
Eugénie after her husband, Napoleon III,
lost the French throne in 1871. Parts of
the movie *El Cid* (1961), starring Charlton Heston, were filmed here.

🛏 Sleeping & Eating

La Vida de Antes　　　　　　HOTEL €€
(☑925 48 06 09; www.lavidadeantes.com; Calle
Colón 2; s/d incl breakfast €55/75; P ✳ @ 🛜 ❄)
The best digs in Consuegra are encased in
a noble old house with tiled floors, antique
furnishings and a pretty patio that evokes a
bygone era. The duplex rooms are particularly cosy and there's interesting art exhibited throughout the building.

El Alfar　　　　　　　　　　SPANISH €€
(☑925 48 18 07; Calle de Valderribas; mains €16-
23; ⊙1-5pm & 8pm-late Fri-Sun, 1-5pm Mon) Consuegra's most ambitious restaurant is also
something of a museum, inhabiting an old
ceramics workshop that was built over the
ruins of the town's ancient Roman circus.
Ruined columns and capitals mingle with a
profusion of pots, plants and trees in the expansive courtyard, while the decor indoors
is equally museumworthy.

It's easy to forget you're in a restaurant –
until the food arrives. The three-course
tasting menu includes La Mancha specialities such as partridge salad, *migas*
(breadcrumbs, often cooked with chorizo
and served with grapes) and a plethora
of local wines (from the world's largest
wine-growing region, no less).

❶ Information

Tourist Office (☑925 47 57 31; www.consue
gra.es; ⊙9am-6pm, to 7pm Jun-Sep) The
tourist office is in the Bolero mill (they all have
names), which is the first you come to as the
road winds up from the town. You can climb
the steps here and see the original windmill
machinery.

There's another tourist office next to the bus
station.

❶ Getting There & Away

There are regular weekday buses (three on
weekends) running between Consuegra and
Toledo (€5.20, one hour) and up to seven buses
daily to Madrid (€10.10, two hours). There's also
a daily connection (€4.50, one hour) to Ciudad
Real.

Campo de Criptana
POP 14,594

One of the most popular stops on the Don
Quijote route, Campo de Criptana is crowned
by 10 windmills visible from kilometres
around. Revered contemporary film-maker
Pedro Almodóvar was born here, but left for
Madrid in his teens, later remarking that in
his conservative provincial town he felt as if
he'd come from another planet.

◉ Sights

While Consuegra might have La Mancha's
most spectacularly sited windmills, Campo de Criptana's cluster of 10 mills on the
northern edge of the town are older, some
dating from the 16th century, and thus have
more credence to support the myth that
Cervantes used them as models for Don
Quijote's 'giants'. One of the windmills has
a ticket office (visits per mill €0.60; ⊙10am-
2pm & 4.30-7pm Tue-Sat) selling admission
to three other mills that hold a variety of
displays (guided tours are offered). All of
the windmills have names. One of them,
Sardinero, sits inside the town in a pretty
whitewashed quarter known as the Barrio
de Albaicín.

🛏 Sleeping & Eating

Hospedería Casa de la Torrecilla　HOTEL €€
(☑926 58 91 30; www.lacasadelatorrecilla.es; Calle
Cardenal Monescillo 17; s/d €45/80; ✳ @ 🛜) The
lovely Hospedería Casa de la Torrecilla has
a vividly patterned and tiled interior patio.
Housed in an early 20th-century nobleman's
house, the rooms have parquet floors and
are spacious and atmospheric.

Cueva La Martina　　　　　　SPANISH €€
(☑926 56 14 76; www.cuevalamartina.com; Ro-
cinante 13; mains €16-20; ⊙1.30-4pm Mon,
1.30-4pm & 8.30-midnight Tue-Sun) The best
place to eat is atmospheric Cueva La Martina, opposite the windmills. The cave-like

dining area is dug into the rock, and there's a breezy upstairs terrace with views over town. Dishes to try include the super simple *asadillo manchego* (a slow-roasted vegetable casserole dominated by red peppers) or the richer poached eggs with truffles and cured ham.

❶ Getting There & Away

Campo de Criptana and Ciudad Real are linked by two buses Monday to Friday and one on Saturday (€8.95, 1¼ hours).

There are four daily trains to Madrid (€16.05, 1½ hours)

Ciudad Real

POP 74,872

Despite being the one-time royal counterpart of Toledo, these days Ciudad Real is an unspectacular Spanish working town. Unless you're on the trail of every last Don Quijote landmark, or possess an interest in provincial Spanish towns where tourists rarely venture, there's probably not enough here to warrant a detour off the main highway.

⊙ Sights

The town centre has a certain charm, with its pedestrianised shopping streets and distinctive Plaza Mayor, complete with carillon clock (topped by Cupid), flamboyant neo-Gothic town-hall facade and modern tiered fountain.

Museo del Quijote
y Biblioteca Cervantina   MUSEUM
(🖉926 20 04 57; Ronda de Alarcos 1; ⊙10am-2pm & 5-8pm Mon-Sat, 10am-2pm Sun) FREE
For true Don Quijote fans, this museum is worth perusing for its audiovisual show – a humorous 3D invocation of the book – and old printing presses and theatre props. It also functions as a Cervantes library, stocked with 3500 Don Quijote books, including some in Esperanto and Braille, with most of them now digitised, and others dating back to 1724. It helps if you speak Spanish. Entry is by guided tour every half-hour.

🛏 Sleeping & Eating

Palacio de la Serna   HOTEL €€
(🖉926 84 22 08; www.hotelpalaciodelaserna. com; Calle Cervantes 18; r €89-140, ste €180-220; P ✳ 🛜 ⊛) Just 20 minutes' drive south of Ciudad Real (and an equivalent distance from Almagro), in the sleepy village of Ballesteros de Calatrava, this superb hotel feels a world away. Set around a courtyard, it combines rural comfort with appealing design; the owner's evocative modern sculptures feature heavily. Rooms are a little avant-garde,

---

THE WINES OF VALDEPEÑAS

From last count, Castilla-La Mancha has nine recognised wine regions: Almansa, Jumila, La Mancha, Manchuela, Mentrida, Mondejar, Ribera del Júcar, Ucles and Valdepeñas. But it's the latter that has the most interesting story.

Situated midway between Madrid and Córdoba, the large and otherwise uninviting town of Valdepeñas offers weary travellers one (and only one) good reason to break the journey. Surrounding the town is what some experts believe to be the largest expanse of vineyards in the world (although much of these belong to the larger, if lesser-known, La Mancha wine region). True aficionados of the humble grape argue that quantity does not easily translate into quality and there's an element of truth to this view – Valdepeñas has historically been to the mass market what La Rioja is to the quality end of the wine trade.

That said, things are changing. You're still more likely to come across Valdepeñas wines in the cheap, cask variety than served in Spain's finest restaurants, but some of Valdepeñas' bodegas have begun making inroads into the quality end of the market. Most of the bodegas offer tours, tastings and short wine courses only by appointment, and charge to boot. Check the websites for details to avoid going thirsty.

Bodegas Arúspide (🖉926 34 70 75; www.aruspide.com; Calle Franci Morales 102; tour €5) Offers tours and a tasting of two or more wines.

Bodega de las Estrellas (🖉926 31 32 48; www.labodegadelasestrellas.com; Calle Unión 82; tour €6-17) Makes organic wine and also has a tour and tasting option that includes a meal in the bodega.

with open showers and numerous thoughtful touches.

There's also a good on-site restaurant.

El Ventero
TAPAS €

(Plaza Mayor 8; tapas from €3.50; ⊙10am-11pm Tue-Sat, 10am-5pm Sun & Mon) Time your chair on the square here to enjoy the carillon clock display (generally noon, 1pm, 2pm, 6pm and 8pm), when Don Quijote, Sancho and Cervantes emerge for a congenial spin around a small stage. The vast menu of *raciones* (large tapas servings) includes *salmorejo* (thick garlicky gazpacho), *almoronía* (similar to ratatouille topped with cheese) and *perdiz roja* (partridge in a sherry sauce).

ⓘ Getting There & Away

From the **bus station** (Carretera Calzada), southwest of the town centre, up to three daily buses head to Toledo (€10.50, two hours) and Madrid (€14.50, 2½ hours).

Most trains linking Madrid with Andalucía stop at Ciudad Real's **train station** (Av Europa), east of the town centre. Regular departures include high-speed services to Madrid (from €27.60, one hour).

Almagro

POP 9100

The theatre and pickled aubergines are Almagro's improbable bedfellows. Almagro is to the theatre what Seville is to flamenco, the spiritual home of the art – at least in Spain – courtesy of its 'golden age' playhouse (Spain's oldest) and all-encompassing theatre museum. Not that you have to be a thespian to appreciate the place. The diminutive town, which gained importance during the Reconquista, might have been designed with 21st-century tourists in mind. Everything of note is a short, traffic-free stroll from its cobbled nexus, Plaza Mayor. Its warped, green-trimmed edifices (below which tapas bars ply the local pickled aubergines) might have you asking: is this the handsomest square in Spain?

◎ Sights

Museo Nacional de Teatro
MUSEUM

(http://museoteatro.mcu.es; Calle de Gran Maestre 2; adult/child €3/free, Sat afternoon & Sun free; ⊙10am-2pm & 4-7pm Mon-Fri, 10am-2pm & 4-6pm Sat, 11am-2pm Sun) Thespian or not, you could spend hours in Almagro's illustrious museum just sifting through the highlights. Theatrical musings include a hand-painted set of playing cards from 1729 found in the nearby Corral de Comedias, a deftly sculpted model of Mérida's Roman theatre, costumes and props relating to *zarzuela* (Spanish mix of theatre, music and dance) and – anchoring it all – a handsome 13th-century courtyard.

Corral de Comedias
HISTORIC BUILDING

(www.corraldecomedias.com; Plaza Mayor 18; adult/child incl English audioguide €3/free; ⊙10am-2pm & 5-8pm Mon-Fri, to 6pm Sat, 10am-12.45pm & 5-8pm Sun) Opening onto the plaza is the oldest theatre in Spain. The 17th-century Corral de Comedias is an evocative tribute to the golden age of Spanish theatre, with rows of wooden balconies facing the original stage, complete with dressing rooms. At various intervals visits become 'theatrised' with costumed actors replacing the audioguide: this costs €1 more. It's still used for performances on Saturday evenings during daylight saving (from the end of March to the end of October); buy tickets via the website.

☞ Tours

Visitas Guiadas a Almagro
WALKING TOUR

(☑609 79 36 54; www.almagrovisitasguiadas.com; Plaza Mayor 41; per person €12) Aside from the standard two-hour Almagro walking tour, it also offers out-of-town tours to Calatrava la Nueva, Tablas de Daimiel and Lagunas de Ruidera.

Alarcos Turismo
WALKING TOUR

(☑926 26 13 82; www.alarcosturismo.com; Calle Mayor de Carnicerías 5; per person €12; ⊙11am & 6.30pm Jul & Aug, 11am & 6pm Jun & Sep, 11am & 5pm Oct-May) Two-hour guided tours of all the major local landmarks. It also runs a small tourist bus (€4) from Tuesday to Sunday.

☆ Festivals & Events

Festival Internacional de Teatro Clásico
THEATRE

(www.festivaldealmagro.com) In July the Corral de Comedias holds a month-long international theatre festival, attracting world-class theatre companies performing, primarily, classical plays.

⌂ Sleeping

Casa Rural Tia Pilar de Almagro
GUESTHOUSE €

(☑926 88 27 24; www.tiapilar.com; Calle Carrascos 1; s/d €40/65; ⚆❄☞❀) This beautiful

Cervantes-era house is full of all sorts of hidden nooks and crannies, including four patios, a lovely common room (with a fancy coffee machine) and a small but elegant swimming pool. Rooms are well heated and/or air-conditioned for an old house and the owners live on-site to provide warm but discreet service.

La Posada de Almagro GUESTHOUSE €
(☑ 926 88 22 44; www.laposadadealmagro.com; Calle Gran Maestre 5; s/d €44/60; ✲ 🕲) A short hop from the Plaza Mayor, this fine inn has simple, tidy rooms with wrought-iron bedheads, thoughtfully decorated walls and tiled bathrooms. Bring earplugs if you're here on a weekend as the noise from the restaurant can be loud and long.

★ La Casa del Rector HOTEL €€
(☑ 926 26 12 59; www.lacasadelrector.com; Calle Pedro Oviedo 8; s/d €85/99; ✲ @ 🕲 ☲) A three-way marriage between modern rooms, 'design' rooms and traditional historical rooms, the Rector is, in a word, magnificent. It's difficult to imagine what taste isn't being catered for in its lush interior set around three courtyards with elegant fountains, retro hipster antiques (sewing machines!) and a streamlined cafe.

Design rooms have wood-floor showers, snazzy coffee machines and electric window blinds. Modern rooms are a little more beige and mainstream. Traditional rooms retain many of the building's original features such as wood beams and heavy tiled floors. To top it all off, there's an on-site spa.

Parador de Almagro HISTORIC HOTEL €€€
(☑ 926 86 01 00; www.parador.es; Ronda de San Francisco 31; r €80-164; 🅿 ✲ @ 🕲 ☲) A sumptuous ivy-clad former convent in a quiet corner of Almagro, this *parador* has a luxurious, old-world charm, despite the mildly incongruous, brightly coloured beams in the rooms.

✕ Eating

Taberna Candilejas SPANISH €
(☑ 654 83 19 77; Plaza Mayor 39; raciones €6-10; ⊙ 9.30am-12.30am Wed-Mon) This boisterous joint makes happy noises from its perch in the corner of Plaza Mayor where it plies *cañas* to the local drinking brigade. But don't dismiss the food, served at several diminutive tables inside. Highlights include unadorned rations of stuffed aubergines and the default peasant food *migas del pastor* (breadcrumbs with chorizo, grapes and a fried egg).

Restaurante Abrasador CASTILIAN €€
(☑ 926 88 26 56; www.abrasador.es; Calle San Agustín 18; tostas €1.50, mains €11.50-25, set menus from €25; ⊙ noon-4pm & 8-11pm Mon, Tue & Thu-Sat, noon-4pm Sun) Thoughtfully prepared cooking dominates the restaurant out the back (snaffle the table next to the open fire in winter if you can), with perfectly grilled meats. Out the front, you'll find some of the most creative tapas in Almagro – the famed local aubergine features prominently and it's our pick of the orders, whatever guise it's in.

ℹ Information

Centro de Recepción de Visitantes (☑ 926 86 07 17; www.ciudad-almagro.com; Calle Ejido de Calatrava; ⊙ 10am-2pm & 5-8pm Tue-Fri, 10am-2pm & 5-7pm Sat, 10am-2pm Sun) Next to the small bus station. Afternoon opening and closing is one hour earlier from November to March.

ℹ Getting There & Away

Buses run to Ciudad Real (€3.65, 30 minutes, up to five daily Monday to Saturday).

There are two daily trains to Madrid (€26.10, 2½ hours); for destinations to the south, change in Ciudad Real (€3.65, 15 minutes, five daily).

WORTH A TRIP

CASTILLO DE CALATRAVA LA NUEVA

This magnificent **castle-monastery** (Calatrava la Nueva; adult/child €2/2.50; ⊙ 11am-2pm & 5.30-8.30pm Tue-Fri, 10am-2pm & 5.30-8.30pm Sat, 10am-2pm & 5-9pm Sun) looms high in the sky some 6km south of the town of Calzada de Calatrava and 30km south of Almagro, from where it once controlled the path into the Sierra Morena and Andalucía. A steep stony road takes you to the top, where you can alternate gawping at expansive views with studying the well-preserved castle church and monastery in closer detail. Seasonal opening hours vary.

Parque Nacional Tablas de Daimiel

Forty kilometres northeast of Ciudad Real, this small wetland national park is great for birdwatching. From the visitor centre (📞926 69 31 18; www.lastablasdedaimiel.com; ⏰9am-7pm Oct-Mar, to 9pm Apr-Sep), which has an exhibition on the fragile local ecosystem, three trails lead out along the lake shore and over boardwalks. From these, and the various observation hides – bring binoculars – you can see an astonishing variety of wildlife, including ducks, geese, kingfishers, flamingos, herons and other waders, tortoises and otters. Early morning and late afternoon are the best times.

The company Visitas Guiadas a Almagro (p220) in Almagro can organise guided visits here.

Alcalá del Júcar

POP 1300

Northeast of Albacete, the deep, tree-filled gorge of Río Júcar makes for a stunning detour. About halfway along the CM3201, the crag-clinging town of Alcalá del Júcar comes into view as you descend via hairpin turns. Its landmark castle (adult/child €2/1.50; ⏰11am-2pm & 5-8pm May-Sep, 11am-2pm & 3-6pm Oct-Apr), dating mostly from the 15th century, towers over the houses that spill down the steep bank of the river gorge. At the foot of the town there's a medieval bridge with Roman origins and a leafy meeting-and-greeting plaza. It's a good destination for young kids, with a large, traffic-free area, and safe paddling in a bend of the river.

Activities here include river trips and local walking trails. Several companies offer a full range of land and water excursions. Avenjúcar (📞967 47 41 34; www.avenjucar.com; Av de la Constitución) tackles adventure activities including wet and dry canyoning and river experiences.

🛏 Sleeping & Eating

Hostal Rambla HOSTAL €
(📞967 47 40 64; www.hostalrambla.es; Paseo Los Robles 2; s/d incl breakfast €50/55; ❄�'🀫) One of several well-priced hotels in Alcalá, Hostal Rambla is by the 'Roman' bridge. Rooms are compact, but it's friendly and well located, and there's a pleasant restaurant with a large terrace, specialising in chargrilled meats served with green peppers and potatoes.

Bodega-Cueva La Asomada BODEGA €
(📞652 18 24 40; Calle de la Asomada 107; mains €7-13; ⏰8pm-midnight Fri, 11am-4pm & 8pm-midnight Sat & Sun) 🌿 Located in a cave and former bodega, La Asomada, at the top of the village, should be sought out by eco folks. Owner Pilar Escusa uses organic produce and prepares delicious seasonal dishes. Reservations essential.

ℹ Information

Tourist Office (📞967 47 30 90; www.turismo castillalamancha.com; Paseo de los Robles 1; ⏰10am-2pm daily, 4-7pm Sat & Sun) The small tourist office has a wealth of information about casas rurales (farmstead accommodation), cave accommodation and activities, including maps showing local walking trails.

ℹ Getting There & Away

There is one daily bus on weekdays only between Albacete and Alcalá (€6.06, 1½ hours). It's run by Emisalba (www.emisalba.com).

THE NORTHEAST

Cuenca

POP 55,738

The setting couldn't be more strategic – or more spectacular. Stacked on a steep promontory at the meeting of two deep river gorges, the old town of Cuenca is natural eye candy. Narrow meandering streets separate tall houses with wooden balconies that literally jut out over the sheer cliffs. Yet, despite its age and Unesco listing, Cuenca has somewhat ironically established itself as a vortex of abstract modern art. Two of its most iconic buildings – including the famed casas colgadas (hanging houses) – have transformed their interiors into modern galleries. It's a theme continued in many of the town's hotels, museums and restaurants.

⊙ Sights

Most of the sights are in the steep-stacked old town perched on a thin promontory between the gorges of Ríos Júcar and Huécar. Just wandering the narrow streets, tunnels and staircases, stopping every now and again to admire the majestic views, is the chief pleasure of Cuenca. The new town spreads out at the base of the hill; this is where you'll find normal Cuenca life with pedestrianised shopping streets and clusters of tapas bars.

★ **Casas Colgadas**   HISTORIC BUILDING

The most striking element of medieval Cuenca, the *casas colgadas* jut out precariously over the steep defile of Río Huécar. Dating from the 14th century, the houses, with their layers of wooden balconies, seem to emerge from the rock as if an extension of the cliffs. The best views of the *casas colgadas* is from the Puente de San Pablo footbridge. Today, the houses host – somewhat improbably – an abstract art museum (p223) founded in the 1960s.

★ **Museo de la Semana Santa**   MUSEUM

(www.msscuenca.org; Calle Andrés de Cabrera 13; adult/child €3/free; ⊘11am-2pm & 4.30-7.30pm Thu-Sat, 11am-2pm Sun; ⊞) This museum is the next best thing to experiencing one of Spain's most spine-tingling Semana Santa parades firsthand. Spread over two floors, the hugely accomplished audiovisual show moves from room to room showing the processions by local brotherhoods against a background of sombre music. After-

wards you are allowed to wander around at leisure, admiring the costumes, crosses and religious iconography.

★ **Museo de Arte Abstracto Español**   MUSEUM

(Museum of Abstract Art; www.march.es/arte/cuenca; Calle Canónigos; adult/concession/child €3/1.50/free; ⊘11am-2pm & 4-6pm Tue-Fri, 11am-2pm & 4-8pm Sat, 11am-2.30pm Sun) From the outside, they look as if they've been sawn off from some high-altitude Tibetan temple, but, from the inside, Cuenca's famous *casas colgadas* have been transformed into a suite of airy, clean-lined galleries displaying some of central Spain's finest abstract art. You can spend hours in here trying to decipher blurry Fernando Zóbel (the museum's founder), bright and direct José Guerrero or the frankly odd works of Catalan Antoni Tàpies.

Catedral   CATHEDRAL

(Plaza Mayor; adult/child €3.80/2, incl Museo Diocesano & audioguide €5; ⊘10am-2pm & 4-5pm Mon-Fri, 10am-6pm Sat, 10am-5pm Sun) Lured in by the impressive old-looking façade (it was actually cleverly rebuilt in neo-Gothic style in 1902), Cuenca's cathedral is well worth a visit – and not just for those attending Mass.

ABSTRACT CUENCA

When Unesco listed Cuenca as a World Heritage site in 1996, it refrained from pushing the merits of its abstract art. But one of the latent joys of this historical city that hangs surreally above two dramatic gorges, is the way it has managed to incorporate modern avant-gardism into its crusty historic core.

Cuenca's penchant for abstract art can be traced back to the 1950s, when a loose collection of locally based artists formed what became known as the 'Cuenca School'. Notable in the group was Fernando Zóbel, a Spanish-Filipino painter and art collector who got together with Cuenca-born engineer-turned-artist Gustavo Torner in 1966 to open the Museo de Arte Abstracto (p223) inside the town's famous hanging houses. It was an inspired choice. Encased in a historical medieval residence, beautifully laid-out exhibits made use of reconfigured minimalist rooms. The museum prospered and others followed. In 1998 Sigüenza-born artist and poet Antonio Pérez opened up an eponymous foundation (p224) in an old Carmelite monastery and stuffed it with works from Warhol to Antoni Tàpies. Seven years later, Torner initiated his own museum, Espacio Torner, in Cuenca's San Pedro convent (the museum is currently on extended hiatus due to funding issues).

But the abstractness extends beyond traditional museums. The brilliant yellow and orange stained glass in Cuenca's 12th-century cathedral (p223) was fashioned by Torner in the early 1990s to create a whimsical hybrid, while, further down the hill in the new town, the concrete and glass Museo de Paleontología (📞650 86 38 61; Río Gritos 5; ⊘10am-2.30pm, 4.30-7pm Tue-Sat; 10am-2.30pm Sun; ⊞) 🅿, with its cube-like display halls, pays more than a passing nod to avant-gardism. You'll even spot abstract influences in the decor of some of Cuenca's hotels and restaurants, the arty interiors of which often belie their medieval outer shells.

Cuenca

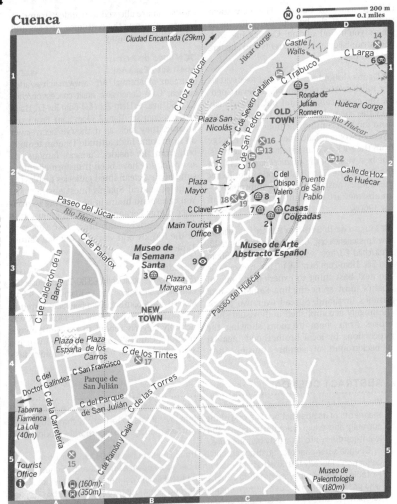

It was built on the site of the main mosque after the city's reconquest by Alfonso VIII in 1177. Highlights within include the Gothic tombs of the Montemayor family, and the chapter house *artesonado* (wooden) ceiling. In typical Cuenca fashion, the unusual abstract stained-glass windows were added in the 20th century.

Túneles de Alfonso VIII   TUNNELS

(Calle Alfonso VIII; guided tour €3.50; ⊘ hours vary) A mole hill of tunnels lies under Cuenca's old town. Over time they have served multiple purposes as aqueducts, crypts and, most recently, air-raid shelters during the civil war. The tunnels have recently been restored and fitted with walkways, lighting and explanatory boards. Tours are guided only and must be booked through the main tourist office (p227).

Fundación Antonio Pérez   GALLERY

(☑ 969 23 06 19; Calle Julián Romero 20; €2; ⊘ 11am-2pm & 5-8pm) This huge modern-art gallery in the labyrinthine ex-Convento de las Carmelitas is a typical Cuenca synthesis of old and new. Stuffed with exhibits that will perplex, inspire and (possibly)

Cuenca

amuse, it is large, but crammed. Antonio Saura is well-represented, as are plenty of other brow-furrowing 1950s and '60s-era innovators.

Mirador VIEWPOINT
Climb to the top of the old town for this fine viewpoint over Cuenca and its plunging gorges.

Museo de Cuenca MUSEUM
(www.patrimoniohistoricoclm.es/museo-de-cuenca; Calle Obispo Valero 12; adult/child €1.20/free, Sat & Sun free; ⊙10am-2pm & 4-7pm Tue-Sat, 10am-2pm Sun) The city's history museum is comprehensive, but heavily weighted towards the pre-medieval age. The story kicks off in the Bronze Age, but the real scoop is Sala 7, stuffed with original Roman statues (including Emperor Augustus), plus various columns and pediments plucked from the nearby archaeological sites at Segóbriga (p230) and Valeria (www.valeria romana.es; adult/child €3/1; ⊙10.30am-2pm & 5.30-8.30pm Apr-Oct, 10.30am-2pm & 3-5pm Mon-Sat, 10am-3pm Sun Nov-Mar). However, post-Renaissance history gets only a light dusting.

Museo Diocesano MUSEUM
(Calle Obispo Valero 1; €2.50, incl cathedral €5; ⊙11am-2pm & 4-7pm Tue-Sat, 11am-2pm Sun Apr-Oct, 11am-2pm & 4-6pm Tue-Sat, 11am-2pm Sun Nov-Mar) Among the usual profusion of religious relics and pious paintings reside some metaphorical rays of light, including faded Flemish tapestries, a couple of distinctive El Grecos and a replica of the Holy Shroud made in 1640.

🎉 Festivals & Events

Semana Santa RELIGIOUS
(www.juntacofradiascuenca.es) Cuenca's Holy Week celebrations are renowned throughout Spain for the eerie, silent processions through the streets of the old town. There's even a town museum (p223) dedicated to the annual event.

🛏 Sleeping

Many of the hotel rooms in the atmospheric old town have top-notch views, so always ask for a room *con vista*. That said, there are some good options in the livelier new town below too. Phone ahead for budget accommodation in the old town, as the owners tend to live elsewhere.

Hostal Tabanqueta HOSTAL €
(☑969 21 40 76; www.hostaltabanqueta.com; Calle Trabuco 13; d €45, apt €50-100; P❄🖥) Up the hill from Plaza Mayor, this friendly spot has free parking nearby and top-of-the-town views. The accommodation is excellent, with heating, stylish tiled bathrooms, attractive artwork and hotel-standard amenities such as toiletries, an espresso machine and hospitality tray with pastries. It also has a number of apartments nearby.

★**Posada de San José** HISTORIC HOTEL €€
(☑969 21 13 00; www.posadasanjose.com; Ronda de Julián Romero 4; s/d €59/85, d with view €97, s/d with shared bathroom €32/45) This 17th-century former choir school retains an extraordinary monastic charm with its labyrinth of rooms, eclectic artwork, uneven floors and original tiles. All rooms are different; cheaper ones are in former priests' cells and share

bathrooms, while more costly doubles combine homey comfort with old-world charm. Several have balconies with dramatic views of the gorge.

Convento del Giraldo
HOTEL €€

(☑969 23 27 00; www.hotelconventodelgiraldo. com; Calle de San Pedro 12; d/ste €66/126; ❄@🅿) Just above the cathedral, this conversion of a 17th-century convent wins points for location and style, though there aren't too many original features left. Nevertheless, the attractive rooms feature dark wooden furniture and big bathrooms, and many feature great views. You can find good discounts online.

Parador de Cuenca
HISTORIC HOTEL €€€

(☑969 23 23 20; www.parador.es; Calle de Hoz de Huécar; d €90-202; 🅿❄🅿🏊) This majestic former convent commands possibly the best views in town of the *casas colgadas* that are suspended on the opposite side of the gorge. The revamped rooms have a luxury corporate feel, while the public areas, including an old cloister, are headily historic with giant tapestries and antiques.

🍴 Eating

The Plaza Mayor (in the old town) and Plaza de España (new town) are the centres of their respective eating zones. There is a good choice in and surrounding both squares.

★ El Bodegón
SPANISH €

(Cerrillo de San Roque A1; menú del día €11; ⊙1-4pm & 8.30-11.30pm Tue-Sun) No frills, great value, lightning-fast service. Up a narrow lane in the new town, this sociable bar could turn out to be the Castilla-La Mancha eating experience that lingers longest in your memory. It's the perfect place to enjoy a long, slow lunch. Try the excellent-value *menú del día* (daily set menu).

San Juan Plaza Mayor
SPANISH €

(Plaza Mayor 5; mains €7-14; ⊙12.30-4pm & 8pm-midnight Tue-Sat, 12.30-4pm Sun) This bright and perennially busy tapas bar on Plaza Mayor has fine cathedral views if you sit outside in the plaza (as most do, even in winter!) and a good selection of bar snacks. The dining room offers a broad range of cheap eats, including a wide selection of rice dishes for two, as well as salads and grilled meats.

GOLD ON A PLATE

Saffron is one of the most sensuous spices in the world: its intense colour, aroma and delicacy are accentuated by a wealth of nuances. It's also among the most expensive – hardly surprising when you consider that it takes some 160,000 flowers to produce just 1kg of commercial saffron.

Spain leads the European saffron market, and La Mancha is the region where the flowers have been grown and cultivated since Moorish times, primarily around Cuenca and Albacete. Visit here in October and the surrounding fields are a sumptuous blanket of purple blooms.

In Spain, saffron most famously appears in traditional paella.

Asador María Morena
SPANISH €€

(☑969 23 88 25; www.asadormariamorena.com; Calle Larga 31; mains €17-24; ⊙1-4pm & 8-11pm) A good all-round restaurant located at the top of the old town with panoramic views over the river gorge, this place will satisfy both romantic diners and those in search of a more casual evening meal. Everything from the goat's cheese salad to the *patatas a lo pobre* (potatoes with onions, garlic and peppers) are given a deft artistic touch.

★ Figón del Huécar
SPANISH €€€

(☑969 24 00 62; www.figondelhuecar.es; Ronda de Julián Romero 6; mains €17-25, set menus €26-36; ⊙1.30-3.30pm & 9-10.30pm Tue-Sat, 1.30-3.30pm Sun) With a romantic terrace offering spectacular views, Figón del Huécar is a highlight of old-town eating. Roast suckling pig, lamb stuffed with raisins, pine nuts and foie gras, and a host of Castilian specialities are presented and served with panache. The house used to be the home of Spanish singer José Luis Perales.

Romera Bistrót
FUSION, SPANISH €€€

(☑626 08 78 32; Calle de los Tintes 19; mains €18-24; ⊙noon-3pm & 8-11pm Mon-Sat) 🚲 Bikes, truffles, sashimi... sound interesting so far? Romero is one of Cuenca's newest restaurants with a short menu that's all over the map: salmon sashimi, black spaghetti, and a foie-gras royale. Everything is executed perfectly in a 10-table, light-filled space that carries the air of a Parisian bistro. To add to the atmosphere (and perhaps the sustainability) there are bike motifs – including (sometimes) bike-shaped pasta.

Drinking & Nightlife

Cuenca is a student town with lively nightlife. Calle San Francisco in the new town has an energetic row of terrace bars with a preclubbing party feel from around 9pm on weekends. There are several more sophisticated venues around Plaza Mayor. For later action, head for the disco-pubs on Calle del Doctor Galíndez, near Plaza de España.

Lolita Lounge Bar BAR
(www.lolitaloungebar.es; Calle Clavel 7; ☺ 7.30pm-late Fri, noon-late Sat & Sun) This slick minimalist bar with lots of steely metal and slate is bang in the historical centre. Cocktails, a huge range of gin, imported beers and a good mix of music attracts the high-heeled and slicked-back-hair set.

Taberna Flamenca La Lola BAR
(☎ 969 69 10 31; www.taberna-flamenca-lalola.es; Sánchez Vera 9; ☺ 7am-4am Thu-Sun, 7am-midnight Mon-Wed) This small tapas bar in the modern part of Cuenca is best visited for its live flamenco, performed on a tiny stage on Friday and Saturday nights at around 10pm.

ℹ Information

Main Tourist Office (☎ 969 24 10 51; http://turismo.cuenca.es; Calle Alfonso VIII 2;

☺10am-2pm & 4.30-7.30pm Mon-Fri, 10am-8pm Sat & Sun) Book here for tours of the medieval Túneles de Alfonso VIII (p224) that honeycomb the old town.

Tourist Office (☎ 969 23 58 15; Av República de Argentina 4; ☺10am-2pm & 5-8pm Mon-Sat, 10am-2pm Sun) In Cuenca's new town.

ℹ Getting There & Away

The Estación de Cuenca (regional train station) and bus station are located almost across from each other, southwest of Calle de Fermín Caballero.

Beware: Cuenca has two train stations. Fast AVE trains (serving Valencia and Madrid) use the supermodern Estación de Cuenca-Fernando Zóbel station, 6km southwest of town. Bus 12 (€1.25, every 30 minutes) links it with the town centre.

BUS

There are up to nine buses daily to Madrid (€15, 2¼ hours) and regular services to other cities in Castilla-La Mancha including Toledo (€14.20, 3¼ hours) and Albacete (€11.55, 2¾ hours).

TRAIN

Numerous daily trains run to Madrid, ranging from slow *regionales* (trains operating within one region, usually stopping all stations; €14.55, three hours) to swift AVEs (€34.80, 55 minutes). The other way, to Valencia, is a similar deal (€16 to €37.60).

Regional trains stop at the Estación de Cuenca near the bus station. Fast AVE trains stop at the Estación de Cuenca-Fernando Zóbel, 6km southwest of the town centre.

WORTH A TRIP

SERRANIA DE CUENCA

Spreading north and east of Cuenca, the Serranía de Cuenca is a heavily wooded and fertile zone of craggy mountains, sandstone gorges and green fields. Ríos Júcar and Huécar flow through the high hinterland, past landscapes well worth exploring with your own transport.

Head out from Cuenca 30km via the CM2105 to extraordinary **Ciudad Encantada** (adult/child €3/free; ☺10am-sunset), where limestone rocks have been eroded into fantastical shapes by nature. The CM2105 continues north via the picturesque village of **Uña**, the crystal-clear waters of **Embalse del Tobar** and past the **Reserva Natural de El Hosquillo**, a protected park where reintroduced brown bears roam wild.

You can return to Cuenca via the CM210, a quiet rural route that passes several traditional villages; **Solán de Cabras** (with summer spa hotel), the source of Spain's trademark blue-bottled water; and **Priego**, a lovely valley town that dates from Roman times and has sights including medieval churches, Roman arches and Moorish towers.

If you're heading on to Sigüenza, track northeast from Beteta to **Molina de Aragón**, a pretty town utterly dominated by one of Spain's most spectacular castles, built by the Moors then embellished after falling into Christian hands.

WORTH A TRIP

PARADOR DE ALARCÓN

South of Cuenca, the **Parador de Alarcón** (Marqués de Villena; ☑ 969 33 03 15; www.parador.es; d from €186; P ❋ 🤖) is one of the grand castle *paradores* (luxurious state-owned hotels) found throughout the country, so you might as well go the whole hog and reserve a room with a four-poster bed and a chaise longue. Regal it might be, but this is actually one of Spain's smallest *paradores* with just 24 rooms. Historic, but intimate.

Pastrana

POP 1054

Pastrana, 42km south of the regional capital of Guadalajara along the CM200, should not be missed. It's an unspoilt place with twisting cobbled streets flanked by honey-coloured stone buildings.

◉ Sights

The heart and soul of the town is the **Plaza de la Hora**, a large square dotted with acacias and fronted by the sturdy **Palacio Ducal**. It's in Pastrana that the one-eyed princess of Éboli, Ana Mendoza de la Cerda, was confined in 1581 for having a love affair with the Spanish king Felipe II's secretary. You can see the caged window of her 'cell', where she died 10 years later, and join a tour on Saturdays at 11.30am (Spanish only €5) run from the tourist office (p228).

Iglesia de Nuestra Señora de la Asunción Museum   MUSEUM
(Colegiata; adult/child €2.50/free; ☉ 11.30am-2pm & 4.30-7pm Tue-Fri, 1-2pm & 4.30-7pm Sun) Walk from the Plaza de la Hora along Calle Mayor and you'll soon reach the massive Iglesia de Nuestra Señora de la Asunción. Inside, the interesting little Museo Parroquial contains the jewels of the princess of Éboli, some exquisite 15th-century Flemish tapestries and even an El Greco.

🛏 Sleeping & Eating

Hotel Palaterna   HOTEL €
(☑ 949 37 01 27; www.hotelpalaterna.com; Plaza de los Cuatro Caños; s/d/ste €50/65/95; ❋ 🤖) Hotel Palaterna is a pleasant, modern hotel overlooking a small square complete with bubbling fountain. Rooms are painted in cool colours, contrasting with dark wood furniture.

Cenador de las Monjas   SPANISH €€€
(☑ 949 37 01 01; www.cenadordelasmonjas.es; Travesia de Ines 1; menus €35-40; ☉ 2-4pm & 9-11pm Fri & Sat, 2-4pm Sun) 🍴 The dining room in the old 16th-century San José monastery offers beautifully prepared Spanish food that is anything but austere; although, abiding by monastic tradition, they grow most of their own vegetables. Sit above a warped tiled floor under a wood-beamed ceiling and indulge in venison meatballs or tuna with a honey glaze.

❶ Information

Tourist Office (☑ 949 37 06 72; www.pastrana.org; Plaza de la Hora 5; ☉ 10am-2pm & 4-7pm Mon-Fri, 10am-2pm & 4-8pm Sat, 10am-2pm Sun) Runs tours on Saturdays dedicated to the one-eyed princess of Éboli, Ana Mendoza de la Cerda.

❶ Getting There & Away

If travelling by public transport from either Madrid or Cuenca, you'll need to take a bus or train to Guadalajara, from where there's a daily bus run by Guadalbus (www.guadalbus.com) to/from Pastrana (€5.50, 1¼ hours).

Sigüenza

POP 4335

Sleepy, historical and filled with the ghosts of a turbulent past, Sigüenza is well worth a detour. The town is built on a low hill cradled by Río Henares and boasts a castle, a cathedral and several excellent restaurants set among twisting lanes of medieval buildings. Start your ambling at the beautiful 16th-century Plaza Mayor.

◉ Sights

★**Catedral**   CATHEDRAL
(☉ 9.30am-2pm & 4-8pm Tue-Sat, noon-5.30pm Sun) Rising up from the heart of the old town is the city's centrepiece – the cathedral. Begun as a Romanesque structure in 1130, work continued for four centuries as the church was progressively expanded and adorned. The largely Gothic result is laced with elements of other styles, from plateresque through to renaissance to Mudéjar. Although the church was heavily damaged during the civil war, it was subsequently re-

Sigüenza

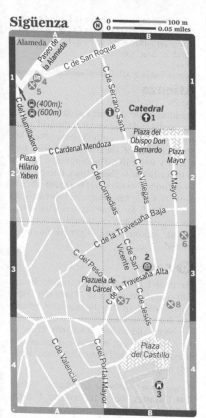

built. The dark interior has a broodingly ancient feel and some fine stained glass pieces, plus an impressive 15th-century altarpiece.

Casa del Doncel
MUSEUM

(San Vicente 1; adult €2; ⊙ 11am-2pm Sat & Sun) This modest museum in a Gothic-Mudéjar mansion is best visited for its guitar-making exhibition, located on the second floor with a mock-up guitar workshop and cache of historical instruments. The other exhibits are a little dowdy.

Castillo
CASTLE

(Plaza del Castillo) Calle Mayor heads south up the hill from the cathedral to a magnificent-looking castle, which was originally built by the Romans and was, in turn, a Moorish *alcázar* (fortress), royal palace, asylum and army barracks. Virtually destroyed during the Spanish Civil War, it was subsequently rebuilt under Franco as a *parador*.

🛏 Sleeping

★ El Doncel
HOTEL €€

(☑ 949 39 00 01; www.eldoncel.com; Paseo de la Alameda 3; d €55-64; 🌬 🤶) With earthy colours, lots of exposed stone, spot lighting, minibars, and marshmallow-soft duvets and pillows, this place is aimed squarely at couples on a romantic weekend away from Madrid. It's comfortable and attractive, and there's an excellent restaurant. Prices drop substantially midweek.

Parador de Sigüenza
HISTORIC HOTEL €€€

(☑ 949 39 01 00; www.parador.es; Plaza del Castillo; d €90-175; 🅿 🌬 🤶) Sigüenza's luxurious *parador* is set in the castle, which dates back to the 12th century and overlooks the town. The magnificent courtyard is a wonderful place to pass the time. The rooms have period furnishings and castle-style windows, so they can be on the dark side; ask for one with a balcony to make the most of the natural light and views.

🍴 Eating

Cafe-Bar Alameda
TAPAS €

(www.alamedatapas.es; Paseo de la Alameda 2; raciones €6-10; ⊙ 10am-midnight) Join the local card players at this down-home bar. Its counter groans with tempting tapas and *pinchos* (canapes), including *caracoles* (snails) and *orejas* (pig's ears) for the intrepid, as well as more digestible, albeit still unusual, choices such as tortilla stuffed with bacon and cheese.

★ Calle Mayor
SPANISH €€

(☑ 949 39 17 48; www.restaurantecallemayor.com; Calle Mayor 21; mains €12-18; ⊙ 1-3.30pm

& 8.30–11pm) A standout meal stop on the hill between the cathedral and castle, Calle Mayor serves traditional dishes such as delicious roast goat or fried lamb's brains, as well as more elaborate creations. It offers excellent value for the quality on offer and a stylish but comfortable dining area to match. Service is correct, if a little on the cold side.

Gurugú de la Plazuela　　　　　TAPAS €€
(www.gurugudelaplazuela.com; Plazuela de la Cárcel; mushroom dishes €12–18; ⊙12.30–4pm & 8–11pm Thu-Sat, 12.30–4pm Sun; ☑) Overlooking the small, atmospheric Plazuela de la Cárcel, the speciality of this historical tavern is mushrooms – lots of them – with some 16 varieties on the menu, prepared all sorts of ways. Other choices include a nice line in game dishes. It holds regular art and photography exhibitions.

Nöla　　　　　　　　FUSION, SPANISH €€€
(☑949 39 32 46; www.nolarestaurante.es; Calle Mayor 41; mains €19–29; ⊙1.30–3.30pm & 8.30–10.30pm Thu-Sat, 1.30–4.30pm Sun) Nöla offers creative interpretations of Castilla-La Mancha recipes in a small but pleasantly intimate space near the castle. This is the spot to come to for modest portions of locally influenced food with a high taste factor.

❶ Information

Tourist Office (☑949 34 70 07; www.turismo castillalamancha.es; Calle Serrano Sanz 9; ⊙10am–2pm & 4–6pm Mon-Thu & Sat, 10am–2pm & 4–8pm Fri, 10am–2pm Sun) Just down the hill from the cathedral. Opens and closes an hour later in the afternoon in summer.

❶ Getting There & Away

Buses are infrequent and mainly serve towns around Sigüenza. They stop on Avenida de Alfonso VI. A better bet are trains.

Five daily regional trains go to Madrid's Chamartín station (€11.85 to €13.60, 1½ to 1¾ hours) via Guadalajara; some go on to Soria in the other direction.

Atienza
POP 479

Standing amid the ruins of Atienza's blustery castle and looking out at the arid plains and low hills that couldn't be anywhere but Spain is one of Castilla-La Mancha best memory souvenirs. The diminutive but romantically atmospheric town doesn't get a lot of foreign visitors, but is a great place to come at weekends (when its museums actually open!) for some aimless wandering. It's situated 30km northwest of Sigüenza and its hilltop castle is visible for miles around

◎ Sights

The main half-timbered square and former 16th-century market place, Plaza del Trigo, is overlooked by the Renaissance Iglesia San Juan Bautista, which has an impressive organ and lavish gilt *retablo*. Three of the diminutive but muscular Romanesque churches hold small museums (open weekends only).

Museo de la Santísima Trinidad　　MUSEUM
(Calle Cervantes; €2; ⊙11.30am–2pm & 4–7pm Sat & Sun) The best of Atienza's three museums is inside the Iglesia de la Santísima Trinidad. Its soaring altarpiece and golden rococo-style side chapel are befitting of a church 10 times the size. Upstairs you'll see a rather eerie 16th-century *catafalque* (coffin platform) painted with skeletons.

Castillo Roquero　　　　　　　　CASTLE
(⊙sunrise-sunset; ☑) **FREE** Now that's what you call a castle! Looking like a natural extension of the crag upon which it sits,

WORTH A TRIP

SEGÓBRIGA

Castilla-La Mancha's best-preserved Roman ruins at Segóbriga (adult/child €5/2.50; ⊙10am–3pm & 4–7pm Tue-Sun Apr-Sep, 10am–6pm Tue-Sun Oct-Mar) may date as far back as the 5th century BC. The highlights are a Roman theatre and amphitheatre on the fringes of the ancient city, looking out over a valley. Other remains include the outlines of a Visigothic basilica and a section of the aqueduct that helped keep the city green in what was otherwise a desert. A small museum (included in the price) has some striking exhibits.

The site is near Saelices, 2km south of the A3 motorway between Madrid and Albacete. From Cuenca, drive west 55km on the N400, then turn south on the CM202.

CAMINO TO ATIENZA

Buses serving the hilltop-hugging town of Atienza are a little thin on the ground; but, for those with strong legs, there's a viable alternative. You can walk to the town on a little-trekked southern branch of the Camino de Santiago through a quintessential Castillan landscape of arid hills punctuated by half-forgotten, semiabandoned villages.

While the hallowed Camino's well-trodden northern route now attracts over a quarter of a million walkers annually, this little-known southern branch – once a highway for pilgrims coming from destinations on Spain's Mediterranean coast – remains largely deserted. A well-signposted 32km section of the route connects the two historic towns of Sigüenza and Atienza, passing through the pinprick but atmospheric villages of Palazuelos, Olmeda de Jadraque and Riofrío del Llano.

To get started, exit Sigüenza via Calle Santa Barbara, passing a football field and crossing a railway line. Then, take the unpaved, vehicle-width track uphill and follow the purple and yellow 'Camino' signs decorated with the famous scarab symbol. The well-marked path is good year-round (weather permitting), but, whichever season you hike, take plenty of food and water. The villages along the way offer little in the way of refreshment.

Atienza's romantically dishevelled *castillo* has Roman, Visigothic and Moorish antecedents. It was finally wrested from the Moors by Christian king Alfonso VI in 1085 and is now a windy ruin enjoying fabulous views over the surrounding *meseta* (plains).

Museo de San Gil
MUSEUM
(Plaza Agustín González; €2; ⊙11.30am-2pm & 4-7pm Sat & Sun) This beautifully laid out museum is in the Romanesque Iglesia de San Gil. The church itself is perhaps the main 'exhibit' with its Mudéjar ceiling and plat-eresque door. Lined up in its naves you'll find religious art along with small sections on archaeology (arrowheads mainly) and palaeontology (fossils).

🛏 Sleeping

Hostal El Mirador
HOSTAL €
(☑949 39 90 38; www.elmiradordeatienza.com; Calle Barruelo; s/d €24/45; ❋🌐) El Mirado, with spotless rooms that are a steal at this price, is a budget option in a modern white-washed building offering great panoramic views over the fields below. The excellent restaurant shares the vistas and serves creative dishes, as well as the standard *cordero* (lamb) and *cabrito* (kid).

★Antiguo Palacio de Atienza
HOTEL €€
(☑949 39 91 80; www.palaciodeatienza.com; Plaza de Agustín González 1; d €49-89; ❋🌐⛲) Want to stay in a palace skilfully updated with well-chosen artworks, comfortable beds and exposed beams fine enough to satisfy the expectations of modern-day princes and princesses (and tourists)? The variation in price relates to the size of the room and whether there's a hot tub in the stylish little bathrooms. Balconies overlook the lawns and pool, and there's a good restaurant.

ℹ Information

Oficina de Turismo (www.atienza.es; Calle Héctor Vázquez 2; ⊙11am-2pm & 4-7pm) The info office also contains a small museum displaying local costumes and paraphernalia relating to the town's customs and festivals.

ℹ Getting There & Away

Buses are scant. A couple leave early in the morning, bound for Madrid (€10, 2¾ hours) and Sigüenza (€3.65, 45 minutes).

Barcelona

Best Places to Eat

➡ Disfrutar (p282)

➡ Cinc Sentits (p282)

➡ Tickets (p285)

➡ Tapas 24 (p282)

➡ Cal Pep (p280)

Best Places to Sleep

➡ DO Reial (p273)

➡ Hotel Casa Fuster (p276)

➡ Hotel Brummell (p277)

➡ Cotton House (p276)

➡ Serras Hotel (p273)

Why Go?

Barcelona is a mix of sunny Mediterranean charm and European urban style, where dedicated hedonists and culture vultures feel equally at home. From Gothic to Gaudí, the city bursts with art and architecture; Catalan cooking is among the country's best; summer sun seekers fill the beaches in and beyond the city; and the bars and clubs heave year-round. From its origins as a middle-ranking Roman town, of which vestiges can be seen today, Barcelona became a medieval trade juggernaut. Its old centre holds one of the greatest concentrations of Gothic architecture in Europe. Beyond this are some of the world's more bizarre buildings: surreal spectacles capped by Antoni Gaudí's Sagrada Família. Barcelona has been breaking ground in art, architecture and style since the late 19th century. From Picasso and Miró to today's modern wonders, Barcelona's racing pulse has barely skipped a beat. Equally busy are the city's avant-garde chefs, who compete with old-time classics for gourmets' attention.

When to Go
Barcelona

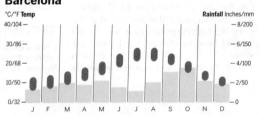

May Plaça del Fòrum rocks during Primavera Sound, a long weekend of outdoor concerts.

Jun Sónar, Europe's biggest celebration of electronic music, is held across the city.

Sep Festes de la Mercè is Barcelona's end-of-summer finale and biggest party.

History

It is thought that Barcelona may have been founded by the Carthaginians in about 230 BC, taking the surname of Hamilcar Barca, Hannibal's father. Roman Barcelona (known as Barcino) covered an area within today's Barri Gòtic and was overshadowed by Tarraco (Tarragona), 90km to the southwest. In the wake of Muslim occupation and then Frankish domination, Guifré el Pilós (Wilfrid the Hairy) founded the house of the Comtes de Barcelona (Counts of Barcelona) in AD 878. In 1137 Count Ramon Berenguer IV married Petronilla, heiress of Aragón, creating a joint state and setting the scene for Catalonia's golden age. Jaume I (1213–76) wrenched the Balearic Islands and Valencia from the Muslims in the 1230s to '40s. Jaume I's son Pere II followed with Sicily in 1282. The accession of the Aragonese noble Fernando to the throne in 1479 augured ill for Barcelona, and his marriage to Queen Isabel of Castilla more still. Catalonia effectively became a subordinate part of the Castilian state. After the War of the Spanish Succession (1702–13), Barcelona fell to the Bourbon king, Felipe V, in September 1714.

Modernisme, Anarchy & the Civil War

The 19th century brought economic resurgence. Wine, cotton, cork and iron industries developed, as did urban working-class poverty and unrest. To ease the crush, Barcelona's medieval walls were demolished in 1854, and in 1869 work began on L'Eixample, an extension of the city beyond Plaça de Catalunya. The flourishing bourgeoisie paid for lavish buildings, many of them in the eclectic Modernisme style, whose leading exponent was Antoni Gaudí. In 1937, a year into the Spanish Civil War, the Catalan communist party (PSUC; Partit Socialista Unificat de Catalunya) took control of the city after fratricidal street battles against anarchists and Trotskyists. George Orwell recorded the events in his classic *Homage to Catalonia*. Barcelona fell to Franco in 1939 and there followed a long period of repression.

From Franco to the Present

Under Franco, Barcelona received a flood of immigrants, chiefly from Andalucía. Some 750,000 people came to Barcelona in the '50s and '60s, and almost as many to the rest of Catalonia. Many lived in appalling conditions. Three years after Franco's death in 1975, a new Spanish constitution created the autonomous community of Catalonia (Catalunya in Catalan; Cataluña in Castilian), with Barcelona as its capital. The 1992 Olympic Games put Barcelona on the map. Under the visionary leadership of popular Catalan Socialist mayor Pasqual Maragall, a burst of public works brought new life to Montjuïc and the once shabby waterfront.

Flush with success after the Olympics makeover, Barcelona continued the revitalisation of formerly run-down neighbourhoods. El Raval, still dodgy in parts, has seen a host of building projects, from the opening of Richard Meier's cutting-edge Macba in 1995 to the Filmoteca de Catalunya in 2012. Further west, the once derelict industrial district of Poble Nou has been reinvented as 22@ (pronounced 'vint-i-dosarroba'), a 200-hectare zone that's a centre for technology and design. Innovative companies and futuristic architecture (such as the brand-new Museu del Disseny) continue to reshape the urban landscape of this ever evolving city.

On other fronts, Catalonia continues to be a trendsetter for the rest of Spain. Barcelona's shared biking program Bicing, launched in 2007, has become a model for sustainable transport initiatives, and the city continues to invest in green energy (particularly in its use of solar power and electric and hybrid vehicles).

Once a great kingdom unto its own, Catalonia has a long independent streak. In 2013, on the Catalan National Day (11 September), hundreds of thousands of separatist supporters formed a 400km human chain across Catalonia. In 2014, a referendum on independence took place, though Spanish judges have said such a vote was illegal and violates the constitution. Whether or not Catalonia will gain its independence, Barcelona will continue to chart its own course ahead.

⊙ Sights

Barcelona could be divided into thematic chunks. In the Ciutat Vella (especially the Barri Gòtic and La Ribera) are the bulk of the city's ancient and medieval splendours. Along with El Raval, on the other side of La Rambla, and Port Vell, where old Barcelona meets the sea, this is the core of the city's life, both by day and by night. Top attractions here include the Museu d'Història de Barcelona, La Catedral and the Museu Picasso.

L'Eixample is where the Modernistas went to town. Attractions here are more

Barcelona Highlights

❶ La Sagrada Família (p251) Marvelling at Antoni Gaudí's still unfolding Modernista masterpiece.

❷ Barri Gòtic (p244) Strolling the narrow medieval lanes of Barcelona's enchanting old quarter.

❸ Palau de la Música Catalana (p245) Seeing a concert in one of Europe's most extravagant concert halls.

❹ Camp Nou (p264) Joining the riotous carnival at an FC Barça match in this hallowed stadium.

❺ Park Güell (p260) Drinking in the views from Gaudí's fabulous creation.

❻ L'Eixample (p251) Dining and drinking amid the architecturally rich streetscape.

❼ Museu Picasso (p249) Discovering Pablo's early masterpieces inside this atmospheric museum.

❽ La Barceloneta (p249) Feasting on fresh seafood, followed by a stroll along the boardwalk.

❾ El Raval (p241) Taking in the nightlife of this bohemian neighbourhood.

❿ Montjuïc (p265) Exploring this hilltop bastion of Romanesque art, a brooding fort, Miró and beautiful gardens.

spread out. Passeig de Gràcia is a concentrated showcase for some of their most outlandish work, but La Sagrada Família, Gaudí's masterpiece, is a long walk (or short metro ride) from there.

Other areas of interest include the beaches and seafood restaurants of the working class district of La Barceloneta. Montjuïc, with its gardens, museums, art galleries and Olympic Games sites, forms a microcosm on its own. Not to be missed are the Museu Nacional d'Art de Catalunya and the Fundació Joan Miró.

Gaudí's Park Güell is just beyond the area of Gràcia, whose narrow lanes and interlocking squares set the scene for much lively nightlife.

Further out, you'll find the amusement park and church of high-up Tibidabo, the wooded hills of Parc de Collserola, FC Barcelona's Camp Nou football stadium and the peaceful haven of the Museu-Monestir de Pedralbes.

◉ La Rambla & Barri Gòtic

The Barri Gòtic is flanked by the mile-long Rambla to the south and the Via Laietana to the north. At its heart is the vast, Gothic cathedral, while some of the city's best museums, such as the Museu d'Història de Barcelona and the Museu Frederic Marès, are within a short walk. Two important squares, useful for orientation, are the Plaça de Sant Jaume, where the government buildings are found, and the handsome, arcaded Plaça Reial.

★ La Rambla   STREET

(Map p238; Ⓜ Catalunya, Liceu, Drassanes) Barcelona's most famous street is both a tourist magnet and a window into Catalan culture, with cultural centres, theatres and intriguing architecture. Set between narrow traffic lanes and flanked by plane trees, the middle of La Rambla is a broad pedestrian boulevard, crowded every day until the wee hours with a wide cross-section of society. A stroll here is pure sensory overload, with souvenir hawkers, buskers, pavement artists, mimes and living statues all part of the ever-changing street scene.

★ La Catedral   CATHEDRAL

(Map p238; ☑ 93 342 82 62; www.catedralbcn.org; Plaça de la Seu; admission free, 'donation entrance' €7, choir €3, roof €3; ⊙ 8am-12.45pm & 5.15-7.30pm Mon-Fri, 8am-8pm Sat & Sun, 'donation entrance' 1-5pm Mon-Sat, 2-5pm Sun; Ⓜ Jaume I) Barcelona's central place of worship presents a magnificent image. The richly decorated main facade, laced with gargoyles and the stone intricacies you would expect of northern European Gothic, sets it quite apart from other churches in Barcelona. The facade was actually added in 1870, although the rest of the building was built between 1298 and 1460. The other facades are sparse in decoration, and the octagonal, flat-roofed towers are a clear reminder that, even here, Catalan Gothic architectural principles prevailed.

★ Museu d'Història de Barcelona   MUSEUM

(MUHBA; Map p238; ☑ 93 256 21 00; www.museuhistoria.bcn.cat; Plaça del Rei; adult/concession/child €7/5/free, 3-8pm Sun & 1st Sun of month free; ⊙ 10am-7pm Tue-Sat, 10am-8pm Sun; Ⓜ Jaume I) One of Barcelona's most fascinating museums takes you back through the centuries to the very foundations of Roman Barcino. You'll stroll over ruins of the old streets, sewers, laundries and wine- and fish-making factories that flourished here following the town's founding by Emperor Augustus around 10 BC. Equally impressive is the building itself, which was once part of the Palau Reial Major (Grand Royal Palace) on Plaça del Rei, among the key locations of medieval princely power in Barcelona.

★ Museu Frederic Marès   MUSEUM

(Map p238; ☑ 93 256 35 00; www.museumares.bcn.cat; Plaça de Sant Iu 5; adult/concession/child €4.20/2.40/free, after 3pm Sun & 1st Sun of month free; ⊙ 10am-7pm Tue-Sat, 11am-8pm Sun; Ⓜ Jaume I) One of the wildest collections of historical curios lies inside this vast medieval complex, once part of the royal palace of the counts of Barcelona. A rather worn coat of arms on the wall indicates that it was also, for a while, the seat of the Spanish Inquisition in Barcelona. Frederic Marès i Deulovol (1893–1991) was a rich sculptor, traveller and obsessive collector, and displays of religious art and vast varieties of bric-a-brac litter the museum.

Plaça de Sant Jaume   SQUARE

(Map p238; Ⓜ Liceu, Jaume I) In the 2000 or so years since the Romans settled here, the area around this square (often remodelled), which started life as the forum, has been the focus of Barcelona's civic life. This is still the central staging area for Barcelona's traditional festivals. Facing each other across the square are the

Palau de la Generalitat (www.president. cat; Plaça de Sant Jaume; ⊙2nd & 4th weekend of month; ⓂJaume I) – the seat of Catalonia's regional government – on the north side and the **Ajuntament** (Casa de la Ciutat; town hall; ☑93 402 70 00; www.barcelona turisme.com; Plaça de Sant Jaume; ⊙10.30am-1.30pm Sun; ⓂJaume I) **FREE** to the south.

Museu d'Idees i Invents de Barcelona MUSEUM
(Museum of Ideas & Inventions; Map p238; ☑93 332 79 30; www.mibamuseum.com; Carrer de la Ciutat 7; adult/concession/child under 4 €8/6/free; ⊙10am-2pm & 4-7pm Tue-Fri, 10am-8pm Sat, to 2pm Sun; ⓂJaume I) Although the price is a bit steep for such a small museum (though they've now introduced a secondary system of €0.20 per minute), the collection makes for an amusing browse over an hour or so. You'll find both brilliant and bizarre inventions on display.

Plaça Reial SQUARE
(Map p238; ⓂLiceu) One of the most photogenic squares in Barcelona, the Plaça Reial is a delightful retreat from the traffic and pedestrian mobs on the nearby Rambla. Numerous eateries, bars and nightspots lie beneath the arcades of 19th-century neoclassical buildings, with a buzz of activity at all hours.

It was created on the site of a convent, one of several destroyed along La Rambla (the street was teeming with religious institutions) in the wake of the Spain-wide disentailment laws that stripped the Church of much of its property. The lamp posts by the central fountain are Antoni Gaudí's first known works in the city.

Temple Romà d'August RUIN
(Map p238; ☑93 256 21 22; Carrer del Paradis 10; ⊙10am-2pm Mon, to 7pm Tue-Sat, to 8pm Sun; ⓂJaume I) **FREE** Opposite the southeast end of La Catedral, narrow Carrer del Paradis leads towards Plaça de Sant Jaume. Inside No 10, an intriguing building with Gothic and baroque touches, are four columns and the architrave of Barcelona's main Roman temple, dedicated to Caesar Augustus and built to worship his imperial highness in the 1st century AD.

Plaça del Rei SQUARE
(Map p238; ⓂJaume I) Plaça del Reia (King's Sq) is a picturesque plaza where Fernando and Isabel received Columbus following his first New World voyage. It is the court-

yard of the former Palau Reial Major. The palace today houses a superb history museum (p236), with significant Roman ruins underground.

Gran Teatre del Liceu ARCHITECTURE
(Map p238; ☑93 485 99 00; www.liceubarcelona. cat; La Rambla 51-59; tour 50min/25min €16/6; ⊙50min tour 9.30am & 10.30am, 25min tour schedule varies; ⓂLiceu) If you can't catch a night at the opera, you can still have a look around one of Europe's greatest opera houses, known to locals as the Liceu. Smaller than Milan's La Scala but bigger than Venice's La Fenice, it can seat up to 2300 people in its grand horseshoe auditorium.

Roman Walls RUIN
(Map p238; ⓂJaume I) From Plaça del Rei it's worth a detour to see the two best surviving stretches of Barcelona's Roman walls, which once boasted 78 towers (as much a matter of prestige as of defence). One section is on the southern side of Plaça de Ramon Berenguer el Gran, with the Capella Reial de Santa Àgata atop. The other is a little further south, by the northern end of Carrer del Sotstinent Navarro.

Plaça de Sant Josep Oriol SQUARE
(Map p238; ⓂLiceu) This small plaza flanking the majestic Església de Santa Maria del Pi (p237) is one of the prettiest in the Barri Gòtic. Its bars and cafes attract buskers and artists and make it a lively place to hang out. It is surrounded by quaint streets, many dotted with appealing cafes, restaurants and shops.

Església de Santa Maria del Pi CHURCH
(Map p238; ☑93 318 47 43; www.basilicadelpi. com; Plaça del Pi; adult/concession/under 6 €4/3/free; ⊙10am-6pm; ⓂLiceu) This striking 14th-century church is a classic of Catalan Gothic, with an imposing facade, a wide interior and a single nave. The simple decor in the main sanctuary contrasts with the gilded chapels and exquisite stained-glass windows that bathe the interior in ethereal light. The beautiful rose window above its entrance is one of the world's largest. Occasional concerts are staged here (classical guitar, choral groups and chamber orchestras).

Sinagoga Major SYNAGOGUE
(Map p238; ☑93 317 07 90; www.callde barcelona.org; Carrer de Marlet 5; ⊙11am-5.30pm Mon-Fri, to 3pm Sat & Sun winter, 10.30am-6.30pm Mon-Fri, to 2.30pm Sat & Sun summer; ⓂLiceu)

Barri Gòtic, La Rambla & El Raval

Ronda de la Universitat

C de Balmes

C de Bergara

Plaça de Catalunya

La Rambla

Av del Portal de l'Àngel

C de Gravina

C de Pelai

C de Riva deneyra

82

C de Jovellanos

Catalunya

C de Santa Anna

C dels Tallers

Catalunya

C dels Tallers

C de la Canuda

28

Plaça de Vicenç Martorell

58

C del Duc de la Victoria

C de Valldonzella

C de les Ramelleres

C del Bonsucces

BARRI GÒTIC

11

46

C d'en Xuclà

Fortuny

C d'en Bot

C de Montalegre

Plaça de Joan Coromines

C d'Elisabets

93

42

MACBA 3

32

C del Notariat

C del Pintor

63

94

C del Petritxol

Plaça dels Àngels

C del Doctor Dou

C del Carme

C d'en Roca

90

C del Cardenal Casañas

61

C de Jerusalem

Rambla de Sant Josep

84

4

C de Ferlandina

C de Joaquín Costa

C del Peu de la Creu

C de les Floristes de la Rambla

Mercat de la Boqueria

Liceu

C de la Lluna

C de les Egipcíaques

10

50

C de la Riera Alta

C de la Riera Baixa

15

40

76

14

C del Carme

C de l'Hospital

EL RAVAL

C de la Junta de Comerç

39

36

C de Sant Rafael

C d'en Robador

C de l'Arc de Sant Agustí

Plaça de Salvador Seguí

75

C de Sant Pau

30

C de la Cera

Rambla del Raval

C de l'Espalter

55

C del Marquès de Barberà

67

C de l'Aurora

52

C de Sant Ramon

C de Sant Pacià

C de la Riereta

C de Sant Oleguer

C de l'Est

C de les Carretes

Plaça de Pere Coromines

C de la Reina Amàlia

53

C de les Tàpies

C del Marquès de Campo Sagrado

Ronda de Sant Pau

C Nou de la Rambla

56

C de les Flors

12

C de l'Om

C d'Aldana

65

C de l'Abat Safont

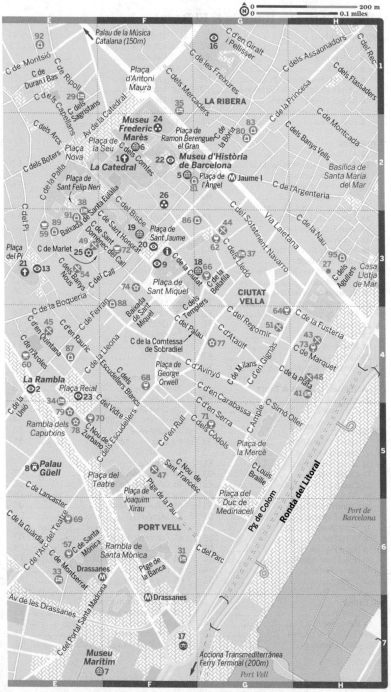

Barri Gòtic, La Rambla & El Raval

EL CALL

One of our favourite places in the Ciutat Vella (Old City) to wander is El Call (pronounced 'kye'), which is the name of the medieval Jewish quarter that flourished here until a tragic pogrom in the 14th century. Today its narrow lanes hide some surprising sites (including an ancient synagogue unearthed in the 1990s and the fragments of a women's bathouse inside the basement of the cafe, Caelum). Some of the old city's most unusual shops are here, selling exquisite antiques, handmade leather products, even kosher wine. Its well-concealed dining rooms and candlelit bars and cafes make a fine destination in the evening.

El Call (which probably derives from the Hebrew word '*kahal*', meaning 'community') is a tiny area, and a little tricky to find. The boundaries are roughly Carrer del Call, Carrer dels Banys Nous, Baixada de Santa Eulàlia and Carrer de Sant Honorat.

Though a handful of Jewish families remained after the bloody pogrom of 1391, the subsequent expulsion of all Jews in the country in the 15th century put an end to the Jewish presence in Barcelona. The Call Menor extended across the modern Carrer de Ferran as far as Baixada de Sant Miquel and Carrer d'en Rauric. The present Església de Sant Jaume on Carrer de Ferran was built on the site of a synagogue.

Even before the pograms of 1391, Jews in Barcelona were not exactly privileged citizens. As in many medieval centres, they were obliged to wear a special identifying mark on their garments and had trouble getting permission to expand their ghetto as El Call's population increased (as many as 4000 people were crammed into the tiny streets of the Call Major).

FREE When an Argentine investor bought a run-down electrician's store with an eye to converting it into central Barcelona's umpteenth bar, he could hardly have known he had stumbled onto the remains of what could be the city's main medieval synagogue (some historians cast doubt on the claim). A guide will explain what is thought to be the significance of the site in various languages.

Mirador de Colom VIEWPOINT
(Map p238; ☎93 302 52 24; www.barcelona turisme.com; Plaça del Portal de la Pau; adult/ concession €6/4; ☺8.30am-8.30pm summer, 8.30am-7.30pm winter; ⓜDrassanes) High above the swirl of traffic on the roundabout below, Columbus keeps permanent watch, pointing vaguely out to the Mediterranean. Built for the Universal Exhibition in 1888, the monument allows you to zip up 60m in a lift for bird's-eye views back up La Rambla and across the ports of Barcelona.

⊙ El Raval

The once down-and-out district of El Raval is still seedy in parts, though it has seen remarkable rejuvenation in recent years, with the addition of cutting-edge museums and cultural centres, including the Richard Meier–designed Museu d'Art Contemporani de Barcelona. Other highlights not to be missed: El Raval's bohemian nightlife and the sprawling culinary delights of Mercat de la Boqueria.

★MACBA ARTS CENTRE
(Museu d'Art Contemporani de Barcelona; Map p238; ☎93 481 33 68; www.macba.cat; Plaça dels Àngels 1; adult/concession/under 12 €10/8/ free; ☺11am-7.30pm Mon & Wed-Fri, 10am-9pm Sat, 10am-3pm Sun & holidays; ⓜUniversitat) Designed by Richard Meier and opened in 1995, MACBA has become the city's foremost contemporary art centre, with captivating exhibitions for the serious art lover. The permanent collection is on the ground floor and dedicates itself to Spanish and Catalan art from the second half of the 20th century, with works by Antoni Tàpies, Joan Brossa and Miquel Barceló, among others, though international artists, such as Paul Klee, Bruce Nauman and John Cage, are also represented.

★Mercat de la Boqueria MARKET
(Map p238; ☎93 412 13 15; www.boqueria.info; La Rambla 91; ☺8am-8.30pm Mon-Sat; ⓜLiceu) Mercat de la Boqueria is possibly La Rambla's most interesting building, not so much for its Modernista-influenced design (it was actually built over a long period, from 1840 to 1914, on the site of the former St Joseph Monastery), but for the action of the food market within.

La Rambla

A TIMELINE

Look beyond the human statues and tourist-swarmed restaurants, and you'll find a fascinating piece of Barcelona history dating back many centuries.

13th century A serpentine seasonal stream (called *ramla* in Arabic) runs outside the city walls. As Barcelona grows, the stream will eventually become an open sewer until it's later paved over.

1500–1800 During this early period, La Rambla was dotted with convents and monasteries, including the baroque **Església de Betlem** ❶, completed in the early 1700s.

1835 The city erupts in anticlericism, with riots and the burning of convents. Along La Rambla, many religious assets are destroyed or seized by the state. This paves the way for new developments, including the **Mercat de la Boqueria** ❷ in 1840, **Gran Teatre del Liceu** ❸ in 1847 and **Plaça Reial** ❹ in 1848.

Teatre Poliorama
Built in 1894 as the seat of the Royal Academy of Sciences and Arts, it later served as a cinema, and a strategic lookout for one communist faction during the Spanish Civil War.

Església de Betlem
Dedicated to the Holy Family, this is the last standing of the many churches once lining La Rambla. Its once sumptuous interior was gutted during the Spanish Civil War.

Font de Canaletes

Via Sepulcral Romana

Plaça del Pi

La Rambla

Palau Moja

Plaça de St Josep Oriol

❼

Centre de la Imatge ❶

Palau de la Virreina

❺

Mercat de la Boqueria
The official name of Barcelona's most photogenic market is El Mercat de Sant Josep, which references the convent of St Josep that once stood here.

❷

Gran Teatre del Liceu
Although badly damaged by fire in 1994, this gorgeous opera house was restored and reborn in 1999, and remains one of Europe's finest theatres.

1883 Architect Josep Vilaseca refurbishes the **Casa Bruno Cuadros** ❺. As Modernisme is sweeping across the city, Vilaseca creates an eclectic work using stained glass, wrought iron, Egyptian imagery and Japanese prints.

1888 Barcelona hosts the Universal Exhibition. The city sees massive urban renewal projects, with the first electric lights coming to La Rambla, and the building of the **Mirador de Colom** ❻.

1936–39 La Rambla becomes the site of bloody street fighting during the Spanish Civil War. British journalist and author George Orwell, who spends three days holed up in the **Teatre Poliorama** ❼ during street battles, later describes the tumultuous days in his excellent book, *Homage to Catalonia*.

Casa Bruno Cuadros
The Casa dels Paraigües (House of Umbrellas) – as it's known locally – prominently advertised its wares, with wall-mounted parasols and an ornate Chinese dragon.

Plaça Reial
Just off La Rambla lies one of Barcelona's prettiest plazas, home to outdoor cafes and bars, palm trees, a gurgling fountain and some unusual lampposts designed by a young Antoni Gaudí.

Mirador de Colom
Southern anchor of La Rambla, this Columbus monument was dedicated in 1888 as part of the Universal Exhibition. You can enjoy fine views from its 60m lookout.

BARRI GÒTIC

La Rambla

Palau Güell

La Rambla

Centre d'Art Santa Mònica

EL RAVAL

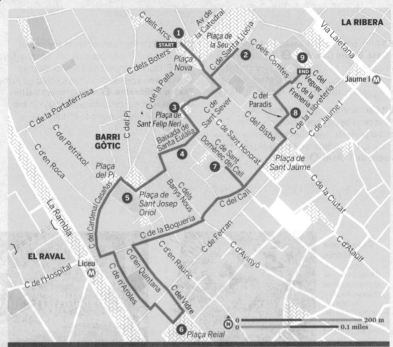

City Walk
Hidden Treasures in the Barri Gòtic

START LA CATEDRAL
END PLAÇA DEL REI
LENGTH 1.5KM; 1½ HOURS

This scenic walk through the Barri Gòtic will take you back in time, from the early days of Roman-era Barcino through to the medieval era.

Before entering the cathedral, have a look at ❶ **three Picasso friezes** on the building facing the square. After noting his signature style, wander through ❷ **La Catedral** (p236); don't miss the cloister with its flock of 13 geese. Leaving the cathedral, enter the former gates of the ancient fortified city and turn right into ❸ **Plaça de Sant Felip Neri**. Note the shrapnel-scarred walls of the old church, damaged by pro-Franco bombers in 1938. A plaque commemorates the victims (mostly children) of the bombing.

Head out of the square and turn right. On this narrow lane, you'll spot a small ❹ **statue of Santa Eulàlia**, one of Barcelona's patron saints who suffered various tortures during her martyrdom. Make your way west to the looming 14th-century ❺ **Església de Sant Maria del Pi** (p237), which is famed for its magnificent rose window. Follow the curving road and zigzag down to ❻ **Plaça Reial** (p237), one of Barcelona's prettiest squares. Flanking the fountain are lamp posts designed by Antoni Gaudí.

Stroll up to Carrer de la Boqueria and turn left on Carrer de Sant Domènec del Call. This leads into the El Call district, once the heart of the medieval Jewish quarter, until the bloody pogrom of 1391. The ❼ **Sinagoga Major** (p237), one of Europe's oldest, was discovered in 1996. Head across Plaça de Sant Jaume and turn left after Carrer del Bisbe. You'll soon pass the entrance to the remnants of a ❽ **Roman Temple**, with four columns hidden in a small courtyard.

The final stop is ❾ **Plaça del Rei** (p237), a picturesque plaza where Fernando and Isabel received Columbus following his first New World voyage. The former palace today houses a superb history museum, with significant Roman ruins underground.

★ Palau Güell
PALACE

(Map p238; ☑93 472 57 75; www.palauguell.cat; Carrer Nou de la Rambla 3-5; adult/concession/under 10 €12/9/free; ⊙10am-8pm Tue-Sun; ⓂDrassanes) Finally reopened in its entirety in 2012 after several years of refurbishment, this is a magnificent example of the early days of Gaudí's fevered architectural imagination. The extraordinary neo-Gothic mansion, one of the few major buildings of that era raised in Ciutat Vella, gives an insight into its maker's prodigious genius.

Centre de Cultura Contemporània de Barcelona
BUILDING

(CCCB; Map p238; ☑93 306 41 00; www.cccb.org; Carrer de Montalegre 5; adult/concession/under 12 for 1 exhibition €6/4/free, 2 exhibitions €8/6/free, Sun 3-8pm free; ⊙11am-8pm Tue-Sun; ⓂUniversitat) A complex of auditoriums, exhibition spaces and conference halls opened here in 1994 in what had been an 18th-century hospice, the Casa de la Caritat. The courtyard, with a vast glass wall on one side, is spectacular. With 4500 sq metres of exhibition space in four separate areas, the centre hosts a constantly changing program of exhibitions, film cycles and other events.

Antic Hospital de la Santa Creu
HISTORIC BUILDING

(Former Hospital of the Holy Cross; Map p238; ☑93 270 16 21; www.bcn.cat; Carrer de l'Hospital 56; ⊙9am-8pm Mon-Fri, to 2pm Sat; ⓂLiceu) Behind La Boqueria stands the Antic Hospital de la Santa Creu, which was once the city's main hospital. Begun in 1401, it functioned until the 1930s, and was considered one of the best in Europe in its medieval heyday – it is famously the place where Antoni Gaudí died in 1926. Today it houses the Biblioteca de Catalunya, and the Institut d'Estudis Catalans (Institute for Catalan Studies). The hospital's Gothic chapel, La Capella (Map p238; ☑93 256 20 44; www.bcn.cat/lacapella; Carrer de l'Hospital; ⊙noon-8pm Tue-Sat, 11am-2pm Sun & holidays; ⓂLiceu) FREE, shows temporary exhibitions.

Església de Sant Pau del Camp
CHURCH

(Map p238; ☑93 441 00 01; Carrer de Sant Pau 101; adult/concession €3/2; ⊙10am-1pm & 4-7pm Mon-Sat; ⓂParal·lel) The best example of Romanesque architecture in the city is the dainty little cloister of this church. Set in a somewhat dusty garden, the 12th-century church also boasts some Visigothic sculptural detail on the main entrance.

REVIVING EL RAVAL

The relocation of the Filmoteca de Catalunya (p292) to the Raval from the neighbourhood of Sarrià is part of the 'Raval Revival', an ongoing project to set up the neighbourhood as one of Spain's most influential cultural centres. As part of the project, representatives from the MACBA, the Gran Teatre del Liceu, the Centre de Cultura Contemporània de Barcelona, the Biblioteca de Catalunya, Arts Santa Mònica, the Virreina Centre de la Imatge, the Institut d'Estudis Catalans and the Filmoteca de Catalunya meet every three months with the aim of creating a cultural network with the Raval as its nucleus. The idea is that these eight institutions will join forces, showing complementary exhibitions, organising cultural events and collaborating in creative projects.

◉ La Ribera

This medieval quarter has a little of everything, from high-end shopping to some of Barcelona's liveliest tapas bars. Key sights include the superb Museu Picasso, the awe-inspiring Gothic Basílica de Santa Maria del Mar and the artfully sculpted Modernista concert hall of Palau de la Música Catalana. For a bit of fresh air, locals head to the manicured gardens of Parc de la Ciutadella.

★ Basílica de Santa Maria del Mar
CHURCH

(☑93 310 23 90; www.santamariadelmarbarcelona.org; Plaça de Santa Maria del Mar; incl guided tour 1-5pm €8; ⊙9am-8pm; ⓂJaume I) At the southwest end of Passeig del Born stands the apse of Barcelona's finest Catalan Gothic church, Santa Maria del Mar (Our Lady of the Sea). Built in the 14th century with record-breaking alacrity for the time (it took just 54 years), the church is remarkable for its architectural harmony and simplicity.

★ Palau de la Música Catalana
ARCHITECTURE

(Map p256; ☑93 295 72 00; www.palaumusica.cat; Carrer de Palau de la Música 4-6; adult/concession/child €18/11/free; ⊙guided tours 10am-3.30pm, to 6pm Easter, Jul & Aug; ⓂUrquinaona) This concert hall is a high point

La Ribera

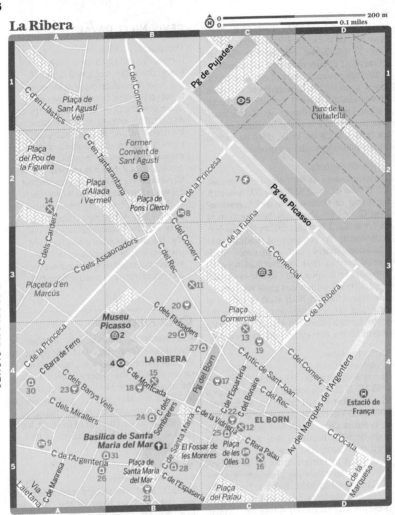

BARCELONA SIGHTS

of Barcelona's Modernista architecture, a symphony in tile, brick, sculpted stone and stained glass. Built by Domènech i Montaner between 1905 and 1908 for the Orfeo Català musical society, it was conceived as a temple for the Catalan Renaixença (Renaissance).

Castell dels Tres Dragons   ARCHITECTURE
(**M** Arc de Triomf) The Passeig de Picasso side of Parc de la Ciutadella is lined by several buildings constructed for, or just before, the Universal Exhibition of 1888. The medieval-looking caprice at the top end is the most engaging. Known as the Castell

dels Tres Dragons (Castle of the Three Dragons), it long housed the Museu de Zoologia, which has since been transferred to the Fòrum area.

Mercat de Santa Caterina   MARKET
(Map p238; ☑93 319 57 40; www.mercatsanta caterina.com; Avinguda de Francesc Cambó 16; ◷7.30am-3.30pm Mon, Wed, Sat, to 8.30pm Tue, Thu, Fri, closed afternoons Jul & Aug; **M** Jaume I) Come shopping for your tomatoes at this extraordinary-looking produce market, designed by Enric Miralles and Benedetta Tagliabue to replace its 19th-century prede-

La Ribera

BARCELONA SIGHTS

cessor. Finished in 2005, it is distinguished by its kaleidoscopic and undulating roof, held up above the bustling produce stands, restaurants, cafes and bars by twisting slender branches of what look like grey steel trees.

Carrer de Montcada STREET
(M Jaume I) An early example of town planning, this medieval high street was driven towards the sea from the road that in the 12th century led northeast from the city walls. It was the city's most coveted address for the merchant classes. The bulk of the great mansions that remain today mostly date to the 14th and 15th centuries.

Born Centre de Cultura i Memòria HISTORIC BUILDING
(☏93 256 68 51; http://elbornculturaimemoria. barcelona.cat; Plaça Comercial 12; centre free, exhibition spaces adult/concession/child €6/4.20/free; ☉10am-8pm Tue-Sun Mar-Sep, 10am-7pm Tue-Sat, to 8pm Sun Oct-Feb; M Barceloneta) Launched to great fanfare in 2013, as part of the events held for the tercentenary of the Catalan defeat in the War of the Spanish Succession, this cultural space is housed in the former Mercat del Born, a handsome 19th-century structure of slatted iron and brick. Excavation in 2001 unearthed remains of whole streets flattened to make way for the much-hated citadel

(ciutadella) – these are now on show on the exposed subterranean level.

Museu de la Xocolata MUSEUM
(☏93 268 78 78; www.museuxocolata.cat; Carrer del Comerç 36; adult/under 7 €6/free; ☉10am-7pm Mon-Sat, 10am-3pm Sun; ♿; M Arc de Triomf) Chocoholics have a hard time containing themselves in this museum dedicated to the fundamental foodstuff – particularly when faced with tempting displays of cocoa-based treats in the cafe at the exit. The displays trace the origins of chocolate, its arrival in Europe, and the many myths and images associated with it. Among the informative stuff and machinery used in the production of chocolate are large chocolate models of emblematic buildings such as La Sagrada Família, along with various characters, local and international.

ℹ️ **ARTICKET BCN**

Barcelona's best bargain for art lovers is the **Articket BCN** (www.articketbcn. org; €30), which gives you entry to six museums for a fraction of what you'd pay if you bought individual tickets. The museums are the MACBA, the CCCB, the Fundació Antoni Tàpies, Fundació Joan Miró, the MNAC and the Museu Picasso.

DON'T MISS

MUSEU PICASSO

The setting alone, in five contiguous medieval stone mansions, makes the Museu Picasso (☏ 93 256 30 00; www.museupicasso.bcn.cat; Carrer de Montcada 15-23; adult/concession/child all collections €14/7.50/free, permanent collection €11/7/free, temporary exhibitions €4.50/3/free, 3-7pm Sun & 1st Sun of month free; ⊙ 9am-7pm Tue, Wed & Fri-Sun, to 9.30pm Thu; Ⓜ Jaume I) unique, and worth the probable queues. The pretty courtyards, galleries and staircases preserved in the first three of these buildings are as delightful as the collection inside.

While the collection concentrates on the artist's formative years – sometimes disappointing for those hoping for a feast of his better-known later works – there is enough material from subsequent periods to give you a thorough impression of the man's versatility and genius. Above all, you come away feeling that Picasso was the true original, always one step ahead of himself (let alone anyone else), in his search for new forms of expression.

The permanent collection is housed in Palau Aguilar, Palau del Baró de Castellet and Palau Meca, all dating to the 14th century. The 18th-century Casa Mauri, built over medieval remains (even some Roman leftovers have been identified), and the adjacent 14th-century Palau Finestres accommodate temporary exhibitions.

The collection, which includes more than 3500 artworks, is strongest on Picasso's earliest years, up until 1904, which is apt considering that the artist spent his formative creative years in Barcelona. Allegedly it was Picasso himself who proposed the museum's creation in 1960, to his friend and personal secretary Jaume Sabartés, a Barcelona native. Three years later, the 'Sabartés Collection' was opened, since a museum bearing Picasso's name would have been met with censorship – Picasso's opposition to the Franco regime was well known. The Museu Picasso we see today opened in 1983. It originally held only Sabartés' personal collection of Picasso's art and a handful of works hanging at the Barcelona Museum of Art, but the collection gradually expanded with donations from Salvador Dalí and Sebastià Junyer Vidal, among others, though the largest part of the present collection came from Picasso himself. His widow, Jacqueline Roque, also donated 41 ceramic pieces and the *Woman with Bonnet* painting after Picasso's death. The original collection still hangs in the Palau Aguilar.

A visit starts with sketches and oils from Picasso's earliest years in Málaga and La Coruña – around 1893–95. Some of his self-portraits and the portraits of his parents, which date from 1896, are evidence enough of his precocious talent. *Retrato de la Tía Pepa* (Portrait of Aunt Pepa), done in Málaga in 1896, shows the incredible maturity of his brush-

Museu del Rei de la Magia   MUSEUM
(Map p256; ☏ 93 318 71 92; www.elreydelamagia. com; Carrer de les Jonqueres 15; adult/concession & child €5/3; ⊙ 11am-2pm & 4-8pm Tue-Sun, closed Sun morning Jul & Aug; 🖴; Ⓜ Urquinaona) This museum is a timeless curio. It is the scene of magic shows, home to collections of material that hark back to the 19th-century origins of the associated magic shop (p294) at Carrer de la Princesa 11, and the place for budding magicians of all ages to enrol in courses. Seeing is believing.

Parc de la Ciutadella   PARK
(Map p250; Passeig de Picasso; 🖴; Ⓜ Arc de Triomf) Come for a stroll, a picnic, a visit to the zoo or to inspect Catalonia's regional parliament, but don't miss a visit to this, the most central green lung in the city. Parc de la Ciutadella is perfect for winding down on a summer day.

Parlament de Catalunya   HISTORIC BUILDING
(Map p250; ☏ 93 304 65 00; www.parlament. cat; ⊙ guided tours 10am-1pm Sat, Sun & holidays; Ⓜ Arc de Triomf) **FREE** Southeast, in the fort's former arsenal, is the regional Parlament de Catalunya. You can join free guided tours, in Catalan and Spanish (Castilian) only, on Saturdays and Sundays; sign up online in advance. The building is open for independent visiting on 11 September from 10am to 7pm. Most interesting is the sweeping Escala d'Honor (Stairway of Honour) and the several solemn halls that lead to the Saló de Sessions, the semicircular auditorium where parliament sits.

Zoo de Barcelona   ZOO
(Map p250; ☏ 902 457 545; www.zoobarcelona. cat; Parc de la Ciutadella; adult/child €19.90/11.95; ⊙ 10am-5.30pm Nov-Mar, 10am-7pm Apr, May, Sep, Oct, 10am-8pm Jun-Aug; 🖴; Ⓜ Barceloneta) The

strokes and his ability to portray character – at the tender age of 15! Picasso painted the enormous *Ciència i caritat* (Science and Charity) in the same year, showcasing his masterful academic techniques of portraiture. His ingeniousness extends to his models too, with his father standing in for the doctor, and a beggar whom he hired off the street along with her offspring, modeling the sick woman and the child. This painting caused the young artist to be noticed in the higher echelons of Spain's art world, when *Ciència i caritat* was awarded an Honorary Mention at the General Fine Arts Exhibition in Madrid in 1897.

In rooms 5–7 hang paintings from his first Paris sojourn, while room 8 is dedicated to the first significant new stage in his development, the Blue Period. *Woman with Bonnet* is an important work from this period, depicting a captive from the Saint-Lazare women's prison and veneral disease hospital that Picasso visited when in Paris – this also sets up the theme of Picasso's fascination with those inhabiting the down-and-out layers of society.

His nocturnal blue-tinted views of *Terrats de Barcelona* (Roofs of Barcelona) and *El foll* (The Madman) are cold and cheerless, yet somehow alive. *Terrats de Barcelona* was painted during his second stint at the 17 Carrer de la Riera Sant Joan studio in 1903 – he painted the city rooftops frequently, from different perspectives in this period. *El foll* shows the artist's interest in the people on the margins of society, and Picasso made many drawings of beggars, the blind and the impoverished elderly throughout 1903 and 1904.

A few cubist paintings pop up in rooms 10 and 11; check the *Glass and Tobacco Packet* still-life painting, a beautiful and simple work. Picasso started to experiment with still life in 1924 – something he'd done before but had not taken to as seriously as he would from here on.

From 1954 to 1962 Picasso was obsessed with the idea of researching and 'rediscovering' the greats, in particular Velázquez. In 1957 he made a series of renditions of the Velázquez' masterpiece, *Las meninas*, now displayed in rooms 12–14. It is as though Picasso has looked at the original Velázquez painting through a prism reflecting all the styles he had worked through until then, creating his own masterpiece in the process. This is a wonderful opportunity to see *Las meninas* in its entirety in this beautiful space.

The last rooms contain his dove paintings, engravings and some 40 ceramic pieces completed throughout the latter years of his unceasingly creative life. You'll see plates and bowls decorated with simple, single-line drawings of fish, owls and other animal shapes, typical for Picasso's daubing on clay.

zoo is a great day out for kids, with 7500 critters that range from geckos to gorillas, lions and elephants – there are more than 400 species, plus picnic areas dotted all around and a wonderful adventure playground. There are pony rides, a petting zoo and a mini-train meandering through the grounds. Thanks to recent advances in legislation prohibiting the use of animals for performances (including circuses and bullfighting) the zoo called time on its dolphin shows in late 2015.

◉ Barceloneta & the Waterfront

The formerly industrial waterfront has experienced a dramatic transformation in the last three decades, with sparkling beaches and seaside bars and restaurants, elegant sculptures, a 4.5km-long boardwalk, ultramodern high-rises and yacht-filled marinas.

Your gateway to the Mediterranean is the gridlike neighbourhood of Barceloneta, an old-fashioned fishing quarter full of traditional seafood eateries.

★ **Museu Marítim**   MUSEUM
(Map p238; ☑ 93 342 99 20; www.mmb.cat; Avinguda de les Drassanes; adult/child €7/3.50, 3-8pm Sun free; ⊙ 10am-8pm; Ⓜ Drassanes) These mighty Gothic shipyards shelter the Museu Marítim, a remarkable relic from Barcelona's days as the seat of a seafaring empire. Highlights include a full-sized replica (made in the 1970s) of Don Juan of Austria's 16th-century flagship, fishing vessels, antique navigation charts and dioramas of the Barcelona waterfront.

Museu d'Història de Catalunya   MUSEUM
(Museum of Catalonian History; Map p250; ☑ 93 225 47 00; www.mhcat.net; Plaça de Pau Vila 3;

La Barceloneta

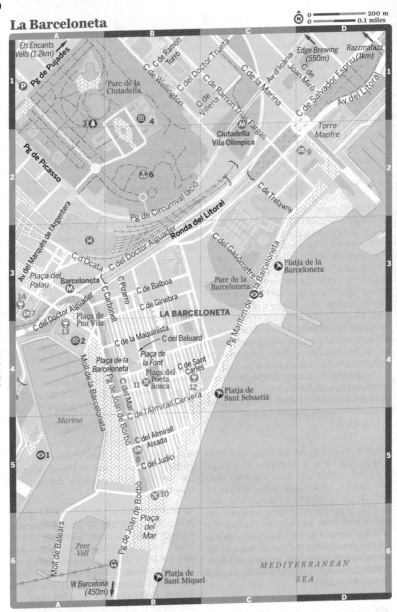

adult/child €4.50/3.50, last Tue of the month Oct-Jun free; ⏱10am-7pm Tue & Thu-Sat, to 8pm Wed, to 2.30pm Sun; Ⓜ Barceloneta) Inside the **Palau de Mar** (Map p250; Plaça de Pau Vila; Ⓜ Barceloneta), this worthwhile museum takes you from the Stone Age through to the early 1980s. It is a busy hotchpotch of dioramas, artefacts, videos, models, documents and interactive bits: all up, an entertaining exploration of 2000 years of Catalan history. Signage is in Catalan/Spanish.

La Barceloneta

Passeig Marítim de la Barceloneta
PROMENADE

(Map p250; Ⓜ Barceloneta, Ciutadella Vila Olímpica) On La Barceloneta's seaward side are the first of Barcelona's beaches, which are popular on summer weekends. The pleasant Passeig Marítim de la Barceloneta, a 1.25km promenade from La Barceloneta to Port Olímpic, is a haunt for strollers and runners, with cyclists zipping by on a separate path nearby.

★ Platjes
BEACH

(⬜ 36, 41, Ⓜ Ciutadella Vila Olímpic, Bogatell, Llacuna, Selva de Mar) A series of pleasant beaches stretches northeast from the Port Olímpic marina. They are largely artificial, but this doesn't stop an estimated seven million bathers from piling in every year!

Edge Brewing
BREWERY

(edgebrewing.com; Carrer de Llull 62; tours including beer tastings €20; ⊙ tours by appointment; Ⓜ Bogatell) Founded by two Americans back in 2013, Edge Brewing has already racked up some impressive awards for its craft beers (among other things it was named top new brewer in the world in 2014 by RateBeer. com). On a brewery tour, you'll get a behind-the-scenes look at Edge's operations, and get to taste some of its classic (like the Hoptimista, an award-winning 6.6% IPA) and seasonal brews (the summertime Apassionada is a passionfruit sour ale).

Museu Can Framis
MUSEUM

(🗗 93 320 87 36; www.fundaciovilacasas.com; Carrer de Roc Boronat 116; adult/student €5/2; ⊙11am-6pm Tue-Sat, to 2pm Sun; Ⓜ Glòries, Llacuna) Set in a former textile factory, this contemporary museum is a showcase for Catalan painting of the past 60 years. The galleries display some 300 works, arranged in thought-provoking ways – with evocative paintings by different artists (sometimes working in different time periods) creating fascinating intersections and collisions.

L'Aquàrium
AQUARIUM

(Map p250; 🗗 93 221 74 74; www.aquariumbcn. com; Moll d'Espanya; adult/child €20/15, dive €300; ⊙ 9.30am-11pm Jul & Aug, to 9pm Sep-Jun; Ⓜ Drassanes) It is hard not to shudder at the sight of a shark gliding above you, displaying its toothy, wide-mouthed grin. But this, the 80m shark tunnel, is the highlight of one of Europe's largest aquariums. It has the world's best Mediterranean collection and plenty of colourful fish from as far off as the Red Sea, the Caribbean and the Great Barrier Reef. All up, some 11,000 fish (including a dozen sharks) of 450 species reside here.

◎ La Sagrada Família & L'Eixample

The elegant, if traffic-filled, district of L'Eixample (pronounced 'lay-sham-pluh') is a showcase for Modernista architecture, including Gaudí's unfinished masterpiece, La Sagrada Família. L'Eixample also has a celebrated dining scene, along with high-end boutiques and wildly diverse nightlife: university party spots, gilded cocktail lounges and the buzzing gay club scene of 'Gaixample' are all part of the mix.

★ La Sagrada Família
CHURCH

(🗗 93 208 04 14; www.sagradafamilia.cat; Carrer de Mallorca 401; adult/concession/under 11 €15/13/free; ⊙ 9am-8pm Apr-Sep, to 6pm Oct-Mar; Ⓜ Sagrada Família) If you have time for only one sightseeing outing, this should be it. La Sagrada Família inspires awe by its sheer verticality, and in the manner of the medieval cathedrals it emulates, it's still under construction after more than 100 years. When completed, the highest tower will be more than half as high again as those that stand today.

Unfinished it may be, but it attracts around 2.8 million visitors a year and is the most visited monument in Spain. The most

La Sagrada Família

A TIMELINE

1882 Francesc del Villar is commissioned to construct a neo-Gothic church.

1883 Antoni Gaudí takes over as chief architect, and plans a far more ambitious church to hold 13,000 faithful.

1926 Death of Gaudí; work continues under Domènec Sugrañes. Much of the **apse** ❶ and **Nativity Facade** ❷ is complete.

1930 Bell towers ❸ of the Nativity Facade completed.

1936 Construction is interrupted by Spanish Civil War; anarchists destroy Gaudí's plans.

1939-40 Architect Francesc de Paula Quintana i Vidal restores the crypt and meticulously reassembles many of Gaudí's lost models, some of which can be seen in the **museum** ❹.

1976 Completion of **Passion Facade** ❺.

1986-2006 Sculptor Josep Subirachs adds sculptural details to the Passion Facade including the panels telling the story of Christ's last days, amid much criticism for employing a style far removed from what was thought typical of Gaudí.

2000 Central nave vault ❻ completed.

2010 Church completely roofed over; Pope Benedict XVI consecrates the church; work begins on a high-speed rail tunnel that will pass beneath the church's **Glory Facade** ❼.

2020s–40s Projected completion date.

TOP TIPS

» **Light** The best light through the stained-glass windows of the Passion Facade bursts through into the heart of the church in the late afternoon.

» **Time** Visit at opening time on weekdays to avoid the worst of the crowds.

» **Views** Head up the Nativity Facade bell towers for the views, as long queues generally await at the Passion Facade towers.

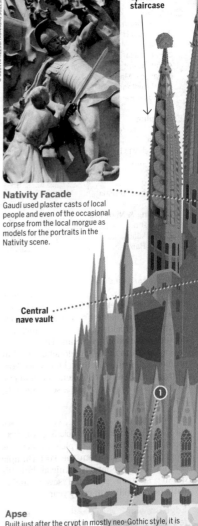

KRZYSZTOF DYDYNSKI/GETTY IMAGES ©

Spiral staircase

Nativity Facade
Gaudí used plaster casts of local people and even of the occasional corpse from the local morgue as models for the portraits in the Nativity scene.

Central nave vault

Apse
Built just after the crypt in mostly neo-Gothic style, it is capped by pinnacles that show a hint of the genius that Gaudí would later deploy in the rest of the church.

JASON WALTMAN/500PX ©

Bell towers
The towers (eight completed) of the three facades represent the 12 Apostles. Lifts whisk visitors up one tower of the Nativity and Passion Facades (the latter gets longer queues) for fine views.

NIKADA/GETTY IMAGES ©

Completed church
Along with the Glory Facade and its four towers, six other towers remain to be completed. They will represent the four Evangelists, the Virgin Mary and, soaring above them all over the transept, a 170m colossus symbolising Christ.

Glory Facade
This will be the most fanciful facade of all, with a narthex boasting 16 hyperboloid lanterns topped by cones that will look something like an organ made of melting ice cream.

Museu Gaudí
Jammed with old photos, drawings and restored plaster models that bring Gaudí's ambitions to life, the museum also houses an extraordinarily complex plumb-line device he used to calculate his constructions.

Escoles de Gaudí

Crypt
The first completed part of the church, the crypt is in largely neo-Gothic style and lies under the transept. Gaudí's burial place here can be seen from the Museu Gaudí.

JEKATERINA NIKITINA/GETTY IMAGES ©

Passion Facade
See the story of Christ's last days from Last Supper to burial in an S-shaped sequence from bottom to top of the facade. Check out the cryptogram in which the numbers always add up to 33, Christ's age at his death.

STEPHEN SAKS/GETTY IMAGES ©

important recent tourist was Pope Benedict XVI, who consecrated the church in a huge ceremony in November 2010.

The Temple Expiatori de la Sagrada Família (Expiatory Temple of the Holy Family) was Antoni Gaudí's all-consuming obsession. Given the commission by a conservative society that wished to build a temple as atonement for the city's sins of modernity, Gaudí saw its completion as his holy mission. As funds dried up, he contributed his own, and in the last years of his life he was never shy of pleading with anyone he thought a likely donor.

Gaudí devised a temple 95m long and 60m wide, able to seat 13,000 people, with a central tower 170m high above the transept (representing Christ) and another 17 towers of 100m or more. The 12 along the three facades represent the Apostles, while the remaining five represent the Virgin Mary and the four evangelists. With his characteristic dislike for straight lines (there were none in nature, he said), Gaudí gave his towers swelling outlines inspired by the weird peaks of the holy mountain Montserrat outside Barcelona, and encrusted them with a tangle of sculpture that seems an outgrowth of the stone.

At Gaudí's death, only the crypt, the apse walls, one portal and one tower had been finished. Three more towers were added by 1930, completing the northeast (Nativity) facade. In 1936 anarchists burned and smashed the interior, including workshops, plans and models. Work began again in 1952, but controversy has always clouded progress. Opponents of the continuation of the project claim that the computer models based on what little of Gaudí's plans survived the anarchists' ire have led to the creation of a monster that has little to do with Gaudí's plans and style. It is a debate that appears to have little hope of resolution. Like or hate what is being done, the fascination it awakens is undeniable.

Guesses on when construction might be complete range from the 2020s to the 2040s. Even before reaching that point, some of the oldest parts of the church, especially the apse, have required restoration work.

Inside, work on roofing over the church was completed in 2010. The roof is held up by a forest of extraordinary angled pillars. As the pillars soar towards the ceiling, they sprout a web of supporting branches, creating the effect of a forest canopy. The tree image is in no way fortuitous – Gaudí envisaged such an effect. Everything was thought through, including the shape and placement of windows to create the mottled effect one would see with sunlight pouring through the branches of a thick forest. The pillars are of four different types of stone. They vary in colour and load-bearing strength, from the soft Montjuïc stone pillars along the lateral aisles through to granite, dark grey basalt and finally burgundy-tinged Iranian porphyry for the key columns at the intersection of the nave and transept. Tribunes built high above the aisles can host two choirs; the main tribune up to 1300 people and the children's tribune up to 300.

The **Nativity Facade** is the artistic pinnacle of the building, mostly created under Gaudí's personal supervision. You can climb high up inside some of the four towers by a combination of lifts and narrow spiral staircases – a vertiginous experience. Do not climb the stairs if you have cardiac or respiratory problems. The towers are destined to hold tubular bells capable of playing complex music at great volume. Their upper parts are decorated with mosaics spelling out 'Sanctus, Sanctus, Sanctus, Hosanna in Excelsis, Amen, Alleluia'. Asked why he lavished so much care on the tops of the spires, which no one would see from close up, Gaudí answered: 'The angels will see them.'

Three sections of the portal represent, from left to right, Hope, Charity and Faith. Among the forest of sculpture on the Charity portal you can see, low down, the manger surrounded by an ox, an ass, the shepherds and kings, and angel musicians. Some 30 different species of plant from around Catalonia are reproduced here, and the faces of the many figures are taken from plaster casts done of local people and the occasional one made from corpses in the local morgue.

Directly above the blue stained-glass window is the Archangel Gabriel's Annunciation to Mary. At the top is a green cypress tree, a refuge in a storm for the white doves of peace dotted over it. The mosaic work at the pinnacle of the towers is made from Murano glass, from Venice.

To the right of the facade is the curious Claustre del Roser, a Gothic-style mini-cloister tacked on to the outside of the church (rather than the classic square enclosure of the great Gothic church monasteries). Once inside, look back to the intricately decorated entrance. On the lower right-hand side you'll notice the sculpture of a reptilian devil handing a terrorist a bomb. Barcelona was regularly rocked by political violence and bombings were frequent in the decades prior to the civil war. The sculpture is one of several on the 'temptations of men and women'.

The southwest Passion Facade, on the theme of Christ's last days and death, was built between 1954 and 1978 based on surviving drawings by Gaudí, with four towers and a large, sculpture-bedecked portal. The sculptor, Josep Subirachs, worked on its decoration from 1986 to 2006. He did not attempt to imitate Gaudí, rather producing angular, controversial images of his own. The main series of sculptures, on three levels, are in an S-shaped sequence, starting with the Last Supper at the bottom left and ending with Christ's burial at the top right. Decorative work on the Passion Facade continues even today, as construction of the Glory Facade moves ahead.

To the right, in front of the Passion Facade, the Escoles de Gaudí is one of his simpler gems. Gaudí built this as a children's school, creating an original, undulating roof of brick that continues to charm architects to this day. Inside is a re-creation of Gaudí's modest office as it was when he died, and explanations of the geometric patterns and plans at the heart of his building techniques.

The Glory Facade is under construction and will, like the others, be crowned by four towers – the total of 12 representing the Twelve Apostles. Gaudí wanted it to be the most magnificent facade of the church. Inside will be the narthex, a kind of foyer made up of 16 'lanterns', a series of hyperboloid forms topped by cones. Further decoration will make the whole building a microcosmic symbol of the Christian church, with Christ represented by a massive 170m central tower above the transept, and the five remaining planned towers symbolising the Virgin Mary and the four evangelists.

Open the same times as the church, the Museu Gaudí, below ground level, includes interesting material on Gaudí's life and other works, as well as models and photos of La Sagrada Família. You can see a good example of his plumb-line models that showed him the stresses and strains he could get away with in construction. A side hall towards the eastern end of the museum leads to a viewing point above the simple crypt in which the genius is buried. The crypt, where Masses are now held, can also be visited from the Carrer de Mallorca side of the church.

Although essentially a building site, the completed sections and museum may be explored at leisure. Guided tours (50 minutes, €9) are offered. Alternatively, pick up an audio tour (€7), for which you need ID. Enter from Carrer de Sardenya and Carrer de la Marina. Once inside, €14 (which includes the audio tour) will get you into lifts that rise

BARCELONA IN...

Two Days

Start with the **Barri Gòtic**. After a stroll along **La Rambla**, wade into the labyrinth to admire **La Catedral** (p236) and the **Museu d'Història de Barcelona** (p236) on historic **Plaça del Rei** (p237). Cross Via Laietana into **La Ribera** for the city's most beloved church, the **Basílica de Santa Maria del Mar** (p245), and the nearby **Museu Picasso** (p249). Round off with a meal and cocktails in the funky **El Born** area.

The following day, start with a walk through Gaudí's unique **Park Güell** (p260), then head for his work in progress, **La Sagrada Família** (p251). Afterwards, head to **El Raval** for dinner at the innovative **Suculent** (p280) followed by drinks at **Bar Marsella** (p285).

Four Days

Start the third day with more Gaudí, visiting **Casa Batlló** (p256) and La Pedrera, followed by beachside relaxation and seafood in **Barceloneta**. Day four should be dedicated to **Montjuïc**, with its museums, galleries, fortress, gardens and Olympic stadium.

One Week

With three extra days, take in **El Raval**, **Gràcia**, a game at **Camp Nou** (p264), **Tibidabo** (p264) views, and the wooded paths of **Collserola** (p264). A tempting one-day excursion is **Montserrat** (p344), Catalonia's 'sacred mountain'. Or spend a day at the beach at **Sitges** (p349).

L'Eixample

up inside the towers in the Nativity and Passion facades. These two facades, each with four sky-scraping towers, are the sides of the church. The main Glory Facade, on which work is under way, closes off the southeast end on Carrer de Mallorca.

★ **Casa Batlló**   ARCHITECTURE

(Map p256; ☎ 973 216 03 06; www.casabatllo. es; Passeig de Gràcia 43; adult/concession/ under 7 €22.50/19.50/free; ⊙ 9am-9pm, last admission 8pm; M Passeig de Gràcia) One of the strangest residential buildings in Europe,

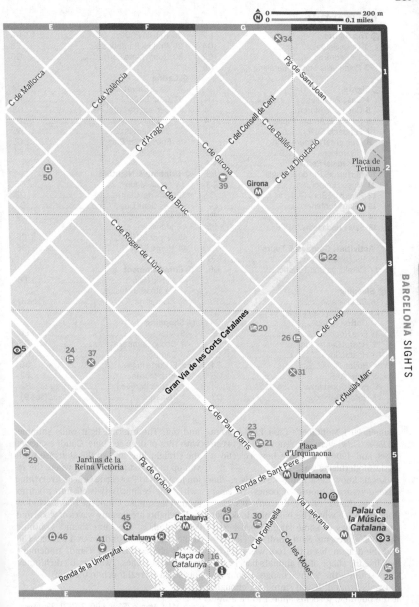

this is Gaudí at his hallucinatory best. The facade, sprinkled with bits of blue, mauve and green tiles and studded with wave-shaped window frames and balconies, rises up to an uneven blue-tiled roof with a solitary tower.

It is one of the three houses on the block between Carrer del Consell de Cent and Carrer d'Aragó that gave it the playful name Manzana de la Discordia, meaning 'Apple (Block) of Discord'. The others are Puig i Cadafalch's Casa Amatller (p259) and

L'Eixample

Domènech i Montaner's Casa Lleó Morera (p259). They were all renovated between 1898 and 1906 and show how eclectic a 'style' Modernisme was.

Locals know Casa Batlló variously as the *casa dels ossos* (house of bones) or *casa del drac* (house of the dragon). It's easy enough to see why. The balconies look like the bony jaws of some strange beast and the roof represents Sant Jordi (St George) and the dragon. Even the roof was built to look like the shape of an animal's back, with shiny scales – the 'spine' changes colour as you walk around. If you stare long enough at the building, it seems almost to be a living being. Before going inside, take a look at the pavement. Each paving piece carries stylised images of an octopus and a starfish, designs that Gaudí originally cooked up for Casa Batlló.

When Gaudí was commissioned to refashion this building, he went to town inside and out. The internal light wells shimmer with tiles of deep sea blue. Gaudí eschewed the straight line, and so the staircase wafts you up to the 1st (main) floor, where the salon looks on to Passeig de Gràcia. Everything swirls: the ceiling is twisted into a vortex around its sunlike lamp; the doors, window and skylights are dreamy waves of wood and coloured glass. The same themes continue in the other rooms and covered terrace. The attic is characterised by Gaudí trademark hyperboloid arches. Twisting, tiled chimney pots add a surreal touch to the roof.

★ **La Pedrera**   ARCHITECTURE
(Casa Milà; Map p256; ☎ 90 220 21 38; www.lapedrera.com; Passeig de Gràcia 92; adult/concession/under 13/under 7 €20.50/16.50/10.25/free; ☉ 9am-8.30pm Mar-Oct, to 6.30pm Nov-Feb; ⓂDiagonal) This undulating beast is another madcap Gaudí masterpiece, built in 1905–10 as a combined apartment and office block.

Formally called Casa Milà, after the businessman who commissioned it, it is better known as La Pedrera (the Quarry) because of its uneven grey stone facade, which ripples around the corner of Carrer de Provença.

Casa Amatller ARCHITECTURE

(Map p256; ☑93 461 74 60; www.amatller. org; Passeig de Gràcia 41; adult/child 6-12/under 6 1hr tour €15/7.50/free, 30min tour €12/7/free; ☉11am-6pm; Ⓜ Passeig de Gràcia) One of Puig i Cadafalch's most striking bits of Modernista fantasy, Casa Amatller combines Gothic window frames with a stepped gable borrowed from Dutch urban architecture. But the busts and reliefs of dragons, knights and other characters dripping off the main facade are pure caprice.

The pillared foyer and staircase lit by stained glass are like the inside of some romantic castle. The building was renovated in 1900 for the chocolate baron and philanthropist Antoni Amatller (1851–1910).

Casa Lleó Morera ARCHITECTURE

(Map p256; ☑93 676 27 33; www.casalleomorera. com; Passeig de Gràcia 35; guided tour adult/concession/under 12 €15/13.50/free, express tour adult/under 12 €12/free; ☉10am-1.30pm & 3-7pm Tue-Sun; Ⓜ Passeig de Gràcia) Domènech i Montaner's 1905 contribution to the Manzana de la Discordia, with Modernista carving outside and a bright, tiled lobby in which floral motifs predominate, is perhaps the least odd-looking of the three main buildings on the block. Since 2014 part of the building has been open to the public (by guided tour only: one-hour tour in English at 11am, and 'express tours' every 30 minutes), so you can appreciate the 1st floor, giddy with swirling sculptures, rich mosaics and whimsical decor.

Museu del Perfum MUSEUM

(Map p256; ☑93 216 701 21; www.museudelperfum. com; Passeig de Gràcia 39; adult/concession €5/3; ☉10.30am-8pm Mon-Fri, 11am-2pm Sat; Ⓜ Passeig de Gràcia) Housed in the back of the Regia perfume store (Map p256; ☑93 216 01 21; www.regia.es; Passeig de Gràcia 39; ☉9.30am-8.30pm Mon-Sat; Ⓜ Passeig de Gràcia), this museum contains oddities from ancient Egyptian and Roman scent receptacles (the latter mostly from the 1st to 3rd centuries AD), to classic eau de cologne bottles – all in all, some 5000 bottles of infinite shapes, sizes and histories. Other items include ancient bronze Etruscan tweezers and little early-19th-century potpourri bowls made of

fine Sèvres porcelain. Also on show are old catalogues and advertising posters.

Fundació Antoni Tàpies GALLERY

(Map p256; ☑93 487 03 15; www.fundaciotapies. org; Carrer d'Aragó 255; adult/concession €7/5.60; ☉10am-7pm Tue-Sun; Ⓜ Passeig de Gràcia) The Fundació Antoni Tàpies is both a pioneering Modernista building (completed in 1885) and the major collection of leading 20th-century Catalan artist Antoni Tàpies. A man known for his esoteric work, Tàpies died in February 2012, aged 88; he left behind a powerful range of paintings and a foundation intended to promote contemporary artists.

Museu del Modernisme Barcelona MUSEUM

(Map p256; ☑93 272 28 96; www.mmbcn.cat; Carrer de Balmes 48; adult/concession/child 6-16/under 6 €10/7/5/free; ☉10.30am-7pm Tue-Sat, to 2pm Sun; Ⓜ Passeig de Gràcia) Housed in a Modernista building, the ground floor seems like a big Modernista furniture showroom. Several items by Antoni Gaudí, including chairs from Casa Batlló and a mirror from Casa Calvet, are supplemented by a host of items by his lesser-known contemporaries, including some typically whimsical, mock medieval pieces by Puig i Cadafalch.

Palau del Baró Quadras ARCHITECTURE

(Map p256; ☑93 467 80 00; www.llull.cat; Avinguda Diagonal 373; ☉8am-8pm Mon-Fri; Ⓜ Diagonal) **FREE** Puig i Cadafalch designed Palau del Baró Quadras (built 1902–06) in an exuberant Gothic-inspired style. The main facade is its most intriguing, with a soaring, glassed-in gallery. Take a closer look at the gargoyles and reliefs – the pair of toothy fish and the sword-wielding knight clearly have the same artistic signature as the architect behind Casa Amatller. Decor inside is eclectic, but dominated by Middle Eastern and East Asian themes.

Recinte Modernista de Sant Pau ARCHITECTURE

(☑93 553 78 01; www.santpaubarcelona.org; Carrer de Sant Antoni Maria Claret 167; adult/concession/under 16 €10/7/free; ☉10am-6.30pm Mon-Sat, to 2.30pm Sun; Ⓜ Sant Pau/Dos de Maig) Domènech i Montaner outdid himself as architect and philanthropist with the Modernista Hospital de la Santa Creu i de Sant Pau, redubbed in 2014 the 'Recinte Modernista'. It was long considered one of the city's most important hospitals, and only recently repurposed, its various spaces becoming cultural centres, offices and something of a monument. The complex, including 16 pavilions – together with the Palau de la Música Catalana, a joint World Heritage site – is lavishly decorated and each pavilion is unique.

Palau Robert   EXHIBITION
(Map p256; ☎93 238 80 91; www.palaurobert. gencat.cat; Passeig de Gràcia 107; ◷10am-8pm Mon-Sat, to 2.30pm Sun; Ⓜ Diagonal) FREE Catalonia's regional tourist office, which holds a huge range of books and leaflets, also serves as an exhibition space, mostly for shows with Catalan themes. In summer concerts are occasionally held in the peaceful gardens at the back of this fine building, or in its main hall.

Casa de les Punxes   ARCHITECTURE
(Casa Terrades; Map p261; Avinguda Diagonal 420; Ⓜ Diagonal) Puig i Cadafalch's Casa Terrades is better known as the Casa de les Punxes (House of Spikes) because of its pointed turrets. This apartment block, completed in 1905, looks like a fairy-tale castle and has the singular attribute of being the only fully detached building in L'Eixample.

Museu Egipci   MUSEUM
(Map p256; ☎93 488 01 88; www.museuegipci. com; Carrer de València 284; adult/concession/ under 15 €11/8/5; ◷10am-2pm & 4-8pm Mon-Fri, 10am-8pm Sat, to 2pm Sun; Ⓜ Passeig de Gràcia) Hotel magnate Jordi Clos has spent much of his life collecting ancient Egyptian artefacts, brought together in this private museum. It's divided into different thematic areas (the pharaoh, religion, funerary practices, mummification, crafts etc) and boasts an interesting variety of exhibits.

Sala Fundación MAPFRE   GALLERY
(Map p256; ☎93 401 26 03; www.fundacionmapfre. org; Carrer de la Diputació 250; adult/student/ under 6 €6/3/free; ◷2-8pm Mon, 10am-8pm Tue-Sat, 11am-7pm Sun; Ⓜ Passeig de Gràcia) FREE Formerly the Fundación Francisco Godia, this stunning, carefully restored Modernista residence was taken over in late 2015 by the charitable cultural arm of Spanish insurance giants MAPFRE as a space for art and photography exhibitions. Housed in the Casa Garriga i Nogués, it is a stunning, carefully restored Modernista residence originally built for a rich banking family by Enric Sagnier in 1902–05.

Palau Montaner   ARCHITECTURE
(Map p256; ☎93 317 76 52; www.fundaciotapies. org; Carrer de Mallorca 278; adult/child €7/free;

◷guided tours 11am Sat; Ⓜ Passeig de Gràcia) Interesting on the outside and made all the more enticing by its gardens, this creation by Domènech i Montaner is spectacular on the inside. Completed in 1896, its central feature is a grand staircase beneath a broad, ornamental skylight. The interior is laden with sculptures (some by Eusebi Arnau), mosaics and fine woodwork. It is currently only open by guided tour, organised by the Fundació Tàpies and in Catalan only.

Fundació Suñol   GALLERY
(Map p256; ☎93 496 10 32; www.fundaciosunol. org; Passeig de Gràcia 98; adult/concession €4/3; ◷11am-2pm & 4-8pm Mon-Fri, 4-8pm Sat; Ⓜ Diagonal) Rotating exhibitions of portions of this private collection of mostly 20th-century art (some 1200 works in total) offer anything from Man Ray's photography to sculptures by Alberto Giacometti. Over two floors, you are most likely to run into Spanish artists, anyone from Picasso to Jaume Plensa, along with a sprinkling of international artists.

⊙ Gràcia & Park Güell

Gràcia was an independent town until the 1890s. Its narrow lanes and picturesque plazas still have a village-like feel, and it has long been a magnet to a young, hip, largely international crowd. Here you'll find well-worn cafes and bars, vintage shops and a smattering of multicultural eateries. On a hill to the north lies the outdoor Modernista storybook of Park Güell, yet another captivating work by Gaudí.

★ Park Güell   PARK
(☎93 409 18 31; www.parkguell.cat; Carrer d'Olot 7; admission to central area adult/child €8/6; ◷8am-9.30pm May-Aug, to 8pm Sep-Apr; ☐24, 32, Ⓜ Lesseps, Vallcarca) North of Gràcia and about 4km from Plaça de Catalunya, Park Güell is where Gaudí turned his hand to landscape gardening. It's a strange, enchanting place where his passion for natural forms really took flight – to the point where the artificial almost seems more natural than the natural.

Park Güell originated in 1900, when Count Eusebi Güell bought a tree-covered hillside (then outside Barcelona) and hired Gaudí to create a miniature city of houses for the wealthy in landscaped grounds. The project was a commercial flop and was abandoned in 1914 – but not before Gaudí had created 3km of roads and walks, steps,

Gràcia

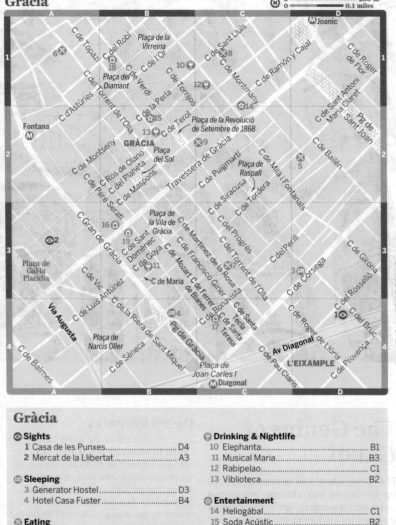

a plaza and two gatehouses in his inimitable manner. In 1922 the city bought the estate for use as a public park.

Just inside the main entrance on Carrer d'Olot, immediately recognisable by the two Hansel-and-Gretel gatehouses, is the park's Centre d'Interpretaciò, in the Pavelló de Consergeria, which is a typically curvaceous former porter's home that hosts a display on Gaudí's building methods and the history of

The Genius of Gaudí

The name Gaudí has become a byword for Barcelona and, through his unique architectural wonders, one of the principal magnets for visitors to the city.

A Catholic & a Catalan

Born in Reus and initially trained in metalwork, Antoni Gaudí i Cornet (1852–1926) personifies, and largely transcends, the Modernisme movement that brought a thunderclap of innovative greatness to turn-of-the-century Barcelona. Gaudí was a devout Catholic and Catalan nationalist, and his creations were a conscious expression of Catalan identity and, in some cases, great piety.

The Masterworks

He devoted much of the latter part of his life to what remains Barcelona's call sign: the unfinished Sagrada Família. His inspiration in the first instance was Gothic, but he also sought to emulate the harmony he observed in nature, eschewing the straight line and favouring curvaceous forms.

Gaudí used complex string models weighted with plumb lines to make his calculations. You can see examples in the upstairs mini-museum in La Pedrera.

The architect's work evokes sinuous movement often with a dreamlike or surreal quality. The private apartment house Casa Batlló is a fine example in which all appears as a riot of the unnaturally natural – or the naturally unnatural. Not only are straight lines eliminated, but the lines between real

1. Casa Batlló (p256)
2. Palau Güell (p245)
3. La Pedrera (p258)

and unreal, sober and dream-drunk, good sense and play are all blurred. Depending on how you look at the facade, you might see St George defeating a dragon, or a series of fleshless sea monsters straining out of the wall.

He seems to have particularly enjoyed himself with rooftops. At La Pedrera and Palau Güell, in particular, he created all sorts of fantastical, multicoloured tile figures as chimney pots looking like anything from *Alice in Wonderland* mushrooms to *Star Wars* imperial troopers.

Saint Gaudí?

Much like his work in progress, La Sagrada Família, Gaudí's story is far from over. In March 2000 the Vatican decided to proceed with the examination of the case for canonising him, and pilgrims already stop by the crypt to pay homage to him. One of the key sculptors at work on the church, the Japanese Etsuro Sotoo, converted to Catholicism because of his passion for Gaudí.

GREATEST HITS

➡ La Sagrada Família (p251), a symphony of religious devotion.

➡ La Pedrera (p258), dubbed 'the Quarry' because of its flowing facade.

➡ Casa Batlló (p256), a fairy-tale dragon.

➡ Park Güell (p260), a park full of Modernista twists.

➡ Palau Güell (p245), one of Gaudí's earliest commissions.

the park. There are nice views from the top floor.

The steps up from the entrance, guarded by a mosaic dragon/lizard (a copy of which you can buy in many downtown souvenir shops), lead to the Sala Hipóstila (aka the Doric Temple). This is a forest of 88 stone columns, some of which lean like mighty trees bent by the weight of time, originally intended as a market. To the left curves a gallery whose twisted stonework columns and roof give the effect of a cloister beneath tree roots – a motif repeated in several places in the park. On top of the Sala Hipóstila is a broad open space whose centrepiece is the Banc de Trencadís, a tiled bench curving sinuously around its perimeter and designed by one of Gaudí's closest colleagues, architect Josep Maria Jujol (1879–1949). With Gaudí, however, there is always more than meets the eye. This giant platform was designed as a kind of catchment area for rainwater washing down the hillside. The water is filtered through a layer of stone and sand, and it drains down through the columns to an underground cistern.

The spired house over to the right is the Casa-Museu Gaudí, where Gaudí lived for most of his last 20 years (1906–26). It contains furniture by him (including items that were once at home in La Pedrera, Casa Batlló and Casa Calvet) and other memorabilia. The house was built in 1904 by Francesc Berenguer i Mestres as a prototype for the 60 or so houses that were originally planned here.

Much of the park is still wooded, but it's laced with pathways. The best views are from the cross-topped Turó del Calvari in the southwest corner.

The walk from metro stop Lesseps is signposted. From the Vallcarca stop, it is marginally shorter and the uphill trek eased by escalators. Bus 24 drops you at an entrance near the top of the park.

The park is extremely popular (it gets an estimated four million visitors a year, about 86% of them tourists). Access is limited to a certain number of people every half-hour, and it's wise to book ahead online (you'll also save a bit on the admission fee).

Gaudí Experience
THEATRE
(☑ 93 285 44 40; Carrer de Larrard 41; adult/child €9/7.50; ⊙ 10.30am-7pm Apr-Sep, to 5pm Oct-Mar; Ⓜ Lesseps, Vallcarca) The 'Gaudí Experience' is a fun-filled Disney-style look at the life and work of Barcelona's favourite son, just

a stone's throw from Park Güell. There are models of his buildings and achingly modern interactive exhibits and touchscreens, but the highlight is the stomach-churning 4D presentation in its tiny screening room. Not recommended for the frail or children aged under six years.

Mercat de la Llibertat
MARKET
(Map p261; ☑ 93 217 09 95; www.mercatllibertat. com; Plaça de la Llibertat 27; ⊙ 8am-8pm Mon-Fri, 8am-3pm Sat; Ⓡ FGC Gràcia) Built in the 1870s, the 'Market of Liberty' was covered over in 1893 in typically fizzy Modernista style, employing generous whirls of wrought iron. It got a considerable facelift in 2009 and has lost some of its aged charm, but the market remains emblematic of the Gràcia district: full of life and all kinds of fresh produce.

◉ Camp Nou, Pedralbes & La Zona Alta

Several of Barcelona's most sacred sights nestle inside the huge expanse beyond L'Eixample. One is the peaceful monastery of Pedralbes; another is the great shrine to Catalan football, Camp Nou. Other attractions include the amusement park and great views atop Tibidabo, the wooded trails of Parc de Collserola, and a kid-friendly science museum.

Camp Nou Experience
MUSEUM
(☑ 902 189900; www.fcbarcelona.com; Gate 9, Avinguda de Joan XXIII; adult/child €23/18; ⊙ 9.30am-7.30pm daily Apr-Sep, 10am-6.30pm Mon-Sat, to 2.30pm Sun Oct-Mar; Ⓜ Palau Reial) A pilgrimage site for football fans from the world, Camp Nou (p292) is one of Barcelona's most hallowed grounds. While nothing compares to the excitement of attending a live match, the Camp Nou Experience is a must for FC Barcelona fans. On this self-guided tour, you'll get an in-depth look at the club, starting with a museum filled with multimedia exhibits, trophies and historical displays, followed by a tour of the stadium.

CosmoCaixa
MUSEUM
(Museu de la Ciència; ☑ 93 212 60 50; www.fundacio. lacaixa.es; Carrer de Isaac Newton 26; adult/child €4/free; ⊙ 10am-8pm Tue-Sun; 🚌 60, Ⓡ FGC Avinguda Tibidabo) Kids (and kids at heart) are fascinated by displays here and this science museum remains one of the city's most popular attractions. The single greatest highlight is the recreation over 1 sq km of

flooded Amazon rainforest (Bosc Inundat). More than 100 species of Amazon flora and fauna (including anacondas, colourful poisonous frogs, and caimans) prosper in this unique, living diorama in which you can even experience a tropical downpour.

Parc d'Atraccions · AMUSEMENT PARK

(☑93 211 79 42; www.tibidabo.cat; Plaça de Tibidabo 3-4; adult/child €30/11; ⊘closed Jan & Feb; ☐T2A from Plaça de Catalunya) The reason most *barcelonins* come up to Tibidabo is for some thrills at this funfair, close to the top funicular station. Here you'll find whirling high-speed rides and high-tech 4D cinema, as well as old-fashioned amusements including an old steam train and the Museu d'Autòmats, with its collection of automated puppets dating as far back as 1880. Check the website for opening times.

Parc de Collserola · PARK

(☑93 280 35 52; www.parcnaturalcollserola.cat; Carretera de l'Església 92; ⊘Centre d'Informació 9.30am-3pm, Can Coll 9.30am-3pm Sun & holidays, closed Jul & Aug; ℝFGC Baixador de Vallvidrera, funicular Funicular de Vallvidrera) *Barcelonins* needing an escape from the city without heading too far into the countryside seek out this extensive, 80-sq-km park in the hills. It is a great place to hike and bike, and bristles with eateries and snack bars. Pick up a map from one of the information centres (such as the Carretera de l'Església 92 location, a short walk from the Baixador de Vallvidrera train station).

Torre de Collserola · VIEWPOINT

(☑93 406 93 54; www.torredecollserola.com; Carretera de Vallvidrera al Tibidabo; adult/child €6/4; ⊘noon-2pm & 3.30-8pm Wed-Sun Jul & Aug, noon-2pm & 3.30-6pm Sat & Sun Sep-Dec & Mar-Jun, closed Jan & Feb; ☐111, Funicular de Vallvidrera) Sir Norman Foster designed the 288m-high Torre de Collserola telecommunications tower, which was completed in 1992. There is an external glass lift to the visitors' observation area, 115m up, from where there are some magnificent views – up to 70km on a clear day. All of Barcelona's TVs and radios receive transmissions from here, and repeater stations across Catalonia are also controlled from this tower.

Jardins del Palau de Pedralbes · PARK

(Avinguda Diagonal 686; ⊘10am-8pm Apr-Oct, to 6pm Nov-Mar; ℳPalau Reial) A few steps from busy Avinguda Diagonal lies this small enchanting green space. Sculptures, fountains, citrus trees, bamboo groves, fragrant eucalyptus, towering cypresses and bougainvillea-covered nooks lie scattered along the paths criss-crossing these peaceful gardens. Among the little-known treasures here are a vine-covered parabolic pergola and a gurgling fountain of Hercules, both designed by Antoni Gaudí.

Museu-Monestir de Pedralbes · MONASTERY

(☑93 256 34 34; monestirpedralbes.bcn.cat; Baixada del Monestir 9; adult/child €5/free, 3-8pm Sun free; ⊘10am-5pm Tue-Fri, to 7pm Sat, to 8pm Sun; ☐22, 63, 64, 75, ℝFGC Reina Elisenda) This peaceful old convent was first opened to the public in 1983 and is now a museum of monastic life (the few remaining nuns have moved into more modern neighbouring buildings). It stands at the top of Avinguda de Pedralbes in a residential area that was countryside until the 20th century, and which remains a divinely quiet corner of Barcelona.

⊙ Montjuïc, Poble Sec & Sant Antoni

The hillside overlooking the port has some of the city's finest art collections: the Museu Nacional d'Art de Catalunya (MNAC), the Fundació Joan Miró and CaixaForum. Other galleries, gardens and an imposing castle form part of the scenery. Just below Montjuïc lies the lively tapas bars and eateries of Poble Sec, while the up-and-coming neighbourhood of Sant Antoni draws the young and hip.

★Museu Nacional d'Art de Catalunya (MNAC) · MUSEUM

(Map p266; ☑93 622 03 76; www.museunacional. cat; Mirador del Palau Nacional; adult/student/child €12/8.40/free, after 3pm Sat & 1st Sun of month free; ⊘10am-8pm Tue-Sat, to 3pm Sun May-Sep, to 6pm Tue-Sat Oct-Apr; ℳEspanya) From across the city, the bombastic neobaroque silhouette of the Palau Nacional (Map p266) can be seen on the slopes of Montjuïc. Built for the 1929 World Exhibition and restored in 2005, it houses a vast collection of mostly Catalan art spanning the early Middle Ages to the early 20th century. The high point is the collection of extraordinary Romanesque frescoes.

★Fundació Joan Miró · MUSEUM

(Map p266; ☑93 443 94 70; www.fmirobcn.org; Parc de Montjuïc; adult/child €12/free; ⊘10am-

Montjuïc & Poble Sec

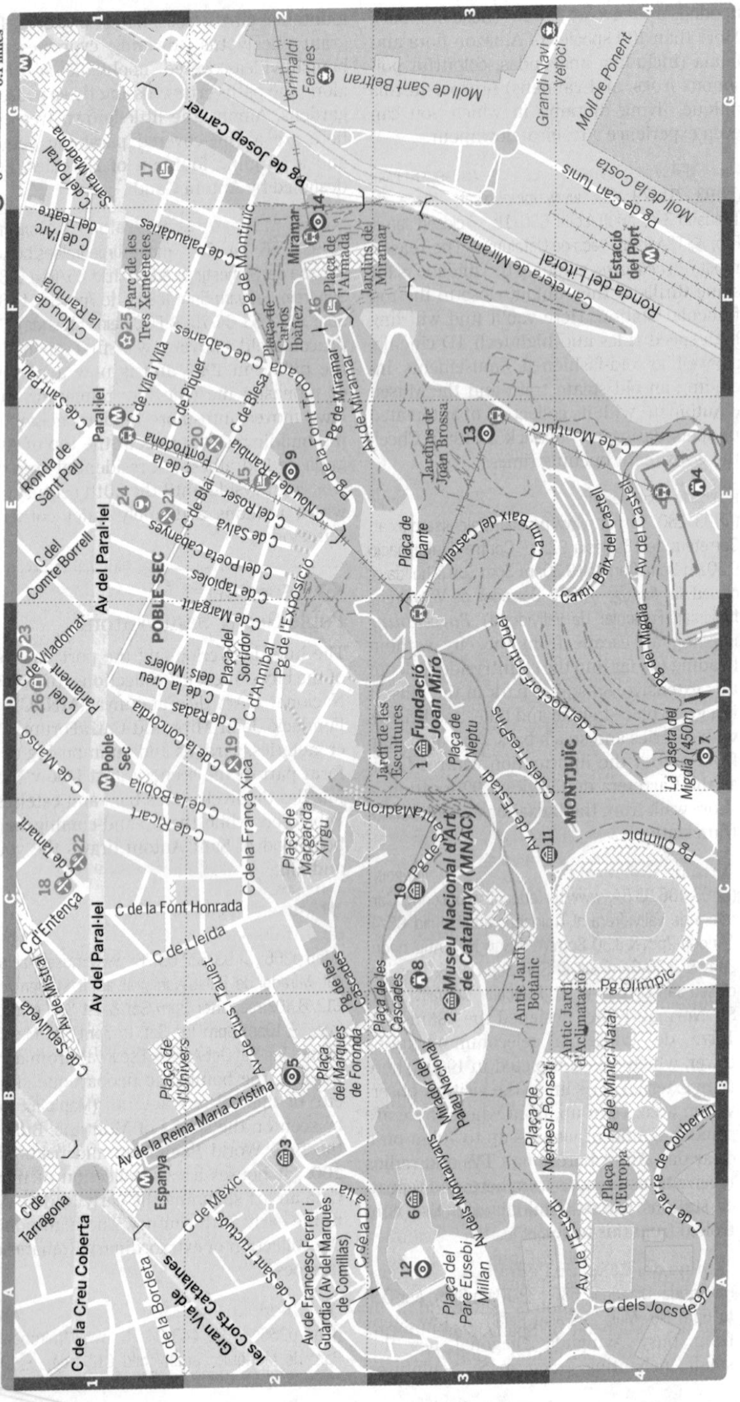

BARCELONA

N

0 —— 200 m
0 —— 0.1 miles

Streets and places:

C de la Creu Coberta
C de Tarragona
C de la Bordeta
Gran Via de les Corts Catalanes
Av del Paral·lel
C de Sepúlveda
C de Mistral (Av de Mistral)
C d'Entença
C de la Font Honrada
C de Lleida
C de Francesc Ferrer i Guàrdia (Av del Marqués de Comillas)
Av de Sant Fructuós
C de Mèxic
C de la D...
Plaça de l'Univers
Plaça del Marqués de Foronda
Av de la Reina Maria Cristina
Espanya
Plaça de les Cascades
Pg de les Cascades
Mirador del Palau Nacional
Av dels Montanyans
Plaça Nacional
Av de Rius i Taulet
Plaça del Pare Eusebi Millan
Plaça de Nemesi Ponsati
Pg de Minici Natal
Plaça d'Europa
C de Pierre de Coubertin
C dels Jocs de 92
Av de l'Estadi
Antic Jardí Botànic
Antic Jardí d'Aclimatació
Pg Olímpic
MONTJUÏC
Museu Nacional d'Art de Catalunya (MNAC)
Pg de Santa Madrona
Plaça de Margarida Xirgu
C de la França Xica
C de Ricart
C de la Bòbila
Poble Sec
C de Radas
C de la Creu
C dels Molers
C de Tapioles
C de Poeta Cabanes
C de la Concòrdia
C de Rius i Taulet
C del Parlament
C de Viladomat
C del Comte Borrell
C de Manso
C de Tamarit
Ronda de Sant Pau
C de Sant Pau
Parallel
Av del Paral·lel
POBLE SEC
C del Margarit
Pg de l'Exposició
C d'Annibal
Plaça del Sortidor
C de Salvà
C de Blai
C del Roser
C de la Font Trobada
Nou de la Rambla
C de la Font
Fontrodona
C de Piquer
C de Blesa
C de Vila i Vilà
Parc de les Tres Xemeneies
C Nou de la Rambla
C de l'Arc del Teatre
Plaça de Raquel Meller
Pg de Josep Carner
Moll de Sant Beltran
Grimaldi Ferries
Grandi Navi Veloci
Moll de Ponent
Moll de Can Tunis
Pg de Can Tunis
Moll de la Costa
Estació del Port
Ronda del Litoral
Carretera de Miramar
Estació de Miramar
Jardins del Miramar
Miramar
Plaça de l'Armada
Av de Miramar
Plaça de Carlos Ibáñez
Plaça de Dante
Jardins de Joan Brossa
Camí Baix del Castell
C de Montjuïc
Camí del Mar
Pg del Mirador
Pg del Migdia
La Caseta del Migdia (450m)
MONTJUÏC
C dels Tarongers
Av de l'Estadi
Plaça de Sant Jordi
Plaça de Neptú
Jardí de les Escultures
Fundació Joan Miró
Av del Castell
C del Doctor Font i Quer
Pg Olímpic

Numbered markers on map:

25 Parc de les Tres Xemeneies
17
14 Miramar
16
13
4
7
1 Fundació Joan Miró
11
10
2 Museu Nacional d'Art de Catalunya (MNAC)
8
5
3
6
12
18
22
23
26
19
9
20
15
21
24

Montjuïc & Poble Sec

8pm Tue-Sat, to 9pm Thu, to 2.30pm Sun & holidays; 55, 150, funicular Paral·lel) Joan Miró, the city's best-known 20th-century artistic progeny, bequeathed this art foundation to his hometown in 1971. Its light-filled buildings, designed by close friend and architect Josep Lluís Sert (who also built Miró's Mallorca studios), are crammed with seminal works, from Miró's earliest timid sketches to paintings from his last years.

Castell de Montjuïc FORTRESS, GARDENS
(Map p266; ☎93 256 44 45; www.bcn.cat/castelldemontjuic; Carretera de Montjuïc 66; adult/child €5/free, after 3pm Sun free; ⊙10am-8pm Apr-Oct, to 6pm Nov-Mar; 150, Telefèric de Montjuïc, Castell de Montjuïc) This forbidding *castell* (castle or fort) dominates the southeastern heights of Montjuïc and enjoys commanding views over the Mediterranean. It dates, in its present form, from the late 17th and 18th centuries. For most of its dark history, it has been used to watch over the city and as a political prison and killing ground.

Poble Espanyol CULTURAL CENTRE
(Map p266; www.poble-espanyol.com; Avinguda de Francesc Ferrer i Guàrdia 13; adult/child €12/7; ⊙9am-8pm Mon, to midnight Tue-Thu & Sun, to 3am Fri & Sat; 13, 23, 150, Ⓜ Espanya) Welcome to Spain! All of it! This 'Spanish Village' is both a cheesy souvenir hunters' haunt and an intriguing scrapbook of Spanish architecture built for the Spanish crafts section of the 1929

World Exhibition. You can meander from Andalucía to the Balearic Islands in the space of a couple of hours, visiting surprisingly good copies of Spain's characteristic buildings.

Font Màgica FOUNTAIN
(Map p266; ☎93 316 10 00; Avinguda de la Reina Maria Cristina; ⊙every 30min 7-9pm Fri & Sat Nov-Mar, 9.30-11pm Thu-Sun Apr-Oct; Ⓜ Espanya) A huge fountain that crowns the long sweep of the Avinguda de la Reina Maria Cristina to the grand facade of the Palau Nacional, Font Màgica is a unique performance in which the water can look like seething fireworks or a mystical cauldron of colour.

Fundació Fran Daurel MUSEUM
(Map p266; www.fundaciofrandaurel.com; Avinguda Francesc Ferrer i Guàrdia 13; ⊙10am-7pm; 13, 23, 150) The Fundació Fran Daurel (in Poble Espanyol) is an eclectic collection of 300 works of art, including sculptures, prints, ceramics and tapestries by modern artists ranging from Picasso and Miró to more contemporary figures, such as Miquel Barceló. The foundation also has a sculpture garden, boasting 27 pieces, nearby the Fundació and within the grounds of Poble Espanyol (look for the Montblanc gate). Frequent temporary exhibitions broaden the offerings further.

CaixaForum GALLERY
(Map p266; ☎93 476 86 00; www.fundacio.lacaixa.es; Avinguda de Francesc Ferrer i Guàrdia 6-8; adult/student & child €4/free, 1st Sun of

BARCELONA SIGHTS

Montjuïc

A ONE-DAY ITINERARY

Montjuïc, perhaps once the site of pre-Roman settlements, is today a hilltop green lung looking over city and sea. Interspersed across varied gardens are major art collections, a fortress, an Olympic stadium and more. A solid one-day itinerary can take in the key spots.

Alight at Espanya metro stop and make for **CaixaForum ❶**, always host to three or four free top-class exhibitions. The nearby **Pavelló Mies van der Rohe ❷** is an intriguing study in 1920s futurist housing by one of the 20th century's greatest architects. Uphill, the Romanesque art collection in the **Museu Nacional d'Art de Catalunya ❸** is a must, and its restaurant is a pleasant lunch stop. Escalators lead further up the hill towards the **Estadi Olímpic ❹**, scene of the 1992 Olympic Games. The road leads east to the **Fundació Joan Miró ❺**, a shrine to the master surrealist's creativity. Contemplate ancient relics in the **Museu d'Arqueologia de Catalunya ❻**, then have a break in the peaceful **Jardins de Mossèn Cinto Verdaguer ❼**, the prettiest on the hill, before taking the cable car to the **Castell de Montjuïc ❽**. If you pick the right day, you can round off with the gorgeously kitsch **La Font Màgica ❾** sound and light show, followed by drinks and dancing in an open-air nightspot in **Poble Espanyol ❿**.

TOP TIPS

» **Moving views** Ride the Transbordador Aeri from Barceloneta for a bird's eye approach to Montjuïc. Or take the Teleféric de Montjuïc cable car to the Castell for more aerial views.

» **Summer fun** The Castell de Montjuïc features outdoor summer cinema and concerts (see http://sala montjuic.org).

» **Beautiful bloomers** Bursting with colour and serenity, the Jardins de Mossèn Cinto Verdaguer are exquisitely laid out with bulbs, especially tulips, and aquatic flowers.

JEAN-PIERRE LESCOURRET/GETTY IMAGES ©

CaixaForum
This former factory and barracks designed by Josep Puig i Cadafalch is an outstanding work of Modernista architecture; like a Lego fantasy in brick.

Piscines Bernat Picornell

Olympic Needle

Poble Espanyol
Amid the rich variety of traditional Spanish architecture created in replica for the 1929 Barcelona World Exhibition, browse the art on show in the Fundació Fran Daurel.

TRAVEL INK/GETTY IMAGES ©

Pavelló Mies van der Rohe
Admire the inventiveness of the great German architect Ludwig Mies van der Rohe in this recreation of his avant garde German pavillion for the 1929 World Exhibition.

a Font Màgica
ake a summer evening to behold the Magic
ountain come to life in a unique 15-minute sound
nd light performance, when the water glows like
cauldron of colour.

PAUL BIRIS/GETTY IMAGES ©

Museu Nacional d'Art de Catalunya
Make a beeline for the Romanesque art selection and the 12th-century
polychrome image of Christ in majesty, which was recovered from the apse
of a country chapel in northwest Catalonia.

Fundació Joan Miró
Take in some of
Joan Miró's giant
canvases, and
discover little-known
works from his early
years in the Sala Joan
Prats and Sala Pilar
Juncosa.

9

3

**Museu
Etnològic**

6

**Teatre
Grec**

5

7

**Museu
Olímpic i
de l'Esport**

4

**Estadi
límpic**

**Jardí
Botànic**

8

Jardins de
Mossèn Cinto
Verdaguer

Castell de Montjuïc
Enjoy the sweeping views of the sea and city from
atop this 17th-century fortress, once a political
prison and long a symbol of oppression.

Museu
d'Arqueologia
de Catalunya
This archaeology
museum, housed in
what was the Graphic
Arts palace during the
1929 World Exhibition,
covers Catalonia and
cultures from else-
where in Spain. Items
range from copies of
pre-Neanderthal skulls
to lovely Carthaginian
necklaces and jewel-
studded Visigothic
crosses.

CULTURA TRAVEL/QUIM ROSER/GETTY IMAGES ©

DON'T MISS

ROMANESQUE TRASURES IN THE MUSEU NACIONAL D'ART DE CATALUNYA

The Romanesque art section in the Museu Nacional d'Art de Catalunya constitutes one of Europe's greatest such collections and is an absolute must for lovers of medieval art – and an excellent place to learn about it for those who have had few previous opportunities. The collection consists mainly of 11th- and 12th-century murals, woodcarvings and altar frontals – painted, bas-relief wooden panels that were forerunners of the elaborate *retablos* (altarpieces) that adorned later churches. Gathered from decaying rural churches in northern Catalonia early last century, they are a surprising treasure of vivid colour, discrediting the idea that medieval churches were bereft of decoration. The two outstanding items are an image of Christ in Majesty, done around 1123 and taken from the apse of the Església de Sant Climent de Taüll in northwest Catalonia, and an apse image of the Virgin Mary and Christ Child from the nearby Església de Santa Maria de Taüll.

month free; ⊙10am-8pm; P; MEspanya) The Caixa building society prides itself on its involvement in (and ownership of) art, in particular all that is contemporary. Its premier art expo space in Barcelona hosts part of the bank's extensive collection from around the globe. The setting is a completely renovated former factory, the Fàbrica Casaramona, an outstanding Modernista brick structure designed by Puig i Cadafalch. From 1940 to 1993 it housed the First Squadron of the police cavalry unit – 120 horses in all.

Museu Etnològic
MUSEUM

(Map p266; www.museuetnologic.bcn.cat; Passeig de Santa Madrona 16-22; adult/child €5/3; ⊙10am-7pm Tue-Sat, to 8pm Sun; ☐55) Barcelona's ethnology museum presents an intriguing permanent collection that delves into the rich heritage of Catalunya. Exhibits cover origin myths, religious festivals, folklore, and the blending of the sacred and the secular (along those lines, don't miss the Nativity scene with that quirky Catalan character *el caganer*, aka 'the crapper').

Museu Olímpic i de l'Esport
MUSEUM

(Map p266; ☏93 292 53 79; www.museu olimpicbcn.com; Avinguda de l'Estadi 60; adult/student €5.10/3.20; ⊙10am-8pm Tue-Sat, 10am-2.30pm Sun; ☐55, 150) The Museu Olímpic i de L'Esport is an information-packed interactive museum dedicated to the history of sport and the Olympic Games. After picking up tickets, you wander down a ramp that snakes below ground level and is lined with displays on the history of sport, starting with the ancients.

Jardí Botànic
GARDENS

(Map p266; www.museuciencies.cat; Carrer del Doctor Font i Quer 2; adult/child €3.50/free, after 3pm Sun free; ⊙10am-7pm Apr-Sep, to 5pm Oct-Mar; ☐55, 150) This botanical garden is dedicated to Mediterranean flora and has a collection of some 40,000 plants and 1500 species that thrive in areas with a climate similar to that of the Mediterranean, such as the Eastern Mediterranean, Spain (including the Balearic and Canary Islands), North Africa, Australia, California, Chile and South Africa.

Telefèric de Montjuïc
CABLE CAR

(Map p266; www.telefericdemontjuic.cat; Av Miramar 30; adult/child one way €8/6.20; ⊙10am-9pm Jun-Sep, to 7pm Oct-May; ☐55, 150) From Estació Parc Montjuïc, this cable car carries you to the Castell de Montjuïc via the *mirador.*

Teleférico del Puerto
CABLE CAR

(Map p266; www.telefericodebarcelona.com; Av de Miramar, Jardins de Miramar; one way/return €11/16.50; ⊙11am-7pm Mar-Oct, to 5:30pm Nov-Feb; ☐50, 153) The quickest way from the beach to the mountain is via the cable car that runs between Torre de Sant Sebastiá in La Barceloneta and the Miramar stop on Montjuïc (from mid-June to mid-September only). From Estació Parc Montjuïc, the separate Telefèric de Montjuïc (p270) cable car carries you to the Castell de Montjuïc via the *mirador* (lookout point).

MUHBA Refugi 307
HISTORIC SITE

(Map p266; ☏93 256 21 22; www.museuhistoria. bcn.cat; Carrer Nou de la Rambla 169; incl tour adult/child €3.40/free; ⊙tours 10.30am, 11.30am & 2.30pm Sun; MParal·lel) Part of the Museu d'Història de Barcelona (MUHBA), this is a shelter that dates back to the days of the Spanish Civil War. Barcelona was the city most heavily bombed from the air during the Spanish Civil War and had more than 1300 air-raid shelters. Local citizens started digging this one under a fold of Montjuïc in March 1937. It's open only on Sundays by tour only.

🏃 Activities

Mediterranean oceanfront and a rambling hilly park overlooking the city make fine settings for a bit of outdoor activity beneath the (generally) sunny skies of Barcelona. For a break from museum-hopping and overindulging at tapas bars, Barcelona has the antidote – running, swimming, cycling or simply pumping fists in the air at a never-dull FC Barça match.

Aire De Barcelona   HAMMAM
(☑ 93 295 57 43; www.airedebarcelona.com; Passeig de Picasso 22; thermal baths & aromatherapy Mon-Thu €31, Fri-Sun €33; ⊙ 10am-10pm Mon-Thu & Sun, 10am-2am Fri & Sat; Ⓜ Arc de Triomf) With low lighting and relaxing perfumes wafting around you, this basement hammam could be the perfect way to end a day. Hot, warm and cold baths, steam baths and options for various massages, including on a slab of hot marble, make for a delicious hour or so. Book ahead and bring a swimming costume.

🎓 Courses

Espai Boisà   COOKING COURSE
(☑ 93 192 60 21; http://espaiboisa.com; Ptge Lluís Pellicer 8; varies; Ⓜ Hospital Clínic) 🍴 Run by a young, multilingual Venezuelan-Catalan couple, this first-rate outfit offers cooking courses on various themes and of various lengths. They emphasise organic, seasonal ingredients from local producers outside of Barcelona – put to good use in dishes including paella, a range of tapas dishes and *crema catalana* (a Catalan version of *crème brûlée*).

Dom's Gastronom Cookery School   COOKING COURSE
(☑ 93 674 51 60; www.domsgastronom.com; Passeig del Roser 43, Valldoreix; 8 hours of classes over 4 days €100) Cordon-bleu chef Dominique Heathcoate runs the full gamut of Catalan, Spanish and French cuisine (and even Asian 'tapas'). It's a one-hour trip to the school from Barcelona's old centre.

☞ Tours

Catalunya Bus Turístic   BUS TOUR
(Map p256; ☑ 93 285 38 32; www.catalunyabusturistic.com; Plaça de Catalunya; Ⓜ Catalunya) Routes include a day in Colònia Güell and Montserrat (€70); Montserrat (€46); Girona and Figueres (€76); and a Penedès wine and *cava* jaunt with three winery tours and lunch (€69). All tours leave at 8.30am or 10.30am (Montserrat) from Plaça de Catalunya.

Barcelona Guide Bureau   TOUR
(☑ 93 315 22 61; www.barcelonaguidebureau.com; Via Laietana 50) Barcelona Guide Bureau places professional guides at the disposal of groups for tailor-made tours of the city. Several languages are catered for. It also offers a series of daily tours, from a five-hour highlights of Barcelona tour (adult/child €62/31, departing at 10am) to a trip to Montserrat, leaving Barcelona at 3pm and lasting about four hours (adult/child €48/24).

Barcelona Walking Tours   WALKING TOUR
(Map p256; ☑ 93 285 38 34; www.barcelonaturisme.com; Plaça de Catalunya 17; Ⓜ Catalunya) The Oficina d'Informació de Turisme de Barcelona organises guided walking tours. One explores the Barri Gòtic (adult/child €16/free; in English 9.30am daily); another follows in Picasso's footsteps (adult/child €22/7, in English 3pm Tuesday, Thursday and Saturday) and winds up at the Museu Picasso; and a third takes in the main jewels of Modernisme (adult/child €16/free, in English 6pm Wednesday and Friday).

My Favourite Things   TOUR
(☑ 637 265405; www.myft.net; tours from €26) Offers tours (with no more than 10 participants) based on numerous themes: street art, shopping, culinary tours, musical journeys and forgotten neighbourhoods are among the offerings. Other activities include flamenco and salsa classes, cooking workshops, and bicycle rides in and out of Barcelona. Some of the more unusual activities cost more and times vary.

CicloTour   BICYCLE TOUR
(Map p238; ☑ 93 317 19 70; www.barcelonaciclotour.com; Carrer dels Tallers 45; tours €22; ⊙ 11am & 4.30pm daily mid-Apr–Oct, 11am Mon-Fri, Sat & Sun 11am & 4.30pm Nov, plus 7.30pm Thu-Sun Jun-Sep, Fri & Sat Oct; Ⓜ Universitat) Daily bike tours around the city's main sights. The evening tour also includes a visit to the Font Màgica.

Barcelona Scooter
DRIVING TOUR

(Map p238; ☑93 221 40 70; www.cooltra.com; Via Laietana 6; tour €50; ⊙3.30pm Thu, 10.30am Sat; MJaume I) Run by Cooltra, Barcelona Scooter offers a three-hour tour by scooter around the city, taking in architectural highlights (La Pedrera, La Sagrada Família) and great views (from Montjuïc). Departure is from the Cooltra rental outlet at 3.30pm on Thursdays and 10.30am on Saturdays.

🎊 Festivals & Events

Festes de Santa Eulàlia
CULTURAL

(www.bcn.cat/santaeulalia) Around 12 February this big winter fest (santaeulalia.bcn. cat) celebrates Barcelona's first patron saint with a week of cultural events, including parades of *gegants* (giants), open-air art installations, theatre, *correfocs* (fire runs) and *castells* (human castles).

Dia de Sant Jordi
CULTURAL

This is the day of Catalonia's patron saint (George) and also the Day of the Book: men give women a rose, women give men a book, publishers launch new titles. Though these days, it's common for women to receive roses *and* books. La Rambla and Plaça de Sant Jaume and other central city streets and squares are filled with book and flower stalls. Celebrated on 23 April.

Primavera Sound
MUSIC

(www.primaverasound.com) For three days in late May or early June, the Parc del Fòrum becomes the centre stage for a host of international DJs and musicians.

Sónar
MUSIC

(www.sonar.es) Usually in mid-June, Sónar is Barcelona's massive celebration of electronic music, with DJs, exhibitions, sound labs, record fairs and urban art. Locations change each year.

La Revetlla de Sant Joan (Verbenas de Sant Joan)
CULTURAL

(Nit de Sant Joan; santjoan.bcn.cat) On 23 June locals hit the packed streets or hold parties at home to celebrate the Revetlla de Sant Joan (St John's Night), which involves drinking and dancing, bonfires and fireworks.

Pride Barcelona
GAY & LESBIAN

(www.pridebarcelona.org) The Barcelona gay-pride festival is a week of celebrations held in late June or early July with a crammed program of culture and concerts, along with the massive gay-pride march on Sunday.

Festa Major de Gràcia
CULTURAL

(www.festamajordegracia.org) Locals compete for the most elaborately decorated street in this popular week-long Gràcia festival held around 15 August. The fest also features free outdoor concerts and performaces, street fairs and other events.

Festes de la Mercè
CULTURAL

(www.bcn.cat/merce) The city's biggest party involves four days of concerts, dancing, *castellers* (human-castle builders), a fireworks display synchronised with the Montjuïc fountains, dances of giants on the Saturday, and *correfocs* – a parade of fireworks-spitting monsters and demons who run with the crowd – spitting dragons and devils from all over Catalonia, on the Sunday. Held around 24 September.

🛏 Sleeping

Barcelona has a wide range of sleeping options, from inexpensive hostels hidden in the old quarter to luxury hotels overlooking the waterfront. The small-scale B&B-style apartment rentals scattered around the city are a good-value choice.

Wherever you stay it's wise to book well ahead. If you plan to travel around holidays such as Christmas, New Year's Eve and Easter, or in summer, reserve a room three or four months ahead of time.

🛏 La Rambla & Barri Gòtic

Alberg Hostel Itaca
HOSTEL €

(Map p238; ☑93 301 97 51; www.itacahostel.com; Carrer de Ripoll 21; dm €30, d without bathroom €76; ✳🛜; MJaume I) A bright, quiet hostel near the cathedral, Itaca has spacious dorms (sleeping six to 10 people) with parquet floors and spring colours, and two doubles. There's a lively, social vibe, and the hostel organises activities (pub crawls, flamenco concerts, free daily walking tours), making it a good option for solo travellers.

Bonic Barcelona
B&B €€

(Map p238; ☑626 053434; www.bonic-barcelona.com; Carrer de Josep Anselm Clavé 9; s/d without bathroom €55/90; ✳🛜; MDrassanes) A small, cosy B&B that has eight rooms in varied styles, with wood or decorative tile floors, tall ceilings and attractive furnishings. Several are bright and cheerfully painted, and some lack exterior windows. Owing to the restrictive layout – all rooms share three bathrooms – maximum occupancy is six or seven guests a night, although groups of friends can book the whole place to themselves.

Vrabac
B&B €€

(Map p238; ☑663 494029; vrabacguesthouse. wordpress.com; Carrer de la Portaferrissa 14; s/d incl breakfast €65/75; ❋☎; ⓜLiceu, Catalunya) In a central location just off La Rambla, Vrabac is set in a beautifully restored heritage building complete with original decorative ceilings, exposed sandstone walls and large oil paintings. Rooms vary in size and features – the best have elegant ceramic tile floors and sizeable balconies with private bathrooms. The cheapest are small and basic, lack a bathroom, and aren't recommended. Cash only.

Serras Hotel
BOUTIQUE HOTEL €€€

(Map p238; ☑93 169 18 68; hoteltheserras barcelona.com; Passeig de Colom 9; r €299; ❋☎☒; ⓜBarceloneta) A fresh and funky five-star that has every comfort – including a rooftop bar with a small dipping pool and a terrific view over the port – but never feels stuffy. Rooms at the front are brighter and have a better view (from the bathtub, in some cases) but rooms at the side are spared the traffic noise.

Hotel Mercer
BOUTIQUE HOTEL €€€

(Map p238; ☑93 310 74 80; www.mercer barcelona.com; Carrer dels Lledó 7; s/d from €430; ⓟ❋☎☒; ⓜJaume I) Set on a narrow medieval lane, Hotel Mercer is one of Barcelona's best new hotels. Famed Spanish architect Rafael Moneo stayed true to the building's original Gothic and even Roman elements while creating lavishly designed rooms, some of which overlook an interior garden. There's a lovely rooftop dip pool, stylish cocktail lounge, tapas bar and restaurant, plus wonderfully peaceful common areas.

DO Reial
BOUTIQUE HOTEL €€€

(Map p238; ☑93 481 36 66; www.hoteldoreial. com; Plaça Reial 1; s/d incl breakfast from €220/270; ❋☎☒; ⓜLiceu) Overlooking the magnificent plaza for which it is named, this 18-room property has handsomely designed rooms with beamed ceilings, wide plank floors and all-important soundproofing. The service is excellent, and the facilities exten-

sive, with a roof terrace (bar in summer), dipping pool, solarium and spa. Its excellent market-to-table restaurants draw in visiting foodies.

Hotel Neri
DESIGN HOTEL €€€

(Map p238; ☑93 304 06 55; www.hotelneri.com; Carrer de Sant Sever 5; d €275; ❋☎; ⓜLiceu) This tranquil hotel occupies a beautifully adapted, centuries-old building backing onto Plaça de Sant Felip Neri. The sandstone walls and timber furnishings lend a sense of history, while the rooms feature cutting-edge technology, including plasma-screen TVs and infrared lights in the stone-clad designer bathrooms. Choose from a menu of sheets and pillows, and sun yourself on the roof deck.

🛏 El Raval

Hotel Peninsular
HOTEL €

(Map p238; ☑93 302 31 38; www.hotelpeninsular. net; Carrer de Sant Pau 34; s/d €40/60; ❋☎; ⓜLiceu) An oasis on the edge of the slightly dicey Barri Xino, this former convent (which was connected by tunnel to the Església de Sant Agustí) has a plant-draped atrium extending its height and most of its length. The 60 rooms are simple, with tiled floors and whitewash, but mostly spacious and well kept. There are some great bargains to be had during quiet periods.

★ Barceló Raval
DESIGN HOTEL €€

(Map p238; ☑93 320 14 90; www.barceloraval. com; Rambla del Raval 17-21; r from €128; ❋☎; ⓜLiceu) Part of the city's plans to pull the El Raval district up by the bootstraps, this oval-shaped designer hotel tower makes a 21st-century splash. The rooftop terrace offers fabulous views and the B-Lounge bar-restaurant is the toast of the town for meals and cocktails. Rooms have slick aesthetics (white with lime green or ruby-red splashes of colour), Nespresso machines and iPod docks.

Chic & Basic Ramblas
DESIGN HOTEL €€

(Map p238; ☑93 302 71 11; www.chicandbasic ramblashotel.com; Passatge Gutenberg 7; r €127-152; ❋☎; ⓜDrassanes) The latest in the Chic & Basic chain is the most riotous to date, with quirky and colourful interiors that hit you from the second you walk in and see a vintage Seat 600 car in the foyer. Note that the name is misleading – the hotel is a couple of blocks into the Raval.

Hotel Sant Agustí
HOTEL €€

(Map p238; ☑ 93 318 16 58; www.hotelsa.com; Plaça de Sant Agustí 3; r €138-155; ❋ 🛜; Ⓜ Liceu) This former 18th-century monastery opened as a hotel in 1840, making it the city's oldest. The location is perfect – a quick stroll off La Rambla on a curious square. Rooms sparkle, and are mostly spacious and light filled. Consider an attic double with sloping ceiling and bird's-eye views.

Casa Camper
DESIGN HOTEL €€€

(Map p238; ☑ 93 342 62 80; www.casacamper. com; Carrer d'Elisabets 11; r €260-310; ❋ 🛜; Ⓜ Catalunya) The massive foyer looks like a contemporary-art museum, but the rooms, decorated in red, black and white, are the real surprise. Most have a sleeping and bathroom area, where you can contemplate the hanging gardens outside your window, with a separate, private sitting room with balcony, TV and hammock located across the corridor.

Hotel España
HOTEL €€€

(Map p238; ☑ 93 550 00 00; www.hotelespanya. com; Carrer de Sant Pau 9-11; r €198-281; ❋ 🛜 ﹖; Ⓜ Liceu) Best known for its wonderful Modernista interiors in the dining rooms and bar, in which architect Domènech i Montaner, sculptor Eusebi Arnau and painter Ramon Casas had a hand, this hotel offers plush, contemporary rooms in a building that still manages to ooze a little history. There's a small plunge pool and sun deck on the roof terrace, along with a bar.

🛏 La Ribera

Pensió 2000
PENSIÓN €

(Map p256; ☑ 93 310 74 66; www.pensio2000. com; Carrer de Sant Pere més Alt 6; d €70-80; ❋ 🛜; Ⓜ Urquinaona) This 1st-floor, family-run place is opposite the anything-but-simple Palau de la Música Catalana. Seven reasonably spacious doubles have mosaic-tiled floors, and after a recent renovation all have private bathrooms. You can eat your breakfast in the little courtyard.

Pensión Francia
HOSTEL €

(☑ 93 319 03 76; www.milisa.com/P.Francia; Carrer de Rera Palau 4; d with/without bathroom €99/60; 🛜; Ⓜ Barceloneta) The homey smell of laundry pervades this quaint little hostel in a great location close to the shore, the Parc de la Ciutadella and the nightlife of El Born. The 11 simple rooms are kept spick and span, with nothing much in the way of frills.

Chic & Basic
DESIGN HOTEL €€

(☑ 93 295 46 52; www.chicandbasic.com/hotel-barcelona-born; Carrer de la Princesa 50; s/d €104/113; ❋ 🛜; Ⓜ Jaume I) This is a very cool hotel indeed, with its 31 spotlessly white rooms and fairy-light curtains that change colour, adding an entirely new atmosphere to the space. The rooms are small, but the ceilings are high and the beds enormous. Many beautiful old features of the original building have been retained, such as the marble staircase.

Hotel Banys Orientals
BOUTIQUE HOTEL €€

(☑ 93 268 84 60; www.hotelbanysorientals.com; Carrer de l'Argenteria 37; s/d €96/118; ❋ 🛜; Ⓜ Jaume I) Book well ahead to get into this magnetically popular designer haunt. Cool blues and aquamarines combine with dark-hued floors to lend this clean-lined, boutique hotel a quiet charm. All rooms, on the small side, look onto the street or back lanes. There are more spacious suites in two other nearby buildings.

Grand Hotel Central
DESIGN HOTEL €€€

(Map p238; ☑ 93 295 79 00; www.grandhotelcentral. com; Via Laietana 30; d €337; 🅿 ❋ 🛜 ﹖; Ⓜ Jaume I) With super-soundproofed rooms no smaller than 21 sq metres, this design hotel, complete with rooftop infinity pool, is one of the standout hotel offerings along Via Laietana. Rooms are decorated in style, with high ceilings, muted colours (beiges, browns and creams), dark wooden floors and subtle lighting.

🛏 Barceloneta & the Waterfront

Amistat Beach Hostel
HOSTEL €

(☑ 93 221 32 81; www.amistatbeachhostel.com; Carrer de l'Amistat 21; dm €21-34; ❋ 🛜; Ⓜ Poblenou) A stylish addition to Poblenou, Amistat has attractively designed common areas, with a beanbag-filled lounge with DJ set-up, a low-lit TV room and a guest kitchen. The rooms themselves, which sleep from four to 12, are clean, but basic – aside from a splash of colour on the ceilings. Friendly staff organise pub crawls, club nights and other events.

H10 Port Vell
BOUTIQUE HOTEL €€

(Map p250; ☑ 93 310 30 65; www.h10hotels.com; Pas de Sota Muralla 9; d from €150; ❋ @ 🛜 ﹖; Ⓜ Barceloneta) The location is excellent at this 58-room hotel within a short stroll of El Born and Barceloneta. Sleek, modern rooms have a trim, minimalist design with black and white bathrooms, and the best rooms (not all) have fine views over the marina. The rooftop terrace is the best feature, with sun loungers, a tiny plunge pool and cocktails by evening.

Hotel 54
HOTEL €€

(Map p250; ☎ 93 225 00 54; www.hotel54barceloneta.es; Passeig de Joan de Borbó 54; s €110-170, d €140-210; ❋@☎; MBarceloneta) Hotel 54 is all about location. Modern rooms, with dark tile floors and designer bathrooms, are sought after for the marina and sunset views. Other rooms look out over the lanes of La Barceloneta. You can also sit on the roof terrace and enjoy the harbour views.

Hotel Arts Barcelona
LUXURY HOTEL €€€

(Map p250; ☎ 93 221 10 00; www.hotelartsbarcelona.com; Marina 19-21; r from €450; P❋@☎❄; MCiutadella Vila Olímpica) Set in a sky-high tower looming above Port Olímpic, this is one of Barcelona's most fashionable hotels. It has more than 480 rooms each kitted out with high-end features (Bang & Olufsen entertainment systems, separate shower and soaking tub), plus unbeatable views. Services range from enticing spa facilities to fine dining in celebrated Enoteca, which has two Michelin stars.

W Barcelona
LUXURY HOTEL €€€

(☎93 295 28 00; www.w-barcelona.com; Plaça de la Rosa del Vents 1; r from €326; P❋@☎❄; ☐17, 39, 57, 64, MBarceloneta) This spinnaker-shaped beach-adjacent tower of glass contains 473 rooms and suites that aim for contemporary-hotel chic. Self-indulgence is a byword and guests can flit between gym, infinity pool (with bar) and spa.

🛏 La Sagrada Família & L'Eixample

Hostal Center Inn
HOTEL €€

(Map p256; ☎ 93 265 25 60; www.centerinnbarcelona.com; Gran Via de les Corts Catalanes 688; s/d €75/85; ❋@☎; MTetuan) Simple rooms with quirky touches – wrought-iron bedsteads, Moroccan mosaic tables on the ample balconies, stripey Tim Burton wallpaper in one room, an antique escritoire in another. The bathrooms carry a vaguely Andalucian flavour. Get a back room if you can, as the Gran Via is noisy.

Five Rooms
BOUTIQUE HOTEL €€

(Map p256; ☎ 93 342 78 80; www.thefiverooms.com; Carrer de Pau Claris 72; s/d from €140/160; ❋☎; MUrquinaona) The Five Rooms is in fact 12 rooms nowadays (standard rooms and suites) in this 1st-floor flat on the border between L'Eixample and the old centre of town. Rooms are all different and features include broad, firm beds, stretches of exposed brick wall, restored mosaic tiles and minimalist decor. There are also two apartments.

Condes de Barcelona
HOTEL €€

(Map p256; ☎ 93 445 00 00; www.condesdebarcelona.com; Passeig de Gràcia 73-75; s/d €160-215; P❋☎❄; MPasseig de Gràcia) The most attractive half of the Condes de Barcelona occupies the 1890s Modernista Casa Enric Batlló. Across the road stands a more modern extension. Clean, designer lines dominate inside each, with luxurious rooms, hardwood floors and architectural touches reminiscent of the Modernista exterior. The rooftop pool is a great place to relax after a hard day's sightseeing.

Hotel Axel
HOTEL €€

(Map p256; ☎ 93 323 93 93; www.axelhotels.com; Carrer d'Aribau 33; s/d from €145; ❋❋☎❄; MUniversitat) Favoured by a mixed fashion and gay set, Axel occupies a sleek corner block and offers modern touches in its 105 designer rooms. A subtle, light colour scheme, plasma TVs and (in the double rooms) king-sized beds are just some of the pluses. Take a break in the rooftop pool, the Finnish sauna or the spa bath.

Hotel Constanza
BOUTIQUE HOTEL €€

(Map p256; ☎ 93 270 19 10; www.hotelconstanza.com; Carrer del Bruc 33; s/d €100/140; ❋☎; MGirona, Urquinaona) This boutique beauty has stolen the hearts of many a visitor to Barcelona. Design touches abound, and little details like flowers in the bathroom add charm. Suites and studios are further options. The terrace is a nice spot to relax for a while, looking over the rooftops of the L'Eixample.

Room Mate Pau
HOTEL €€

(Map p256; ☎ 93 343 63 00; pau.room-matehotels.com; Carrer de Fontanella 7; s/d €160; ❋☎; MUrquinaona, Catalunya) Just a short stroll from Plaça de Catalunya, Room Mate Pau sits somewhere between upscale hostel and boutique hotel. The rooms are small and minimalist, but cleverly designed (with good mattresses and USB-connected flatscreen TVs). The enticing interior terrace with bar draws a young and hip crowd.

Praktik Rambla BOUTIQUE HOTEL €€
(Map p256; ☎93 343 66 90; www.hotelpraktikrambla.com; Rambla de Catalunya 27; s/d €110-135; ❄📶; Ⓜ Passeig de Gràcia) This Modernista gem hides a gorgeous little boutique number. While the high ceilings and the bulk of the original tile floors have been maintained, the 43 rooms have daring ceramic touches, spot lighting and contemporary art. There is a chilled reading area and deck-style lounge terrace. The handy location on a tree-lined boulevard is an added plus.

Hostal Oliva HOSTAL €€
(Map p256; ☎93 488 01 62; www.hostaloliva.com; Passeig de Gràcia 32; s/d €55/95, without bathroom €41/71; ❄📶; Ⓜ Passeig de Gràcia) A picturesque antique lift wheezes its way up to this 4th-floor *hostal*, a terrific, reliable cheapie in one of the city's most expensive neighbourhoods. Some of the single rooms can barely fit a bed but the doubles are big enough, and light and airy (some with tiled floors, others with parquet and dark old wardrobes).

Hostal Goya HOSTAL €€
(Map p256; ☎93 302 25 65; www.hostalgoya.com; Carrer de Pau Claris 74; s/d from €105; ❄📶; Ⓜ Urquinaona) The Goya is a modestly priced gem on the chichi side of L'Eixample. Rooms have a light colour scheme that varies from one to another. In the bathrooms, the original mosaic floors have largely been retained, and combined with contemporary design features. The more expensive doubles have a balcony.

Cotton House HOTEL €€€
(Map p256; ☎93 450 50 45; www.hotelcottonhouse.com; Gran Via de les Corts Catalanes 670; r from €332; ❄📶; Ⓜ Urquinaona) An exceptionally splendid new addition to the city's luxury hotels, situated in the former headquarters of the Cottonmakers' Guild, something which is alluded to throughout, from the huge sprays of cotton bolls in the jaw-dropping lobby to the room names (Damask, Taffeta etc). There's even a space off the library where you can select fabric and have a shirt made.

Hotel Majèstic HOTEL €€€
(Map p256; ☎93 488 17 17; www.hotelmajestic.es; Passeig de Gràcia 68; s/d €330; P❄📶🏊; Ⓜ Passeig de Gràcia) This sprawling, central option has the charm of a great European hotel. The rooftop pool is superb for views and relaxing, or you can pamper yourself in the spa after a workout in the gym. The standard rooms (no singles) are smallish but comfortable and come with marble bathrooms.

Gràcia & Park Güell

★**Casa Gràcia** HOSTEL €
(Map p256; ☎93 174 05 28; www.casagraciabcn.com; Passeig de Gràcia 116; dm/s/d from €27/90/103; ❄@📶; Ⓜ Diagonal) A hostel with a difference, the tasteful Casa Gràcia has raised the bar for budget accommodation. There are some enticing common spaces, including a terrace, a library nook, and an artfully decorated lounge – not to mention a restaurant and DJ-fueled bar on hand.

Generator Hostel HOSTEL €€
(Map p261; ☎93 220 03 77; generatorhostels.com; Carrer de Còrsega 373; dm/d from €28/111; Ⓜ Verdaguer, Diagonal) Part of the design-forward Generator brand, this stylish hostel has much to recommend it, including a quirky bar made from reclaimed lumber and recycled elevator parts and festooned with an explosion of paper lanterns. The rooms themselves are quite simple if adequately equipped – unless you opt for the penthouse room with a terrace offering panoramic views over the city.

Hotel Casa Fuster DESIGN HOTEL €€€
(Map p261; ☎93 255 30 00; www.hotelcasafuster.com; Passeig de Gràcia 132; r from €262; P❄@📶🏊; Ⓜ Diagonal) This sumptuous Modernista mansion, built in 1908–11, is one of Barcelona's most luxurious hotels. Standard rooms are plush, if small. Period features have been restored at considerable cost and complemented with hydro-massage tubs, plasma TVs and king-size beds. The rooftop terrace (with pool) offers spectacular views.

Camp Nou, Pedralbes & La Zona Alta

Inout Hostel HOSTEL €
(☎93 280 09 85; www.inouthostel.com; Major del Rectoret 2; dm €22; ❄@📶🏊; Ⓡ FGC Baixador de Vallvidrera) 🌿 One of Spain's most extraordinary hostels, Inout is a beautifully located property with a strong social ethos. Over 90% of staff here have disabilities. It's a friendly and welcoming place with extensive facilities, including an enticing pool, sports courts, and a low-key restaurant with panoramic views. It's a 12-minute uphill

walk from the FGC Baixador de Vallvidrera station.

Hotel Pol & Grace
BOUTIQUE HOTEL €€

(☑ 93 415 40 00; www.polgracehotel.es; Carrer de Guillem Tell 49; r from €120; ✳ ⋒; ◪ FGC Molina, Sant Gervasi) This stylish new hotel has appealing, uniquely designed rooms, revolving around Barcelona themes (images and artefacts that celebrate a Catalan festival, key architectural icons, gastronomy, etc). There's also a handsomely designed lounge where guests can unwind, and a roof terrace is in the works.

ABaC Barcelona
LUXURY HOTEL €€€

(☑ 93 319 66 00; www.abacbarcelona.com; Avinguda del Tibidabo 1; d from €253; ✳ @ ⋒; ◪ FGC Avinguda Tibidabo) This uberstylish hotel in Sant Gervasi receives high marks for its beautifully designed rooms, kitted out with Bang & Olufsen TVs, rainfall shower heads, Jacuzzi tubs with aromatherapy and luxury bed linens. A lovely spa and one of the city's best restaurants (p284) (with two Michelin stars) add to the appeal.

🛏 Montjuïc, Poble Sec & Sant Antoni

Tailor's Hostel
HOSTEL €

(☑ 93 250 56 84; www.tailors-hostel.com; Carrer de Sepúlveda 146; dm €24-30; ✳ ⋒; ◪ Urgell, Sant Antoni) Decorated like a mid-20th-century tailor's shop, this popular hostel has uncommon style, with old sewing machines, lovingly framed brassieres and vintage fixtures adorning the common areas. Aside from admiring the aesthetics, there's much afoot at Tailor's: you can shoot a round on the old billiards table, mingle with other guests in the comfy lounge, or join one of the many activities on offer.

Pars Teatro Hostel
HOSTEL €

(Map p266; ☑ 93 443 94 66; www.teatrohostel.com; Carrer d'Albareda 12; dm €25-35; ⋒; ◪ Drassanes) True to name, Teatro Hostel has a theatrically decorated interior: old photos of actors of yesteryear hang on the walls of the vintage-filled main lounge, above an old row of velvety theatre seats. Rooms are less exciting, but clean and well-maintained, and the hostel organises dinners, beach parties and other activities. Friendly staff.

★ Hotel Brummell
BOUTIQUE HOTEL €€

(Map p266; ☑ 93 125 86 22; www.hotelbrummell.com; Carrer Nou de la Rambla 174; d from €150; ✳ ⋒ ⌕; ◪ Paral·lel) This stylish addition to Barcelona has been turning heads since its 2015 opening. It's a thoughtfully designed hotel with a creative soul and great atmosphere. The 20 rooms are bright with a cheerful, minimalist design, and the best of the bunch have sizable terraces with views and even outdoor soaking tubs. The smallest (the Brummell Classic rooms) feel a little tight.

Hotel Market
BOUTIQUE HOTEL €€

(☑ 93 325 12 05; www.andilanahotels.com; Carrer del Comte Borrell 68; r €130; ✳ @ ⋒; ◪ Sant Antoni) Attractively located in a renovated building along a narrow lane just north of the grand old Sant Antoni market, this place has an air of simple chic, with wide plank floors, oversized armoires, bold art prints and nicely designed bathrooms (stone basins, rain showers). Some rooms have tiny (two-seat) balconies.

Hotel Miramar
HOTEL €€€

(Map p266; ☑ 93 281 16 00; www.hotelmiramarbarcelona.com; Plaça de Carlos Ibáñez 3; r €230; ✳ ⋒ ⌕; ⌹ 50, 150) Welcome to the only hotel on Montjuïc, a designer five-star job. Local architect Oscar Tusquets took the shell of a building built for the 1929 World Fair and later the Barcelona HQ of Spanish national TV (1959–83), and created this hilltop configuration where all rooms have broad balconies and views over the port, city or park.

🍴 Eating

Barcelona has a celebrated food scene fuelled by a combination of world-class chefs, imaginative recipes and magnificent ingredients fresh from farms and the sea. Catalan culinary masterminds like Ferran Adrià and Carles Abellan have become international icons, reinventing the concept of haute cuisine, while classic old-world Catalan recipes continue to earn accolades in dining rooms and tapas bars across the city.

🍴 La Rambla & Barri Gòtic

First things first: skip the strip. La Rambla is fine for people-watching, but no great shakes for the palate. Instead, venture off into the streets that wind into the Barri Gòtic and your belly (and wallet) will be eternally grateful. Inside the medieval labyrinth, choices abound. If you had to pinpoint any one area, it would be the eastern half of the *barri* (neighbourhood) near Via Laietana on the narrow streets above the

CATALAN COOKING

New Catalan Cuisine

Avant-garde chefs have made Catalonia famous throughout the world for their food laboratories, their commitment to food as art and their crazy riffs on the themes of traditional local cooking.

Here the notion of gourmet cuisine is deconstructed as chefs transform liquids and solid foods into foams, create 'ice cream' of classic ingredients by means of liquid nitrogen, freeze-dry foods to make concentrated powders and employ spherification to create unusual and artful morsels. This alchemical cookery is known as molecular gastronomy, and invention is the keystone of this technique.

Diners may encounter olive oil 'caviar', 'snow' made of gazpacho with anchovies, jellified Parmesan turned into spaghetti, and countless other concoctions.

The dining rooms themselves also offer a reconfiguration of the five-star dining experience. Restaurateurs generally aim to create warm and buzzing spaces, with artful design flourishes, and without the stuffiness and formality typically associated with high-end dining.

Classic Catalan Cuisine

Traditional Catalan recipes showcase the great produce of the Mediterranean: fish, prawns, cuttlefish, clams, pork, rabbit, game, first-rate olive oil, peppers and loads of garlic. Classic dishes also feature unusual pairings (seafood with meat, fruit with fowl): cuttlefish with chickpeas, cured pork with caviar, rabbit with prawns, goose with pears.

Great Catalan restaurants can be found in nearly every neighbourhood around town. The settings can be a huge part of the appeal – with candle-lit medieval chambers in the Ciutat Vella and Modernista design in L'Eixample setting the stage for a memorable feast. Although there are plenty of high-end places in this city, foodie-minded *barcelonins* aren't averse to eating at humbler, less elegant places – which sometimes cook up the best meals.

cathedral (around Carrer de les Magdalenes) and between Plaça de Sant Jaume and the waterfront. Here you'll find a huddle of old-time tapas bars as well as innovative newcomers.

La Plata   TAPAS €
(Map p238; ☑ 93 315 10 09; www.barlaplata.com; Carrer de la Mercè 28; tapas €2.50-5; ☺ 9am-3.30pm & 6.30-11.30pm Mon-Sat; Ⓜ Jaume I) Tucked away on a narrow lane near the waterfront, La Plata is a humble but well-loved bodega that serves just three plates: *pescadito frito* (small fried fish), *butifarra* (sausage) and tomato salad. Add in the drinkable, affordable wines (€1.10 per glass) and you have the makings of a fine pre-dinner tapas spot.

Xurreria   CHURROS €
(Map p238; ☑ 93 318 76 91; Carrer dels Banys Nous 8; cone €1.20; ☺ 7.30am-1.30pm & 3.30-8.15pm; Ⓜ Jaume I) It doesn't look much from the outside, but this brightly lit street joint is Barcelona's best spot for paper cones of piping-hot churros – long batter sticks fried and sprinkled with sugar and best enjoyed dunked in hot chocolate.

★ La Vinateria del Call   SPANISH €€
(Map p238; ☑ 93 302 60 92; www.lavinateria delcall.com; Carrer de Sant Domènec del Call 9; small plates €7-12; ☺ 7.30pm-1am; Ⓜ Jaume I) In a magical setting in the former Jewish quarter, this tiny jewel box of a restaurant (recently extended to add another dining room) serves up tasty Iberian dishes including Galician octopus, cider-cooked chorizo and the Catalan *escalivada* (roasted peppers, aubergine and onions) with anchovies. Portions are small and made for sharing, and there's a good and affordable selection of wines.

★ Cafè de l'Acadèmia   CATALAN €€
(Map p238; ☑ 93 319 82 53; Carrer dels Lledó 1; mains €14-18; ☺ 1-3.30pm & 8-11pm Mon-Fri; 🛜; Ⓜ Jaume I) Expect a mix of traditional Catalan dishes with the occasional creative twist. At lunchtime, local Ajuntament (town hall) office workers pounce on the *menú del día* (daily set menu; €14.30). In

the evening it is rather more romantic, as low lighting emphasises the intimacy of the beamed ceiling and stone walls. On warm days you can also dine on the pretty square at the front.

Federal   CAFE €€
(Map p238; ☑ 93 280 81 71; www.federalcafe.es; Passatge de la Pau 11; mains €9-12; ☺ 9am-midnight Mon-Thu, to 1am Fri & Sat, 9am-5.30pm Sun; ☎; M Drassanes) Don't be intimidated by the industrial chic, the sea of open MacBooks or the stack of design mags – this branch of the Poble Sec Federal mothership is incredibly welcoming, with healthy, hearty and good-value food. Choose a salad and a topping (poached eggs, strips of chicken) or a yellow curry, say, and follow it up with a moist slab of carrot cake.

Belmonte   TAPAS €€
(Map p238; ☑ 93 310 76 84; Carrer de la Mercè 29; tapas €4-10, mains €12; ☺ 8pm-midnight Tue-Sat, plus 1-3.30pm Sat; ☎; M Jaume I) This tiny tapas joint in the southern reaches of Barri Gòtic whips up beautifully prepared small plates – including an excellent *truita* (tortilla), rich *patatons a la sal* (salted new potatoes with *romesco* sauce) and tender *carpaccio de pop* (octopus carpaccio). Wash it down with the housemade *vermut* (vermouth).

Milk   BRUNCH €€
(Map p238; ☑ 93 268 09 22; www.milkbarcelona. com; Carrer d'en Gignàs 21; mains €8-12; ☺ 9am-2am Sun-Thu, to 3am Fri & Sat; ☎; M Jaume I) Also known to many as an enticing cocktail spot, Irish-run Milk's key role for Barcelona night owls is providing morning-after brunches (served till 4.30pm). Avoid direct sunlight and tuck into pancakes, eggs Benedict and other hangover dishes in a cosy lounge-like setting complete with ornate wallpaper, framed prints on the wall and cushion-lined seating. The musical selection is also notable.

Can Culleretes   CATALAN €€
(Map p238; ☑ 93 317 30 22; www.culleretes. com; Carrer Quintana 5; mains €10-17; ☺ 1.30-4pm & 9-11pm Tue-Sat, 1.30-4pm Sun; M Liceu) Founded in 1786, Barcelona's oldest restaurant is still going strong, with tourists and locals flocking here to enjoy its rambling interior, old-fashioned tile-filled decor, and enormous helpings of traditional Catalan food, including fresh seafood and fragrant, sticky stews.

✖ El Raval

For contrast alone, El Raval is possibly the most interesting part of the old city. Timeless classics of Barcelona dining are scattered across what was long the old city's poorest *barri* (district), and since the late 1990s, battalions of hip new eateries and artsy restaurants can be found in the area around the MACBA. Some of the cheapest eats in town, full of character, lurk along El Raval's streets. From Carrer de Sant Pau north towards Carrer de Pelai, the university and Ronda de Sant Antoni is where you'll find most of these haunts.

Elisabets   CATALAN €
(Map p238; ☑ 93 317 58 26; Carrer d'Elisabets 2-4; mains €8-10, menú del día €10.85; ☺ 7.30am-11.30pm Mon-Sat Sep-Jul; M Catalunya) This unassuming restaurant is popular for no-nonsense local fare. The walls are dotted with old radio sets and the *menú del día* (daily set menu) varies daily. If you prefer *a la carta*, try the *ragú de jabalí* (wild boar stew) and finish with *mel i mató* (Catalan dessert made from cheese and honey).

Sésamo   VEGETARIAN €
(☑ 93 441 64 11; Carrer de Sant Antoni Abat 52; tapas €6; ☺ 8pm-midnight Tue-Sun; ✍; M Sant Antoni) Widely held to be the best vegie restaurant in the city (admittedly not as great an accolade as it might be elsewhere), Sésamo is a cosy, fun place. The menu is mainly tapas, and most people go for the seven-course tapas menu (€25, wine included), but there are a few more substantial dishes. Nice touches include the home-baked bread and cakes.

★ Mam i Teca   CATALAN €€
(Map p238; ☑ 93 441 33 35; Carrer de la Lluna 4; mains €9-12; ☺ 1-4pm & 8pm-midnight Mon, Wed-Fri & Sun, 8pm-midnight Sat; M Sant Antoni) A tiny place with half a dozen tables, Mam i Teca is as much a lifestyle choice as a restaurant. Locals drop in and hang at the bar, and diners are treated to Catalan dishes made with locally sourced products and that adhere to Slow Food principles (such as cod fried in olive oil with garlic and red pepper, or pork ribs with chickpeas).

★ Bar Pinotxo   TAPAS €€
(Map p238; www.pinotxobar.com; Mercat de la Boqueria; mains €8-17; ☺ 6am-4pm Mon-Sat; M Liceu) Bar Pinotxo is arguably La Boqueria's, and even Barcelona's, best tapas bar. It sits

BARCELONA EATING

among the half-dozen or so informal eateries within the market, and the popular owner, Juanito, might serve up chickpeas with pine nuts and raisins, a soft mix of potato and spinach sprinkled with salt, soft baby squid with cannellini beans, or a quivering cube of caramel-sweet pork belly.

Suculent
CATALAN €€

(Map p238; ☑ 93 443 65 79; www.suculent.com; Rambla del Raval 43; mains €13-21; ☺ 1-4pm & 8.30-11.30pm Wed-Sun; Ⓜ Liceu) Michelin-starred chef Carles Abellan adds to his stable with this old-style bistro, which showcases the best of Catalan cuisine. From the cod brandade to the oxtail stew with truffled sweet potato, only the best ingredients are used. Be warned that the prices can mount up a bit, but this is a great place to sample regional highlights.

El Quim
TAPAS €€

(Map p238; ☑ 93 301 98 10; www.elquimdelaboqueria.com; Mercat de la Boqueria; ☺ 7am-4pm Tue-Thu, to 5pm Fri & Sat; Ⓜ Liceu) This classic counter bar in the Mercat de la Boqueria is ideal for trying traditional Catalan dishes such as fried eggs with baby squid (the house speciality) or *escalivada* (smoky grilled vegetables). Daily specials are prepared using whatever is in season, and might include artichoke chips or sautéd wild mushrooms.

🍴 La Ribera

If you'd mentioned El Born (El Borne in Spanish) in the early 1990s, you wouldn't have raised much interest. Now the area is peppered with bars, dance dives, groovy designer stores and restaurants. You'll find avant-garde chefs playing with fusion and technology cheek by jowl with no-nonsense matrons serving up traditional comfort food, and you'll also find an increasing number of multicultural restaurants.

Paradiso
SMOKERY €

(☑ 639 310671; www.rooftopsmokehouse.com; Carrer de Rera Palau 4; mains €8; ☺ cocktail bar 7pm-2am Sun-Thu, to 3am Fri & Sat, pastrami bar noon-2am Sun-Thu, to 3am Fri & Sat; Ⓜ Barceloneta) A kind of Narnia-in-reverse, Paradiso is fronted with a snowy-white space, not much bigger than a wardrobe, and in itself reason enough to linger, with pastrami sandwiches, smoked duck and other home-cured delights from the Rooftop Smokehouse team, best known for their food trucks.

Bormuth
TAPAS €

(☑ 93 310 21 86; Carrer del Rec 31; tapas from €4; ☺ 1pm-midnight; ☎; Ⓜ Jaume I) Opened on the pedestrian Carrer del Rec in 2013, Bormuth has tapped into the vogue for old-school tapas with modern-times service and decor, and serves all the old favourites – *patatas bravas, ensaladilla* (Russian salad), tortilla – along with some less predictable and superbly prepared numbers (try the chargrilled red pepper with black pudding).

Euskal Etxea
TAPAS €

(☑ 93 310 21 85; Placeta de Montcada 1; tapas €1.95; ☺ 10am-12.30am Sun-Thu, to 1am Fri & Sat; Ⓜ Jaume I) Barcelona has plenty of Basque and pseudo-Basque eateries, but this is the real deal. It captures the feel of San Sebastián better than many of its newer competitors. Choose your *pintxos* (Basque tapas piled on slices of bread), sip *txacoli* (Basque white wine), and keep the toothpicks so the staff can count them up and work out your bill.

★ El Atril
INTERNATIONAL €€

(☑ 93 310 12 20; www.atrilbarcelona.com; Carrer dels Carders 23; mains €11-15; ☺ noon-midnight Mon-Thu, to 1am Fri & Sat, 11.30am-11.30pm Sun; ☎; Ⓜ Jaume I) Aussie owner Brenden is influenced by culinary flavours from all over the globe, so while you'll see plenty of tapas (the *patatas bravas* are recommended for their homemade sauce), you'll also find kangaroo fillet, salmon and date rolls with mascarpone, chargrilled turkey with fried yucca, and plenty more.

★ Casa Delfín
CATALAN €€

(☑ 93 319 50 88; www.tallerdetapas.com; Passeig del Born 36; mains €10-15; ☺ 8am-midnight Sun-Thu, to 1am Fri & Sat; ☎; Ⓜ Barceloneta) One of Barcelona's culinary delights, Casa Delfín is everything you dream of when you think of Catalan (and Mediterranean) cooking. Start with the tangy and sweet *calçots* (a cross between a leek and an onion; February and March only) or salt-strewn *padron* peppers, moving on to grilled sardines speckled with parsley, then tackle the meaty monkfish roasted in white wine and garlic.

Cal Pep
TAPAS €€

(☑ 93 310 79 61; www.calpep.com; Plaça de les Olles 8; mains €13-20; ☺ 7.30-11.30pm Mon, 1-3.45pm & 7.30-11.30pm Tue-Sat, closed last 3 weeks Aug; Ⓜ Barceloneta) It's getting a foot in the door of this legendary fish restaurant that's the problem – there can be queues out into the square. And if you want one of the five tables out the back, you'll need to call ahead. Most people are happy elbowing their way to the bar for some of the tastiest seafood tapas in town.

✘ Barceloneta & the Waterfront

For good food and atmosphere, head to La Barceloneta, the lanes of which bristle with everything from good-natured, noisy tapas bars to upmarket seafood restaurants. Almost all options shut on Sunday and Monday evenings. The Port Olímpic marina is lined with restaurants and tapas bars, popular in spring and summer but mostly underwhelming. A more upmarket series of places huddles at the northeast end of Platja de la Barceloneta – it's hard to beat the sea and palm-tree backdrop. Otherwise, the search for culinary curios will take you behind the scenes in Poblenou, which has a growing number of appealing options.

★ **La Cova Fumada**   TAPAS €
(Map p250; ☑ 93 221 40 61; Carrer del Baluard 56; tapas €4-8; ⊙ 9am-3.20pm Mon-Wed, 9am-3.20pm & 6-8.15pm Thu & Fri, 9am-1pm Sat; Ⓜ Barceloneta) There's no sign and the setting is decidedly downmarket, but this tiny, buzzing family-run tapas spot always packs in a crowd. The secret? Mouthwatering *pulpo* (octopus), *calamar, sardinias* and 15 or so other small plates cooked to perfection in the small open kitchen. The *bombas* (potato croquettes served with *alioli*) and grilled *carxofes* (artichokes) are good, but everything is amazingly fresh.

Can Dendê   AMERICAN €
(☑ 646 325551; Carrer de la Ciutat de Granada 44; mains €6-11; ⊙ 8.30am-5pm Mon-Fri, from 10.30am Sat & Sun; Ⓜ Llacuna) An eclectic crowd gathers at this bright, bohemian Brazilian-run eatery in Poblenou. Anytime brunch is the culinary star here, and you can tuck into eggs Benedict with smoked salmon, fluffy pancakes or pulled pork sandwiches while watching the cooks in action and listening to the mix of sounds at play – Latin tropicalia, American grooves, plus the various languages spoken at neighbouring tables.

★ **Can Recasens**   CATALAN €€
(☑ 93 300 81 23; Rambla del Poblenou 102; mains €7-15; ⊙ 9pm-1am Mon-Fri & 1-4pm & 9pm-1am Sat; Ⓜ Poblenou) One of Poblenou's most romantic settings, Can Recasens hides a warren of warmly lit rooms full of oil paintings, flickering candles, fairy lights and baskets of fruit. The food is outstanding, with a mix of salads, fondues, smoked meats, cheeses, and open-faced sandwiches piled high with delicacies like wild mushrooms and brie, *escalivada* (grilled vegetables) and gruyere, and spicy chorizo.

El 58   TAPAS €€
(Le cinquante huit; Rambla del Poblenou 58; sharing plates €4-11; ⊙ 1.30pm-midnight Tue-Sat; Ⓜ Llacuna) This French-Catalan eatery serves imaginative, beautifully prepared tapas dishes that earn rave reviews from both locals and expats. Solo diners can grab a seat at the marble-topped front bar and get dining tips from the friendly multilingual baristas. The back dining room with its exposed brick walls, industrial light fixtures and curious artworks is a lively place to linger over a long meal.

Kaiku   SEAFOOD €€
(Map p250; ☑ 93 221 90 82; www.restaurantkaiku.cat; Plaça del Mar 1; mains for 2 €28-36; ⊙ 1-3.30pm Tue-Sun; Ⓜ Barceloneta) Overlooking the waterfront at the south end of Barceloneta, Kaiku has a solid reputation for its creative seafood plates. Mouth-watering ingredients are sourced from the nearby fish market, and artfully prepared in dishes such as crayfish with mint, swordfish carpaccio with avocado and sundried tomatoes, chilli-smeared tuna with green apples and mushrooms, and the outstanding rice dishes for two.

✘ La Sagrada Família & L'Eixample

Most of this huge area's many varied and enticing restaurants are concentrated in the Quadrat d'Or between Carrer de Pau Claris and Carrer de Muntaner, Avinguda Diagonal and Gran Via de les Corts Catalanes. There is no shortage of perfectly acceptable bar-restaurants (often with street-side tables) that offer reasonable *menús del dia* (daily set menus) and stock-standard dishes *a la carta*. In among these places are sprinkled real finds, offering both local and international cuisine.

Copasetic   CAFE €
(☑ 93 532 76 66; www.copaseticbarcelona.com; Carrer de la Diputació 55; mains €8-12; ⊙ 10.30am-midnight Tue & Wed, to 1am Thu, to 2am Fri & Sat, to 5.30pm Sun; 🔊 ⌀; Ⓜ Rocafort) A fun and friendly cafe, decked out with retro furniture. The menu holds plenty for

everyone, whether your thing is eggs Benedict, wild-berry tartlets or a juicy fat burger. There are lots of vegetarian, gluten-free and organic options, and superb (and reasonably priced) brunches on weekends. Wednesday night is ladies' night, with cheap cocktails. Lunch *menús* (Tuesday to Friday) cost between €9.50 and €11.

★ Tapas 24   TAPAS €€

(Map p256; ☑93 488 09 77; www.carlesabellan. com; Carrer de la Diputació 269; tapas €4-9; ⊙9am-midnight; 🛜; Ⓜ Passeig de Gràcia) Carles Abellan, master of the now-defunct Comerç 24 in La Ribera, runs this basement tapas haven known for its gourmet versions of old faves. Specials include the *bikini* (toasted ham and cheese sandwich – here the ham is cured and the truffle makes all the difference) and a thick black *arròs negre de sípia* (squid-ink black rice).

★ Cerveseria Catalana   TAPAS €€

(Map p256; ☑93 216 03 68; Carrer de Mallorca 236; tapas €4-11; ⊙8am-1.30am Mon-Fri, 9am-1.30am Sat & Sun; Ⓜ Passeig de Gràcia) The 'Catalan Brewery' is good for breakfast, lunch and dinner. Come for your morning coffee and croissant, or enjoy the abundance of tapas and *montaditos* (canapés) at lunch. You can sit at the bar, on the pavement terrace or in the restaurant at the back. The variety of hot tapas, salads and other snacks draws a well-dressed crowd of locals and outsiders.

Chicha Limoná   MEDITERRANEAN, PIZZERIA €€

(Map p256; ☑93 277 64 03; www.chichalimona. com; Passeig de Sant Joan 80; mains €10-16; ⊙8.30am-1am Tue-Thu, 8.30am-2am Fri, 9.30am-2am Sat, 9.30am-5pm Sun; 🛜; Ⓜ Tetuan) Passeig de Sant Joan has become the newest haunt for the hussar-moustached, turned-up-cigarette-pants brigade, and bright, bustling Chicha Limoná has provided them with somewhere great to eat. Grilled octopus with quince jelly, pork with apple compote and pear tatin with crème anglaise are among the oft-changing dishes (set menu €12.90), along with homemade pizzas.

Entrepanes Díaz   SANDWICHES €€

(Map p256; ☑93 415 75 82; Carrer de Pau Claris 189; sandwiches €6-8, salads €12; ⊙11am-midnight Tue-Sat, 11am-6pm Sun; Ⓜ Diagonal) A new concept in upmarket gourmet sandwiches, from roast beef to suckling pig, along with sharing plates of Spanish specialities such as sea urchins and shrimp fritters, in a sparkling old-style bar. The policy of only hiring experienced waiters over 50 lends a certain gravitas to the operation and some especially charming service.

Cata 1.81   TAPAS €€

(Map p256; ☑93 323 68 18; www.cata181. com; Carrer de València 181; tapas €5.50-8; ⊙6pm-midnight Mon-Sat; Ⓜ Passeig de Gràcia) A beautifully designed venue (with lots of small lights, some trapped in birdcages), this is the place to come for fine wines and dainty gourmet dishes like *raviolis amb bacallà* (salt-cod dumplings) or *truita de patates i tòfona negre* (thick potato tortilla with a delicate trace of black truffle). The best idea is to choose from one of several tasting-menu options.

★ Cinc Sentits   INTERNATIONAL €€€

(Map p256; ☑93 323 94 90; www.cincsentits. com; Carrer d'Aribau 58; tasting menus €100/120; ⊙1.30-3pm & 8.30-10pm Tue-Sat; Ⓜ Passeig de Gràcia) Enter the realm of the 'Five Senses' to indulge in a jaw-dropping tasting menu consisting of a series of small, experimental dishes (there is no à la carte, although dishes can be tweaked to suit diners' requests). There is a lunch *menú* for €55.

Casa Calvet   CATALAN €€€

(Map p256; ☑93 412 40 12; www.casacalvet. es; Carrer de Casp 48; mains €28-31; ⊙1-3.30pm & 8.30-11pm Mon-Sat; Ⓜ Urquinaona) An early Gaudí masterpiece loaded with his trademark curvy features houses a swish restaurant (just to the right of the building's main entrance). Dress up and ask for an intimate *taula cabina* (wooden booth). You could opt for scallops and razor clams with pesto and buckwheat, or venison with juniper and porcini sauce.

★ Disfrutar   MODERN EUROPEAN €€€

(☑93 348 68 96; www.en.disfrutarbarcelona.com; Carrer de Vilarroel 163; tasting menus €75/105/135; ⊙1-4pm & 8-11pm Tue-Sat; Ⓜ Hospital Clínic) In its first few months of life, Disfrutar rose stratospherically to become the city's finest restaurant – book now while it's still possible to get a table. Run by alumni of Ferran Adrià's game-changing El Bulli restaurant, it operates along similar lines.

Nothing is as it seems, from red and green peppers that are actually chocolate ganache coated in, respectively, chilli and mint-flavoured gelatine, to an iced hare consommé in a brandy snifter.

The decor is fabulously on point, with latticed brickwork and trademark geometric ceramics from Catalan design team Equipo Creativo, and the service is faultless.

✖ Gràcia & Park Güell

Spread across this busy quarter are all sorts of enticing options, from simple tapas bars to top-class seafood. Gràcia is loaded with Middle Eastern and other ethnic restaurants, many of which are upbeat and good value. Several classic Catalan taverns tick along nicely with a strong local following. There's little of interest, however, around Park Güell.

Chivuo's
SANDWICHES €

(Map p261; ☑93 218 51 34; www.chivuos.com; Carrer del Torrent de l'Olla 175; sandwiches €7-9; ⏱1-5pm & 7pm-midnight Mon-Fri, 6pm-midnight Sat; Ⓜ Lesseps, Fontana) Satisfying grilled sandwiches and delicious craft brews make a fine pair at this buzzing little snack den in Gràcia. A mostly local crowd comes for the slow-roasted pork, tuna melts, bacon-covered burgers and 'philli cheese steaks' – best ordered with *fritas* (chips). The rotating selection of eight craft brews includes mostly Catalan and Spanish brews, including excellent ales from Barcelona-based Edge Brewing (p251).

La Panxa del Bisbe
TAPAS €€

(☑93 213 70 49; Carrer del Torrent de les Flors 156; tapas €8-14, tasting menus from €30; ⏱1.30-3.30pm & 8.30pm-midnight Tue-Sat; Ⓜ Joanic) With low lighting and an artfully minimalist interior, the 'Bishop's Belly' serves up creative tapas that earn high praise from the mostly local crowd. Feast on grilled razor clams, foie gras with pine nuts and pumpkin, tender morsels of tuna tataki or *picanya* (grilled rump steak) served with chips and Béarnaise sauce.

El Glop
CATALAN €€

(Map p261; ☑93 213 70 58; www.elglop.com; Carrer de Sant Lluís 24; mains €7-20; ⏱1pm-midnight Mon-Fri, from noon Sat & Sun; Ⓜ Joanic) This raucous eatery is decked out in country Catalan fashion, with gingham tablecloths and no-nonsense, slap-up meals. The secret is hearty serves of simple dishes, such as *cordero a la brasa* (grilled lamb), *paella de pescado y marisco* (fish and seafood paella), and appetisers like *berenjenas rellenas* (stuffed aubergines) or *calçots* (spring onions) in winter.

Cal Boter
CATALAN €€

(Map p261; ☑93 458 84 62; www.restaurant calboter.com; Carrer de Tordera 62; mains €8-15; ⏱1-4pm & 9pm-midnight Tue-Sat, 1-4pm Sun & Mon; Ⓜ Joanic) Families and noisy groups of pals are drawn to this classic eatery for *cargols a la llauna* (snails sautéed in a tin dish), *filet de bou amb salsa de foie* (a thick clump of tender beef drowned in an orange and foie gras sauce), and other Catalan specialities.

Con Gracia
FUSION €€€

(Map p261; ☑93 238 02 01; www.congracia. es; Carrer de Martínez de la Rosa 8; set menu €65, with wine pairing €95; ⏱7-11pm Tue-Sat; Ⓜ Diagonal) This teeny hideaway (seating about 20 in total) is a hive of originality, producing delicately balanced Mediterranean cuisine with Asian touches. On offer is a regularly changing surprise tasting menu or the set 'traditional' one, with dishes such as squid stuffed with *jamón ibérico* and black truffle, and juicy black angus steak. Book ahead.

✖ Camp Nou, Pedralbes & La Zona Alta

Some of the grandest kitchens in the city are scattered across La Zona Alta, from Tibidabo across Sant Gervasi (as far down as Avinguda Diagonal, west of Gràcia) to Pedralbes. Plenty of places of all cuisines and qualities abound, often tucked away in quiet, unassuming residential streets far from anything of interest to tourists. Eating in La Zona Alta can be both a culinary and, with a couple of notable exceptions, a genuinely local experience.

Comaxurros
CHURROS €

(☑93 417 94 05; Carrer de Muntaner 562; churros from €2; ⏱4.30-8.30pm Tue, 9am-2pm & 5-8.30pm Wed-Sun; Ⓡ FGC El Putxet) At this eye-catching little cafe, brought to you by Barcelona's famous *pastelería* Canals, the humble churro receives a dramatic makeover: it's fried in olive oil to crispy (healthier) perfection and served with unique fillings and toppings (pistachio, strawberry sauce, dark chocolate). You'll even find savoury churros – with cheese, mushrooms and *jamón ibérico* (Iberian ham), among other delicacies.

Bar Tomàs
TAPAS €

(☑93 203 10 77; Carrer Major de Sarrià 49; tapas €2.50-5.50; ⏱noon-4pm & 6-10pm Mon-Sat; Ⓡ FGC Sarrià) Many *barcelonins* have long claimed that Bar Tomàs is by far the best

BARCELONA EATING

place in the city for *patatas bravas* (potato chunks in a slightly spicy tomato sauce). Despite the fluorescent lights and friendly but gruff service, folks from all walks of life pile in, particularly for lunch on weekends.

La Molina
CATALAN €€

(☑93 417 11 24; Passeig de Sant Gervasi 65; mains €11-17; ☺1pm-12.30am Mon-Fri, 11am-5pm Sat & Sun; ℝFGC Avinguda Tibidabo) La Molina looks like a typical tapas bar at first glance – pavement tables, nondescript bar in front – but head to the back room and you'll discover one of the great unsung Catalan restaurants in the neighbourhood.

Dishes are made with care and beautifully presented in inventive combinations such as foie gras with duck egg and potatoes, grilled octopus with Galician potatoes, and chickpeas with calamari and blood sausage.

ABaC
CATALAN €€€

(☑93 319 66 00; www.abacbarcelona.com; Avinguda del Tibidabo 1; mains €45-75, tasting menus €135-165; ☺1.30-4pm & 8.30-11pm Tue-Sat; ℝFGC Av Tibidabo) Led by celebrated chef Jordi Cruz, ABaC offers one of Barcelona's most memorable dining experiences (and also one of its priciest). Expect creative, mouthwatering perfection in dishes like sea urchin curry with lime, guinea fowl with Norway lobster, and roasted sea bass with artichokes and oysters.

Via Veneto
CATALAN €€€

(☑93 200 72 44; www.viavenetorestaurant.com; Carrer de Ganduxer 10; mains €31-43, tasting menus €85-125; ☺1-3.30pm Mon-Fri, 1-3.30pm & 8-11.30pm Mon-Sat, closed Aug; ℝFGC La Bonanova) Dalí used to regularly waltz into this high-society eatery after it opened in 1967. The vaguely art-deco setting (note the oval mirrors), orange-rose tablecloths, leather chairs and fine cutlery may cater to more conservative souls, but the painter was here for the kitchen exploits.

✖ Montjuïc, Poble Sec & Sant Antoni

Montjuïc has limited eating options, for the obvious reason that it is mostly parks and gardens. In Poble Sec, however, you'll turn up all sorts of creative eating and drinking spots, from historic taverns offering Catalan classics to a handful of smart, new-wave eateries, while equally creative Sant Antoni is the place for new cafe openings.

Escribà
DESSERTS €

(☑93 454 75 35; www.escriba.es; Gran Via de les Corts Catalanes 546; pastries from €2; ☺8.30am-3pm & 5-9.30pm Mon-Fri, 8.30am-8.30pm Sat & Sun; Ⓜ Urgell) Antoni Escribà carries forward a family tradition (since 1906) of melting *barcelonins'* hearts with remarkable pastries and criminal chocolate creations. Try the Easter *bunyols de xocolata* (little round pastry balls filled with chocolate cream). Escribà has another branch (p293) in a Modernista setting at La Rambla.

★ Palo Cortao
TAPAS €€

(Map p266; ☑93 188 90 67; www.palocortao.es; Carrer de Nou de la Rambla 14; mains €10-15; ☺8pm-1am Tue-Sun & 1-5pm Sat & Sun; Ⓜ Paral·lel) Palo Cortao has a solid reputation for its beautifully executed seafood and meat dishes, served at fair prices. Highlights include octopus with white bean hummus, skirt steak with foie armagnac, and tuna tataki tempura. You can order half sizes of all plates – which will allow you to try more dishes.

★ Quimet i Quimet
TAPAS €€

(Map p266; ☑93 442 31 42; Carrer del Poeta Cabanyes 25; tapas €4-10, montaditos around €3; ☺noon-4pm & 7-10.30pm Mon-Fri, noon-4pm Sat; Ⓜ Paral·lel) Quimet i Quimet is a family-run business that has been passed down from generation to generation. There's barely space to swing a *calamar* in this bottle-lined, standing-room-only place, but it is a treat for the palate, with *montaditos* (tapas on a slice of bread) made to order.

Casa Xica
FUSION €€

(Map p266; ☑93 600 58 58; Carrer de la França Xica 20; sharing plates €9-15; ☺1.30-3pm & 8.30-11.30pm Mon-Sat; Ⓜ Poble Sec) On the parlour floor of an old house, Casa Xica is a casual, but artfully designed space that fuses elements of the Far East with fresh Catalan ingredients (owners Marc and Raquel lived and travelled in Asia).

Tonka
INTERNATIONAL €€

(Map p238; ☑93 127 05 44; www.tonkabar.com; Carrer del Marquès de Campo Sagrado 27; ☺5pm-midnight Tue-Fri, from 10am Sat & Sun; 🖥🍴; Ⓜ Sant Antoni, Poble Sec) It's hard not to fall for this charming neighbourhood eatery. Fresh-cut flowers in vermouth jars, groovy music and a spray of colourful art prints on the wall set the stage for dining on delicious organic and veg-friendly dishes with Asian and Latin American accents.

Bodega 1900

TAPAS €€

(Map p266; ☑93 325 26 59; www.bodega1900. com; Carrer de Tamarit 91; tapas €5-14; ⊙noon-4pm & 7-11.30pm; MSant Antoni) The latest venture from the world-famous Adrià brothers, Bodega 1900 mimics an old-school tapas and vermouth bar, but this is no ordinary spit-and-sawdust joint serving *patatas bravas* and tortilla. Witness, for example, the *mollete de calamars,* probably the best squid sandwich in the world, hot from the pan and served with chipotle mayonnaise, kimchi and lemon zest; or the 'spherified' false olives.

★Tickets

MODERN SPANISH €€€

(Map p266; ☑606 225545; www.ticketsbar.es; Avinguda del Paral·lel 164; tapas €5-27; ⊙6.30-10.30pm Tue-Fri, 1-3pm & 7-10.30pm Sat, closed Aug; MParal·lel) This is, literally, one of the sizzling tickets in the restaurant world, a tapas bar opened by Ferran Adrià, of the legendary El Bulli, and his brother Albert. And unlike El Bulli, it's an affordable venture – if you can book a table, that is: you can only book online, and two months in advance (or call for last-minute cancellations).

It's a fairly flamboyant and modern affair in terms of decor, playing with circus images and theatre lights, while the food veers towards the deliciously surreal in concoctions like spherical olives, 'airbaguette' with dry aged Rubia Gallega beef, or the wild carrot cone with cardamom yoghurt, sugared sesame and carrot ice cream. The seafood bar serves 14 varieties of oysters, with caviar, borscht and other unusual toppings.

🍷 Drinking & Nightlife

Barcelona is a nightlife-lovers' town, with an enticing spread of candlelit wine bars, old-school taverns, stylish lounges and kaleidoscopic nightclubs where the party continues until daybreak. For something a little more sedate, the city's atmospheric cafes and teahouses make a fine retreat when the skies turn grey.

🍷 La Rambla & Barri Gòtic

★Ginger

COCKTAIL BAR

(Map p238; ☑93 310 53 09; www.ginger.cat; Carrer de Palma de Sant Just 1; ⊙7.30pm-2.30am Tue-Thu, 7.30pm-3am Fri & Sat; MJaume I) Tucked away just off peaceful Plaça de Sant Just, Ginger is an art deco–style multilevel drinking den with low lighting, finely crafted cocktails and good ambient sounds (provided by vinyl-spinning DJs some nights). It's a mellow spot that's great for sipping wine and sampling from the gourmet tapas menu.

L'Ascensor

BAR

(Map p238; ☑93 318 53 47; Carrer de la Bellafila 3; ⊙6pm-2.30am Sun-Thu, to 3am Fri & Sat; 🐾; MJaume I) Named after the lift (elevator) doors that serve as the front door, this elegant drinking den with its vaulted brick ceilings, vintage mirrors and marble-topped bar gathers a faithful crowd that comes for old-fashioned cocktails and lively conversation against a soundtrack of up-tempo jazz and funk.

Ocaña

BAR

(Map p238; ☑93 676 48 14; www.ocana.cat; Plaça Reial 13; ⊙noon-2.30am Mon-Fri, 11am-2.30am Sat & Sun; 🐾; MLiceu) Named after a flamboyant artist who once lived on Plaça Reial, Ocaña is a beautifully designed space with chandeliers and plush furnishings. Have a seat on the terrace and watch the passing people parade, or head downstairs to the Moorish-inspired Apotheke bar or the chic lounge a few steps away, where DJs spin for a mix of beauties and bohemians on weekend nights.

Sor Rita

BAR

(Map p238; ☑93 176 62 66; www.sorritabar. es; Carrer de la Mercè 27; ⊙7pm-3am Sun-Thu, to 3.30am Fri & Sat; 🐾; MJaume I) A lover of all things kitsch, Sor Rita is pure eye candy, from its leopard-print wallpaper to its high-heel-festooned ceiling and deliciously irreverent decorations inspired by the films of Almodóvar. It's a fun and festive scene, with special-event nights including tarot readings on Mondays, €5 all-you-can-eat snack

---

THE GREEN FAIRY

Bar Marsella (Map p238; ☑93 442 72 63; Carrer de Sant Pau 65; ⊙10pm-2.30am Mon-Thu, 10pm-3am Fri & Sat; MLiceu) has been in business since 1820, and has served the likes of Hemingway, who was known to slump here over an *absenta* (absinthe). The bar still specialises in absinthe, a drink to be treated with respect. Your glass comes with a lump of sugar, a fork and a little bottle of mineral water. Hold the sugar on the fork, over your glass, and drip the water onto the sugar so that it dissolves into the absinthe, which turns yellow. The result should give you a warm glow.

buffets on Tuesdays, karaoke or cabaret on Wednesdays and gin specials on Thursdays.

Polaroid
BAR

(Map p238; ☑ 93 186 66 69; www.polaroidbar.es; Carrer dels Còdols 29; ⏰ 7pm-2.30am Sun-Thu, to 3am Fri & Sat; Ⓜ Drassanes) For a dash of 1980s nostalgia, Polaroid is a blast from the past, with its wall-mounted VHS tapes, old film posters, comic-book-covered tables, action-figure displays and other kitschy decor. Not surprisingly, it draws a fun, unpretentious crowd who comes for cheap *cañas* (draught beer), mojitos and free popcorn.

La Cerveteca
BAR

(Map p238; www.lacerveteca.com; Carrer d'en Gignàs 25; ⏰ 6pm-midnight Tue-Fri, noon-3.30pm & 6pm-midnight Sat, noon-3.30pm Sun; Ⓜ Jaume I) An unmissable stop for beer lovers, La Cerveteca serves an impressive variety of global craft brews. In addition to scores of bottled beers, there's a frequent rotation of what's on draught. Cheeses, *jamón ibérico* and other charcuterie selections are on hand, including *cecina* (cured horse meat).

Marula Café
BAR

(Map p238; ☑ 93 318 76 90; www.marulacafe.com; Carrer dels Escudellers 49; ⏰ 11pm-6am Wed-Sun; Ⓜ Liceu) A fantastic find in the heart of the Barri Gòtic, Marula will transport you to the 1970s and the best in funk and soul. James Brown fans will think they've died and gone to heaven. It's not, however, a monothematic place and DJs slip in other tunes, from breakbeat to house. Samba and other Brazilian dance sounds also penetrate here.

Cafè de l'Òpera
CAFE

(Map p238; ☑ 93 317 75 85; www.cafeoperabcn.com; La Rambla 74; ⏰ 8.30am-2.30am; 📶; Ⓜ Liceu) Opposite the Gran Teatre del Liceu is La Rambla's most intriguing cafe. Operating since 1929, it is pleasant enough for an early evening libation or coffee and croissants. Head upstairs for an elevated seat above the busy boulevard. Can you be tempted by the *cafè de l'Òpera* (coffee with chocolate mousse)?

BEST CAFES

Some of Barcelona's most atmospheric cafes lie hidden in the cobbled lanes of the Ciutat Vella. A round-up of our favourite spots for a pick-me-up:

Salterio (Map p238; Carrer de Sant Domènec del Call 4; ⏰ 11am-midnight, to 1am Fri & Sat; 📶; Ⓜ Jaume I) A wonderfully photogenic candlelit spot tucked down a tiny lane in El Call, Salterio serves refreshing teas, Turkish coffee, authentic mint teas and snacks amid stone walls, incense and ambient Middle Eastern music. If hunger strikes, try the *sardo* (grilled flat-bread covered with pesto, cheese or other toppings).

Caelum (Map p238; ☑ 93 302 69 93; www.caelumbarcelona.com; Carrer de la Palla 8; ⏰ 10.30am-8.30pm Mon-Thu, to 11pm Fri & Sat, to 9pm Sun; Ⓜ Liceu) Centuries of heavenly gastronomic tradition from across Spain are concentrated in this exquisite medieval space in the heart of the city. The upstairs cafe is a dainty setting for decadent cakes and pastries, while descending into the underground chamber with its stone walls and flickering candles is like stepping into the Middle Ages.

Granja M Viader (Map p238; ☑ 93 318 34 86; www.granjaviader.cat; Carrer d'en Xuclà 6; ⏰ 9am-1.30pm & 5-9pm Mon-Sat; Ⓜ Liceu) For more than a century, people have flocked down this alley to get to the cups of homemade hot chocolate and whipped cream (ask for a *suís*) ladled out in this classic Catalan-style milk-bar-cum-deli. The Viader clan invented Cacaolat, a forerunner of kids' powdered-chocolate beverages. The interior here is delightfully vintage and the atmosphere always upbeat.

La Nena (Map p261; ☑ 93 285 14 76; www.chocolaterialanena.com; Carrer de Ramon y Cajal 36; desserts from €4.50; ⏰ 9am-10pm; 🛒; Ⓜ Fontana) A French team has created this delightfully chaotic space for indulging in cups of *suïssos* (rich hot chocolate) served with a plate of heavy homemade whipped cream and *melindros* (spongy sweet biscuits), fine desserts and even a few savoury dishes (including crêpes). The place is strewn with books, and you can help yourself to the board games on the shelves.

The area out the back is designed to keep kids busy, with toys, books and a blackboard with chalk, making it an ideal family rest stop.

El Raval

★ La Confitería
BAR

(Map p238; Carrer de Sant Pau 128; ⊙7.30pm-2.30am Mon-Thu, 6pm-3.30am Fri, 5pm-3.30am Sat, 12.45pm-2.45am Sun; ⓂParal·lel) This is a trip into the 19th century. Until the 1980s it was a confectioner's shop, and although the original cabinets are now lined with booze, the look of the place barely changed with its conversion into a laid-back bar. A quiet enough spot for a house *vermut* (€3; add your own soda) in the early evening.

Casa Almirall
BAR

(Map p238; www.casaalmirall.com; Carrer de Joaquín Costa 33; ⊙6pm-2.30am Mon-Thu, 6.30pm-3am Fri, noon-3am Sat, noon-12.30am Sun; ⓂUniversitat) In business since the 1860s, this unchanged corner bar is dark and intriguing, with Modernista decor and a mixed clientele. There are some great original pieces in here, such as the marble counter, and the cast-iron statue of the muse of the Universal Exposition, held in Barcelona in 1888.

Moog
CLUB

(Map p238; www.masimas.com/moog; Carrer de l'Arc del Teatre 3; ⊙midnight-5am Mon-Thu & Sun, to 6am Fri & Sat; ⓂDrassanes) This fun and minuscule club is a standing favourite with the downtown crowd. In the main dance area, DJs dish out house, techno and electro, while upstairs you can groove to a nice blend of indie and occasional classic-pop throwbacks. Admission is €5.

Bar Pastís
BAR

(Map p238; www.barpastis.com; Carrer de Santa Mònica 4; ⊙7.30pm-2am; ⓂDrassanes) A French cabaret theme (with lots of Piaf in the background) dominates this tiny, cluttered classic. It's been going, on and off, since the end of WWII. You'll need to be in here before 9pm to have any hope of sitting, getting near the bar or anything much else. On some nights it features live acts, usually performing French *chansons*.

London Bar
BAR

(Map p238; Carrer Nou de la Rambla 34-36; ⊙6pm-3am Mon-Thu & Sun, 6pm-3.30am Fri & Sat; ⓂLiceu) Open since 1909, this Modernista bar started as a hang-out for circus hands and was later frequented by the likes of Picasso, Miró and Hemingway. Today it fills to the brim with punters at the long front bar and rickety old tables. On occasion you can attend concerts at the small stage right up the back.

Boadas
COCKTAIL BAR

(Map p238; www.boadascocktails.com; Carrer dels Tallers 1; ⊙noon-2am Mon-Thu, noon-3am Fri & Sat; ⓂCatalunya) One of the city's oldest cocktail bars, Boadas is famed for its daiquiris. Bow-tied waiters have been serving up unique, drinkable creations since Miguel Boadas opened it in 1933 – in fact Miró and Hemingway both drank here. Miguel was born in Havana, where he was the first barman at the immortal La Floridita.

La Ribera

Guzzo
COCKTAIL BAR

(☑93 667 00 36; www.guzzo.es; Plaça Comercial 10; ⊙6pm-3am Tue-Thu, to 3.30am Fri & Sat, noon-3am Sun; ⓐ; ⓂBarceloneta) A swish but relaxed cocktail bar, run by much-loved Barcelona DJ Fred Guzzo, who is often to be found at the decks, spinning his delicious selection of funk, soul and rare groove. You'll also find frequent live-music acts of consistently decent quality, and a funky atmosphere at almost any time of day.

Rubí
BAR

(☑647 773707; Carrer dels Banys Vells 6; ⊙7.30pm-2.30am Sun-Thu, to 3am Fri & Sat; ⓂJaume I) With its boudoir lighting and cheap mojitos, Rubí is where the Born's *cognoscenti* head for a nightcap – or several. It's a narrow, cosy space – push through to the back where you might just get one of the coveted tables, with superior bar food, from Vietnamese rolls to more traditional selections of cheese and ham.

El Born Bar
BAR

(☑93 319 53 33; Passeig del Born 26; ⊙10am-2am Mon-Sat, noon-1.30am Sun; ⓐ; ⓂJaume I) El Born Bar effortlessly attracts everyone from cool thirty-somethings from all over town to locals who pass judgment on Passeig del Born's passing parade. Its staying power depends on a good selection of beers, spirits, and *empanadas* and other snacks.

Mudanzas
BAR

(☑93 319 11 37; Carrer de la Vidrieria 15; ⊙10am-2am Sun-Thu, to 3am Fri & Sat; ⓐ; ⓂJaume I) This was one of the first bars to get things into gear in El Born and it still attracts a faithful crowd. With its chequered floor and marble-topped tables, it's an attractive, lively place for a beer and perhaps a sandwich or a tapa. It also has a nice line in rums and malt whisky.

Juanra Falces
COCKTAIL BAR

(☑ 93 310 10 27; Carrer del Rec 24; ⊘ 8pm-3am Tue-Sat, 10pm-3am Sun & Mon; Ⓜ Jaume I) Transport yourself to a Humphrey Bogart movie in this narrow little bar, formerly (and still, at least among the locals) known as Gimlet. White-jacketed bar staff with all the appropriate aplomb will whip you up a gimlet or any other classic cocktail (around €10) that your heart desires.

La Vinya del Senyor
WINE BAR

(☑ 93 310 33 79; www.lavinyadelsenyor.com; Plaça de Santa Maria del Mar 5; ⊘ noon-1am Mon-Thu, noon-2am Fri & Sat, noon-midnight Sun; ☎; Ⓜ Jaume I) Relax on the *terrassa*, which lies in the shadow of the Basílica de Santa Maria del Mar, or crowd inside at the tiny bar. The wine list is as long as *War and Peace* and there's a table upstairs for those who opt to sample by the bottle rather than the glass.

🍷 Barceloneta & the Waterfront

Absenta
BAR

(Map p250; www.absentabar.es; Carrer de Sant Carles 36; ⊘ 7pm-1am Tue & Wed, from 11am Thu-Mon; Ⓜ Barceloneta) Decorated with old paintings, vintage lamps and curious sculpture (including a dangling butterfly woman and face-painted TVs), this whimsical and creative drinking den takes its liquor seriously. Stop in for the house-made vermouth or for more bite try one of the many absinthes on hand. Just go easy: with an alcohol content of 50% to 90%, these spirits have kick!

Can Paixano
WINE BAR

(Map p250; ☑ 93 310 08 39; Carrer de la Reina Cristina 7; ⊘ 9am-10.30pm Mon-Sat; Ⓜ Barceloneta) This lofty old champagne bar (also called La Xampanyeria) has long been run on a winning formula. The standard poison is bubbly rosé in elegant little glasses, com-

---

CAVA BARS

Cava bars tend to be more about the festive ambience than the actual drinking of *cava*, a sparkling white or rosé, most of which is produced in Catalonia's Penedès region. The most famous *cava* bars are **El Xampanyet** (☑ 93 319 70 03; Carrer de Montcada 22; ⊘ noon-4pm & 7-11pm Tue-Sat, noon-4pm Sun; Ⓜ Jaume I) in La Ribera and **Can Paixano** (p288) in Barceloneta.

---

bined with bite-sized *bocadillos* (filled rolls) and tapas (€3 to €7). Note that this place is usually jammed to the rafters, and elbowing your way to the bar can be a titanic struggle.

BlackLab
MICROBREWERY

(Map p250; ☑ 93 221 83 60; www.blacklab.es; Plaça Pau Vila 1; ⊘ noon-1.30am; Ⓜ Barceloneta) Inside the historic Palau de Mar, BlackLab was Barcelona's first brewhouse to open way back in 2014. With 20 taps (including 18 housemade brews, including saisons, double IPAs and dry stouts), it's an impressive operation, and the brewmasters are constantly experimenting with new flavours.

La Cervecita Nuestra de Cada Día
BAR

(Carrer de Llull 184; ⊘ 5.30-9.30pm Sun & Mon, 11.30am-2pm & 5.30-9.30pm Tue-Sat; Ⓜ Llacuna) Equal parts beer shop and craft brew bar, La Cervicita has a changing selection of unique beers from around Europe and the USA. You might stumble across a Catalan sour fruit beer, a rare English stout, a potent Belgian triple ale or half a dozen other drafts on hand – plus many more varieties by the bottle.

Espai Joliu
CAFE

(Carrer Badajoz 95; ⊘ 9am-7pm Mon-Fri; ☎; Ⓜ Llacuna) Further proof that Poblenou is fast becoming the Brooklyn of Barcelona are places like Espai Joliu, a charming little space with art mags, handmade stationery and ceramics sold up front and a peaceful cafe (blonde wood tables, melodic indie rock) tucked up the steps at the back.

🍷 La Sagrada Família & L'Eixample

★ Monvínic
WINE BAR

(Map p256; ☑ 93 272 61 87; www.monvinic.com; Carrer de la Diputació 249; ⊘ 1-11pm Tue-Fri, 7-11pm Mon & Sat; Ⓜ Passeig de Gràcia) Apparently considered unmissable by El Bulli's sommelier, Monvínic is an ode, a rhapsody even, to wine loving. The interactive wine list sits on the bar for you to browse, on a digital tablet similar to an iPad, and boasts more than 3000 varieties.

★ Dry Martini
BAR

(☑ 93 217 50 80; www.drymartiniorg.com; Carrer d'Aribau 162-166; ⊘ 1pm-2.30am Mon-Thu, 6pm-3am Fri & Sat, 7pm-2.30am Sun; Ⓜ Diagonal) Waiters with a knowing smile will attend to your cocktail needs and make uncannily good suggestions, but the house drink, taken at the bar or in one of the plush green leather banquettes, is a safe bet. The gin and tonic comes in an enormous mug-sized glass – one will take you most of the night.

Napar BCN
BREWERY

(Map p256; ☑606 546467; www.naparbcn.com; Carrer de la Diputació 223; ⊙noon-midnight Tue-Thu, to 2am Fri & Sat, noon-5pm Sun; ☎; Ⓜ Universitat) The latest bar to open as part of Barcelona's burgeoning craft-beer scene, Napar has 12 beers on tap, six of which are beers brewed on-site, including a mix of IPAs, pale ale and stout. There's also an accomplished list of bottled beers. It's a stunning space, with a gleaming steampunk aesthetic, and serves some excellent food should hunger strike.

Milano
COCKTAIL BAR

(Map p256; ☑93 112 71 50; www.camparimilano.com; Ronda de la Universitat 35; ⊙noon-2.30am Mon-Sat, 6pm-2.30am Sun; Ⓜ Catalunya) An absolute gem of hidden Barcelona nightlife, Milano is a subterranean old-school cocktail bar with velvet banquettes and glass-fronted cabinets, presided over by white-jacketed waiters, and completely invisible from street level. Check the website for details on occasional live music.

Cafè del Centre
CAFE

(Map p256; ☑93 488 11 01; Carrer de Girona 69; ⊙10am-midnight Mon-Fri, noon-midnight Sat; ☎; Ⓜ Girona) Step back a century in this cafe, in business since 1873. The wooden bar extends down the right side as you enter, fronted by a slew of marble-topped tables and wooden chairs. It exudes an almost melancholy air by day but gets busy at night. Staff pride themselves on stocking 50 beers, and there is a lunchtime *menú* for €11.

Les Gens Que J'Aime
BAR

(Map p256; ☑93 215 68 79; www.lesgensque jaime.com; Carrer de València 286; ⊙6pm-2.30am Sun-Thu, 7pm-3am Fri & Sat; Ⓜ Passeig de Gràcia) This intimate basement relic of the 1960s follows a deceptively simple formula: chilled jazz music in the background, minimal lighting from an assortment of flea-market lamps and a cosy, cramped scattering of red-velvet-backed lounges around tiny dark tables.

🍷 Gràcia & Park Güell

Rabipelao
COCKTAIL BAR

(Map p261; ☑93 182 50 35; www.elrabipelao.com; Carrer del Torrent d'En Vidalet 22; ⊙7pm-2am Mon-Sat, 1-4pm & 7pm-2am Sun; Ⓜ Joanic, Fon-

tana) An anchor of Gràcia's nightlife, Rabipelao is a celebratory space with a spinning disco ball and DJs spinning driving salsa beats. Patrons aside, there's much to look at here: a silent film plays in one corner beyond the red velvety wallpaper-covered walls and there's a richly hued mural above the bar – not to mention the tropical cocktails (mojitos and caipirinhas) and snacks (arepas, ceviche).

Elephanta
BAR

(Map p261; ☑93 237 69 06; http://elephanta.cat; Carrer del Torrent d'en Vidalet 37; ⊙6pm-1.30am Mon-Wed, to 2.30am Thu-Sat, 5-10pm Sun; Ⓜ Joanic, Fontana) This friendly and petite cocktail bar is a fine place to catch up with a friend. It has an old-fashioned vibe, with long plush green banquettes and art-lined walls and a five-seat bar topped with old vintage wooden stools.

Gin is the drink of choice, with more than 40 varieties on hand, and the cocktails are deftly mixed (though be patient, these things take time).

Viblioteca
WINE BAR

(Map p261; ☑93 284 42 02; www.viblioteca.com; Carrer de Vallfogona 12; ⊙6pm-1am Mon-Sat, 7pm-midnight Sun; Ⓜ Fontana) If the smell of ripe cheese doesn't rock your boat, this is not the place for you – a glass cabinet piled high with the stuff assaults your olfactory nerves as you walk into this small, white, cleverly designed space. The real speciality at Viblioteca, however, is wine, and you can choose from 150 mostly local labels, many of them available by the glass.

Musical Maria
BAR

(Map p261; ☑93 501 04 60; Carrer de Maria 5; ⊙9pm-2.30am; ☎; Ⓜ Diagonal) Even the music hasn't changed since this place got going in the late 1970s. Those longing for rock 'n' roll crowd into this animated bar, listen to old hits and knock back beers. Out the back there's a pool table and the bar serves pretty much all the variants of the local Estrella Damm brew.

🍷 Camp Nou, Pedralbes & La Zona Alta

El Maravillas
COCKTAIL BAR

(☑93 360 73 78; Plaça de la Concòrdia 15; ⊙noon-midnight Mon-Thu, to 2am Fri & Sat; Ⓜ Maria Cristina) Overlooking the peaceful Plaça de la Concòrdia, El Maravillas feels like a secret hideaway – especially if you've just arrived from the crowded lanes of the *ciutat vella* (old city). The glittering bar has just a few tables, with outdoor seating on the square when the weather warms. Creative cocktails, good Spanish red wines and easy-drinking vermouths are the drinks of choice.

Dô Bar   BAR
(☑93 209 18 88; www.do-bcn.com; Carrer de Santaló 30, entrance on l'Avenir; ⊙7pm-1am Mon-Thu, 8pm-1am Fri & Sat; ℝFGC Muntaner) This neighbourhood charmer has a warm and inviting interior, where friends gather over tall wooden tables to enjoy excellent gin and tonics, wines by the glass, craft beer and satisfying small plates (anchovies, mussels, tacos, charcuterie). On warm nights, arrive early for one of the terrace tables out the front.

Mirablau   BAR
(☑93 418 58 79; www.mirablaubcn.com; Plaça del Doctor Andreu; ⊙11am-4.30am Mon-Thu, 10am-4.30am Fri-Sun; ℝFGC Avinguda Tibidabo) Gaze out over the entire city from this privileged balcony restaurant on the way up to Tibidabo. Wander downstairs to join the folk in the tiny dance space. In summer you can step out on to the even smaller terrace for a breather.

Bikini   CLUB
(☑93 322 08 00; www.bikinibcn.com; Avinguda Diagonal 547; €10-25; ⊙midnight-6am Thu-Sat; ⬛6, 7, 33, 34, 63, 67, 68, ⓂEntença) This old star of the Barcelona nightlife scene has been keeping the beat since the darkest days of Franco. Every possible kind of music gets a run, from Latin and Brazilian beats to 1980s disco, depending on the night and the space you choose.

🍷 Montjuïc, Poble Sec & Sant Antoni

★**La Caseta del Migdia**   BAR
(☑617 956572; www.lacaseta.org; Mirador del Migdia; ⊙8pm-1am Wed-Fri, from noon Sat & Sun, weekends only in winter; ⬛150) The effort of getting to what is, for all intents and purposes, a simple *chiringuito* (makeshift cafe-bar) is worth it. Stare out to sea over a beer or coffee by day. As sunset approaches the atmosphere changes, as lounge music (from samba to funk) wafts out over the hillside. Drinks aside, you can also order barbecue, fired up on the outdoor grills.

GAY & LESBIAN BARCELONA

Although somewhat overshadowed by the beachy gay mecca of Sitges up the coast, Barcelona still has a lively gay scene. Gay bars, clubs and cafes are mostly concentrated around the 'Gaixample', between Carrer de Muntaner and Carrer de Balmes, around Carrer del Consell de Cent.

For information, pick up a copy of Shanguide (www.shangay.com), available in many gay bars and shops. Other sources of info include www.60by80.com, www.visitbarcelonagay.com and www.guiagaybarcelona.es.

Arena Madre (Map p256; ☑93 487 83 42; www.grupoarena.com; Carrer de Balmes 32; Sun-Fri €6, Sat €12; ⊙12.30-5am; ⓂPasseig de Gràcia) Popular with a hot young crowd, Arena Madre is one of the top clubs in town for boys seeking boys. Mainly electronic and house, with a striptease show on Monday, handbag on Thursday, and live shows throughout the week. Heteros are welcome but a minority.

Metro (☑93 323 52 27; www.metrodiscobcn.com; Carrer de Sepúlveda 185; before 2am from €6, after 2am €20; ⊙12.15am-5.30am; ⓂUniversitat) Metro attracts a casual gay crowd with its two dance floors, three bars and very dark room. Keep an eye out for shows and parties, which can range from parades of models to bingo nights (on Thursday nights, with sometimes-interesting prizes), plus the occasional striptease.

To save cash, come before 2am, though you're likely to be drinking all by your lonesome, as Metro doesn't fill up till late.

Punto BCN (Map p256; ☑93 451 91 52; www.grupoarena.com; Carrer de Muntaner 63-65; ⊙6pm-2.30am Sun-Thu, to 3am Fri & Sat; ⓂUniversitat) It's an oldie but a goody. A big bar over two levels with a slightly older crowd, this place fills to bursting on Friday and Saturday nights with its blend of Spanish pop and dance. It's a friendly early stop on a gay night out, and you can shoot a round of pool if you feel so inclined.

Bar Calders
BAR

(Map p266; ☑ 93 329 93 49; Carrer del Parlament 25; ⊙ 5pm-2am Mon-Fri, 11am-2.30am Sat, 11am-midnight Sun; Ⓜ Sant Antoni) It bills itself as a wine bar, but actually the wine selection at Bar Calders is its weak point. As an all-day cafe and tapas bar, however, it's unbeatable, with a few tables outside on a tiny pedestrian lane, and has become the favoured meeting point for the neighbourhood's boho element.

El Rouge
BAR

(Map p266; ☑ 666 251556; Carrer del Poeta Cabanyes 21; ⊙ 11pm-2am Mon, 8pm-2am Tue & Thu, 10pm-3am Fri & Sat; ☏; Ⓜ Poble Sec) Decadence is the word that springs to mind in this bordello-red lounge-cocktail bar, with acid jazz, drum and bass and other sounds drifting along in the background. The walls are laden with heavy-framed paintings, dim lamps and mirrors, and no two chairs are alike. You can sometimes catch DJs, risqué poetry soirées, cabaret shows or even nights of tango dancing.

Bacanal
CAFE

(Carrer de Sepúlveda 164; ⊙ 9am-midnight Mon & Wed-Fri, 10am-2am Sat, 10am-8.30pm Sun; ☏; Ⓜ Urgell) This decidedly hip neighbourhood cafe invites lingering, with its spacious light-filled interior, artwork-lined walls and thoughtful touches (flowers on the tables) – never mind the concrete floors and columns. A mix of laptop users and chatterers stay fuelled on good coffees, smoothies, craft beers, wines, sandwiches and low-playing grooves.

Bar Olimpia
BAR

(Map p238; ☑ 606 200800; Carrer d'Aldana 11; ⊙ 7pm-1am Wed & Thu, to 2.30am Fri & Sat, 6-11pm Sun; Ⓜ Paral·lel) This great little neighbourhood bar is a little slice of Barcelona history. It was here (and on the surrounding block), where the popular Olimpia Theatre Circus once performed way back in the 1930s. Today the vaguely retro bar draws a diverse crowd, who come for house-made vermouth, snacks (like quesadillas, cheese plates, tuna tartare), and satisfying gin and tonics.

☆ Entertainment

☆ La Rambla & Barri Gòtic

Gran Teatre del Liceu
THEATRE, LIVE MUSIC

(Map p238; ☑ 93 485 99 00; www.liceubarcelona. com; La Rambla 51-59; ⊙ box office 9.30am-8pm Mon-Fri, 9.30am-6pm Sat & Sun; Ⓜ Liceu) Barcelona's grand old opera house, restored after fire in 1994, is one of the most technologically advanced theatres in the world. To take a seat in the grand auditorium, returned to all its 19th-century glory but with the very latest in acoustics, is to be transported to another age.

El Paraigua
LIVE MUSIC

(Map p238; ☑ 93 302 11 31; www.elparaigua.com; Carrer del Pas de l'Ensenyança 2; ⊙ noon-midnight Sun-Wed, to 2am Thu, to 3am Fri & Sat; Ⓜ Liceu) A tiny chocolate box of dark tinted Modernisme, the 'Umbrella' has been serving up drinks since the 1960s. The turn-of-the-20th-century decor was transferred here from a shop knocked down elsewhere in the district and cobbled back together to create this cosy locale.

Jamboree
LIVE MUSIC

(Map p238; ☑ 93 319 17 89; www.masimas. com/jamboree; Plaça Reial 17; €12-20; ⊙ 8pm-6am; Ⓜ Liceu) For over half a century, Jamboree has been bringing joy to the jivers of Barcelona, with high-calibre acts featuring jazz trios, blues, Afrobeats, Latin beats and big-band sounds. Two concerts held most nights of the week (at 8pm and 10pm), after which Jamboree morphs into a DJ-spinning club at midnight. WTF jam sessions are held Mondays (with entrance a mere €5).

Sala Tarantos
FLAMENCO

(Map p238; ☑ 93 304 12 10; www.masimas.com/ tarantos; Plaça Reial 17; €15; ⊙ shows 8.30pm, 9.30pm & 10.30pm; Ⓜ Liceu) Since 1963, this basement locale has been the stage for up-and-coming flamenco groups performing in Barcelona. These days Tarantos has become a mostly tourist-centric affair, with half-hour shows held three times a night. Still, it's a good introduction to flamenco, and not a bad setting for a drink.

Harlem Jazz Club
JAZZ

(Map p238; ☑ 93 310 07 55; www.harlemjazzclub. es; Carrer de la Comtessa de Sobradiel 8; €6-10; ⊙ 10.30pm-3am Sun & Tue-Thu, to 5am Fri & Sat; Ⓜ Liceu) This narrow, old-city dive is one of the best spots in town for jazz, as well as funk, Latin, blues and gypsy jazz. It attracts a mixed crowd who maintains a respectful silence during the acts. Most concerts start around 10pm. Get in early if you want a seat in front of the stage.

☆ El Raval

★ Filmoteca de Catalunya
CINEMA

(Map p238; ☎93 567 10 70; www.filmoteca.cat; Plaça de Salvador Seguí 1-9; adult/concession €4/3; ⊙screenings 5-10pm, ticket office 10am-3pm & 4-9.30pm Tue-Sun; Ⓜ Liceu) After almost a decade in the planning, the Filmoteca de Catalunya – Catalonia's national cinema – moved into this modern 6000-sq-metre building in 2012. It's a glass, metal and concrete beast that hulks in the midst of the most louche part of the Raval, but the building's interior shouts revival, with light and space, wall-to-wall windows, skylights and glass panels that let the sun in.

Jazz Sí Club
LIVE MUSIC

(☎93 329 00 20; www.tallerdemusics.com; Carrer de Requesens 2; €4-10, incl drink; ⊙8.30-11pm Tue-Sat, 6.30-10pm Sun; Ⓜ Sant Antoni) A cramped little bar run by the Taller de Músics (Musicians' Workshop) serves as the stage for a varied program of jazz jams through to some good flamenco (Friday and Saturday nights). Thursday night is Cuban night, Tuesday and Sunday are rock, and the rest are devoted to jazz and/or blues sessions. Concerts start around 9pm but the jam sessions can get going earlier.

☆ La Ribera

★ Palau de la Música Catalana
CLASSICAL MUSIC

(Map p256; ☎93 295 72 00; www.palaumusica.cat; Carrer de Palau de la Música 4-6; from €15; ⊙box office 9.30am-9pm Mon-Sat, 10am-3pm Sun; Ⓜ Urquinaona) A feast for the eyes, this Modernista confection is also the city's most traditional venue for classical and choral music, although it has a wide-ranging program, including flamenco, pop and – particularly – jazz. Just being here for a performance is an experience. In the foyer, its tiled pillars all a-glitter, sip a pre-concert tipple.

☆ Barceloneta & the Waterfront

Razzmatazz
LIVE MUSIC

(☎93 320 82 00; www.salarazzmatazz.com; Carrer de Pamplona 88; €15-40; ⊙9pm-4am; Ⓜ Marina, Bogatell) Bands from far and wide occasionally create scenes of near hysteria in this, one of the city's classic live-music and clubbing venues. Bands can appear throughout the week (check the website), with different start times. On weekends the live music then gives way to club sounds.

☆ La Sagrada Família & L'Eixample

Music Hall
CONCERT VENUE

(Map p256; ☎93 238 07 22; www.musichall.es; Rambla de Catalunya 2-4; varies; ⊙7.30pm-midnight; Ⓜ Catalunya) The early-evening incarnation of City Hall, this former theatre is the perfect size and shape for live music, holding a crowd of around 500. The acoustics are also great and the layout means everyone gets a good view of the stage.

☆ Gràcia & Park Güell

Soda Acústic
LIVE MUSIC

(Map p261; ☎93 016 55 90; www.facebook.com/sodacustic; Carrer de les Guilleries 6; from €3; ⊙8pm-2.30am Wed-Sun; Ⓜ Fontana) This low-lit modern space stages an eclectic lineup of bands and performing artists. Jazz, Balkan swing, Latin rhythms and plenty of experimental, not easily classifiable musicians all receive their due. The acoustics are excellent. Check its Facebook page for upcoming shows.

Heliogàbal
LIVE MUSIC

(Map p261; www.heliogabal.com; Carrer de Ramón i Cajal 80; ⊙9.30pm-3am Wed-Sat; Ⓜ Joanic) This compact bar is a veritable hive of cultural activity where you never quite know what to expect. Aside from art exhibitions and poetry readings, you will be pleasantly surprised by the eclectic live-music program. Jazz groups are often followed by open jam sessions, and experimental music of all colours gets a run.

☆ Camp Nou, Pedralbes & La Zona Alta

Camp Nou
FOOTBALL

(☎902 189900; www.fcbarcelona.com; Carrer d'Arístides Maillol; Ⓜ Palau Reial) Among Barcelona's most-visited sites is the massive stadium of Camp Nou (which means New Field in Catalan), home to the legendary Futbol Club Barcelona. Attending a game amid the roar of the crowds is an unforgettable experience. Football fans who aren't able to see a game can get a taste of all the excitement at the Camp Nou Experience (p264), which includes a visit to interactive galleries and a tour of the stadium. The season runs from September to May.

ℹ️ SEEING AN FC BARCELONA MATCH

Tickets to FC Barcelona matches are available at Camp Nou, online (through FC Barcelona's official website), and through various city locations. Tourist offices sell them – the branch at Plaça de Catalunya is a centrally located option – as do FC Botiga stores. Tickets can cost anything from €39 to upwards of €250, depending on the seat and match. On match day the ticket windows (at gates 9 and 15) open from 9.15am until kick off. Tickets are not usually available for matches with Real Madrid.

You will almost definitely find scalpers lurking near the ticket windows. They are often club members and can sometimes get you in at a significant reduction. Don't pay until you are safely seated.

☆ Montjuïc, Poble Sec & Sant Antoni

Sala Apolo
LIVE MUSIC

(Map p266; ☏ 93 441 40 01; www.sala-apolo.com; Carrer Nou de la Rambla 113; club €12-18, concerts vary; ⊕ 12.30am-5am Mon-Thu, 12.30am-6am Fri & Sat; Ⓜ Paral·lel) This is a fine old theatre, where red velvet dominates and you feel as though you're in a movie-set dancehall scene featuring Eliot Ness. 'Nasty Mondays' and 'Crappy Tuesdays' are aimed at a diehard, we-never-stop-dancing crowd. Earlier in the evening, concerts generally take place here and in 'La 2', a smaller auditorium downstairs.

Tastes are as eclectic as possible, from local bands and burlesque shows to big-name international acts.

🛍️ Shopping

If your doctor has prescribed an intense round of retail therapy to deal with the blues, then Barcelona is the place. Across Ciutat Vella (Barri Gòtic, El Raval and La Ribera), L'Eixample and Gràcia is spread a thick mantle of boutiques, historic shops, original one-off stores, gourmet corners, wine dens and more designer labels than you can shake your gold card at. You name it, you'll find it here.

🛍️ La Rambla & Barri Gòtic

A handful of interesting shops dots La Rambla, but the real fun starts inside the labyrinth. Young fashion on Carrer d'Avinyó, a mixed bag on Avinguda del Portal de l'Àngel, some cute old shops on Carrer de la Dagueria and lots of exploring in tight old lanes awaits.

Torrons Vicens
FOOD

(Map p238; ☏ 93 304 37 36; www.vicens.com; Carrer del Petritxol 15; ⊕ 10am-8.30pm Mon-Sat, 11am-8pm Sun; Ⓜ Liceu) You can find the *turrón* (nougat) treat year-round at Torrons Vicens, which has been selling its signature sweets since 1775.

Sabater Hermanos
BEAUTY

(Map p238; ☏ 93 301 98 32; www.shnos.com.ar; Plaça de Sant Felip Neri 1; ⊕ 10.30am-9pm; Ⓜ Jaume I) This fragrant little shop sells handcrafted soaps of all sizes. Varieties like fig, cinnamon, grapefruit and chocolate smell good enough to eat, while sandalwood, magnolia, mint, cedar and jasmine add spice to any sink or bathtub.

Escribà
FOOD & DRINK

(Map p238; ☏ 93 301 60 27; www.escriba.es; La Rambla 83; ⊕ 9am-10pm; 🖥; Ⓜ Liceu) Chocolates, dainty pastries and mouth-watering cakes can be lapped up behind the Modernista mosaic facade here or taken away for private, guilt-ridden consumption. This Barcelona favourite is owned by the Escribà family, a name synonymous with sinfully good sweet things. More than that, it adds a touch of authenticity to La Rambla.

Formatgeria La Seu
FOOD

(Map p238; ☏ 93 412 65 48; www.formatgerialaseu.com; Carrer de la Dagueria 16; ⊕ 10am-2pm & 5-8pm Tue-Sat, closed Aug; Ⓜ Jaume I) Dedicated to artisan cheeses from all across Spain, this small shop is run by the oh-so-knowledgeable Katherine McLaughlin and is the antithesis of mass production – it sells only the best from small-scale farmers and the stock changes regularly. Wine and cheese tastings in the cosy room at the back are fun.

L'Arca
VINTAGE, CLOTHING

(Map p238; ☏ 93 302 15 98; www.larca.es; Carrer dels Banys Nous 20; ⊕ 11am-2pm & 4.30-8.30pm Mon-Sat; Ⓜ Liceu) Step inside this enchanting shop for a glimpse of beautifully crafted apparel from the past, including

18th-century embroidered silk vests, elaborate silk kimonos, and wedding dresses and shawls from the 1920s. Thanks to its incredible collection, it has provided clothing for films including *Titanic, Talk to Her* and *Perfume.*

Cereria Subirà
HOMEWARES

(Map p238; 93 315 26 06; Baixada de la Llibreteria 7; 9.30am-1.30pm & 4-8pm Mon-Thu, 9.30am-8pm Fri, 10am-8pm Sat; Jaume I) Even if you're not interested in myriad mounds of colourful wax, pop in just so you've been to the oldest shop in Barcelona. Cereria Subirà has been churning out candles since 1761 and at this address since the 19th century; the interior has a beautifully baroque quality, with a picturesque *Gone With the Wind* staircase.

Herboristeria del Rei
BEAUTY

(Map p238; 93 318 05 12; www.herboristeriadelrei.com; Carrer del Vidre 1; 2-8.30pm Mon, 10am-8.30pm Tue-Sat; Liceu) Once patronised by Queen Isabel II, this timeless corner store flogs all sorts of weird and wonderful herbs, spices and medicinal plants. It's been doing so since 1823 and the decor has barely changed since the 1860s. However, some of the products have, and you'll find anything from fragrant soaps to massage oil nowadays.

Film director Tom Tykwer shot scenes from *Perfume: The Story of a Murderer* here.

Taller de Marionetas Travi
MARIONETTES

(Map p238; 93 412 66 92; www.marionetastravi.com; Carrer de n'Amargós 4; noon-8pm Mon-Sat; Urquinaona) Opened in the 1970s, this atmospheric shop sells beautifully handcrafted marionettes. Don Quijote, Sancho and other iconic Spanish figures are on hand, as well as unusual works from other parts of the world – including rare Sicilian puppets and pieces from Myanmar (Burma), Indonesia and elsewhere.

La Manual Alpargatera
SHOES

(Map p238; 93 301 01 72; lamanualalpargatera.es; Carrer d'Avinyó 7; 9.30am-1.30pm & 4.30-8pm Mon-Fri, from 10am Sat; Liceu) Clients from Salvador Dalí to Jean Paul Gaultier have ordered a pair of *espadrilles* (rope-soled canvas shoes) from this famous store. The shop was founded just after the Spanish Civil War, though the roots of the simple shoe design date back hundreds of years and originated in the Catalan Pyrenees.

El Raval

El Raval boasts a handful of art galleries around MACBA, along with a burgeoning second-hand and vintage-clothes scene on Carrer de la Riera Baixa. Carrer dels Tallers is one of the city's main music strips.

★ Les Topettes
BEAUTY

(Map p238; 93 500 55 64; www.lestopettes.com; Carrer de Joaquín Costa 33; 11am-2pm & 4-9pm Tue-Sat; Universitat) It's a sign of the times that such a chic little temple to soap and perfume can exist in the Raval. The items in Les Topettes' collection have been picked for their designs as much as the products themselves, and you'll find gorgeously packaged scents, candles and unguents from Diptyque, Cowshed and L'Artisan Parfumeur, among others.

Teranyina
ARTS & CRAFTS

(Map p238; www.textilteranyina.com; Carrer del Notariat 10; 11am-3pm & 5-8pm Mon-Fri; Catalunya) Artist Teresa Rosa Aguayo runs this textile workshop in the heart of the artsy bit of El Raval. You can join courses at the loom, admire some of the rugs and other works that Teresa has created, and, of course, buy them.

La Ribera

The former commercial heart of medieval Barcelona is today still home to a cornucopia of old-style specialist food and drink shops, a veritable feast of aroma and atmosphere. They have been joined, since the late 1990s, by a raft of hip little fashion stores.

El Rei de la Màgia
MAGIC

(Map p238; 93 319 39 20; www.elreydelamagia.com; Carrer de la Princesa 11; 10.30am-2pm & 4-7.30pm Mon-Sat; Jaume I) For more than 100 years, the people behind this box of tricks have been keeping locals both astounded and amused. Should you decide to stay in Barcelona and make a living as a magician, this is the place to buy levitation brooms, glasses of disappearing milk and decks of magic cards.

Hofmann Pastisseria
FOOD

(93 268 82 21; www.hofmann-bcn.com; Carrer dels Flassaders 44; 9am-2pm & 3.30-8pm Mon-Thu, 9am-8.30pm Fri & Sat, 9am-2.30pm Sun; Barceloneta) With its painted wooden cabinets, this bite-sized gourmet patisserie, linked to the prestigious Hofmann cooking school, has an air of timelessness. Choose between jars of delicious chocolates, the renowned croissants (in various flavours) and more dangerous pastries, or an array of cakes and other sweet treats.

El Magnífico
COFFEE

(☑ 93 319 39 75; www.cafeselmagnifico.com; Carrer de l'Argenteria 64; ◷ 10am-8pm Mon-Sat; Ⓜ Jaume I) All sorts of coffee has been roasted here since the early 20th century. The variety of coffee (and tea) available is remarkable – and the aromas hit you as you walk in. Across the road, the same people run the exquisite tea shop **Sans i Sans** (☑ 93 310 25 18; Carrer de l'Argenteria 59; ◷ 10am-8pm Mon-Sat; Ⓜ Jaume I).

Casa Gispert
FOOD

(☑ 93 319 75 35; www.casagispert.com; Carrer dels Sombrerers 23; ◷ 10am-2pm & 4-8pm Mon-Sat; Ⓜ Jaume I) The wonderful, atmospheric and wood-fronted Casa Gispert has been toasting nuts and selling all manner of dried fruit since 1851. Pots and jars piled high on the shelves contain an unending variety of crunchy tidbits: some roasted, some honeyed, all of them moreish. Your order is shouted over to the till, along with the price, in a display of old-world accounting.

Vila Viniteca
WINE

(Map p238; ☑ 902 327777; www.vilaviniteca.es; Carrer dels Agullers 7; ◷ 8.30am-8.30pm Mon-Sat; Ⓜ Jaume I) One of the best wine stores in Barcelona (and there are a few...), this place has been searching out the best local and imported wines since 1932. On a couple of November evenings it organises what has become an almost riotous wine-tasting event in Carrer dels Agullers and surrounding lanes, at which cellars from around Spain present their young new wines.

At No 9 it has another store devoted to gourmet food products.

Loisaida
CLOTHING, ANTIQUES

(☑ 93 295 54 92; www.loisaidabcn.com; Carrer dels Flassaders 42; ◷ 11am-9pm Mon-Sat, 11am-2pm & 4-8pm Sun; Ⓜ Jaume I) A sight in its own right, housed in what was once the coach house and stables for the Royal Mint, Loisaida (from the Spanglish for 'Lower East Side') is a deceptively large emporium of colourful, retro and somewhat preppy clothing for men and women, costume jewellery, music from the 1940s and '50s and some covetable antiques.

Arlequí Màscares
ARTS & CRAFTS

(Map p238; ☑ 93 268 27 52; www.arlequimask.com; Carrer de la Princesa 7; ◷ 10.30am-8.30pm Mon-Sat, 10.30am-3pm & 4-7.30pm Sun; Ⓜ Jaume I) A wonderful little oasis of originality, this shop specialises in masks for costume and decoration. Some of the pieces are superb, while stock also includes a beautiful range of decorative boxes in Catalan themes, and some old-style marionettes.

Nu Sabates
SHOES, ACCESSORIES

(☑ 93 268 03 83; www.nusabates.com; Carrer dels Cotoners 14; ◷ 11am-9pm Mon-Sat; Ⓜ Jaume I) A couple of modern-day Catalan cobblers have put together some original handmade leather shoes for men and women (and a handful of bags and other leather items) in their friendly and stylish locale, which is enlivened by some inspired musical selections.

Olisoliva
FOOD

(Map p238; ☑ 93 268 14 72; www.olisoliva.com; Mercat de Santa Caterina; ◷ 9.30am-3.30pm Mon, Wed & Sat, to 8.30pm Tue & Thu; Ⓜ Jaume I) Inside the Mercat de Santa Caterina, this simple, glassed-in store is stacked with olive oils and vinegars from all over Spain. Taste some of the products before deciding. Some of the best olive oils come from southern Spain. The range of vinegars is astounding too.

Custo Barcelona
FASHION

(☑ 93 268 78 93; www.custo.com; Plaça de les Olles 7; ◷ 10am-9pm Mon-Sat, noon-8pm Sun; Ⓜ Barceloneta) The psychedelic decor and casual atmosphere lend this avant-garde Barcelona fashion store a youthful edge. Custo presents daring new women's and men's collections each year on the New York catwalks. The dazzling colours and cut of everything from dinner jackets to hot pants are for the uninhibited. It has three other stores around town.

La Botifarreria
FOOD

(☑ 93 319 91 23; www.labotifarreria.com; Carrer de Santa Maria 4; ◷ 8.30am-2.30pm & 5-8.30pm Mon-Sat; Ⓜ Jaume I) Say it with a sausage! Although this delightful deli sells all sorts of goodies, the mainstay is an astounding variety of handcrafted sausages – the *botifarra*. Not just the regular pork variety either – these sausages are stuffed with anything from green pepper and whisky to apple curry.

BARCELONA SHOPPING

🛍 Barceloneta & the Waterfront

Aside from several weekend markets and the mall mayhem of Maremàgnum, there aren't many shopping options along the waterfront.

Els Encants Vells   MARKET
(Fira de Bellcaire; ☑ 93 246 30 30; www.encantsbcn.com; Plaça de les Glòries Catalanes; ⊘ 9am-8pm Mon, Wed, Fri & Sat; Ⓜ Glòries) In a gleaming open-sided complex near Plaça de les Glòries Catalanes, the 'Old Charms' flea market is the biggest of its kind in Barcelona. Over 500 vendors ply their wares beneath massive mirror-like panels. It's all here, from antique furniture through to second-hand clothes. A lot of it is junk, but occasionally you'll stumble across a *ganga* (bargain).

System Action   CLOTHING
(☑ 93 225 79 90; systemaction.es; Carrer de Pere IV 122; ⊘ 10am-7pm Mon-Sat; Ⓜ Llacuna) If you like discovering local producers, then look no further than this outlet store on Pere IV. Though System Action has stores all across Catalunya (and in Madrid), its design headquarters are a few blocks south in a former Poblenou ice factory. Fashions are feminine but rugged, and you'll find good basics here. Very wearable scarves, sweaters, skirts and even shoes.

Prices are reasonable – especially when sales are underway.

🛍 La Sagrada Família & L'Eixample

Most of the city's classy shopping spreads across the heart of L'Eixample, in particular along Passeig de Gràcia, Rambla de Catalunya and adjacent streets. All about are dotted a surprising array of speciality stores, selling anything from gloves to glues.

El Corte Inglés   DEPARTMENT STORE
(Map p256; ☑ 93 306 38 00; www.elcorteingles.es; Plaça de Catalunya 14; ⊘ 9.30am-9.30pm Mon-Sat; Ⓜ Catalunya) This is now the city's only department store, with everything you'd expect, from computers to cushions, and high fashion to homewares. It's famous for its decent customer service (though this isn't always the case in Spain). El Corte Inglés has other branches, including at **Portal de l'Àngel 19-21** (Map p238; Portal de l'Àngel 19-21; ⊘ 9.30am-9.30pm Mon-Sat; Ⓜ Catalunya), **Avinguda Diagonal 617** (☑ 93 366 71 00; www.elcorteingles.es; Avinguda Diagonal 617;

⊘ 9.30am-9.30pm Mon-Sat; Ⓜ Maria Cristina), and **Avinguda Diagonal 471-473** (☑ 93 493 48 00; www.elcorteingles.es; Avinguda Diagonal 471-473; ⊘ 9.30am-9.30pm Mon-Sat; Ⓜ Hospital Clínic) near Plaça de Francesc Macià.

The top floor is occupied by a so-so restaurant with fabulous city views.

Cacao Sampaka   FOOD
(Map p256; ☑ 93 272 08 33; www.cacaosampaka.com; Carrer del Consell de Cent 292; ⊘ 9am-9pm Mon-Sat; Ⓜ Passeig de Gràcia) Chocoholics will be convinced they have died and passed on to a better place. Load up in the shop or head for the bar out the back where you can have a classic *xocolata* (hot chocolate) and munch on exquisite chocolate cakes, tarts, ice cream, sweets and sandwiches. The bonbons make particularly good presents.

Altaïr   BOOKS
(Map p256; ☑ 93 342 71 71; www.altair.es; Gran Via de les Corts Catalanes 616; ⊘ 10am-8.30pm Mon-Sat; 🕿; Ⓜ Catalunya) Enter a wonderland of travel in this extensive bookshop, which is a mecca for guidebooks, maps, travel literature and all sorts of other books likely to induce a severe case of itchy feet. It has a travellers' noticeboard and, downstairs, a travel agent.

Norma Comics   BOOKS
(☑ 93 244 81 25; www.normacomics.com; Passeig de Sant Joan 7-9; ⊘ 10.30am-8.30pm Mon-Sat; Ⓜ Arc de Triomf) With a huge range of comics, both Spanish and international, this is Spain's biggest dealer – everything from Tintin to some of the weirdest sci-fi and sex comics can be found here. Also on show are armies of model superheroes and other characters produced by fevered imaginations. Kids from nine to 99 can be seen snapping up items to add to their collections.

FNAC   DEPARTMENT STORE
(Map p238; ☑ 902 100 632; www.fnac.es; El Triangle, Plaça de Catalunya 4; ⊘ 10am-9.30pm Mon-Sat; Ⓜ Catalunya) FNAC, the French book, CD and electronics emporium, has a couple of branches around town, but this is the biggest.

Lurdes Bergada   CLOTHING
(Map p256; ☑ 93 218 48 51; www.lurdesbergada.es; Rambla de Catalunya 112; ⊘ 10.30am-8.30pm Mon-Sat; Ⓜ Diagonal) Lurdes Bergada is a boutique run by mother-and-son designer team Lurdes Bergada and Syngman Cucala. The classy men's and women's fashions use natural fibres and have attracted a cult following.

Camper   SHOES

(Map p256; ☑ 93 215 63 90; www.camper.com; Carrer de València 249; ☉ 10am-9pm Mon-Sat; Ⓜ Passeig de Gràcia) What started as a modest Mallorcan family business (the island has a long shoemaking tradition) has, over the decades, and particularly with the success of the 'bowling shoe' in the '90s, become the Clarks of Spain. The shoes, from the eminently sensible to the stylishly fashionable, are known for solid reliability and are sold all over the world.

It now has shops all over Barcelona.

Joan Múrria   FOOD

(Map p256; ☑ 93 215 57 89; www.murria.cat; Carrer de Roger de Llúria 85; ☉ 9am-2pm & 5-8pm Mon-Fri; Ⓜ Passeig de Gràcia) Ramon Casas designed the century-old Modernista shopfront advertisements featured at this culinary temple. For a century the gluttonous have trembled at this altar of speciality food goods from around Catalonia and beyond.

🔒 Gràcia & Park Güell

A wander along the narrow lanes of Gràcia turns up all sorts of surprises, mostly tiny enterprises producing a variety of pretty garments and trinkets. These places tend to come and go, so you never quite know what you might find. Carrer de Verdi has plenty of interesting boutiques.

Amapola Vegan Shop   CLOTHING

(Map p261; ☑ 93 010 62 73; www.amapolavegan shop.com; Travessera de Gràcia 129; ☉ 11am-2.30pm & 5-8.30pm Mon-Sat; Ⓜ Fontana, Diagonal) A shop with a heart of gold, Amapola proves that you need not toss your ethics aside in the quest for stylish clothing and accessories. You'll find sleek leather alternatives for wallets, hand bags and messenger bags by Matt & Nat, dainty ballerina-style flats by Victoria and elegant scarves by Barts.

Lady Loquita   CLOTHING

(Map p261; ☑ 93 217 82 92; www.ladyloquita. com; Travessera de Gràcia 126; ☉ 11am-2pm & 5-8.30pm Mon-Sat; Ⓜ Fontana) Lady Loquita is a hip little shop, where you can browse through light summer dresses by Tiralahilacha, evening wear by Japamala and handmade jewellery by local design label Klimbim. There are also whimsical odds and ends: dinner plates with dog people portraits and digital prints on wood by About Paola.

La Festival   WINE

(Map p261; ☑ 93 023 22 81; Carrer de Verdi 67; ☉ 5.30-9.30pm Mon, 10.30am-9.30pm Tue-Sat, 11am-2pm Sun; Ⓜ Fontana) This handsomely designed shop earns high marks for its knowledgeable (and English-speaking) staff who can give you a wealth of information about the many excellent wines for sale here. Most bottles are from Spanish producers, though there are a few French options, and some organic as well as biodynamic wines.

You can also refill your bottle with wine or vermouth from one of the casks at the front, starting at €3 a bottle.

Bodega Bonavista   WINE

(Map p261; ☑ 93 218 81 99; Carrer de Bonavista 10; ☉ 10am-2.30pm & 5-9pm Mon-Fri, noon-3pm & 6-9pm Sat, noon-3pm Sun; Ⓜ Fontana) An excellent little neighbourhood wine shop that endeavours to seek out great wines at reasonable prices. The stock is mostly from Catalonia and elsewhere in Spain, but there's also a good selection from France. The Bonavista also acts as a deli, and there are some especially good cheeses.

🔒 Camp Nou, Pedralbes & La Zona Alta

Although many of Barcelona's better-off folks descend from the 'High Zone' to L'Eixample to shop, there are still plenty of trendy little boutiques scattered around La Zona Alta.

Labperfum   BEAUTY

(Carrer de Santaló 45; ☉ 11am-2pm & 5-8pm Mon-Sat; Ⓡ FGC Muntaner) This tiny shop looks like an old apothecary, with its shelves lined with pretty glass bottles. What's for sale are extraordinary fragrances (for men and women) made in-house. Scents diverge from run-of-the-mill Obsession, with varieties like tobacco, black orchid and leather. You can also buy scented candles, soaps and creams. Beautiful packaging and fair prices (starting at €14 for 50ml).

FC Botiga Megastore   SOUVENIRS

(☑ 93 409 02 71; www.fcbmegastore.com; Gate 9, off Avinguda Joan de XXIII; ☉ 10am-7pm Mon-Sat, to 3pm Sun; Ⓜ Palau Reial, Collblanc) This sprawling three-storey shop in Camp Nou (p292) has footballs, shirts, scarves, socks, wallets, bags, sneakers, smartphone covers – pretty much anything you can think of – all featuring Barça's famous red-and-blue insignia.

Oriol Balaguer
FOOD

(☑93 201 18 46; www.oriolbalaguer.com; Plaça de Sant Gregori Taumaturg 2; ⊙10am-2pm & 5-9pm Mon-Sat; ⏚FGC La Bonanova) Oriol Balaguer whips up magnificent sweet creations, doled out in their museumlike shop.

🅿 Montjuïc, Poble Sec & Sant Antoni

Shopping options are fairly limited among these neighbourhoods. Sant Antoni offers the best exploring for shoppers, with a famed food market, and a growing number of second-hand shops and galleries sprinkled on its tree-lined streets. The streets near Carrer del Parlament are the best place to roam.

Galeri
ARTS

(Map p266; ☑93 124 13 30; Carrer de Viladomat 27; ⊙11am-2pm & 5-9pm Tue-Sat; ⓜPoble Sec) This boxy, brightly lit gallery sells prints by Catalan artists as well as unusual graphic T-shirts, canvas bags and small ceramics – delicate conversation pieces, just small enough to fit in a carry-on. There are also a few original paintings and sculptures, from an ever-changing collection.

Mercat de Sant Antoni
MARKET

(☑93 426 35 21; www.mercatdesantantoni.com; Carrer de Comte d'Urgell 1; ⊙7am-2.30pm & 5-8.30pm Mon-Thu, 7am-8.30pm Fri & Sat; ⓜSant Antoni) Just beyond the western edge of El Raval is Mercat de Sant Antoni, a glorious old iron and brick building that has been undergoing renovation since 2009. In the meantime, a huge marquee has been erected alongside to house a food market. The secondhand book market still takes place alongside on Sunday mornings.

The latest estimates for the market's re-opening was slated for the end of 2017.

ℹ Information

MEDICAL SERVICES

Farmàcia Castells Soler (☑93 487 61 45; www.farmaciacastells.com; Passeig de Gràcia 90; ⊙24hr; ⓜDiagonal)

Farmàcia Clapés (☑93 301 28 43; www.farmaciaclapes.com/tienda; La Rambla 98; ⊙24hr; ⓜLiceu)

Farmàcia Torres (☑93 453 92 20; www.farmaciaabierta24h.com; Carrer d'Aribau 62; ⊙24hr; ⏚FGC Provença)

Hospital Clínic (☑93 227 54 00; www.hospitalclinic.org; Carrer de Villarroel 170; ⓜHospital Clínic)

Hospital Dos de Maig (☑93 507 27 00; www.csi.cat; Carrer del Dos de Maig 301; ⓜSant Pau/Dos de Maig)

TOURIST INFORMATION

Several tourist offices operate in Barcelona. A couple of general information telephone numbers worth bearing in mind are ☑010 and ☑012. The first is for Barcelona and the other is for all Catalonia (run by the Generalitat). You sometimes strike English speakers, although for the most part operators are Catalan/Spanish bilingual. In addition to tourist offices, information booths operate at Estació del Nord bus station and at Portal de la Pau, at the foot of the Mirador de Colom at the port end of La Rambla. Others set up at various points in the city centre in summer.

El Prat Airport (⊙8.30am-8.30pm)

Estació Sants (Estació Sants; ⊙8am-8pm; ⏚Estació Sants)

Palau Robert Regional Tourist Office (Map p256; ☑93 238 80 91; www.palaurobert.gencat.cat; Passeig de Gràcia 107; ⊙10am-8pm Mon-Sat, to 2.30pm Sun; ⓜDiagonal) Offers a host of material on Catalonia, audiovisual resources, a bookshop and a branch of Turisme Juvenil de Catalunya (for youth travel).

Plaça de Catalunya (Map p256; ☑93 285 38 34; www.barcelonaturisme.com; Plaça de Catalunya 17; ⊙9.30am-9.30pm; ⓜCatalunya)

Plaça Sant Jaume (Map p238; ☑93 285 38 32; Carrer de la Ciutat 2; ⊙8.30am-8.30pm Mon-Fri, 9am-7pm Sat, 9am-2pm Sun & holidays; ⓜJaume I)

> ### ⓘ WARNING: KEEP AN EYE ON YOUR VALUABLES
>
> Every year aggrieved readers write in with tales of woe from Barcelona. Petty crime and theft, with tourists as the prey of choice, are a problem, so you need to take a few common-sense precautions. Thieves and pickpockets operate on airport trains and the metro, especially around stops popular with tourists (such as La Sagrada Família). The Old City (Ciutat Vella) is the pickpockets' and bag-snatchers' prime hunting ground. Take special care on and around La Rambla. Prostitutes working the lower (waterfront) end often do a double trade in wallet snatching.

❶ Getting There & Away

AIR

After Madrid, Barcelona is Spain's busiest international transport hub and a host of airlines, including many budget carriers, fly directly to Barcelona from around Europe. Ryanair uses Girona and Reus airports (buses link Barcelona to both). Iberia, Air Europa, Spanair and Vueling all have dense networks across the country and, while flights can be costly, you can save considerable time by flying from Barcelona to distant cities like Seville or Málaga.

Barcelona's **El Prat airport** (📞 902 404704; www.aena.es) lies 17km southwest of Plaça de Catalunya at El Prat de Llobregat.

BOAT

Barcelona has ferry connections to the Balearic Islands and Italy.

Passenger and vehicular ferries operated by **Acciona Trasmediterránea** (📞 902 454645; www.trasmediterranea.es; Ⓜ Drassanes) to/from the Balearic Islands dock around the **Moll de Barcelona wharf** in Port Vell.

Grandi Navi Veloci (Map p266; 📞 in Italy +39 010 209 4591; www1.gnv.it; Ⓜ Drassanes) runs high-speed, luxury ferries three (sometimes more) days a week between Genoa and Barcelona. The journey takes 18 hours. Ticket prices vary wildly depending on season and how far in advance you purchase them. The same company runs a similar number of ferries between Barcelona and Tangier, Morocco (voyage time about 26 hours).

Grimaldi Ferries (Map p266; 📞 902 53 13 33, in Italy 📞 39 081 496 444; www.grimaldi-lines.com; Ⓜ Drassanes) operates similar services from Barcelona to Civitavecchia (near Rome, 20½ hours, six to seven times a week), Livorno (Tuscany, 19½ hours, three times a week) and Porto Torres (Sardinia, 12 hours, daily).

BUS

Barcelona is well-connected by bus to other parts of Spain, as well as to major European cities.

Long-distance buses leave from **Estació del Nord** (📞 902 26 06 06; www.barcelonanord.cat; Carrer d'Ali Bei 80; Ⓜ Arc de Triomf). A plethora of companies service different parts of Spain; many come under the umbrella of **Alsa** (📞 902 422242; www.alsa.es). For other companies, ask at the bus station. There are frequent services to Madrid, Valencia and Zaragoza (20 or more a day) and several daily departures to distant destinations such as Burgos, Santiago de Compostela and Seville.

CAR & MOTORCYCLE

➡ Vehicles must be roadworthy, registered and have third-party insurance.

➡ Ask your insurer for a European Accident Statement form, which can simplify matters in the event of an accident.

➡ A European breakdown assistance policy is a good investment.

➡ EU national driver's licences are accepted, as are those from some other non-EU countries (like Switzerland). Otherwise, an international driving licence is a good idea.

TRAIN

The main train station in Barcelona is **Estació Sants** (Plaça dels Països Catalans; Ⓜ Estació Sants), located 2.5km west of La Rambla. Direct overnight trains from Paris, Geneva, Milan and Zurich arrive here.

Train is the most convenient overland option for reaching Barcelona from major Spanish centres like Madrid and Valencia. It can be a long haul from other parts of Europe – budget flights frequently offer a saving in time and money.

A network of *rodalies/cercanías* serves towns around Barcelona (and the airport). Contact **Renfe** (📞 902 320320; www.renfe.es). Eighteen high-speed Tren de Alta Velocidad Española (AVE) trains between Madrid and Barcelona run daily in each direction, nine of them in under three hours.

❶ Getting Around

Barcelona has abundant options for getting around town. The excellent metro can get you most places, with buses and trams filling in the gaps. Taxis are the best option late at night.

BUS

Transports Metropolitans de Barcelona (TMB; 📞 93 298 70 00; www.tmb.net) buses run along most city routes every few minutes between 5am and 6.30am to between around 10pm and 11pm. Many routes pass through Plaça de Catalunya and/or Plaça de la Universitat. After 11pm a reduced network of yellow *nitbusos* (night buses) runs until 3am or 5am. All *nitbus* routes pass through Plaça de Catalunya and most run every 30 to 45 minutes.

A hop-on, hop-off **Bus Turístic** (📞 93 298 70 00; www.barcelonabusturistic.cat/en; day ticket adult/child €28/16; ⏱ 9am-8pm) run by TMB, with audio guides in 10 languages, operates from Plaça de Catalunya and Plaça del Porta de la Pau. It covers three circuits (44 stops), linking virtually all the city's main sights.

CAR & MOTORCYCLE

With the convenience of public transport and the high price of parking in the city, it's unwise to drive in Barcelona. However, if you're planning a road trip outside the city, a car is handy.

Avis, Europcar, National/Atesa and Hertz have desks at El Prat airport, Estació Sants and

Estació del Nord. Rental outlets in Barcelona include the following:

Avis (☑ 93 344 37 00; www.avis.com; Carrer de Còrsega 293-295; Ⓜ Diagonal)

Cooltra (☑ 93 221 40 70; www.cooltra.com; Via Laietana 6; ⏱10am-7pm; Ⓜ Barceloneta) You can rent scooters here for around €35 (plus insurance). Cooltra also organises scooter tours.

Europcar (☑ 93 302 05 43; www.europcar. com; Gran Via de les Corts Catalanes 680; Ⓜ Girona)

Hertz (☑ 902 998707; www.hertz.com; Carrer de Viriat 45; Ⓜ Sants Estació)

MondoRent (☑ 93 295 32 68; www.mondorent. com; Passeig de Joan de Borbó 80-84; ⏱10am-7pm; Ⓜ Barceloneta) Rents scooters as well as electric bikes.

National/Atesa (☑ 93 323 07 01; www.enter-prise.es; Carrer de Muntaner 45; Ⓜ Universitat)

METRO

The easy-to-use **TMB Metro** (p299) system has 11 numbered and colour-coded lines. It runs from 5am to midnight Sunday to Thursday and holidays, from 5am to 2am on Friday and days immediately preceding holidays, and 24 hours on Saturday.

Ongoing work to expand the metro continues on several lines. Lines 9 and 10 will eventually connect with the airport (2016 at the earliest).

Suburban trains run by the **Ferrocarrils de la Generalitat de Catalunya** (FGC; ☑ 900 901515; www.fgc.net) include a couple of useful city lines. All lines heading north from Plaça de Catalunya stop at Carrer de Provença and Grà-cia. One of these lines (L7) goes to Tibidabo and another (L6 to Reina Elisenda) has a stop near the Monestir de Pedralbes. Most trains from Plaça de Catalunya continue beyond Barcelona to Sant Cugat, Sabadell and Terrassa. Other FGC lines head west from Plaça d'Espanya, including one for Manresa that is handy for the trip to Montserrat.

Depending on the line, these trains run from about 5am (with only one or two services before 6am) to 11pm or midnight Sunday to Thursday, and from 5am to about 1am Friday and Saturday.

TAXI

Taxis charge €2.10 flag fall plus meter charges of €1.03 per kilometre (€1.30 from 8pm to 8am and all day on weekends). A further €3.10 is added for all trips to/from the airport, and €1 for luggage bigger than 55cm x 35cm x 35cm. The trip from Estació Sants to Plaça de Catalunya, about 3km, costs about €11. You can flag a taxi down in the streets or call one:

Fonotaxi (☑ 93 300 11 00)

Radio Taxi 033 (☑ 93 303 30 33; http://radio taxi033.com)

The call-out charge is €3.40 (€4.20 at night and on weekends). In many taxis it is possible to pay with a credit card and, if you have a local tele-phone number, you can join the T033 Ràdio taxi service for booking taxis online (www.radio taxi033.com, in Spanish). You can also book online at www.catalunyataxi.com.

Taxi Amic (☑ 93 420 80 88; www.taxi-amic-adaptat.com) is a special taxi service for people with disabilities or difficult situations (such as transport of big objects). Book at least 24 hours in advance if possible.

TRAM

There are a handful of **tram lines** (☑ 900 701 181; www.tram.cat) in the city. All standard transport passes are valid. A scenic option is the *tramvia blau* (blue tram), which runs up to the foot of Tibidabo.

T1, T2 and T3 Run into the suburbs of greater Barcelona from Plaça de Francesc Macià and are of limited interest to visitors.

T4 Runs from behind the zoo (near the Ciuta-della Vila Olímpica metro stop) to Sant Adrià via Glòries and the Fòrum.

T5 Runs from Glòries to Badalona (Gorg stop).

T6 Runs from Badalona (Gorg) to Sant Adrià.

Catalonia

Best Places to Eat

➜ El Celler de Can Roca (p316)

➜ Cal Ton (p355)

➜ La Cuina de Can Simon (p303)

➜ El Jardinet (p344)

➜ Can Ventura (p335)

Best Places to Sleep

➜ Mil Estrelles (p315)

➜ Parador Ducs de Cardona (p347)

➜ Hotel Durán (p324)

➜ Hotel Els Caçadors (p333)

➜ Villa Paulita (p334)

Why Go?

Catalonia feels distinct from the rest of Spain, and its four provinces enclose an impressive wealth of natural splendour. Pyrenean peaks loom above meadows and fertile vineyards, plains are pock-marked with volcanic cones, and rocky coves punctuate sandy beaches.

The Costa Brava's shores are its biggest lure, though travellers will also discover medieval architecture and Jewish history in Girona and Besalú, and Salvador Dalí's gloriously surreal 'theatre-museum' in Figueres.

For adventure, head north where the Pyrenees rise to 3000m peaks. Here, hiking trails weave among valleys and lonely villages are crowned with Romanesque churches and monasteries. Stepping even further back in time, the Roman and Greek ruins of Tarragona and Empúries are among Spain's most impressive. And an entirely different landscape awaits in the Delta de l'Ebre's shimmering wetlands, home to flocks of pirouetting flamingos.

When to Go
Tarragona

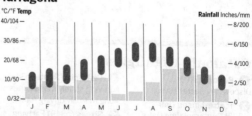

May The Costa Brava's beaches are free from crowds, though the water is a little chilly.

Sep The Catalan Pyrenees are aflame in autumnal colours, and the hiking is perfect.

Oct–Nov The museums and galleries of the Dalí circuit are at their quiet best.

FRANCE

Puig Neulós
(1250m)

Vielha Salardú
Pica d'Estats
(3143m) **ANDORRA
LA VELLA** Portbou
Espot
Pico de Aneto
(3404m) Llavorsí Puigcerdà Llívia La Jonquera Garriguella Portlligat
Boí 3 Rialp Bellver de Ribes de Beget Figueres Roses Cadaqués
Parc Nacional Sort Cerdanya Freser 2 Castelló L'Escala
d'Aigüestortes i La Seu La Molina Besalú d'Empúries Illes
Estany de Sant Maurici d'Urgell & Masella Ripoll Olot 8 Santa Pau Verges 9 Medes
Parc Natural Púbol 1 Begur
del Cadí-Moixeró Sant Joan Parc Natural de la Girona 6 Tamariu
Tremp Berga de les Zona Volcànica de Peratallada Palafrugell
Àger Abadesses la Garrotxa Riu Ter Llafranc
CATALONIA Vic Santa Coloma
Solsona de Farners Sant Feliu
Ponts Cardona Lloret de Guíxols
Balaguer de Mar Tossa de Mar
Manresa Sant Celoni Blanes
Reial Monestir Monestir de Granollers
de Santa Maria Montserrat A-P7
Lleida de Vallbona de Igualada Terrassa Mataró
les Monges Premià de Mar
Cistercian Reial Monestir Sant
Route 4 de Santes Creus Sadurní
Reial Monestir de A-P2 d'Anoia **Barcelona**
Santa Maria de Poblet Vilafranca Castelldefels
Montblanc del Penedès 5 **Sitges**
TARRAGONA Valls Vilanova i
Reus la Geltrú
Móra la Nova Altafulla
10 **Tarragona**
Gandesa PortAventura
N-420 Castell
de Miravet MEDITERRANEAN
SEA
A-P7
Tortosa Deltebre Riumar
Amposta 7 **Delta de l'Ebre**
A-P7 Parc Natural Delta
Sant Carles de l'Ebre
de la Ràpita

0 ———— 50 km
N 0 ———— 25 miles

Catalonia Highlights

1 Begur (p310)
Discovering secret coves.

2 Teatre-Museu Dalí
(p322) Contemplating Dalí's
theatre of the absurd in Figueres.

**3 Parc Nacional
d'Aigüestortes i Estany
de Sant Maurici** (p339)
Conquering the trails in
Catalonia's sole national park.

4 Cistercian Route (p348)
Admiring stately monasteries
along this hilly driving route.

5 Sitges (p349) Partying
hard in this upbeat, gay-
friendly seaside town.

6 Girona (p312) Exploring
medieval laneways and
thrilling museums.

7 Delta de l'Ebre (p359)

Watching flocks of flamingos
turn the skies pink.

8 Olot (p326) Feeling a
rumble beneath your feet in
volcano-carved hills.

9 Illes Medes (p317) Diving into a marine wonderland.

10 Tarragona (p355)
Gawking at Roman ruins right
in the centre of a lively city.

COSTA BRAVA

Stretching north to the French border, the Costa Brava, or 'rugged coast', is by far the prettiest of Spain's three principal holiday coasts. Though you'll find plenty of tourism development and English breakfasts, there are also unspoiled coves, charming seaside towns with quality restaurants, spectacular scenery, and some of Spain's best diving around the protected Illes Medes.

Nestling in the hilly backcountry – green and covered in umbrella pine in the south, barer and browner in the north – are charming stone villages and the towering monastery of Sant Pere de Rodes. A little further inland are the bigger towns of Girona, with its sizeable and strikingly well-preserved medieval centre, and Figueres, famous for its bizarre Teatre-Museu Dalí, foremost of a series of sites associated with the eccentric surrealist artist Salvador Dalí.

The coastal settlements are very – and we mean very – quiet in winter.

Tossa de Mar

POP 5681

Tossa de Mar curves around a boat-speckled bay, guarded by a headland crowned with impressive defensive medieval walls and towers. Tourism has bolted a larger, modern extension onto this picturesque village of crooked, narrow streets, though its old town and clifftop views retain their magic.

Tossa was one of the first places on the Costa Brava to attract foreign visitors: a small colony of artists and writers gravitated towards what painter Marc Chagall dubbed 'Blue Paradise' in the 1930s. It was made famous by Ava Gardner in the 1951 film *Pandora and the Flying Dutchman*; you'll find a statue of the silver-screen queen along the path towards the lighthouse.

In July and August it's hard to reach the water's edge without tripping over oily limbs. Out of high season it is still an enchanting place to visit, though many attractions and amenities limit their hours or close shop entirely.

Sights

Far de Tossa LIGHTHOUSE

(adult/child €3/1.50; ⊙10am-8pm Apr-Oct, to 6pm Tue-Sun Nov-Mar) Mont Guardí is crowned with this 1919 lighthouse, beneath which there's a 20-minute walk-through display on the history of lighthouses and life inside

them. Concerts are held in the glow of the lighthouse during July and August (additional charges apply).

Sleeping

Hotel Hermes HOSTAL €

(☑972 34 02 96; www.hotelhermes-tossademar. com; Avinguda de Ferràn Agulló 6; s/d/tr/q €38/60/75/90; ⊙Easter-Oct; @🖥🛋) Rooms at this friendly guesthouse are a steal, considering the location one block from the bus station. There's a good quality cafe downstairs, cheery service and a rooftop Jacuzzi.

★**Cap d'Or** HOSTAL €€

(☑972 34 00 81; www.hotelcapdor.com; Passeig del Mar 1; s/d/q incl breakfast €69/112/179; ⊙Easter-Oct; 🖳🖥) Rub up against the town's history in this family-run spot right in front of the town walls. Rooms are lovingly decorated in an array of pastel tones, each with its own medley of vintage-feel picture frames and cutesy marine miscellany. The best of them look straight onto the beach.

Hotel Diana HOTEL €€

(☑972 34 18 86; www.hotelesdante.com; Plaça d'Espanya 6; d/ste incl breakfast from €80/120; ⊙Apr-Oct; 🅿🖳🖥) Fronting Platja Gran, this artistic hotel in a 1906 mansion is lavished with Modernista fittings fashioned by one of Gaudí's architectural disciples. Stained glass, wrought-iron furnishings and vintage-style headboards infuse the place with an old-world glamour, and many rooms have divine beach views. Off-site parking is an additional €10 to €20.

Eating

Restaurant Bahia SEAFOOD €€

(☑972 34 03 22; www.restaurantbahiatossa.com; Passeig del Mar 19; mains €13; ⊙1-3.30pm & 7-10.30pm) Grilled sardines and pans of paella crowd the tables of this charming seafood place. The interior is decorated with local ceramics and tables spilling onto the road allow a glimpse of the beach.

★**La Cuina de Can Simon** CATALAN €€€

(☑972 34 12 69; http://restaurantcansimon.com; Carrer del Portal 24; mains €22-35, tasting menus €68-98; ⊙1-3.30pm Wed-Sun, 8-10.30pm Wed-Sat) This is the standout star of a slew of restaurants hugging the old wall along Carrer del Portal. Within a former fisherman's stone house, La Cuina de Can Simon credits its innovative dishes to a dual heritage: the owner's grandfathers were a fisherman and

MODERNIST CEMETERY

Even if you're not usually lured by the dark side, this extraordinary cemetery (Camí del Repòs 1; ☉8am-8pm Apr-Oct, 8am-6pm Nov-Mar) is more like a modernist sculpture gallery than a sombre memorial site. Tombs are trimmed with Gothic tracery, topped with dragons clutching skulls, or shaped like maidens ecstatically wreathed in roses. Opened in 1901, the cemetery has artworks from Catalan sculptors and architects including Josep Puig i Cadafalch and Vicenç Artigas. The cemetery is northwest of central Lloret de Mar, and just 200m south of the tourist office.

an artist. Flavoursome fusions such as tuna with wasabi gnocchi, or crunchy pineapple with cinnamon ice cream, are money well spent. Opens daily in summer.

Drinking & Nightlife

Bar El Far de Tossa   COCKTAIL BAR
(Mont Guardí; ☉11am-late) Perched on Mont Guardí next to the lighthouse is this bar with a terrace overhanging a steep drop. Views of cliffs speckled with cacti plummeting towards the inky sea can inspire vertigo, so take the edge off with a cocktail (€8.50). Its 'Ava Gardner' is a blend of strawberry, vodka and Cointreau; but you're here for the best views in town, rather than the mixology.

Information

Tourist Office (☎972 34 01 08; www.info tossa.com; Avinguda del Pelegrí 25; ☉10am-2pm & 4-7pm Mon-Sat) Next to the bus station. During high season it opens from 9am to 9pm.

Getting There & Away

Sarfa (www.sarfa.com) runs to/from Barcelona's Estació del Nord (€12.15, 1¼ hours, five to seven daily) and also has direct airport services. The bus station is next to the tourist office.

The C32 *autopista* connects Tossa to Barcelona, while the picturesque GI682 snakes spectacularly 23km northeast to Sant Feliu de Guíxols.

Sant Feliu de Guíxols

POP 21,810
Grip your steering wheel along 23 magnificent kilometres of snaking roads eastwards

from Tossa de Mar. The reward is reaching Sant Feliu de Guíxols, a beach town with more than its fair share of historical architecture. Most impressive is the 10th-century monastery, but there are remnants of centuries past in the lanes that jut out from Plaça del Mercat. Sant Feliu also has an attractive waterside promenade, and walking trails that are well signposted from its sandy beach.

Sights

Centuries of history echo among the walls of Sant Feliu de Guíxols' narrow laneways. Look out for Carrer de la Notaria, a late-18th-century street that survived mysterious arson attempts. Admirers of architecture may also wish to check out Plaça del Mercat, where the town's market hall was built in 1929.

Information

Tourist Office (☉9.30am-2pm & 4-7pm Mon-Fri, 10am-8pm Sat & Sun) With info on Sant Feliu de Guíxols and the rest of the Costa Brava, this office is part of the monastery complex, near the Porta Ferrada. It operates extended hours during high summer.

Getting There & Away

Sarfa buses reach Sant Feliu de Guíxols from Barcelona (€15.40, 1½ hours, seven daily), Girona (€8.30, two hours, three daily) and Palafrugell (€3.10, 50 minutes, 12 to 15 daily).

Palafrugell & Around

Halfway up the coast from Barcelona to the French border begins one of the most beautiful stretches of the Costa Brava. The town of Palafrugell, 4km inland, is the main access point for a cluster of enticing beach spots. Calella de Palafrugell, Llafranc and Tamariu, one-time fishing villages squeezed into small bays, are three of the Costa Brava's most charming, low-key resorts.

Begur, 7km northeast of Palafrugell, is a handsomely conserved, castle-topped village with a cluster of less-developed beaches nearby. Inland, seek out charming Pals and the fabulous village of Peratallada.

Palafrugell

POP 22,763
Palafrugell is the main transport, shopping and service hub for the stretch of Costa Bra-

Costa Brava

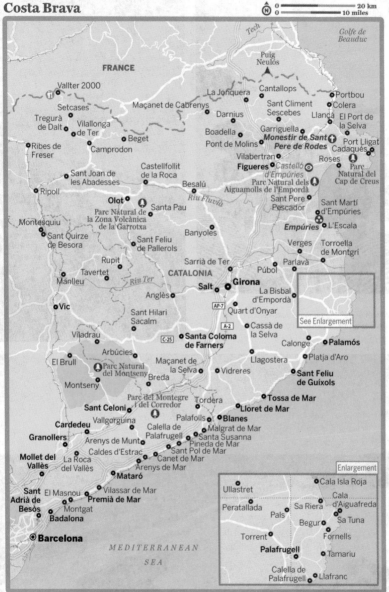

va extending from Calella de Palafrugell to Begur. But this inland town is more than a way station en route to the beach. There are artistic and cultural treasures to uncover in Plaça Can Mario, plus one of the region's most striking Gothic churches.

Sights

Museu del Suro   MUSEUM
(www.museudelsuro.cat; Carrer de Begur; adult/child €3/1.50; ⊙10am-2pm & 5-8pm Mon-Sat, 10am-2pm Sun) This surprisingly large and modern museum within an old factory has

MEL STUART/GETTY IMAGES ©

1. Fornells, Costa Brava 2. Cabo de Gata, Almería
3. Costa de la Luz 4. Praia As Catedrais, Galicia

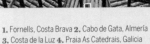

DOMINGO LEIVA/GETTY IMAGES ©

Spain's Best Beaches

Spaniards argue for hours about which is their district's finest beach, so picking favourites from 5000km of coastline is a controversial, albeit mighty pleasurable, task. The Mediterranean's gentle strands and pretty coves contrast with the rougher beauty of the Atlantic coasts.

Illas Cíes (p537) A protected archipelago off Galicia, with beaches so stunning you'll gasp in disbelief. The finest, Praia das Rodas, is only accessible by boat.

Aiguablava/Fornells (p310) Neighbouring Costa Brava coves near Begur, so divine that we couldn't choose between them.

Cabo de Gata (p722) A series of stunning beaches, all distinct, on this memorable peninsula in Almería province.

Playa de Torimbia (p486) Walking down to this sheltered fingernail-shaped cove laid out below you is an Asturian classic near Llanes. Clothing optional.

Playa del Silencio (p488) Backed by a natural rock amphitheatre, this Asturian jewel between Cudillero and Luarca is hard to beat.

Playa de la Concha (p417) A scallop-shaped stretch of sand in the heart of San Sebastián, and possibly Europe's finest city beach.

Bolonia A stretch of pristine sand, the finest of Andalucía's unspoiled Costa de la Luz (p632). Nearby Zahara de los Atunes and Playa de los Lances are spectacular, too.

Playa de los Eucaliptos Wild, long and windy, this spot near Amposta in Catalonia's Delta de l'Ebre (p359) is perfect for beachcombers, kiteboarding and wakeboarding.

Praia As Catedrais (p525) The unearthly rock formations at this Galician strand near Ribadeo are such a drawcard that daily numbers are limited.

THE CHANGING FORTUNES OF CATALONIA

Like many European nations, the kingdom of Spain was cobbled together, by a series of conquests and dynastic alliances, from what were once separate states. Though the last of these was over 500 years ago, folk in the peninsula still tend to identify more strongly with their ancestral village or local region – the *patria chica* ('small fatherland') than with the nation as a whole. There are separatist movements in many parts of the peninsula but especially in two regions: the Basque country and Catalonia.

Away from the big cities and Costa Brava, Catalonia feels as if you've entered a separate country. Virtually no Spanish is spoken and the red-and-yellow flag of the region flutters from the balconies. The overall feeling, as expressed by an oft-encountered piece of graffiti, is that 'Catalonia is not Spain'.

The genesis of Catalonia began when the Franks, under Charlemagne, pushed back the Moors in the 8th and 9th centuries. The Catalan golden age began in the early 12th century when Ramon Berenguer III, who already controlled Catalonia and parts of southern France, launched the region's first seagoing fleet. In 1137 his successor, Ramon Berenguer IV, was betrothed to the one-year-old heiress to the Aragonese throne, thereby giving Catalonia sufficient power to expand its empire out into the Mediterranean but joining it to another crown. When Fernando became king of Aragón in 1479 having already married Isabel, Queen of Castile, Spain was more or less created. Catalonia resented its new subordinate status but could do little to overturn it. After backing the losing side in the War of Spanish Succession (1702–14), Barcelona rose up against the Spanish crown, whose armies besieged the city from March 1713 until 11 September 1714. The victorious Felipe V abolished Catalan privileges, built a huge fort (the Ciutadella) to watch over the city, banned writing and teaching in the Catalan language, and farmed out Catalonia's colonies to other European powers.

Trade again flourished from Barcelona in the centuries that followed, and by the late 19th and early 20th centuries there were growing calls for greater self-governance to go with the city's burgeoning economic power. However, after the civil war ended in 1939, pro-republic Catalonia was treated harshly by victorious General Franco. Reprisals and purges resulted in the shootings of at least 35,000 people. Over time, the use of Catalan in public was banned and all street and town names were changed into Spanish, which became the only permitted language in schools and the media. Self-government was returned after Franco's death in 1975 though the sense of grievance remains.

Recent decades have seen Catalan culture flourish: you'll see this reflected in the re-emergence of traditional festivals and dances, the prevalence of Catalan flags on many facades and the near-universal use of Catalan in public. Unlike, for example, the Basque country, there is no real sense of ethnic identity in Catalonia. For Catalans, their language is the key to their identity.

The issue of independence from Spain has been at the forefront of Catalan politics for years, and in recent times has snowballed with regular demonstrations and events. The 2014 Catalan poll in favour of independence was declared illegal by Madrid. In September 2015, pro-independence coalition Junts Pel Sí ('Together for yes') won over 39% of voters in Catalan parliamentary elections. The question of Catalan independence dominated discourse about the elections, which were treated by many as an unofficial referendum. At time of research, the Catalan parliament was formulating a plan to exit by 2017, to a furious response in Madrid.

Some Catalans feel their taxes subsidise the rest of the nation, and tough economic times have exacerbated this feeling. But the very fact that Catalonia is such a valuable asset makes the central government very unwilling to let it go and, constitutionally at least, a Catalan secession would have to be approved by nationwide referendum: an unlikely scenario.

audiovisual displays detailing Catalonia's cork industry. Cork cutting and branding machinery, cork transport, and other mysteries are unveiled, while coats of arms made entirely of cork number among the more peculiar sights. The examination station with microscopes might seem like overkill for cork novices, but this museum offers a worthwhile glimpse of an industry critical to Palafrugell.

ℹ Information

Tourist Office (☑972 30 02 28; www.visit palafrugell.cat; Avenida de la Generalitat 33; ◷10am-1pm & 4-7pm Mon-Sat, 10am-1pm Sun) The tourist office is just off the C66 highway en route to central Palafrugell. It operates longer hours in high season.

ℹ Getting There & Away

Sarfa buses run between Palafrugell and Barcelona (€18.50, 2¼ hours, seven daily) and Girona (€6.50, one hour, at least 12 daily).

Calella de Palafrugell

POP 747

The whitewashed buildings of Calella, the southernmost of Palafrugell's crown jewels, are strung Aegean-style around a bay of rocky points and small, pretty beaches, with a few fishing boats hauled up on the sand. Though deservedly well known for its beauteous bay, Calella has resisted the temptation to sprawl, and has an agreeably hidden feel, despite being merrily full of visitors in summer.

◉ Sights & Activities

In addition to lingering on one of the beaches, you can stroll along pretty **coastal footpaths** northeast to Llafranc (30 minutes) and beyond, or south to Platja del Golfet beach, close to Cap Roig (about 40 minutes).

✸ Festivals & Events

Festival de Cap Roig   MUSIC
(www.caproigfestival.com) Excellent music festival held at the Jardins de Cap Roig around mid-July to late August, featuring all kinds of music from rock to jazz, and big, big names.

Cantada d'Havaneres   MUSIC
(havanerescalella.cat) *Havaneres* are melancholy Caribbean sea shanties that became popular among Costa Brava sailors in the 19th century, when Catalonia maintained busy links with Cuba. These folksy concerts in July are traditionally accompanied by the drinking of *cremat* – a rum, coffee, sugar, lemon and cinnamon concoction that you set alight briefly before quaffing.

🍽 Sleeping & Eating

★**Hotel Mediterrani**   BOUTIQUE HOTEL €€€
(☑972 61 45 00; www.hotelmediterrani.com; Carrer Lladó 55; s €135, d €160-210; ◷Apr-Oct; P❄🐾) Swish, arty rooms decked out in placid creams, with breathtaking views of a hidden sliver of sand and an aquamarine sea, make this hotel at the southern end of town very hard to beat.

Xabec   CATALAN €€
(☑972 61 46 10; www.restaurantxabec.com; Carrer de Lladó 6; mains €12-18; ◷1-3.30pm & 8-11pm Fri-Wed Easter-Oct) Follow the metal boat sign on Carrer de Lladó towards delectable local fare, including squid-ink risotto and Catalan sausage. The interior, decorated with fishing nets and cannons, manages to strike an agreeable balance between chintzy and chic.

ℹ Information

Tourist Office (☑972 61 44 75; www.visitpala frugell.cat; Carrer de les Voltes 6; ◷10am-8pm) By the beachfront strip; opens shorter hours in low season.

ℹ Getting There & Away

Buses from Palafrugell serve Calella (€1.70, four daily – more in summer, 20 minutes).

Llafranc

POP 320

Barely 2km northeast of Calella de Palafrugell, and now merging with it along the roads set back from the rocky coast between them, upmarket Llafranc has a small bay and a long, handsome stretch of sand, cupped on either side by pine-dotted craggy coastline.

◉ Sights & Activities

The GR92 path links Llafranc with the other nearby coastal villages – these are short, spectacular walks. There are plenty of easy walks that you can complete wearing your beach sandals; ask at the tourist office for details. There are also good diving excursions available.

★**Cap de Sant Sebastià**   VIEWPOINT
This magical spot up east of town offers fabulous views in both directions and out to sea. There's a **lighthouse** here, as well as a 15th-century **watch tower** and chapel now incorporated into romantic Hotel El Far. You'll also find the ruins of a pre-Roman

Iberian settlement with multilingual explanatory panels. It's a 40-minute walk up: follow the steps from the harbour and the road up to the right. You can continue from here to Tamariu (one hour).

Sleeping & Eating

Hostal Celimar   HOSTAL €€
(☑972 30 13 74; www.hostalcelimar.com; Carrer de Carudo 12-14; s/d/tr/q €55/75/90/120; ☺Mar-Oct; 🛜) This crimson-painted *hostal*, barely a stumble from the beach, is hard to miss. It offers immaculate white-walled rooms and spotless bathrooms, and has a pleasant downstairs bar with a nautical theme. It's friendly, no-frills and a marvellous deal for the price.

Hotel El Far   HOTEL €€€
(☑972 30 16 39; www.elfar.com; Cap de Sant Sebastià; r €225-290; ☺mid-Feb–Dec; 🅿🍽🛜) A happy marriage between secluded clifftop luxury and excellent local seafood can be found here. Each room has its own large balcony affording superb sea views and the restaurant beneath serves up fresh seafood and rice dishes (the *fideuà* are particularly good). The walkway around the hotel has panoramic views of Llafranc's glowing coast.

Chez Tomás   FRENCH €€
(☑972 30 62 15; Carrer de Lluís Marquès Carbó 2; mains €14-23; ☺7.45-10.30pm Jun-Sep, 1-4pm & 8-11.30pm Fri-Sun Mar-May & Oct) Tuck into Iberian pork cheek in red wine, fried rabbit, duck in port, and a host of other delights of land and sea, all prepared with a pinch of French flair at this charming restaurant tucked away on the beachfront strip.

Casamar   CATALAN €€€
(☑972 30 01 04; www.hotelcasamar.net; Carrer del Nero 3; mains €20-26; ☺1.30-3.30pm Tue-Sun, 8.30-10.30pm Tue-Sat Apr-Dec) Winningly located on a headland overlooking the bay and harbour, this orange-hued hotel has a top-notch restaurant serving classy seafood and artfully selected ingredients in a welcoming atmosphere. There's a degustation menu, complete with cocktails, for €72. Find it via the stairs leading upwards from the southern end of the beach.

ⓘ Information

Tourist Office (Passeig de Cipsela; ☺10am-8pm) A kiosk at the western end of the beach; opens shorter hours in low season.

ⓘ Getting There & Away

Buses from Palafrugell serve Llafranc (€1.90, 20 minutes, six daily – more in summer).

Tamariu
POP 290

Four kilometres north up the coast from Llafranc, quiet Tamariu is a fabulous, small, crescent-shaped cove redolent with the scent of pine. Its beach has some of the most translucent waters on Spain's Mediterranean coast.

Sleeping & Eating

Hotel Tamariu   HOTEL €€
(☑972 62 00 31; www.tamariu.com; Passeig del Mar 2; s/d from €102/120; ☺Mar-Oct; 🍽🛜) A former fishermen's tavern, the Hotel Tamariu has been family-run for four generations. It has spacious rooms in nautical navy and white, each with a balcony offering vine-draped views of this tiny beach town. Rates include breakfast.

El Clot dels Mussols   SEAFOOD €€
(Passeig del Mar 2; mains €14-20) Attached to Hotel Tamariu, El Clot dels Mussols is a top spot for seafood, with tables overlooking the turquoise waves that lash the shore.

ⓘ Getting There & Away

Sarfa buses run to Palafrugell (€1.80, 15 minutes, four daily) from mid-June to mid-September only. Parking in the village is a nightmare during summer.

Begur
POP 3994

Crowned by a 10th-century castle, with sublime coast glistening in its surrounds, Begur is one of the loveliest spots along the Costa Brava. This fairytale town, 7km northeast of Palafrugell, has a tempting array of restaurants, soothing spa hotels, and modernist mansions that add a splash of colour among the stone streets of its medieval centre.

From Begur, attractive winding roads run down to Aiguablava, Fornells, Sa Tuna and Aiguafreda, where you'll discover pocket-sized coves hemmed in by pine trees. A *bus platges* (beach bus) service runs in summertime from Begur's Plaça de Forgas.

◎ Sights

Castell de Begur CASTLE
(⊘24hr) **FREE** There is little to explore aside from the ragged ruins of this antique castle, in much the same state as when it was wrecked by Spanish troops to impede the advance of Napoleon's army in 1810. Clearly signposted from central Begur, a steep walk leads to the ramparts, with breathtaking views over hills that roll towards the Mediterranean Sea. The Elizabeth Taylor film *Suddenly, Last Summer* was shot at the castle in 1959.

🛏 Sleeping & Eating

★ Hotel Classic HISTORIC HOTEL **€€**
(📞 656 906995; www.hotelclassicbegur.com; Carrer de Pi i Ralló 3; d €90-160; 🕸 🞲) This truly authentic hotel, right in the core of Begur's old town, has managed to preserve original paintwork befitting the mid-19th century building it inhabits. All 10 rooms in this 1857 building are impeccably decorated in vintage styles linked to notable dates in the town's history, from stone-walled havens to Modernista chambers awash in pastel blue and coral. Access to the small but luxurious spa is included. The hotel is open year-round.

Cluc Hotel BOUTIQUE HOTEL **€€€**
(📞 972 62 48 59; www.cluc.cat; Carrer del Metge Pi 8; d €149; 🕸 🞲) This ravishing stone building harbours one of the trendiest, yet friendliest, places to stay in Begur's old town. Rooms are a little small, but they are decorated in pleasing vintage style. There's an honesty bar and relaxing library area too. Rates include breakfast.

Sa Caleta CATALAN **€€**
(Carrer de Pi i Ralló 2; mains €10-18; ⊘1-4.30pm & 7pm-midnight Thu-Mon) The motherly owner-chef here prefers to let her fresh seafood flavours do the talking: there are few pretensions but plenty of quality. Generously proportioned dishes include several daily fish specials, generous pans of paella and quality steaks.

ⓘ Information

Tourist Office (📞 972 62 45 20; www.visit begur.com; Avinguda del Onze de Setembre 7; ⊘9am-2pm & 4-9pm Mon-Fri, from 10am Sat & Sun) This helpful tourist office in Begur operates shorter hours in the low season.

WORTH A TRIP

CASTELL DE PÚBOL

If you're intrigued by artist Salvador Dalí, the Castell de Púbol (www. salvador-dali.org; Plaça de Gala Dalí; adult/ concession €8/6; ⊘10am-5pm Tue-Sun mid-Mar–Dec) is an essential piece of the puzzle. Between Girona and Palafrugell (22km northwest of the latter, south of the C66), this castle was Dalí's gift to his wife and muse Gala. The Gothic and Renaissance building, with creepers tracing its walls, spiral stone staircases and a shady garden, was decorated according to Gala's tastes. Nonetheless there are surrealist touches such as the grimacing anglerfish fountain and a sofa shaped like pouting lips.

ⓘ Getting There & Away

Sarfa buses run to Barcelona (€19.50, two to 2¼ hours, three daily) via Palafrugell (€1.70, 15 minutes). There's also a Girona service (€8.35, 1½ hours, one daily on weekdays).

Peratallada

POP 430
As soon as you set foot in heart-stoppingly pretty Peratallada, there can be no doubt why this fortified medieval town is beloved by Barcelona day trippers and French tourists alike. Pale archways, cobbled squares and sandstone buildings strung with ivy create an impression of fairytale romance, though most of the town's historic buildings can only be admired from outside. The old town's many visitors are well catered for by a plethora of good restaurants, as well as handicraft and clothing shops that beckon from laneways snaking among the crumbling walls.

🛏 Sleeping & Eating

★ El Cau del Papibou HOTEL **€€**
(📞 972 63 47 16; http://hotelelcaudelpapibou.com; Carrer Major 10; d €100-125; ⊘Mar-Jan; 🞲) Colourful rooms with rustic views sit above a tapas restaurant at this friendly, characterful spot in the centre of town.

La Riera CATALAN **€€**
(📞 972 63 41 42; www.lariera.es; Plaça de les Voltes 3; mains €12-20; ⊘1-3.30pm & 8-10.30pm Wed-Mon) This sophisticated eatery within an esteemed old town *hostal* simmers up an

excellent range of rice dishes, from simple seafood paella to *arròs de llamàntol* (lobster on rice), as well as earthy roasted meats such as slow-cooked lamb and grilled duck.

ⓘ Information

Oficina de Turisme (☏972 64 55 21; www. forallac.cat; Plaça Castell 3; ☺9am-8pm; ☎) Doubling as a cafe, most of the info at this little tourist office is self-service, but it has a good selection of maps and leaflets.

ⓘ Getting There & Away

Weekday buses run from Palafrugell (€3.35, 50 minutes) and Begur (€2.25, 40 minutes, two daily) to Peratallada. There is also a weekday bus from Girona (€5, 55 minutes, one daily).

Girona

POP 97,227

Northern Catalonia's largest city is a jewellery box of museums, galleries and Gothic churches, strung around a tangle of cobbled lanes and medieval walls. Reflections of Modernista mansions shimmer in the Riu Onyar, which demarcates the historic centre on its right bank from the gleaming commercial centre on the left.

The Roman town of Gerunda lay on Vía Augusta, the highway from Cádiz all the way to the Pyrenees. Taken from the Muslims by the Franks in the late 8th century, Girona became the capital of one of Catalonia's most important counties, falling under the sway of Barcelona in the late 9th century.

Girona's wealth in medieval times produced many fine Romanesque and Gothic buildings that have survived repeated attacks and sieges. There are also traces of a Jewish community that flourished in Girona until their expulsion in 1492. These cultural riches are packed into Girona's walkable centre. With Catalonia's most diverse nightlife and dining scene outside Barcelona, Girona makes a delicious distraction for a few days, before you're helplessly drawn to the coast.

◉ Sights

★ Catedral
CATHEDRAL
(www.catedraldegirona.org; Plaça de la Catedral; adult/student incl Basílica de Sant Feliu €7/5, Sun free; ☺10am-7.30pm Apr-Oct, 10am-6.30pm Nov-Mar) Towering over a flight of 86 steps rising from Plaça de la Catedral, this edifice is

ⓘ GIRONAMUSEUS CARD

The GironaMuseus card (www.girona museus.cat) covers six Girona museums including the Museu d'Història dels Jueus de Girona, Museu d'Art, Museu d'Història de Girona, Monestir de Sant Pere de Galligants and the Museu del Cinema. It provides useful savings – you pay the full entrance fee at the first museum you visit and then get a 50% discount at the remainder. It's valid for six months.

far more ancient than its billowing baroque facade suggests. Built over an old Roman forum, parts of the cathedral's foundations date from the 5th century. Today, Gothic styling – built over the Romanesque church during the 14th century – dominates, though a fine, double-columned Romanesque cloister dates from the 12th century. It's a surprisingly formidable sight to explore, but an audio guide is included in the price.

★ Museu d'Història dels Jueus de Girona
MUSEUM
(www.girona.cat/call; Carrer de la Força 8; adult/child €4/free; ☺10am-6pm Mon-Sat, to 2pm Sun) Until 1492 Girona was home to Catalonia's second most important medieval Jewish community (after Barcelona), and one of the finest Jewish quarters in the country. The Call was centred on the narrow Carrer de la Força for 600 years, until relentless persecution forced the Jews out of Spain. This excellent museum shows genuine pride in Girona's Jewish heritage without shying away from the less salubrious aspects, such as persecution by the Inquisition and forced conversions.

Museu del Cinema
MUSEUM
(www.museudelcinema.cat; Carrer de Sèquia 1; adult/child €5/free; ☺10am-6pm Tue-Fri, 10am-8pm Sat, 11am-3pm Sun; ☝) There is much more to this museum than the silver screen. Displays examine the reasons why humanity longs to indulge its imagination, probing the origins of visual storytelling, such as Chinese and Indian shadow puppets. It's a whistle-stop tour taking in the invention of the camera obscura, the 19th-century debut of the Lumière brothers, and optical illusions using mirrors and trickery of light. There is a vast assortment of displays to poke, play with and peer through.

Museu d'Art
GALLERY

(www.museuart.com; Plaça de la Catedral 12; admission €4.50; ⊙10am-7pm Tue-Sat May-Sep, to 6pm Oct-Apr, 10am-2pm Sun) Next door to the cathedral, in the 12th- to 16th-century Palau Episcopal, this art museum impresses with the scale and variety of its collection. Around 8500 pieces of art, mostly from this region, make up the collection, which ranges from Romanesque woodcarvings and stained-glass tables to modernist paintings of the city by Mela Mutter and early-20th-century sculptures by influential Rafael Masó i Valentí.

Monestir de Sant Pere de Galligants
MONASTERY

(www.mac.cat; Carrer de Santa Llúcia; adult/child €4.50/3.50; ⊙10am-6pm Tue-Sat, 10am-2pm Sun) This beautiful 11th- and 12th-century Romanesque Benedictine monastery has a sublime bell tower and a lovely cloister featuring otherworldly animals and mythical creatures on the capitals of its double columns – there are some great ones in the church too. It's also home to the Museu Arqueològic (Carrer de Santa Llúcia; incl with Monestir entry; ⊙10am-6pm Tue-Sat, 10am-2pm Sun). Weekday opening hours from June to September run until 7pm.

Passeig Arqueològic
WALLS

(Passeig de la Muralla; ⊙10am-8pm) FREE A walk along Girona's medieval walls is a wonderful way to appreciate the city landscape from above. There are several points of access, the most popular being across the street from the Banys Àrabs, where steps lead up into some heavenly gardens where town and plants merge into one organic masterpiece. The southernmost part of the wall ends right near Plaça de Catalunya.

Museu d'Història de Girona
MUSEUM

(www.girona.cat/museuciutat; Carrer de la Força 27; adult/student/child €4/2/free; ⊙10.30am-5.30pm Tue-Sat, to 1.30pm Sun) This museum's setting within 18th-century cloisters lends an appropriately antique feel to your journey from Roman Girona to the present day. Standout displays include an exhibition illuminating the 3rd- to 4th-century Can Pau Birol mosaic, which depicts a lively circus scene with charioteers, and an explanation of the siege of Girona by Napoleonic troops. Many pieces on display are copies rather than originals, making this a place to unpeel the layers of Girona's history rather than goggle at sculpture and art.

Basílica de Sant Feliu
CHURCH

(Plaça de Sant Feliu; adult/student incl Catedral €7/5, Sun free; ⊙10am-5.30pm Mon-Sat, 1-5.30pm Sun) Just downhill from the cathedral is Girona's second great church, with its landmark truncated bell tower. The nave is majestic with Gothic ribbed vaulting, while St Narcissus, the patron of the city, is venerated in an enormous marble-and-jasper, late-baroque side chapel. Underneath his reclining form you see scenes from his life including the conversion of women, martyrdom and expelling of an evil genie. To the side is the Gothic sepulchre, dating from 1328, that previously held his remains. A

GIRONA'S JEWS

In its 13th-century heyday, Girona was home to one of Catalonia's largest Jewish communities, who lived by and large peacefully alongside their Christian neighbours, gaining in prosperity and contributing to fields as diverse as astronomy and medicine.

Nevertheless the Jewish community came under attack, especially during the later crusades of the 12th and 13th centuries. The Call – a maze of tiny alleys, surrounded by a stone wall – went from refuge to ghetto as Jews were gradually confined to their tiny corner of the town. Especially stomach-churning were the 'Disputes', rigged debates intended to ridicule pillars of the Jewish community against the supposedly superior logic of Christians. The spin of the day reported that these debates led to mass conversions, but the likelier story is that Jews converted out of heavy pressure and fear. Slander against Jews became increasingly grotesque, with tales of murdered Christian infants.

Things came to a head during a riot in 1391, when a mob broke into the ghetto, massacring 40 residents. Since the Jews were still under the king's protection, troops were sent in and the survivors were confined to the Galligants Tower 'for their own safety' for 17 weeks, only to find their houses and possessions destroyed when they came out. Many converted to Christianity during the 15th century. In 1492 those who remained were expelled from Spain, ending a story that had been over 1500 years in the making.

Girona

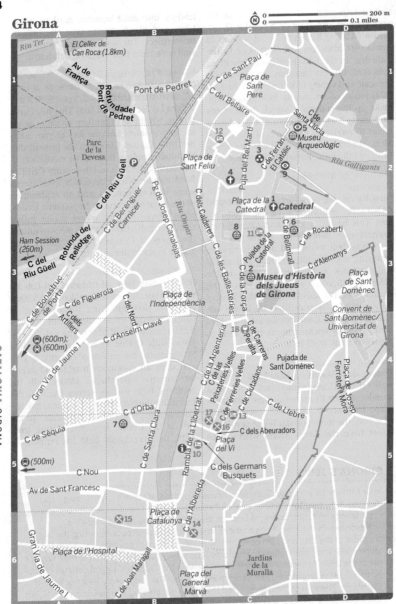

0   200 m
0   0.1 miles

CATALONIA GIRONA

decent audio guide tour is included with admission.

Banys Àrabs   RUIN
(www.banysarabs.cat; Carrer de Ferràn el Catòlic; adult/child €2/1; ⏰10am-7pm Mon-Sat, to 2pm Sun Apr-Sep, 10am-2pm daily Oct-Mar) Although modelled on earlier Muslim and Roman bathhouses, the Banys Àrabs are a finely preserved, 12th-century Christian affair in Romanesque style. The baths contain an *apodyterium* (changing room), followed

Girona

by a *frigidarium* and *tepidarium* (with respectively cold and warm water) and a *caldarium* (a kind of sauna) heated by an underfloor furnace.

🛌 Sleeping

The most atmospheric accommodation choices are in the old town, and there's a good sprinkling of apartments for rent and hostels too. Don't rule out digs on the west bank of the river, Girona's commercial side: it may not be as charming as the east bank, but there are some good quality hotels within walking distance of the best sights.

Pensió Viladomat PENSION €
(972 20 31 76; www.pensioviladomat.cat; Carrer dels Ciutadans 5; s/d without bathroom €24/40, d/tr with bathroom €50/68; 🛜) This is one of the nicest of the cheaper *pensiones* (small hotels) scattered about the southern end of the old town. It has simple, modernised, well-maintained rooms.

⭐ **Mil Estrelles** BOUTIQUE HOTEL €€
(972 59 67 07; www.milestrelles.com; La Bastida, Borgonyà; d €110-179; P ❄ 🛜) 🌿 Stargazers and lovers shouldn't miss Mil Estrelles, a unique hotel 16km north of Girona. Fabulously combining old stone and modern plastic, it offers lovably rustic rooms in a noble historical farmhouse, as well as cute chambers in clear plastic bubbles dotted about the garden, perfect for spotting constellations from the comfort of your double bed.

⭐ **Bells Oficis** B&B €€
(972 22 81 70; www.bellsoficis.com; Carrer dels Germans Busquets 2; r incl breakfast €55-91; ❄🛜) A lovingly restored, 19th-century flat just by the Rambla in the heart of Girona makes a

stylish and ultra-welcoming place to stop. It's the former home of Catalan artist Jaume Busquets i Mollera, and retains period details in each of the five individually styled rooms. Some rooms share bathrooms, while those with en suite have no bathroom door. The largest room has ample room for four people.

Casa Cúndaro BOUTIQUE HOTEL €€
(972 22 35 83; www.casacundaro.com; Pujada de la Catedral 7; d/q €60/90, apt €70-90; ❄🛜) The understated exterior of this medieval Jewish house hides five sumptuous rooms and four self-catering apartments – all combining original exposed stone walls and antique doors with modern luxuries. You couldn't wish for a more characterful base. Its location right next to the cathedral is either a boon or a bane, depending on whether you enjoy the sound of church bells. Reserve well in advance.

⭐ **Hotel Llegendes de Girona Catedral** HOTEL €€€
(972 22 09 05; www.llegendeshotel.com; Carrer Portal de la Barca 4; d €137-299; P ❄🛜) Each of the 15 rooms within this restored 18th-century building has been decorated according to a different Catalan legend or theme. It's a pleasing fusion of ancient and modern, with comfortable beds and huge rain showers. Some rooms have gorgeous cathedral views. Book ahead for the decadent 'Eros suite', boasting a tantric sex sofa (with a handy instruction manual).

✖ Eating

+Cub CAFE €
(www.mescub.cat; Carrer de l'Albereda 15; mains €10-14; ⏰8am-9pm Mon-Thu, 8am-midnight Fri, 9am-midnight Sat; 🛜✎) This trendy cafe-bar

is as good for a takeaway coffee as it is for a full-blown nosh on speciality burgers and vegie crêpes. Thirst-quenchers include fresh fruit-juice combos and shakes, and they have a range of Scottish, German and other beers, plus local Moska homebrew.

Nu
CATALAN €€

(📋972 22 52 30; www.nurestaurant.cat; Carrer d'Abeuradors 4; mains €16-18; ⊙1.15-3.45pm & 8.15-10.45pm Mon-Sat; 🐾) Sleek and confident, this handsome contemporary old-town spot has innovative, top-notch plates prepared in view by the friendly team. Flavour combinations keep things interesting: sample tuna *tataki* with red fruit glaze, tandoori pork cheeks with mango, and orange flower crème brulée. Great value for this quality.

Occi
FUSION €€

(📋972 22 71 54; www.restaurantocci.com; Carrer dels Mercaders 3; mains €15-23; ⊙1-3.30pm & 8.30-11pm, closed Wed) With elegant contemporary styling and quality glassware and service, Occi has many elements of a pricier place but remains accessible and welcoming. The menu incorporates Catalan, French and Asian influences, such as squid lavished with *romesco* (pepper and nut) sauce and bite-sized tuna heaped with wasabi. Reserve ahead as the day it closes can vary.

L'Alqueria
SPANISH, CATALAN €€

(📋972 22 18 82; www.restaurantalqueria.com; Carrer de la Ginesta 8; mains €14-20; ⊙1-4pm Tue-Sun, 9-11pm Wed-Sat) This smart minimalist *arrocería* serves the finest *arròs negre* (rice cooked in cuttlefish ink) and *arròs a la catalan* in the city, as well as around 20 other superbly executed rice dishes, including paellas. Eat your heart out, Valencia! It's wise to book ahead for dinner, though it also offers takeaway.

★El Celler de Can Roca
CATALAN €€€

(📋972 22 21 57; www.cellercanroca.com; Calle Can Sunyer 48; degustation menus €150-180; ⊙1-4pm & 8.30-11pm Wed-Sat, 8.30-11pm Sun) Ever-changing avant-garde takes on Catalan dishes have catapulted El Celler to global fame. Named the best restaurant in the world in 2015 by The World's 50 Best, each year brings new innovations from molecular gastronomy to multi-sensory food-art interplay to sci-fi dessert trolleys, all with mama's home cooking as the core inspiration.

Run by three brothers, El Celler de Can Roca is set in a refurbished country house, 2km northwest of central Girona. Book online 11 months in advance or put your name on the standby list.

🍷 Drinking & Nightlife

Ham Session
WINE BAR

(📋682 189023; http://donjamon.cat; Carrer del Riu Güell 18; ⊙9.30pm-2am Thu-Sat) Wine, late nights and uncompromisingly good Iberico ham: together at last. Nocturnal grazers will find heaven at this gourmet-focused wine bar, which pairs fine wines with a seemingly endless buffet of local cheeses and freshly carved ham. Book ahead to assure your spot at seats surrounding wine barrels.

Lola Cafè
BAR

(monapartgrup.com/lolacafe; Carrer de la Força 7; ⊙7pm-3am Wed-Sat) Baroque-style gilt mirrors and intimate tables for two make this a sultry night among the cobbled lanes of Girona's medieval town. Dance into the night to live rumba (Wednesday and Thursday

---

WHAT'S COOKING IN CATALONIA?

Cuina Catalana rivals Basque cuisine as Spain's best, drawing ingredients from *mar i muntanya* (sea and mountain). It has come a long way since medieval recipes for roast cat with garlic: its essence now lies in its sauces for meat and fish. There are five main types: *sofregit*, of fried onion, tomato and garlic; *samfaina*, *sofregit* plus red pepper and aubergine or zucchini (courgette); *picada*, based on ground almonds, usually with garlic, parsley, pine nuts or hazelnuts, and sometimes breadcrumbs; *allioli*, garlic pounded with olive oil and egg yolk to make a mayonnaise; and *romesco*, an almond, tomato, olive oil, garlic and vinegar sauce, also used as a salad dressing.

Calçots, which are a type of long spring onion, are delicious as a starter with *romesco* sauce and are in season in late winter/early spring. This is when Catalans get together for a *calçotada*, the local version of a barbecue.

Catalans seem to live on *pa amb tomàquet*, bread slices rubbed with tomato, olive oil and garlic.

evenings) or their regular mash-up of '80s and '90s pop, and stay hydrated with caipirinhas, mojitos and more.

ℹ️ Information

Tourist Office (📞 972 22 65 75; www.girona. cat/turisme; Rambla de la Llibertat 1; ⊗ 9am-8pm Mon-Fri, 9am-2pm & 4-8pm Sat, 9am-2pm Sun) Multilingual and helpful tourist information spot by the river.

ℹ️ Getting There & Away

AIR

Girona-Costa Brava airport (www.girona-air port.net), a Ryanair hub, is located 11km south of the centre, with Sagalés (www.sagales. com) connecting it to Girona's main bus/train station (€2.75, 30 minutes, hourly), as well as Barcelona's Estació del Nord (one way/return €16/25, 1¼ hours). Other direct bus services run to various Costa Brava destinations, including Lloret de Mar (€10, 35 minutes). A **taxi** (📞 672 081830, 636 431300) to central Girona costs around €27 during the day and €35 at night.

BUS

Teisa (www.teisa-bus.com) runs from Girona to Besalú (€4.10 to €4.70, one hour, four to 12 daily) and Olot (€7.45 to €8.50, 1½ hours, four to 15 daily). Sarfa (www.sarfa.com) serves Cadaqués (€10.80, 1¾ hours, one on weekdays) and other coastal destinations. The **bus station** (📞 972 21 23 19; Plaça d'Espanya) is next to the train station.

TRAIN

Girona is on the train line between Barcelona (€11.25 to €16.20, 40 minutes to 1¼ hours, up to 24 daily), Figueres (€4.10 to €5.45, 30 minutes, two to three daily) and Portbou, on the French border (€6.15 to €8.25, one hour, one daily). There are several through trains to France and beyond.

ℹ️ Getting Around

The experience of parking in Girona is alluded to in the *Book of Revelations* (probably). Underground car parks are demonically expensive, while free places are snapped up quickly. There is some free parking around Carrer Josep Morató i Grau, just south of the historic centre. If you're desperate for somewhere to dump the car, there's free parking galore off the Carrer de Sant Gregori roundabout near El Celler de Can Roca, a 30-minute walk northwest of the centre.

L'Estartit & the Illes Medes

L'Estartit, 6km east of Torroella de Montgrí, has a long, wide beach of fine sand and a flashy St-Tropez vibe along its palm-lined boardwalk. But it's the diving that draws travellers to this pretty stretch of Catalonia's Mediterranean coast. The protected Illes Medes, a spectacular group of rocky islets barely 1km offshore, are home to some of the most abundant marine life in coastal Spain.

🏃 Activities

Illes Medes   DIVING

The range of depths (down to 50m) and underwater cavities and tunnels contribute much to the allure of the Illes Medes, seven islets off L'Estartit beach. Since being gazetted as a *reserva natural submarina* in 1983, marine life has thrived here, making this archipelago Spain's most popular destination for snorkellers and divers. Kiosks by the harbour, at the northern end of L'Estartit beach, offer snorkelling and glass-bottomed boat trips to the islands.

🛏️ Sleeping

⭐ **Les Medes**   CAMPGROUND €

(📞 972 75 18 05; www.campinglesmedes.com; Paratge Camp de l'Arbre, L'Estartit; site €21.70 plus per adult €9.30, bungalows from €93.50; 🅿️ 🛜 ❄️) This is one of Catalonia's best campsites, open year-round and set in a leafy location 2km south of L'Estartit and 800m from the seaside. There is a sauna as well as three pools (one for grown-ups only), bike rental, laundry facilities and even massages available.

Hotel Les Illes   HOTEL €€

(📞 972 75 12 39; www.hotellesilles.com; Carrer de Les Illes 55, L'Estartit; s/d/tr incl breakfast €78/128/139; ⊗ mid-Mar–mid-Nov; ❄️ 🛜) This white, bright, family-friendly divers' hangout behind the harbour is a top pick if you want to venture beneath the waves. Rooms are functional though unremarkable; the best reason to stay is to make use of their diving centre. In operation for more than 30 years, it's a good option for team excursions, diving lessons and gear hire. Full board is available and some rooms sleep up to five guests.

ℹ️ Information

Tourist Office (📞 972 75 19 10; www.visit estartit.com; Passeig Marítim, L'Estartit; ⏰ 9am-1pm & 3-6pm Mon-Fri, 10am-2pm Sat & Sun) At the northern end of Passeig Marítim, this tourist office has lists of L'Estartit's scuba diving outfits. Opening hours vary seasonally.

ℹ️ Getting There & Away

L'Estartit is easily reached from Torroella de Montgrí (€1.70, 10 minutes, 16 daily on weekends, five daily on weekends) via the Ampsa bus network.

L'Escala

POP 10,143

At the southern end of the 16km Golf de Roses is L'Escala, a resort town with a difference. Yes, summer brings sun-worshippers to amble along its sea front, lick ice cream on sandy beaches and clink glasses of *tinto de verano* (a summer punch of red wine and sparkling water). But merry L'Escala is also the access point to the Greco-Roman site Empúries, set in a northerly neighbourhood 1km beyond the bustling town. This sprawling ancient city, behind a near-virgin beach facing the Mediterranean, is worthy of exploration both for its remarkable ruins and picturesque setting.

🅾️ Sights

⭐ **Empúries**　　　ARCHAEOLOGICAL SITE

(📞 972 77 02 08; www.mac.cat; adult/child €5/free; ⏰ 10am-8pm Jun-Sep, to 5pm Oct-May, closed Mon Nov-Feb) Exploring this evocative archaeological site and its accompanying museum allows you to immerse yourself in a strategic Greek, and later Roman, trading port. A lively audio guide commentary (included in the price) unravels the history of the Greek town in the lower part of the site, before leading you to the Roman town, with its reconstructed forum. The museum exhibits the top finds, including a statue of Asclepius, god of medicine, dating to the 2nd century BC.

🛏️ Sleeping & Eating

Can Miquel　　　HOTEL €€

(📞 972 77 14 52; www.canmiquel.com; Platja de Montgó; s/d incl breakfast €104/130; ⏰ Mar-Nov; 🅿️❄️📶🏊) Four kilometres southeast of central L'Escala behind a pretty cove beach, this rather severe-looking building features plain rooms and top-class staff. There's a good pool area, tennis courts, and a fish restaurant.

Hostal Spa Empúries　　BOUTIQUE HOTEL €€€

(📞 972 77 02 07; www.hostalempuries.com; Platja del Portitxol; d from €166; 🅿️❄️📶) 🍴 This stylish year-round hotel next to the Roman ruins fronts a sandy splash of ocean. Some rooms are beach-coloured and the mosaic bathrooms clearly take their inspiration from the ruins; the rooms in the new wing, with rain showers and enormous beds, are particularly comfortable. The two restaurants specialise in creative Mediterranean and seafood dishes using local produce.

In high summer, a minimum stay of a few nights may apply. Prices tumble during the off season.

⭐ **La Gruta**　　　FUSION €€€

(📞 972 77 62 11; www.restaurantlagruta.com; Carrer del Pintor Enric Serra 15; 3-course menu €29; ⏰ 12.30-3.30pm Mon-Sat, 8pm-10.30pm Tue-Sat) A fusion of French and Spanish flavours, spiced with occasional Indian flair, fill plates at this innovative spot. Think steak with light tandoori spices, truffled *oeuf cocotte* (French-style baked egg) and duck marinaded in ginger, plus patisserie items and a rainbow of iced desserts.

ℹ️ Information

Tourist Office (📞 972 77 06 03; www.lescala. cat; Plaça de les Escoles 1; ⏰ 9am-1pm & 4-7pm Mon-Fri, 10am-1pm & 4-7pm Sat, 10am-1pm Sun) L'Escala's tourist office is conveniently located down the street from where the bus drops visitors. It operates shorter hours during the low season.

ℹ️ Getting There & Away

Sarfa has daily buses from Barcelona (€21.70, three hours, three daily), Girona (€6.40, one hour, two to five daily) and Figueres (€4.95, one hour, two to four daily). Arriving in town, buses will drop you on Avinguda Girona, just down the street from the tourist office.

Castelló d'Empúries

POP 11,473

This town once presided over Empúries, a medieval Catalan county that maintained a large degree of independence up to the 14th century. Modern Castelló d'Empúries maintains the imperious aura of a former capital, but these days its cobbled lanes are trodden less by counts and more by affable locals and the odd tourist.

Traces of Castelló d'Empúries' history can be found in the impressive Basílica de Santa

SANT MARTÍ D'EMPÚRIES

Size isn't everything. Though minuscule, walled Sant Martí d'Empúries impresses with its glorious shores and medieval history. Until 1079 it was the seat of Empúries county before its vulnerability to pirate attacks prompted a power shift. These days it makes a wonderful excursion from L'Escala (5km south) or Castelló d'Empúries (12km north). Sand beaches extend just beyond the walls of its historical centre. The main square, flanked by a broad sandstone church, is packed with more than its fair share of excellent restaurants.

Getting There & Away

Rodalies trains run from Barcelona's Estació Sants to Sant Sadurní (€4.10, 45 minutes, half-hourly). By car, take the A2 north from Barcelona follow signs west at Martorell.

María and well-preserved Gothic Convent de Sant Domènec. The town also makes a superb base for lovers of the outdoors. Nearby Parc Natural dels Aiguamolls de l'Empordà is superb for bird watching and has a number of easy hikes, while wind-blown (but otherwise peaceful) beaches lie just 5km east.

◉ Sights

**Parc Natural dels
Aiguamolls de l'Empordà** PARK
(GIV6216 Sant Pere Pescador–Castelló d'Empúries Km 4.2; parking motorbike or car €5, van €10; ⊙El Cortalet information centre 9.30am-2pm & 3.30-7pm high season, to 4pm low season) The remnants of the mighty marshes that once covered the whole coastal plain here are preserved in this natural park, a key site for migrating birds. The March–May and August–October migration periods bring big increases in the numbers of wading birds. Keen twitchers may drop their binoculars in the excitement of glimpsing flamingo, bee eater, glossy ibis, spoonbill, rare black stork and more than 300 other species passing through the area (some 90 of which nest here).

Ecomuseu-Farinera MUSEUM
(www.ecomuseu-farinera.org; Carrer de Sant Francesc 5; adult/under 14 €3.70/2.65; ⊙10am-2pm & 4-7pm Mon-Sat, 10.30am-1.30pm Sun) In its heyday, this *farinera* (flour factory) was producing 20,000kg of the white stuff each day. Even if milling innovations aren't your thing, a wander in this museum takes you on a surprisingly diverting journey from sheaf to loaf, with huge turbines to gawp at, plus a hypnotic soundtrack of hydraulics. There is a kids' trail to guide young visitors around the museum.

🛏 Sleeping & Eating

★**Hotel Casa Clara** HOSTAL €€
(☑972 25 02 15; www.hostalcasaclara.com; Plaça de les Monges; s/d/tr €65/75/100; P❋🐾) Genial service and quaint, cosy rooms make this colourful *hostal* a splendid midrange option right in the heart of old-town Castelló d'Empúries. All seven spacious, tiled rooms feature natural light, an individual colour scheme and comfortable beds. There is a pleasant lounge and terrace area with board games and books, and the attached restaurant features a changing menu of flavoursome Catalan fare (three courses €15).

Hotel Moneda HOTEL €€€
(☑972 15 86 02; www.hoteldelamoneda.com; Plaça de la Moneda; d €88-276; ⊙Mar-Nov; P❋🐾🖳) This 18th-century luxury mansion makes an enticing couples' retreat. Low-slung medieval archways provide an intimate old-world atmosphere, while rooms are awash in bright primary colours. There's a little swimming pool, Andalusian-style Jacuzzi and sexy touches such as *cava* (sparkling wine) on arrival and slippers to pad around the enormous rooms. Leave the kids at home for this one.

Les Voltes CATALAN €€
(Plaça dels Homes 4; mains €12-15; ⊙1-3.30pm Wed-Sun, 8.30pm-10.30pm Wed-Sat) As pleasant for a glass of *tinto de verano* (red wine and soda) as for a full-blown feast of barbecued pork, Les Voltes spreads from a cavernous stone-walled interior onto atmospheric Plaça dels Homes. The service is cordial and the tablecloths are white, but the outdoor terrace is casual enough to stay for a snack.

CATALONIA CASTELLÓ D'EMPÚRIES

ⓘ Getting There & Away

Sarfa runs buses to Figueres (€1.70, 15 minutes, 18 daily on weekdays, one on weekends), Cadaqués (€4.20, 50 minutes, six weekdays, one weekends) and Barcelona's Estació del Nord (€20.75, two hours, two on weekdays, one on weekends).

Cadaqués

POP 2820

Cadaqués gleams above the cobalt-blue waters of a rocky bay on Catalonia's most easterly outcrop. This whitewashed village owes its allure in part to its windswept pebble beaches and meandering lanes, and the easy-going atmosphere that draws throngs of summer visitors. But it's the artist Salvador Dalí who truly gave Cadaqués its sparkle.

The artist spent family holidays here during his youth, and lived much of his later life at nearby Port Lligat. Thanks to Dalí and other luminaries, such as his friend Federico García Lorca, Cadaqués pulled in a celebrity crowd and still does. A visit in 1929 by the poet Paul Éluard and his Russian wife, Gala, caused an earthquake in Dalí's life: he ran off to Paris with Gala (who was to become his lifelong obsession and, later, his wife) and joined the Surrealist movement.

Summer in Cadaqués is very busy, so an advance booking can make or break a trip. September is less crowded, but tourist amenities begin to slumber from mid-October. There can also be sea storms at this time of year, bringing autumn breaks to an abrupt and soggy halt.

◉ Sights

Casa Museu Dalí   MUSEUM

(☑ 972 25 10 15; www.salvador-dali.org; adult/under 8yr €11/free; ☉ 10.30am-6pm Tue-Sun, closed Jan–mid-Feb) Located by a peaceful cove in Port Lligat, a tiny fishing settlement a 20-minute walk from Cadaqués, the Casa Museu Dalí was the residence and sanctuary of Salvador Dalí. This splendid whitewashed structure is a mishmash of cottages and sunny terraces, linked together by narrow labyrinthine corridors and containing an assortment of offbeat furnishings. Access is by semi-guided tour only. It's essential to book ahead, by phone or via the website.

Dalí lived in this magnificent seaside complex with his wife Gala from 1930 to 1982. The cottage was originally a mere fisherman's hut, but it was steadily altered and enlarged by its owners. Every corner reveals a new and wondrous folly or *objet d'art*: a taxidermied polar bear with jewellery to rival Mr T's, stuffed swans (something of an obsession for the artist) perched on bookshelves, and the womb-like Oval Room. The artist's workshop and the boudoir-like resting room for models are especially interesting. Meanwhile Dalí's bedroom still has a suspended mirror, positioned to ensure he was the first person to see the glint of sunrise each morning. If the Teatre-Museu Dalí in Figueres is the mask that the showman presented to the world, then this is an intimate glimpse of Dalí's actual face.

It's open longer hours in the high season.

Museu de Cadaqués   MUSEUM

(Carrer de Narcís Monturiol 15; adult/child €4/3; ☉ 10am-8pm daily Jul-Sep, 10.30am-1.30pm & 4-7pm Mon-Sat Apr-Jun & Oct) Salvador Dalí often features strongly in the temporary exhibitions displayed here, as do his con-

---

WORTH A TRIP

THE COSTA BRAVA WAY

The 255km-long stretch of cliffs, coves, rocky promontories and pine groves that make up the signposted Costa Brava Way, stretching from Blanes to Colliure in France, unsurprisingly offers some of the best walks in Catalonia, ranging from gentle rambles to high-octane scrambles (or one long, demanding hike if you want to do the whole thing). For the most part, the trail follows the established GR92, but also includes a number of coastal deviations.

A choice route is **Cadaqués to the Cap de Creus Lighthouse** (2½ hours), a relatively easy walk that begins in the centre of Cadaqués, then passes Portlligat, continuing along windswept, scrub-covered, rocky ground past several isolated beaches before it reaches the lighthouse.

temporaries, also connected to Cadaqués, such as Picasso. It opens roughly Easter to October, but this depends on the yearly exhibition.

Beaches

Cadaqués' main beach, and several others along the nearby coast, are small, with more pebbles than sand, but their picturesqueness and beautiful blue waters make up for that. Overlooking Platja Llané, to the south of the town centre, is Dalí's parents' holiday home. All the beaches around here experience strong winds, so caution is recommended. Even in high summer, swimming can be far from relaxing.

Sleeping

Hotel Llane Petit
HOTEL €€

(☑972 25 10 20; www.llanepetit.com; Carrer del Dr Bartomeus 37; d €118-191; ☺mid-Mar–Oct; P❋❀☲) Thirty-seven rooms fitted out in the bright, nautical style beloved of Cadaqués fill this four-storey place overlooking a pocket-sized pebbled beach. The location is splendid and most of the rooms have a generous balcony to sit on. Breakfast (€12) and parking (€10 to €15) cost extra. Prices drop by up to 30% outside high season.

Hostal Vehí
HOSTAL €€

(☑972 25 84 70; www.hostalvehi.com; Carrer de l'Església 6; d with bathroom €60-90; ☺Mar-Nov; ❋❀) In the heart of the old town, this family-run guesthouse has clean-as-a-whistle rooms with homey touches such as floral duvets and wood furnishings. Superior doubles are vast, with pleasant views over Cadaqués' coral-coloured rooftops. It's a pain to walk to if you have a lot of luggage (and cars can't access this part of the old town), but it's the best midrange deal in town. Book way ahead for July and August.

L'Horta d'en Rahola
BOUTIQUE HOTEL €€€

(☑972 25 10 49; www.hortacadaques.com; Carrer Sant Vicens 1; d €125-200; ☺Mar-Dec; P❋❀) Just by the roundabout at the entrance to the village, this luminous family-run place is a characterful conversion of a 17th-century farmhouse, with a garden growing vegetables and fruit. The seven rooms, all different, are light and bright with a marine feel. There's a restaurant, personal service is excellent and you're made to feel very welcome.

MONESTIR DE SANT PERE DE RODES

Combine views of a deep-blue Mediterranean and the menacing peaks of the Pyrenees with a spectacular piece of Romanesque architecture. The resulting sensory overload is the Monestir de Sant Pere de Rodes (☑972 38 75 59; adult/under 8s €4.50/free, Tue free; ☺10am-7pm Tue & Thu-Sat, to 8pm Wed, 10am-2.30pm Tue-Sun Oct-May), which sits 500m up in the hills southwest of El Port de la Selva. Founded in the 9th century, it became the most powerful monastery in the county of Empúries. The great triple-naved, barrel-vaulted basilica is flanked by the square Torre de Sant Miquel bell tower and a two-level cloister.

Eating

Es Baluard
SEAFOOD €€

(☑972 25 81 83; www.esbaluard-cadaques.net; Carrer de la Riba Nemesi Llorens; mains €16-22; ☺1-3.30pm & 8.30-11pm) There may be roe deer carpaccio and salt-sprinkled grilled asparagus on the menu, but the family behind Es Baluard clearly worships at the throne of Poseidon. Fish dishes such as *anchoas de Cadaqués* (anchovies from Cadaqués) and *suquet de peix* (local fish stew) dominate the menu. Plus there is a formidable selection of desserts including syrup-soaked figs and cream cheese ice cream with orange marmalade.

Casa Nun
SEAFOOD €€

(☑972 25 88 56; Plaça des Portitxó 6; mains €15-25; ☺12.30-3.30pm & 7.30-11pm daily Apr-Oct, Sat & Sun Nov-Mar) Head for the cute upstairs dining area or take one of the few tables outside overlooking the port. Everything is prepared with care, from the seafood dominating the menu to generous steaks and a little dessert selection with *tarta de limón* and homemade flans.

ℹ Information

Tourist Office (☑972 25 83 15; www.visit cadaques.org; Carrer del Cotxe 2; ☺9am-1pm & 3-6pm Mon-Thu, to 7pm Fri & Sat, 10am-1pm Sun) Near where the main road meets the water, this tourist info place opens longer hours in the high season.

DALÍ

One of the 20th century's most recognisable icons, Salvador Dalí (1904–89) could have had the term 'larger than life' invented for him. He then would probably have decorated it with pink pineapples.

Born in Figueres, Dalí's surrealist trajectory through the often-serious landscape of 20th-century Spain brought him into contact and collaboration with figures such as Pablo Picasso, Luís Buñuel, Federico García Lorca and (controversially) Franco. A raft of foreign celebrities flocked to be seen in his extravagant company. He turned his hand to everything from film-making to architecture to literature.

Self-consciously eccentric and a constant source of memorable soundbites, he was nevertheless in some ways a conservative figure and devout Catholic. His long relationship with his Russian wife Gala provided the stable foundation that his whirligig life revolved around.

The celebrity, the extraordinarily prolific output and, let's face it, the comedy moustache tend to pull focus from the fact that he was an artist of the highest calibre. In his paintings, Dalí's surrealism is often far more profound than it seems at first glance. The floppy clocks of his most famous work, *The Persistence of Memory*, are interpreted by some as a reference to the flexibility of time proposed by Einstein. His *Christ of St John of the Cross* combines expert composition, symbol-laden Renaissance-style imagery and a nostalgic, almost elegiac view of the Catalan coast that he so loved.

❶ Getting There & Away

Sarfa buses connect Cadaqués to Barcelona (€24.50, 2¾ hours, one to two weekdays, plus weekends in summer), Figueres (€5.50, one hour, four weekdays) via Castelló d'Empúries, and Girona (€10.80, 1¾ hours, one weekdays).

Cap de Creus

Cap de Creus is the most easterly point of the Spanish mainland and is a place of sublime, rugged beauty, battered by the merciless *tramuntana* wind and reachable by a lonely, 8km-long road that winds its way through the moonscapes. With a steep, rocky coastline indented by coves of turquoise water, it's an especially wonderful place to be at dawn or sunset.

The odd-shaped rocks, barren plateaux and deserted shorelines that litter Dalí's famous paintings were not just a product of his fertile imagination. This is the landscape that inspired the artist, which he described as a 'grandiose geological delirium'. See if you can find the huge rock that morphed into the subject of his painting *The Great Masturbator*, half-way between the main road and the lighthouse at the top.

❶ Getting There & Away

Cap de Creus is most easily accessed by car, along an 8km winding gravel road from Cadaqués via Port Lligat.

Figueres

POP 45,444

Twelve kilometres inland from Catalonia's glistening Golf de Roses lies Figueres, birthplace of Salvador Dalí and now home to the artist's flamboyant theatre-museum. Although Dalí's career took him to Madrid, Barcelona, Paris and the USA, Figueres remained close to his heart; so in the 1960s and '70s he created the extraordinary Teatre-Museu Dalí – a monument to surrealism and a legacy that outshines any other Spanish artist, both in terms of popularity and sheer flamboyance. Whatever your feelings about this complex, egocentric man, this museum is worth every cent and minute you can spare.

Beyond this star attraction, busy Figueres has a couple of interesting museums, pleasant shopping streets around Carrer de Peralada, and a whopping 18th-century fortress. It's well worth staying to see the city breathe after Dalí day-trippers board their buses at sundown.

◉ Sights

★ Teatre-Museu Dalí   MUSEUM
(www.salvador-dali.org; Plaça de Gala i Salvador Dalí 5; adult/child under 9yr incl Museu de l'Empordà €12/free; ⊙9am-8pm Tue-Sun Jul-Sep, 10.30am-6pm Tue-Sun Oct-Jun, closed Mon) The first name that comes into your head when you lay your

eyes on this red castle-like building, topped with giant eggs and stylised Oscar-like statues and studded with plaster-covered croissants, is Dalí. An entirely appropriate final resting place for the master of surrealism, it has assured his immortality. Exhibits within these walls range from enormous installations - like *Taxi Plujós* (Rainy Taxi), an early Cadillac, surmounted by statues – to the more discreet, such as a tiny mysterious room with a mirrored flamingo.

'Theatre-museum' is an apt label for this trip through the incredibly fertile imagination of one of the great showmen of the 20th century. Between 1961 and 1974 Salvador Dalí converted Figueres' former municipal theatre, ruined by a fire at the end of the civil war in 1939, into the Teatre-Museu Dalí. It's full of surprises, tricks and illusions, and contains a substantial portion of Dalí's life's work, though you won't find his most famous pieces here: they are scattered around the world.

Even outside, the building aims to surprise, from its entrance watched over by medieval suits of armour balancing baguettes on their heads, to bizarre sculptures outside the entrance on Plaça de Gala i Salvador Dalí, to the pink wall along Pujada del Castell. The Torre Galatea, added in 1983, is where Dalí spent his final years.

Choice exhibits include Taxi Plujós (*Rainy Taxi*), composed of an early Cadillac, surmounted by statues. Put a coin in the slot and water washes all over the occupant of the car. The Sala de Peixateries (Fishmongers' Hall) holds a collection of Dalí oils, including the famous Autoretrat Tou amb Tall de Bacon Fregit (*Soft Self-Portrait with Fried Bacon*) and Retrat de Picasso (*Portrait of Picasso*). Beneath the former stage of the theatre is the crypt with Dalí's plain tomb, located at 'the spiritual centre of Europe' as Dalí modestly described it.

Gala, Dalí's wife and lifelong muse, is seen throughout – from the Gala Mirando el Mar Mediterráneo (*Gala Looking at the Mediterranean Sea*) on the 2nd level, which also appears to be a portrait of Abraham Lincoln from afar, to the classic Leda Atómica (*Atomic Leda*).

After you've seen the more notorious pieces, such as climbing the stairs in the famous Mae West Room, see if you can find a turtle with a gold coin balanced on its back, peepholes into a tiny mysterious room with a mirrored flamingo amid fake plants, and Dalí's heavenly reimagining of the Sistine Chapel in the Palace of the Wind Room.

A separate entrance (same ticket and opening times) leads into Dalí Joies, a collection of 37 jewels, designed by Dalí. He designed these on paper (his first commission was in 1941) and the jewellery was made by specialists in New York. Each piece, ranging from the disconcerting Ull del Temps (Eye of Time) through to the Cor Reial (Royal Heart), is unique.

Castell de Sant Ferran
FORT

(www.lesfortalesescatalanes.info; adult/child €3/free; ☉10.30am-6pm Apr–mid-Jul, 10.30am-8pm mid-Jul–mid-Sep, 10.30am-3pm Oct-Mar) This sturdy 18th-century fortress commands the surrounding plains from a low hill 1km northwest of the centre. The complex is a wonder of military engineering: it sprawls over 32 hectares, with the capacity for 6000 men to march within its walls and snooze in military barracks that are on display today. The admission fee includes a clanking audio guide (nearly as old as the castle) to help navigate the site. Book ahead for group guided tours (€10 to €15 per person). Opening hours vary seasonally.

Museu del Joguet
MUSEUM

(www.mjc.cat; Carrer de Sant Pere 1; adult/child €6/free; ☉10am-6pm Tue-Sat, 11am-2pm Sun, closed Jan) This museum has more than 3500 toys from throughout the ages – from the earliest board games involving coloured stones to ball-in-a-cup to intricate dolls' houses to 1920s dolls with baleful stares that may haunt your dreams to Catalonia- and Valencia-made religious processions of tiny figures. It's a mesmerising display, with plenty to amuse the kids... that is, unless you're

---

ⓘ VISITING THE TEATRE-MUSEU DALÍ

The Teatre-Museu Dalí is Spain's most visited museum outside Madrid, so it's worthwhile double-checking the opening hours (it's closed on Mondays) and reserving tickets online in advance. In August the museum opens at night from 10pm to 12.30am (admission €13, bookings essential).

The biggest crowds arrive during weekends and on public holidays. Arrive early to avoid long queues.

the kind to associate blank-eyed Victorian dolls with horror movies. Admission is half-price if you flash a Teatre-Museu Dalí ticket.

Museu de l'Empordà · MUSEUM

(www.museuemporda.org; La Rambla 2; adult/child €4/free; ⊙ 11am-8pm Tue-Sat, to 2pm Sun) Across four floors, this local museum time travels from ancient amphorae to 7th-century sculptures to rotating installations of contemporary art. The region's culture and history are presented in a rather fragmented way, but it's an enjoyable romp. The 17th-century religious art is especially worthy of attention. There are signs in Spanish and Catalan, plus explanation on laminated cards in English and French. Admission is free with a Teatre-Museu Dalí ticket.

🛏 Sleeping

Hostel Figueres · HOSTEL €

(☑ 630 680575; www.hostelfigueres.com; Carrer dels Tints 22; dm/d €19/59; ☜) This fresh-faced newcomer to Figueres' accommodation scene opened in June 2015 and is exactly the backpacker hideaway the city sorely needed. The 14-bed dorm is clean and airy, with fans to keep things cool. Staff positively fizz with recommendations, plus they can arrange bike hire. The hostel is fitted with a communal kitchen, lounge room, lockers, hand-washing station for clothes, and there's towel hire (€1).

Hotel Ronda · HOTEL €

(☑ 972 50 39 11; www.hotelrondafigueres.com; Avinguda Salvador Dali 17; s/d/tr from €42/55/72; 🅿❄☜) Located 2.5km south of the centre, Hotel Ronda is best suited to travellers with their own wheels. For drivers it's perfectly positioned on the main road for day trips out of town to Girona or L'Estartit and the coast. Rooms have a business feel but are very comfortable with near-blackout curtains. Underground parking is included in the price, a true blessing in traffic-choked Figueres.

⭐ Hotel Durán · HOTEL €€

(☑ 972 50 12 50; www.hotelduran.com; Carrer de Lasauca 5; d from €75; 🅿❄☜) For absolute immersion in the Dalí legend, a stay at this mid-19th-century hotel is a must. The artist and his wife were frequent guests here, and there's a fitting blend of old-style elegance with contemporary design and surrealist touches. Rooms are modern and great value, while the restaurant has the opulence of a royal banquet hall.

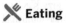 Eating

Sidrería Txot's · CATALAN, BASQUE €

(www.sidreriatxots.com; Avinguda Salvador Dalí 114; mains €10; ⊙ noon-midnight; ☜) Perch on a wooden seat and watch your Basque cider poured from on high from the barrel – the way it's supposed to be – before tucking into cold and hot *pintxos* (Basque tapas), tasty burgers, cured meats, cheeses and salads, as well as dishes such as chorizo in cider and L'Escala anchovies on toast. The kitchen's open all afternoon – handy for a post-Dalí meal.

El Motel · CATALAN €€€

(Hotel Empordà; ☑ 972 50 05 62; www.elmotel.cat; Avinguda Salvador Dalí i Domènech 170; tasting menu €39.70; ⊙ 7.30-11am, 12.45-3.45pm & 9-11pm; 🅿☜) Jaume Subirós, the chef and owner of this hotel-restaurant on a busy road 1km north of the centre, is a seminal figure of the transition from traditional Catalan home cooking to the polished, innovative affair it is today. Highlights are such dishes as sea urchins from Cadaqués, cod with truffle and calf's cheek in red wine. There are also appealing rooms in which to sleep off the gastronomic indulgence (single €94, double €109, suite €140).

WORTH A TRIP

CENTRE DE REPRODUCCIÓ DE TORTUGUES DE L'ALBERA

For 21 years, the little wildlife sanctuary Centre de Reproducció de Tortugues de l'Albera (☑ 972 55 22 45; www.tortugues.cat; Garriguella; admission €6; ⊙ 10am-1pm & 3-5pm Tue-Sat, 10am-1pm Sun late Mar-Oct; 🐾) has been a haven for Hermann's tortoises, and a force for educating people about these little armoured tanks of the Pyrenees. There's an introductory film (Catalana, Spanish, English, French or German) explaining menaces to the region's tortoises, but the biggest thrill is a stroll around the boardwalk outside, to peep at scores of critters ambling among rocks and flower beds. The sanctuary is just north of Garriguella, a teeny town 15km northeast of Figueres.

MUSEU MEMORIAL DE L'EXILI

Museu Memorial de l'Exili (www.museuexili.cat; Carrer Major 43-47, La Jonquera; adult/child €4/free; ⏰ 10am-6pm Tue-Sat, 10am-2pm Sun) Anyone familiar with Picasso's *Guernica* already has a tiny insight into the horror of civilian suffering during Spain's Civil War. This museum traces the experiences of Catalonian people exiled and persecuted during this era. This thought-provoking museum is aptly located in the town of La Jonquera, close to the Spain–France border where many were forced to flee. It explains the build-up to the Spanish Civil War through photographs, an informative audio guide, and haunting art installations.

For those who survived physical displacement, imprisonment and brutal purges, the psychological wounds continued long after the death of Franco. This museum encourages visitors to think beyond the Spanish Civil War, and to explore the concept of emotional and mental exile more deeply in the context of other global conflicts. The museum is 19km north of Figueres.

ℹ️ Information

Tourist Office (☎ 972 50 31 55; http://visitfigueres.cat; Plaça del Sol; ⏰ 9.30am-2pm & 4-6pm Tue-Sat, 10am-2pm Sun & Mon) On the busy main road slicing Figueres is this handy information place. It opens longer hours in high season.

ℹ️ Getting There & Away

Sarfa buses serve Cadaqués (€5.50, one to 1½ hours, four on weekdays) via Castelló d'Empúries.

There are half-hourly train connections to Girona (€4.10 to €5.45, 30 minutes) and Barcelona (€12 to €16, 1¾ to 2½ hours). Hourly trains chug towards Portbou (€3.40, 30 minutes) for connections across the French border.

Besalú

POP 2400

The broad but elegant 12th-century Pont Fortificat (Fortified Bridge) over Río Fluvià in medieval Besalú, with its two tower gates and heavy portcullis, is an arresting sight, leading you into the coiled maze of cobbled narrow streets that make up the core of this delightfully well-preserved town. Following a succession of Roman, Visigothic and Muslim rulers, during the 10th and 11th centuries Besalú was the capital of an independent county that stretched as far west as Cerdanya before it came under Barcelona's control in 1111. Today it's a favourite day-trip destination from Girona, with a steady stream of visitors roaming the ramparts and exploring Besalú's Jewish history.

👁️ Sights

⭐ Pont Fortificat

BRIDGE

Besalú's fortified stone bridge is so old, it strains memory. The first records of the bridge date to 1075, though periodic modifications have bolstered its defensive structure. It was bombed in 1939 during the Spanish Civil War and repaired soon after. Today this pale sandstone bridge, with its sturdy tower and portcullis, is a vantage point for the loveliest views of medieval Besalú.

Micromundi

MUSEUM

(www.museuminiaturesbesalu.com; Plaça Prat de Sant Pere 15; adult/child €4.90/2.50; ⏰ 10am-8pm daily Apr-Oct, 10am-3pm Tue-Fri, to 8pm Sat & Sun Nov-Mar; 👶) Prepare to squint with increasing intensity as you enter this peculiar museum opposite Monestir de Sant Pere. Peer through a magnifying glass at jewellery, figurines and tiny dioramas from around the world, including ants wielding parasols, Lilliputian re-creations of the siege of Troy, and retina-spraining Mexican skulls. The third of the museum's three rooms has a row of microscopes above creations invisible to the naked eye, including Besalú's bridge on a pin's head and camels passing through the eye of a needle.

Jewish Square

RUIN

(Baixada de Mikwe; guided tours €2.20) Besalú's thriving Jewish community fled the town in 1436 after relentless Christian persecution. They left behind a miqvé (ritual bath) dating from the 12th century, a rare survivor of its kind in Spain, which was only rediscovered in 1964. It sits down by the river inside a vaulted stone chamber, around which remnants of the 13th-century synagogue were unearthed during excavations in 2005. Access to the miqvé is by guided tour, but you can see the square and ruin exterior independently.

🛏 Sleeping & Eating

3 Arcs
HOTEL €€

(☑972 59 16 78; www.hotel3arcs.com; Carrer Ganganell 15; s/d/tr €73/84/99; ❄🗑) As the name suggests, you'll know this place by the slender stone archways adjoining this fine old-town building. Its 12 simple rooms are compact and modern, and set within a refurbished historic building. There is a pleasant downstairs bakery and friendly management. Prices are up to 20% lower outside high season.

Els Jardins de la Martana
HOTEL €€

(☑972 59 00 09; www.lamartana.com; Carrer del Pont Vell 2; s/d/tr €70/112/135; 🅿❄🗑) This charming, family-run hotel, set in a mansion dating from 1910, is on the out-of-town end of the grand old bridge. The 10 rooms have tiled floors, high ceilings and balconies, and many offer views across the bridge to the town. There's a beautiful terrace and gardens, a noble library with fireplace, and various family rooms positioned around a dedicated kids' play area. It could do with a spruce up, but is lovable and very friendly.

Restaurant La Cúria Reial
CATALAN €€

(☑972 59 02 63; www.curiareial.com; Plaça Llibertat 8-9; mains €12; ⊙1-3.30pm & 8.30-10.30pm Wed-Mon) Whether dining beneath the arches in its snug stone interior or out on the terrace overlooking the bridge, an atmospheric experience is assured at Cúria Reial. The menu, spanning market fare and *cuina volcànica* from the fertile Garrotxa hills, delights with tasty lunch menus (€18.50), juicy grilled fish and lavish desserts, such as jasmine ice cream served in chilled melon soup.

Pont Vell
CATALAN €€

(☑972 59 10 27; www.restaurantpontvell.com; Pont Vell 26; mains €15-24; ⊙1-3.30pm Wed-Mon, 8.30pm-10.30pm Wed-Sat, closed late Dec-late Jan) The views to the old bridge (after which the restaurant is named) are enough to tempt you to take a seat here, even without considering the wide-ranging menu full of locally sourced delights, such as home-made terrines, ox tail in red wine, and cannelloni of guineafowl and truffles.

ℹ Information

Tourist Office (☑972 59 12 40; www.besalu. cat; Carrer del Pont 1; ⊙10am-1.30pm daily, 4-7pm Mon-Sat) Across the bridge from the centre.

ℹ Getting There & Away

Teisa buses (www.teisa-bus.com) run to Barcelona (€15.40, 1¾ hours, three to four daily), Olot (€3.45, 30 minutes, eight to 13 daily), Figueres (€3.45 to €4, 30 minutes, two to three daily) and Girona (€4.10 to €4.70, one hour, four to 12 daily).

The N260 road from Figueres to Olot meets the C66 from Girona at Besalú.

THE PYRENEES

Catalonia's Pyrenees are more than an all-season adventure playground. Certainly, the Val d'Aran draws skiers and snowboarders in winter, with resorts ranging from red-carpet to family-friendly. Summer and autumn lure droves of hikers to the jewel-like lakes and valleys of the Parc Nacional d'Aigüestortes i Estany de Sant Maurici and the climbing terrain of the Serra del Cadí.

But there is also Catalan heritage to be discovered amid the breathtaking scenery. Centuries-old monasteries slumber in these mountains, meaning treks in the Pyrenees are as likely to bypass ruined Romanesque churches as offer a valley panorama. Tastebuds yearning for more than hiking fodder will find satisfaction in the rich gastronomy of Garrotxa's volcanic zone. Beyond the big-ticket sights and major resorts, Catalonia's Pyrenees conceal a raw beauty that awaits discovery.

Olot

POP 972 / ELEV 443M

If you perceive a rumbling sensation during your travels in Olot, it might be more than your belly bemoaning that over-sized *crema catalana*. More than 100 small earthquakes set Catalonia trembling each year, though most are barely perceptible. The scenery in Garrotxa, a lush region of cone-shaped hills spreading from regional capital Olot, was chiselled by more extreme geological activity 70,000 years ago.

Olot is a good base for exploring the area. The town spreads over a large area, with

OUT & ABOUT IN THE PYRENEES

The Catalan Pyrenees provide magnificent walking and trekking. You can undertake strolls of a few hours, or day walks that can be strung together into treks of several days. Nearly all can be done without camping gear, with nights spent in villages or *refugis* (no-frills mountain shelters).

Most of the *refugis* are run by two Barcelona mountain clubs, the Federació d'Entitats Excursionistes de Catalunya (FEEC; www.feec.org) and the Centre Excursionista de Catalunya (CEC; www.cec.cat), which also provide info on trails. A night in a *refugi* costs around €12.50 to €18. Moderately priced meals (around €15 to €20) are sometimes available in high season. It's worth calling ahead to assure your place (in summer, *refugis* can fill up, and in shoulder season, many are closed) and to ask if cooking facilities are available.

The coast-to-coast **GR11 long-distance trail network** traverses the entire Pyrenees from Cap de Creus on the Costa Brava to Hondarribia on the Bay of Biscay. The tougher **HRP (Haute Randonnée Pyrénéenne**, recommended only for the hardiest and most experienced trekkers, takes you higher up into the mountains, crossing the Spanish–French border several times.

The season for walking in the high Pyrenees is from late June to early October. Always be prepared for fast-changing conditions, no matter when you go.

Local advice from tourist offices, park rangers, mountain *refugis* and other walkers is invaluable. Dedicated hiking maps are essential.

There's boundless scope for climbing – Pedraforca in the Serra del Cadí offers some of the most exciting ascents.

---

broad, tree-lined boulevards, but the medieval centre is agreeably walkable.

◉ Sights

Four hills of volcanic origin stand sentry on the fringes of Olot. Walk up **Volcà del Montsacopa**, 500m north of the centre, or **Volcà de la Garrinada**, 1km northeast of the centre, both of which are volcanic craters.

A combined museum ticket grants access to both the Museu dels Volcans and Museu Comarcal de la Garrotxa (€4).

🏃 Activities

Vol de Coloms   BALLOONING
(☎972 68 02 55; www.voldecoloms.cat; flights from €170) These hot-air-balloon trips over Garrotxa's hills are a memorable way to experience the scale of the volcano-carved scenery. Flights last about 90 minutes and include *cava*, a snack and a flight certificate to prove your bravery.

🛏 Sleeping

★ Can Blanc   CASA RURAL €€
(☎972 27 60 20; www.canblanc.es; Passatges de la Deu; s/d/tr incl breakfast €62/100/130; P❄🛜🏊) This secluded place on the southern edge of Olot is surrounded by parkland. Colourful, modern-rustic rooms come in a range of shapes and sizes. The gardens

and pool will put a smile on your face on hot summer days and a great breakfast is thrown in. Ask for directions to the next-door La Deu restaurant, as people are more likely to know it.

Hotel La Perla   HOTEL €€
(☎972 26 23 26; www.laperlahotels.com; Carretera la Deu 9; s/d/apt from €40/70/83; P❄🛜) This family-friendly hotel complex, 2km south of central Olot, has pleasant rooms and apartments, some with terraces, plus a soothing outdoor area with a babbling volcanic stone fountain. There are play areas and games rooms to keep kids busy and a friendly restaurant with changing set menus brimming with simple local produce. The location is quiet, but it's only a 400m walk to Parc Nou and the volcano museum.

🍴 Eating

La Deu   CUINA VOLCÀNICA €€
(☎972 26 10 04; www.ladeu.es; Carretera la Deu; mains €10-23; ⊙1-4pm & 8.30-10.30pm Mon-Sat, 1-4pm Sun; P🛜) Down a tree-lined road with a volcanic stone fountain gushing merrily in its outdoor dining area, this family-run restaurant has been perfecting its filling local cuisine since the 19th century. There's huge variety, including the likes of slow-cooked lamb, pork with sweet chestnuts and cod lashed with local honey.

VOLCANIC CUISINE

In Olot and around, a dedicated group of chefs proudly carries on the *cuina volcànica* culinary tradition, which stems from the exceptionally fertile volcanic soil, responsible for a bounty of locally grown produce that forms the base of this hearty cuisine. Ingredients include black radishes, wild mushrooms, Santa Pau beans, *ratafia* (liquor with aromatic herbs, sometimes flavoured with walnut) and *piumoc* (dry pork sausage).

★ Les Cols   CUINA VOLCÀNICA €€€

(✆972 26 92 09; www.lescols.com; Carretera de la Canya; degustation €85; ⏰1-3.30pm & 8.30-10.30pm Wed-Sat, 1-3.30pm Tue & Sun) Set in a converted 19th century *masia*, Les Cols is 2km northeast of central Olot. Inside, the decor has a 21st-century edge, with iron and glass walls, a chilled-out ambience and gourmet ambitions. Dishes with local products are prepared with a silken touch, from chicken and duck to wild boar.

❶ Information

Casal dels Volcans (✆972 26 62 02; http://parcsnaturals.gencat.cat/ca/garrotxa; Parc Nou, Avinguda de Santa Coloma; ⏰10am-2pm & 4-6pm Mon-Sat, 10am-2pm Sun) Information about the Parc Natural de la Zona Volcànica de la Garrotxa.

Tourist Office (✆972 26 01 41; www.turismeolot.cat; Carrer Doctor Fàbregas 6; ⏰10am-1pm & 4-7pm Mon-Sat, 10am-2pm Sun) This brand-new tourist information centre has a slick, modern interior (tread carefully over that glass floor) and multilingual staff armed with maps and informative pamphlets galore.

❶ Getting There & Away

Teisa (www.teisa-bus.com) runs buses to/from Barcelona (€13.60 to €18.50, two to 2¼ hours, three to seven daily) and Girona via Besalú (€3.45, 45 minutes, seven to 12 daily). The easiest approach by car from Barcelona is by the AP7 and C63.

Parc Natural de la Zona Volcànica de la Garrotxa

The hills around Olot are volcanic in origin, making up the 120 sq km Parc Natural de la Zona Volcànica de la Garrotxa. Volcanic eruptions began here about 350,000 years ago, but the last one was 11,500 years ago. As the African and Eurasian tectonic plates nudge ever closer (at a rate of 2cm per year), the occasional mild earthquake still sends a shiver across Garrotxa. But the volcanoes have long snoozed under a blanket of meadows and oak forests.

The park completely surrounds Olot but the most interesting area is between Olot and the village of Santa Pau, 10km southeast. In the park there are about 40 volcanic cones, up to 160m high and 1.5km wide. Together with the lush vegetation, a result of fertile soils and a damp climate, these create a landscape of verdant beauty. Between the woods are crop fields, a few hamlets and scattered old stone farmhouses and Romanesque churches.

◉ Sights

Monestir de
Sant Joan les Fonts   MONASTERY

(www.turismesantjoanlesfonts.com; Sant Joan les Fonts; ⏰noon-2pm summer, noon-2pm Sat & Sun Sep-May) FREE This riverside monastery is tucked away at the northern end of Sant Joan les Fonts, 9km north of Olot. The church, with its distinctive bulge and stone belltower, dates to the 12th century. While opening hours to this imposing building are limited, its broad Romanesque form makes for a pleasant view if you want to pause between Olot and the dramatic cliffs of Castellfollit de la Roca.

🏃 Activities

There are 28 hiking routes around the natural park, most of which are clearly signposted. A number of easy walking trails lead directly from the car parks near Olot and Santa Pau to the volcanic cones. Inquire at the park information office Casal dels Volcans (p328) in Olot, where you can collect helpful hiking maps and info on trails. The basalt lava flows near the town of Sant Joan les Fonts are an especially stunning place to walk.

🛏 Sleeping

The biggest choice of accommodation is in Olot. Smaller towns Sant Joan les Fonts, Castellfollit de la Roca and Santa Pau each have a handful of guesthouses, plus there are camp sites within the natural-park area itself.

Camping Lava Ecològic CAMPGROUND €
(📞972 68 03 58; www.campinglava.com; Carretera Olot-Santa Pau, Km 7; car & tent/adult/child
€17/8/7; 🅿@🏊) This campground within
Garrotxa's *parc natural* has solid amenities,
including laundry facilities, hot showers and
internet, plus ample outdoor space, a pool
(summer only) and easy access to activities
including hiking trails and horse riding. For
those who abhor the great outdoors, there
are bungalows that sleep up to six people
(from €72).

Pensión Mont Roc PENSION €
(📞972 29 41 06; Carretera Olot-Girona, Castellfollit de la Roca; 🅿❄🛜) This relaxing guesthouse with snug rooms and somewhat
old-fashioned decor has an unbeatable view
of the town of Castellfollit de la Roca tee-
tering on the edge of a cliff. The restaurant
downstairs serves Catalan cuisine overlooking the spectacular scenery.

ⓘ Getting There & Away

Teisa (www.teisa-bus.com) runs buses from
Garrotxa's main hub Olot to Barcelona (€13.60
to €18.50, two to 2¼ hours, three to seven daily)
and Girona via Besalú (€3.45, 45 minutes, seven
to 12 daily). The easiest approach by car from
Barcelona is by the AP7 and C63 towards Olot.

ⓘ Getting Around

Garrotxa is best explored by rental car or bicycle. Public transport around the region is light,
but Teisa runs buses from Olot to Castellfollit
de la Roca via Sant Joan de les Fonts (€1.70, 15
minutes, two daily).

Ripoll

POP 10,751 / ELEV 691M

With an impressive monastery at Ripoll's
heart, and another close by in tiny Sant Joan
de les Abadesses, this otherwise unremarkable town is a worthy stopover for admirers
of Romanesque art.

Ripoll can claim, with some justice, to
be the birthplace of Catalonia. In the 9th
century it was the power base from which
local strongman Guifré el Pilós (Wilfred the
Hairy) succeeded in uniting several counties
of the Frankish March along the southern
side of the Pyrenees. Guifré went on to become the first in a line of hereditary counts
of Barcelona. To encourage repopulation of
the Pyrenean valleys, he founded the Monestir de Santa Maria, the most powerful
monastery of medieval Catalonia – and was
buried there after death.

Ripoll is well situated for rambling the
dormant volcanoes of Garrotxa, 30km east,
or the vertiginous hiking and skiing terrain
around the Vall de Ribes, 13km north.

⊙ Sights

⭐**Monestir de Santa Maria** MONASTERY
(www.monestirderipoll.cat; Plaça de l'Abat Oliba;
adult/child €5.50/2.75; ⊙10am-2pm & 4-7pm
Mon-Sat, 10am-2pm Sun Apr-Sep, 10am-1.30pm &
3.30-6pm Mon-Sat, 10am-2pm Sun Oct-Mar) Consecrated in AD 888, the Monestir de Santa
Maria was Catalonia's spiritual and cultural
heart from the mid-10th to mid-11th centuries. The five-naved basilica was adorned

CATALONIA RIPOLL

DON'T MISS

DRAGONS, GIANTS & BIG HEADS

Fire and fireworks play a big part in many Spanish festivals, but Catalonia adds a special
twist with the *correfoc* (fire-running), in which devil and dragon figures run through the
streets spitting fireworks at the crowds.

Correfocs are often part of the *festa major*, a town or village's main annual festival,
which usually takes place in July or August. Part of the *festa major* fun are the *sardana*
(Catalonia's national folk dance) and *gegants*, splendidly attired 5m-high giants that
parade through the streets or dance in the squares. Giants tend to come in male-
and-female pairs, such as a medieval king and queen. Almost every town and village
has its own pair, or up to six pairs, of giants. They're accompanied by grotesque 'dwarfs'
(known as *capsgrossos*, or 'big-heads').

On La Nit de Sant Joan (23 June), big bonfires burn at crossroads and town
squares in a combined midsummer and St John's Eve celebration, and fireworks ex-
plode all night. The supreme fire festival is the Patum in Berga, 30km west of Ripoll. An
evening of dancing and firework-spitting angels, devils, mulelike monsters, dwarfs, giants
and men covered in grass culminates in a mass frenzy of fire and smoke. Patum happens
on Corpus Christi (the Thursday 60 days after Easter Sunday).

Hiking the Pyrenees

The Pyrenees aren't Europe's highest mountains, but they might just be their most formidable. The craggy behemoths stretch from the Bay of Biscay to the Mediterranean like a giant unbroken wall with barely a low-level pass to break them. Spectacular for many reasons, not least the abundance of powerful waterfalls, they act like a siren's call for hikers.

The GR11

Anyone who has spent any time hiking in the Spanish Pyrenees will likely be on first-name terms with Gran Recorrido 11 (GR11), the region's most comprehensive long-distance footpath. It parallels the range in its entirety from Cap de Creus on the Costa Brava to Hondarribia on the Bay of Biscay. Measuring approximately 820km in length and with a cumulative elevation gain equivalent to five Mt Everests, most people sensibly elect to tackle the trail in short hops. Well-trammelled sections pass through the Valle de Ordesa near Torla and the Valle de Vallibierna close to Benasque.

Hiking Bases

The Spanish Pyrenees' two national parks, Ordesa y Monte Perdido in Aragón and Aigüestortes i Estany de Sant Maurici in Catalonia have a particularly high concentration of good hiking trails, with accommodation available in *refugios* (mountain shelters) or nearby villages. The former park is home to 3355m-high Monte Perdido, a tough ascent for well-equipped climbers, as well as easier hiking options such as the grunt up to the French frontier at Brecha de Rolando, or the popular Circo de Soaso, an

1. Hiker on the Gran Recorrido 11 long-distance footpath
2. Parque Nacional de Ordesa y Monte Perdido (p380)
3. Parc Nacional d'Aigüestortes i Estany de Sant Maurici (p339)

attractive day-hike to a waterfall. If you're super-fit, you can walk across Catalonia's Aigüestortes i Estany de Sant Maurici in one day along the show-stopping 25km Espot–Boí (east-west traverse). You'll need several days to complete the 55km **Carros de Foc** (www.carrosdefoc.cat) that links all nine of the park's *refugios*.

Other good hiking bases with places to stay and a nearby network of trails include the villages of Hecho and Torla in Aragon, or Taüll and Olot in Catalonia. The latter has good, family-friendly walking terrain.

Practicalities

The best time for walking is mid-June to early September, though the more popular parks and paths can be crowded in midsummer. The weather can be unpredictable, so walkers should always be prepared for extreme conditions. However,

since this is Europe (rather than Alaska), you're never too far from a village with basic shops and accommodation.

Dotted throughout the mountains are *refugios*. Some are staffed and serve meals, while others provide shelter only. At holiday times staffed *refugios* are often full, so unless you've booked ahead, be prepared to camp. The **Federación Aragonesa de Montañismo** (www.fam. es) in Zaragoza can provide information, and a FAM card will get you substantial discounts on *refugio* stays. For information on *refugios* in Catalonia, try the Barcelona-based **Federacio Enitats Excursionistes da Catalunya** (www.feec.org). **Editorial Alpina** (www.editorialalpina.com) produce excellent maps for walkers. For a definitive guide to the GR11, check out the Cicerone Guide *The GR11 Trail – La Senda* by Brian Johnson (2014).

SANT JOAN DE LES ABADESSE

Who gallops through the hills around Monestir de Sant Joan de les Abadesses (www.monestirsantjoanabadesses.cat; Plaça de l'Abadia; admission €3; ⏰10am-2pm & 4-6pm Mon-Sat Mar-Oct, 10am-2pm Mon-Sat Nov-Feb) on stormy nights, engulfed in flames and accompanied by ravenous black dogs? If you believe the stories, it's the legendary cursed Count Arnau, whose association with the Monestir de Sant Joan de les Abadesses has bequeathed it a heritage of brooding fairytales alongside its centuries of spiritual activity. The monastery is worth a visit for both its architectural treasures and the count's legend, richly illustrated in a permanent display.

Getting There & Away

Sant Joan de les Abadesses is 10km east of Ripoll on the N260 to Olot; there is a small free car park for tourists just north of the main road, signposted as you enter the town centre.

Teisa (www.teisa-bus.com) operates buses more than hourly weekdays and two-hourly at weekends from Ripoll (€1.95, 15 minutes).

---

in about 1100 with a stone portal that ranks among the most splendid Romanesque art in Spain. The well restored basilica interior has admirable floor mosaics, a display about the Bibles of Ripoll (rare illustrated manuscripts created between 1008 and 1020), plus the tomb of Guifré el Pilós, who founded the monastery.

🛏 Sleeping

Hostal Ripollès   HOSTAL €

(☑972 70 02 15; www.hostaldelripolles.com; Plaça Nova 11; s/d/tr from €33/47/66; 🛜) Within the town's medieval heart, this family establishment has decent en-suite rooms above a restaurant that whips up pizza, pasta and regional dishes. The decor may be grandmotherly, but the atmosphere is friendly and the location is excellent, mere steps from Ripoll's monastery and main square.

La Trobada   HOTEL €€

(☑972 70 23 53; www.latrobadahotel.com; Passeig del Compositor Honorat Vilamanyà 4; s/d/tr €40/65/85; 🅿🛜) Clean, simple and with polite, eager-to-please staff, La Trobada has Ripoll's most comfortable accommodation. Rooms are plain but well maintained, and many offer fine views towards the Monestir de Santa Maria. The restaurant downstairs serves simple Catalan fare for lunch and dinner. La Trobada is less than five minutes' walk from central Ripoll.

ℹ Information

Tourist Office (☑972 70 23 51; www.ripoll. cat/turisme; Plaça del Abat Oliba; ⏰10am-1.30pm & 3.30-6pm Mon-Sat, to 7pm summer, 10am-2pm Sun) Next door to the Monestir de Santa Maria. Opening hours vary seasonally.

ℹ Getting There & Away

Daily rodalies trains (line R3) run from Ripoll to Barcelona (€8.40, two hours, 12 to 16 daily) via Vic (€4.10, 40 minutes). Heading north from Ripoll, trains reach Ribes de Freser (€2.50, 20 minutes, up to seven daily) and Puigcerdà (€4.90, one hour, seven daily).

Vall de Núria & Ribes de Freser

A trio of little towns populate the Vall de Ribes and Vall de Núria, southeast of Cerdanya and north of Ripoll. Here spectacular ragged hills, pine forests and plummeting dales are squeezed between the Serra Cavallera and Serra de Montgrony ranges, rippling north to the Capçaleres del Ter i del Freser mountains.

Sheltered within the Vall de Ribes is the small but well-equipped town of Ribes de Freser, 13km north of Ripoll. A further 6km north lies Queralbs, a charming stone village perched at an altitude of 1180m. Beyond here, and accessible only by *cremallera* (rack railway), is Núria (1960m to 2252m). This lofty valley holds the sanctuary of the Mare de Déu de Núria icon, though in winter it draws as many winter-sports devotees as pilgrims. Reaching Núria by *cremallera* is a worthy day trip for its views alone: the train rattles past lichen-streaked rubble, waterfalls, patches of forest, and gaping valleys.

◉ Sights

★ Santuari de la Mare de Déu   CHURCH
(www.valldenuria.cat; Núria; ⊙8am-6.30pm)
FREE The sanctuary (1911) sits incongruously in the centre of a building (now a hotel)
that emits an unfortunate boarding-school
vibe. A pastel-painted passageway trimmed
with gold leads visitors from the main
church to the upper level, housing the Mare
de Déu de Núria behind a glass screen above
the altar. Mary, with a regal expression, sits
in star-spangled robes, clasping a grown-up
Jesus. The icon is in 12th-century Romanesque style, despite believers insisting that
Sant Gil sculpted it back in AD 700.

⚘ Activities

Núria Ski Resort   SKIING
(☑972 73 20 20; www.valldenuria.cat/hivern; day
lift pass with train adult/child €27/20.20; ⊙Dec-
Mar; ♠) In winter, Núria transforms into
a small-scale ski resort with 11 short runs.
Much of the terrain is geared towards beginners, though there are two red (intermediate) and black (advanced) slopes to keep
more experienced skiers and boarders busy
for an afternoon. There's also a separate
kids' activity area with tobogganing in winter and pony rides in summer.

🛌 Sleeping

Alberg Pic de l'Àliga   HOSTEL €
(☑972 73 20 48; www.xanascat.cat; Núria; dm
under/over 30yr incl breakfast €23/28; ⊙Jan-Sep)
Fancy a cheap sleep 2120m above sea level? This youth hostel in a spacious lodge is
perched at the top of the *telecabina* (cable
car) leading up from the Hotel Vall de Núria.
Dorm rooms sleep from three to 18 people
and it has a bar, board games and a common
room for mingling with other travellers.

The cable car (€1.50) runs from
9am to 6pm daily (to 7pm mid-July to
mid-September).

★ Hotel Els Caçadors   HOTEL €€
(☑972 72 70 77; www.cacadors.com; Carrer de
Balandrau 24, Ribes de Freser; s/d from €61/82;
⊙Dec-Oct; P✳🖘) Family-run since 1920,
this local institution has ample rooms in
three grades: 'bronze' has warm beige tones
and wood fittings, 'silver' ramps up the comfort with hydromassage tubs (some with
skylights for star-gazing), while 'gold' rooms
and suites are the most luxurious, aimed
at romantic getaways. There is a top-floor
lounge plus a deck where the Jacuzzi offers
mountain views.

Hostal les Roquetes   HOSTAL €€
(☑972 72 73 69; www.hostalroquetes.com; Carretera de Ribes 5, Queralbs; d €66-78; P🖘) This
comforting and scenically situated guesthouse is a few paces above the train station
in Queralbs, a great location for walking
or day trips up to Núria via the funicular.
Rooms are sizeable and clean, some with a
little terrace and inspiring mountain views.
Half-board options are available from the
restaurant downstairs.

ℹ Information

Núria Tourist Office (☑972 73 20 20; www.
valldenuria.com; Núria; ⊙8.30am-4.45pm)
This tourist info place within Núria's sanctuary
is open extended hours during high season.

Ribes de Freser Tourist Office (☑972 72 77
28; www.valldeiribes.cat; Carretera de Bruguera
2, Ribes de Freser; ⊙10am-2pm & 4-6pm Tue-
Thu, 10am-2pm & 4-7pm Fri & Sat, 10am-2pm
Sun) At the southern entrance to town, this
tourist information office offers advice on cultural sights, transport and trail maps. Opening
hours vary seasonally.

ℹ Getting There & Away

There are two train stations in Ribes de Freser.
Ribes-Enllaç, just south of town, has connecting
trains to Barcelona (€9.10, two to 2½ hours,
seven daily) and Ripoll (€2.50, 20 minutes,
seven daily).

The more centrally located Ribes-Vila is a **cremallera** (☑973 73 20 20; www.valldenuria.cat;
Ribes-Núria 1-way/return adult €14.25/22.80,
child €8.55/13.70) stop between lower station
Ribes-Enllaç and Queralbs, along the line to
Núria (which isn't reachable by car). These
trains run from Ribes de Freser to Núria via
Queralbs six to 12 times a day (35 minutes, 20
from Queralbs), depending on the season. There
are car parks at Ribes-Enllaç and Queralbs if you
are making a day trip to Núria via *cremallera*.

Cerdanya

Cerdanya, along with French Cerdagne
across the border, occupies a low-lying
green basin between the higher reaches of
the Pyrenees to the east and west. Although
Cerdanya and Cerdagne, once a single Catalan county, were divided by the Treaty of the
Pyrenees in 1659, Catalan is spoken on both
sides of the border and Spain flows seamlessly into France.

Puigcerdà

POP 8761 / ELEV 1202M

Barely 2km from France, Puigcerdà (puh-cher-*da*) dates back to the 12th century – not that you'd know it, since it lost most of its historical buildings during the civil war. The town's not much more than a way-station, but it's a jolly one, teeming with hikers in summer and used as a base by skiers during the winter season. A dozen Spanish, Andorran and French ski resorts lie within 45km.

Sights

Estany de Puigcerdà
LAKE

The *estany* (lake) in the north of town was created during the 13th century for irrigation purposes. Today it's a superb spot for a stroll: rowing boats and birdlife bob across its surface in summer, while winter amplifies the majesty of the snow-streaked mountains visible from the shore. The lake is surrounded by turn-of-the-20th-century summer houses, built by wealthy Barcelona families.

Església de Santa Maria
TOWER

(Plaça de Santa Maria) Only the tower remains of the 17th-century Església de Santa Maria. Nonetheless this stocky Romanesque structure dominates lively Plaça Santa Maria, and a tourist information office is within.

Sleeping

Sant Marc
CASA RURAL €€

(972 88 00 07; www.santmarc.es; Camí de Sant Marc 34; d/f from €81/145; P🐾🛜🏊) Extensive tree-lined grounds and down-filled duvets on plush beds greet you at this *casa rural* 2km south of Puigcerdà's town centre. The wood-floored rooms are spacious and decorated in soothing creams and the stone-walled restaurant specialises in dishes that make maximum use of local meats and cheeses. It has ample outdoor space to snooze in, horses to ride, and a bottle of *cava* in your room comes as standard. Book at least a couple of days ahead.

★ Villa Paulita
HISTORIC HOTEL €€€

(972 88 46 22; www.villapaulitahotel.com; Avinguda Pons i Gasch 15; d €110-200; P@🛜🏊) The fairytale towers of this bright-red 19th-century manor house signal the town's most charming and luxurious accommodation. It offers a good spa complex (included),

friendly and professional service, and an excellent restaurant with vistas over the lake. Check the website for seasonal closures.

Eating

Pop a button for local speciality *trinxat*, a fried flan of potato and cabbage, garnished with strips of crisp pork belly. *Cargols* (snails) are also popular in this region. For its size, Puigcerdà has a very good selection of fine dining and casual tapas options, many of which cluster around Plaça Santa Maria and along Carrer Alfons I.

La Caixeta
TAPAS €

(www.facebook.com/caixetabistro; Carrer Querol 22; dishes €4-12; ⊙11am-2am Wed-Mon) You're never quite sure which side of the border you're on here. A cheerful cafe-bar with artful hipster decor, this place does cupcakes and cocktails, as well as generous glasses of French wine, and deli-style tapas that run from foie gras and camembert to Catalan charcuterie.

★ TapaNyam
CATALAN €€

(972 88 23 60; http://tapanyam.es; Plaça de l'Alguer 2; mains €8-12; ⊙1-11pm Wed-Sun, to 5pm Mon) Pair crisp sauvignon blanc with equally invigorating views at TapaNyam. Outdoor diners at this friendly restaurant can enjoy a panorama of Puigcerdà's slate rooftops and green meadows that stretch right to the Pyrenees. Feast on local favourites like *trinxat* (potato and cabbage with a pork garnish), grilled snails or rabbit with garlic mayonnaise, or graze on tapas of mussels, octopus and mountain cheeses; whatever your hunger level, you're sure to raise a glass to the tremendous view.

El Caliu
CATALAN €€

(972 14 08 25; Carrer Alfons 1; mains €8-14; ⊙1-3.30pm & 8.30-11pm Thu-Mon, 1-3pm Tue) Dishes at this well-respected restaurant have an emphasis on local ingredients; try the Catalan-style pizza with goat's cheese, confit duck or *pastís de bolets*, a rich pâté of seasonal mushrooms.

Information

Tourist Office (972 88 05 42; Plaça Santa Maria; ⊙9.30am-1.30pm & 4.30-7.30pm Mon-Fri, 10am-1.30pm & 5-7.30pm Sat, 10am-1.30pm Sun) Friendly tourist office in central Puigcerdà, located within a historic tower.

❶ Getting There & Away

The bus and train stations are at the foot of the hill, just southwest of central Puigcerdà.

ALSA (www.alsa.es) buses run to/from Barcelona (€20.40, three hours, one or two daily) and La Seu d'Urgell (€6.90, one hour, four to six daily).

From Barcelona, the C16 approaches Puigcerdà through the Túnel del Cadí. Puigcerdà is also reachable via the picturesque N260 from Ribes de Freser. The main crossing into France is at Bourg-Madame, immediately east of Puigcerdà.

Rodalies trains run from Barcelona to Puigcerdà (€12, 2½ to three hours, six daily) via Vic, Ripoll and Ribes de Freser. Four to five a day continue across the border to Latour-de-Carol, where you can connect to the French network.

Llívia

POP 1536 / ELEV 1224M

Look twice at your map of the Spain–France border. Just 6km northeast of Puigcerdà, amid verdant meadows and little French villages, is Llívia, a tiny bastion of Catalonia beyond the main border between France and Spain. Under the 1659 Treaty of the Pyrenees, Spain ceded 33 villages to France, but Llívia was a 'town' and so, together with the 13 sq km of its municipality, remained a Spanish possession. Much more than just a cartographical oddity, this small town has a charming medieval centre and more excellent restaurants than you might expect for its size. The majority of visitors arrive to hike the hills during summer, and to access ski resorts on the Spanish and French sides of the Pyrenees.

◉ Sights

Llívia's few sights lie in its tiny medieval nucleus near the top of town, including the entertaining Museu Municipal and the 15th-century Gothic Església de Mara de Déu dels Àngels, which has three defensive towers around it. The ruined castle above the town is little more than wall remnants; find hiking trail maps for the surrounding area in the tourist office.

Museu Municipal   MUSEUM
(Carrer dels Forns 4; adult/child €3/1; ◎10am-6pm Tue-Fri, 10am-8pm Sat, 10am-2pm Sun) Inside what's alleged to be the world's oldest pharmacy building (dating to 1415) unfurls the region's history from Neolithic to modern day. The highlight is a curiosity chest of mortars and pestles, ancient maps and bottles of unguents linked to the medieval pharmacy.

🛏 Sleeping & Eating

Hotel Esquirol   HOTEL €€
(☑972 89 63 03; www.hotelesquirol.net; Avinguda Catalunya; s/d €60/70) This excellent hotel has the feel of a mountain lodge, with stone walls, wooden eaves and the odd pair of historic skis adorning the walls, but it's only 300m from the town centre. Hotel Esquirol's 19 rooms have a homey feel, many with wooden ceilings and floral quilts, while the service is efficient but friendly. Book ahead on the website for discounts.

★ Can Ventura   CATALAN €€
(☑972 89 61 78; www.canventura.com; Plaça Major 1; mains €14-20; ◎1.30-3.30pm & 8-10.30pm Wed-Sun) Beautifully prepared Catalan food with a whisper of French flair. Aptly for a restaurant within a 1791 building, traditional Catalan flavours have pride of place, like grilled octopus, slow-cooked lamb and smoky *trinxat*, but you'll also taste hints of Asian fusion. Desserts like a silky mousse of *fromage blanc* (sweet white cheese) and

CATALONIA CERDANYA

WORTH A TRIP

SERRA DEL CADÍ

The spectacular Serra del Cadí offers a string of picturesque villages and mountains that offer excellent walking for those suitably equipped and experienced. The range's most spectacular peak is **Pedraforca** ('Stone Pitchfork', 2497m), which offers the most challenging rock climbing in Catalonia, while the main Cadí range, part of **Parc Natural Cadí-Moixeró**, has a number of staffed refuges in the park for serious multiday hikes.

The villages used as jumping-off points for exploring the area are strung along the picturesque B400, which runs west from the Barcelona-bound C16 from Puigcerdà to La Seu d'Urgell on the C14. These include **Saldes**, **Gósol**, picturesque **Josa del Cadí,** and **Tuixent**. The valley makes a spectacular drive too, a longer but super-scenic route between Puigcerdà and La Seu d'Urgell.

bilberries, or steamy chocolate fondant, are an irresistible finish.

ⓘ Getting There & Away

Four to eight ALSA (www.alsa.es) buses run from Puigcerdà to Llívia daily (€1.70, 20 minutes).

La Molina & Masella

These ski resorts lie either side of Tosa d'Alp (2537m), 15km south of Puigcerdà, and are linked by the Alp 2500 lift. La Molina and Masella Ski Resorts (www.lamolina.cat; day lift pass adult/child €41/31; ⊙9am-4pm late Nov-late Apr) have a combined total of 135km of runs of all grades at altitudes of 1600m to over 2500m. Rental equipment and ski schools are available at both resorts; La Molina is better for beginners. Lift passes cover the whole area. In the summer, La Molina caters to adrenalin junkies with its mountain-bike park, quad-biking and more.

🛏 Sleeping

Alberg Mare de Déu de les Neus HOSTEL €
(☑972 89 20 12; www.xanascat.cat; La Molina; dm under/over 30 incl breakfast €18/22; ⓟ@🏠) At the bottom part of La Molina, near the train station and 4km from the slopes, this handy youth hostel is far and away the cheapest place to stay. Rooms range from twin to eight-bed dorms; there's a small supplement for en-suite dorms. The atmosphere is efficient though convivial. There are ski lockers and you can buy hot meals. Call ahead: the timing of seasonal closures can vary.

Hotel Adserà HOTEL €€
(☑972 89 20 01; www.hoteladsera.com; Carrer Pere Adserà, La Molina; s/d/tr/q incl breakfast €78/130/162/195; ⊙Nov-Easter & Jul-Aug; ⓟ@🏠🏊) This homey hotel in a stone building offers a personal touch and historic charm unlike many of the region's resort choices. Just 2.5km below the slopes, this hotel is an excellent choice for families with its rotating daily activities for kids, plus a games room, garden and pool. Rooms are compact and simple, and the staff are bursting not only with skiing advice (ask about piste pass discounts) but suggestions for summer activities too.

ⓘ Getting There & Away

In the ski season there's a bus service from Puigcerdà to the ski area plus infrequent daily services from Llívia via Puigcerdà to La Molina's telecabina (cable car; 7.40am), and regular buses from La Molina town (€2) up to the slopes. The easiest driving route from Barcelona is by the C58 toll road and the C16 through the Túnel del Cadí.

La Seu d'Urgell

POP 12,366 / ELEV 691M

The lively valley town of La Seu d'Urgell (la *se*-u dur-*zhey*) is Spain's gateway to Andorra, 10km to the north. La Seu has an attractive medieval centre, watched over by an admirable Romanesque cathedral. When the Franks evicted the Muslims from this part of the Pyrenees in the early 9th century, they made La Seu a bishopric and capital of the counts of Urgell; it remains an important market and cathedral town.

ⓞ Sights

★**Catedral de Santa Maria & Museu Diocesà** CATHEDRAL, MUSEUM
(adult/child €3/free; ⊙10am-1.30pm year-round, plus 4-6pm mid-Mar–May & mid-Sep–Oct, 4-7.30pm Jun–mid-Sep) Dominating La Seu d'Urgell's old town on the southern side of Plaça dels Oms is the 12th-century Catedral de Santa Maria. This pale sandstone cathedral complex is one of Catalonia's outstanding Romanesque buildings. Its neat cloister is rich in characterful carved capitals depicting mythical beasts and grimacing gargoyles. The superb attached museum (which follows the cathedral's opening hours) has a wealth of Romanesque frescoes from various churches, as well as a copy of the 10th-century Beatus de Liébana, king among medieval illustrated manuscripts.

🛏 Sleeping

Casa Rural La Vall del Cadí CASA RURAL €
(☑973 35 03 90; www.valldelcadi.com; Carretera de Tuixén; s/d €49/55; ⓟ❄🏠) Barely a 1km walk south of the centre and across the Segre River, you are in another, protected, bucolic world in this stone country house on a working family-run farm (and it smells as such!). Cosy rooms, with terracotta floors, iron bedsteads and, in some cases, timber ceiling beams, have a nice winter detail – underfloor heating. Some rooms share bathrooms.

Hotel Andria HISTORIC HOTEL €€
(☑973 35 03 00; www.hotelandria.com; Passeig Joan Brudieu 24; s/d incl breakfast from €66/88; ⓟ❄🏠) This welcoming hotel in a building

dating to 1876 has a more refreshing feel than its competition, with a flower garden, terrace and romantic restaurant. Rooms vary in size but are all comfortable, with a charming decor of wooden beams and antique fittings. With advance warning, the hotel's excellent restaurant can cater admirably for dietary requirements from vegetarian to gluten-free.

Parador de La Seu d'Urgell HISTORIC HOTEL €€
(☑ 973 35 20 00; www.parador.es; Carrer de Sant Domènec 6; d from €80) While not as palatial as some of Spain's *paradores* (state-run hotels in heritage buildings), this pleasing hotel has plain, modern rooms surrounding an elegant cloister, whose stone archways are illuminated pink and green at night. Right by La Seu d'Urgell's cathedral, there's no better location to soak up the atmosphere of the medieval town centre.

Eating

Restaurant Ignasi CREPERIE, FRENCH €€
(restaurant.ignasi@hotmail.com; Carrer de Capdevila 17; mains €10-14; ⊙ 1-4pm & 8.30-10.30pm Tue-Sun) This lively restaurant within brightly coloured walls has *galettes* (buckwheat pancakes) as its speciality, along with French mountain favourites like *tartiflette* (a bake of potatoes, onions, bacon and rich Reblochon cheese) and risotto of meaty boletus mushrooms. Service can be slow in this popular spot, but it's always with a smile.

Les Tres Portes CATALAN €€
(Avinguda Joan Garriga i Massó 7; mains €8-19; ⊙ 1.15-3.30pm & 8.30-10.30pm Thu-Sun) Fill your belly with seasonal flavours, small tasting plates of Andalucian squid and *patatas bravas* (potatoes in a spicy tomato sauce), or a hearty range of Catalan favourites like *cargols* (snails) and grilled rabbit. The restaurant interior is warm and brightly decorated, while the tranquil garden is perfect for summer dining.

Drinking & Nightlife

Glops COCKTAIL BAR
(www.glops.com.es; Carrer Canonges 64; ⊙ 5.30pm-12.30am Tue-Thu, 5.30pm-2.45am Fri & Sat, 5-11.30pm Sun) This delightful cocktail bar is an enjoyably edgy contrast to the medieval centre of La Seu d'Urgell. Neon lights brighten the stone walls, decorated with miscellany from antique cameras and hand-drawn caricatures of the staff to African masks and fairy lights. But the wonderful mixed drinks (€5 to €8) will seize your attention, from inventive mojitos to gin cocktails piled high with forest fruits.

ℹ Information

Tourist Office (☑ 973 35 15 11; www.turisme seu.com; Carrer Major 8; ⊙ 10am-2pm & 4-7pm Mon-Sat, 10am-1pm Sun) Helpful office across the street from the cathedral has a leaflet on historical walks and a display on city history. Extended hours in high season.

ℹ Getting There & Away

The bus station is on the northern edge of the old town. ALSA (www.alsa.es) runs buses to Barcelona (€28.25, three to 3½ hours, five daily), Puigcerdà (€6.90, one hour, four to six daily) and Lleida (€19.25, 2¼ hours, two to three daily).

Pallars Sobirà

The Riu Noguera Pallaresa tumbles south from the heights of the Val d'Aran, the pristine scenery of Pallars Sobirà extending from both sides. West of the river lies the Parc Nacional Aigüestortes i Estany de Sant Maurici; to its east, the vast Parc Natural de

CATALONIA PALLARS SOBIRÀ

WORTH A TRIP

ANDORRA

If you're on the lookout for great hiking or skiing, are keen to stock up on duty-free booze, smokes or electronics, or just want to say you've been in a different country, then the curious nation of Andorra, just 10km north of Seu d'Urgell, is for you. At only 468 sq km, it's one of Europe's smallest countries and, though it has a democratic parliament, the nominal heads of state are two co-princes: the bishop of Urgell in Spain, and the President of France. Catalan is the official tongue, though Spanish, French and, due to a large immigrant workforce, Portuguese are widely spoken. Regular buses run from Seu d'Urgell to the busy capital, Andorra la Vella. If driving, make sure to fuel up in Andorra, as it's significantly cheaper. There's rarely any passport control, though you may well be stopped by customs on the way back into Spain, so don't go over the duty-free limit.

l'Alt Pirineu, spangled with lonely Romanesque churches among which weave hiking trails.

The river itself draws rafters and other adventure-sports enthusiasts to the small towns along its banks, principally (from north to south) Llavorsí, Rialp and Sort. Each of these towns is well-equipped with accommodation, cafes and restaurants, though outside the March to October season, they are very quiet.

Activities

The Riu Noguera Pallaresa's grade IV drops attract a constant stream of white-water fans between mid-March and mid-October. It's usually at its best in May and June.

The best stretch is the 12km from Llavorsí to Rialp, on which the standard raft outing costs around €41 per person for two hours. Longer rides to Sort and beyond will cost more, and Sort is the jumping-off point for the river's tougher grade IV rapids.

In Llavorsí, there are several rafting operators, most of whom offer a full range of summer activities including kayaking, canyoning, horse riding, rock-climbing and canoeing as well as some winter programs. Operators include Roc Roi (973 62 20 35; www.rocroi.com; Plaça Biuse 8, Llavorsí; 1hr rafting from €38; mid-Mar–mid-Oct), Rafting Llavorsí (973 62 21 58; http://raftingllavorsi.cat; Camí de Riberies, Llavorsí; half-day rafting €60) and, for more experienced rafters, Yeti Emotions (973 62 22 01; www.yetiemotions.com; Carrer de Borda Era d'Alfons, Llavorsí). For rafting, bring your own swimming costume

WORTH A TRIP

PYRENEAN BACK ROADS

As beautiful and dramatic as Vall de la Noguera Pallaresa and Val d'Aran are, they can certainly feel rather overrun in summertime by rafters and hikers. If you're looking for solitude and adventure off the beaten track, take the B-roads up into the hills northeast of Llavorsí and Esterri d'Àneu, or else north of Vielha, leading to some remote and, in parts, tough mountain-walking country along and across the Andorran and French borders. Highlights include glacial lakes and the ascent of the Pica d'Estats (3143m), the highest peak in Catalonia.

and towel and a change of clothes; other equipment provided.

Skipallars SKIING

(973 62 11 99; www.skipallars.cat; day pass from €25.60) The ski areas of Port Ainé and Espot, both in the Pallars Sobirà region of the Pyrenees, have 70km of piste to ski or snowboard. A single ski pass allows access to both, plus the Tavascan area in the Parc Natural de l'Alt Pirineu.

Sleeping

Hotel Victor HOTEL €

(973 62 03 79; www.hotel-victor.es; Avenida Flora Cadena 35, Rialp; d/tr incl breakfast €64/92;) Located in central Rialp on the main road running between Llavorsí and Sort, family-run Hotel Victor is as good a base for summer rafters as for winter ski trips. Rooms are clean, cosy and jazzily furbished. Staff can help arrange ski passes, and ski storage is available.

Hostal Noguera HOSTAL €

(973 62 20 12; www.hostalnoguera.info; Carretera Vall d'Aran, Llavorsí; s/d €34/60;) This stone building, on the southern edge of the village, has pleasant rooms overlooking the river, whose cascading noise will lull you to sleep. The downstairs restaurant has unremarkable but filling local specialities like fried eggs swimming in ratatouille, spicy Cuban-style rice and grilled meats.

Hotel Pessets HOTEL €€

(973 62 00 00; www.hotelpessets.com; Avinguda de la Diputació 3, Sort; d/ste incl breakfast from €99/130;) At this wellness-focused hotel, lodgings range from simple neutral-toned double rooms to chic suites with naturalist prints and wood-panelled ceilings. The highlights are the spa area complete with both indoor and outdoor pools (though the latter is seasonal) and a private outdoor chill-out area with mountain views.

Information

Tourist Office (973 62 10 02; www.pallarssobira.info; Camí de la Cabanera, Sort; 10am-2pm Sun-Thu, 10am-2pm & 4-7pm Fri & Sat) The main tourist office for the area is in Sort. This information centre is packed to the rafters with all the maps and trail info you'll ever need, supplied by helpful, multilingual staff.

Parc Nacional d'Aigüestortes i Estany de Sant Maurici

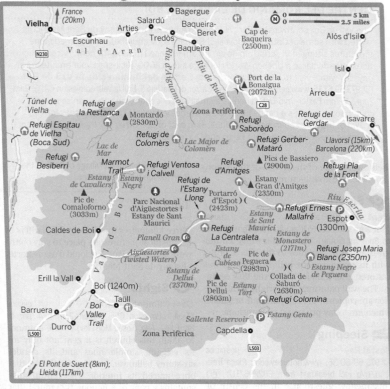

ⓘ Getting There & Away

ALSA (www.alsa.es) runs buses to Llavorsí via Sort and Rialp from Barcelona (€36, one daily, five hours) and Lleida (€11.60, three to four daily, three hours). On-demand transport runs between La Seu d'Urgell and Sort (€4, twice daily, one hour). Call **Viatges Matí** (📞689 495777) to book this.

Parc Nacional d'Aigüestortes i Estany de Sant Maurici & Around

Catalonia's only national park extends 20km east to west, and only 9km from north to south. But the rugged terrain within this small area sparkles with more than 400 lakes and countless streams and waterfalls, combined with a backdrop of pine and fir forests, and open bush and grassland, bedecked with wildflowers in spring and fringed with scarlet leaves in autumn.

Created by glacial action over two million years, the park is essentially two east–west valleys at 1600m to 2000m altitudes lined by jagged 2600m to 2900m peaks of granite and slate.

The national park lies at the core of a wider wilderness area. The outer limit is known as the *zona periférica* and includes some magnificent high country to the north and south.

The main approaches are via the village of **Espot**, 4km east of the park and 8km away from **Estany de Sant Maurici** lake, and **Vall de Boí**, part of its western sector.

Boí

POP 973

The valley location of petite Boí draws trekkers and winter-sports lovers, while its

DON'T MISS

CENTRE DEL ROMÀNIC DE LA VALL DE BOÍ

The Vall de Boí, southwest of Parc Nacional d'Aigüestortes i Estany de Sant Maurici, is dotted with some of Catalonia's loveliest Romanesque churches – unadorned stone structures sitting in the crisp alpine air. Together these 11th- to 14th-century constructions were declared a Unesco World Heritage site in 2000. Kick-start your architectural odyssey with a visit to interpretation centre **Centre del Romànic de la Vall de Boí** (☑ 973 69 67 15; www.centreromanic.com; Carrer del Batalló 5, Erill la Vall; admission €2; ☻ 9am-2pm & 5-7pm Easter–mid-Oct). There is a small art collection, you can organise guided church tours, and it's a handy place to buy combined tickets (three churches for €7).

Two of the finest churches are in Taüll, 3km east of Boí. Other worthwhile Romanesque churches are at Barruera (Sant Feliu) and Durro (Nativitat).

belltower is one of the jewels of the region's Romanesque architecture.

◉ Sights

Sant Joan de Boí   CHURCH

(Boí; admission €2; ☻ 10am-2pm & 4-7pm Dec-Oct, to 8pm Jul & Aug) This 11th-century church gives an air of romance to the village of Boí with its angular stone belltower, which was restored after a major fire in the 13th century. The wall paintings that brighten the interior are copies of the Romanesque originals, which are today preserved in Barcelona.

🛏 Sleeping

Hostal Pey   HOSTAL €€

(☑ 973 69 60 36; www.hotelpey.com; Plaça Treio 4; d/tr/q incl breakfast from €82/96/117; 🅿) This mellow guesthouse in the centre of Boí has comfy, home-style rooms and a decent restaurant, plus ski storage and staff brimming with local advice. Book ahead; it's popular.

❶ Information

National Park Information Office (☑ 973 69 61 89; Carrer de les Graieres 2, Boí; ☻ 9am-2pm & 3.30-5.45pm Mon-Sat, 9am-2pm Sun) Find trekking and winter-sports information at this tourism hub.

❶ Getting There & Away

Buses between Barcelona/Lleida and Vielha stop at El Pont de Suert year-round. From here a daily bus runs to Boí (€1 to €1.75, 25 minutes), leaving in the afternoon on weekdays and in the morning on weekends. In summer, there's a daily park bus connecting Espot with Boí via Vielha.

There are also nine-person **taxis** (☑ 973 69 63 14; www.taxisvalldeboi.com; Plaça del Treio, Boí; 1-way Boí to Estany de Sant Maurici adult/child €5.25/3.25; ☻ 8am-7pm summer, 9am-6pm

rest of yr) between the village of Boí and the Parc Nacional d'Aigüestortes.

Taüll

POP 260

Three kilometres uphill from Boí, Taüll is by far the most picturesque place to stay on the west side of the Parc Nacional d'Aigüestortes i Estany de Sant Maurici.

◉ Sights

Sant Climent de Taüll   CHURCH

(Taüll; admission €5; ☻ 10am-2pm & 4-7pm, to 8pm Jul & Aug, closed Mon Nov) At the entrance to Taüll, this church is a gem not only for its elegant, simple lines and its slender six-storey belltower, but also for the art that once graced its interior. The central apse contains a copy of a famous 1123 mural that now resides in Barcelona's Museu Nacional d'Art de Catalunya. At the church's centre is a Pantocrator (Christ figure), whose rich Mozarabic-influenced colours, and expressive but superhuman features, have become a virtual emblem of Catalan Romanesque art. An audiovisual presentation gives background.

Santa Maria de Taüll   CHURCH

(Taüll; ☻ 10am-7pm) **FREE** Up in the old village centre of Taüll and crowned with a five-storey tower, the original artwork from this 11th-century church has been whisked away to Barcelona (like many of the churches in the region).

🏃 Activities

Boí-Taüll Ski Resort   SKIING

(www.boitaullresort.com; day-pass adult/child €39/29; ☻ Dec-early Apr) High up at altitudes from 2020m to 2751m, this medium-sized ski resort has 45km of pistes, including a few slopes suitable for beginners and plenty more to please intermediate and advanced skiers and snowboarders. There is also a freestyle area and snowpark for practising those jumps.

🛏 Sleeping & Eating

★ Alberg Taüll
HOSTEL €

(☎973 69 62 52; www.alberguetaull.com; Avenida Feixanes 5, Taüll; dm €23, d €38-48, ste €95; P 🛜) This is everything a hostel should be: the stylish rooms feature large beds with orthopaedic mattresses, there's underfloor heating for those crisp mornings, and the common area has a large map of the park to help you plan out your hikes. Families are welcome and there's good walking advice. Sheets and a towel cost an extra €4.50. Cheaper midweek; prices include breakfast.

Santa Maria
BOUTIQUE HOTEL €€

(☎973 69 61 70; www.taull.com; Plaça Cap del Riu 3, Taüll; s/d incl breakfast €75/94; P 🛜) Through a shady entrance a grand stone archway leads into the quiet courtyard of this rambling country haven with rose-draped balcony, run by congenial hosts. The rooms are tastefully furnished and the building, all stonework with a timber-and-slate roof, oozes timeless character. There's wi-fi in common areas. The hotel closes throughout November.

Sedona
INTERNATIONAL €

(☎973 69 62 54; Les Feixes 2, Taüll; main €10; ⊙noon-4pm & 7-11.30pm Tue-Sun; 🛜 🍴) Catalan fish dishes, Tex-Mex and mixed tapas pile the plates at this food and après-ski hangout.

❶ Getting There & Away

Buses reach Vielha from Barcelona (€34.87, five to six hours, seven daily) and Lleida (€13.87, 2½ to three hours, four or five daily) stop at El Pont de Suert year-round. From here, irregular local buses reach Taüll. Driving is a much better option.

Espot

POP 357

Scenic Espot is an excellent gateway to exploring the Parc Nacional d'Aigüestortes i Estany de Sant Maurici, which begins 4km west of this little town. Stone buildings add charm to Espot, which is well-equipped with places to eat and stay, while mountain views from the town centre will make you eager to lace up your hiking boots.

🛏 Sleeping & Eating

★ Roca Blanca
HOTEL €€

(☎973 62 41 56; www.hotelrocablanca.com; Carrer Església; d/ste incl breakfast €90/125; ⊙mid-Nov-end Oct; P 🛜) This cheerful hotel is beautifully well-maintained, from its 16 spacious rooms with modern bathrooms to the polished lounge with fireplace – also home to a dopey St Bernard named Homer Simpson. Contemporary art adorns the walls, and service is attentive and personal. It also has a gym, sauna, and relaxing garden space for you to rest your quads after a day spent hiking or skiing.

Restaurant Juquim
CATALAN €€

(☎973 62 40 09; Plaça San Martí 1; mains €11-20; ⊙12.45-4pm & 7.30-10.30pm, closed Tue mid-Oct-May) This popular spot on the main square has a varied menu concentrating largely on filling country food, with generous winter warmers like pig's trotters slathered in garlic and olive oil, or *civet de senglar* (wild boar stew). The adjacent bar (open 8am to 11pm Thursday to Tuesday) does simpler fare and sandwiches.

❶ Information

National Park Information Office (☎973 62 40 36; www.gencat.cat/parcs/aiguestortes; Carrer de Sant Maurici 5, Espot; ⊙9am-2pm & 3.30-5.45pm Mon-Sat, 9am-2pm Sun) Find hiking tips, maps, transport advice and more in this helpful tourist office in Espot.

❶ Getting There & Away

ALSA (www.alsa.es) buses from Barcelona (€38.50, five hours, one daily) and Lleida (€13.10, three hours, three daily) to Esterri d'Àneu stop at the Espot turn-off on the C13. From there it's a 7km uphill walk to Espot.

You can visit the Parc Nacional d'Aigüestortes with a little help from a fleet of 25 **4WDs** (☎973 62 41 05; www.taxisespot.com; 1-way Espot to Estany de Sant Maurici adult/child €5.25/3.25; ⊙8am-7pm summer, 9am-6pm rest of year) with fixed-rate tours to the park, lake and beyond.

Val d'Aran

Catalonia's northernmost region, famous for its plunging valleys and snowy peaks, is an adventure playground for skiers and snowboarders. Baqueira-Beret's pistes lure the winter-sports jet-set. Meanwhile, charming villages like Salardú enchant hikers with views of cloud-scraping mountains. From Aran's pretty side valleys, walkers can go over the mountains in any direction, notably southward to the Parc Nacional d'Aigüestortes i Estany de Sant Maurici.

It wasn't always this way: the Val d'Aran was an inaccessible outpost until the 1948 completion of a tunnel connecting the valley's main town Vielha to the rest of Spain. A surge of tourism development followed, allowing the world to experience this spectacular region of tumbling valleys dotted with stone-and-slate villages, many with notable Romanesque churches.

Thanks in part to its geography, Aran's native language is not Catalan but Aranese (*Aranés*), which is a dialect of Occitan or the *langue d'oc*, the old Romance language of southern France.

Vielha

POP 5474 / ELEV 974M

A sprawl of stone-and-slate houses, winter-sports shops and holiday apartments make up hectic Vielha, often used as a base for exploring the Val d'Aran. While it doesn't have the charisma of the valley's smaller towns, Vielha's tiny centre, anchored by the distinctive spire of Sant Miquèu church, is packed with rustic restaurants, especially along the banks of the gushing Riu Garona. Vielha's outdoor-gear shops, supermarkets and accommodation choices make it a good place to circle your wagons before hiking or skiing. It's best to have your own wheels: the Vall de Boí's trekking terrain is a 20-minute drive south, while Baqueira's ski resorts are 20 minutes east.

🛏 Sleeping & Eating

⭐ **Hotel El Ciervo** BOUTIQUE HOTEL €€
(☑ 973 64 01 65; www.hotelelciervo.net; Plaça de Sant Orenç 3; s/d incl breakfast €45/72; ☺ closed May–mid-Jun & mid-Oct–Nov; 🛜) Right in the centre of Vielha, this exceptionally welcoming hotel, a real departure from the mundane ski-town norm, feels like an alpine fairytale, with an exterior covered in paintings of trees and forest creatures and a delightfully cosy interior full of decorative touches. Each lovely room varies in style and feel but includes a hydromassage tub, and the breakfast spread is excellent. Good value, and even better midweek.

Hotel Ço de Pierra HOTEL €€
(☑ 973 64 13 34; www.hotelpierra.com; Carrèr Major 25; d incl breakfast €65-90; 🛜) In Betrén, a timeless village tacked on to the eastern end of Vielha's sprawl (1km walk from the centre of town), this gorgeous place respects the stone-and-slate pattern of traditional housing and its 10 rooms combine stone, timber and terracotta for warmth.

Restaurant Gustavo (Era Móla) CATALAN, FRENCH €€
(Carrèr de Marrèc 14; mains €14-19; ☺ 8-11pm Mon-Tue & Thu-Fri, 1-3.30pm & 8-11.30pm Sat & Sun Dec-Apr & Jul-Sep) One of the best restaurants in town. Expect carefully prepared local cooking with a heavy French hand, and savour the *solomillo de cerdo al Calvados* (pork fillet bathed in Calvados) and artistically arranged desserts.

ℹ Information

Tourist Office (☑ 973 64 01 10; www.visitval daran.com; Carrèr de Sarriulèra 10; ☺ 10am-1.30pm & 4.30-8pm Mon-Sat) This tourist-information point near Vielha's Sant Miquèu church operates longer hours in high season.

ℹ Getting There & Around

Buses reach Vielha from Barcelona (€34.87, five to six hours, seven daily) and Lleida (€13.87, 2½ three hours, four or five daily).

ALSA (www.alsa.es) runs regular buses from Vielha up the valley as far as Baqueira. Most travellers explore the region by car, though parking can be a problem. If you have no luck in the centre, there are often spaces north of the Mercadona supermarket along Avinguda Baile Calbeto Barra.

Arties

POP 400 / ELEV 1143M

Seven kilometres east of Vielha, this fetching village sits astride the confluence of the Garona and Valarties rivers. Arties' proximity to the upmarket Baqueira-Beret-Bonaigua ski area (just 6km east) has allowed upmarket hotels to flourish. The village snoozes outside peak summer and winter seasons, but is a pretty place to stop year-round: the balconies of its stone houses overflow with flowers while Romanesque **Església de Santa Maria**, with its three-storey belfry and triple apse, stands proudly in their midst.

ℹ Getting There & Away

Buses reach Arties from Vielha (€1.10, 20 minutes, hourly), via Salardú.

Salardú

POP 580 / ELEV 1267M

Glamorous Arties is 3km to its west, chic ski area Baqueira is 3km east, yet pint-sized Salardú retains a more rugged, outdoorsy ambience than its neighbours. Salardú welcomes hikers with its decent budget and midrange digs. The village's architectural highlight is the jaw-strainingly lovely Romanesque Sant Andreu church; don't miss exploring inside. The even dinkier village of Bagergue, a tranquil spot well suited to solitary treks and boasting glorious mountain views, lies 2km to Salardú's northeast.

◉ Sights

Església de Sant Andrèu   CHURCH
(Salardú; ⊙10am-2pm & 4-7pm) Within the remarkably colourful frescoed walls of this 12th- and 13th-century church, gaze upon the haunting form of the Crist de Salardú. This gaunt wooden sculpture of Jesus on the cross dates to the 13th century. Until 1649, Sant Andreu's sturdy belltower was a castle keep, though only the church and some ruined exterior castle walls remain today.

⌷ Sleeping

Refugi Rosta   REFUGE €
(☑973 64 53 08; www.refugirosta.com; Plaça Major 3; dm/d incl breakfast €26.50/73; ℙ⌆) Pyrenean mountain *refugis* are special, convivial places, and this creaky old building is one of the most characterful. There are no luxuries but there's plenty of good cheer, and the dormitories, with their typical side-by-side sleeping, are comfortable enough. Bring a sleeping bag or hire sheets and towels. The restaurant serves a cheap and hearty set menu.

Hotel Seixes   HOTEL €€
(☑973 64 54 06; www.seixes.com; Bagergue; s/d/tr/ste from €44/69/99/130; ⊙Apr-Nov; ℙ⌆) This hikers' favourite is situated within the sound of the pealing bell of Sant Feliu church in Bagergue, 2km north of Salardú. Its 17 rooms are comfortable though simple, and the location will appeal to nature lovers and solitude seekers. Staff are knowledgeable about local trekking routes.

❶ Getting There & Away

Buses reach Salardú from Vielha (€1.10, 20 minutes, hourly).

WORTH A TRIP

CATALONIA'S TOP SKI RESORT

Pound the pistes at **Baqueira-Beret-Bonaigua Ski Resort** (www.baqueira.es; day lift pass adult/child €49/27.50; ⊙late Nov-early Apr), Catalonia's top winter-sports resort, beloved of Spanish royals, European celebrities and loyal skiers. Its quality lift system gives access to pistes totalling around 150km (larger than any other Spanish resort), amid fine scenery at between 1500m and 2510m.

CENTRAL CATALONIA

Vic

POP 41,956

This feisty Catalonian town combines dreamy medieval architecture with youthful energy. Remarkably restored Roman ruins and jazzy Modernista houses add to a spirited mix of architectural styles, while Plaça Major smoulders with a palette of ochre and brick-red mansions. The old quarter has meandering laneways that bypass chapels and cosy restaurants.

Despite its resolutely Catalan political outlook, the town is very multicultural; meanwhile its university keeps an activist buzz in the air. A day trip from Barcelona is enough to take in Vic's cathedral and the superb museum, plus a restaurant or two, but a longer stay allows time to get lost amid the street art and medieval alleyways.

◉ Sights

Plaça Major, the largest square in Catalonia, has a pleasing medley of medieval, baroque and Modernista architecture. A crop of cafes spill onto the square. It's also the site of Vic's twice-weekly **market** (Tuesday and Saturday mornings), which sells local food and cheap clothing. Around it swirl the narrow streets of medieval Vic, lined with mansions, churches and a 1st-century **Roman temple**, painstakingly restored during the 19th and 20th centuries.

★ Museu Episcopal   GALLERY
(www.museuepiscopalvic.com; Plaça Bisbe Oliba 3; adult/child over 10 €7/3.50; ⊙10am-1pm & 3-6pm Tue-Fri, 10am-7pm Sat, 10am-2pm Sun) This museum holds a marvellous collection

of Romanesque and Gothic art, second only to the Museu Nacional d'Art de Catalunya collection in Barcelona. The Romanesque collection depicts some strikingly gory images – from saints being beheaded or tortured to the Archangel Michael spearing a devil through his jaw. The Gothic collection contains works by such key figures as Lluís Borrassà and Jaume Huguet. Opens longer hours in high season. Arrive one hour before closing time to visit.

Catedral de Sant Pere   CATHEDRAL

(Plaça de la Catedral; adult/child €2/free; ⊙10am-1pm & 4-7pm) Centuries of styles clash in Vic's impressive cathedral. Most of the neoclassical exterior was built during the 18th century, but the Romanesque belltower is one of few remnants dating to the 11th century. Within, the Stations of the Cross are animated in colourful World War II–era frescoes, while Corinthian columns glow bronze in the darkness. Entrance to the cathedral itself is free – the listed prices apply to the cloisters, crypt and *retaule* (altarpiece).

🎆 Festivals & Events

Mercat de Ram   EASTER MARKET

(www.vicfires.cat) In the week running up to Palm Sunday, Plaça Major hosts the Mercat del Ram (Palm Market, a tradition that goes back to AD 875), selling palms and laurels. This agricultural fiesta showcases everything from tractors to equestrian displays, as well as local cheeses by the cartful. Rambla del Carme and Rambla del Passeig along the northern border of the old town fill with stalls selling cured meats, cheeses, *coca* (Easter cake) and other fantastic regional produce.

Mercat de Música Viva   MUSIC

(www.mmvv.net) The town hosts the Mercat de Música Viva, a big if somewhat chaotic event, over several days in late September in which Catalan, national and foreign acts of various schools of Latin rock, pop and jazz get together to jam in locations around the city. Plan in advance via the website or find the information point off Plaça Major.

🛏 Sleeping

Estació del Nord   HOTEL €

(☑935 16 62 92; www.estaciodelnord.com; Plaça de l'Estació 4; s/d €50/60; [P][❄][🛜]) Lodgings above a train station seldom inspire, but this family-run hotel goes against expectations. The owners are warm and accommodating,

but they run a tight ship: rooms are immaculately clean, service is efficient, and the 14 rooms are well-maintained and soundproofed. There's free parking at a location nearby.

Seminari Allotjaments   GUESTHOUSE €€

(☑938 86 15 55; www.seminarivic.cat; Ronda Francesc Camprodon 2; s/d/tr/q incl breakfast €56/71/83/110; [P][❄][🛜]) Everything functions like clockwork at this modern guesthouse within a former seminary, 500m north of Vic's Plaça Major. Rooms are furnished simply and decorated in bold primary colours, spread across a cavernous seminary complex surrounding a courtyard (ideal for pensive strolls). It has a student ambience, but it's spotless, the staff are helpful and there is on-site parking (€7).

★ El Jardinet   CATALAN €€

(☑938 86 28 77; www.eljardinetdevic.com; Carrer de Corretgers 8; mains €18-23; ⊙1-3.30pm & 8.30-11pm Tue-Sat, 1-3.30pm Sun; [🛜]) This warm-hearted restaurant has been perfecting Catalan cuisine since 1980, making it one of the best choices in town. There's an exceedingly good choice of mains, including a tower of *trinxat* and salads draped in melting goat's cheese. The artistically presented desserts resemble a surrealist sketch. Diners can choose between El Jardinet's minimalist interior or outdoor space.

❶ Information

Tourist Office (☑938 86 20 91; www.victurisme.cat; Plaça del Pes; ⊙10am-2pm & 4-8pm Mon-Fri, 10am-2pm & 4-7pm Sat, 10.30am-1.30pm Sun) Just off Plaça Major within the town hall building, this tourist office has friendly, multilingual staff who can offer a host of suggestions about exploring Vic and the surrounding area. The interior also has some exhibits on Catalan culture plus a small selection of souvenirs.

❶ Getting There & Away

Regular rodalies trains (line R3) run from Barcelona (€6.15, one to 1½ hours).

Montserrat

Montserrat, 50km northwest of Barcelona, is at the heart of Catalan identity for its mountain, monastery and the natural park weaving among its distinctive rock formations. Montserrat mountain is instantly recognisable for its rock formations, sculpted over millennia by wind and frost. These turrets of rock, a coarse conglomerate of limestone and eroded fragments, extend like gnarled fingers from its 1236m-high bulk. More than halfway up the mountain lies the Benedictine Monestir de Montserrat, home to the Black Virgin, one of Spain's most revered icons. Extending from this sacred spot is the Parc Natural de de la Muntanya de Montserrat, superlative hiking terrain where brooks tumble into ravines and lookout points boast panoramas of rocky pillars

Montserrat (often used interchangeably to mean the monastery and mountain) is a very popular day-trip from Barcelona. The monastery complex throngs with visitors, but serenity can be found on the walking trails or by staying overnight.

History

The monastery (p345) – Spain's second most important pilgrimage centre after Santiago – was founded in 1025. Most of the complex was built around the Virgen de Montserrat, a stunning icon dating to the 12th century (though traditionalists declare it was carved by St Luke and hidden by St Peter in the mountains). The monastery was wrecked by Napoleon's troops in 1811, then largely abandoned as a result of anti-clerical legislation in the 1830s, and slowly rebuilt from 1858. Today a community of a few dozen monks lives here. Pilgrims come from far and wide to venerate the Virgen de Montserrat, affectionately known as La Moreneta ('the Little Brown One' or 'the Black Madonna'), a Romanesque dark wooden sculpture of a regal-looking Mary holding the infant Jesus on her lap, holding a globe, which pilgrims come to touch. She has been Catalonia's patroness since 1881 and her blessing is particularly sought by newlyweds. Colourful legends have sprung up around this holy place, including a folk tale that described jagged Montserrat mountain as sawn by angels to make a throne for the Virgin Mary.

Sights

Monestir de Montserrat MONASTERY
(www.abadiamontserrat.net; basilica 7.30-10.30am & 12.15-6.15pm) Catalonia's most renowned monastery was founded in 1025 to commemorate visions of the Virgin Mary, accompanied by celestial light and a chorus of holy music, experienced by shepherds. The monastery complex encompasses two

blocks: on one side, the basilica and monastery buildings (housing a religious community of more than 100), and on the other, facilities for tourists and pilgrims. Admirable monastery architecture in Plaça de Santa Maria includes a gleaming late-19th-century facade depicting St George and St Benedict in relief, and 15th-century cloisters.

Basilica CHURCH
(www.abadiamontserrat.net; 7.30am-8pm) FREE The open courtyard in front of the basilica immediately sets an impressive tone, with marbled floors and art nouveau–style frescoes visible between elegant archways. The basilica's brick facade features carvings of Christ and the 12 Apostles, dating to the early 20th century. Beyond its heavy doors, the interior glitters with white marble and gold, a blend of Renaissance and Catalan styles.

Cambril de la Mare de Déu CHURCH
(7-10.30am & 12.15-6.15pm) FREE Follow signs to the Cambril de la Mare de Déu to the right of Montserrat's main basilica entrance to see the 'Black Virgin', a revered 12th-century statue of the Virgin Mary with Jesus seated on her knee.

Museu de Montserrat MUSEUM
(www.museudemontserrat.com; Plaça de Santa Maria; adult/student €7/6, €11 with Espai Audiovisual; 10am-5.45pm Mon-Fri, 10am-6.45pm Sat & Sun) This museum has an excellent collection, ranging from an Egyptian mummy and Gothic altarpieces to fine canvases by Caravaggio, El Greco, Picasso and several Impressionists, as well as a comprehensive collection of 20th-century classic Catalan art and some fantastic Orthodox icons.

Activities

Beyond the touristic hubbub surrounding Montserrat's monastery and basilica, there's tranquillity to be found in the web of walking trails across the mountain. Take the **Funicular de Sant Joan** (1-way/return €2.40/3.70; every 20min 10am-4.50pm) for the first 250m uphill from the monastery; alternatively, it's a 45-minute walk along the road between the funicular's bottom and top stations. From the top, it's a further 20-minute stroll (signposted) to the Sant Joan chapel, with fine westward views.

More exciting is the one-hour walk northwest, along a path marked with some blobs of yellow paint, to Montserrat's highest peak, Sant Jeroni, from where there's a sheer drop on the north face. The walk takes you across the upper part of the mountain, with a close-up experience of some of the rock pillars. Before setting out, check ahead with the Information Office (p346) regarding weather and trail conditions, wear good walking boots, and bring water.

🛏 Sleeping

Hotel Abat Cisneros   HOTEL €€
(✆938 77 77 01; www.montserratvisita.com; s/d incl breakfast €63.75/109.90; 🅿🛜) The only hotel in the monastery complex has a superb location next to the basilica. Rooms are comfortable though simple; some make up for the spartan decor with views overlooking Plaça de Santa Maria. There are also inexpensive basic apartments and family packages available. Its restaurant serves imaginative Catalonian dishes (mains €17 to €20).

☆ Entertainment

Escolanía de Montserrat   CHORAL MUSIC
(www.escolania.cat; ⊗performances 1pm Mon-Thu, 11am Sun, 6.45pm Sun-Thu) The clear voices of one of Europe's oldest boys' choirs have echoed through the basilica since the 14th century. The choir performs briefly on most days (except school holidays), singing *Virolai*, written by Catalonia's national poet Jacint Verdaguer, and *Salve Regina*. The 53 *escolanets*, aged between nine and 14, go to boarding school in Montserrat and must endure a two-year selection process to join the choir. Check performance times on the website.

ℹ Information

Information Office (✆938 77 77 77; www. montserratvisita.com; ⊗9am-5.45pm Mon-Fri, 9am-8pm Sat & Sun) Located in the monastery, this information point has details on the monastery complex and walking trails around Montserrat. Hours vary by season.

ℹ Getting There & Away

The R5 line trains operated by FGC (www.fgc. net) run half-hourly to hourly from Barcelona's Plaça d'Espanya station. Services start at 6.36am (one hour), but take the 8.36am to connect with the first AERI **cable car** (✆938 35 00 05; www.aerimontserrat.com; 1-way/return €7/10; ⊗9.40am-7pm, closed mid-late Jan) from the Montserrat Aeri stop (every 15 minutes from 9.40am to 7pm, five minutes, operating

shorter hours from November to February). Alternatively take the **cremallera** (✆902 31 20 20; www.cremallerademontserrat.com; 1-way/ return €6.30/10) train up to the monastery from the following R5 stop, Monistrol de Montserrat. There are various train/*cremallera* combo tickets available.

By car, take the C16 from Barcelona, then the C58 shortly after Terrassa, followed by the C55 to Monistrol de Montserrat. You can leave your vehicle at the free car park and take the *cremallera* up to the top or drive up and park (cars €6.50).

Cardona
POP 4921

Long before arrival, you spy in the distance the outline of an impregnable 18th-century fortress high above Cardona. Once ruled by the self-styled 'Lords of Salt', who brought Cardona wealth by mining the Muntanya de Sal (mountain of salt), today the castle (now housing a *parador* – a sumptuous state-owned hotel) lures tourists to admire its stocky watchtowers and Romanesque church. Aside from this standout attraction, Cardona is a sleepy place, best experienced as an atmospheric day-trip or stopover between Barcelona and the Pyrenees.

◉ Sights

Castell de Cardona   CASTLE
FREE Visible long before entering Cardona, this fortress tops a hill that broods above the modern town. From this strategic position, centuries of noblemen have kept a watchful eye over Cardona's *Muntanya de Sal* (Salt Mountain), the 'white gold' that gave Cardona its wealth. The ramparts have panoramic views of the vast Lleida plain; the loftiest vantage point is the Torre de la Minyona. It's free to wander around the castle, but sights within the complex have separate admission charges.

Església de Sant Vicenç   CHURCH
(Castell de Cardona; adult/child €3.50/2.50; ⊗10am-1pm & 3-5pm Tue-Sun, to 7pm Jun-Sep) This Romanesque church within Cardona's castle complex has an elegant stone-walled interior. The vaulted crypt, dedicated to St James, is a stopping point for pilgrims plying the French Way of St James route to Santiago de Compostela. Buy tickets to the church in the tourist information booth within the castle complex and staff will unlock the door.

🛏 Sleeping & Eating

⭐ **Parador Ducs de Cardona** HISTORIC HOTEL €€

(📞938 69 12 75; www.parador.es; d incl breakfast €115; P ✱ @ 🛜) Rooms are within an adjoining modern building, but that doesn't dim the magic of staying at this *parador* within the medieval Castell de Cardona. Lodgings are large and comfortable, many with exceptional views over Cardona. Common areas are resplendent with antique furnishings and display cases of historic finery. The highlight is breakfasting under the Gothic arches of a converted monks' refectory.

⭐ **La Volta del Rector** MODERN EUROPEAN €€€

(📞938 69 16 37; http://lavoltadelrector.cat; Carrer de les Flors 4; mains from €18; ⊘1.30-3pm & 8-11pm Tue-Sun; 🍴) Dine like a duke in the heart of medieval Cardona. Twelfth-century stone walls mix with wild violet decor at La Volta del Rector, where the atmosphere is rustic, romantic and hip all at once. Dishes, from grills to wild game and salmon carpaccio, are whipped up with flair, while a wine list of the region's best drops is accompanied by enthusiastic recommendations.

ℹ Getting There & Away

Cardona is served by ALSA buses from Barcelona (€12.85, two hours, two to four daily) and Manresa (€4.40, one hour, hourly Monday to Friday, three daily at weekends).

The bus station is just north of the tourist office by the side of the BV3001 road.

Lleida

POP 138,416

Lleida's battletorn history has faded into memory, replaced by a pacey, workaday vibe. During the 14th and 15th centuries, this arid, inland city was a centre of economic activity, fed in part by Jewish and Muslim communities. Culture and art flourished, thanks to surrounding monasteries and a university founded in 1300. Relics of the holy cloth and thorns made Lleida's cathedral a revered stopping point on the Way of St James pilgrimage route.

Battle lines were drawn here across Catalonia's history, with Lleida nearly always backing the losing side. The old town was reduced to rubble during the War of the Spanish Succession. The conquerors built a citadel to protect their new acquisitions, only for it to be sacked by the French in 1812.

CATALONIA'S HUMAN CASTLES

Among the strangest spectacles in Catalonia are *castells*, or human 'castles'. This sport originated in Valls, 20km north of Tarragona, in the 18th century and has since spread to other parts of the region. It involves teams of *castellers* standing on each other's shoulders with a death-defying child scrambling up the side of the human tower to perch at the top before the whole structure gracefully disassembles itself. Towers can reach up to nine levels high – don't try this at home. For the most spectacular *castells*, pay a visit to Tarragona's Festival of Santa Tecla (p357) in mid-September.

The fortress-cathedral crowning the city, La Seu Vella, evokes Lleida's former grandeur, while a scattering of museums and Modernista buildings offer reasons to linger.

👁 Sights

⭐ **La Seu Vella** CATHEDRAL

(www.turoseuvella.cat; cathedral/cathedral plus tower €7/5; ⊘10am-1.30pm & 3-5.30pm Tue-Fri, 10am-5.30pm Sat, 10am-3pm Sun) Lleida's 'old cathedral', enclosed within a later fortress complex, towers above the city from its commanding hilltop location. Work began on the cathedral in 1203, though today it is a masterpiece of the Transitional style, with bold Romanesque forms complemented by Gothic vaults and elaborate tracery. The octagonal bell tower, crowned with Gothic flourishes, rises at the southwest end of the beautiful cloisters, a forest of slender columns from which you can gaze at expansive views over Lleida.

Church of Sant Llorenç CHURCH

(Plaça Sant Josep; ⊘9.30am-12.30pm & 5-8pm Mon-Fri, 10am-1.30pm & 5-8pm Sat & Sun) FREE This well-refurbished 12th-century Romanesque church is worth admiring for its elegant octagonal belltower and the gargoyles leaping from its eaves.

Museu de Lleida MUSEUM

(www.museudelleida.cat; Carrer del Sant Crist 1; adult/child €5/2.50; ⊘10am-2pm & 4-6pm Tue-Thu & Sat, 10am-2pm Fri & Sun) This expansive museum brings together artefacts reaching back to the Stone Age, through

CATALONIA LLEIDA

CISTERCIAN ROUTE

A combined ticket gives access to three monasteries on the Cistercian Route (Ruta del Cister; www.larutadelcister.info; combined 3-monastery ticket €12), plus discounts on other regional museums. Tackling all three in a single day-trip from Tarragona is doable if you start early, but it requires careful timing: some visits are by irregular guided tours only. Start with Santa Maria de Poblet (whose long lunch hour can disrupt day-trip schedules), before heading to Reial Monestir de Santes Creus. Finish with Santa Maria de Vallbona de les Monges, the latest closing of the trio.

Reial Monestir de Santes Creus (Plaça de Jaume el Just, Santes Creus; adult/senior & student €4.50/3.50; ⊙10am-6.30pm Jun-Sep, 10am-5pm Oct-May) An atmosphere of awe descends before entering the monastery, in broad Plaça de Sant Bernat Calbó: its mix of architectural styles spans six centuries, including retired monks' quarters and an ornamental 18th-century fountain. Behind the monastery's Romanesque and Gothic facade lies a 14th-century sandstone cloister, a 12th-century chapter house whose ceiling ripples with rib-shaped vaults, a cavernous dormitory, and royal apartments where the comtes-reis (count-kings; rulers of the joint state of Catalonia and Aragón) often stayed. There's also a church, whose construction began in the 12th century.

Reial Monestir de Santa Maria de Poblet (www.poblet.cat; Vimbodí-Poblet; adult/student €7.50/4.50; ⊙10am-12.30pm & 3-5.30pm Mon-Sat, 10.30am-12.30pm & 3-5.30pm Sun) The largest monastery of the Cistercian Route, Unesco-listed Santa Maria de Poblet was founded by monks from southern France in 1150. It rose rapidly to become Catalonia's most powerful monastery. Highlights include the mostly Gothic main cloister and the alabaster sculptural treasures of the Panteón de los Reyes (Kings' Pantheon). The raised alabaster sarcophagi contain such greats as Jaume I (the conqueror of Mallorca and Valencia) and Pere III. Entry is strictly by semi-guided tours (Catalan and Spanish), which operate every 20 minutes during opening hours.

Reial Monestir de Santa Maria de Vallbona de les Monges (⌨973 33 02 66; www.monestirvallbona.cat; Carrer Major, Vallbona de les Monges; adult/child €4/1; ⊙10.30am-1.30pm & 4.30-6.45pm Tue-Sat, noon-1.30pm & 4.30-6.45pm Sun Mar-Oct, closes 5.30pm rest of year) A dozen monges (nuns) still live and pray at this 12th-century institution, the only women's monastery along the Cistercian Route. The monastery has undergone years of restoration, which has finally cleared up most of the remaining civil-war damage. Queen Violant of Hungary, a queen consort of Aragon and formidable political influencer, is entombed within (note the bilingual plaque outside the monastery in Catalan and Hungarian). Visits are by guided tour (Spanish or Catalan).

Fèlix Hotel (⌨977 60 90 90; http://felixhotel.net; Ctra N240, Km 17, Valls; s/d €54/62; P🐾) This comfortable, if slightly creaky, hotel has rooms as cosy and ample as the welcome. It's well located for monastery-hopping along the Cistercian Route and also makes an excellent alternative to staying in central Tarragona (with free parking to boot). Fèlix Hotel is 17km north of Tarragona in quiet Valls.

Roman remains and medieval art into the 19th century. Highlights include the atmospherically lit collection of medieval religious sculptures and the delicate 1st- to 5th-century mosaics from the El Romeral mansion, a patchwork of peacock feathers and leaves.

Castell de Gardeny CASTLE
(Turó de Gardeny; adult/child €2.60/1.60; ⊙10am-1.30pm Sat & Sun) The Knights Templar built a monastery complex here short-

ly after Lleida was taken from the Muslims in 1149. It was later expanded into a fortress in the 17th century. Today you can still see the original Romanesque Església de Santa Maria de Gardeny and a hefty tower. An imaginative audiovisual display (in Spanish or Catalan) lends visitors insight into the monastic life of the Knights Templar.

This historic site is a 2km walk southwest from La Seu Vella.

Museu d'Art Jaume Morera   GALLERY
(http://mmorera.paeria.es; ⊙noon-2pm & 5-8pm Tue-Sat, 11am-2pm Sun) **FREE** This impressive collection of Catalan art focuses particularly on work by Lleida-associated artists, such as the surrealist sculptures by Leandre Cristòfol, with excellent temporary photography exhibitions held here as well.

★ Festivals & Events

Aplec del Cargol   FOOD
(http://aplec.org; ⊙late May) Munch on molluscs at Lleida's annual snail-eating festival.

🛏 Sleeping & Eating

Hotel Real   HOTEL €
(☑973 23 94 05; www.hotelreallleida.com; Avinguda de Blondel 22; r €41-56; P❈🔊) A modern mid-rise place, business-oriented Hotel Real overlooks the river near the train and bus stations. The rooms are bright and clean; the better ones have generous balconies and all have decent bathrooms. Very good value.

Hotel Zenit   HOTEL €€
(☑973 22 91 91; http://lleida.zenithoteles.com; Carrer General Brito 21; d/tr from €62/82; P❈🔊) This business-focused hotel is somewhat bland, but makes up for it with comfortable rooms in a simple palette of beige and white, good wi-fi speed, and helpful multilingual staff. It's well-located to explore the city, with La Seu Vella and Lleida's museums barely a 10-minute stroll from the hotel. Parking costs an additional €10.

El Cau de Sant Llorenç   CATALAN €€
(☑973 28 91 63; www.elcaudesantllorenc.com; Plaça Sant Josep 4; mains €14-19; ⊙1-3.30pm & 9-11.30pm Tue-Sat, 1-3.30pm Sun) On a quiet night, it's all rather hush-hush in this old-town corner. But once you get buzzed in, it's as if you've entered a private club: excellent service, elegant contemporary decor and smartly presented modern Catalan cuisine.

★ **l'estel de la Mercè**   CATALAN, FUSION €€€
(☑973 28 80 08; www.lesteldelamerce.com; Carrer Cardenal Cisneros 30; mains €16-25; ⊙1-4pm & 8.30-11.30pm Wed-Sat, 1-4pm Tue & Sun) A 1.5km walk from central Lleida, this sleek fine-dining place creates fusion dishes using fresh seasonal produce. Feast on the likes of crispy suckling pig terrine with orange and cloves, Asian-inspired fish dishes like tuna on crispy rice, and strawberries flambéed with pepper.

ℹ Information

Tourist Office (☑973 70 03 19; www.turisme delleida.cat; Carrer Major 31; ⊙10am-1.30pm & 4-7pm Mon-Sat, 10am-1pm Sun) This friendly tourist office on the main pedestrian street has maps and local tips galore. There's another branch in the cathedral complex, whose opening hours follow those of La Seu Vella (10am to 1.30pm and 4pm to 7pm Monday to Saturday, 10am to 1pm Sunday).

ℹ Getting There & Away

From the centrally located **bus station** (off Avenida Blondel), southwest of the old town, off Avenida Blondel, regular services include Zaragoza (€11.38, 1¾ to 2½ hours, three to five daily), Barcelona and El Prat airport (€21, two to 3¼ hours, 12 to 18 daily); Vielha (€13.87, 2½ to three hours, seven to nine daily) and La Seu d'Urgell (€19.25, 2¼ hours, four daily).

Regular trains reach Barcelona from Lleida (€17.65 to €42.60, one hour), with some proceeding to Madrid (€51.15 to €123.20, two hours, 10 daily) via Zaragoza (€14.85 to €27.10, one hour).

COSTA DAURADA & AROUND

Sitges

POP 28,171

Just 35km along the coast southwest of Barcelona, Sitges sizzles with beach life, nightclubs and an enviable clutch of festivals. Sitges has been a resort town since the 19th century, and was a key location for the Modernisme movement, which paved the way for the likes of Picasso. These days it's Spain's most famous gay holiday destination. In July and August the town cranks up the volume to become one big beach party, while Carnaval unbridles Sitges' hedonistic side. But despite bacchanalian nightlife, Sitges remains a classy destination: its array of galleries and museums belie its small size, there's a good sprinkling of upmarket restaurants in its historic centre, and an October film festival draws culture fiends from miles around. The town is quieter during the off-season, but you can still experience a taste of nightlife and culture.

◉ Sights

The most beautiful part of Sitges is the headland area, where noble Modernista palaces

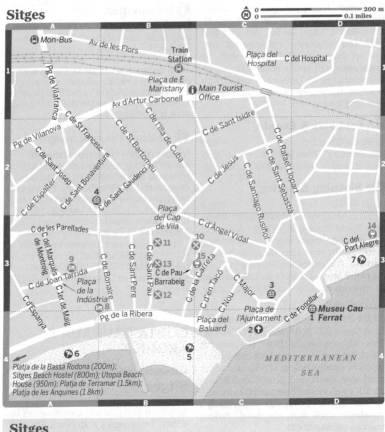

Sitges

Sitges

and mansions strike poses in the streets around the striking Església de Sant Bartomeu i Santa Tecla (p351), with the blue sea as a backdrop.

★ **Museu Cau Ferrat**   MUSEUM
(www.museusdesitges.cat; Carrer de Fonollar; incl Museu Maricel adult/reduced €10/7; ☺10am-7pm Tue-Sun) Built in the 1890s as a house-cum-studio by artist Santiago Rusiñol, a pioneer of the Modernisme movement, this mansion is crammed with his own art and that of his contemporaries, including his friend Picasso, as well as his own collection of ancient relics and antiques. The visual feast is piled

high, from Grecian urns and a 15th-century baptismal font to 18th-century tilework that glitters all the way to the floral-painted wood-beamed ceiling.

Fundació Stämpfli Art Contemporani
GALLERY

(www.fundacio-stampfli.org; Plaça de l'Ajuntament 13; adult/child €5/3.50; ⏰3.30-7pm Fri, 10am-2pm & 5-7pm Sat, 11am-3pm Sun) Within an old wood-beamed fish-market building is this slick 20th-century art gallery. White-washed walls and shiny tiled floors draw all eyes to the primary colours of bold pop art and modern art within. Pucker up for Peter Stämpfli's *Rouge baiser* (an enormous cerise pair of lips), alongside works by Arroyo, Cueco and other greats. The lower floor has rotating temporary exhibitions. The museum runs extended hours in high season.

Museu Romàntic
MUSEUM

(www.museusdesitges.cat; Carrer de Sant Gaudenci 1) Housed in a late-18th-century Can Llopis mansion, this faded museum recreates with its furnishings and dioramas the lifestyle of a 19th-century Catalan landowning family. Closed for renovations during our visit, the museum was due to reopen in 2016.

Església de Sant Bartomeu i Santa Tecla
CHURCH

(Plaça de l'Ajuntament) Sitges' most striking landmark is this 17th-century parish church, sitting proudly on a rocky elevation that separates the 2km-long main beach to the southwest from the smaller, quieter Platja de Sant Sebastià to the northeast. Opening hours vary.

🏖 Beaches

The main beach is flanked by the attractive seafront Passeig Maritim, dotted with *chiringuitos* (beachside bars) and divided into nine sections with different names by a series of breakwaters. West of the centre, Anquines and Terramar beaches have paddleboat rental and deck chairs during the summer. East of the headland find St Sebastià, Balmins and fine brown-sanded D'aiguadolç beaches. Though Bassa Rodona used to be the unofficial 'gay beach', gay sunbathers are now spread out pretty evenly, while Balmins is the sheltered bay favoured by nudists.

Platja de la Ribera
BEACH

One of Sitges' more popular places to soak up the sun.

Platja de la Fragata
BEACH

Lively Sitges beach close to Sant Bartomeu church.

🎎 Festivals & Events

Carnaval
CARNIVAL

(www.carnavaldesitges.com) Carnaval in Sitges is a week-long booze-soaked riot made for extroverts and exhibitionists, complete with masked balls and capped by extravagant gay parades held on the Sunday and the Tuesday night, featuring flamboyantly dressed drag queens, giant sound systems and a wild all-night party with bars staying open until dawn. Dates change from year to year; check the website.

Festa Major
TOWN FESTIVAL

(www.sitgesfestamajor.cat) The town's Festa Major, held over six days in mid-August in honour of Sitges' patron saint, features a huge fireworks display on the 23rd as well as numerous processions, *sardanas* (*sardanes* in Catalan; traditional dances) and fire-breathing beasts.

International Film Festival
FILM

(Festival Internacional de Cinema Fantàstic de Catalunya; www.sitgesfilmfestival.com) Early October brings the world's best festival of fantasy and horror films. Cutting-edge sci-fi and blood-curdling cinema is shown in venues across Sitges. Book tickets for individual showings if possible, as the best sell out in advance. But you can still rock up to ticket booths and get lucky on the day.

🛏 Sleeping

Utopia Beach House
HOSTEL, HOTEL €

(☑938 11 11 36; www.utopiasitges.com; Carrer Socias 22; dm/d from €12/32; 🛜) Tucked away from Passeig Maritim and a short walk from the beach, this bubbly place has a choice of pastel-painted dorm rooms, double rooms with private bathrooms, and apartments (available from June to September). It has a cheerful bar area amid a leafy garden, a colourful hangout lounge with mini-library, laundry facilities (€3), noticeboards with local tips, and everything you need for a fun-packed stay.

Parrots Hotel
HOTEL €€

(☑938 94 13 50; www.parrotshotel.com; Calle de Joan Tarrida 16; d €99-130; ⏰mid-Feb–Oct;

❋ @ 🛜) It's hard to miss this bright-blue gay hotel. Courteous staff usher you towards thoroughly modern rooms with cable TV and air-con, there are balconies for people-watching, and a sauna to get steamy in. It's right in the heart of the action.

Sitges Beach Hostel
HOSTEL €€

(📳 938 94 62 74; www.sitgesbeachhostel.com; Calle Anselm Clavé 9; dm/d €35/66; ☉ mid-Jan-mid-Dec; ❋ 🛜) This breezy place sits near the beach, a five-minute walk west of the centre. Comfortable dorms are pricey, but you get plenty for your euro, with cheap meals available, plenty of outdoor terrace and balcony space to relax in, plus a sociable lounge.

Hotel Platjador
HOTEL €€

(📳 938 94 50 54; www.hotelsitges.com; Passeig de la Ribera 35; s/d €107/134; ❋ @ 🛜 ❄) This welcoming seafront hotel has fabulous rooms (many with balconies) featuring enormous plush beds and mountains of pillows. It has an indoor pool and there's a rooftop bar overlooking the sea. It's superb value off-season.

✖ Eating

Lady Green
VEGETARIAN €€

(Carrer de Sant Pau 11; mains €9-12; ☉ 7-11pm Wed & Fri, 1-4pm & 7-11pm Thu, Sat & Sun; 📳) Zucchini noodles glistening with pesto, zesty Mexican platters and delectable American-style cheesecake: this vegetarian cafe will satisfy even the most demanding tastebuds with inventive meat-free dishes and wonderful desserts. There are also choices for vegan and gluten-free diners, plus a range of invigorating fresh juices and smoothies.

El Pou
TAPAS €€

(www.elpoudesitges.com; Carrer de Sant Pau 5; dishes €4-10; ☉ 1.30-4pm & 8-11.30pm Thu-Sun, 8-11.30pm Mon & Wed; 🛜) Tiny Wagyu beef burgers, meatballs with cuttlefish, and classics like anchovies and local cheese crowd tables at this friendly gourmet tapas place. The presentation delights the eye as much as the flavours delight the palate.

La Salseta
CATALAN €€

(📳 938 11 04 19; www.lasalseta.com; Carrer de Sant Pau 35; mains €12-19; ☉ 1-3.30pm & 8.30-11.30pm Wed-Sat, Tue & Sun 1-3.30pm) 🍃 Slow food and seasonal produce dominate the menu of this homey restaurant, with crisp pig's feet with Catalan blood sausage, succulent Penedès chicken and a range of paella dishes the highlights of a thoroughly satisfying menu.

eF & Gi
FUSION €€€

(📳 938 11 33 07; Carrer Major 33; mains €18-25; ☉ 1-4pm & 8-11.30pm Wed-Mon Mar-Jan; 🛜) Fabio and Greg (eF & Gi) are not afraid to experiment and the results are startlingly good: the mostly Mediterranean menu, with touches of Asian inspiration, throws out such delights as chargrilled beef infused with lemongrass and kaffir lime, and tuna loin encrusted with peanuts and kalamata olives with mango chutney. Don't skip the dessert, either.

☕ Drinking & Nightlife

Much of Sitges' nightlife happens on one short pedestrian strip packed night-long in summer: Carrer 1er de Maig aka Calle del Pecado (Sin Street), Plaça de la Indústria and Carrer Marquès de Montroig, all in a

---

CATALAN WINE

Throughout two-and-a-half millennia of wine production, it's safe to say Catalonia has had time to finesse its local drops. With the days of Roman vineyards and medieval monastery wine-making long past, modern Catalonia now has 12 *denominaciones de origen* (DO) and has birthed boozy innovations like sparkling *cava*.

Penedès' wine country is justly famous for these Champagne-style sparkling wines, ranging in taste from dry and flinty to sweet, plus fruity whites from Macabeo, Xarel·lo and other varietals. Other notable wine-making zones include Priorat, which produces aromatic, full-bodied reds, particularly from *cariñena* (carignan) and *garnacha* (grenache) grapes, and Costers del Segre, which comprises several fairly distinct subregions and produces quality whites and reds from a wide variety of grapes including macabeo, chardonnay, monastrell and cabernet sauvignon. The Raimat subregion is particularly worthy of attention. Wine tourism here has seen recent investment, with new routes allowing you to tour vineyards by jeep or bicycle; learn more on www.catalunya.com/what-to-do/enoturism.

short line off the seafront, though most bars shut by around 3.30am. All-night revellers are drawn to the clubs just outside of town; the popular ones change name regularly, but you'll soon find out what is trendy this summer.

★ **Casablanca**   BAR
(Carrer Pau Barrabeig 5; ⊙8pm-2am Thu-Sat, Tue-Sun in high season) This cocktail-driven bar exudes nostalgia with its old-timey soundtrack, bygone Hollywood stars crowding its walls and vintage furnishings. A selection of classy cocktails are stirred with aplomb by seasoned staff who extend an exuberant welcome to newcomers.

★ **Bar Voramar**   BAR
(www.pub-voramar.com; Carrer del Port Alegre 55; ⊙4.30pm-1am Thu-Tue) On Platja de Sant Sebastià, this is a fabulous old-time bar decked out like a ship playing flamenco, jazz and more. It does brilliant caipirinhas, mojitos and more. The chummy booth seating is a Sitges classic.

ℹ Information

Main Tourist Office (☑938 94 42 51; www. sitgestur.cat; Plaça de E Maristany 2; ⊙10am-2pm & 4-6.30pm Mon-Sat, 10am-2pm Sun) Information office by the train station. Opens until 8pm during high season (except Sundays).

ℹ Getting There & Away

From about 5am to 10pm regular R2 rodalies trains run to Barcelona's Passeig de Gràcia and Estació Sants (€4.10, 45 minutes). You can reach Barcelona airport by changing at El Prat de Llobregat. **Buses** (www.monbus.cat) also run to the airport from Passeig de Vilafranca (€6.50, 35 minutes, half-hourly to hourly).

Penedès Wine Country

Some of Spain's finest wines come from the Penedès plains southwest of Barcelona. Sant Sadurní d'Anoia, located about 35km west of Barcelona, is the capital of *cava*, a sparkling, champagne-style wine popular worldwide, and glugged across Spain, particularly at Christmas. Vilafranca del Penedès, 12km further southwest, is an attractive historical town and the heart of the Penedès Denominació de Origen (DO; Denomination of Origin) region, which produces noteworthy light whites and some very tasty reds.

Sant Sadurní d'Anoia
POP 12,590

One hundred or so wineries around Sant Sadurní make it the centre of *cava*, made by the same method as French champagne. Beyond the popping corks in Sant Sadurní's surrounds, the town is a sleepy place, though it has a rich calendar of food and wine festivals.

🏃 Activities

Freixenet   WINERY
(☑938 91 70 96; www.freixenet.com; Carrer de Joan Sala 2, Sant Sadurní d'Anoia; adult/child 9-17 €7.50/4.50; ⊙1½hr tours 10am-1pm & 3-4.30pm Mon-Thu, 10am-1pm Fri-Sun) The biggest *cava*-producing company, easily accessible next to the Sant Sadurní train station. Book ahead for visits that include a tour of its 1920s cellar, a spin on the tourist train around the property and samples of its *cava*. If you don't book a tour, you can still sample top fizz and platters of ham and nibbles in the atmospheric tasting room.

ℹ Information

Tourist Office (☑938 91 31 88; http:// turismesantsadurni.com; Carrer Hospital 23; ⊙9.15am-2.45pm & 4-6.30pm Tue-Fri, 10am-2pm & 4.30-7pm Sat, 10am-2pm Sun) Learn about food festivals and book winery tours and more at this information office.

ℹ Getting There & Away

Rodalies trains run from Barcelona's Estació Sants to Sant Sadurní (€4.10, 45 minutes, half-hourly). By car, take the A2 north from Barcelona follow signs west at Martorell.

Vilafranca del Penedès
POP 39,221

To experience Penedès wine country without attaching yourself to a long guided tour or renting a car (a burden, if you want to sip greedily), base yourself in Vilafranca. Livelier than Sant Sadurní, the town spreads over quite an area, but its centre has uplifting medieval architecture and a seam of truly excellent restaurants with wine lists to match. Vineyard excursions are easy to organise from here, and the town makes a charming (though fattening) weekend break.

◉ Sights

Vinseum   MUSEUM
(Museu de les Cultures del Vi de Catalunya; www. vinseum.cat; Plaça de Jaume I 5; adult/child €7/4;

TASTING IN PENEDES

It's easier to get around the wine country if you have your own wheels, though several companies run tours of the wineries from Barcelona (which can be a good option, if you're intent on serious wine sampling). Visitors are welcome to tour several of the region's wineries, though advance booking is essential in most places. The more enthusiastic ones will show you how *cava* and/or other wines are made and finish off with a glass or two. Tours generally last about 1½ hours and some may only be in Catalan and/ or Spanish.

Browse www.dopenedes.es and www.enoturismepenedes.cat for more wine-tourism options.

Codorníu (☑ 93 891 33 42; www.codorniu.es; Avinguda de Jaume Codorníu, Sant Sadurní d'Anoia; adult/child €9/6; ☺ 9am-5pm Mon-Fri, to 1pm Sat & Sun) There is no more glorious spot to quaff sparkling wine than the vaulted interior of Codorníu's palatial Modernista headquarters, at the entry to Sant Sadurní d'Anoia when coming by road from Barcelona. Codorníu's wine-making activities are said to be documented right back to the 16th century. Manuel Raventós, credited with bringing this wine-maker into the big time during the late 19th century, was the first to create sparkling Spanish wine by the Champagne method back in 1872.

Giró Ribot (☑ 938 97 40 50; www.giroribot.es; Finca el Pont) The magnificent farm buildings ooze centuries of tradition. This winery uses mostly local grape varieties to produce a limited range of fine *cava* and wines (including muscat). Visits are seasonal and must be booked in advance. Prices depend on the experience. The winery is 7km north of Vilafranca, just beyond the village of Santa Fe del Penedès.

Jean León (☑ 938 17 76 90; www.jeanleon.com; Camí Mas de Rovira, Torrelavit; adult/child €10.25/free; ☺ 9am-5pm Mon-Fri, 9am-1pm Sat & Sun) Since 1963 this winery has been using cabernet sauvignon and other French varietals to create various high-quality wines. Visits to this wonderfully scenic vineyard are multilingual but must be booked in advance.

Torres (☑ 938 17 73 30; www.torres.es; vineyard tour adult/child €7.80/5.50; ☺ 9am-4pm Mon-Sat, to noon Sun & holidays) Just 2km northwest of Vilafranca on the BP2121, this is the area's premier winemaker, with a family wine-making tradition dating from the 17th century. It revolutionised Spanish wine-making in the 1960s by introducing temperature-controlled, stainless-steel technology and French grape varieties. Torres produces an array of reds and whites of all qualities, using many grape varieties.

☺ 10am-7pm Tue-Sat, 10am-2pm Sun) Set down your *cava* glass for a moment and school yourself on the history and cultural significance of wine in Penedès. This 17,000-item collection pores over ancient vine-cultivation techniques, and offers interesting detail on the evolution of wine-making in the area. Outside summer, the museum closes for lunch between 2pm and 4pm.

Tours

Catalunya Bus Turístic (p271) conducts day tours that include visits to three bodegas, cheese and wine matching and tapas.

⭐ **El Molí Tours** CYCLING, WINERY TOUR
(☑ 938 97 22 07; www.elmolitours.com; Torreles de Foix; half-day €70) This highly recommended tour company, headed by the indomitable Paddy, arranges all manner of tours around wine country – from luxury gourmet day tours to numerous cycling options, such as half-/full-day guided bike tours that include lunch and *cava* sampling.

Sleeping & Eating

Mercer Casa Torner i Güell BOUTIQUE HOTEL €€
(☑ 938 17 47 55; www.casatorneriguell.com; Calle Rambla de Sant Francesc 26; d/ste from €100/140) The voluminous rooms at this central hotel have a sleek feel, with a mix of monochrome, mauve and faux-leather furnishings, while the bar area and reception are achingly glamorous. The result is somewhere between trendy and romantic, and it's all ideally located to explore Vilafranca's excellent restaurants.

El Convent
CATALAN €€

(☑ 931 69 43 84; Carrer de la Fruita 12; mains €10-15; ⊙ 9am-1pm & 6.30pm-12.30am Tue-Fri, 9am-4pm & 7pm-midnight Sat) This warren-like tavern has fantastically good-value set menus (three courses €20) packed with well-executed Catalan specials. Temptations range from juicy Iberico pork steaks to cloud-like desserts of yoghurt and fruit.

★ Cal Ton
CATALAN €€€

(☑ 938 90 37 41; www.restaurantcalton.com; Carrer Casal 8; mains €16-24; ⊙ 1-4pm & 8.30-10.30pm Tue-Sat, 1-4pm Sun) An evening of gastronomic wonder awaits at Cal Ton. From feather-light potato and prawn ravioli to spider crab rice, meals at this crisp, modern restaurant exhaust superlatives. Meanwhile the unpretentious yet knowledgeable service ensures the perfect local wine to complement any dish. The quivering chocolate fondant with passionfruit ice cream enjoys top billing on the dessert menu.

ⓘ Information

Tourist Office (☑ 938 18 12 54; www.turisme vilafranca.com; Carrer Hermenegild Clascar 2; ⊙ 3-6pm Mon, 9.30am-1.30pm & 3-6pm Tue-Sat, 10am-1pm Sun) This information hub provides tips on visiting some of the smaller wineries in the area. Afternoon opening in summer is 4pm to 7pm.

ⓘ Getting There & Away

Rodalies trains run from Barcelona's Estació Sants to Vilafranca (€4.90, 55 minutes). By car, take the A2 north from Barcelona follow signs west at Martorell.

Tarragona

POP 132,199

In this effervescent port city, Roman history collides with beaches, nightlife and a food scene that perfumes the air with freshly grilled seafood. The biggest lure is the wealth of ruins in Spain's second most important Roman site, including mosaic-packed museums and a seaside amphitheatre. A roll-call of excellent places to eat gives you good reason to linger in the knot of lanes in the medieval centre, flanked by a broad cathedral with Gothic flourishes. Tarragona is also a gateway to the Costa Daurada's sparkling beaches and the feast of Modernisme architecture in nearby Reus.

History

Tarragona was first occupied by the Romans, who called it Tarraco, in 218 BC; prior to that the area was first settled by Iberians, followed by Carthaginians. Scipio launched his successful military endeavours from here, and in 27 BC Augustus made it the capital of his new Tarraconensis province (roughly all modern Spain) and stayed until 25 BC, directing campaigns. During its Roman heyday Tarragona was home to over 200,000 people, and though abandoned when the Muslims arrived in AD 714, the city was reborn as the seat of a Christian archbishopric in the 11th century.

◉ Sights

★ Catedral de Tarragona
CATHEDRAL

(www.catedraldetarragona.com; Plaça de la Seu; adult/child €5/3; ⊙ 10am-7pm Mon-Sat mid-Mar–Oct, 10am-5pm Mon-Fri, 10am-7pm Sat Nov–mid-Mar) Sitting grandly atop town, Tarragona's cathedral has both Romanesque and Gothic features, as typified by the main facade. The cloister has Gothic vaulting and Romanesque carved capitals, one of which shows rats conducting a cat's funeral...until the cat comes back to life! It's a lesson about passions seemingly lying dormant until they reveal themselves. Chambers off the cloister incorporate the Museu Diocesà, with its large collection extending from Roman hairpins to some lovely 12th- to 14th-century polychrome woodcarvings of a breastfeeding Virgin.

★ Museu Nacional Arqueològic de Tarragona
MUSEUM

(www.mnat.cat; Plaça del Rei 5; adult/child €4.50/free; ⊙ 9.30am-6pm Tue-Sat, to 8.30pm Jun-Sep, 10am-2pm Sun) This excellent museum does justice to the cultural and material wealth of Roman Tarraco. The mosaic collection traces the changing trends – from simple black-and-white designs to complex full-colour creations; a highlight is the large, almost complete *Mosaic de Peixos de la Pineda*, showing fish and sea creatures. Explanation in the museum is in Catalan and Spanish, but there is a multilingual audio guide included in the price.

Museu d'Història de Tarragona
RUIN

(MHT; www.museutgn.com; adult/child per site €3.30/free, all sites €11.05/free; ⊙ sites 9am-9pm Tue-Sat, 10am-3pm Sun Easter-Sep, 9am-7pm Tue-Sat, 9am-3pm Sun Oct-Easter) The Museu

Tarragona

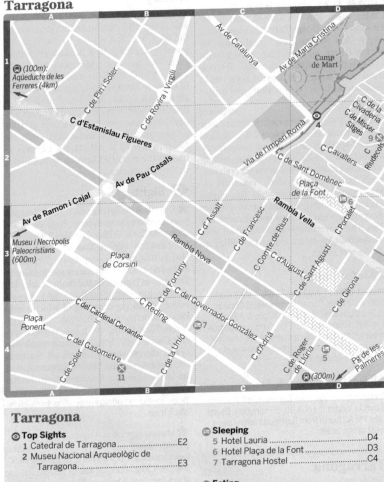

Tarragona

◎ Top Sights
1	Catedral de Tarragona	E2
2	Museu Nacional Arqueològic de Tarragona	E3

◎ Sights
3	Amfiteatre Romà	E4
4	Passeig Arqueològic Muralles	D2

🛏 Sleeping
5	Hotel Lauria	D4
6	Hotel Plaça de la Font	D3
7	Tarragona Hostel	C4

🍴 Eating
8	AQ	E1
9	Arcs Restaurant	D2
10	Ares	F2
11	Barquet	B4

d'Història de Tarragona consists of various separate Unesco World Heritage Roman sites, as well as some other historic buildings around town: Forùm Provincial Pretori i Circ Romans, Amfiteatre Romà, Passeig Arqueològic Muralles and Fòrum de la Colònia. Buy a combined ticket and get exploring.

Amfiteatre Romà
RUIN

(Parc de l'Anfiteatre; adult/child €3.30/free; ⏰9am-9pm Tue-Sat, 10am-3pm Sun Easter-Sep, 10am-7pm Tue-Sat, 10am-3pm Sun Oct-Easter) Near the beach is this well-preserved amphitheatre, where gladiators hacked away at each other, or wild animals. In its arena are the remains of 6th- and 12th-century churches built to commemorate the martyrdom of the Christian bishop Fructuosus and two deacons, believed to have been burnt alive here in AD 259. Much of the amphitheatre was picked to bits, the stone used

to build the port, so what you see now is a partial reconstruction.

Passeig Arqueològic Muralles   WALLS

(adult/child €3.30/free; ☉ sites 9am-9pm Tue-Sat, 10am-3pm Sun Easter-Sep, 10am-7pm Tue-Sat, 10am-3pm Sun Oct-Easter) A peaceful walk takes you around part of the perimeter of the old town between two lines of city walls. The inner ones are mainly Roman and date back to the 3rd century BC, while the outer ones were put up by the British in 1709 during the War of the Spanish Succession. The early stretches are a mighty 4m thick. Prepare to be awed by the gateways built by the Iberians and clamber up onto the battlements from the doorway to the right of the entrance for all-encompassing views of the city.

The walk starts from the Portal del Roser where Avenida Catalunya touches the old town.

Aqüeducte de les Ferreres   BRIDGE

(Pont del Diable; ☉ 9am-dusk) **FREE** This aqueduct sits in a tangle of dusty pathways and glades 4km north of central Tarragona, just off the AP7 freeway (near where it intersects with the N240). It is a fine stretch of two-tiered aqueduct (217m long and 27m high), along which you can totter to the other side. Bus 5 to Sant Salvador from Plaça Imperial de Tàrraco, running every 10 to 20 minutes, will take you close, and you can walk back to the city along the river (about 90 minutes).

Museu i Necròpolis Paleocristians   RUIN

(Avinguda de Ramón i Cajal 80; adult/child €4.50/ free; ☉ 9.30am-1.30pm & 3-5.30pm Tue-Sat, 10am-2pm Sun) This vast Roman-Christian city of the dead on the western edge of town consists of over 2000 elaborate tombs. It was used from the 3rd century AD onwards, thus attesting to Rome's conversion to Christianity. The museum features curious funereal objects and sarcophagi. Entry is free if you have already purchased a ticket to the Museu Nacional Arqueològic de Tarragona (p355). It opens extended hours in high season.

PortAventura   AMUSEMENT PARK

(www.portaventura.es; adult/child €45/39; ☉ 10am-7pm or 8pm, to midnight Jul & Aug; 🚼) A massive, blockbuster amusement park, PortAventura lies 7km west of Tarragona. Divided into themed sections, the park has plenty of exhilarating rides and numerous shows to keep all ages happy. The park complex boasts Shambhala, Europe's highest rollercoaster, as well as Costa Caribe Aquatic Park, a water world that includes some fear-inducing slides. There are various combined and multiday tickets available, and themed on-site accommodation that suits families with young kids.

🎉 Festivals & Events

Festival de Santa Tecla   STREET CARNIVAL

(www.tarragonaturisme.cat/es/eventos/santa-tecla; Tarragona) This colourful 10-day festival brings *castells*, or human 'castles', to the centre of Tarragona. Teams of *castellers* stand on each other's shoulders to build towers up to nine levels high. Watch the spectacle along Rambla Nova and stick around for the fireworks after sundown.

CATALONIA TARRAGONA

🛌 Sleeping

Tarragona Hostel
HOSTEL €

(☑877 05 58 96; www.tarragonahostel.com; Carrer de la Unió; dm/d €12/30; 🛜) All the backpacker essentials are well-executed at this dead-centre hostel with chirpy staff. Choose from eight-bed dorms or a double room, and avail yourself of free wi-fi, a comfy common room, shared kitchen and laundry facilities (€4).

Hotel Plaça de la Font
HOTEL €€

(☑977 24 61 34; www.hotelpdelafont.com; Plaça de la Font 26; s/d €55/75; ❄🛜) Comfortable modern rooms, decorated in individual styles with photos of Tarragona monuments, fill this cheerful hotel on popular Plaça de la Font. Rooms at the front are pretty well soundproofed from the sociable murmur below and have tiny balconies for people-watching. Breakfast is an extra €5.

Hotel Sant Jordi
HOTEL €€

(☑977 20 75 15; www.hotelsantjordi.info; Avinguda Vía Augusta 185; s/d €68/79; P❄🛜) The reception's decor screams 1970s, but this hotel, 2.5km northeast of central Tarragona by the appealing Savinosa beach, has spotless, comfortable rooms with balconies. The old world, caring atmosphere makes it far cosier than it appears at first glance. The hotel closes for a month in mid-November.

Hotel Lauria
HOTEL €€

(☑977 23 67 12; www.hotel-lauria.com; Rambla Nova 20; s/d incl breakfast €65/77; P❄🛜🏊) Right on the Rambla Nova near where it ends at a balcony overlooking the sea, this smart hotel offers great-value modern rooms with welcome splashes of colour, large bathrooms and a small swimming pool. The rooms at the back are less exposed to the noise from the Rambla.

🍴 Eating

Ares
CATALAN, SPANISH €€

(http://aresrestaurant.com; Plaça del Forum; mains €10-12; ⊙1-4pm & 8.30-11.30pm Wed-Sun) Amid a riot of colourful, exuberant Modernista decor, the welcome from this husband-and-wife team guarantees a good atmosphere for dining. Some classic Catalan dishes take their place alongside quality ingredients from across Spain: Asturian cheeses, Galician seafood, Burgos black pudding. Quality and quantity are both praiseworthy.

Barquet
SEAFOOD €€

(☑977 24 00 23; www.restaurantbarquet.com; Carrer del Gasometre 16; mains €11-18; ⊙1-3.30pm & 9-10.30pm Tue-Sat, 1-3.30pm Mon) This popular neighbourhood restaurant is a short downhill stroll from the centre. It's deservedly famous for its excellent rice dishes bursting with maritime flavour, and also has great *raciones* (large plates) of seafood. Don't be fooled by the nautical warehouse interior, fish dishes and jewel-like desserts are executed with finesse.

AQ
MEDITERRANEAN, FUSION €€

(☑977 21 59 54; www.aq-restaurant.com; Carrer de les Coques 7; mains €11-20; ⊙1.30-3.30pm & 8.30-11pm Tue-Sat) The crisp interior design of this stone-walled restaurant promises fine dining, and AQ amply delivers. Its impeccably crafted fusion dishes – taking inspiration from Catalan, Italian and Asian cuisines – are playfully executed. Treat your tastebuds to Iberico pork burgers, squid carbonara or chop suey lobster. The three-course lunch menu (€19.80) is excellent value.

Arcs Restaurant
CATALAN €€€

(☑977 21 80 40; www.restaurantarcs.com; Carrer de Misser Sitges 13; mains €18-22; ⊙1-4pm & 8.30-11pm Tue-Sat) Inside a medieval cavern decorated with bright contemporary art, feast on Mediterranean dishes that follow the seasons. Sample duck with a gin and tonic cream, salmon tataki with wasabi, or the always-excellent catch of the day. Leave room for desserts that please the eye as much as the tastebuds.

ℹ️ Information

Tourist Office (☑977 25 07 95; www.tarragonaturisme.es; Carrer Major 39; ⊙10am-2pm & 3-5pm Mon-Fri, to 7pm Sat, 10am-2pm Sun) Good place for booking guided tours of the city. Opens extended hours in high season.

ℹ️ Getting There & Away

Eleven kilometres northwest from Tarragona, Reus airport is used by Ryanair, with flights to London, Dublin, Brussels and Frankfurt Hahn among others. Buses (usually timed for flights) run from Tarragona's bus station (20 minutes, €3) as well as from Barcelona (1¾ hours, €15).

The **bus station** (Plaça Imperial Tarraco) is 1.5km northwest of the old town along Rambla Nova. Destinations include Barcelona (€8.80, 1½ hours, up to 16 daily), Lleida (€5.25, 1¾ hours, three to five daily) and Valencia (€22, three to 4½ hours, six daily).

If checking train times online (www.renfe.com), be wary of two differently located stations in Tarragona. The local train station (Tarragona) is a 10-minute walk from the old town near the beach. There are departures to Barcelona (€8.05 to €20.80, one to 1½ hours, every 30 minutes) and Valencia (€15.20 to €31, two to 3½ hours, 19 daily).

A second out-of-town train station, Camp de Tarragona, lies 10km north of the centre (a 20-minute taxi ride away). There are frequent high-speed trains to Barcelona (€17.30 to €36.50, 35 minutes) and Lleida (€12 to €20, 30 minutes). Make use of hotel transfers if arriving here late at night, as taxis can be erratic.

Delta de L'Ebre

The Delta de l'Ebre, a 20km-long bulge of silt-formed land near Catalonia's southern border, is laced by waterways that melt into the Balearic Sea. Flamingos and ibis strut in reed-fringed lagoons, dune-backed beaches are lashed by the wind, and marshes reflect sunsets like mirrors.

Seventy-eight square kilometres of this wild and exposed place is the Parc Natural Delta de l'Ebre, northern Spain's most important waterbird habitat. Migration season (October and November) sees the bird population peak, but birds are also numerous in winter and spring. The park's flat expanse of waterside trails is ideal for cyclists and ramblers. Exploring this remote and rural landscape, with its whitewashed farmhouses marooned among rice paddies and purple herons posing in ponds, lingers in the memory.

Scruffy, sprawling Deltebre is at the centre of the delta, but push on to smaller villages like Riumar, at the delta's easternmost point, or Poblenou del Delta.

⊙ Sights

Ecomuseu MUSEUM
(Carrer de Dr Martí Buera 22, Deltebre; admission €2; ⊙10am-2pm & 3-6pm Mon-Sat, 10am-2pm Sun) This engaging open-air museum shines a light on the delta's ecosystems and traditional trades, such as fishing and rice cultivation. The garden's wooden boardwalks weave past local flora, fishermen's tools and even a *llagut*, an early 20th-century boat used to haul more than 350 sacks of rice at a time. There is also an aquarium offering a glimpse of the freshwater denizens of the

GAUDÍ CENTRE

Reus, 14km west of Tarragona, is the birthplace of visionary architect Antoni Gaudí. Though none of Gaudí's buildings can be found in Reus, he was inspired by many of the historic structures in his home town. The superb **Gaudí Centre** (www.gaudicentre.cat; Plaça del Mercadal 3, Reus; adult/child €9/5; ⊙10am-2pm & 4-7pm Mon-Sat, 11am-2pm Sun; ☞) gives a thorough introduction to the man and his global influence through engaging multilingual and audiovisual displays. The inspiration Gaudí found in nature, as well as his thoughtfulness and humility, are portrayed alongside touchable scale models of his designs.

delta. The museum opens shorter hours in low season.

🛏 Sleeping

⭐ **Mas del Tancat** CASA RURAL €
(☑656 901014; masdeltancat@gmail.com; Camí dels Panissos; d/q €55/90; 🅿❄☞) A historic farmhouse, Mas del Tancat has just five rooms with iron bedsteads, calming colour schemes and an ebullient welcome. Sitting by the waters of the delta, with farm animals wandering through the grounds, it is a tranquil escape and home-cooked dinners are available on request. Leave Amposta on the TV3405 towards Sant Jaume and turn right to Els Panissos just after the 3km sign.

⭐ **Masia Tinet** CASA RURAL €€
(☑977 48 93 89; www.masiatinet.com; Barrio Lepanto 13, Deltebre; d incl breakfast €71.50; 🅿❄☞🏊) Rooms at this cushy, family-run guesthouse are elegant but rustic, with bare brick walls, wooden beams and high ceilings. The lounge area has rocking chairs and a bar run on the honour system. There's a garden with deck chairs, so you can watch the sun set over marshlands speckled with birdlife, plus there's a small pool. Breakfasts are a banquet of homemade preserves and fresh produce, and service has a personal touch.

L'Algadir del Delta HOTEL €€
(☑977 74 45 59; www.hotelalgadirdelta.com; Ronda dels Pins 27-29, Poblenou del Delta; s/d incl breakfast €100/136; ⊙Feb-Dec; 🅿❄☞🏊) With great birdwatching on the hotel doorstep,

CASTELL DE MIRAVET

Castell de Miravet (adult/child €3.50/2.30; ◷10am-5.30pm Tue-Sun, to 8pm summer), southern Catalonia's finest castle, is at Miravet, 6km off the N420, 60km west of Tarragona. Built in the 11th century, it was reconquered then given to the Templars. It's a formidable stronghold, with incredibly solid walls, and it towers above the pretty village that cascades down a hill on the banks of the Ebro. Opening hours vary seasonally.

this sleek, friendly, modern place in this tranquil village in the heart of the delta makes a top base. Rooms are contemporary, stylish and comfortable. There's a pleasant pool area and the hotel loans bikes to help you explore. The restaurant is also a worthy place to sample local cuisine.

✖ Eating

★ Mas Prades   CATALAN €€
(☑977 05 90 84; www.masdeprades.cat; Carretera T340, Km 8, Deltebre; mains €12-22; ◷1-3.30pm & 8-11pm Tue-Sun, weekends only Nov-Mar; ⛄) Gourmets come all the way down from Barcelona to this revamped country house to sample its superb delta cuisine. There is a range of lunch menus from three to five courses (€18 to €35), each of which makes a lip-smacking introduction to local delicacies like tender mussels roasted in garlic butter, baby squid, sizzling platters of rabbit and chicken, and the classic delta rice with wild duck.

Casa Nuri   SEAFOOD €€
(☑977 48 01 28; www.restaurantnuri.com; Final Goles de Ebre, Riumar; mains €13-20; ◷10am-10pm Apr-Oct) Locals fill this riverfront place, thanks to its reputation for superb local seafood like razor clams, rice glistening with squid ink, and just-caught sea bream. It's close to the booking office for Creuers Delta Ebre. Opens shorter hours in low season.

ⓘ Information

Centre d'Informació (☑977 48 96 79; www.turismedeltebre.com; Carrer de Dr Martí Buera 22, Deltebre; ◷10am-2pm & 3-6pm Mon-Sat, 10am-2pm Sun) The Centre d'Informació is housed in the same complex as the local eco-museum. Pick up maps of the region and brochures on cycle routes here.

ⓘ Getting There & Away

Weekday Hife (www.hife.es) buses head to the delta towns from Tarragona (€12.64, one to two hours, four daily) and Tortosa (€3.90, 30 minutes to one hour, up to 18 daily).

ⓘ Getting Around

If you don't reach the Delta de l'Ebre with your own wheels, consider renting a bike: the area sprawls and has extremely limited public transport.

Tortosa

POP 33,932

Arid Tortosa, 70km south of Tarragona and inland from the fertile Delta de l'Ebre, is experiencing a quiet tourism renaissance. It's a sleepy town, for sure; but with a neck-straining castle, otherworldly sculpture garden and architectural gems spanning Gothic to Modernista styles, it's carving a small niche for itself as a destination for cultural weekend breaks.

Tortosa was a battleground between medieval Christian and Muslim Spain. More recently, Tortosa was also on the front line between Nationalists and Republicans during the civil war and the site of an epic battle, which wrecked much of its medieval centre and cost over 35,000 lives. The town is also suffused with Jewish history that dates back to the 6th century; pick up a pamphlet in the tourist office to uncover Jewish Tortosa.

The town is a convenient base for daytrips to Miravet Castle or Gandesa's Centre d'Estudis de la Batalla de l'Ebre.

⊙ Sights

Jardins del Príncep   PARK
(adult/child €3/2; ◷10am-1.30pm & 4.30-7.30pm Tue-Sat, 10am-1.30pm Sun) In the grounds of a former 19th-century spa, this carefully manicured sculpture garden is a thought-provoking and uplifting place to explore. The statues purport to illustrate the motives and destiny of humankind (a rather broad artistic theme). Nevertheless, there are plenty of intriguing sculptures, among them an eye-popping tower of nude figures.

Museu de Tortosa   MUSEUM
(www.museudetortosa.cat; admission €3; ◷10am-1.30pm & 5-8.30pm Tue-Sat, 11am-1.30pm Sun) Within a splendid blue Modernista building, decorated with gold trim and white checkerboard designs, lies this rather minimalist town museum. The 1908 building

is worth ogling: formerly a city slaughter-house, its design has delicate Moorish elements. Within, the museum does a great job of contextualising the area's history, from traces of early Iberian settlement through to the disorder and revolution from the 18th century onwards. From October to April, the museum operates afternoon hours of 4pm to 7pm.

Castell de la Suda
CASTLE, RUIN

(⊙24hr) FREE Wandering around this 10th-century fortress is murder on your footwear: trails seem to lead nowhere, and you have to contend with steep and unfinished stairways. Despite the access issues, the castle is an enjoyable ramble, especially for the lofty views over Tortosa. Near the entrance to the adjoining *parador*, you'll find a small Islamic cemetery.

Catedral de Santa Maria
CATHEDRAL

(Carrer Portal del Palau; adult/child €3/2; ⊙10am-1.30pm & 4.30-7pm Mon-Sat, 11am-2pm Sun) This Gothic cathedral seizes attention with its many turrets and with gargoyles jutting from every eave.

🛏 Sleeping & Eating

Parador de Tortosa
HISTORIC HOTEL €€

(☑977 44 44 50; www.parador.es; Castell de le Suda; d from €95; P✷🗶🗘) Tortosa's formidable fortress encloses a *parador* (historic state-run hotel), allowing you to repose in medieval surroundings overlooking vertiginous views of the town.

★ Xampu-Xampany
TAPAS €€

(www.xampu-xampany.com; Avinguda Catalunya 41; mains €11-16; ⊙9am-8pm Mon-Fri, 9am-midnight Sat) This upmarket bar-restaurant on Tortosa's left bank stocks regional favourites, allowing you to snack on ham, sheep's cheese and tomato-slathered bread until late. Alternatively, fill up on the menu of well-presented Catalan classics, washed down with local wine.

ℹ Information

Tourist Information (☑977 44 96 48; www.tortosaturisme.cat; Rambla Felip Pedrell 3; ⊙10am-1.30pm & 4.30-7.30pm Tue-Sat, 10am-1.30pm Sun) Get info, tips and the Tortosa Card at this tourist office next to the Museu de Tortosa.

ℹ Getting There & Away

Trains reach Tortosa from Tarragona (€8.05, one to 1½ hours, three daily) and Valencia (€15.30, three hours, four daily). If visiting by car, find parking near the tourist office.

CATALONIA TORTOSA

Aragón

Best Places to Eat

→ Restaurante Méli Mélo (p368)

→ La Barrica (p394)

→ La Cocina del Principal (p373)

→ Restaurante Canteré (p374)

→ Restaurante Callizo (p383)

Best Places to Sleep

→ Hotel los Siete Reyes (p382)

→ Parador de Sos del Rey Católico (p373)

→ Hotel Sauce (p368)

→ La Casa del Tío Americano (p397)

→ Hotel Barosse (p378)

Why Go?

Welcome to one of the twin building blocks of contemporary Spain. When Aragonese king Ferdinand II married his powerful Castillan counterpart Isabella in 1476, history was made and modern Spain as we now know it got its raison d'être.

Aragón encompasses a dramatic sweep of land, from the Pyrenees with their sober Romanesque churches and culture barely touched by the Moorish invasion, to the southern city of Teruel, where fertile Islamic-Christian intermingling threw up some of the best Mudéjar architecture in Iberia.

The counterweight in the middle is Zaragoza, a graceful, but perennially underrated Iberian metropolis nestled in the Ebro River valley that hosted Expo 2008 and is still riding in its slipstream.

Loaded with diversity, wider Aragón satisfies many tastes, including outdoor adventurers (canyoning is popular), lovers of Mudéjar architectonics, and aesthetes infatuated with the artistic genius of Goya. Behind the scenes, it quietly protects some of the finest medieval villages in Spain.

When to Go
Zaragoza

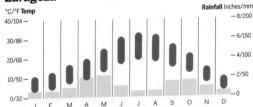

Feb Teruel's Fiesta Medieval returns you to the Middle Ages.

Mid-Jun–early Sep The best time to hike the high country of the Aragonese Pyrenees.

Oct Zaragoza's Fiestas del Pilar combine the sacred with the city's famed love of revelry.

Aragón Highlights

1 Parque Nacional de Ordesa y Monte Perdido (p380) Hiking to the French frontier in this national park, pride of the Pyrenees.

2 Sos del Rey Católico (p372) Ambling over the cobblestones in the foothills of the Pyrenees.

3 Albarracín (p396)

Having medieval Moorish hallucinations among the pink-hued houses.

4 Zaragoza (p364) Discovering the buzzing city above ground and the glorious, ruined, Roman one beneath.

5 Teruel (p392) Admiring Mudéjar and Moderismo architecture in this surprising town.

6 Hecho (p374) Walking a section of the GR11 or stepping onto the Camino de Santiago near this Pyrenees village.

7 Alquézar (p384) Plunging down a ravine in Spain's canyoning capital.

8 Castillo de Loarre (p389) Visiting this fairytale castle with panoramic views.

ZARAGOZA

POP 679,624

The ethereal image of the multi-domed Basílica de Nuestra Señora de Pilar reflected in the Río Ebro at dawn is reason alone to visit Zaragoza, one of Spain's most underrated regional capitals. Stay after sunrise and the reasons to linger quickly stack up. Spain's fifth largest city is loaded with creatively displayed Roman remains, a turreted castle with an interior like a mini-Alhambra, and the epoch-defining art of Francisco de Goya, the genius painter who was born nearby in 1746.

And there's more! Zaragoza's most recent moment in the spotlight came in 2008 when it hosted the World Expo. Infrastructure from the event has added much to the city's cultural repertoire. A stroll around the riverside northwest of the city centre will reveal space-age bridges, a plush new bus and railway station, and the largest freshwater aquarium in Europe.

History

The Romans founded Caesaraugusta (from which 'Zaragoza' is derived) in 14 BC. As many as 25,000 people migrated to the city whose river traffic brought the known world to the banks of Río Ebro. The city prospered for almost three centuries, but its subsequent decline was confirmed in AD 472 when the city was overrun by the Visigoths. In Islamic times, Zaragoza was capital of the Upper March, one of Al-Andalus' frontier territories. In 1118, it fell to Alfonso I, ruler of the expanding Christian kingdom of Aragón, and immediately became its capital. In the centuries that followed, Zaragoza grew to become one of inland Spain's most important economic and cultural hubs and a city popular with Catholic pilgrims. It is now Spain's fifth-largest city and, since the 2008 Expo, has greatly improved its modern infrastructure.

ARAGÓN ZARAGOZA

Zaragoza

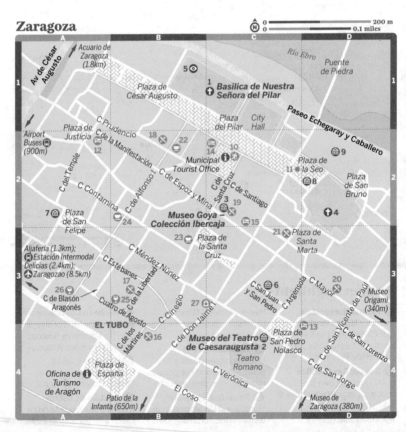

Sights

The great eras of the city's layered history – Roman, Islamic and Christian – have all left enduring monuments in Zaragoza.

★ Aljafería   PALACE

(Calle de los Diputados; admission €5, Sun free; ⊙10am-2pm & 4-6.30pm Mon-Sat, 10am-2pm Sun) The Aljafería is Spain's finest Islamic-era edifice outside Andalucía. Built as a pleasure palace for Zaragoza's Islamic rulers in the 11th century, it underwent its first alterations in 1118 when the city passed into Christian hands. In the 1490s, the Catholic Monarchs, Fernando and Isabel, tacked on their own palace, whereafter the Aljafería fell into decay. Twentieth-century restorations brought the building back to life, and in 1987 Aragón's regional parliament was established here. Tours take place throughout the day (multilingual in July and August).

Inside the main gate, cross the rather dull introductory courtyard into a second, the Patio de Santa Isabel, once the central courtyard of the Islamic palace. Here you're confronted by the delicate interwoven arches typical of the geometric mastery of Islamic architecture. Opening off the stunning northern porch is a small, octagonal oratorio (prayer room), with a magnificent horseshoe-arched doorway leading into its mihrab (prayer niche indicating the direction of Mecca). The finely chiselled floral motifs, Arabic inscriptions from the Quran and a pleasingly simple cupola are fine examples of Islamic art.

Moving upstairs, you pass through rooms of the Palacio Mudéjar, then to the Catholic Monarchs' palace, which, as though by way of riposte to the Islamic finery below, contains some exquisite Mudéjar coffered ceilings, especially in the lavish Salón del Trono (Throne Room).

★ Museo Goya – Colección Ibercaja   MUSEUM

(www.museogoya.ibercaja.es; Calle de Espoz y Mina 23; admission without/with audioguide €4/6; ⊙10am-2pm & 4-8pm Mon-Sat, 10am-2pm Sun) Outside of Madrid's Museo del Prado, this excellent museum contains what is arguably, the best expose of the work of one of Spain's most revered artists. A recent refurbishment (and renaming) has only enhanced its credentials. The place is exceedingly well laid-out with each of its three floors carrying a different theme.

The first floor amasses some of the art that influenced Goya. The second exhibits the man himself through his paintings and prints. Four complete sets of his prints are included, most notably the groundbreaking but sometimes grotesque, *Los Desastres de la Guerra* (Disasters of War). The top floor investigates Goya's massive influence by

ARAGÓN ZARAGOZA

CAESARAUGUSTA – A CITY UNDERGROUND

Underneath modern Zaragoza's streets lies a parallel universe little known to unversed outsiders. It tells the story of Caesaraugusta, a Roman town founded in the year 14 BC that once reigned as one of Iberia's most illustrious and strategically important colonies before being ignominiously sacked by the Visigoths in AD 472.

Left to rot as medieval Zaragoza grew up around it, Caesaraugusta lay buried and forgotten for over 1500 years. It was only in the 1990s that its crumbling remnants were resuscitated and given new life in a brilliant quartet of inter-related museums. Hidden in four subterranean exhibition spaces are the Museo del Foro de Caesaraugusta with remains of a Roman forum; the Museo del Puerto Fluvial, an erstwhile river dock; the Museo de las Termas Públicas containing some public baths; and – best of all – the Museo del Teatro de Caesaraugusta, a 600-seat theatre that was once one of the largest in Iberia.

While the ruins might be – well – 'ruins' compared to better preserved Roman sites in Mérida and Tarragona, the genius of Zaragoza's museums lies in their layout and creative extras. Well-curated exhibition chambers combine mock-ups of how things used to look with clever multimedia exhibits loaded with theatrical panache. The pièce de résistance is the Roman theatre, protected by a huge polycarbonate roof and best viewed through panoramic glass windows from an adjacent Interpretive Centre.

A joint ticket for all four museums can be procured for €7 and is a fantastic investment. Situated in close proximity to each other, they can all easily be visited in the same day.

tracking through the work of his imitators and followers.

★ Museo del Teatro de Caesaraugusta   MUSEUM

(Calle de San Jorge 12; adult/child €4/free; ⊙10am-2pm & 5-9pm Tue-Sat, 10am-2.30pm Sun) The finest in the quartet of Zaragoza's Roman museums was discovered during the excavation of a building site in 1972. The crumbling but precious theatre once seated 6000 spectators, and great efforts have been made to help visitors reconstruct the edifice's former splendour, including evening projections of a virtual performance (May to October) and an entertaining audiovisual production. The theatre is visible from the surrounding streets and an on-site cafe. The all-round aesthetics are fabulous.

★ Basílica de Nuestra Señora del Pilar   CHURCH

(Plaza del Pilar; ⊙6.45am-8.30pm Mon-Sat, to 9.30pm Sun) FREE Brace yourself for this great baroque cavern of Catholicism. The faithful believe that it was here on 2 January AD 40 that Santiago saw the Virgin Mary descend atop a marble *pilar* (pillar). A chapel was built around the remaining pillar, followed by a series of ever more grandiose churches, culminating in the enormous basilica. A lift (admission €3; ⊙10am-2pm & 4-6pm Mon-Fri, 10am-2pm Sat) whisks you most of the way up the north tower from where

you climb to a superb viewpoint over the domes and city.

Museo Diocesano   MUSEUM

(✆976 39 94 88; www.mudiz.com; Paseo Echegaray y Caballero 102; admission €5; ⊙10am-2pm & 5-9pm Tue-Sat, 10am-2pm Sun) Church museums can sometimes be boring emporiums of anonymous sacred art, but not this one. Slick multimedia exhibits set an arty tone which is continued as you navigate through a skilfully laid out trajectory that takes in the older elements of the palace, learning about Roman forums and the locally venerated Virgin of Pilar. The top floor is a Renaissance feast with paintings by the two local Francsicos, Goya and Bayeu.

Museo de Zaragoza   MUSEUM

(www.museodezaragoza.es; Plaza de los Sitios 6; ⊙10am-2pm & 5-8pm Tue-Sat, 10am-2pm Sun) FREE Devoted to archaeology and fine arts, the city museum displays artifacts from prehistoric to Islamic times, with some exceptional mosaics from Roman Caesaraugusta. The upper floor contains 15 paintings by Goya and more than two dozen of his etchings. It's 400m south of the Teatro Romano.

La Seo   CATHEDRAL

(Catedral de San Salvador; Plaza de la Seo; adult/child €4/free; ⊙10am-2pm, 6-6.30pm Tue-Fri, 10am-12.30pm & 4-6.30pm Sat, 10am-noon & 4-6.30pm Sun) Dominating the eastern end of Plaza del Pilar, La Seo was built between the 12th and 17th centuries and displays a fabulous spread of architectural styles from Romanesque to baroque. The cathedral stands on the site of Islamic Zaragoza's main mosque (which in turn stood upon the temple of the Roman forum). The admission price includes entry to La Seo's **Museo de Tapices** (Plaza de la Seo; ⊙10am-2pm & 4-6.30pm Mon-Fri, 10am-12.30pm & 4-6.30pm Sat, 10am-noon & 4-6.30pm Sun), a collection of 14th- to 17th-century Flemish and French tapestries considered the best of its kind in the world.

Museo del Foro de Caesaraugusta   MUSEUM

(Plaza de la Seo 2; adult/child €3/free; ⊙10am-2pm & 5-9pm Tue-Sat, 10am-2.30pm Sun) The trapezoidal building on Plaza de la Seo is the entrance to an excellent reconstruction of part of Roman Caesaraugusta's forum, now well below ground level. The remains of porticoes, shops, a great *cloaca* (sewer) system, and a limited collection of artefacts from the 1st century AD are on display. An interesting multilingual 15-minute audiovisual show breathes life into it all and culminates with a clever 'talking head' of a statue.

Acuario de Zaragoza   AQUARIUM

(☑976 07 66 06; www.acuariodezaragoza.com; Av José Atarés; adult/child €14/7; ⊙10am-8pm; 🅿🚼) Built for the 2008 Expo, Zaragoza's aquarium is the largest in Europe and the third largest in world. Its theme is 'river systems' and it focuses on five of the world's great rivers from the Amazon to – closer to home – the Ebro (the facility sits on its banks). There are plenty of fish, reptiles and other animals to see, plus explanatory boards in Spanish and English. Located a couple of kilometres from the city centre on the old Expo site, it rarely gets crowded.

Museo Origami   MUSEUM

(www.emoz.es; Centro de Historias, Plaza San Agustín 2; adult/concession/child under 12 €3/1.50/free; ⊙10am-2pm & 5-9pm Tue-Sat, 10am-2.30pm Sun; 🚼) Open since November 2013, this museum devoted to 'the art of folding paper' is the first of its kind in Europe and continues to attract worldwide interest from origami aficionados. Temporary exhibitions covering some six galleries are of a staggeringly high standard.

Patio de la Infanta   GALLERY

(Calle San Ignacio de Loyola 16; ⊙9am-2pm & 5-9pm Mon-Fri, 10am-2pm & 5-9pm Sat, 11am-2pm Sun) **FREE** This exhibition space houses the Ibercaja bank's collection of paintings, and puts on many temporary exhibitions. However, the real star is the lovely plateresque (15th- and 16th-century Spanish baroque) courtyard whose ornate columns carved with human figures are reminiscent of Guadalajara's Palacio de los Duques del Infantado. It's 600m south of Plaza de España.

Museo de Pablo Gargallo   GALLERY

(Plaza de San Felipe 3; adult/child €4/free; ⊙10am-2pm & 5-9pm Tue-Sat, 10am-2.30pm Sun) Within the wonderfully restored 17th-century Palacio Argillo is a representative display of sculptures by Pablo Gargallo (1881–1934), a friend of Picasso and recognised as Aragón's most gifted artistic son after Goya.

Museo de las Termas Públicas   MUSEUM

(Roman Baths; Calle San Juan y San Pedro 3-7; adult/child €3/free; ⊙10am-2pm & 5-9pm Tue-Sat, 10am-2.30pm Sun) The smallest of Zaragoza's Roman museums displays the subterranean remains of the city's one-time bathhouse. The ruined pool is not particularly compelling in itself, but it is given extra oomph by

---

❶ ZARAGOZA – CHEAP & EASY

The **Zaragoza Card** (24/48/72hr €18/21/24; www.zaragozacard.com) offers free entry to several monuments and museums, travel on the Tourist Bus and discounts on hotels, restaurants, public transport and car hire, including:

Tourist Bus (Bus Turístico; ☑976 20 12 00; www.zaragozaturismo.es; day tour/night tour €8/11) Hop-on, hop-off sightseeing bus that does two 75-minute city circuits daily in summer.

Guided Tours (www.zaragozaturismo.es; tours €5.50-13) A selection of gastronomic, cultural and architectural walking tours. Book through the tourist office.

BiziZaragoza (☑902 319 931; www.bizizaragoza.com; 3-day card €5) Public bike-sharing scheme with 2600 bicycles available at 130 docking stations spread around the city. You can procure a three-day subscription for €5.28, after which the first 30 minutes of each ride you take is free.

DON'T MISS

FOLLOW THE GOYA TRAIL

Francisco José de Goya y Lucientes, better known as the master painter Goya, was born in Aragón and his work can be seen all over his native region.

Casa Natal de Goya (p370), Fuendetodos

Museo del Grabado de Goya (p371), Fuendetodos

Ermita de la Fuente (p370), Muel

Museo Goya – Colección Ibercaja (p365), Zaragoza

Museo de Zaragoza (p366), Zaragoza

Basílica de Nuestra Señora del Pilar (p366), Zaragoza

Museo de Huesca (p388), Huesca

technological gadgets and an audiovisual show that reconstructs the baths to their former 1st century BC glory. Also on display here is a strangely intimate line of communal public latrines dating from an even earlier Roman era.

Festivals & Events

Fiestas del Pilar RELIGIOUS
Zaragoza's biggest event is a week of full-on celebrations (religious and otherwise) honouring its patron saint, peaking on 12 October, the Día de Nuestra Señora del Pilar.

Sleeping

Hostal el Descanso HOSTAL €
(☑976 29 17 41; Calle de San Lorenzo 2; s/d without bathroom €18/25; 🛜) This welcoming place combines a terrific location overlooking a pretty plaza near the Roman theatre with simple, bright rooms with washbasins. It feels exactly like a family home, probably because it is.

★**Hotel Sauce** BOUTIQUE HOTEL €€
(☑976 20 50 50; www.hotelsauce.com; Calle de Espoz y Mina 33; s from €45, d €51-66; ❉🛜) This chic, small hotel with a great central location has a hip feel thanks largely to its white wicker, painted furniture, stripy fabrics and tasteful watercolours on the walls. The superior rooms are well worth the few euros extra. There's a thoroughly pleasant 24-hour coffee shop/cafe on the ground floor with a cake display case that's rarely left empty.

Catalonia El Pilar HOTEL €€
(☑976 20 58 58; www.hoteles-catalonia.com; Calle de la Manifestación 16; r from €69; ❉@🛜) Ten-out-of-10 for the facade, a magnificent Modernista construction that has been artfully renovated to house this eminently comfortable contemporary hotel. Inside, rooms are spacious and decorated in restful muted earth tones with elegant marble-clad bathrooms. Some of the beds are king-size.

There's also a small gym – unusual in city centre hotels in Spain.

Sabinas APARTMENT €€
(☑976 20 47 10; www.sabinas.es; Calle de Espoz y Mina 33; apt €79-85; ❉🛜) A variety of three- to four-person apartments all equipped with microwaves and fridges. The contemporary style is clean-lined and modern and some have fantastic basilica views. There are three locations all within a block of each other. Key pick-up and contact is at the reception of the nearby Hotel Sauce.

Hotel Pilar Plaza HOTEL €€
(☑976 39 42 50; www.hotelpilarplaza.es; Plaza del Pilar 11; s/d incl breakfast from €75/85; ❉🛜) The Goya museum might be around the corner, but this basilica-facing hotel (recently placed under new management) prefers to exhibit edgier art by the likes of Banksy (a copy of his '*Girl with a Balloon*' decorates the staircase). The boutique rooms are seriously white; so white they are almost clinical (although not many hospital rooms have chandeliers or hydromassage showers, it's true).

Bonus: there's a small Mudejar-style spa.

Eating

Head to the tangle of lanes in El Tubo, north of Plaza de España, for one of Spain's richest gatherings of tapas bars.

★**Restaurante Méli Mélo** TAPAS €
(☑976294695;www.restaurantemelimelozaragoza. com; Calle Mayor 45; tapas €2-5; ⏱1-5pm & 8pm-midnight Mon-Sat, 1-5pm Sun) Typically, *pintxos* are Basque-style tapas presented on small slices of bread, but in Méli Mélo they are stacked up so high they look like mini-skyscrapers topped with creative arrangements of cured hams, breaded cod, octopus and aubergine. Come here at 8pm before the rush and you'll see a veritable Manhattan of *pintxos* lined up on the bar all ready for tasting.

Casa Pascualillo   CONTEMPORARY TAPAS €
(Calle de la Libertad 5; tapas from €1.60, mains €5-
14; ☺noon-4pm & 7-11pm Tue-Sat, noon-4.30pm
Sun) The bar groans under the weight of its
unique tapas like El Pascualillo, a 'small' *bocadillo* (filled roll) of *jamón*, oyster mushrooms and onion. Take your pick – like
Zaragozans have been doing here since
1939. There's also an informal restaurant attached – the sort of place where razor-thin
septuagenarians dine alone on three-course
lunches.

Churrería la Fama   CHURROS €
(Calle Prudencio; chocolate & 4 churros €3.10;
☺8am-1pm & 5-9.30pm; 🖶) Zaragoza does
the best churros (deep-fried doughnut-like
snack) in the region and La Fama is *the*
place to enjoy them dipped in a glass of
thick hot chocolate.

Los Xarmientos   ARAGONESE €€
(☑976 29 90 48; Calle Espoz y Mina 25; mains €12-
19; ☺1-4pm & 8-11.30pm Wed-Sat, 1-4pm Tue &
Sun) Aragonese meat dishes are a speciality
at this artfully designed restaurant. It styles
itself as a *parrilla*, meaning the dishes are
cooked on a barbecue-style grill. It's a fine
place to sample the local *ternasco* (lamb),
Aragon's most emblematic dish, served here
with a jacket potato on the side.

Casa Lac   CONTEMPORARY TAPAS €€
(☑976 29 90 25; Calle de los Mártires 12; mains
from €12; ☺12.15-4pm & 8.15pm-midnight Mon-
Sat, 12.15-8.15pm Sun) The grand old lady of
the Zaragoza dining scene, Casa Lac pays
homage to the 19th century; it opened in
1825 and is reputedly the oldest licensed restaurant in Spain. The downstairs bar is dedicated to avant-garde tapas like artichoke
hearts with foie gras and crispy fried cod
in a red-pepper sauce. Try the tapas tasting
menu for €6.50 to €8.

Tragantua   TAPAS, SEAFOOD €€
(Plaza Santa Marta; mains €12-20; ☺12.30-4pm
& 8pm-12.30am) Locals flock here for reportedly the best *croquetas de jamón* (ham croquettes) in town. Other popular mini bites
include *bola de bacalau* (breadcrumbed
cod), while more substantial tentacle-waving
teasers include stewed baby octopus and the
sizeable *langostino* (lobster) *de Vinaroz*.
The ambience is comfortably traditional.

🍸 Drinking & Nightlife

Calle del Temple, southwest of Plaza del Pilar, is the spiritual home of Zaragoza's roar-

ing nightlife. This is where the city's considerable student population heads out to party
with more bars lined up cheek to jowl than
anywhere else in Aragón. Nothing gets moving before midnight.

Café Botanico   CAFE
(Calle de Santiago 5; ☺9am-1pm Mon-Wed, 9am-
2am Thu & Fri, 10am-2am Sat, 10am-11pm Sun;
🛜) Café Botanico combines a florist (think
plenty of greenery, including fragrant herbs)
and a cafe serving great coffee, a tea menu
and some truly delicious cakes. Thanks, in
part, to its central location, it is perennially
popular. It also runs the contemporary art
gallery next door.

Zen Gong Café   LOUNGE
(www.cafegong.com; Calle de Alfonso I 13; ☺7am-
2am Sun-Thu, 8am-4.30am Fri & Sat; 🛜) The
Gong wouldn't look out of place in Madrid or Barcelona, with stylish decor,
weird-and-wonderful lighting and a breadth
of atmospheres, from breakfast cafe to
lunchtime wine bar and then a venue for
pop, house and even drag acts by night.

Gran Café de Zaragoza   CAFE
(Calle de Alfonso I 25; ☺8.30am-10pm Sun-Thu,
9am-2.30am Fri & Sat; 🛜) This Zaragoza institution evokes the grand old cafes of Spain's
past with a gold-plated facade and refreshing lack of laptops. That said, it's a place to
be seen by young and old alike and the elegant salon is a good place for morning coffee
or afternoon churros 'n' chocolate.

Café Praga   CAFE
(Plaza de la Santa Cruz 13; ☺9am-1am Mon-Thu,
10am-3am Sat & Sun) One of Zaragoza's favourite cafes, Praga has a front-row seat on

---

LOCAL KNOWLEDGE

TAKE A RIVERSIDE STROLL

The restoration of the riverbank for
Expo 2008 has created footpaths
on either side of the Río Ebro linked
by some eye-catching bridges both
super-modern and old. Take your binoculars as it's superb birdwatching territory with herons, kingfishers, sandpipers,
gulls, swallows, swifts, egrets, wagtails
and many more species to be spied
on or near the water. Equally evocative
is the sight of the Basilica de Nuestra
Señora del Pilar reflected perfectly in
the river at dawn or dusk.

one of the city's most agreeable plazas, and there's occasional live music in the main bar.

Rock & Blues Café MUSIC BAR
(www.rockandbluescafe.com; Cuatro de Agosto 5-9; ⊙3pm-2.30am) Rock 'n' roll paraphernalia, paying homage to the likes of Jimi Hendrix and Jim Morrison, set the tone for the music and style of this longstanding favourite. There's live pop, rock or blues most Thursdays at 10pm. It's a fascinating and atmospheric spot, open late on weekends.

🛍 Shopping

Fantoba CHOCOLATES
(www.fantoba.com; Calle de Don Jaime I 21; ⊙10am-10pm) This fabulous shop dates from 1856 and is decorated with elaborately packaged sweets, ranging from cream-filled cakes and mini-macaroons to wonderfully ornate chocolate stiletto shoes, plus handmade chocolates, marzipan fruits and exquisite tins of biscuits.

ℹ Information

Municipal Tourist Office (☑976 20 12 00; www.zaragozaturismo.es; Plaza del Pilar; ⊙9am-9pm mid-Jun–mid-Oct, 10am-8pm mid-Oct–mid-Jun; 🖥) Has branch offices around town, including the train station.

Oficina de Turismo de Aragón (☑976 28 21 81; www.turismodearagon.com; Plaza de España 1; ⊙9am-2pm & 5-8pm Mon-Fri, from 10am Sat & Sun; 🖥) Has plenty of brochures on the province.

ℹ Getting There & Away

AIR
Zaragoza airport (☑976 71 23 00; www.zaragoza-airport.com). 10km west of the city, has direct Ryanair (www.ryanair.com) flights to/from London (Stansted), Brussels (Charleroi), Paris (Beauvais), Milan (Bergamo), Lanzarote and Seville. Vueling (www.vueling.

WORTH A TRIP

GOYA FRESCOES
A small church in the town of Muel, the **Ermita de la Virgen de la Fuente** (Avenida Virgen de la Fuente; ⊙9am-8pm), is notable because it contains some paintings of the saints undertaken by a young Goya. The village is 30km south of Zaragoza.

com) and Air Europa (www.aireuropa.com) also operate seasonal flights to the Canary Islands.

BUS
Dozens of bus lines fan out across Spain from the bus station attached to the Estación Intermodal Delicias train station. It's 3km northwest of the city centre.

Alosa (☑902 21 07 00; www.alosa.es) Up to 12 buses to/from Huesca (€7.80, one hour). To Jaca (€15.90, 2½ hours, four daily).

ALSA (☑902 42 22 42; www.alsa.es) Frequent daily buses to/from Madrid (from €16.65, 3¾ hours) and Barcelona (€15.75, 3¾ hours).

TRAIN
Zaragoza's futuristic **Estación Intermodal Delicias** (www.renfe.com; Calle Rioja 33) is connected by almost hourly high-speed AVE services to Madrid (€63.20, 1¼ hours) and Barcelona (€71.50, from 1½ hours). Other destinations include Huesca (from €7.15, one hour), Jaca (€14.85, 3½ hours) and Teruel (€20.10, 2¼ hours).

ℹ Getting Around

BUS
Airport buses (☑902 36 00 65; tickets €1.70) run to/from Paseo María Agustín and Avenida César Augusto via the bus/train station every half-hour (hourly on Sunday).

Buses 34 and 51 travel between Plaza España and the Estación Intermodal Delicias.

TRAM
The C1 **tram** (www.urbandezaragoza.es; tickets €1.35) line runs through the centre of town from Plaza de España to Plaza de Bambola due south.

CENTRAL ARAGÓN

Fuendetodos
POP 170

Located some 23km east of Cariñena along the A220 lies the tiny village of Fuendetodos where Francisco José de Goya y Lucientes (Goya) was born in 1746.

⦿ Sights

Casa Natal de Goya MUSEUM
(www.fundacionfuendetodosgoya.org; Calle Zuloaga 3; incl Museo del Grabado de Goya €3; ⊙11am-2pm & 4-7pm Tue-Sun) This humble birthplace of Goya stayed in his family until the early 20th century, when it was purchased by the Basque painter, Ignacio Zuloaga. Destroyed

WORTH A TRIP

MONASTERIO DE PIEDRA

The one-time Cistercian Monasterio de Piedra (☎902 19 60 52; www.monasteriopiedra. com; park & monastery adult/child €15.50/11, monastery €8; ⊙ park 9am-7pm, monastery 10am-1pm & 3-7pm), 28km southwest of Calatayud, dates from the 13th century but was abandoned in the 1830s. Subsequent owners laid out the ground as a formal wooded park full of caves and waterfalls, the latter fed by Río Piedra. It's a wonderful place for a family day out, although it can get overrun on summer weekends. Incorporated into the complex is the Hotel Monasterio de Piedra.

On Tuesday, Thursday, Saturday and Sunday, Automóviles Zaragoza runs a 9am bus from Zaragoza to the monastery (€14, 2½ hours) via Calatayud, returning at 5pm.

during the civil war, the house was subsequently restored with furniture and exhibits relating to Goya's life and times.

Museo del Grabado de Goya
MUSEUM

(Calle Zuloaga; incl Casa Natal de Goya €3; ⊙ 11am-2pm & 4-7pm Tue-Sun) One hundred metres down the road from Goya's birthplace, this museum contains an important collection of the artist's engravings. There are four series including the famously satirical *Los Caprichos* and the bullfighting-themed *La Tauromaquia*.

ℹ Getting There & Away

Up to four buses daily head to Fuendetodos (€6.75, one hour) from Zaragoza.

Tarazona

POP 10,865

A journeyman town for most travellers, Tarazona rewards the curious with its strong Jewish heritage, an oversized cathedral (an unusual Gothic-Mudéjar hybrid), one of Spain's oldest bullrings and the bizarre Cipotegato festival, when a brave local dressed as a harlequin gets pelted with tomatoes by boisterous crowds every August.

◎ Sights

Judería
AREA

Tarazona has one of Spain's best preserved Jewish quarters, guarded atmospherically by its *casas colgadas* (hanging houses) that jut out over the streets below. While there are no real monuments to visit per se, the Judería has an easy-to-follow walking route with points of interest marked on explanatory boards along the way. Over 70 Jewish families lived here from the 12th to the 15th centuries, centred around a tight web of

streets around Calle Jubería and Rúa Alta de Bécquer.

Catedral Santa María de la Huerta
CATHEDRAL

(Plaza de la Seo; admission €4; ⊙ 11am-2pm & 4-7pm Tue-Sat, 11am-2pm & 4-6pm Sun) This magnificent cathedral dates from 1158 but was rebuilt in the 15th to 16th centuries. It reopened in 2011 after 30 years of restoration work. Elements from its French-Gothic roots can be observed in the frescoes in the high altar, Mudéjar influences can be seen in the intricate masonry, Renaissance artwork is reflected in the decorative chancel and carved altars, while the main portal and retrochoir display paintings from the baroque era.

Palacio Episcopal
PALACE

(Bishop's Palace; Plaza Palacio; ⊙ 11.30am-2.30pm & 4.30-7.30pm Tue-Sat, 11.30am-2.30pm & 4.30-6.30pm Sun) FREE On the site of an ancient Muslim citadel and, subsequently, the residence of several Aragonese kings, the imposing 16th-century Bishop's Palace took well over a century to build. Its exterior has a striking series of perfectly proportioned arches while, within, highlights include a series of 16th-century episcopal portraits and a magnificent Mudéjar coffered ceiling (two more are missing – purchased by William Randolph Hearst for his California 'castle' in the early 20th century).

Ayuntamiento
HISTORIC BUILDING

(Town Hall; Plaza de España) The town hall's 16th century façade is a storybook of engravings. The larger etchings are of mythical beings – you'll spot Hercules on the left – while running along the full length of the façade is a depiction of the coronation procession of Spanish King Carlos V in Bologna in 1530.

WORTH A TRIP

WINE MUSEUM

Just south of Zaragoza lies one of Spain's oldest DOs (Denominación de Origen; protected wine-growing regions), in operation since 1932. The so-called Campo de Cariñena is centred on the town of Cariñena where you'll find the Museo del Vino (Wine Museum; www.docarinena.com; Camino de la Platera 7; admission €1.50; ⏰10am-2pm & 4-6pm Tue-Sat, 11am-2pm Sun) hosted in an old 1918-vintage warehouse. It gives a good overview of the region's wine-growing history. Cariñena is just off the A-23 motorway between Zaragoza and Teruel.

⭐ Festivals & Events

Cipotegato
CULTURAL

In a country known for its bizarre festivals, Tarazona's Cipotegato takes the weirdness to a new level. Celebrated on August 27th, the star of the show is a hapless harlequin dressed in a red, green and yellow costume who runs through the main square while getting pelted with tomatoes by practically everyone in town.

The festival is descended from an old town tradition whereby every year a prisoner was given the chance to win his/her freedom by trying to out-run a stone-throwing mob. Somewhere along the line the stones were replaced by tomatoes, and the prisoner was reincarnated as a harlequin.

🛌 Sleeping & Eating

Hostal Santa Agueda
HOSTAL €

(☎976 64 00 54; www.santaagueda.com; Visconti 26; s/d incl breakfast from €35/49.50; ❄🐶) Just off Plaza San Francisco, this 200-year-old home has attractive rooms with wooden beams and a cheery decor. The little breakfast room is a glorious shrine to local girl Raquel Meller, Aragón's queen of popular song during the early 20th century. You'll hear her crooning over your croissants.

Hotel Condes de Visconti
HOTEL €€

(☎976 64 49 08; www.condesdevisconti.com; Visconti 15; d/ste from €65/75; P❄@) Beautiful rooms, mostly with colourful individual decor, plus a preserved Renaissance patio, make this 16th-century former palace a fine stopover. It also has a cafe and good old-fashioned service.

Saboya 21
ARAGONESE €€

(☎976 64 24 90; www.restaurantesaboya21.com; Marrodán 34; mains €14-20; ⏰1-4pm Tue-Sun, plus 9.30-11pm Fri & Sat; 🐶) Talented young chef, José Tazueco whips up a selection of culinary treats that zap traditional ingredients with a creative flair. Expect artistically presented plates and dishes like *ensalada de pato* (duck salad) *con piña colada* or artichokes stuffed with goose liver pâté. It's perched above a more informal cafe called Amadeo I. Reservations recommended.

ℹ Information

Tourist Office (☎976 64 00 74; www.tarazona.es; Plaza San Francisco 1; city tours €5-9.50; ⏰9.30am-2pm & 4-7pm Mon-Fri, 10am-2pm & 4-7pm Sat, 10am-2pm Sun) Organises guided tours, in Spanish, of the city, with an optional extra of the cathedral.

ℹ Getting There & Away

Up to 10 **Therpasa** (☎976 64 11 00; www.therpasa.es) buses run daily to/from Zaragoza (€7.90, 1¼ hours) and Soria (€6.10, one hour).

THE ARAGONESE PYRENEES

Sos del Rey Católico
POP 650 / ELEV 625M

If King Ferdinand II of Aragon were reincarnated in the 21st century, he'd probably still recognise his modest birthplace in Sos del Rey Católico. Take away the petrol station and the smattering of parked Peugeots and Fiats, and little has changed in this small, tightly-packed hilltop village since 1452 when the future king of a united Spain was born in the Sada palace. Legend has it that Ferdinand's mother risked going into labor by travelling on horseback from nearby Navarra (5km away as the crow flies), purely to ensure her son was born Aragonese.

Royalty aside, Sos is a fine place to soak up the tranquil essence of Aragonese village life (the Parador is well worth a splurge!). When you've finished having historical hallucinations in its labyrinthine streets, you can investigate the intricate network of mossy walking paths that dissolve into the surrounding countryside.

⊙ Sights

Casa Palacio de Seda
HISTORIC BUILDING

(Plaza de la Hispanidad; adult/child €2.90/1.90, incl tour of village €4.90/2.90; ⊙10am-1pm & 4-7pm Tue-Fri, 10am-2pm & 4-7pm Sat & Sun) Fernando II de Aragn is said to have been born in this building in 1452. It's an impressive noble mansion, which now contains an interpretative centre, with fine exhibits on the history of Sos and the life of the king. The tourist office (p374), also housed here, runs guided tours of the building.

Iglesia de San Esteban
CHURCH

(admission €1; ⊙10am-1pm & 3.30-5.30pm) This Gothic church with a weathered Romanesque portal, has a deliciously gloomy crypt decorated with medieval frescos.

Castillo de la Peña Feliciano
RUIN

The 12th-century watchtower is all that remains of the castle that once guarded the frontier between the two Christian kingdoms of Aragón and Navarra. Climb up for the views of the countryside in all directions.

🛏 Sleeping

Hostal las Coronas
HOSTAL €

(☑948 88 84 08; www.hostallascoronas.com; Calle Pons Sorolla 2; r €65-70) Run by friendly Fernando, this *hostal* has modest rustic-style rooms. Request number 3 with its spa shower and balcony overlooking Sos' hauntingly hemmed-in plaza. The downstairs bar serves tapas (€2 to €6) and breakfast (€6).

Ruta del Tiempo
HOTEL €€

(☑948 88 82 95; www.rutadeltiempo.es; Calle Larraldía 1; incl breakfast s €50, d €70-118; ⊙Mar-Oct; ❋🌐) Evocatively located under the arches, rooms on the 1st floor are themed around three Aragonese kings, while the four 2nd-floor rooms have decorations dedicated to four different continents. They're all good, but spacious 'Asia' and 'Africa' are the best rooms.

Casa del Infanzón
BOUTIQUE HOTEL €€

(☑605 94 05 36; www.casadelinfanzon.com; Calle Coliseo 3; d/ste €59/68; ❋🌐) In the heart of the Jewish quarter, this is a great deal with aesthetically furnished rooms sporting plush fabrics, a soothing colour scheme and spacious bathrooms. Several rooms have small terraces and the ample breakfast (€6.50) includes homemade breads, local *jamón* and eggs prepared to order. There is a cosy salon with a fireplace.

⭐ Parador de Sos del Rey Católico
HOTEL €€€

(☑948 88 80 11; www.parador.es; Calle Arquitecto Sainz de Vicuña 1; r from €142; ⊙15 Feb-1 Jan; Ⓟ❋🌐) This is what a Parador experience is all about: a lovingly restored historic building overlooking Sos where you can hole up with a book, sink sangrias on the restaurant terrace, or just lie back and enjoy the expansive views from your suitably regal bedroom. There's a terrific restaurant (set menus €32) serving a changing menu of regional specialities.

🍴 Eating

⭐ La Cocina del Principal
ARAGONESE €€

(☑948 88 83 48; www.lacocinadelprincipal.com; Calle Fernando el Católico 13; mains €14-17.50; ⊙1.30-3.30pm & 8.30-10.30pm Tue-Sat) Generally hailed as the best food in town, this place wins plaudits for its rib-eye steak, apple-doused veal, and pig's trotters. The setting, inside a typically medieval Sos house, is enhanced by some interesting art, including a graffiti-etched rendering of Goya's '3rd of May' masterpiece hung up on the stairway.

Vinacua
ARAGONESE €€

(www.vinacua.com; Calle Goya 24; mains €8-16, set menus €12-20; ⊙1-3.30pm & 9-11pm Mon-Fri, 1.30-3.30pm Sat & Sun; 🌐) Hearty local cuisine is served in a contemporary space with raspberry-pink walls and glossy-black furnishings. The menu includes rabbit with snails, garbanzo bean stew, grilled meats

---

WORTH A TRIP

THE DIY FRESCO

The **Sanctuario de la Misericordia** (admission €1; ⊙10am-2pm & 4.30-8pm Apr-Oct, 10.30am-1.30pm & 3.30-7pm Nov-Mar) near Borja, 45km southeast of Tarazona, attracted worldwide media attention in August 2012 after an 81-year-old amateur artist botched the restoration of a 20th-century religious painting called *Ecce Homo* in the local church. The result (subsequently dubbed 'potato Jesus') went viral on the internet, an incident which, ironically, brought prosperity to the town through tourism. Visitors are charged €1 admission to view the painting which has been reproduced on advertising banners and copied by modern pop artists.

and, for lightweights, some excellent salads with toppings like warm goat's cheese or partridge and pâté.

Shopping

Morrico Fino FOOD
(Calle Fernando el Católico 14; ⏰10am-1.30pm & 5-8pm) One of several tiny shops selling tasty regional food products found hidden in Sos' lanes.

ⓘ Information

Tourist Office (☏948 88 85 24; Plaza Hispanidad; ⏰10am-2pm & 4-8pm) Housed in the Casa Palacio de Seda, the tourist office runs twice-daily guided tours (one/two hours €2.90/4.90) of the village on weekends.

ⓘ Getting There & Away

An **Autobuses CincoVillas** (☏976 70 05 90; www.autobusescincovillas.com) bus departs from Zaragoza (2½ hours, €10.50) for Sos at 5pm Monday to Friday. It returns from Sos at 7am.

Around Sos del Rey Católico

From just north of Sos, the engaging A1601 begins its 34km-long snaking journey west and then northwest en route to the N240. It passes the pretty villages of Navardún and Urriés, before climbing over the Sierra de Peña Musera and down to the gorgeous abandoned village of Ruesta – medieval murals from the ruined church here can be viewed at Jaca's fine Museo Diocesano (p377). The final stretch passes some unusual rock formations and wheat fields, with fine views of the hilltop village of Milanos away to the east.

Valles de Echo & Ansó

The verdant Hecho and Ansó valleys are mountain magic at its best, beginning with gentle climbs through the valleys and the accumulating charms of old stone villages punctuating slopes of dense mixed woods of beech, pine, rowan, elm and hazel. As the valleys narrow to the north, 2000m-plus peaks rise triumphantly at their heads.

ⓘ Getting There & Away

A bus to Jaca leaves Ansó at 6.30am, Siresa at 6.53am and Echo at 7am, Monday to Saturday, returning from Jaca at 6.50pm. A good road links Ansó and Echo, a distance of about 12km.

Hecho

POP 630 / ELEV 833M
There probably isn't a more pleasant spot from which to launch lung-stretching sorties into the Pyrenees than humble Hecho, an attractive warren of solid stone houses with steep roofs and flower-decked balconies.

◉ Sights

The helpful tourist office (p375) also contains the small **Museo de Arte Contemporáneo**, a basement art gallery of changing exhibitions. Alongside is the **Museo de Escultura al Aire Libre y Pinturas Contemporánea** (www.hecho.es; Carretera Oza; ⏰10am-1.30pm & 5.30-8pm Mon-Sat, 10am-1.30pm Sun) 🆓, a hillside sculpture park. At the heart of the village is the endearing **Museo Etnológico Casa Mazo** (www.hecho.es; Calle Aire; admission €1.50; ⏰10.30am-1.30pm & 5-8pm), with a terrific display of photographs of villagers from the 1920s and 1930s.

🛏 Sleeping & Eating

Casa Blasquico HOTEL €
(☏974 37 50 50; www.casablasquico.es; Plaza de la Fuente 1; d/tr €55/74; ⏰closed 1st half Sep & Jan; ❀🐕🛜) The best place to stay in town, the charming Casa Blasquico has six rooms. With its flower boxes, gables and woody decor, it might have been plucked straight out of the Swiss Alps.

★**Restaurante Canteré** SPANISH €€
(☏974 37 52 14; www.cantere.es; Calle Aire 1; set menú €20.50; ⏰noon-4pm & 8-11pm) Hake and octupus? Tuna and wasabi? Carpaccio? These are not things you'd normally expect in an isolated mountain village. Canteré is a homey restaurant in Hecho's main square with a menu to rival Paris' Latin Quarter. Not that there's any Parisian pretension here. Indeed, the service and ambiance couldn't be more down-to-earth (and athletic). The desserts are equally fabulous.

Best food in the Aragonese Pyrenees? It's got to be a contender.

Restaurante Gaby ARAGONESE €€
(☏974 37 50 07; www.casablasquico.es; Plaza de la Fuente 1; mains €9-19; ⏰1.30-3.30pm & 8.30-10pm; 🛜) This much-lauded restaurant, downstairs in Casa Blasquico, is a delightful place to eat, with an intimate wood-beamed

DON'T MISS

SKIING ARAGÓN
••••••••••••••••••••••••••••••••

Aragón is one of Spain's premier ski destinations. The following are the major ski stations:

Candanchú (☑974 37 31 94; www.candanchu.com) Around 59km of widely varied pistes, 28km north of Jaca.

Astún (☑974 37 30 88; www.astun.com) The Pyrenees' most modern resort with its own purpose-built ski village; it's 3km east of Candanchú.

Panticosa (☑974 48 72 48; www.formigal-panticosa.com; ⊞) The smallest of Aragón's five Pyrenees-based ski resorts, Panticosa occupies a pleasant perch at the confluence of two picturesque valleys.

Formigal (☑974 49 00 00; www.formigal-panticosa.com) The antidote to nearby Panticosa, Formigal is Aragón's largest ski resort with 137km-worth of pistes strongly biased towards expert skiers; accessible from the A136 north of Sabiñago.

Cerler & Ampriu (☑974 55 10 12; www.cerler.com) This resort is closely affiliated to the nearby town of Benasque and thus enjoys bags of eating/sleeping and après-ski options. Its 72km of pistes drop from a high point of 2650m.

dining room plus a small outside terrace overlooking the cobbles. There is an extensive wine list and specialities include *crepes de setas* (wild mushroom crepes) and *conejo a la montañesa* (rabbit stew).

ℹ Information

Tourist Office (☑974 37 55 05; www.valledehecho.net; Carretera Oza; ☉10am-1.30pm & 5.30-8pm Jul-Oct, Sat & Sun only Nov-Jun)

Selva de Oza

This top end of the Valle de Echo is particularly beautiful; the rutted road runs parallel to Río Aragón Subordán as it bubbles its way through thick woodlands. Around 7km beyond Siresa, the road squeezes through the Boca del Infierno (Hell's Mouth), while about 14km from Siresa the paved road ends, shortly after it connects with the GR11 path en route between Candanchú and Zuriza. You can partake in zip-lining at the kid-friendly Bosque de Oza (☑974 37 54 21; ⊞) at the end of the road, or go off in search of neolithic *dolmens* (burial chambers) and an ancient stone circle on a handful of short treks.

It's possible to walk from Hecho to Selva de Oza on the Aragonese branch of the Camino de Santiago (which closely parallels the road).

Ansó

POP 480 / ELEV 860M

Ansó takes you even further into a world of high places and harmony. The rough-hewn stone houses here are in grey stone, with red-tiled roofs. Some walls are whitewashed, making a pleasing chequerboard pattern. Forested slopes climb ever upwards from where Ansó straggles along a low escarpment above a partly covered streambed. A grid of narrow streets surrounds the main square, Plaza Mayor.

🍽 Sleeping & Eating

Hostal Kimboa   HOSTAL €
(☑974 37 01 84; www.hostalkimboa.com; Paseo Chapitel 24; s/d incl breakfast €45/55) A charming family-owned small hotel in the centre of town with pleasant pine-furnished rooms above a good restaurant specialising in traditional grilled meats (mains €8 to €10), plus a popular bar with outside terrace.

Posada Magoria   HOTEL €
(☑974 37 00 49; http://posadamagoria.com; Calle Milagros 32; d €55-60; ☜) Adjoining the lofty rough-walled church, the delightful Posada Magoria is crammed with vintage character and lovingly kept by a family with lots of local knowledge. The kitchen *comedor* (dining room) serves up an excellent €12 *menú* of organically sourced vegetarian dishes (try the nettle soup if it's on offer).

Maiberal   ARAGONESE €€
(☑974 37 01 74; www.restaurantemaiberal.es; Calle Arrigo 1; mains €8-12; ☉11am-4pm Mon, Tue & Thu, 11am-4pm & 7-11pm Fri-Sun) A friendly, authentic place serving comfort food like free-range roasted chicken in a creamy mushroom sauce. There are delectable tapas, *tostas*

(toasts with toppings) and *raciones* (large serving), as well.

ℹ️ Information

Tourist Office (📞 974 37 02 25; Plaza Mayor; 🕐10am-2pm & 5-8pm daily Jul & Aug, Sat & Sun Sep-Jun) Offers free guided tours of the village.

Siresa

POP 130 / ELEV 850M

A couple of kilometres north of Echo, Siresa is another village as captivating as it is tiny.

◉ Sights

Iglesia de San Pedro CHURCH
(admission €1.50; 🕐11am-1pm & 5-7pm Thu-Tue, 11am-1pm Wed) This thick-walled 11th-century church is the town's centrepiece; it originally comprised of one of Aragón's earliest monasteries. The cavernous interior is suitably austere.

🛏️ Sleeping

Hotel Usón HOTEL €
(📞974 37 53 58; www.hoteluson.com; s/d/apt from €40/50/65; 🕐Easter-Oct; 🅿️🛜) There's perfect peace in fabulous surroundings at the Hotel Usón, high in the Echo valley, 5km north of Siresa on the road to the Selva de Oza. Popular with birdwatchers and walkers, the restaurant offers hearty home-cooked meals.

Hotel Castillo d'Acher HOTEL €
(📞974 37 53 13; www.castillodacher.com; Plaza Mayor; d €50; 🛜) This hotel has a pleasant mix of rooms, some rather old-fashioned, others pine-clad and modern. The owners also offer a *casa rural* (village accommodation; minimum one week stay). The spacious in-house restaurant does a good *menú del día* (daily set menu; €12).

Valle de Zuriza

This narrow valley, which runs for 15km north of Ansó, follows the Río Jeral and leads high into remote Pyrenean corners where raptors circle high above. Where the paved road ends, wonderful walking trails such as the GR11 take over.

ℹ️ Getting There & Away

A bus will get you only as far as Ansó. You'll need a car and – beyond that – your legs, to navigate the Zuriza.

Santa Cruz de la Serós

POP 140

Santa Cruz de la Serós is a pretty village 4km south of the N240. It is primarily used as a gateway to what is, arguably, Aragón's most fascinating monastery – the Monasterio de San Juan de la Peña.

◉ Sights

★Monasterio de San Juan de la Peña MONASTERY
(Old Monastery; www.monasteriosanjuan.com; Monasterio Viejo only/Monasteries Viejo & Nuevo €7/12; 🕐10am-2pm & 3-8pm Jun-Aug, shorter hours Sep-May) San Juan de la Peña is a religious complex comprising of two monasteries. A fire in 1675 led the monks to abandon the original 10th century Monasterio Viejo and build a new one, the Monasterio Nuevo, in brick further up the hill. Despite once being one of the most important medieval monasteries in Aragon with various Grail legends associated with it, both places had been abandoned by the mid-19th century. They have since been rehabilitated and merit a detour (stick to the Monasterio Viejo if you're short on time).

From the village of Santa Cruz de la Serós, a winding road climbs the Sierra de la Peña 7km to the Monasterio Viejo (Old Monastery), tucked protectively under an overhanging lip of rock at a bend in the road. Its highlight is a Romanesque cloister, with marvellous carved 12th- and 13th-century capitals depicting Genesis and the life of Christ. The first three kings of Aragón – Ramiro I (1036–64), Sancho Ramírez (1064–94) and Pedro I (1094–1104) – are among those buried here.

The Monasterio Nuevo (New Monastery) is a dual-towered red-bricked building located roughly 1.5km further up the road. It hosts the Monastery Interpretation Centre built over the monastery's 17th century ruins and the Kingdom of Aragón Interpretation Centre devoted to the kings of Aragón. The former has a glass-paneled floor and slightly cheesy life-sized models of monks, while the latter plays a audiovisual show about Aragon's steely monarchs.

Tickets for the monasteries are sold at the Monasterio Nuevo and, during the summer, this is where you'll have to park. A semi-regular bus shuttles down to the Monasterio Viejo and back.

🛏 Sleeping & Eating

Hostelería Santa Cruz
HOSTAL €

(📞974 36 19 75; www.santacruzdelaseros.com; Calle Ordana; s/d from €50.50/62.50; 📶) Near the church in Santa Cruz de la Serós, this is a beautiful place with friendly service and lovely rooms overlooking the village square. Its restaurant serves a good *menú del día* (€12).

❶ Getting There & Away

There's no public transport to the monastery. For walkers, a stiff 4km marked path (the GR65.3.2) leads up from Santa Cruz to the Monasterio Viejo. With an ascent of 350m, it takes about 1½ hours.

Jaca

POP 13,250 / ELEV 820M

A gateway to the western valleys of the Aragonese Pyrenees, Jaca has a compact and attractive old town dotted with remnants of its past as the capital of the nascent 11th-century Aragón kingdom. These include an unusual fortress and a sturdy cathedral, while the town also has some great places to eat. On winter weekends, après-ski funsters provide a lively soundtrack.

◉ Sights

There are some lovely old buildings in the streets of the *casco historico* (old town) that fans out south of the cathedral, including the 15th-century **Torre del Reloj** (Plaza del Marqués de la Cadena) and the charming little **Ermita de Sarsa** (Avenida Oroel), moved here in 1972 from an abandoned Pyrenean village

★ Museo Diocesano
MUSEUM

(Museum of Sacred Art; www.diocesisdejaca.org; Plaza de la Catedral; adult/concession €6/4.50; ⊙10am-1.30pm & 4-7pm Tue-Sat, 10am-1.30pm Sun) Jaca's excellent Museo Diocesano (accessed from the cathedral) is a kind of mini version of Barcelona's Museu Nacional d'Art de Catalunya. Its speciality (and highlight) is a set of 11th century religious murals rescued from the Romanesque church of Bagues in the Pyrenees and displayed in rooms surrounding the church's old cloister. The rest of the exhibits are by no means ballast. Check out the musical instruments and the ingenious binoculars in the cloister that show you how it used to look.

Museo de Miniaturas Militares
MUSEUM

(Museum of Military Miniatures; www.museomini aturasjaca.es; adult/child €6/4) The thought of a model soldier museum might not sound particularly enticing to anyone over the age of 10, but think again. The 3D battle scenes displayed in these interconnecting rooms offer a pictorial history lesson, from neolithic spear-throwers to Franco's fascist tanks.

Catedral de San Pedro
CATHEDRAL

(Plaza de la Catedral; ⊙11.30am-1.30pm & 4.15-8pm) **FREE** Jaca's 11th-century cathedral is a formidable building, its imposing facade typical of the sturdy stone architecture of northern Aragón. It was once more gracefully French Romanesque in style, but a Gothic overhaul in the 16th century bequeathed a hybrid look. The interior retains some fine features, in particular the side chapel dedicated to Santa Orosia, the city's patron saint, whose martyrdom is depicted in a series of mysterious murals.

ARAGÓN JACA

WHAT'S COOKING IN ARAGÓN?

The kitchens and tables of Aragón are dominated by meat. The region's cold, harsh winds create the ideal conditions for curing *jamón* (ham), a top tapa here; some of the best can be found in the storied cafe-cum-deli Pastelería Muñoz (p395) in Teruel's Plaza Torico. Likewise, another meaty favourite, *jarretes* (hock of ham or shanks) is available in simple village restaurants like Torla's La Brecha (p381), while heartier *ternasco* (suckling lamb) is generally served as a steak or ribs with potatoes – try it at Los Xarmientos (p369) in Zaragoza.

Other popular dishes include *conejo a la montañesa* (rabbit mountain-style) served with gusto at Hecho's Restaurante Gaby (p374) while (phew!) vegetarians can seek out tasty *pochas viudas* (white-bean stew with peppers, tomatoes and onion), a popular starter at restaurants like La Cocina del Principal (p373) in Sos del Rey Católico.

With France just up the road, it's no surprise, perhaps, that *caracoles* (snails) are an Aragonese speciality. Try them!

Ciudadela
FORTRESS

(Citadel; www.ciudadeladejaca.es; Calle del Primer Viernes de Mayo; adult/child €6/4; ⊙ 11am-2pm & 5-8pm Tue-Sun) The star-shaped, 16th-century citadel is Spain's only extant pentagonal fortress and one of only two in Europe. It now houses an army academy, but visits are permitted, with 40-minute multilingual guided tours. The citadel also hosts the Museo de Miniaturas Militares (p377). While a toy solider museum might not sound particularly enticing to anyone over the age of 10, the 3D battle scenes displayed in these interconnecting rooms offer a pictorial history lesson from neolithic spear-throwers to Franco's fascist tanks.

A combined ticket for the museum and citadel costs €10/8.

⭐ Festivals & Events

Fiesta de Santa Orosia
RELIGIOUS

Jaca puts on its party gear for the week-long Fiesta de Santa Orosia, which revolves around the saint's day of 25 June.

Festival Folklórico de los Pirineos
FOLKLORE

(www.festivaljaca.es) This folklore festival held in late July and early August (on odd-numbered years), provides 1½ weeks of international music, dance, crafts and theatre.

🛏️ Sleeping

Hostal París
HOSTAL €

(☑ 974 36 10 20; www.hostalparisjaca.com; Plaza de San Pedro 5; s/d without bathroom from €32/42; 🛜) Close to the cathedral, this friendly, central option has high ceilings, creaky floorboards, spotless, ample-sized rooms and smart, shared bathrooms (seven bathrooms for 20 rooms). Many rooms overlook the square. Breakfast is available for a minimal extra cost.

⭐ Hotel Barosse
BOUTIQUE HOTEL €€

(☑ 974 36 05 82; www.barosse.com; incl breakfast s €72-136, d €115-170; ❄️🛜) In the quiet hamlet of Barós, 2km south of Jaca, Hotel Barosse has six individually styled rooms with lovely attention to detail, from exposed stone walls and splashes of colour to fine bathroom packages of goodies. There's a reading room, garden, an on-site Jacuzzi and sauna, and fine views of the Pyrenees. The owner, José is a wonderful host (and chef). It's adults only.

🍴 Eating

⭐ La Tasca de Ana
CONTEMPORARY TAPAS €

(Calle de Ramiro I 3; tapas from €3; ⊙ 7-11.30pm Mon-Fri, 12.30-3.30pm & 7-11.30pm Sat & Sun; 🛜) One of Aragón's best tapas bars – hence the crowds – La Tasca has tempting options lined up along the bar, more choices cooked to order and a carefully chosen list of local wines. Check out its *tapas mas solicitados* (most popular orders) listed on the blackboard. Top contenders include the *tostada* (toast) topped with goat's cheese and blueberries.

Gorbea
TAPAS €€

(www.bargorbea.com; Calle Mayor 24; pinchos from €2, miniaturas €5; ⊙ noon-4pm & 7-11.30pm) An upbeat contemporary bar with excellent Basque-style *pinchos* (snacks), *miniaturas* (small dishes) like *kokotyas al pil pil* (hake in a chilli-spiced sauce), plus good size *raciones* to share.

Restaurante El Portón
ARAGONESE €€

(☑ 974 35 58 54; Plaza de la Cadena 1; mains €15-28; ⊙ 1.30-4pm & 8.30pm-midnight Thu-Tue) Located in a little tree-shaded plaza, this classy venue serves haute-cuisine versions of Aragonese fare. Foie gras is something of a speciality – try the bison stuffed with foie gras. Reservations essential.

🛍️ Shopping

Confitería Echeto
FOOD

(Plaza de la Catedral 4; ⊙ 9.30am-2.30pm & 4.30-9pm Mon-Sat) In business since 1890 (take a peek at the original National cash register), the cakes here are unmatched in town. Also sells fancy tins of speciality sweets.

ℹ️ Information

Tourist Office (☑ 974 36 00 98; Plaza de San Pedro 11-13; ⊙ 9am-1.30pm & 4.30-7.30pm Mon-Sat)

ℹ️ Getting There & Away

BUS

Regular Alosa (www.alosa.es) buses go to Huesca (€7.80, 1¼ hours, nine daily) and Zaragoza (€15.90, 2¼ hours, ten daily) from the central **bus station** (☑ 974 35 50 60; Plaza de Biscós).

TRAIN

Twice daily trains go to Huesca (€8.10, two hours) and Zaragoza (€15, two hours).

HIKING ROUTES

The Parque Nacional de Ordesa y Monte Perdido (p380) equals walking trails (http://senderos.turismodearagon.com). Pick up a copy of the Senderos maps and descriptions for the four sectors (Ordesa, Añisclo, Escuaín and Pineta) from any of the information offices. The star walk is probably the hike through the Valle de Ordesa to Circo de Soaso.

Circo de Soaso A classic day walk and one of park's most popular. Starting in Pradera de Ordesa two hours' walk (or a short drive) from Torla, the GR11 path follows the Valle de Ordesa to Circo de Soaso, a rocky balcony with the centrepiece Cola de Caballo (Horsetail) waterfall. Allow six to seven hours for the 16km round-trip.

Refugio de Góriz & Monte Perdido Fit walkers can continue beyond the turn-around on the Circo de Soaso to walk and climb a series of steep switchbacks (part of the GR11) to the Circo itself. Beyond here the path continues up to the Refugio de Góriz, at 2200m, the main base camp for ascents of Monte Pedido. Be warned, Monte Perdido is a serious undertaking that requires mountaineering skills, crampons and ice axes.

Faja Racón, Circo de Cotatuero & Faja Canarellos This summer-only walk takes you along spectacular high-level paths on the north flank of the Valle de Ordesa. It starts in Pradera de Ordesa with a turn-around at the classic Pyrenean waterfall Cascada de Cotatuero.

Brecha de Rolando The Brecha de Rolando (Roldán; 2807m) is a dramatic, breezy gap in the mountain wall on the French frontier. To reach it, you first have to follow the Faja Racón, Circo de Cotatuero & Faja Canarellos hike up to the Circo de Colatuero. The cool-headed may then climb part of the wall of the Circo by the Clavijas de Cotatuero, a set of 32 iron pegs hammered into the rock. From here you are about 2½ hours' march from the Brecha de Rolando.

Puerto de Bujaruelo Just north of the village of Torla on the road to Pradera de Ordesa, the GR11 branches north in a 6km arc up the very pretty Valle de Bujaruelo to San Nicolás de Bujaruelo. From here an east–northeast path leads in about three hours (with a 950m ascent) up to the Puerto de Bujaruelo on the border with France.

Cañón de Añisclo The Cañón de Añisclo is a gaping wound in the earth's fabric. Energetic walkers who have made it to the Refugio de Góriz can descend the gorge from the north, from where numerous trails fan out into the mountains. From the south, the trail starts at a car park at Ereta de Biés and pitches north along a forest road by the Río Beliós before the trees part and canyon and mountain views open out. The turn-around point is at the powerful Fuen Blanca waterfall.

Balcón de Pineta This challenging day-hike begins close to the Parador Nacional de Bielsa just outside the northeastern border of the park. After the waterfalls of the Cascadas del Cinca, it climbs via a series of steep switchbacks up to the 'Pineta Balcony' for stunning glacier and mountain views. Allow eight to 10 hours round-trip and a cumulative elevation of 1200m.

Valle de Tena

From the regional centre of Biescas, north of Sabiñánigo, the A136 climbs gently towards the French border.

Leading deep into the mountains, a narrow road up the Valle de Tena runs 8km past the ski resort of Panticosa to the Panticosa Resort, a large leisure complex with two four-star hotels, several restaurants, a thermal spa (☑ 974 48 71 61; www.balneariodepanticosa.com; baths/massages from €21/40;

⊙ 11am-midnight) and various other facilities, some realised, some still in planning. The setting, by a lake in an enclosed valley high in the Pyrennes, is stunning, but the complex which mixes Belle Epoque architecture with super-modern tends to divide opinion between convenience-seeking tourists (who like it) and mountain purists (who don't).

Returning to the main A136, Sallent de Gállego, 3.5km north of the Panticosa turn-off, is a lovely stone village with a bubbling brook running through it.

🛏 Sleeping

Hotel Continental   HOTEL €€
(www.panticosa.com; r from €96; P ✳ @ 🛜) One
of two hotels that form part of the Panticosa
Resort, the Continental is encased in a curvaceous super-modern building. The facility
is huge, with an adjacent spa and four different restaurants.

❶ Getting There & Away

From Jaca, one or two daily buses wind over to
Panticosa and Formigal (€5.25, two hours).

The N260 leaves the valley at Biescas and
follows a pretty route to Torla and Aínsa.

Parque Nacional de Ordesa y Monte Perdido

This is where the Spanish Pyrenees really take your breath away. At the heart of
it all is a dragon's back of limestone peaks
skirting the French border, with a southeastward spur. Monte Perdido (3348m),
the third-highest peak in the Pyrenees, is
in the park. Deep valleys slice down from
the high ground. Most were carved by gla-
ciers and at their heads lie bowl-like glacial
circos (cirques) backed by spectacular cur-
tain walls of rock. Chief among the valleys
are Pineta (east), Escuaín (southeast), Bellos (south), Ordesa (southwest), Bujaruelo
(west) and Gavarnie (north, in France).

Along with Picos de Europa, Ordesa y
Monte Perdido is the oldest national park in
Spain, created in 1918.

🛏 Sleeping

Refugio Góriz   HUT €
(🛜 974 34 12 01; www.goriz.es; bed/full-board/half-
board €16.80/40.10/52.20) The Spanish Pyrenees' star refuge is located in the shadow of
Monte Perdido, for which it acts as an unofficial base-camp. Open year-round, it sits
at the crossroads of an enviable network of
paths. The quickest route in is from Pradera
de Ordesa (four hours on foot). Beds are in
shared dorms and they serve breakfast and
dinner as well as offering a picnic lunch.

Camping is permitted outside between
sunset and sunrise only.

❶ Information

MAPS

If you're keen to traverse the park along the
GR11, Editorial Alpina (www.editorialalpina.com)
produces excellent maps for walkers. Another
good reference is the guidebook *Through the
Spanish Pyrenees: GR11 – A Trekking Guidebook*
by Paul Lucia and available from Cicerone Press
(www.cicerone.co.uk).

RULES & REGULATIONS

Bivouacing is allowed only above certain altitudes (1800m to 2500m, depending on the
sector); ask at one of the information centres for
details. Swimming in rivers or lakes, mountain
biking, fishing and lighting fires are banned.

TOURIST INFORMATION

Centro de Visitantes de Torla (🛜 974 48 64
72; Torla; ⏱ 9am-2pm & 4.15-7pm Apr-Oct,
8am-3pm Nov-Mar)

Bielsa (🛜 974 50 10 43; Bielsa; ⏱ 8am-3pm &
4.15-7pm Apr-Oct, 8am-3pm Nov-Mar; 🛜)

Centro de Visitantes de Tella (🛜 974 48 64
72; Tella; ⏱ 9am-2pm & 4.15-7pm daily Apr-Oct,
Sat & Sun Nov-Mar)

Escalona (🛜 974 50 51 31; Escalona; ⏱ 8am-
3pm & 4.15-7pm Apr-Oct, 8am-3pm Nov-Mar)

❶ Getting There & Away

The main entry point into the park is **Torla**, 3km
south of the southwest corner of the national
park. It's perfectly practical to walk in from here.

From **Escalona**, 11km north of Aínsa on the
A138, a minor paved road heads northwest
across to **Sarvisé**. This road crosses the park's
southern tip, with a narrow, sinuous section
winding up the dramatic Bellos valley and giving
access to walks in the spectacular Cañón de
Añisclo (the upper reaches of the Bellos valley).

From **Bielsa**, a 12km paved road runs up the
Valle de Pineta in the park's northeastern corner, where you'll find one of Spain's more isolated Parador hotels.

Private vehicles may not drive from Torla to
Pradera de Ordesa during Easter week and July
to mid-September. During these periods a shuttle bus (one way/return €3/4.50) runs between
Torla's Centro de Visitantes and Pradera de
Ordesa. A maximum of 1800 people are allowed
in this sector of the park at any one time.

During the same periods, a one-way system
is enforced on part of the Escalona–Sarvisé
road. From the Puyarruego turn-off, 2km out of
Escalona, to a point about 1km after the road
diverges from the Bellos valley, only northwest-
ward traffic is allowed. Southeastward traffic
uses an alternative, more southerly road.

Torla

POP 320

Torla is a lovely Alpine-style village of
stone houses with slate roofs, although

Parque Nacional de Ordesa y Monte Perdido

it does get overrun in July and August. Walkers use Torla as a gateway to the national park, but the town's setting is also delightful, with the houses clustered above Río Ara under the a backdrop of the national park's mountains. In your ramblings around town, make for the 13th-century Iglesia de San Salvador; there are fine views to be had from the small park on the church's northern side.

🛏 Sleeping

Hotel Villa de Torla   HOTEL €€

(☑974 48 61 56; www.hotelvilladetorla.com; Plaza de Aragón 1; s/d/tr €50/70/90; 🏊) The rooms here are tidy – some are spacious and stylish, others have floral bedspreads and look a little tired. But the undoubted highlight is the swimming pool and the bar terrace, from where there are lovely views. There's also a Jacuzzi and small gym.

Casa de San Martín   HISTORIC HOTEL €€€

(☑974 50 31 05; www.casadesanmartin.com; s/d from €132/165; ☺Mar-Nov; 🅿❄🐾) Along a dirt track 5km off the main Torla–Aínsa road (take the sign for San Martín de la Solana), Casa de San Martín is a stunning rural retreat. The handsome stone house has been beautifully renovated and the rooms are temples to good taste, without being overdone. Meals (set menus €38.50) are exceptional and the setting is tranquil and picturesque.

🍽 Eating

La Brecha   ARAGONESE €

(☑974 48 62 21; www.lucienbriet.com; Calle Francia; mains €8-10; ☺1.30-4pm & 8-10.30pm) Simple homestyle dishes like *jarretes* (hock of ham) are the speciality of this bustling local bar and restaurant. Don't forget to try the homemade *pacharan* (traditional local liquour said to help with digestion). Open all year – another bonus.

Restaurante el Duende ARAGONESE €€
(☑974 48 60 32; www.elduenderestaurante.com; Calle de la Iglesia; mains €15-22; ☺1.30-3.30pm & 8-10.30pm) Food you'll want to photograph served out of a building you'll probably want to photograph too – Duende just might inspire that mythical spirit flamenco aficionados know as *duende*. Encased in 19th-century building made from local stone and serving a variety fantastic meats right off the grill, it's undoubtedly the best restaurant in town.

❶ Getting There & Away

One daily bus operated by **Alosa** (☑902 21 07 00; www.alosa.es) connects Torla to Aínsa (€4.30, one hour).

Aínsa

POP 2230

The beautiful hilltop village of medieval Aínsa, which stands above the small modern town of the same name, is one of Aragón's gems, a medieval masterpiece hewn from uneven stone. From its perch, you'll have commanding panoramic views of the mountains, particularly the great rock bastion of La Peña Montañesa.

◉ Sights

Castle CASTLE
(☺7am-11pm) **FREE** The castle and fortifications off the western end of the Plaza de San Salvador mostly date from the 1600s, though the main tower is 11th century; there are some reasonable views from the wall. It contains an Ecomuseo (p382) on Pyrenean fauna with an aviary that is 'home' to various rescued birds of prey, including the majestic *quebrantahuesos* (bearded vulture), and the **Espacio del Geoparque de Sobrarbe** (www.geoparquepirineos.com; ☺9.30am-2pm & 4.30-7.30pm) **FREE** with displays on the region's intriguing geology, as well as good views from the tower.

Ecomuseo MUSEUM
(admission €4; ☺11am-2pm & 4-8pm) The largest of the castle's four towers has been made into an Ecomuseo which you enter through a shop on the ground floor. There are three components: an expo space spread over three floors that explains the flora and fauna of the Pyrenees; a multimedia room with an eagle's-eye film about the mountains; and a giant aviary in the main part of the tower that is 'home' to various rescued birds of prey, including the majestic *quebrantahuesos* (bearded vulture).

Iglesia de Santa María CHURCH
(belfry admission €1; ☺belfry 11am-1.30pm & 4-7pm Sat & Sun) Aínsa's main church – austere and sober by Spanish standards – bears all the hallmarks of unadulterated Romanesque. Few embellishments mark its thick, bare walls which date from the 11th century. Don't leave without exploring the crypt and the belfry.

✵ Festivals & Events

Festival Internacional de Música MUSIC
(www.festivalcastillodeainsa.com) In July, Aínsa hosts this month-long festival with predominantly Spanish and a few international music acts in the castle grounds.

▦ Sleeping

Albergue Mora de Nuei HOSTEL €
(☑974 51 06 14; www.alberguemoradenuei.com; Calle del Portal de Abajo 2; dm/d €17/50; ⓐ) At the lower end of the old town, facing onto Plaza de San Salvador, this fine place is one of Aragón's best hostels. Rooms are colourful, there's a roof terrace, an atmospheric basement bar, good food, and a regular calendar of live music and other cultural events. There's one double room with private bathroom; the rest are six to 10-bed dorms.

★ Hotel los Siete Reyes HOTEL €€
(☑974 50 06 81; www.lossietereyes.com; Plaza Mayor; d €70-120; ❋ⓐ) Tucked under an arcade in Ainsa's ancient main square and exhibiting a style perhaps best described as historical-boutique, the Siete Reyes offers seven rooms fit for seven kings (and queens). Modern art hangs on old stone walls and mood lighting shines from ceilings crossed by wooden beams.

Posada Real HOTEL €€
(☑974 50 09 77; www.posadareal.com; Plaza Mayor 6; d from €70; ❋ⓐ) A tastefully renovated noble mansion, this *posada* (inn) has large rooms and exposed wooden beams; some rooms have four-poster beds and/or good views. It's a few steps down off Plaza Mayor.

✕ Eating

L'Alfil TAPAS €
(Calle Traversa; raciones €5.80-18.50; ☺11am-4pm & 7pm-midnight Thu-Tue May-Oct, shorter hours

Nov-Apr) This pretty little cafe-bar, with floral accompaniment to its outside tables, is in a side street along from the church. It has a whole heap of *raciones* that are more creative than you'll find elsewhere, from ostrich chorizo, snails and deer sausage to wild-boar pâté and cured duck. Also specialises in local herbal liquors.

Bodegas del Sobrarbe ARAGONESE €€
(☑974 50 02 37; www.bodegasdelsobrarbe.com; Plaza Mayor 2; mains €18-22; ☺noon-4pm & 8-11pm) Unless you're a vegetarian, you won't want to wave *adiós* to Aragon before you've tasted the local lamb, known as *ternasco*, which is slow-roasted and best served with some Pyrenean mushrooms and/or *patatas a lo pobre* (potatoes sauteed with onions and garlic). Bodegas del Sobrarbe overlooking Aínsa's archaic main square is a fine place to try it.

⭐**Restaurante Callizo** CONTEMPORARY SPANISH €€€
(☑974 50 03 85; Plaza Mayor; set menus €25-42; ☺1-3pm & 7-11pm Tue-Sat, 1-4pm Sun) Tap a local and they'll probably tell you this is the best place in town, if not the region. It pulls off that difficult trick off marrying Aragonese tradition with modern gastronomic theatre. The result: a true eating experience, especially if you opt for the five-course tasting menu. Typical dishes include wild boar and roast suckling lamb, as well as a few fish dishes.

🛈 Information

Municipal Tourist Office (☑974 50 07 67; www.ainsasobrarbe.net; Avenida Pirenáica 1; ☺10am-2pm & 4-7:30pm) Located in the new town down the hill.

Regional Tourist Office (☑974 50 05 12; www.turismosobrarbe.com; Plaza del Castillo 1, Torre Nordeste; ☺9:30am-2pm & 4-7pm Sun-Thu, 9.30am-2pm & 4.30-7.30pm Sun) Definitely the best tourist office with bags of info and extremely helpful staff. It's located within the castle walls inside one of the four towers.

🛈 Getting There & Away

Alosa (☑902 21 07 00; www.alosa.es) runs daily buses to/from Barbastro (€5.85, one hour) and Torla (€4.30, one hour).

Benasque

POP 2240 / ELEV 1140M

Aragón's northeastern corner is crammed with the highest and shapeliest peaks in the Pyrenees, and Benasque, a comparatively modern Alpine-style town, is perfectly sited to serve as gateway to the high valleys. Even in midsummer, these epic mountains can be capped with snow and ice. Northeast of Benasque, the Pyrenees' highest peak, the Pico de Aneto (3404m), towers above the massif.

🤿 Activities

Sin Fronteras ADVENTURE SPORTS
(☑974 55 01 77; www.sinfronterasadventure.com; Carretera Benasque 1; 🚐) A slew of summer activities with an emphasis on rafting, canyoning (including kid-appropriate routes) and the increasingly popular *via ferratas* (fixed protection climbing routes).

Meridiano Cero ADVENTURE SPORTS
(www.guiaspirineos.com; Benasque) A local operator which offers guides and courses in everything from skiing to mountain climbing. Book through the comprehensive website.

Compañía de Guías Valle de Benasque ADVENTURE SPORTS
(☑974 55 14 25; www.guiasbenasque.com; Avenida de Francia) This company has an impressive 20 years of experience and offers a range of activities and courses for both summer and winter, including hiking, skiing, snowboarding and rock climbing. It can also supply all the necessary kit and equipment.

🛌 Sleeping & Eating

⭐**Hotel Aneto** HOTEL €€
(☑974 55 10 61; www.hotelesvalero.com; Avenida de Francia 4; d incl breakfast from €104; ☺Jun-Mar; 🅿❄@🛜🏊) The streamlined, super-modern Aneto is a cut above your cosy ski lodge with a wide selection of rooms, from the snazzy to the positively luxurious.

DON'T MISS

WHITEWATER RAFTING

Southwest of Benasque, the village of Campo is a major centre for whitewater rafting on the Río Ésera which is sometimes regulated by opening one of the local river dams. Operators line Campo's main street. One good choice is Sin Fronteras, which also offers kayaking and canoeing.

Bonuses include a small indoor swimming pool, free parking, a great lobby bar and filling breakfasts. Staff pull off that magic amalgamation of ultra-professionalism but thoroughly warm service.

Hotel Avenida HOTEL €€
(☎974 55 11 26; www.h-avenida.com; Avenida de los Tilos 14; d/tr/q €74/81/99; 🛜) Rooms are small but clean in this typical ski lodge hotel with a woody decor and gabled roof. There's a restaurant attached and there are triple and quadruple room options for families and/or groups.

El Veedor de Viandas ARAGONESE €€
(www.elveedordeviandas.com; Avenida Los Tilos; pinchos €1.70, mains €8-12; ⊙noon-3.30pm & 6-11pm Thu-Tue) A welcoming informal space combining a gourmet deli, bodega, tapas bar and restaurant. *Pinchos* and *tostadas* have innovative toppings like *manzana con foie* (apple and pâté) and oyster mushrooms with bacon and garlic mayonnaise. Plus there are salads, carpaccios, egg-based dishes and belly-filling *cazuelitas* (mini-stews).

Restaurante el Fogaril ARAGONESE €€
(☎974 55 16 12; Calle Mayor 5; mains €12-20; ⊙1-4pm & 8.30-10.30pm) Part of the adjacent and popular Hotel Ciria, this elegant restaurant serves outstanding Aragonese fare. Its specialities include young venison and stuffed partridge, *cozal* (small deer) and freshwater fish.

🛍 Shopping

Barrabés OUTDOOR EQUIPMENT
(www.barrabes.com; Avenida de Francia; ⊙10.30am-1.30pm & 4.30-9pm) This really is the one-stop sports store in town, selling equipment and sportswear for just about every activity you can think of. It also carries a good range of guides and maps, and has an online shopping option.

ℹ Information

Tourist Office (☎974 55 12 89; www.turismobenasque.com; Calle San Sebastián; ⊙9.30am-1pm & 4.30-8pm)

ℹ Getting There & Away

Two buses daily operate Monday to Saturday, and one runs on Sunday, from Huesca (€13.35, 2½ hours).

Upper Ésera Valley & Maladeta Massif

North of Benasque, the A139 continues paved for about 12km. About 10km from Benasque, a side road leads 6km east along the pretty upper Ésera valley, ending at La Besurta, with a hut selling drinks and some food.

Hospital de Benasque (☎974 55 20 12; www.llanosdelhospital.com; s/d incl breakfast from €67/86; 🅿@🛜), just 2.5km shy of the French border, is a large mountain lodge surrounded by handsome peaks. There's a bar, restaurant, spa and wellness centre, and rooms have a comfortable luxurious feel. Cross-country skiing is popular in the winter.

South of La Besurta is the great 3308m Maladeta massif, a superb challenge for experienced climbers and culminating in Pico de Aneto (3404m), the highest peak in the Pyrenees.

ℹ Getting There & Away

Unless you're on a long-distance hiking trip, you'll need your own wheels to penetrate this far into the mountains.

The A139 north of Benasque is your gateway.

Alquézar

POP 300 / ELEV 670M

Like so many Aragonese villages, Alquézar jumps out at you unexpectedly. You'll barely guess its magnificence until you're virtually inside its tight labyrinth of streets overlooked by the steep cliffs of the plunging Rio Vero gorge. Aesthetic beauty aside, Alquézar reigns as Aragon's (and Spain's) canyoning capital, with multiple companies offering adventure trips into the surrounding Sierra de Guara, a sparsely-populated limestone massif in the foothills of the Pyrenees.

◉ Sights

Colegiata de Santa María CASTLE, MONASTERY
(admission €2.50; ⊙11am-1.30pm & 4.30-7.30pm) Alquézar is crowned by this large castle-monastery. Originally built as an *alcázar* (fortress) by the Arabs in the 9th century, it was conquered and replaced by an Augustinian monastery in 1099. Remnants are still visible. The columns within its delicate cloister are crowned by carved capitals depicting biblical scenes, and the walls

are covered with spellbinding murals. On the upper level is a museum of sacred art.

Activities

The main canyoning season is mid-June to mid-September and prices, which vary depending on the number of people and the graded difficulty of the trip, generally include gear, guide and insurance – prices start at around €39 for a day-trip. Most of the agencies also offer rafting, trekking, rock climbing and *via ferratas*. Recommended places are lined up in a row at the entrance to the village.

Avalancha ADVENTURE SPORTS
(☎974 31 82 99; www.avalancha.org; Arrabal; ⊙8am-9pm) Activities include trekking for €50/80 per half/full day and rock climbing for €120 per half day. A day's canyoning is €39 to €49 depending on group size.

Vertientes ADVENTURE SPORTS
(☎974 31 83 54; www.vertientesaventura.com; San Hipólito) Offers rafting from €37, canyoning from €68 and half-day treks from €58.

Guías Boira ADVENTURE SPORTS
(☎974 31 89 74; www.guiasboira.com; San Hipólito) Offers two-day canyoning packages for €82.

Sleeping

Albergue Rural de Guara HOSTEL €
(☎974 31 83 96; www.albergueruraldeguara.com; Calle Pilaseras; dm €15.50, breakfast €5.50) This cheerfully run *albergue* is perched up above the village with fine views from the surrounds. Rooms are shared dorms. Staff can arrange picnic lunches (€8). Breakfast is an extra €5.50.

Hotel Maribel BOUTIQUE HOTEL €€
(☎974 31 89 79; www.hotelmaribel.es; Calle Arrabal; d incl breakfast €120-150; ⊙Feb-Dec; ❄📶) This boutique hotel has plenty of charm and, while the decor won't be to everyone's taste (following a wine theme and ranging from gorgeous to vaguely kitsch), every room is supremely comfortable. If there's no-one at reception, try the nearby Restaurante Casa Gervasio.

Hotel Villa de Alquézar HOTEL €€
(☎974 31 84 16; www.villadealquezar.com; Calle Pedro Arenal Cavero 12; s/d incl breakfast €65/79; P📶) This is a lovely place with plenty of style in its airy rooms; several sport great views and there are period touches throughout. The most expensive rooms on the top floor are large and have wonderful covered balconies – they're perfect for watching the sun set over town while nursing a bottle of Somontano wine.

The hotel usually shuts from Christmas to the end of January.

Eating

L'Artica CAFE €
(☎974 31 88 69; www.panaderialartica.com; Iglesia 1; pizzas €7-12; ⊙8am-8pm) There's not much new in the old town of Alquézar, except this nascent bakery cum cafe cum restaurant opened by a well-established local family in 2014. Split over two floors with terraces that literally hang over the village's spectacular gorge, L'Artica is decked out bistro-style with creamy furniture and cabinets displaying musical instruments.

La Marmita ARAGONESE €€
(☎974 31 89 56; www.lamarmitadeguara.com; Avenida San Hipólito; menú del día €22.50; ⊙2-4pm & 7-10pm) Located at the entrance to the village, with views of the Colegiata looking like Harry Potter's Hogwarts atop its crag. Choose between piled-high *pinchos* in the bar or the more expansive *menú del día* in the dining room. A speciality is *caracoles* (snails). If this sounds a mite indigestible, there are innovative takes on standard favourites, like baked cod with potatoes and truffles.

★**Casa Pardina** ARAGONESE €€€
(☎974 31 84 25; www.casapardina.com; Calle Medio; set menus €28; ⊙1.30-3pm & 8-10pm May-Oct) A very special restaurant where the food exudes contemporary creativity and the setting (in the family home of the owner) is all soothing stone work, twinkling chandeliers, summer terraces and views that could have sprung from the pages of *National Geographic*. The menu is subtle yet classy with dishes like oxtail with chestnuts, and stewed venison with dates and honey. Reservations recommended.

Information

Tourist Office (☎974 31 89 40; www.alquezar.org; Calle Arrabal; ⊙9am-2pm & 5-8:30pm Sun-Fri, 9am-2pm Sat) Runs guided tours (€3.50) three times daily in summer and can arrange audioguides (€4).

Getting There & Away

There are two daily buses to Alquézar from Barbastro (€2.75) Monday to Saturday. Check

J.D. DALLET/GETTY IMAGES ©

1. Sos del Rey Católico (p372) **2.** Albarracín (p396)
3. Alquézar (p384) **4.** Iglesia de Santa María (p382), Aínsa

JUAN/JOFOTOS/GETTY IMAGES ©

Villages of Aragón

Few regions can rival Aragón for its spread of charming villages. Most are built in the sturdy stone typical of the region, with terracotta and slate roofs. And their settings – against a backdrop of Pyrenean peaks or hidden in isolated corners of the south – are as beguiling as the architecture.

Albarracín (p396)

One of Spain's most beautiful villages, which would look equally at home in southern Italy, Albarracín combines time-worn streets in shades of ochre and dusky rose with a dramatic setting. The views from the castle or the precipitous walls high on a ridge will stay with you long after you leave.

Aínsa (p382)

There's no more beautifully preserved historic centre in Aragón and after the sun sets the crowds go home and silence reigns. Aínsa's stunning laneways, porticoed Plaza Mayor and views of the Pyrenees from the village's hilltop perch are simply wonderful.

Alquézar (p384)

A centre for canyoning and other high-octane pursuits, Alquézar's alter ego is a tranquil village that, from above, resembles a Tuscan hill town.

Sos del Rey Católico (p372)

Uniformly cobblestoned streets, the whiff of Spanish legend and a perch high above the madding crowd make Sos a memorable stop en route to or from the Pyrenees.

Daroca (p390)

Just when you think Aragón's southern badlands have little to offer, Daroca embraces you within its walls, which encircle the town high on the ridgelines.

with the tourist office for times – it doubles as the local school bus and times change during holidays.

Huesca

POP 52,440

The hard-working provincial capital of Huesca doesn't delay many travellers, but those that do hang around can blow the dust off Spain's oldest grocery store, a multifarious museum juxtaposing Neolithic remains with paintings by Goya, and an eye-opening lesson in Gothic and Romanesque architecture courtesy of two medieval churches.

◎ Sights

Iglesia de San Pedro El Viejo　　　CHURCH
(Plaza de San Pedro; adult/concession €2.50/1.50; ◎10am-1.30pm & 4.30-6pm Mon-Sat, 11am-12.15pm & 1-2pm Sun) The church of San Pedro is one of the oldest and most important Romanesque structures in Spain, dating from the early 1100s. It's particularly noted for its hexagonal tower, open cloister adorned with 38 beautifully carved Romanesque capitals, and mausoleum containing the remains of two Aragonese kings (and brothers), Alfonso I (1073–1134) and Ramiro II (1086–37).

Catedral de Santa María　　　CATHEDRAL
(Plaza de la Catedral; cathedral free, museum & tower €4; ◎cathedral hours vary, museum & tower 10.30am-2pm & 4-8pm Mon-Fri, 10.30am-2pm Sat) This Gothic cathedral is one of Aragón's great surprises. The richly carved main portal dates from 1300, the attached Museo Diocesano contains some extraordinary frescos and painted altarpieces, and the stately interior features a superb, 16th-century alabaster *retablo* (altarpiece) by Damián Forment showing scenes from Christ's crucifixion. To round off your visit, climb the 180 steps of the bell tower for 360-degree views all the way to the Pyrenees.

Museo de Huesca　　　MUSEUM
(Plaza Universidad 1; ◎10am-2pm & 5-8pm Tue-Sat, 10am-2pm Sun) FREE The octagonal city museum with its pretty courtyard contains a well-displayed collection (labels in Spanish only) covering the archaeology of Huesca province and progressing onto early modern art, including eight works by Goya.

🛏 Sleeping & Eating

Hostal Lizana　　　HOTEL €
(🖉974 22 07 76; www.hostallizana.com; Plaza de Lizana 6; s/d/tr €25/40/54; 🖥) Bargain basement, family-run hotel with a good central location and friendly staff. There are two 'wings' both overlooking the same square. Adjacent parking costs €7.

La Posada de la Luna　　　BOUTIQUE HOTEL €€
(🖉974 24 08 57; www.posadadelaluna.com; Calle Joaquin Costa 10; s/d €61/69; 🅿🌀🖥) This attractive small hotel incorporates some original features of old Huesca architecture with a whimsical but contemporary feel (with whispers of Gaudí), designer bathrooms and hydromassage showers. It's a comfortable, charming place, although some of the rooms are on the small side.

Bar Da Vinci　　　TAPAS €
(🖉974 22 53 53; Calle del Padre Huesca 13; raciones €4-11; ◎9am-midnight) If you want a quick tapas session rather than a sit-down gourmet meal, follow Huesca's renaissance men and women to Da Vinci's in the ebullient tapas bar strip of Calle del Padre Huesca. Serving tasty morsels or bigger *raciones* in a congenial setting, it's a popular abode. Should the tables fill up there's plenty of standing room at the bar.

El Origen　　　ARAGONESE €€€
(🖉974 22 97 45; Plaza del Justicia 4; set menus €15-40; ◎11am-4pm & 8-11pm Thu-Tue) 🖉 Ignore the inauspicious setting on this somewhat drab modern square as this restaurant is an oasis of elegance and fine dining, with set menus that vary from traditional Aragonese to more innovative and contemporary. Ecological produce is used as far as possible. Reservations recommended.

🛍 Shopping

Ultramarinos La Confianza　　　FOOD & DRINK
(🖉974 22 26 32; Plaza Luís López Allue 8; ◎9am-2pm & 5-9.15pm) It won't take you long to deduce that La Confianza is the oldest grocery shop in Spain. With its tiled floors, elegant mirrors and old-fashioned shelves stacked high behind the counter, it looks pretty much the same as it must have done at its inception in 1871. Pop in and buy some deluxe biscuits as an appetising souvenir.

ℹ Information

Tourist Office (🖉974 29 21 70; www.huesca turismo.com; Plaza López Allué 1; ◎9am-2pm

& 4-8pm) This excellent office runs daily guided tours of the historic centre (adult/child €2/1) at 11am on weekends year-round and daily from mid-June until mid-September. There are also bus tours (adult/child €5/free) at 9am daily in July and August to the Castillo de Loarre, Los Mallos and the Sierra de Guara.

ⓘ Getting There & Away

BUS

Alosa (📞 974 21 07 00; www.alosa.es) runs buses to/from Zaragoza (€7.80, 1¼ hours, half-hourly), Jaca (€7.80, 1¼ hours, seven daily), Barbastro (€4.65, 50 minutes, nine daily) and a twice-daily service Monday to Saturday to Benasque (€13.35, 2¾ hours), running once on Sunday.

TRAIN

Seven trains a day run to/from Zaragoza (from €7.15, one hour), including one high-speed AVE services (€10, 40 minutes). There are also AVE services to/from Madrid (€57.20, 2¼ hours, one daily), as well as services to Jaca (€8.25, 2¼ hours, two daily).

Loarre

POP 370

The small agricultural village of Loarre, situated 30km northwest of Huesca, is famous for one reason only – the Castillo de Loarre, a multi-towered Reconquista-era castle.

⊙ Sights

Castillo de Loarre   CASTLE
(www.castillodeloarre.es; with/without tour €5.50/3.90; ⊙10am-8pm Jun-Aug, 10am-7pm Mar-Jun, Sep & Oct, 11am-5:30pm Nov-Feb; P 🚻) This evocative castle broods above the southern plains across which Islamic raiders once rode. Raised in the 11th century by Sancho III of Navarra and Sancho Ramírez of Aragón, its resemblance to a crusader cas-

tle has considerable resonance with those times. Although the dungeons and towers are no longer open to visitors for safety reasons, there is still plenty to see, including a Romanesque chapel and crypt.

The castle is a 5km drive or a 2km, one-hour, uphill walk by the PR-HU105 footpath, from the village of Loarre, 35km northwest of Huesca.

Birdwatchers note that this is also an excellent spot to spy griffon and Egyptian vultures and red kite circling overhead.

ⓘ Getting There & Away

There are two daily buses linking Loarre with Huesca (€3.50, 40 minutes).

Fraga

POP 15,000

The rural town of Fraga in the relentless flatlands between Zaragoza and the Mediterranean coast is the unlikely locale for Florida 135 (p389), the temple of Spanish techno.

🍷 Drinking & Nightlife

Florida 135   CLUB
(www.f135.com; Calle Sotet 2; admission €13; ⊙11.30pm-7.30am Sat) There's Ibiza and there's ....Fraga, a rural village 120km east of Zaragoza that hosts Florida 135, the temple of Spanish techno. The windowless 3000-sq-metre, graffiti-strewn space is the most recent incarnation of a dance hall that's been going since 1942. Busloads of clubbers arrive for the club's main Saturday-night sessions.

ⓘ Getting There & Away

There are at least three buses a day to Zaragoza (€9.10, 2¼ hours) run by Agreda (www.agredasa.es).

ARAGÓN'S WINE (DOC) REGIONS

Aragón has four Denominación de Origen Calificada (DOC) wine regions.

Somontano The most prestigious wine-producing region. Produces reds, whites and rosés. Better known labels include Enate and Viñas del Vero.

Calatayud Well-known for its big and bold red wine, Calatayud Superior, made from garnacho grapes from 50-year-old vines.

Campo de Borja Famed for its powerful aromatic red wines using soley garnacho grapes, as well as its sweet and fruity Moscatel.

Cariñena Known for its signature oak-aged reds, dry whites from the macabeo grapes, fruity *rosados* and sweet moscatel.

Somontano Wine Region

Somontano is Aragón's most prestigious wine-growing region. Centred on the town of Barbastro, Somontano has more than 30 vineyards producing reds, whites and rosés from 13 different types of foreign and local grape varieties.

The **tourist office** (📞 974 30 83 50; www.turismosomontano.es; Avenida de la Merced 64; ⊙ 10am-2pm & 4-7.30pm Tue-Sat Sep-Jun, daily Jul & Aug) in Barbastro has brochures in Spanish, English and French outlining the various wineries that can be visited for sales, tours and/or tastings. Always ring ahead to arrange a time – the tourist office will help you make the calls if you turn up in person.

Part of the same complex as the tourist office, the **Espacio de Vino** is an interpretation centre devoted to Somontano wines with audiovisual displays, interactive grape-aroma displays and occasional wine tastings (per person €10). Attached to the tourist office is also a wine shop. Both places keep the same hours as the tourist office.

Another excellent resource is the website www.rutadelvinosomontano.com, which maps out possible wine itineraries through the region. The website also has details of the **Bus del Vino Somontano**, a monthly all-day bus tour of selected bodegas from Zaragoza/Huesca (€29/27).

ⓘ Getting There & Away

Alosa (p383) runs daily buses from Barbastro to Aínsa (€5.85, one hour).

THE SOUTH

Daroca

POP 2310

The old walled town of Daroca is the meeting point of two different Aragóns: the Romanesque north and the Mudéjar south. This cultural crossover is etched onto the town's buildings which mix distinct Romanesque and Mudéjar elements like sedimentary rock on the same building

Ringed by medieval walls, Daroca once sported 114 towers, though only a handful remain. Since many of its old buildings are only viewable from the outside, it's best to look upon Daroca as a kind of giant alfresco museum. Procure a map from the tourist office and go on a self-guided walking tour. Explanatory boards (in English and Spanish) piece together the history and help decipher the unusual architectural fusion.

◉ Sights

Iglesia de San Juan CHURCH
(Paseo de San Juan) Not generally open to the public, but no matter... What makes this church important (and interesting) is the delineation of its architecture. On the semi-circular apse, you can clearly see the line where the original Romanesque builders switched from grey stone to terracotta brick and finished building the church in a Mudéjar style. The switch came in the middle of the 13th century, making this one of the earliest examples of Mudéjar architecture in Aragon.

Colegiata de Santa María de los Sagrados Corporales CHURCH
(⊙ 11am-1pm & 5.30-7.30pm Tue-Sat, 5.30-7.30pm Sun) FREE The pretty Plaza de España, at the top of the village, is dominated by this ornate Romanesque Mudéjar Renaissance–style church, which boasts a lavish interior and organ. The 16th-century Gothic Puerta del Perdón rounds out the church's impressive portfolio of European architectural styles. Overall, it's one of Daroca's most appealing (and unexpected) gems.

Iglesia de San Miguel CHURCH
Up the hill west of the town centre, this 12th-century church is an austerely beautiful masterpiece of Romanesque architecture, but its greatest treasures are the Gothic frescos within. Sadly, the church is kept closed, except for guided tours run by the tourist office or for concerts during the town's festivals.

☞ Tours

Guided Walks WALKING TOUR
(tours €2-4; ⊙ guided tours 11am & 6pm Tue-Sun) The best of the self-guided walks offered by the tourist office is the 45-minute Ruta Monumental, which gives a wonderful feel for the town and is well signposted. The other is the two-hour Ruta del Castillo y Las Murallas, a far more strenuous undertaking that climbs up to and follows the walls. You

can either go it alone with an easy-to-follow map or join a guided walk.

Festivals & Events

Festival Internacional
de Música Antigua   MEDIEVAL
In the first two weeks of August, Daroca hosts the International Festival of Medieval Music in the two main churches.

Feria Medieval   MEDIEVAL
During the last week of July, Calle Mayor is closed to traffic, locals don their medieval finery, and concerts mark the Medieval Festival.

Sleeping & Eating

La Posada del Almudí   HOTEL €€
(☑976 80 06 06; www.posadadelalmudi.es; Calle Grajera 5; s/d/q incl breakfast €45/65/120; ❄🖵) A one-time 16th-century palace, this lovely old place exudes charm. The rooms in the main building have been lovingly restored, retaining the original beams, while across the lane are more contemporary rooms, with stylish black-and-white decor and parquet floors. Rooms on the 3rd floor have great views of the Iglesia de San Miguel.

The restaurant (mains €15 to €18, set menu €12.50) offers good local cuisine and has a delightful terrace overlooking the traditional walled garden. The adjacent tapas bar is the best in town and serves glorious *pinchos*.

Hotel Cien Balcones   HOTEL €€
(☑976 54 50 71; www.cienbalcones.com; Calle Mayor 88; s/d incl breakfast from €56/72; P❄🖵) This contemporary three-star hotel has large, designer rooms, modern bathrooms and bold colour schemes throughout. There's an excellent restaurant (mains from €9) and a cafe that serves up cheap *raciones*, *bocadillos* and pizza with outside seating in the attractive central courtyard.

Café Imperio Colmado   CAFE €
(☑976 80 01 56; Mayor 157; snacks €2-6; ⊙9am-11.30pm Mon-Fri, 9am-12.30am Sat & Sun) One of Daroca's more interesting cafes and new in 2014, this place also acts as a purveyor of local products including fine groceries and wine (there's a tasting room out back). The decor mixes Marilyn Monroe posters with a handful of electric organs – presumably put there for show. Good for coffee and a sandwich.

ℹ Information

Tourist Office (☑976 80 01 29; Calle Mayor 44; ⊙10am-2pm & 4-8pm) Come here for the essential town maps marked with self-guided walking tours. It also shows a short informative video of Daroca's history (in Spanish).

ℹ Getting There & Away

Buses stop outside the Mesón Félix bar, at Calle Mayor 104. Three daily buses run to Zaragoza (€6.85, 1½ hours) and Teruel (€5.45, 1¾ hours), Monday to Saturday.

Laguna de Gallocanta

Some 20km south of Daroca, this is Spain's largest natural lake, with an area of about 15 sq km (though it can almost dry up in summer). It's a winter home for tens of thousands of cranes, as well as many other kinds of waterfowl – more than 260 bird species have been recorded here. The cranes arrive in mid-October and leave for the return flight to their breeding grounds in Scandinavia in March. Unpaved tracks of 36km in total encircle the lake, passing a series of hides and observation points – the tracks can be driven in normal vehicles except after heavy rain. Take binoculars.

Sleeping

Allucant   HOSTAL €
(☑976 80 31 37; www.allucant.com; Calle San Vicente; dm €13, d with/without bathroom from €45/30; P🖵) Serious twitchers will feel right at home at this simple but well-run birdwatching base in the village of Gallocanta. Meals (€9 to €12) and picnic lunches (€7) can be arranged. The place also acts as an informal cultural centre with regular art exhibitions and courses available, ranging from photography to painting.

ℹ Information

Centro de Interpretación Laguna de Gallocanta (☑978 73 40 31; Carr. A-1507; ⊙10am-8pm Tue-Sun) Information and exhibitions, along the Tornos–Bello road near the southeast corner of the lake.

ℹ Getting There & Away

There are a couple of daily buses from Daroca to the village of Gallocanta (€1.45, 20 minutes), but you really need your own wheels to explore the *laguna* (lake) properly.

Teruel

POP 35,840 / ELEV 917M

The town of Teruel is synonymous with Mudéjar architecture. Nowhere else in Spain – with the possible exception of Seville – is this glamorous amalgamation of Islamic craft and Christian taste in such evidence. The hallmarks – terracotta bricks, glazed tiles and ornate wooden ceilings – are crafted skilfully into the town's towers and churches, four of which are Unesco-listed. There's also smatterings of a Mudéjar revival from the early 20th century personified in the Escalinata, an elaborate staircase near the station.

Ironically, Teruel never had a strong Islamic presence. A Moorish fort existed here from the 10th century onwards, but the city itself was founded in 1171 by the conquering Christian king, Alfonso II. In subsequent centuries, Teruel floundered as a forgotten outpost set in Aragon's isolated southern highlands. Its most famous historical moment was also its most tragic. The battle of Teruel in 1937–38, documented by American writer and journalist, Ernest Hemingway, was one of the bloodiest in the Spanish Civil War, claiming over 140,000 lives.

◉ Sights

★ **Fundación Amantes**   MUSEUM, CHURCH
(www.amantesdeteruel.es; Calle Matías Abad 3; combined ticket €9; ☉10am-2pm & 4-8pm) Teruel's finest sight offers various ticket options, but the full-on four-part guided tour of the mausoleum, church, tower and cloister/garden is well worth it. You'll begin in the somewhat curious Mausoleo de los Amantes (Mausoleum of the Lovers) which pulls out the stops on the city's famous legend of Isabel and Juan Diego. Here they lie in modern alabaster tombs, sculpted by Juan de Ávalos, with their hands almost (but not quite) touching. Around this centrepiece a predictably sentimental audiovisual exhibition has been shaped featuring music and theatre.

From here you'll progress to the 14th-century Iglesia de San Pedro, with its impossibly ornate ceiling covered in gold stars (added in the early 20th century) and baroque high altar. The simple cloisters and adjoining gardens comprise act three. For a final flourish you are led up the Torre de San Pedro, one of Teruel's four Mudéjar towers. You can enjoy the fine views over Teruel in full panorama – an unusual high-level arched walkway circumnavigates the roof of the church.

★ **Catedral de Santa María de Mediavilla**   CATHEDRAL
(Plaza de la Catedral; adult/child incl Museo de Arte Sacro €3/2; ☉11am-2pm & 4-8pm) Teruel's cathedral is a rich example of the Mudéjar imagination at work with its kaleidoscopic brickwork and colourful ceramic tiles. The superb 13th-century bell tower has hints of the Romanesque in its detail. Inside, the astounding (and neck craning) Mudéjar ceiling of the nave is covered with paintings that add up to a medieval cosmography – from musical instruments

---

THE LOVERS OF TERUEL

In the early 13th century, Juan Diego de Marcilla and Isabel de Segura fell in love, but, in the manner of other star-crossed historical lovers, there was a catch: Isabel was the only daughter of a wealthy family, while poor old Juan Diego was, well, poor. Juan Diego convinced Isabel's reluctant father to postpone plans for Isabel's marriage to someone more appropriate for five years, during which time Juan Diego would seek his fortune. Not waiting a second longer than the five years, Isabel's father married off his daughter in 1217, only for Juan Diego to return, triumphant, immediately after the wedding. He begged Isabel for a kiss, which she refused, condemning Juan Diego to die of a broken heart. A final twist saw Isabel attend the funeral in mourning, whereupon she gave Juan Diego the kiss he had craved in life. Isabel promptly died and the two lovers were buried together.

It has long been thought that the two bodies in Teruel's mausoleum are those of Isabel and Juan Diego. For years they were displayed rather distastefully as mummies in a glass case before being placed in their more dignified alabaster tombs in 1955. Stoking the romance of the legend further, recent carbon-testing has verified that both bodies did indeed die in the early 13th century of natural causes. Broken hearts?

Teruel

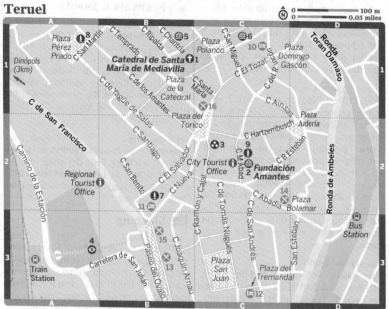

Teruel

◎ Top Sights

◎ Sights

◎ Sleeping

◎ Eating

and hunting scenes to coats of arms and Christ's crucifixion.

La Escalinata
STAIRCASE

(Paseo del Óvalo) This grand staircase that connects the Paseo del Óvalo to the train station is a masterpiece of neo-Mudéjar monumental architecture redolent of Seville's Plaza de España. First built in 1920, it was painstakingly restored in the early 21st century. Along with the redesigned Paseo del Óvalo, La Escalinata has won numerous awards for urban redesign. There's a lift back up to the Paseo.

Torre de San Martín
TOWER

(Calle San Martín) Although you can't climb it, Torre de San Martín, the northwestern gate of the old city, is almost as beautiful as the Torre de El Salvador. Completed in 1316, it was incorporated into the city's walls in the 16th century.

Torre de El Salvador
TOWER, MUSEUM

(www.teruelmudejar.com; Calle El Salvador; adult/concession €2.50/1.80; ☉11am-2pm & 4.30-7.30pm) The most impressive of Teruel's Mudéjar towers is the Torre de El Salvador, an early-14th-century extravaganza of brick and ceramics built around an older Islamic minaret. You climb the narrow stairways and passageways, and along the way you'll find exhibits on Mudéjar art and architecture on three different floors. The views from the summit are Teruel's best.

Museo de Arte Sacro   MUSEUM

(☑ 978 61 99 50; Plaza Francés de Aranda 3; adult/child incl cathedral €3/2; ⊙10am-2pm & 4-8pm Mon-Sat) Adjacent to the cathedral, the Museo de Arte Sacro is housed in the stately Palacio Episcopal and has two floors of superb religious paintings and sculptures dating from the 12th century, as well as some ornate 16th-century bishops' vestments. There are also several wood panels from the cathedral's extraordinary Mudéjar ceiling that have been damaged by woodworm (or similar) but which still display their vibrant design.

Museo Provincial   MUSEUM

(Plaza Polanco; ⊙10am-2pm & 4-7pm Tue-Fri, 10am-2pm Sat & Sun) FREE Teruel's Museo Provincial is housed in the 16th-century Renaissance Casa de la Comunidad. The archaeological sections are a highlight, plus there's a huge Roman mosaic laid out on the top floor. On the ground floor there are changing exhibitions of contemporary art.

Aljibe Fondero   RUIN

(www.aljibemedieval.com; Calle Ramón y Cajal; adult/concession €1.30/1; ⊙11am-2pm & 5-7pm) Off the southeastern corner of Plaza del Torico is the entrance to the Aljibe, a 14th-century underground water-storage facility. In addition to showcasing the remnants of the cisterns, there are audiovisual presentations on medieval Teruel, in Spanish.

Activities

Dinópolis   AMUSEMENT PARK

(www.dinopolis.com; Poligano Los Planos; adult/child €28/22; ⊙10am-8pm, ticket office closes 6pm; 🚼) The region around Teruel has unveiled a wealth of dinosaur remains. Notwithstanding this big-box complex is more of a dinosaur theme park than a pulse-raiser for serious paleontologists. It's 3km southwest of the town centre, well signposted just off the Valencia road. Exhibits include a train through time, 3D and 4D animations, and an excellent museum, among other attractions. Kids will obviously love it. Check website for off-season opening times.

 ## Festivals & Events

Fiesta Medieval   MEDIEVAL

(www.bodasdeisabel.com) On the weekend closest to 14 February, Teruel's inhabitants don medieval dress for the Fiesta Medieval, also known as the Bodas de Isabel de Segura. There are medieval markets and food stalls, but the centrepiece is the re-enactment of Los Amantes (the Diego and Isabel legend).

Feria del Ángel   LOCAL FIESTA

(www.vaquillas.es) Popularly known as La Vaquilla, the weeklong Feria del Ángel revolves around 10 July, the Día de San Cristóbal (St Christopher's Day) which commemorates Teruel's founding.

Sleeping

Fonda del Tozal   INN €

(☑ 978 60 21 73; Calle del Rincón 5; s/d €30/40; 🖧) Dating from the 16th century and one of the oldest inns in Spain, the rooms here vary considerably but all have a real sense of the past with beams, solid furniture and ancient floor tiles. In some rooms, the paintwork has been stripped back in places to reveal the original faintly patterned plasterwork beneath.

★ Hotel el Mudayyan   BOUTIQUE HOTEL €€

(☑ 978 62 30 42; www.elmudayyan.com; Calle Nueva 18; s €55-70, d €70-90; 🌐🖧) The recently expanded Mudayyan is pretty unique. Modern, clean-lined, comfortable rooms are a given, but pushing the boat out further is a ground-floor *teteria* (Moorish tea room), fantastic buffet breakfasts sweetened with thick hot chocolate (all for only €5), and a secret subterranean tunnel dating from the 16th century that leads to the church next door. Staff will happily give you a tour.

Hotel Teruel Plaza   HOTEL €€

(☑ 978 60 86 55; Plaza del Tremandal 3; s/d from €49/80; 🌐🖧) Under new management, this central hotel has benefited from a refurbishment. Rooms are spacious with sofas or armchairs and have neon-style spot lighting in vivid colours, The smart bathrooms are done out in blue and ochre tiling.

Eating

★ La Barrica   TAPAS €

(Calle Abadia 5; tapas €2-3; ⊙9.30am-3.30pm & 8-11pm Mon & Wed-Fri, noon-3.30pm & 8-11pm Sat & Sun) The Battica is *pintxo* (Basque

ARAGONESE MUDÉJAR – THE ULTIMATE IN CHRISTIAN-ISLAMIC FUSION

Many Spanish buildings are hybrids, but few cityscapes can equal the dynamic Christian-Islamic hybridisation of Teruel, Spain's capital of Mudéjar.

Mudéjar is an architectural style unique to Spain that arose out of the peculiar history of the Reconquista which saw towns and villages fall successively back into Christian hands between the mid-700s and 1492. Skilled Muslim architects living in the newly conquered lands were used by the Christians to design their new buildings, applying Islamic building techniques to a basic Christian model.

Different nuances of Mudéjar can been seen all over Spain, but the style reached its apex between the 13th and 16th centuries in a rough triangle of land between Teruel, Zaragoza and Tarazona. The regional inspiration probably came from Zaragoza's Aljafería (p365), a Moorish palace decked out a little like Granada's Alhambra, that had been taken over and fortified by Christian king, Alfonso I in 1118.

Aragonese Mudéjar borrowed heavily from Romanesque, but used terracotta brick rather than grey stone as its main building material. In some towns, such as Daroca, Romanesque and Mudéjar styles are stacked on top of one another in the same building like sedimentary rock. In Teruel, a purer form of Mudéjar is manifested in a splendid quartet of rectangular church towers adorned with graceful arches and decorated with glazed tiles laid out in geometric patterns. The impression is not a million miles from the Almohad minarets of Morocco.

Mudéjar had died out by the 17th century, but it re-emerged briefly in the 1920s in Teruel, reinvigorated by Gaudí-inspired modernists such as Pau Monguió (who also designed many of Teruel's art nouveau buildings). The sweeping Escalinata (p393) and the decorative portico on the cathedral both date from this period.

Teruel's Mudéjar architecture was listed by Unesco in 1986 and, in 2001, the protection was extended to include monuments in Zaragoza, Tobed, Cervera de la Cañada and Calatayud.

tapas) heaven. Trouble is, quite a lot of people know it. Arrive promptly at 8pm if you want a seat and order a glass of wine to go with one of the delicate little *pintxo* treats, which are displayed like Goyesca art on top of small pieces of toasted bread. One or two will serve as a tasty prelude to dinner.

Bar Gregori
TAPAS €

(Paseo del Óvalo 6; mains €6-13; ☻7.30am-midnight) You can simplify the menu at Gregori by fishing out its two best down-to-earth dishes. The meatballs, doused in a thick sauce and often displayed in a paella pan on top of the bar; and the sardines, grilled to perfection and plonked on a plate with a slice of lemon and some olive oil. All you need to know.

Pastelería Muñoz
CAFE, DELI €

(☐ 978 60 11 30; www.dulcesdeteruel.es; Plaza Carlos Castel (Torico); cakes €2-4; ☻9.30am-2pm & 5.30-9pm Mon-Sat, 10am-2pm Sun) In operation since 1855, Muñoz is a storied old deli cum patisserie cum cafe that plies revered local products including that all important Teruel cured ham, along with some rather inviting fresh pastries. Come *merienda* time (afternoon snack; 5pm-ish), the place is usually packed to the rafters with families guarding pushchairs and wine-sipping pensioners who look like they've been coming here for snacks since... well, 1855.

Don't leave without trying a piece of carrot cake.

Mesón Óvalo
ARAGONESE €€

(☐ 978 61 82 35; Paseo del Óvalo 8; mains €14-19; ☻1-4pm & 8-11pm Tue-Sat, 1-4pm Sun) There's a strong emphasis on regional Aragonese cuisine at this pleasant place, with meat and game dishes to the fore. One fine local speciality is *jarretes* (hock of lamb stewed with wild mushrooms), a dish that dates back to the period when Muslims ruled this part of Spain.

❶ Information

City Tourist Office (☐ 978 62 41 05; Plaza de los Amantes 6; ☻10am-2pm & 4-8pm Sep-Jul, 10am-8pm Aug) Ask here for audioguides (€2) to the old city, and pick up the *Teruel Ruta*

Europea del Modernismo which maps out 17 unusual art nouveau buildings around town.

Regional Tourist Office (☑ 978 64 14 61; Calle de San Francisco 1; ◷ 9am-2pm & 4.30-7pm) Information about the wider Aragón region.

ℹ Getting There & Away

From Teruel's **bus station** (☑ 978 61 07 89; www.estacionbus-teruel.com), there are regular buses to/from Zaragoza (€11, two to three hours).

Teruel is on the railway between Zaragoza (€20.10, two hours) and Valencia (€18.10, 2½ hours). The station is located at the foot of the magnificent sweeping Escalinata.

Albarracín

POP 1100 / ELEV 1180M

The pink-hued medieval houses of Albarracín are like nothing else in Spain. So authentic are its twisting, narrow streets with their overhanging wooden balconies that one half expects Don Quijote and Sancho Panza to appear from around a blind corner. You can argue all day about Spain's prettiest village, but Albarracín, with its rocky outcrop setting, elegantly ruined castle and peculiar Moorish history (from 1012 to 1104, it was the seat of a tiny Islamic state ruled by the Berber Banu Razin dynasty with links to Córdoba), is definitely a contender.

The village is 38km west of Teruel and well worth an over-nighter if your itinerary allows.

◎ Sights

Many of Albarracín sights are managed by the Fundación Santa María de Albarracín and can only be visited on a guided tour (although the rules can vary according to season). Make their office by the cathedral your first port of call.

Muralla   CITY WALL

Albarracín's highest point, the **Torre del Andador** (Walkway Tower) dates from the 9th century; the surrounding walls, draped steeply over a hill, are more recent and date from the 11th or 12th century. It's a stiff climb to the summit, but pretty essential if you want to see the town spread out below you in a panorama unchanged since the Middle Ages.

Castle   CASTLE

(Castillo; admission €2.50; ◷ guided tours 1pm & 4pm) Crowning the old town, this fascinating castle, with 11 towers and an area of 3600 sq metres, dates from the 9th century when Albarracín was an important Islamic military post. In private hands until 2005, the archaeological digs have revealed fascinating insights into the town's history. All is explained on the hour-long, Spanish-language tour (buy your tickets at the Museo de Albarracín); contact the Centro de Información to arrange English-language tours.

Museo de Juguetes   MUSEUM

(www.museodejuguetes.com; Calle Medio 2; adult/child €3/1.50; ◷ 11am-2pm & 4-7pm Tue-Sat, 11am-2pm Sun Mar-Dec; 🐾) Albarracín's toy museum is a fascinating journey through the historical world of toys – the kids will love it. It's down the hill, around 500m east of the tourist office. Note: it's closed in January and February.

Museo Diocesano   MUSEUM

(admission €2.50; ◷ 10.30am-2pm & 4-7pm) The Palacio Episcopal (Bishop's Palace), backing onto the cathedral, houses a rich collection of religious art and is a cut above your average church museum. The 15th- to 17th-century tapestries in particular stand out, as does a strange glass salt-holder in the shape of a fish.

Catedral del Salvador   CATHEDRAL

With its cupola typical of the Spanish Levant, Albarracín's cathedral is one of the signature monuments of the village skyline; within its dusty entrails there is an elaborate gilded altarpiece and some very unique wall frescoes. Restoration is ongoing, but you can get in on a guided tour from Fundación Santa María de Albarracín (p396).

Museo de Albarracín   MUSEUM

(Calle San Juan; admission €2.50; ◷ 10.30am-1pm & 5-7pm) In the old city hospital, this interesting museum is devoted to the town's Islamic heritage, with numerous finds from the archaeological digs in the castle. Opposite the museum's entrance, the 17th-century Ermita de San Juan was built on the site of Albarracín's former synagogue.

☞ Tours

Fundación Santa María de Albarracín   WALKING TOUR

(☑ 978 70 40 35; http://fundacionsantamariadealbarracin.com; Calle de la Catedral; tours €3.50; ◷ 10am-2pm & 4-8pm Mon-Sat, 10am-2pm & 4-7pm Sun) ✐ This commendable non-profit is responsible for much of the ongoing renovations in the town and coordinates visits to the five main monuments, namely the cathedral, the castillo, the Museo de Albarracín, the Museo Diocesano and the Torre Blanca. It also organises 1½-hour guided walks three to four times daily (less in winter). Call into the office by the cathedral to best coordinate your visit.

El Andador WALKING TOUR
(☑ 978 70 03 81; www.elandadoralbarracin.es; Calle de la Catedral 4; tours €3.50) El Andador offers 1½-hour walks through Albarracín two to six times daily. It also offers tours in English.

🛏 Sleeping

Meson del Gallo HOTEL €
(☑ 978 71 00 32; Calle Los Puentes 1; r €45; ❄ 🐾) Opened in January 2014 at the entrance to the village, this hotel is the result of an aesthetic *reforma* (restoration) of three traditional village houses. Behind the village-like blush-rose facade, the light, contemporary rooms with wicker furniture exceed initial expectations. The bathrooms are small but swish with stone-coloured mosaic tiling and hydromassage showers, and there's a lovely local downstairs restaurant

Posada del Adarve HOTEL €
(☑ 978 70 03 04; www.posadadeladarve.com; Calle Portal de Molina 23; s €30, d €50-75; @ 🐾) An Albarracín townhouse by the Portal de Molina (Molina Gateway), this prettily restored hotel has beautifully decorated, if small, rooms, friendly service and a homey, intimate feel.

★ La Casa del Tío Americano HOTEL €€
(☑ 978 71 01 25; www.lacasadeltioamericano.com; Calle Los Palacios 9; s/d incl breakfast €80/95; 🐾) A wonderful small hotel, 'The House of the American Uncle' proclaims brightly painted rooms, some with exposed stone walls and friendly, impeccable service. The views of the village from the breakfast terrace (and from rooms 2 and 3) are magnificent. A welcoming glass of champagne is a lovely touch, and the generous breakfast features local cheese, honey and ham.

La Casona del Ajimez HOTEL €€
(☑ 978 71 03 21; www.casonadelajimez.com; Calle de San Juan 2; d €76; 🐾) Like other lovingly restored Albarracín small hotels, this place has warm and charming decor, and fine views from some rooms. It's at the southern end of town, near the cathedral.

Casa de Santiago HOTEL €€
(☑ 978 70 03 16; www.casadesantiago.net; Subida a las Torres 11; d/ste €70/95; 🐾) A beautiful place with lots of exposed wood and tiled floors, and charming service to go with it, the Casa lies at the heart of the old town a few steps up from Plaza Mayor. You step off the street into an immediate comfort zone.

🍴 Eating

La Alcazaba ARAGONESE €
(☑ 610 21 55 56; Portal de Molina 10; mains €5-12; ☺ 11am-3.30pm & 8-10.30pm Tue-Sun) Close to the main square and usually open when other more seasonal places close, the Alcazaba's cosy cave-like interior fits right in with the historical atmosphere of Albarracín. The menu doesn't stray too far from home with rabbit, trout wrapped in cured ham and Navarra asparagus.

★ Tiempo de Ensueño CONTEMPORARY SPANISH €€
(☑ 978 70 40 70; www.tiempodeensuenyo.com; Calle Palacios 1B; mains €19-25; ☺ 1-4pm & 7-11pm Tue-Sun) This high-class restaurant has a sleek, light-filled dining room, attentive but discreet service, and food that you'll remember long after you've left. Spanish nouvelle cuisine in all its innovative guises makes an appearance here with a changing menu, as well as a book-length wine list, mineral-water menu, choice of olive oils, welcome cocktail and, above all, exquisite tastes.

Rincon del Chorro ARAGONESE €€
(Calle Chorro 5; menú degustación €24.90, mains €9-15; ☺ 1-4pm & 8.15-11pm Fri-Sun) Traditional dishes from Albarracín are the show stoppers here, including heartwarming stews like *jerigota* (a ratatouille-style dish), oxtail and white beans with partridge and wild mushrooms. The comfort food theme reaches a high note with desserts like chocolate fondant and pumpkin and almond pie.

🍷 Drinking & Nightlife

El Molino del Gato BAR
(Calle San Antonio 4; ☺ 3pm-3am Thu-Tue Sep-Jun, noon-3pm Jul & Aug) Just behind the tourist office, this outstanding bar is the place to drink in Albarracín. Built around a 15th-century mill, it has water gushing beneath a glass panel in the floor and the outdoor tables are fine places to nurse a drink; there are more than 25 types of beer. The bar also hosts regular contemporary art exhibitions.

Shopping

Sierra de Albarracín FOOD

(www.quesodealbarracin.es; Calle Rubiales 1; ⊙10am-2pm & 4-7pm Mon-Fri, to 8pm Sat & Sun) You'll see the respected local cheeses labelled as Sierra de Albarracín in small shops all over the village, but why not go straight to the source? The owner's shop is around 3km away on the road out of town to Gea de Albarracín, and has the full range of sheep and goat's cheese. You can try most varieties before you buy.

Information

Tourist Office (☑978 71 02 62; Calle San Antonio; ⊙10am-2pm & 4-8pm Mon-Sat, to 7pm Sun) On the main road at the gateway to the old town.

Getting There & Away

Buses travel once daily between Teruel and Albarracín (€4.40, 45 minutes).

Around Albarracín

The hills around Albarracín conceal some easy-to-view, if sometimes faint, examples of prehistoric rock art, some of which date back 7000 years. In addition to animal representations (livestock, horses), you'll see some archaic matchstick-like human figures.

To get to the protected area, follow the signs from Albarracín's tourist office for the *pinturas rupestres* (rock paintings). The main car park (with a picnic area and children's play area) is 5.5km from Albarracín. Three well-signposted walking trails of between 2.3km and 3km (45 minutes to 1¼ hours) lead out through coniferous woods punctuated by huge mushroom-like rock formations. A fourth trail leaves from another car park 700m back down the road towards Albarracín. If you only have time for one trail, make it the 2.5km **Sendero del Arrastradero**, which leads to the iconic **Abrigo del Arquero de los Callejones**, a perfectly rendered human archer seemingly caught in flight scrawled underneath a trippy mushroom-shaped rock. There are other drawings round about (all protected by metal bars) and a serendipitous lookout.

Sights

Roman Aqueduct RUIN

The road between Gea de Albarracín and Albarracín (18km) is shadowed by traces of an ancient Roman aqueduct. Signs point to the most accessible sections, and there's a Centro de Interpretación in Gea Albarracín which explains in more depth the history and role of the aquaduct.

Closed at the time of research for repair work.

Activities

Jamones Bronchales TOUR

(☑978 70 13 13; www.jamonesbronchales.com; ⊙10am-2pm & 5-8pm Mon-Sat) **FREE** Teruel's *jamón* is widely respected throughout Spain, and Jamones Bronchales, in the village of Bronchales, 29km northwest of Albarracín, runs tours (minimum 15 people) of its drying operations and shows how the *jamón* is prepared. You can also buy the end product here.

Getting There & Away

You'll need your own wheels to get to the rock paintings. Alternatively, you can walk there. A trail leads out from Albarracín. It's about 5km.

Bilbao, Basque Country & La Rioja

Best Places to Eat

➡ Arzak (p424)

➡ La Cuchara de San Telmo (p425) Mina Restaurante (p413) La Fábrica (p423)

➡ Bar Torrecilla (p450)

Best Places to Sleep

➡ Hotel Marqués de Riscal (p455)

➡ Hotel Zubieta (p416)

➡ Miró Hotel (p408)

➡ Pensión Aida (p422)

➡ La Casa de los Arquillos (p434)

Why Go?

The jade hills and drizzle-filled skies of this pocket of Spain are quite a contrast to the popular image of the country. The Basques, the people who inhabit this corner, also consider themselves different. They claim to be the oldest Europeans and to speak the original European language. Whether or not this is actually the case remains unproven, but what is beyond doubt is that they live in a land of exceptional beauty and diversity. There are mountains watched over by almost forgotten gods, cultural museums and art galleries, street parties a million people strong and, arguably, the best food in Spain.

Leave the rugged north behind and feel the temperature rise as you hit the open, classically Spanish plains south of Pamplona. Here you enter the world of Navarra and La Rioja. It's a region awash with glorious wine, sunburst colours, dreamy landscapes, medieval monasteries and enticing wine towns.

When to Go
Bilbao

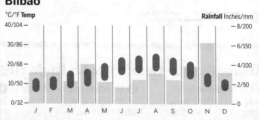

May Spring brings crowds, and a bustling modern art scene, in the museums and galleries of Bilbao.

Jul–Sep Lively San Sebastián at its best and, unless you're skiing, the best time to visit the Pyrenees.

Sep Harvest festivals bring festivity and free-flowing wine to the villages of La Rioja.

Bilbao, Basque Country & La Rioja Highlights

1 San Sebastián (p417)
Playing on a perfect beach, gorging on fabulous *pintxos* (Basque tapas), dancing all night and dreaming of staying forever in stylish San Sebastián.

2 Bilbao (p401) Finding artistic inspiration at the Museo Guggenheim Bilbao and in exceptional galleries.

3 Mundaka (p415) Catching a ride in the home of the best waves in Europe.

4 La Rioja (p448) Learning the secrets of a good drop in the museums and vineyards of La Rioja.

5 Olite (p444) and **Ujué** (p445) Rolling back the years in medieval fortress towns.

6 Navarran Pyrenees (p441) Climbing mist-shrouded slopes haunted by witches and vultures.

7 Pamplona (p436) Pretending you're Hemingway during the Sanfermines week of debauchery in Pamplona.

BASQUE COUNTRY

No matter where you've just come from, be it the hot, southern plains of Spain or gentle and pristine France, the Basque Country is different. Known to Basques as Euskadi or Euskal Herria ('the land of Basque Speakers') and called El Pais Vasco in Spanish, this is where mountain peaks reach for the sky and sublime rocky coves are battered by mighty Atlantic swells. It's a place that demands exploration beyond the delightful and cosmopolitan main cities of Bilbao, Vitoria and San Sebastián. You travel through the Basque Country always curious, and frequently rewarded.

History

No one quite knows where the Basque people came from (they have no migration myth in their oral history), but their presence here is believed to predate even the earliest known migrations. The Romans left the hilly Basque Country more or less to itself, but the expansionist Castilian crown gained sovereignty over Basque territories during the Middle Ages (1000–1450), although with considerable difficulty; Navarra constituted a separate kingdom until 1512. Even when they came within the Castilian orbit, Navarra and the three other Basque provinces (Guipúzkoa, Vizcaya and Álava) extracted broad autonomy arrangements, known as the *fueros* (the ancient laws of the Basques).

After the Second Carlist War in 1876, all provinces except Navarra were stripped of their coveted *fueros,* thereby fuelling nascent Basque nationalism. Yet, although the Partido Nacionalista Vasco (PNV; Basque Nationalist Party) was established in 1894, support was never uniform as all Basque provinces included a considerable Castilian contingent.

When the Republican government in Madrid proposed the possibility of home rule (self-government) to the Basques in 1936, both Gupúzkoa and Vizcaya took up the offer. When the Spanish Civil War erupted, conservative rural Navarra and Álava supported Franco, while Vizcaya and Gupúzkoa sided with the Republicans, a decision they paid a high price for in the four decades that followed.

It was during the Franco days that Euskadi Ta Askatasuna (ETA; Basque Homeland and Freedom) was first born. It was originally set up to fight against the Franco regime, which suppressed the Basques through banning the language and almost all forms of Basque culture. After the death of Franco, ETA called for nothing less than total independence and continued its bloody fight against the Spanish government until, in October 2011, the group announced a 'definitive cessation of its armed activity'.

Bilbao

POP 346,575

Bilbao isn't the kind of city that knocks you out with its physical beauty – head on over to San Sebastián for that particular pleasure – but it's a city that slowly wins you over. Bilbao, after all, has had a tough upbringing. Surrounded for years by an environment of heavy industry and industrial wastelands, its riverfront landscapes and quirky architecture were hardly recognised or appreciated by travellers on their way to more pleasant destinations. But Bilbao's graft paid off when a few wise investments left it with a shimmering titanium landmark, the Museo Guggenheim Bilbao – and a horde of art world types from around the world started coming to see what all the fuss was about.

The *Botxo* (Hole), as it's fondly known to its inhabitants, has now matured into its role of major European art centre. But at heart it remains a hard-working town, and one that has real character. It's this down-to-earth soul, rather than its plethora of art galleries, that is the real attraction of the vital, exciting and cultured city of Bilbao.

⊙ Sights

★ Museo Guggenheim Bilbao   GALLERY
(www.guggenheim-bilbao.es; Avenida Abandoibarra 2; adult/student/child from €13/7.50/free; ⊙10am-8pm, closed Mon Sep-Jun) Opened in September 1997, The shimmering Museo Guggenheim Bilbao is one of modern architecture's iconic buildings. It almost single-handedly lifted Bilbao out of its post-industrial depression and into the 21st century – and with sensation. It boosted the city's already inspired regeneration, stimulated further development and

> ### ℹ ARTEAN PASS
>
> The Artean Pass is a joint ticket for the Museo Guggenheim Bilbao (p401) and the Museo de Bellas Artes (p405), which offers significant savings. It's available from either museum.

Bilbao

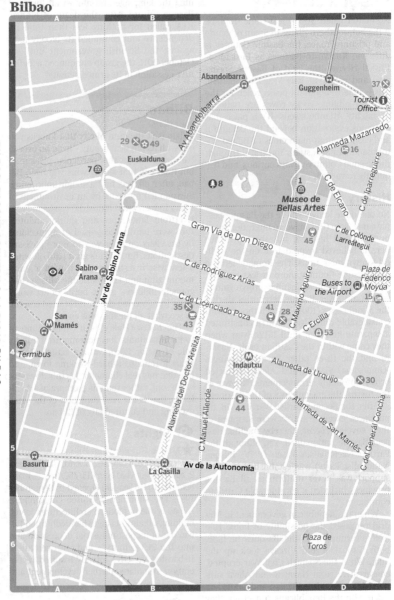

placed Bilbao firmly in the international art and tourism spotlight.

Some might say, probably quite rightly, that structure overwhelms function here and that the museum is more famous for its architecture than its content. But Canadian architect Frank Gehry's inspired use of flowing canopies, cliffs, promontories, ship shapes, towers and flying fins is irresistible.

Gehry designed the museum with historical and geographical contexts in mind. The site was an industrial wasteland, part

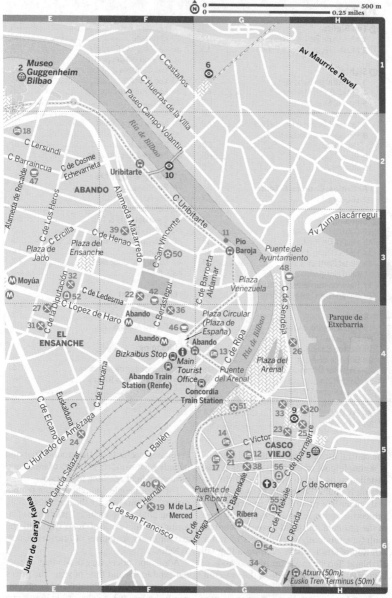

of Bilbao's wretched and decaying warehouse district on the banks of the Ría del Nervión. The city's historical industries of shipbuilding and fishing reflected Gehry's own interests, not least his engagement with industrial materials in previous works. The gleaming titanium tiles that sheathe most of the building like giant herring scales are said to have been inspired by the architect's childhood fascination with fish.

Other artists have added their touch to as well. Lying between the glass buttresses of

Bilbao

the central atrium and the Ría del Nervión is a simple pool of water that emits a mist installation by Fuyiko Nakaya. Near the riverbank is Louise Bourgeois' *Maman*, a skeletal spider-like canopy said to symbolise a protective embrace. In the open area west of the museum, the child-favourite fountain sculpture randomly fires off jets of water. Jeff Koons' kitsch whimsy *Puppy*, a 12m-tall Highland Terrier made up of thousands of begonias, is on the city side of the museum. Bilbao has hung on to 'El Poop', who was supposed to be a passing attraction as part of a world tour. *Bilbaínos* will tell you that El Poop came first – and then they had to build a kennel behind it.

Heading inside, the interior of the Museo Guggenheim Bilbao is purposefully vast. The cathedral-like atrium is more than 45m high, with light pouring in through the glass cliffs.

Permanent exhibits fill the ground floor and include such wonders as mazes of metal and phrases of light reaching for the skies.

For most people, though, it is the temporary exhibitions that are the main attraction. During 2014, these included exhibitions featuring the life work of Yoko Ono and the extraordinary sculptures of Brazilian Ernesto Neto.

Admission prices vary depending on special exhibitions and time of year. The prices listed here are the maximum (and most common); the last ticket sales are half an hour before closing. Free guided tours in Spanish take place at 12.30pm and 5pm; sign up half an hour before at the information desk. Tours can be conducted in other languages but you must ask at the information desk beforehand. Groups are limited to 20 (and there needs to be a minimum of eight), so get there early. It's also possible to organise private group tours with advance request in Spanish, English, French and German, among others. The museum is equipped with specially adapted magnetic loop PDA video guides for those with hearing impairments. Excellent self-guided audio tours in various languages are free with admission and there is also a special children's audio guide. Entry queues can be horrendous, with wet summer days and Easter almost guaranteeing you a wait of over an hour. The museum is wheelchair accessible.

★ **Museo de Bellas Artes**   GALLERY
(www.museobilbao.com; Plaza del Museo 2; adult/student/child €7/5/free, Wed free; ◷10am-8pm Wed-Mon) The Museo de Bellas Artes houses a compelling collection that includes everything from Gothic sculptures to 20th-century pop art. There are three main subcollections: classical art, with works by Murillo, Zurbarán, El Greco, Goya and van Dyck; contemporary art, featuring works by Gauguin, Francis Bacon and Anthony Caro; and Basque art, with works of the great sculptors Jorge Oteiza and Eduardo Chillida, and strong paintings by the likes of Ignacio Zuloaga and Juan de Echevarría.

Casco Viejo   OLD TOWN
The compact Casco Viejo, Bilbao's atmospheric old quarter, is full of charming streets, boisterous bars and plenty of quirky and independent shops. At the heart of the Casco are Bilbao's original seven streets, Las Siete Calles, which date from the 1400s.

The 14th-century Gothic **Catedral de Santiago** (Plaza de Santiago; ◷10am-1pm & 5-7.30pm Tue-Sat, 10am-1pm Sun & holidays) has a splendid Renaissance portico and pretty little cloister. Further north, the 19th-century arcaded **Plaza Nueva** is a rewarding *pintxo* (Basque tapas) haunt. There's a lively Sunday-morning **flea market** here, which is full of secondhand book and record stalls, and pet 'shops' selling chirpy birds (some kept in old-fashioned wooden cages), fluffy mice and tiny baby terrapins. Elsewhere in the market, children and adults alike swap and barter football cards and old stamps from countries you've never heard of; in between weave street performers and waiters with trays piled high. The market is much more subdued in winter. A sweeter-smelling **flower market** takes place on Sunday mornings in the nearby **Plaza del Arenal**.

Euskal Museoa   MUSEUM
(Museo Vasco; www.euskal-museoa.org/es/hasiera; Plaza Miguel Unamuno 4; adult/child €3/free, Thu free; ◷10am-7pm Mon & Wed-Fri, 10am-1.30pm & 4-7pm Sat, 10am-2pm Sun) This is probably the most complete museum of Basque culture and history in all of Spain. The story begins in prehistory; from this murky period the displays bound rapidly up to the modern age, in the process explaining just how long the Basques have called this corner of the world home.

Museo Marítimo Ría de Bilbao   MUSEUM
(www.museomaritimobilbao.org; Muelle Ramón de la Sota 1; adult/student & child/under 6yr €6/3.50/free; ◷10am-8pm Tue-Sun, to 6pm Mon-Fri Oct-Mar) This space-age maritime museum, appropriately sited down on the waterfront, uses bright and well-thought-out displays to bring the watery depths of Bilbao and Basque maritime history to life. There's an

---

CITY TOURS

There are a number of different city tours available. Some are general-interest tours, others focus on specific aspects of the city such as architecture or food. The following are recommended.

Bilbao tourist office (☑944 79 57 60; www.bilbaoturismo.net; Plaza Circular 1; ◷9am-9pm; ☏) Organises 1½-hour walking tours covering either the old town or the architecture in the newer parts of town. At busy times tours can run with more frequency.

Bilboats (☑946 42 41 57; www.bilboats.com; Plaza Pío Baroja; adult/child from €12/7) Runs boat cruises along the Nervión several times a day.

Bilbao Greeters (www.bilbaogreeters.com; adult €12) One of the more original, and interesting, ways to see the city and get to know a local is through the Bilbao Greeters organisation. Essentially a local person gives you a tour of the city showing you their favourite sights, places to hang out and, of course, *pintxo* (Basque tapas) bars. You need to reserve through the website at least a fortnight in advance.

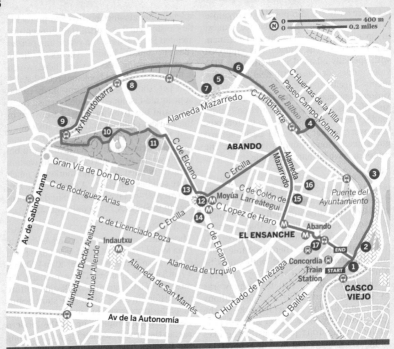

🏃 Walking Tour
Architecture and River Views

START TEATRO ARRIAGA
FINISH TEATRO ARRIAGA
LENGTH ABOUT 4KM; THREE HOURS

One of the pleasures of a visit to Bilbao is just walking around admiring its crazy mix of architectural styles and the riverside walkways.

Start at the baroque **❶ Teatro Arriaga**, on the edge of the Casco Vieja, which was built in 1890. Follow the river through the **❷ Plaza del Arenal** and pass by the grand **❸ ayuntamiento** (town hall), dating from the late 19th century. Continue upriver along the Paseo Campo Volantín, which is lined with buildings covering a range of styles. Cross over the **❹ Puente Zubizuri**; this wave-like bridge was designed by Santiago Calatrava and is the most striking bridge in the city.

Arriving on the other side of the river turn right and carry on up the waterfront towards the most famous building in the city, the **❺ Museo Guggenheim Bilbao** (p401). It's hard to unhinge your eyes from the museum, but do be sure to check out the

spider-like **❻ Maman** and **❼ Puppy**, the sweetest-smelling dog you ever did see.

Continue walking along the river past numerous sculptures. On your left is the **❽ Iberdrola tower**, a 165m glass office block, the tallest building in the region. Eventually you arrive at the modern **❾ Euskalduna Palace**. Turn left and enjoy the stroll through the whimsical **❿ Parque de Doña Casilda de Iturrizar**, pass by the **⓫ Museo de Bellas Artes** (p405) and head down Calle de Elcano to **⓬ Plaza de Federico Moyúa**, which marks the centre of the new town. This square is lined by impressive buildings including, on your right, the early-20th-century Flemish-style **⓭ Palacio de Chávarri** and, opposite, the oh-so-grand **⓮ Hotel Carlton** (p408). Turn down Calle Ercilla, then right down Alameda Mazarredo until you come to the pretty **⓯ Jardines Albia**, overlooked by the 16th-century church **⓰ Iglesia San Vicente Mátir**. Cut down to Calle López de Haro and, passing the art-nouveau facade of the **⓱ FEVE train station**, cross the Puente del Arenal to arrive back at the start of the walk.

outdoor section where children (and nautically inclined grown-ups) can clamber about a range of boats pretending to be pirates and sailors, in addition to frequent temporary exhibitions.

Estadio San Mamés
STADIUM

(www.athletic-club.eus) Bilbao's modern football stadium, home of local team Athletic Bilbao, overlooks the river to the east of the city centre. It's within easy walking distance of the San Mamés metro station. Work is ongoing on the stadium's club museum, which is expected to open in 2016.

Zubizuri
BRIDGE

The most striking of the modern bridges that span the Ría del Nervión, the Zubizuri (Basque for 'White Bridge') has become an iconic feature of Bilbao's cityscape since its completion in 1997. Designed by Spanish architect Santiago Calatrava, it has a curved walkway suspended under a flowing white arch to which it's attached by a series of steel spokes.

Funicular de Artxanda
FUNICULAR

(Plaza Funicular; adult/child €0.95/0.31; ⏰ 7.15am-11pm Mon-Sat, 8.15am-10pm Sun Jun-Sep, closes earlier Oct-May) Bilbao is a city hemmed in by hills and mountains, resting in a tight valley. For a breathtaking view over the city and the wild Basque mountains beyond, take a trip on the funicular railway that has creaked and moaned its way up the steep slope to the summit of Artxanda for nearly a century.

🎊 Festivals & Events

Carnaval
CARNIVAL

Carnaval (February) is celebrated with vigour in Bilbao.

Bilbao BBK Live
MUSIC

(www.bilbaobbklive.com) Bilbao's biggest musical event is Bilbao BBK Live, which takes place over three days in mid-July.

Aste Nagusia
CULTURAL

(www.astenagusia.com) Bilbao's grandest fiesta begins on the first Saturday after 15 August. It has a full program of cultural events over 10 days.

🛏 Sleeping

Bilbao welcomes quite a lot of tourists and the most popular hotels and guesthouses can get booked up early in high season, so it pays to book as far ahead as possible. The Bilbao tourism authority has a very useful reservations department (☑ 902 87 72 98; www.bilbaoreservas.com).

Casual Bilbao Gurea
PENSIÓN €

(☑ 944 16 32 99; www.casualhoteles.com; Calle de Bidebarrieta 14; s/d from €42/48; 🛜) The family-run Gurea has arty, modern rooms with wooden floors and large bathrooms (most of which have bath tubs) and exceptionally friendly staff. Add it all up and you get what is easily one of the best deals in the old town.

BILBAO, BASQUE COUNTRY & LA RIOJA BILBAO

LOCAL KNOWLEDGE

THE ART OF EATING PINTXOS

Just rolling the word *pintxo* (Basque tapas) around your tongue defines the essence of this cheerful, cheeky little slice of Basque cuisine. The perfect *pintxo* should have exquisite taste, texture and appearance and should be savoured in two elegant bites. The Basque version of a tapa, the *pintxo* transcends the commonplace by the sheer panache of its culinary campiness. In San Sebastián especially, Basque chefs have refined the *pintxo* to an art form.

Many *pintxos* are bedded on small pieces of bread or on tiny half-baguettes, upon which towering creations are constructed, often melded with flavoursome mayonnaise and then pinned in place by large toothpicks. Some bars specialise in seafood, with much use of marinated anchovies, prawns and strips of squid, all topped with anything from chopped crab to pâté. Others deal in pepper or mushroom delicacies, or simply offer a mix of everything. And the choice isn't normally limited to what's on the bar top in front of you: many of the best *pintxos* are the hot ones you need to order. These are normally chalked up on a blackboard on the wall somewhere.

Locals tend to just eat one or two of the house specials at each bar before moving on somewhere else. When it comes to ordering, tell the barman what you want first and never just help yourself to a *pintxo* off the counter!

Miró Hotel DESIGN HOTEL €€

(⌂ 946 61 18 80; www.mirohotelbilbao.com; Alameda Mazarredo 77; d from €137; ❄ @ ☎) This hip hotel, facing the Museo Guggenheim Bilbao, is the passion project of fashion designer Antonio Miró. It's filled with modern photography and art, quirky books, and minimalist decor – a perfect fit with an arty city.

Pensión Iturrienea Ostatua BOUTIQUE HOTEL €€

(⌂ 944 16 15 00; www.iturrieneaostatua.com; Calle de Santa María 14; r €60-80; ☎) One of Bilbao's more eccentric hotels, Pensión Iturrienea Ostatua has a unique look: part farmyard and part old-fashioned toy shop, mixing floral wallpaper and brightly painted railings with black and white-tiled floors. It sounds unusual, but the aesthetic works — located on one of the charming pedestrian streets in the historic center, it's a traveller's favourite.

Hotel Bilbao Jardines BOUTIQUE HOTEL €€

(⌂ 944 79 42 10; www.hotelbilbaojardines.com; Calle Jardines 9; s/d from €55/70; ❄ ☎) Though this hotel has a faintly institutional look from the outside, and the green-hued interior decor is somewhat dated, it's a good-value place to stay in the Casco Viejo (Old Town). Guest rooms are light-filled and guests can borrow bicycles for free.

Hostal Begoña GUESTHOUSE €€

(⌂ 944 23 01 34; www.hostalbegona.com; Calle de la Amistad 2; s/d from €46/60; P @ ☎) Friendly Begoña has guest rooms decorated with modern artwork, wrought-iron beds, and colourful tiled bathrooms. The cosy common areas have plenty of books and information about local culture and attractions. It's a great place to meet other travellers, too.

Hotel Carlton HISTORIC HOTEL €€€

(⌂ 944 16 22 00; www.hotelcarlton.es; Plaza de Frederico Moyúa 2; d from €182; P ❄ @ ☎) Style, class and sophistication: at Hotel Carlton, sitting proudly in a prominent position on Plaza Federico Moyúa, it's old-fashioned glamour with a retro twist all the way. The elegant building, constructed between 1919 and 1926, was the work of Bilbao architect Manuel María Smith.

Silken Gran Hotel Domine DESIGN HOTEL €€€

(⌂ 944 25 33 00; www.granhoteldominebilbao. com; Alameda Mazarredo 61; d from €255; P ❄ @ ☎) If money's no object, check into this stellar showpiece of the Silken chain. It's modern chic all the way, with spacious guest rooms and luxe bathrooms – there are views of the Museo Guggenheim Bilbao from some of the pricier suites – and breakfast served on the hotel's lovely rooftop terrace.

✖ Eating

In the world of trade and commerce, the Basques are an outward-looking lot, but when it comes to food they refuse to believe that any other people could possibly match their culinary skills (and they may well have a point). This means that eating out in Bilbao is generally a choice of Basque, Basque or Basque food. Still, life could be worse and there are some terrific places to eat.

The porticoed Plaza Nueva is a good spot for coffee and people-watching, especially in summer.

El Puertito SEAFOOD €

(⌂ 944 02 62 54; Calle de Licenciado Poza 22, cnr Calle Maestro Garcia Rivero; oysters €1-3.30; ⊙ 10am-10pm) On warm summer evenings, wine-sipping crowds congregate at this small bar to enjoy an oyster or six. Aficionados can choose from a chalked-up menu of French and Galician oysters, while amateurs can simply ask the knowledgeable, English-speaking staff for their recommendations.

La Mary Restaurante BASQUE €

(www.lamaryrestaurant.com; Plaza de Arriquíbar 3; menú del día €9.95, mains €7.95-9.95; ⊙ 1-4pm & 8-11.30pm) From the outside this looks like quite a swanky place, but in fact it's very casual. To enjoy the bargain lunch menú you'll need to arrive early; otherwise, count on joining the queue of locals waiting for a table. It might not be the best quality in town, but it's probably the best value.

Rio-Oja BASQUE €

(⌂ 944 15 08 71; www.rio-oja.com; Calle de Perro 4; mains €7-12; ⊙ 9am-11pm Tue-Sun) An institution that shouldn't be missed. It specialises in light Basque seafood and heavy inland fare, but for most visitors the snails, sheep brains or squid floating in pools of ink are the makings of a culinary adventure story they'll be recounting for years. Don't worry, though: it really does taste much better than it sounds.

★ Casa Rufo BASQUE €€

(⌂ 944 43 21 72; www.casarufo.com; Hurtado de Amézaga 5; mains €10-15; ⊙ 1.30-4pm & 8.30-11pm Mon-Sat) Despite the emergence of numerous glitzy restaurants that are temples to haute cuisine, this resolutely old-fashioned place, with its shelves full of dusty bottles

PINTXO BARS IN BILBAO

Although it lacks San Sebastián's stellar reputation for *pintxos* (Basque tapas), prices are generally slightly lower here (all charge from around €2.50 per *pintxo*) and the quality is about equal. There are literally hundreds of *pintxo* bars throughout Bilbao, but the Plaza Nueva on the edge of the Casco Viejo offers especially rich pickings, as do Calle de Perro and Calle Jardines. Some of the city's standouts, in no particular order:

Bar Gure Toki (Plaza Nueva 12; pintxos from €2.50) With a subtle but simple line in creative *pintxos* including some made with ostrich.

Café-Bar Bilbao (Plaza Nueva 6; pintxos from €2.50; ⊘7am-11pm Mon-Fri, 9am-11.30pm Sat, 10am-3pm Sun) Cool blue southern tile work and warm northern atmosphere.

Casa Victor Montes (⊘944 15 70 67; www.victormontesbilbao.com; Plaza Nueva 8; mains €15, pintxos from €2.50; ⊘10.30am-11pm Mon-Thu, 10.30am-midnight Fri & Sun) As well known for its *pintxos* as its full meals.

Sorginzulo (Plaza Nueva 12; pintxos from €2.50; ⊘9.30am-12.30am) A matchbox-sized bar with an exemplary spread of *pintxos*. The house special is calamari but it's only served on weekends.

Berton Sasibil (Calle Jardines 8; pintxos from €2.50; ⊘8.30am-midnight Mon-Sat, 10am-4pm Sun) Here you can watch informative films on the crafting of the same superb *pintxos* that you're munching on.

Claudio: La Feria del Jamón (Calle Iparragirre 9-18; pintxos from €2.50; ⊘10am-2pm & 5-9pm Mon-Fri, 10am-2pm & 6-9.30pm Sat) A creaky old place full of ancient furnishings. As you'll guess from the name and the dozens of legs of ham hanging from the ceiling, it's all about pigs. Opposite the bar, it has a shop selling hams to take away.

La Viña del Ensanche (⊘944 15 56 15; www.lavinadelensanche.com; Calle de la Diputación 10; pintxos from €2.50, menú €30; ⊘8.30am-11pm Mon-Fri, noon-1am Sat) Hundreds of bottles of wine line the walls of this outstanding *pintxos* bar. And when we say outstanding, we mean that it could well be the best place to eat *pintxos* in the city.

Museo del Vino (Calle de Ledesma 10; pintxos from €2.50; ⊘1-5pm & 8-11pm Mon-Fri) Tiled white interior, Gaudiesque windows, delicous octopus *pintxos* and an excellent wine selection (as you'd hope with a name like this). This place makes us smile.

Bitoque de Albia (www.bitoque.net; Alameda Mazarredo 6; pintxos from €2.50; ⊘1.30-4pm Mon-Wed, 1.30-4pm & 8.30-11.15pm Thu-Sat) Award-winning modern *pintxos* bar serving such unclassic dishes as minituare red tuna burgers, salmon sushi and clams with wild mushrooms. It also offers a *pintxos* tasting menu (€12).

El Globo (www.barelglobo.com; Calle de Diputación 8; pintxos from €2.50; ⊘8am-11pm Mon-Thu, 8am-midnight Fri & Sat) This is an unassuming but popular bar with favourites such as *txangurro gratinado* (spider crab).

Los Candiles (Calle de Diputación 1; pintxos from €2.50; ⊘7am-10pm Mon-Sat) A narrow, low-key little bar, with some subtle *pintxos* filled with the taste of the sea.

Mugi (www.mugiardotxoko.es; Licenciado Poza 55; pintxos from €2.50; ⊘7am-midnight Mon-Sat, noon-midnight Sun) Widely regarded *pintxo* bar. It can get so busy that you might have to stand outside.

of top-quality olive oil and wine, still stands out as one of the best places to eat traditional Basque food in Bilbao. The house special is steak – lovingly cooked over hot coals.

⭐ **Agape Restaurante** BASQUE €€
(⊘944 16 05 06; www.restauranteagape.com; Calle de Hernani 13; menú del día €12.20, menús €14.80-36; ⊘1-4pm Sun-Wed, 1-4pm & 8.30-11.30pm Thu-Sat) With a solid reputation among locals for good-value meals that don't sacrifice quality, this is a great place for a slice of real Bilbao culinary life. It's well away from the standard tourist circuit, but is worth the short walk.

El Txoko Berria
BASQUE €€

(944 79 42 98; http://eltxokoberria.com; Calle de Bidebarrieta 14; mains €8-16; ⊙1-4pm & 7.30-11pm) This welcoming restaurant is a good bet for honest, earthy local cuisine. Take a seat in the handsome dining room and dig into staples such as cod *Bizkaina* style (with a sweet, slightly spicy pepper sauce) and grilled meats.

Los Fueros
BASQUE €€

(944 15 30 47; www.losfueros.com; Calle Fueros 6; pintxos €5-6, mains €12-16; ⊙noon-midnight Mon & Wed-Sat, to 4pm Tue & Sun) Seafood stars at this backstreet bar-restaurant near Plaza Nueva, appearing in time-honoured crowd-pleasers like grilled prawns and fried hake with pepper mayonnaise. The bar is smarter than many Old Town places, decked out in contemporary mosaic-tiling and cool Mediterranean blues.

Zortziko Restaurante
CONTEMPORARY BASQUE €€€

(944 23 97 43; www.zortziko.es; Alameda Mazarredo 17; menús from €85, mains €22-39; ⊙1-3.30pm & 9.30-11pm Tue-Sat;) Michelin-starred chef Daniel García presents immaculate modern Basque cuisine in a formal 1920s-style French dining room. The highly inventive menu changes frequently, but might include such delicacies as grilled scallops with liquid potatoes and truffles or, and here's one you don't see cropping up all that much, pigeon ice-cream.

If the food inspires your taste buds, then sign up for one of his occasional cooking courses (€40).

Nerua Guggenheim Bilbao
CONTEMPORARY BASQUE €€€

(944 00 04 30; www.neruaguggenheimbilbao.com; tasting menu from €65, mains €30-35; ⊙1-3pm & 8.30-9.30pm Thu-Sat, 1-3pm Tue, Wed & Sun) The Museo Guggenheim Bilbao's modernist, chic, and very white restaurant is under the direction of Michelin-starred chef Josean Alija (a disciple of Ferran Adria). Needless to say, the *nueva cocina vasca* (Basque nouvelle cuisine) is breathtaking – even the olives are vintage classics: all come from 1000-year-old olive trees!

Reservations are essential. If the gourmet restaurant is too much for you, try the museum's Bistró, which has *menús* from €20.

Drinking & Nightlife

In the Casco Viejo, around Calles Barrenkale, Ronda and de Somera, there are plenty of terrific hole-in-the-wall, no-nonsense bars with a generally youthful crowd.

Across the river, in the web of streets around Muelle Marzana and Bilbao la Vieja, are scores more little bars and clubs. This is gritty Bilbao as it used to be in the days before the arty makeover. It's both a Basque heartland and the centre of the city's ethnic community. The many bars around here are normally welcoming, but one or two can be

---

BILBAO CAFES

Bilbao has some classic cafes in which to enjoy a caffeine shot and a sweet snack. Styles range from frusty and old fashioned to modern and flash. Here's our pick of the crop.

Café Iruña (cnr Calles de Colón de Larreátegui & Berástegui; ⊙7am-1am Mon-Thu, 7am-2am Fri, 9am-1am Sat, noon-1am Sun) Ornate Moorish style and a century of gossip are the defining characteristics of this grande old dame. It's the perfect place to indulge in a bit of people-watching. Dont miss the delicous *pinchos morunos* (spicy kebabs).

La Granja (Plaza Circular 3; ⊙7.30am-12.30am Mon-Fri, 10.30am-1.30am Sat) With its period furnishings and polished wooden bar top, this place, which first opened its doors in 1926, is another of Bilbao's old time-warp cafes.

Opila (Calle de Sendeja 4) Fantastic patisserie and cafe. Downstairs is all art-deco furnishings and glass display cabinets and upstairs is way more up to the moment.

Mami Lou Cupcake (www.mamiloucupcake.com; Calle Barraincua 7; ⊙11am-8.30pm Mon-Sat) Relive your childhood at this cute little cafe with 1950s deco and colourful home-made cupcakes.

Casa del Café & Té (Alaveda Doctor Areliza 22; ⊙9am-9pm Mon-Fri, 9am-2pm & 5-9pm Sat) This cute little blue teashop sells tea leaves to take away or you can sit and sup your brew in-situ.

a bit seedy. It's not a great idea for women to walk here alone at night.

There are plenty of clubs and live venues in Bilbao, and the vibe is friendly and generally easy-going. Venues' websites usually have details of upcoming gigs.

Bilbao offers regular performances of dance, opera and drama at the city's principal theatre and the Kafe Antzokia. Check the theatre websites for current information.

Cotton Club CLUB
(944 10 49 51; www.cottonclubbilbao.es; Calle de Gregorio de la Revilla 25; 8.30pm-3am Tue & Wed, to 5am Thu, to 6.30am Fri & Sat, 7pm-1.30am Sun) A historic Bilbao nightspot, the Cotton Club draws a mixed crowd to its DJ-stoked nights and regular gigs – mainly blues, jazz and rock . It's a tiny place so prepare to get up close with your fellow revellers.

Geo Cocktail Lounge COCKTAIL BAR
(944 66 84 42; Calle Maximo Aguirre 12; 3pm-1.30am Tue-Sun) For a refined post-dinner cocktail, search out this lounge bar in the area south of the Museo Guggenheim Bilbao. Expect subdued lighting, low-key tunes and expertly crafted cocktails.

Bar Nashville BAR
(944 05 55 06; Calle de Licenciado Poza 24; 8am-1am Mon-Thu, to 2.30am Fri, noon-2.30am Sat) In the dressy, bar-heavy area around Calle de Licenciado Poza, this casual neighbourhood hangout is decidedly unpretentious. The colours of local football team, Athletic Bilbao, hang in the window, as chatty drinkers of all ages cram into the narrow, eclectically decorated interior.

Badulake CLUB
(www.badulakebilbao.com; Calle Hernani 10; 9.30pm-5am Thu, to 6am Fri, midnight-6am Sat) A well-known address on Bilbao's nightlife scene, Badulake bursts to life on Thursdays when Las Fellini, a local cabaret act, ham it up in front of a largely gay audience. On Friday and Saturday nights the fun is fuelled by '80s disco, mainstream pop and DJ-spun electronica.

☆ Entertainment

There are plenty of clubs and live venues in Bilbao, and the vibe is friendly and generally easy-going. Venues' websites usually have details of upcoming gigs.

Bilbao offers regular performances of dance, opera and drama at the city's principal theatre and the Kafe Antzokia. Check the theatre websites for current information.

★Kafe Antzokia LIVE MUSIC
(944 24 46 25; www.kafeantzokia.com; Calle San Vicente 2) This is the vibrant heart of contemporary Basque Bilbao, featuring international rock, blues and reggae, as well as the cream of Basque rock-pop. Weekend concerts run from 10pm to 1am, followed by DJs until 5am. During the day it's a cafe, restaurant and cultural centre all rolled into one and has a programme of exciting events.

🛍 Shopping

For major department stores and big-name fashion labels trawl the streets of El Ensanche. For more one of a kind, independent boutiques, Casco Viejo is the place to look (although even here the chain shops are increasingly making their presence felt).

Bilbao is also a great place for food shopping (of course!).

Vaho ACCESSORIES
(www.vaho.ws; Calle Correo 25; 11am-2.30pm & 5-8.30pm Mon-Sat) Street fashion goes green at this hip bag store where everything is made from material recycled from old advertising banners. The resulting satchels, messenger bags, wallets and the like are bright and bold with loud, in-your-face designs.

Mercado de la Ribera MARKET
(Calle de la Rlbera) Overlooking the river, the Mercado de la Ribera is supposedly one of the largest covered food markets in Spain. It's had a recent makeover which has sanitised it somewhat, but many of the city's top chefs still come here to select fresh produce each morning.

Arrese FOOD
(www.arrese.biz; Calle Lopez de Haro 24; 9am-9pm Mon-Sat, 9am-3pm & 5-9pm Sun) With 160 years of baking experience you'd hope the cakes at this little patissiere would taste divine, but frankly, they're even better than expected.

Txorierri FOOD
(Calle Artekale 19; 10am-2pm & 4-8pm Mon-Sat) High-quality deli selling the full tummy-pleasing array of local culinary delicacies.

Chocolates de Mendaro FOOD
(www.chocolatesdemendaro.com; Calle de Licenciado Poza 16; ⏰10am-2pm & 4-8pm Mon-Sat)
This old-time chocolate shop created its first chocolate treats way back in 1850 and is hands down the best place to ruin a diet in Bilbao.

ℹ Information

Bilbao's friendly tourist-office staffers are extremely helpful, well informed and, above all, enthusiastic about their city. At all offices ask for the free bimonthly *Bilbao Guía*, with its entertainment listings plus tips on restaurants, bars and nightlife.

At the newly opened, state-of-the-art **main tourist office** (p405) there's free wi-fi access, a bank of touch-screen information computers and, best of all, some humans to help answer questions. There are also branches at the **airport** (📞 944 71 03 01; www.bilbaoturismo.net; Bilbao Airport; ⏰9am-9pm Mon-Sat, 9am-3pm Sun) and the **Museo Guggenheim Bilbao** (www.bilbaoturismo.net; Alameda Mazarredo 66; ⏰10am-7pm daily, to 3pm Sun Sep-Jun).

ℹ Getting There & Away

AIR

Bilbao's **airport** (BIO; 📞 902 404 704; www.aena.es) is near Sondika, to the northeast of the city. A number of European flag carriers serve the city. Of the budget airlines, **EasyJet** (www.easyjet.com) and **Vueling** (www.vueling.com) cover the widest range of destinations.

BUS

Bilbao's main bus station, **Termibus** (📞 944 39 50 77; Gurtubay 1, San Mamés), is west of the centre. There are regular services to the following destinations:

DESTINATION	FARE	DURATION
Barcelona	€50	7-8hr
Biarritz (France)	€19.48	3hr
Logroño	€14	2¾hr
Madrid	€34	4¾hr
Oñati	€6.50	1¼hr
Pamplona	€18	2¾hr
San Sebastián	€9	1hr
Santander	€9	1¼hr
Vitoria	€9	1½hr

Bizkaibus travels to destinations throughout the rural Basque Country, including coastal communities such as Mundaka and Gernika (€2.50). Euskotren buses serve Lekeitio (€6.65).

TRAIN

The Abando train station is just across the river from Plaza Arriaga and the Casco Viejo. There are frequent trains to the following destinations:

DESTINATION	FARE	DURATION
Barcelona	from €19.60	6¾hr
Burgos	from €7	3hr
Madrid	from €20	5hr
Valladolid	from €12.55	4hr

Nearby is the **Concordia train station**, with its handsome art-nouveau facade of wrought iron and tiles. It is used by the **FEVE** (www.feve.es), a formerly private rail company that was recently purchased by RENFE. It has trains running west into Cantabria. There are three daily trains to Santander (from €12.55, three hours) where you can change for stations in Asturias.

The **Atxuri train station** is just upriver from Casco Viejo. From here, **Eusko Tren/Ferrocarril Vasco** (www.euskotren.es) operates services every half-hour to the following:

DESTINATION	FARE	DURATION
Bermeo	€3.70	1½hr
Guernica	€3.70	1hr
Mundaka	€3.70	1½hr

ℹ Getting Around

TO/FROM THE AIRPORT

The **airport bus** (Bizkaibus A3247; €1.45) departs from a stand on the extreme right as you leave arrivals. It runs through the northwestern section of the city, passing the Museo Guggenheim Bilbao, stopping at Plaza de Federico Moyúa and terminating at the Termibus (bus station). It runs from the airport every 20 minutes in summer and every 30 minutes in winter from 6.20am to midnight. There is also a direct hourly bus from the airport to San Sebastián (€16.85, 1¼ hours). It runs from 7.45am to 11.45pm.

Taxis from the airport to the Casco Viejo cost about €23 to €30 depending on traffic.

METRO

There are metro stations at all the main focal points of El Ensanche and at Casco Viejo. Tickets start at €1.65. The metro runs to the north coast from a number of stations on both sides of the river and makes it easy to get to the beaches closest to Bilbao.

TRAM

Bilbao's Eusko Tren tramline is a boon to locals and visitors alike. It runs to and fro between Basurtu, in the southwest of the city, and the Atxuri train station. Stops include the Termibus station, the Museo Guggenheim Bilbao and Teatro Arriaga by the Casco Viejo. Tickets cost €1.50 and need to be validated in the machine next to the ticket dispenser before boarding.

Around Bilbao

Guernica

POP 16,800

Guernica (Basque: Gernika) is a state of mind. At a glance it seems no more than a modern and non-too-attractive country town. Apparently, prior to the morning of 26 April 1937, Guernica wasn't quite so ugly, but the horrifying events of that day meant that the town was later reconstructed as fast as possible with little regard for aesthetics.

The reasons Franco wished to destroy Guernica are pretty clear. The Spanish Civil War was raging and World War II was looming on the horizon. Franco's Nationalist troops were advancing across Spain, but the Basques, who had their own autonomous regional government consisting of supporters of the Left and Basque nationalists, stood opposed to Franco and Guernica was the final town between the Nationalists and the capture of Bilbao. What's harder to understand is why Hitler got involved, but it's generally thought that the Nazis wanted to test the concept of 'terror bombing' on civilian targets. So when Franco asked Hitler for some help he was only too happy to oblige. On that fateful April morning planes from Hitler's Condor Legion flew backwards

SHINING STARS

Basque Country is widely considered one of the world's most exciting culinary destinations. More than forty restaurants in the region have earned Michelin stars, with the highest concentration in San Sebastián. While serious foodies plan entire trips around a gourmet evening at one of Basque Country's three-star venues – like the famed Martín Berasategui Restaurant (p424) or Arzak (p424), both located just outside of San Sebastián – one-star restaurants are usually more affordable and accessible to travellers. Here are a few of our favourites. Reservations, of course, are recommended and/or required.

Alameda (☑943 64 27 89; www.restaurantealameda.net; Calle Minasoroeta 1, Hondarribia; tasting menus €38-80; ☉1-3.30pm & 8-11pm, closed evenings Sun, Mon & Tue) Located in the quaint coastal town of Hondarribia, Alameda started out as a simple tavern. The restaurant, specialising in traditional Basque cuisine made with locally sourced ingredients, still has a cosy, intimate feel, but now it's a dining destination worth a detour. Request terrace seating on a nice day.

Mina (☑944 79 59 38; www.restaurantemina.es; Muelle Marzana; tasting menu €60-110; ☉2-3.30pm & 9-10.30pm Wed-Sat, 2-3.30pm Sun & Tue) This riverside dining institution, off the beaten path in a neighborhood of Bilbao that's rarely frequented by tourists, is known for its culinary creativity. The menu swings toward the avant-garde: a popular dessert is frozen 'seawater' with seaweed and lemon sorbet.

Kokotxa (☑943 42 19 04; www.restaurantekokotxa.com; Calle del Campanario 11; mains €25-31, menús from €60; ☉1.30-3.30pm & 8.45-11pm Tue-Sat) Wander down a quiet alley in San Sebastián's historic centre to find charming Kokotxa. The chefs do their daily shopping at the city's colourful fish and produce market, creating special menú de mercado (market menus) – fresh, unique, and always changing.

Etxanobe (☑944 42 10 71; http://etxanobe.com; Avenida Abandoibarra 4; mains €20-37, menús €75-88; ☉1-4pm & 7.45pm-midnight Mon-Sat) Occupying an unusual location on the third floor of a concert venue in Bilbao, Etxanobe does tasting menus with a view over the city. It's a great place to try traditionally prepared Basque meat dishes.

Mugaritz (☑943 52 24 55; www.mugaritz.com; Aldura Aldea 20, Errenteria; tasting menu €185; ☉12.30-2.30pm & 8-9.30pm, closed Sun dinner, Mon & Tue lunch) Drive into the hills south of San Sebastián for an unforgettable dining experience: a 24-course tasting menu with edible cutlery. It's considered one of the best restaurants in the world – you'll need to plan ahead – but at the moment it has two Michelin stars, not three, making it slightly more accessible for the time being.

and forwards over the town demonstrating their newfound concept of saturation bombing. In the space of a few hours, the town was destroyed and many people were left dead or injured. Exactly how many people were killed remains hard to quantify, with figures ranging from a couple of hundred to well over a thousand. The Museo de la Paz de Gernika claims that around 250 civilians were killed and several hundred injured. What makes the bombings even more shocking is that it wasn't the first time this had happened. Just days earlier, the nearby town of Durango suffered a similar fate, but that time the world had simply not believed what it was being told.

Aside from blocking the path to Bilbao, Guernica may also have been targeted by Franco because of its symbolic value to the Basques. It's the ancient seat of Basque democracy and the site at which the Basque parliament met beneath the branches of a sacred oak tree from medieval times until 1876. Today the original oak is nothing but a stump, but the Tree of Guernica lives on in the form of a young oak tree.

The tragedy of Guernica gained international resonance with Picasso's iconic painting *Guernica,* which has come to symbolise the violence of the 20th century. A copy of the painting now hangs in the entrance hall of the UN headquarters in New York, while the original hangs in the Centro de Arte Reina Sofía (p92) in Madrid.

⊙ Sights

Museo de la Paz de Gernika   MUSEUM
(Guernica Peace Museum; ☑ 946 27 02 13; www.museodelapaz.org; Plaza Foru 1; adult/child €5/3; ⊙10am-7pm Tue-Sat, 10am-2pm Sun Mar-Sep, shorter hours rest of yr) Guernica's seminal experience is a visit to the peace museum,

where audiovisual displays calmly reveal the horror of war and hatred, both in the Basque Country and around the world. Displays are in Basque, but guided tours in other languages are available: log onto the website and fill out the visitor's booking form ahead of your visit.

Parque de los Pueblos de Europa   PARK
(Allende Salazar) The Parque de los Pueblos de Europa contains a couple of typically curvaceous sculptures by Henry Moore and other works by renowned Basque sculptor Eduardo Chillida. The park leads to the attractive Casa de Juntas, where the provincial government has met since 1979. Nearby is the Tree of Guernica, under which the Basque parliament met from medieval times to 1876.

Cuevas de Santimamiñe   ART
(☑944 65 16 57; www.santimamiñe.com; adult/child €5/3; ⊙10am-5.30pm Apr-Oct, 10am-1pm Tue-Sun Nov-Mar) The walls of this cave system, a short way northeast of Guernica, are decorated with around fifty different Neolithic paintings depicting bison, horses, rhinos and the like. Only reproductions are on display, however.

Museo de Euskal Herría   MUSEUM
(☑946 25 54 51; Allende Salazar 5; adult/child €3/1.50; ⊙10am-2pm & 4-7pm Tue-Sat, 10.30am-2.30pm Sun) Housed in the beautiful 18th-century Palacio de Montefuerte, this museum contains a comprehensive exhibition on Basque history and culture, with fine old maps, engravings and a range of other documents and portraits.

✖ Eating

There are plenty of bars in Guernica serving good *pintxos,* and several restaurants

---

WORTH A TRIP

SAN JUAN DE GAZTELUGATXE

On the road between the small towns of Bakio and Bermeo is one of the most photographed features of the Basque coast: the small island of San Juan de Gaztelugatxe. Attached to the mainland by a short causeway this rocky isle is topped by a hermitage (⊙ hours vary). The island is named after St John the Baptist whom local tradition holds visited the island; his footprint is still visible near the top of the 200-odd steps that lead up to the hermitage.

The island is the goal of pilgrimages on June 24th, July 31st and August 29th. Legend has it that by ringing the bell outside the hermitage thirteen times you will be granted a wish and banish bad spirits. And if you don't believe in such things then the spectacular views along the coast should prove reward enough for the walk out here.

offering set menus that cater to day-trippers from Bilbao visiting Guernica's caves or museums.

Zallo Barri
BASQUE €€

(☑ 946 25 18 00; www.zallobarri.com; Juan Calzada 79; mains €15-22; ☺ noon-3.30pm Sun-Thu, noon-3.30pm & 8-11pm Fri & Sat) Locals will tell you that this dining institution is the best place in town for authentic Basque cuisine.

❶ Information

Tourist Office (☑ 946 25 58 92; www.gernika-lumo.org; Artekalea 8; ☺ 10am-2pm & 4-7pm Mon-Sat, 10am-2pm Sun) This helpful office has friendly multilingual staff.

❶ Getting There & Away

Guernica is an easy day trip from Bilbao by ET/FV train from Atxuri train station (€3.10, one hour). Trains run every half-hour; buses also make the journey.

Mundaka
POP 1900

Universally regarded as the home of the best wave in Europe, Mundaka is a name of legend for surfers across the world. The wave breaks on a perfectly tapering sandbar formed by the outflow of the Río Urdaibai and, on a good day, offers heavy, barrelling lefts that can reel off for hundreds of metres. Fantastic for experienced surfers, Mundaka is not a place for novices to take to the waves.

Despite all the focus being on the waves, Mundaka remains a resolutely Basque port with a pretty main square and harbour area.

🛏 Sleeping & Eating

Hotel Atalaya
HOTEL €€

(☑ 946 17 70 00; www.atalayahotel.es; Kalea Itxaropena 1; s/d €98/122; 🅿 🛜) This grand hotel is in a lovely old building near the waterfront and has clean and reliable rooms, many with terraces facing the sea. Unfortunately, like everywhere in Mundaka, it's a bit overpriced.

El Puerto
CAFE €

(www.hotelelpuerto.com; Portu 1; snacks €3-6; ☺ 11am-late) The shady terrace at Hotel El Puerto, a stately blue and white building facing the harbour, is a good place to stop for a coffee, a glass of wine, or a cheap bite to eat.

❶ Information

Tourist Office (☑ 946 17 72 01; www.mundaka.org; Kepa Deuna; ☺ 10.30am-1.30pm & 4-7pm Tue-Sat, 11am-2pm Sun) A small tourist office.

❶ Getting There & Away

Buses and ET/FV trains between Bilbao and Bermeo (€3.10, one hour) stop here. You can also catch a Bizkaibus bus from Bilbao (€2.50, one hour).

Central Basque Coast

The coast road from Bilbao to San Sebastián is a glorious journey past spectacular seascapes, with cove after cove stretching and verdant fields suddenly ending where cliffs plunge into the sea.

Getaria
POP 2,725

The attractive medieval fishing settlement of Getaria is a world away from nearby cosmopolitan San Sebastián and is a much better place to get a feel for coastal Basque culture. The old village tilts gently downhill to a baby-sized harbour, at the end of which is a forested island known as El Ratón (the Mouse), on account of its similarity to a mouse (this similarity is easiest to see after several strong drinks!).

It might have been this giant mouse that first encouraged the town's most famous son, the sailor Juan Sebastián Elcano, to take to the ocean waves. His adventures eventually culminated in him becoming the first man to sail around the world, after the captain of his ship, Magellan, died halfway through the endeavour.

Getaria has a short but very pleasant beach next to the town's busy harbour, which is almost totally sheltered from all but the heaviest Atlantic swells. Its safe bathing makes it an ideal family beach. If you're more a culture vulture than a bronzed god or goddess, get your kicks at the new **Cristóbal Balenciaga Museoa** (www.cristobalbalenciagamuseoa.com; adult/child/under 9yr €10/7/free; ☺ 10am-7pm Jul & Aug, shorter hr Sep-Jun). Local boy Cristóbal became one of the big names in fashion design in the 1950s and '60s and this impressive museum showcases some of his best works.

Just 2km further east, along a coastal road that battles with cliffs, ocean waves

WORTH A TRIP

PUENTE COLGANTE

A worthwhile stop en route to the beaches is the Unesco World Heritage–listed Puente Colgante (Vizcaya Bridge; www.puente-colgante.com; per person €0.40, walkway €9, guided tour €45; ☺5am-10pm, walkway 10am-7pm Nov-Mar, to 8pm Mon-Thu, to 9pm Fri Apr-Oct; Ⓜ Areeta, Portugalete), designed by Alberto Palacio, a disciple of Gustave Eiffel (he of Parisian tower fame). Opening in 1893, it was the world's first transporter bridge and links the suburbs of Getxo and Portugalete. A platform, suspended from the actual bridge high above, is loaded with up to six cars plus foot passengers; it then glides silently over Río Nervión to the other bank. The nearest metro stop from Bilbao is Areeta or Portugalete.

and several cavelike tunnels, is Zarautz, which consists of a 2.5km-long soft sand beach backed by a largely modern strip of tower blocks. The beach, which is one of the longest in the Basque Country, has some of the most consistent surfing conditions in the area, and a number of surf schools will help you 'hang ten'.

◉ Sights

★ Iglesia de San Salvador   CHURCH
(☑943 14 07 51; Calle Nagusia 39; ☺9:30am-7pm) With its unusual shape, sloping wooden floors, and nautical atmosphere, Getaria's striking 15th-century Gothic church is well worth a stop. Features worth noting include the gravestone of the great navigator Juan Sebastián Elcano , who was baptized here, and an underground passage (Katrapona, not open to the public) that leads to Getaria's harbor.

🍴 Sleeping & Eating

Hotel Itxas-Gain   HOTEL €€
(☑943 14 10 35; www.hotelitxasgain.com; St San Roque 1, Getaria; s €50, d €70-125; 🕿) A short walk from two beaches, the Hotel Itxas-Gain is a great deal with a mixture of room types: some have little balconies and whirlpool baths that overlook the whirlpool-like ocean. Weather permitting, breakfast is served in the peaceful gardens.

Elkano   BASQUE €€€
(☑943 14 00 24; www.restauranteelkano.com; Calle Herrerieta 2; tasting menu €75; ☺1-3.30pm & 8-10.30pm Wed-Mon) In Getaria, a seaside village about 20km from San Sebastián, Elkano is a superb seafood restaurant that has been thrilling diners for years. Its speciality is seasonal fish prepared with disarming simplicity, such as its show-stopping chargrilled *robaballo* (turbot).

❶ Getting There & Away

Buses run regularly to Getaria (€2.35, one hour) from San Sebastián's bus station – you can also board these buses on Av Libertad in San Sebastián, closer to the beach. In Getaria, the buses stop on the main road, outside the tourist office, on the edge of the historic quarter and within easy walking distance of the port (downhill) and the Balenciaga museum (uphill).

Lekeitio
POP 7305

Bustling Lekeitio is gorgeous. The attractive old core is centred on the unnaturally large and slightly out-of-place late-Gothic Iglesia de Santa María de la Asunción and a busy harbour lined by multicoloured, half-timbered old buildings – some of which house fine seafood restaurants and *pintxo* bars. But for most visitors, it's the two beaches that are the main draw. The one just east of the river, with a small rocky mound of an island offshore, is one of the finest beaches in the Basque Country. In many ways the town is like a miniature version of San Sebastián, but for the moment at least, Lekeitio remains a fairly low-key and predominately Spanish and French holiday town.

🍴 Sleeping & Eating

★ Hotel Zubieta   BOUTIQUE HOTEL €€
(☑946 84 30 30; www.hotelzubieta.com; Atea; d from €95; 🅿🕿) A gorgeous and romantic boutique hotel, five minutes' walk from the centre of town, which is filled with memories of upper-class 18th-century life. It sits within beautiful flower gardens and is surrounded by spring-blossoming cherry trees.

Hotel Palacio Oxangoiti   BOUTIQUE HOTEL €€
(☑944 65 05 55; www.oxangoiti.net; Gamarra 2; d from €99; 🕿) This lovely 16th-century 'palace' is now a seven-room boutique hotel.

It's filled with the smells of ancient polished wood and elegantly combines old and new to produce a very memorable place to stay. The hotel is right in the centre of town and next to the church, so be prepared for some bell clanging after 8am.

Taberna Bar Lumentza
PINTXOS €

(www.lumentza.com; Buenaventura Zapirain 3; pintxos €2-5; ⊙ noon-late Tue-Sun) A big hit with the locals, this no-fuss *pintxos* bar is tucked away in the side streets. Try the octopus cooked on the *plancha* (grill) washed down with a glass of wine or two.

❶ Information

Tourist Office (☑ 946 84 40 17; Plaza Independencia; ⊙ 10am-2pm & 4-8pm)

❶ Getting There & Away

Bizkaibus buses (€3.50) leave from Calle Hurtado de Amézaga, by Bilbao's Abando train station, about eight times a day (except Sunday) and goes via Guernica and Elantxobe. Buses also run four times daily from Lekeitio to San Sebastián (€6.65). Drivers take note: finding a parking space can be borderline impossible in the summer.

San Sebastián

POP 186,130

It's impossible to lay eyes on stunning San Sebastián (Basque: Donostia) and not fall madly in love. This city is cool and happening by night, charming and well mannered by day. It's a city filled with people that love to indulge – and with Michelin stars apparently falling from the heavens onto its restaurants, not to mention *pintxo* (tapas) culture almost unmatched anywhere else in Spain, San Sebastián frequently tops lists of the world's best places to eat.

Just as good as the food is the summertime fun in the sun. For its setting, form and attitude, Playa de la Concha is the equal of any city beach in Europe. Then there's Playa de Gros (also known as Playa de la Zurriola), with its surfers and sultry beach-goers. As the sun falls on another sweltering summer's day, you'll sit back with a drink and an artistic *pintxo* and realise that, yes, you too are in love with San Sebastián.

San Sebastián has four main centres of action. The lively Parte Vieja (old town) lies across the neck of Monte Urgull, the bay's eastern headland, and is where the most popular *pintxo* bars and many of the cheap lodgings are to be found. South of the Parte Vieja is the commercial and shopping district, the Área Romántica, its handsome grid of late-19th-century buildings extending from behind Playa de la Concha to the banks of Río Urumea. On the east side of the river is the district of Gros, a pleasant enclave that, with its relaxed ambience and the surfing beach of Playa de Gros, makes a cheerful alternative to the honeypots on the west side of the river. Right at the opposite, western end, of the city is Playa de Ondarreta (essentially a continuation of Playa de la Concha), a very upmarket district known as a millionaires' belt on account of its lavish holiday homes.

◉ Sights

★ Playa de la Concha
BEACH

Fulfilling almost every idea of how a perfect city beach should be formed, Playa de la Concha (and its westerly extension, Playa de Ondarreta), is easily among the best city beaches in Europe. Throughout the long summer months a fiesta atmosphere prevails, with thousands of tanned and toned bodies spread across the sands. The swimming is almost always safe.

★ Aquarium
AQUARIUM

(www.aquariumss.com; Plaza Carlos Blasco de Imaz 1; adult/child €13/6.50; ⊙ 10am-9pm Jul & Aug, 10am-8pm Mon-Fri, 10am-9pm Sat & Sun Easter-Jun & Sep, shorter hours rest of year) Fear for your life as huge sharks bear down behind glass panes, or gaze in disbelief at tripped-out fluoro jellyfish. The highlights of a visit to the city's excellent aquarium are the cinema-screen-sized deep-ocean and coral-reef exhibits and the long tunnel, around which swim monsters of the deep. The aquarium also contains a maritime museum section. Allow at least 1½ hours for a visit.

★ Parque de Cristina Enea
PARK

(Paseo Duque de Manda) Created by the Duke of Mandas in honour of his wife, the Parque de Cristina Enea is a favourite escape for locals. This formal park, the most attractive in the city, contains ornamental plants, ducks and peacocks, and open lawns.

Isla de Santa Clara
ISLAND

About 700m from Playa de la Concha, this island is accessible by **boats** (www.motoras delaisla.com; Lasta Plaza; normal boat €4,

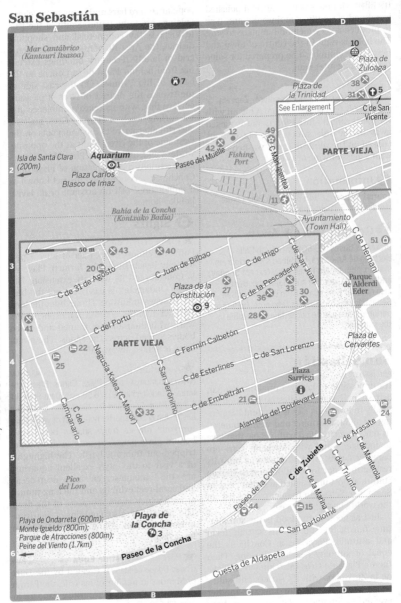

Map of San Sebastián (Parte Vieja)

- Mar Cantábrico (Kantauri Itsasoa)
- 7
- 10
- Plaza de Zuloaga
- Plaza de la Trinidad
- 38
- 31
- 5
- See Enlargement
- C de San Vicente
- PARTE VIEJA
- 49
- 12
- 42
- Paseo del Muelle
- Fishing Port
- C Mari Jaenttea
- Aquarium 1
- Plaza Carlos Blasco de Imaz
- Isla de Santa Clara (200m)
- 11
- Bahía de la Concha (Kontxako Badía)
- Ayuntamiento (Town Hall)
- C de Hernani
- 51
- 43
- 40
- C de Iñigo
- C de San Juan
- Parque de Alderdi Eder
- 0 50 m
- 20
- C de 31 de Agosto
- C Juan de Bilbao
- Plaza de la Constitución
- 27
- C de la Pescadería
- 33
- 36
- 30
- 9
- 28
- C del Portu
- PARTE VIEJA
- Plaza de Cervantes
- 41
- 22
- 25
- Nagusia Kalea (C Mayor)
- C Fermín Calbetón
- C de San Lorenzo
- C San Jerónimo
- C de Esterlines
- Plaza Sarriegi
- C del Campanario
- C de Embeltrán
- 21
- 16
- 24
- 32
- Alameda del Boulevard
- C de Zubieta
- C de Arasate
- C de Manterola
- C del Triunfo
- C de la Marina
- Pico del Loro
- 44
- 15
- Playa de la Concha
- 3
- Paseo de la Concha
- Playa de Ondarreta (600m); Monte Igueldo (800m); Parque de Atracciones (800m); Peine del Viento (1.7km)
- Paseo de la Concha
- Cuesta de Aldapeta
- C San Bartolomé

glass-bottom boat €6; ⏱10am-8pm Jun-Sep) that run every half-hour from the fishing port. At low tide the island gains its own tiny beach and you can climb its forested paths to a small lighthouse. There are also picnic tables and a simple cafe.

Playa de Gros   BEACH
(Playa de la Zurriola) Less popular than nearby Playa de la Concha, but just as showy, Playa de Gros is the city's main surf beach. Though swimming here is more dangerous,

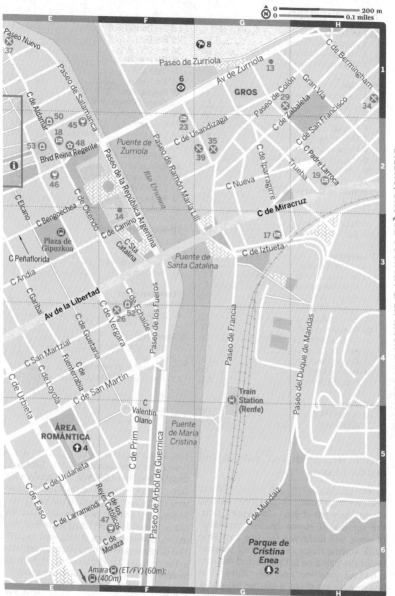

it has more of a local vibe. It's located east of Río Urumea.

Playa de Ondarreta
BEACH

Playa de Ondarreta, the western extension of the renowned Playa de la Concha, has a less glam, more genteel atmosphere. It's long been popular with the city's most wealthy visitors and residents (look for the former royal summer palace of Miramar that overlooks the beach). Blue and white

San Sebastián

striped canvas beach 'huts' and volleyball nets dot the sands.

Monte Igueldo   VIEWPOINT
(www.monteigueldo.es; ⊙10am-10pm Jun-Sep, shorter hours rest of year) The views from the summit of Monte Igueldo, just west of town, will make you feel like a circling hawk staring down over the vast panorama of the Bahía de la Concha and the surrounding coastline and mountains. The best way to get there is via the old-world funicular railway (www.monteigueldo.es; Plaza del Funicular; return adult/child €3.15/2.35; ⊙10am-9pm Jun-Aug, shorter hours rest of yr) to the Parque de Atracciones (www.monteigueldo.es; admission €2.20; ⊙11.15am-2pm & 4-8pm Mon-Fri, to 8.30pm Sat & Sun Jul-Sep, shorter hours rest of year), a slightly tacky theme park at the top of the hill.

San Telmo Museoa   MUSEUM
(www.santelmomuseoa.com; Plaza Zuloaga 1; adult/student/child €6/3/free; ⊙10am-8pm Tue-Sun) Although it's one of the newest museums in the Basque Country, the San Telmo Museoa has actually been around since the 1920s. It was closed for many years, but after major renovation work it reopened in 2011. The displays range from historical artifacts to the squiggly lines of modern art, with all pieces reflecting Basque culture and society.

Monte Urgull   CASTLE, PARK
You can walk to the summit of Monte Urgull, topped by the low castle walls of the Castillo de la Mota and a grand statue of Christ, by taking a path from Plaza de Zuloaga or from behind the aquarium. The views are breathtaking and the shady parkland on the way up is a peaceful retreat from the city.

Iglesia de San Vicente
CHURCH

(Calle de San Vicente 3; ⊙9am-1pm & 5-8pm Mon-Fri) Lording it over the Parte Vieja, this striking church is thought to be the oldest building in San Sebastián. Its origins date to the 12th century, but it was rebuilt in its current Gothic form in the early 1500s. The towering facade gives onto an echoing vaulted interior, featuring an elaborate gold altarpiece and a 19th-century French organ. Also impressive are the stained glass rose windows.

Peine del Viento
SCULPTURE

A symbol of the city, the *Peine del Viento* (Wind Comb) sculpture, which sits at the far western end of the Bahía de la Concha, below Monte Igueldo, is the work of the famous Basque sculptor Eduardo Chillida and architect Luis Peña Ganchegui.

Plaza de la Constitución
PLAZA

(Plaza de la Constitución) One of the most attractive city squares in the Basque country, the Plaza de la Constitución sits at the heart of the old town. The square dates from 1813 but sits on the site of an older square. It was once used as a bullring; the balconies of the fringing houses were rented to spectators.

Catedral del Buen Pastor de San Sebastián
CATHEDRAL

(Urdaneta 12) The dominant building of the new town is the city cathedral, proudly overlooking a busy plaza. The cathedral was consecrated in 1897 and has a 75m-high bell tower. Under the foundation stone of the cathedral is a lead box containing pictures of the Spanish royal family and the pope at the time of construction.

Kursaal
BUILDING

(☑943 00 30 00; www.kursaal.eus; Zurriola Hiribidea 1) Designed by Rafael Moneo, the Kursaal is one of the city's most beloved, and noteworthy buildings. Consisting of two cubes made of translucent glass, the structure, which serves as San Sebastián's cultural and conference centre, was designed to represent two beached rocks. A lively array of musical and cultural events are held here year-round.

Courses & Tours

San Sebastián Food
TOUR, COOKING COURSE

(☑943 42 11 43; www.sansebastianfood.com; Hotel Maria Cristina, Paseo de la República Argentina 4) The highly recommended San Sebastián Food runs an array of *pintxo* tasting tours (from €95) and cookery courses (from €145) in and around the city, as well as wine tastings (from €45). The shop/booking office also sells an array of high-quality local food and drink products.

Sabores de San Sebastián
TOUR

(Flavours of San Sebastián; ☑902 44 34 42; www.sansebastianreservas.com; tour €18; ⊙11.30am Tue & Thu Jul & Aug) The tourist office runs the Sabores de San Sebastián, a two-hour tour (in Spanish and English, French tours are available on request) of some of the city's *pintxo* haunts. Tours are also held with less frequency outside high season – contact the tourist office for dates.

Catamarán Ciudad San Sebastián
BOAT TOUR

(www.ciudadsansebastian.com; Paseo del Muelle 14; adult/child €9/5; ⊙noon-8pm Jul-Aug, shorter hours Sep-Jun) Boat tours of the bay and out onto the open ocean on a motorised catamaran run hourly (except at 3pm) in the summer.

Pukas
SURFING

(☑943 32 00 68; www.pukassurf.com; Paseo de Zurriola 24) Playa de Gros, with its generally mellow and easy waves, is a good place for learners to come to grips with surfing. Aspiring surfers should drop by Pukas, where lessons and board and wetsuit hire are available. Prices vary depending on group size and lesson length, but start at €64 for a weekend course comprising a 1½-hour lesson each day.

Festivals & Events

Carnaval
CARNIVAL

Carnaval (February or March – dates change) is a big event in San Sebastián, but nearby Tolosa goes even more berserk.

Heineken Jazzaldia
JAZZ

(www.heinekenjazzaldia.com) Big-name acts converge for the San Sebastián jazz festival in July.

Semana Grande
SUMMER FESTIVAL

Semana Grande is the big summer festival in mid-August.

Film Festival
FILM

(www.sansebastianfestival.com) The world-renowned, two-week film festival has been an annual fixture in the second half of September since 1957.

🛏 Sleeping

Accommodation standards in San Sebastián are generally good, but prices are high and availability in high season is very tight. In fact, with the city's increasing popularity, many of the better places are booked up for July and August months in advance. If you do turn up without a booking, head to the tourist office, which keeps a list of available rooms.

Pensión Altair
PENSIÓN €€

(☑ 943 29 31 33; www.pension-altair.com; Calle Padre Larroca 3; s/d €62/88; ❄ @ 🛜) This *pensión* is in a beautifully restored town house, with unusual church-worthy arched windows and modern, minimalist rooms that are a world away from the fusty decor of the old-town *pensione*s. Interior rooms lack the grandiose windows but are much larger.

Reception is closed between 1.30pm and 5pm.

Pensión Amaiur
BOUTIQUE HOTEL €€

(☑ 943 42 96 54; www.pensionamaiur.com; Calle de 31 de Agosto 44; d with/without bathroom €60/75; @ 🛜) A top-notch guesthouse in a prime old-town location, Amaiur has bright floral wallpapers and bathrooms tiled in Andalucían blue and white. The best rooms are those that overlook the main street, where you can sit on a little balcony and be completely enveloped in blushing red flowers. Some rooms share bathrooms.

Pensión Régil
PENSIÓN €€

(☑ 943 42 71 43; www.pensionregil.com; Calle de Easo 9; s/d €70/82; 🛜) You'll hardly find a better deal in San Sebastián in high season. Guest rooms aren't anything special, but they're tidy, and they all have private bathrooms – and the location is close to Playa de la Concha.

Pensión Aldamar
HOTEL €€

(☑ 943 43 01 43; www.pensionaldamar.com; Aldamar 2; d from €80; ❄ 🛜) This smart *pensión* offers superb modern rooms with white decor and stone walls, some of which have little balconies from which to watch the theatre of street life below. It's a big step up in quality from many of the other old-town *pensione*s.

Pensión Artea Narrica
PENSIÓN €€

(☑ 943 45 51 00; www.pensionarteanarrika.com; Calle de Narrica 3; d from €75; ❄ 🛜) Recent-ly renovated, this place doesn't look like much from the outside, but actually offers some of the nicer, and better value, beds in the old town. Rooms have something of a farmhouse look with exposed wooden roof beams and stone walls, but the furnishings are modern.

Pensión Kursaal
BOUTIQUE HOTEL €€

(☑ 943 29 26 66; www.pensionkursaal.com; Peña y Goñi 2; d from €70; ❄ @ 🛜) With a rattling 1930s-style lift and massive, wall-sized photos, this excellent *pensión*, full of light and colour, is a mix of old and new. Guest rooms have a refined look; some have interesting views.

Pensión Aida
PENSIÓN €€

(☑ 943 32 78 00; www.pensionesconencanto.com; Calle de Iztueta 9; s/d €75/92; ❄ @ 🛜) The owners of this excellent *pensión* read the rule book on what makes a good hotel and have complied exactly. The rooms are bright and bold, full of exposed stone, and the communal area, with soft sofas and plenty of information, is a big plus.

Hostal Alemana
BOUTIQUE HOTEL €€

(☑ 943 46 25 44; www.hostalalemana.com; Calle de San Martín 53; s/d from €66/77; 🅿 🛜) With a great location just a few sandy footsteps from the beach, this smart hotel has opted for the white, minimalist look, countered with stylish black-and-white photos, all of which works very well and makes the rooms feel light and airy. The charming Belle Époque exterior only adds to the appeal.

Pensión Edorta
BOUTIQUE HOTEL €€

(☑ 943 42 37 73; www.pensionedorta.com; Calle del Puerto 15; r €90-100, r without bathroom €65-70; 🛜) A fine *pensión* with rooms that are all tarted up in brash modern colours, but with a salute to the past in the stone walls and ceilings. It's very well cared for and well situated.

Cheaper rooms share bathrooms.

Hotel de Londres y de Inglaterra
HISTORIC HOTEL €€€

(☑ 943 44 07 70; www.hlondres.com; Calle de Zubieta 2; d from €238; 🅿 ❄ 🛜) Sitting pretty on the beachfront, Hotel de Londres y de Inglaterra (Hotel of London and England) is as proper as it sounds. Queen Isabel II set the tone for this hotel well over a century ago, and things have stayed pretty regal ever since. The place exudes elegance; some rooms have stunning views over Playa de la Concha.

Hotel Maria Cristina — HISTORIC HOTEL €€€

(☎ 943 43 76 00; www.starwoodhotels.com; Paseo de la República Argentina 4; d from €500; P ❄ @ 🛜) Audrey Hepburn stayed here – as did Coco Chanel, Alfred Hitchcock, and Mick Jagger, to name a few. The palatial Maria Cristina, now a member of the Starwood Collection, dominates the riverfront skyline at sunset. Glamorous and impeccably maintained, with huge and luxurious rooms, it's still a favourite with royalty and Hollywood stars.

Pensión Ur-Alde — PENSIÓN €€€

(☎ 943 42 25 81; www.ur-alde.com; Calle del Puerto 17; d €200; ❄ 🛜) This excellent *pensión* has interestingly decorated rooms: each was inspired by a different world city, from Amsterdam to Rio de Janeiro. The location is excellent and the owners are extremely helpful in helping travellers plan excursions in the region.

 Eating

With 16 Michelin stars (including three restaurants with the coveted three stars), San Sebastián stands atop a pedestal as one of the culinary capitals of the planet. As if that alone weren't enough, the city is overflowing with bars – almost all of which have bar tops weighed down under a mountain of *pintxos* that almost every Spaniard will (sometimes grudgingly) tell you are the best in country. These statistics alone make San Sebastián's CV look pretty impressive. But it's not just us who thinks this: a raft of the world's best chefs, including such luminaries as Catalan super-chef Ferran Adrià, have said that San Sebastián is quite possibly the best place on the entire planet to eat.

Ramuntxo Berri — BASQUE €

(Calle Peña y Goñi 10; mains €10-14, menú del día €11.50; ⊙ 9am-4.30pm & 7pm-midnight Mon-Sat, 9am-5pm Sun) Anyone else smell a bargain? The well-prepared dishes served here, which are largely traditional Basque, would cost double the price if this restaurant were located in the old town. It's so popular with locals at lunchtime you might have to queue for a table.

It also has a good array of *pintxos*; don't miss the *foie con manzana* (liver with apple).

Holly Burger — BURGERS €

(Calle de la Pescadería 6; burgers €5-7.50; ⊙ 1-4pm & 7.30-11.30pm; 🖶) Homemade gourmet burgers with names like Heaven Can Wait (though if you eat too many burgers, it probably won't) and Passion Red. There's also a good strong helping of vegie burgers and even gluten-free ones.

Antonio Bar — PINTXOS €

(www.antoniobar.com; Calle de Vergara 3; pintxos from €2.50) One of the best *pintxos* bars in the new city, Bar Antonio packs them in for house specials like prawn ravioli; the peppers are also worth fawning over. It's small place that from the outside looks more like the sort of cafe you'd get in a train station waiting room.

★ La Fábrica — MODERN BASQUE €€

(☎ 943 98 05 81; www.restaurantelafabrica.es; Calle del Puerto 17; mains €15-20, menús from €25; ⊙ 12.30-4pm & 7.30-11.30pm Mon-Fri, 1-4pm & 8-11pm Sat-Sun) The red-brick interior walls and white tablecloths lend an air of class to this restaurant, whose modern takes on Basque classics have been

LOCAL KNOWLEDGE

TXOKO

Peek through the keyholes of enough Basque doors and eventually you'll come across an unusual sight: a large room full of men, and only men, seated around a table bending under the weight of food and drink. This is *Txoko* (Basque Gastronomic Society) and it is an almost exclusively male preserve. The men who come here (who often wouldn't be seen dead in the kitchen at home) are normally highly accomplished amateur chefs who take turns cooking their own speciality for the critical consumption of the other members. It's often said that the best Basque food is to be found at the *Txoko*. Recently a few women have started to enter the *Txoko*, but only as guests and even then they are never allowed into the kitchen when the cooking is in process in case they distract the men. Women are, however, let into the kitchen afterwards – to do the washing up!

making waves with San Sebastián locals over the last couple of years. At just €25, the multi-dish tasting *menú* is about the best-value deal in the city. Advance reservations are essential.

Restaurante Alberto SEAFOOD €€

(☑ 943 42 88 84; Calle de 31 de Agosto 19; mains €12-15, menús €15; ☺ noon-4pm & 7pm-midnight Thu-Tue) A charming old seafood restaurant with a fishmonger-style window display of the day's catch. It's small and friendly, and the pocket-sized dining room feels like it was once someone's living room. The food is earthy (well, salty) and good, and the service swift.

Txuleta PINTXOS €€

(☑ 943 44 10 07; www.txuletarestaurante.com; Plaza de la Trinidad 2; pintxos €3, mains €11-24; ☺ noon-4pm & 7-11.30pm, closed Mon evening & Tue) Those in the know come to Txuleta for the meat. A *txuleta* is a cut of beef and this is the place to sample some wonderful melt-in-your mouth examples – try the *pintxo txuleta* (€3), a mini-kebab of three bite-sized chunks of tender beef. There's also a restaurant serving a full menu of steaks and seafood.

Kaskazuri SEAFOOD €€

(☑ 943 42 08 94; http://kaskazuri.com; Paseo de Salamanca 14; menús from €19; ☺ 1-3.30pm & 8.30-11pm) Upmarket Basque seafood is all the rage in this flash restaurant, which is built on a raised platform allowing views of the former home of your dinner. It cooks up a storm with the €19 *menú del día* (daily set menu).

Restaurante Mariñela SEAFOOD €€

(☑ 943 42 13 88; www.marinela-igeldo.com; Paseo del Muelle; mains €10-18; ☺ 1-4pm & 9pm-midnight Tue-Sat, 1-4pm Sun) You pay for the fabulous harbourfront setting, but the location guarantees that the fish is so fresh it may flop back off your plate and swim away. There are several similar neighbouring places.

Bar Nestor BASQUE €€

(☑ 943 42 48 73; http://barnestor.com; Calle de la Pescadería 11; steak from €14; ☺ noon-4pm & 7pm-midnight) It would be very easy to overlook this dated-looking bar, but for those in the know this place has exceptional steaks, best when enjoyed alongside grilled green peppers. It's very popular and there's very

little space, so get there when it opens to ensure you get a table.

Arzak CONTEMPORARY BASQUE €€€

(☑ 943 27 84 65; www.arzak.info; Avenida Alcalde Jose Elosegui 273; meals around €195; ☺ Tue-Sat, closed Nov & late Jun) With three shining Michelin stars, acclaimed chef Juan Mari Arzak is king when it comes to *nueva cocina vasca* and his restaurant is considered one of the best in the world. Arzak is now assisted by his daughter Elena, and they never cease to innovate. Reservations, well in advance, are obligatory.

The restaurant is located just east of San Sebastián.

Martín Berasategui Restaurant BASQUE €€€

(☑ 943 36 64 71; www.martinberasategui.com; Calle Loidi 4, Lasarte-Oria; tasting menu €195; ☺ Wed-Sun lunch) This superlative restaurant, about 9km southwest of San Sebastián, is considered by foodies to be one of the best restaurants in the world. The chef, Martín Berasategui, approaches cuisine as a science and the results are tastes you never knew existed. Reserve well ahead.

Akelañe BASQUE €€€

(☑ 943 31 12 09; www.akelarre.net; Paseo Padre Orcolaga 56; tasting menu €170; ☺ 1-3.30pm & 8.30-11pm Tue-Sat Jul-Dec, Wed-Sat Jan-Jun) This is where chef Pedro Subijana creates cuisine that is a feast for all five senses. As with most of the region's top *nueva cocina vasca* restaurants, the emphasis here is on using fresh, local produce and turning it into something totally unexpected. It's in the suburb of Igeldo just west of the city.

🍷 Drinking & Nightlife

It would be hard to imagine a town with more bars than San Sebastián. Most of the city's bars mutate through the day from calm morning-coffee hangouts to *pintxo*-laden delights, before finally finishing up as noisy bars full of writhing, sweaty bodies. Nights in San Sebastián start late and go on until well into the wee hours.

Pub Drop PUB

(Reyes Católicos 18; ☺ 3pm-midnight Mon-Wed, 11am-midnight Thu & Sun, to 4am Fri & Sat) One of a number of haunts on a popular drinking strip near the cathedral, this shabby-chic bar is the place to get to grips with the local beer. There are up to 50 craft ales on offer, including several strong,

BEST PINTXO BARS IN SAN SEBASTIÁN

The following *pintxo* bars all charge between €2.50 to €3.50 for one *pintxo*. Not so bad if you just take one, but is one ever enough?

La Cuchara de San Telmo (www.lacucharadesantelmo.com; Calle de 31 de Agosto 28; pintxos from €2.50; ⏱7.30-11pm Tue, noon-3.30pm & 7.30-11pm Wed-Sun) This unfussy, hidden-away (and hard to find) bar offers miniature *nueva cocina vasca* (Basque nouvelle cuisine) from a supremely creative kitchen. Unlike many San Sebastián bars this one doesn't have any *pintxos* laid out on the bar top; instead you must order from the blackboard menu behind the counter. Don't miss delights such as *carrílera de ternera al vino tinto* (calf cheeks in red wine), with meat so tender it starts to dissolve almost before it's past your lips.

Bar Borda Berri (Calle Fermín Calbetón 12; pintxos from €2.50; ⏱noon-midnight) You won't find any *pintxos* sprawled across the counter of this outstanding little bar. Instead you must order them freshly made from the blackboard menu behind the bar. The bar staff are happy to offer advice on the day's best choice, but otherwise the house specials are pigs' ears and delicious calf cheeks.

Bergara Bar (www.pinchosbergara.es; General Artetxe 8; pintxos from €2.50; ⏱9am-11pm) The Bergara Bar, which sits on the edge of a busy square, is one of the most highly re-garded *pintxo* bars in Gros, a growing powerhouse in the *pintxo*-bar stakes, and has a mouth-watering array of delights piled onto the bar counter as well as others chalked up on the board.

Astelena (Calle de Iñigo 1; pintxos from €2.50; ⏱1-4.30pm & 8-11pm Tue & Thu-Sat, 1-4.30pm Wed) The *pintxos* draped across the counter in this bar, tucked into the corner of Plaza de la Constitución, stand out. Many of them are a fusion of Basque and Asian inspirations, but the best of all are perhaps the foie-gras-based treats. The great positioning means that prices are slightly elevated.

Bar Goiz-Argi (Calle de Fermín Calbetón 4; pintxos from €2.50; ⏱9.30am-3.30pm & 6.30-11.30pm Wed-Sun, 9.30-3.30pm Mon) *Gambas a la plancha* (prawns cooked on a hotplate) are the house speciality. Sounds simple, we know, but never have we tasted prawns cooked quite as perfectly as this.

La Mejíllonera (Calle del Puerto 15; pintxos from €2.50; ⏱11.30am-3pm & 6-11pm) If you thought mussels only came with garlic sauce, come here to discover mussels (from €3.50) by the thousand in all their glorious forms. Mussels not for you? Opt for the calamari and *patatas bravas* (fried potatoes with a spicy tomato and mayo sauce). We promise you won't regret it.

Bar Nagusía (Nagusía Kalea 4; pintxos from €2.50) This bar, reminiscent of old San Se-bastián, has a counter that groans under the weight of its *pintxos*. You'll be groaning after a few as well – in sheer pleasure.

Bodega Donostiarra (www.bodegadonostiarra.com; Calle de Peña y Goñi 13; pintxos from €2.50, mains €9; ⏱9.30am-midnight Mon-Sat) The stone walls, pot plants and window orna-ments give this place a real old-fashioned French bistro look, but at the same time it feels very up to date and modern. Although initial impressions make you think the food will be very high class, it's actually best regarded for humble *jamón* (cured ham), chorizo and tortilla. It also has a long wine list (and an attached wine shop).

Bar Martinez (Calle 31 de Agosto 13; pintxos from €2.50; ⏱9.30am-11pm Tue-Sun, Fri & Sat open late) This small bar, with dusty bottles of wine stacked up, has won awards for its *morros de bacalao* (delicate slices of cod balanced atop a piece of bread) and is one of the more character-laden places to dip into some *pintxos*.

Bar Diz (Calle Zabaleta 17; pintxos from €2.50; ⏱8am-late) In beach-blessed Gros, tiny Bar Diz has massively good *pintxos* (and the breakfast isn't bad either), and other foreign tourists are rare, so it's a totally local affair. If you're hungry opt for a *ración* (large plate).

hoppy brews from the aptly-named Basque Brewing project.

Museo del Whisky
BAR

(www.museodelwhisky.com; Alameda Boulevard 5; ⊙3.30pm-3.30am) Appropriately named, this piano bar is full of bottles of Scotland's finest (3400 bottles to be exact) as well as a museum's worth of whisky-related knick-knacks – old bottles, tacky mugs and glasses, and a nice, dusty atmosphere.

Be Bop
BAR, CLUB

(www.barbebop.com; Paseo de Salamanca 3; ⊙8pm-3am) This long-standing and snazzy jazz bar has occasional live performances. It attracts a slightly older crowd than some of the old-town bars and on weekends it jams till dawn.

Bataplan Disco
CLUB

(☑943 47 36 01; www.bataplandisco.com; Paseo de la Concha; ⊙club midnight-7am Thu-Sat, terrace 2pm-2.30am Jun-Sep) San Sebastián's top club, a classic disco housed in a grand seafront complex, sets the stage for memorable beach-side partying. The club action kicks in late, but in summer you can warm up with a drink or two on the street-level terrace. Note that door selection can be arbitrary and groups of men might have trouble getting in.

☆ Entertainment

Altxerri Jazz Bar
LIVE MUSIC

(www.altxerri.eu; Blvd Reina Regente 2; ⊙4pm-3am) This jazz and blues temple has regular live gigs by local and international stars. Jamming sessions take over on the nights with no gig; there's also an in-house art gallery.

Etxekalte
JAZZ

(www.etxekalte.com; Calle Mari Igentea; ⊙6pm-4am Tue-Thu & Sun, 6pm-5am Fri & Sat) A late-night haunt near the harbour, which moves to dance music and grooves to jazz. There's a guest DJ most weeks.

🛍 Shopping

The Parte Vieja is awash with small independent boutiques, while the Área Romántica has all your brand-name and chain-store favourites.

Benegas
BEAUTY

(Calle de Garibay 12; ⊙10am-1.15pm & 4-8pm Mon-Sat) A historic perfume shop stocking leading international brands and in-house creations such as the herby, fruit-scented Benegas cologne. You'll also find make-up and gents' grooming products.

Aitor Lasa
FOOD

(www.aitorlasa.com; Calle de Aldamar 12) This high-quality deli is the place to stock up on the ingredients for a gourmet picnic you'll never forget. It specialises in cheeses, mushrooms and other seasonal products.

Chocolates de Mendaro
FOOD

(www.chocolatesdemendaro.com; Calle de Echaide 6; ⊙10am-2pm & 4-8pm) We dare you to walk past this fabulous old chocolate shop and resist the temptation to walk inside.

Mercado de la Bretxa
MARKET

(Alameda del Boulevard) On the east side of the Parte Vieja, Mercado de la Bretxa is where every chef in the old town comes to get the freshest produce. It's a good place to stock up on picnic supplies and the heaped stalls are a worthwhile sight in thier own right.

ⓘ Information

Oficina de Turismo (☑943 48 11 66; www.sansebastianturismo.com; Alameda del Boulevard 8; ⊙9am-8pm Mon-Sat, 10am-7pm Sun Jul-Sep, shorter hours rest of year) This friendly office offers comprehensive information on the city and the Basque Country in general.

ⓘ Getting There & Away

AIR

The city's **airport** (☑free call 902 404704; www.aena.es) is 22km out of town, near Hondarribia. There are regular flights to Madrid and Barcelona and occasional charters to other major European cities. Biarritz, just over the border in France, is served by Ryanair and EasyJet, among various other budget airlines, and is generally much cheaper to fly into.

BUS

The main bus stop is a 20-minute walk south of the Parte Vieja, between Plaza de Pío XII and the river. Local buses 28 and 26 connect the bus station with Alameda del Boulevard (€1.65, 10 minutes), but it's also a pleasant stroll into the historic center from here, especially if you walk along the river. There's no real station here, but all the bus companies have offices and ticket booths near the bus stop.

There are daily bus services to the following:

DESTINATION	FARE	DURATION
Biarritz (France)	from €6.75	1¼hr
Bilbao	from €3.30	1hr
Bilbao airport	€16.85	1¼hr
Madrid	from €36	5-6hr
Pamplona	from €7.80	1hr
Vitoria	from €6.20	1½hr

TRAIN

The main **Renfe train station** (Paseo de Francia) is just across Río Urumea, on a line linking Paris to Madrid. There are several services daily to Madrid (from €27, 5½ hours) and two to Barcelona (from €19.25, six hours).

For France you must first go to the Spanish/French border town of Irún (or sometimes trains go as far as Hendaye; Renfe from €2.25, 25 minutes), which is also served by Eusko Tren/Ferrocarril Vasco (www.euskotren.es), and change there. Trains depart every half-hour from Amara train station, about 1km south of the city centre, and also stop in Pasajes (from €1.50, 12 minutes) and Irún/Hendaye (ET/FV €1.70, 25 minutes). Another ET/FV railway line heads west to Bilbao via Zarautz, Zumaia and Durango, but it's painfully slow, so the bus is usually a better plan.

ℹ️ Getting Around

Buses to Hondarribia (€2.35, 45 minutes) and the airport (€2.35, 45 minutes) depart from Plaza de Gupúzcoa.

Around San Sebastián

Pasajes

POP 16,080

Pasajes (Basque: Pasaia), where Río Oiartzun meets the Atlantic, is the largest port in the province of Gupúzcoa. The main street and the area immediately around the central square are lined with pretty houses and colourful balconies, and are well worth a half-day's exploration. Highlights are the great seafood restaurants and the spectacular entrance to the port, through a keyhole-like split in the cliff face – even more impressive when a huge container ship passes through it.

From Pasajes you could, the following day, continue over the giant whaleback mountain of Jaizkibel (547m), which though not technically very high has views to make you feel you've just conquered a Himalayan peak! This walk takes a full day and is fairly hard going. The tourist office in San Sebastián can supply route details.

👁️ Sights

Casa Museo Victor Hugo   MUSEUM
(📞943 34 15 56; Calle Donibane 63, Pasajes; ⏰9am-2pm & 4-7pm Jul & Aug, 10am-2pm & 4-6pm rest of year) **FREE** French author Victor Hugo spent the summer of 1843 in Pasajes, lodging at this typical waterfront house and working on his travelogue *En Voyage, Alpes et Pyrénées*. The second floor retains a smattering of period furniture and various prints and first editions; the first floor is home to Pasajes' tourist office (p430).

Faro de la Plata   LIGHTHOUSE
(Pasajes) It's quite a climb above the town, but the views from around the lighthouse (closed to the public) are worth the effort. This is especially so when a large cargo ship slips through the cliff walls that form the entrance to the narrow but perfect port of Pasajes.

🏃 Activities

Coastal Path   HIKING
The nicest way of getting between San Sebastián and Pasaia is to walk along the coastal path that wends its way over the cliffs between the two towns. There are lovely sea views, unusual cliff formations and, halfway along, a hidden beach that tempts when its hot. Ask at San Sebastián tourist office (p426) for route information. It takes 2½ to 3 hours.

🍴 Eating

Restaurante Ziaboga Jatetxea   SEAFOOD €€
(📞943 51 03 95; www.ziabogapasaia.com; Calle Donibane 91, Pasajes; menús €20-50, mains €16-21; ⏰1-4pm Tue-Thu & Sun, 1-4pm & 8-11pm Fri & Sat) Pasajes is full of excellent seafood restaurants, but Ziaboga Jatetxea (there's a linguistic challenge for you) is one of the best. And with a weekday lunch *menú* of just €20, it's also very good value. The crab dishes are legendary.

Casa Cámara   SEAFOOD €€€
(📞943 52 36 99; www.casacamara.com; Calle San Juan 79, Pasajes; menús €37-78; ⏰1.30-4pm & 8.30-11pm Tue-Sun) Managed by the same family for generations, Casa Cámara is built half on stilts over the Bay of Pasajes. The bulk of the menu is seafood based and the cooking is assured and traditional. The lobsters live

Basque Culture

The Basques are different. They have inhabited their corner of Spain and France seemingly forever. While many aspects of their unique culture are hidden from curious eyes, the following are visible to any visitor.

Pelota

The national sport of the Basque country is *pelota vasca*, and every village in the region has its own court – normally backing up against the village church. Pelota can be played in several different ways: bare-handed, with small wooden rackets, or with a long hand-basket called *chistera*, with which the player can throw the ball at speeds of up to 300km/h. It's possible to see pelota matches throughout the region during summer.

Lauburu

The most visible symbol of Basque culture is *lauburu*, the Basque cross. The meaning of this symbol is lost in the mists of time – some say it represents the four old regions of the Basque Country, others that it represents spirit, life, consciousness and form – but today many regard it as a symbol of prosperity, hence its appearance in modern jewellery and above house doors. It is also used to signify life and death and is found on old headstones.

Traditional Basque Games

Basque sports aren't just limited to pelota: there are also log cutting, stone lifting, bale tossing and tug of war. Most stemmed from the day-to-day activities of the region's farmers and

1. Sanfermines festival
2. A pelota player with a
chistera 3. *Lauburu*, the
Basque cross

fishers. Although most of these skills are no longer used on a daily basis, the sports are kept alive at numerous fiestas.

Bulls & Fiestas

No other Basque festival is as famous as Sanfermines (p437), with its legendary *encierro* (running of the bulls) in Pamplona. The original purpose of the *encierro* was to transfer bulls from the corrals where they would have spent the night to the bullring where they would fight. Sometime in the 14th century someone worked out that the quickest and 'easiest' way to do this was to chase the bulls out of the corrals and into the ring. It was only a small step from that to the full-blown carnage of Pamplona's Sanfermines.

Traditional Dress

Basque festivals are a good time to see traditional Basque dress and dance. It's said that there are around 400 different Basque dances, many of which have their own special kind of dress.

Basque Language

Victor Hugo described the Basque language as a 'country', and it would be a rare Basque who'd disagree with him. The language, known as Euskara, is the oldest in Europe and has no known connection to any Indo-European languages. Suppressed by Franco, Basque was subsequently recognised as one of Spain's official languages, and it has become the language of choice among a growing number of young Basques.

WORTH A TRIP

SANTUARIO DE LOYOLA

Just outside Azpeitia (12km south of the A8 motorway along the GI631) lies the portentous Santuario de Loyola (www.santuariodeloyola.org; adult/child €3/free; ⏱10am-noon & 4-7pm), dedicated to St Ignatius, the founder of the Jesuit order. The dark, sooty basilica, laden with grey marble and plenty of carved ornamentation, is monstrous rather than attractive. The house where the saint was born in 1490 is preserved in one of the two wings of the sanctuary. Weekends are the most interesting times to come; the sanctuary fills up with pilgrims.

in a cage lowered down through a hole in the middle of the dining area straight into the sea.

ℹ Information

Tourist Office (☎943 34 15 56; Calle Donibane 63, Pasajes; ⏱9am-2pm & 4-7pm Jul & Aug, 10am-2pm & 4-6pm rest of year)

ℹ Getting There & Away

Pasajes is practically a suburb of San Sebastián; numerous buses (€1.45, 25 minutes) ply the route between them.

For a much more enjoyable way of getting there, though, you can walk over the cliffs from San Sebastián. The walk takes about 2½ to three hours and passes through patches of forest and past the occasional idyllic beach and strange rock formations covered in seabirds and then descends to Pasajes, which you reach by taking the small ferry boat across the inlet.

Hondarribia

POP 16,890

Lethargic Hondarribia (Castilian: Fuenterrabía), staring across the estuary to France, has a heavy Gallic fragrance, a charming *casco antiguo* (old city) and, in contrast to the quiet old city, a buzzing beach scene.

You enter the *casco* through an archway at the top of Calle San Compostela to reach the pretty Plaza de Gipuzkoa. Head straight on to Calle San Nicolás and go left to reach the bigger Plaza de Armas and the Gothic Iglesia de Santa María de la Asunción (Calle Mayor, Hondarribia).

For La Marina, head the other way from the archway. This is Hondarribia's most picturesque quarter. Its main street, Calle San Pedro, is flanked by typical fishermen's houses, with facades painted bright green or blue and wooden balconies gaily decorated with flower boxes.

The beach is about 1km from the town. Lined by bars and restaurants, it's not the prettiest stretch of coastline, but it does offer some of the calmest waters in the entire region.

◉ Sights

Monte Jaizkibel   MOUNTAIN
(Hondarribia) Monte Jaizkibel is a giant slab of rock that acts as a defensive wall, protecting the inland towns and fields from the angry, invading ocean. A very strenuous walking trail (about 20km) and a car-taxing road wend their way up the mountain to a ruined fortress and spectacular views. From here you can walk all the way to Pasajes.

Castillo de Carlos V   CASTLE
(Plaza de Armas 14) Today it's a government-run hotel, but for over a thousand years this castle hosted knights and kings. Its position atop the old town hill gave it a commanding view over the strategic Bidasoa estuary, which has long marked the Spain–France border. Poke your head into the reception lobby to admire the medieval decor.

⌖ Sleeping & Eating

Hotel San Nikolás   HOTEL €€
(☎943 64 42 78; www.hotelsannikolas.es; Plaza de Armas 6; s €83, d €109-127; ☎) Located inside a charming old building on the main plaza, in the heart of Hondarribia's historic center, this small hotel is an enjoyable spot to stay for a night or two.

Parador de Hondarribia   HISTORIC HOTEL €€€
(☎943 64 55 00; www.parador.es; Plaza de Armas 14; d from €228; P❋@☎) It's not every day that the opportunity to sleep in a thousand-year-old fortress guarding the boundaries of Spain arises. This sumptuous offering from the Parador chain has modern guest rooms with hard-wood floors and stone walls, many with sea views. But the place to be at sunset is one of the castle's courtyards or terraces, glass of wine in hand.

La Hermandad de Pescadores   SEAFOOD €€
(☎943 64 27 38; http://hermandaddepescadores.com; Calle Zuloaga 12, Hondarribia; mains €18-

21; ⊘1-3.30pm & 8-11pm, closed evenings Mon & Sun) Locals in the know travel from San Sebastián to eat at this historic Hondarribia restaurant. Housed in a traditional white-and-blue cottage, it serves an array of seafood classics but is best known for its *sopa de pescado* (fish soup), said by some to be the best in the area.

Arroka Berri
BASQUE €€

(☑943 64 27 12; www.arrokaberri.com; Calle Higer Bidea 6, Hondarribia; mains €15-25; ⊘1-3.30pm & 8-11pm) Arroka Berri isn't yet well known outside of town, but we're certain that news of its fabulous cuisine will one day spread far and wide. As with many trend-setting Basque restaurants, this one takes high-quality local produce and turns old-fashioned recipes on their head with a fun, theatrical twist. Unusually, it's open every day.

⊙ Information

Tourist Office (☑943 64 36 77; www.hondarribia.org; Plaza de Armas 9; ⊘9.30am-7.30pm daily Jul–mid-Sep, shorter hours rest of year)

⊙ Getting There & Away

Buses run frequently to nearby Irún and on to San Sebastián (€2.50, one hour); catch them from Sabin Arana.

Oñati
POP 11,280

With a flurry of magnificent architecture and a number of interesting sites scattered through the surrounding green hills, the small, and resolutely Basque town of Oñati is a great place to get to know the rural Basque heartland. Many visitors pass through on their way to or from the nearby Santuario de Arantzazu (p431).

⊙ Sights

Iglesia de San Miguel
CHURCH

(☑943 78 34 53; Avenida de Unibertsitate 2; ⊘hours vary) This late-Gothic confection has a cloister built over the river. The church faces onto the main square, Foruen Enparantza, dominated by the eye-catching baroque *ayuntamiento* (town hall). Contact the tourist office for guided tours.

Universidad
de Sancti Spiritus
HISTORIC BUILDING

(Avenida de la Universidad 8; ⊘closed on holidays) Oñati's number-one attraction is the Renaissance treasure of the Universidad de Sancti Spiritus. Built in the 16th century, it was the first university in the Basque Country and, until its closure in 1902, alumni here were schooled in philosophy, law and medicine. The Mudéjar courtyard is worth a look.

Monastery of Bidaurreta
MONASTERY

(☑943 78 34 53; Kalea Lazarraga; ⊘hours vary) Founded in 1510, this monastery contains a beautiful baroque altarpiece. It's at the opposite end of town from the tourist office and Iglesia de San Miguel. Hours aren't regular; contact the tourist office for the latest details.

⊫ Sleeping

Oñati doesn't get a lot of tourists staying overnight. But the countryside around town is awash in *casas rurales* – ask at the tourist office for a list.

Ongí Hotela
HOTEL €

(☑943 71 82 85; www.hotelongi.com; Calle Zaharra 19; s/d €42/56; ❋⍟) A basic but central place with sparkling-clean rooms and friendly service.

⊙ Information

Tourist Office (☑943 78 34 53; Calle San Juan 14; ⊘10am-2pm & 3.30-7.30pm Mon-Fri, 10am-2pm & 4-6.30pm Sat, 10am-2pm Sun)

⊙ Getting There & Away

PESA buses serve Oñati from many destinations in Basque Country, including Bilbao (€6.65, 45 minutes to one hour).

WORTH A TRIP

SANTUARIO DE ARANTZAZU

About 10km south of Oñati, the **Santuario de Arantzazu** (☑943 78 09 51; www.arantzazu.org; Barrio de Arantzazu 8) is a busy Christian pilgrimage site that's a fabulous conflation of piety and avant-garde art. The sanctuary was built in the 1960s on the site where, in 1468, a shepherd found a statue of the Virgin under a hawthorn bush. The sanctuary's design is based on this. The overwhelming impression of the building is of spiky towers and halls guarded by fourteen chiselled apostles and, in the crypt, a devil-red Christ.

Vitoria

POP 242,100 / ELEV 512M

Vitoria (Basque: Gasteiz) has a habit of falling off the radar, yet it's actually the capital of not just the southern Basque province of Álava (Basque: Araba) but also the entire Basque Country. Maybe it was given this honour precisely because it is so forgotten, but if that's the case, prepare for a pleasant surprise. With an art gallery whose contents frequently surpass those of the more famous Bilbao galleries, a delightful old quarter, dozens of great *pintxo* bars and restaurants, a large student contingent and a friendly local population, you have the makings of a lovely city.

⊙ Sights

At the base of Vitoria's medieval Casco Viejo is the delightful Plaza de la Virgen Blanca. It's lorded over by the 14th-century Iglesia de San Miguel (Plaza de la Virgén Blanca; ⊙10.30am-1pm & 5.30-7pm Mon-Fri), whose statue of the Virgen Blanca, the city's patron saint, lends its name to the plaza below.

The 14th-century Iglesia de San Pedro Apóstol (☑945 25 41 93; Fundadora de las Siervas de Jesús) is the city's oldest church and has a fabulous Gothic frontispiece on its eastern facade.

★ **Artium** MUSEUM

(☑945 20 90 00; www.artium.org; Calle de Francia 24; adult/child €6/free, by donation Wed; ⊙11am-2pm & 5-8pm Tue-Fri, 11am-8pm Sat & Sun; ☑) Unlike some more famous Basque art galleries, Vitoria's palace of modern art doesn't need to dress to impress. It's daring, eccentric and challenging in a way other museums could never get away with.

The large subterranean galleries are filled with engrossing pieces by Basque, Spanish and international artists, displaying some fairly intense modernist work. Over the years we've seen exhibitions featuring 'art' that many would describe as borderline pornography, children's drawings depicting suicide and even a grainy, bloody video of a woman having her hymen sewn back up to make her a virgin again. Yes, this is art designed to shock. Guided tours, in Spanish, run several times a day. After digesting the art, sample some of the cuisine at the much-praised Cube Café (www.cubeartium.com; Calle de Francia 24, Centro Museo Artium; menú del día €15; ⊙9am-11.30pm Mon-Thu, 9am-2am Fri, 10am-2am Sat, 11am-11.30pm Sun) inside the museum.

Anillo Verde PARK

Ringing the city is the Anillo Verde (Green Belt), the pride of Vitoria. A series of interconnecting parks, ponds and marshes linked to one other by cycle paths, this is one of the reasons Vitoria was named the European Green Capital in 2012. The most important of these green areas is the Parque de Salburúa (Salburúa Park). Several outfitters rent bicycles (€7/12 for 2/4 hours); Vitoria Bikes (p434) also runs guided bike tours (from €18 to 25.)

Bibat MUSEUM

(☑945 20 90 00; Calle de la Cuchillería/Aiztogile Kalea 54; adult/student/child €3/1/free; ⊙10am-2pm & 4-6.30pm Tue-Fri, 10am-2pm Sat, 11am-2pm Sun) The Museo de Arqueología and the Museo Fournier de Naipes (☑945 18 19 20; Calle de la Cuchillería 54; adult/student/child €3/1/free; ⊙10am-2pm & 4-6.30pm Tue-Fri, 10am-2pm Sat, 11am-2pm Sun) are combined into one museum known as Bibat. The Museo de Arqueología has giant TV screens that bring the dim and distant past to life. The eccentric Museo Fournier de Naipes has an impressive collection of historic presses and playing cards, including some of the oldest European decks.

Catedral de Santa María CATHEDRAL

(☑945 25 51 35; www.catedralvitoria.eus; Plaza Santa Maria; ⊙10am-2pm & 4-7pm) At the summit of the old town and dominating its skyline is the medieval Catedral de Santa María. For a number of years the cathedral has been undergoing a lengthy restoration project. There are excellent guided tours that provide insight into the excitement of restoration and give you a taste not just of the past and future of the cathedral but of the city as a whole.

Museo de Bellas Artes GALLERY

(Paseo de Fray Francisco 8; adult/student/child €3/1/free; ⊙10am-2pm & 4-6.30pm Tue-Fri, 10am-2pm Sat & 5-8pm Sat, 11am-2pm Sun) Housed in an astoundingly ornate building, the absorbing Museo de Bellas Artes has Basque paintings and sculpture from the 18th and 19th centuries. The works of local son Fernando de Amaríca are on display and reflect an engaging romanticism that manages to mix drama with great warmth of colour and composition.

Catedral de María Inmaculada CATHEDRAL

(Calle de Monseñor Cadena y Eleta) Vitoria's cathedral might look old, but in fact it only

Vitoria

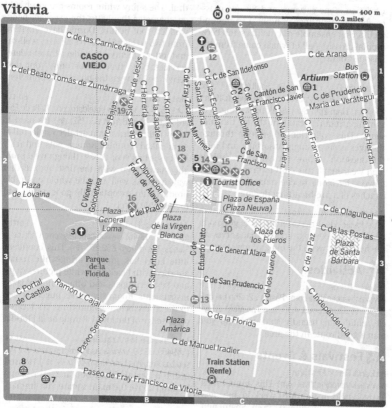

BILBAO, BASQUE COUNTRY & LA RIOJA VITORIA

Vitoria

ⓞ Top Sights
1 Artium	D1

ⓞ Sights
2 Bibat	C1
3 Catedral de María Inmaculada	A3
4 Catedral de Santa María	C1
5 Iglesia de San Miguel	C2
6 Iglesia de San Pedro Apóstol	B2
7 Museo de Armería	A4
8 Museo de Bellas Artes	A4
Museo Fournier de Naipes	(see 2)
9 Paseo de los Arquillos	C2

ⓞ Activities, Courses & Tours
10 Vitoria Bikes	C3

🛏 Sleeping
11 Abba Jazz Hotel	B3
12 Albergue de la Catedral	C1
13 Hotel Dato	C3
La Casa de los Arquillos	(see 5)

🍴 Eating
14 Arkupe	C2
15 Asador Matxete	C2
16 Asador Sagartoki	B2
17 Bar El Tabanco	B2
Cube Artium	(see 1)
18 La Malquerida	B2
19 Restaurante El Clarete	B1
20 Toloño	C2

dates from the early 1970s. There are some impressive, fairly adventurous stained-glass windows and a neck-stretchingly high nave. More interesting, though, is the attached

Museo Diocesano de Arte Sacro (Calle de Monseñor Cadena y Eleta; adult/student/child €3/1/free; ⏰ 11am-2pm & 4-6.30pm Tue-Fri, 11am-2pm Sat & Sun), which contains some early

Christian stone carvings and Basque crosses, detailed paintings of biblical scenes and a glittering ensemble of crucifixes and ceremonial crosses – all of which come from the Basque Country.

Museo de Armería
MUSEUM

(Paseo de Fray Francisco 3; adult/student/child €3/1/free; ⊙10am-2pm & 4-6.30pm Tue-Fri, 10am-2pm Sat, 11am-2pm Sun) Seeking a knight in shining armour? Head straight for this museum. This collection of armour through the ages is surprisingly absorbing and begs the question of how on earth the gallant men wearing all this stuff even managed to move – let alone rescue damsels from the clutches of a fire-breathing dragon.

Paseo de los Arquillos
HISTORIC BUILDING

The Paseo de los Arquillos is a gorgeous neo-classical covered arcade that serves as the border between the old and new towns.

🏃 Activities

Vitoria Bikes
BICYCLE TOUR

(www.activateenalava.com; Postas 32; 2hr/full day €7/15; ⊙10am-2pm & 4.30-8pm Thu-Mon) Bicycle rental. The friendly staff can help you plan a good route in the area.

🎉 Festivals & Events

Azkena Rock Festival
MUSIC

(www.azkenarockfestival.com) This annual rock festival, held in the third week in July, features musical headliners from Spain and abroad, plus audio-visual events and outdoor cinema.

Jazz Festival
MUSIC

(www.jazzvitoria.com) This mid-July festival attracts numerous national and international acts.

Fiestas de la Virgen Blanca
CITY FESTIVAL

The calm sophistication of Vitoria takes a back seat on August 4 to 8 during the boisterous Fiestas de la Virgen Blanca. Fireworks, bullfights, concerts and street dancing are preceded by the symbolic descent of Celedón, a Basque effigy that flies down on strings from the Iglesia de San Miguel into the plaza below.

🛏 Sleeping

Albergue de la Catedral
HOSTEL €

(☑945 27 59 55; www.alberguecatedral.com; Calle de la Cuchillería 87; under 25yr/over 25yr dm from €16/18, d from €40; @ 🛜) This hip hostel is virtually built into the walls of the cathedral. The shiny white rooms are given added character thanks to the exposed, bendy wooden roof beams. Dorms have anything from two to eight beds. It's all very well-run and offers plenty of budget-travel-related services. Note that there's only front desk reception between the hours of 1pm to 9pm.

Hotel Dato
HOTEL €

(☑945 14 72 30; www.hoteldato.com; Calle de Eduardo Dato 28; s/d from €36/52; 🛜) It's hard to know if the extravagant art-deco style, full of semi-naked nymphs, Roman pots and frilly fittings is kitsch or classy (though we'd probably have to go with the first one). Either way, it works well and the whole ensemble produces an exceptionally good value and memorable hotel.

Abba Jazz Hotel
HOTEL €

(☑945 10 13 46; www.abbahotels.com; Calle de la Florida 7; s/d from €62/67; 🛜) This confident little hotel has small, searing-white rooms adorned with black-and-white pictures of piano keys, trumpets and other suitably jazzy instruments. Room size varies hugely, so ask to see a few before committing. It's located on the edge of the lovely Parque de la Florida.

La Casa de los Arquillos
B&B €€

(☑945 15 12 59; www.lacasadelosarquillos.com; Paseo Los Arquillos 1; s/d from €70/79; 🛜) Housed inside a beautiful old building in a prime location above the main square, this immaculate bed and breakfast takes its youthful inspiration from the artwork in the Artium: each room is individually decorated in a highly original, and often eccentric, style.

🍴 Eating

Internationally Vitoria might not have the same culinary cachet as San Sebastián, but among in-the-know Spaniards this is a city with serious culinary pedigree. How serious? Well, in 2014 it was awarded the title of *Capital Nacional de la Gastronomia* (National Gastronomic Capital) on account of its stellar array of *pintxo* bars and highly creative chefs. What makes Vitoria even more enticing as a foodie destination is that unlike San Sebastián, where the price of *pintxos* is starting to get a bit silly, eating out here is very affordable. Even more so on Thursday evenings when many bars offer a *pintxo* and drink for €1 to €2.

Bar El Tabanco
PINTXOS €

(www.eltabanco.es; Calle de la Korrería 46; pintxos from €2; ⊙7-11.30pm Tue-Fri, 12.30-4pm &

7-11.30pm Sat-Sun) Taking its cue, in terms of both decoration and food, from the steamy southern region of Andalucía, this is another ever busy, ever reliable *pintxo* bar.

Toloño
PINTXOS €

(Calle de San Francisco 3; pintxos from €2, set lunch €13; ⊙11am-1.30pm & 5-8pm Tue-Sat) This bar has won awards for its creative *pintxos*; the house specials often involve creative takes on local mushrooms. It's a large bar, so there's normally somewhere to sit down, plus a small outdoor space that's a charming spot to people-watch.

La Malquerida
PINTXOS €

(Calle de la Correría 10; pintxos from €2; ⊙10am-10.30pm Mon-Thu, 10am-midnight Fri & Sat) A fantastic *pintxo* bar hidden away under the shadows of the church spires. Many locals consider it the best in town.

Asador Sagartoki
PINTXOS €

(www.sagartoki.com; Calle del Prado 18; mains €8-12, set menu €42; ⊙10am-11pm Mon-Fri, 9am-midnight Sat-Sun) A marvellous *pintxo* bar and *sidrería* (cider house) that has one of the most creative menus around and an atmosphere to go with it. The house specials, which have won awards, are the tortilla and the fried-egg *pintxos*. Sit back and marvel as the bar staff orchestrate jets of cider from big barrels to the glasses in their outstretched hands.

Asador Matxete
STEAK €€

(☑945 13 18 21; www.matxete.com; Plaza de Matxete 4-5; mains €15-20; ⊙noon-11pm Tue-Sat, noon-6pm Sun) There are two types of *asador* (restaurants specialising in barbecued meat): smoky old farmhouse-like places that haven't changed in decades, and sleek new urban remakes. This one falls into the second category and it produces gourmet steaks served up with flair. It's delightfully situated on a quiet old town plaza and has a lovely summer terrace.

Arkupe
BASQUE €€€

(☑945 23 00 80; www.restaurantearkupe.com; Calle Mateo Benigno de Moraza 13; mains €15-2,1menús €40-47; ⊙1.30-3.30pm & 8.30-11pm) For modern, creative Basque cooking, check out stylish Arkupe, just around the corner from the main plaza. There's an extensive wine list, with all the offerings racked up against the back wall. Reserve in advance for meals. It's also a great place to stop for people-watching and quick drink

WHAT'S COOKING IN THE BASQUE COUNTRY, NAVARRA AND LA RIOJA?

Food and drink is almost the cornerstone of life in this part of Spain. Basque food is generally considered about the best in the country, and the wines of La Rioja are the finest in Spain. Seafood is big on the coast: *bacalao al pil-pil* (salted cod and garlic in an olive-oil emulsion) and *chipirones en su tinta* (baby squid served in its own ink) are both popular. Further into the hills and mountains people tuck into *chuleton de buey* (steaks – never less than massive). Look out also for fine mountain cheese in the Pyrenees and tiny elvers (young eels) on the coast (although nowadays a substitute is often used due to the rarity of elvers).

or bite, standing at one of the high outdoor tables.

Restaurante El Clarete
BASQUE €€€

(☑945 26 38 74; Cercas Bajas 18; menús €25-50; ⊙1.30-3.30pm Mon-Wed, 1.30-3.30pm & 9-11pm Thu-Sat) This appealing restaurant offers good set *menús* featuring fresh, original takes on classic Basque cuisine and smart wine pairings. The easygoing atmosphere and fairly low prices keep it busy with locals.

Drinking & Nightlife

There's a strong politico-arty vibe in the Casco Viejo, where a lively student cadre keeps things swerving with creative street posters and action. The main action is at Calle de la Cuchillería/Aiztogile and neighbouring Cantón de San Francísco Javier, both of which are packed with busy bars that attract a wide range of age groups. There's a heavy Basque nationalist atmosphere in some bars.

Information

Tourist Office (☑945 16 15 98; www.vitoria-gasteiz.org/turismo; Plaza de España 1; ⊙10am-8pm Jul-Sep, shorter hours Oct-Jun) In the central square of the old town. It can organise guided tours of the city, including fascinating tours taking in the numerous giant wall murals of the city and tours out to the extensive green spaces and birdwatching sites that fringe the city.

BILBAO, BASQUE COUNTRY & LA RIOJA VITORIA

❶ Getting There & Away

There are car parks by the train station, by the Artium, and just east of the cathedral.

Vitoria's **bus station** (Calle de los Herrán) has regular services to the following:

DESTINATION	FARE	DURATION
Barcelona	from €21.50	7hr
Bilbao	€6.30	1¼hr
Madrid	€27	4½hr
Pamplona	€7.50-€8.50	1¾hr
San Sebastián	€12	1¼hr

Trains go to the following:

DESTINATION	FARE	DURATION	FREQUENCY
Barcelona	from €31	5hr	1 daily
Madrid	from €41	4-6hr	5 daily
Pamplona	from €6	1hr	5 daily
San Sebastián	from €12	1¾hr	up to 10 daily

NAVARRA

Several Spains intersect in Navarra (Nafarroa in Basque). The soft greens and bracing climate of the Navarran Pyrenees lie like a cool compress across the sun-struck brow of the south, which is all stark plains, cereal crops and vineyards, sliced by high sierras with cockscombs of raw limestone. Navarra is also pilgrim territory: for centuries the faithful have used the pass at Roncesvalles to cross from France on their way to Santiago de Compostela (p507).

Navarra was historically the heartland of the Basques, but dynastic struggles and trimming due to reactionary politics, including Francoism, has left it as a semi-autonomous province, with the north being Basque by nature while the south leans towards Castilian Spain. The centre hangs somewhere in between and Navarra seems intrinsically uncommitted to the vision of a Basque future.

The Navarran capital, Pamplona, tends to grab the headlines with its world-famous running of the bulls, but the region's real charm is in its spectacularly diverse landscapes and its peppering of small towns and villages that seem to melt into the landscape.

Pamplona

POP 196,100 / ELEV 456M

Senses are heightened in Pamplona (Basque: Iruña), capital of the fiercely independent Kingdom of Navarra, alert constantly to the fearful sound of thundering bulls clattering like tanks down cobbled streets and causing mayhem and bloodshed along the way. Of course, visit outside the eight days in July when the legendary festival of Sanfermines takes over the minds and souls of a million people and the closest you'll come to a bloodthirsty bull is in a photograph. For those who do dare venture here outside fiesta time, despite the overriding feeling that you're the only one who missed the party, you will find Pamplona a fascinating place. And for those of you who come during fiesta week? Welcome to one of the biggest and most famous festivals in the world – if you hadn't drunk so much, it would have been a week you would remember forever!

◎ Sights

★**Museo de Navarra** MUSEUM
(☎848 42 89 26; www.cfnavarra.es/cultura/museo; Calle Cuesta de Santo Domingo 47; adult/student/child €2/1/free, free Sat afternoon & Sun; ⏱9.30am-2pm & 5-7pm Tue-Sat, 11am-2pm Sun) Housed in a former medieval hospital, this superb museum has an eclectic collection of archaeological finds (including a number of fantastic Roman mosaics unearthed mainly in southern Navarra), as well as a selection of art, including Goya's *Marqués de San Adrián*. Labelling is in Spanish only, but foreign translation leaflets are available.

Catedral de Santa María CATHEDRAL
(www.catedraldepamplona.com; Calle Dormitalería; adult/child €5/3; ⏱10:30am-5pm Mon-Sat) Pamplona's main cathedral stands on a rise just inside the city ramparts amid a dark thicket of narrow streets. The cathedral is a late-medieval Gothic gem spoiled only by its rather dull neoclassical facade, an 18th-century appendage. The vast interior reveals some fine artefacts, including a silver-plated Virgin and the splendid 15th-century tomb of Carlos III of Navarra and his wife Doña Leonor. The real joy is the

Pamplona

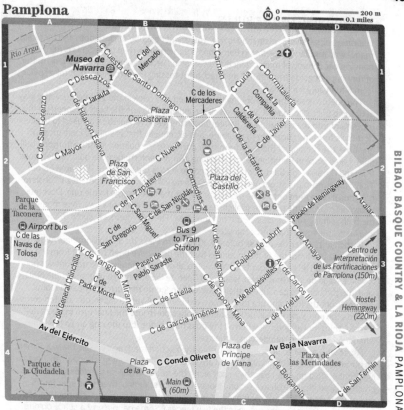

Pamplona

Gothic **cloister**, where there is marvellous delicacy in the stonework.

Ciudadela   FORTRESS
(Avenida del Ejército) The walls and bulwarks of the grand fortified citadel, the star-shaped Ciudadela, were built between 1571 and 1645 under the direction of King Felipe II. It's considered one of the best examples of military architecture from the Spanish Renaissance. The former moats and bastions now host cultural performances and sporting events.

Centro de Interpretación de las
Fortificaciones de Pamplona   CITY WALLS
(Interpretation Center of the Fortifications of Pamplona; ☎ 948 21 15 54; www.murallasdepamplona. com; cnr Calles Arrieta & Aralar; adult/child €3/1.50; ☉ 11am-2pm & 5-7pm Tue-Sun Apr-Oct,

THE RUNNING OF THE BULLS

Liberated, obsessive or plain mad is how you might describe aficionados (and there are many) who regularly take part in Pamplona's Sanfermines (Fiesta de San Fermín), a nonstop cacophony of music, dance, fireworks and processions – and the small matter of running alongside a handful of agitated, horn-tossing *toros* (bulls) – that takes place from 6 to 14 July each year.

The bullrun is said to have originally developed way back in the 14th century as a way of herding bulls into market, with the seller running alongside the bulls to speed up their movement into the marketplace. In later times the same technique was used to transport bulls from the corrals to the bullring, and essentially that is still the case today. *El encierro*, the running of the bulls from their corrals to the bullring for the afternoon bullfight, takes place in Pamplona every morning during Sanfermines. Six bulls are let loose from the Coralillos de Santo Domingo to charge across the square of the same name. They continue up the street, veering onto Calle de los Mercaderes from Plaza Consistorial, then sweep right onto Calle de la Estafeta for the final charge to the ring. Devotees, known as *mozos* (the brave or foolish, depending on your point of view), race madly with the bulls, aiming to keep close – but not too close. The total course is some 825m long and lasts little more than three minutes.

Participants enter the course before 7.30am from Plaza de Santo Domingo. At 8am two rockets are fired: the first announces that the bulls have been released from the corrals; the second lets participants know they're all out and running. The first danger point is where Calle de los Mercaderes leads into Calle de la Estafeta. Here many of the bulls skid into the barriers because of their headlong speed on the turn. They can become isolated from the herd and are then always dangerous. A very treacherous stretch comes towards the end, where Calle de la Estafeta slopes down into the final turn to Plaza de Toros. A third rocket goes off when all the bulls have made it to the ring and a final one when they have been rounded up in the stalls.

Those who prefer to be spectators rather than action men (and we use the word 'men' on purpose here as, technically, women are forbidden from running, although an increasing number do it anyway) bag their spot along the route early. A space doesn't mean an uninterrupted view because a second 'security' fence stands between the spectators and runners, blocking much of the view (only police, medical staff and other authorised people can enter the space between the two fences). Some people rent a space on one of the house balconies overlooking the course. Others watch the runners and bulls race out of the entrance tunnel and into the bullring by buying a ticket for a seat in the ring. Whatever the vantage point, it's all over in a few blurred seconds.

Each evening a traditional bullfight is held. Sanfermines winds up at midnight on 14 July with a candlelit procession, known as the Pobre de Mí (Poor Me), which starts from Plaza Consistorial.

Concern has grown about the high numbers of people taking part in recent *encierros*. Since records began in 1924, 16 people have died during Pamplona's bullrun. Many of those who run are full of bravado (and/or drink) and have little idea of what they're doing. The number of injuries differs from year to year, but serious injuries are common (usually due to goring, but also from pile ups of participants) and deaths not unheard of. On top of the dangers to runners, the bulls themselves are all destined to die in the bull ring and that aspect of the running, as well as the stress of the run itself and the possibility of the bulls slipping and injuring themselves in the stampede, have led to animal welfare groups condemning the spectacle as a cruel tradition.

shorter hours rest of yr) If these walls could talk. This excellent interpretation center, located in the Fortín de San Bartolomé, explains the design and function of Pamplona's original fortifications, whose construction dates from the 16th century. It's still considered one of the best preserved bastions in Europe. Among the many curiosities in the museum: centuries-old graffiti, most likely created by guardsmen.

🛏 Sleeping

During Sanfermines, hotels raise their rates mercilessly – all quadruple their normal rack rates and many increase them fivefold – and it can be near impossible to get a room without reserving between six months and a year in advance. The tourist office maintains a list of private houses with rooms to rent during this period, and touts hang around the bus and train stations offering rooms. With numerous 'San Fermín' buses arriving from all nearby Spanish and French cities, it's actually not a bad idea to stay in a different town altogether and catch a ride on the party buses. Ask local tourist offices for details of departure times and costs.

At any other time of year, Pamplona is packed with good-value accommodation and it's rarely worth booking ahead.

Hostal Arriazu HOTEL €
(☎948 21 02 02; www.hostalarriazu.com; Calle Comedias 14; s/d €59/64; ☎) Falling somewhere between a budget *pensión* and a midrange hotel, this good-value option is located in a former theatre. The rooms are pleasingly old-fashioned, though the en-suite bathrooms are perfectly modern. There's also a pretty courtyard and an appealing lounge area.

Hostel Hemingway HOSTEL €
(☎948 98 38 84; www.hostelhemingway.com; Calle Amaya 26; dm €17-20, s/d from €35/42; @☎) This well-run hostel, located a few minutes' walk from the old town, was renovated in 2013. Clean and friendly, with a communal kitchen, it's a great budget pick. It's just off Avenida de Carlos III.

Hotel Castillo de Javier HOTEL €€
(☎948 20 30 40; www.hotelcastillodejavier.com; Calle de San Nicolás 50; s from €45, d €63-69; ✳☎) Though it's located on a busy street, lined with shops and restaurants and always noisy at night, this small hotel has surprisingly quiet rooms thanks to double-glazed doors and windows. Some rooms have balconies, ideal for people-watching, though cheaper rooms have rather less inspiring views.

Hotel Europa HOTEL €€
(☎948 22 18 00; www.hreuropa.com; Espoz y Mina 11; s/d from €67/73; ☎) Though the building is better-known for its restaurant, the sleek Europa also features several floors of modern hotel rooms. Note that the most economical accommodations are tiny and windowless, but the location is tough to beat.

★**Palacio Guendulain** HISTORIC HOTEL €€€
(☎948 22 55 22; www.palacioguendulain.com; Calle de Zapatería 53; d from €155; Ⓟ✳☎) To call this stunning hotel, inside the converted former home of the viceroy of New Granada, sumptuous is an understatement. On arrival, you're greeted by a museum-piece 17th-century carriage and a collection of classic cars being guarded by the viceroy's private chapel. The rooms contain *Princess and the Pea*–soft beds, enormous showers and regal armchairs.

🍴 Eating

Pamplona is filled with good restaurants and bars, many serving Basque cuisine and *pintxos*, others serving traditional Navarran dishes.

★**Bar Gaucho** PINTXOS €
(www.cafebargaucho.com; Espoz y Mina 7; pintxos €2-3.50; ☺7am-3pm & 6.30-11pm) This bustling bar serves multi-award-winning *pintxos* that, despite some serious competition, many a local will tell you are the finest in the city.

Casa Otaño BASQUE €€
(☎948 22 50 95; www.casaotano.com; Calle de San Nicolás 5; mains €15-18, menú del día €18; ☺1-4pm & 9-11pm Mon-Sat) It may be a little pricier than many on this street, but Casa Otaño is worth the expense. Excellent dishes range from the locally caught trout to succulent duck. The relatively formal atmosphere is softened by the dazzling array of pink and red flowers spilling off the balcony.

Restaurante Europa BASQUE, SPANISH €€€
(☎948 22 18 00; Espoz y Mina 11, Hotel Europa; mains €22-28, menús €47-62; ☺1-3.30pm & 9-11pm Mon-Sat) There's fine formal dining to be had in this modern white-tablecloth restaurant. Meals consist of very traditional Navarran and Basque dishes and the walls are lined with photos of the good, great or just plain glam Spanish celebrities who have eaten here.

🍷 Drinking & Nightlife

Pamplona's resident student population ensures a lively after-dark scene year-round. There's a strong Basque vibe in the bars

DON'T MISS

CAFÉ IRUÑA

Hemingway was here. Opened on the eve of Sanfermines in 1888, Café Iruña's (www.cafeiruna.com; Plaza del Castillo 44; ⊘ 8am-midnight Mon-Thu, 9am-midnight Fri-Sun) dominant position, powerful sense of history and frilly belle époque decor make this by far the most famous and popular watering hole in the city. In addition to a long list of wine and spirits, it also has a good range of pintxos and light meals.

around Calle Carmen and Calle de la Caldererería and up towards the cathedral. The area opposite the bullring on Paseo de Hemingway is also home to a few more bars and clubs. Larger nightclubs are found a walk or short taxi ride south and west of the old city centre, in the direction of the university. The doors at these places are usually open after 11pm Thursday to Saturday and the cover charge tends to be around €8 to €12, depending on the the night.

ℹ️ Information

The extremely well-organised **tourist information office** (☑ 848 42 04 20; www.turismo.navarra.es; Avenida da Roncesvalles 4; ⊘ 9am-7pm Mon-Fri, 10am-2pm & 4-7pm Sat, 10am-2pm Sun), just opposite the statue of the bulls in the new town, has plenty of information about the city and Navarra. There are a couple of summer-only tourist info booths scattered throughout the city.

ℹ️ Getting There & Away

AIR

Pamplona's **airport** (☑ free call 902 404704), about 7km south of the city, has regular flights to Madrid, Barcelona and a few other Spanish cities. **Bus 16** (€1.35) travels between the city (from the bus station and Calle de las Navas de Tolosa) and the suburb of Noáia, from where it's about a 200m walk to the airport. A taxi costs about €15-20.

BUS

From the **main bus station** (☑ 902 02 36 51; www.estaciondeautobusesdepamplona.com; Ave de Yanguas y Miranda 2), buses leave for most towns throughout Navarra, although service is restricted on Sunday.

Regular bus services travel to the following:

DESTINATION	FARE	DURATION
Bilbao	€15	2¾hr
Logroño	€9.20	1¾hr
San Sebastián	€7.80	1hr
Vitoria	€7.58-8.50	1¼-2hr

Regional destinations include the following:

DESTINATION	FARE	DURATION	FREQUENCY
Estella	€4.30	1hr	10 daily
Olite	€3.50	¾hr	16 daily

TRAIN

Pamplona's train station is linked to the city centre by **bus 9** from Paseo de Sarasate every 15 minutes. Tickets are also sold at the **Renfe agency** (Calle de Estella 8; ⊘ 9am-1.30pm & 4.30-7.30pm Mon-Fri, 9am-1pm Sat).

Note that it's much quicker to take the bus to San Sebastián. Trains run to/from the following:

DESTINATION	FARE	DURATION	FREQUENCY
Madrid	from €29	3hr	4 daily
San Sebastián	from €15	2hr	2 daily
Tudela	from €9	1hr	5 daily
Vitoria	from €6	1hr	4 daily

Around Pamplona

Javier

POP 112 / ELEV 448M

Tiny Javier (Xavier), 11km northeast of Sangüesa, is a quiet rural village set in gentle green countryside. It's utterly dominated by a childhood-fantasy castle that is so perfectly preserved you half expect the drawbridge to come crashing down and a knight in armour to gallop out on a white steed to challenge you. As well as being an inspiration for fairytale dreams, this is also the birthplace of the patron saint of Navarra, San Francisco Xavier, who was born in the village in 1506. Xavier spent much of his life travelling, preaching, teaching and healing in Asia. Today his body lies in a miraculous state of preservation in a cathedral in Goa, India.

◉ Sights

Castillo de Javier
CASTLE

(☑948 88 40 24; €2.75; ☺10am-1.30pm & 3.30-6.30pm) This tenth-century castle, strategically located on the border between the kingdoms of Navarra and Aragón, is Javier's main attraction. Inside, there's a small museum dedicated to San Francisco Xavier, the patron saint of Navarra, who was born in the village in 1506.

🛏 Sleeping

Hotel Xabier
HOTEL €

(☑948 88 40 06; www.hotelxabier.com; Zona turística; d/tr €56/71; 🅿🛜) If you want to sleep near the castle, stay at the red-brick, ivy-clad Hotel Xabier. You can peer out of your window on a moonlit night and look for ghosts flitting around the castle keep.

ⓘ Getting There & Away

Most travellers come here by car. Several daily buses serve Sangüesa from Pamplona's bus station; Javier is a short taxi ride away. Tafallesa buses also go directly to Javier, usually once a day, from Pamplona's bus station.

The Navarran Pyrenees

Awash in greens and often concealed in mists, the rolling hills, ribboned cliffs, clammy forests and snow-plastered mountains that make up the Navarran Pyrenees are a playground for outdoor enthusiasts and pilgrims on the Camino de Santiago. Despite being firmly Basque in history, culture and outlook, there is something of a different feeling to the tiny towns and villages that hug these slopes. Perhaps it's their proximity to France, but in general they seem somehow more prim and proper than many of the lowland towns. This only adds to the charm of exploring what are, without doubt, some of the most delightful and least exploited mountains in western Europe.

Driving through this beautiful region is a pleasure. As you bear northeast out of Pamplona on the N135 and ascend into the Pyrenees, the yellows, browns and olive greens of lower Navarra begin to give way to more-luxuriant vegetation before the mountains thunder up to great Pyrenean heights, following the path of the Camino de Santiago.

Happy wanderers on wheels can drift around a network of quiet country roads in the area, stopping in pretty villages along the way. A couple of kilometres south of Burguete, the NA140 branches off east to Garralda. Push on to Arive, a charming hamlet, from where you could continue east to the Valle del Salazar, or go south along Río Irati. Another option is to take a loop northeast through the beautiful Selva de Irati (www.selvadeirati.com; car parking €5) forest, with its thousands of beech trees that turn the slopes a flaming orange every autumn and invite exploration on foot (from the parking area several well-marked trails lead off for anything from 2km to 8.2km return). Eventually this route will link you up with the Valle del Salazar at Ochagavía. If you stick to the NA140 between Arive and Ochagavía, Abaurregaina and Jaurrieta are particularly picturesque.

Valle del Baztán

This is rural Basque Country at its most typical, a landscape of splotchy reds and greens. Minor roads take you in and out of charming little villages, such as Arraioz, known for the fortified Casa Jaureguizar; and Ziga, with its 16th-century church.

Just beyond Irurita on the N121B is the valley's biggest town, Elizondo, given an urban

---

WORTH A TRIP

SIERRA DE ARALAR

One of Navarra's many natural parks, the scenic Sierra de Aralar offers pleasant walking and dramatic drives. There's not much to Lekunberri, the area's main town, except a gaggle of solid Basque farmhouses in the old quarter and an ever-growing estate of soulless modern housing beyond.

For most, the main reason for visiting Lekunberri is to travel the bendy back road NA1510, which leads southwest through a tasty tapestry of mixed deciduous and evergreen forests to culminate (after 21km) at the Santuario de San Miguel de Aralar (www.aralarkosanmigel.info; Monte Aralar; ☺10am-2pm & 4-6pm) FREE.

The tourist office (☑948 50 72 04; www.plazaola.org; Plazaola 21, Lekunberri; ☺10am-2pm Tue-Sun) here is very helpful and can advise on the numerous fantastic walks the area offers.

air by its tall half-timbered buildings. It's a good base for exploring the area.

Beyond Elizondo, the NA2600 road meanders dreamily amid picturesque farms, villages and hills before climbing sharply to the French border pass of Puerto de Izpegui, where the world becomes a spectacular collision of crags, peaks and valleys. At the pass, you can stop for a short, sharp hike up to the top of Mt Izpegui.

The N121B continues northwards to the Puerto de Otxondo and the border crossing into France at Dantxarinea. Just before the border, a minor road veers west to the almost overly pretty village of Zugarramurdi.

◎ Sights

La Cueva de Zugarramurdi CAVE
(www.turismozugarramurdi.com; adult/child €4/2; ⊙10.30am-8pm Jul & Aug, shorter hours rest of year) According to the Inquisition, these caves (also known as Cuevas de Las Brujas, or Caves of the Witches) were once the scene of evil debauchery. True to form, inquisitors tortured and burned scores of alleged witches here.

Museo de las Brujas MUSEUM
(www.turismozugarramurdi.com; adult/child €4.50/2; ⊙11am-7.30pm mid-Jul–mid-Sep) Playing on the flying-broomstick theme of the Cueva de Zugarramurdi, this museum is a fascinating dip into the mysterious cauldron of witchcraft in the Pyrenees.

⌂ Sleeping

Antxitónea Hostal HOSTAL €€
(☑948 58 18 07; www.antxitonea.com; Braulío Iriarte 16; d/tr from €64/90; ☎) This well-run *hostal* has plain rooms with flower-bedecked balconies, some with river views. The attached restaurant is worth a stop.

❶ Getting There & Away

Most travellers drive here. Zugarramurdi is located about 80km north of Pamplona via N121A.

Burguete
POP 260

A steady stream of pilgrims on the Camino de Santiago pass through this quaint 12th-century town. The main road runs tightly between neat, whitewashed houses with bare cornerstones at Burguete (Basque: Auritz), lending a more sober French air to things. Despite lacking the history, it actually makes a better night's halt than nearby Roncesvalles.

⌂ Sleeping & Eating

Camping Urrobi CAMPGROUND €
(☑948 76 02 00; www.campingurrobi.com; site/bungalow for up to three €18/73; ⊙Apr-Oct; ℗⬤❄) Campers will be happy at this riverside campsite a few kilometres south of town. It also has a hostel and bungalows.

Hotel Rural Loizu HOTEL €€
(☑948 76 00 08; www.loizu.com; Calle de San Nicolás 13; s/d €63/87; ⊙Apr-Dec; ℗⬤) This is a pleasant country hotel whose upper rooms have attractive beams and exposed stone walls. Downstairs, there's a good restaurant.

❶ Getting There & Away

Most visitors arrive by car or on foot, but there's also regular bus service to Pamplona (€4, one hour).

Roncesvalles
POP 33

History hangs heavily in the air of Roncesvalles (Basque: Orreaga). Legend has it that it was here that the armies of Charlemagne were defeated and Roland, commander of Charlemagne's rearguard, was killed by Basque tribes in 778. This is an event celebrated in the epic 11th-century poem *Chanson de Roland* (Song of Roland) and is still talked about by today's Basques. In addition to violence and bloodshed, though, Roncesvalles has long been a key point on the road to Santiago de Compostela, and today Camino pilgrims continue to give thanks at the famous monastery for a successful crossing of the Pyrenees, one of the hardest parts of the Camino de Santiago.

The main event here is the monastery complex (☑948 79 04 80; www.roncesvalles.es; church free; guided tours adult/child €4.30/2.50; ⊙10am-2pm & 3.30-7pm Apr-Oct, shorter hours Nov-Mar), which contains a number of different buildings of interest.

◎ Sights

Real Colegiata de Santa María CHURCH
(☑948 79 04 80; ⊙9am-8.30pm) FREE
The 13th-century Gothic Real Colegiata de Santa María, a good example of Navarran Gothic architecture, contains a much-revered, silver-covered statue of the Virgin beneath a modernist-looking canopy worthy of Frank Gehry.

🛏 Sleeping

Casa de Beneficiados
HOTEL €€

(✏️948 76 01 05; www.casadebeneficiados.com; Orreaga-Roncesvalles; apt for 2/3 €80/115; ⊘ mid-Mar–Dec; 📶) In a former life this was an 18th-century monks' residence. Today it's comfortable and utterly modern, with bicycle rental, laundry facilities, free wi-fi and luggage storage.

ℹ️ Getting There & Away

Many travellers arrive on foot or by car, but you can also get to Roncesvalles by bus from Pamplona (€6, one hour).

Ochagavía
POP 584

This charming Pyrenean town lying astride narrow Río Zatoya sets itself quite apart from the villages further south. Grey stone, slate and cobblestones dominate the old centre, which straddles a bubbling stream crossed by a pleasant medieval bridge. The town's sober dignity is reinforced by the looming presence of the Iglesia de San Juan Evangelista.

🛏 Sleeping & Eating

Hostal Casa Sario
HOTEL €

(✏️948 89 01 87; www.casasario.com; Llana 11, Jaurrieta; s/d €47/64; 📶) This sweet little rural hotel, in the heart of the nearby village of Jaurrieta, has simple wood-floored rooms and a busy bar-restaurant downstairs.

★Hotel Rural Auñamendi
HOTEL €€

(✏️948 89 01 89; www.hotelruralaunamendi.com; Urrutia 23; d/t €75/95; 📶) After extensive renovations in 2014, this lovely hotel is a top pick for its bright, spacious rooms, comfortable public spaces, and coffee bar with outdoor terrace seating.

Asador Sideria Kixkia
BASQUE €€

(www.kixkia.com; Urrutia 59; menús €25-33; ⊘ 1-3.30pm & 9-11pm) There are plenty of places to eat in the area, but it's hard to beat the earthy, rural atmosphere and filling mountain food of the Asador Sideria Kixkia at the southern end of the village.

ℹ️ Getting There & Away

ALSA buses go from Pamplona to Ochagavía (€9,20, 1½ hours).

To reach France, take the NA140 northeast from Ochagavía into the Sierra de Abodi and cross at the Puerto de Larrau (1585m), a majestically bleak pass.

Valle del Roncal

Navarra's most beautiful mountain area is around Roncal and this easternmost valley, made up of seven villages, is an alternative route for leaving or entering the Navarran Pyrenees.

BURGUI
POP 230

The gateway to this part of the Pyrenees is Burgui – an enchanting huddle of stone houses built beside a clear, gushing stream (the Río Esca) bursting with frogs and fish and crossed via a humpbacked Roman bridge.

🛏 Sleeping

Hostal El Almadiero
HOSTAL €€

(✏️948 47 70 86; www.almadiero.com; Plaza Padre Tomás de Burgui 1; d from €64; 📶) In the heart of the village, this pleasant *hostal rural* has bright, cosy rooms with 19th-century charm and mod cons like hot water.

ℹ️ Getting There & Away

Burgui isn't well served by public transport. The village is roughly a one-hour drive east of Pamplona via A21.

RONCAL
POP 272

The largest centre along this road, though still firmly a village, Roncal is a place of cobblestone alleyways that twist and turn between dark stone houses and meander down to a river full of trout.

ISABA
POP 475

Lording it over the other villages in the valley, lofty Isaba, lying above the confluence of Ríos Belagua and Uztárroz, is another popular base for walkers and skiers. Heading north out of town towards the French border the scenery becomes ever more spectacular. The road starts off confined between mountain peaks before suddenly opening out into high Alpine pastures with a backdrop of the most majestic mountains in the western Pyrenees. Approaching the French border the road corkscrews up and up to the pass of Roncalia where you'll find a small ski resort. Beyond is France and another, larger ski resort, Pierre St Martin.

There are signed walking trails on both sides of the border.

Sleeping

Hostal Lola
HOTEL €€

(☑948 89 30 12; www.hostal-lola.com; Mendigatxa 17; d €70; ☎) This family-run place hidden down a narrow side alley offers probably the best value for money and has rooms loaded with desks, sofas and big beds. There's a nice flower-hemmed terrace and a decent restaurant. The only drawback is that the walls are so thin you can pretty much hear everything your neighbours are up to.

Hostal Ezkaurre
HOSTAL €€€

(☑948 89 33 03; www.hostalezkaurre.es; Garagardoia 14; d €189; ☎) A delightful rainbow-tinged small hotel at the northern edge of village. While the rooms are quite sober, the common areas, including a library and lounge, are cosy and stylish.

Information

Tourist Office (☑948 89 32 51; www.vallederoncal.es; Barrio Izargentea 28; ☺10am-2pm & 4-8pm Mon-Sat, 10am-2pm Sun)

Getting There & Away

Most travellers arrive here in their own cars, but you could also take a La Tallafesa bus from Pamplona to nearby Uztárroz (€4.50, two hours) and then hire a taxi into Isaba.

Southern Navarra

Olite

POP 3890 / ELEV 365M

The turrets and spires of Olite are filled with stories of kings and queens, brave knights and beautiful princesses – it's as if it has burst off the pages of a fairytale. Though it might seem a little hard to believe today, this quiet village was once the home of the royal families of Navarra, and the walled old quarter is crowded with their memories.

Founded by the Romans (parts of the town wall date back to Roman times), Olite first attracted the attention of royalty in 1276. However, it didn't really take off until it caught the fancy of King Carlos III (Carlos the Noble) in the 15th century, when he embarked on a series of daring building projects.

Sights

Palacio Real
CASTLE

(Castillo de Olite; www.guiartenavarra.com; adult/child €3.50/2; ☺10am-8pm Jul-Aug, 10am-7pm Mon-Fri, 10am-8pm Sat & Sun May-Jun & Sep, shorter hours Oct-Apr) It's Carlos III that we must thank for the exceptional Palacio Real, which towers over the village. Back in Carlos' day, the inhabitants of the castle included not just princes and jesters but also lions, giraffes and other exotic pets, as well as Babylon-inspired hanging gardens. Today, though the princes and lions are sadly missing, some of the hanging gardens remain.

Integrated into the castle is the Iglesia de Santa María la Real, which has a superbly detailed Gothic portal. There are guided tours of both buildings; check with the ticket office for times; otherwise an audio guide to the castle is €1.

Museo de la Viña y el Vino de Navarra
MUSEUM

(www.guiartenavarra.com; Plaza de los Teobaldos 10; adult/child €3.50/2; ☺10am-2pm & 4-6pm Mon-Sat, 10am-2pm Sun Mar-Oct, shorter hours Nov-Feb) Don't miss this museum, which is a fascinating journey through wine and wine culture. Everything is well labelled and laid out and some fascinating facts are revealed. For instance, did you know that Noah (the one of the Ark fame) was apparently the first human ever to get drunk? It's in the same building as the tourist office.

Galerías Subterráneas
MUSEUM

(Plaza Carlos III; adult/child €1.50/1; ☺11am-1pm Tue-Fri, 11am-2pm & 5-7pm Sat, Sun & public holidays) These underground galleries, whose origin and use remain something of a mystery, contain a small museum explaining the town's medieval life (in Spanish). These basically illustrate that if you were rich, then life was one jolly round of food and wine – and if you weren't, well, life was tough.

Laguna de Pitillas
LAKE

The lakes and marshes that make up the Laguna de Pitillas are one of the top birding sites in Navarra. Now a protected Ramsar wetland site of international importance, the Laguna de Pitillas provides a home for around 160 permanent and migratory species, including marsh harriers, great bitterns and even ospreys.

To get there, take the N121 south of Olite and then turn off down the NA5330.

🛏 Sleeping & Eating

Hotel Merindad de Olite   HISTORIC HOTEL €€
(☑948 74 07 35; www.merindaddeolitehoteles. com; Rúa de la Judería 11; s €58-68, d €68-78; ❄🛜) Built almost into the old town walls, this charming place has small but comfortable rooms and masses of medieval style. Get in fast because it fills quickly.

Hotel el Juglar   BOUTIQUE HOTEL €€
(☑948 74 18 55; www.merindaddeolitehoteles. com; Rúa Romana 39; d €88-128; P❄🛜🏊) A few minutes' walk into the new suburbs. The handful of rooms here are all slightly different from one another – some have big round whirlpool baths, some old-fashioned stone baths, and others elaborate walk-in showers. All have four-poster beds and lots of fancy decorations, and there's a pool to cool off in on a hot summer day.

⭐Parador de Olite   HISTORIC HOTEL €€
(☑948 74 00 00; www.parador.es; Plaza de los Teobaldos 2; r from €120; ❄@) Situated in a wing of the castle (though the cheaper rooms are in a newer extension), this offering from the Parador chain is in a sumptuous, atmospheric class of its own. Though there might be good rooms available elsewhere in town for considerably fewer euros, they don't come with a castle attached.

ℹ Information

Tourist Office (☑948 74 17 03; Plaza de los Teobaldos 10; ⊙10am-2pm & 4-7pm Mon-Sat, 10am-2pm Sun) Olite has a friendly and helpful tourist office, in the same building as the wine museum.

ℹ Getting There & Away

Up to 16 buses a day run between Olite and Pamplona (€3.50, 45 minutes). The bus from Pamplona drops passengers near the entrance to the walled city. Heading back to the city, catch the bus outside Olite's historic area, at the bus shelters on the road to Pamplona.

Ujué

POP 198

Balancing atop a hill criss-crossed with terraced fields, the tiny village of Ujué, some 18km east of Olite and overlooking the plains of southern Navarra, is a perfect example of a fortified medieval village. Today the almost immaculately preserved village is sleepy and pretty, with steep, narrow streets tumbling down the hillside.

The village plays host to a fascinating *romería* (pilgrimage) on the first Sunday after St Mark's Day (25 April), when hundreds of people walk through the night from Tudela to celebrate Mass in the village church.

⊙ Sights

Iglesia-fortaleza de Santa María de Ujué   CHURCH
(San Isidro 8; admission by donation; ⊙10am-6pm) A fortified church of mixed Romanesque-Gothic style, Iglesia de Santa María contains a rare statue of the Black Virgin, which is said to have been discovered by a shepherd who was led to the statue by a dove. In addition to the Virgin, the church also contains the heart of Carlos II.

🍴 Eating

Mesón las Migas   SPANISH €€
(☑948 73 90 44; www.mesonlasmigas.es; Villeta 19; mains €10-18; ⊙1-3.30pm & 8-10pm mid-Jul–Aug, 1-3.30pm weekends only rest of year) Serving traditional south Navarran food, this is the best place to eat. Try the hunks of meat cooked over an open wood fire and don't miss the house special, *migas de pastor* (fried breadcrumbs with herbs and chorizo).

ℹ Getting There & Away

Most travellers arrive by car. If you're taking the bus from Pamplona, you'll make a connection in Tafalla or Olite, both roughly 20km east of the village.

Parque Natural de las Bárdenas Reales

In a region largely dominated by wet mountain slopes, the last thing you'd expect to find is a sunburnt desert. The Bárdenas Reales are badlands, the dramatic landscape shaped by the forces of water, wind, and erosion.

There are plenty of hiking and cycling trails through the park, though many are only vaguely signposted.

There's a **park information office** (☑948 83 03 08; www.bardenasreales.es; Km 6 military zone rd; ⊙9am-2pm & 3-5pm Apr-Aug, shorter hours rest of year) on the main route into the park from Arguedas, which can supply

Camino Francés in Navarra & La Rioja

information on driving, cycling and walking routes. Otherwise, the tourist office in Olite has information.

🛏 Sleeping

Hotel Aire de Bardenas BOUTIQUE HOTEL €€€
(📞948 11 66 66; www.airedebardenas.com; Ctra de Ejea, Km 1, Tudela; d €203-269; 🅿❄🛜🏊) Humble shipping crates transformed into a stylish boutique hotel. All rooms have luxurious amenities; many also each feature views over an expanse of semi-desert. There's great service, a swimming pool, and a superb in-house restaurant (mains €14 to €22). It's situated several kilometres east of Tudela, just off the NA125.

ℹ Getting There & Away

There's no public transport to the park; drive or take a bus or train to nearby Tudela.

Puente de la Reina

POP 2810 / ELEV 421M

The chief calling card of Puente la Reina (Basque: Gares), 22km southwest of Pamplona on the A12, is the spectacular six-arched medieval bridge that dominates the western end of town, but Puente la Reina rewards on many other levels. A key stop on the Camino de Santiago, the town's pretty streets throng with the ghosts of a multitude of pilgrims. Their first stop here was at the late-Romanesque Iglesia del Crucifijo, erected by the Knights Templars and still containing one of the finest Gothic crucifixes in existence. And just a short way out of town is one of the prettiest chapels along the

whole Camino. Throw into this mix some fine places to stay and, in the nearby countryside, a ruined Roman city and the result is a fine place to be based for a day or so.

◉ Sights

Santa María de Eunate CHURCH
(www.santamariadeeunate.es; Carretera de Campanas; ⏰10.30am-1pm & 5.30-8pm Tue-Sun, shorter hours in winter) Surrounded by cornfields and brushed by wild flowers, the near perfect octagonal Romanesque chapel of Santa María de Eunate is one of the most picturesque chapels along the whole Camino. Dating from around the 12th century its origins – and the reason why it's located in the middle of nowhere – are something of a mystery. The chapel is 2km southeast of Muruzábal, which is itself 5km northeast of Puente la Reina.

🛏 Sleeping

Hotel Rural El Cerco BOUTIQUE HOTEL €€
(📞948 34 12 69; www.elcerco.es; Rodrigo Ximénez de Rada 36; s/d €50/75; 🛜) At the eastern end of the old quarter, this hotel is one of the most charming places to stay in town. It's housed in an antique building, smartly transformed into a stylish, small boutique hotel with exposed stone walls and wooden roof beams.

ℹ Getting There & Away

Frequent buses (€4.30, one hour) run between Pamplona's bus station and Estella; they all stop along the main road in the village of Puente la Reina.

Estella

POP 14,130 / ELEV 483M

Estella (Basque: Lizarra) was known as 'La Bella' in medieval times because of the splendour of its monuments and buildings, and though the city has lost some of its beauty to modern suburbs, its historic centre is still thoroughly charming. During the 11th century, Estella became a main reception point for the growing flood of pilgrims along the Camino de Santiago. Today most visitors are continuing that same plodding tradition.

◉ Sights

Iglesia de San Pedro de la Rúa   CHURCH
(☑948 55 00 70; ⊙10am-1.30pm & 6-7pm Mon-Sat, 9.45am-12.30pm Sun, shorter hours in winter)
This 12th-century church is the most important monument in Estella. Its cloisters are a fine example of Romanesque sculptural work.

Museo Gustavo de Maeztu   PALACE
(www.museogustavodemaeztu.com; San Nicolás 1, Palacio de los Reyes; ⊙9.30am-1pm Tue-Fri, 11am-2pm Sat-Sun) FREE Adjacent to the tourist office is the **Palacio de los Reyes**, a rare example of Romanesque civil construction. It houses a museum with an intriguing collection of paintings by Gustavo de Maeztu y Whitney (1887–1947), who was of Cuban-English parentage but emphatically Basque in upbringing and identity. Landscapes, portraits and full-bodied nudes reflect Maeztu's engaging sensual romanticism.

THE CAMINO IN NAVARRA & LA RIOJA

At the gates of Spain, Navarra is the first Spanish leg of the journey to Santiago de Compostela for walkers on the Camino Francés route. The opening section, which crosses over the Pyrenees, is also one of the most spectacular parts of the entire Camino.

Roncesvalles to Pamplona

From the **Puerto de Ibañeta**, the Camino dramatically enters Spain and drops down to **Roncesvalles**. Dominated by its great, imposing abbey, Roncesvalles admirably sets the tone for this extraordinary route. Inside the heavily restored 13th-century Gothic church, you'll find the first statue of Santiago dressed as a pilgrim (with scallop shells and staff).

Pamplona became an official stop along the Camino in the 11th century, cementing its prosperity. Just inside the cathedral's bland neoclassical facade are the pure, soaring lines of the 14th-century Gothic interior.

Pamplona to Logroño & Beyond

Heading west out of Pamplona via Zariquiegui and the Sierra del Perdón, pilgrims reach **Puente la Reina**, where the Camino Aragonés, coming from the east, joins up with the Camino Francés.

Estella, the next stop, contains exceptional monumental Romanesque architecture: the outstanding portal of the Iglesia de San Miguel; the cloister of the Iglesia de San Pedro de la Rúa; and the Palacio de los Reyes de Navarra.

Outside Estella, evergreen oaks and vineyards fill undulating landscapes until a long, barren stretch leads through the sleepy towns of **Los Arcos**, **Sansol** and **Torres del Río**. In hillside Torres you'll find another remarkably intact eight-sided Romanesque chapel, the Iglesia del Santo Sepulcro.

The great Río Ebro marks the entrance to **Logroño** and explains its wealth and size. The dour Gothic Iglesia de Santiago houses a large Renaissance altarpiece depicting unusual scenes from the saint's life, including run-ins with the wicked necromancer Hermogenes.

Nájera literally grew out of the town's red cliff wall when King Ramiro discovered a miraculous statue of the Virgin in one of the cliff's caves in the 11th century.

Santo Domingo de la Calzada is one of the road's most captivating places. It is named for its energetic 11th-century founder, Santo Domingo, who cleared forests, built roadways, a bridge, a pilgrim's hospice and a church, and performed many wondrous miracles depicted masterfully in Hispano-Flemish paintings in the cathedral.

Iglesia de San Miguel
CHURCH

(📞 948 55 04 31; Plaza San Miguel; ⊙ hours vary) Across the river and overlooking the town is the Iglesia de San Miguel, with a fine Romanesque north door.

⚜ Festivals & Events

Carrera del Encierro
FAIR

In the end of July through the first week of August, Estella hosts a week-long *feria* (fair) with its own *encierro* (running of the bulls).

🛏 Sleeping & Eating

Hotel Tximista
DESIGN HOTEL €€

(📞 948 55 58 70; www.sanvirilahoteles.com/tximista; Zaldu 15; s/d €80/95; 🅿 ❄ 🛜) This striking modern hotel, built into and out of an old watermill, mixes rusty old industrial cogs and wheels from the mill with poppy-red artwork. Rooms are comfortable, although some suffer from road noise, and there's a nice garden overlooking the gurgling river.

Hospedería Chapitel
HOTEL €€

(📞 948 55 10 90; www.hospederiachapitel.com; Chapitel 1; s/d from €75/100; 🅿 🛜) Estela's most stylish sleeping option. Though there aren't many common spaces, guest rooms and suites are spacious and quaint.

Asador Astarriaga
SPANISH €€

(www.asadorastarriaga.com; Plaza de Los Fueros 12; mains €10-17; ⊙ 10am-1.30pm & 8pm-midnight Mon-Sat, 10am-1.30pm Sun) With outdoor seating on the main square, this restaurant is popular with Galicia-bound pilgrims. The menu focuses on steaks and seafood.

ℹ Getting There & Away

Buses leave from the **bus station** (Plaza Coronación) for Pamplona (€4.30, one hour), 10 daily Monday to Friday, and six daily on weekends.

LA RIOJA

Get out the *copas* (glasses) for La Rioja and some of the best red wines produced in the country. Wine goes well with the region's ochre earth and vast blue skies, which seem far more Mediterranean than the Basque greens further north. In fact, it's hard not to feel as if you're in a different country altogether. The bulk of the vineyards line Río Ebro around the town of Haro, but some also extend into neighbouring Navarra and the Basque province of Álava. This diverse region offers more than just the pleasures of the grape, though, and a few days here can see you mixing it up in lively towns and quiet pilgrim churches, and even hunting for the remains of giant reptiles.

Logroño
POP 151.960

Logroño is a stately wine country town with a heart of tree-studded squares, narrow streets and hidden corners. There are few monuments here, but perhaps more importantly to some, a great selection of *pintxos* (Basque tapas) bars. In fact, Logroño is quickly gaining a culinary reputation to rival anywhere in Spain.

⊙ Sights

A stroll around the old town and down to the river is a thoroughly pleasant way to spend an afternoon.

★ Museo de la Rioja
MUSEUM

(📞 941 29 12 59; www.larioja.org; Plaza San Agustín 23; ⊙ 10am-2pm & 4-9pm Tue-Sat, 10am-2pm Sun) FREE In both Spanish and English, this superb museum in the centre of Logroño takes you on a wild romp through Riojan history and culture – from the days when dinner was killed with arrows to recreations of the kitchens that many a Spanish *abuela* (grandmother) grew up using.

Catedral de Santa María de la Redonda
CATHEDRAL

(Calle de Portales; ⊙ 8am-1pm & 6-8.45pm Mon-Sat, 9am-2pm & 6.30-8.45pm Sun) The Catedral de Santa María de la Redonda started life as a Gothic church before maturing into a full-blown cathedral in the 16th century.

Iglesia de San Bartolomé
CHURCH

(Calle de Rodríguez Paterna) The impressive main entrance to this 13th-century church has a splendid portico of deeply receding borders and an expressive collection of statuary.

🏃 Activities

Rioja Trek
WINE

(📞 941 58 73 54; www.riojatrek.com; wine experience €28 per person) Based in the small village

Logroño

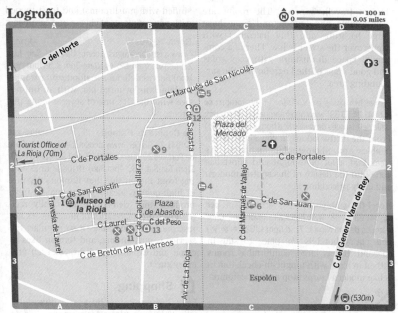

of Fuenmayor (10 minutes west of Logroño) Rioja Trek offers three-hour wine 'experiences' where you visit a vineyard and bodega and participate in the process of actually making some wine yourself (and keeping the bottle afterwards).

The same people also run well-priced wine-tasting courses, family-friendly wine related activities and, as the name would suggest, guided hikes along some of La Rioja's fabulous mountain trails.

🎊 Festivals & Events

Actual   CULTURAL
A program of cultural, musical and artistic events in the first week of January.

Feast of San Bernabé   FEAST DAY
The Feast of San Bernabé commemorates the French siege of Logroño in 1521 on 11 June.

Fiesta de San Mateo   CULTURAL
Logroño's week-long Fiesta de San Mateo starts on the Saturday before 21 September and doubles as a harvest festival, during which all of La Rioja comes to town to watch the grape-crushing ceremonies in the Espolón and to drink ample quantities of wine.

Logroño

🛏 Sleeping

Hostal La Numantina   PENSIÓN €
(☑ 941 25 14 11; www.hostalnumantina.com; Calle de Sagasta 4; s/d from €33/54; 🛜) This professional operation caters perfectly (almost perfectly – the wi-fi signal is weak) to the

budget traveller's needs. The rooms are comfortable and homey, and some have large bathtubs and tiny balconies with views over the street below. There's a communal space downstairs with cosy sofas and good maps of the Logroño and the surrounding area.

Hotel Marqués de Vallejo DESIGN HOTEL €€
(☏ 941 24 83 33; www.hotelmarquesdevallejo.com; Calle del Marqués de Vallejo 8; d from €96; P ❋ ☎) From the driftwood art to cow skins, beach pebbles and photographic highlights, it's clear that a lot of thought and effort has gone into the design of this stylish, modern and fairly priced hotel.

Hotel Calle Mayor BOUTIQUE HOTEL €€€
(☏ 941 23 23 68; www.hotelcallemayor.com; Calle Marqués de San Nicolás 71; d from €102; P ❋ ☎) This classy hotel is *the* place to stay in Logroño. It has large, comfortable rooms bathed in light, with tongue-in-cheek touches like modern lamps atop ancient columns.

🍴 Eating

Make no mistake about it: Logroño is a foodie's delight. There are a number of very good restaurants and then there are the *pintxos* – few cities have such a dense concentration of excellent *pintxo* bars. Most of the action takes place on Calle Laurel and Calle de San Juan. *Pintxos* cost around €2 to €4, and most of the *pintxo* bars are open from about 8pm through to midnight, except on Mondays.

Bar Torrecilla PINTXOS €
(Calle Laurel 15; pintxos from €2; ☉1-4pm & 8-11pm) The best *pintxos* in town? You be the judge. Go for the pyramid of *jamón* or the mini-burgers, or anything else that strikes your fancy, at this modern bar on buzzing Calle del Laurel.

La Taberna del Laurel PINTXOS €
(Calle Laurel 7; pintxos from €2; ☉noon-4pm & 8pm-late) The speciality at La Taberna del Laurel is *patatas bravas* (potatoes in a spicy tomato sauce). They're not just good: they're divine. The restaurant takes its name from its location on Calle del Laurel, informally known as the 'street of *pintxos*'.

La Taberna de Baco PINTXOS €
(Calle de San Agustín 10; pintxos from €2) This popular bar has a list of around 40 different *pintxos,* including *bombitas* (potatoes

stuffed with mushrooms) and toast topped with pâté, apple, goat cheese and caramel.

Bar A Tu Gusto PINTXOS €
(www.gastrobaratugusto.com; Calle de San Juan 21; pintxos from €2; ☉10am-3pm & 5-11pm Wed-Mon) Serves delicious seafood *pintxos* in an Andalucian-flavoured bar, with an impressive wine list. It's one of several along this street.

La Cocina de Ramon SPANISH €€€
(☏941 28 98 08; www.lacocinaderamon.es; Calle de Portales 30; menús €28-37; ☉1.30-4pm & 8.30-11pm Tue-Sat, 1.30-4pm Sun) It looks unassuming from the outside, but Ramon's mixture of high-quality, locally grown market-fresh produce and tried-and-tested family recipes gives this place a lot of fans. But it's not just the food that makes it so popular: the service is outstanding, and Ramon likes to come and explain the dishes to each and every guest.

🛍 Shopping

Félix Barbero Botas Rioja HANDICRAFTS
(http://botasrioja.artesaniadelarioja.org; Calle de Sagasta 8; ☉10am-2pm & 4-8pm Mon-Sat) Maintaining a dying craft, Félix Barbero handmakes the classic Spanish animal skin wine carriers in which farmers carried their daily rations of wine while working in the fields. The standard one-litre model starts around €22.

Vinos El Peso WINE
(Calle del Peso 1; ☉9.30am-2pm Mon-Sat) There are countless wine outlets in town, but this one is excellent. In addition to local varietals, it's a good place to pick up some *vermút* (vermouth) de la Rioja.

ℹ Information

Tourist Office of La Rioja (☏941 29 12 60; www.lariojaturismo.com; Calle de Portales 50; ☉9am-2pm & 5-8pm Mon-Fri, 10am-2pm & 5-8pm Sat, 10am-2pm & 5-7pm Sun Jul-Sep, shorter hours Oct-Jun) This office can provide lots of information on both the city and La Rioja in general.

ℹ Getting There & Away

If you arrive at the train or **bus station** (☏941 23 59 83; Av de España 1), first head up Avenida de España and then Calle del General Vara de Rey until you reach the Espolón, a large, park-like square lavished with plane trees (and with an underground car park). The Casco Viejo starts just to the north.

Buses go to the following:

DESTINATION	FARE	DURATION
Bilbao	€14	2¾hr
Haro	€6	40 minutes
Pamplona	€9	1¾hr
Santo Domingo de la Calzada	€3.50	¾hr
Vitoria	€9	2¼hr

By train, Logroño is regularly connected to the following:

DESTINATION	FARE	DURATION
Bilbao	from €13.50	2½hr
Burgos	from €13	1¾hr
Madrid	from €31	3¼hr
Zaragoza	from €14	2½hr

West of Logroño

San Millán de Cogolla

POP 305 / ELEV 733M

About 16km southwest of Nájera, the hamlet of San Millán de Cogolla, home to only a few hundred people, is set in a lush valley. Like Nájera, San Millán de Cogolla has a long and fascinating Jewish history that dates back to the tenth century. But most people come here to see two remarkable monasteries that helped give birth to the Castilian language. On account of their linguistic heritage and artistic beauty, they have been recognised by Unesco as World Heritage sites.

◉ Sights

Monasterio de Suso MONASTERY

(☑941 37 30 82; www.monasteriodesanmillan. com/suso; €4; ⊙9.30am-1.30pm & 3.30-6.30pm Tue-Sun) Built above the caves where San Millán once lived, the Monasterio de Suso was consecrated in the 10th century. It's believed that in the 13th century a monk named Gonzalo de Berceo wrote the first Castilian words here. It can only be visited on a guided tour. Tickets must be bought in advance and include a short bus ride up to the monastery.

You can reserve tickets by calling ahead, or you can pick them up at the very helpful tourist office at the Monasterio de Yuso. Maps detailing short walks in the region can also be obtained at the tourist office.

Monasterio de Yuso MONASTERY

(☑941 37 30 49; www.monasteriodesanmillan. com; adult/child €6/2; ⊙10am-1.30pm & 4-6.30pm Tue-Sun) The Monasterio de Yuso, sometimes called El Escorial de La Rioja, contains numerous treasures in its museum. You can only visit as part of a guided tour (in Spanish only; non-Spanish speakers will be given an information sheet in English and French). Tours last 50 minutes and run every half-hour or so. In August it's also open on Mondays.

❶ Getting There & Away

Most travellers drive here. The village is located about an hour's drive west of La Rioja via A12.

Santo Domingo de la Calzada

POP 6520 / ELEV 630M

Santo Domingo is small-town Spain at its very best. A large number of the inhabitants continue to live in the partially walled old quarter, a labyrinth of medieval streets where the past is alive and the sense of community is strong. It's the kind of place where you can be certain that the baker knows all his customers by name and that everyone will turn up for María's christening. Santiago-bound pilgrims have long been a part of the fabric of this town, and that tradition continues to this day, with most visitors being foot-weary pilgrims. All this helps to make Santo Domingo one of the most enjoyable places in La Rioja.

◉ Sights

Catedral de Santo Domingo de la Calzada CATHEDRAL

(www.catedralsantodomingo.es; Plaza del Santo 4; adult/student/child €4/3/free; ⊙10am-8.30pm Mon-Fri, 9am-7.10pm Sat, 9am-12.20pm & 1.45-7.10pm Sun Apr-Oct, shorter hours Nov-Mar) The morose, monumental cathedral and its attached museum glitter with the gold that attests to the great wealth the Camino has bestowed on otherwise backwater towns. An audioguide to the cathedral and its treasures is €1. Guided tours, including a nighttime tour, are also available.

The cathedral's most eccentric feature is the white rooster and hen that forage in a glass-fronted cage opposite the entrance to the crypt (look up!). Their presence celebrates a long-standing legend, the Miracle of the Rooster, which tells of a young man who was unfairly executed only to recover

WORTH A TRIP

HOTEL VIURA

A modern architectural landmark in wine country, the Hotel Viura (☑945 60 90 00; www.hotelviura.com; Mayor, Villabuena de Álava; d from €128; P ❋ ☎) appears to be, on first glance, a collection of metallic, multi-coloured boxes piled haphazardly on the hillside. On closer investigation, its a sleek designer hotel that stands in whimsical contrast to the traditional village of Villabuena de Álava. Service and amenities are top-rate; it's a truly unique place to stay.

miraculously, while the broiled cock and hen on the plate of his judge suddenly leapt up and chickened off, fully fledged.

🛏 Sleeping

Hostal R Pedro I   HOTEL €
(☑941 34 11 60; www.hostalpedroprimero.es; San Roque 9; s/d €45/56; ☎) This carefully renovated town house, which has terracotta-coloured rooms with wooden roof beams and entirely modern bathrooms, is a terrific deal.

Parador de Santo Domingo de la Calzada   HISTORIC HOTEL €€
(☑941 34 03 00; www.parador.es; Plaza del Santo 3; r from €125; P ☎) The Parador Santo Domingo is the antithesis of the town's general air of piety. Occupying a 12th-century former hospital, opposite the cathedral, this palatial hotel offers anything but a frugal medieval-like existence. The in-house restaurant is reliably good.

Parador Santo Domingo Bernado de Fresneda   HOTEL €€
(☑941 34 11 50; www.parador.es; Plaza de San Francisco 1; d from €90; P ☎) Just on the edge of the old town is the Parador Santo Domingo Bernado de Fresneda, which occupies a former convent and pilgrim hostel. With its divine beds and opulent rooms, it's now a pretty luxurious place to stay.

ℹ Getting There & Away

Frequent buses run to Nájera (€1.60, thirty minutes) and onward to Logroño. The bus stop, where you'll find posted bus schedules, is located on Avenida Juan Carlos I (also known as Calle San Roque), just across the street from the historic centre.

La Rioja Wine Region

La Rioja wine rolls on and off the tongue with ease, by name as well as by taste. All wine fanciers know the famous wines of La Rioja, where the vine has been cultivated since Roman times. The region is classic vine country and vineyards cover the hinterland of Río Ebro. On the river's north bank, the region is part of the Basque Country and is known as La Rioja Alavesa.

Haro

POP 11,530 / ELEV 426M

Despite its fame in the wine world, there's not much of a heady bouquet to Haro, the capital of La Rioja's wine-producing region. But the town has a cheerful pace and the compact old quarter, leading off Plaza de la Paz, has some intriguing alleyways with bars and wine shops aplenty.

There are plenty of wine bodegas in the vicinity of the town, some of which are open to visitors (almost always with advance reservation). The tourist office keeps a full list.

🏃 Activities

Bodegas Muga   WINERY
(☑941 30 60 60; www.bodegasmuga.com; Barrio de la Estación; winery tour €10; ⊙tours by reservation Mon-Sat) Just after the railway bridge on the way out of town, this bodega is particularly receptive and gives daily guided tours (except Sunday) and tastings in Spanish. Although technically you should book in advance in high season, you can often just turn up and join a tour.

🎉 Festivals & Events

Batalla del Vino   WINE
(www.batalladelvino.com) On June 29 the otherwise mild-mannered citizens of Haro go temporarily berserk during the *Batalla del Vino* (Wine Battle), squirting and chucking wine all over each other in the name of San Juan, San Felices and San Pedro. Plenty of it goes down the right way, too.

🛏 Sleeping

Hotel Arrope   HOTEL €€
(☑941 30 40 25; www.hotelarrope.com; Virgén de la Vega 31; d from €83; ❋ ☎) This town-centre hotel has a young-and-cool attitude, which is quite unexpected in conservative Haro. The

EXPERIENCE THE WEALTH OF THE GRAPE

The humble grape has created great wealth for some of the villages around La Rioja. Proof of this are some of the extravagant bodegas and hotels that have sprung up in recent years in what otherwise appear to be backwater farming communities.

Visit the following to see what we mean, but first, a few basics: wine categories in La Rioja are termed Young, Crianza, Reserva and Gran Reserva. Young wines are in their first or second year and are inevitably a touch 'fresh'. Crianzas must have matured into their third year and have spent at least one year in the cask, followed by a few months resting in the bottle. Reservas pay homage to the best vintages and must mature for at least three full years in cask and bottle, with at least one year in the cask. Gran Reservas depend on the very best vintages and are matured for at least two years in the cask followed by three years in the bottle. These are the 'velvet' wines.

Getting thirsty? Let's hit the wine roads. When the owner of the Bodegas Marqués de Riscal, in the village of Elciego, decided he wanted to create something special, he didn't hold back. The result is the spectacular Frank Gehry–designed **Hotel Marqués de Riscal** (p455). Costing around €85 million, the building is a flamboyant wave of multicoloured titanium sheets that stands in utter contrast to the village behind. The building is having a radical effect on the surrounding countryside and has led to more tourists, more jobs, more wine sales and more money appearing in the hands of locals. Casual visitors are not, however, welcome at the hotel. If you want a closer look, you have three options. The easiest is to join one of the bodega's **wine tours** (p455) – there's at least one English language tour a day, but it's best to book in advance. You won't get inside the building, but you will get to see its exterior from some distance. A much closer look can be obtained by reserving a table at one of the two superb in-house restaurants: the Michelin-approved **Restaurante Marqués de Riscal** (p455) or the **Bistró 1860** (p455). For the most intimate look at the building, you'll need to reserve a room for the night, but be prepared to part with some serious cash!

Just a couple of kilometres to the north of Laguardia is the **Bodegas Ysios** (p455). Designed by Santiago Calatrava as a 'temple dedicated to wine', it's wave-like roof made of aluminium and cedar wood matches the flow of the rocky mountains behind it. It looks its best at night when pools of light flow out of it. Daily tours of the bodega are an excellent introduction to wine production. The 4pm tour on Saturdays is in English.

There are several other, somewhat less confronting, wine cellars around Laguardia that can be visited, often with advance notice only – contact the tourist office in Laguardia for details. **Bodegas Palacio** (p455) is only 1km from Laguardia on the Elciego road; reservations are not essential but are a good idea (especially out of season). The same bodega also runs excellent wine courses. The beginners' wine-tasting course (€30) runs monthly throughout the year, except August and January. Advance reservations are essential. There's also a hotel attached to the complex, but compared to options in Laguardia, it lacks character.

Also just outside Laguardia is the **Centro Temático del Vino Villa Lucia** (p454), a wine museum and shop selling high-quality wine from a variety of small, local producers. Museum visits are by guided tour only and finish with a 4D film and wine tasting.

It's worth noting that buried under the houses of Laguardia are numerous small wine bodegas, some of which are open to the public. Ask at the tourist office for details.

No matter how good Riojan wines are don't forget that other parts of this corner of Spain produce some high-quality wines as well. Southern and western Navarra produce some superb wines, which easily rival those of La Rioja (indeed in places only a matter of metres separates the vineyards of La Rioja from those of Navarra). The Basque country proper isn't as well regarded, but the hills around the small coastal town of Getaria produce a memorable, crisp white wine known as *txakoli* (Basque white wine), and the area south of Vitoria is known as Rioja Alava, and that alone probably gives you a clue to the quality of wine produced there.

attached bar-cafe, with a large terrace, is a very pleasant place for a glass of wine and some small plates.

Hotel Los Agustinos
HISTORIC HOTEL €€

(☑941 31 13 08; www.hotellosagustinos.com; San Agustín 2; d from €94; P ✳ ☎) History hangs in the air of this stately hotel, set in a 14th-century convent. Rooms could use an update, but the stunning covered courtyard is a wonderful place to linger over a glass of wine. The hotel's restaurant (menus from €39) is also highly excellent.

❶ Information

Tourist Office (☑941 30 35 80; www.haro turismo.org; San Martín 26; ☉10am-2pm & 4-7pm Mon-Sat, 10am-2pm Sun mid-Jun–Sep, 10am-2pm Mon-Fri, 10am-2pm & 4-6pm Sat Oct–mid-Jun) A couple of hundred metres along the road from Plaza de la Paz.

❶ Getting There & Away

Regular trains connect Haro with Logroño (from €5.95, 40 minutes).

Buses additionally serve Logroño, Nájera, Vitoria, Bilbao, Santo Domingo de la Calzada and Laguardia. The bus station, which has a small indoor space with a cafe, is located 4-5 blocks south of the historic centre. Walk along Avenida de la Rioja to get there.

Briones

POP 900 / ELEV 501M

One man's dream has put the small, obscenely quaint village of Briones firmly on the Spanish wine and tourism map. The sunset-gold village crawls gently up a hillside and offers commanding views over the surrounding vine-carpeted plains. Here you'll find the fantastic Vivanco (p454). Over several floors and numerous rooms, you will learn all about the history and culture of wine and the various processes that go into its production. View the world's largest collection of corkscrews, then sample a few varietals at the winery.

◉ Sights

Vivanco
MUSEUM

(Museo de la Cultura del Vino; www.vivancocultura devino.es; Carretera Nacional, Km 232; guided winery and museum visit with wine tasting €20; ☉11am-6pm Tue-Fri & Sun, 10am-8pm Sat Jul-Aug, shorter hours rest of year) A must for wine lovers. Tour the winery before or after a visit to the excellent **Museo de la Cultura del Vino** (Museum of the Culture of Wine), where you'll learn all about the history and culture of wine and the various processes that go into its production. All of this is done through interesting displays brought to life with the latest in technology. The treasures on display include Picasso-designed wine jugs, Roman and Byzantine mosaics, and wine-inspired religious artifacts.

🛏 Sleeping

Los Calaos de Briones
HOTEL €

(☑941 32 21 31; www.loscalaosdebriones.com; San Juan 13; d from €65; ☎) Rest your wine-heavy head at this lovely hotel. Some rooms suitably romantic four-poster beds. The attached restaurant, in an old wine cellar, is stuffed with excellent locally inspired cuisine (mains €12 to €15).

❶ Getting There & Away

Briones is located between Haro and Logroño. Autobuses Gimenez runs frequent buses from Logroño to Briones (€3.10, 50 minutes), continuing onward to Haro. In Briones, the bus stops on the edge of town, just off the highway.

Laguardia

POP 1520 / ELEV 557M

It's easy to spin back the wheels of time in the medieval fortress town of Laguardia, or the 'Guard of Navarra' as it was once appropriately known, sitting proudly on its rocky hilltop. The walled old quarter, which makes up most of the town, is virtually traffic-free and is a sheer joy to wander around. As well as memories of long-lost yesterdays, the town further entices visitors with its wine-producing present and striking scenery.

◉ Sights

Maybe the most impressive feature of the town is the castle-like **Puerta de San Juan**, one of the most stunning city gates in Spain.

Centro Temático del Vino Villa Lucía
MUSEUM

(☑945 60 00 32; www.villa-lucia.com; Carretera de Logroño; tour inc tasting €11; ☉11am-6.30pm Tue-Fri, 10.15am-6.30pm Sat, 11am-12.30pm Sun) Just outside Laguardia is this impressive wine museum and shop selling high-quality vino from small local producers. Museum

MARQUÉS DE RISCAL

When the owner of Elciego's Bodegas Marqués de Riscal decided he wanted to create something special, he didn't hold back. The result is the spectacular Frank Gehry–designed Hotel Marqués de Riscal (☑ 945 18 08 80; www.hotel-marquesderiscal.com; Calle Torrea 1, Elciego; r from €330; P ✳ 🛜). Costing around €85 million, the building is a flamboyant wave of multicoloured titanium sheets that stand in utter contrast to the village behind.

The building is having a radical effect on the surrounding countryside and has led to more tourists, more jobs, more wine sales and more income for the local economy. Casual visitors are not welcome at the hotel, however. If you want a closer look, you have three options. The easiest is to join one of the bodega's wine tours – it's necessary to book in advance. You won't get inside the building, but you will get to see its exterior from some distance. A much closer look can be obtained by reserving a table at one of the two superb in-house restaurants: the Michelin-approved Restaurante Marqués de Riscal or the Bistró 1860. For the most intimate look at the building, of course, you'll need to reserve a room for the night.

Elciego (Eltziego in Basque, and on some road signs) is located 25km northwest of Logroño via N232A.

Tours

Wine Tours (Vinos de los Herederos del Marqués de Riscal; ☑ 945 18 08 88; www.marquesderiscal.com; Hotel Marqués de Riscal, Calle Torrea 1, Elciego; tour €12) A winery offering guided visits; adjacent to the Hotel Marqués de Riscal.

Eating

Bistró 1860 (☑ 945 18 08 80; Hotel Marqués de Riscal, Calle Torrea 1, Elciego; mains €18-25) One of several stylish restaurants at the Hotel Marqués de Riscal.

Restaurante Marqués de Riscal (☑ 945 18 08 80; Hotel Marqués de Riscal, Calle Torrea 1, Elciego; mains €24-30) The elegant headlining restaurant at the Marqués de Riscal hotel and winery.

BILBAO, BASQUE COUNTRY & LA RIOJA LAGUARDIA

visits are by guided tour only and include a tasting.

Bodegas Ysios   WINERY
(☑ 941 27 99 00; www.ysios.com; Camino de la Hoya; per person €12; ☺ tours 11am, 1pm & 4pm Mon-Fri, 11am & 1pm Sat & Sun) Just a couple of kilometres to the north of Laguardia is the Bodegas Ysios. Designed by Santiago Calatrava as a 'temple dedicated to wine', it features an aluminium wave for a roof and a cedar exterior that blends into the mountainous backdrop. It looks its best at night when pools of light flow out of it.

Daily tours of the bodega are an excellent introduction to wine production; book ahead.

**Iglesia de Santa María
de los Reyes**   CHURCH
(☑ 945 60 08 45; Travesía Mayor 1; tour €2; ☺ guided tours 11.15am, 12.15pm, 1.15pm, 5pm and 6.30pm Mon-Fri in summer) The impressive

Iglesia de Santa María de los Reyes has a breathtaking late-14th-century Gothic doorway, adorned with beautiful sculptures of the disciples and other motifs. If the church doors are locked, pop down to the tourist office where you can get a key. Otherwise, guided tours (in Spanish) run throughout the day in summer.

🏃 Activities

Bodegas Palacio   WINERY
(☑ 945 60 01 51; www.bodegaspalacio.com; Carretera de Elciego; tour €5; ☺ tours 1pm, other times by appointment) Bodegas Palacio, only 1km from Laguardia on the Elciego road, runs tours in Spanish, English and German (Monday to Saturday). Reservations are not essential, but they are a good idea, especially out of season. The same bodega also runs excellent wine courses. Check the website for more information.

🛏 Sleeping

Laguardia is an increasingly popular week-end-break destination with Spaniards and French visitors. In season it may be wise to book ahead.

Posada Mayor de Migueloa
HISTORIC HOTEL €€

(☑945 600 187; www.mayordemigueloa.com; Mayor de Migueloa 20; s/d incl breakfast €99/105; ❋🛜) For the ultimate in gracious La Rioja living, this old mansion-hotel with its rickety rooms full of polished wood is irresistible. Under the hotel is a small wine bodega (guided visits for non-guests €5).

Castillo el Collado
HISTORIC HOTEL €€€

(☑945 62 12 00; www.hotelcollado.com; Paseo el Collado 1; d €125-185; 🛜) Like a whimsical Disney dream castle this place, which from the outside is all sturdy turrets and pretty flower gardens, is a truly unique and charming place to stay. Also onsite: a great restaurant, a cosy tavern, and a wine bar with stained glass windows overlooking the old walls of Laguardia, all open to the public.

Hospedería de los Parajes
HISTORIC HOTEL €€€

(☑945 62 11 30; www.hospederiadelosparajes.com; Calle Mayor 46-48; s/d from €121/132; ❋@🛜) Extraordinarily plush rooms that combine a bit of today with a dollop of yesteryear. Rooms are stuffed with antiques, cowskin rugs and ever-glaring statues. The beds are divinely comfortably, the showers have rustic stone floors and the service is top-notch.

🍴 Eating

★ Restaurante Amelibia
SPANISH €€

(☑945 62 12 07; www.restauranteamelibia.com; Barbacana 14; menú del día €17; ⊙1-3.30pm Sun-Mon & Wed-Thu, 1-3.30pm & 9-10.30pm Fri-Sat) This classy restaurant is one of Laguardia's highlights: stare out the windows at a view over the scorched plains and distant mountain ridges while dining on sublime traditional Spanish cuisine – the meat dishes in particular are of exquisitely high quality.

Castillo el Collado Restaurant
SPANISH €€

(www.hotelcollado.com; Paseo El Collado 1; menus from €25) There's an old-world feeling to the place, and classic Riojan dishes like roasted suckling pig. There's also an English-language menu, and, naturally, a great wine selection.

ℹ Information

Tourist Office (☑945 60 08 45; www.laguardia-alava.com; Calle Mayor 52; ⊙10am-2pm & 4-7pm Mon-Fri, 10am-2pm & 5-7pm Sat, 10.45am-2pm Sun) Has a list of local bodegas that can be visited.

ℹ Getting There & Away

Eight or nine daily buses leave Logroño for Vitoria (€8, 1½ hours), stopping in Laguardia (€3, 25 to 30 minutes) on the way. There's no bus station: buses stop at the covered shelters along the main road that runs through town, near the lookout point.

Cantabria & Asturias

Best Places to Eat

➡ Solórzano (p462)

➡ La Conveniente (p462)

➡ La Cabaña (p467)

➡ Gloria (p479)

➡ Arbidel (p484)

Best Places to Sleep

➡ Los Balcones del Arte (p462)

➡ Casa del Marqués (p469)

➡ La Posada de Babel (p485)

➡ La Casona de Amandi (p483)

➡ CAEaCLAVELES (p485)

Why Go?

You can traverse either of these two regions from north to south in little more than an hour. But don't. The coastline is a sequence of sheer cliffs, beautiful beaches and small fishing ports. Behind it, gorgeously green river valleys dotted with stone-built villages rise to the 2000m-plus mountain wall of the Cordillera Cantábrica, which reaches majestic heights in the Picos de Europa. The beauty is endless and ever-changing. The damp climate makes sure that you'll eat and drink well too: on offer are quality meat, local cheeses, and cider from Asturias' apple orchards, as well as the fruits of the sea. And travellers with a feel for history will be in their element: early humans painted some of the world's most magnificent prehistoric art at Altamira and elsewhere, and it was at Covadonga in Asturias that the seed of the Spanish nation first sprouted 1300 years ago.

When to Go
Oviedo

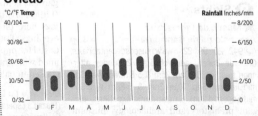

May, Jun & Sep	Late Jul	Late Aug
May, Jun & Sep Best time: temperatures are up, rainfall and prices are down, crowds are away.	**Late Jul** Santander's Semana Grande brings the summer fun.	**Late Aug** Join thousands of tipplers at Gijón's Fiesta de la Sidra Natural (Natural Cider Festival).

CANTABRIA

For modern travellers, Cantabria offers a bit of everything. The coastline is a sequence of soft cliffs, beautiful beaches and colourful fishing ports; summer seaside days are perfectly possible (unreliable weather permitting). The inland mountains – sliced up by deep, multibranched valleys connected only by steep passes – are sprinkled with sleepy towns and villages and prove a feast for the eyes, whether you drive the country roads or walk the trails.

Lively capital Santander provides a slice of urban life, with buzzing beaches and bodegas. Santillana del Mar and Comillas entice with their medieval and Modernista trappings. The prehistoric art of Altamira, El Castillo and Covalanas caves is some of the oldest and very best in the world, and Cantabria's rugged ranges culminate in the abrupt mountain walls of the Picos de Europa in the west.

Santander

POP 130,603

The belle-époque elegance of El Sardinero aside, modern Santander is not the most beautiful of cities. A huge fire raged through the centre back in 1941, leaving little that's old or quaint. But Cantabria's capital is an engaging one, nonetheless, making the most of its setting along the northern side of the handsome Bahía de Santander. It's a lively spot to spend a night or two, with fine urban beaches, busy shopping streets, a heaving bar and restaurant scene, plenty of surf, and some intriguing cultural attractions. It's a popular summer holiday resort for Spaniards.

◉ Sights

★ Museo de Prehistoria y Arqueología de Cantabria   MUSEUM

(☏942 20 99 22; www.museosdecantabria.es; Calle de Bailén; adult/child €5/2 Sunday afternoon free; ☺10.30am-2pm & 5-8.30pm Wed-Sun mid-Jun–mid-Sep, 10am-2pm & 5-8pm Wed-Sun mid-Sep–mid-Jun) Santander's excellent, elegant prehistory and archaeology museum showcases Cantabria's immense archaeological wealth, with explanatory matter in French, English and Spanish. The detailed, interactive multimedia displays range from early hominid remains to giant steles (stone disks) carved by the pre-Roman Cantabrians, a replica Roman patio, prehistoric cave art and the medieval Spanish kingdoms of Asturias and León.

★ Península de la Magdalena   PARK

(☺8am-9pm) At the eastern tip of the bay, this sprawling parkland is perfect for a stroll and popular with picnickers. Kids will enjoy the resident seals and penguins, the replica Spanish galleons, and the little train that choo-choos around the headland (adult/child €2.15/1.45). The views of nearby beaches across the crashing sea are sensational.

Palacio de la Magdalena   PALACE

(☏942 20 30 84; www.palaciomagdalena.com; Península de la Magdalena; tours €3; ☺tours hourly 11am-1pm & 4-6pm Mon-Fri, hourly 10am-noon Sat & Sun) The eclectically styled, English-inspired palace crowning the Península de la Magdalena was built between 1908 and 1912 as a gift from the city to the royal family, which used it every summer until 1930. Detailed 45-minute guided tours (in Spanish) lead you past oak floors, bronze chandeliers, surprisingly simple bedrooms, a chestnut-wood-carved staircase and the king's former study. Visits are reduced in summer, when the palace hosts the Universidad Internacional Menéndez Pelayo (www.uimp.es), a global get-together for specialists in all sorts of disciplines.

Jardines & Paseo de Pereda   PARK, PROMENADE

(Pereda's Gardens; Paseo de Pereda) The pretty, recently refurbished Jardines de Pereda are named after 19th-century Cantabrian writer José María de Pereda, whose seminal work, Escenas Montañesas, is sculpted here in bronze and stone.

The bayside promenade fronting these gardens continues east to the Puerto Chico (Little Port) marina. Half the city strolls or jogs here on summer (and, often, winter) evenings. Both Paseo de Pereda and Calle Castelar, opposite the Puerto Chico, are lined with grand buildings flaunting typical glassed-in balconies.

Mercado La Esperanza   MARKET

(Plaza La Esperanza; ☺8am-2pm & 5-7.30pm Mon-Fri, 8am-2pm Sat) Behind the city hall, in the western part of central Santander, you'll find the 19th-century cast-iron Mercado La Esperanza, a colourful market with masses of fish and seafood downstairs, and meat, cheese, fruit and orujo (firewater) from Potes (in the Picos de Europa) upstairs.

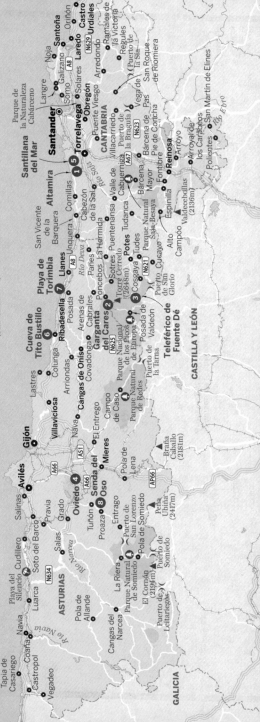

Cantabria & Asturias Highlights

1 Altamira (p470) Marvelling at the artistic genius of these renowned cave paintings.

2 Garganta del Cares (p499) Walking the dramatic gorge of Garganta del Cares.

3 Teleférico de Fuente Dé (p503) Riding the cable car to the superb heights of the Picos de Europa.

4 Oviedo (p476) Delighting in the grace of Oviedo's cathedral and hitting *el bulevar de la sidra*.

5 Santillana del Mar (p469) Letting this medieval beauty bewitch you with its charms.

6 Cueva de Tito Bustillo (p484) Admiring some of Spain's oldest and most exquisite cave art in Ribadesella.

7 Playa de Torimbia (p486) Bathing at this spectacular, secluded strand of golden sand.

8 Senda del Oso (p490) Cycling the course of a former mine railway and meeting its bears.

Santander

0 0
0.1 miles
200 m

Peninsula de la Magdalena (2km);
Escuela de Surf Sardinero (2.4km);
Playa del Sardinero (2.4km)

C Castelar
C Gamazo

Puerto Chico

C de Tetuán

C de San Emeterio

C de Casimiro Sainz

Paseo de Menéndez Pelayo

C de Bonifaz

11

13

C de la Peña Herbosa

C Gándara

C del Sol

C de Vallicergo

C de Santa Lucía

C de Lope de Vega

C de Hernán Cortés

C de Ataúlfo Argenta

Paseo de Pereda

Bahía de Santander

Estación Marítima

Los Reginas

Playa del Puntal (2.5km);
Playa de Somo (5km)

Pasaje Nieves

Pasaje Lituca

Plaza de Cañadío

10

12

C de Gómez Oreña

C de Daoíz y Velarde

Plaza de Pombo

Buses to El Sardinero

C del Río de la Pila

Arrabal

C del Medio

C de Marcelino Sanz de Sautuola

C de Bailén

Pasaje Inés

Paseo de Pereda

Museo de Prehistoria y Arqueología de Cantabria

C del Río de la Pila

C de San José

Pasaje Ana

1

4

Buses to El Sardinero

C Vista Alegre

C de Guevara

C de Rualasal

C de Juan de Herrera

C de San Francisco

C Aldeana

Plaza del Príncipe

C de Somorrostro

Plaza Alfonso XIII

C Cubo

Plaza la Esperanza

6

5

Av de Calvo Sotelo

C de

2 3

17

C del Jesús de Monasterio

Plaza del Obispo José Eguino y Trecu

C de Cádiz

C Navas de Tolosa

C de Méndez Núñez

C de Caldezón de la Barca

C de Antonio López

C de Cervantes

C de Cisneros

C de Gravina

C de Rubio

C Alta

C de Rodríguez

C Castilla

Bus Station

Train Station (Renfe)

Train Station (FEVE)

C Magallanes

8

C Túnel Burgos

Puente Viesgo (28km);
Santillana del Mar (28km)

(5km)

Santander

Catedral de la Asunción CATHEDRAL

(☑ 942 22 60 24; Plaza del Obispo José Eguino y Trecu; admission by donation; ⊙ 10am-1pm & 4.30-7pm Mon-Fri, to 8pm Sat, 10am-1.30pm & 5-9pm Sun) Santander's serene cathedral is composed of two Gothic churches, one above the other. The 14th-century **upper church**, off which is a 15th-century cloister, was extensively rebuilt after a 1941 fire, and contains the tomb of celebrated local scholar Marcelino Menéndez Pelayo. In the lower, 13th-century **Iglesia del Santísimo Cristo** (Iglesia Vieja; ☑ 942 21 15 63; Calle de Somorrostro; ⊙ 8am-1pm & 4-8pm Jun-Sep, 8am-1pm & 5-8pm Oct-May), glass floors reveal excavated remains of Roman Santander. Displayed nearby are silver vessels containing the skulls of the early Christian martyrs San Emeterio and San Celedonio, Santander's patron saints.

⛱ Beaches

Playa del Sardinero BEACH

El Sardinero's 1.5km-long strand of gorgeous golden sand faces the open sea, north of the Península de la Magdalena. It's backed by some of Santander's most expensive real estate, including emblematic early-20th-century creations such as the Gran Casino. Surfers emerge in force along Sardinero when the waves are right, mainly in autumn and winter, when they can reach 1.5m. Buses 1 and 2 (€1.30) run east to Sardinero from the Jardines de Pereda in the centre.

Playa del Puntal BEACH

A 2km-long finger of sand jutting out across the bay towards Santander, roughly opposite the Península de la Magdalena, El Puntal is idyllic on calm days (but beware the currents). A couple of popular *chiringuitos* (beach bars) open up here over summer. Weather permitting, passenger ferries (€4 return) sail over about every 30 minutes from 10.30am to 7.30pm, May to October, from the **Estación Marítima Los Reginas** (☑ 942 21 67 53; www.losreginas.com; Paseo Marítimo).

Playa de Somo BEACH

Across the bay from Santander, and just beyond Playa del Puntal (p461), Playa de Somo is a beautiful gold-tinged beach with, usually, pretty good surf. A year-round ferry (one way/return €2.70/4.85, 30 minutes) runs to Somo from the Estación Marítima Los Reginas (p461) every 30 or 60 minutes from 8.30am to 7.30pm.

🎓 Courses

Escuela de Surf Sardinero SURFING

(☑ 942 27 03 01; www.escueladesurfsardinero.com; Balneario de la Primera Playa del Sardinero; per person 2hr group class incl board, wetsuit & transport €30-35, board/wetsuit rental per day €25/12; ⊙ Mar-Nov) Perfectly placed in the middle of Playa del Sardinero, this well-organised surf school and shop offers surfing classes run in Spanish, English and French. Depending on conditions, sessions might run in Liencres, 10km west. SUP classes (two hours €30) are also available.

Escuela Cántabra de Surf SURFING

(☑ 942 51 06 15, 609 482823; www.escuelacantabra desurf.com; Calle Isla de Mouro 10, Somo; board/wetsuit rental per half-day €15/8, per person 2hr group class incl board & wetsuit €30; ⊙ daily mid-Mar–mid-Nov, weekends only mid-Nov–mid-Mar) Based in Somo, across the bay from central Santander, this well-established surf school has been leading surf-lovers into the waves for 25 years, with classes run in English, Spanish or Italian and a range of surf camps and courses. Also does SUP group sessions (two hours €50).

🎉 Festivals & Events

Festival Internacional de Santander MUSIC

(FIS; www.festivalsantander.com) Santander's sweeping summer musical season in August covers everything from opera, piano and jazz to ballet.

Semana Grande
FIESTA
(www.semanagrandesantander.com; ⊙late Jul)
Santander's big summer fiesta, a week of fun
around 25 July.

🛏 Sleeping

Hostal La Mexicana
HOSTAL €
(☑942 22 23 54; www.hostallamexicana.com; Calle
de Juan de Herrera 3; s €41-50, d €55-65, q €75-95;
🛜) A welcoming, well-kept and well-run
38-room *hostal* (budget hotel) on a mostly traffic-free shopping street in central
Santander. Rooms have a solid, old-fashioned
style full of florals, but they are perfectly
comfy. There are interconnecting rooms for
families. Breakfast (€3) available.

⭐ Los Balcones del Arte
BOUTIQUE HOTEL €€
(☑942 03 65 47; www.losbalconesdelarte.com;
5th fl, Plaza del Príncipe 2; 1-bedroom apt €90-140,
2-bedroom apt €120-190; P🛜) Four stunning
contemporary-design apartments grace the
top floor of this beautifully renovated, su-
percentral building, right beside the Plaza
Porticada. Each is impeccably designed in
its own elegant character, with antique furniture, fun fabrics, splashes of bold detail
and fully kitted-out kitchens (including Nespresso machines). Shimmery-blue snakeskin
wallpaper decorates one-bedroom 'Argenta';
four-person 'Puerto' features leopard-print
cushions, a gold-themed bedroom and a sea-
view balcony.

Jardín Secreto
BOUTIQUE HOTEL €€
(☑942 07 07 14; www.jardinsecretosantander.com;
Calle de Cisneros 37; r €55-80; ⊜🛜) Named
for its little back garden, this is a charming
six-room world of its own spread across a

WORTH A TRIP

THE CHEESE MAKER

From Selaya, 35km south of Santander,
signs direct you to family-run **Queseria
La Jarradilla** (☑942 59 03 42, 652
779660; www.quesoslajarradilla.com; Barce-
nilla 246, Tezanos de Villacarriedo; ⊙tours
noon Sat, shop 11am-2pm & 4.30-6.30pm
Mon-Sat, 11am-2pm Sun), where you can
taste, purchase and find out all about
the soft, young cheeses of the Valles
Pasiegos (the Pas, Pisueña and Miera
valleys), one of Cantabria's most traditional rural areas. Tours run once a week
and can be in English (depending on
demand), but the shop is usually open.

---

two-centuries-old house near the city centre.
It's run by an on-the-ball brother-and-sister
team, and designed by their mother in a
stylish, contemporary blend of silvers, greys
and pastels with exposed stone, brick and
wood. Top-floor rooms 3 and 4 have tiny
garden-facing terraces.

Hotel Bahía
HOTEL €€€
(☑942 20 50 00; www.hotelbahiasantander.com;
Calle de Cádiz 22; s €79-169, d €89-199, q €119-219;
P❄🛜) Central Santander's top hotel, opposite the UK ferry port, is looking exquisite after a refurb. Large, very comfortable
rooms are done up in sparkly silvers and
creams, with elegant, minimalist style and
rich floor carpets. Some have sea views;
others overlook the cathedral or the street
below. Cosy kids' bunks are a nice touch for
family rooms and service is professional
and friendly.

🍴 Eating

Casa Lita
TAPAS €
(☑942 36 48 30; www.casalita.es; Paseo de Pereda
37; pinchos €2.50; ⊙noon-late) Pack into 'the
house of *pinchos*' amid crowds of stylish
santanderinos and brick walls plastered
with early-20th-century Santander posters. You'll be lucky to score a table. Classic
Iberian ham and local cheese *raciones* put
in an appearance, while inventive contemporary creations, such as miniburgers and
pumpkin-and-leek quiche, keep flavours
exciting. There are even a few Cantabrian
artisan beers.

⭐ Solórzano
TAPAS, CANTABRIAN €€
(☑942 22 27 24; www.barsolorzano.com; Calle de
la Peña Herbosa 17; raciones €5-14; ⊙12.30-4pm
& 8.30-11.30pm Mon & Wed-Fri, 12.30pm-late Sat,
12.30-4pm Sun) Between slinky red booths,
mirrored walls and black-and-white tiled
floors, always-busy Solórzano serves up simple yet elegantly presented Cantabrian *raciones* to a soothing jazz soundtrack. Local
cheeses arrive on wax paper and the house
chips feature *mejillones* (mussels). This self-
styled *vermuteria* also knocks up luscious
liquid mixes starring artisan vermouth from
all over Spain.

⭐ La Conveniente
TAPAS, TABLAS €€
(☑942 21 28 87; Calle de Gómez Oreña 9; raciones
& tablas €6-20; ⊙7pm-midnight Mon-Sat) This
cavernous bodega has soaring stone walls,
wooden pillars and more wine bottles than
you'll ever have seen in one place. Squeeze

WHAT'S COOKING IN CANTABRIA & ASTURIAS?

The most traditional Cantabrian and Asturian food is simple peasant fare, fuelled by the surrounding mountains and sea. Green mountain pastures yield not only good meats but a whole array of tasty cheeses, while fresh seafood abounds in the Bay of Biscay. Meat-eaters will be in their element, although vegetarians might struggle.

Cocido montañés Inland Cantabria's dish par excellence: a filling stew of white beans, cabbage, potato, chorizo, black pudding and, sometimes, port.

Fabada asturiana No dish better represents Asturias' taste for simplicity than the humble *fabada*, a hearty bean dish jazzed up with meat and sausage. For a taste of this classic favourite, head to Oviedo's Gloria (p479).

Ultra-tangy blue cheeses from the Picos de Europa King of Asturian cheeses is the powerful – but surprisingly moreish – bluey-green *queso de Cabrales*, made from untreated cow's milk, or a blend of cow's and goat's and sheep's milk, and matured in mountain caves. It often pops up in meat sauces or poured on top of potatoes (*patatas al Cabrales*). To sample local cheeses, order a *tabla de quesos* (platter of cheeses) at any sophisticated city eatery.

Seafood There is a wealth of fresh seafood in Cantabria and Asturias, while inland rivers provide trout, salmon and eels. You can go with good old, top-quality traditional fish preparations or explore a world of 'new concept' seafood at the Real Balneario de Salinas (p487), near Avilés.

Cachopo Asturias' *cachopo* (breaded veal stuffed with ham, cheese and vegetables) is a carnivore's dream. Dig in at Tierra Astur (p479) in Oviedo.

CANTABRIA & ASTURIAS SANTANDER

into the tramlike front enclosure, line up for the vast dining room or just snack at the bar. The food offerings are straightforward – *tablas* (platters) of cheese, *embutidos* (sausages), ham, pâtés – and servings are generous. Arrive by 8.30pm for a table.

Cañadío CONTEMPORARY CANTABRIAN €€€
(942 31 41 49; www.restaurantecanadio.com; Calle de Gómez Oreña 15; raciones €9-14, mains €18-25; ☺1-4pm & 9pm-midnight Mon-Sat; 🐾) A tastefully contemporary spot with art on the red walls, comfy booths and timber floors, Cañadío offers top-notch creative cooking with local inspiration. Hake is prepared in a variety of styles, the deep-fried goat's cheese salad is delicious and there's usually a traditional Cantabrian special. Or you can join the crowds in the front bar for very tempting *pinchos*.

🍷 Drinking & Nightlife

Plaza de Cañadío and Calles de Daoíz y Velarde and Hernán Cortés have plenty of popular *bares de copas* (drinks bars), where you can chat over beer, cocktails, spirits and wine. Calle de Santa Lucía, Calle del Sol and, in particular, the upper half of Calle del Río de la Pila teem with more bohemian bars. Paseo de Pereda and its eastward continuation, Calle Castelar, are dotted with cafes.

ℹ️ Information

Oficina de Turismo de Cantabria (942 31 07 08; www.turismodecantabria.com; Calle de Hernán Cortés 4; ☺9am-9pm) Inside the Mercado del Este.

Oficina de Turismo Municipal (☎942 20 30 00; www.santanderspain.info; Jardines de Pereda; ☺9am-9pm Jun-Sep, to 7pm Mon-Fri, 10am-7pm Sat, 10am-2pm Sun Oct-May) A summer branch operates at El Sardinero mid-June to mid-September.

ℹ️ Getting There & Away

AIR

Santander airport (942 20 21 00; www.aena.es; Avenida de Parayas) is 5km south of town, at Parayas. Half-hourly buses run to/from Santander's bus station (€2.50, 15 minutes) between 6.30am and 11pm daily.

Airlines and destinations:

Iberia (www.iberia.com) Madrid.

Ryanair (www.ryanair.com) Barcelona, Brussels (Charleroi), Dublin, Edinburgh, London (Stansted), Málaga, Milan (Bergamo), Rome (Ciampino).

Vueling (www.vueling.com) Barcelona.

BOAT

Brittany Ferries (www.brittany-ferries.co.uk) runs three weekly car ferries, including one no-frills service, from Portsmouth, UK (24 to 32 hours), and one from Plymouth, UK (20 hours). Fares vary enormously. A standard return trip for two adults and a car, with two-berth interior cabins, booked in February, costs around UK£900 for travel in July or August, or UK£550 in October, from either UK port. Taking the no-frills Portsmouth ferry, a similar deal (also with two-berth interior cabins), costs approximately UK£700 for July and UK£380 for October.

BUS

ALSA (✆902 422242; www.alsa.es) is the major company operating from Santander's **bus station** (✆942 21 19 95; Calle Navas de Tolosa).

DESTINATION	FARE	DURATION	MINIMUM FREQUENCY
Bilbao	€7-15	1¼-1¾hr	16 daily
Madrid	€25-36	5-6¼hr	6 daily
Oviedo	€8-28	2¼-3¼hr	13 daily
San Sebastián	€13-29	2½-3hr	11 daily

TRAIN

There are two train stations, beside each other on Calle de Rodríguez: **FEVE** (✆902 320320; www.renfe.com/viajeros/feve) serves destinations along Spain's northern coast, while **Renfe** (✆902 320320; www.renfe.com) serves destinations to the south.

Bilbao (€8.90, three hours, three FEVE trains daily)

Madrid (€26 to €43, four to six hours, three to five long-distance Renfe trains daily) Via Reinosa, Palencia and Valladolid.

Oviedo (€16, five hours, two FEVE trains daily) Via San Vicente de la Barquera, Llanes, Ribadesella and Arriondas.

❶ Getting Around

BOAT

Regular ferries link central Santander with the beaches of El Puntal (return €4) and Somo (one way/return €2.70/4.85), on the opposite side of the bay, departing from the **Estación Marítima Los Reginas** (p461).

BUS

Central Santander is easy to explore on foot, but urban buses 1 and 2 are handy for getting to/from El Sardinero (€1.30); they stop on Avenida de Calvo Sotelo near the main post office and at the Jardines de Pereda.

Around Santander

There are some worthwhile attractions around Santander, all within easy reach of the city: beautiful surf-mad beaches, one of Spain's finest wildlife parks and some of the world's oldest prehistoric cave art.

Parque de la Naturaleza Cabárceno   ZOO
(✆942 56 37 36, 902 210112; www.parquede cabarceno.com; adult/child €30/19; ⊙9.30am-7pm Jul & Aug, to 6pm Mar-Jun, Sep, Oct & weekends, to 5pm weekdays Nov-Feb; ⓟ) This open-air zoo, 17km south of Santander, is a curious but successful experiment: a free-range home on the site of former open-cut mines for everything from rhinos, wallabies, gorillas, dromedaries and lynxes to endangered Cantabrian brown bears. You'll need a car and about three hours or so to tour its 14km of roadways. The park's much-awaited *teleférico* (cable car) is due to open in early 2016. From

---

WORTH A TRIP

CUEVAS DE MONTE CASTILLO

Of the four Unesco World Heritage–listed Cuevas de Monte Castillo (✆942 59 84 25; http://cuevas.culturadecantabria.com; adult/child per cave €3/1.50; ⊙9.30am-2.30pm & 3.30-7.30pm Tue-Sun, reduced hours & closed Tue mid-Sep–mid-Jun; ⓟ), 2km south of Puente Viesgo, two – El Castillo and Las Monedas – are open for 45-minute guided visits (in Spanish). Booking ahead is highly recommended, especially for the more spectacular El Castillo, which contains Europe's most ancient cave art. As you explore 500m into the cave, you'll see art almost as breathtaking as that of Cantabria's famous Cueva de Altamira – and unlike at Altamira, this is the genuine article rather than a replica.

Five to eight daily buses run to Puente Viesgo from Santander (€2.30, 40 minutes).

BEACHES AROUND SANTANDER

Playas de Langre (P) The two gorgeously wild golden beaches of Langre are backed by cliffs topped with rolling green fields, and often have surfable waves. Most beach-goers head for Langre La Grande, although the smaller adjacent Langre La Pequeña is more protected. It's a 30km drive east of Santander: round the bay to Somo, then head east on the CA141 for 4km, then 2km north to Langre; the beaches (signposted) are another 500m northeast.

Playa de Valdearenas (Playa de Liencres; P) Protected by the pine-filled Parque Natural de las Dunas de Liencres, this exquisite 3km-long, gold-tinged beach has a delightful natural feel and is hugely popular with surfers and beach-lovers alike. It's a 16km drive west of Santander. Take the A67 west for 11km, then the CA231 north for 4km; it's signposted.

Santander, take the N623 towards Burgos, then the S30 southeast and follow signs to Cabárceno.

Eastern Cantabria

The 95km stretch of coast between Santander and Bilbao (Basque Country) offers citizens of both cities several seaside escapes. While the towns are less attractive than those on Cantabria's western coast, some of the beaches are divine. Inland, a sea of green awaits in the Valles Pasiegos and the Alto Asón district of southeastern Cantabria.

Santoña

POP 10,811

The laid-back fishing port of Santoña, 42km east of Santander, is famed for its anchovies, which are bottled or tinned here with olive oil to preserve them. North of town lies the beautiful Playa de Berria.

◉ Sights

Playa de Berria   BEACH

Head 2.5km north along the CA141 to Playa de Berria, a magnificent sweep of blonde sand and crashing surf on the open sea, linked to Santoña by frequent buses (€1.45, five minutes).

Fuerte de San Martín   FORTRESS

(Calle Monte; ⊙ 11am-2pm & 6-9pm mid-Jun–Aug) Santoña is dominated by two fortresses, the most accessible of which is the imposing horseshoe-shaped Fuerte de San Martín, built in the early 17th century but much remodelled since. It's at the eastern end of the seafront promenade. Further east, reached by foot, is the abandoned Fuerte de San Carlos.

🛏 Sleeping

Hotel Juan de la Cosa   HOTEL €€

(☎ 942 66 12 38; www.hoteljuandelacosa.com; Playa de Berria 14; s €57-120, d €62-134, q €93-170; ⊙ Easter-Oct; P ❄ ☎ ☒) Hotel Juan de la Cosa may be in an unsympathetic-looking building, but about two-thirds of its spacious, blue-hued, maritime-inspired rooms have beach views. It also offers a good restaurant with a seafood emphasis and plain self-catering apartments designed for families.

❶ Information

Oficina de Turismo de Santoña (☎ 942 66 00 66; www.turismosantona.com; Calle Santander 5; ⊙ 10am-2pm & 5-8pm mid-Jun–mid-Sep, 9am-4pm Mon-Fri, 10am-2pm Sat mid-Sep–mid-Jun) A summer information booth also opens on the seafront promenade from mid-June to August.

❶ Getting There & Away

BOAT

From March to November, **Excursiones Marítimas** (☎ 637 584164; www.excursiones maritimas.com; ⊙ 9am-9pm mid-Jul–mid-Sep, 9am-7pm Mon-Fri, to 8pm Sat & Sun Mar–mid-Jul & mid-Sep–Nov) runs a shuttle ferry from Santoña across the estuary to the northwestern end of Laredo beach (return €3.50). From June to September, there's also a ferry to central Laredo several times daily (return €10).

BUS

ALSA (☎ 902 422242; www.alsa.es) and **Autobuses Palomera** (☎ 942 88 06 11; www.autobusespalomera.com) serve Santoña's **bus station** (Calle Marinos de Santoña). Sixteen buses run between Santoña and Santander

(€4.25, one hour) Monday to Friday; 10 on Saturday, eight on Sunday. There are also seven to 13 buses daily to Laredo (€1.80, 30 minutes), from where there are services to Castro Urdiales.

Castro Urdiales & Around

POP 25,137

Just 31km west of Bilbao (Basque Country) and 26km east of Laredo, Castro Urdiales is a lively, attractive seafront town with a pretty harbour, a tangle of narrow lanes making up its medieval core and a dramatically Gothic church perched above. The town played an important part as one of the Cuatro Villas de la Costa, a group of four major medieval ports that were united in 1779 as Cantabria province (the others were Santander, Laredo and San Vicente de la Barquera).

Off the A8 motorway en route between Laredo and Castro Urdiales, you'll find Playas de Oriñón and Sonabia, two golden beaches that are well worth a stop. Both are accessed by the same minor road; Sonabia (not signposted) is 1.7km beyond Oriñón.

◎ Sights

Iglesia de Santa María de la Asunción
CHURCH

(⊙10am-noon & 4-6pm Mon-Fri, 10am-noon Sat, hours vary) The haughty Gothic jumble that is the Iglesia de Santa María de la Asunción stands out spectacularly above Castro Urdiales' harbour. It was built in 1208, but additions continued until almost the 20th century. The church shares its little headland with the ruins of what was for centuries the town's defensive bastion, now support-

ing a lighthouse, and a much-reworked one-arched medieval bridge.

🛏 Sleeping & Eating

Ardigales 11
BOUTIQUE HOTEL €€

(☑942 78 16 16; www.pensionardigales11.com; Calle de Ardigales 11; s €48-56, d €70-90, q €100-120; ❈ �🀫) Behind a solid stone exterior, on old-town Castro's main bar street, hides this somewhat futuristic hotel, with 11 slick modern rooms decked out in tasteful blacks, whites and greys. Downstairs, soft-neon lights brighten up the cosy lounge area, complete with its own bar.

Hotel Las Rocas
HOTEL €€

(☑942 86 04 00; www.lasrocashotel.com; Calle Flavióbriga 1; s/d €90/120; P ❈ 🀫) Just back from Playa de Brazomar, long-standing Las Rocas offers contemporary-style rooms adorned with floral fabrics, soft pastels and a touch of colourful art, many with large glassed-in galleries and beach views. Breakfast (€11) is a big buffet spread with extra dishes cooked to order.

ⓘ Information

Oficina de Turismo (☑942 87 15 12; www.turismocastrourdiales.net; Parque Amestoy; ⊙9am-9pm Jul & Aug, 9.30am-2pm & 4-7pm Sep-Jun) On the seafront.

ⓘ Getting There & Away

ALSA (☑902 422242; www.alsa.es) runs at least eight buses daily to Santander (€6.40, one hour) via Laredo from Castro's **bus station** (Calle Leonardo Rucabado 42). Buses to Bilbao (€2.75, 45 minutes) leave half-hourly from 6am to 10pm (hourly on Sunday), making various

WORTH A TRIP

LAREDO

Laredo, 46km east of Santander, is a ridiculously popular Spanish beach resort. Its sandy, 5km-long Playa de Salvé, across the bay from Santoña, is backed by ugly 20th-century building blocks. But, at the eastern end of town, the evocative cobbled streets of the old Puebla Vieja slope down dramatically from La Atalaya hill, packed with busy bars and restaurants.

At the eastern end of town is a **tourist office** (☑942 61 10 96; www.laredoturismo.es; Alameda Miramar; ⊙9am-9pm Jul–mid-Sep, 9.30am-2pm & 4-7pm mid-Sep–Jun).

Getting There & Away

ALSA (☑902 422242; www.alsa.es) runs at least 17 buses daily between Laredo and Santander (€4.25, 40 minutes) and Bilbao (€3.59, 50 minutes) from the **bus station** (Calle Reconquista de Sevilla 1). There are also at least 15 buses daily to Castro Urdiales (€2.15, 15 to 40 minutes).

stops including at Calle La Ronda 52, half a block from the seafront.

There's no public transport to Playas de Oriñón and Sonabia, so you'll need your own wheels.

Southern Cantabria

Fine panoramas of high peaks and deep river valleys flanked by patchwork quilts of green await the traveller venturing into the Cantabrian interior. Every imaginable shade of green seems to have been employed to set this stage, strewn with warm stone villages and held together by a network of narrow country roads. The area's major town is Reinosa.

Reinosa & Around

POP 9605 / ELEV 851M

Southern Cantabria's main town, 70km south of Santander, is an unexceptional place, but Reinosa has plenty of curiosities nearby, including the remains of Cantabria's most important Roman settlement, an impressive collection of rock-cut and Romanesque churches, and the source of one of Spain's mightiest rivers, the Río Ebro.

◉ Sights

Nacimiento del Río Ebro SPRING

(Fontibre; ℗) Spain's most voluminous river, the Río Ebro, starts life at this serene tree-shaded spring, 5km northwest of Reinosa. It's a stunning, peaceful spot, with deep-turquoise water, a tiny shrine and a few ducks splashing around. From here, the Ebro meanders 930km southeast via Logroño (La Rioja) and Zaragoza (Aragón) to meet the Mediterranean.

Colegiata de San Pedro CHURCH

(☑ 636 268256; Cervatos; ◷ by appointment) The 12th-century Colegiata de San Pedro in Cervatos, 5km south of Reinosa, is one of Cantabria's finest Romanesque churches, with rare erotic carvings on its corbels.

Arqueositio Cántabro-Romano de Camesa-Rebolledo ARCHAEOLOGICAL SITE

(☑ 942 59 84 25; http://centros.culturadecantabria. com; Mataporquera; combined ticket with Julióbriga adult/child €3/1.50; ◷ 10.30am-2.30pm & 3.30-7.30pm Tue-Sun mid-Jun–mid-Sep, reduced hours mid-Sep–mid-Jun; ℗) This fascinating triple-epoch excavation site of a Roman villa buried beneath a Visigothic necropolis and a medieval graveyard sits just outside Mata-

porquera, 20km south of Reinosa. Visits are by 45-minute guided tour, in Spanish.

Julióbriga RUIN

(☑ 942 59 84 25; http://centros.culturade cantabria.com; Retortillo; adult/child €3/1.50; ◷ 10.30am-2.30pm & 3.30-7.30pm Tue-Sun mid-Jun–mid-Sep, reduced hours mid-Sep–mid-Jun; ℗) The remains of Cantabria's most significant Roman town, Julióbriga, lie 5km east of Reinoisa. Julióbriga peaked in the 1st and 2nd centuries, before being abandoned in the 3rd century. Guided visits lead you through the Museo Domus, a full-scale recreation of a Roman house, but you're free to explore the rest of the site, including its 12th-century Romanesque church, independently.

🛏 Sleeping & Eating

Villa Rosa HOTEL €€

(☑ 942 75 47 47; www.villarosa.com; Calle de los Héroes de la Guardia Civil 4; s/d incl breakfast €50/70; 🛜) Set in a charmingly restored, century-old Modernista building, pale-pink Villa Rosa looks more like something you'd expect to see in central Europe. Most of its 12 very comfy and colourful rooms have an inviting period feel (with suitably modern facilities). Rates include a one-hour spa session. It's handily close to the train and bus stations, at the southwestern end of Reinosa.

La Cabaña CONTEMPORARY CANTABRIAN €€

(☑ 942 75 08 37; Calle de Juan José Ruano 4; mains €8-20; ◷ 1.30-4pm & 9-11pm Wed-Sun, 1.30-4pm Mon; 🌱) A Madrid-trained chef heads up this friendly eatery specialising in fun local-inspired concoctions that manage to be inventive without turning excessively modern. Lovingly created dishes focus on meat grills, huge salads and delicious homemade pastas (a rare find in these parts). The ravioli is a four-cheese extravaganza, with pungent Picos de Europa cheeses, while mushrooms arrive battered in locally loved Orzales bread.

ⓘ Information

Oficina de Turismo (☑ 942 75 52 15; www.sur decantabria.es; Avenida del Puente de Carlos III 23; ◷ 9.30am-2.30pm & 4-7pm Jul & Aug, 9.30am-2.30pm Mon-Sat Sep-Jun)

ⓘ Getting There & Away

BUS

At least six daily buses run between Reinosa's **bus station** (Avenida de Castilla) and Santander (€6.50, 1¼ hours). Two daily buses head south to

CANTABRIA & ASTURIAS CANTABRIA & ASTURIAS REINOSA & AROUND

TOURING THE EBRO'S ROCK-CUT CHURCHES

Spain's most voluminous river, the Ebro, rises at Fontibre (5km northwest of Reinosa), fills the Embalse del Ebro reservoir to the east, then meanders south and east into Castilla y León. Its course is strung with some fascinating, picturesque stops. You can follow it on the GR99 long-distance footpath or on minor roads out of Reinosa.

From Reinosa, head east along the CA730 – visiting Roman Julióbriga (p467) en route, if you fancy – to Arroyo, where you turn south on the CA735 and follow signs to the Santuario de Montesclaros (☎942 77 05 50; Ctra CA741; ⏱hours vary; P), a monastery with a fine site overlooking the Ebro valley and a history going back to at least the 12th century. From here, follow the CA741 southwest to Arroyal de los Carabeos (via a fantastic viewpoint across to the monastery), then head south on the CA272 to a roundabout where it meets the CA273. Nine kilometres west on the CA273 is the remarkable Iglesia Rupestre de Santa María de Valverde (Santa María de Valverde; ⏱10am-2pm & 4-7pm Tue-Sun mid-Jun–mid-Sep, Mass 1pm Sun mid-Sep–mid-Jun). This beautiful, multiarched church, hewn from the living rock, is the most impressive of several *iglesias rupestres* (rock-cut churches) in this area, dating from probably the 7th to 10th centuries, the early days of Christianity in the region. Beside the church, the Centro de Interpretación del Rupestre (☎942 77 61 46; Santa María de Valverde; adult/child €1/free; ⏱10am-2pm & 4-7pm Tue-Sun mid-Jun–mid-Sep, reduced hours rest of year) tells the story of the area's curious rock-church phenomenon through photos, maps, video and multimedia – well worth a visit, even if you don't understand Spanish, and full of useful information. From here, head back east and continue to Campo de Ebro, where the tiny rock-cut Ermita de Santa Eulalia is hidden behind a 17th-century church beside the main road. Just 3km east lies Polientes, the area's biggest village, which has a bank, petrol station (self-service with credit cards only) and a few places to stay, of which the pick is homey, flower-filled Posada El Cuartelillo Viejo (☎942 77 61 51; www.elcuartelilloviejo.com; Ctra General 31, Polientes; r incl breakfast €50-65; ⏱Apr-Oct; 🖥).

East of Polientes, along the CA275, you'll find the finest of the area's other rock-cut churches. First comes a little rock-cut roadside church in Cadalso, then the dramatic two-level church at Arroyuelos. Across the Ebro from Arroyuelos, San Martín de Elines is well worth a detour for its exquisite Romanesque church. Finally, the small but wonderfully sited El Tobazo cave-church is part of a small group of caves towards the top of the Ebro gorge east of Arroyuelos. To find it, cross the bridge into Villaescusa del Ebro, 2.5km east of Arroyuelos, turn immediately left and follow the track for 900m to a grassy clearing on the right. From here you have a 700m uphill walk, starting from the far corner of the clearing. A beautiful waterfall (appearing as a moss-covered, cave-pocked cliff after prolonged dry weather) comes into view about halfway up, with the cave-church just above it to the right.

Except for Santa María in July and August, all these churches are usually locked (though they're striking from the outside too). You'll need to contact the helpful Oficina de Turismo de Valderredible (☎942 77 61 46; www.valderredible.es; Avenida de Cantabria; ⏱10am-2pm & 4.30-8.30pm Mon-Sat, 10am-2pm Sun) in Polientes in advance to arrange visits.

From Villaescusa del Ebro, the CA275 continues along the Ebro gorge to Orbaneja del Castillo in Castilla y León.

Palencia (€6.85, two hours), Valladolid (€9.32, 2¾ hours), Salamanca (€15, two hours) and Madrid (€30, five hours).

TRAIN

Six daily Renfe *cercanías* (suburban trains) go between Reinosa and Santander (€5.15, 1½ hours). A few daily trains go south to Palencia, Valladolid, Salamanca and Madrid.

ℹ Getting Around

The best (and, usually, only) way to visit the main sights in the area is with your own vehicle.

Western Cantabria

Cantabria's most exquisite (and most popular) villages are strung like pearls across the green-cloaked coastline west of Santander.

First comes medieval beauty Santillana del Mar, with the prehistoric wonders of the Cueva de Altamira closeby; then Comillas and its unexpected Modernista architecture; and, finally, handsome San Vicente de la Barquera, with its pretty port.

Santillana del Mar

POP 980

They say Santillana is the town of the three lies – not holy (santi), flat (llana) or by the sea (del mar). This medieval jewel is in such a perfect state of preservation, with its bright cobbled streets, flower-filled balconies and tanned stone and brick buildings huddling in a muddle of centuries of history, that it seems too good to be true. It's a film set, surely? Well, no. People still live here, passing their grand precious houses down from generation to generation. In summer, the streets get busy with curious visitors.

Strict town-planning rules were first introduced back in 1575, and today they include the stipulation that only residents or guests in hotels with garages may bring vehicles into the old heart of town. Other hotel guests may drive to unload luggage and must then return to the car park at the town entrance.

Santillana is a bijou in its own right, but also makes the obvious base for visiting nearby Altamira (p470).

◎ Sights

Colegiata de Santa Juliana　　CHURCH
(Plaza del Abad Francisco Navarro; adult/child €3/free; ◷10am-1.30pm & 4-7.30pm, closed Mon Oct-Jun) A stroll along Santillana's cobbled main street, past solemn 15th- to 18th-century nobles' houses, leads you to this beautiful 12th-century Romanesque ex-monastery. The big drawcard is the cloister, a formidable storehouse of Romanesque handiwork, with the capitals of its columns finely carved into a huge variety of figures. The monastery originally grew up around the relics of Santa Juliana, a 3rd-century Christian martyr from Turkey (and the real source of the name Santillana), whose sepulchre stands in the centre of the church.

⌂ Sleeping

★ Casa del Organista　　HOTEL €€
(☑942 84 03 52; www.casadelorganista.com; Calle de Los Hornos 4; s €65-75, d €80-95; ◷closed 1st half Jan; ℗☜) The 14 rooms at this elegant 18th-century house, once home to the Colegiata de Santa Juliana's organist, are particularly attractive, with plush rugs, antique furniture and plenty of exposed oak beams and stonework. Some have balconies looking towards the colegiata or across red-tiled roofs. Expect a warm welcome and excellent breakfasts (€6).

La Casona de los Güelitos　　RURAL HOTEL €€
(☑942 82 19 15; www.lacasonadelosguelitos.com; Barrio Vispieres 8; r €70-105; ℗☜) This wonderfully welcoming, family-run hotel occupies a gorgeously restored 17th-century house adorned with tangles of bougainvillea, 2.5km south of Santillana. Each of the 11 homey, delicately styled rooms bursts with a statement colour, incorporating original wood and stone features and pretty countryside views. Hot-red room 9, with its private balcony, perches above the entrance. Excellent breakfasts (€5) involve delicious multi-flavoured oven-fresh breads.

★ Casa del Marqués　　HISTORIC HOTEL €€€
(☑942 81 88 88; www.hotelcasadelmarques.com; Calle del Cantón 24; r €85-190; ◷early Mar-early Dec; ℗❋☜) Feel like the lord or lady of the manor in this 15th-century Gothic mansion, once home to the Marqués de Santillana. Exposed timber beams, thick stone walls and cool terracotta floors contribute to the atmosphere of the 15 sumptuous, all different rooms (some surprisingly modern). Three 1st-floor chambers overlook gorgeous gardens. The owners are proud of their 700-year-old banister, made from a single tree.

✗ Eating

Los Blasones　　CANTABRIAN €€
(☑942 81 80 70; Plaza La Gándara 8; tapas €2.50, mains €16-24; ◷1-4pm & 8-10.30pm Mar-Sep, 1-4pm Sat-Thu Oct-Feb) A warm yellow dining room lined with chestnut wood, Los Blasones has been proudly dishing up the usual Cantabrian selection since 1970. Hearty offerings from the open-plan kitchen include cocido montañés, giant beef chops and fresh fish of the day, plus a choice of three-course set menus (€16 to €25).

Restaurante Gran Duque　　CANTABRIAN €€
(☑942 84 03 86; www.granduque.com; Calle del Escultor Jesús Otero 7; mains €15-19; ◷1-3.30pm & 8-10.30pm, closed Sun & Mon lunch Sep-May) The food is high-quality local fare and what sets it apart is the setting, a grand stone house

with noble trappings and lovely decorative touches such as the exposed brick and beams. There's a reasonable balance of surf and turf options including *mariscadas* for two (seafood feasts; from €50) and a decent €19 *menú del día,* available for lunch and dinner.

ℹ Information

Oficina Regional de Turismo (☑ 942 81 82 51, 942 81 88 12; Calle del Escultor Jesús Otero; ☺ 9am-9pm Jul–mid-Sep, 9.30am-2pm & 4-7pm mid-Sep–Jun)

ℹ Getting There & Away

Autobuses La Cantábrica (☑ 942 72 08 22; www.lacantabrica.net) runs three or more daily buses from Santander to Santillana (€2.65, 40 minutes), continuing to Comillas (20 minutes) and San Vicente de la Barquera (40 minutes). Buses stop by Campo del Revolgo, just south of the main road.

Altamira

Spain's finest prehistoric art, the wonderful paintings of bison, horses, deer and other animals in the Cueva de Altamira, 2.5km southwest of Santillana del Mar, was discovered in 1879 by Cantabrian historian and scientist Marcelino Sanz de Sautuola and his eight-year-old daughter María Justina. By 2002, Altamira had attracted so many visitors that the cave was closed to prevent deterioration of the art, but a replica cave in the museum here now enables everyone to appreciate the inspired, 13,000- to 35,000-year-old paintings. These magical carbon-and-ochre illustrations are particularly special for depicting completely coloured-in beasts, rather than animal outlines (as in other Cantabrian caves).

In 2014 the Altamira authorities started trialling experimental visits into the real Altamira cave, the first time that the general public had been allowed into the original cave since 2002. The trials have proved a huge success and now, each Friday morning, five lucky visitors are randomly selected to enter the real cave for 37 minutes, on the same day. People entering the museum before 10.30am on Friday will be offered an application form if interested.

The much-awaited 2016 film *Altamira,* starring Antonio Banderas as Sautuola, tells the story of this discovery and the ensuing controversy over the paintings' authenticity.

◉ Sights

★ **Museo de Altamira**   MUSEUM
(☑ 942 81 88 15; http://museodealtamira.mcu.es; Avenida Marcelino Sanz de Sautuola, Santillana del Mar; adult/child, EU senior or EU student €3/free, Sun, from 2.30pm Sat free; ☺ 9.30am-8pm Tue-Sat May-Oct, to 6pm Tue-Sat Nov-Apr, to 3pm Sun & holidays year-round; P ♿) The museum's highlight is the Neocueva, a dazzling, full-sized re-creation of the real Cueva de Altamira's most interesting chamber, the Sala de Polícromos (Polychrome Hall), which is covered in exquisite 15,000-year-old ochre-and-black bison paintings created using the natural rock relief. Other excellent English- and Spanish-language displays cover prehistoric humanity and cave art around the world, from Altamira to Australia. The museum is incredibly popular (264,000 visitors in 2015), so it's best to reserve tickets in advance, especially for Easter, July, August and September.

⌂ Sleeping

The most obvious base for exploring Altamira is beautiful, cobbled Santillana del Mar, 2.5km northeast, which has an excellent array of accommodation mostly set inside grand historical homes.

ℹ Getting There & Away

Those without vehicles must walk or take a taxi (€5) to Altamira from Santillana del Mar, 2.5km northeast.

Comillas

POP 1818

Sixteen kilometres west of Santillana through verdant countryside, Comillas is set across hilltops crowned by some of the most original and beautiful buildings in Cantabria. For these, the town is indebted to the first Marqués de Comillas (1817–1883), who was born here as plain Antonio López, made a fortune in Cuba as a tobacco planter, shipowner, banker and slave trader, and then returned to commission leading Catalan Modernista architects to jazz up his hometown in the late 19th century. This, in turn, prompted the construction of other quirky mansions in Comillas. And there's more too: a lovely golden beach, a tiny fishing port and a pleasant, cobbled old centre.

⊙ Sights

★ Palacio de Sobrellano   HISTORIC BUILDING

(☑942 72 03 39; http://centros.culturade cantabria.com; Barrio de Sobrellano; adult/child €3/1.50, grounds free; ☺9.30am-2.30pm & 3.30-7.30pm Tue-Sun mid-Jun–mid-Sep, reduced hours mid-Sep–mid-Jun) In hillside parkland stands the Marqués de Comillas' fabulous neo-Gothic palace. With this 1888 building, Modernista architect Joan Martorell truly managed to out-Gothic real Gothic. On the 25-minute guided tour (in Spanish), you'll see the grand lounge featuring ornate wood-carved fireplaces with Gaudí-designed dragons, the elaborate dining room with its gold-wood *artesonado* (ceiling of interlaced beams with decorative insertions), beautiful stained-glass windows and vibrant original murals detailing the marquis' story. Martorell also designed the marquis' majestic family tomb, next door.

★ Playa de Oyambre   BEACH

(🅿) The 2km-long soft-blonde Playa de Oyambre, 5km west of Comillas, is a sandy dream protected by the Parque Natural Oyambre. It has some surfable waves, a couple of year-round campgrounds and a dash of intriguing history for being the emergency landing spot of the first ever USA–Spain flight in 1929.

★ Capricho de Gaudí   ARCHITECTURE

(☑942 72 03 65; www.elcaprichodegaudi. com; Barrio de Sobrellano; adult/child €5/2.50; ☺10.30am-9pm Jul & Aug, to 8pm Mar-Jun & Oct, to 5.30pm Nov-Feb, closed 1 week Jan) Antoni Gaudí left few reminders of his genius beyond Catalonia, but, of those that he did, the 1885 Gaudí Caprice is easily the most flamboyant. This brick building, one of Gaudí's earliest works and originally a summer playpad for the Marqués de Comillas' sister-in-law's brother, is striped all over the outside with ceramic bands of alternating sunflowers and green leaves. The elegant interior is comparatively restrained, with quirky touches including *artesonado* ceilings (interlaced beams with decorative insertions), stained-glass windows and slim spiral staircases.

Fuente de los Tres Caños   FOUNTAIN

(Calle de Joaquín del Piélago) In the heart of town, this elaborate triple-tiered fountain and lamp post was created in 1899 by Modernista Lluís Domènech i Montaner and decorated with intricate floral motifs.

Antigua Universidad Pontificia   ARCHITECTURE

(☑630 256767; Calle de Manuel Noriega; adult/child €3.50/free, car €2; ☺10am-1pm & 5-8pm, closed afternoons Oct-May; 🅿) Modernista architects Joan Martorell, Cristóbal Cascante and Lluís Domènech i Montaner all had a hand in this complex 1892 former seminary, with Domènech i Montaner contributing its medieval flavour. It's now an international Spanish language and culture study centre, the **Centro Universitario CIESE-Comillas** (☑942 71 55 00; www.fundacioncomillas.es; Calle de Manuel Noriega). Visits to its elaborate interiors and patios are guided in Spanish; from June to September, the 6pm tour is in English. Access to the grounds is free (unless you take a car in).

🛏 Sleeping & Eating

Hotel Marina de Campíos   BOUTIQUE HOTEL €€

(☑607 441647, 942 72 27 54; www.hotelmarina decampios.wix.com/marinadecampios; Calle del General Piélagos 14; r incl breakfast €95-135; ☺Jun-Sep; ✳☀🐕) This bright-red, 19th-century house, a few steps from Comillas' central plaza, has been revamped into a classy contemporary hotel with 19 boldly styled rooms, most sporting curtained beds, patterned walls and the names of famous operas. Out the back, there's a lovely inner patio, with a piano bar and snack spot opening onto it. Outside summer the hotel opens only some weekends; check ahead.

Hostal Esmeralda   HOSTAL €€

(☑942 72 00 97; www.hostalesmeralda.com; Calle de Antonio López 7; s/d €60/80; 🐕) Just east of the town centre, Esmeralda is a handsomely restored 1874 stone building with large, old-fashioned but tasteful rooms, comfy beds, splashes of colourful decor and plenty of character. It's well run by the fourth generation of the family that built it. Skip the overpriced breakfast. Rates dive outside August.

Restaurante Gurea   CANTABRIAN, BASQUE €

(☑942 72 24 46; Calle Ignacio Fernández de Castro 11; mains €8-14, menú €14.50; ☺1-3.45pm & 8.15-11pm, closed Tue dinner & Wed) This friendly, elegant restaurant and social bar, hidden in a small street a few blocks east of the town centre, dishes up Basque-Cantabrian fare and can throw together excellent salads and *raciones*. There's a varied *menú especial* (€24) and a set menu for two (€50), available for lunch or dinner.

1. *Sidra* (cider) 2. Scenery at Playa del Silencio (p488), Cudillero 3. Cave paintings, Altamira (p470) 4. Picos de Europa (p494)

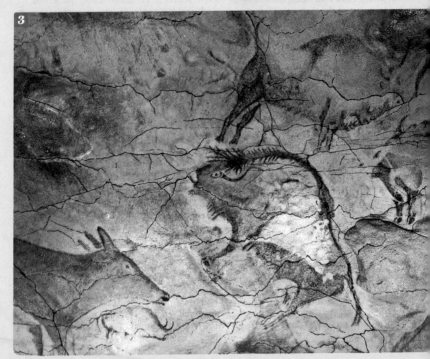

RAINER MIRAU/GETTY IMAGES ©

Surprises of the North

The small northern regions of Cantabria and Asturias are a delightful discovery. Green valleys stretch down from snow-topped peaks to beautiful beaches. Locals drink cider and eat fantastic seafood and cheese, and the region's fascinating history begins with some of the world's most outstanding cave art.

Spectacular Peaks

Rising majestically only 15km inland, the Picos de Europa mark the greatest, most dramatic heights of the Cordillera Cantábrica, with enough awe-inspiring mountainscapes to make them arguably the finest hill-walking country in Spain. You can ramble past high-level lakes, peer over kilometre-high precipices or traverse the magnificent Garganta del Cares gorge (p499).

Legendary Cider Bars

In a region that rolls out 80% of Spanish cider, Asturias' boisterous, fabulously fun *sidrerías* (cider bars) are a way of local life. There's no greater pleasure than knocking back a fizzing *culín* (cider shot), expertly poured from high above into a low-held glass (p481).

Ancient Cave Art

Humanity's first accomplished art was painted, drawn and engraved on the walls of European caves by Stone Age hunter-gatherers between about 39,000 and 10,000 BC, and reached some of its greatest artistic genius at the World Heritage–listed caves of Altamira (p470), Monte Castillo (p464) and Covalanas in Cantabria.

Glorious Beaches

Wild, rugged and unspoilt, the hundreds of secluded sandy stretches and mysterious coves that line the 550km-long Cantabrian and Asturian coast are some of Spain's most beautiful and breathtaking beaches, and when the waves are up, the region's surf scene comes alive.

Volotea (www.volotea.com) Ibiza, Málaga, Seville and Valencia.

Vueling Airlines (www.vueling.com) Barcelona, London (Gatwick) and Málaga.

ALSA (☑ 902 422242; www.alsa.es) is the major company operating from Oviedo's **bus station** (☑ 985 96 96 96; www.estacionde autobusesdeoviedo.com; Calle de Pepe Cosmen), 700m north of the central Campo de San Francisco.

DESTINATION	FARE	DURATION	FREQUENCY
Avilés	€2.55	30min-1hr	every 15-30min, 6.30am-10.30pm
Cangas de Onís	€7.05	1½hr	7-13 daily
Gijón	€2.50	30min	every 10-30min, 6.30am-10.30pm
Llanes	€11	1¾-2¾hr	10-11 daily
Madrid	€24-57	5-6hr	12-13 daily
Ribadesella	€8.10	1¼-1¾hr	6-8 daily
Santander	€10-27	2¼-3hr	9-12 daily
Santiago de Compostela	€30	4½-5½hr	3-4 daily

TRAIN

Oviedo's one **train station** (Avenida de Santander) serves both train companies: **Renfe** (☑ 902 320320; www.renfe.com), for destinations to the south, and **FEVE** (☑ 902 320320; www.renfe.com/viajeros/feve), on the upper floor, for destinations along Spain's north coast.

Cudillero (€3.30, 1¼ hours, three direct FEVE trains daily)

Gijón (€3.40, 33 minutes, half-hourly or hourly Renfe *cercanías* 6.38am to 10.45pm)

León (€9.90 to €20, two hours, five to six Renfe trains daily)

Llanes (€8.55, 2¾ hours, three to four FEVE trains daily) Via Arriondas (€5.15, 1¾ hours) and Ribadesella (€6.65, two hours).

Luarca (€7.40, 2½ hours, two FEVE trains daily) Continues into Galicia to Ferrol (€24, 7¼ hours).

Madrid (€32 to €54, 4¼ to six hours, six to eight Renfe trains daily)

Santander (€16, five hours, two FEVE trains daily) Via Arriondas, Llanes and Ribadesella.

ⓘ Getting Around

Bus A2 (€1.20) runs up to the Monte Naranco monuments from the northern end of Calle Uría, near the train station; bus A1 runs back into town. **Transportes Unidos de Asturias** (www.tua.es) is a handy source for Oviedo's urban buses.

Gijón

POP 259,867

Bigger, grittier and gutsier than Oviedo, seaside Gijón (khi-*hon*) produces iron, steel and chemicals, and is the main loading terminal for Asturian coal. It's also Asturias' largest city. But Gijón has emerged like a phoenix from its industrial roots, having given itself a thorough face-lift with pedestrianised streets, parks, seafront walks, cultural attractions and lively eating, drinking and shopping scenes. It's a surprisingly engaging city, and a party and beach hot spot too, with endless summer entertainment. Though it's no quaint Asturian fishing port, Gijón sure knows how to live.

Gijón's ancient core is concentrated on the headland known as Cimadevilla, the old fishermen's quarter. The harmonious, porticoed Plaza Mayor marks the southern end of this promontory. To the west stretch the Puerto Deportivo (marina) and the broad golden Playa de Poniente, while to the south is the busy, more modern, 19th- to 20th-century city centre, bounded on its eastern side by Playa de San Lorenzo.

◉ Sights

Plaza de Jovellanos   SQUARE
An enticing web of narrow lanes and small squares wraps itself around the landward side of Cimadevilla, though the area was significantly damaged during the civil war. The Plaza de Jovellanos is dominated by the home of Gijón's most celebrated scion, the 18th-century Enlightenment politician Gaspar Melchor de Jovellanos. It's now the Museo Casa Natal de Jovellanos (☑ 985 18 51 52; http://museos.gijon.es; Plaza de Jovellanos; ⊙ 10am-2pm & 5-7.30pm Tue-Sun) **FREE**, housing artwork by Asturian creatives including Gijón-born painter Evaristo Valle. A section of Gijón's Roman walls and towers has been reconstructed stretching west from the plaza.

✦ Festivals & Events

Fiesta de la Sidra Natural   DRINK
(Natural Cider Festival) Gijón's cider festival in late August includes brewery tours, free tastings and an annual attempt on the world

THE ART OF CIDER DRINKING

Asturian cider is served *escanciada:* poured from a bottle held high overhead into a glass held low, which gives it some fizz. Don't worry, you don't have to do this yourself – bar staff will flaunt their own skills by not even looking at the glass or bottle as they pour, probably chatting to somebody else over their shoulder at the same time. A shot of cider, about one-fifth of a glass, is known as a *culete* or *culín;* immediately knock it back in one go (leaving a tiny bit in the glass), before the fizz dissipates.

Every Asturian town has plenty of *sidrerías* (cider bars) and the epicentre of the scene is Oviedo's el bulevar de la sidra (p479), lined with a dozen jam-packed *sidrerías*.

Asturias churns out 80% of Spanish cider: anything up to 45 million litres a year, depending on the apple harvest. About 95% of this is consumed in Asturias itself. Apples are reaped in autumn and crushed to a pulp (about three-quarters of which winds up as apple juice). The cider is fermented in *pipes* (barrels) kept in *llagares* (the places where the cider is made) over winter. It takes about 800kg of apples to fill a 450L *pipa,* which makes 600 bottles. Traditionally, the *pipes* were transported to *chigres* (cider taverns) and drinkers would be served direct from the *pipa.* The *chigre* is dying out, though, and most cider now comes in bottles in *sidrerías*.

Since 2002, a Denomination of Origin (DO) Sidra de Asturias has been established for 22 Asturian ciders, which meet particular technical and quality standards, but this is certainly not to say that non-DO ciders cannot be as good.

The main cider-producing region is east of Oviedo, centred on Gijón, Nava, Villaviciosa and Siero. Find out more at Comarca de la Sidra (www.lacomarcadelasidra.com).

record number of people simultaneously pouring cider (8564 in 2015), which happens on Playa de Poniente.

Semana Grande SUMMER FESTIVAL
The biggest of all Gijón fiestas, with concerts, dance sessions, fireworks and plenty of partying across the city's plazas, streets and beaches. Held early to mid August.

🛏 Sleeping

Parador Molino Viejo HOTEL €€
(☑985 37 05 11; www.parador.es; Avenida Torcuato Fernández Miranda, Parque de Isabel la Católica; r €115-160; 🅿🛜) Gijón's *parador* (luxury state-owned hotel) isn't Spain's most lavish, but it does have a beautiful, tranquil setting inside a revamped watermill amid plenty of greenery, 2km southeast of Cimadevilla. Rooms are classy and comfy, with floral curtains, varnished-wood floors and all the usual *parador* trimmings.

Hotel Central HOTEL €€
(☑985 09 86 51; www.hotelcentralasturias.com; Plaza del Humedal 4; s €45-50, d €60-70; 🛜🅱) The warm, family-run Central may feel a little dated here and there, but it's by far one of Gijón's most characterful hotels, tucked away in its own fluffy-cushioned world 900m south of Cimadevilla near the bus station. There are just nine smallish but homey

rooms, in a fuss-free, white-and-cream boutique style. Breakfast (€5) is served in the snug lounge.

Hotel Pasaje HOTEL €€
(☑985 34 49 15; www.hotelpasaje.es; Calle del Marqués de San Esteban 3; s/d €60/95; 🛜) A pleasant, friendly, family-owned hotel with good, clean, bright rooms, many enjoying sea views. It's conveniently and centrally located facing the Puerto Deportivo, staff are a wonderful source of local information and there's a handy on-site cafe.

🍴 Eating

The most atmospheric area to eat is Cimadevilla, though the newer city centre also offers plenty of choice. Newly pedestrianised Calle Begoña, on *la ruta de los vinos,* is popular for tapas and wine.

Rawcoco HEALTH FOOD €
(☑620 963877; www.rawcoco.es; Calle de San Bernardo 36; dishes €4-8; ⊙8.30am-9.30pm Mon-Fri, 9.30am-9.30pm Sat & Sun; 🍴) A refreshing novelty for Asturias, this chic modern 'green bar' with neo-rustic decor whips up delicious fresh juices, creative smoothies (try a 'healthy skin' blend of ginger, avocado, cucumber and pineapple) and a selection of teas and coffees, alongside tasty health-focused bites such as wholemeal

sandwiches, 'superfood' breakfast bowls (muesli, fruit, yoghurt) and crunchy salads.

La Galana   SIDRERÍA, ASTURIAN **€€**
(☑ 985 17 24 29; www.restauranteasturianolagalana. es; Plaza Mayor 10; mains & raciones €15-24; ⊙ 1.30-4pm & 8pm-midnight; ☑) The front bar is a boisterous *sidrería* for snacking on tapas (€6.50 to €16) accompanied by free-flowing cider. For a smarter dining experience, head to the spacious back dining room with ceilings covered in murals. Fish, such as wild sea bass or *pixín* (anglerfish) with clams, is the strong suit. It also does excellent vegetarian dishes, including giant veg-tempura platters and beautifully prepared salads.

Casa Gerardo   ASTURIAN **€€€**
(☑ 985 88 77 97; www.restaurantecasagerardo. es; Carretera AS19, Km 9, Prendes; mains €19-35, set menus €60-120; ⊙ 1-3.45pm Tue-Thu & Sun, 1-3.45pm & 9-10.45pm Fri & Sat; P) About 12km west of Gijón, this stone-fronted modern-rustic house has been serving top-quality local cooking since 1882. Five generations of the Morán family have refined their art to the point of snagging a Michelin star. The *fabada*, fish and shellfish are famously delectable. To best sample the Morán blend of tradition and innovation, go for one of the set menus.

Drinking & Nightlife

Hit the *sidrerías* (cider bars) in Cimadevilla, along Cuesta del Cholo (Tránsito de las Ballenas) and around town. Further up in Cimadevilla, a bustling student scene flourishes around the Plaza Corrada. South of Cimadevilla, lively bars abound along *la ruta de los vinos* (Calles del Buen Suceso, Santa Rosa and Begoña). Naútico, near Playa de San Lorenzo, and Fomento, parallel to Playa de Poniente, host plenty more drinking spots.

Varsovia   COCKTAIL BAR
(www.varsoviagijon.com; Calle de Cabrales 18; ⊙ 4pm-1.30am Sun-Thu, to 4am Fri & Sat) Bottles tower up to the ceiling at this sensational, split-level, open-stone-walled cocktail bar, whose mixologist Borja Cortina was named Spain's best 2015 bartender. Soak up the Playa de San Lorenzo scene through huge arched windows while sipping ambitious liquid creations like rum-based 'Purple' with violet liqueur or perhaps a more conventional watermelon martini.

ⓘ Information

Gijón Turismo (☑ 985 34 17 71; www.gijon. info; Espigón Central de Fomento; ⊙ 10am-9pm Aug, 10am-2.30pm & 4.30-7.30pm Sep-Jul) The main tourist office, on a Puerto Deportivo pier, is very helpful. A summer information booth also opens at Playa de San Lorenzo from May to September.

ⓘ Getting There & Away

BUS

Buses fan out across Asturias and beyond from the **ALSA bus station** (☑ 902 422242; www. alsa.es; Calle de Magnus Blikstad).

DESTINATION	FARE	DURATION	FREQUENCY
Aeropuerto de Asturias	€8	45min	hourly 6am-8pm & 9.30pm
Oviedo	€2.50	30min	every 10-20min, 6.30am-10.30pm
Ribadesella	€7	1¾hr	7-10 daily
Santander	€15	2¾-3¾hr	12-15 daily

TRAIN

All **Renfe** (☑ 902 320320; www.renfe.com) and **FEVE** (☑ 902 320320; www.renfe.com/viajeros/feve) trains depart from the **Estación Sanz Crespo** (Calle de Sanz Crespo), 1km west of the city centre. Destinations include Cudillero (€3.30, 1¾ hours, five to 10 direct FEVE trains daily) and Oviedo (€3.40, 30 minutes, two to three Renfe *cercanías* hourly 6am to 11.30pm).

Change at Pravia or Oviedo for most other FEVE destinations. Renfe also has several daily trains to León (€13, 2½ hours) and Madrid (€33, five hours).

East Coast

Mostly Spanish holidaymakers seek out a summer spot on the beaches and coves along the Asturian coast east of Gijón, backed by the Picos de Europa, which rise only 15km inland.

Playa de Gulpiyuri   BEACH
(Naves) More a sight than a sunbathing spot, this magical, 50m-long hidden cove framed by cliffs and greenery is one of Spain's most famous inland beaches. It doesn't front the sea, but you can hear waves sloshing through underwater tunnels to reach its gold-toned sands. To get here, turn north off the AS263 or A8 at the eastern end of

Naves – the beach is 500m north, with the final 300m on foot. You can also walk here from Playa de San Antolín, 1.5km southeast.

Villaviciosa & Around

POP 6386 (VILLAVICIOSA)

About 27km east of Gijón, Villaviciosa rivals Nava as Asturias' cider capital. Apart from the Romanesque Iglesia de Santa María, its pretty little town centre is mostly a child of the 18th century.

◎ Sights

Playa de Rodiles   BEACH
(**P**) The beautiful, broad golden sands of 1km-long Playa de Rodiles, backed by pines and eucalyptus trees, front the sea at the mouth of the Ría de Villaviciosa, 11km north of Villaviciosa. Surfers might catch a wave here in late summer.

Museo del Jurásico de Asturias   MUSEUM
(MUJA; ✆ 902 306600; www.museojurasicoasturias. com; Rasa de San Telmo, Colunga; adult/senior & child €7.24/4.70, Wed free; ⊙ 10.30am-8pm Jul & Aug, 10am-2.30pm & 3.30-6pm Wed-Fri, 10.30am-2.30pm & 4-7pm Sat & Sun Feb-Jun & Sep-Dec; **P**) Dotted with Jurassic-era dinosaur fossils, the Asturian coastline between Gijón and Ribadesella is known as *La costa de la los dinosaurios* (The Dinosaur Coast). Asturias' popular claw-shaped Jurassic museum, 18km east of Villaviciosa and 24km west of Ribadesella, takes you through 4.5 billion years of prehistory with dinosaur footprints, fossils and bones and 20 giant dinosaur replicas. The pair of mating tyrannosaurus is more than 12m high.

Iglesia de San Salvador de Valdediós   CHURCH
(✆ 670 242372; www.monasteriovaldedios.com; Valdediós; adult/child €3/1.25; ⊙ 10am-2pm & 4.30-7.30pm Tue-Sun Apr-Sep, 11am-1.30pm Tue-Sun Oct-Mar) The area surrounding Villaviciosa is sprinkled with ancient churches. Don't miss this beautifully preserved triple-naved AD 893 church, built as part of a palace complex for Alfonso III in the old Kingdom of Asturias' unique pre-Romanesque style. It's 9km southwest of Villaviciosa, well signposted off the AS267 to Pola de Siero.

☞ Tours

El Gaitero   BREWERY TOUR
(✆ 985 89 01 00; www.sidraelgaitero.com; La Espuncia; tours free; ⊙ 10am-1.15pm & 4-6.15pm Mon-Fri, 10am-1.15pm Sat mid-May–mid-Sep, 10am-

1.15pm & 4-7pm Thu-Sun mid-Sep–mid-May) For the full-blown cider experience, tour the long-standing El Gaitero cider-brewing bodegas, 2km northeast of central Villaviciosa on the N632. Set up in 1890, El Gaitero now produces up to 27 million bottles of cider a year. One-hour guided visits (in Spanish) include a free tasting session and the detailed museum. Advance bookings recommended.

🍽 Sleeping & Eating

★ La Casona de Amandi   COUNTRY HOUSE €€
(✆ 985 89 01 30; www.lacasonadeamandi.com; Calle de San Juan 6, Amandi; s €65-90, d €85-130, all incl breakfast; **P** 🛜) The most attractive lodgings in the Villaviciosa area are at this exquisite 19th-century farmhouse surrounded by tranquil lawn gardens, 1.5km south of Villaviciosa, where a warm welcome awaits. Wonderfully comfy rooms, all of which ooze their own character and vary in size, contain antique beds, plenty of pillows, hand-painted furnishings and organic soaps, and floors are original chestnut. Dinner available on request.

La Ballera   SIDRERÍA, ASTURIAN €
(✆ 985 89 00 09; Calle General Campomanes 18; menú €10, mains €7-14; ⊙ 11.30am-late Fri-Wed) This boisterous town-centre *sidrería* is as authentically Asturian as it gets: check-print paper tablecloths, earthy traditional fare (*fabada, patatas al Cabrales*, meaty mains), a good-value *menú del día* and, of course, nonstop pours of cider.

❶ Information

Oficina de Turismo de Villaviciosa (✆ 985 89 17 59; www.turismovillaviciosa.es; Calle Agua 29; ⊙ 10.30am-2pm & 4-7.30pm Wed-Sun Apr-Sep, 10.30am-2pm & 4-7.30pm Tue-Sat Oct-Mar) Inside the 16th-century Casa de los Hevia.

❶ Getting There & Away

ALSA (✆ 902 422242; www.alsa.es) has seven or more buses daily to Oviedo (€4.30, 35 minutes to one hour) and Ribadesella (€3.90, 35 minutes to one hour), and 13 or more to Gijón (€3, 25 minutes to one hour).

Ribadsella & Around

POP 2796 (RIBADESELLA)

Split in two by the Río Sella's estuary, Ribadesella is a low-key fishing town and lively beach resort. Its two halves are joined by the long, low Sella bridge. The western part (where most hotels are) has an expansive golden beach, Playa de Santa Marina, while the older part of town and fishing harbour are on the eastern side. Between Ribadesella and Llanes, 28km east along the coast, more than 20 sandy beaches and pretty coves await discovery.

Unless you've booked far ahead, it's best to stay away from Ribadesella on the first weekend of August, when the whole place goes mad for the Descenso Internacional del Sella canoeing festival.

◎ Sights

★ **Cueva de Tito Bustillo**   CAVE
(☑985 18 58 60, reservations 902 306600; www.centrotitobustillo.com; Avenida de Tito Bustillo; incl Centro de Arte Rupestre adult/senior, student & child €7.34/5.30, Wed free; ⏰10.15am-5pm mid-Mar–Oct; ℗) To admire some of Spain's finest cave art, including superb horse paintings probably done around 15,000 to 10,000 BC, visit this World Heritage–listed cave, 300m south of the western end of the Sella bridge. Daily visitor numbers are limited, so online or phone reservations are essential. Even if you miss the cave itself, the modern **Centro de Arte Rupestre Tito Bustillo** (adult/senior, student & child €5.30/3.16, Wed free; ⏰10am-7pm Wed-Sun Jul & Aug, reduced hours Sep-Jun; ℗), 200m south, is well worth a visit for its displays, video and replicas.

✨ Festivals & Events

Descenso Internacional del Sella   CANOEING
The Río Sella is at its busiest on the first Saturday after 2 August, when 1500 professional paddlers (followed by many more fun paddlers) head downriver to Ribadesella from Arriondas in the Descenso Internacional del Sella, an international kayaking/canoeing event that kicked off in 1930.

🛏 Sleeping

El Jardín de Eugenia   BOUTIQUE HOTEL €€
(☑985 86 08 05; www.eljardindeugenia.com; Calle del Palacio Valdés 22; r incl breakfast €100-130; 🛜) Popular with returnees, Eugenia's is a fine, friendly, family-run boutique pad occupying a 100-year-old house. Hand-painted floral-themed murals embellish each of the 14 individually designed, Asian-inspired rooms – all comfy, characterful and full of dark-wood furniture. We love the cream-washed top-floor rooms, with sloping wood-beamed ceilings and

mini-chandeliers. Other perks: homemade breakfasts, free bikes, laundry service and a summer lounge terrace.

Villa Rosario   HISTORIC HOTEL €€€
(☑985 86 00 90; www.hotelvillarosario.com; Calle de Dionisio Ruisánchez 3-6; r €60-220; ⏰Mar–mid-Jan; ℗❄@🛜) Set inside a century-old *casa de indianos* (house built by a returned colonist), this luxurious history-filled hotel overlooks Playa de Santa Marina. Interiors are tastefully styled with marble floors, rich-toned carpets and an original cherry-wood staircase, while white-on-white rooms are fashionably contemporary and minimalist. Go for a room in the original *palacete*, rather than the smart but less characterful Villa Rosario II block.

🍴 Eating

The lively waterfront *sidrerías* on the eastern side of the Río Sella are a good bet for seafood. Ribadesella also has some excellent top-end restaurants.

Carroceu   SIDRERÍA, ASTURIAN €
(☑985 86 14 19; Calle Marqués de Argüelles 25; dishes €7-14; ⏰1-4pm & 8pm-midnight Fri-Wed) A popular choice in central Ribadesella, this laid-back, stone-walled *sidrería* is perfect for snacking on simple seafood-focused tapas like deep-fried calamari, steamed cockles and tuna-stuffed onions, plus Asturian cheese and meat *raciones*.

★ **Arbidel**   CONTEMPORARY ASTURIAN €€€
(☑985 86 14 40; www.arbidel.com; Calle Oscura 1; mains €23-35, set menus €40-70; ⏰1.30-4pm & 8.30-11pm Wed-Sat, 1.30-4pm Tue & Sun, closed Jan) Tucked into an old-town corner, much-loved Michelin-starred Arbidel is famous for chef Jaime Uz' reinvention of classic Asturian flavours and ingredients with a distinctly modern flair – at non-exorbitant prices (relatively speaking). Exquisitely prepped local-inspired delights might feature green-apple gazpacho, baked *pixín* (anglerfish) with squid noodles or a giant beef chop for two, but the good-value degustation menus are the way to go.

ℹ Information

Oficina de Turismo de Ribadesella (☑985 86 00 38; www.ribadesella.es; Paseo Princesa Letizia; ⏰10am-2pm & 4-8pm Jul & Aug, 10am-2pm & 4-6.30pm Tue-Sat, 11am-2pm Sun Sep-Jun) At the eastern end of the Sella bridge.

❶ Getting There & Away

BUS

ALSA (☑ 902 422242; www.alsa.es) buses depart from the **bus station** (Avenida del Palacio Valdés), 300m south of the Sella bridge, east of the river.

DESTINATION	FARE	DURATION	MINIMUM FREQUENCY
Gijón	€6.90	1½-1¾hr	6 daily
Llanes	€2.80	35min	7 daily
Oviedo	€8.10	1-1½	6 daily
Santander	€8.06	1½-2½	2 daily

TRAIN

Three or four FEVE trains run daily to/from Oviedo (€6.65, two hours), Arriondas (€1.85, 30 minutes) and Llanes (€2.55, 40 minutes), and two to/from Santander (€9.65, three hours).

Llanes & Around

POP 4427 (LLANES)

Inhabited since ancient times, Llanes was for a long time an independent-minded town and whaling port with its own charter, awarded by Alfonso IX of León in 1206. Today, with a small medieval centre, a bustling harbour and some sensational beaches within easy reach, it's one of northern Spain's more popular holiday destinations – a handy base for the Asturias coast (Ribadesella is just 28km west), with the Picos de Europa close at hand, if not particularly exciting in itself.

◉ Sights

Bufones de Arenillas　　　LANDMARK
(Puertas de Vidiago) From Puertas de Vidiago, 6km east of Llanes on the N634, signs past the church lead you 2km (along a bumpy track) to the Bufones de Arenillas, a dozen geyser-style jets of seawater, which are pumped up through holes in the earth by the pressure of seawater. With heavy seas, some jets can spurt a spectacular 20m high (it's dangerous to get too close). When seas are calm, you'll just hear air and water whooshing eerily through the tunnels below.

Cueva del Pindal　　　CAVE
(☑ 608 175284; http://artepaleoliticoenasturias. com; Pimiango; adult/senior & child €3.13/1.62, Wed free; ⊙ 10am-4pm Wed-Sun) The World Heritage–listed Cueva del Pindal, 2km northeast of Pimiango (past a spectacular coastal lookout), contains 31 Palaeolithic paintings and engravings of animals, mostly ochre, including bison, horses and rare depictions of a mammoth and a fish. It's not in the same league as Cantabria's Altamira or Ribadesella's Tito Bustillo caves, but it was the first prehistoric cave art discovered in Asturias. With its setting among wooded sea-cliffs, close to a 16th-century chapel, ruined Romanesque monastery and interpretation centre, it's an appealing visit.

Cave visits must be booked by phone at least one day ahead; a maximum of six groups of 20 can enter each day and children under seven are not allowed. It's signposted off the N634, 21km east of Llanes.

🛏 Sleeping

★ **CAEaCLAVELES**　　　DESIGN HOTEL €€
(☑ 984 09 40 10, 658 110774; www.caeaclaveles. com; La Pereda; s €95-120, d €100-140; 🅿 🕸 🛜) Absolutely not what you'd expect in countryside Asturias, this exquisitely contemporary five-room design pad with a chic urban feel is built to resemble a little hill. The slim, curvy, low-rise structure doubles up as its warm artist-owner's home-studio: her creations adorn the walls. Alluring, airy doubles channel cool minimalism, splashed with rich colours and flooded with light through floor-to-ceiling windows.

★ **La Posada de Babel**　　　DESIGN HOTEL €€
(☑ 985 40 25 25; www.laposadadebabel.com; La Pereda; s €65-90, d €95-165; ⊙ mid-Mar–mid-Dec; 🅿 🛜 🕸) 🍃 About 4km south of Llanes, this unique spot combines striking modern architecture and bold design with sprawling lawns and a relaxed yet civilised vibe, all inspired by its owners' extended Asia travels. The 12 different rooms occupy four contrasting buildings, including one in a typical Asturian *hórreo* (grain store) on stone stilts. The kitchen (breakfast €5, dinner €28) emphasises market-fresh and organic food.

🍴 Eating

Plenty of lively *marisquerías* (seafood eateries) and *sidrerías* line Calles Mayor and Manuel Cué, so finding a place to tuck into sea critters and wash them down with cascades of cider is no problem.

Restaurante Siete Puertas　　　SEAFOOD €€
(☑ 686 859412, 985 40 27 51; Calle de Manuel Cué 7; mains €15-30, menús €12-30; ⊙ 1-4pm & 8-11pm, closed Mon-Thu & Sun dinner Nov-Mar) The Siete Puertas is a cut above your average Llanes restaurant, with neat white tablecloths,

WORTH A TRIP

BEACHES AROUND LLANES

More than 20 sandy stretches and concealed coves lie scattered along the dramatic coastline between Llanes and Ribadesella, 28km west.

Playa de Torimbia (Niembro) This beautiful gold-blonde crescent bounded by rocky headlands and a bowl of green hills, 9km west of Llanes, is truly spectacular. It's also a particularly popular nudist beach. Turn off the AS263 at Posada to reach Niembro (2km), from where it's a further 2km to the beach; it's well signposted through Niembro's narrow streets. You have to walk the last kilometre or so, which keeps the crowds down.

Playa de Toranda (Niembro) About 8km west of Llanes, Playa de Toranda is dramatically backed by fields and a forested headland. To get here, turn off the AS263 at Posada and head 2km northwest to Niembro; the beach is 500m beyond Niembro and well signed.

Playa de la Ballota A particularly attractive 350m-long beach 4.5km east of Llanes, hemmed in by green cliffs and signposted down a dirt track from the LLN2 Cué–Andrín road.

efficient service, a canopied summer terrace and elegantly prepared local dishes. Fish and homemade desserts are its fortes, and there's a variety of *menús* to suit different budgets.

ℹ Information

Oficina de Turismo (☑ 985 40 01 64; www.llanes.es; Calle Marqués de Canillejas, Antigua Lonja; ⊙10am-2pm & 5-9pm mid-Jun–mid-Sep, 10am-2pm & 4-6.30pm Mon-Sat, 10am-2pm Sun mid-Sep–mid-Jun) The tourist office can tell you about plenty of good walking routes in the area, including the 5000km E9 coastal path that passes through here on its journey from Russia to Portugal.

ℹ Getting There & Away

BUS

ALSA (☑ 902 422242; www.alsa.es) operates from the **bus station** (☑ 985 40 24 85; Calle Bolera).

DESTINATION	FARE	DURATION	FREQUENCY
Arriondas	€4.60	1-1½hr	5-7 daily
Gijón	€8.80	1-1¾hr	4-5 daily
Oviedo	€11	1¼-2¼hr	11-12 daily
Ribadesella	€2.80	20-40min	7-11 daily
San Vicente de la Barquera	€2.30	30min	4-7 daily
Santander	€6	1½-2hr	4-8 daily

TRAIN

Three or four FEVE trains arrive daily from Oviedo (€8.55, three hours), Arriondas (€4, one hour) and Ribadesella (€2.55, 40 minutes), two of them continuing to Santander (€7.80, 2¼ hours).

West Coast

The cliffs of Cabo Peñas, 20km northwest of Gijón, mark the start of the western half of Asturias' coast, which includes its most northerly and highest (almost 100m) points. The industrial steel-producing town of Avilés is a world away from the peaceful, colourful fishing ports of Cudillero and Luarca, to its west. Further west, you'll reach Galicia. Gorgeous sandy stretches and towering cliffs dot this entire coastline.

Avilés

POP 75,744

Avilés, 29km west of Gijón and 34km north of Oviedo, is an old estuary port and steel-making town. The historic core's elegant colonnaded streets and its central Plaza de España, fronted by two fine 17th-century buildings, make for a lovely stroll, and there are some good, authentic Asturian restaurants to enjoy in town. While you're here, you might catch one of the occasional innovative, independent Spanish and global music, theatre, cinema or art events at the Centro Cultural Internacional Oscar Niemeyer.

◉ Sights

Centro Cultural Internacional Oscar Niemeyer   CULTURAL CENTRE
(Centro Niemeyer; ☑ 984 83 50 31; www.niemeyercenter.org; Avenida del Zinc; tours adult/child

€3/2; ⊙10am-9.30pm Jul & Aug, to 7.30pm Sep-Jun, tours 5pm Wed-Fri, 12.30pm & 5pm Sat & Sun) This multifaceted international cultural centre, founded in 2011 on once-industrial land just east across the river from the city centre, was designed by Brazilian architect Oscar Niemeyer (the creator of Brasilia) as a gift to Asturias and as a cultural nexus between the Iberian Peninsula and Latin America. The bold-white complex now hosts a range of independent avant-garde theatre, music, cinema, literature and art shows. Informative one-hour guided tours (in Spanish) take in the auditorium and dome, detailing Niemeyer's work both here and elsewhere.

🛌 Sleeping

Hotel Palacio Valdés　　HOTEL €€
(☑984 11 21 11; www.hotelpalaciovaldes.com; Calle Llano Ponte 4; r €60-140; 🛜) Business-smart comfort is the theme at this polished, modern hotel set inside a revamped townhouse, 200m northeast of the Plaza de España. Front rooms have classic glassed-in balconies with views across the river to the Centro Niemeyer, while top-floor slanted-ceiling digs are styled as attics. Nonsmokers, avoid the 2nd floor.

Hotel Don Pedro　　HOTEL €€
(☑985 51 22 88; www.hdonpedro.com; Calle de La Fruta 22; s €50-70, d €65-80, tr €75-90; 🛜) Just off the central Plaza de España, Hotel Don Pedro has attractive, comfy rooms with exposed stone or brick, velvet sofas, rich colour schemes and rugs on wooden floors.

🍴 Eating

Aviles' historic centre is filled with bubbly bars and restaurants, though the area's standout restaurant, the Real Balneario de Salinas (p487), is 5.5km northwest of town in the seaside suburb of Salinas.

Casa Tataguyo　　ASTURIAN €€
(☑985 56 48 15; www.tataguyo.com; Plaza del Carbayedo 6; mains €10-22, lunch menú €16-22; ⊙1-4pm & 8pm-late) Tucked into a busy restaurant-lined plaza, Tataguyo has being going strong since the 1840s. Feast on delectable classic meat- and fish-focused Asturian fare, including frills-free *cocidos* (stews) and *lechazo al horno* (roast young lamb), or keep it light with platters of cold meats and cheeses and piled-high salads. The

high-quality, three-course lunchtime *menú*, with wine, is popular.

⭐**Real Balneario de Salinas**　　ASTURIAN, SEAFOOD €€€
(☑985 51 86 13; www.realbalneario.com; Avenida de Juan Sitges 3, Salinas; mains €26-34, menús €50-88; ⊙1-3.30pm & 8-11.30pm Tue-Sat, 1-3.30pm Sun, closed mid-Jan–mid-Feb) Serious food lovers, head to the seaside suburb of Real Balneario de Salinas, 5.5km northwest of central Avilés. Opened as a beachside bathing centre by King Alfonso XIII in 1916, it's a top seafood restaurant today. Choose from traditional or creative 'new concept' fish and shellfish preparations, plus some very tempting desserts. Lobster is a current favourite, while the long-standing speciality is champagne sea bass.

ℹ️ Information

Oficina de Turismo (☑985 54 43 25; www.aviles.es; Calle de Ruiz Gómez 21; ⊙10am-8pm Jul–mid-Sep, 10am-2pm & 4.30-6.30pm Mon-Fri, 10.30am-2.30pm Sat & Sun mid-Sep–Jun) Just off the main Plaza de España.

ℹ️ Getting There & Away

BUS

From the **bus station** (Avenida Telares), 800m north of the central Plaza de España, **ALSA** (☑902 422242; www.alsa.es) buses run frequently to Oviedo (€2.55, 30 to 60 minutes, at least 37 buses daily) and Gijón (€2.40 to €3, 30 to 45 minutes, at least 27 buses daily).

TRAIN

From the FEVE station on Avenida Telares, 700m north of the Plaza de España, trains head to Gijón (€1.95, 40 minutes, at least 31 times daily), some with connections there for Oviedo (€3.30, 1½ hours).

Cudillero

POP 1355

Cudillero, 60km northwest of Oviedo, is the most picturesque fishing village on the Asturian coast – and it knows it. The houses, painted in a rainbow of pastels, cascade down to a tiny port on a narrow inlet. Despite its touristy feel, Cudillero is reasonably relaxed and makes an appealing stop, even in mid-August when every room in town is taken. The surrounding coastline is a dramatic sequence of sheer cliffs and fine beaches.

◉ Sights

Playa del Silencio   BEACH
(Castañeras) This is one of Spain's most beautiful beaches: a long, silver, sandy cove backed by a natural rock amphitheatre. It isn't particularly good for swimming due to underwater rocks, but it's a stunning spot for a stroll and, weather permitting, some sun-soaking. It's 15km west of Cudillero: take the A8 west, then exit 441 for Santa Marina, and head west on the N632 to Castañeras, from where the beach is signposted. The last 500m down is on foot.

Playa de Aguilar   BEACH
(Muros de Nalón; P) The nearest beach to Cudillero is the fine, sandy Playa de Aguilar, 5km east on the AS317 from El Pito to Muros de Nalón. Immediately east and accessed by a short path from the joint car park lies tiny, cliff-framed Playa de Xiró.

Mirador de La Garita-Atalaya   VIEWPOINT
A tangle of narrow, sloping, twisting streets threads up to this battered lookout point perched high above the harbour.

🍴 Sleeping & Eating

Albergue Cudillero   HOSTEL €
(☑689 232532, 985 59 02 04; www.albergue cudillero.com; El Pito; dm €17.50-20; P 🐾) Aimed at Camino de Santiago pilgrims but open to everyone, these two spotless, modern, red-walled four-person dorms are set back from the road in El Pito, 2km south of Cudillero's port. Sheets, blankets and individual lockers are provided, along with towel rental (€1). There's a small fully equipped communal kitchen, with summer tables outside.

Hotel Casa Prendes   HOTEL €€
(☑985 59 15 00; www.hotelcasaprendes.com; Calle San José 4-8; r €75-90; 🐾) A brilliantly maintained townhouse hotel just back from Cudillero's harbour, offering nine comfy, stone-walled rooms with colourful curtains and flower-print bedspreads, attentive service and a small private breakfast cafe. The owners also rent seven apartments nearby.

El Faro   SEAFOOD €€
(☑985 59 15 32; Calle del Riofrío 4; mains €14-23; ☺10am-4pm & 8pm-midnight Thu-Tue) Though it doesn't enjoy sea views, El Faro is a smart, attractive eatery tucked one street back from the port. Stone, timber, colourful artwork and cool cream decor create a welcoming atmosphere in which to dig into fish of the day, *merluza* (hake) in a variety of styles, fish-filled salads, *parrilladas de marisco* (mixed grilled shellfish) or *arroz caldoso* (seafood and rice stew).

❶ Information

Oficina de Turismo de Cudillero (☑985 59 13 77, town hall 985 59 00 03; www.cudillero. es; Puerto del Oeste; ☺10am-2pm & 4-7.30pm Jul & Aug, 11am-2pm & 4-6pm Jun & Sep, 10am-3pm Mon-Sat Oct-May) By the port. On low-season weekdays, it operates from the *ayuntamiento* (town hall), just behind the port.

❶ Getting There & Away

CAR
The only place to park is at the port, in front of the tourist office.

BUS
From the bus station, at the top of the hill 800m from the port, three or more daily buses go to Gijón (€5.60, 1¼ hours) via Avilés (€3.20, 45 minutes), where you can connect for Oviedo.

TRAIN
The FEVE train station is 2km inland from the port: trains to Gijón (€3.30, 1½ to two hours) run about hourly until 6pm (fewer on weekends); for Oviedo (€3.30, 1½ to 2¼ hours) you usually change at Pravia.

Luarca & Around
POP 5013

Marginally less scenic than its rival coastal town Cudillero, Luarca has a similar setting in a deep valley running down to an expansive harbour full of colourful fishing boats. It's a handy base for some good nearby beaches and the last major Asturian stop before you enter Galicia to the west.

◉ Sights

Ermita de la Regalina   CHAPEL, VIEWPOINT
(Cadavedo) Spectacularly positioned on a grassy headland fringed by jagged cliffs, sandy beaches and crashing seas, 16km east of Luarca, this delicate little blue-and-white chapel is absolutely worth finding for the sensational views alone. A couple of typical stilted Asturian *hórreos* (grain stores) complete the panorama. From Luarca, head 13km east on the A8, take exit 451 for Cadavedo and follow signs to Playa de Cadavedo, then Ermita de la Regalina.

Castro de Coaña
ARCHAEOLOGICAL SITE

(☑985 97 84 01; www.castrosdeasturias.es; Coaña; adult/senior, student & child €3.13/1.62, Wed free; ⊙10.30am-5.30pm Wed-Sun, to 3.30pm Oct-Mar; P) The town of Coaña lies 4km inland from the port of Navia, 19km west of Luarca. Two kilometres south, the hillside Castro de Coaña is one of northern Spain's best-preserved Celtic settlements, dating back to the 4th century BC and well worth visiting.

Playa de Barayo
BEACH

(Barayo; P) Part of a protected nature reserve, Playa de Barayo is a good sandy beach in a pretty bay at the mouth of a river winding through wetlands and dunes. Turn off the N634 11km west of central Luarca onto the NV2 towards Puerto de Vega; after 800m turn right towards Vigo (1.5km) and follow signs. From the car park, the beach is accessible by a well-marked 30-minute hike.

Cabo Busto
CAPE

(Busto) Twelve kilometres east of Luarca, wind-lashed Cabo Busto gives you an idea of the Asturian coast's wildness as waves crash onto its rocky cliffs below a 19th-century lighthouse. The coastal views are fantastic.

Playa de Cueva
BEACH

(Cueva; P) Soft 600m-long Playa de Cueva, 7km east of Luarca on the old N634 coast road, is one of the district's top beaches, with cliffs, caves, a river and occasional decent surf. It's signposted.

🛏 Sleeping & Eating

Hotel La Colmena
HOTEL €

(☑985 64 02 78; www.lacolmena.com; Calle de Uría 2; s/d €45/65; 🛜) La Colmena's 16 rooms are a tad more comfortable and stylish than the ugly exterior facing Plaza de Alfonso X suggests. They have some attractive touches, such as dark parquet floors, high ceilings and tall windows, though the showers and singles are a bit of a squeeze. There's an on-site cafe.

★3 Cabos
RURAL HOTEL €€

(☑985 92 42 52; www.hotelrural3cabos.com; Ctra de El Vallín, Km 4; s €95, d €105-125, all incl breakfast; ⊙closed early Jan-early Feb; P@🛜) A beautiful contemporary conversion of a 120-year-old farmhouse, 3 Cabos enjoys fabulous panoramas from its elevated inland site. Its six exquisitely designed, well-equipped rooms feature open-stone walls, comfy beds and spacious bathrooms. Best are the top-floor, sea-facing attic-design

rooms, with original timber beams. The panoramic bar-restaurant (breakfast and dinner; mains €16 to €22) focuses on fresh local products, including gluten-free and vegie options.

Restaurante Sport
SEAFOOD €€€

(☑985 64 10 78, 639 700607; www.facebook.com/sportrestaurante; Calle de Rivero 9; tapas €4-8, mains €14-30; ⊙noon-4pm & 8pm-midnight, closed Sun & Wed night Oct-May, closed early Jan-early Feb) This reliable seafood restaurant, facing the river a few steps back from the harbour, has been delighting customers with its daily changing menu of local fish and shellfish since the 1950s. Choose from tasty tapas or sample *percebes,* a northwest Spain delicacy, sold at €6 per 100g (when available). Anything *del pincho* has been caught with a rod and line.

❶ Information

Oficina Municipal de Turismo de Luarca (☑985 64 00 83; www.turismoluarca.com; Plaza Alfonso X; ⊙10.30am-2pm & 4-7.15pm Mar-Aug, 1.30am-2pm & 4-7.15pm Tue-Sat Sep-Feb)

❶ Getting There & Away

BUS

At least four daily **ALSA** (☑902 422242; www.alsa.es) buses run east to Oviedo (€10, 1¼ to 1¾ hours) and west to Ribadeo (€7, 1¾ hours) in Galicia, from Calle García Prieto.

TRAIN

The FEVE train station is 800m south of the town centre. Two trains run daily east to Cudillero (€3.60, 1¼ hours) and Oviedo (€7.40, 2½ hours), and west to Ribadeo (€4.75, 1½ hours) and as far as Ferrol (€16.35, 4½ hours) in Galicia.

Inland Western Asturias

There's some gorgeous country in southwest Asturias. Even just driving through on alternative routes into Castilla y León can be rewarding, such as the AS228 via the 1587m Puerto Ventana, the AS227 via the beautiful 1486m Puerto de Somiedo or the AS213 via the 1525m Puerto de Leitariegos – all scenic mountain roads crossing dramatic passes.

Most people head off biking along the popular Senda del Oso cycling and hiking path, where you stand a high chance of spotting four Cantabrian brown bears in a hillside enclosure. Further west, the green-covered valleys of the Parque Natural de Somiedo Unesco-listed biosphere reserve lie well off the beaten track.

Senda del Oso

The Senda del Oso (Path of the Bear) is a 20km cycling and walking track along the course of a former mine railway between the villages of Tuñón and Entrago, southwest of Oviedo. With easy gradients, it runs through increasingly spectacular valley scenery into deep, narrow canyons, with several bridges and more than 30 tunnels. It also offers the high probability of seeing Cantabrian brown bears in a large enclosure at Cercado Osero (which is probably as close as you'll ever get to them), and it's a fun outing with (or without) the kids. A more recently opened branch track southeast from Caranga to Santa Marina in the Valle de Quirós has increased the total rideable track to 36km.

👁 Sights

★ **Cercado Osero** PARK

(☑985 96 30 60; www.osodeasturias.es) ⏺ About 5.5km south of Tuñón (or a 1.1km walk south from the Área Recreativa Buyera), the Senda del Oso cycling and hiking path reaches the Cercado Osero, a 40,000-sq-metre hillside compound home to three female Cantabrian brown bears: Paca, Tola and Molina. The two older bears, Paca and Tola, were orphaned as cubs by a hunter in 1989. Since 2008, they have spent their time in a second 7000-sq-metre enclosure just below the path at the same spot.

Parque de la Prehistoria MUSEUM

(☑985 76 47 39, 902 306600; www.parquedela prehistoria.es; San Salvador de Alesga; adult/senior & child €6.12/3.57; ⏺10am-2.30pm & 4-8pm Jul & Aug, reduced hours Sep-Jun; ℗) Four kilometres south of Entrago, the Parque de la Prehistoria is well worth a visit for its excellent introduction to Spanish and European cave art. It includes replicas of Asturias' World Heritage–listed Tito Bustillo and Candamo caves and France's Niaux cave, along with a good museum-gallery that explains much of the what, when, who, how and why of Europe's Palaeolithic cave-art phenomenon.

Casa del Oso INTERPRETATION CENTRE

(☑985 96 30 60; www.osodeasturias.es; Proaza; ⏺10am-2pm & 4-6pm) Proaza's Casa del Oso is the headquarters of the Fundación Oso de Asturias, which runs the Paca-Tola bear conservation project, and has exhibits on Spanish brown bears. It also doubles up as the tourist office, offering info on the Senda del Oso and other local activities.

🛈 Getting There & Away

Pullmans Llaneza (☑985 46 58 78; www. pullmansllaneza.com) runs three or four daily

---

THERE'S A BEAR IN THERE

The wild mountain area of southwest Asturias and northwestern Castilla y León, including the Parque Natural de Somiedo, is the main stronghold of Spain's biggest animal, the brown bear *(oso pardo)*. Bear numbers in the Cordillera Cantábrica have climbed to more than 200 from as low as 70 in the mid-1990s, including a smaller population of 30 to 40 in a separate easterly area straddling southeast Asturias, southwest Cantabria and northern Castilla y León. Killing bears has been illegal in Spain since 1973, but only since the 1990s have concerted plans for bear recovery been carried out. Experts are heartened by the fact there has been at least one recent case of interbreeding between the western and eastern groups.

This lumbering beast can reach 300kg and live 25 to 30 years, and has traditionally been disliked by farmers – despite being almost entirely vegetarian. Public support has played a big part in its recent recovery in the Cordillera Cantábrica, which owes a lot to the celebrated bears of Asturias' Senda del Oso (above), southwest of Oviedo. Experts warn that the bear is not yet completely out of the woods – illegal snares set for wild boar and poisoned bait put out for wolves continue to pose serious threats, as do forest fires, new roads and ski stations, which reduce the bears' habitat and mobility, while poaching has claimed the lives of at least two bears in the last few years.

You can see bears in semi-liberty at the Cercado Osero (above) on the Senda del Oso. The Fundación Oso Pardo (www.fundacionosopardo.org) is Spain's major resource and advocate for brown bears and its Centro de Interpretación 'Somiedo y El Oso' (right), in Pola de Somiedo, is a good place to brush up on bear facts.

buses from Oviedo bus station to Tuñón (€2, 30 minutes), Proaza (€2, 45 minutes) and Entrago (€2.50, one hour), terminating at San Martín, 1km beyond Entrago and 3km before the Parque de la Prehistoria.

Parque Natural de Somiedo

If you fancy exploring beautiful mountain country that few foreigners reach, head for this 291-sq-km Unesco-listed biosphere reserve on the northern flank of the Cordillera Cantábrica. Composed chiefly of five valleys descending from the Cordillera's 2000m-plus heights, the park combines thick woodlands, rocky mountains and high pastures dotted with *brañas* (groups of now largely abandoned *cabanas de teito* – thatched herders' shelters). It's also a key stronghold of Spain's bear population.

The main population centre is plain Pola de Somiedo (70km southwest of Oviedo), which has a bank, an ATM, a supermarket, a petrol station and the park's **Centro de Interpretación** (☑ 985 76 37 58; www.parquenaturalsomiedo.es; Pola de Somiedo; ⊗10am-2pm & 4-7pm Tue-Sat, 10am-2pm Sun). Valle de Lago, a wonderful 8km drive southeast of Pola de Somiedo that winds and climbs to about 1300m, is another base, with good walking.

◎ Sights

Centro de Interpretación 'Somiedo y El Oso'　INTERPRETATION CENTRE
(☑ 942 23 49 00, 985 76 34 06; www.fundacionosopardo.org; Pola de Somiedo; adult/child €3/1; ⊗11am-2pm & 5-9pm mid-Jun–mid-Sep, 11am-2pm & 4-7pm Sat & Sun late Apr–mid-Jun & mid-Sep–Oct) Run by the Fundación Oso Pardo, this exposition is a good place to brush up on facts about Northern Spain's brown bears, with informative displays and videos (in Spanish) that include details about the species' continuous battle for survival.

🏃 Activities

One of Somiedo's best (and most popular) walking areas is the **Valle de Lago**, whose upper reaches contain glacial lakes and high summer pastures. Here the **Ruta de Valle de Lago** (6km, around 2½ hours one way) trail leads to Asturias' most expansive lake. You must leave vehicles in Valle de Lago village.

Other good walks include the **La Peral–Villar de Vildas** route in the upper Pigüeña valley (13km, around five hours one way), which passes one of the largest and

best-preserved *brañas,* La Pornacal, and the challenging ascent of **El Cornón** (2194m), the park's highest peak (14km, around nine hours return).

🛏 Sleeping

Braña La Code　CABIN €€
(☑ 985 76 37 76, 606 721125; www.campinglagosdesomiedo.com; Valle de Lago; d cabin €88, each extra person €15; Ⓟ🛈) This quirky spot in Valle de Lago village offers accommodation in six shaggy-roofed, local-style *cabanas de teito,* built with traditional materials but significantly more comfortable than the real thing (including bathrooms, TVs and kitchenettes). It shares a simple bar-restaurant with the agreeably rustic adjoining **Camping Lagos de Somiedo** (☑ 985 76 37 76, 606 721125; www.campinglagosdesomiedo.com; Valle de Lago; sites per 2 people, car & tent €23; ⊗Easter & Jun-Sep; Ⓟ🛈).

Auriz　APARTMENT €€
(☑ 619 320001; www.auriz.es; Pola de Somiedo; apt for 2/4/6 €70/120/160; ⊗closed mid-Jan–early Feb; Ⓟ🛈🛈) Six excellent, modern, two-floor, three-bedroom apartments with kitchens and wood-burning stoves, all bursting with colour, beside a trout stream just off the road to Valle de Lago on the eastern side of Pola de Somiedo.

Palacio de Flórez-Estrada　HISTORIC HOTEL €€
(☑ 985 763709, 616 170018; www.florezestrada.com; Pola de Somiedo; s/d/ste incl breakfast €70/90/110, apt €70; ⊗Apr-Oct; Ⓟ🛈🛈) A gorgeous olde-worlde riverside mansion in sprawling gardens just off the road to Valle de Lago, on the eastern side of Pola de Somiedo. Cosy rooms are spread across a 15th-century tower, simple meals are served and the owner hosts an array of cultural events and yoga retreats. The four two-person apartments, inside revamped stables on the same pretty site, are open year-round.

❶ Getting There & Away

BUS

An **ALSA** (☑ 902 422242; www.alsa.es) bus departs Oviedo bus station for Pola de Somiedo (€8.75, two hours) at 5pm Monday to Friday and 10am on weekends, returning from Pola at 6.45am (5.30pm on weekends).

CAR

With your own wheels, you can approach Somiedo from the Senda del Oso area by the

Wild Spain

Spain is one of Europe's best destinations for watching wildlife. Most of the excitement surrounds the three flagship species – the Iberian lynx, the Iberian wolf and the brown bear – but birdwatchers also rave about the twitching possibilities in Spain. Other possibilities include whale-watching off the south coast, especially from Tarifa, and Europe's only primates, the Barbary macaques, in Gibraltar.

Iberian Lynx

The beautiful *lince ibérico* (Iberian lynx), the most endangered wild cat species on Earth, once inhabited large areas of the peninsula, but numbers fell below 100 at the beginning of the 21st century. A captive-breeding program and the reintroduction of captive-bred lynx into the wild have seen the wild population reach an estimated 320 individuals, with a further 150 in captivity.

The two remaining lynx populations are in Andalucía: the Parque Nacional de Doñana (with around 80 lynxes); and the Sierra Morena (nearly 250) spread across the Guadalmellato (northeast of Córdoba), Guarrizas (northeast of Linares) and Andújar-Cardeña (north of Andújar) regions.

Iberian Wolf

Spain's population of *lobo ibérico* (Iberian wolf) has been stable at between 2000 and 2500 for a few years now, up from a low of around 500 in 1970. Though officially protected, wolves are still considered an enemy by many country people and the hunting of wolves is still permitted in some areas. The species is found in small populations across the

and Cangas' second river, the Río Güeña. There are plenty more eating options on and around central Calle de San Pelayo.

★ **El Molín de la Pedrera** ASTURIAN €€
(☑ 985 84 91 09; www.elmolin.com; Calle del Río Güeña 2; mains €12-20; ☺ noon-4.30pm & 8.30-11.30pm Thu-Mon, noon-4.30pm Tue) This good-value, stone-and-brick-walled family-run eatery wins with both its traditional Asturian dishes such as *fabada* (bean, meat and sausage stew), *tortos de maíz* (maize cakes) and locally sourced cheese platters, as well as its more creative efforts such as Cabrales-cheese-and-hazelnut filo parcels and delicious homemade desserts. Excellent meat dishes, welcoming service and good wines round out a top dining experience.

La Sifonería ASTURIAN €€
(☑ 985 84 90 55; www.lasifoneria.net; Calle de San Pelayo 28; dishes €8-15; ☺ 1-4pm & 8pm-midnight Thu-Mon, 8pm-midnight Wed) Crammed with ancient cider-making siphons, blue-and-white-tiled walls and photos of the friendly cider-pouring owners, this wonderfully down-to-earth tapas spot is perfect for tucking into uncomplicated Asturian cooking at good prices. Try Cabrales cheese croquettes, *tortos* (maize cakes) and a variety of *revueltos* (scrambled-egg dishes), or heartier classics such as *cachopo* (stuffed breaded veal). There's just a handful of bench-style tables.

❶ Information

Oficina de Turismo (☑ 985 84 80 05; www.cangasdeonis.com; Avenida de Covadonga 1; ☺ 10am-8pm Jul & Aug, 10am-2pm & 4-7pm Mon-Sat, 10am-2pm Sun Sep-Jun)
Centro de Información Casa Dago (p494) Offers Picos hiking info and free guided walks from July to September (bookings recommended).

❶ Getting There & Away

ALSA (☑ 902 42 22 42; www.alsa.es) runs at least seven daily buses from Oviedo to Cangas (€6.35 to €7.05, 1½ hours) and back, all stopping in Arriondas en route. Cangas' bus station is in the Barrio La Pedrera on the northern side of the Río Güeña, linked by a footbridge to the town centre.

An alternative to the buses is to take a taxi. There are regular taxis that stick to the better roads, such as Taxitur (p495) in Cangas.

Covadonga
POP 45 / ELEVATION 260M

The importance of Covadonga, 10km southeast of Cangas de Onís, lies in what it represents, though it's also a spectacular spot with a striking 19th-century basilica (p497) tucked between soaring mountains. Somewhere hereabouts, in approximately AD 722, the Muslims received their first defeat in Spain, at the hands of the Visigothic nobleman (and, later, Asturian king) Pelayo – an event considered to mark the beginning of the 800-year Reconquista. It's believed that, before battle, the Virgin appeared to Pelayo's warriors in a hillside cave here, and Covadonga is still an object of pilgrimage today.

◉ Sights

Basílica de Covadonga CHURCH
(☺ 9am-7pm, hours vary) **FREE** Covadonga's original wooden church burnt down in 1777 and a landslide destroyed much of the settlement in the 19th century. The main church, the Basílica de Covadonga, is a neo-Romanesque affair built between 1877 and 1901.

Santa Cueva RELIGIOUS SITE
(☺ 9am-7pm, hours vary) **FREE** In this cave, now with a chapel installed, the Virgin supposedly appeared to Pelayo's warriors before their AD 722 victory over the Muslims. Weekends and summers see long queues of the faithful and curious lining up to enter. The cave's two tombs are claimed to be those of Pelayo himself, his daughter Hermesinda and her husband Alfonso I.

❶ Getting There & Away

Three or more **ALSA** (☑ 902 42 22 42; www.alsa.es) buses daily run from Cangas de Onís to Covadonga (€1.50, 15 minutes). From late July to mid-September, a shuttle-bus service (€1.50) operates to Covadonga from four car parks (per vehicle €2) in Cangas de Onís (beside the bus station) and along the road between there and Covadonga.

Lagos de Covadonga

Don't let summer crowds deter you from continuing 12km uphill past Covadonga to these two beautiful little lakes, set against jaunty (often snow-topped) peaks. Most day trippers don't get past patting a few cows' noses and snapping some photos, so walking here is as delightful as anywhere else in the Picos.

En route, about 8km uphill from Covadonga, the Mirador de la Reina is worth a stop for its dramatic panoramas across hills to the Bay of Biscay.

Lago de Enol is the first lake you reach, with the main car park and an info point just beyond it (downhill). It's linked to Lago de la Ercina, 1km away, not only by the paved road but also by a footpath (part of the PRPNPE2) via the Centro de Visitantes Pedro Pidal (⊙10am-6pm Easter & mid-Jul–mid-Sep), which has displays on Picos flora and fauna.

When mist descends, the lakes, surrounded by the green pastures and bald rock that characterise this part of the Picos, take on an eerie appearance.

Activities

The Lagos de Covadonga are the starting point for several fine walks.

Walking Routes

A marked loop walk, the Ruta de los Lagos (PRPNPE2; 5.7km, about 2½ hours), takes in the two lakes, the Centro de Visitantes Pedro Pidal (p498) and an old mine, the Minas de Buferrera. About 400m south of Lago de Enol, the route passes the Refugio Vega de Enol (Casa de Pastores; ☑630 45 14 75, 984 09 08 35; Lago de Enol; dm €12, half-board €28; ⊙year-round; 🛜🐾), whose 16 bunks are the nearest accommodation to the lakes. It has a hot shower, serves good food (mains €8 to €15) and is reachable by vehicle.

Two other relatively easy trails from the lakes will take you slightly further afield. The PRPNPE4 leads 7.6km southeast from Lago de la Ercina, with an ascent of 610m, to the Vega de Ario, where the Refugio Vega de Ario (Refugio Marqués de Villaviciosa; ☑656 84 30 95, 649 72 19 71, 984 09 20 00; www.refugiovegadeario.es; dm adult/child €14/8, half-board €28; ⊙Easter & Jun-Oct) has 40 bunks and meal service. The reward for about three hours' effort in getting there is magnificent views across the Garganta del Cares to the Picos' Macizo Central.

The PRPNPE5 leads you roughly south from Lago de Enol to the 68-bed Refugio de Vegarredonda (☑985 92 29 52, 626 343366; www.vegarredondaremis.com; dm adult/child €14/8; ⊙Mar-Nov) at 1410m, with meal service, and on to the Mirador de Ordiales, a lookout point over a 1km sheer drop into the Valle de Angón. It's a 10km (about a 3½-hour) walk each way – relatively easy along a mule track as far as the *refugio*, then a little more challenging on up to the *mirador*. Track conditions permitting, drivers can save about 40 minutes by driving as far as the Pandecarmen car park, 2km south of Lago de Enol.

❶ Getting There & Away

BUS

From late July to mid-September, a shuttle-bus service (day ticket adult/child €8/3.50) operates to the Lagos de Covadonga from four car parks (per vehicle €2) in Cangas de Onís (beside the bus station) and along the road between there and Covadonga.

CAR

To avoid traffic chaos from late July to mid-September and during some other major holidays, private vehicles cannot drive up from Covadonga to the Lagos de Covadonga from about 8.30am to 8pm. They can, however, drive up to the lakes before 8.30am or after 8pm and, once up, drive down any time.

TAXI

A regular taxi costs €30 one way from Cangas de Onís to the Lagos de Covadonga, or €44 round trip with one hour's waiting time at the lakes. From late July to early September and during some other major holidays, **Taxitur** (p495) operates a round-trip service (€11 per adult, €5 per child) in eight-passenger vehicles.

Central Picos

The star attraction of the Picos' central massif is the gorge that divides it from the western Macizo El Cornión. The popular Garganta del Cares (Cares Gorge) trail through it gets busy in summer, but the walk is always an exhilarating experience. This part of the Picos, however, also has plenty of less heavily tramped paths and climbing challenges. Arenas de Cabrales, on the AS114 between Cangas de Onís and Panes, is a popular base, but Poncebos, Sotres, Bulnes and Caín also offer facilities.

Arenas de Cabrales

POP 809 / ELEV 135M

Arenas de Cabrales (also Las Arenas) lies at the confluence of the bubbling Ríos Cares and Casaño, 30km east of Cangas de Onís. The busy main road is lined with hotels, restaurants and bars, and just off it is a little tangle of quiet squares and back lanes. Arenas is a popular base for walking the spectacular Garganta del Cares gorge.

⊙ Sights

Cueva-Exposición Cabrales   MUSEUM
(☑985 84 67 02; www.fundacioncabrales.com;
Ctra AS264; adult/child €4.50/3; ⊙10.15am-
1.15pm & 4.15-7.15pm Apr-Sep, to 6.15pm Oct-Mar)
Learn all about and sample the fine smelly
Cabrales cheese at Arenas' Cueva-Exposición
Cabrales, a cheese-cave museum 500m
south of the centre on the Poncebos road.
Forty-minute guided visits are in Spanish
and, occasionally, English.

🏃 Activities

Arenas is a good access point for the popular
Garganta del Cares walk, which begins 6km
south at Poncebos. Cheese-making tours are
a hit here too; check with the local tourist office and the one in Cangas de Onís (p496)
to find out which makers welcome visitors.

🛏 Sleeping & Eating

La Portiella del Llosu   CASA RURAL €
(☑646 866780, 984 11 24 34; www.llosu.es;
Pandiello; r incl breakfast €60; ☎) Set against
magnificent valley and Picos panoramas
in peaceful Pandiello, 10km northwest of
Arenas, this is a delightfully rustic restoration of a 16th-century home. The five
warm-coloured rooms (with views) come
furnished with antiques and family heirlooms, such as hand-painted cupboards and
ceramic-bowl sinks, spruced up by the hospitable owners. Breakfasts are homemade.

It's 2km from the Pandiello turnoff just
east of Ortiguero.

Restaurante Cares   ASTURIAN €€
(☑985 84 66 28; cafecares-ast@hotmail.com;
Calle Mayor; mains €8.75-20, menús €15-25;
⊙1-3.30pm & 8-11.30pm Jul–mid-Sep, 1-3.30pm
Tue-Thu & Sun, 1-3.30pm & 8-11.30pm Fri & Sat
mid-Sep–Jun, hours vary; ☑🅿) On the main
road, beside the Poncebos junction, the
Cares is one of the best-value restaurants
for miles. It does well-priced lunch and dinner *menús*, including a vegetarian *menú* (a
rare breed in northern Spain), plus *platos
combinados* (meat/eggs with chips and
veg), kids' meals, à la carte fish and meats,
and a choice of hearty Asturian *cachopo*
(ham-and-cheese-stuffed breaded veal).

ℹ Information

Oficina de Turismo (☑985 84 64 84; www.
cabrales.es; Calle Mayor; ⊙10am-2pm & 4-7pm
Tue-Sun Easter & Jun–mid-Sep, hours vary) In

the middle of town, opposite the Poncebos road
junction.

ℹ Getting There & Away

Two or more daily **ALSA** (☑902 42 22 42;
www.alsa.es) buses run from Cangas de Onís
to Arenas (€2.95, 40 minutes) and back. Two
buses daily, Monday to Friday only, link Arenas
with Llanes (€3.45, one hour, or €6.50, 1¾
hours). Buses stop next to the tourist office, in
the middle of town at the junction of the Poncebos road.

Garganta del Cares

Traversed by the Río Cares, the magnificent
1km-deep, 10km-long Garganta del Cares
gorge separates the Picos' western massif
from its central sibling. This dramatic limestone canyon extends between Poncebos,
6km south of Arenas de Cabrales in Asturias, and Caín in Castilla y León. People flock
here year-round, but especially in summer,
to walk the insanely popular Ruta del Cares
(p499) (PRPNPE3), carved high into and
through the rugged walls of the gorge between the two villages.

🏃 Activities

⭐**Garganta del Cares Walk**   WALKING
(Ruta del Cares; PRPNPE3) You can walk
Spain's favourite trail, the 10km Ruta del
Cares, in either direction, but by heading
from north (Poncebos) to south (Caín)
you'll save its finest stretches for last.
The beginning involves a steady climb in
the gorge's wide, mostly bare early stages.
From the top end of Poncebos, follow the
'Ruta del Cares' sign pointing uphill 700m
along the road. After 3km, you'll reach
some abandoned houses. Just a little further and you're over the highest point of
the walk.

ℹ Getting There & Away

From about mid-July to early September, **ALSA**
(☑902 42 22 42; www.alsa.es) runs two or
three morning buses from Cangas de Onís to
Caín (€8, two hours), starting back from Caín
to Cangas in early or mid-afternoon; and two
or three afternoon/early evening buses from
Cangas to Poncebos (€4.50, 45 minutes) via
Arenas de Cabrales, and back. These schedules
enable you to take a bus from Cangas to Caín,
walk the Garganta del Cares north from Caín to
Poncebos, and get a bus back from Poncebos to
Cangas, all in one day.

CANTABRIA & ASTURIAS GARGANTA DEL CARES

There is a similar service from León via Posada de Valdeón to Caín in the morning and back from Poncebos to Posada de Valdeón and León in the afternoon (€20 for the León–Caín and Poncebos–León round trip).

A number of agencies in Picos towns will transport you to either end of the walk and pick you up at the other end, usually for around €115 for up to four people. At extra cost, some will add on 4WD tours into the Picos.

Bulnes

POP 24 / ELEV 647M

The rust-roofed hamlet of Bulnes, inaccessible by road, sits high up a side valley off the Cares gorge, south of Poncebos. You can reach it by a quite strenuous, 5km uphill walk (about two hours) from Poncebos or aboard the Funicular de Bulnes (☑985 84 68 00; one way/return adult €17/22, child €4.30/6.60; ⊘10.30am-8pm Easter & mid-Jun–mid-Sep, 10am-12.30pm & 2-6pm rest of year), a tunnel railway that climbs steeply for over 2km inside the mountain from its lower station just below Poncebos. At the top of this thrill-inducing ride, tiny Bulnes sits in a pretty, secluded valley surrounded on all sides by towering rocky peaks.

You can also approach Bulnes from the east by walking about 2.5km (one hour) down from the Collado de Pandébano.

Bulnes is divided into two parts: the upper Barrio del Castillo and the lower La Villa. All amenities are in La Villa.

🏃 Activities

Roadless Bulnes sits on some good walking routes for those who don't mind plenty of up and down.

Walking Routes

The PRPNPE19 trail comes up from Poncebos in a relatively strenuous 5km, with an ascent of about 500m (about two hours), then continues even more demandingly 4km southward with over 1100m of ascent, often on stony slopes, up to the Refugio Vega de Urriello (☑638 27 80 41, 650 78 03 81, 984 09 09 81; www.refugiodeurriellu.com; dm adult/child €14/8; ⊘year-round) beneath the mighty El Naranjo de Bulnes. Or you can head 2.5km east uphill from Bulnes to the Collado de Pandébano pass, where the PRPNPE21 provides an easier (though not easy) approach to the Refugio Vega de Urriello. From the Collado, you can also descend 4km eastward to Sotres in about one hour.

🛏 Sleeping & Eating

La Casa del Chiflón   CASA RURAL €
(☑985 84 59 43; www.lacasadelchiflon.com; s/d incl breakfast €45/60; ⊘Easter & Jun–mid-Oct; ☏) An attractive stone-walled casa rural (village accommodation) with six snug rooms, efficient management and a riverside restaurant, in the lower half of Bulnes.

Bar Bulnes   SPANISH €
(☑985 84 59 34; raciones €5-11; ⊘10am-8pm Easter & Jul-Sep, 10am-6pm rest of year, closed Mon-Fri Jan & Feb) You'll find good home cooking and enormous Cabrales cheese bocadillos (filled rolls) at sweet, simple Bar Bulnes, in the lower half of Bulnes.

❶ Getting There & Away

The Funicular de Bulnes (p500) makes the seven-minute trip between Poncebos and Bulnes every half-hour in both directions.

Sotres

POP 112 / ELEV 1045M

A side road twists and turns 11km from Poncebos up to little Sotres, the highest village in the Picos and the starting point for a number of good walks.

🏃 Activities

Sotres is the start (or end) point for a number of good walks.

Walking Routes

A popular route goes east to the village of Tresviso and on down to Urdón, on the Potes–Panes road. As far as Tresviso (10km) it's a paved road, but the final 7km is a dramatic walking trail, the Ruta Urdón-Tresviso (PRPNPE30), snaking 850m down to the Desfiladero de la Hermida gorge. Doing this in the upward direction, starting from Urdón, is at least as popular.

Many walkers head west from Sotres to the Collado de Pandébano pass, a 4km (one to 1½ hour) walk on the far side of the Duje valley. At Pandébano the 2519m rock finger called El Naranjo de Bulnes (Pico Urriello) comes into view – an emblem of the Picos de Europa and a classic challenge for climbers. Few walkers can resist the temptation to get even closer to El Naranjo. From Pandébano, it's 5km (about three hours), with 700m of ascent, up the PRPNPE21 trail to the Vega de Urriello (1953m), at the foot of the mountain. Here the 96-bunk Refugio Vega de Urriello (p500) is attended year-round (weather permitting), with meal service. Otherwise, you can descend 2.5km (about one hour) west from Pandébano to Bulnes.

You can also walk south from Sotres along 4WD tracks to the Hotel Áliva (☑942 73 09 99; www.cantur.com; s/d/tr €50/80/95; ⊗mid-Jun–mid-Oct) or Espinama in the southeast of the national park.

❶ Getting There & Away

The only ways to reach Sotres are to drive up the winding, 11km paved road from Poncebos; to walk (from Urdón, Tresviso, Bulnes or elsewhere); or to approach from the south (Hotel Áliva or Espinama) on a 4WD trip. A taxi from Arenas de Cabrales costs about €20.

Eastern Picos

The AS114 east from Cangas de Onís and Arenas de Cabrales in Asturias meets the N621, running south from the coast, at the humdrum town of Panes. South of Panes, the N621 follows the Río Deva upstream through the impressive Desfiladero de la Hermida gorge. You cross into Cantabria at Urdón, 2km north of the hamlet of La Hermida, then continue 18km south to Potes, the major base and activity hub for the eastern Picos. About 23km west of Potes lies Fuente Dé, with its cable car providing the main Picos access point in this area.

Potes & Around

POP 1405 / ELEV 291M

Overrun in peak periods, but still lively and delightful in its cobbled old town, Potes is a hugely popular staging post on the southeastern edge of the Picos, with the Macizo Ándara rising close at hand. Potes is effectively the 'capital' of Liébana, a beautifully verdant and historic valley area lying between the Picos and the main spine of the Cordillera Cantábrica.

◉ Sights

The heart of Potes is a cluster of bridges, towers and charming backstreets restored in traditional slate, wood and red tile after considerable damage during the civil war. The Centro de Visitantes Sotama (p494), 2km north of Potes, has excellent displays on Picos de Europa wildlife, history and geology, as well as on Beato de Liébana and Romanesque architecture.

Monasterio de Santo Toribio de Liébana
MONASTERY

(☑942 73 05 50; www.santotoribiodeliebana.org; ⊗10am-1pm & 4-7pm May-Sep, to 6pm Oct-Apr; ℗) FREE Christian refugees, fleeing from Muslim-occupied Spain to Liébana in the 8th century, brought with them the Lígnum Crucis, purportedly the single biggest chunk of Christ's cross and featuring the hole made by the nail that passed through Christ's left hand. The Santo Toribio Monastery, 3km west of Potes, has housed this holy relic ever since. The monastery is also famous for being the home of 8th-century medieval monk and theologian Beato de Liébana, celebrated across Europe for his *Commentary on the Apocalypse*.

Iglesia de Santa María de Lebeña
CHURCH

(Lebeña; adult/child €1.50/free; ⊗10am-1.30pm & 4-7.30pm Tue-Sun Jun-Sep, to 6pm Oct-May; ℗) Nine kilometres northeast of Potes, the fascinating Iglesia de Santa María de Lebeña dates back to the 9th or 10th century. The horseshoe arches are a telltale sign of its Mozarabic style – rare this far north in Spain. The floral motifs on its columns are Visigothic, while below the main 18th-century *retablo* (altarpiece) stands a Celtic stone engraving. Apparently, the yew tree outside (reduced to a sad stump by a storm in 2007) was planted 1000 years ago.

⚹ Activities

The Potes area provides good access to Fuente Dé. Potes is the main base for all eastern Picos activities, with several agencies offering a host of options: mountain biking (rental half/full day €15/25, guided trips €40 to €60), horse riding (one/1½/2½ hours €20/25/30), climbing (€40 to over €300), canyoning (€30 to €40) and tandem paragliding (half-hour €100). You can also take cheese-making and *orujo*-making tours.

El Coterón
DISTILLERY

(☑942 73 08 76; www.elcoteron.com; Arguébanes; ⊗tours 10.30am & 4pm Mon-Fri, noon & 4pm Sat & Sun) FREE Several Potes-area *orujo*-makers have opened their doors to visitors, revealing the secret behind this strong local liquor. About 5km northwest of Potes, El Coterón is a small family-run *orujo* distillery offering informative tours (sometimes in English) of their facilities and, of course, the chance to taste and purchase products at the original source. Visit in October or November to

CANTABRIA & ASTURIAS POTES & AROUND

POTES FIREWATER

The potent liquor *orujo*, made from leftover grape pressings, is drunk throughout northern Spain and is something of a Potes speciality. People here like to drink it as an after-dinner aperitif as part of a herbal tea called *té de roca* or *té de puerto*. Plenty of shops around town sell *orujo*, including varieties flavoured with honey, fruits and herbs, and most will offer you tastings if you're thinking of buying.

Potes' fun-filled Fiesta del Orujo (p502) kicks off on the second weekend in November, and involves practically every bar in town setting up a stall selling *orujo* shots for a few cents, the proceeds of which go to charity.

Several Potes-area *orujo*-makers have recently swung open their doors to visitors. About 5km northwest of Potes, El Coterón (p501) is a small family-run *orujo* distillery offering informative tours (sometimes in English) of their facilities and, of course, the chance to taste and purchase products at the source. Visit in October or November to witness the apples being picked and pressed. Bookings recommended.

witness the apples being picked and pressed. Bookings recommended.

Quesería Alles FOOD
(📞 616 29 84 00, 942 73 31 53; www.quesopicon.es; Bejes; ⏰ 10am-1pm & 4-7pm) FREE If you're keen on Cantabria's super-pungent blue Picón cheese, head 20km north of Potes to tiny Bejes (582m; signposted off the N621), where you can tour and taste at one of the region's most successful *queserías* (cheese makers). Detailed Spanish-language tours take in the cheese-making process and facilities and, if you enquire ahead, possibly the local cheese-maturing cave too.

🎊 Festivals & Events

Fiesta del Orujo DRINK
(www.fiestadelorujo.es) Honouring the potent locally made liquor *orujo*, Potes' fun-filled Fiesta del Orujo kicks off on the second weekend in November and involves practically every bar in town setting up a stall selling *orujo* shots for a few cents, the proceeds of which go to charity.

🛏 Sleeping & Eating

⭐ **La Casa de las Chimeneas** APARTMENT €€
(📞 942 73 63 00; www.lacasadelaschimeneas.es; Plaza Mayor, Tudes; 1-bedroom apt €75-105, 2-bedroom apt €115-155; 🅿 🛜 ☷) In a pretty hillside hamlet stands this old English-Spanish–owned farmstead converted into eight comfy, well-equipped and characterful apartments, most on two or three levels. Each apartment has its own theme, detailed by intricate, hand-painted, medieval-inspired murals. Enjoy the curved infinity pool, games room, fabulous Picos panoramas and light bites at

their equally original Taberna del Inglés (⏰ hrs vary).

⭐ **Posada San Pelayo** COUNTRY HOUSE €€
(📞 942 73 32 10; www.posadasanpelayo.com; San Pelayo; s €55-66, d €71-88; 🅿 🛜 ☷) About 5km west of Potes, Posada San Pelayo is a beautiful, welcoming, family-run rural hotel of recent construction in traditional country style. Spacious modern-rustic rooms, many with timber terraces, are done up in cheerful earthy colours and there are plenty of cosy common areas, a winter fire and a gorgeous garden and pool with exquisite mountain views. Breakfast (€6.60) is good.

Asador Llorente CANTABRIAN €€
(📞 942 73 81 65; Calle de San Roque 1, Potes; mains €8-18; ⏰ 1-4pm & 8.30-11.30pm, closed Tue Sep-Jul) For super-generous helpings of fresh, high-quality local food, head upstairs to this warm, wood-beamed loft-like space with Picos photos and a tiny trickling fountain. Carnivores are in for a treat: try the Liébana speciality *cocido lebaniego* (a filling stew of chickpeas, potato, greens, chorizo, black pudding, bacon and beef) or tuck into a half-kilogram *chuletón* (giant beef chop). Crisp salads are tasty too.

El Bodegón CANTABRIAN, ASTURIAN €€
(📞 942 73 02 47; Calle de San Roque; mains €9-17; ⏰ 1-4pm & 8pm-midnight Jun-Aug, closed Wed Sep-May) Snack on *raciones* of Cantabrian cheeses, Galician-style octopus or cured meats in the lively, dimly lit bar or settle into the elegant, stone-walled, wood-beamed restaurant for traditional mountain fare such as *fabada* (bean and sausage stew), *cachopo* (stuffed breaded veal) and *solomillo al Cabrales* (tenderloin with Cabrales cheese sauce).

ℹ Information

Oficina de Turismo (☎942 73 07 87; turismo potes@yahoo.es; Plaza de la Independencia; ☺10am-2pm & 4-8pm Jul–mid-Sep, to 6pm mid-Sep–Jun) In the deconsecrated 14th-century, rustic Gothic Iglesia de San Vicente.

Centro de Visitantes Sotama (p494) Info on Picos hiking routes; about 2km north of Potes.

ℹ Getting There & Away

From Santander, **Autobuses Palomera** (☎942 88 06 11; www.autobusespalomera.com) travels via San Vicente de la Barquera, Panes, Urdón and Lebeña to Potes (€8.30, 2½ hours), and back again one to three times daily.

Fuente Dé & Around

POP 8 (FUENTE DÉ) / ELEV 1078M

Tiny, dramatic Fuente Dé lies at the foot of the stark southern wall of the Picos' Macizo Central. It's composed of two hotels and a campground huddled around the ridiculously popular Teleférico de Fuente Dé (p503), from the top of which walkers and climbers can make their way deeper into the central massif. The winding CA185 from Potes to Fuente Dé is a beautiful 23km trip.

◉ Sights

★ **Teleférico de Fuente Dé**   CABLE CAR
(☎942 73 66 10; www.cantur.com; Fuente Dé; adult/child return €16/6; ☺9am-8pm Easter & Jul–mid-Sep, 10am-6pm mid-Sep–Jun, closed 2nd half Jan; P) In just four minutes, the spine-tingling Teleférico de Fuente Dé whisks visitors 753m up to the top of the sheer southern wall of the Picos' central massif (1823m), from where hikers and climbers can venture further in. Cable cars depart every 20 minutes, weather permitting. You can check online for updates, but it's better to phone. Be warned that during high season (especially August) you can wait over an hour for a cable-car place, in both directions. Luckily there are cafes at either end.

Casa del Oso   INTERPRETATION CENTRE
(☎942 23 49 00; www.fundacionosopardo.org; Parador de Fuente Dé, Fuente Dé; adult/child €3/1; ☺11am-7pm mid-Jun–mid-Sep, 11am-6pm Sat & Sun mid-Apr–mid-Jun & mid-Sep–Oct; P) Fuente Dé's Casa del Oso is run by the Fundación

Oso Pardo, Spain's main brown bear advocate, and has interactive exhibits and documentaries on endangered Cantabrian brown bears.

🏃 Activities

There are some fantastic walks starting from the top of the Teleférico de Fuente Dé. Fuente Dé's hotels also offer 4WD trips into the mountains (around €100).

Walking Routes

It's an easy 3.5km, one-hour walk from the top of the Teleférico de Fuente Dé (p503) to the Hotel Áliva (p501), where you'll find refreshments. From the hotel, two 4WD tracks descend into the valley that separates the central massif from its eastern cousin. One heads north to Sotres via Vegas de Sotres (about 9km or two hours' walking). The other winds 7km south down to Espinama on the CA185 (about 2½ hours' walking). The PRPNPE24, popular for its contrasting landscapes, starts off along the Hotel Áliva–Espinama track then branches off about halfway down to return to Fuente Dé (11km, about 3¼ hours from the hotel).

Other possibilities for the suitably prepared include making your way across the massif to El Naranjo de Bulnes (Pico Urriello; the Picos' emblem) or climbing Peña Vieja (2613m). These require proper equipment and experience – Peña Vieja has claimed more lives than any other mountain in the Picos. Less challenging is the PRP-NPE23, a route of 5.5km northwest from the Teleférico de Fuente Dé, passing below Peña Vieja to the Collado de Horcados Rojos pass, which opens up spectacular panoramas including El Naranjo de Bulnes, with an ascent of 500m. Allow about 4½ hours there and back.

There are also some relatively gentle valley walking trails starting from villages on or not far from the CA185 such as Espinama, Mogrovejo or Brez.

🛏 Sleeping & Eating

Fuente Dé has a campground and two hotels including an ugly *parador*. The 23km-long CA185 between Potes and Fuente Dé is dotted with attractive rural hotels, *hostales* (budget hotels) and campgrounds. There are particularly good options in Espinama and Cosgaya, 3.5km and 10km southeast of Fuente Dé respectively.

★ **Hotel del Oso** HOTEL €€
(☎ 942 73 30 18; www.hoteldeloso.com; Cosgaya; s €63-71, d €78-89, q €116-130; ⊙ closed Jan; P 🛜 ≋) The gorgeous, long-standing Hotel del Oso comprises majestic twin stone houses facing each other across the Río Deva and the road. Spacious rustic-style rooms with timber floors and floral decor are very inviting, the restaurant (p504) is one of the area's finest, with top-quality meat, stews and desserts, and there's a lovely pool. It's 13km southwest of Potes or 10km southeast of Fuente Dé.

Hotel Rebeco HOTEL €€
(☎ 942 73 66 01; www.hotelrebeco.com; Fuente Dé; s/d €55/71; ⊙ closed Jan, variable; P 🛜) Many of the 30 rooms in this handsome, warm stone lodge have mountain views and 11 include loft levels that are perfect for kids. You can't help but admire owner Conchi Cuesta's tapestries. It has a good, reasonably priced **restaurant** (☎ 942 73 66 01; www. hotelrebeco.com; Fuente Dé; raciones €10-16, mains €6-20; ⊙ 1-10.30pm, closed Jan, variable; 🛜) and a roaring winter fire, and organises 4WD outings into the Picos (around €100, maximum six people).

★ **Hotel del Oso** CANTABRIAN €€
(☎ 942 73 30 18; www.hoteldeloso.com; Cosgaya; mains €13 to €24, menú €20; ⊙ 1-3.45pm & 8.30-10.30pm, closed Jan; P) One of the region's outstanding restaurants, the flower-fringed Hotel del Oso has been pleasing the public with its fantastic *cocido montañés* (stewed white beans, cabbage, potato, chorizo, black pudding and, sometimes, port) and its local variation, *cocido lebaniego* (stewed chickpeas, potato, greens, chorizo, black pudding, bacon and beef), for more than 30 years. It's also particularly good for top-quality meats and desserts – but it's all delicious.

❶ Getting There & Away

From July to mid-September there is a bus service once or twice daily run by **Autobuses Palomera** (☎ 942 88 06 11; www.autobusespalomera.com) between Potes and Fuente Dé (30 minutes, €1.75). A taxi from Potes to Fuente Dé costs about €25.

Santiago de Compostela & Galicia

Best Places to Eat

➡ El Silabario (p539)

➡ Restaurante Paprica (p545)

➡ O Curro da Parra (p512)

➡ Abastos 2.0 (p512)

➡ Adega O Bebedeiro (p520)

Best Places to Sleep

➡ Casa de Trillo (p516)

➡ Hotel Herbeira (p523)

➡ Hotel Costa Vella (p511)

➡ Parador Hostal dos Reis Católicos (p512)

➡ Hotel Mar da Ardora (p515)

➡ Casa do Castelo de Andrade (p522)

Why Go?

Galicia, a unique region with its own language and distinctive culture, is home to Santiago de Compostela, the goal of several hundred thousand people who set out yearly on the storied Camino de Santiago pilgrim trail. Santiago is one of Spain's most beautiful and magical cities, and an exceptionally good reason for any traveller, pilgrim or not, to make their way to Spain's northwestern corner.

But Galicia is much more than Santiago. The wild coastline is frayed up and down its 1200km length by majestic *rías* (coastal inlets), and strung with cliffs, beaches, islands and fishing ports that bring in indisputably the best seafood in Spain. Inland is a labyrinth of deep-green valleys and hills, speckled with stone-built villages, aged monasteries, vineyards and farms that put top-quality meat on Galician tables. Nor is Santiago Galicia's only exciting city: A Coruña, Vigo and Lugo are all contemporary cultural hubs with heady nocturnal scenes.

When to Go
Santiago de Compostela

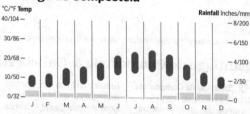

Jun & Sep No peak-season crowds or prices but (hopefully) decent weather.

Jul & Aug If you're aiming for some beach time, your best chance of sunny weather is now.

24 Jul Spectacular fireworks launch Santiago de Compostela's celebration of the Día de Santiago.

Santiago de Compostela & Galicia Highlights

❶ Santiago de Compostela (p507) Soaking up the incomparable atmosphere and history of this fascinating city.

❷ Costa da Morte (p515) Exploring the capes, beaches and lighthouses north of Cabo Fisterra, Spain's 'Land's End'.

❸ Seafood and wine (p538)

Feasting on fresh fish, octopus with Galician wines anywhere along the coast, as at A Guarda.

❹ Beach time (p524) Choosing from popular and busy, or remote and dramatic like Praia do Picón.

❺ Cliffs and capes of the Rías Altas (p524) Standing

atop Europe's highest ocean cliffs at the Garita de Herbeira.

❻ Illas Cíes (p537) Sailing to pristine beaches and trails of these spectacular islands.

❼ Ribeira Sacra (p543) Meandering in the wineries, woodlands and canyons of the 'Holy Riverbank'.

SANTIAGO DE COMPOSTELA

POP 80,000

Locals say the arcaded, stone streets of Santiago de Compostela – the final stop on the epic Camino de Santiago pilgrimage trail – are at their most beautiful in the rain, when the Old Town glistens. Most would agree, however, that it's hard to catch Santiago in a bad pose. Whether you're wandering the streets of the Old Town, nibbling on tapas in the taverns, or gazing down at the rooftops from atop the cathedral, Santiago seduces.

Today more than 250,000 Camino de Santiago pilgrims and countless thousands of other visitors journey here each year. The biggest numbers hit the city in July and August, but Santiago has a festive atmosphere throughout the warmer half of the year. If you'd like to enjoy the place less than jam-packed, May, June and September are good months to come.

History

The faithful believe that Santiago Apóstol (St James the Apostle, one of Christ's closest disciples) preached in Galicia and, after his execution in Palestine, was brought back by stone boat and buried here. The tomb was supposedly rediscovered in about the AD820s by a religious hermit, Pelayo, following a guiding star (hence, it's thought, 'Compostela' – from the Latin *campus stellae*, field of the star). Asturian king Alfonso II had a church erected above the holy remains, pilgrims began flocking to it, Alfonso III replaced it with a bigger church in pre-Romanesque style in the 890s, and by the 11th century the pilgrimage along the Camino de Santiago was a major European phenomenon, bringing a flood of funds into the city. Building of the magnificent cathedral we see today began in 1075, and Bishop Diego Xelmírez obtained archbishopric status for Santiago in 1100 and added numerous other churches in the 12th century. The following centuries, however, were marked by squabbling between rival nobles, and Santiago gradually slipped into the background.

Only since the 1980s, as capital of the autonomous region of Galicia and a rediscovered tourist and pilgrimage destination, has the city been revitalised.

◎ Sights

The magnificent cathedral and Praza do Obradoiro are the natural starting points and focus for exploring Santiago. The Old Town

in which they sit – a roughly oval-shaped area bounded by the line of the medieval city walls – is where almost everything of interest is found and its stone-paved streets are a delight to wander, with plenty of cafes, bars and restaurants to drop in on as you go.

Praza de Galicia marks the boundary between the Old Town and the Ensanche (Extension), the 20th-century shopping and residential area to its south.

★ Catedral de Santiago de Compostela

CATHEDRAL

(www.catedraldesantiago.es; Praza do Obradoiro; ⊙7am-8.30pm) The grand heart of Santiago, the cathedral soars above the city centre in a splendid jumble of spires and sculpture. Built piecemeal over several centuries, its beauty is a mix of the original Romanesque structure (constructed between 1075 and 1211) and later Gothic and baroque flourishes. The tomb of Santiago beneath the main altar is a magnet for all who come to the cathedral. The artistic high point is the Pórtico de la Gloria inside the west entrance, featuring 200 masterly Romanesque sculptures.

Over the centuries the cathedral has suffered some wear and tear from water seepage, settlement and humidity, and a current restoration program means that you may well find much of the main (western) facade and the Pórtico de la Gloria covered in scaffolding. It's hoped that work on the Pórtico de la Gloria will finish by late 2017, but until then access to it will be restricted to a limited number of guided visits daily: check with the cathedral's Visitor Reception Centre (p514) for current information on these.

The cathedral we see today is actually the fourth church to stand on this spot. It has a traditional Latin-cross layout and three naves. The lavish baroque western facade facing Praza do Obradoiro was erected in the 18th century, replacing the weather-damaged Romanesque one. This is traditionally the cathedral's main entrance, but it's currently closed because of the restoration works. Most people therefore enter the cathedral through the south door on Praza das Praterías (beneath the only facade that conserves its original Romanesque structure). Inside, the fantastically elaborate, churrigueresque Altar Mayor (High Altar) rises up from the central crossing where the transepts intersect the nave, with the long main nave stretching away to the west, flanked by majestic rows of Romanesque arches.

Santiago de Compostela

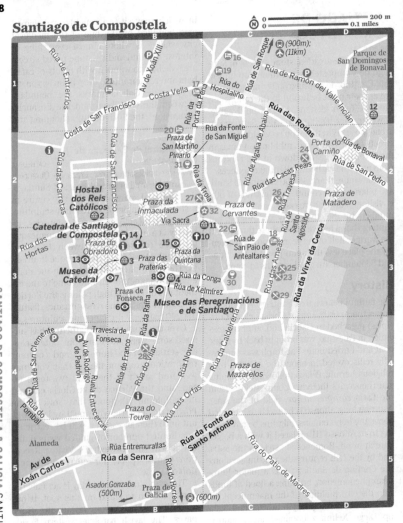

SANTIAGO DE COMPOSTELA & GALICIA SANTIAGO DE COMPOSTELA

From the right side of the ambulatory (walkway) that runs round behind the Altar Mayor, a small staircase leads up to a statue of Santiago that has watched over the cathedral since its consecration in 1211. The faithful queue up to kiss or embrace the statue. From here you emerge on the left side, then descend some steps into the **Cripta Apostólica**, where we are assured Santiago's remains lie, inside a large 19th-century silver casket. Behind the Altar Mayor is the **Puerta Santa** (Holy Door; Praza das Praterías), which opens onto Praza da Quintana and is cracked open only in holy years (next in 2021).

A special pilgrims' Mass is usually celebrated at the High Altar at noon daily, with other High Altar Masses at 7.30pm and 9am or 10am. Touristic visits are discouraged during Mass.

For some wonderful views of the cathedral's interior from its upper storeys, and over the city from the cathedral roof, it's worth taking a **cathedral rooftop tour** (☏ 902 557812; www.catedraldesantiago. es; adult/senior, pilgrim, unemployed & student/child €12/10/free, combined ticket with Museo da Catedral €15/12/free; ⊙ tours hourly 10am-1pm & 4-6pm or 7pm; ⛪).

Santiago de Compostela

The artistically unparalleled **Pórtico de la Gloria** (Galician: Porta da Gloria) stands just inside the cathedral's Obradoiro entrance, at the west end of the nave. If you're unable to see the Pórtico itself because of restoration works, you can at least visit an exhibition on it, which is being maintained for the duration of the restoration in the **Pazo de Xelmírez** (Praza do Obradoiro; ⊙9am-8pm Apr-Oct, 10am-8pm Nov-Mar) adjoining the cathedral (access to the Pazo is included in tickets for the Museo da Catedral and the rooftop tour). The Pórtico features 200 Romanesque sculptures by Maestro Mateo, who was placed in charge of the cathedral-building program in the late 12th century. These detailed, inspired and remarkably lifelike sculptures add up to a comprehensive review of major figures from the Bible, with the Old Testament and its prophets on the north side, the New Testament and Apostles on the south, and glory and resurrection depicted in the central archway.

The main figure in the central archway is a throned, resurrected Christ, surrounded by the four Evangelists plus angels and symbols of Jesus' passion. In an arc above are the 24 musicians said in Revelations to sit around the heavenly throne. Below Christ's feet is Santiago, and below him

Hercules (holding open the mouths of two lions). Visitors arriving in the cathedral traditionally said a brief prayer while placing their fingers in five holes above Hercules' head, created by the repetition of this very act by millions of faithful over the centuries. On the other side of the central pillar is a sculpture of Maestro Mateo. For centuries, tradition called for visitors to bump heads with the maestro to acquire some of his genius. These countless knocks led to Mateo's notably flat nose, and both he and Hercules were blocked off behind metal barriers even before the Pórtico acquired its recent scaffold covering.

Among the Old Testament prophets, the very bright smile on Daniel's face is, according to one legend, caused by the tightly dressed figure of Queen Esther on the pillar opposite him. Legend also has it that Esther's stone breasts were originally much larger, but were filed down on orders of a disapproving bishop – to which townspeople responded by inventing Galicia's cone-shaped *tetilla* (nipple) cheese in Esther's honour.

★**Museo da Catedral**　　　　MUSEUM
(Colección Permanente; www.catedraldesantiago.es; Praza do Obradoiro; adult/senior, pilgrim, unemployed & student/child €6/4/free; ⊙9am-8pm

DON'T MISS

EXPLORING AROUND THE CATHEDRAL

The cathedral is surrounded by handsome plazas that invite you to wander through them.

Praza do Obradoiro

The grand square in front of the cathedral's west facade earned its name (Workshop Sq) from the stonemasons' workshops set up here while the cathedral was being built. It's free of both traffic and cafes and has a unique, magical atmosphere.

Stretching across the northern end of the *praza*, the Hostal dos Reis Católicos (adult/child €3/free; ☉ noon-2pm & 4-6pm Sun-Fri) was built in the early 16th century by order of the Catholic Monarchs, Isabel and Fernando, as a recuperation centre for exhausted pilgrims. Today it's a *parador* (luxurious state-owned hotel) and shelters well-heeled travellers instead, but its four courtyards and some other areas are open to visitors: the self-guided tour, with leaflet and over 40 information panels, is well worthwhile.

Along the western side of the *praza* stretches the elegant 18th-century Pazo de Raxoi, now Santiago's city hall. At the south end stands the Colegio de San Xerome, a former college for the poor that is now the rectorate of Santiago University. This 17th-century building has a 15th-century Romanesque/Gothic portal, which was transferred from the college's previous building.

Praza de Fonseca

South of the cathedral, stop in cafe-lined Praza de Fonseca to look into the Colexio de Fonseca (☉ 10am-8.30pm Mon-Sat) with its beautiful Renaissance courtyard; this was the original seat of Santiago's university (founded in 1495) and now houses the university's main library. Its Gothic chapel and Salón Artesonado, either side of the entrance, house assorted temporary exhibitions.

Praza das Praterías

'Silversmiths' Sq' is marked by the elegant Fuente de los Caballos (Fountain of the Horses) fountain (1825), a popular photo op, with the cathedral's Romanesque south portal at the top of the steps. Curiously, the baroque Casa do Cabildo, on the lower side of the square, is no more than a 3m-deep facade, erected in the 1750s to embellish the plaza.

Praza da Quintana

Outside the cathedral's east end, Praza da Quintana is lined by the long, stark wall of the Mosteiro de San Paio de Antealtares, founded in the 9th century for the monks who looked after Santiago's relics (now a convent). Its Museo de Arte Sacra (Vía Sacra 5; €1.50; ☉ 10.30am-1.30pm & 4-7pm Mon-Sat, 4-7pm Sun), accessed through the convent church at the top of the plaza steps, contains the original altar raised over those relics. The cathedral's Puerta Santa (p508), opening on to Praza Quintana, is opened only in holy years (next in 2021): it's flanked by 24 Romanesque sculptures of biblical figures that were once part of the cathedral's original stone choir, created by Maestro Mateo and his team in the late 12th century.

Praza da Inmaculada

Praza da Inmaculada, on the cathedral's north side, is where most pilgrims arriving in Santiago first set eyes on the cathedral. Opposite looms the huge, austerely baroque Mosteiro de San Martiño Pinario, now a seminary.

Apr-Oct, 10am-8pm Nov-Mar) The Museo da Catedral spreads over four floors and includes the cathedral's large, 16th-century, Gothic/plateresque cloister. You'll see a sizeable section of Maestro Mateo's original carved stone choir (destroyed in 1604 but recently pieced back together), an impressive collection of religious art (including the *botafumeiros,* in the 2nd-floor library), the lavishly decorated 18th-century *sala capitular* (chapter house), a room of tapestries woven from designs by Goya, and, off the cloister, the Panteón de Reyes, with tombs of kings of medieval León.

★ **Museo das Peregrinacións e de Santiago** MUSEUM
(http://museoperegrinacions.xunta.gal; Praza das Praterías; adult/pilgrim & student/senior & child €2.40/1.20/free, Sat afternoon & Sun free; ⊙9.30am-8.30pm Tue-Sat, 10.15am-2.45pm Sun) Recently installed in a newly converted premises on Praza das Praterías, the brightly displayed Museum of Pilgrimages & Santiago gives fascinating insights into the phenomenon of Santiago (man and city) down the centuries. Much of the explanatory material is in English as well as Spanish and Galician. There are also great close-up views of some of the cathedral's towers from the 3rd-floor windows.

Museo do Pobo Galego MUSEUM
(Galician Folk Museum; www.museodopobo.gal; Rúa San Domingos de Bonaval; adult/senior & student/child €3/1/free, Sun free; ⊙10.30am-2pm & 4-7.30pm Tue-Sat, 11am-2pm Sun) A short walk northeast of the Old Town, this former convent houses extensive and interesting exhibits on Galician life and arts ranging from fishing boats and bagpipes to traditional costumes and antique printing presses.

✶ Festivals & Events

Fiestas del Apóstol Santiago CULTURAL, RELIGIOUS
(Fiestas of the Apostle St James) Two weeks of music, parades and other festivities surround the Día de Santiago (Feast of St James; 25 July), which is simultaneously Galicia's 'national' day. Celebrations peak in a truly spectacular lasers-and-fireworks display, the Fuegos del Apóstol, on Praza do Obradoiro on the night of 24 July.

🛏 Sleeping

From hostels for pilgrims and backpackers to chic boutique lodgings and historic luxury hotels, Santiago has hundreds of lodgings at all price levels. Even so, the best-value and most central places can fill up weeks ahead in summer, especially July and August.

The Last Stamp HOSTEL €
(El Último Sello; ☑981 563 525; www.thelaststamp.es; Rúa Preguntoiro 10; dm €18-20; ⊙closed late Dec-late Feb; @�📶) A purpose-designed hostel, the Last Stamp occupies a 300-year-old, five-storey house (with lift) in the heart of the Old Town. The cleverly designed dorms feature semi-private modules with ultra-solid bunks, good mattresses and individual reading lights. Some rooms enjoy cathedral views.

Bathrooms and kitchen are good and big – and Camino-themed murals add a bit of fun.

Pensión da Estrela PENSIÓN €
(☑981 576 924; www.pensiondaestrela.com; Praza de San Martíño Pinario 5; s/d €40/50; 📶) There are just six smallish rooms here but they're bright, colourful and clean, and four overlook a quiet plaza. The welcome is warm, with nice touches like neatly rolled towels and a bag of sweets, and there's a small kitchen with free tea and coffee.

★ **Hotel Costa Vella** BOUTIQUE HOTEL €€
(☑981 569 530; www.costavella.com; Rúa da Porta da Pena 17; s/d €59/81; ❄📶) Tranquil, thoughtfully designed rooms (some with typically Galician *galerías* – glassed-in balconies), a friendly welcome, super-helpful management and staff, and a lovely garden cafe (p512) make this family-run hotel in an old stone house a wonderful option – and the €6 breakfast is substantial.

Moure Hotel DESIGN HOTEL €€
(☑981 583 637; http://mourehotel.com; Rúa dos Loureiros 6; s/d incl breakfast €85/99; ⊙closed Jan; ❄@📶) An award-winning conversion of a 19th-century building, the Moure will please anyone who likes a bit of adventure and innovation in their hotel design. The many clever contemporary touches in use of space, light and materials range from the solid steel stair-rail running the full four-storey height of the building to bathtubs with views or set outdoors on private patios.

Hotel Pazo de Altamira BOUTIQUE HOTEL €€
(☑981 558 542; www.pazodealtamira.com; Rúa Altamira 18; r €80-95, breakfast €8; ⊙closed Jan & Feb; ❄📶) A former noble mansion just steps from the bustling Mercado de Abastos, the Altamira provides 16 very appealing, bright, white rooms with real wood floors, comfy beds, bathtubs and in many cases their own *galerías*. The hotel is also home to the excellent **Café de Altamira** (Rúa das Ameas 9; mains €12-16, lunch menú Mon-Fri €16; ⊙1.30-3.45pm & 8.30-11.15pm Mon-Sat; 📶).

Altaïr Hotel BOUTIQUE HOTEL €€
(☑981 554 712; http://altairhotel.net; Rúa dos Loureiros 12; s/d €75/110, breakfast €8.50; ⊙closed Jan; 📶) In what's termed a 'neo-rustic' style, the Altaïr combines traditional stone walls and solid oak floors with cosy comfort, attentive staff, soft furnishings and splashes of contemporary design. The super-colourful Carlos Sansegundo canvas hung in the

SANTIAGO DE COMPOSTELA & GALICIA SANTIAGO DE COMPOSTELA

bar-breakfast area is a masterstroke! Some great city views from the rooms too.

★ Parador Hostal dos Reis Católicos
HISTORIC HOTEL €€€

(☑981 582 200; www.parador.es; Praza do Obradoiro 1; r incl breakfast €166-294, ste from €347; ⊞❄@🖾) Opened in 1509 as a pilgrims' hostel, and with a claim to be the world's oldest hotel, this palatial *parador* occupies a wonderful building that is one of Santiago's major monuments in its own right, just steps from the cathedral. Even standard rooms are regal, with canopied beds, wooden floors, original art and generously sized bathrooms with bathtubs and big glass showers.

★ San Francisco Hotel Monumento
HISTORIC HOTEL €€€

(☑981 581 634; www.sanfranciscohm.com; Campillo San Francisco 3; s €105-110, d €154-198, breakfast €16; ⊞❄@🖾🏊) The three cloister-courtyards and the low-lit hallways with their stone door frames recall the hotel's former life as a Franciscan monastery (mostly dating from the 18th century). But the rooms, minimalist, modern and spacious, are all about contemporary comfort, and there's a great indoor pool as well as a huge grassy garden and very spacious common areas.

✖ Eating

Central Santiago is packed with eateries and most do their job pretty well. The many lining Rúa do Franco cater chiefly to a not particularly discriminating tourist market, and you'll find the most enticing options elsewhere. Don't leave Santiago without trying a *tarta de Santiago,* the city's famed almond cake.

★ Café Hotel Costa Vella
CAFE €

(Rúa da Porta da Pena 17; breakfast €2.60-4.30; ⊙8am-11pm; 🖾) The garden cafe of Hotel Costa Vella (p511) is the most delightful spot for breakfast (or a drink later in the day), with its fountain, a scattering of statuary, and beautiful flowering and fruit trees. And if the weather takes a Santiago-esque rainy turn, you can still enjoy it from the glass pavilion or the *galería.*

★ Mercado de Abastos
MARKET €

(www.mercadodeabastosdesantiago.com; Rúa das Ameas 5-8; ⊙7am-2pm Mon-Sat) 🍃 Santiago's food market is a fascinating, always lively scene, very clean, and with masses of fresh produce from the seas and countryside attractively displayed at 300-odd stalls. Stock up on *tetilla* cheese, cured meats, sausage, fruit and *empanada* (pastry pie) for a picnic. **Pulpería Sanjurjo** (small plate €8; ⊙11.30am-3.30pm Tue-Sat approx Apr-Oct, Thu-Sat Nov-Mar) in the southern alley sells wooden plates of delicious *pulpo á feira* (Galicia's favourite octopus dish), which you can take to any nearby bar and enjoy with a drink. Or buy seafood or meat and have it cooked up on the spot for €4 per person at hugely popular **Mariscomanía** (Stall 81; ⊙9am-3pm Tue-Sat) (no octopus or fish though). One part of the market is reserved for villagers and stallholders selling the produce of their orchards or vegetable gardens.

La Flor
SEAFOOD €

(Rúa das Casas Reais 25; dishes €7-10; ⊙11.30am-12.30am Mon-Thu, 11.30am-2.15am Fri & Sat; 🖾🍴) La Flor is not just a fashionable, buzzy bar for drinks and good music but also a place where you can eat an eclectic range of creative and not too heavy dishes from vegetable lasagne to chicken fingers, homemade burgers or rocket-and-goat-cheese salad – all amid a uniquely random melange of art, *objets* and hanging lamps.

O Gato Negro
RACIONES €

(Rúa da Raíña; raciones €4-18; ⊙12.30-3pm & 7.30-11pm Tue-Sat, 12.30-3pm Sun) Marked by a green door and a black-cat sign, this classic and often packed Old Town haunt serves platefuls (no tapas) of ham, cheese, peppers, *empanada* and all manner of seafood to those lucky enough to get one of its five tables and the rest of the crowd standing in the narrow bar and outside the door.

★ Abastos 2.0
CONTEMPORARY GALICIAN €€

(☑654 015937; www.abastosdouspuntocero.es; Rúa das Ameas 3; dishes €3-12, menú €21; ⊙noon-3.30pm & 8-11pm Mon-Sat) This highly original and incredibly popular marketside eatery offers new dishes concocted daily from the market's offerings. Go for small individual items, or plates to share, or a six-item *menú* that adds up to a meal for €21. The seafood is generally fantastic, but whatever you order you're likely to love the great tastes and delicate presentation – if you can get a seat!

★ O Curro da Parra
CONTEMPORARY GALICIAN €€

(www.ocurrodaparra.com; Rúa do Curro da Parra 7; mains €10-18, tapas & starters €6-13; ⊙1.30-3.30pm & 8.30-11.30pm Tue-Sun) With a neat little stone-walled dining room upstairs and a narrow tapas and wine bar below, always-busy Curro da Parra serves a broad range of tasty, thoughtfully created, market-fresh fare. You might go for crunchy prawn-and-soft-cheese rolls with passion-fruit sauce, or the free-range chicken skewers with mayonnaise-style *grebiche* sauce – or just ask about the fish and seafood of the day.

O Filandón
TAPAS, RACIONES €€

(Rúa Acibechería 6; raciones €15-20, medias raciones €10-12; ⊙1-4pm & 8pm-1am, to 2am Fri & Sat) Squeeze past the cheese-shop counter into the thin, cellar-like bar area behind, where you'll receive exceedingly generous free *pinchos* (snacks) with drinks, and can order *empanadas* or plates of ham, sausage, cured meats, cheese, peppers or anchovies. Thousands of notes and words of wisdom scribbled by past clients dangle from the walls, and a welcoming log fire burns on chilly winter evenings.

Asador Gonzaba
GRILL €€€

(☑981 594 874; Rúa Nova de Abaixo 17; mains €15-30; ⊙noon-5pm & 8pm-midnight, closed Sun evening) For a Galician meat feast, wander a little south out of the Old Town to this classic grill house where the clientele is mostly local. Nothing fancy about the decor: the focus is on the meat, specifically *chuletón*, a top-quality giant beef chop weighing as much as 1kg. Service is friendly and there's also good grilled fish or octopus for less carnivorous appetites.

Drinking & Nightlife

On summer evenings every streetside nook in the Old Town is filled with people relaxing over tapas and drinks. The liveliest bar area lies east of the cathedral. Santiago's large student population comes out in full force approaching midnight, Thursday to Saturday. Later, people gravitate towards clubs along Rúas da República Arxentina and Nova de Abaixo, in the new town.

★ Pub Atlántico
BAR

(☑981 572 152; Rúa da Fonte de San Miguel 9; ⊙typically 5.30pm-3am or later, in winter may open 9pm & close Sun & Mon) This buzzing two-floor bar pulls in an artsy, mostly 20s and 30s crowd, with excellent gin and tonics and cocktails, and a great soundtrack ranging from Cajun blues to Spanish indie.

Modus Vivendi
PUB

(Praza de Feixóo 1; ⊙6pm-4am, from 1pm Jul & Aug) In the stables of an 18th-century mansion, Modus Vivendi attracts all types and hosts regular varied live music, DJs and exhibitions. It serves local craft beers, caipirinhas, mojitos and more, and is reckoned to be Galicia's oldest 'pub' (since 1972).

☆ Entertainment

★ Casa das Crechas
LIVE MUSIC

(www.facebook.com/casadascrechas; Vía Sacra 3; ⊙5pm-late Tue-Sun) There's no better place for Celtic and other live music. Head to the tightly packed downstairs bar about 10.30pm most Wednesdays from September to mid-June for terrific Galician folk jam sessions (admission €1). Musicians from Portugal, Brazil and elsewhere also play

---

PIPERS & FIDDLERS

Galician folk music has much in common with Celtic traditions in Brittany, Ireland and Scotland, and the haunting sounds of the *gaita* (bagpipe), violin, *bombo* (a big drum) and accordion-like *zanfona* provide the soundtrack to many events.

The most sure-fire spot for hearing a Galician piper is the passageway between Praza do Obradoiro and Praza da Inmaculada in Santiago de Compostela, a day-long haunt of local folk buskers. The best place to catch a live group on a regular basis is Santiago's Casa das Crechas. Several Celtic music festivals liven up the summer months. The biggest and best is the four-day Festival Ortigueira (www.festivaldeortigueira.com) at Ortigueira in the Rías Altas in mid-July, which attracts bands and musicians from several countries and tens of thousands of music lovers. Other annual festivals well worth seeking out include the Festival Intercéltico do Morrazo in Moaña (Ría de Vigo) on a weekend in July or August, and the Festa da Carballeira (www.festadacarballeira.com), on the first Saturday of August at Zas (Costa da Morte).

Leading *gaiteros* (bagpipers) and other folkies are popular heroes in Galicia. If you fancy tuning into this soulful, quintessentially Galician cultural scene, look out for gigs by piper and multi-instrumentalist Carlos Núñez, pipers Xosé Manuel Budiño or Susana Seivane, piper/singer Mercedes Peón, singer Uxía, harpist and *zanfona*- and bouzouki-player Roi Casal, or groups Luar Na Lubre or Milladoiro.

here (there's live music about three nights a week), and there are often DJ sessions on Friday and Saturday.

ℹ️ Information

Cathedral Visitor Reception Centre (☎ 902 557812; www.catedraldesantiago.es; Praza do Obradoiro; ☺ 9am-8pm Apr-Oct, 10am-8pm Nov-Mar) Buy tickets for Museo da Catedral and cathedral rooftop tours here. It's set in the crypt beneath the steps of the cathedral's Obradoiro facade.

Centro Internacional de Acollida aos Peregrinos (☎ 981 568 846; http://peregrinos santiago.es; Rúa das Carrretas 33; 8am-9pm Apr-Oct, 10am-7pm Nov-Mar) People who have covered at least the last 100km of the Camino de Santiago on foot or horseback, or the last 200km by bicycle, for religious or similar reasons, can obtain their 'Compostela' certificate to prove it here. The website has a good deal of useful info for pilgrims arriving in Santiago.

Oficina de Turismo de Galicia (☎ 981 584 081; www.turgalicia.es; Rúa do Vilar 30-32; ☺ 9am-8pm Mon-Fri, 10am-8pm Sat, 10am-3pm Sun Easter–mid-Oct, 10.30am-7pm Mon-Sat mid-Oct–Easter) The scoop on all things Galicia.

Turismo de Santiago (☎ 981 555 129; www.santiagoturismo.com; Rúa do Vilar 63; ☺ 9am-9pm approx Apr-Oct, 9am-7pm Mon-Fri, 9am-2pm & 4-7pm Sat & Sun Nov-Mar) The efficient main municipal tourist office.

ℹ️ Getting There & Away

AIR

Santiago's **Lavacolla airport** (☎ 981 547 501; www.aena.es) is 11km east of the city. Direct flights (some only operating during variable summer months) include the following:

Aer Lingus (www.aerlingus.com) Dublin.

EasyJet (www.easyjet.com) Basel-Mulhouse, Geneva, London (Gatwick), Rome.

Iberia (www.iberia.com) Barcelona, Bilbao, Madrid.

Ryanair (www.ryanair.com) Barcelona, Frankfurt (Hahn), London (Stansted), Madrid, Málaga, Milan (Bergamo), Seville, Valencia.

Swiss (www.swiss.com) Zurich.

Turkish Airlines (www.turkishairlines.com) Istanbul.

Vueling Airlines (www.vueling.com) Amsterdam, Barcelona, Berlin, Brussels, London (Gatwick), Málaga, Paris, Rome, Valencia, Zurich.

BUS

The **bus station** (☎ 981 542 416; Praza de Camilo Díaz Baliño; 📶) is about a 20-minute walk northeast of the city centre. **Castromil-Monbus**

(☎ 902 292900; www.monbus.es) runs to many places in Galicia; **Empresa Freire** (www.empre safreire.com) and **ALSA** (☎ 902 422242; www.alsa.es) operate to Lugo; ALSA serves destinations outside Galicia.

DESTINATION	FARE (€)	DURATION	MINIMUM FREQUENCY
A Coruña	7.80	1-1½hr	12 daily
Cambados	5.60	1½hr	2 daily
Ferrol	10	1½hr	5 daily
Fisterra	15	2-3hr	3 daily
León	30	6hr	1 daily
Lugo	9.45-13	1½-2¾hr	11 daily
Madrid	46-57	8-10hr	3 daily
Ourense	12	2hr	5 daily
Oviedo	30-42	4½-6¾hr	3 daily
Pontevedra	6.40	1-1½hr	11 daily
Porto (Portugal)	33	3¼hr	1 daily
Santander	50	8-10hr	3 daily

TRAIN

The **train station** (Rúa do Hórreo) is about a 15-minute walk south from the Old Town. All trains are run by Renfe (☎ 902 320320; www.renfe.com), which has a **ticket office** (Rúa do Vilar 3; ☺ 3.30-8pm Mon, 9.30am-2pm & 3.30-8pm Tue-Fri, 9.30am-2pm Sat) in the Old Town as well as at the station. There is high-speed service to A Coruña and Ourense, and high-speed AVE service to/from Madrid is due to start in 2018.

DESTINATION	FARE (€)	DURATION	MINIMUM FREQUENCY
A Coruña	6.10-13	30-40min	19 daily
Madrid	17-36	5¼hr	2 daily
Ourense	6-20	35-45min	9 daily
Pontevedra	6.10-7.35	35min-1hr	15 daily
Vigo	9.25-11	50min-1½hr	15 daily

COSTA DA MORTE

Rocky headlands, winding inlets, small fishing towns, plunging cliffs, wide sweeping bays and many a remote, sandy beach – this is the eerily beautiful 'Coast of Death'. One of the most enchanting parts of Galicia, this relatively isolated and unspoilt shore runs from

Muros, at the mouth of the Ría de Muros y Noia, round to Caión, just before A Coruña. It's a coast of legends, like the one about villagers who used to put out lamps to lure passing ships on to deadly rocks. This treacherous coast has certainly seen a lot of shipwrecks, and the idyllic landscape can undergo a rapid transformation when ocean mists blow in.

Fisterra & Around

POP 2800 (FISTERRA)

The fishing port of Fisterra has a picturesque harbour, fine views across the Ría de Corcubión, and some good beaches within a few kilometres, but the main reason throngs of people head here is to continue out to Cabo Fisterra. This beautiful, windswept cape is the western edge of Spain, at least in popular imagination (the real westernmost point is Cabo Touriñán, 20km north) and the end point of an ever more popular 89km extension of the Camino de Santiago.

Fisterra gets busier by the year with Camino travellers and tourists drawn to this oddly magnetic corner of Spain.

◉ Sights

★ Cabo Fisterra   CAPE

(Cabo Finisterre; P) Panoramic Cabo Fisterra is a 3.5km drive or walk south of Fisterra town. It's topped by a lighthouse (not open to visitors but with an intermittently open tourist information office on its ground floor). Camino de Santiago pilgrims ending their journeys here ritually burn smelly socks, T-shirts and the like on the rocks just past the lighthouse.

Praia da Mar de Fora   BEACH

The spectacular beach Praia da Mar de Fora, over on the ocean (western) side of the Fisterra peninsula, is reachable via an 800m walk from the top of the town (but with strong winds and waves, it's not recommended for swimming).

⌂ Sleeping & Eating

Hostel Albergue Oceanus   HOSTEL €

(☑609 821302; oceanusfinisterre@gmail.com; Rúa Santa Catalina 1; dm €12; ❈@🛜) New in 2015 and well situated on the Santiago side of the town centre, Oceanus is thoughtfully designed, with its one big 36-bunk dorm divided into separate sections in a sort of boat-cabin style, and reading lights and electric plugs for each bunk. There are good,

clean, large showers, a laundry room, bikes to rent and a bright kitchen/dining area.

★ Hotel Mar da Ardora   DESIGN HOTEL €€

(☑667 641304; www.hotelmardaardora.com; Rúa Atalaia 15; s/d incl breakfast & spa €99/110; ☺closed late Dec-end Jan; P@🛜⊠) ⌀ This delightful little family-run hotel sits at the top of town, with fantastic westward ocean views from the big windows and terraces of its six rooms. Everything is in impeccably contemporary but comfortable style, from the cubist architecture to the soothing white/grey/silver colour schemes. Downstairs is an excellent spa/gym with solar-heated pool and Turkish bath.

O Pirata   SEAFOOD €

(Paseo de Calafigueira; raciones €7-12; ☺noon-11pm Tue-Sun Feb-Nov) With just half a dozen tables but a nice view over the harbour and a short but sweet menu, O Pirata serves up the freshest of fish and seafood at good prices. Try one of its 'portions' of mixed fish and/or seafood (€12.50 to €20).

O Centolo   SEAFOOD €€

(www.centolo.com; Paseo da Ribeira; mains €10-25, menús €12-38; ☺9am-2am, closed mid-Dec–mid-Feb; 🛜) A cut above most other harbourfront eateries, the Centolo provides well-prepared fish and shellfish, with good, friendly service, in its downstairs cafe and upstairs restaurant, both with big windows looking over the harbour.

❶ Information

Oficina Municipal de Turismo (☑981 740 781; www.concellofisterra.com; Rúa Real 2; ☺2-11pm) Inside the municipal pilgrims' hostel, 50m uphill from the harbour car park.

❶ Getting There & Away

Monbus (www.monbus.es) runs three to five daily buses to/from Santiago de Compostela (€15, two to three hours) via Muros, Carnota, O Pindo and Cée. Monbus can get you from Fisterra to Muxía or Camariñas with a transfer at Cée (Monday to Friday only, and schedules involve an hour or two of waiting in Cée). Autocares Vázquez (www.autocaresvazquez.net) runs up to five buses to/from A Coruña (€15, 2¼ hours).

Muxía & Around

POP (MUXÍA) 1600

The stone-built fishing village of Muxía, on the south side of the Ría de Camariñas, is a

BRING YOUR UMBRELLA

Swept by one rainy front after another from the Atlantic, Galicia has, overall, twice as much rain as the Spanish national average. Galicians have more than 100 words to describe different nuances of precipitation, from *babuxa* (a species of drizzle) to *xistra* (a type of shower) to *treboada* (a thunderstorm). June to August are the least rainy months. If you haven't brought an umbrella, don't panic – every Galician town has specialist umbrella shops: just ask for the nearest *paragüería* (par-ag-wer-ee-ah).

beloved pilgrimage spot thanks to the belief that the Virgin Mary appeared to Santiago (St James) while he was preaching here. Trails to Muxía are becoming ever more popular as extensions of the Camino de Santiago, and Muxía is experiencing something of a tourism boom as a result.

The coast south from Muxía is spectacular and can be toured by vehicle or on foot. Highlights include the sheltered beach **Praia de Lourido** (🏖), the picturesque rocky cape **Cabo Touriñán** (P 🏖) and the surf beach **Praia de Nemiña**.

Another picturesque fishing village, Camariñas, is only 4km northeast of Muxía across the Ría de Camariñas – but 24km by road. Fortunately it's a pretty drive, with the inviting beach **Praia do Lago**, the *hórreo*-studded hamlet **Leis** and the riverside village of **Cereixo** along the way.

⊙ Sights & Activities

Muxía is the goal of increasingly popular pilgrim trails from Santiago de Compostela and Fisterra. The route from Santiago de Compostela (87km) diverges from the Santiago–Fisterra route just west of Hospital village, 60km from Santiago. A separate 29km route links Muxía with Fisterra.

The Ruta do Solpor de Europa walking trail follows the spectacular coast south from Muxía to Praia de Nemiña.

Santuario da Virxe da Barca   CHURCH
(P) This 18th-century church on the rocky seashore at the north end of town marks the spot where (legend attests) the Virgin Mary arrived in a stone boat and appeared to Santiago (St James) while he was preaching here.

🛏 Sleeping & Eating

★ Bela Muxía   HOSTEL €
(☑ 687 798222; www.belamuxia.com; Rúa da Encarnación 30, Muxía; dm €12-15, d €40-50; ⊙ closed 1 month Jan or Feb; @ 🛜) Exceptionally comfortable and stylish, this designer hostel features bright, hotel-standard private rooms with bathroom, as well as spacious dorms with good mattresses, reading lights and electrical plugs for each bunk, and plenty of showers and toilets. Common areas, including the kitchen-dining area, are spacious and well designed, and there are some great panoramas from the upper floors.

★ Casa de Trillo   COUNTRY HOUSE €€
(☑ 981 727 778; www.casadetrillo.com; Santa Mariña; s €60-74, d €75-92, apt for 2 €95, all incl breakfast; ⊙ closed 8-25 Jan; P @ 🛜) Deep in typically Galician countryside at Santa Mariña, about 8km south of Muxía (well signposted along the country lanes), this charming 16th-century manor house has a lot of history, lovely gardens, cosy, well-appointed rooms and home-grown food. It's a marvellous base for exploring the area or just relaxing, and the hospitable owners can answer your every question.

A de Loló   SEAFOOD €€
(Rúa Virxe da Barca 37; raciones & mains €7-18, menús €9.50-25; ⊙ 12.30-4.30pm & 7.30-11pm mid-Feb–late Dec; 🖉) With an emphasis on the freshest of local ingredients and seafood in particular, this is one of Muxía's top restaurants. There's an unusually good range of vegetarian options too.

❶ Getting There & Away

Hefe SL (www.grupoferrin.com) runs two daily buses from Santiago de Compostela to Muxía and vice-versa. **Autocares Vázquez** (http://autocaresvazquez.net) operates buses from Muxía to Camariñas and A Coruña at 6am Monday to Friday and 6.10pm on Sunday, and from A Coruña to Muxía at 3pm Monday to Saturday.

Camariñas & Around

POP 2600 (CAMARIÑAS)

The fishing village of Camariñas, wrapped around its colourful harbour, is known for its fine traditional lacework, which can be viewed at several specialist shops and the **Museo do Encaixe** (Lace Museum; Praza Insuela; €2; ⊙ 11am-2pm & 5-7pm Tue-Sun Apr-Aug).

The rugged coast between Camariñas and Camelle, to the northeast, is one of the most beautiful stretches of the Costa da Morte and you can drive, ride or walk it along the Ruta Litoral of around 25km.

Camelle village has no outstanding charm, but it does have two touching mementoes of 'Man' (Manfred Gnädinger), an eccentric long-time German resident who died in 2002: the Xardín-Museo do Alemán, beside the pier, and the Museo Man de Camelle (☑ 981 710 224; www.mandecamelle. com; Rúa do Peirao, Camelle; ☉ 11am-1pm & 4-7pm Tue-Sun mid-Jun–mid-Sep, 11am-1pm & 4-7pm Sat & Sun mid-Sep–mid-Jun; P) FREE, back along the waterfront.

Praia de Traba is a lovely 4km walk east along the coast from Camelle.

Sleeping & Eating

Hotel Puerto Arnela   HOTEL €
(☑ 981 737 240; www.hotelpuertoarnela.es; Plaza del Carmen 20, Camariñas; r incl breakfast €60; ☎) A stone manor house facing the harbour with appealing country-style rooms and a restaurant (p517) serving good, uncomplicated shellfish, fish and meat.

★**Lugar do Cotariño**   CASA RURAL €€
(☑ 639 638634; www.docotarino.com; Camariñas; r incl breakfast €95-110; ☉closed late Dec–mid-Jan; P@☎) A labour of love for its owners, this beautifully reconstructed 400-year-old farmstead sits in verdant countryside 1km out of Camariñas. The seven rooms are homey and pretty in perfect country style, the two 'specials' in the main house being especially large and appealing. The lovely garden includes two ancient stone *hórreos*.

Restaurante Puerto Arnela   GALICIAN €€
(Plaza del Carmen 20, Camariñas; mains €6-15; ☉1-4pm & 9-11.30pm, closed Mon & evenings Tue-Thu & Sun Sep-Jun) The restaurant at Hotel Puerto Arnela serves up excellent shellfish, grilled fish, *caldeiradas* (fish stews) and meat dishes – nothing too fancy, just good ingredients prepared simply and well.

❶ Getting There & Away

Autocares Vázquez buses run to A Coruña (€11.75, 1½ hours) at 6.30am Monday to Friday and at 6.40pm on Sundays. From A Coruña to Camariñas, there is direct service only on Saturdays (departing at 3.30pm) and Sundays and holidays (2.30pm and 5pm). These buses continue from Camariñas to Muxía (€3.20, 30 minutes) at 5.55pm on Saturdays, and 4.25pm and 6.45pm on Sundays and holidays.

Laxe & Around

POP 1800 (LAXE)

A bay beach runs along the lively waterfront of the port of Laxe, and the 15th-century Gothic church of Santa María da Atalaia stands guard over the harbour. Much of this area's appeal lies beyond the town. Laxe's tourist office and its website (in Spanish and Galician) have information on walks in the area, including the 8km coastal walk to Praia de Traba via the surf beach Praia de Soesto.

For a fascinating archaeological outing, drive 7km east on the AC429 to As Grelas, then 2.4km south on the AC430 to find the turn-off for the Castro A Cidá de Borneiro, a pre-Roman *castro* amid thick woodlands. One kilometre further along the AC430, turn right along the DP1404 and go 1km to the Dolmen de Dombate (☉10am-8pm mid-Mar–Sep, 10am-7pm Oct–mid-Mar, guided tours every 30min 11am-2pm & 4-8pm Jul-Sep, 10.30am-2pm & 4-6.30pm Fri-Sun Oct–mid-Mar, 11am-2pm & 4-8pm Thu-Sun mid-Mar–Jun; P) FREE, a large, well-preserved prehistoric tomb dubbed the 'megalithic cathedral of Galicia' and recently encased in a protective pavilion.

❶ Information

Tourist Office (☑ 981 706 965; www.concello delaxe.com/turismo; Avenida Cesáreo Pondal 26; ☉9am-3pm Mon-Fri) Laxe's tourist office has information on walks in the area, including a coastal walk west to Praia de Traba via the surf beach Praia de Soesto.

❶ Getting There & Away

Laxe is linked to A Coruña by two or more daily Vázquez buses (€9 to €10, 1¼ to two hours).

RÍAS ALTAS

In few places do land and sea meet in such abrupt beauty. The untamed beaches, towering cliffs and powerful waves of the Rías Altas (the eastern half of Galicia's north coast) are more dramatic than the landscapes of the Rías Baixas. They're also far less touristed, making an ideal destination for travellers yearning to get off the heavily beaten path. Add in the allure of cultured, maritime A Coruña, medieval towns including Betanzos and Pontedeume, several lively little fishing ports and the backdrop of a green, farmhouse-studded countryside, and you'll wonder why more visitors don't journey north.

A Coruña

G | F | E | D | C | B | A

Ría de A Coruña

Paseo Marítimo

Aquarium Finisterrae (1.3km);
Torre de Hércules (2.4km)

Torre de Hércules (1.7km)

Adega O Bebedeiro (300m)

MOOM 57 (750m);
Museo Nacional de Ciencia y Tecnología (1.25km)

Ensenada del Orzán

Playa del Orzán

Av de Pedro Barrié de la Maza

Puerto de A Coruña

Dársena de la Marina

CIUDAD VIEJA

C de la Maestranza

C de San Francisco

Paseo del Parrote

Paseo Marítimo

Paseo de la Dársena

Puerta Real

Av de Montoto

Plaza del General Azcárraga

C Zapatería

Turismo de A Coruña

Plaza de María Pita

C de la Trompeta

C del Capitán Troncoso

C de San Agustín
C de la Florida
C de la Franja
C de Riego de Agua

Plaza de España

C de la Torre
C de San Roque

C del Hospital
C de Zalaeta

C Barrera

C Ciega
C Canalejo
C del Sol
C del Orzán
C de San Andrés
C de la Galera
C Cordelería
C Cancela
C Estrella
R Nueva
C de General Mola
C de Colinas
C Santa Catalina
C Cordelería

Av de la Marina

Jardines de Méndez Núñez

Av del Alférez Provisional

Comandante Cañanes

Plaza Pontevedra

C de la Alameda
C Juana de Vega
C San
C Durán Loriga

C de Juan Flórez

Compostela

Zara (150m)

Rosaleda

(1.5km);
(1.6km);
(8km)

N

200 m
0.1 miles

A Coruña

POP 214,000

A Coruña (Castilian: La Coruña) is a port city and beachy hot spot; a cultural hub and a busy commercial centre; a historic city and a proud modern metropolis with a fine food scene and buzzing nightlife – all in all, an intriguing place to discover that is too often overlooked by travellers.

The city occupies a particularly contorted corner of the Galician coast. The centre sits on an isthmus straddled by the port on its southeast side and the main ocean beaches on the northwest. An irregularly shaped peninsula extends 2km north out to the city's World Heritage–listed Roman lighthouse, the Torre de Hércules. The Paseo Marítimo, a wonderful 13km walkway and bike path, runs all the way from the port, around the peninsula, along the ocean beaches and on out to the west.

Sights

Torre de Hércules   LIGHTHOUSE
(www.torredeherculesacoruna.com; Avenida de Navarra; adult/senior & child €3/1.50, Mon free; ☉10am-9pm Jun-Sep, 10am-6pm Oct-May; ℗) The World Heritage–listed 'Tower of Hercules' sits near the windy northern tip of the city. Legend attributes its construction to one of the labours of Hercules, but it was actually the Romans who originally built this lighthouse in the 1st century AD – a beacon on what was then the furthest edge of the civilised world. Climb the 234 steps for great panoramas of the city and coast. Buses 3 and 5 run here from Puerta Real near Plaza de María Pita.

Aquarium Finisterrae   AQUARIUM
(☑981 189 842; www.mc2coruna.org/aquarium; Paseo Marítimo 34; adult/senior & child €10/4; ☉10am-6pm Mon-Fri, 11am-8pm Sat & Sun Jan-Apr, 10am-7pm Mon-Fri, 11am-8pm Sat & Sun May, Jun & Sep-Dec, 10am-9pm Jul & Aug; ℗♿) Kids love the seal colony and the underwater Nautilus room (surrounded by sharks and 50 other fish species) at this excellent aquarium on the city's northern headland. The focus is on the marine life of Galicia's coasts and the Atlantic.

Museo Nacional de Ciencia y Tecnología   MUSEUM
(www.muncyt.es; Plaza del Museo Nacional 1; ☉11am-8pm Tue-Sat, 11am-3pm Sun Jul–mid-Sep, 10am-5pm Tue-Fri, 11am-7pm Sat, 11am-3pm Sun mid-Sep–Jun; ♿) FREE Not just for techies, A Coruña's innovative National Science and Technology Museum will engage everybody. You'll see the first computer used in Spain (a monstrous IBM 650 bought by the railway company Renfe in 1959), and the entire front section of a Boeing 747. Perhaps most fascinating is the room displaying innovations from every year of the 20th century – a 1965 SEAT 600 (the tiny car that 'got Spain motoring'), a Sony PlayStation (1994), a 1946 state-of-the-art pencil sharpener and much more.

Ciudad Vieja

Shady plazas, charming old churches, hilly cobbled lanes and a good smattering of cafes and bars fill A Coruña's compact old city. Start your explorations at stately Plaza de María Pita and make your way through the labyrinth to the 16th-century Castillo de San Antón, the fort guarding the entrance to the port, which now houses the Museo Arqueológico e Histórico (☑981 189 850; Paseo Marítimo; adult/senior & child €2/1, Sat free; ☉10am-9pm Tue-Sat, 10am-3pm Sun Jul & Aug, 10am-7.30pm Tue-Sat, 10am-2.30pm Sun Sep-Jun).

Interesting stops en route include the Iglesia de Santiago (Calle de Santiago), Casa Museo María Pita (Calle Herrerías 28; ☉10.30am-2pm & 5.30-8pm Tue-Sat, 10.30am-2pm Sun) FREE and Xardín de San Carlos (Calle de San Francisco).

🛏️ Sleeping

Lois
HOTEL €

(📞 981 212 269; www.loisestrella.com; Calle Estrella 40; s €40-45, d €50-70, breakfast €8; ❄️🛜) The recently revamped Lois is a class above other budget hotels with its comfy and stylish rooms in contemporary greys and whites, up-to-date bathrooms, and its own stone-walled restaurant. The four singles are a squeeze but the seven doubles are a good size and all with their own *galerías*.

Blue Coruña Hotel
HOTEL €€

(📞 881 888 555; www.hotelbluecoruna.com; Calle de Juana de Vega 7; s €81-100, d €90-125, breakfast €9-10; ❄️🛜) One of the newest hotels in town, the contemporary-style Blue has every room themed to a different world city, with a unique mural. Everything is bright, comfortable and convenient, with up-to-date fittings like touch-on/touch-off lamps, good bathrooms with rain shower heads and nonsteam and magnifying mirrors. Standard singles are a bit small, but doubles and superior singles are b-i-g.

Meliá María Pita
HOTEL €€€

(📞 981 205 000; http://melia.com; Avenida Pedro Barrié de la Maza 3; s €106-139, d €135-200, incl breakfast; 🅿️❄️🛜) This classy 183-room hotel boasts a big, glittery lobby, good eating options, plenty of private parking, and spacious, recently renovated rooms in attractive greys, silvers and whites – but its biggest plus is the location just across the street from Playa del Orzán and the glorious beach views from the upper floors. All superior rooms and some standards ('classic') have beach views.

🍴 Eating

Tapa Negra
CONTEMPORARY TAPAS €

(Calle Barrera 32; tapas €2-3, raciones €6-14; ⊙1-4pm & 7pm-2.30am) Tapa Negra's black, white and red decor suggests a little creativity, and this popular spot delivers with tasty combinations such as croquettes of Cabrales cheese and *revuelto de pulpo, grelos y langostinos* (scrambled eggs with octopus, greens and prawns).

⭐ Adega O Bebedeiro
GALICIAN €€

(📞 981 210 609; www.adegaobebedeiro.com; Calle de Ángel Rebollo 34; mains €14-25; ⊙1.30-4pm & 8pm-midnight Tue-Sat, 1.30-4pm Sun) It's on a humble street on the northern headland and it looks a dump from outside, but the inside is rustically neat with a conversation-inspiring assortment of Galician bric-a-brac. The food is classic home-style cooking with some inventive touches, like scallop-stuffed sea bass in puff pastry, or Galician beef entrecôte with goat's cheese, all in generous quantities. Packed on weekends.

Pablo Gallego
CONTEMPORARY GALICIAN €€

(📞 981 208 888; www.pablogallego.com; Calle del Capitán Troncoso 4; mains €8-23; ⊙1-4pm & 9pm-midnight Mon-Sat, 1-4pm Sun) This fine restaurant prepares artful 21st-century dishes with traditional Galician market ingredients. Try smoked sardines with guacamole or its speciality barbecued pork knuckles, or maybe just the fish or shellfish of the day.

Pulpeira de Melide
SEAFOOD €€

(Plaza de España 16; raciones €8-16; ⊙12.30-4pm & 7.30pm-midnight Tue-Sun) Frequently packed, this informal bar-cum-restaurant is one of the very best places to enjoy that quintessential Galician favourite, *pulpo á feira* (tender octopus slices with paprika, olive oil and boiled potatoes). The potato omelette is pretty good too, and there's a daily selection of other market-fresh seafood if you fancy something other than octopus.

🍷 Drinking & Nightlife

A Coruña buzzes with taverns, bars and clubs. Before midnight, head to Plaza de María Pita for low-key drinks or navigate the taverns and tapas bars in the lanes to its west. From Thursday to Saturday, dozens of pubs and music bars in **Los Cantones Village** (Avenida del Alférez Provisional) and the streets behind Playa del Orzán party till 3am or 4am.

MOOM 57
CLUB

(www.facebook.com/moom57; Paseo de Ronda 57; ⊙5.30pm-2am Mon-Wed, 5.30pm-4am Thu, 5.30pm-6.30am Fri & Sat, 4-10pm Sun) Highly popular MOOM has well-designed pub, disco and terrace spaces, with great bay views from the terrace, which is a fine place for a drink from late afternoon any day. The DJs really get into the groove with house, pop and hip-hop after 3am Friday and Saturday nights, but there are often also live bands around midnight the same nights.

🛍️ Shopping

Zara
FASHION

(Calle de Juan Flórez 64-66; ⊙10am-9pm Mon-Sat) The first-ever Zara boutique sits in A Coruña's main shopping area at the southwest end of the isthmus. Opened in 1975 by local clothesmaker Amancio Ortega, it's now one of more than 2000 Zara shops scattered all around the world – but the Inditex group, of which Zara is now part, still has its headquarters in Arteixo on A Coruña's outskirts.

ⓘ Information

Turismo de A Coruña (☑ 981 923 093; www. turismocoruna.com; Plaza de María Pita 6; ◷ 9am-8.30pm Mon-Fri, 10am-2pm & 4-8pm Sat, 10am-7pm Sun) The very helpful and professional main city tourist office, with information in several languages.

ⓘ Getting There & Away

AIR

From A Coruña's **Alvedro airport** (☑ 981 187 200; www.aena.es), 8km south of the city centre, **Iberia** (www.iberia.com) and **Air Europa** (www.aireuropa.com) both fly several times daily to Madrid; **Vueling Airlines** (www.vueling. com) flies daily to London (Heathrow) and Barcelona, and several times weekly to Seville and Bilbao; and **TAP Portugal** (www.flytap.com) flies to Lisbon five times weekly.

BUS

From the **bus station** (☑ 981 184 335; Calle de Caballeros), 2km south of the city centre, Castromil-Monbus heads south to Santiago de Compostela (€7.80, one to 1½ hours, 13 or more daily) and beyond. **Arriva** (☑ 981 311 213; www. arriva.es) serves Ferrol, the Rías Altas, Lugo and Ourense; **Autocares Vázquez** (☑ 981 148 470; http://autocaresvazquez.net) serves the Costa da Morte; and ALSA heads to Madrid and destinations in Asturias, Cantabria, the Basque Country and Castilla y León.

TRAIN

The **train station** (Plaza de San Cristóbal) is 2km south of the city centre.

DESTINATION	FARE (€)	DURATION	MINIMUM FREQUENCY
Ferrol	4.50-6.10	1¼-2½hr	5 daily
León	10-33	5-6hr	4 daily
Lugo	10-11	1½-2hr	3 daily
Madrid	30-53	5½-11hr	3 daily
Pontevedra	10-16	1-1¾hr	13 daily
Santiago de Compostela	6-16	30-40min	21 daily

Trains to the Rías Altas, Asturias, Cantabria and the Basque Country are operated by **FEVE** (www.renfe.com/viajeros/feve) and start from Ferrol.

ⓘ Getting Around

Buses (€1.50) run every half-hour (hourly on Saturdays and Sundays) from about 7.15am to 9.45pm between the airport and Puerta Real in the city centre.

Local bus 5 runs from the train station to Puerta Real in the city centre, and back to the station from Plaza de España. Buses 1, 1A and 4 run from the bus station to the city centre: returning, take bus 1 or 1A from Puerta Real or bus 4 from Plaza de España. Rides cost €1.30.

Betanzos

POP 10,400

Once a thriving estuary port rivalling A Coruña, Betanzos has a well-preserved medieval Old Town that harmoniously combines galleried houses, small, old-fashioned shops and some monumental architecture, and is renowned for its welcoming taverns with local wines and good food.

⊙ Sights

Old Town   OLD TOWN
Take Rúa Castro up from the central plaza into the oldest part of town. Handsome Praza da Constitución is flanked by a couple of appealing cafes along with the Romanesque/Gothic **Igrexa de Santiago**, whose main portico was inspired by Santiago de Compostela's Pórtico de la Gloria. A short stroll northeast, two beautiful Gothic churches, **Santa María do Azougue** and **San Francisco**, stand almost side by side opposite the municipal market. San Francisco is full of particularly fine stone carving.

🛏 Sleeping & Eating

Hotel Garelos   HOTEL €€
(☑ 981 775 930; www.hotelgarelos.com; Calle Alfonso IX 8; s €50-60, d €70-90, incl breakfast; 🅿❄🛜) Hotel Garelos, 150m down from Praza dos Irmáns García Naviera, has spick-and-span rooms with comfy beds, parquet floors and original watercolours, and rates include a generous buffet breakfast.

O Pote   GALICIAN €
(www.mesonopote.com; Travesía do Progreso 9; raciones €4-15, menús del día €11-26; ◷ 1-4pm & 8-11pm, closed Sun & Tue evenings; 🛜) The tempting options at this tavern include a classic *tortilla de Betanzos*, and the famous omelette is also part of the terrific *menús del día*.

ℹ Getting There & Away

BUS

Arriva buses head to/from A Coruña (€2.20, 40 minutes) about hourly, 8am to 10pm. Four or more Arriva buses head to Pontedeume (€2.50, 30 minutes) and a few to Ferrol, Lugo and Viveiro. All buses stop in Praza dos Irmáns García Naveira.

TRAIN

Betanzos Cidade train station is northwest of the town centre, across the Río Mendo. At least four trains go daily to/from A Coruña (€4, 40 to 50 minutes) and Pontedeume (€2.25, 15 minutes).

Pontedeume

POP 4500

This hillside town overlooks the Eume estuary, where fishing boats bob. The Old Town is an appealing combination of handsome galleried houses, narrow cobbled streets and occasional open plazas, liberally sprinkled with taverns and tapas bars. Several parallel narrow streets climb up from the main road, the central one being the porticoed Rúa Real.

🍴 Sleeping & Eating

⭐ Casa do Castelo de Andrade
COUNTRY HOUSE €€

(☑ 981 433 839; www.casteloandrade.com; Lugar Castelo de Andrade; r €105-130 late Jul-early Sep, €80-110 rest of year; ⊘ closed mid-Oct–Mar; ℗ 🛜) The area's most enticing sleeping option is this enchanting rural hotel 7km southeast of town. It's a pretty stone farmhouse in enormous grounds, with 10 immaculate, all different, olde-worlde-style rooms, and the owner is a mine of helpful information about the area.

Zas
GALICIAN €

(Travesía Real 2; tapas €2.50-8, raciones €5-16; ⊘ 12.15-4.30pm & 7.30-11pm Wed-Mon) You'll find some of the town's best eats in this small, wood-panelled bar, in a narrow street off Rúa Real, cooking up simple but perfect Galician classics such as *pulpo á feira*, steamed cockles, *percebes* (goose barnacles),

---

WHAT'S COOKING IN SANTIAGO DE COMPOSTELA & GALICIA?

With the produce of the ocean, coastline and rich inland pastures all readily to hand, Galician food bursts with exceptional variety and freshness, and a new wave of creative Galician chefs is producing some wonderful taste experiences in innovative restaurants all over the region.

Pulpo á feira Galicia's signature dish (known as *pulpo a la gallega* elsewhere in Spain): tender slices of octopus tentacle sprinkled with olive oil and paprika, with *cachelos* (boiled potatoes) the perfect accompaniment. It's available almost everywhere that serves food, but most Galicians agree that the best *pulpo á feira* is cooked in the inland town of O Carballiño, 30km northwest of Ourense. Cooks here invented the recipe in the Middle Ages, when the local monastery received copious supplies of octopus from tenants on its coastal properties. Around 70,000 people pile into O Carballiño on the second Sunday of August for the Festa do Pulpo de O Carballiño (p541).

Percebes Galicia's favourite shellfish delicacy, pulled off coastal rocks between waves at low tide (a sometimes dangerous pursuit) and looking like miniature dragon claws. The Rías Altas town of Cedeira is famed for its rich *percebes* and Taberna Praza do Peixe (p523) is one of the best spots to try them.

Chuletón A giant beef chop that can weigh 1kg or more – perfect at Santiago de Compostela's Asador Gonzaba (p513).

Queso tetilla Cone-shaped 'nipple cheese', made from Galician cow's milk, is gentler on the tastebuds than many Spanish cheeses. Browse the varieties at Santiago de Compostela's Mercado de Abastos (p512).

Nova cociña galega Talented Galician chefs are concocting delightful innovative dishes based on the best seasonal ingredients in creative preparations. A bunch of them have banded together in a loose association called Grupo Nove (www.nove.biz). Three of the best will serve you meals to remember at El Silabario (p539) in Tui, Eirado da Leña (p532) in Pontevedra and Lugo's Restaurante Paprica (p545).

and *raxo* and *zorza* (both bite-sized chunks of marinated pork).

ℹ️ Getting There & Away

Buses and trains between A Coruña, Betanzos and Ferrol stop here.

Cedeira & Around

POP 4600 (CEDEIRA)

The coast north of the naval port of Ferrol is studded with small maritime towns and pretty beaches. The best base is the fishing port and very low-key resort of Cedeira, tucked into a sheltered *ría* (coastal inlet).

The cute, tiny old town sits on the west bank of the little Río Condomiñas, while Praia da Magdalena fronts the modern, eastern side of town. Around the headland to the south (a 7km drive) is the much more appealing Praia de Vilarrube, a long, sandy beach with shallow waters between two river mouths, in a protected area of dunes and wetlands.

Ferrol itself is a transport hub (among other things, it's the western terminus of the FEVE railway along the coast to the Basque Country), but has little to detain you.

🏃 Activities

Praia de Pantín   SURFING

(🏄) This beach 12km south of Cedeira has a great right-hander for surfers. Over six days in late August or early September, it hosts the Pantín Classic (www.pantinclassic.com), a qualifying event in the World Surf League. From about late June to early September, several surf schools operate here, charging around €30 per two-hour class or €100 for a course of five two-hour classes.

Ruta dos Peiraos   FISHING

This scenic 14km walking route heads out to the holy hamlet of San Andrés de Teixido, north of Cedeira. For the most spectacular part, along the tops of Atlantic cliffs, you can drive to Trasmonte village, 5km along the route, and start there (this also avoids the mostly uphill section from Cedeira to Trasmonte).

🛌 Sleeping & Eating

⭐ **Hotel Herbeira**   DESIGN HOTEL €€

(☑ 981 492 167; www.hotelherbeira.com; Cordobelas; s €88-100, d €100-122, breakfast €7.15; ⊗ closed 22 Dec-12 Jan; 🅿 ❄ @ 🛜 ⛱) As sleek as Galicia gets, this welcoming, family-run hotel boasts

16 large, contemporary rooms with glassed-in galleries, well-equipped bathrooms and stunning views over the *ría* – a perfect combination of design, comfort and practicality. There's a beautiful pool at the front and and a nice, bright cafe for breakfast.

Casa Cordobelas   COUNTRY HOUSE €€

(☑ 981 480 607; www.cordobelas.com; Cordobelas; s/d €55/72, 1-/2-bedroom apt €83/110, breakfast €5.50; ⊗ closed mid-Dec–mid-Jan; 🅿 🛜) A charming stone-built property run by a friendly family, comprising four converted, century-old, village houses with seven comfortable, spacious, rustic-style rooms, and a lovely garden.

Mesón Muiño Kilowatio   TAPAS, RACIONES €€

(Rúa do Mariñeiro 9; tapas €4-9, raciones €8-17; ⊗ noon-11pm, closed Mon-Thu Oct-Mar) This tiny bar packs 'em in for generous servings of fish, seafood, *raxo* and *zorza* (versions of chopped grilled pork), and other Galician delights, at good prices.

Taberna Praza do Peixe   SEAFOOD €€

(Rúa do Mariñeiro 1; raciones €6-16; ⊗ 10.30am-4pm & 7.30-11pm) This bar-cum-restaurant popular with locals, just west of the river, is one of the best places in town for fish and seafood. Savour Cedeira's famous *percebes,* or its tasty version of the local speciality *rape a cedeiresa* (breaded monkfish in a tomato-and-white-wine sauce).

ℹ️ Information

Tourist Office (☑ 981 482 187; Avenida de Castelao 18; ⊗ 10.30am-2pm & 5-8pm Mon-Fri, 11am-2pm Sat) A helpful place on the main road in the new part of town.

ℹ️ Getting There & Away

By bus from the south, you'll need to get to Ferrol, then take a Monbus bus from Praza de Galicia to Cedeira (€3.25, one hour, five daily Monday to Friday, two daily Saturday and Sunday). Cedeira's bus station is on Rúa Deportes, just off the main road, Avenida Castelao, 700m southeast of the Río Condomiñas.

Cabo Ortegal & Around

The wild, rugged coastline for which the Rías Altas are famous begins above Cedeira. No public transport serves the main places of interest, but if you have wheels (and, even better, time for some walks), Galicia's northwestern corner is a spectacular place to explore, with lush forests, vertigo-inducing cliffs, stunning oceanscapes and horses roaming free over the hills.

◉ Sights

★ Garita de Herbeira
VIEWPOINT

(Ⓟ) From San Andrés de Teixido the DP2205 winds up and across the Serra da Capelada towards Cariño for incredible views. Six kilometres from San Andrés is the must-see Garita de Herbeira, a naval lookout post built in 1805, 615m above sea level and the best place to be wowed over southern Europe's highest ocean cliffs.

★ Cabo Ortegal
CAPE

(Ⓟ) Four kilometres north of the workaday fishing town of Cariño looms the mother of Spanish capes, Cabo Ortegal, where the Atlantic Ocean meets the Bay of Biscay. Great stone shafts drop sheer into the ocean from such a height that the waves crashing on the rocks below seem pitifully benign. Os Tres Aguillóns, three jagged rocky islets, provide a home to hundreds of marine birds, and with binoculars you might spot dolphins or whales.

🛏 Sleeping & Eating

San Andrés de Teixido has several cafes, where you can sample the area's famed *percebes*: the minimum serve is usually 250g, costing anything from €8 upwards. Cariño has several restaurants and bars with food.

Muíño das Cañotas
COUNTRY HOUSE €€

(☏ 981 420 181; www.muinodascanotas.es; A Ortigueira 10; r incl breakfast €65-85; Ⓟ 🛰) Charming Muíño das Cañotas, in a pretty little valley just off the DP6121, 2km south of Cariño, has five beautiful rooms in a converted 14th-century watermill. It's well signposted.

Mesón O Barómetro
GALICIAN €

(Rúa Fraga Iribarne 23, Cariño; raciones €6-12; ⊙1-4pm & 8.30pm-midnight Wed-Mon) A good choice for well-priced fish, seafood and Galician meat dishes, with half a dozen tables in the bar and a small dining room inside. A good range of Galician wines too.

❶ Getting There & Away

Arriva (www.arriva.es) runs three buses each way, Monday to Friday only, between Cariño and Mera (20 minutes, €1.40), 10km south.

Some of these services connect at Mera with Arriva buses along the AC862 between Ferrol and Viveiro. From Cedeira, the 1pm (Monday to Friday) Arriva bus to Mera connects with the 1.30pm Mera–Cariño bus.

Bares Peninsula

The Bares Peninsula is a marvellously scenic spur of land jutting north into the Bay of Biscay, with walking trails, beaches and a few delightfully low-key spots to stay over.

The road along the peninsula leaves the AC862 Hwy at O Barqueiro, a storybook fishing village where slate-roofed, white houses cascade down to the port. For an even quieter base, push north to tiny Porto de Bares, on a lovely half-moon of sand lapped by the *ría's* waters.

Take a walk to the panoramic Punta da Estaca de Bares, Spain's most northerly point, and, a few kilometres southwest, enjoy the vistas from the bench known as the 'Best Bank of the World' (Ⓟ) overlooking the spectacular Acantilados de Loiba cliffs and little-known beaches, such as Praia do Picón (Ⓟ).

Further west, a short detour off the AC862 leads to the small but pretty Praia de Santo António in Porto de Espasante.

🛏 Sleeping & Eating

Hospedaxe Porto Mar
HOSTAL €

(☏ 981 414 023; www.portomar.eu; Calle Feliciano Armada, Porto de Bares; s/d €35/45; 🛰) The only accommodation in Porto de Bares itself is the 18 smallish but clean and cosy rooms (half of them sea-facing) at Hospedaxe Porto Mar. The amiable owners also run one of the three seafood-focused eateries by the beach, O Centro.

Semáforo de Bares
HOTEL €€

(☏ 699 943584, 981 417 147; www.hotelsemaforodebares.com; r €66-120, ste €180, incl breakfast; ⊙closed 2nd half Feb & 2nd half Oct; Ⓟ 🛰) For a treat, book a room in this maritime-signalling station turned contemporary hotel, whose six rooms (the best are quite indulgent) sit 3km above the village on a panoramic hilltop.

O Centro
GALICIAN €€

(Porto de Bares; raciones €9-20; ⊙9.30am-midnight) A good spot for a wide variety of shellfish, fish and Galician meat grills, just above the beach at Porto de Bares.

Restaurante La Marina SEAFOOD €€
(Porto de Bares; mains €12-24; ⊙10am-midnight) With a panoramic dining room overlooking Porto de Bares' beach, Restaurante La Marina does great seafood paellas as well as a host of other maritime fare.

Getting There & Away

A few daily FEVE trains and Arriva buses, on Ferrol–Viveiro routes, serve O Barqueiro.

Viveiro

POP 7400

This town at the mouth of the Río Landro has a well-preserved historic quarter of stone buildings and stone-paved streets (several of them pedestrian-only), where outward appearances haven't changed a great deal since Viveiro was rebuilt after a 1540 fire. It's famous for its elaborate Semana Santa celebrations, when the town fills with processions and decorations. Check out the Gothic **Igrexa de Santiago** (Rúa de Cervantes; ⊙11.30am-1pm & 6.30-8.30pm) and the 12th-century Romanesque **Igrexa de Santa María do Campo** (Rúa de Felipe Prieto; ⊙7.30am-8.30pm Mon-Sat, 11am-1.30pm & 5.30-7pm Sun). The 4km drive up to **Mirador San Roque** rewards with expansive panoramas.

Playa de Area is a fine, 1.2km-long stretch of sand with a semi-built-up backdrop on the Ría de Viveiro, 5km north of town by the LU862. Five kilometres beyond – by the LUP2610 winding through woodlands or the well-signposted Camino Natural da Ruta do Cantábrico walking trail – is the lovely, less-frequented **Praia de Esteiro**, with waves that are good for beginner (and sometimes more experienced) surfers.

Sleeping & Eating

Hotel Vila HOTEL €
(☎982 561 331; www.hotel-vila.es; Rúa Nicolás Cora Montenegro 57; s/d €27/45; ⊙closed late Dec-late Jan; P ☎) Just down from FEVE's Viveiro Apeadero station, this well-kept little one-star hotel has neat, recently redecorated and refurnished rooms. Manager Magdalena speaks fluent English.

Hotel Ego HOTEL €€€
(☎982 560 987; www.hotelego.es; Playa de Area; s €110, d €143-165, ste €193-275; P ✱ ☎ ≋) The excellent, contemporary-style Hotel Ego is 5km north of Viveiro on the Ribadeo road, overlooking Playa de Area beach. Most of its 45 ample rooms have sea views and balconies, and the adjacent Restaurante Nito (p525) is one of the area's best eateries.

La Quinta SEAFOOD, GRILL €€
(Rúa Pastor Díaz 66; mains €11-23; ⊙1-4pm & 8pm-midnight; ☎) On a pedestrian street running south from Praza Maior, La Quinta specialises in top-class grilled meats but is also good for fish and seafood, with good service. The prettily decorated main dining room is upstairs, but you can also have tapas or *raciones* in the ground-floor bar.

Restaurante Nito SEAFOOD €€
(Playa de Area; mains €12-35; ⊙1.30-4pm & 8pm-midnight) Adjacent to Hotel Ego, overlooking Playa de Area, the Nito is one of the coast's finest eateries, providing quality meat, fish and shellfish, and fine vistas.

Getting There & Away

A few Arriva buses fan out to Lugo and along the Rías Altas as far as A Coruña and Ribadeo. The bus station is on the waterfront street Avenida Ramón Canosa, just north of the Old Town.

FEVE trains from Ferrol to Oviedo stop here.

Ribadeo

POP 6800

This lively port town on the Ría de Ribadeo, which separates Galicia from Asturias, is a sun-seeker magnet in summer. The Old Town between Praza de España and the harbour is an attractive mix of handsome old galleried and stone houses. For a beach you'll have to head out of town, but **Praia As Catedrais** (Cathedrals Beach; P ♿), 10km away, is one of Galicia's most spectacular strands.

An excellent, well-marked walking and bike trail, the **Camiño Natural da Ruta do Cantábrico**, runs 133km west along the coast from Ribadeo to O Vicedo, west of Viveiro. The first 3km, from Ribadeo's central Praza de España to the Illa Pancha lighthouse, make a nice *ría*-side leg stretch. From Illa Pancha, the route continues 17km along a beautiful length of coast to Praia As Catedrais, via the tiny fishing village of **Rinlo**, which has several good seafood eateries.

Sleeping & Eating

Hotel Rolle HOTEL €€
(☎982 120 670; www.hotelrolle.com; Rúa de Ingeniero Schulz 6; r incl breakfast €95; ✱ @ ☎) Just two blocks from Praza de España, the

Rolle has spacious, attractive rooms in a rustically modern style, with nice, up-to-date bathrooms and plenty of exposed stone and wood. The owner is happy to tell you about things to see and do in the area.

Parador de Ribadeo LUXURY HOTEL €€€

(☑982 128 825; www.parador.es; Rúa de Amador Fernández 7; s €137-233, d €154-250, incl breakfast; P🛜) For views, you can't beat this *parador* (luxurious state-owned hotel), where most of the 47 fairly formal rooms have their own *galerías* with *ría* vistas.

La Botellería MODERN SPANISH €€

(Rúa de San Francisco 24; mains €9-18; ⊙noon-4pm & 7.30pm-midnight Tue-Sun) Head to this convivial bar or its pretty white-tabled dining room, near Praza de España, for good wine and original and tasty dishes like tuna tartare with guacamole and mango sauce, or banana and chorizo croquettes with mint sauce.

ⓘ Information

Tourist Office (☑982 128 689; http://turismo.ribadeo.gal; Praza de España; ⊙10am-2pm & 4-8pm, closed Sun Sep-Jun) Get the scoop on everything here.

ⓘ Getting There & Away

BUS

At least four daily buses head to Luarca, Oviedo and (Monday to Friday only) Viveiro, and there's daily service to Lugo, A Coruña and Santiago de Compostela. The bus station is on Avenida Rosalía de Castro, about 500m north of Praza de España.

TRAIN

Multistop FEVE trains operate to/from Oviedo (€12, 3½ hours, two daily) and Ferrol (€11, three hours, four daily).

Parque Natural Fragas do Eume

East of Pontedeume, the valley of the Río Eume is home to Europe's best-preserved Atlantic coastal forest, with beautiful deciduous woodlands and species of rare relict ferns. The 91-sq-km Parque Natural Fragas do Eume has a helpful visitors centre, the Centro de Interpretación (☑981 432 528; ⊙10am-2pm & 4-8pm, closed afternoons Mon-Fri mid-Sep–mid-Jun), 6km from Pontedeume on the DP6902 Caaveiro road. Next door, Restaurante Andarubel (☑981 433 969; www.facebook.com/andarubel.fragasdoeume; mains

€8-21; ⊙1-4pm & 8.30-11pm, closed Jan–mid-Feb, Mon-Fri Nov, Dec & mid-Feb–May) rents bikes (€5/8/12 per one/two/four hours) and kayaks (€6 per person per hour).

A paved road and an off-road path lead along the thickly forested valley to the beautifully sited old Mosteiro de Caaveiro (⊙tours hourly 11.15am-2.15pm & 4.15-6.15pm, closed Mon-Thu Mar–mid-Jun) FREE, 8km from the visitors centre. With time and a vehicle it's well worth venturing into the less frequented eastern part of the park: the A Capela–Monfero road gives access to several well-marked walking trails of a few kilometres each – particularly scenic is the 6.5km Camiño dos Cerqueiros loop above the Encoro do Eume reservoir.

ⓘ Getting There & Away

There's no public transport to the visitors centre or anywhere else in the park, so you need your own wheels, or at least a taxi from Pontedeume.

RÍAS BAIXAS

Wide beaches and relatively calm waters have made the Rías Baixas (Castilian: Rías Bajas) Galicia's most popular holiday destination. The Rías de Muros y Noia, de Arousa, de Pontevedra and de Vigo – Galicia's four longest *rías* (coastal inlets) – boast way more towns, villages, hotels and restaurants than other stretches of the Galician coast, which obscures some of their natural beauty. Still, the mix of pretty villages, sandy beaches and good eating options, especially the wonderful seafood, keep most people happy. Throw in lovely old Pontevedra, the big-city feel of lively Vigo, the quaint albariño wine capital Cambados and trips to offshore islands like the magnificent Illas Cíes, and you have a tempting travel cocktail.

Ría de Arousa

The Ría de Arousa is home to the appealing olde-worlde village of Cambados, 'capital' of the albariño wine country, and also to one of the Rías Baixas' busiest tourist towns, ugly but lively O Grove.

Cambados

POP 6900

The capital of the albariño wine country, famed for its fruity whites, the pretty little *ría*-side town of Cambados makes a pleasant base for touring the Rías Baixas. Its compact core of old streets is lined by stone architecture dotted with inviting taverns and eateries.

👁 Sights

You can visit and taste at 10 different **wineries** in the Cambados municipality (in the town and up to 6km outside – see www.cambadosenoturismo.com for information) and more than 20 others within about 12km (see www.rutadelvinoriasbaixas.com). The best-known wineries are outside town, but there are two small and interesting ones in the Pazo de Fefiñáns, which lines two sides of broad Praza de Fefiñáns at the northern end of the town centre. Cambados' tourist office (p528) has details on all visitable wineries. It's always advisable to call ahead to wineries, to check that someone will be available to attend you.

⭐ Gil Armada   MANSION, WINERY
(☑660 078252; http://bodegagilarmada.com; Praza de Fefiñáns; tours €5-13; ☉tours noon, 1pm, 6pm, 7pm Jun-Sep, noon & 5.30pm Oct-May, closed Sun afternoon) Gil Armada is a small family-run winery housed in the handsome, 17th-century Pazo de Fefiñáns. A variety of absorbing guided tours are offered: the basic one-hour version covers the main rooms of the historic house, with some fascinating antiques and art, its distillery and its lovely, vast gardens with 150-year-old vines and an ancient woodland. The more expensive options (up to two hours) include a visit to the panoramic tower and a wine-tasting.

Igrexa de Santa Mariña Dozo   CHURCH
(Rúa do Castro; ☉sunrise-sunset) **FREE** Pay a visit to this ruined 15th-century church beside the Museo Etnográfico e do Viño. It's now roofless but still has its four semicircular roof arches intact, and is surrounded by a well-kept cemetery with elaborate graves – quite spooky at dusk! Just beyond, **Monte de A Pastora** park provides expansive views over the Ría de Arousa.

Museo Etnográfico e do Viño   MUSEUM
(Ethnographic & Wine Museum; Rúa Os Olmos; adult/senior & child incl Museo do Muiño de Mareas da Seca & Casa Museo Ramón Cabanillas €3.20/1.60; ☉10am-2pm & 5-8pm Tue-Sat, 10am-2pm Sun, afternoon closing 6.30pm Nov-May) Cambados' main museum focuses on al-

Rías Baixas

bariño wine – not only its production and history but also the culture that goes with it.

Martín Códax   WINERY
(☑986 526 040; www.martincodax.com; Rúa Burgáns 91, Vilariño; tours incl tasting of 1/2/3/4 wines €3/5/10/15, incl vineyard & tasting of 3/4 wines €15/25; ☉tours hourly 11am-1pm & 5-7pm Mon-Fri, 11am-1pm Sat Apr-Oct, hourly 11am-1pm & 4.30pm Mon-Fri Nov-Mar; P) Galicia's best-known winery is only a short drive east of Cambados; a variety of tours from 45 minutes to three hours are offered, including tasting of up to four wines. Some include vineyard visits.

Bodegas del Palacio de Fefiñanes WINERY
(☑986 542 204; www.fefinanes.com; Praza de Fefiñáns; visits incl tasting per person €5-12, minimum per group €25-48; ☉10am-1pm & 4-7pm Mon-Fri) This small establishment, one of two wineries in the handsome, 17th-century

Pazo de Fefiñáns, produces some quality, garlanded albariño wines.

⭐ Festivals & Events

Fiesta del Albariño WINE
(http://fiestadelalbarino.es) Concerts, fireworks and exhibitions accompany the consumption of huge quantities of wine and tapas during the Fiesta del Albariño, on the first Sunday of August and the four preceding days.

🛏 Sleeping & Eating

Hotel Real Ribadomar BOUTIQUE HOTEL €€
(☑986 524 404; www.hotelrealribadomar.com; Rúa Real 8; s €50-80, d €80-125, incl breakfast; ❄🕾) A charmingly renovated central townhouse with pretty rooms combining exposed stone and attractive wallpaper, fresh white linen on soft beds, gleaming bathrooms and homey touches, including ribbon-wrapped towels and baskets of pot-pourri.

Pazo A Capitana COUNTRY HOUSE €€
(☑986 520 513; www.pazoacapitana.com; Rúa Sabugueiro 46; s €59-70, d €70-90, incl breakfast; ⊗closed mid-Dec–mid-Jan; 🅿❄🕾) This 17th-century country house on the edge of town is a lovely sleeping option, with stately rooms, beautiful, expansive gardens and an on-site winery with four century-old stone presses.

Rincón del Tío Paco GALICIAN €
(Rúa San Gregorio 2; tapas & raciones €3-12; ⊗9am-midnight) This welcoming bar at the entrance to Rúa Príncipe serves up quality grilled meats as well as straightforward but tasty seafood and fish.

Vago Viños GALICIAN €€
(Rúa Príncipe; dishes €7-16; ⊗noon-4pm & 8pm-midnight Wed-Mon) A change from Cambados' prevailing mode of cutely traditional taverns and tapas bars, contemporary-style Vago Viños has not a single exposed stone or wood beam in sight. The cuisine is delicious and mildly adventurous too – dishes like prawns with wild mushrooms and soy sauce, warm shellfish or vegetable salads, and excellent burgers with Galician Arzúa cheese. Good wines too.

ℹ Information

Oficina Municipal de Turismo (☑986 520 786; www.cambados.es; Edificio Exposalnés, Paseo da Calzada; ⊗10am-2pm & 5-8pm Jun-Sep, 10am-2pm & 4.30-7.30pm Tue-Sat, 10.30am-2pm Sun Oct-May) Helpful office between the bus station and Old Town.

GALICIAN WINES

There's no better accompaniment to Galician food than Galician wines, which have a character all their own. Best known are the fruity whites from the albariño grape, which constitute more than 90% of the wine produced in the **Rías Baixas** Denominación de Origen (DO), located near Galicia's southwestern coast and along the lower Río Miño. Albariño's surge in popularity in the last couple of decades has, to some palates, yielded some wines that are *too* sweet and fruity. A good traditional albariño should have the aroma of a green apple and a slightly sour taste.

Encouraged by albariño's success, vintners elsewhere in Galicia are innovating, expanding and producing some top-class wines. Many of the best reds come from the native mencía grape, and winemakers are reviving other native Galician grapes that almost disappeared in the 19th-century phylloxera plague – among them the white godello and the red brancellao and merenzao.

Galicia's other DOs:

Ribeiro From the Ribadavia area in southern Galicia, Ribeiro produces some very good whites, mostly from the treixadura grape.

Ribeira Sacra In the southeast, yielding rich reds from mencía grapes grown on the amazingly steep hillsides above the Río Sil.

Monterrei In the warmest, driest part of southeast Galicia, bordering Portugal, Monterrei turns out both reds and whites: Crego e Monaguillo produces very drinkable mencía reds and fruity godello whites.

Valdeorras This southeastern region bordering Castilla y León produces, among others, godello whites and mencía and brancellao reds.

ℹ Getting There & Away

The bus station is on Avenida de Galicia, 300m south of the Old Town. Castromil runs to/from Santiago de Compostela (€5.60, 1½ hours) at least twice daily and O Grove (€2.50, 40 minutes) at least three times. **Autocares Cuiña** (www.autocarescuina.com) runs to/from Pontevedra (€3.15, one hour) at least four times daily.

O Grove

POP 7100

More than two-dozen sandy beaches make this seaside town and the relatively unspoilt peninsula surrounding it a buzzing summer destination. The O Grove–Sanxenxo area is Galicia's biggest magnet for Spanish summer beach tourism, and the towns are not pretty, but there are certainly some fine, if far from deserted, beaches.

◉ Sights

★ Praia A Lanzada   BEACH

(P 🚻) Dune-backed Praia A Lanzada sweeps a spectacular 2.3km along the west side of the low-lying isthmus leading to O Grove. It's Galicia's most splendid stretch of sand, and enticingly natural, but not exactly deserted, as the mammoth car parks attest.

Illa de Sálvora   ISLAND

(🚻) This interesting small island, part of the Parque Nacional de las Islas Atlánticas de Galicia, has a mainly rocky coast, a lighthouse, an abandoned village and an old fish-salting-plant-cum-mansion. Four-hour trips (adult/child €20/10) go from O Grove most days from about July to mid-September with **Cruceros Rías Baixas** (☑986 731 343; www.crucerosriasbaixas.com; 🚻) or **Cruceros do Ulla** (☑986 731 818; www.crucerosdoulla.com; 🚻). They include a guided walk and a little beach time.

🎉 Festivals & Events

Festa do Marisco   FOOD

O Grove is famous for its shellfish and in early or mid-October it stages the 10-day Festa do Marisco seafood festival, with regattas, concerts and other diversions, as well as the consumption of a huge amount of shellfish and albariño wine.

🛏 Sleeping & Eating

Hotel Samar   HOTEL €€

(☑986 738 378; www.samarhotel.com; Carretera de San Vicente do Mar; r incl breakfast €100-170; ⊘Easter–mid-Oct; P ❄ 🕿) The only hotel with direct access to Praia A Lanzada, welcoming Samar looks right along the spectacular beach from its elevated perch at the northern end. The 14 large, pine-furnished rooms, most with king-size beds, all have their own terraces and many enjoy beach views. The included breakfast is substantial.

Hotel La Noyesa   HOTEL €€

(☑986 730 923; www.hotelnoyesa.com; Plaza de Arriba 4; s €50-65, d €65-80, incl breakfast; ⊘closed mid-Dec–mid-Feb; P ❄ @ 🕿 🐾) Situated 150m inland from Praza do Corgo, which spreads out by the harbour and fish market, the Noyesa offers spacious, bright, clean rooms, and **Hotel Noyesa Plaza** (☑986 730 923; www.hotelnoyesa.com; Plaza de Arriba 5; s €50-65, d €65-80, incl breakfast; ⊘closed mid-Dec–mid-Feb), with a more contemporary touch across the street, is part of the same business with the same prices. They may require a two-night minimum at peak periods.

Beiramar   SEAFOOD €€

(☑986 731 081; Avenida Beiramar 30; mains €12-30; ⊘1-4pm & 8-11.30pm Tue-Sat, 1-4pm Sun, closed Nov) Among the slew of eateries facing the seafront, the Beiramar is a superior option with its big white tablecloths and classy but contemporary feel. It specialises in quality fish and seafood but also does good Galician beef grills, and has a good wine list with a Galician emphasis.

El Rincón de Norat   SPANISH €€

(Avenida Luis Casáis 22; mains €15-30; ⊘7am-midnight) This popular tapas and wine bar and restaurant in the Norat Marina Hotel & Spa building serves some tasty and nicely presented dishes, naturally with an emphasis on seafood.

ℹ Getting There & Away

The **Estación de Autobuses y Catamaranes** (Avenida Beiramar), a combined bus station and boat-trip terminal, stands on the seafront road. Monbus runs at least nine buses daily to Pontevedra (€4.25, 1¼ hours) via Sanxenxo, and Castromil runs two or more to Santiago de Compostela (€7.40, 1¼ hours) via Cambados.

Padrón

POP 7000

As the story goes, the town of Padrón, on the Río Sar 20km south of Santiago de Compostela, is where St James' (Santiago's) corpse landed in Galicia on arrival from Palestine in its stone boat. Padrón is also known for its tiny green peppers, *pimientos de padrón,* which were imported from Mexico by 16th-century Franciscan friars and are now grown all around town. When fried up and sprinkled with coarse salt, they're one of Spain's favourite tapas. Just beware of the odd very spicy one. Padrón was also the home town of two of Galicia's most famous writers – Galicia's 'national poet' Rosalía de Castro (1837–85) and Nobel Prize–winning novelist Camilo José Cela (1916–2002).

The town has a neat little old centre of stone houses and stone-paved streets. The more modern areas surrounding this are good examples of how dreary 20th-century Galician urban development could be.

◎ Sights

Igrexa de Santiago   CHURCH
(◷10am-1pm & 5-7pm) Padrón is the last stop before Santiago de Compostela on the Camino Portugués pilgrim route, and pilgrims make a beeline for the Igrexa de Santiago, next to the Ponte do Carme over the Río Sar. Beneath the church's high altar stands a Roman sacrificial altar that gave the town its name – the Pedrón (Big Stone). According to legend, the boat bearing Santiago's body was moored to the Pedrón on arrival.

❶ Getting There & Away

Castromil (www.monbus.es) runs at least five buses daily to/from Santiago de Compostela (€2.10, 30 minutes), five to/from Pontevedra (€4.15, 50 minutes) and two to/from Cambados (€3.35, one hour). **Arriva** (www.arriva.es) provides slightly more frequent service from Santiago.

At least nine daily trains run from Santiago de Compostela (€3.20, 15 minutes) and six or more from Pontevedra (€5.20, 40 minutes).

Pontevedra

POP 62,000

Pontevedra is an inviting, small, riverside city that combines history, culture and style into a lively base for exploring the Rías Baixas. The interlocking lanes and plazas of the compact Old Town are abuzz with shops, markets, cafes and tapas bars.

Back in the 16th century, Pontevedra had somewhat greater significance as Galicia's biggest city and an important port. Columbus' flagship, the *Santa María,* was built here, and indeed many locals are convinced

that Columbus himself was not Genoese as is commonly believed, but was really a Pontevedra nobleman called Pedro Madruga, who for obscure reasons faked his own death and took on a new identity.

◎ Sights

An excellent museum and some unusual old churches are well worth devoting time to, but really it's the Old Town as a whole that is Pontevedra's star turn. It's a pleasure just to wander round its narrow, mainly pedestrianised streets linking more than a dozen plazas. Praza da Leña is a particularly quaint nook.

★ **Edificio Sarmiento**   MUSEUM
(Rúa Sarmiento) The Edificio Sarmiento, pride of the Museo de Pontevedra, occupies a recently renovated 18th-century college. Its absorbing collection ranges over Galician Sargadelos ceramics, modern art (including a few works by Picasso, Miró, Dalí and Tapiès), statues of prophets from the original facade of Santiago de Compostela cathedral, and prehistoric Galician gold jewellery, petroglyphs and carvings.

Museo de Pontevedra   MUSEUM
(☑986 851 455; www.museo.depo.es; ◷10am-9pm Tue-Sat, 11am-2pm Sun) FREE Pontevedra's eclectic museum is scattered over five city-centre buildings. At research time, three were closed for restoration, leaving you with just the two newest and most interesting sections – the recently built Sexto Edificio (Rúa de Padre Amoedo) and the adjoining Edificio Sarmiento (p530) in a renovated 18th-century Jesuit college.

Praza da Ferrería   SQUARE
Praza da Ferrería has the best selection of cafes in town and is the hub of Pontevedra social life. It's overlooked by the Igrexa de San Francisco (◷7.30am-12.45pm & 5.15-8.15pm Mon-Fri, 7.30am-1.45pm Sat & Sun), said to have been founded in the 13th century by St Francis of Assisi when on pilgrimage to Santiago (the main portico remains from the original church). Just off the plaza, you can't miss the distinctive curved facade of the Santuario da Virxe Peregrina (Praza da Peregrina; ◷9am-2pm & 4-9pm), an 18th-century caprice with a distinctly Portuguese flavour.

Basílica de Santa María a Maior   CHURCH
(Praza de Alonso de Fonseca; ◷10am-1.30pm & 5-9pm, except during Mass) Pontevedra's most

Pontevedra

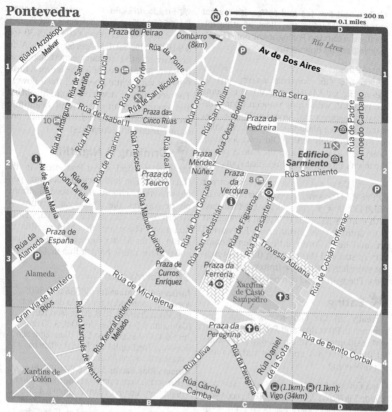

Pontevedra

impressive church is a beautiful, mainly late-Gothic affair, with some plateresque and Portuguese Manueline influences, built by Pontevedra's sailors' guild in the 16th century. Busts of Christopher Columbus and that other great empire-builder Hernán Cortés flank the rosette window on the elaborate western facade, a plateresque work by Cornelius de Holanda and Juan Noble.

🛏 Sleeping

Slow City Hostel　　　　　　　　HOSTEL €
(📞 631 062896; www.slowcityhostelpontevedra. com; Rúa da Amargura 5; dm/d €17/40; ☺ closed Nov; 🛜) Run by a welcoming, well-travelled local couple, Slow City has one spacious dorm with six solid and comfy bunks, and two neat, spotless, all-white private doubles. With an excellent Old Town location, a good

kitchen and free tea and coffee, it's a great option for all budget travellers, whether following the Camino Portugués or not. There's bicycle parking downstairs.

Hotel Rúas
HOTEL €

(986 846 416; www.hotelruas.net; Rúa de Figueroa 35; s/d €44/60; ❄@🛜) The rooms are pleasant, with shiny wooden floors, unfussy furnishings and large bathrooms, and some have nice plaza views – excellent value for this absolutely central Old Town location. Reception is amiable and the cafe is one of the town's most popular breakfast spots.

Parador Casa del Barón
HISTORIC HOTEL €€

(986 855 800; www.parador.es; Rúa do Barón 19; r €110-130; P❄🛜) This elegant refurbished 16th-century palace is equipped throughout with antique-style furniture and historical art, and has a lovely little garden. Rooms vary in size and those facing the street may get some late-night noise from weekend parties. The wi-fi signal can be feeble.

✖ Eating

Virtually all the Old Town's plazas, and streets like Rúas Real and Princesa, are lined with restaurants and bars doing good-value set lunches by day and tapas and *raciones* in the evening.

Casa Fidel O Pulpeiro
SEAFOOD €

(Rúa de San Nicolás 7; raciones €6-12; ☺noon-4pm & 8-11pm Thu-Tue) Fidel's has been serving up perfectly done *pulpo á feira*, Galicia's quintessential octopus dish of tender tentacle slices with paprika and olive oil (ask for some *cachelos*, sliced boiled potatoes, to accompany it), for more than 50 years. But this simple, spotless eatery with its pine tables and white paper tablecloths also offers plenty of shellfish, *empanadas*, omelettes and meat dishes if you fancy something different.

A Ultramar
FUSION €€

(986 857 266; http://laultramar.es; Rúa de Padre Amoedo Carballo 1-3; dishes €7-25; ☺12.30-4pm & 8pm-midnight Tue-Sat, 12.30-4pm Sun) Stylishly contemporary in both cuisine and design, Ultramar was opened in 2015 by Pepe Vieira, who has a Michelin-starred restaurant out towards Sanxenxo. The mostly medium-sized dishes run from good burgers with Arzúa parmesan to Mexican-style beef tacos with spicy chipotle sauce or Chinese-style *jiaozi* shrimp-and-leek dumplings. And there's a choice of fashionable vermouths as well as selected wines.

★ Eirado da Leña
GALICIAN, FUSION €€€

(986 860 225; www.eiradoeventos.com; Praza da Leña 3; mains €22-25, menús €40-55; ☺1.30-4pm & 9-11.30pm Tue-Sat, 1.30-4pm Sun & Mon) A deliciously creative culinary experience in an intimate little stone-walled restaurant, tastefully set with white linen and fresh flowers. The set *menús*, available both lunchtime and evening, comprise several beautifully presented courses, served with a smile and some curious little surprises!

Drinking & Nightlife

It's hard to find a bar-less street in the Old Town. For laid-back drinks and people-watching, choose from several atmospheric squares, like Prazas da Verdura, do Teucro or da Leña, or the tapas bars along Rúa Real. There are also bars on Rúa do Barón, or for heftier *marcha* (action), head down to the music bars of Rúa de Charino.

❶ Information

Turismo de Pontevedra (986 090 890; www.visit-pontevedra.gal; Praza da Verdura; ☺9.30am-2pm & 4.30-8.30pm Mon-Sat, 10am-2pm & 5-8pm Sun Jun-Oct, 9.30am-2pm & 4.30-7.30pm Mon-Sat, 10am-2pm Sun Nov-May) The helpful city tourist office has a convenient central location.

Turismo Rías Baixas (986 804 100; http://turismoriasbaixas.com; Praza de Santa María; ☺9am-9pm Mon-Fri, 10am-2.30pm & 4.30-8pm Sat & Sun mid-Jun–mid-Sep, 9am-8pm Mon-Fri, 10am-2pm & 4-7pm Sat, 10am-2pm Sun mid-Sep–mid-Jun) Information on all of Pontevedra province.

❶ Getting There & Away

BUS

The **bus station** (986 852 408; www.autobusespontevedra.com; Rúa da Estación) is about 1.5km southeast of the Old Town. Castromil-Monbus goes at least 18 times daily to Vigo (€3 to €3.55, 30 minutes to one hour), 13 or more times to Santiago de Compostela (€6.40, one to 1½ hours) and twice or more to Ourense (€11, two hours). Buses also run to Sanxenxo, O Grove, Cambados, Padrón, Bueu, Tui and Lugo.

TRAIN

Pontevedra's **train station** (Rúa Eduardo Pondal), across the roundabout from the bus station, has roughly hourly services, from 7am or 8am to 10pm or 11pm, to Santiago de Compostela (€6.10 to €7.35, 35 minutes to one hour), A Coruña (€14 to €16, one to 1¾ hours) and Vigo (€3.65, 15 to 30 minutes).

GALICIA SEAFOOD TIPS

Galician seafood is plentiful, fresh, and may well be the best you have ever tasted. Almost every restaurant and bar has several seafood specialities on the menu. Shellfish fans will delight over the variety of *ameixas* (clams), *mexillons* (mussels), *vieiras* (scallops), *zamburiñas* and *volandeiras* (types of small scallop), *berberechos* (cockles) and *navajas* (razor clams). But Galicia's ultimate crustacean delicacy is the much-prized *percebes* (goose barnacles), which bear a disconcerting resemblance to fingernails or claws: to eat them you hold the 'claw' end, twist off the other end and eat the soft, succulent bit inside!

Other delicacies include various crabs, from little *nécoras* and *santiaguiños* to huge *centollos* (spider crabs) and the enormous *buey del mar* ('ox of the sea'), and the *bogavante* or *lubrigante* (European lobster), with two enormous claws.

Shellfish in restaurants are often priced by weight: around 250g per person usually makes a fair serving.

While mussels, oysters and some fish are farmed, most crabs are caught wild. Look for *salvaje* (wild) or *del pincho* (rod-caught) on menus to identify nonfarmed fish.

Ría de Pontevedra

The small, old city of Pontevedra sits at the head of the *ría* and is one of the Rías Baixas' most appealing urban experiences. The shores of the *ría* are quite built-up till you get towards their outer ends where you'll find some decent beaches. On the north shore, the Sanxenxo area, together with O Grove a little further north, forms Galicia's busiest summer beach tourism zone.

Combarro

POP 1300

Near Pontevedra on the *ría's* north shore, Combarro has a particularly quaint old quarter that is worth a meal stop on your way through. A jumble of *hórreos* (traditional stone grain stores) stands right on the waterside, with a smattering of waterside restaurants, and behind them is a web of crooked lanes (some of them hewn directly out of the rock bed) dotted with *cruceiros* (stone crucifixes; a traditional Galician art form). It can, however, get extremely busy in high summer.

ⓘ Getting There & Away

Combarro is on the Pontevedra–Sanxenxo bus route.

Sanxenxo

POP 2300

Sanxenxo (Castilian: Sangenjo) has been dubbed the 'Marbella of Galicia' and it does have a thing or two in common with some of Spain's Mediterranean resorts in the summer season: a busy leisure port, a long buzzing waterfront, and streets of mostly ugly 20th-century buildings packed with eateries and tourist accommodation. The tourism here, however, is almost exclusively Spanish.

Praia de Silgar is a fine, sandy and busy beach, stretching west from the shiny marina development in the middle of the seafront, which also contains a tourist office (p534) and a large car park. Further west, towards Portonovo, dune-backed Praia de Baltar is a bit quieter, as is Praia de Areas, 3km east.

🛏 Sleeping & Eating

Hotel Rotilio   HOTEL **€€**
(☑986 720 200; www.hotelrotilio.com; Avenida do Porto 7; s €66-76, d €102-126, breakfast €10; ⊙closed mid-Oct–mid-Mar; ❋🄰) Stylish and comfortable Hotel Rotilio overlooks both Praia de Silgar and the marina. Run by the third generation of the same family, it has 39 bright, pretty rooms, all with sea views and unusual silk paintings by local fine-arts students. There's a five-night minimum stay from mid-July to the end of August.

La Taberna de Rotilio   CONTEMPORARY GALICIAN **€€€**
(dishes €11-25; ⊙2-4pm & 9-11pm, closed mid-Oct–mid-Mar, Sun night & Mon Mar-Jun, Sep & Oct) Right in the centre of things, La Taberna de Rotilio serves up terrific Galician seafood and meat with a creative touch to many of the dishes, such as spider-crab cannelloni or spinach-stuffed seabass. Choose between the main dining room or the informal gastrobar downstairs.

ℹ Information

Tourist Office (☎ 986 720 285; www.turis modesanxenxo.com; Porto Juan Carlos I; ⏱10am-2pm & 4-8.30pm Mon-Sat, 10am-2pm Sun Jul–mid-Sep, 9.30am-2pm & 4-7pm Tue-Sat mid-Sep–Jun) In the marina complex on the central beachfront.

ℹ Getting There & Away

Buses between Pontevedra and O Grove (more than 20 a day in summer) stop in Sanxenxo.

Illa de Ons

In summer you can get well away from urban civilisation (if not all other tourists) by hopping on a boat to vehicle-free Illa de Ons at the mouth of the Ría de Pontevedra and part of the Parque Nacional de las Islas Atlánticas de Galicia. The island is 5.6km long with one tiny village, several sandy beaches, cliffs, ruins, four walking trails (circuits of between 1km and 8km) and rich bird life.

🛏 Sleeping

Camping Isla de Ons   CAMPGROUND €
(☎986 441 678; www.isladeons.net; per adult/child €6/4, rentals per tent/sleeping bag/air bed €6/5/5; ⏱Easter-Sep) This campground, reopened in 2016 after a complete revamp, is at Chan de Pólvora, about 600m west from the boat jetty. It has camping space for more than 200 people, and a restaurant. Reserve ahead by phone or through the website.

Casa Acuña   PENSIÓN, APARTMENT €€
(☎986 441 678; www.isladeons.net; d incl breakfast €65-85, apt for 2 €95-105, apt for 4 €125-155; ⏱May-Sep) You can stay in bright rooms or apartments (reservations strongly advised) at Casa Acuña in Ons village.

ℹ Getting There & Away

Three companies, **Cruceros Rías Baixas** (www.crucerosriasbaixas.com) and **Naviera Mar de Ons** (www.mardeons.es) and **Cruceros Islas de Ons** (www.islasdeons.com), sail to Ons from Sanxenxo and/or nearby Portonovo during the summer season. There are several sailings daily by one or more of these companies from about late June to late September. The trip takes 45 minutes one way; return fares are €12 to €16 for adults and €6 or €7 for children. There are also sailings from Bueu, on the south side of the Ría de Pontevedra, for most of the season.

Ría de Vigo

The far end of the *ria's* north shore is one of the least populated and most scenic parts of the Rías Baixas. The peaceful village of Hío draws visitors for a look at Galicia's most famous *cruceiro* (stone crucifix; a traditional Galician art form), the **Cruceiro de Hío** (ℙ).

Several sandy beaches are within easy reach of Hío, including 800m-long **Praia Areabrava**, 3km north. But the area's greatest gem is the rocky promontory **Cabo de Home** (ℙ), whose walking trails, beaches, panoramic Iron Age *castro* and spectacular views of the Illas Cíes make it a great place to spend a day or half-day.

🛏 Sleeping & Eating

A Casa de Aldán   HOTEL €€
(☎986 328 732; www.acasadealdan.net; Avenida José Graña 20, Aldán; s €71, d €110-149, incl breakfast; 🐾) This clever, highly original conversion of a 19th-century fish-salting plant overlooks the fishing harbour in the village of Aldán. Thick stone walls combine with contemporary cedar furnishings and good, modern bathrooms in 13 sizeable, bright rooms, and there's a lovely walled garden. It's advisable to reserve or at least call ahead.

Restaurante Hotel Doade   SEAFOOD €€
(mains €10-30; ⏱1-4.30pm & 8.30-11.30pm Tue-Sun, closed Nov) The excellent restaurant in Hotel Doade focuses on *ría*-fresh seafood, with oven-baked fish a speciality.

ℹ Getting There & Away

Naviera Mar de Ons (www.mardeons.es) operates hourly ferries from Vigo's **Estación Marítima de Ría** (Ferry Port; Rúa Cánovas del Castillo 3) to Cangas (€2.20, 20 minutes) on the north side of the *ría*. From Cangas, **Autobuses Cerqueiro** (www.autobusescerqueiro.es) runs to Aldán (€1.40, 10 minutes) at least seven times daily (continuing to Bueu on the Ría de Pontevedra), to Hío (€1.40, 15 minutes) three or four times daily except Sunday, and to Donón (€1.40, 25 minutes) at 11.30am Monday to Saturday. The Donón bus comes straight back so there's no return service till the next morning.

Drivers from Vigo can cross the *ría* on the Puente de Rande bridge then head west along the north shore.

Vigo

POP 200,000

Depending on where you point your lens, Vigo is a historic and cultured city or a gritty industrial port. Home to Europe's largest fishing fleet, this is an axis of commerce in northern Spain. Yet its central areas are very walkable and full of intriguing nooks, and it's the main gateway to the beautiful Illas Cíes. Above all, Vigo is a welcoming and confident city whose citizens really know how to enjoy life, especially after dark in the many buzzing tapas bars, restaurants, music bars and clubs.

The Casco Vello (Old Town) climbs uphill from the cruise-ship port; the heart of the modern city spreads east from here, with Praza de Compostela a welcome green space in its midst.

◎ Sights

At the heart of the jumbled lanes of the Casco Vello is elegant Praza da Constitución, a perfect spot for a drink. Head down Rúa dos Cesteiros, with its quaint wicker shops, and you'll reach the Old Town's main church, the Igrexa de Santa María (Praza da Igrexa). Just below here is Rúa Pescadería, famed for its oyster shuckers.

Praia de Samil   BEACH
(⛱) A long swath of sandy beaches stretches southwest of the city. Best is 1.2km-long Praia de Samil, beginning about 5km from the city centre. It's backed by a long promenade and has great views of the Illas Cíes. Several buses run from the city centre.

Centro de Visitantes
Illas Atlánticas   INTERPRETATION CENTRE
(Rúa da Palma 4; ⊙10am-2pm & 4.30-7.30pm Tue-Sat, 11am-2pm Sun) FREE This centre in the Old Town presents photos, information and an attractive audiovisual display on the nature and history of the Illas Cíes in the mouth of the Ría de Vigo and the Ons, Sálvora and Cortegada archipelagos further north, which together comprise the Parque Nacional de las Islas Atlánticas de Galicia (Atlantic Islands of Galicia National Park; www.iatlanticas.es) ⚑.

Museo de Arte
Contemporánea de Vigo   MUSEUM
(Marco; www.marcovigo.com; Rúa do Príncipe 54; ⊙11am-2.30pm & 5-9pm Tue-Sat, 11am-2.30pm Sun) FREE Vigo is something of a modern art centre, with several museums and galleries to prove it. The Contemporary Art Museum is the number-one venue for exhibitions ranging from painting and sculpture to fashion and design.

🛏 Sleeping

Hotel Náutico   HOTEL €
(☑986 122 440; www.hotelnautico.net; Rúa Luis Taboada 28; s/d €33/45, incl breakfast €35/50; 🛜) A friendly budget hotel near Praza de Compostela, with a clean, crisp style and a pleasant nautical look. Rooms are on the small side, but cosy. It has a good deal on parking in a nearby car park – €8 per 24 hours.

Hotel América   HOTEL €€
(☑986 438 922; www.hoteles-silken.com; Rúa de Pablo Morillo 6; r €84-115, incl breakfast €101-132; 🅿❄@🛜) The América gets a big thumbs-up for its well-equipped, spacious rooms with tasteful modern art and elegantly muted colour schemes, its friendly, efficient staff and its quiet sidestreet location near the waterfront. Nearly all the 47 rooms are exterior facing, and the breakfast is a good buffet-style affair, served on the roof terrace in summer.

Gran Hotel Nagari   LUXURY HOTEL €€€
(☑986 211 111; www.granhotelnagari.com; Praza de Compostela 21; r €152-165, incl breakfast & spa €195-206; 🅿❄🛜🏊) Luxurious Nagari has a welcome and personal feel to its contemporary design and service. Rooms boast remote-controlled colour-changing lighting and temperature control, giant-headed showers, hi-tech coffee makers and big-screen smart TVs, and there's a rooftop pool and spa with fabulous views.

🍴 Eating

Good restaurants, tapas bars and cafes are scattered all over the central area, and beyond. The narrow lanes of the Old Town, especially around Praza da Constitución, and the Praza de Compostela area all have plenty of options.

Rúa Pescadería   SEAFOOD €
(Rúa das Ostras; oysters per dozen €12-15) Short Rúa Pescadería, in the lower part of the Old Town, is jammed with people tucking into fresh seafood. From about 10am until 4pm you can buy oysters from the ostreras (shuckers) here, and sit down to eat them with a drink at one of the restaurants. Oysters and albariño wine are Vigo's traditional Sunday-morning hangover cure.

Follas Novas GALICIAN €€

(☑ 986 229 306; Rúa de Serafín Avendaño 10; mains €11-17; ⊘ 1.15-3.45pm & 8.15-11.45pm Mon-Sat) It's well worth venturing a little out of the city centre for the top-class fare at this small, unpretentious restaurant, about 400m east of Praza de Compostela. But it's advisable to reserve as it fills up super-fast. Attentive, friendly service complements the excellent preparations of quality fresh ingredients.

Taverna da Curuxa CONTEMPORARY GALICIAN €€

(☑ 986 436 526; Rúa dos Cesteiros 7; mains €7-13; ⊘ 1-4.45pm & 8.30-11.45pm Wed-Sun; ☑) This atmospheric stone tavern just off Praza da Constitución mixes the traditional and contemporary in decor and menu. Try one of its seafood rice dishes in clay pots, or an entrecôte steak, or go for vegetable lasagne or an avocado-and-smoked-trout salad. It's worth booking for dinner.

Drinking & Nightlife

For early evening drinks, the bars around Praza da Constitución in the Old Town and Praza de Compostela are enticing. From around 11pm the action shifts east to the music bars and pubs along Rúas de Areal and Rosalía de Castro. The more alternative party area, after about midnight, is the Churruca district about 1km southeast of the Old Town.

Cervexería Nós BAR

(www.cervexanos.es; Rúa da Palma 3; ⊘ 6pm-1am Tue-Thu, noon-4pm & 6pm-3am Fri & Sat, noon-4pm & 6pm-midnight Sun) This lively Old Town craft-beer bar has its own and international beers on tap, and dozens more bottled varieties.

Van Gogh Café BAR

(Rúa de Rosalía de Castro 28; ⊘ 7am-2am or later) One of Vigo's nocturnal classics, Van Gogh is always busy by night with a completely mixed-ages crowd. There's a loungey area and small open-air patio up the steps at the back of the long main bar with its colourful array of well over 100 bottles to pour your drinks from.

☆ Entertainment

La Fábrica de Chocolate Club LIVE MUSIC

(www.facebook.com/lafabricadechocolateclub.vigo; Rúa Rogelio Abalde 22; ⊘ 10.30pm-4.30am Thu-Sat) This club is one of northern Spain's top venues for live indie and rock bands, with a couple of gigs weekly, usually at 10pm Friday and Saturday.

La Iguana Club LIVE MUSIC

(www.facebook.com/laiguanaclub; Rúa de Churruca 14; ⊘ midnight-5am Tue-Sat night, opens earlier for live gigs) A great venue for live rock and related bands for over quarter of a century, with gigs most Friday and Saturday nights.

ℹ Information

Oficina de Turismo de Vigo (☑ 986 224 757; www.turismodevigo.org; Estación Marítima de Ría, Rúa Cánovas del Castillo 3; ⊘ 10am-5pm) Helpful tourist office, in the ferry terminal.

ℹ Getting There & Away

AIR

Vigo's **Peinador airport** (☑ 902 404704; www. aena.es), 9km east of the city centre, has direct flights to/from London Luton (Iberia twice weekly, mid-July to late September), Madrid (Iberia and Air Europa), Barcelona (Vueling and Rya-nair), Bilbao (Iberia), Málaga (Air Europa), Dublin (Ryanair) and Bologna, Italy (Ryanair).

BOAT

Ferries to the Illas Cíes and Cangas leave from the **Estación Marítima de Ría** (p534).

BUS

The **bus station** (☑ 986 373 411; Avenida de Madrid 57) is 2km southeast of the Old Town. **Castromil-Monbus** (www.monbus.es) makes several trips daily to all main Galician cities, including Pontevedra (€3, 30 minutes), Santiago de Compostela (€9.35, 1½ hours) and Ourense (€11, 1½ hours), and the coastal towns of southwest Galicia. **Avanza** (www.avanzabus.com) runs to/from Madrid (€43 to €47, 7¼ to nine hours) at least four times daily. **Autna** (www. autna.com) runs at least twice daily to/from Porto, Portugal (€12, 2½ hours), with connections there for Lisbon.

TRAIN

Vigo has two stations. Most trains use **Vigo-Guixar train station** (Rúa Areal), 1km east of the Old Town, but about half of those going to/from Pontevedra, Santiago de Compostela and A Coruña use **Vigo-Urzáiz train station** (Praza da Estación), 1km southeast of the Old Town. Trains run at least 15 times daily to Pontevedra (€3.20 to €3.60, 20 to 40 minutes) and Santiago de Compostela (€9.25 to €11, 50 minutes to 1½ hours), and six or more times to Ourense (€10 to €20, 1½ to two hours). There's also service to Ribadavia, Tui, Valença (Portugal), A Coruña, León, Madrid and elsewhere.

ℹ Getting Around

Vitrasa (☑ 986 29 16 00; www.vitrasa.es) runs city buses (€1.32 per ride). Bus C9A runs between the central Rúa Policarpo Sanz and the airport; the bus station and Vigo-Guixar train station are linked to the city centre by bus C2 (to/from Porta do Sol). Bus 4C runs between the bus station and Rúa Policarpo Sanz.

Illas Cíes

The Illas Cíes, three spectacular islands that form a beautiful bird sanctuary and are home to some of Galicia's most privileged beaches, are a 45-minute, 14km ferry ride from Vigo. This small archipelago forms a 6km breakwater that protects the Ría de Vigo from the Atlantic's fury and is the main attraction of the Parque Nacional de las Islas Atlánticas de Galicia (p535).

This is an ideal spot for lolling on pristine sandy beaches, such as the 1km-long, lagoon-backed crescent of Praia das Rodas, joining the northern Illa de Monteagudo to the central Illa do Faro, or nudist Praia das Figueiras. Walking trails skirt the shores and climb up to spectacular high lookouts, like the Ruta Monte Faro.

🏃 Activities

Ruta Monte Faro   FISHING
This walking trail leads up to a viewpoint with the most impressive panoramas – cliffs, beaches, ocean and the whole Ría de Vigo. It's a 7.4km round trip from the main jetty at the north end of Praia das Rodas.

🛌 Sleeping

Camping Islas Cíes   CAMPGROUND €
(☑ 986 438 358; www.campingislascies.com; adult/child/tent €8.25/6.20/8.50, 2/4-person tent & bed rental per night €49/75) Public boat service to the Illas Cíes only goes during Semana Santa, on weekends from then to the end of May, and daily from June to early September. To stay overnight you must camp at Camping Illas Cíes. The campground has a restaurant and supermarket, and a capacity of 800 people – often filled in August. There is a two-night minimum stay in July and August.

ⓘ Information

Illas Cíes Camping Office (☑ 986 438 358; Estación Marítima de Ría, Vigo; ⊙ 8.30am-1.30pm & 3.30-7.30pm) For camping in July or August, or at any time if you want to rent a tent, you must reserve in advance, online or at the camping office in the Estación Marítima de Ría in Vigo. If you reserve online you must

show a printout of your reservation at the camping office in Vigo (if you are sailing from there) or when you board the ferry in Cangas or Bueu.

ⓘ Getting There & Away

Public boats to the Cíes (round trip adult/child €19/6) normally only sail during Semana Santa (Holy Week), on weekends and holidays in May, daily from June to late September, and on the first two weekends of October. They are operated, weather permitting, by three companies. **Naviera Mar de Ons** (☑ 986 225 272; www.mardeons.es) runs at least four daily trips (10 in July and August) from Vigo's Estación Marítima de Ría, four or more from Cangas, and four or more (in Semana Santa, July and August only) from Baiona; **Nabia Naviera** (www.piratasdenabia.com) makes up to five trips a day from Vigo, three from Cangas and three (July and August only) from Baiona; and **Cruceros Rías Baixas** (http://crucerosriasbaixas.com) runs three daily trips from Vigo, from July to mid-September.

THE SOUTHWEST

Galicia's southwest corner is home to three towns that all make enjoyable stops on a circuit of the region or a journey to or from Portugal – the historic port and resort Baiona, the pretty fishing town A Guarda and the riverside cathedral town Tui.

Baiona

POP 2900

Baiona (Castilian: Bayona) is a popular resort with its own little place in history: the shining moment came on 1 March 1493, when one of Columbus' small fleet, the *Pinta,* stopped in for supplies, bearing the remarkable news that the explorer had made it to the Indies (in fact, the West Indies). Then an important trading port, Baiona was later eclipsed by Vigo – but there's still a hefty reminder of its old importance in the shape of the stout defensive walls, towers and gun batteries of Monte Boi promontory jutting out from the town's waterfront.

A tangle of inviting lanes, with a handful of 16th- and 17th-century houses and chapels, makes up Baiona's casco histórico (historic centre), behind the harbourfront road, Rúa Elduayen. Four kilometres east of town is the magnificent sweep of Praia América at Nigrán.

⊙ Sights

Fortaleza de Monterreal FORTRESS
(Sep-Jun free, pedestrian/car incl occupants €1/5 Jul & Aug; ⊙ 10am-10pm Jul & Aug, 10am-7pm Sep-Jun; P ⛺) You can't miss the pine-covered promontory Monte Boi, dominated by the Fortaleza de Monterreal. The fortress, erected between the 11th and 17th centuries, is protected by an impregnable 3km circle of walls. An enticing 40-minute walking trail loops the promontory's rocky shoreline, which is broken up by a few small beaches.

🛏 Sleeping & Eating

Hotel Cais HOTEL €€
(☑ 986 355 643; hotelr.cais@gmail.com; Rúa Alférez Barreiro 3; s/d €55/65; ⊙ closed Sun-Thu Jan & Feb; 🛜) Little Cais has a couple of rooms facing the harbour, but rooms at the side or back are likely to be quieter. All have bright white bedding and paintwork, and there's a convenient cafe downstairs.

Parador de Baiona LUXURY HOTEL €€€
(☑ 986 355 000; www.parador.es; Monterreal; s/d incl breakfast from €145/165; P ✳ 🛜 ⛱) This privileged *parador,* inside Monte Boi's fortress enclosure, was built in 1967 but in medieval-castle style with big stone blocks and wood-beamed ceilings. Suits of armour stand in the lobby, while the best rooms boast canopied beds and wonderful views.

Taberna Mendoza GALICIAN €€
(Rúa Elduayen 1; mains €10-24; ⊙ noon-4pm & 8.30-11.30pm; 🛜) A cut above most other harbour-facing eateries, the Mendoza offers a choice between an informal bar area serving *raciones* and tapas and a stone-walled sit-down restaurant, all with efficient service and picture windows. Maritime fare like the grilled *zamburiñas* (small scallops) or wild *lubina* (seabass) is always a solid choice, but equally good is the inland produce such as *tiras* (strips) of Galician entrecôte.

❶ Information

Tourist Office (☑ 986 687 067; www.turismodebaiona.com; Paseo da Ribeira; ⊙ 10am-2pm & 4-8pm Feb-Nov, 11am-1.30pm & 3.30-5.30pm Dec & Jan) Helpful office on the approach to the Monte Boi promontory.

❶ Getting There & Away

ATSA buses run to and from Vigo (€2.20, 45 minutes) every 30 or 60 minutes till 9pm. Just a couple a day go south to A Guarda (€3.25, 45 minutes). Catch buses at stops on the harbour-front road, Rúa Elduayen.

A Guarda

POP 6200

A fishing port just north of where the Río Miño spills into the Atlantic, A Guarda (Castilian: La Guardia) has a pretty harbour and some excellent seafood restaurants, but its unique draw is the hill Monte de Santa Trega (p538), rising just outside town. You can drive or walk up to its magnificently panoramic summit. Another fine walking path runs 3km south from A Guarda's harbour along the coast to the heads of the Miño.

⊙ Sights

★ **Monte de Santa Trega** HILL
(adult/child in vehicle Tue-Sun Feb-Dec €1/0.50, other times free; P ⛺) A Guarda's unique draw is the beautiful Monte de Santa Trega, whose 341m summit is a 4km drive or 2km uphill walk (the PRG122) from town. On the way up, poke around the partly restored Iron Age Castro de Santa Trega. At the top, you'll find a 16th-century chapel, an interesting small archaeological museum (⊙ 10am-8pm Tue-Sun Apr-Sep, 11am-5pm Oct-Mar; P) FREE on *castro* culture, a couple of cafes and souvenir stalls – and truly majestic panoramas up the Miño, across to Portugal and out over the Atlantic.

Castelo de Santa Cruz FORT
(Avenida de Santo Domingo de Guzmán; ⊙ 10am-9pm Apr-Sep, 10am-6pm Oct-Mar; P ⛺) FREE This fort with four arrowhead-shaped corner bastions makes an interesting visit in the town. Built to defend A Guarda against the Portuguese in the 17th century, it was opened to the public in 2014.

🛏 Sleeping & Eating

★ **Hotel Convento de San Benito** HISTORIC HOTEL €€
(☑ 986 611 166; www.hotelsanbenito.es; Praza de San Bieito; s €55-58, d €65-96, breakfast €6; ⊙ closed Jan; P ✳ 🛜) A real treat, Hotel Convento de San Benito is housed in a 16th-century convent down by the harbour. Its 33 elegant rooms are romantic, individually decorated, very comfortable and very well kept, and the whole place is like a mini-museum with fascinating antiques, paintings, sculptures, books and manuscripts strewn all over the place.

Casa Chupa Ovos
SEAFOOD €€

(☑986 611 015; Rúa La Roda 24; mains & raciones €7.50-18; ☺1-4.30pm & 7.30-11.45pm Thu-Tue) It's up a flight of steps from the harbourfront street Rúa do Porto, and it doesn't have a sea view, but Chupa Ovos is a firm favourite with locals and visitors alike for its perfectly prepared fresh seafood, friendly and prompt service, bright atmosphere and good wines.

❶ Getting There & Away

A **ferry** (☑986 611 526; car/bicycle incl driver/rider €3/1, car/foot passenger €1; ☺about hourly 9.30am-1.30pm & 3.30-9.15pm Mon-Fri, from 10.30am Sat & Sun Jul-Aug, about hourly 10.30am-1.30pm & 3.30-8.15pm Tue-Fri, from 11.30am Sat & Sun Sep-Jun) crosses the Miño from Camposancos, 2km south of A Guarda, to Caminha, Portugal.

ATSA buses run to/from Vigo (€5.10, 80 minutes) every 30 or 60 minutes until 7pm (fewer on weekends). Most go via Tui, but two or three daily go via Baiona. Buses stop on the main street through the town centre, Avenida de Galicia.

Tui

POP 6000

Sitting above the broad Río Miño 25m inland, the border town of Tui (Castilian: Tuy) draws Portuguese and Spanish day trippers with its lively bar scene, tightly packed medieval centre and magnificent cathedral. It's well worth strolling round the Old Town and down to the Paseo Fluvial, a riverside path that heads 1km down the Miño almost to the two-level, 19th-century **Puente Internacional** (railway above, road below), which crosses the Miño to Portugal's equally appealing Valença.

◉ Sights

★**Catedral de Santa Maria**
CATHEDRAL

(adult/child €3/free; ☺10am-12.30pm & 4-7pm Sep-Jun, 10am-2pm & 4-9pm Jul & Aug) The highlight of the Old Town is the fortress-like Catedral de Santa Maria, which reigns over Praza de San Fernando. Begun in the 12th century, it reflects a stoic Romanesque style in most of its construction, although the ornate main portal is reckoned the earliest work of Gothic sculpture on the Iberian Peninsula. Admission covers the lovely Gothic cloister, the 15th-century tower and the gardens with river views, as well as the main nave and chapels.

🍴 Sleeping & Eating

O Novo Cabalo Furado
HOSTAL €

(☑986 604 445; www.cabalofurado.com; Rúa Seijas 3; s/d/apt €40/60/80; 🛜) The rooms and apartments at this superior Old Town *hostal* are simple but inviting, with all-wood furnishings and sparkling bathrooms. Advance reservations are essential from November to February.

Hotel A Torre do Xudeu
HISTORIC HOTEL €€

(☑986 603 535; www.atorredoxudeu.es; Rúa Tide 3; r incl breakfast €65-80; ☺closed mid-Dec–Feb; 🅿🛜) A lovely 1746 mansion with thick stone walls and a pretty garden, the atmospheric 'Jew's Tower' has just six beautifully looked-after rooms in a fairly formal style, with large bathrooms. Several rooms look across the Río Miño to Portugal.

La Pizarra del Silabario
CONTEMPORARY GALICIAN €€

(Rúa Colón; raciones €8-21, lunch menús Mon-Fri €9-14; ☺1.30-4pm & 8.30-11pm) This gastrobar enables you to sample the taste sensations of the adjoining restaurant El Silabario (p539) on a tighter budget.

★**El Silabario**
CONTEMPORARY GALICIAN €€€

(☑986 607 000; www.restaurantesilabario.com; Rúa Colón 11; mains €25-35, menús €29-84; ☺1.30-4pm & 9-11.30pm Tue-Sat, 1.30-4pm Sun; 🛜) Silabario converts market-fresh ingredients into delicious, frequently changing flavour combinations – the likes of duck-and-wild-mushroom pancakes or rod-caught hake with a soya *pil-pil* (chili, garlic and olive oil). An enormous wine list and picture windows looking across to Portugal enhance the experience. You can sample Silabario taste sensations on a budget at the adjoining gastrobar La Pizarra del Silabario.

❶ Information

Oficina Municipal de Turismo (☑677 418405; www.concellotui.org; Praza de San Fernando; ☺10am-8pm daily Jul-Sep, shorter hours Tue-Sun Oct-Jun) Very helpful and informative office in front of the cathedral.

❶ Getting There & Away

ATSA buses to Vigo (€3.30, 40 minutes) and A Guarda (€3.25, 40 minutes), both every 30 or 60 minutes until 7.45pm or later (fewer services on weekends), stop on Paseo de Calvo Sotelo, in front of Hostal Generosa.

THE EAST

Although often overshadowed by Galicia's glorious coastline and the better-known attractions of Santiago de Compostela, eastern Galicia is a treasure trove of enticing provincial cities, lovely landscapes, wine-growing regions and old-fashioned rural enclaves – perfect territory for travellers who like digging out their own gems.

Ourense

POP 99,900

Galicia's third-largest city has a spruced-up labyrinth of a historic quarter, a lively tapas scene and tempting riverside thermal baths. An oddly beguiling place, Ourense (Castilian: Orense) first came into its own as a trading centre in the 11th century. The broad Río Miño runs east–west across the city, crossed by several bridges, including the elegant, stone-built, part-Roman, part-medieval Ponte Vella (Old Bridge) and the soaring concrete-and-metal Ponte do Milenio (Millennium Bridge) that opened in 2001. The central area, including the compact Old Town, rises south of the river.

◉ Sights

The Old Town unfolds around 12th-century Catedral de San Martiño (Rúa de Juan de Austria; ⊙11.30am-1pm & 5-7.30pm Mon-Sat, 5-7.30pm Sun), in a maze of narrow streets and small plazas that are a pleasure to wander. The largest square is sloping Praza Maior, rimmed by old stone buildings with cafes under the arcades and the classical-facaded Casa do Concello (City Hall) at its foot.

Claustro de San Francisco CONVENT
(Rúa Emilia Pardo Bazán; ⊙11.30am-1.30pm & 6.30-9.30pm Tue-Sat, 11.30am-1.30pm Sun, plus 5-8pm Sun mid-Oct–May) FREE The capitals of the 63 arches of the lovely 14th-century Claustro de San Francisco are carved with a fascinating collection of people, animals, imaginary creatures and Galician plants – well worth a visit, and the attendant may give you a free tour.

⚡ Activities

A Chavasqueira
Open-Air Pools THERMAL POOL
(⊙9am-9pm) FREE A Chavasqueira pools, right on the riverbank, are the closest to the city centre of Ourense's open-air riverside thermal pools. You can walk there in 20

to 30 minutes from the Old Town, or take the Tren das Termas (www.urbanosdeourense.es; one way €0.85; ⊙hourly 10am-1pm & 4-8pm, reduced frequency Oct-May), a mini-train from Praza Maior.

Muiño da Vega Open-Air Pools THERMAL POOL
(⊙9am-9pm) FREE These four relatively large (up to 15m long) pools are the most enticing of Ourense's free open-air thermal pools, sitting in a pleasantly green spot on the bank of the Miño about 5km northwest of the city centre.

Termas Chavasqueira THERMAL POOL
(www.termaschavasqueira.com; adult €4; ⊙9am-11.30pm or later Tue-Sun) Closest of the privately run pools to the city centre are the Termas Chavasqueira, with four warm pools and one cold one, plus two saunas, massage service and a cafe. You can walk there from the Old Town in 20 to 30 minutes or take the Tren das Termas from Praza Maior.

🛏 Sleeping

Hotel Irixo HOTEL €
(☑988 254 620; info@hotelirixo.es; Rúa dos Irmáns Villar 15; s/d €35/50; ☏) On a small Old Town square, the Irixo provides plain, neat, clean rooms renovated a few years ago, though only a few look out on the street. Singles can be tight.

Hotel Carrís Cardenal Quevedo HOTEL €€
(☑988 375 523; www.carrishoteles.com; Rúa Cardenal Quevedo 28; r from €71; P ❄ ☏) Aimed at both leisure and business travellers, the Cardenal Quevedo offers comfy but pretty standard contemporary chain-hotel rooms in greys, browns and whites. There are bathtubs in all rooms and breakfast is available. It's a 600m walk north from the heart of the Old Town.

🍴 Eating

Ir de tapeo (going for tapas) is a way of life in Ourense, and streets near the cathedral including Fornos, Paz, Lepanto, Viriato, San Miguel and Praza do Ferro brim with taverns where having to push and shove your way to the bar is a sign of quality. Tapas start at €1.20 and are nearly always washed down with a glass of local wine.

Tapería O Enxebre GALICIAN €
(Rúa Lepanto 14; items €4-15; ⊙noon-4pm & 7.30pm-midnight Tue-Sun) A relatively calm Old Town option where you can sit down for small or medium-sized servings of many

tasty offerings ranging from *pulpo á feira* or *solomillo* (tenderloin) to *tostas* (slices of toasted bread) topped with quail egg, bacon and caramelised onion. It has a decent choice of Galician and other wines too.

Síbaris 2.0
MODERN SPANISH €€
(Local 7, Rúa Santo Domingo 15; dishes €8-13, lunch menú €11; ☺11am-midnight Mon-Sat) Síbaris is not just a restaurant with a flavoursome contemporary twist on Spanish fare but also a well-stocked wine shop and Galician specialist deli (cheeses and hams, of course, but also lampreys in oil, crab paté and sea-urchin caviar). The frequently changing menu might include seafood ravioli or truffled chicken with roast vegies or a scrumptious apple crumble with raspberry ice cream.

A Taberna
GALICIAN €€
(Rúa Julio Prieto 32; mains €14-22; ☺1-4pm & 9pm-midnight Tue-Sat, 1-4pm Sun, closed Semana Santa & last 3 weeks Aug) Reminiscent of a countryside inn with its wood beams and shelves of decorative crockery, A Taberna serves up first-class traditional Galician seafood and meat dishes with a few tasty twists, such as its venison tournedos with blueberries or the grilled scallops with sea-urchin caviar. It's 500m south of the cathedral.

ℹ Information

Oficina Municipal de Turismo (☎988 36 60 64; www.turismodeourense.com; Calle Isabel La Católica 2; ☺9am-2pm & 4-8pm Mon-Fri, 11am-2pm Sat & Sun) A very helpful place beneath the Xardinillos Padre Feijóo park, just off pedestrianised Rúa do Paseo.

ℹ Getting There & Away

BUS

From Ourense's **bus station** (☎988 216 027; Carretera de Vigo 1), 2km northwest of the city centre, Monbus runs to Santiago (€9, 1½ to two hours, four or more daily), Vigo (€11, 1½ to two hours, six or more daily), Pontevedra (€11, two hours, two or more daily) and Lugo (€9.40, 1¾ hours, two or more daily). Arriva heads to A Coruña (€18, three hours, four daily). **Avanza** (www.avanzabus.com) journeys to Madrid (€37 to €42, six to seven hours, six daily).

TRAIN

The **train station** (Avenida de Marín) is 500m north of the Río Miño. Renfe runs to Santiago (€11 to €20, 40 minutes to 1¾ hours, 12 daily), Vigo (€12 to €25, 1½ to 2½ hours, 15 daily), León (€9.15 to €26, four to 4½ hours, four daily) and elsewhere.

DON'T MISS

FESTA DO PULPO DE O CARBALLIÑO

Most Galicians agree that the best *pulpo á feira* (Galicia's signature octopus dish) is cooked in the town of O Carballiño, 30km northwest of Ourense. Around 70,000 people pile into O Carballiño on the second Sunday of August for the Festa do Pulpo de O Carballiño (www.festadopulpodocarballino.es).

Cooks here invented the recipe in the Middle Ages, when the local monastery received copious supplies of octopus from tenants on its coastal properties.

Ribadavia & the Ribeiro Wine Region

POP 3200 (RIBADAVIA)

The headquarters of the Ribeiro Denominación de Origen (DO), which produces some of Galicia's best white wines, Ribadavia sits beside the Río Avia 30km west of Ourense in a region of verdant, rolling hills dotted with vineyards and old stone villages. The town's little historic centre is an enticing maze of narrow streets lined with heavy stone arcades and broken up by diminutive plazas; within this in medieval times was Galicia's largest Jewish quarter, centred on Rúa Merelles Caulla.

◉ Sights

More than 20 wineries in the area are open for visits. Winemaking in the Ribeiro area began with the Romans and was revived by medieval monks. Back in the 16th century, Ribeiro wine was popular in England. The Ribeiro Denominación de Origen (DO) has its origins in Ribadavia's Municipal Ordinances of 1579, laying down rules for the production and provenance of Ribeiro wine. Ribeiro's following is growing again today as vintners develop some quality wines often with indigenous grapes and/or organic production processes. The Treixadura grape is the basis of most Ribeiro whites.

Most wineries require a phone call in advance of your visit: staff at Ribadavia's tourist office really know their wineries and can help arrange visits and advise on the pros and cons of different wineries according to your interests (traditional or modern architecture, autochthonous grape varieties, quality of welcome and explanation, prize-winning wines, ecological values...). For further information on the Ribeiro wine area, check www.rutadelvinoribeiro.com and http://ribeiro.es.

Bodega Castro Rei   WINERY

(✓988 472 069; www.bodegacastrorei.com; 1hr tour €3; ⊙tours 11.30am, 12.30pm, 6pm & 7pm mid-Jun–mid-Sep, by appointment rest of year) Castro Rei offers summer visits without prior booking to its pretty, walled vineyard, just a 500m walk from the town centre, with a wine tasting and snack. Meet at Ribeiro e Xamón shop on Praza Maior a few minutes before the start time.

Bodega Viña Meín   WINERY

(✓676 358763; www.vinamein.com; ⊙9am-1pm & 3.30-6.30pm Mon-Fri, by reservation; P) `FREE` This medium-size winery adjoining the Viña Meín country hotel produces more than 100,000 bottles annually of good reds and whites from indigenous Galician grapes grown on 19 hectares of vineyards around the Avia valley. It has a lovely bright modern tasting room for you to sample its vintages.

Bodega Casal de Armán   WINERY

(✓638 043335; www.casaldearman.net; O Cotiño, San Andrés; incl tasting €5; ⊙visits by reservation 1pm, 6pm & 8pm Tue-Sun Nov-Aug; P) Adjoining the Casal de Armán country hotel and restaurant, set among vineyards 6km northeast of Ribadavia, this winery produces both white and red wines. Visits for hotel and restaurant guests are normally free of charge.

Castelo dos Sarmento   CASTLE

(Castelo dos Condes; Rúa Progreso; adult/child incl Museo Sefardí & audioguide €3.50/free; ⊙10.30am-2.30pm & 5-8pm, closed afternoons Sun year-round & Mon-Fri Oct-May) The large, chiefly 15th-century castle of the Counts of Ribadavia is one of Galicia's biggest medieval castles. Tickets are sold at the tourist office.

Museo Sefardí   MUSEUM

(Centro de Información Xudía de Galicia; Praza Maior 7; adult/child incl Castelo dos Sarmento & audioguide €3.50/free; ⊙10.30am-2.30pm & 5-8pm, closed afternoons Sun year-round & Mon-Fri Oct-May) Above the tourist office on the lovely main square, this centre has exhibits, in Galician, on the Jews of Galicia since their expulsion from Spain in 1492.

🏃 Activities

Paseo Fluvial   FISHING

Relax with a stroll along this riverside path beside the Ríos Avia and Miño. You can access it by steps down from Praza Buxán, next to Praza Madalena: it's 600m to the Avia's confluence with the much bigger Miño, then 1.8km along the Miño to the path's end.

🎊 Festivals & Events

Feira do Viño do Ribeiro   WINE

Ribadavia parties on the first weekend in May with this big wine festival.

🛏 Sleeping & Eating

Viña Meín   COUNTRY HOUSE €

(✓617 326385; www.vinamein.com; Meín, San Clodio; d incl breakfast €60; ⊙closed Nov-May; P🛜🏊) Viña Meín, in a beautiful part of the Avia valley about 10km north of Ribadavia, is a delightful six-room old-stone country guesthouse run by a friendly family, with a medium-sized on-site winery producing good whites and reds from indigenous Galician grapes.

★ Casal de Armán   COUNTRY HOUSE €€

(✓680 979763; www.casaldearman.net; O Cotiño, San Andrés; r incl breakfast €75-90; P🛜) You can kill several birds with one stone at this dignified country house in a lovely elevated position overlooking the countryside. The six cosy rooms feature plenty of exposed stone and toiletries made from grape extract! Also here are a rustic-chic restaurant serving excellent traditional Galician food (reservations advised at weekends), and a winery with free visits for restaurant or hotel guests.

It's 6km northeast of Ribadavia.

Casal de Armán Restaurant   GALICIAN €€

(✓988 491809; O Cotiño, San Andrés; mains €14-19; ⊙1-3.30pm & 9-11pm Tue-Sun, closed dinner Tue-Thu & Sun mid-Oct–May; P) The rustic-chic restaurant at this lovely country hotel serves excellent Galician fare with occasional creative twists (eg beef tenderloin with vegetable couscous). Reservations advised for weekends.

ℹ Information

Tourist Office (✓988 471 275; http://ribadaviaturismo.weebly.com; Praza Maior 7; ⊙10.30am-2.30pm & 5-8pm, closed afternoons Sun year-round & Mon-Fri Oct-May) Very helpful office in an old mansion of the Counts of Ribadavia on the lovely main square.

❶ Getting There & Away

At least three buses and two trains run daily to Ourense and Vigo from stations in the east of town, just across the Río Avia.

Ribeira Sacra

Northeast of Ourense, along the Ríos Sil and Miño, unfold the unique natural beauty and cultural heritage of the Ribeira Sacra (Sacred Riverbank), so called for the many medieval monasteries founded here after early Christian hermits and monks were drawn to this remote area. Apart from historic buildings and beautiful scenery – particularly spectacular along the Cañón do Sil (Sil Canyon) – the area offers good walking and mountain-bike trails, winery visits (Ribeira Sacra is one of Galicia's five wine DOs) and boat trips along the rivers.

The area is poorly served by public transport, but it makes for a marvellous driving trip. A good route is to head from Ourense to Monforte de Lemos via the Mosteiro de San Pedro de Rocas, Mosteiro de Santo Estevo, Parada de Sil and Castro Caldelas. Try to give yourself at least two days to make the most of what the area has to offer.

Parada de Sil & Around

The village of Parada de Sil sits on the plateau high above the Cañón do Sil, 22km east

of Luintra. From the village, separate side roads lead 1km to the spectacular **Balcóns de Madrid** viewpoint and 4km down to the lovely **Mosteiro de Santa Cristina de Ribas de Sil** (interior €1; ⊙ exterior 24hr, interior hours variable; **P**). Part of the PRG98 walking trail heads down to the monastery and back up to the viewpoint in a loop of about 10km from the village.

Another great walking trail in the area, combining a beautiful wooded river canyon and several upland villages, is the **Ruta Cañón do Río Mao** (PRG177).

🛏 Sleeping

Reitoral de Chandrexa   CASA RURAL **€**
(☑ 988 208 099; www.chandrexa.com; Chandrexa; d €48-58; ⊙ closed mid-Dec–mid-Jan; **P** 🐾) 🐾
A charming little guesthouse occupying the former curate's house next to Santa María de Chandrexa church, and serving excellent organic breakfasts (€5.50) and dinners (€12-plus), with many ingredients from its own garden. The three comfy rooms have stone walls, wood floors and ceilings, and good bathrooms, and there's a cosy farmhouse-style dining-cum-sitting room.

Albergue A Fábrica da Luz   HOSTEL **€**
(☑ 988 984 990; http://afabricadaluz.com; OU0605 Km 5.7; dm/d incl breakfast €17/34; ⊙ daily Jun-Sep, Sat, Sun & holidays Semana Santa-May & Oct-early Dec; **P** 🐾) Housed in a recently converted small hydroelectric station in the

---

WORTH A TRIP

LUINTRA & AROUND

Two of the Ribeira Sacra's most impressive and contrasting monasteries stand a few kilometres either side of the village of Luintra, about 25km northeast of Ourense. They make a fine pair of first stops if you're starting out on a Ribeira Sacra tour from Ourense.

Mosteiro de San Pedro de Rocas (www.centrointerpretacionribeirasacra.com; ⊙ 10.30am-1.45pm & 4-7.45pm daily Apr-Sep, 10.30am-1.45pm & 4-6pm Tue-Sun Oct-Mar; **P**) Founded in AD 573, this enchanting mini-monastery 11km south of Luintra contains three cave chapels, originally carved out of the rock as retreats for early hermits, plus a number of rock-cut graves from the 10th century and later. The adjacent interpretation centre and tourist information office has interesting displays on the Ribeira Sacra. You can also take a lovely walk along the Camiño Real (PRG4), a 9km circuit trail that loops through this area of dense woods and rocky crags.

Mosteiro de Santo Estevo (⊙ closed early Dec-early Feb; **P**) The enormous Mosteiro de Santo Estevo, on the steep, thickly wooded, valley side above the Río Sil, dates from the 12th century and has three magnificent cloisters (one Romanesque/Gothic, two Renaissance), an originally Romanesque church and an 18th-century baroque facade. It's now a **hotel** (☑ 988 010 110; www.parador.es; Santo Estevo; r from €110; ⊙ closed early Dec-early Feb; **P** ❋ 🐾), but everyone is free to wander round the main monumental parts and eat in the cafe or restaurant.

beautiful leafy canyon of the Río Mao (a tributary of the Río Sil), this is a well-run and welcoming place to stay. The two 14-bunk dorms and two double rooms (sharing bathrooms) are clean and well kept, and good, inexpensive food is available.

ⓘ Getting There & Away

The OU0508 runs 22km along the wooded hillsides above the Cañon do Sil from Luintra to Parada de Sil, passing the turn-offs for Santo Estevo and the Embarcadoiro de Santo Estevo.

Castro de Caldelas

The hilltop village of Castro Caldelas, with its cobbled streets and old stone houses with Galician *galerías* and well-tended flower boxes, is an ideal spot to spend the night, 52km east of Ourense. Explore the old quarter at the top of the village, crowned by a panoramic 14th-century castle (€2; ⊙10am-2pm & 4-7pm; Ⓟ ♿).

From Castro Caldelas, the OU903 winds 10km northward down to the Sil Canyon then becomes the LU903 climbing the north side of the gorge, cutting across almost vertical vineyards en route towards Monforte de Lemos. Interesting wineries to visit on this route include Ponte da Boga (✆988 203 306; www.pontedaboga.es; ⊙11am-2.30pm & 4-8pm Easter-Oct, 9am-1.30pm & 3-6pm Mon-Fri Nov-Easter; Ⓟ) FREE, Adega Algueira (✆982 410 299; www.adegaalgueira.com; tour incl tasting €5; ⊙tours 11am, 1pm & 5pm Apr-Oct, 1pm Nov-Mar; Ⓟ) and Regina Viarum (✆619 009777; www.reginaviarum.es; tour incl tasting €1-5; ⊙tours 11am, noon, 1pm, 1.45pm, 4.30pm, 5pm, 6pm & 7.15pm daily Jun-Oct, 11am, noon, 1pm, 4.30pm, 5.30pm & 6.30pm Thu-Sun Nov-May; Ⓟ) – these last two are both located at Doade, a few kilometres up the hill on the north side of the canyon.

From the bridge over the Sil, you can take 1½- to two-hour cruises on the 16-passenger Brandan (✆982 410 299; www.adegaalgueira.com; adult/child €15/7; ⊙11am, 12.30pm, 5pm & 6.30pm Apr-Oct; ♿) or larger boats operated by the Diputación de Lugo (✆982 260 196; www.lugoterra.com; Embarcadeiro de Doade; adult/senior & child €9/5; ⊙11.30am, 5pm & 7pm daily Jun-Sep, 11.30am & 4pm Wed-Sun Oct-May; ♿).

🛏 Sleeping

Hotel Casa de Caldelas HOTEL €
(✆988 203 197; www.hotelcasadecaldelas.com; Praza do Prado 5, Castro Caldelas; s €30-40, d €40-

55, incl breakfast; ☎) Snug, up-to-date rooms in a handsome 18th-century stone house on the village's main square make this small, welcoming hotel a great find. The bathrooms are snug but have good contemporary fittings.

ⓘ Getting There & Away

The direct road from Ourense is the OU536, but the more scenic route is via Luintra and Parada de Sil. From Parada de Sil, follow the OU0605 eastwards, passing waterfalls, impossibly steep vineyards, stone villages and occasional jaw-dropping vistas of the gorge below. After 14km, turn left into lost-in-time Cristosende and continue 2km to A Teixeira, then follow the signs 10km to Castro Caldelas.

Lugo
POP 90,000

The grand Roman walls encircling old Lugo are considered the best preserved of their kind in the world and are the number-one reason visitors land here. Within the fortress is a beautifully preserved labyrinth of streets and squares, most of them traffic-free and ideal for strolling, with plenty of interesting things to see and a terrific tapas-bar scene. Lucus Augusti was a major town of Roman Gallaecia and modern Lugo is a quiet but very engaging city, with a good number of other Roman remains besides the walls.

⊙ Sights

★ **Roman Walls** WALLS
(⊙24hr; ♿) FREE The path running right round the top of the World Heritage–listed Roman walls is to Lugo what a maritime promenade is to a seaside resort: a place to jog, take an evening stroll, see and be seen. The walls, erected in the 3rd century AD, make a 2.2km loop around the Old Town, rise 15m high and are studded with 85 stout towers. They failed, however, to save Lugo from being taken by the Suevi in 460 and the Muslims three centuries later.

Catedral de Santa María CATHEDRAL
(✆982 231 038; Praza Pio XII; ⊙8.25am-8.45pm) The cathedral, inspired by Santiago de Compostela's, was begun in 1129, though work continued for centuries, yielding an aesthetic mix of styles ranging from Romanesque (as in the transepts) to neoclassical (the main facade). It's a serene building that merits a close look.

Camino Francés in Galicia

Museo Provincial MUSEUM
(www.museolugo.org; Praza da Soidade; ⊙9am-
9pm Mon-Fri, 10.30am-2pm & 4.30-8pm Sat,
11am-2pm Sun) **FREE** Lugo's main museum
includes parts of the Gothic Convento de
San Francisco and is one of Galicia's best
and biggest museums. Collections range
from pre-Roman gold jewellery and Roman
mosaics to Galician Sargadelos ceramics and
art from the 15th to 20th centuries.

Casa dos Mosaicos ARCHAEOLOGICAL SITE
(Rúa de Doutor Castro 20-22; ⊙11am-1.30pm &
4-7.30pm Tue-Sat, 11am-2pm Sun Jun-Sep, 11.30am-
1.30pm & 5-7pm Thu-Sat, 11.30am-1.30pm Sun
Oct-May) **FREE** These remains of a Roman
mansion sit beneath an Old Town street,
with some beautiful, wonderfully preserved
mosaics and murals.

★ Festivals & Events

Arde Lucus HISTORICAL
(www.ardelucus.com; ▣) Around 600,000 people pack into Lugo over three or four days in
mid-June, as the city returns to its Roman
roots with this festival featuring chariot races, gladiator fights, a whole lot of Roman
costume and much more.

🛏 Sleeping

Hostal-Albergue Lucus HOSTAL, HOSTEL €
(☑608 072819; www.lucushostal.com; Rúa
Rei Don García 1, 1ºB; dm €15, s €25-28, d €30-
40, breakfast €3.50; 🐾) New in 2015, this
is a spick-and-span, bright and friendly
place that offers both four-bed dorms and
private rooms with bathroom. It's a 10-
minute walk from the Roman walls or the

bus station, and has a cafe as well as a
guest kitchen.

Orbán e Sangro BOUTIQUE HOTEL €€€
(Hotel Pazo de Orbán; ☑982 240 217; www.pazode-
orban.es; Travesía do Miño 6; r €88-220, incl breakfast €110-238; 🅿❄🐾) The 12 rooms of this
welcoming hotel, in an 18th-century mansion just inside the city walls, are regal, with
rich linen, antique furnishings, designer
bathrooms and huge 2.15m beds with latex
mattresses. The hotel serves a great 'ecological' breakfast, is full of intriguing art and
antiques, and has its own tavern in a highly
original early-20th-century style.

🍴 Eating

The Old Town, especially Rúa da Cruz, Rúa
Nova and Praza do Campo, north of the cathedral, is liberally endowed with inviting
bar-restaurants serving both tapas and main
dishes. Many offer two free tapas with each
drink: one selected by the bar, the other chosen by you from a list recited verbally (usually at high speed!) by bar staff.

Las Cinco Vigas TAPAS €
(Rúa da Cruz 9; raciones €4-12; ⊙9am-midnight
Wed-Mon) Always one of the busiest tapas bars,
with a mixed crowd enjoying terrific free tapas, including a great *terneira al vino tinto*
(veal in red wine) – also available as *raciones*
if you want more than a few mouthfuls.

**★Restaurante
Paprica** CONTEMPORARY GALICIAN €€
(www.paprica.es; Rúa das Noreas 10; mains €18-
26; ⊙1.30-3.45pm & 9-11pm, closed Mon night &
Sun Jun–mid-Sep, Sun night & Mon mid-Oct–May)

WORTH A TRIP

CAMINOS DE GALICIA

All of the Caminos de Santiago converge in Galicia, their shared goal. About 65% of pilgrims arrive by the Camino Francés from the Pyrenees, cresting the hills on the border of Castilla y León, then striding west for the final 154km across welcome green countryside to Santiago de Compostela. But growing numbers also reach Santiago by the Camino Portugués (entering Galicia from Portugal at Tui or A Guarda), Camino del Norte/de la Costa (along the coast from the Basque Country through Cantabria and Asturias), Vía de la Plata (from Andalucía), Camino Primitivo (from Oviedo via Lugo) or Camino Inglés (from A Coruña or Ferrol).

Tiny O Cebreiro, where the Camino Francés enters Galicia, is 1300m high and marks the top of the route's longest, hardest climb. About half the buildings here are bar-restaurants (many offering cheap set menus) or *pensiones* or pilgrims' hostels: among them are dotted several *pallozas* (circular, thatched dwellings of a type known in rural Galicia since pre-Roman times, where families shared living space with their livestock). The nicest accommodation is the five wood-beamed, stone-walled rooms in the main building of Hotel Cebreiro (☑982 367 182; www.hotelcebreiro.com; s/d €40/50; 🛜) (reservations advised for summer).

In Triacastela, 19km downhill from O Cebreiro, the *camino* divides, with both paths reuniting later in Sarria. The longer (25km) southern route passes through Samos, a village built around the very fine Benedictine Mosteiro de Samos (☑982 546 046; www.abadiadesamos.com; tours €3; ⊙tours every 30 or 60min 9am-8pm Apr-Oct, 10am-2pm & 4-7pm Nov-Mar; 🅿). This monastery has two beautiful big cloisters (one Gothic, with distinctly unmonastic Greek nymphs adorning its fountain, the other neoclassical and filled with roses). Samos has plenty of inexpensive lodgings, but it's well worth continuing 3.5km west to the welcoming Casa de Díaz (☑982 547 070; www.casadediaz.com; d €44-54; ⊙closed Nov-Mar; 🅿@🛜🖾), an 18th-century farmhouse turned rural hotel at Vilachá. It has 12 comfy rooms in olde-worlde style.

People undertaking just the last 100km of the *camino* usually start 12km west of Samos at Sarria (actually 114km from Santiago). From here the *camino* winds through village after village, across forests and fields, then descends steeply to Portomarín, above the Río Miño. After a tough 25km stretch to Palas de Rei, the next 15km to Melide follows some lovely rural lanes. From Melide, 53km remain through woodlands, villages, countryside and, at the end, city streets. The *camino* approaches central Santiago along Rúa de San Pedro and arrives in Praza da Inmaculada on the northern side of the cathedral. Most pilgrims take a few more steps down through an archway to emerge on magnificent Praza do Obradoiro, before the cathedral's famous western facade.

If you're touring Galicia rather than *camino*-ing it, the 30km from O Cebreiro to Samos make a marvellous side trip. Drivers entering Galicia along the A6 from Astorga can turn off into Pedrafita do Cebreiro, then follow the LU633 4km south up to O Cebreiro. The road from there to Samos winds down through green countryside with great long-distance views, frequently criss-crossing the camino.

The talented young team here turns out excellent and satisfying creative dishes based on time-honoured Galician ingredients of fresh fish, shellfish and vegetables and quality meat – a contemporary experience enhanced by the clean-lined, unfussy decor. You can eat light in the bar or sit down to á la carte meals or a set menu. Everything is delicious, including the desserts!

A Nosa Terra TAPAS, RACIONES €€
(http://currunchoanosaterra.com; Rúa Nova 8; mains €9-18; ⊙1-4pm & 9pm-midnight) An inviting classic on the Rúa Nova tapas trail, with a long list of wines by the glass. Stand in the narrow bar area for tapas and drinks, or sit at tables in the back for seafood salads, *raciones* of scallops or pork *solomillo* (tenderloin) in blue-cheese sauce.

ⓘ Information

Oficina de Turismo de Galicia (☑982 231 361; www.turismo.gal; Rúa do Miño 12; ⊙9.30am-2pm & 4.30-7pm Mon-Fri, 11am-1.30pm Sat) Information on all parts of Galicia, with an interpretation centre on the Camino de Santiago in Lugo.

Oficina Municipal de Turismo (☑982 251 658; http://lugo.gal; Praza do Campo 11; ⊙11am-6pm, closed 2-4pm Mon-Wed, longer hours Jun–mid-Oct) Helpful office in the Centro de Interpretación de la Muralla.

❶ Getting There & Away

BUS

From the **bus station** (☑982 223 985; Praza da Constitución), just outside the southern walls, Empresa Freire runs to Santiago de Compostela (€10, 1½ to two hours, five or more daily), and Arriva to A Coruña (€11, 1¼ to two hours, five or more daily). Other services head to Monforte de Lemos, Ourense, Pontevedra, Ferrol, Viveiro, Ribadeo, Ponferrada, León, Madrid, Asturias and beyond.

TRAIN

Renfe trains head at least three times daily to A Coruña (€10 to €11, 1¾ hours) and Monforte de Lemos (€6 to €15, one hour), and once daily to Madrid (€30 to €35, seven hours).

Verín

POP 10,200

The small town of Verín, on the main road into southern Galicia from the rest of Spain, the A52, is worth a stop for one major reason – the spectacular Castillo de Monterrei, towering on a hilltop just outside town.

Verín is also the headquarters of the up-and-coming Monterrei wine Denominación de Origen (DO; www.domonterrei.com, www.rutadelvinomonterrei.com).

◎ Sights

Castillo de Monterrei　　　　　　CASTLE
(☑tours 646 777341; ⊙10.30am-7pm; ⓘ) FREE
Looming on a hilltop just outside Verín, the doughty, mainly 15th-century Castillo

de Monterrei was a keystone of the defence of Spain's border with Portugal in turbulent centuries past. The castle has recently been converted into a luxurious *parador* hotel, but the mighty keep, which towers over the rest of the complex, is open to anyone to visit, as is the cafe. Free guided visits of the whole castle are given (in English if requested) every hour or two from 10.30am to 6pm.

From Verín head 2km west along the OU115, then go 3km up the signposted road to the castle.

⌦ Sleeping

Parador de Verín　　　　HERITAGE HOTEL €€
(☑988 410 075; www.parador.es; r €85-98, breakfast per person €16; P❋🛜🏊) Built in the 20th century in the style of a Galician *pazo* (palace/mansion) of yesteryear, Parador de Verín is a little less luxurious than the *parador* in the castle itself, but enjoys views almost as good and is still a very comfortable place to stay. In 2016 it was only open from July to September but that may change.

Parador Castillo de Monterrei　　HISTORIC HOTEL €€€
(☑988 029 230; www.parador.es; s/d incl breakfast €131/147; ⊙Feb-early Dec; P🛜🏊) This recently opened *parador* in a 500-year-old castle is a lovely mix of historic atmosphere and contemporary comfort, with superb views from 12 luxurious, brand-new rooms.

❶ Getting There & Away

The Hwy A52 linking Ourense with Puebla de Sanabria in Castilla y León (and, beyond there, Zamora, Valladolid and Madrid) runs just south of Verín. Monbus has at least five daily buses to/from Ourense (€7.60, 1½ hours).

Extremadura

Best Places to Eat

- ➡ Atrio (p553)
- ➡ La Rebotica (p571)
- ➡ La Cacharrería (p553)
- ➡ Villa Xarahiz (p562)
- ➡ Tábula Calda (p569)
- ➡ Nardi (p563)

Best Places to Sleep

- ➡ Atrio (p553)
- ➡ El Jardín del Convento (p563)
- ➡ La Flor de Al-Andalus (p568)
- ➡ Posada Dos Orillas (p557)
- ➡ Hospedería del Real Monasterio (p559)
- ➡ Haldón Country (p562)

Why Go?

Exploring Extremadura is a journey into the heart of old Spain, from the country's finest Roman ruins to mysterious medieval cities and time-worn villages. Mérida, Cáceres and Trujillo rank among Spain's most beautifully preserved historical settlements. *Extremeño* hamlets have a timeless charm, from the remote northern hills to sacred eastern Guadalupe and seductive Zafra on the cusp of Andalucía in the south.

Few foreign travellers make it this far. Spaniards, however, know Extremadura as a place to sample some of inland Spain's best food: roasted meats, the pungent, creamy Torta del Casar cheese and the finest Monesterio *jamón* (ham).

This is a region of broad blue skies and vast swathes of sparsely populated land with isolated farmhouses and crumbling hilltop castles. And yet, city sophistication fills Mérida and Cáceres. Wooded sierras rise along the northern, eastern and southern fringes, while the raptor-rich Parque Nacional de Monfragüe is arguably Extremadura's most dramatic corner.

When to Go

Caceres

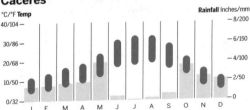

Mar–Apr The Valle del Jerte becomes a spectacular white sea of cherry blossom.	**Jul–Aug** Mérida's 2000-year-old Roman theatre hosts the Festival Internacional de Teatro Clásico.	**Sep** Prime time to visit: fewer tourists and good weather, without the intense summer heat.

Extremadura Highlights

1 Cáceres (p549) Exploring the Ciudad Monumental's magical cobbled streets and packed tapas bars.

2 Mérida (p565) Clambering over Spain's finest Roman ruins.

3 Trujillo (p555) Travelling to the medieval hometown of some of Latin America's most infamous conquistadors.

4 Zafra (p570) Feasting on tapas beneath the Plaza Grande's palms, then sleeping in a castle.

5 Parque Nacional de Monfragüe (p564) Spotting majestic birds of prey wheeling above the Tajo.

6 Guadalupe (p558) Admiring the fabulous art and architecture at Guadalupe's extraordinary monastery.

7 Alcántara (p555) Checking out the mighty, impressive Roman bridge over the Tajo.

8 La Vera (p561) Exploring half-timbered villages and rushing rivers, then marvelling at the cherry blossom of the adjacent Valle del Jerte.

9 Granadilla (p564) Pacing the quiet lanes of this restored historic museum village.

10 Monesterio (p572) Learning all about Spain's favourite food at the Museo del Jamón, and then tasting it.

Cáceres

POP 95,617

The Ciudad Monumental (Monumental City) of provincial capital Cáceres is truly extraordinary. Narrow cobbled streets twist and climb among ancient stone walls lined with palaces, mansions, arches and churches, while the skyline is decorated with turrets, spires, gargoyles and enormous

Cáceres

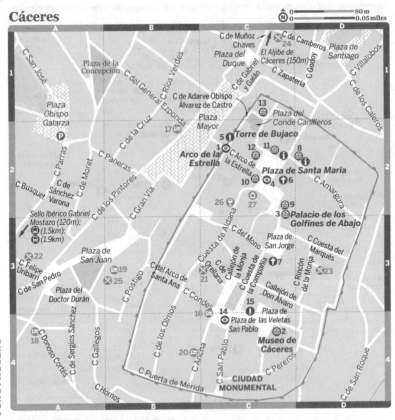

EXTREMADURA CÁCERES

storks' nests. Protected by defensive walls, it has survived almost intact from its 16th-century period of splendour. At dusk or after dark, when the crowds have gone, you'll feel like you've stepped back into the Middle Ages.

Stretching at its feet, the lively, arcaded Plaza Mayor is one of Spain's most beautiful public squares.

⊙ Sights

The Ciudad Monumental's name captures it all. Fuelled particularly by wealth brought from the Americas, the churches, palaces and towers are hugely impressive and beautiful. Few people actually live here now and there are just a handful of bars, cafes and restaurants. If you're lucky (as we always seem to be), a flamenco singer might be busking in one of the squares, adding to the magic.

⊙ Plaza de Santa María & Around

Most visitors approach the stunning Ciudad Monumental from the Plaza Mayor, passing under the 18th-century Arco de la Estrella (Calle Arco de la Estrella) onto the Plaza de Santa María. Notable facades on the Plaza de Santa María include the Palacio Episcopal (Bishop's Palace), the Palacio de Mayoralgo and the Palacio de Ovando, all in 16th-century Renaissance style.

As you wander further into the Ciudad Monumental to the southeast, you'll pass the Renaissance-style Palacio de la Diputación.

★ Torre de Bujaco   TOWER
(927 24 67 89; Plaza Mayor; adult/child €2.50/free; ⊙10am-2pm & 5.30-8.30pm Tue-Sun, afternoons Tue-Sun Oct-Apr 4.30-7.30pm) As you head up the steps to the Ciudad Monumental from

Cáceres

the Plaza Mayor, turn left to climb the 12th-century, 25m-high Torre de Bujaco, home to an interpretative display on Cáceres' history. Up on the rooftop there's a fabulous stork's-eye view over the Plaza Mayor. From here, you can also walk across the top of the 18th-century Arco de la Estrella.

Concatedral de Santa María CATHEDRAL
(Plaza de Santa María; admission €1; ⊙10am-2pm & 5-8pm Mon-Sat, 10am-12.45pm & 5-6.30pm Sun) This 15th-century Gothic cathedral creates an impressive opening scene for the Ciudad Monumental. Inside, you'll find a magnificent carved 16th-century cedar altarpiece, fine noble tombs and chapels, and a museum. Beautiful colourful murals (including dragons) adorn the vaulted ceiling above the altarpiece. Climb the bell tower for old-town views.

Palacio de Carvajal HISTORIC BUILDING
(☎927 25 55 97; Calle Amargura 1; ⊙8am-8.45pm Mon-Fri, 10am-1.45pm & 5-7.45pm Sat, 10am-1.45pm Sun) FREE Just off the northeastern corner of the main Plaza de Santa María stands this late-15th-century mansion. The building was abandoned after fires tore through in the 19th century. Now restored, it houses a modern display on the province's attractions and the helpful regional tourist office (p554).

Palacio Toledo-Moctezuma HISTORIC BUILDING
(Plaza del Conde Canilleros) Just north of the Plaza de Santa María lies the domed 16th-century Palacio Toledo-Moctezuma,

once home to Isabel Moctezuma, daughter of the Aztec emperor Moctezuma II, who was brought to Cáceres as a conquistador's bride. The palace now contains the municipal archives.

⦿ Plaza de San Jorge

The compact Plaza de San Jorge lies southeast of the main Plaza de Santa María, overlooked by an 18th-century church.

★Palacio de los Golfines de Abajo HISTORIC BUILDING
(☎927 21 80 51; www.palaciogolfinesdeabajo.com; Plaza de los Golfines; adult/senior/child €2.5/1.5/free; ⊙tours hourly 10am-1pm & 5-7pm Tue-Sat, 1am-1pm Sun, afternoons Tue-Sat Oct-Apr 4.30-6.30pm) The sumptuous home of Cáceres' prominent Golfín family has been beautifully restored. Built piecemeal between the 14th and 20th centuries, it's crammed with historical treasures: original 17th-century tapestries and armoury murals, a 19th-century bust of Alfonso XII, a signed 1485 troops request from the Reyes Católicos (Catholic Monarchs) to their Golfín stewards. But it's the detailed, theatrical tours (Spanish, English, French or Portuguese), through four richly decorated lounges, an extravagant chapel and a fascinating documents room, that make it a standout.

Iglesia de San Francisco Javier CHURCH
(Iglesia de la Preciosa Sangre; Plaza de San Jorge; adult/child €1/free; ⊙10am-2pm & 5-8pm, afternoons Oct-Apr 4.30-7.30pm) An 18th-century

EXTREMADURA CÁCERES

Jesuit church with a baroque facade that rises above the Plaza de San Jorge. You can climb its towers for glorious old-town views.

◉ Plaza de San Mateo & Around

From the lower part of the old town, Calle Cuesta de la Compañía climbs to Plaza de San Mateo – the summit of the Ciudad Monumental.

Torre de las Cigüeñas   TOWER

(Tower of the Storks; Plaza de San Pablo) Sandwiched between the Plaza de San Mateo and the Plaza de las Veletas, at the top of the old town, this is the only Cáceres tower to retain its battlements: the rest were lopped off in the late 15th century under orders from Isabel la Católica.

★ Museo de Cáceres   MUSEUM

(☑927 01 08 77; Plaza de las Veletas; non-EU/EU citizens €1.20/free; ☺9am-3pm & 5-8.30pm Tue-Sat, 10.15am-2.30pm Sun, afternoons Tue-Sat Oct-Apr 4-7.30pm) The excellent Museo de Cáceres, spread across 12 buildings in a 16th-century mansion built over an evocative 12th-century *aljibe* (cistern), is the only surviving element of Cáceres' Moorish castle. The impressive archaeological section includes an elegant stone boar dated to the 4th to 2nd centuries BC, while the equally appealing fine-arts display (behind the main museum; open only in the mornings) showcases works by such greats as Picasso, Miró, Tàpies and El Greco.

★ Activities

El Aljibe de Cáceres   HAMMAM

(☑927 22 32 56; www.elaljibedecaceres.com; Calle de Peña 5; sessions from €20; ☺10am-2pm & 6-10pm Tue-Sun) This luxurious re-creation of the Moorish-style bath experience combines soothing architecture and a range of treatments. The basic thermal bath pass includes aromatherapy and herbal tea, but you can also throw in a range of massages (from €27).

☞ Tours

★ Cuentatrovas de Cordel   WALKING TOUR

(☑666 836332, 667 283187; www.cuentatrovas. com; adult €10, child over/under 10 €5/free) Guides and other actors dress up in period costume and take you on a tour with a difference through the Ciudad Monumental. It's fun, informative (for Spanish speakers) and very much recommended. Times vary, with after-dark tours their speciality, departing from the Arco de la Estrella. There's also an ornithology-focused tour.

★ Festivals & Events

Fiesta de San Jorge   LOCAL FIESTA

On April 22 and 23 Cáceres celebrates the Fiesta de San Jorge, in honour of its patron saint, with shows, fireworks, competitions, a recreation of a Christian-Moorish battle and a giant dragon on the Plaza Mayor.

WOMAD   WORLD MUSIC

(World of Music, Arts & Dance; www.womad.org) For three fiesta-fuelled days in mid-May, Cáceres stages a long-running edition of WOMAD, with international bands playing in the old city's squares.

▭ Sleeping

Hotel Don Carlos   HOTEL €

(☑927 22 55 27; www.hoteldoncarloscaceres. com; Calle Donoso Cortés 15; s €36-42, d €52-74; ℗�ⓢ) Rooms are elegantly decorated in a simple countryside style at this small, welcoming hotel, carefully created with bare brick and stone from a long-abandoned, early-19th-century house. There are two artists among the owner's family, hence plenty of original artwork.

★ Hotel Casa Don Fernando   BOUTIQUE HOTEL €€

(☑927 21 42 79, 927 62 71 76; www.casadon fernando.com; Plaza Mayor 30; s €52-71, d €59-81; ℗❋ⓢ) Cáceres' smartest midrange choice sits on Plaza Mayor right opposite the Arco de la Estrella. Boutique-style rooms, spread over four floors, are tastefully modern, with gleaming bathrooms through glass doors. Pricier 'superiors' enjoy the best plaza views (though weekend nights can be noisy), and attic-style top-floor rooms are good for families. Service hits that perfect professional yet friendly note.

NH Collection Palacio de Oquendo   HISTORIC HOTEL €€

(☑927 21 58 00; www.nh-collection.com; Plaza de San Juan 11; s €64-120, d €68-140; ❋ⓢ) Classy, spacious cream-coated rooms, complete with coffee kits, chunky mattresses, soothing lighting and stylish modern bathrooms, await within this beautifully revamped 16th-century palace. Best are the balcony rooms with views across the Plaza de San Juan. Step into on-site Tapería Yuste for deliciously inventive tapas.

Parador de Cáceres
HISTORIC HOTEL €€

(☑927 21 17 59; www.parador.es; Calle Ancha 6; r €95-138; P☀@🛜) A substantial makeover has given this old-town conglomeration of 14th-century Gothic palaces swish, modern interiors, with bedrooms and bathrooms displaying a distinctively non-medieval level of style and comfort. Superior rooms are standouts: one sporting original arched red-brick ceilings, another fantastic Ciudad Monumental views. You should specify if you'd like a double bed (most rooms are twins).

★ Atrio
BOUTIQUE HOTEL €€€

(☑927 24 29 28; http://restauranteatrio.com; Plaza de San Mateo 1; d without/with dinner €350/560; P☀🛜▦) Impeccably sleek modern styling, sultry white-on-white rooms and some serious pieces of original contemporary art dominate this fabulous fusion of five-star boutique hotel and one of Spain's most garlanded restaurants. The old-town location is exquisite, with panoramic Cáceres views from the orange-tree–lined rooftop pools and terrace. Throw in top-notch personal service and it's obvious why Atrio is considered Extremadura's finest hotel.

🍴 Eating

Los Siete Jardines
CAFE €

(☑927 21 73 36; www.facebook.com/los-siete-jardines-621720017929398; Calle Rincón de la Monja 9; breakfast €2.50; ⊙10am-late Tue-Sun) Lost in the old-town maze, Los Siete Jardines triples as contemporary art gallery, cultural hub and bohemian-feel breakfast spot. Tuck into coffee, freshly squeezed orange juice and *jamón*-topped toast in the back garden, with Cáceres' monuments towering around, or soak up the scene through floor-to-ceiling windows from the brick-and-stone-clad interior.

★ La Cacharrería
TAPAS €€

(☑927 03 07 23; lacacharreria@live.com; Calle de Orellana 1; tapas €4.50, raciones €10-14.50; ⊙restaurant 12.30-4pm & 8.30-midnight Thu-Mon, cafe 4pm-1.30am Thu-Sat, 4-11pm Sun; 🖐) Local flavours and ingredients combine in exquisite, international-inspired concoctions at this packed-out, minimalist-design tapas bar tucked into an old-town house. *Solomillo* (tenderloin) in Torta del Casar cheese arrives in martini glasses. Delicious guacamole, hummus, felafel and 'salsiki' are a godsend for vegetarians. No

advance reservations: get here by 1.45pm or 8.30pm.

Tapería Yuste
TAPAS €€

(☑927 21 58 00; www.nh-collection.com; Plaza de San Juan 11-13; tapas €4.25, raciones €8-17; ⊙1-4pm & 8pm-midnight) This elegant all-white dining room offers an unconventionally refined sit-down tapas experience, with fresh flowers on white-clothed tables and modern art adorning the walls. Carefully crafted gourmet delights – from hearty pumpkin soup and gnocchi in Torta del Casar cheese to Iberian ham *pizarras* (boards) – blend contemporary flair and local flavours in single-tapa format. There are plenty of sharing platters, too.

Madruelo
CONTEMPORARY SPANISH €€

(☑927 24 36 76; www.madruelo.com; Calle de Camberos 2; mains €14-20; ⊙1.30-4pm & 9.15pm-midnight Wed-Sat, 1.30-4pm Sun-Tue) This popular, intimate and soberly decorated restaurant is where *cacereños* in the know go for high-class, modern Spanish cuisine at a fair price. Excellent grilled meats with a choice of sauces are complemented by rices, salads, soups, *bacalao* (cod) dishes, local cheese and meat platters, plus the odd flourish from elsewhere in the Mediterranean such as moussaka.

★ Atrio
CONTEMPORARY SPANISH €€€

(☑927 24 29 28; http://restauranteatrio.com; Plaza de San Mateo 1; menús €129-139; ⊙2-4pm & 8.30-11pm; 🖐) With a stunning location in the heart of old-town Cáceres, this is Extremadura's top restaurant. Chic contemporary design and service that's both formal and friendly back up the wonderful, inventive culinary creations. The focus is on local produce of the highest quality, via a 12- to 13-course degustation menu. Vegetarian and gluten-free menus available with advance notice. Bookings essential.

🍸 Drinking & Nightlife

★ Las Claras
BEER HALL

(Plaza de la Soledad; ⊙noon-late Fri-Sun, 5pm-late Mon-Thu) Tapping into Extremadura's slowly growing craft-beer scene, character-packed Las Claras pours its own homegrown brew alongside an impressive collection of local and international artisan labels (by bottle) and giant G&Ts. Plastered across the yellow-washed walls are hand-painted murals of customers and friends. A bubbly mixed crowd spills onto the pretty plaza outside.

EXTREMADURA'S HOME OF CHEESE

Extremadura may be well known for its *jamón*, but its smooth Torta del Casar cheese is equally celebrated in Spanish culinary circles. Casar de Cáceres, 12km north of Cáceres and well signposted off the N630 to Plasencia, is where this regional treasure was born and is still produced.

Sights

Museo del Queso (☑927 29 00 81; Calle Barrionuevo Bajo 7; ⊙10am-2pm Tue-Sat) This small museum is dedicated to Extremadura's beloved Torta del Casar, a pungent, creamy cheese that's aged for 40 days and eaten most often as a spread on *tostas* (topped toast), but also pops up with a steak or, nowadays, in creative modern concoctions.

Eating

Don't leave town without sampling that much-loved Torta del Casar; the main street is lined with shops selling it.

Getting There & Away

If you don't have your own wheels, Norbabus (☑927 23 48 08; www.norbabus.com) runs eight buses daily Monday to Friday (two on Saturday) between Casar de Cáceres and Cáceres bus station (€1.80, 20 minutes).

El Corral de las Cigüeñas   BAR, CAFE
(☑927 21 64 25; www.elcorralcc.com; Cuesta de Aldana 6; ⊙7.30am-1pm Mon-Wed, 7.30am-1.30pm & 7pm-late Thu & Fri, 5.30pm-late Sat & Sun) Las Cigüeñas' secluded courtyard, with its lofty palm trees and ivy-covered walls just inside the Ciudad Monumental, is the perfect spot for a quiet cocktail in relaxing surroundings. There's often live music; check the website. It also does breakfast (€2.40 to €3.40).

Shopping

Centro de Artesanía Casa
Moraga   HANDICRAFTS
(Plaza de Santa María; ⊙10am-2pm & 4.30-7.30pm) This government-run emporium showcases local *extremeño* handicrafts, including leather, pottery, jewellery and wood-carving.

Sello Ibérico Gabriel Mostazo   FOOD & DRINK
(☑927 24 28 81; www.mostazo.es; Calle de San Antón 6; ⊙9.30am-2pm & 5-8.30pm Mon-Sat, 10am-2pm Sun) One of the best delis in town, with plenty of cheeses, *jamón*, wines and fresh and tinned local products.

❶ Information

Oficina de Turismo (☑927 11 12 22, 674 301332; www.turismoextremadura.com; Plaza de Santa María; ⊙10am-2pm & 5.30-8.30pm Jun-Sep, 10am-2pm & 4.30-7.30pm Oct-May)

Oficina de Turismo Regional (☑927 25 55 97; www.turismocaceres.org; Palacio Carvajal, Calle Amargura 1; ⊙8am-8.45pm Mon-Fri, 10am-1.45pm & 5-7.45pm Sat, 10am-1.45pm Sun) Covers Cáceres city and province; very helpful.

❶ Getting There & Away

BUS

The **bus station** (☑927 23 25 50; www.estacion autobuses.es; Calle Túnez 1) is 2km southwest of the old town.

DESTINATION	FARE	DURATION	FREQUENCY
Badajoz	€4.30	1¼hr	3-6 daily
Madrid (normal/ express)	€23/ 30	3¾/4½hr	6-9/1-2 daily
Mérida	€5.71	1hr	2-3 daily
Plasencia	€7.95	1¼hr	1-5 daily
Trujillo	€3.67	45min	4-8 daily

TRAIN

From the train station, 2.5km southwest of the old town, at least four trains daily run to/from Madrid (€28 to €33, 3¾ hours to 4¼ hours), Mérida (€6.10 to €7.35, one hour) and Plasencia (€5.20 to €6.05, one hour).

❶ Getting Around

Bus L8 from outside the bus station (400m east of the train station) runs to/from the central Plaza Obispo Galarza.

Valencia de Alcántara

POP 5699

Pretty Valencia de Alcántara is 7km east of the Portuguese border and was even captured by Portugal from 1644 to 1668. Its well-preserved old centre is a curious labyrinth of whitewashed houses, churches and mansions.

The surrounding countryside is known for its cork industry and some 40 ancient dolmens (stone circles of prehistoric monoliths).

ⓘ Information

Oficina de Turismo (☑ 927 58 21 84; www.valenciadealcantara.es; Plaza Gregorio Bravo; ⊙10am-2pm Tue-Sun year-round, 4.30-7.30pm Tue-Fri Jul-Sep, to 6.30pm Tue-Fri Oct-Jun)

ⓘ Getting There & Away

Norbabus (☑ 927 23 48 08; www.norbabus.com) runs two buses daily Monday to Friday between Valencia de Alcántara and Cáceres (€11, 1¼ hours).

Alcántara

POP 1571

Alcántara is Arabic for 'the Bridge', and sure enough, below this remote Extremaduran town, a spectacular Roman bridge extends across the Río Tajo. The town itself retains old walls, a ruined castle of Moorish origin, several imposing mansions and churches, and the enormous Renaissance Convento de San Benito (☑ 927 39 00 80; Calle Trajano; ⊙tours hourly 10.15am-1.15pm, 4.30pm & 5.45pm Mon-Fri, from 11.15am Sat & Sun, closed Sun afternoon) FREE.

🛏 Sleeping

Hospedería Conventual de Alcántara HISTORIC HOTEL €€ (☑ 927 39 06 38; www.hospederiasdeextremadura.es; Ctra del Poblado Iberdrola; r incl breakfast €71-105; P❄🛜🅿🐕) On the eastern edge of town, this comfortable and stylish modern hotel enjoys a marvellous setting in a 15th-century monastery turned flour factory. It offers bright rooms bursting with colour.

ⓘ Information

Oficina de Turismo de Alcántara (☑ 927 39 08 63; www.alcantara.es; Avenida de Mérida 21; ⊙10am-2pm & 4.30-6.30pm Mon-Fri, 10.30am-2.30pm Sat & Sun)

ⓘ Getting There & Away

Mirat (☑ 927 23 33 54; www.mirat-transportes.es) runs four buses Monday to Friday to/from Cáceres (€6.50, 1½ hours).

Trujillo

POP 9510

The historic core of Trujillo is one of the best-preserved (and most beautiful) medieval towns in Spain. Beginning in the Plaza Mayor, its splendour extends up the hillside into a labyrinth of mansions, leafy courtyards, fruit gardens, quiet plazas, churches and convents enclosed within 900m of walls circling the upper town. It all dates to the 16th century, when Trujillo's favourite sons returned home from the Americas as wealthy conquistadors.

Whether bathed in the warm light of a summer sunset or shrouded in winter mists, Trujillo can feel truly magical. This, of course, also makes it pretty popular.

◉ Sights

Don't miss the less-visited western end of the upper old town, with its cobbles, palaces and flower-filled plazas. Keep an eye out for multi-monument passes (four sights €4.70), available through the tourist office (p558).

★ Plaza Mayor SQUARE

Trujillo's main square is is one of Spain's most spectacular plazas, surrounded by baroque and Renaissance stone buildings sporting intricately carved facades, topped with a skyline of towers, turrets, cupolas, crenellations and nesting storks.

A large, bronze equestrian statue of the conquistador Francisco Pizarro by American sculptor Charles Rumsey dominates the plaza. But all is not as it seems. Apparently Rumsey originally sculpted it as a statue of Hernán Cortés to present to Mexico, but Mexico, which takes a dim view of Cortés, declined it, so it was given to Trujillo as Pizarro instead.

On the south side of the plaza, carved images of Pizarro and his lover Inés Yupanqui (sister of the Inca emperor Atahualpa) adorn the corner of the 16th-century Palacio de la Conquista (Plaza Mayor). To the right is their daughter Francisca Pizarro Yupanqui with her husband (and uncle), Hernando Pizarro. The mansion was built in the 1560s for Hernando and Francisca after Hernando (the only Pizarro brother not to die a bloody death in Peru) emerged from 20 years in jail for murder. Higher up, a bas-relief carving shows the Pizarro family shield (two bears and a pine tree), the walls of Cuzco (in present-day Peru) and Pizarro's ships.

Off the plaza's northeastern corner lies the 16th-century **Palacio de los Duques de San Carlos** (Palacio de los Carvajal Vargas; Plaza Mayor), with its sober classical patio, grand granite staircase and distinctive brick chimneys built in Mudéjar style (though some say they represent New World cultures conquered by Spain). Nowadays it's a convent for the Jerónimo order.

★ **Castillo de Trujillo** CASTLE

(adult/child €1.40/free; ⊙10am-2pm & 5-8pm, afternoons Oct-Mar 4-7pm) Occupying the town's 600m-high summit, Trujillo's fairytale castle is of 10th-century Islamic origin (note the horseshoe arch just inside the entrance) and was later strengthened by the Christians. Patrol the battlements for magnificent sweeping views (sunset views are exquisite), visit the derelict *aljibe* (cistern) and climb to the hermitage of Our Lady of the Victory, Trujillo's patron. A 50-cent coin makes her spin around in her alcove; you can also spot her above the entrance gate as you approach.

★ **Iglesia de Santa María la Mayor** CHURCH

(Plaza de Santa María; adult/child €1.80/free; ⊙10.30am-2pm & 5-7.30pm, afternoons Oct-Mar 4-7pm) This 13th-century church is a stunner. It has a mainly Gothic nave and an 18th-century, 106-step tower that you can climb for fabulous views across Trujillo, the castle and the sprawling countryside.

ℹ️ **TOURS**

Informative, fast-paced two-hour guided tours of Trujillo (in Spanish) leave from the tourist office (p558) daily at 11am and 5.30pm (4.30pm in winter). Tickets cost €7 (kids free) and take in the Castillo de Trujillo, Iglesia de Santa María la Mayor, Casa-Museo de Pizarro, Iglesia de Santiago, Aljibe Hispano-Musulmán (otherwise off limits) and Plaza Mayor. Tickets also entitle you to free entry into the Iglesia de San Martín and the Torre del Alfiler. Tours may run in other languages with advance bookings.

The church's magnificent altarpiece includes 25 brilliantly coloured 15th-century paintings by Spanish artist Fernando Gallego in the Hispano-Flemish style, depicting scenes from the lives of Mary and Christ. The beautiful Romanesque **Torre Julia** should be open to visitors by the time you read this.

Aljibe de Altamirano MONUMENT

(Plazuela de Altamirano) This quiet, evocative 10th-century *aljibe* (cistern) is remarkable for its triple-naved format featuring six arches sculpted from granite. It's currently only accessible on the tourist office's guided tour.

Casa-Museo de Pizarro MUSEUM

(Calle del Convento de las Jerónimas; adult/child €1.40/free; ⊙10am-2pm & 5-8pm, afternoons Oct-Mar 4-7pm) High in the upper old town (and signposted from the Puerta de Santiago), this small museum occupies a 15th-century home believed to have belonged to the Pizarro family. It includes period furniture, various knick-knacks from the Pizarro boys' conquests, a handy Pizarro family tree and, upstairs, historical displays (in Spanish and, in parts, English) detailing Spanish conquests in the Americas.

Iglesia de San Martín CHURCH

(Plaza Mayor; adult/child €1.40/free; ⊙10am-2pm & 5-7.30pm, afternoons Oct-Mar 4-6.30pm) Trujillo's 16th-century Iglesia de San Martín looms over the Plaza Mayor, with delicate Gothic ceiling tracing in its single nave, striking stained-glass windows, a 1724 altarpiece and a grand 18th-century organ. Climb up to the choir loft (right as you enter) for the best view.

Iglesia de Santiago CHURCH

(Plaza de Santiago; adult/child €1.40/free; ⊙10am-2pm & 5-8pm, afternoons Oct-Mar 4-7pm) To the right of the grand Puerta de Santiago, and into the walled town, stands the Iglesia de Santiago, Trujillo's oldest church, founded in the 13th century by the Knights of Santiago (look for their scallop-shell emblem).

🎊 **Festivals & Events**

Feria del Queso FOOD

(www.feriadelquesotrujillo.es) Cheesemakers from all over Spain (and beyond) converge on the Plaza Mayor for Trujillo's pungent cheese fair. Late April to early May.

EXTREMADURA & THE AMERICAS

The *extremeños* jumped at the opportunities presented by Columbus' 1492 discovery of the Americas – hardly surprising given that Extremadura was one of Spain's poorest regions.

In 1501, Fray Nicolás de Ovando from Cáceres was named governor of all the Indies. Among the 2500 followers who joined him in his Caribbean capital of Santo Domingo, many were from Extremadura, including Francisco Pizarro, illegitimate son of a minor noble family from Trujillo. In 1504, Hernán Cortés, from a similar family in Medellín, arrived in Santo Domingo.

Both young men prospered. Cortés took part in the conquest of Cuba in 1511 and settled there. Pizarro, in 1513, accompanied Vasco Núñez de Balboa (from Jerez de los Caballeros) to Darién (Panama), where they 'discovered' the Pacific Ocean. In 1519, Cortés led a small expedition to what's now Mexico, rumoured to be full of gold and silver. By 1524, with combined fortitude, cunning, luck and ruthlessness, Cortés and his band had subdued the Aztec empire.

Pizarro returned to Spain and, before returning to the New World, visited Trujillo, where he received a hero's welcome and collected his four half-brothers, as well as other relatives and friends. Their expedition set off from present-day Panama in 1531, with just 180 men and 37 horses, and managed to capture the Inca emperor Atahualpa, despite the 30,000-strong Inca army. Pizarro demanded an enormous ransom, which was paid, but Trujillo's finest went ahead and executed Atahualpa anyway. The Inca empire, with its capital in Cuzco and extending from present-day Colombia to Chile, soon fell to a combination of casual brutality, broken alliances, cynical realpolitik and civil war between Pizarro and his longtime ally, Diego de Almagro. Pizarro was eventually assassinated in 1541 by the executed Almagro's son and is buried in the cathedral of Lima, Peru. Of the Pizarro brothers, only Hernando returned to Spain alive.

About 600 people of Trujillo made their way to the Americas in the 16th century, so it's no surprise that there are more than 20 other Trujillo towns in Central and South America. Conquistadors and colonists from all over Spain also took with them the cult of the Virgen de Guadalupe (p558) in eastern Extremadura, which remains widespread throughout Latin America.

Sleeping

★ El Mirador de las Monjas   HOTEL €
(☏ 927 65 92 23; www.elmiradordelasmonjas.com; Plaza de Santiago 4; r incl breakfast €50-65; ❋) High in the old town, this super-friendly six-room *hostería* (small hotel) has bright, spotless, modern rooms decorated in a minimalist-chic style with lots of creams and whites and gorgeous, gleaming bathrooms. Upstairs rooms with sloping ceilings and pretty vistas are slightly better than those below, but all are outrageously good value and there's a quality restaurant (☏ 927 65 92 23; www.elmiradordelasmonjas.com; Plaza de Santiago 4; mains €10-19; ⊙1-3.30pm & 8-10pm Easter-Aug, 1-3.30pm & 8-10pm Fri & Sat, 1-3.30pm Mon, Thu & Sun Sep, Oct & Mar, closed Nov-Feb; ☎) attached.

★ Posada Dos Orillas   HISTORIC HOTEL €
(☏ 927 65 90 79; www.dosorillas.com; Calle de Cambrones 6; d €60-65; ☎) In a fantastic old-town corner, this tastefully renovated 15th-century mansion oozes character. The 13 comfy rooms replicate Spanish colonial taste and are named for countries containing towns called Trujillo. Twin-room 'Extremadura' has glimpses of Santa María church from its bathroom. Nights are deliciously quiet, while personal service from the welcoming owners couldn't be better. Breakfast, often in the patio, costs €3.

Finca Santa Marta   COUNTRY HOUSE €€
(☏ 927 31 92 03; www.fincasantamarta.com; Pago San Clemente; s €55-65, d €65-85, ste €110-135, incl breakfast; P ☎ ❋ ❋) All countryside comfort and rustic charm, this Spanish-Dutch-owned country home lies in olive and almond groves, 14km southeast of Trujillo. There are 13 comfy, flowery, all-different rooms – one occupies restored stables. 'Suites', with big sharing balconies, sleep four. Cosy lounges, 100-year-old tiles, wide-open gardens and a turquoise-toned pool add to the appeal. It's signposted off the EX208, south of Km 89.

NH Palacio de Santa Marta
HOTEL €€

(☑ 927 65 91 90; www.nh-hotels.com; Calle de los Ballesteros 6; d standard/premium from €60/90; ▣※🛜🅿) Just above Plaza Mayor, the refurbished 16th-century Santa Marta Palace combines slick, modern, wood-floored chambers (featuring tea/coffee kits and big bathrooms) with beautiful original features such as exposed stone walls and high ceilings. There's a summer-only pool with views across Trujillo's rooftops. For prime vistas over the square, book a superior room. Spacious room 208, with its little pillared balcony, is stunning.

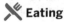 Eating

Mesón La Troya
SPANISH €

(☑ 927 32 13 64; www.mesonlatroya.com; Plaza Mayor 10; mains €6.50-17, set menu €15; ⏱ 1-4pm & 8-11pm; 🍴) Famous across Spain for its copious servings of no-frills *comida casera* (home-style cooking), Troya enjoys a prime location on Trujillo's main square. The food is decent, but it's more about quantity. You'll be directed to one of several dining areas, where plates of tortilla, chorizo and lettuce-and-tomato salad materialise before you've even ordered your three-course *menú*. Weekend queues stretch out the door.

El 7 de Sillerías
SPANISH €€

(☑ 927 32 18 56; www.el7desillerias.com; Calle Sillerías 7; raciones €9-20, mains €10-20; ⏱ noon-late Wed-Mon; 🛜🍴) With a friendly local buzz, snug wood-beamed interior and elegantly presented traditional fare, this cafe-bar-restaurant just southeast off the Plaza Mayor is the pick of Trujillo's eateries. Tasty menu choices include Extremaduran *jamón*/cheese boards, plenty of Iberian pork and huge *parrilladas de verduras* (grilled vegetable platters). The cafe-bar area dishes out *raciones* (large plate servings), *bocadillos* (filled rolls) and *tostas* (topped toast).

❶ Information

Oficina de Turismo (☑ 927 32 26 77; www.turismotrujillo.com; Plaza Mayor; ⏱ 10am-2pm & 5-8pm Apr-Sep, 10am-2pm & 4-7pm Oct-Mar) Right on the Plaza Mayor; leads excellent guided tours (p556) of Trujillo.

❶ Getting There & Away

The **bus station** (☑ 927 32 12 02; Avenida de Extremadura) is 1km south of the Plaza Mayor.

DESTINATION	FARE	DURATION	FREQUENCY
Badajoz (normal/ express)	€12/ 20	2/1¾hr	5/3 daily
Cáceres	€3.65	¾hr	5-6 daily
Madrid (normal/ express)	€19/ 31	3½/2¾hr	9/3 daily
Mérida	€9.03	1½hr	2 daily

Guadalupe
POP 2013

Centred on its palatial monastery, a treasure-trove of art, architecture and history, the sparkling white village of Guadalupe is a hugely popular pilgrimage centre. It's also a worthy destination in its own right, a bright jewel set in the green crown of the surrounding ranges and ridges of the Sierra de Villuercas (part of the Geoparque Villuercas, Ibores y Jara). These hushed hills offer plenty of good walks, through thick woods of chestnut, oak and cork meshed with olive groves and vineyards.

◉ Sights

★ **Real Monasterio de Santa María de Guadalupe**
MONASTERY, CHURCH

(☑ 927 36 70 00; www.monasterioguadalupe.com; Plaza de Santa María de Guadalupe; church free, monastery by guided tour adult/child €5/2; ⏱ church 9am-7.30pm, monastery 9.30am-1pm & 3.30-6.30pm) Guadalupe's renowned monastery is located, according to legend, on the spot where, in the early 14th century, a shepherd found an effigy of the Virgin, hidden years earlier by Christians fleeing the Muslims. A sumptuous church-monastery was built on the site, drawing pilgrims from across the world ever since. Now cared for by nine Franciscan monks, it remains one of Spain's most important pilgrimage sites, especially for South American and Filipino Catholics. The building is an architectural delight, crammed with historical riches.

🎆 Festivals & Events

Fiesta de la Virgen de Guadalupe
RELIGIOUS

Guadalupe honours its beloved Virgen de Guadalupe in September with an intricate ceremony that sees the Virgin's image re-

GUADALUPE HIKES

Ruta de Isabel la Católica (PRCC242) A splendid walking option is to take a Miajadas- or Cáceres-bound bus to the village of Cañamero, southwest of Guadalupe, and hike back along a well-signed 15km trail that retraces the steps of pilgrims coming to Guadalupe from the south – including the Reyes Católicos (Catholic Monarchs) Isabel and Fernando, after the 1492 fall of Moorish Granada. Allow about four hours.

Ruta de las Ermitas This three-hour hike, one of the less challenging walking routes accessible from Guadalupe, loops 10km past bridges, churches and a dramatic, disused viaduct, then back into town. Its final stretch links with the longer-distance Ruta de Isabel la Católica.

moved from its usual *camarín* (chamber), dressed in special jewels and temporarily displayed to the public. A statue is paraded around on the evening of the 6th and again on the 8th (which also happens to be Extremadura's regional feast day).

🛌 Sleeping

Posada del Rincón   INN **€**
(☑927 36 71 14; www.posadadelrincon.com; Plaza de Santa María de Guadalupe 11; s €40, d €50-60; ❄🐾) Behind the misleadingly tucked-away facade on Guadalupe's main square, this sparkling up-to-date *posada* sprawls back into 20 comfy, rustic-design rooms around a pretty patio. Exposed stone and brick, and terracotta-tiled floors pop up everywhere. The top-floor attic-style room 12 has rooftop windows that open up your very own monastery views. Interconnecting rooms are handy for families.

⭐**Hospedería del Real Monasterio**   HISTORIC HOTEL **€€**
(☑927 36 70 00; www.hotelhospederiamonasterio guadalupe.com; Plaza de Juan Carlos I; s €50-57, d/tr €72/95; ⊙closed approx mid-Jan–mid-Feb; 🅿❄🐾) Centred on the Real Monasterio's beautiful Gothic cloister (now housing a bar and cafe), this old-fashioned hotel lets you live it up in a national monument without paying *parador*-style prices. High-ceilinged rooms are darkish and venerable but comfortable and full of character. There's a sumptuous flower-filled patio just off the lobby, plus a good restaurant, and the whole place is thick with history.

Parador de Guadalupe   HISTORIC HOTEL **€€**
(☑927 36 70 75; www.parador.es; Calle Marqués de la Romana 12; r €95-114; 🅿❄🐾🏊) Guadalupe's *parador* (luxurious state-owned hotel) occupies a converted 15th-century hospital and

16th-century religious school opposite the monastery. Spacious rooms are tastefully decorated and the cobbled courtyard is delightful, with its central fountain, lemon and orange trees and surrounding cloister-like colonnade with arches. There's a gorgeous summer-only pool, along with a smart (if slightly overpriced) restaurant.

🍴 Eating

Hospedería del Real Monasterio   SPANISH **€€**
(☑927 36 70 00; www.hotelhospederiamonasterio guadalupe.com; Plaza de Juan Carlos I; raciones €6-20, mains €8-22; ⊙1-3pm & 9-10.30pm, closed approx mid-Jan–mid-Feb; 🅿) Dine grandly under the arches of the magnificent Gothic cloister or in the lavish dining hall, rich with 17th-century timber furnishings and antique ceramics. There's a competent range of both meat and fish dishes and classic *raciones*, and most of the desserts are homemade. Three-course *menús* (€15 to €17) keep things simple.

Parador de Guadalupe   EXTREMADURAN **€€€**
(☑927 36 70 75; www.parador.es; Calle Marqués de la Romana 12; mains €18-22, set menu €22-35; ⊙8-11am, 1.30-4pm & 8.30-11pm) Set inside a reworked 15th-century hospital, the *parador*'s smart, slightly overpriced restaurant serves refined Extremaduran fare by changing seasonal menu. In summer, sit outside in the orange-tree–dotted courtyard, its pretty fountain tinkling away in the background.

ℹ️ Information

Oficina de Turismo de Guadalupe (☑675 286987, 927 15 41 28; www.oficinadeturismo guadalupe.blogspot.co.uk; Plaza de Santa María de Guadalupe; ⊙10am-2pm & 4-7pm) On the main square, opposite the monastery.

EXTREMADURA GUADALUPE

ⓘ Getting There & Away

Buses stop on Avenida Conde de Barcelona, near the town hall, 200m south of the Plaza de Santa María de Guadalupe. **Mirat** (☑927 23 33 54; www.mirat-transportes.es) runs two services Monday to Friday (one on Sunday) to/from Cáceres (€12, 2½ hours) via Trujillo. **Samar** (☑902 25 70 25; www.samar.es) has one to two daily buses to/from Madrid (€18, four hours).

Plasencia

POP 40,755

This pleasant, bustling town is the natural hub of northern Extremadura. Rising above a bend of the Río Jerte, it retains long sections of its defensive walls, though they're tricky to spot once you're actually in town. The attractive old quarter of narrow streets, Romanesque churches, stately stone palaces and buzzing tapas bars is worth exploring. Plasencia is also a good base for ventures into the nearby La Vera (p561) and Ambroz (p562) valleys.

◉ Sights

Catedral de Plasencia   CATHEDRAL
(☑927 42 44 06; Plaza de la Catedral; admission €4; ⊙11am-2pm & 4-7pm Tue-Sun) Plasencia's magnificent cathedral is two-in-one. The 16th-century Catedral Nueva is a Gothic-Renaissance blend with a handsome plateresque facade, a soaring 17th-century *retablo* (altarpiece) and intricate walnut-carved choir stalls featuring seats dedicated to the Reyes Católicos (Catholic Monarchs). Within the Romanesque Catedral Vieja are 13th-century cloisters surrounding a fountain and lemon trees. The octagonal Capilla de San Pablo has a dramatic 1569 Caravaggio painting of John the Baptist, a religious museum and, out the front, the arched Romanesque doorway.

Palacio del Marquesado de Mirabel   MANSION
(☑927 41 07 01; Plaza de San Vicente Ferrer; adult/child €4/free; ⊙10.30am-2pm & 4-6pm) Dating to the 15th century, this is one of Plasencia's most majestic civil buildings. Enter through the fine, columned two-floor Renaissance patio, then head upstairs to a 1555 bust of Carlos I, a grand 16th-century reception hall and chapel, and an Italian-inspired hanging garden overlooking the plaza. Ring the doorbell to get inside; info is in Spanish, English and Portuguese.

Plaza Mayor   SQUARE
Plasencia life flows through the lively, arcaded Plaza Mayor: meeting place of 10 streets, home to plenty of bar-restaurants and scene of a Tuesday farmers market since the 12th century. The jaunty figure striking the hour atop the Gothic town hall is El Abuelo Mayorga, a 1970s replica of the 13th-century original and the unofficial symbol of the town. The town hall also sports a Carlos I coat of arms.

🛏 Sleeping & Eating

★**Palacio Carvajal Girón**   HISTORIC HOTEL €€
(☑927 42 63 26; www.palaciocarvajalgiron.com; Plaza Ansano 1; r €95-155; ��P꘍ꔮꘌ) An impressive conversion job has transformed this formerly ruined palace in the heart of the old town into a chic address. Rooms have modern fittings, fresh white decor, plus original features, including fireplaces. The top-floor attic-style standard rooms have sloping ceilings and in-room concrete baths or showers, while the swish 1st-floor suite has an XXL bathroom with original tilework.

Parador de Plasencia   HISTORIC HOTEL €€€
(☑927 42 58 70; www.parador.es; Plaza de San Vicente Ferrer; r €100-165; ⓟP꘍ꔮꘌ) One of

---

WHAT'S COOKING IN EXTREMADURA?

➡ *Migas extremeñas* (breadcrumbs fried with garlic, peppers and pork) at Mesón La Troya (p558)

➡ *Caldereta de cabrito* (stewed kid) at Villa Xarahiz (p562)

➡ *Cochinillo asado* (roast suckling pig) at La Tahona (☑620 389991; www.asadorlatahonadecaceres.com; Calle Felipe Uribarri 4; tapas €6, raciones €12-22, mains €15-25; ⊙1-4pm & 8-11pm)

➡ Torta del Casar (a strong, creamy cheese served on toast) at La Bodeguilla (p569)

➡ *Jamón ibérico* (Iberian ham), anywhere, but especially the bars of Monesterio (p572)

EXTREMADURA PLASENCIA

Extremadura's finest, Plasencia's *parador* is a classic – oozing the atmosphere and austerity of its 15th-century convent roots, with massive stone columns, soaring ceilings and a traditional Renaissance cloister. The 66 rooms are far from monastic, luxuriously furnished with rugs, rich fabrics, wood-carved bedheads, red-velvet curtains and varnished terracotta floors. The on-site bar occupies an old bodega.

★ **Casa Juan**   EXTREMADURAN €€
(☑927 42 40 42; www.restaurantecasajuan.com; Calle de las Arenillas 2; mains €13-18; ☉1.30-4pm & 8.30-11pm, closed Jan; 🅿) Tucked down a quiet old-town lane, welcoming Casa Juan does well-prepared *extremeño* meat dishes (such as roast suckling pig) plus some tasty vegetarian and gluten-free bites. Start with locally made olive oil and bread, then try the homemade Torta del Casar gratin or the expertly hung local *retinto* beef. Fairly priced wines from around Spain seal an excellent deal.

Succo   CONTEMPORARY SPANISH €€
(☑927 41 29 32; www.restaurantesucco.es; Calle Vidrieras 7; mains €10-19; ☉9am-late Mon-Sat, to 4pm Sun; 🐝) In the heart of Plasencia's eating area, just off the Plaza Mayor, this urban-chic tapas bar plates up delectable inventive tapas and *raciones*, delicately presented at tall white tables or in the bamboo-dotted dining room. The *huevos rotos* (smashed eggs) with *jamón* and *patatas panaderas* (potatoes with tomato and onion) gets a big thumbs up, as does the friendly service.

🍷 Drinking & Nightlife

La Puerta de Tannhäuser   CAFE
(☑927 41 17 97; www.facebook.com/la-puerta-de-tannhäuser-librería-café-espacio-arte-y-ocio-plasencia-112471498834919; Rua Zapatería 22; ☉11am-2pm & 5-9pm; 🐝🅿) Not what you'd expect in old-town Plasencia, Extremadura's first cafe-bookshop is warm, friendly and an absolute delight. Relax at hot-red tables over carefully concocted coffees or lovingly chosen wines, and soak up the creative vibe. There's an extensive stock of Spanish-language books, plus regular literary events.

ℹ Information

Oficina de Turismo (☑927 42 38 43; www.plasencia.es; Calle Santa Clara 4; ☉7.45am-3pm & 4-7pm Mon-Fri, 10am-2pm & 4-7pm Sat & Sun) Information on Plasencia and northern Extremadura.

ℹ Getting There & Away

BUS

The **bus station** (☑927 41 45 50; Calle de Tornavacas 2) is 1km east of the Plaza Mayor. Destinations include the following:

Cáceres (€5.15, 50 minutes, one to four daily)

Madrid (€18 to €19, 3½ hours, two to three daily)

Salamanca (€9.72, 1½ to 2¼ hours, seven to eight daily)

Buses also serve smaller destinations around northern Extremadura.

TRAIN

The train station is off Avenida de España (the Cáceres road), 1km southwest of town. Trains depart up to four times daily from Plasencia for Madrid (€23 to €28, 2¾ hours), Cáceres (€5.20 to €6, one hour) and Mérida (€12 to €15, two hours).

La Vera

Surrounded by the Sierras de Tormantos and Gredos, with mountains often still capped with snow as late as May, Extremadura's fertile La Vera region produces raspberries, asparagus and, above all, *pimentón* (paprika), sold in charming old-fashioned tins and with a distinctive smoky flavour. Typical, too, are half-timbered houses leaning at odd angles, their overhanging upper storeys supported by timber or stone pillars. With its gurgling streams and easily manageable roads, La Vera makes a great driving tour from Plasencia.

◎ Sights

★ **Monasterio de Yuste**   MONASTERY
(☑902 04 44 54; www.patrimonionacional.es; Ctra de Yuste, Cuacos de Yuste; adult/child €7/4, audio guide €4; ☉10am-8pm Apr-Sep, to 6pm Oct-Mar; 🅿) In a lovely shady setting 1.5km northwest of Cuacos de Yuste, this monastery is where Carlos I of Spain (Charles I; also known as Carlos V of Austria) came in 1557 to prepare for death after abdicating his emperorship over much of Western and Central Europe. It's a soulful, evocative place amid the forested hills, and a tranquil counterpoint to the grandeur of so many formerly royal buildings elsewhere in Spain.

Puente Romano   BRIDGE
(Madrigal de la Vera) This impressive Roman-origin bridge stands about 1km east of Madrigal, just north off the EX203 road

EASTER SUFFERING

At midnight on Good Friday eve, Valverde hosts one of Spain's most bizarre religious festivities, Los Empalaos ('the Impaled'). Penitent locals strap their arms to a beam, their near-naked bodies wrapped tight with 60m-long cords from waist to fingertips. Barefoot, veiled, with two swords strapped to their backs and wearing crowns of thorns, these 'walking crucifixes' follow a painful Way of the Cross.

and practically in Castilla y León. In warm weather, the river below is a popular swimming spot.

Sleeping

★ Haldón Country   HOTEL €€

(927 57 10 04; www.hotelhaldoncountry.com; Finca El Haldón, Robledillo de la Vera; s/d incl breakfast €79/90; P※🕲🛋) This exquisite, welcoming rural hotel, just off the main road between Jarandilla and Villanueva, is a haven of peace and relaxation. Set in extensive grounds, it has airy, light modern rooms (plus a few older-style rooms) with original art. The atrium holds a heated pool and small spa. It was closed for renovations at research, due to reopen in August 2016.

★ Parador de Jarandilla   HISTORIC HOTEL €€

(927 56 01 17; www.parador.es; Avenida de García Prieto 1, Jarandilla de la Vera; r €85-109; P※🕲🛋) Be king of the castle at this 15th-century castle-turned-hotel with a warm, welcoming feel. Carlos I stayed here for a few months while waiting for his monastery digs to be completed. Within the stout walls and turrets lie period-furnished rooms that are wonderfully comfy without going ostentatiously grand, plus a classic courtyard where you can dine royally from the restaurant menu.

La Vera de Yuste   CASA RURAL €€

(927 17 22 89; www.laveradeyuste.com; Calle Teodoro Perianes 17, Cuacos de Yuste; s/d incl breakfast €50/70; ※) This beauty is set in two typical 18th-century village houses near Cuacos de Yuste's Plaza Mayor. The wood-beamed rooms have chunky rustic furniture and the garden is a delight, surrounded by rose bushes with a small courtyard and vegetable patch.

Eating

★ Villa Xarahiz   SPANISH €€

(927 66 51 50; www.villaxarahiz.com; Ctra EX203, Km 32.8, Jaraíz de la Vera; mains €8-15; ⊙1.30-3.45pm & 9-10.45pm Tue-Sat, 1.30-3.45pm Sun; 🕲🛋) Offering spectacular sierra views from the terrace and the upmarket wood-beamed dining room, this hotel restaurant 1km north of Jaraíz is one of La Vera's best bets for Spanish wines and smart regional food, featuring local peppers, *caldereta de cabrito* (stewed kid), *cochinito frito al ajo* (garlic-fried suckling pig) and other quality Extremadura produce. The €12 weekday lunch *menú* is a hit.

Parador de Jarandilla   SPANISH €€

(927 56 01 17; www.parador.es; Avenida de García Prieto 1, Jarandilla de la Vera; mains €18-20; ⊙1.30-4pm & 8.30-11pm; P🕲🛋) Dine in regal style on elegant Extremaduran dishes and fine Spanish wines inside the chunky walls of Jarandilla's 15th-century castle, where you can sit outside in the romantic palm-studded courtyard.

ℹ Information

Oficina de Turismo de Jarandilla de la Vera (927 56 04 60; www.jarandilla.com; Avenida Soledad Vega Ortiz, Jarandilla de la Vera; ⊙10am-2pm & 4.30-7.30pm Tue-Sat, 10am-2pm Sun) The most useful of a number of tourist offices dotted around La Vera.

Oficina de Turismo de Villanueva de la Vera (927 56 70 31; www.villanuevadelavera. es; Avenida de la Vera, Villanueva de la Vera; ⊙10am-4pm Mon & Thu, 10am-6pm Fri & Sat, 10.30am-6.30pm Sun) On the main road.

ℹ Getting There & Away

Mirat (927 23 33 54; www.mirat-transportes. es) runs three buses Monday to Friday from Plasencia to Jarandilla (€6, one hour) via Jaraíz (€4, 50 minutes) and lower La Vera villages, and one on Sunday. Some continue further up the valley. There's also one daily bus Monday to Friday and Sunday between Cáceres and Jarandilla (€15, 2¼ hours).

Self-drivers can cross north into the Valle del Jerte via the winding CC17 over the 1269m Puerto de Piornal.

Valle del Ambroz

This broad valley northwest of the Valle del Jerte and northeast of Plasencia is split by the Vía de la Plata and the A66 motorway. It has a friendly feel and some intriguing sights, most notably the ghost village of Granadilla, the ruined Roman city of Cáparra and lively Hervás, with its beautifully preserved Jewish Quarter.

Hervás

POP 4194

Hervás, 45km northeast of Plasencia, is a lively and handsome town with a picturesque old quarter and some excellent restaurants. It makes a great base for exploring the Valle del Ambroz.

◉ Sights

Barrio Judío　　　　　　　　　　AREA

Hervás houses Extremadura's best surviving *barrio judío* (Jewish quarter), whose narrow streets extend down to the river. This neighbourhood thrived until the 1492 expulsion of the Jews, when most families fled to Portugal. Seek out, in particular, Calle Rabilero. For fine views, climb up to the Iglesia de Santa María, on the site of a ruined Templar castle.

Museo Pérez Comendador-Leroux　　GALLERY

(☑ 927 48 16 55; www.mpcl.net; Calle Asensio Neila 5; ⊙ 4-8pm Tue, 11am-2pm & 4-8pm Wed-Fri, 10.30am-2pm Sat & Sun) FREE Within an impressive 18th-century mansion, the Museo Pérez Comendador-Leroux houses works by Hervás-born, 20th-century sculptor Enrique Pérez Comendador and his wife, the French painter Magdalena Leroux. Among 650 pieces on display are Leroux's colourful Rome-focused watercolours, plus sculptures of Leroux and a series of *extremeño* conquistadors by Comendador and early versions of his statue of San Pedro de Alcántara displayed at Concatedral de Santa María (p551) in Cáceres.

🛏 Sleeping & Eating

★ El Jardín del Convento　　HOTEL **€€**

(☑ 660 452292, 927 48 11 61; www.eljardindelconvento.com; Plaza del Convento 22; r €50-85, cottage €100-115; ✱ ☎) Bordering the Jewish quarter, this is one of Extremadura's most fabulous hotels. The gorgeous garden – all roses, vegetables and tranquil seating – makes for rural yet stylish relaxation. All-different rooms are full of character, with wooden floors, open-stone walls, elegant period furniture and, for some, a big wooden balcony. Breakfast (€7.50) is a dream of homemade jams, cakes and other local treats.

La Bodeguita　　　　　　　SPANISH **€**

(☑ 676 782828; Calle Relator González 2; raciones €3.50-7; ⊙ noon-4pm & 8-11pm Wed-Mon) Beautiful traditional dishes make busy little La Bodeguita an excellent choice for a fuss-free feed. Grilled prawns, chorizo tortilla, *pulpo a la gallega* (Galician-style octopus) and light fresh salads await you – after, of course, your complimentary tapa. It's a simple, bubbly spot amid a cluster of old-quarter houses.

★ Nardi　　　CONTEMPORARY EXTREMADURAN **€€**

(☑ 927 48 13 23; www.restaurantenardi.com; Calle Braulio Navas 19; raciones €8-14, mains €15-20; ⊙ 1.30-4pm & 8.30-11pm Wed-Mon; ☑ ⓗ) Nardi impresses with rich, classic dishes given a contemporary zing, served in a warm, elegant dining room with wood beams, yellow walls and rustic art. Extremaduran meats, such as *solomillo ibérico de bellota* (Iberian pork tenderloin), are the focus, but it has excellent vegetarian options too, including salads, pumpkin soup and stir-fried boletus (mushrooms) with truffle foam, plus a kids' menu.

ⓘ Information

Oficina de Turismo de Hervás (☑ 927 47 36 18; www.turismodehervas.com; Calle Braulio Navas 6; ⊙ 10am-2pm & 4.30-7.30pm Tue-Sun) Good information on Hervás and the Valle del Ambroz.

EXTREMADURA VALLE DEL AMBROZ

WORTH A TRIP

YACIMIENTO ROMANO DE CÁPARRA

Unearthed in 1929, the fascinating, substantial remains of the once-splendid Roman city of Cáparra (☑ 927 19 94 85; Ctra CC13.3; Ⓟ) mostly date to around the 1st century. Initially favoured for its strategic location on the Vía de la Plata, the city fell into decay in the 4th century and was eventually deserted. Wander the 14-hectare site to spot its crumbled walls, gates, forum, thermal baths and amphitheatre. Most impressive of all is the wonderfully preserved, late-1st-century Arco de Cáparra, a four-arch granite gateway.

GRANADILLA

About 25km west of Hervás, the ghost village of Granadilla (Ctra CC168; ⊙10am-1.30pm & 4-8pm Tue-Sun Apr-Oct, afternoons 4-6pm Tue-Sun Nov-Mar; 🅿) is a beguiling reminder of how Extremadura's villages must have looked before modernisation. Founded by the Moors in the 9th century but abandoned in the 1960s when the nearby dam was built, Granadilla's traditional architecture has been painstakingly restored since the 1980s as part of a government educational project. Enter through the narrow Puerta de Villa, overlooked by the sturdy 15th-century castle, which you can climb for brilliant panoramas.

ⓘ Getting There & Away

Cevesa (☑902 39 31 32; www.cevesa.es) runs one bus daily Monday to Friday between Hervás and Plasencia (€3.30, one hour), continuing to Cáceres (€8.45, 2¼ hours).

Parque Nacional de Monfragüe

Spain's 14th national park is a dramatic, hilly 180-sq-km paradise for birdwatchers (and other nature lovers). Straddling the Tajo valley, it's home to spectacular colonies of raptors and more than 75% of Spain's protected species. Among some 175 feathered varieties are around 300 pairs of black vultures (the largest concentration of Europe's biggest bird of prey) and populations of two other rare large birds: the Spanish imperial eagle (12 pairs) and the black stork (30 pairs). Deer, otters, genets, badgers, rabbits, foxes and wild boar are other inhabitants.

The best time to visit is between March and October, since many bird species winter in Africa.

The pretty hamlet of Villareal de San Carlos, from where most hiking trails leave, is the most convenient base. There are also amenities in Torrejón el Rubio, on the south side of the park.

◉ Sights

★**Castillo de Monfragüe** CASTLE

The hilltop Castillo de Monfragüe, a ruined 9th-century Islamic fort, has sweeping 360-degree views across the park, with birds swooshing by above and below. It's signposted up a steep winding road off the EX208, 8km south of Villareal de San Carlos. The castle can also be reached via an attractive 8km, 1½-hour walk from Villareal, along the so-called Ruta Roja (Red Route).

★**Mirador Salto del Gitano** VIEWPOINT

(🅿) Arguably the most spectacular spot in the national park is the Mirador Salto del Gitano. From this lookout point, 5km south of Villareal along the EX208, there are stunning views across the Río Tajo gorge to the Peña Falcón crag, home to a colony of circling Griffon vultures. The 8km 'Ruta Roja' walk between Villareal and the Castillo de Monfragüe passes through here.

🏃 Activities

Monfragüe Vivo BIRDWATCHING, ADVENTURE SPORTS

(☑927 45 94 75, 620 941778; www.monfraguevivo.com) Birdwatching tours and a variety of park activities, including walking, kayaking and jeep trips, with local guides.

EN-RUTA Rutas por Monfragüe BIRDWATCHING

(☑927 40 41 13, 605 898154; www.rutaspormonfrague.com) A range of birdwatching, walking and jeep excursions into the park.

Birding Extremadura BIRDWATCHING

(☑927 31 93 49; www.birdingextremadura.com) Birdwatching trips run by British ornithologist Martin Kelsey.

🛏 Sleeping & Eating

Casa Rural Monfragüe CASA RURAL €

(☑927 19 90 02; www.monfraguerural.com; Calle de Villareal 15, Villareal de San Carlos; s/d incl breakfast €39/55; ❋🛜) This light-filled *casa rural* (village accommodation) has six large, brightly painted rooms filled with floral prints in a lovely stone building directly opposite the park's information centre. There's an attractive bar-restaurant downstairs serving classic Extremaduran fare. It rents bikes (€20) and binoculars (€5), arranges tours and has several similar rooms just down the road.

Hospedería Parque de Monfragüe
HOTEL €€

(☑927 45 52 78; www.hospederiasdeextremadura. es; Ctra EX208, Km 39, Torrejón el Rubio; d €71-95, q €104-114, all incl breakfast; P❖@❖☀) ⚑ This tranquil four-star hotel, 1km north of Torrejón el Rubio, looks out across the plains to the national park and is partly run on solar power and bioenergy. Freshly revamped dark-turquoise and varnished-wood rooms come with desks, squeaky floors and tile-covered bathrooms. Duplexes are good for families, and there's a decent restaurant.

Paraíso de los Sentidos
EXTREMADURAN €€

(☑927 45 52 78; www.hospederiasdeextremadura. es; Hospedería Parque de Monfragüe, Ctra EX208, Km 39, Torrejón el Rubio; mains €15-20, set menu €15-25; ❨8-10.45am, 1.30-4pm & 8.30-11pm) A classy hotel restaurant that does a decent job of refined Extremaduran dishes in a bright peaceful setting. It's 1km north of Torrejón el Rubio on the EX208.

Restaurante Monfragüe
EXTREMADURAN €€

(☑927 19 90 02; www.monfraguerural.com; Calle de Villareal 15, Villareal de San Carlos; mains €10-20, set menu €9; ❨1-4pm & 8-10pm) This lively bar-restaurant attached to an excellent *casa rural* plates up classic meat-heavy Extremaduran fare, including *caldereta de cabrito* (stewed kid), *raciones* of *jamón* and Torta del Casar gratin.

ⓘ Information

Centro de Interpretación del Parque Nacional de Monfragüe (Villareal de San Carlos; ❨9.30am-7.30pm Jul-Sep, 9.30am-6pm Oct-Jun, from 9am Sat & Sun all year) With displays on local history, fauna and flora, this is the perfect introduction to the park.

Centro de Visitantes (☑927 19 91 34; www. magrama.gob.es/es/red-parques-nacionales/ nuestros-parques/monfrague; Villareal de San Carlos; ❨9.30am-7.30pm Jul-Sep, 9.30am-6pm Oct-Jun, from 9am Sat & Sun all year) The park's main information centre advises on hikes and birdwatching spots. It also organises free two-hour guided hikes at 9am on Friday, Saturday and Sunday (minimum three people; phone ahead).

Monfragüe Bird Center (☑927 19 95 79; www. centrosurmonfrague.com; Monfragüe Centro de Visitantes Sur, Torrejón el Rubio; ❨ hours vary) Maps and advice on birdwatching spots, plus Spanish-language displays on local birds, migration patterns and, next door, Monfragüe's prehistoric cave art.

Oficina de Turismo de Torrejón el Rubio (☑927 45 52 92; www.torrejonelrubio.com; Calle Madroño 1, Torrejón el Rubio; ❨10am-2pm & 4-6pm Tue, Wed & Sun, to 7pm Thu-Sat) On the main road; helpful on hiking, birdwatching and other park activities.

ⓘ Getting There & Away

BUS

Public transport through the park is limited. **Emiz** (☑607 514078, 927 24 72 21; www.emiz. es) runs one bus daily Monday to Friday in each direction between Plasencia and Torrejón el Rubio (€3.95, 45 minutes), stopping in Villareal de San Carlos. There's also one bus on Monday and Friday between Torrejón el Rubio and Trujillo (45 minutes).

TRAIN

The nearest train station is at Monfragüe, 18km north of Villareal de San Carlos.

Mérida

POP 58,971

Mérida, capital of Extremadura, was once also capital of the Roman province of Lusitania (as Emerita Augusta, founded 25 BC) and is still home to the most impressive and extensive Roman ruins in all Spain. The ruins lie sprinkled around town, often appearing in the most unlikely corners, and one can only wonder what still lies buried beneath the lively, modern city.

◉ Sights

★ Teatro Romano
RUIN

(Paseo Álvarez Sáez de Buruaga; entry by combined ticket adult/concession/child €12/6/free; ❨9am-9pm Apr-Sep, 9.30am-6.30pm Oct-Mar) Mérida's most spectacular Roman monument, and the only one to once again fulfil its original function (by hosting performances during the Festival Internacional de Teatro Clásico (p568) in summer), the Teatro Romano is the city's indisputable highlight. It was built around 15 BC to seat 6000 spectators. The adjoining (slightly less dazzling) **Anfiteatro** (Paseo Álvarez Sáez de Buruaga; entry by combined ticket adult/concession/child €12/6/free; ❨9am-9pm Apr-Sep, 9.30am-6.30pm Oct-Mar) opened in 8 BC for gladiatorial contests and held 14,000; the gladiator-versus-lion fresco in the Museo Nacional de Arte Romano (p567) was taken from here.

Mérida

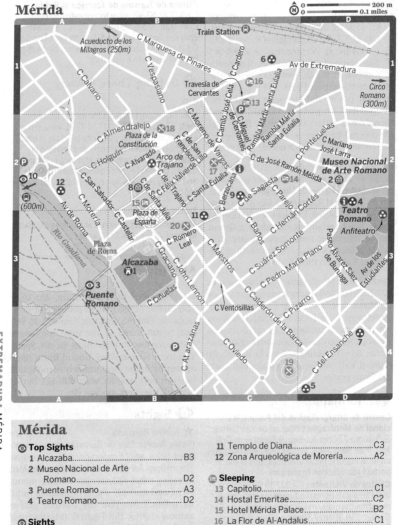

EXTREMADURA MÉRIDA

Mérida

★ **Puente Romano**   BRIDGE

Don't miss the extraordinarily powerful spectacle of the Puente Romano spanning the Río Guadiana. At 792m in length with 60 granite arches, it's one of the longest bridges built by the Romans. It was constructed in 25 BC when Emerita Augusta (modern-day Mérida) was founded, and then partly restored in the 17th century. The 20th-century **Puente Lusitania**, a sleek suspension bridge designed by Santiago Calatrava, mirrors it to the northwest. The best Roman bridge views are from the Alcazaba's south-western ramparts.

★ Museo Nacional de Arte Romano   MUSEUM

(☎924 31 16 90; http://museoarteromano.mcu.es; Calle de José Ramón Mélida; adult/child €3/free, EU seniors & students free, after 2pm Sat & all day Sun free; ☺9.30am-8pm Tue-Sat, 10am-3pm Sun Apr-Sep, 9.30am-6.30pm Tue-Sat, 10am-3pm Sun Oct-Mar) Even if you visit only a handful of Mérida's sights, make sure one of them is this fabulous museum, which has a superb three-floor collection of statues, busts, mosaics, frescoes, coins, pottery and other Roman artefacts, all beautifully displayed alongside information panels in Spanish and English. Designed by Navarran architect Rafael Moneo, the soaring arched brick structure makes a stunning home for the collection, its walls hung with some of the largest, most beautiful mosaics.

★ Alcazaba   FORTRESS

(Calle Graciano; entry by combined ticket adult/concession/child €12/6/free; ☺9am-9pm Apr-Sep, 9.30am-6.30pm Oct-Mar) This large Islamic fort was built in the mid-9th century on a site already occupied by the Romans and Visigoths, probably becoming the first ever *alcazaba* in Al-Andalus. In the middle of the sprawling complex, its pretty goldfish-populated *aljibe* (cistern) reuses Visigothic marble, flower motifs and stone slabs, while the ramparts look out over the Puente Romano and the Río Guadiana. The 15th-century monastery in the northeast corner now serves as regional government offices.

Circo Romano   RUIN

(Avenida Juan Carlos I; entry by combined ticket adult/concession/child €12/6/free; ☺9am-9pm Apr–late-Oct, 9.30am-2pm & 4-6.30pm late–Oct–Mar) The 1st-century Circo Romano could accommodate 30,000 spectators. Discovered in the 16th century, its remains represent the only surviving hippodrome of its kind in Spain. In the attached interpretive centre you can read (in Spanish) all about Diocles, a champion *auriga* (horse and chariot racer) who served his apprenticeship in Mérida before going on to the big league in Rome.

Cripta de Santa Eulalia   RUIN, CHURCH

(Avenida de Extremadura; entry by combined ticket adult/concession/child €12/6/free; ☺9am-9.30pm Apr-Sep, 9.30am-2pm & 4-6.30pm Oct-Mar) This basilica was built in the 5th century in honour of Mérida's patron saint, who is said to have been martyred in the 4th century. It was then reconstructed in the 13th century. The modern-day church is closed to the public, but, beside it, a museum and excavated areas allow you to identify Roman houses, a 4th-century Christian cemetery and the original 5th-century church.

Acueducto de los Milagros   RUIN

(Calle Marquesa de Pinares) Built between the 1st century BC and the 3rd century, the 830m-long Acueducto de los Milagros once supplied Roman Mérida with water from the dam at Lago Proserpina, 6km north of town. It's now highly favoured by nesting storks.

Casa del Mitreo   RUIN

(Calle Oviedo; entry by combined ticket adult/concession/child €12/6/free; ☺9am-9pm Apr-Oct, 9.30am-2pm & 4-6.30pm Nov-Mar) Beside Mérida's Plaza de Toros, the Casa del Mitreo is a late-1st- or 2nd-century Roman house with a well-preserved fresco and several intricate mosaics. Among the mosaics you'll find the partial but beautiful remains of the 3rd-century *mosaico cosmológico* (with its bright colours and allegories about the creation of the world), which was damaged by a fire. The Casa del Mitreo is connected by footpath to the adjacent Los Columbarios (Calle del Ensanche; entry by combined ticket adult/concession/child €12/6/free; ☺9am-9pm Apr-Oct, 9.30am-2pm & 4-6.30pm Nov-Mar) Roman funeral site.

Templo de Diana   RUIN

(Calle de Sagasta) Inaccurately named, for it's now known to have been dedicated to the Imperial cult, this 1st-century-BC temple stood in the municipal forum, where the city government was based. It was constructed on the site of an earlier Moorish building and parts were later incorporated into a 16th-century mansion built within it. The forum's restored Pórtico del Foro is 100m northeast up Calle de Sagasta.

Arco de Trajano   RUIN

(Calle de Trajano) This imposing 15m-high granite archway isn't known to have anything to do with Trajan, but it was situated on one of Mérida's main Roman streets and, in its original marble-covered form, may have served as an entrance to a sacred area.

Museo de Arte Visigodo   MUSEUM

(Calle de Santa Julia; ☺9.30am-8pm Apr-Sep, 9.30am-6.30pm Tue-Sat, 10am-3pm Sun Oct-Mar)

ⓘ COMBINED TICKET

Admission to most of Mérida's Roman sites is via a combined ticket (€12 for adults, €6 for students and pensioners, free for children under 12). It covers admission to the Teatro Romano and Anfiteatro, Casa del Anfiteatro (if/when it reopens), Los Columbarios, Casa del Mitreo, Alcazaba, Circo Romano, Cripta de Santa Eulalia and the Zona Arqueológica de Morería. The Museo Nacional de Arte Romano is not included. The ticket allows you one entry to each sight, has no time limit and can be bought at any of the sights except the Zona Arqueológica de Morería.

FREE Many of the Visigothic objects unearthed in Mérida are exhibited in this archaeological museum, set inside a 16th-century church-convent just off the Plaza de España. It's a fascinating (Spanish-language) insight into a little-known period of Spanish history. In a little side-room, there's a stone-carved Moorish inscription dating the Alcazaba's 835 foundation.

Zona Arqueológica de Morería   RUIN
(Avenida de Roma; entry by combined ticket adult/concession/child €12/6/free; ☺9.30am-2pm & 5-7.30pm Apr-Sep, 9.30am-2pm & 4-6.30pm Oct-Mar) This excavated Moorish quarter contains the remains of a cemetery, walls, houses dating from Roman to post-Islamic times and the foundations of a 4th-century, 4m-wide Roman gate.

✦ Festivals & Events

Festival Internacional de Teatro
Clásico   THEATRE
(www.festivaldemerida.es; admission €12-39; ☺Jul-Aug) This prestigious summer festival, held at Mérida's Roman theatre and amphitheatre, features Greek and more recent drama classics, plus music, photography and dance. It starts at 10.45pm most nights.

🛏 Sleeping

★ La Flor de Al-Andalus   HOSTAL €
(☑924 31 33 56; www.laflordeal-andalus.es; Avenida de Extremadura 6; s €35-45, d €45-52; ❄🤍) If only all *hostales* were this good value. A self-appointed 'boutique *hostal*', La Flor de Al-Andalus has 18 comfy, colourful rooms beautifully decorated in Andalucian style

(with elegant tiles, elaborate mirrors and hanging lanterns), plus friendly service and a convenient location within walking distance of Mérida's main sights. Try to avoid ground-floor rooms by reception.

Capitolio   APARTMENT €
(☑924 30 31 63; www.capitolio.es; Travesía de Cervantes 2; s/d from €50/60; ℗❄🤍) These gorgeously styled modern miniapartments in a handy central location have equipped kitchens, plus plenty of space, light and sparkle. The individual colour schemes alternate between elegantly sober and minimalist and luxuriantly colourful, with full-wall flower photographs, asymmetric bedheads or slogan-covered pillows. Whichever version you choose, it's excellent value.

★ Hostal Emeritae   HOSTAL €€
(☑924 30 31 83; www.hostalemeritae.com; Calle de Sagasta 40; s €30-40, d €42-70, tr €56-70; ℗❄🤍) Just six months old at research time, this fabulous new arrival has a relaxed feel enhanced by cosy, contemporary rooms drenched in fresh whites and creams. Top-floor 'superior doubles', with soft-toned art and private balconies, are worth that little extra, and there's a tasteful purple-and-grey-themed communal patio. Breakfast (€1.50) is available.

Aqua Libera   CASA RURAL €€
(☑924 31 00 32; www.aqualibera.com; Calle Cáceres 26, Aljucén; r without/with breakfast €69/79; ☺Mar-Dec; 🤍🏊🛁) For a Mérida-area sleep with a Roman-inspired twist, seek out this thoughtfully restored townhouse turned thermal baths and homey adults-only country hotel in little Aljucén, 16km north of Mérida. Expect poolside recliners, candlelit corridors, flower-lined gardens, Roman-style mosaics, columned courtyards and elaborate Roman-themed meals (€30). There are just four bright, welcoming rooms, three with colour-tiled kitchenettes.

Hotel Mérida Palace   HISTORIC HOTEL €€€
(☑924 38 38 00; www.meridapalace.com; Plaza de España 19; r €74-187; ℗❄🤍🏊) Set across two linked 18th- and 19th-century buildings flanking the palm-dotted Plaza de España, Mérida Palace is smart, efficient and wonderfully characterful. Swish pastel-painted rooms sport Roman-themed touches such as mosaic-print bedheads, black-and-white ancient-Mérida drawings and decorative Roman coins. Enter

through the beautiful arched, blue-toned atrium and, in summer, enjoy the rooftop pool overlooking the plaza's palms and fountain.

✕ Eating

Mercado San Albín   TAPAS €
(www.facebook.com/mercado-san-albin-plaza-de-toros-de-merida-969421809796174; Plaza de Toros, Calle Oviedo; tapas €4-10; ⊙noon-4pm & 9pm-midnight) The halls of Mérida's red-washed 20th-century bullring have been transformed into a busy tapas-style hangout. In each alcove, individual stalls deliver their own specialities, with everything from *jamón* and croquettes to cocktails and cakes making an appearance. Mix and match and and sit wherever you like.

★ La Bodeguilla   SPANISH €€
(☑924 31 88 54; Calle Moreno de Vargas 5; mains €10-22, set menu from €10; ⊙8am-midnight) A real local favourite, packed-out La Bodeguilla ticks all the right boxes – friendly service, well-priced food and a refreshingly varied menu that spans the full range of *extremeño* and wider specialities (grilled meats, creative salads, rice and pasta dishes, plus everything else from scrambles to local Torta del Casar cheese on toast). Chef-owner Emilio keeps things ticking. Lunchtime bookings essential.

★ Tábula Calda   SPANISH €€
(☑924 30 49 50; www.tabulacalda.com; Calle Romero Leal 11; mains €12-19, set menu €14-27; ⊙1-4.30pm & 8pm-midnight) 🍴 This inviting yellow-washed space, filled with tilework and greenery, serves well-priced, quality meals encompassing Spain's favourite staples. Everything either comes from its garden or is sourced from within 100km of the kitchen. Before your food arrives, you'll enjoy a complimentary tapa, house salad (orange, sugar and olive oil, reflecting the family's Jewish roots) and olives. Manuel is a welcoming host.

La Carbonería   CONTEMPORARY SPANISH €€
(☑924 30 29 83; www.facebook.com/pages/la-carboneria-mérida/379770068793001; Plaza de la Constitución 4; mains €9-22; ⊙1pm-late; 🐾) Blue-and-white mosaic floors open the show at this modern and elegant grilled-meats specialist. Fresh giant salads (with serving tongs!) and enormous *jamón* or cheese platters are designed for sharing, while the stars of the menu are the par-ticularly succulent Iberian meat mains. All this, plus friendly waiters and a long list of Extremaduran wines, draws a smart, mixed local crowd.

ℹ Information

Oficina de Turismo (☑924 38 01 91; www.turismomerida.org; Calle Santa Eulalia 64; ⊙9am-2pm & 4.30-8pm Mon-Sat) At the top (northeast) end of Mérida's main shopping street.

Oficina de Turismo (Teatro Romano) (☑924 33 07 22; www.turismomerida.org; Paseo Álvarez Sáez de Buruaga; ⊙9am-7.30pm) Next to the Roman theatre.

ℹ Getting There & Away

BUS

Buses depart from the **bus station** (☑924 37 14 04; Avenida de la Libertad), across the river via the Puente Lusitana.

DESTINATION	FARE	DURATION	FREQUENCY
Badajoz	€5.12	1hr	3-8 daily
Cáceres	€5.71	1hr	2-3 daily
Lisbon	€32	4hr	1 daily
Madrid (normal/ express)	€26/ 39	5/4hr	4/3 daily
Seville	€15	2¾hr	5 daily
Zafra	€5.30	1¼hr	5-8 daily

TRAIN

From the station, just off Avenida de Extremadura, trains run to Madrid (€31 to €47, 4½ to eight hours, six or seven daily), Cáceres (€6.10 to €7.35, one hour, four to five daily), Seville (€20, 3¾ hours, one daily) and Zafra (€6.10 to €7.35, 45 minutes, one to three daily).

Alburquerque

POP 5486

This small, pretty town, 40km north of Badajoz, is mainly worth a visit for its wonderfully preserved Castillo de Luna.

⊙ Sights

Castillo de Luna   CASTLE
(⊙tours 11am, noon, 1pm, 4pm & 5pm) **FREE** Looming large above little Alburquerque is the intact Castillo de Luna. The centrepiece of a complex frontier defence system of forts, the castle was built on the site of its Muslim predecessor in the 13th century

and subsequently expanded. From the top of the five-sided 15th-century defensive tower, views take in the Portuguese border (the Portuguese actually took the town for a few years in the early 18th century). You'll walk across the 10m-high drawbridge, then explore the grand castle digs.

ⓘ Getting There & Away

Alburquerque is served by four buses Monday to Friday (one on Saturday) from Badajoz (€3.76, 45 minutes to one hour).

Olivenza

POP 12,090

Pretty, intriguing Olivenza, 27km southwest of Badajoz, clings to its Portuguese heritage – it has only been Spanish since 1801. The town's cobbled ancient core is distinctive for its whitewashed houses, impressive churches and castle, typical turreted defensive walls and taste for beautiful blue-and-white ceramic tilework, which you'll spot immediately on street signs.

🛏 Sleeping & Eating

Hotel Palacio de Arteaga　　　　HOTEL €€
(☑924 49 11 29; www.palacioarteaga.com; Calle Moreno Nieto 5; s €55-70, d €66-119, incl breakfast; ❄ 🛜) Bursting with colour and character, this gorgeous historical conversion in the heart of town features comfy, spacious, modern rooms around an elaborate patio. Made-to-order breakfasts are a wonderful touch.

Casa Maila　　　　EXTREMADURAN, TAPAS €€
(☑924 49 15 05; Calle Colón 3; tapas €3-4, mains €12-18; ⊙noon-midnight Tue-Sun, to 4pm Mon) Refreshingly down to earth, friendly Casa Maila is excellent for both delicious tapas and *raciones* and more elaborate, mostly meaty mains, on the edge of bubbly Plaza de España.

ⓘ Information

Oficina de Turismo (☑924 49 01 51; www.olivenzavirtual.com; Plaza Santa María del Castillo 15; ⊙10am-2pm & 5-7pm Tue-Sat, afternoons Oct-Apr 4-6pm, 10am-2pm Sun all year)

ⓘ Getting There & Away

From the **bus station** (☑924 49 05 31; Calle Avelino Palma Brioa), there are buses to/from Badajoz (€1.88, 25 minutes) almost hourly Monday to Friday and twice on Saturday.

Zafra

POP 16,828

Looking for all the world like an Andalucian *pueblo blanco* (white village), gleaming-white Zafra is a serene, attractive stop along the A66 between Seville and Mérida. Affectionately labelled *'Sevilla la chica'* ('the little Seville') for its similarities with Andalucía's capital, Zafra was originally a Muslim settlement. Its narrow streets are lined with baroque churches, old-fashioned shops, glassed-in balconies and traditional houses decorated by overflowing bougainvillea and hot-pink splashes of geraniums. The newer part of town isn't all that enthralling, but Zafra's historic core is a beauty.

⊙ Sights

Zafra's 15th-century castle, a blend of Gothic, Mudéjar and Renaissance architecture, is now the luxurious Parador de Zafra (p571) and dominates the town. The Plaza Grande and the adjoining Plaza Chica, both beautifully arcaded and bordered by tapas bars, are the places to soak up Zafra life. The southwestern end of Plaza Grande, with its palm trees and centuries-old homes, is one of Extremadura's prettiest. Guarding the western entry point to the old town is the Puerta de Jerez, part of Zafra's 15th-century wall.

Convento de Santa Clara　　　　CONVENT
(☑924 55 14 87; www.museozafra.es; Calle Sevilla 30; ⊙10am-2pm Tue-Sun mid-Jun–mid-Oct, 11am-2pm & 5-6.30pm Tue-Sun mid-Oct–mid-Jun) FREE Tucked away off Zafra's main shopping street, this imposing 15th-century Mudéjar convent was originally designed as a holy resting place for the powerful local Feria dynasty. It's still a working convent with cloistered nuns. Visitors can, however, explore the detailed on-site museum, with its interesting (Spanish-language) insights into the sisters' lives and Zafra's history. Visits include the gilded chapel, where Jane Dormer, (1538-1612) lady-in-waiting to Mary I of England and wife of the first Duque de Feria, is buried.

Bodegas Medina　　　　WINERY
(☑924 57 50 60; www.bodegasmedina.net; Calle Cestería 4; tour without/with tasting €6/12; ⊙tours

10.30am & noon Mon-Fri, 11am & 12.30pm Sat & Sun) Extremadura's only wine DO (Denominación de Origen) is Ribera del Guadiana. On the western fringe of Zafra's old town, you can tour and taste on 45- to 90-minute visits at one of the DO's most prominent southern wineries, Bodegas Medina, which produces reds, whites, rosés and cava. Bookings recommended.

Iglesia de la Candelaria CHURCH

(Calle Tetuán; ⊙11am-2pm & 6-7pm Tue-Thu, 11am-2pm Fri, 11am-2pm & 5-7pm Sat) FREE This 16th-century church is worth a look for its fine altarpieces, featuring works by Francisco de Zurbarán.

⭐ Festivals & Events

Feria de San Miguel FIESTA

(Feria Internacional Ganadera; www.figzafra.es) Zafra's big annual fiesta happens in conjunction with the town's renowned cattle fair, which has been going strong since the 15th century. Late September to early October.

🛏 Sleeping

⭐ Hotel Plaza Grande HOTEL €

(📞924 56 31 63; www.hotelplazagrande.es; Calle Pasteleros 2; s €30-36, d €45, incl breakfast; 🅿✳🎧) Right on the Plaza Grande, this friendly, sparkling gem of a hotel is an excellent deal. Elegant modern-rustic decor accentuates terracotta with cream paintwork, exposed brick, floral prints and soft pastels. Go for room 108, with its corner balconies overlooking the plaza; room 208 is the same but with windows instead of balconies. The lively downstairs cafe-restaurant (📞924 56 31 63; www.hotelplazagrande.es; Calle Pasteleros 2; tapas €4.50-6, raciones €9-18, mains €14-20; ⊙12.30pm-midnight; 🎧🍴) is reliably good.

Parador de Zafra HISTORIC HOTEL €€

(📞924 55 45 40; www.parador.es; Plaza Corazón de María 7; r €80-100, ste €120-180; 🅿✳🎧🏊) They say a person's home is their castle: at this gorgeously restored 15th-century fortress, it's the reverse. Beyond the exquisite marble-pillared Renaissance patio, airy rooms come richly decorated with burgundy-coloured fabrics and antiques. Ivy and turrets surround the secluded pool, and the restaurant is excellent. Guests can climb up to the battlements for Zafra's finest views.

Hotel Huerta Honda HOTEL €€

(📞924 55 41 00; www.hotelhuertahonda. com; Calle López Asme 30; s/d/superior/ste €55/62/85/120; 🅿➧✳🎧🏊) Whichever room type you go for, the rich-orange-and-yellow Huerta Honda is a classy choice, with top-notch service. Standards and superiors are bland but comfy, contemporary and tastefully styled in browns and beiges. 'Gran Clase' rooms are sumptuous suites with neo-Moorish decor, wood-carved ceilings, four-poster beds, tiled bathrooms and antiques. Ask for a room overlooking the bougainvillea-draped courtyard and Zafra's castle.

🍴 Eating

Gastro-Bar Baraka TAPAS €

(Plaza Grande 20; tapas €3-4, raciones €6.50-10; ⊙7pm-midnight Mon-Wed, 7pm-3am Thu, 1pm-3am Fri-Sun) Gastro-Bar Baraka adds a touch of urban flair to Plaza Grande's classic charm. Dishes range from creative *tostas* (toasted bread with toppings; €6.50) and outstanding tapas to more substantial *raciones* (Torta del Casar, *jamón*, honey-fried aubergine), meat-focused mains and in-season mushroom specials. Enjoy on a balmy summer evening with a glass of local wine in the lamplit plaza – bliss.

⭐ La Rebotica SPANISH €€

(📞924 55 42 89; www.lareboticazafra.com; Calle Boticas 12; mains €15-21; ⊙1.30-4pm & 8.30pm-midnight Tue-Sat, 1.30-4pm Sun; 🎧) This refined restaurant in the heart of Zafra's old town delivers with its traditional meaty menu and subtly sophisticated setting among wall mirrors, leather chairs and yellow-washed walls. Dine on elegantly prepared *rabo de toro* (oxtail) and five different pork dishes, plus a few seafood or vegie options; finish with outstanding desserts such as chocolate mousse with strawberry sorbet. Reservations recommended.

Parador de Zafra SPANISH €€

(📞924 55 45 40; www.parador.es; Plaza Corazón de María 7; mains €12-20, set menu €25; ⊙7-11am, 1.30-4pm & 8.30-11pm mid-Dec–Oct) For an intimate, upscale dinner, enjoy refined *extremeño* cooking and a selection of seasonal *menús* overlooking the magnificent Renaissance courtyard inside Zafra's revamped 15th-century castle.

MONESTERIO

Since the completion of the A66 motorway, many bypassed towns have disappeared into quiet obscurity, but not Monesterio: this is one of Spain's (and certainly Extremadura's) most celebrated sources of *jamón* (ham).

Museo del Jamón (☑ 924 51 67 37; www.museodeljamondemonesterio.com; Paseo de Extremadura 314; ☉ 9.30am-2pm & 5.30-8pm Mon-Sat, 10am-2pm Sun, afternoons Mon-Sat Oct-Jun 4.30-7pm; Ⓟ) Occupying pride of place at the southern end of Monesterio, the excellent Museo del Jamón is arguably the best of its kind in Spain. Displays, interactive exhibits and videos starring local ham producers (all in Spanish) take visitors through the process of *jamón* production, from types of Iberian pigs and their ideal habitats to the *matanza* (killing of the pigs) and the curing process. English-language audioguides provided.

Getting There & Away

Three to seven buses run daily between Monesterio and Zafra (€3.59, 40 minutes).

🛍 Shopping

Joaquín Luna   FOOD

(☑ 924 55 05 37; www.joaquinluna.com; Plaza de España 10; ☉10am-2pm & 5-8pm Mon-Fri, 10am-1.30pm Sat) An outlet for one of Extremadura's well-respected producers of *jamón* and other cured meats, plus local cheeses. Also does tasty €1 *pulguitas* (mini filled rolls) packed with *jamón* or Torta del Casar.

ℹ Information

Oficina de Turismo (☑ 924 55 10 36; www.visitzafra.com; Plaza de España; ☉10am-2pm & 5.30-7.30pm Mon-Fri, 10am-2pm Sat & Sun, afternoons Mon-Fri Oct-May 4.30-6.30pm) On the southern edge of the old town.

ℹ Getting There & Away

Zafra's **bus station** (☑ 924 55 39 07; Carretera Badajoz-Granada 4) is 1km northeast of the old town. Destinations include the following:

Badajoz (€6.69, two hours, four to nine daily)

Cáceres (€10, 1¾ to 2¼ hours, six daily)

Mérida (€5.30, 1¼ hours, four to 10 daily)

Seville (€12, 1¾ hours, four to six daily)

Around Zafra

From Zafra, roads head southwest into northern Huelva province (Andalucía) through the rolling Sierra de Aracena and southeast into the Parque Natural Sierra Norte de Sevilla (Andalucía).

Quiet **Burguillos del Cerro**, 19km southwest of Zafra, is overlooked by a 15th-century **castle** atop a grassy hill.

Fregenal de la Sierra, 40km southwest of Zafra, is appealing for its churches, noble homes, bullring and 13th-century castle, **Castillo Templario** (Plaza de la Constitución, Frenegal de la Sierra; ☉10am-2.45pm & 5-7pm) FREE.

Walled, hilly and handsome **Jerez de los Caballeros**, 42km southwest of Zafra, was a cradle of conquistadors. Attractions here include the 13th-century **Templars' castle** (Plaza del Ayuntamiento, Jerez de los Caballeros; ☉8am-10pm) FREE, plus several stunning churches, three with towers emulating Seville's Giralda.

About 19km northwest of Zafra, little **Feria** rose to fame in the 14th century as home of the formidable local Feria dynasty. With its sensational hilltop perch, the refurbished 15th-century **castle** (☑ 685 147292; Feria; adult/child €4/2; ☉11.30am-1.30pm & 5.30-8.30pm mid-Mar–mid-Sep, 11am-2pm & 4-6pm mid-Sep–mid-Mar) is a regional highlight.

ℹ Information

Oficina de Turismo de Frenegal de la Sierra (☑ 924 70 00 00; www.frenegaldelasierra.es; Calle El Rollo 1, Frenegal de la Sierra; ☉10am-2.45pm & 6-8pm Jul-Aug, 10am-2.45pm & 5-7pm Sep-Jun)

Oficina de Turismo de Jerez de los Caballeros (☑ 924 73 03 72; www.jerezcaballeros.es; Plaza de la Constitución 4, Jerez de los Caballeros; ☉8am-3pm & 5-7pm Mon-Fri, 9.30am-2.30pm Sat & Sun Jul-Sep; 4.30-6.30pm Mon-Fri Oct-Jun)

Badajoz

POP 149,892

Just 5km east of Portugal, the scruffy, sprawling, industrial city of Badajoz is hardly Extremadura's prettiest or most interesting, but it's a lively enough stop, and the historic centre and hilltop Alcazaba are well worth a visit if you're in the area.

◉ Sights

★ Alcazaba
FORTRESS

(⊙24hr; P) FREE Badajoz' majestic 12th-century, 8-hectare Alcazaba, the largest in Spain, lords over the city above the Plaza Alta. Guarding all is the Torre de Espantaperros (⊙by guided tour 10.30am 1st Sat of month) FREE (Scare-Dogs Tower), symbol of Badajoz, constructed by the Moors and topped by a 16th-century Mudéjar bell tower wrapped around an older original. Within the fort, a refurbished Renaissance palace houses the Museo Arqueológico Provincial (☑924 00 19 08; Plaza José Álvarez y Sáenz de Buruaga; ⊙10am-3pm Tue-Sun) FREE, crammed with artefacts from prehistoric to Roman, Islamic and medieval Christian periods.

Plaza Alta
SQUARE

At the top of the old town, beneath the walls of the Alcazaba, is the unusual Plaza Alta, dating to 1681, framed on its east side by the strikingly bold, deep-red-and-white, Moorish-inspired Casas Coloradas.

⚑ Festivals & Events

Carnaval
CARNIVAL

(www.carnavalbadajoz.es) Held in February, Badajoz' colour-bursting Carnaval celebrations and street parties have been kicking on since (at least) the 19th century and are among Spain's most elaborate and popular.

⟷ Sleeping & Eating

Hotel San Marcos
HOTEL €

(☑924 22 95 18; www.hotelsanmarcos.es; Calle Meléndez Valdés 53; s €32-51, d €37-56; P ❄ 🛜) Polished service and excellent facilities make this superfriendly, vanilla-scented city-centre hotel top value. Rooms are a good size, with plenty of light, plus fridges, safes and, for some, balconies. Bathrooms are sleek and modern; many feature hydromassage showers.

NH Gran Hotel Casino Extremadura
HOTEL €€

(☑924 28 44 02; www.nh-hotels.com; Avenida Adolfo Díaz Ambrona 11; r €57-118; P ❄ 🛜) Several of Badajoz' classiest hotel picks are just across the Río Guadiana, a short walk west of the old town. This swish, sprawling complex sports modern, elegant, business-style rooms decked out in smart dark woods, with desks and in-room espresso machines. It offers an on-site spa and gym, plus a friendly yet professional welcome.

El Claustro
TAPAS €€

(☑924 20 17 21; Plaza de Cervantes 13A; tapas €2.50-4, raciones €8-15; ⊙noon-midnight) El Claustro's stylish stone-clad interior, filled with edgy artwork and gold-trimmed mirrors, is fronted by a lively tapas bar serving generous, innovative snacks. The chandelier-lit dining room behind dishes up larger portions in (slightly) more formal surrounds and there are a few open-air tables out on Plaza de Cervantes.

ℹ Information

Oficina de Turismo Casas Mudéjares (☑924 29 13 69; www.turismobadajoz.es; Plaza de San José 18; ⊙10am-2pm & 5-7.30pm Mon-Fri, 10am-2pm Sat) Right below the Alcazaba.

Oficina Municipal de Turismo (☑924 22 49 81; www.turismobadajoz.es; Paseo de San Juan; ⊙10am-2pm & 5.30-8pm Mon-Sat, 10am-2pm Sun, afternoons Mon-Sat Oct-Jun 5-7.30pm) Just off the main Plaza de España.

ℹ Getting There & Away

Buses leave from the **bus station** (☑924 25 86 61; Calle José Rebollo López), 1.5km south of the main Plaza de España.

DESTINATION	FARE	DURATION	FREQUENCY
Cáceres	€5.15	1¼hr	3-6 daily
Lisbon	€25	2½hr	2-3 daily
Madrid (normal/ express)	€31/ 43	4¾/5¾hr	5/2 daily
Mérida	€5.14	50min	3-7 daily
Seville	€17	3½hr	2-4 daily
Zafra	€6.69	1¼hr	5-7 daily

Seville & Andalucía's Hill Towns

Why Go?

A parched region fertile with culture, a conquered land that went on to conquer, a fiercely traditional place that has accepted rapid modernisation: western Andalucía has multiple faces. Here, in the cradle of quintessential Spain, the questions are often as intriguing as the answers. Who first concocted flamenco? How did tapas become a national obsession? Could Cádiz be Europe's oldest settlement? Are those really Christopher Columbus' bones inside Seville cathedral? And where on earth did the audacious builders of Córdoba's Mezquita get their divine inspiration from? Putting together the missing pieces of the puzzle is what makes travel in the region the glorious adventure that it is. Seville is western Andalucía's Holy Grail, Córdoba deserves more than a day trip, while the white towns will lure you into quieter rural areas and perhaps inspire you to visit the region's only national park amid the bird-rich wetlands of Doñana.

Best Places to Eat

➜ La Pepona (p595)

➜ Bar-Restaurante Eslava (p596)

➜ Jesús Carrión (p609)

➜ El Jardín del Califa (p634)

Best Places to Sleep

➜ V... (p633)

➜ Hotel Casa 1800 (p592)

➜ El Molino del Santo (p638)

➜ Casa Olea (p652)

When to Go

Seville

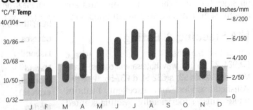

°C/°F Temp	Rainfall Inches/mm
40/104 —	— 8/200
30/86 —	— 6/150
20/68 —	— 4/100
10/50 —	— 2/50
0/32 —	— 0

J F M A M J J A S O N D

Apr Sombre Semana Santa processions are followed by the exuberance of the spring fairs.

May Relatively cool weather. Many towns and villages celebrate *romerías* (pilgrimages).

Late Sep The heat diminishes, the crowds go home – but it's still warm enough for the beach.

SEVILLE

POP 703,000 / ELEV 30M

Some cities have looks, other cities have personality. The *sevillanos* – lucky devils – get both, courtesy of their flamboyant, charismatic, ever-evolving Andalucian metropolis founded, according to myth, 3000 years ago by the Greek god Hercules. Drenched for most of the year in spirit-enriching sunlight, this is a city of feelings as much as sights, with different seasons prompting vastly contrasting moods: solemn for Semana Santa, flirtatious for the spring fiesta and soporific for the gasping heat of summer.

Like all great cities, Seville has historical layers. Roman ruins testify the settlement's earliest face, memories of the Moorish era flicker like medieval engravings in the Santa Cruz quarter, while the riverside Arenal reeks of lost colonial glory. Yet, one of the most remarkable things about modern Seville is its ability to adapt and etch fresh new brushstrokes onto an ancient canvas.

History

Founded by the Romans, the city of Seville didn't really flower until the Moorish Almoravid period, which began in 1085. They were replaced by the Almohads in the 12th century; Caliph Yacub Yusuf made Seville capital of the Almohad realm and built a great mosque where Seville's cathedral now stands. But Almohad power dwindled after the disastrous defeat of Las Navas de Tolosa in 1212, and Castilla's Fernando III (El Santo; the Saint) went on to capture Seville in 1248.

Fernando brought 24,000 settlers to Seville and by the 14th century it was the most important Castilian city. Seville's biggest break was Columbus' discovery of the Americas in 1492. In 1503 the city was awarded an official monopoly on Spanish trade with the new-found continent. It rapidly became one of the biggest, richest and most cosmopolitan cities on earth.

But it was not to last. A plague in 1649 caused the death of half the city's population, and as the 17th century wore on, the Río Guadalquivir became more silted and less navigable. In 1717 the Casa de la Contratación (Contracting House; the government office controlling commerce with the Americas) was transferred to Cádiz.

The beginnings of industry in the mid-19th century saw the first bridge across the Guadalquivir, the Puente de Triana (or Puente de Isabel II), built in 1852, and the old Almohad walls were knocked down in 1869 to let the city expand. In 1936 Seville fell very quickly to the Nationalists at the start of the Spanish Civil War, despite resistance in working-class areas (which brought savage reprisals).

Things have been looking up since the 1980s when Seville was named capital of the newly autonomous Andalucía (over the last quarter-century a number of provinces in Spain have been given a certain amount of autonomy from Madrid). Seville's economy was steadily improving with a mix of tourism, commerce, technology and industry in the early 2000s. Then, in 2008, the financial crisis hit the city with a sharp jolt, as it did in the rest of Andalucía. Although big metropolitan projects such as the Metropol Parasol continued, the economic situation hit rock bottom in 2012 with sky-high unemployment and serious recession. The last three years have been more optimistic with growth returning to the Spanish economy, although unemployment in Seville province still hovers stubbornly above 30%.

◉ Sights

◉ Catedral & Around

Catedral & Giralda　　　　　CATHEDRAL
(Map p584; www.catedraldesevilla.es; adult/child €9/free; ⊙11am-3.30pm Mon, 11am-5pm Tue-Sat, 2.30-6pm Sun) Seville's immense cathedral, one of the largest Christian churches in the world, is awe-inspiring in its scale and sheer majesty. It stands on the site of the great 12th-century Almohad mosque, with the mosque's minaret (the Giralda) still towering beside it.

After Seville fell to the Christians in 1248, the mosque was used as a church until 1401. Then, in view of its decaying state, the church authorities decided to knock it down and start again. Legend has it that they wanted to construct a church so large future generations will think they were mad. When it was completed in 1502 after one hundred years of hard labour, the Catedral de Santa María de la Sede, as it is officially known, was (and remains) the largest church in the world by volume and pretty much defines the word 'Gothic'. It is also a veritable art gallery replete with notable works by Zurbarán, Murillo, Goya and others.

Seville & Andalucía's Hill Towns Highlights

❶ Jerez de la Frontera (p621) Watching a spontaneous flamenco performance in a backstreet bar in one of flamenco's true homes.

❷ Seville (p575) Exploring Andalucía's most beguiling city with its fabulous monuments, creative tapas bars and passionate spirit.

❸ Córdoba (p639) Tackling the tangle of Moorish streets in the *judería* on your way to the sublime Mezquita.

❹ Zuheros (p651) Following the kilometre markers along the Vía Verde de la Subbética on your way to this spectacular white town.

❺ Sanlúcar de Barrameda (p619) Realising you quite like sherry if it's accompanied by fresh-from-the-ocean seafood in the town's Bajo de Guía.

❻ Vía Verde de la Sierra (p633) Seeing griffon vultures nesting on high crags along this fantastic route.

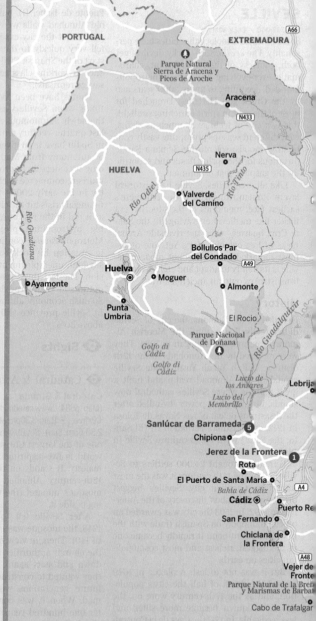

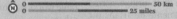

Seville

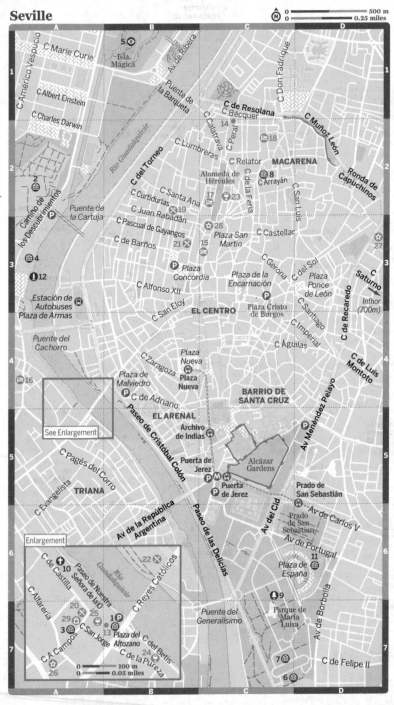

N

0 — 500 m
0 — 0.25 miles

A **B** **C** **D**

C Marie Curie
C Américo Vespucio
C Albert Einstein
C Charles Darwin

5

Isla
Mágica

Puente de
la Barqueta

Av de Ribera

C de Resolana

C Bécquer
14
C Peral
18

MACARENA

Río Guadalquivir

C del Torneo

C Lumbreras

C Calatrava

C Relator

8
C Arrayán

Ronda de
Capuchinos

C Muñoz León

C de Don Fadrique

2

Camino de
los Descubrimientos

Puente de
la Cartuja

C Santa Ana
C Curtidurías
C Juan Rabadán
19
C Pascual de Gayangos
21
C de Barños
15

Alameda de
Hércules
17
23
C de la Feria

28

Plaza San
Martín

C San Luis

C Castellar

C Gerona

C del Sol

Plaza
Ponce
de León

27

C
Saturno

4
12

Plaza
Concordia
C Alfonso XII

C San Eloy

Plaza de la
Encarnación

Plaza Cristo
de Burgos

C Santiago

C de Recaredo

Inthor
(700m)

3

Estación de
Autobuses
Plaza de Armas

EL CENTRO

C Imperial

C Águilas

C de Luis
Montoto

4

Puente del
Cachorro

16

Plaza de
Malviedro

C Zaragoza
C de Adriano

Plaza
Nueva

Plaza
Nueva

BARRIO DE
SANTA CRUZ

Av de Menéndez Pelayo

Paseo de Cristóbal Colón

EL ARENAL

Archivo
de Indias

Alcázar
Gardens

5

C Pagés del Corro

TRIANA

C Evangelista

Puerta de
Jerez

Puerta
de Jerez

Prado de
San Sebastián

Prado
de San
Sebastián

Av del Cid

Av de Carlos V

6

Av de la República
Argentina

Paseo de las Delicias

Av de Portugal

11
Plaza de
España

9

Parque de
María Luisa

Av de Borbolla

Enlargement

Río Guadalquivir

22

C de Castilla
10
Paseo de Nuestra
Señora de la O

C Reyes Católicos

Puente del
Generalísimo

C Alfarería
20
25
29
1
3
C San Jorge
13
Plaza del
Altozano

C A Campos
26
C del Betis
24
C de la Pureza

7

7
6
C de Felipe II

0 — 100 m
0 — 0.05 miles

See Enlargement

Seville

➡ **Exterior**

From close up, the bulky exterior of the cathedral with its Gothic embellishments gives hints of the treasures within. Pause to look at the **Puerta del Perdón** on Calle Alemanes, a legacy of the Islamic mosque.

➡ **Sala del Pabellón**

Selected treasures from the cathedral's art collection are exhibited in this room, the first after the ticket office. Much of what's displayed here, as elsewhere in the cathedral, is the work of masters from Seville's 17th-century artistic Golden Age.

➡ **Southern & Northern Chapels**

The chapels along the southern and northern sides of the cathedral hold more riches of sculpture and painting. Near the western end of the northern side is the **Capilla de San Antonio**, housing Murillo's humungous 1656 canvas depicting the vision of St Anthony of Padua. The painting was victim of a daring art heist in 1874.

➡ **Tomb of Christopher Columbus**

Inside the **Puerta del Príncipe** (Door of the Prince) stands the monumental tomb of Christopher Columbus (Cristóbal Colón in Spanish) – the subject of a continuous riddle – containing what were long believed to be the great explorer's bones, brought here from Cuba in 1898.

Columbus died in 1506 in Valladolid, in northern Spain. His remains lay at La Cartuja monastery in Seville before being moved to Hispaniola in 1536. Even though there were suggestions that the bones kept in Seville's cathedral were possibly those of his son Diego (who was buried with his father in Santo Domingo, Hispaniola), recent DNA tests seemed to finally prove that it really is Christopher Columbus lying in that box. Yet, unfortunately, to confuse matters further, the researchers also say that the bones in Santo Domingo could also be real, since Columbus' body was moved several times after his death. It seems that even death couldn't dampen the great explorer's urge to travel.

➡ **Capilla Mayor**

East of the choir is the Capilla Mayor (Main Chapel). Its Gothic retable is the jewel of the cathedral and reckoned to be the biggest altarpiece in the world. Begun by Flemish sculptor Pieter Dancart in 1482 and finished by others in 1564, this sea of gilt and polychromed wood holds more than 1000 carved biblical figures. At the centre of the lowest level is the tiny 13th-century silver-plated cedar image of the Virgen de la Sede (Virgin of the See), patron of the cathedral.

Seville Cathedral

In 1402, the inspired architects of Seville set out on one of the most grandiose building projects in medieval history. Their aim was to shock and amaze future generations with the size and magnificence of the building. It took until 1506 to complete the project, but 500 years later Seville Cathedral is still the largest Gothic cathedral in the world.

WHAT TO LOOK FOR

To avoid getting lost, orient yourself by the main highlights. Directly inside the southern (main) entrance is the grand **Tomb of Columbus ❶**. Turn right here and head into the southeastern corner to uncover some major art treasures: a Goya in the Sacristía de los Cálices, a Zurbarán in the **Sacristía Mayor ❷**, and Murillo's shining *Immaculada* in the Sala Capitular. Skirt the cathedral's eastern wall taking a look inside the **Capilla Real ❸** with its important royal tombs. By now it's impossible to avoid the lure of the **Capilla Mayor ❹** with its fantastical altarpiece. Hidden over in the northwest corner is the **Capilla de San Antonio ❺** with a legendary Murillo. That huge doorway almost in front of you is the rarely opened **Puerta de la Asunción ❻**. Make for the **Giralda ❼** next, stealing admiring looks at the high, vaulted ceiling on the way. After looking down on the cathedral's immense footprint, descend and depart via the **Patio de los Naranjos ❽**.

TOP TIPS

» **Pace yourself** Don't visit the Alcázar and Cathedral on the same day. There is far too much to take in.

» **Viewpoints** Take time to admire the cathedral from the outside. It's particularly stunning at night from the Plaza Virgen de los Reyes, and from across the river in Triana.

Capilla Mayor
Behold! The cathedral's main focal point contains its greatest treasure, a magnificent gold-plated altarpiece depicting various scenes in the life of Christ. It constitutes the life's work of one man, Flemish artist Pieter Dancart.

Patio de los Naranjos
Inhale the perfume of 60 Sevillan orange trees in a cool patio bordered by fortress-like walls – a surviving remnant of the original 12th-century mosque. Exit is gained via the horseshoe-shaped Puerta del Perdón.

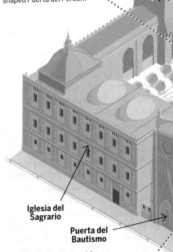

Puerta del Perdón

Iglesia del Sagrario

Puerta del Bautismo

Puerta de la Asunción
Located on the western side of the cathedral and also known as the Puerta Mayor, these huge, rarely opened doors are pushed back during Semana Santa to allow solemn processions of Catholic *hermandades* (brotherhoods) to pass through.

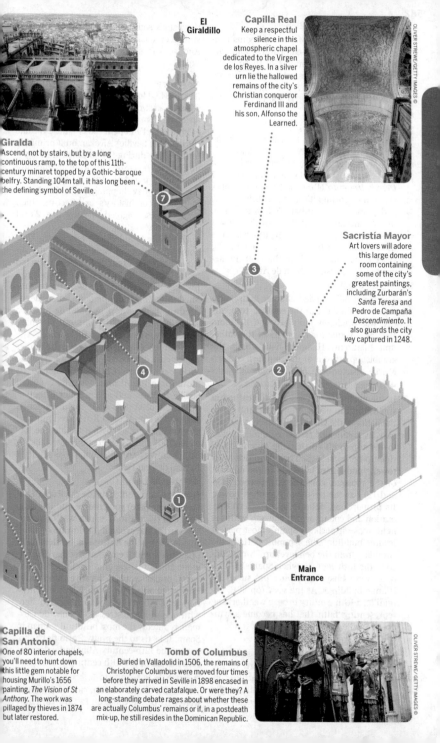

El Giraldillo

Capilla Real
Keep a respectful silence in this atmospheric chapel dedicated to the Virgen de los Reyes. In a silver urn lie the hallowed remains of the city's Christian conqueror Ferdinand III and his son, Alfonso the Learned.

Giralda
Ascend, not by stairs, but by a long continuous ramp, to the top of this 11th-century minaret topped by a Gothic-baroque belfry. Standing 104m tall, it has long been the defining symbol of Seville.

Sacristía Mayor
Art lovers will adore this large domed room containing some of the city's greatest paintings, including Zurbarán's *Santa Teresa* and Pedro de Campaña *Descendimiento*. It also guards the city key captured in 1248.

Main Entrance

Capilla de San Antonio
One of 80 interior chapels, you'll need to hunt down this little gem notable for housing Murillo's 1656 painting, *The Vision of St Anthony*. The work was pillaged by thieves in 1874 but later restored.

Tomb of Columbus
Buried in Valladolid in 1506, the remains of Christopher Columbus were moved four times before they arrived in Seville in 1898 encased in an elaborately carved catafalque. Or were they? A long-standing debate rages about whether these are actually Columbus' remains or if, in a postdeath mix-up, he still resides in the Dominican Republic.

OLIVER STREWE/GETTY IMAGES ©

➡ Sacristía de los Cálices

South of the Capilla Mayor are rooms containing some of the cathedral's main art treasures. The westernmost of these is the Sacristy of the Chalices, where Francisco de Goya's painting of the Seville martyrs, *Santas Justa y Rufina* (1817), hangs above the altar.

➡ Sacristía Mayor

This large room with a finely carved stone dome was created between 1528 and 1547: the arch over its portal has carvings of 16th-century foods. Pedro de Campaña's 1547 *Descendimiento* (Descent from the Cross), above the central altar at the southern end, and Francisco de Zurbarán's *Santa Teresa,* to its right, are two of the cathedral's most precious paintings. The room's centrepiece is the Custodia de Juan de Arfe, a huge 475kg silver monstrance made in the 1580s by Renaissance metalsmith Juan de Arfe.

➡ Sala Capitular

The beautifully domed chapter house, also called the Cabildo, in the southeastern corner, was originally built between 1558 and 1592 as a venue for meetings of the cathedral hierarchy. Hanging high above the archbishop's throne at the southern end is a Murillo masterpiece, *La inmaculada.*

➡ Giralda

In the northeastern corner of the cathedral you'll find the passage for the climb up to the belfry of the Giralda. The ascent is quite easy, as a series of ramps goes all the way to the top, built so that the guards could ride up on horseback. The decorative brick tower stands 104m tall and was the minaret of the mosque, constructed between 1184 and 1198 at the height of Almohad power. Its proportions, delicate brick-pattern decoration and colour, which changes with the light, make it perhaps Spain's most perfect Islamic building. The top-most parts of the Giralda – from the bell level up – were added in the 16th century, when Spanish Christians were busy 'improving on' surviving Islamic buildings. At the very top is El Giraldillo, a 16th-century bronze weathervane representing 'faith' that has become a symbol of Seville.

➡ Patio de los Naranjos

Outside the cathedral's northern side, this patio was originally the courtyard of the mosque. It's planted with *66 naranjos* (orange trees), and a Visigothic fountain sits in the centre. Hanging from the ceiling in the patio's southeastern corner is a replica stuffed crocodile – the original was a gift to Alfonso X from the Sultan of Egypt around 1260.

★ Alcázar   CASTLE
(Map p584; ☑ tours 954 50 23 24; www.alcazarsevilla.org; adult/child €9.50/free; ☉ 9.30am-7pm Apr-Sep, to 5pm Oct-Mar) If heaven really *does* exist, then let's hope it looks a little bit like the inside of Seville's Alcázar. Built primarily in the 1300s during the so-called 'dark ages' in Europe, the castle's intricate architecture is anything but dark. Indeed, compared to our modern-day shopping malls, the Alcázar marks one of history's architectural high points. Unesco agreed, making it a World Heritage site in 1987.

Originally founded as a fort for the Cordoban governors of Seville in 913, the Alcázar has been expanded or reconstructed many times in its 11 centuries of existence. In the 11th century Seville's prosperous Muslim *taifa* (small kingdom) rulers developed the original fort by building a palace called Al-Muwarak (the Blessed) in what's now the western part of the Alcázar. The 12th-century Almohad rulers added another palace east of this, around what's now the Patio del Crucero. Christian Fernando III moved into the Alcázar when he captured Seville in 1248, and several later Christian monarchs used it as their main residence. Fernando's son Alfonso X replaced much of the Almohad palace with a Gothic one. Between 1364 and 1366 Pedro I created the Alcázar's crown jewel, the sumptuous Mudéjar Palacio de Don Pedro.

➡ Patio del León

From the ticket office inside the Puerta del León (Lion Gate) you emerge into the Patio del León (Lion Patio), which was the garrison yard of the original Al-Muwarak palace. Just off here is the Sala de la Justicia (Hall of Justice), with beautiful Mudéjar plasterwork and an *artesonado* (ceiling of interlaced beams with decorative insertions). This room was built in the 1340s by Christian king Alfonso XI, who disported here with one of his mistresses, Leonor de Guzmán, reputedly the most beautiful woman in Spain. It leads to the pretty Patio del Yeso, part of the 12th-century Almohad palace reconstructed in the 19th century.

➡ Patio de la Montería

The rooms on the western side of this patio were part of the Casa de la Contratación

(Contracting House), founded by the Catholic Monarchs in 1503 to control trade with Spain's American colonies. The **Salón del Almirante** (Admiral's Hall) houses 19th- and 20th-century paintings showing historical events and personages associated with Seville. The room off its northern end has an international collection of beautiful, elaborate fans. The **Sala de Audiencias** (Audience Hall) is hung with tapestry representations of the shields of Spanish admirals and Alejo Fernández' landmark 1530s painting *Virgen de los mareantes* (Virgin of the Navigators).

➡ **Cuarto Real Alto**

The Alcázar is still a royal palace. In 1995 it staged the wedding feast of Infanta Elena, daughter of King Juan Carlos I, after her marriage in Seville's cathedral. The **Cuarto Real Alto** (Upper Royal Quarters), the rooms used by the Spanish royal family on their visits to Seville, are open for (heavily subscribed) tours (€4.50) several times a day; some are in Spanish, some in English. It's essential to book ahead for a place. Highlights of the tour include the 14th-century **Salón de Audiencias**, still the monarch's reception room, and Pedro I's bedroom, with marvellous Mudéjar tiles and plasterwork.

➡ **Palacio de Don Pedro**

Posterity owes Pedro I a big thank you for creating this palace (also called the Palacio Mudéjar), the single most stunning architectural feature in Seville.

Though at odds with many of his fellow Christians, Pedro had a long-standing alliance with the Muslim emir of Granada, Mohammed V, the man responsible for much of the Alhambra's finest decoration. So in 1364, when Pedro decided to build a new palace within the Alcázar, Mohammed sent along many of his best artisans. These were joined by others from Seville and Toledo. Their work, drawing on the Islamic traditions of the Almohads and caliphal Córdoba, is a unique synthesis of Iberian Islamic art.

Inscriptions on the palace's facade, facing the Patio de la Montería, encapsulate the collaborative nature of the enterprise. While one announces in Spanish that the building's creator was 'the very high, noble and conquering Don Pedro, by the grace of God king of Castilla and León', another proclaims repeatedly in Arabic that 'there is no conqueror but Allah'.

At the heart of the palace is the wonderful **Patio de las Doncellas** (Patio of the Maidens), surrounded by beautiful arches, plasterwork and tiling. The sunken garden in the centre was uncovered by archaeologists in 2004 from beneath a 16th-century marble covering.

The **Alcoba Real** (Royal Quarters), on the northern side of the patio, has stunningly beautiful ceilings and wonderful plaster- and tilework. Its rear room was probably the monarch's summer bedroom.

From here you can move west into the little **Patio de las Muñecas** (Patio of the Dolls), the heart of the palace's private quarters, featuring delicate Granada-style decoration; indeed, plasterwork was actually brought here from the Alhambra in the 19th century, when the mezzanine and top gallery were added for Queen Isabel II. The **Cuarto del Príncipe** (Prince's Room), to its north, has a superb wooden cupola ceiling trying to re-create a starlit night sky.

The spectacular **Salón de Embajadores** (Hall of Ambassadors), at the western end of the Patio de las Doncellas, was the throne room of Pedro I's palace. The room's fabulous wooden dome of multiple star patterns, symbolising the universe, was added in 1427. The dome's shape gives the room its alternative name, **Sala de la Media Naranja** (Hall of the Half Orange).

On the western side of the Salón de Embajadores, the beautiful Arco de Pavones, named after its peacock motifs, leads into the **Salón del Techo de Felipe II**, with a Renaissance ceiling (1589–91).

➡ **Salones de Carlos V**

Reached via a staircase at the southeastern corner of the Patio de las Doncellas, these are the much remodelled rooms of Alfonso X's 13th-century Gothic palace. The rooms are now named after the 16th-century Spanish king Carlos I, using his title as Holy Roman Emperor, Charles V.

➡ **Patio del Crucero**

This patio outside the Salones de Carlos V was originally the upper storey of the patio of the 12th-century Almohad palace. Initially it consisted only of raised walkways along the four sides and two cross-walkways that met in the middle. Below grew orange trees, whose fruit could be plucked at hand height by the lucky folk strolling along the walkways. The patio's lower level was built over in the 18th century after earthquake damage.

SEVILLE & ANDALUCÍA'S HILL TOWNS

Central Seville

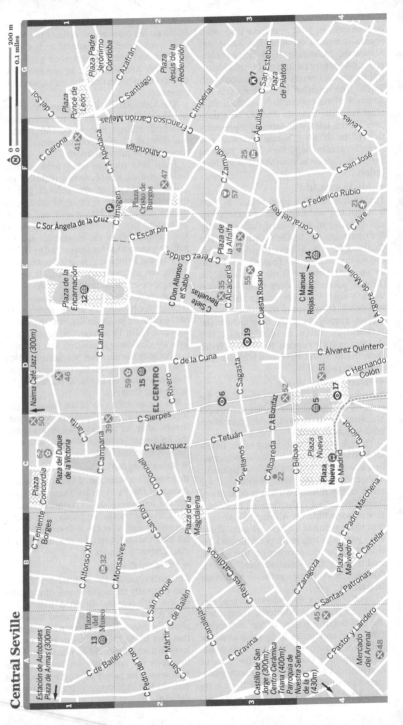

0 0 200 m
0 0.1 miles

Estación de Autobuses
Plaza de Armas (300m)

Naíma Café Jazz (300m)

C del Sol

Plaza Ponce de León

Plaza Padre Jerónimo Córdoba

C Azafrán

C Santiago

Plaza Jesús de la Redención

C Francisco Carrión Mejías

C Imperial

41

C Gerona

C Apodaca

C A Apodaca

C Alhóndiga

7

C San Esteban

Plaza de Pilatos

C Águilas

C Levíes

25

C Zamudio

C San José

57

C Federico Rubio

21

C Aire

C Corral del Rey

Plaza Cristo de Burgos

47

C Imagen

C Sor Ángela de la Cruz

C Escarpín

C Pérez Galdós

Plaza de la Alfalfa

43

C Argote de Molina

Plaza de la Encarnación

12

C Laraña

Don Alonso el Sabio

C Siete Revueltas

35

C Alcaicería

55

C Cuesta Rosario

14

C Manuel Rojas Marcos

19

C de la Cuna

C Sagasta

51

C Álvarez Quintero

C Hernando Colón

46

59

15

EL CENTRO

C Rivero

6

C Sierpes

52

5

17

C Tetuán

C A Bonifaz

C Bilbao

C Madrid

Plaza Nueva

50

39

C Tarifa

C Campana

Plaza del Duque de la Victoria

Plaza de la Concordia

62

C Teniente Borges

C Velázquez

C Jovellanos

C Albareda

22

Plaza Nueva

C J G Vinci

C Padre Marchena

C O'Donnell

C León

C Alfonso XII

32

C Monsalves

C San Roque

Plaza de la Magdalena

C Reyes Católicos

Plaza de Malviedro

C Castelar

Plaza del Museo

13

C de Bailén

C P Mártir

C de Bailén

C Canalejas

C Gravina

C Santas Patronas

C Zaragoza

45

C de Bailén

C Pedro del Toro

C San Eloy

Castillo de San Jorge (300m);
Centro Cerámica
Triana (400m);
Parroquia de
Nuestra Señora
de la O (430m)

Mercado del Arenal

48

C Pastory y Landero

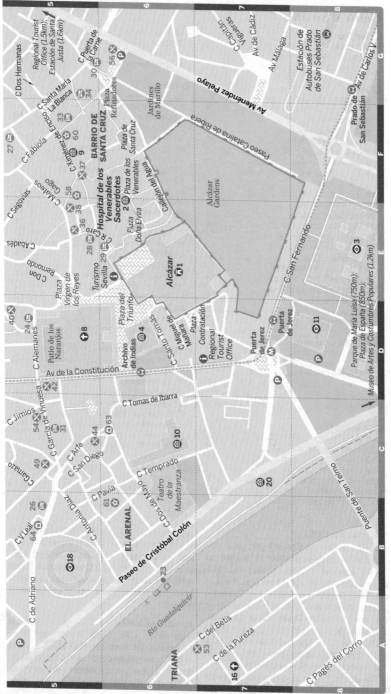

Central Seville

➡ Gardens & Exit

From the Salones de Carlos V you can go out into the Alcázar's large somnolent gardens. Formal gardens with pools and fountains sit closest to the palace. From one, the Jardín de la Danza (Garden of the Dance), a passage runs beneath the Salones de Carlos V to the Baños de Doña María de Padilla (María de Padilla Baths). These are the vaults beneath the Patio del Crucero – originally that patio's lower level – with a grotto that replaced the patio's original pool.

The gardens' most arresting feature is the Galería de Grutesco, a raised gallery with porticoes fashioned in the 16th century out of an old Muslim-era wall. There is also a fun hedge maze, which will delight children. The gardens to the east, beyond a long wall, are 20th-century creations, but don't hold that against them – they are heavenly indeed.

Archivo de Indias   MUSEUM
(Map p584; Calle Santo Tomás; ⊙9.30am-4.45pm Mon-Sat, 10am-2pm Sun) **FREE** Housed in the former Casa de la Contratación (Contracting House) on the western side of Plaza del Triunfo, the Archivo de Indias has, since

1785, been the main archive of Spain's American empire, with 80 million pages of documents dating from 1492 to the end of the empire in the 19th century – a most effective statement of Spain's power and influence during its Golden Age.

Barrio de Santa Cruz

Seville's medieval *judería* (Jewish quarter), east of the cathedral and Alcázar, is today a tangle of atmospheric, winding streets and lovely plant-decked plazas perfumed with orange blossom. Among its most characteristic plazas is Plaza de Santa Cruz, which gives the *barrio* (district) its name. Nearby, Plaza de Doña Elvira is perhaps the most romantic small square in Andalucía, especially in the evening.

★ Hospital de los Venerables Sacerdotes   GALLERY

(Map p584; ☎ 954 56 26 96; www.focus.abengoa.es; Plaza de los Venerables 8; adult/child €5.50/2.75, Sun afternoon free; ◷10am-2pm & 4-8pm) Inside this 17th-century baroque mansion once used as a hospice for ageing priests, you'll find one of Seville's greatest and most admirable art collections. The on-site Centro Velázquez was founded in 2007 by the local Focus-Abengoa Foundation with the intention of reviving Seville's erstwhile artistic glory. Its collection of masterpieces anchored by Diego Velázquez' *Santa Rufina* is one of the best and most concise art lessons the city has to offer. The excellent audio commentary explains how medieval darkness morphed into Velázquezian realism.

Centro de Interpretación Judería de Sevilla   MUSEUM

(Map p584; ☎ 954 04 70 89; www.juderiadesevilla.es; Calle Ximenez de Enciso; €6.50; ◷10.30am-3.30pm & 5-8pm Mon-Sat, 10.30am-7pm Sun) A reinterpretation of Seville's weighty Jewish history has been long overdue and what better place to start than in the city's former Jewish quarter. This newish museum is in an old Sephardic Jewish house in the higgledy-piggledy Santa Cruz quarter, the one-time Jewish neighbourhood that never recovered from a brutal pogrom and massacre in 1391. The events of the pogrom and other historical happenings are catalogued inside, along with a few surviving mementos including documents, costumes and books. It's small but poignant.

◉ El Centro

As the name suggests, this is Seville's centre, and the densely packed zone of narrow streets and squares north of the cathedral is the heart of the Seville shopping world, as well as the home of some excellent bars and restaurants.

Casa de la Memoria   CULTURAL CENTRE

(Map p584; ☎ 954 56 06 70; www.casadelamemoria.es; Calle Cuna 6; €3; ◷10.30am-6.30pm) Lucid memories will be hard to shake off after visiting the Casa de la Memoria, especially if you stay for an evening flamenco show. This flamenco cultural centre inhabits the former stables of the adjacent Palacio de la Condesa de Lebrija. A suite of exposition rooms display revolving flamenco exhibits. An exposé of Seville's Cafe Cantantes was showing at last visit. It is the only centre of its kind in Seville.

Museo del Baile Flamenco   MUSEUM

(Map p584; www.museoflamenco.com; Calle Manuel Rojas Marcos 3; adult/seniors & students €10/8; ◷10am-7pm) The brainchild of *sevillano* flamenco dancer Cristina Hoyos, this museum spread over three floors of an 18th-century palace makes a noble effort to showcase the mysterious art with sketches, paintings and photos of erstwhile (and contemporary) flamenco greats, plus a collection of dresses and shawls. Even better than that are the fantastic nightly concerts (7pm; €20) in the on-site courtyard.

Plaza de San Francisco   SQUARE

(Map p584) Plaza de San Francisco has been Seville's main public square since the 16th century. The southern end of the Ayuntamiento (Town Hall; Map p584; Plaza de San Francisco) here is encrusted with lovely Renaissance carving from the 1520–30s.

Calle Sierpes   STREET

(Map p584) Pedestrianised Calle Sierpes, heading north from the Plaza de San Francisco, and the parallel Calle Tetuán/Velázquez are the hub of Seville's fanciest shopping zone. This being Andalucía, it's busiest in the evenings between about 6pm and 9pm.

Palacio de la Condesa de Lebrija   MUSEUM, PALACE

(Map p584; Calle Cuna 8; ground fl €5, whole bldg €8, ground fl 9am-noon Wed free; ◷10.30am-7.30pm Mon-Fri, 10am-2pm & 4-6pm Sat, 10am-

2pm Sun) This 16th-century mansion, a block east of Calle Sierpes, has a rich collection of art and artisanry and a beautiful Renaissance-Mudéjar courtyard. The late Countess of Lebrija was an archaeologist, and she remodelled the house in 1914, filling many of the rooms with treasures from her travels.

Plaza del Salvador
SQUARE

(Map p584) This plaza, which has a few popular bars, was once the forum of Roman Hispalis. It's dominated by the **Parroquia del Divino Salvador**, a big baroque church built between 1674 and 1712 on the site of Muslim Ishbiliya's main mosque.

Casa de Pilatos
PALACE

(Map p584; ☏954 22 52 98; www.fundacion-medinaceli.org; Plaza de Pilatos; ground fl €6, whole house €8; ☺9am-7pm Apr-Oct, to 6pm Nov-Mar) The haunting Casa de Pilatos, which is still occupied by the ducal Medinaceli family, is one of the city's most glorious mansions. It's a mixture of Mudéjar, Gothic and Renaissance styles, with some beautiful tilework and *artesonados* (ceilings of interlaced beams with decorative insertions). The overall effect is like a poor man's Alcázar.

Museo de Bellas Artes
GALLERY

(Fine Arts Museum; Map p584; Plaza del Museo 9; €1.50, EU citizens free; ☺10am-8.30pm Tue-Sat, to 5pm Sun) Housed in the beautiful former Convento de la Merced, Seville's Museo de Bellas Artes does full justice to Seville's leading role in Spain's 17th-century artistic Siglo de Oro (Golden Age). Much of the work here is of the dark, brooding religious type.

Metropol Parasol
MUSEUM

(Map p584; www.metropolsevilla.com; Plaza de la Encarnación; €3; ☺10.30am-midnight Sun-Thu, to 1am Fri & Sat) Smarting with the audacity of a modern-day Eiffel Tower, the opinion-dividing Metropol Parasol, which opened in March 2011 in the Plaza de la Encarnación, claims to be the largest wooden building in the world. Its undulating honeycombed roof is held up by five giant mushroom-like pillars, earning it the local nickname *Las Setas de la Encarnación* (the mushrooms of Plaza de la Encarnación).

◉ El Arenal & Triana

Colonising *caballeros* (gentlemen) made rich on New World gold once stalked the streets of El Arenal on the banks of the Río Guadalquivir, watched over by Spanish galleons offloading their American booty. There's no port here today, but the compact quarter retains plenty of rambunctious bars and a seafaring spirit.

The legendary barrio of Triana sits on the west bank of the Río Guadalquivir. This atmospheric quarter was once home to many of Seville's most quintessential characters and it still hosts some of its most poignant sights.

Torre del Oro
MUSEUM

(Map p584; Paseo de Cristóbal Colón; €3, Mon free; ☺9.30am-6.45pm Mon-Fri, 10.30am-6.45pm Sat & Sun) This 13th-century Almohad watchtower by the river supposedly had a dome covered in golden tiles, hence its name, 'Tower of Gold'. Today, it hosts a small **maritime museum** spread over two floors and a rooftop viewing platform.

The tower was also once used to store the booty siphoned off the colonial coffers by the returning conquistadors from Mexico and Peru. Since then it has become one of the most recognisable architectural symbols of Seville.

Hospital de la Caridad
GALLERY

(Map p584; Calle Temprado 3; €5; ☺9am-1pm & 3.30-7pm Mon-Sat, 9am-12.30pm Sun) The Hospital de la Caridad, a large sturdy building one block east of the river, was once a hospice for the elderly. It was founded by Miguel de Mañara, by legend a notorious libertine who changed his ways after seeing a vision of his own funeral procession. Its main set piece is its gilded chapel decorated profusely by several Golden Age painters and sculptors, most notably Murillo and Roldán.

Plaza de Toros de la Real Maestranza
BULLRING, MUSEUM

(Map p584; ☏954 22 45 77; www.realmaestranza.com; Paseo de Cristóbal Colón 12; tours adult/child €7/4; ☺half-hourly 9.30am-8pm, to 3pm bullfight days) In the world of bullfighting, Seville's bullring is the Old Trafford and Camp Nou. In other words, if you're selected to fight here then you've made it. In addition to being regarded as a building of almost religious significance to fans, it's also the oldest ring in Spain (building began in 1758) and it was here, along with the bullring in Ronda, that bullfighting on foot began in the 18th century.

TRIANA – THE OUTSIDER NEIGHBOURHOOD INSIDE SEVILLE

To fully understand the modern montage that makes up Seville, there are several essential pilgrimages. Arguably, the most important is to Triana, the neighbourhood situated on the west bank of the Río Guadalquivir, a place whose past is littered with stories of sailors, ceramicists, bullfighters, flamenco artists, religious zealotry and a strong working-class identity.

Triana's 'outsider' reputation was first cemented in the Middle Ages when it was labelled *extramuros* (outside the walls) by Seville's authorities, a place where 'undesirables' were sent to live. In 1481 infamy was established when the seat of the Inquisition Court was set up in the Castillo de San Jorge on the banks of the Guadalquivir, from where it began trying suspected religious deviants for heresy. The outsider myth burgeoned in the 15th century as itinerant Roma people drifted in from the east and started to put down roots, an influx that gave Triana much of its musical personality.

By the 19th century, Triana's interlinked Roma families were producing the finest bullfighters and flamenco singers of the age. The neighbourhood also began to supplement its long-established fishing industry with pottery and tile-making using thick clay dug out of the banks of the Guadalquivir.

Most of Seville's Roma were resettled in Seville's new suburbs in the 1960s, a move that altered the demographics of Triana, but not its essence. Unlike the more sanitised Santa Cruz quarter, Triana has kept much of its authenticity. Its outdoor living room in summer is the bar-filled **Calle del Betis** overlooking the river, while its kitchen is the fish-biased **Mercado de Triana**. The quarter's religious devotion can be glimpsed in numerous churches, most notably the Gothic-Mudéjar **Parroquia de Santa Ana** (Map p584; Calle de la Pureza 80; donation €1.50; ⊙10.30am-1.30pm Mon-Fri, 4.40-6.30pm Tue & Wed), Triana's so-called 'cathedral', and the baroque **Parroquia de Nuestra Señora de la O** (Map p578; Calle Castilla 30).

Castillo de San Jorge
MUSEUM

(Map p578; ☑954 33 22 40; Plaza del Altozano; ⊙9am-1.30pm & 3.30-8pm Mon-Fri, 10am-2pm Sat & Sun) **FREE** 'Nobody expects the Spanish Inquisition!' Monty Python once quipped, but in Seville it's not so easy to escape the trauma. After all, this is where the Inquisition Court held its first ever council, in the infamous Castillo de San Jorge in 1481, an act that ignited 325 years of fear and terror. When the Inquisition fires were finally doused in the early 1800s, the castle was destroyed and a market built over the top – but its foundations were rediscovered in 1990.

Centro Cerámica Triana
MUSEUM

(Map p578; Antillano Campos 14; €2.10; ⊙10am-2pm & 5-8pm Mon-Sat, 10am-3pm Sun) Triana's – and Seville's – newest museum is an attempt to rekindle the flames that once lit the kilns of the neighbourhood's erstwhile ceramic industry. It cleverly mixes the methodology and history of ceramic production with the wider history of Triana and its people.

⊙ South of the Centre

South of Santa Cruz and El Centro, the city opens out into expansive parks and broad streets which in recent years have been reclaimed by trams, bikes and strollers.

Antigua Fábrica de Tabacos
UNIVERSITY

(Map p584; Calle San Fernando; ⊙8am-9.30pm Mon-Fri, to 2pm Sat, free tours 11am Mon-Thu) **FREE** Seville's massive former tobacco factory – workplace of Bizet's passionate fictional heroine, Carmen – was built in the 18th century and has the second-largest building footprint in Spain after El Escorial. It's now the buzzing campus to the University of Seville. You can wander in at will or partake in a free tour at 11am Monday to Thursday. Meet in the main lobby.

Hotel Alfonso XIII
LANDMARK

(Map p584; Calle San Fernando 2) As much a monument as it is an accommodation option, and certainly more affordable if you come for a cup of coffee as opposed to a room, this striking only-in-Seville hotel – conceived as the most luxurious in Europe when it was built in 1928 – was constructed in tandem with the Plaza de España for the 1929 world fair. The style is classic neo-Mudéjar with glazed tiles and terracotta bricks.

Parque de María Luisa   PARK

(Map p578; ⊘ 8am-10pm Sep-Jun, to midnight Jul & Aug; 🚻 👶) The lungs of central Seville are the dreamy Parque de María Luisa, which is a delightful place to escape from the noise of the city, with duck ponds, snoozing *sevillanos* and paths snaking under the trees.

If you'd rather continue your cultural education than commune with the flowers, the park contains a couple of sites that'll keep you smiling. Curving round the Plaza de España, with its fountains and mini-canals, is the most grandiose of the buildings built for the 1929 Exposición Iberoamericana. It's a brick-and-tile confection showcasing Seville tilework at its gaudiest, displaying a map and historical scene for each Spanish province. You can hire row boats here to ply the canals from only €5.

The Museo Arqueológico (€1.50, EU citizens free; ⊘ 10am-8.30pm Tue-Sat, to 5pm Sun), at the southern end of the park, is an unexpected depository of Roman sculptures, mosaics and statues – much of it gathered from Itálica. There is also a room of gold jewellery from the mysterious Tartessos culture.

Opposite is the Museo de Artes y Costumbres Populares (🗐 954 23 25 76; €1.50, EU citizens free; ⊘ 10am-8.30pm Tue-Sat, to 5pm Sun), with a spotlight on the ceramic tiles produced in a factory founded by Englishman Charles Pickman, in the former monastery of Cartuja in 1840.

The park is a great place for children to run off some steam; they'll enjoy feeding the doves in the plaza by the museum at the southern end of the park. Four-person quad bikes are available to rent for €12 per half-hour.

🛈 SEVILLA CARD

The Sevilla Card (24/48/72hr €30/48/64; www.sevillacard.es) allows discounted access to city sights, tours, and some shops and restaurants. Purchase online.

◉ North of the Centre

North of El Centro lies the youthful Alameda de Hércules, a long rectangular plaza, and the adjacent Maracena district centred on its famous church. Facing it across the river is Isla Cartuja, site of the 1992 Expo.

Centro de la
Interpretación Mudéjar   MUSEUM

(Map p578; Plaza Calderón de la Barca; ⊘ 10am-2pm & 5-8pm Mon-Fri, 10am-2pm Sat) FREE The Mudéjar architectural style, which long defined Seville, has a shrine to its importance encased within one of Seville's textbook-Mudéjar buildings, the Palacio de Los Marqueses de la Algaba (Plaza Calderón de la Barca). The small on-site museum with collected Mudéjar relics from the 12th to 20th centuries gets a little lost in the wonderfully restored mansion with its dreamy courtyard, but the captions (in Spanish and English) do a good job of explaining the nuances of the complex Mudéjar style.

Isla Mágica   AMUSEMENT PARK

(Map p578; 🗐 902 161716; www.islamagica.es; adult/child €29/20; ⊘ high season around 11am-10pm, closed Dec-Mar; 🚻) This Disney-goes-Spanish-colonial amusement park provides a great, if expensive, day out for kids and all lovers of white-knuckle rides. Hours vary by season – see the website. Buses C1 and C2 run to Isla Mágica.

El Pabellon de la Navegación   MUSEUM

(Map p578; www.pabellondelanavegacion.es; Camino de los Descubrimientos 2; adult/child €4.90/3.50; ⊘ 11am-8.30pm Tue-Sat, to 3pm Sun; 🚻) This boxy modern pavilion on the banks of the Río Guadalquivir opened in 2012 and revived a previous navigation museum that lasted from the 1992 Expo until 1999. Its permanent collection is split into four parts – navigation, mariners, shipboard life and historical views of Seville – and although its exhibits are interactive and kid-friendly, for an adult they might be a little underwhelming. The ticket includes a ride up the adjacent Torre Schindler (Map p578; ⊘ 9am-7pm Apr-Oct, to 6pm Nov-Mar).

Conjunto Monumental
de la Cartuja   MONASTERY, ART GALLERY

(Cartuja Monastery; Map p578; 🗐 955 03 70 70; www.caac.es; complete visit €3, monument or temporary exhibitions €1.80, free 7-9pm Tue-Fri & all day Sat; ⊘ 11am-9pm Tue-Sat, to 3pm Sun) This historic but offbeat art gallery was once a monastery, then a ceramics factory, but today is home to the **Centro Andaluz de Arte Contemporáneo**.

Founded in 1399, the Conjunto Monumental de la Cartuja became the favourite *sevillano* lodging place for Christopher Columbus, who prayed in its chapel before his trip to the Americas and whose remains lay here for more than two decades in 1530–40.

Activities

Aire Baños Árabes
HAMMAM

(Map p584; ☑955 01 00 25; www.airedesevilla. com; Calle Aire 15; bath/bath with massage €26/41; ⊙every 2hr 10am-midnight) Jumping on the *hammam* bandwagon, Seville's Arabic-style baths win prizes for tranquil atmosphere, historic setting (in the Barrio de Santa Cruz) and Moroccan *riad*-style decor – living proof that those Moors knew a thing or two about how to relax. It's best to book baths and massages one day in advance.

Courses

Seville is a great city in which to hang around for a while and learn a new skill. Many visitors from overseas join a Spanish language course and there are dozens of schools offering courses.

If learning a language is just too scholarly, then how about learning how to shimmy with the best of them? Seville has many dance and flamenco schools open to visitors staying a while.

CLIC
LANGUAGE COURSE

(Map p584; ☑954 50 21 31; www.clic.es; Calle Albareda 19) A well-established language centre headquartered in a pleasant house with a good social scene and adjacent library. Courses for children, adults and seniors. Prices are approximately €125 for 10 lessons.

Taller Andaluz de Cocina
COOKING COURSE

(Map p578; ☑672 162621; www.tallerandaluzde cocina.com; Mercado de Triana; 3hr course €45) This recently established company in Triana market offers Spanish-Andaluz cooking courses three to four times a week at 11am. The three-hour courses use local market ingredients and include tasting afterwards. It also runs free market tours on selective days at 10.30am. Check the calendar on the website.

Taller Flamenco
FLAMENCO COURSE, LANGUAGE COURSE

(Map p578; ☑954 56 42 34; www.tallerflamenco. com; Calle Peral 49) Offers one-week packages with the possibility of being taught in groups or on a one-to-one basis. It also offers Spanish language classes.

Fundación Cristina Heeren de Arte Flamenco
FLAMENCO COURSE

(☑954 21 70 58; www.flamencoheeren.com; Avenida de Jerez 2) This is by far the best-known flamenco school and offers long-term courses in all flamenco arts; also offers one-month intensive summer courses.

Tours

★ Pancho Tours
CULTURAL TOUR

(Map p584; ☑664 642 904; www.panchotours. com) FREE The best walking tours in the city? Join in and see – they're free, although you're welcome to tip the hard-working guide who'll furnish you with an encyclopedia's worth of anecdotes, stories, myths and theories about Seville's fascinating past. Tours kick off daily, normally at 11am – check the website for exact details. Pancho also offers bike tours (€25) and nightlife tours (€10 to €15).

Past View
TOUR

(Map p584; ☑954 32 66 46; www.pastview.es; Plaza de la Encarnación; tours €15; ⊙10.30am & 1pm; ⊞) This ingenious augmented-reality video tour takes you on a guided walk using 3D video glasses that re-create scenes from the past in the actual locations they happened. The ticket office and starting point is in the Metropol Parasol (p588) and the two-hour walk (with a guide) proceeds through Seville's main sights to the Torre del Oro.

Cruceros Turísticos Torre del Oro
BOAT TOUR

(Map p584; ☑954 56 16 92; www.cruceros torredeloro.com; adult/child under 14yr €16/free) One-hour sightseeing river cruises run every half-hour from 11am, departing from the river bank by the Torre del Oro. Last departure can range from 6pm in winter to 10pm in summer.

Festivals & Events

Feria de Abril
SPRING FAIR

The April fair, held in the second half of the month (sometimes edging into May), is the jolly counterpart to the sombre Semana

Santa. The biggest and most colourful of all Andalucía's ferias (fairs) is less invasive (and also less inclusive) than the Easter celebration. It takes place on El Real de la Feria, in the Los Remedios area west of the Río Guadalquivir.

Semana Santa　　　　　　HOLY WEEK
(www.semana-santa.org) Every day from Palm Sunday to Easter Sunday, large, life-sized *pasos* (sculptural representations of events from Christ's Passion) are carried from Seville's churches through the streets to the cathedral, accompanied by processions that may take more than an hour to pass. The processions are organised by more than 50 different *hermandades* or *cofradías* (brotherhoods, some of which include women).

The climax of the week is in the *madrugada* (early hours) of Good Friday, when some of the most respected brotherhoods file through the city. The costume worn by the marching penitents consists of a full robe and a conical hat with slits cut for the eyes. The regalia was incongruously copied by America's Ku Klux Klan.

Procession schedules are widely available during Semana Santa, or see the Semana Santa website. Arrive near the cathedral in the early evening for a better view.

Bienal de Flamenco　　　　　FLAMENCO
(www.labienal.com) Most of the big names of the flamenco world participate in this major flamenco festival. Held in September in even-numbered years.

🛏 Sleeping

There's a good range of places to stay in all three of the most attractive areas – Barrio de Santa Cruz (within walking distance of Prado de San Sebastián bus station), El Arenal and El Centro (both convenient for Plaza de Armas bus station).

Room rates are for each establishment's high season – typically from March to June and again in September and October. During Semana Santa and the Feria de Abril rates are doubled – at least! – and sell out completely. Book well ahead at this time.

🛏 Barrio de Santa Cruz

Pensión San Pancracio　　　　PENSIÓN €
(Map p584; ☑ 954 41 31 04; Plaza de las Cruces 9; d €50, s/d/tr with shared bathroom €33/36/52) A rare budget option in Santa Cruz, this old,

rambling family house has plenty of different room options (all cheap) and a pleasant flower-bedizened patio-lobby. Friendly staff make up for the lack of luxury. The compromise: shared bathrooms.

★ Hotel Amadeus　　　　　HOTEL €€
(Map p584; ☑ 954 50 14 43; www.hotelamadeus sevilla.com; Calle Farnesio 6; s/d €100/114; P❋🛜) Just when you thought you couldn't find hotels with pianos in the rooms anymore, along came Hotel Amadeus. It's run by an engaging musical family in the old *judería* (Jewish quarter) – several of the astutely decorated rooms come complete with soundproof walls and upright pianos, ensuring you don't miss out on your daily practice.

Hotel Puerta de Sevilla　　　HOTEL €€
(Map p584; ☑ 954 98 72 70; www.hotelpuertade sevilla.com; Calle Puerta de la Carne 2; s/d €50/70; P❋@🛜) This superfriendly – and super-positioned – hotel is a great mix of the chintz and the stylish. In the lobby there's an indoor water feature lined with superb Seville tilework. The rooms are all flower-patterned textiles, wrought-iron beds and pastel wallpaper. It also features an unbeatable people-watching roof terrace.

Un Patio en Santa Cruz　　　HOTEL €€
(Map p584; ☑ 954 53 94 13; www.patiosanta cruz.com; Calle Doncellas 15; s €65-85, d €65-120; ❋🛜) Feeling more like an art gallery than a hotel, this place has starched white walls coated in loud works of art, strange sculptures and preserved plants. The rooms are immensely comfortable, staff are friendly, and there's a cool rooftop terrace with mosaic Moroccan tables. It's easily one of the hippest and best-value hotels in town.

Hotel Palacio Alcázar　　BOUTIQUE HOTEL €€
(Map p584; ☑ 954 50 21 90; www.hotelpalacio alcazar.com; Plaza de Alianza 12; s €65, d €76-108; ❋@🛜) 🌿 Fresh, white minimalism in the lush *barrio* of Santa Cruz, Palacio Alcázar is a recent addition to Seville's oldest quarter. It sports 12 lovely rooms and an equally lovely roof-terrace tapas bar where you call the waiter by ringing a bell on your table.

★ Hotel Casa 1800　　　LUXURY HOTEL €€€
(Map p584; ☑ 954 56 18 00; www.hotelcasa 1800sevilla.com; Calle Rodrigo Caro 6; r from €195; ❋@🛜) Reigning as number one in Seville's 'favourite hotel' charts is this positively regal Santa Cruz pile where the word *casa* (house)

is taken seriously. This really is your home away from home (albeit a posh one), with charming staff catering for your every need. Historic highlights include a complimentary afternoon-tea buffet, plus a quartet of penthouse garden suites with Giralda views.

🛏 El Centro

Oasis Backpackers' Hostel HOSTEL €
(Map p584; ☎955 26 26 96; www.oasissevilla. com; Calle Almirante Ulloa 1; dm/d incl breakfast €15/50; ▣@◈🖥) It's not often you get to backpack in a palace. A veritable oasis in the busy city-centre district, this place is a friendly welcoming hostel set in a palatial 19th-century mansion with some private room options, a cafe-bar and a rooftop deck with a small pool.

Hotel Abanico HOTEL €€
(Map p584; ☎954 21 32 07; www.hotelabanico. com; Calle Águilas 17; s/d €86/90; ▣◈) If you want to wake up and know instantly that you're in Seville, book into this underdog hotel where the distinctive tilework, wrought-iron balconies and radiant religious art have Seville written all over them.

Hotel Boutique Doña Lola BOUTIQUE HOTEL €€
(Map p578; ☎954 91 52 75; www.donalolasevilla. com; Calle Amor de Dios 19; s/d €79/87; ▣◈) Hidden improbably in a rather ordinary tenement in El Centro, Doña Lola is a little haven of modernity and well-positioned for sorties pretty much everywhere. The reception area resembles a psychedelic chess board. Rooms are smallish and surgically clean, making good use of the limited space.

EME Catedral Hotel LUXURY HOTEL €€€
(Map p584; ☎954 56 00 00; www.emecatedral hotel.com; Calle de los Alemanes 27; d/ste from €250/446; ▣@◈🖥) Take 14 fine old *sevillano* houses and knock them into one. Bring in a top designer and one of Seville's most respected chefs. Carve out a *hammam,* a rooftop pool, four restaurants, including Santo Restaurante, and slick, striking rooms with red accents. Then stick it all nose-to-nose with the largest Gothic cathedral in the world.

🛏 El Arenal & Triana

★ Hotel Adriano HOTEL €€
(Map p584; ☎954 29 38 00; www.adrianohotel. com; Calle Adriano 12; s/d €65/75; ▣◈) A solid Arenal option with great staff, rooms with attractive *sevillano* features and one of the best coffee shops in Seville out front.

Hotel Simón HOTEL €€
(Map p584; ☎954 22 66 60; www.hotelsimon sevilla.com; Calle García de Vinuesa 19; s/d €88/125; ▣@) This well-used but grand 18th-century Sevillan house in El Arenal has an ornate patio and quiet, old-fashioned rooms, some of them embellished with rich *azulejo* tilework. Character and location are its two hallmarks (it's 100m from the cathedral). You won't find better at this price.

Hotel Monte Triana HOTEL €€
(Map p578; ☎954 34 31 11; www.hotelesmonte. com; Clara de Jesús Montero 24; d from €79; ▣◈) Staying in Triana has its advantages, aside from the fact that you're within fish-throwing distance of Seville's most soulful quarter. The businesslike Monte Triana has spacious rooms, a 42-car garage (a luxury in Seville), a fitness room (ditto), and its own bar and cafe. You can even choose your own pillow stuffing – latex, feather or viscoelastic.

🛏 North of the Centre

Hotel Sacristía de Santa Ana BOUTIQUE HOTEL €€
(Map p578; ☎954 91 57 22; www.hotelsacristia. com; Alameda de Hércules 22; d from €95; ▣◈) Possibly the best deal in Seville, this delightful hotel is located on the Alameda. It's great for visiting neighbouring bars and restaurants, and the hotel itself is a heavenly place with a small fountain surrounded by bonsai trees greeting you in the central courtyard. Away from the courtyard are old-fashioned rooms with big arty bedheads, circular baths and cascading showers.

Hotel San Gil HOTEL €€
(Map p578; ☎954 90 68 11; www.hotelsangil. com; Calle Parras 28; s/d €96/119; ▣◈🖥) Shoehorned at the northern end of the Macarena neighbourhood, San Gil's slightly out-of-the-way location is balanced by its proximity to the nightlife of the Alameda de Hércules. The nearby web of bike lanes provides a good excuse to get acquainted with the Sevici bike-sharing scheme. An ostentatiously tiled lobby fronts plain but modern rooms with large beds and ample space.

🍴 Eating

Seville produces Andalucía's most inventive tapas – end of story – and, if you're not enamoured with the new culinary alchemists, there are plenty of decent salt-of-the-earth tapas bars, too.

Mercado del Arenal (Map p584; Calle Pastor y Landero) and **Mercado de la Encarnación** (Map p584; Plaza de la Encarnación) are central Seville's two food markets. The Encarnación, which mainly sells fruit, vegies and fish, is located under the giant mushroom pillars of the Metropol Parasol (p588).

Barrio de Santa Cruz

Bodega Santa Cruz   TAPAS €
(Map p584; Calle Mateos Gago; tapas €2; ⊙11.30am-midnight) This forever-crowded bodega is where eating tapas becomes a physical contact sport. Watch out for flying elbows and admire those dexterous waiters who bob and weave like prizefighters amid the chaos. The fiercely traditional tapas are best enjoyed alfresco with a cold beer as you watch marching armies of Santa Cruz tourists go squeezing past.

Café Bar Las Teresas   TAPAS €
(Map p584; Calle Santa Teresa 2; tapas €3; ⊙10am-midnight) The hanging hams look as ancient as the bar itself, a sinuous wraparound affair with just enough room for two stout waiters to pass carrying precariously balanced tapas plates. The atmosphere is dark but not dingy, the food highly traditional, and the crowd an integrated mix of tourists and Santa Cruz locals.

Vinería San Telmo   TAPAS €€
(Map p584; ☑954 41 06 00; www.vineriasantelmo.com; Paseo Catalina de Ribera 4; tapas €3.50, medias raciones €10; ⊙1-4.30pm & 8pm-midnight)

San Telmo invented the *rascacielo* (skyscraper) tapa, an 'Empire State' of tomatoes, aubergine, goat's cheese and smoked salmon. If this and other creative nuggets such as foie gras with quail's eggs and lychees, or exquisitely cooked bricks of tuna, don't make you drool with expectation then you're probably dead.

Casa Tomate   TAPAS €€
(Map p584; ☑954 22 04 21; Calle Mateos Gago 24; tapas €3-4, raciones €12; ⊙9am-midnight) Hams swing from ceiling hooks, old feria posters are etched with art-nouveau and art-deco designs, and outdoor blackboards relay what's cooking in the kitchen of Casa Tomate on Santa Cruz' most intense tourist strip. The staff recommend dishes like garlic prawns and pork sirloin in a white-wine-and-pine-nut sauce, and who are you to argue?

El Centro

Plaza de la Alfalfa is the hub of the tapas scene and has some excellent bars.

★**Redhouse Art & Food**   INTERNATIONAL €
(Map p584; ☑661 615 646; www.redhouse-espace.com; Calle Amor de Dios 7; snacks from €4; ⊙11.30am-12.30am Tue-Sun; 🛜) It's hard to classify Redhouse. With its mismatched chairs and abstract wall art, it's flirting with hipster territory, yet inside you'll find families, seniors, college geeks and the obviously not-so-hip enjoying a whole variety of food from casual coffee to romantic meals. Whatever you opt for, save room for the best homemade cakes in Andalucía.

LOCAL KNOWLEDGE

WHAT'S COOKING IN SEVILLE & ANDALUCÍA'S HILL TOWNS?

Pescaíto Frito The nose doesn't lie and you'll need it in Cádiz to lead you to the best fried fish. There's an abundance of good seafood restaurants in the city, but the best – if you follow the crowds – is Freiduría Las Flores (p615), where take-out cones of assorted battered fish are scooped fresh out of the fryer.

Solomillo al Whisky This rich tapa – pork sirloin cooked in a garlic, lemon and whisky sauce – is a speciality in Seville.

Salmorejo Córdoba's take on cold gazpacho soup is rich, orange in colour and – unlike gazpacho – too thick to drink.

Jamón Ibérico The champagne of Spain's cured meats is produced from black Iberian pigs that roam freely in the Sierra de Aracena (in Huelva province) feeding mainly on acorns.

Bar Europa
TAPAS €

(Map p584; ☎954 22 13 54; www.bareuropa.info; Calle Siete Revueltas 35; tapas €3, media raciones €6-8; ⏰8am-1am) An old-school bar with no pretensions that's been knocking out tapas since 1925. Notwithstanding, Europa isn't afraid to experiment. Its signature tapa is the *quesadilla los balanchares gratinada sobre manzana* which turns a boring old Granny Smith apple into a taste sensation by covering it in goat's cheese and laying it on a bed of strawberries.

Horno de San Buenaventura
CAFE €

(Map p584; www.hornosanbuenaventura.com; Avenida de la Constitución; pastries from €1; ⏰7.30am-10pm Mon-Fri, 8am-10pm Sat & Sun) There are actually two of these gilded pastry/coffee/snack bars in Seville, one here on Avenida de la Constitución opposite the cathedral and the other (inferior one) at the Plaza de la Alfalfa (Map p584; Plaza de Alfalfa; ⏰9am-9pm) All kinds of fare are on show, though it's probably best for its lazy continental breakfasts (yes, the service can be slow) or a spontaneous late-night cake fix.

Confitería La Campana
CAFE, BAKERY €

(Map p584; www.confiterialacampana.com; cnr Calles Sierpes & Martín Villa; large cakes from €7; ⏰8am-10pm) A bakery and cafe with the words 'institution' written all over it, La Campana has been heaving with sugar addicts since 1885. Workers and the elite alike storm Seville's most popular bakery for the *yema* (soft, crumbly biscuit cake wrapped like a toffee), or a delicious *nata* (custard cake) that quivers under the glass.

★ La Pepona
TAPAS, MODERN €€

(Map p584; ☎954 21 50 26; Javier Lasso de la Vega 1; tapas €3.50-6.50; ⏰1.30-4.30pm & 8pm-midnight Mon-Sat) One of the best newcomer restaurants of 2014, La Pepona gets all the basics right, from the bread (doorstop-sized rustic slices), to the service (fast but discreet), to the decor (clean Ikea lines and lots of wood). Oscar status is achieved with the food, which falls firmly into the nouveau tapas camp.

Try the goat with yoghurt, couscous and mint – an epic amalgamation of Iberia and Morocco.

The Room
INTERNATIONAL €€

(Map p584; ☎619 200 946; www.theroomart cuisine.com; Calle Cuesta del Rosario 15; tapas €2.75-5; ⏰noon-4.30pm & 8pm-1am; 🐾) Another new 'art-cuisine' place, The Room sticks its succinct menu on a blackboard and circumnavigates the globe with everything from British-style fish and chips to pad thai noodles, Peruvian ceviche and Italian risotto. The interior is megacasual with Chaplin movies often projected onto a wall.

Los Coloniales
CONTEMPORARY ANDALUCIAN €€

(Map p584; www.tabernacoloniales.es; cnr Calle Dormitorio & Plaza Cristo de Burgos; mains €10-12; ⏰12.30pm-midnight) The quiet ones are always the best. It might not look like much from the outside, but Los Coloniales is something very special. The quality plates line up like models on a catwalk: *chorizo a la asturiana*, a divine spicy sausage in an onion sauce served on a bed of lightly fried potato; eggplants in honey; and pork tenderloin *al whisky* (a whisky-flavoured sauce).

There is another inferior, more touristy branch, Taberna Los Coloniales (Map p584; Calle Jimios), near the cathedral.

La Azotea
FUSION, ANDALUCIAN €€

(Map p578; ☎955 11 67 48; Jesús del Gran Poder 31; raciones €10; ⏰1.30-4.30pm & 8.30pm-midnight Thu-Mon) The latest word in *nueva cocina* comes from Azotea whose proliferating empire – there are now four branches – testifies to a growing legend. The decor is Ikea-friendly, staff wear black, and the *raciones* (full servings of tapas items), which are sweetened and spiced with panache, arrive like pieces of art in a variety of plates, dishes and boxes.

Robles Laredo
CONTEMPORARY SPANISH €€

(Map p584; www.casa-robles.com; Plaza de San Francisco; raciones €9-12; ⏰11am-1am Sun-Wed, to 2am Thu-Sat) This small Italianate cafe-restaurant is fairly dwarfed by its two huge chandeliers and a vast collection of delicate desserts displayed in glass cases. The tapas are equally refined. Try the foie gras, beef burgers with truffle sauce, or oysters and whitebait.

El Rinconcillo
TAPAS €€

(Map p584; ☎954 22 31 83; www.elrinconcillo.es; Calle Gerona 40; tapas €3, raciones €12; ⏰1pm-1.30am) Some say the Rinconcillo is resting on its laurels. Maybe so; but, with more than 345 years of history, there are a lot to rest on. Seville's oldest bar first opened in 1670, when the Inquisition was raging and tapas were still just tops you screwed on bottles.

Come here for the sense of history rather than for the food, but stay for the *ortiguillas fritas* (fried sea anemones) and a saucerful of the biggest olives you've ever seen.

Restaurante Albarama
TAPAS €€

(Map p584; ☎954 22 97 84; www.restaurante albarama.com; Plaza de San Francisco 5; tapas €5.50; ⊙1-4.15pm & 8.15-11.45pm) A long, slim restaurant usually inhabited with plenty of long, slim people who tuck into tapas that are more about quality than quantity. Come here to enjoy the true beauty of tapas – the opportunity to taste a small sample of fancy food without breaking the bank.

Egaña Santo Restaurante
BASQUE, FUSION €€€

(Map p584; ☎954 21 28 73; www.eganagastro group.com; Calle Argote de Molina 29; mains €24-38; ⊙12.30-4pm & 8pm-late Wed-Sat & Mon, 12.30-4pm Sun) The former stomping ground of Michelin-starred Basque chef Martin Berasategui has changed hands and is now ruled over by another Basque, Josemari Egaña, a man with a long history on the Seville culinary scene. It's affiliated with the posh EME Catedral Hotel (p593) next to the cathedral, and the food remains headily experimental with a passing nod to Andalucian tradition.

Foie gras escalopes and roast octopus headline a menu doused in the elegance of Basque cuisine.

✖ El Arenal & Triana

Mercado Lonja del Barranco
INTERNATIONAL €

(Map p578; www.mercadodelbarranco.com; Calle Arjona; snacks €5-12; ⊙10am-midnight Sun-Thu, to 2am Fri & Sat) 🍴 Fabulous new food court in an Eiffel-esque structure near the Isabel II bridge, with posh stalls stashed with the full cornucopia of *sevillano* food products. Float through the stalls and load up on cakes, fried fish, beer, miniburgers and tapas. There are plenty of nooks and crannies filled with shared tables. It's a mouth-watering and highly sociable experience.

Casa Cuesta
CONTEMPORARY SPANISH €

(Map p578; ☎954 33 33 37; www.casacuesta.net; Calle de Castilla 3-5; mains €10; ⊙12.30-4.30pm & 8pm-12.30am) Massive glass windows look out onto a crowded plaza, mirrors artfully reflect framed bullfighting posters and flamenco iconography, and gleaming gold beer pumps furnish a wooden bar shielding bottles that look older than most of the clientele. Casa Cuesta has that wonderful sensation of *sevillano* authenticity.

★ La Brunilda
TAPAS €€

(Map p584; ☎954 22 04 81; Calle Galera 5; tapas €3.50-6.50; ⊙1-4pm & 8.30-11.30pm Tue-Sat, 1-4pm Sun) Seville's crown as Andalucía's tapas capital is regularly attacked by well-armed rivals from the provinces, meaning it constantly has to reinvent itself and offer up fresh competition. Enter La Brunilda, a newish font of fusion tapas sandwiched into an inconspicuous backstreet in the Arenal quarter where everything – including the food, staff and clientele – is pretty.

Mesón Cinco Jotas
TAPAS €€

(Map p584; www.mesoncincojotas.com; Calle Castelar 1; medias raciones €10; ⊙8am-midnight Mon-Fri, from noon Sat & Sun) In the world of *jamón* (ham) making, if you are awarded Cinco Jotas (Five Js) for your *jamón*, it's like getting an Oscar. The owner of this place, Sánchez Romero Carvajal, is the biggest producer of Jabugo ham, and has a great selection on offer.

T de Triana
ANDALUCIAN €€

(Map p584; ☎954 33 12 03; Calle del Betis 20; ⊙8pm-2am) The T is Triana being itself: simple fish-biased tapas, walls full of history, *fútbol* on the big screen whenever local boys Sevilla or Real Betis are playing, and live, gutsy flamenco shows every Friday night at 10pm.

Infanta
ANDALUCIAN €€€

(Map p584; ☎954 56 15 54; www.infantasevilla. es; Calle Arfe 34-36; mains €16-24; ⊙12.30-5pm & 8pm-midnight Mon-Sat, 12.30-5pm Sun) A one-time spit and sawdust Arenal tapas bar that has moved around the corner and reinvented itself as something a little slicker and 'nouveau'. Nonetheless, the bright interior includes some beautiful throwback architectural features and the food never strays far from local ingredients. For a break from tapas, try the on-site sit-down restaurant with a full à la carte menu.

✖ North of the Centre

★ Bar-Restaurante Eslava
FUSION, ANDALUCIAN €€

(Map p578; www.espacioeslava.com; Calle Eslava 3; medias raciones €9-13; ⊙12.30pm-midnight Tue-Sat, 12.30-4.30pm Sun) A legend in its own dinnertime, Eslava shirks the traditional tile-work and bullfighting posters of tapas-bar lore and delivers where it matters: fine food backed up with equally fine service.

There's a 'nouvelle' tinge to the memorable *costillas a la miel* (pork ribs in a honey and rosemary glaze) and vegetable strudel in a cheese sauce, but there's nothing snobby about the atmosphere, which is local and pretty fanatical after 9pm. An equally good restaurant (with shared kitchen) sits next door.

 ## Drinking & Nightlife

Bars usually open from 6pm to 2am on weekdays and 8pm to 4am on weekends. Drinking and partying get going as late as midnight on Friday and Saturday (daily when it's hot), upping the tempo as the night goes on.

In summer dozens of *terrazas de verano* (summer terraces; temporary, open-air, late-night bars), many of them with live music and plenty of room to dance, spring up along both banks of the river. They change names and ambience from year to year.

Drinking neighbourhoods are legion. Classic spots include drinks on the banks of the Río Guadalquivir in Triana (the wall along Calle del Betis forms a fantastic makeshift bar), Plaza de la Alfalfa (cocktail and dive bars), the Barrio de Santa Cruz and the Alameda de Hércules. The latter is the hub for young *sevillanos* and the city's gay nightlife.

Cervezas Taifa MICROBREWERY
(Map p578; ✆954 04 27 31; www.cervezastaifa.es; Mercado de Triana 36; ☺7.30am-3pm Mon-Fri, 12.30pm-5pm Sat & Sun) A tiny nano-brewery in Triana market, Taifa is at the forefront of Andalucía's newborn craft-beer movement that is slowly challenging the monopoly of Cruzcampo et al (Cruzcampo is Spain's bestselling beer). Its diminutive market stall (equivalent to that of a small fruit stall) also serves as a factory, shop and bar.

El Garlochi BAR
(Map p584; Calle Boteros 4; ☺10pm-6am) Dedicated entirely to the iconography, smells and sounds of Semana Santa, the ultracamp El Garlochi is a true marvel. Taste the rather revolting sounding cocktail, Sangre de Cristo (Blood of Christ) or Agua de Sevilla, both heavily laced with vodka, whisky and grenadine, and pray they open more bars like this.

Café de la Prensa BAR
(Map p578; ✆954 00 29 69; Calle del Betis 8; ☺3pm-2.30am Mon-Thu, 2pm-3.30am Fri-Sun) Calle del Betis is second only to the Alameda

de Hércules as a communal Seville watering hole and Café de la Prensa is a fine place to kick off a riverside bar crawl. You can sit inside and stare at walls covered in old newspapers or squeeze outside for better views of the river with the Giralda beckoning in the background.

Bulebar Café BAR
(Map p578; ✆954 90 19 54; Alameda de Hércules 83; ☺9am-2am) This place gets pretty *caliente* (hot) at night but is pleasantly chilled in the early evening, with friendly staff. Don't write off its spirit-reviving alfresco breakfasts that pitch earlybirds with up-all-nighters. It's in the uber-cool Alameda de Hércules.

☆ Entertainment

★**Sevilla de Ópera** THEATRE
(Map p584; ✆955 29 46 61; www.sevilladeopera.com; Mercado del Arenal, Calle Pastor y Landero; ☺shows 9pm Fri & Sat) Seville has served as the fictional setting for countless operas, so it made sense when in 2012 a group of opera singers and enthusiasts decided to initiate the Sevilla de Ópera club. The setting in the Arenal market is like a kind of 'Opera *tablao*' with shows designed to make the music more accessible.

Teatro Duque La Imperdible THEATRE
(Map p584; ✆954 38 82 19; www.imperdible.org; Plaza del Duque de la Victoria; adult/child €12/5) This epicentre of experimental arts stages lots of contemporary dance, theatre and flamenco, usually around 9pm. The bar here also hosts varied music events from around 11pm Thursday to Saturday.

Naima Café Jazz JAZZ
(Map p578; ✆954 38 24 85; Calle Trajano 47; ☺live performances from 11pm Sat & Sun) Very mellow bar with live jazz most nights, Naima is so small you'll probably find yourself squeezed in next to the drummer with a hi-hat crashing inches from your nose.

Flamenco

★**Casa de la Memoria** FLAMENCO
(Map p584; ✆954 56 06 70; www.casadelamemoria.es; Calle Cuna 6; €18; ☺shows 7.30pm & 9pm) Neither a *tablao* (choreographed flamenco show) nor a private *peña* (club, usually of flamenco aficionados), this cultural centre offers what are, without doubt, the most intimate and authentic nightly flamenco shows in Seville. It's accommodated in

the old stables of the Palacio de la Condesa de Lebrija.

It's perennially popular and space is limited to 100, so reserve tickets a day or so in advance by calling or visiting the venue.

Tablao El Arenal   FLAMENCO
(Map p584; www.tablaoelarenal.com; Calle Rodo 7; admission with drink/dinner €38/72; ⊗ restaurant from 7pm, shows 8pm & 10pm) Of all the places in Seville that offer flamenco 'dinner shows', this is one of the best. With a seating capacity of 100 in an old-school tavern, it lacks the grit and – invariably – *duende* (flamenco spirit) of the *peñas*, although you can't fault the skill of the performers. Tickets include one drink. Skip the food.

Casa de la Guitarra   FLAMENCO
(Map p584; ☑ 954 22 40 93; Calle Mesón del Moro 12; adult/child €17/10; ⊗ shows 7.30pm & 9pm) Tiny newish flamenco-only venue in Santa Cruz (no food or drinks served) where a miscued step from the performing dancers would land them in the front row of the audience. Glass display cases filled with guitars of erstwhile flamenco greats adorn the walls.

La Casa del Flamenco   FLAMENCO
(Map p584; ☑ 954 50 05 95; www.lacasadelflamencosevilla.com; Calle Ximénez de Enciso, 28; adult/child €18/10; ⊗ 8.30pm) When Seville's Casa de la Memoria (p597) moved its flamenco venue to El Centro in 2012, its former location - a beautiful patio in an old Sephardic Jewish mansion in Santa Cruz - was filled by La Casa del Flamenco. Fortunately, not much else has changed and the performances on a stage hemmed in by seating on three sides are mesmerising.

Casa Anselma   FLAMENCO
(Map p578; Calle Pagés del Corro 49; ⊗ midnight-late Mon-Sat) True, the music is often more folkloric than flamenco, but Casa Anselma is the antithesis of a touristy flamenco *tablao*, with cheek-to-jowl crowds, zero amplification and spontaneous outbreaks of dexterous dancing. Beware: there's no sign, just a doorway embellished with *azulejos*.

Anselma is in Triana, about 200m from the western side of the Puente de Isabel II.

El Palacio Andaluz   FLAMENCO
(Map p578; ☑ 954 53 47 20; www.elpalacioandaluz.com; Calle de María Auxiliadora; admission with drink/dinner €38/76; ⊗ shows 7pm & 9.30pm)

The purists will, no doubt, tell you that these highly choreographed performances in a 400-seat theatre are for tourists, but go along anyway and decide for yourself. You may be surprised. The Palacio's performers are absolute masters of their art with talent to write home about. What a show!

🔒 Shopping

Shopping in Seville is a major pastime, and shopping for clothes is at the top of the list for any *sevillano*. Shoes fetishists beware: Seville possibly has the densest quota of shoe shops on the planet.

Calles Sierpes, Velázquez/Tetuán and Cuna have retained their charm with a host of small shops selling everything from polka-dot *trajes de flamenca* (flamenco dresses) to antique fans. Most shops open between 9am and 9pm, but expect it to be ghostly quiet between 2pm and 5pm when they close for siesta.

For a more alternative choice of shops, head for Calles Amor de Dios and Doctor Letamendi, close to Alameda de Hércules.

Triana is famous for its pottery and tile-making. A dozen shops and workshops still sell charming and artistic ceramics on the corner of Calles Alfarería and Antillano Campos.

Padilla Crespo   ACCESSORIES, CLOTHING
(Map p584; ☑ 954 21 29 88; Calle Adriano 18B; ⊗ 10am-8.30pm Mon-Sat) If you're really immersing yourself in the culture, you can pick up your wide-brimmed hat and riding outfit for the Feria de Abril right here.

Cerámica Santa Ana   CERAMICS
(Map p578; ☑ 954 33 39 90; Calle San Jorge 31; ⊗ 10am-8.30pm Mon-Fri, to 3pm Sat) Seville specialises in distinctive *azulejos* and they are best seen in Triana. Cerámica Santa Ana has been around for more than 50 years and the shop itself almost qualifies as a tourist attraction.

El Postigo   MARKET
(Map p584; cnr Calles Arfe & Dos de Mayo; ⊗ 11am-2pm & 4-8pm) This covered arts and crafts market in the Arenal houses a few shops selling everything from pottery and textiles to silverware.

ⓘ Information

Inhfor (☑ 954 54 19 52; Estación Santa Justa; ⊗ 8am-10pm, closes for lunch Sat & Sun) Independent tourist office at the train station.

Regional Tourist Office (Map p584; Avenida de la Constitución 21; ⊙9am-7pm Mon-Fri, 10am-2pm & 3-7pm Sat, 10am-2pm Sun, closed holidays) The Constitución office is well informed but often very busy. There is also a branch at the airport (☑954 44 91 28; Aeropuerto San Pablo; ⊙9am-8.30pm Mon-Fri, 10am-6pm Sat, 10am-2pm Sun, closed holidays).

Turismo Sevilla (Map p584; www.turismo-sevilla.org; Plaza del Triunfo 1; ⊙10.30am-7pm Mon-Fri) Information on all of Sevilla province.

ⓘ Getting There & Away

AIR

Seville's **airport** (SVQ; ☑954 44 90 00; www.aena.es) has a fair range of international and domestic flights.

Numerous international carriers fly in and out of Seville; carrier and schedule information changes frequently, so it's best to check with specific airlines or major online booking agents.

BUS

Seville has two main bus stations serving different destinations and bus companies. Plaza de Armas is the larger of the two.

Estación de Autobuses Plaza de Armas (Map p578; www.autobusesplazadearmas.es; Avenida del Cristo de la Expiración) The main HQ for Spain's intercity bus company, Alsa, linking to other major cities in Andalucía including Málaga (€19, three hours, eight daily), Granada (€23, three hours, nine daily), Córdoba (€12, two hours, seven daily) and Almería (€37, 5½ hours, three daily). Damas runs buses to Huelva province and Eurolines has international services to Germany, Belgium, France and beyond.

Estación de Autobuses Prado de San Sebastián (Map p584; Plaza San Sebastián) Primarily home to smaller companies running buses to lesser towns in western Andalucía. Of note are Amarillos serving the provinces of Sevilla, Cádiz and parts of Málaga and Comes who run to some of the harder-to-reach 'white towns'.

TRAIN

Seville's **Estación Santa Justa** (☑902 43 23 43; Avenida Kansas City) is 1.5km northeast of the centre.

High-speed AVE trains go to/from Madrid (from €79, 2½ hours, 20 daily) and Córdoba (from €30, 40 minutes, 30 daily). Slower trains head to Cádiz (€16, 1¾ hours, 15 daily), Huelva (€12, 1½ hours, three daily), Granada (€30, three hours, four daily) and Málaga (€44, two hours, 11 daily).

ⓘ Getting Around

Seville offers a multitude of ways to get around, though walking still has to be the best option, especially in the centre. The **Sevici bike-sharing scheme** has made cycling easy and bike lanes are now almost as ubiquitous as pavements. The tram has recently been extended to the station of San Bernardo but its routes are still limited. Buses are more useful than the metro to link the main tourist sights. The recent 'greening' of the city has made driving increasingly difficult as whole roads in the city centre are now permanently closed to traffic; park on the periphery.

TO/FROM THE AIRPORT

The EA bus (€4) makes the trip between the airport and the city centre roughly every 20 to 30 minutes throughout the day. The service is reduced slightly on Sundays, as well as very early in the morning and late in the evening. The first bus from the airport to the city is at 5.45am and the last at 12.15am. From the city to the airport the first bus is at 5.15am and the last at 12.45am. It runs to/from the Plaza de Armas bus station via Santa Justa train station, the Prado de San Sebastián bus station and the Torre del Oro.

A taxi costs a set €22 with a charge of €1 per bag from the airport to the centre, but going the other way you'll be lucky to pay less than €25. There's a €3 to €4 surcharge late at night, and on weekends and holidays.

BUS

Buses C1, C2, C3 and C4 do useful circular routes linking the main transport terminals and the city centre. The standard ticket is €1.40 but a range of passes are available (from stations and kiosks next to stops) if you're likely to use buses a lot.

CAR & MOTORCYCLE

If you like getting hot, sweaty, frustrated, angry and sometimes frightened, then you'll enjoy driving in Seville. If you don't, then avoid picking up your hire car until after you leave the city. Car crime is rampant – never leave anything in your car. There are numerous underground car parks (many marked on the relevant maps), which cost around €18 per 24 hours.

METRO

Seville's **metro system** (www.sevilla21.com/metro) connects Ciudad Expo with Olivar de Quinto (this line isn't that useful for visitors). Three more lines are due for completion by 2017. The standard ticket is €1.35. A one-day travel card costs €4.50.

TRAM

Tranvia (www.tussam.es) is the city's sleek tram service, first introduced in 2007. Two parallel lines run in pollution-free bliss between Plaza Nueva, Avenida de la Constitucíon, Puerta de Jerez, San Sebastián and San Bernardo. The standard ticket is €1.40 but a range of other passes are also available.

SEVILLE PROVINCE

Just northwest of Seville you'll find the Roman ruins of Itálica, at Santiponce. To the east, the flat and fertile farmlands of La Campiña stretch into the fiery distance, a land of huge agricultural estates belonging to a few landowners, dotted with romantic old towns like Carmona, Osuna and Écija. Heading north, you'll hit the tranquil, largely untouristed hills of the Sierra Norte de Sevilla.

Carmona

POP 23,200 / ELEV 250M

Perched on a low hill 35km east of Seville, overlooking a hazy *vega* (valley) that sizzles in the summer heat, and dotted with ancient palaces and majestic monuments, Carmona comes as a surprise highlight of western Andalucía.

This strategic site was important as long ago as Carthaginian times. The Romans laid out a street plan that survives to this day: the Via Augusta, running from Rome to Cádiz, entered Carmona by the eastern Puerta de Córdoba and left by the western Puerta de Sevilla (both of which are still standing strong). The Muslims built a strong defensive wall around Carmona, but the town fell in 1247 to Fernando III. Later on, Mudéjar and Christian artisans constructed grand churches, convents and mansions.

Sights

From the Puerta de Sevilla, it's an easy stroll through the best of old-town Carmona. Inside the **town hall** (☎954 14 00 11; Calle El Salvador; free; ⊙8am-3pm Mon-Fri) FREE is a large, very fine Roman mosaic of the gorgon Medusa.

★Necrópolis Romana HISTORIC SITE
(Roman cemetery; ☎600 143632; www.museosdeandalucia.es; Avenida de Jorge Bonsor 9; ⊙9am-7pm Tue-Sat & 9am-3.30pm Sun Apr-May, 9am-3.30pm Tue-Sun Jun–mid-Sep, 9am-5.30pm Tue-Sat & 9am-3.30pm Sun mid-Sep–Mar) FREE On the southwestern edge of Carmona lie the remains of a Roman city of the dead. A dozen or more family tombs, some elaborate and many-chambered, were hewn into the rock here in the 1st and 2nd centuries AD. Most of the inhabitants were cremated, and in the tombs are wall niches for the boxlike stone urns. You can enter the huge Tumba de Servilia, the tomb of a family of Hispano-Roman VIPs, and climb down into several others.

Alcázar de la Puerta de Sevilla GATE
(adult/child €2/1, free Mon; ⊙10am-6pm Mon-Sat, to 3pm Sun) The impressive main gate of Carmona's old town is one element of a fortification that had already been standing for five centuries when the Romans reinforced it and built a temple on top. The Muslim Almohads added an *aljibe* (cistern) to the upper patio, which remains a hawklike perch from which to admire the typically Andalucian tableau of white cubes and soaring spires.

Iglesia Prioral de Santa María de la Asunción CHURCH
(☎954 19 14 82; Plaza Marqués de las Torres; €3; ⊙9.30am-2pm & 5.30-6.30pm Tue-Fri, to 2pm Sat) This splendid church was built mainly in the 15th and 16th centuries on the site of the former main mosque. The Patio de los Naranjos by which you enter has a Visigothic calendar carved into one of its pillars. Inside, the plateresque altar is detailed to an almost perverse degree, with 20 panels of biblical scenes framed by gilt-scrolled columns.

Sleeping

Hostal Comercio HOSTAL €
(☎954 14 00 18; hostalcomercio@hotmail.com; Calle Torre del Oro 56; s/d €35/50; ❄📶) Just inside the Puerta de Sevilla, the long-standing, old-fashioned Comercio provides 14 spiffy, simple rooms around a plant-filled patio with Mudéjar-style arches. Unpretentious decor is matched by friendly service, cultivated over generations.

El Rincón de las Descalzas BOUTIQUE HOTEL €€
(☎954 19 11 72; www.elrincondelasdescalzas.com; Calle de las Descalzas 1; incl breakfast s €52, d €66-82; ❄📶) Tucked into a quiet old-town corner, this stylishly revamped 18th-century home offers 13 elegant rooms in all different colours, rambling up around orange-toned patios with fountains. All have their own quirk (exposed stone walls, 100-year-old

wood-carved beds); some are noticeably nicer, and 'Antífona', with its raised bath and brick arches, is a great choice.

Parador de Carmona   HISTORIC HOTEL €€€
(☑ 954 14 10 10; www.parador.es; Calle Alcázar; r €188; P❄@🛜🏊) With jaw-dropping, unexpected views of the surrounding valley roasting under the Sevillan sun, Carmona's luxuriously equipped *parador* (top-end state-owned hotel) feels even more sumptuous for the ruined Alcázar in its grounds. Most of the smart, shiny-terracotta-floored rooms overlook the plains. The beautiful dining room serves a three-course €33 *menú*, or just pop in for coffee: the terrace is divine. Best rates online.

🍴 Eating

Molino de la Romera   TAPAS €€
(☑ 954 14 20 00; www.molinodelaromera.com; Calle Sor Ángela de la Cruz 8; mains €17-20; ⏰ 1-4pm & 8-11pm Tue-Sat, 1-4pm Sun) Housed in a cosy 15th-century olive-oil mill with wonderful views across the *vega,* this popular restaurant serves hearty, well-prepped meals with a splash of contemporary flair. Traditional Andalucian flavours rule (try the Carmona spinach), but tasty novel variations include fish flambéed in vodka, and *secreto ibérico* (a succulent section of Iberian pork loin) with candied pumpkin.

Bar Goya   TAPAS, RACIONES €€
(Calle Prim 2; raciones €5-12; ⏰ 8am-11pm Sat-Mon & Thu, 8am-3pm Tue, noon-11pm Fri; 🖬) From the kitchens of this ever-crammed bar on Plaza de San Fernando comes forth a fabulous array of tasty tapas. Apart from such carnivores' faves as *carrillada* (pigs' cheeks) and *menudo* (tripe), chef Isabel offers pure vegetarian treats such as *alboronía* (a delicious veg stew) and an excellent Carmona spinach (blended with chickpeas).

ℹ Information

Tourist Office (☑ 954 19 09 55; www.turismo.carmona.org; Alcázar de la Puerta de Sevilla; ⏰ 10am-6pm Mon-Sat, to 3pm Sun)

ℹ Getting There & Away

BUS

Monday to Friday, **Casal** (www.autocarescasal.com) runs hourly buses to Seville (€2.80, one hour) from the **stop** on Paseo del Estatuto, less often on weekends. **Alsa** (www.alsa.es) has three daily buses to Córdoba (€9.72, 1½ hours) via Écija (€4.71, 35 minutes) from the car park next to the Puerta de Sevilla.

Écija

POP 38,700 / ELEV 110M

Easily the least visited of the Campiña towns, Écija for that very reason offers a genuine insight into Andalucian urban life. Crammed with Gothic-Mudéjar palaces and churches, the towers of which glitter in the sun, this is *la ciudad de las torres* (the city of towers). To the Romans, it was Colonia Augusta Firma Astigi, one of the main cities of their Iberian realm, which struck it rich supplying far-flung markets with olive oil. Roman remains lie strewn

DON'T MISS

ÉCIJA'S CHURCHES & BELL TOWERS

Écija's spire-studded townscape is a constant reminder of its prosperous past, though some structures toppled as a result of Lisbon's great earthquake in 1755. One of the finest towers belongs to the Giralda-like **Iglesia de Santa María** (Plaza de Santa María; ⏰ 9.30am-1.30pm & 5-8.30pm Mon-Sat, 9.30am-1.30pm Sun), just off Plaza de España, while that of the **Iglesia de San Juan** (Plaza de San Juan; €2; ⏰ 10.30am-1.30pm & 4-7pm Tue-Sat, 10.30am-1.30pm Sun) rises like a frosted wedding cake a few blocks northeast (this is the only bell tower you can climb). The Gothic-Mudéjar **Iglesia de San Pablo-Santo Domingo** (Plaza de Santo Domingo; ⏰ 6.30-7.30pm Tue-Fri, 7-8pm Sat, 11.30am-12.30pm & 7-8pm Sun), north of the square, is startlingly strung with a gigantic set of rosary beads.

The **Parroquia Mayor de Santa Cruz** (Plazuela de Nuestra Señora del Valle; ⏰ 10am-1pm & 4-8pm Tue-Sat, 10am-1pm & 6-9pm Sun), four blocks north of Plaza de España, was once the town's principal mosque and still has traces of Islamic features and some Arabic inscriptions. Beyond a roofless atrium is an interior crammed with sacred paraphernalia and baroque silverwork. A sarcophagus in front of the altar dates from the early Christian period, with a chiselled likeness of Daniel flanked by a pair of lions.

across town, including under the main plaza.

Écija is 53km east of Carmona on the A4 between Córdoba and Seville. Try to avoid July and August, when temperatures soar to a suffocating 45°C and Écija sizzles as *la sartén de Andalucía* (the frying pan of Andalucía).

◉ Sights

The centre of life is the cafe-lined Plaza de España, otherwise known as El Salón (the parlour), around which sprawls the old quarter.

Museo Histórico Municipal   MUSEUM
(☑ 954 83 04 31; http://museo.ecija.es; Plaza de la Constitución 1; ⊘ 10am-2pm Tue-Sun Jun-Sep, 10am-1.30pm & 4.30-6.30pm Tue-Sat, 10am-3pm Sun Oct-May) **FREE** The 18th-century Palacio de Benamejí houses the city's impressive history museum. Pride of place goes to the best Roman finds from the area, including a marble sculpture of an Amazon (legendary female warrior). The upper level features a hall devoted to six fantastically preserved Roman mosaics, some unearthed beneath Écija's central square, with one tableau depicting the 'birth' of wine. If you ask, someone will lead you up to the mirador (lookout), which has wonderful panoramic city views.

Palacio de Peñaflor   PALACE
(Calle Emilio Castelar 26) The huge 18th-century 'Palace of the Long Balconies', 300m east of Plaza de España, is Écija's most iconic image. Though the interior is closed indefinitely for potential renovations, the curved, fresco-lined facade is bewitching enough, morning or evening.

🛌 Sleeping & Eating

Hotel Palacio de los Granados   HISTORIC HOTEL €€
(☑ 955 90 53 44; www.palaciogranados.com; Calle de Emilio Castelar 42; d/ste incl breakfast €88/110; 🅿 ❅ 🛜 ☻) This small palace, some sections of which date back to the 16th century, has been carefully restored by its architect owner. Lavishly furnished chambers surround a quiet patio. From central Plaza de España, go south on Avenida Miguel de Cervantes, then 450m east on Calle de Emilio Castelar.

Hispania   TAPAS €€
(☑ 954 83 26 05; www.hispaniacafe.com; Pasaje Virgen de Soterraño; tapas €2-5, mains €10-16; ⊘ noon-4pm & 8.30pm-1am Tue-Sun) Stylish, friendly and packed with *ecijanos*, this side-street operation has a bold colour scheme that matches its experimental kitchen. The innovative chefs just keep coming up with new creations that give classic Spanish cooking a contemporary zing, whether they're doing tapas, *bocatas* (sandwiches), desserts or *revueltos* (scrambled egg dishes). Book ahead Thursday to Saturday.

ⓘ Information

Tourist Office (☑ 955 90 29 33; www.turismo ecija.com; Calle Elvira 1; ⊘ 9am-3pm & 5-7pm)

ⓘ Getting There & Away

Alsa (www.alsa.es) buses depart from the **bus station** (Avenida del Gil) for Carmona (€4.71, 35 minutes, two daily), Córdoba (€5.01, one hour, five daily) and Seville (€7.32, 1¼ hours, three daily).

WORTH A TRIP

ITÁLICA

Itálica (☑ 955 12 38 47; www.museosdeandalucia.es; Avenida de Extremadura 2; €1.50, EU citizens free; ⊘ 9am-3.30pm Tue-Sun mid-Jun–mid-Sep, 9am-5.30pm Tue-Sat & 9am-3.30pm Sun mid-Sep–mid-Jun; 🅿) was the first Roman town in Spain, founded in 206 BC. It was the birthplace of the 2nd-century AD Roman emperor Trajan, and probably of his adopted son and successor Hadrian (he of the wall across northern England). Although emperors are fairly rare here today, what remains of those times are broad paved streets and ruins of houses built around patios of beautiful mosaics. Itálica also contains one of the biggest Roman **amphitheatres** in the world (seating 20,000 spectators).

HUELVA PROVINCE

To fixed-itinerary travellers, Huelva province is that nodule of land 'on the way to Portugal'. To those willing to drag their heels a little, it's home to the region's best cured ham, its most evocative fandangos, and Spain's largest and most ebullient *romería* (pilgrimage). Throw in some British-influenced mining heritage, Christopher Columbus memorabilia, and what is possibly Spain's most revered national park, and you've got the makings of an Andalucian break well outside the standard mould.

Huelva

POP 147,000

The capital of Huelva province is a modern, unpretentious industrial port set between the Odiel and Tinto estuaries. Despite its unpromising approaches and slightly grimy feel, central Huelva is a lively enough place, and the city's people – called *choqueros* because of their supposed preference for the locally abundant *chocos* (cuttlefish) – are noted for their warmth.

Huelva's history dates back 3000 years to the Phoenician town of Onuba. Onuba's river-mouth location made it a natural base for exporting inland minerals to the Mediterranean. The town was devastated by the 1755 Lisbon earthquake, but later grew when British company Rio Tinto developed mines in the province's interior in the 1870s. Today Huelva has a sizeable fishing fleet and a heavy dose of petrochemical industry (introduced in the 1950s by Franco).

◎ Sights

Muelle-Embarcadero
de Mineral de Río Tinto   HISTORIC SITE
An odd legacy of the area's mining history, this impressive iron pier curves out into the Odiel estuary 500m south of the port. It was designed for the Rio Tinto company in the 1870s by British engineer George Barclay Bruce. Equipped with boardwalks on upper and lower levels, it makes for a delightful stroll or jog to admire the harbour and ships. It's 1km southwest of Plaza de las Monjas.

Museo de Huelva   MUSEUM
(☑959 65 04 24; www.museosdeandalucia.es; Alameda Sundheim 13; ⊙9am-3.30pm Tue-Sat, 10am-5pm Sun Jun–mid-Sep, 9am-7.30pm Tue-Sat, 9am-3.30pm Sun mid-Sep–May) FREE This excellent town museum is stuffed with his-

tory and art. The permanent ground-floor exhibition concentrates on the province's impressive archaeological pedigree, with interesting items culled from its Roman and mining history; don't miss the blue-toned 16th-century *azulejos* from nearby walled-town Niebla.

🎎 Festivals & Events

Fiestas Colombinas   HISTORICAL
In the first week of August, Huelva celebrates Columbus' departure for the Americas (3 August 1492) with this six-day festival of music, dance, cultural events and bullfighting.

🛏 Sleeping & Eating

Hotel Familia Conde   BUSINESS HOTEL €
(☑959 28 24 00; www.hotelfamiliaconde.com; Alameda Sundheim 14; s/d €52/60; 🅿@🛜) True, it's housed in a soulless block, but this central business-class operation is efficiently run with friendly service, and the airy, fresh-smelling rooms have gleaming bold-coloured bathrooms. It's a few steps east of the cafe-lined Gran Vía (Avenida Martín Alonso Pinzón).

Hotel Monte Conquero   BUSINESS HOTEL €€
(☑959 28 55 00; www.hotelesmonte.com; Avenida Pablo Rada 10; r from €65; 🅿🛜) Catering to the business set, this impeccably maintained hotel is probably your best bet in Huelva. Bright-red banisters draped in greenery liven up the lobby and staff are charmingly efficient. 'Executive' women's rooms feature complimentary haircare and beauty kits, and all 162 rooms are smartly outfitted with dark-wood desks, crisp white sheets and those all-important back-up internet cables.

Restaurante Juan José   ANDALUCIAN €
(☑959 26 38 57; Calle Villamundaka 1; tapas €2-3, raciones €8-14; ⊙6.30am-6pm & 8pm-midnight Mon-Sat) It's 1.5km northeast of Plaza de las Monjas, but Huelva's crowds regularly pack into this humble establishment for its fabulously gooey *tortilla de patatas* (potato-and-onion omelette). The tuna (fresh from Isla Cristina) and *carne mechada* (meat stuffed with pepper and ham) are tasty, too. Arrive before 2pm to snag a lunch table.

Azabache   TAPAS €€
(☑959 25 75 28; www.restauranteazabache.com; Calle Vázquez López 22; raciones €6-16; ⊙8am-11pm Mon-Fri, to 4pm Sat) After a taste of traditional Huelva? Squeeze into this narrow

tiled tapas bar where busy, helpful waiters are quick to deliver cheese and *jamón* platters, plus scrambled *gurumelos* (local wild mushrooms), fried *chocos* and fresh fish specials.

ⓘ Information

Regional Tourist Office (www.turismohuelva. org; Calle Jesús Nazareno 21; ◷9am-7.30pm Mon-Fri, 9.30am-3pm Sat & Sun) Helpful on the whole province.

Tourist Office (☑959 54 18 17; Plaza de las Monjas; ◷10am-2pm & 5-8.30pm Mon-Fri, to 2pm Sat)

ⓘ Getting There & Away

Most buses from the **bus station** (Calle Doctor Rubio) are operated by **Damas** (☑959 25 69 00; www.damas-sa.es). Destinations include Almonte (for El Rocío), Aracena, Isla Cristina, La Rábida, Moguer, Matalascañas, Palos de la Frontera, Seville and Faro (Portugal). Frequency is reduced on Saturday, Sunday and public holidays.

Renfe (☑902 43 23 43; www.renfe.com) runs three train services to Seville (€12, 1½ hours) and one high-speed ALVIA train to Córdoba (€38, 1¾ hours) and Madrid (€72, 3¾ hours) daily.

Lugares Colombinos

The 'Columbian Sites' are the three townships of La Rábida, Palos de la Frontera and Moguer, along the eastern bank of the Tinto estuary. All three played a key role in Columbus' preparation for his journey of discovery and can be visited in a fun day trip from Huelva, Doñana or Huelva's eastern coast. As the countless greenhouses suggest, this is Spain's main strawberry-growing region (Huelva province produces 90% of Spain's crop).

La Rábida

POP 500

◉ Sights

Muelle de las Carabelas　　HISTORIC SITE (Wharf of the Caravels; €3.55; ◷10am-9pm Tue-Sun mid-Jun–mid-Sep, 9.30am-7.30pm Tue-Sun mid-Sep–mid-Jun; ℗) On the waterfront below the Monasterio de la Rábida is this pseudo 15th-century quayside, where you can board replicas of Columbus' tiny three-ship fleet. The ships are moored behind an interesting museum covering the history of the great explorer's journeys.

Monasterio de la Rábida　　MONASTERY (☑959 35 04 11; www.monasteriodelarabida.com; Paraje de la Rábida; €3; ◷10am-1pm & 4-7pm Tue-Sun; ℗) In the pretty, peaceful village of La Rábida, don't miss this 14th- and 15th-century Franciscan monastery, visited several times by Columbus before his great voyage of discovery.

Palos de la Frontera

POP 5300

It was from the port of Palos de la Frontera that Columbus and his merry band set sail into the unknown. The town provided the explorer with two of his ships, two captains (Martín Alonso Pinzón and Vicente Yáñez Pinzón) and more than half his crew.

◉ Sights

Iglesia de San Jorge　　CHURCH (Calle Fray Juan Pérez) Towards the northern end of Calle Colón is this 15th-century Gothic-Mudéjar church, where Columbus and his sailors took communion before embarking on their great expedition. Water for their ships came from La Fontanilla well nearby.

Casa Museo Martín Alonso Pinzón　　MUSEUM (☑959 10 00 41; Calle Colón 24; €1; ◷10am-2pm Mon-Fri) The former home of the *Pinta*'s captain now houses a permanent exhibition on Palos' crucial contribution to Columbus' famous first expedition.

✗ Eating

El Bodegón　　GRILL, ANDALUCIAN €€ (☑959 53 11 05; Calle Rábida 46; mains €12-25; ◷noon-4pm & 8.30-11.30pm Wed-Mon) Stop to take on supplies at this noisy, atmospheric grotto of a restaurant, which cooks up fish and meat on wood-fired grills.

Moguer

POP 14,300

The sleepy whitewashed town of Moguer, 8km northeast of Palos de la Frontera on the A494, is where Columbus' ship, the *Niña*, was built. The main Columbus site in town is the 14th-century **Monasterio de Santa Clara** (☑959 37 01 07; www.mon asteriodesantaclara.com; Plaza de las Monjas; guided tours €3.50; ◷tours 10.30am, 11.30am & 12.30pm Tue-Sun & 4.30pm, 5.30pm & 6.30pm Tue-Sat), with a lovely Mudéjar cloister and an impressive collection of Renaissance religious art; Columbus spent a night of vigil and prayer here after returning from his first voyage in March 1493. Visits are by guided tour.

Hotel Plaza Escribano (☑959 37 30 63; www.hotelplazaescribano.com; Plaza Escribano 5; s/d €39/56; P❀🐾) is a friendly, modern hotel in Moguer's historic core. Large, stylish rooms are splashed in pastels that complement bright bedspreads; there's a small library for guests plus a cute courtyard and lots of lively tiling.

About 300m southwest of the central Plaza del Cabildo, **Mesón El Lobito** (☑959 37 06 60; Calle Rábida 31; mains €7-19; ⊙10.30am-5pm & 8.30pm-midnight) dishes up huge, great-value platters of traditional country fare in a cavernous *bodega* (wine cellar); grilled fish and meats come fresh from the open log fire.

There's an excellent **tourist office** (☑959 37 18 98; Calle Andalucía 17; ⊙10am-2pm & 5-7pm Tue-Sat) inside the Teatro.

Parque Nacional de Doñana

The World Heritage–listed Parque Nacional de Doñana is a place of haunting natural beauty and exotic horizons, where flocks of flamingos tinge the evening skies pink above one of Europe's most extensive wetlands (the Guadalquivir delta), huge herds of deer and boar flit through *coto* (woodlands), and the elusive Iberian lynx battles for survival. Here, in the largest roadless region in Western Europe, and Spain's most celebrated national park, you can literally taste the scent of nature at her most raw and powerful.

The 542-sq-km national park extends 30km along or close to the Atlantic coast and up to 25km inland. Much of the perimeter is bordered by the separate **Parque Natural de Doñana**, under less strict protection, which forms a 538-sq-km buffer for the national park. The two *parques* together provide a refuge for 360 bird species and 37 types of mammal, including endangered species such as the Iberian lynx and Spanish imperial eagle (nine breeding pairs). They're also a crucial habitat for half a million migrating birds.

Since its establishment in 1969, the national park has been under pressure from tourism operators, farmers, hunters, developers and builders who oppose the restrictions on land use. Ecologists, for their part, argue that Doñana is increasingly hemmed in by tourism and agricultural schemes, roads and other infrastructure that threaten to deplete its water supplies and cut it off from other undeveloped areas.

Some resident lynxes have been run over attempting to cross roads around Doñana (Spain lost 20 lynxes in road accidents in 2014). On the bright side, lynx numbers in the Doñana area now stand at around 80 to 100 individuals, despite a disastrous slump in numbers of its main prey, the rabbit, which led to park authorities introducing 10,000 new rabbits into the area in 2015. There's also an increasingly successful captive breeding program – up to 27 breeding pairs in 2015 (check out www.lynxexsitu.es). The Centro de Visitantes El Acebuche (p606) streams a live video of lynxes in its nearby breeding centre, but you can't visit them.

Access to the interior of the national park is restricted, although anyone can walk or cycle along the 28km Atlantic beach between Matalascañas and the mouth of the Río Guadalquivir (which can be crossed by boat from Sanlúcar de Barrameda in Cádiz province), as long as they do not stray inland.

The only way to visit the national park is by guided jeep tour with one of three licensed companies: Cooperativa Marismas del Rocío (p606), from the Centro de Visitantes El Acebuche; Doñana Reservas (p606), from El Rocío; and **Visitas Doñana** (☑956 36 38 13; www.visitasdonana.com; Bajo de Guía; tours €35; ⊙9am-7pm), from Sanlúcar de Barrameda, in Cádiz province.

National Park Tours

Four-hour, land-based trips in 20- to 30-person all-terrain vehicles are the only way to get inside the national park from the western side. The experience can feel a bit theme park–like, but guides have plenty of in-depth information to share. You can pretty much count on seeing deer and wild boar, though ornithologists may be disappointed by the limited birdwatching opportunities, and you'd be very lucky to spot a lynx.

During spring, summer and holidays, book at least a month ahead, but otherwise a week is usually sufficient notice. Bring binoculars (if you like), drinking water and mosquito repellent (except in winter). English-, German- and French-speaking guides are normally available if you ask in advance.

Cooperativa Marismas del Rocío WILDLIFE TOUR

(☑959 43 04 32; www.donanavisitas.es; Centro de Visitantes El Acebuche; tours €29.50) Runs four-hour tours of the national park in 20- to 30-person all-terrain vehicles, departing from the **Centro de Visitantes El Acebuche**. Tours traverse 75km of the southern part of the park and cover all the major ecosystems – coast, dunes, marshes and Mediterranean forest. Trips start with a long beach drive, then head inland.

Doñana Nature WILDLIFE TOUR

(☑959 44 21 60; www.donana-nature.com; Calle Las Carretas 10, El Rocío; tours per person €28) Runs half-day, general interest tours of the Parque Natural de Doñana at 8am and 3pm daily (binoculars provided). Specialised ornithological and photographic trips are also offered. English-speaking guides available on request.

Doñana Reservas WILDLIFE TOUR

(☑959 44 24 74; www.donanareservas.com; Avenida de la Canaliega, El Rocío; tours per person €28) Runs four-hour tours in 20- to 30-person all-terrain vehicles, focusing on the marshes and woods in the northern section of the park, and including a stop at the Centro de Visitantes José Antonio Valverde (usually an excellent birdwatching spot). Recent reports of lynx sightings.

ℹ Information

The park has seven information points.
Centro de Visitantes El Acebuche (☑959 43 96 29; ☺8am–9pm Apr–mid-Sep, to 7pm mid-Sep–Mar) Twelve kilometres south of El Rocío on the A483, then 1.6km west, El Acebuche is the national park's main visitor centre. It has paths to birdwatching hides and a live film of Iberian lynxes at its breeding centre.
Centro de Visitantes El Acebrón (☑671 593138; ☺9am-3pm & 4-7pm) Located 6km along a minor paved road west from the Centro de Visitantes La Rocina, this centre offers a Doñana information counter and an ethnographic exhibition on the park inside a palatial 1960s residence, plus walking paths.
Centro de Visitantes La Rocina (☑959 43 95 69; ☺9am-3pm & 4-7pm) Beside the A483, 1km south of El Rocío. Has a national park information desk and walking paths.

ℹ Getting There & Away

You cannot enter the park in your own vehicle.
Damas (www.damas-sa.es) runs eight to 10 buses daily between El Rocío and Matalascañas, which stop at the El Acebuche turn-off on the A483 on request. Some tour companies will pick you up from Matalascañas with advance notice.

El Rocío

El Rocío, the most significant town in the vicinity of the Parque Nacional de Doñana, surprises first-timers. Its streets, unpaved and covered in sand, are lined with colourfully decked-out single-storey houses with sweeping verandahs, left empty half the time. But this is no ghost town: these are the well-tended properties of 115 *hermandades* (brotherhoods), whose pilgrims converge on the town every Pentecost (Whitsunday) weekend for the Romería del Rocío, Spain's largest religious festival. And at most weekends, the *hermandades* arrive in a flurry of festive fun for other ceremonies.

Beyond its uniquely exotic ambience, El Rocío impresses with its striking setting in front of luminous Doñana *marismas* (wetlands), where herds of deer drink at dawn and, at certain times of year, pink flocks of flamingos gather in massive numbers.

Whether it's the play of light on the marshes, an old woman praying to the Virgin at the Ermita, or a girl passing by in a sultry flamenco dress, there's always something to catch the eye on El Rocío's dusky, sand-blown streets.

◉ Sights

Ermita del Rocío CHURCH

(☺8am-9pm Apr-Sep, to 7pm Oct-Mar) A striking splash of white at the heart of the town, the Ermita del Rocío was built in its present form in 1964. This is the permanent home of the celebrated Nuestra Señora del Rocío (Our Lady of El Rocío), a small wooden image of the Virgin dressed in long, jewelled robes, which normally stands above the main altar.

People arrive to see the Virgin every day of the year, and especially on weekends, when El Rocío's brotherhoods often gather for colourful celebrations.

🏃 Activities

The marshlands in front of El Rocío, which have water most of the year, offer some of the best bird- and beast-watching in the entire Doñana region. Deer and horses graze in the shallows and you may be lucky enough to spot a big pink cloud of flamingos wheel-

DON'T MISS

SPAIN'S GREATEST RELIGIOUS PILGRIMAGE: ROMERÍA DEL ROCÍO

Every Pentecost (Whitsunday) weekend, seven weeks after Easter, El Rocío transforms from a quiet backwater into an explosive mess of noise, colour and passion. This is the culmination of Spain's biggest religious pilgrimage, the **Romería del Rocío**, which draws up to a million joyous pilgrims.

The focus of all this revelry is the tiny image of Nuestra Señora del Rocío (Our Lady of El Rocío), which was found in a marshland tree by a hunter from Almonte village back in the 13th century. When he stopped for a rest on the way home, the Virgin magically returned to the tree. Before long, a chapel was built on the site of the tree (El Rocío) and pilgrims started arriving.

Solemn is the last word you'd apply to this quintessentially Andalucian event. Participants dress in their finest Andalucian costume and sing, drink, dance, laugh and romance their way to El Rocío. Most belong to the 115 *hermandades* (brotherhoods) who arrive from towns all across southern Spain on foot, horseback and in colourfully decorated covered wagons.

The weekend reaches an ecstatic climax in the very early hours of Monday. Members of the Almonte *hermandad*, which claims the Virgin as its own, barge into the church and bear her out on a float. Violent struggles ensue as others battle for the honour of carrying La Paloma Blanca (the White Dove). The crush and chaos are immense, but somehow the Virgin is carried round to each of the *hermandad* buildings before finally being returned to the church in the afternoon. Upcoming dates: 4 June 2017, 20 May 2018 and 9 June 2019.

ing through the sky. Pack a pair of binoculars and stroll the waterfront promenade.

Francisco Bernis Birdwatching Centre BIRDWATCHING
(📞959 44 23 72; www.seo.org; ⊗9am-2pm & 4-6pm Tue-Sun) **FREE** About 700m east of the Ermita along the waterfront, this birdwatching facility backs on to the marshes. Flamingos, glossy ibis, spoonbills and more can be observed through the rear windows or from the observation deck with high-power binoculars (free). Experts here can help you identify species and inform you about visiting migratory birds and where to see them.

Doñana a Caballo HORSE RIDING
(📞674 219568; www.donanaacaballo.com; Avenida de la Canaliega, El Rocío; per 1hr/2hr/half-day €20/30/60) Guided horse rides for all levels through the Coto del Rey woodlands east of El Rocío.

🛌 Sleeping & Eating

Hotels get booked up to a year ahead for the Romería del Rocío.

Hotel Toruño HOTEL €€
(📞959 44 23 23; www.toruno.es; Plaza Acebuchal 22; s/d incl breakfast €48/67; P❋🅰) About 350m east of the Ermita, this brilliantly

white villa stands right by the *marismas*, where you can spot flamingos going through their morning beauty routine. Inside, tile murals continue the ornithological theme – even in the shower! Rooms are bright and cosy, but only a few actually overlook the marshes. Breakfast is in the wonderful restaurant, opposite.

Hotel La Malvasía HOTEL €€
(📞959 44 38 70; www.lamalvasiahotel.com; Calle Sanlúcar 38; s/d €66/94; ❋🅰) This idyllic hotel occupies a grand *casa señorial* (manor house) overlooking the marshes at the eastern end of town. Rooms are crushed with character including rustic tiled floors, vintage El Rocío photos and floral-patterned iron bedsteads. Top-level units make great bird-viewing perches.

★ Restaurante Toruño ANDALUCIAN €€
(📞959 44 24 22; www.toruno.es; Plaza Acebuchal 22; mains €12-20; ⊗8am-midnight; 🖋) With its traditional Andalucian atmosphere, authentically good food and huge portions, this is El Rocío's one must-try restaurant. A highlight on the menu is the free-range *mostrenca* calf, unique to Doñana; for non-carnivores, the huge grilled veg *parrillada* is fantastic. On warm evenings dine in front of the restaurant by the 1000-year-old *acebuche* tree.

ℹ Information

Tourist Office (☎ 959 44 23 50; www.
turismoalmonte.com; Calle Muñoz Pavón;
⊙ 9.30am-2pm) Inside the town hall.

ℹ Getting There & Away

Damas (www.damas-sa.es) buses run from
Seville's Plaza de Armas to El Rocío (€6.36, 1½
hours, two daily), continuing to Matalascañas.
From Huelva, take a Damas bus to Almonte,
then another to El Rocío (eight daily).

Minas de Riotinto

POP 3260 / ELEV 420M

Tucked away on the southern fringe of
Huelva's Sierra Morena is one of the world's
oldest mining districts; even King Solo-
mon of faraway Jerusalem is said to have
mined gold here for his famous temple. The
Romans were digging up silver by the 4th
century BC, but the mines were then left
largely untouched until the British Rio Tinto company transformed the area into one
of the world's key copper-mining centres in
the 1870s (leading, incidentally, to the foundation of Spain's first football club here).
The mines were sold back to Spain in 1954.
Though the miners clocked off for the last
time in 2001, it's still a fascinating place to
explore, with a superb museum, and the opportunity to visit the old mines and ride the
mine railway.

The Río Tinto itself rises a few kilometres northeast of town, its name ('red
river') stemming from the deep red-brown
hue produced by the reaction of its acidic
waters with the abundant iron and copper
ores.

◉ Sights

Peña de Hierro   MINE
(☎ 959 59 00 25; www.parquemineroderiotinto.
es; adult/child €8/7; ⊙ 10.30am-3pm & 4-7pm)
These are old copper and sulphur mines
3km north of Nerva (6km east of Minas de
Riotinto). Here you see the source of the Río
Tinto and a 65m-deep opencast mine, and
are taken into a 200m-long underground
mine gallery. There are three guaranteed
daily visits but schedules vary, so it's essential to book ahead through the Museo Minero (by phone or online).

Museo Minero   MUSEUM
(☎ 959 59 00 25; www.parquemineroderiotinto.es;
Plaza Ernest Lluch; adult/child €4/3; ⊙ 10.30am-

3pm & 4-7pm; P) Riotinto's mining museum
is a figurative goldmine for devotees of industrial archaeology, taking you through the
area's unique history from the megalithic
tombs of the 3rd millennium BC to the Roman and British colonial eras, the 1888 *año
de los tiros* (year of the gunshots) upheaval
and finally the closure of the mines in 2001.
The tour includes an elaborate 200m-long
re-creation of a Roman mine.

🏃 Activities

Ferrocarril Turístico-Minero   TRAIN TOUR
(☎ 959 59 00 25; www.parquemineroderiotinto.es;
adult/child €10/9; ⊙ 1.30pm & 5.30pm mid-Jul–
mid-Sep, 1.30pm mid-Sep–mid-Jul, closed Mon-Fri
Nov-Jan) A fun way to see the area (especially with children) is to ride the old mining
train, running 22km (round trip) through
the surreal landscape in restored early
20th-century carriages. The train parallels
the river for the entire journey, so you can
appreciate its constantly shifting hues. It's
mandatory to book ahead. Tickets may be
purchased either at the town's museum or
the railway station.

ℹ Getting There & Away

Damas (www.damas-sa.es) runs five daily
buses between Minas de Riotinto and Huelva
(€6.88, 1¾ hours) Monday to Friday, three on
weekends.

Aracena & Around

POP 6700 / ELEV 730M

Sparkling white in its mountain bowl, the
thriving old market town of Aracena is an
appealingly lively place that's wrapped like
a ribbon around a medieval church and ruined castle. With a stash of good places to
eat and sleep, it makes an ideal Sierra de
Aracena base.

◉ Sights

Plaza Alta   SQUARE
The handsome, cobbled Plaza Alta was originally the centre of the town. Here stands
the elegant 15th-century Cabildo Viejo, the
former town hall, with a grand Renaissance
doorway.

Castillo   CASTLE
Dramatically dominating the town are
the tumbling, hilltop ruins of the *castillo*,
an atmospheric fortification built by the
kingdoms of Portugal and Castilla in the

12th century. Right beside is the Iglesia Prioral de Nuestra Señora del Mayor Dolor (◷10am-5pm, to 7.30pm Jul & Aug), a Gothic-Mudéjar hybrid built about a century later with attractive brick tracery on the tower, noted for its distinctive Islamic influence. Both are reached via a steep lane from Plaza Alta.

Museo del Jamón
MUSEUM

(Gran Vía; adult/child €3.50/2.50; ◷10.45am-2.15pm & 3.30-7pm) The *jamón* for which the sierra is famed gets due recognition in this modern museum. You'll learn why the acorn-fed Iberian pig gives such succulent meat, about the importance of the native pastures in which they are reared, and about traditional and contemporary methods of slaughter and curing. One room is devoted to local wild mushrooms.

A discount is available when combined with the ticket for the Gruta de las Maravillas.

Gruta de las Maravillas
CAVE

(Cave of Marvels; ☑663 937876; Calle Pozo de la Nieve; tours adult/child €8.50/6; ◷10am-1.30pm & 3-6pm) Beneath the town's castle hill is a web of caves and tunnels carved from the karstic topography. An extraordinary 1km route takes you through 12 chambers and past six underground lakes, all beautifully illuminated and filled with weird and wonderful rock formations, which provided a backdrop for the film *Journey to the Center of the Earth.*

Activities

The hills and mountains around Aracena offer some of the most beautiful, and least known, walking country in Andalucía. Any time of year is a good time to hike here but spring, when the meadows are awash with wildflowers and carnival-coloured butterflies, is the best time to hit the trails. The Centro de Visitantes Cabildo Viejo (☑959 12 95 53; Plaza Alta; ◷9.30am-2pm Thu-Sun) can recommend walks of varying difficulty and give you basic maps; the tourist office (p610) sells a good map with dozens of suggested hikes.

Linares de la Sierra Walk
HIKING

This sublime and fairly gentle 5km, two-hour ramble takes you down a verdant valley to beautifully sleepy Linares de la Sierra. The signposted path (PRA48) is easy to find off the HU8105 on the southwestern edge of Aracena, 500m beyond the municipal swimming pool.

Sleeping & Eating

Molino del Bombo
BOUTIQUE HOTEL €

(☑959 12 84 78; www.molinodelbombo.com; Calle Ancha 4; s/d €36/60; ❄☎) Though of recent vintage, the top-of-town Bombo has a rustic style that blends in with Aracena's time-worn architecture. Bright rooms have wonderfully comfy, pillow-laden beds, plus frescoes and exposed stone and brick designs; some bathrooms are done up as picturesque grottoes. The cosy salon and courtyard with trickling fountain are perfect for lounging.

Hotel Convento Aracena
HISTORIC HOTEL €€

(☑959 12 68 99; www.hotelconventoaracena. es; Calle Jesús y María 19; s €84-130, d €94-145; ⓟ❄☎⊗) Glossy, straight-lined, modern rooms contrast with flourishes of original Andalucian baroque architecture at this recently converted 17th-century convent, your finest option in Aracena town. Room 9 is fabulously set in the church dome. Enjoy the on-site spa, good sierra cuisine, and year-round saltwater pool, with gorgeous village views and summer bar.

★ Rincón de Juan
TAPAS €

(Calle José Nogales; tapas €1.80-3, raciones €7-10; ◷7.30am-4pm & 6.30pm-midnight Mon-Sat, 7.30am-4pm Sun) It's standing room only at this wedge-shaped, stone-walled corner bar, indisputably the top tapas spot in town. Iberian ham is the star attraction and forms the basis for a variety of *montaditos* (small stuffed rolls) and *rebanadas* (sliced loaves for several people). The local goat's cheese is always a good bet.

★ Jesús Carrión
TAPAS €€

(☑959 46 31 88; www.jesuscarrionrestaurante. com; Calle Pozo de la Nieve 35; tapas €5-9, mains €10-17; ◷1-4.30pm & 8-11pm Thu-Sat, 1-4.30pm Wed & Sun; ☎⊉) Devoted chef Jesús heads up the creative kitchen at this wonderful family-run restaurant, which is causing quite the stir with its lovingly prepared, contemporary twists on traditional Aracena dishes. Try the Iberian ham carpaccio or the local boletus-mushroom risotto. Homemade breads come straight from the oven and salads are deliciously fresh – not a tinned vegetable in sight!

ℹ️ Information

Tourist Office (☑ 663 937877; www.aracena. es; Calle Pozo de la Nieve; ⊙10am-2pm & 4-6pm) Opposite the Gruta de las Maravillas; sells a good walking map.

ℹ️ Getting There & Away

The **bus station** (Avenida de Sevilla) is 700m southeast of Plaza del Marqués de Aracena. **Damas** (www.damas-sa.es) runs one morning and two afternoon buses (one on Sunday) from Seville (€7.46, 1¼ hours), continuing to Cortegana via Alájar or Jabugo. From Huelva, there are two afternoon departures Monday to Friday, one at weekends (€11, three hours). There's also local service between Aracena and Cortegana via Linares, Alájar and Almonaster la Real.

CÁDIZ PROVINCE

If you had to break off one part of Andalucía to demonstrate to aliens what it looked like, you'd probably choose Cádiz province. Emblematic regional highlights are part of the furniture here: thrillingly sited white towns, craggy mountains, endless olives trees, flamenco in its purist incarnation, the original (and best) fortified sherry, the cradle of Andalucian horse culture, and festivals galore. Stuffed in among all of this condensed culture are two expansive natural parks that cover an unbroken tract of land that runs from Olvera in the north to Algeciras in the south. The same line once marked the blurred frontier between Christian Spain and Moorish Granada, and the ancient border is flecked with huddled white towns, many of them given a 'de la Frontera' suffix testifying to their volatile but fascinating history.

Cádiz

POP 121,700

You could write several weighty tomes about Cádiz and still fall miles short of nailing its essence. Old age accounts for much of the complexity. Cádiz is generally considered to be the oldest continuously inhabited settlement in Europe, founded as Gadir by the Phoenicians in about 1100 BC. Now well into its fourth millennium, the ancient centre, surrounded almost entirely by water, is a romantic jumble of sinuous streets where Atlantic waves crash against eroded sea walls, salty beaches teem with sun-worshippers, and cheerful taverns echo with the sounds of cawing gulls and frying fish.

Spain's first liberal constitution (La Pepa) was signed here in 1812, while the city's distinctive urban model provided an identikit for fortified Spanish colonial cities in the Americas. Indeed, the port – with its crenellated sea walls and chunky forts – is heavily reminiscent of Cuba's Havana or Puerto Rico's San Juan.

Enamoured return visitors talk fondly of Cádiz' seafood, sands and stash of intriguing monuments and museums. More importantly, they gush happily about the *gaditanos* (people from Cádiz), an upfront, sociable bunch whose crazy Carnaval (p613) is an exercise in ironic humour and whose upbeat *alegrías* (flamenco songs) will bring warmth to your heart.

👁️ Sights

To understand Cádiz, first you need to befriend its *barrios* (districts). The old city is split into classic quarters: the Barrio del Pópulo, home of the cathedral, and nexus of the once prosperous medieval settlement; Barrio de Santa María, the old Roma and flamenco quarter; Barrio de la Viña, a former vineyard that became the city's main fishing quarter and Carnaval epicentre; and Barrio del Mentidero (said to take its name from the many rumours spread on its streets) in the northwest.

⭐ **Catedral de Cádiz**   CATHEDRAL
(☑ 956 28 61 54; Plaza de la Catedral; adult/child €5/3; ⊙10am-6pm Mon-Sat, 1.30-6pm Sun) Cádiz' beautiful yellow-domed cathedral is an impressively proportioned baroque-neoclassical construction, best appreciated from seafront Campo del Sur in the evening sun. Though commissioned in 1716, the project wasn't finished until 1838, by which time neoclassical elements (the dome, towers and main facade) had diluted architect Vicente Acero's original baroque plan.

⭐ **Museo de Cádiz**   MUSEUM
(www.museosdeandalucia.es; Plaza de Mina; €1.50, EU citizens free; ⊙9am-3.30pm Tue-Sun mid-Jun–mid-Sep, 9am-7.30pm Tue-Sat & 9am-3.30pm Sun mid-Sep–mid-Jun) Yes, it's a bit dusty, but the Museo de Cádiz is the province's top museum. Stars of the ground-floor archaeology section are two Phoenician marble sarcophagi carved in human likeness, along with lots of headless Roman statues and a giant marble Emperor Trajan

(with head) from the Baelo Claudia (p634) ruins. Upstairs, the excellent fine arts collection displays 18 superb 17th-century canvases of saints, angels and monks by Francisco de Zurbarán.

Casa del Obispo
MUSEUM

(www.lacasadelobispo.com; Plaza de Fray Félix; adult/child €5/4; ⊙10am-8pm, to 6pm mid-Sep–mid-Jun) Outside the cathedral's eastern exterior wall, this expansive museum of glass walkways over 1500 sq metres of excavated ruins takes you through Cádiz' eventful history, from the 8th century BC to the 18th century. It served as a Phoenician funerary complex, Roman temple and mosque, before becoming the city's Episcopal Palace in the 16th century. It was closed temporarily at research time: enquire at the tourist office (p616).

Plaza de San Juan de Dios
SQUARE

Glammed up for the 200th anniversary of the 1812 constitution, cafe-lined Plaza San Juan de Dios is dominated by the grand, neoclassical *ayuntamiento* (town hall) built around 1800.

Centro de Interpretación del Teatro Romano
INTERPRETATION CENTRE

(Calle Mesón 12; ⊙11am-5pm Mon-Sat, 10am-2pm Sun Apr-Sep, closed the first Monday of each month; 10am-4.30pm Mon-Sat, 10am-2pm Sun Oct-Mar) FREE On the seaward edge of the Barrio del Pópulo is Cádiz' Roman theatre. Though the theatre itself is closed for renovation works, you can see parts of it at this adjacent, recently reopened interpretation centre.

Museo de las Cortes de Cádiz
MUSEUM

(Calle Santa Inés 9; ⊙9am-6pm Tue-Fri, to 2pm Sat & Sun) FREE The remodelled Museo de las Cortes de Cádiz is full of memorabilia of the revolutionary 1812 Cádiz parliament. One exhibit jumps out at you: the huge, marvellously detailed model of 18th-century Cádiz, made in mahogany and ivory by Alfonso Ximénez between 1777 and 1779.

Puerta de Tierra
GATE

(Land Gate; ⊙10am-6pm Tue-Sun) FREE The imposing 18th-century Puerta de Tierra guards the southeastern (and only land) entry to Cádiz' old town. You can wander the upper fortifications and defence tower, where Spanish- and English-language panels detail visible sights and the evolution of Cádiz' complex fortification system.

Torre Tavira
TOWER

(www.torretavira.com; Calle Marqués del Real Tesoro 10; €6; ⊙10am-8pm, to 6pm Oct-Apr) Northwest of Plaza de Topete, the Torre Tavira opens up dramatic panoramas of Cádiz and has a camera obscura that projects live, moving images of the city on to a screen (sessions every 30 minutes).

Castillo de San Sebastián
FORT, MUSEUM

(Paseo Fernando Quiñones; adult/child €2/free; ⊙9.30am-5pm) After centuries as a military installation, this polygonal fort built in 1706 on a small islet joined by a stone walkway to Playa de la Caleta has finally opened its doors as historic-sight-cum-exhibition-centre. Its bulky walls and walkways are replete with city views. Opening hours may vary as renovations meander on.

Plaza de Topete
SQUARE

About 250m northwest of the cathedral, this triangular plaza is one of Cádiz' most intimate. Bright with flowers, it's usually talked about as Plaza de las Flores (Square of the Flowers). Right beside is the revamped **Mercado Central de Abastos** (Plaza de la Libertad; ⊙9am-3pm), built in 1837 and the oldest covered market in Spain.

🏃 Activities

Playa de la Victoria
BEACH

Often overshadowed by the city's historical riches, Cádiz' beaches are Copacabana-like in their size, vibe and beauty. This fine, wide strip of Atlantic sand starts 1km south of the Puerta de Tierra and stretches 4km back along the peninsula.

Take bus 1 (Plaza España-Cortadura; €1.10) from Plaza de España, or walk or jog along the promenade from the Barrio de Santa María.

Playa de la Caleta
BEACH

Hugging the western side of the Barrio de la Viña, this small, popular city beach catches the eye with its mock-Moorish *balneario* (bathhouse). It's flanked by two forts: the Castillo de San Sebastián (p611), for centuries a military installation, and the star-shaped **Castillo de Santa Catalina** (📞956 22 63 33; Calle Antonio Burgos; ⊙11am-7pm, to 8.30pm Mar-Oct) FREE, built after the 1596 Anglo-Dutch sacking of the city.

Mimicking Ursula Andress in *Dr. No*, Halle Berry famously strode out of the sea here in an orange bikini in the 2002 James Bond film *Die Another Day*.

Cádiz

Courses

Gadir Escuela Internacional de Español LANGUAGE COURSE
(📞956 26 05 57; www.gadir.net; Calle Pérgolas 5) About 300m southeast of the Puerta de Tierra, this long-established school has a wide range of classes in small, specialised groups.

K2 Internacional LANGUAGE COURSE
(📞956 21 26 46; www.k2internacional.com; Plaza Mentidero 19) Based in the Barrio

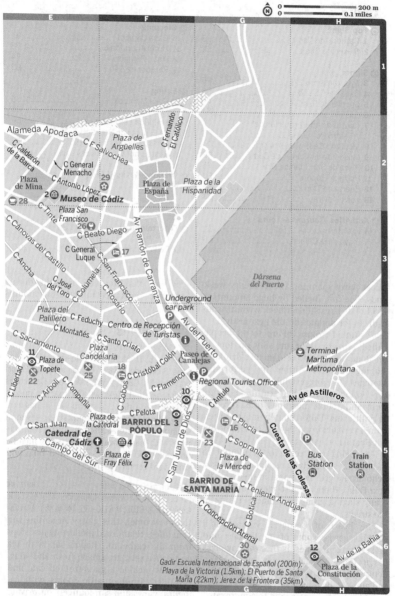

del Mentidero, this school offers special courses for people over 50 years old. The school also organises a range of flamenco, cooking and even surf courses, as well as accommodation.

✯✯ Festivals & Events

Carnaval
CARNIVAL

No other Spanish city celebrates Carnaval with as much spirit, dedication and humour as Cádiz. Here it becomes a 10-day singing, dancing and drinking fancy-dress

Cádiz

street party spanning two February weekends. The fun, fuelled by huge amounts of alcohol, is irresistible. Check www.turismo.cadiz.es for updates on the next festival.

Costumed groups of up to 45 people, called *murgas,* tour the city on foot or on floats and tractors, dancing, drinking, singing satirical ditties or performing sketches. The biggest hits are the 12-person *chirigotas* with their scathing humour, irony and double meanings, often directed at politicians. Unfortunately most of their famed verbal wit will be lost on all but fluent Spanish speakers.

This being carefree Cádiz, in addition to the 300 or so officially recognised *murgas* (who are judged by a panel in the Gran Teatro Falla), there are also plenty of *ilegales* – any singing group that fancies taking to the streets.

The heart of Carnaval, where you'll stumble across some of the liveliest and most drunken scenes, is the working-class Barrio de la Viña, between the Mercado Central de Abastos and Playa de la Caleta, and along Calle Ancha and around Plaza de Topete, where *ilegales* tend to congregate.

Typically, the first weekend sees the mass arrival of nonlocal partygoers, while the second weekend is when the *gaditanos* (people from Cádiz) really come out to play. Surprisingly, things can be quiet midweek.

If you plan to sleep in Cádiz during Carnaval, book accommodation months ahead.

🛏 Sleeping

★ Casa Caracol   HOSTEL €
(📞956 26 11 66; www.hostel-casacaracol.com; Calle Suárez de Salazar 4; hammock/dm/d incl breakfast €10/18/40; @ 🟢) 🌿 Casa Caracol is Cádiz' original old-town backpacker hostel. Friendly as only Cádiz can be, it has colourful bunk dorms for four, six or seven, a sociable communal kitchen, and a roof terrace with hammocks. Other perks include home-cooked dinners, yoga, and bike and surfboard rental. No lift.

Hotel Patagonia Sur   HOTEL €€
(📞856 17 46 47; www.hotelpatagoniasur.es; Calle Cobos 11; s €105, d €110-135; ✳ @ 🟢) A relative newcomer, this glossy Argentine-run gem offers clean-lined modernity just steps from the cathedral. Rooms, all with tea and coffee sets, are smart, fresh and snug. Bonuses include a glass-fronted cafe and sun-filled 5th-floor attic rooms with cathedral views and sun-loungers on private terraces.

Hotel Argantonio   HOTEL €€
(📞956 21 16 40; www.hotelargantonio.com; Calle Argantonio 3; incl breakfast s €75-95, d €100-125; ✳ @ 🟢) This character-filled, small-is-beautiful hotel in Cádiz' old quarter

sparkles with its hand-painted and wood-carved doors, colourfully tiled floors adorning bedrooms, bathrooms and corridors, and intricate Moorish arch and fountain in the lobby. The 1st floor is Mudéjar, the 2nd 'colonial romantic', the 3rd a mix. Tucked away on the roof is a lounge terrace.

★ **Parador de Cádiz** HOTEL €€€
(🖉956 22 69 05; www.parador.es; Avenida Duque de Nájera 9; incl breakfast s €192-272, d €210-290; 🅿🖥🌊) Bold, beautiful and right beside Playa de la Caleta, the so-called Parador Atlántico contrasts with Andalucía's other *paradores* (luxurious state-owned hotels) in that it's super-modern and built from scratch. Bright reds and blues throw character into the sleek, contemporary rooms with balcony and floor-to-ceiling windows. Choose from four sea-view swimming pools.

✖ Eating

Just as the air in Jerez de la Frontera is thick with sherry, Cádiz smells unforgettably of fresh fish. Calle Virgen de la Palma, in the Barrio de la Viña, is the city's go-to seafood street, where fantastic fish restaurants plate up the day's catch at alfresco tables. Calles Plocia and Sopranis, off Plaza de San Juan de Dios, are the gourmet eat-streets.

★ **Casa Manteca** TAPAS €
(🖉956 21 36 03; Calle Corralón de los Carros 66; tapas €2.50; ⊙noon-4pm & 8.30pm-12.30am, closed Sun & Mon evenings approx Nov-Mar) The hub of La Viña's Carnaval fun, with every inch of its walls covered in flamenco, bullfighting and Carnaval memorabilia, Casa Manteca is a *barrio* classic full of old tapas faves. Ask the chatty waiters for a tapa of mussels or *chicharrones* (pressed pork dressed with a squeeze of lemon), and it'll fly across the bar on wax paper.

Restaurant Café Royalty CAFE €
(🖉956 07 80 65; www.caferoyalty.com; Plaza Candelaria; snacks €12-20, restaurant €33-55; ⊙9am-midnight Jun-Sep, 11am-11pm Oct-May) Originally opened in 1912 on the centenary of the 1812 constitution, the Royalty was once a discussion corner for the intellectuals of the day, including beloved *gaditano* composer Manuel de Falla. The cafe closed in the 1930s, but thanks to an inspired renovation project overseen by a local *gaditano* it reopened in 2012, 100 years after its initial inauguration.

Freiduría Las Flores SEAFOOD €
(🖉956 22 61 12; Plaza de Topete 4; tapas €1.50, raciones €6-8; ⊙noon-4.30pm & 8.30pm-midnight) Cádiz' addiction to fried fish reaches new heights here. If it comes from the sea, chances are it's been fried and dished up at Las Flores as tapa, *media ración* (larger tapas serving) or *ración* (full-plate serving), or in an improvised paper cup, fish-and-chips style. If you can't choose, try a *surtido* (mixed fry-up). Don't count on a table.

★ **La Esquina de Sopranis** TAPAS €€
(🖉956 26 58 42; www.sopranis.es; Calle Sopranis 5; tapas €1.50-5.50; ⊙1-4pm & 8.30-11.30pm Tue-Sat, 1-4pm Sun; 🌿) One of those bubbly, contemporary tapas places you'll never want to leave, packed-out Sopranis blends casual and sophisticated to perfection. The food is equally exquisite. Local seasonal ingredients are thrown together in beautifully presented creative combos, like mini *solomillo* (pork sirloin) with chorizo sauce or market-fresh *timbal de verduras* (vegetable stack). Our top pick: the melt-in-the-mouth cheeses.

Arrocería La Pepa SPANISH, SEAFOOD €€
(🖉956 26 38 21; www.restaurantelapepa.es; Paseo Marítimo 14; paella per person €12-15; ⊙1.30-4pm & 8.30-11pm Thu-Sat, 1.30-4pm Sun-Wed) For a decent paella, leave the old town behind and head 3km southeast along Playa de la Victoria – take an appetite-inducing oceanside stroll or jog, or a quick ride on bus 1 to Estadio (Plaza España-Cortadura; €1.10). The fish in La Pepa's seafood paella tastes like it's just jumped 100m from the Atlantic on to your plate.

Mesón Criollo SEAFOOD €€
(www.mesoncriollo.com; cnr Calles Virgen de la Palma & Lubet; mains €7-14; ⊙noon-4pm & 8-11.30pm, closed Sun-Tue & Wed night Oct-Feb) Amid La Viña's countless fish restaurants, this one stands out for its prawns, fish brochettes and – if you happen to arrive at the right time – individual paella. Sit out on the palm-studded street at tapas time and you'll feel like there's a permanent carnival going on in what is Cadiz' primary Carnaval quarter.

El Faro SEAFOOD €€€
(🖉956 21 10 68; www.elfarodecadiz.com; Calle San Félix 15; mains €16-25; ⊙1-4pm & 8.30-11.30pm) Ask any *gaditano* for their favourite Cádiz restaurant and there's a high chance they'll choose El Faro, at once jam-packed tapas

bar and upmarket restaurant decorated with pretty ceramics. Seafood is why people come here, although the *rabo de toro* (oxtail) has its devotees.

If any place in this relaxed city has a dress code, it's El Faro, but even here it only extends to banning swimsuits...

Drinking & Nightlife

With limitations on outdoor drinking spaces and enforced closing times, Cádiz nightlife isn't quite what it used to be, but there are still plenty of places to find after-dark fun.

In the old city, the Plaza de Mina–Plaza San Francisco–Plaza de España triangle is the centre of the late-night bar scene, especially Calle Beato Diego; things get going around midnight, but can be quiet early in the week. More bars are scattered around the Barrio del Pópulo, east of the cathedral. Punta San Felipe (La Punta), on the northern side of the harbour, has a string of drinks/dance bars packed with a youngish crowd from about 3am to 6am Thursday to Saturday.

Cádiz' other nocturnal haunt, particularly in summer, is down along Playa de la Victoria and the Paseo Marítimo, on and around Calle Muñoz Arenillas near the Hotel Playa Victoria (about 2.5km south of the Puerta de Tierra).

Tetería El Oasis
TEAHOUSE

(Calle San José 6; ⊙5pm-midnight Mon-Fri, 4pm-2am Sat) Find dark nooks under the red and orange lace curtains and sip discreetly on a Darjeeling in a state of contemplative meditation – until the belly dancers arrive (Friday, 11pm)!

Nahu
BAR

(www.nahucadiz.es; Calle Beato Diego 8; ⊙4pm-3am Mon-Sat; 🕾) Stylish student-oriented cocktail bar with mood lighting, Moroccan lamps and chill-out sofas. At its best when you're perched at the bar, G&T in hand, but good for coffee and wi-fi too. DJ sessions Friday or Saturday.

Quilla
CAFE, WINE BAR

(www.quilla.es; Playa de la Caleta; ⊙10am-11pm; 🕾) A bookish cafe-bar encased in what appears to be the rusty hulk of an old ship overlooking Playa de la Caleta, with coffee, pastries, tapas, wine, art expos and *gratis* sunsets. Opening hours spill over in summer.

⭐ Entertainment

Cádiz helped invent flamenco and subtly nurtured the talent of Andalucía's finest classical composer, Manuel de Falla, and this weighty musical legacy is ingrained in the city's entertainment scene.

⭐ Peña Flamenca La Perla
FLAMENCO

(📞956 25 91 01; www.laperladecadiz.es; Calle Carlos Ollero; €3) Paint-peeled La Perla, set romantically next to the crashing Atlantic surf off Calle Concepción Arenal in the Barrio de Santa María, hosts flamenco at 10pm most Fridays, more often in spring and summer, for an audience full of aficionados. It's an unforgettable experience.

La Cava
FLAMENCO

(📞956 21 18 66; www.flamencolacava.com; Calle Antonio López 16; €22, with dinner €37; ⊙Mar-Dec) Cádiz' main *tablao* (choreographed flamenco show) happens in a rustically bedecked tavern with drinks and dinner on Tuesdays (April to November), Thursdays and Saturdays at 9.30pm.

ℹ Information

Centro de Recepción de Turistas (📞956 24 10 01; www.turismo.cadiz.es; Paseo de Canalejas; ⊙9am-6.30pm Mon-Fri, to 5pm Sat & Sun) Near the bus and train stations.

Regional Tourist Office (📞956 20 31 91; Avenida Ramón de Carranza; ⊙9am-7.30pm Mon-Fri, 9.30am-3pm Sat & Sun)

ℹ Getting There & Away

BOAT

From the **Terminal Marítima Metropolitana**, 17 daily catamarans (www.cmtbc.es) leave Monday to Friday for El Puerto de Santa María (€2.65, 30 minutes); there are six on Saturday, five on Sunday.

BUS

All out-of-town buses currently leave from the provisional **bus station** (📞956 80 70 59; Plaza Sevilla), next to the train station. Cádiz' new bus station, on Avenida Astilleros on the east side of the train station, is due to be completed in late 2015; all services are likely to switch to the new station once it opens.

Most buses are operated by **Comes** (www.tgcomes.es) or **Los Amarillos** (📞902 210317; www.samar.es). The **Consorcio de Transportes Bahía de Cádiz** (📞856 10 04 95; www.cmtbc.es) runs buses between Jerez de la Frontera airport and Cádiz, via Jerez city.

DESTINATION	FARE	DURATION	FREQUENCY
Arcos de la Frontera	€7.25	1½hr	1-4 daily
El Bosque	€8.80	2½hr	2-4 daily
El Puerto de Santa María	€2.65	45min	hourly
Granada	€36	5¼hr	4 daily
Jerez de la Frontera	€3.75	50min	3-7 daily
Málaga	€28	4½hr	4 daily
Ronda	€16	3½hr	1-2 daily
Sanlúcar de Barrameda	€5	1hr	5-10 daily
Seville	€13	1¾hr	9 daily
Tarifa	€9.91	1¾hr	7 daily
Vejer de la Frontera	€5.67	1½hr	5-7 daily

CAR & MOTORCYCLE

The AP4 motorway from Seville to Puerto Real on the eastern side of the Bahía de Cádiz carries a €7.25 toll.

TRAIN

From the train station, on the southeastern edge of the old town, trains go to/from El Puerto de Santa María (€3.40, 35 minutes, 23 daily), Jerez de la Frontera (€4.05 to €6.05, 45 minutes, 33 daily) and Seville (€16 to €24, 1¾ hours, 15 daily). Three or four daily high-speed ALVIA trains go to Madrid (€74, 4½ hours).

El Puerto de Santa María

POP 88,700

When you're surrounded by such cultural luminaries as Cádiz, Jerez de la Frontera and Seville, it's easy to get lost in the small print; such is the fate of El Puerto de Santa María, despite its collection of well-known icons. Osborne sherry, with its famous bull logo (which has become the national symbol of Spain), was founded and retains its HQ here, as do half a dozen other sherry bodegas. With its abundance of good beaches, sherry bodegas, elaborate cuisine, weighty bullfighting legacy and smattering of architectural heirlooms, El Puerto can seem like southern Andalucía in microcosm. It's an easy day trip from Cádiz or Jerez.

◉ Sights

⭐ **Bodegas Osborne**   SHERRY BODEGA

(☑956 86 91 00; www.osborne.es; Calle los Moros 7; tours €8; ⊙tours noon & 12.30pm, in English & 10.30am) Creator of the legendary black-bull logo still exhibited on life-sized billboards all over Spain (now without the name), Osborne, the best known of El Puerto's sherry wineries, was set up – with no intentional irony – by an Englishman, Thomas Osborne Mann, in 1772. It remains one of Spain's oldest companies run continuously by the same family.

The gorgeous whitewashed bodega, hidden in flower-fringed gardens, adds extra tours from June to mid-September. Book ahead.

Bodegas Gutiérrez Colosía   SHERRY BODEGA

(☑956 85 28 52; www.gutierrezcolosia.com; Avenida de la Bajamar 40; tours €6; ⊙tours 12.15pm Mon-Fri, 1pm Sat) No bookings needed for English-, Spanish- or German-language tours of this intimate, family-run sherry bodega, right beside the catamaran dock. Visits end with a five-wine tasting, which can include tapas and flamenco on request. Timings vary.

Castillo de San Marcos   CASTLE

(☑627 569335; servicios.turisticos@caballero.es; Plaza Alfonso X El Sabio; adult/child €6/3, free Tue; ⊙tours hourly 11.30am-1.30pm Tue, 10.30am-1.30pm Thu & Sat) Heavily restored in the 20th century, El Puerto's fine castle was constructed over an Islamic mosque by Alfonso X of Castilla after he took the town in 1260. The old mosque inside, now converted into a church, is the highlight. Tuesday tours require bookings; Thursday and Saturday tours end with a sherry tasting (the castle is owned by Bodegas Caballero); all 11.30am sessions are in English.

Plaza de Toros   BULLRING

(www.plazadetorospuertosantamaria.es; Plaza Elías Ahuja; €4; ⊙10am-2pm & 5-7pm Tue-Fri, 10am-2pm Sat; ℗) Four blocks southwest of Plaza de España is El Puerto's grand Plaza de Toros, built in 1880 with room for 15,000 spectators and still one of Andalucía's most important bullrings. Entry is from Calle Valdés.

Iglesia Mayor Prioral   CHURCH

(⊙8.30am-1pm Mon-Fri, 8.30am-12.30pm & 6-9pm Sat & Sun) El Puerto's most splendid church, the 15th- to 18th-century Iglesia Mayor Prioral, dominates Plaza de España.

✦ Festivals & Events

Festividad Virgen del Carmen   RELIGIOUS

On July 16, fisherfolk Andalucía-wide pay homage to their patron; El Puerto parades the Virgin's image along the Río Guadalete.

Feria de Primavera
y Fiestas del Vino Fino   WINE
(Spring Fair) Around 200,000 half-bottles of *fino* (dry, straw-coloured sherry) are drunk during this six-day fiesta (April/May).

🛌 Sleeping

El Baobab Hostel   HOSTEL €
(☑956 54 21 23; www.casabaobab.es; Calle Pagador 37; dm €18-20, s €22-30, d €45-55; ❄🖥🌐) Facing the Plaza de Toros in a converted 19th-century building, this small, six-room hostel is El Puerto's best budget choice with a homey, friendly feel, tastefully done interiors and communal kitchen and bathrooms.

★Palacio San Bartolomé   LUXURY HOTEL €€€
(☑956 85 09 46; www.palaciosanbartolome. com; Calle San Bartolomé 21; s €54-98, d €78-195; ❄@🌐) Every now and again along comes a hotel that blows away even the most jaded hotel reviewer. Fancy a room with its own mini swimming pool, sauna, Jacuzzi, bathrobes and deckchairs? It's all yours for €198 at the deftly designed, welcoming San Bart, set in a former palace.

🍴 Eating

El Puerto is famous for its outstanding seafood and tapas bars. Look along the central Calles Luna and Misericordia, Calle Ribera del Marisco to the north, and Avenidas de la Bajamar and Aramburu de Mora to the south.

Romerijo   SEAFOOD €
(☑956 54 12 54; www.romerijo.com; Ribera del Marisco 1; seafood per 250g from €4.50, raciones €8-12; ⏱11am-11.30pm) A huge, always-busy El Puerto institution, Romerijo has three sections: one boiling seafood, another (opposite) frying it, and the third a *cervecería* (beer bar). Buy by the quarter-kilo in paper cones. The *freiduría* (fried-fish shop) closes 4pm to 7pm.

★Mesón del Asador   SPANISH, GRILL €€
(www.mesondelasador.com; Calle Misericordia 2; tapas €2-3, mains €10-20; ⏱12.30-4pm & 8pm-midnight) It's a measure of El Puerto's gastronomic nous that, in such a seafood-orientated town, there's a meat restaurant that could compete with any Buenos Aires steakhouse. The power of the Mesón's delivery is in the smell that hits you the moment you open the door – chargrilled beef and pork sizzling away on mini-barbecues

brought to your table. Try the chorizo or the chicken brochette.

El Faro del Puerto   ANDALUCIAN, SEAFOOD €€
(☑956 87 09 52; www.elfarodelpuerto.com; Ctra de Fuentebravía Km 0.5; tapas €6-10, mains €17-22; ⏱1-4.30pm & 9-11pm Mon-Sat, 1-4.30pm Sun; 🚗) El Faro is worth hunting down for its traditional-with-a-hint-of-innovation take on local seafood, excellent wine list, and classically smart, multiroom setting inside an old *casa señorial* (manor house). The tuna tartare is a highlight. The (cheaper) bar/tapas menu has good vegetarian and gluten-free choices. It's on the roundabout at the northwest end of Calle Valdés.

Aponiente   SEAFOOD €€€
(☑956 85 18 70; www.aponiente.com; Calle Francisco Cossi Ochoa; 7-course menu €165; ⏱1.45-2.45pm & 8.45-9.45pm Tue-Fri, Mon-Sat in Jul & Aug) Audacious is the word for the bold experimentation of leading Spanish chef Angel León, whose seafood-biased *nueva cocina* menu has won a cavalcade of awards including two Michelin stars and a 2011 plug from the *New York Times* as one of 10 restaurants in the world 'worth a plane ride'.

The restaurant splits local opinion in traditional El Puerto. Some snort at its prices and pretension, others salivate at the thought of fish 'chorizo', yeast-fermented mackerel and creamy rice with microseaweeds. It recently relocated to a restored 18th-century tide mill, featuring marine-inspired interior design.

🍷 Drinking & Nightlife

Bodega Obregón   BAR
(Calle Zarza 51; ⏱9am-3pm & 6-9pm Mon-Fri, 9am-4pm Sat, 10am-3pm Sun) Think sherry's just a drink for grandmas? Come and have your illusions blown to pieces at this spit-and-sawdust-style bar where the sweet stuff is siphoned from woody barrels. The home-cooked Saturday-lunch *guisos* (stews) are a local favourite.

☆ Entertainment

Peña Flamenca Tomás El Nitri   FLAMENCO
(☑956 54 32 37; Calle Diego Niño 1) This good honest *peña*, with the air of a foot-stomping, 19th-century flamenco bar, showcases some truly amazing guitarists, singers and dancers in a club full of regulars. Shows are usually on Saturday nights.

ℹ️ Information

Tourist Office (☑ 956 48 37 15; www.turismo elpuerto.com; Plaza de Alfonso X El Sabio 9; ⊙ 10am-2pm & 6-8pm Mon-Sat, 10am-2pm Sun)

ℹ️ Getting There & Away

BOAT

The **catamaran** (www.cmtbc.es) leaves from in front of the Hotel Santa María for Cádiz (€2.65, 30 minutes) 16 times daily Monday to Friday, five on weekends.

BUS

El Puerto has two bus stops. Buses to Cádiz (€2.65, 45 minutes, hourly), Jerez de la Frontera (€1.60, 20 minutes, two to seven daily) and Sanlúcar de Barrameda (€1.90, 25 minutes, 13 daily) go from the bus stop outside the Plaza de Toros. Buses to Seville (€10, 1¾ hours, two daily) go from outside the train station.

TRAIN

From the train station at the northeast end of town, frequent trains go to/from Jerez de la Frontera (€2, 10 minutes), Cádiz (€3.40, 35 minutes) and Seville (€14, 1¼ hours).

Sanlúcar de Barrameda

POP 67,300

Sanlúcar is one of those lesser-known Andalucian towns that will pleasantly surprise you. Firstly, there's the gastronomy: Sanlúcar cooks up some of the region's best seafood on a hallowed waterside strip called Bajo de Guía. Secondly, Sanlúcar's unique location at the northern tip of the esteemed sherry triangle enables its earthy bodegas, nestled in the somnolent, monument-strewn old town, to produce the much-admired one-of-a-kind *manzanilla* (chamomile-coloured sherry). Thirdly, plonked at the mouth of the Río Guadalquivir estuary, Sanlúcar provides a quieter, less trammelled entry point into the ethereal Parque Nacional de Doñana than the popular western access points in Huelva province.

As if that wasn't enough, the town harbours a proud nautical history. Both Christopher Columbus, on his third sojourn, and Portuguese mariner Ferdinand Magellan struck out from here on their voyages of discovery. Don't miss out.

👁️ Sights

⭐ Bodegas Barbadillo
WINERY

(☑ 956 38 55 00; www.barbadillo.com; Calle Sevilla; tours €6; ⊙ tours noon & 1pm Tue-Sat, noon Sun, in English 11am Tue-Sat) Barbadillo was the first family to bottle Sanlúcar's famous *manzanilla* and also produces one of Spain's most popular *vinos*. Bodega tours end with a tasting. Also in this 19th-century building is the informative **Museo de la Manzanilla** (⊙ 10am-3pm Tue & Thu-Sat, 10am-6pm Wed, 11am-2pm Sun) **FREE**, which traces the 200-year history of *manzanilla*.

Palacio de Orleans y Borbón
PALACE

(cnr Calles Cuesta de Belén & Caballeros; ⊙ 10am-1.30pm Mon-Fri) **FREE** From central Plaza del Cabildo, cross Calle Ancha and head up Calle Bretones, which becomes Calle Cuesta de Belén. At the top you'll come to this beautiful neo-Mudéjar old-town palace, built as a 19th-century summer home for the aristocratic Montpensier family. It's now Sanlúcar's town hall; you can only visit the gardens.

Palacio de los Duques de Medina Sidonia
PALACE

(☑ 956 36 01 61; www.fcmedinasidonia.com; Plaza Condes de Niebla 1; €5; ⊙ tours noon Tue-Fri, 11.30am & noon Sun) Just off Calle Caballeros, this was the rambling home of the aristocratic family that once owned more of Spain than anyone else. The mostly 17th-century house bursts with antiques, and paintings by Goya, Zurbarán and other Spanish greats. Stop for coffee and cake in its old-world **cafe** (Plaza Condes de Niebla 1; cakes €2-3.50; ⊙ 9am-9pm Tue-Sun, 9am-1pm & 4-8.30pm Mon).

Castillo de Santiago
CASTLE

(☑ 956 92 35 00; www.castillodesantiago.com; Plaza del Castillo de Santiago; adult/child €6/4; ⊙ 10am-2.30pm Tue-Sat, 11am-2.30pm Sun) Surrounded by Barbadillo's bodegas, Sanlúcar's restored 15th-century castle has great views from its hexagonal Torre del Homenaje (keep). The story goes that Isabel la Católica first saw the sea from here. Entry to the Patio de Armas and its restaurant is free.

Iglesia de Nuestra Señora de la O
CHURCH

(Plaza de la Paz; ⊙ mass 7pm Mon & Wed-Fri, 9am, noon & 7pm Sun) Fronting the old town's Calle Caballeros, this medieval church stands out among Sanlúcar's many others for its fine 1360s Gothic-Mudéjar portal and its rich interior decoration, particularly the Mudéjar *artesonado* (ceiling of interlaced beams with decorative inserts).

Activities

Sanlúcar is a potential base for exploring the Parque Nacional de Doñana (p605), which glistens just across the Río Guadalquivir.

Trips here are run by the licensed Visitas Doñana (p605), whose boat, the *Real Fernando*, chugs up the river for wildlife viewing. Your first option is a three-hour boat/jeep combination, which goes 30km through the park's dunes, marshlands and pine forests in 20-person 4WD vehicles. There's usually one trip in the morning and another in the afternoon. The second (less interesting) option is a hop-on-hop-off ferry tour with a little walking. You can book and find out more about Doñana at the **Centro de Visitantes Fábrica de Hielo** (📞 956 38 65 77; Bajo de Guía; ⏲ 9am-7pm). Trips depart from Bajo de Guía. It's best to reserve a week ahead.

Viajes Doñana (📞 956 36 25 40; viajesdonana@hotmail.com; Calle San Juan 20; tours €35; ⏲ 9am-2pm & 5-8.30pm Mon-Fri, 10.30am-2pm Sat) agency books the same trips.

Festivals & Events

Feria de la Manzanilla   WINE

A big *manzanilla*-fuelled fair kicks off Sanlúcar's summer in late May or early June.

Carreras de Caballos   HORSES

(www.carrerassanlucar.es) Two horse-race meetings held almost every year since 1845, on the beaches beside the Guadalquivir estuary in August.

Sleeping

⭐ **Hostal Alcoba**   HOTEL €€

(📞 956 38 31 09; www.hostalalcoba.es; Calle Alcoba 26; s €70-80, d €80-90; 🅿❄🛜🏊) The beautifully quirky but stylish 11-room Alcoba, with a slick, modernist courtyard complete with loungers, pool and hammocks, looks like something that architect Frank Lloyd Wright might have conceived. Skilfully put together (and run), it's a genius design creation that's somehow wonderfully homey, functional and central (just off the northeastern end of Calle Ancha), all at the same time.

Hotel Posada de Palacio   HISTORIC HOTEL €€

(📞 956 36 50 60; www.posadadepalacio.com; Calle Caballeros 11; d incl breakfast €88-174; ⏲ Mar-Oct; ❄🛜) Plant-filled patios, high ceilings, gracious historical charm and 18th-century luxury add up to one of the most elegantly characterful places to stay in this region.

Each room is different – tiled floors, brick arches, loft-like set-ups – but the superior doubles are standouts. There's antique furniture, but it's never too overdone.

Hotel Barrameda   HOTEL €€

(📞 956 38 58 78; www.hotelbarrameda.com; Calle Ancha 10; s €70-85, d €68-90; ❄🛜) This gleaming, 40-room hotel overlooks the tapas bar fun on Plaza del Cabildo, and makes an excellent, central choice for the sparkling modern rooms in its new wing (some with little terraces), ground-floor patio, marble floors and super-efficient service. Rates drop outside July and August.

Eating

Strung out along **Bajo de Guía**, 750m northeast of the centre, is one of Andalucía's most famous eating strips, once a fishing village and now a haven of high-quality seafood restaurants that revel in their simplicity. The undisputed speciality is *arroz caldoso a la marinera* (seafood rice); the local *langostinos* (king prawns) are another favourite.

⭐ **Casa Balbino**   TAPAS, SEAFOOD €

(www.casabalbino.com; Plaza del Cabildo 11; tapas €2-3; ⏲ noon-5pm & 6-11.30pm) It doesn't matter when you arrive, Casa Balbino is always overflowing with people, drawn in by its fantastic seafood tapas. Whether you're perched at the bar, tucked into a corner or lucky enough to score one of the outdoor plaza tables, you'll have to elbow your way to the front and shout your order to a waiter, who'll shout back and hand over your dish.

The options are endless, but the *tortillas de camarones* (crisp shrimp fritters), fried-egg-topped *tagarninas* (thistles) and *langostinos a la plancha* (grilled king prawns) are exquisite.

⭐ **Poma**   SEAFOOD €€

(📞 956 36 51 53; www.restaurantepoma.com; Bajo de Guía 6; mains €10-16; ⏲ 1-4.30pm & 7.30pm-midnight) You could kick a football on Bajo de Guía and guarantee it'd land on a decent plate of fish, but you should probably aim for Poma, where the *frito variado* (€14) comes with five different varieties of lightly fried species plucked out of the nearby sea and river.

Casa Bigote   SEAFOOD €€€

(📞 956 36 26 96; www.restaurantecasabigote.com; Bajo de Guía 10; mains €12-20; ⏲ 12.30-4pm & 8pm-midnight Mon-Sat) Classier than most places, Casa Bigote is the most renowned of Bajo de Guía's seafood-only restaurants. Waiters flit back and forth across a small lane to its permanently packed tapas bar on the corner opposite.

ⓘ Information

Oficina de Información Turística (☏956 36 61 10; www.sanlucarturismo.com; Avenida Calzada Duquesa Isabel; ☉10am-2pm & 4-6pm)

ⓘ Getting There & Away

From the **bus station** (Avenida de la Estación), **Los Amarillos** (☏902 21 03 17; www.losamarillos.es) goes hourly to/from El Puerto de Santa María (€2.17, 30 minutes), Cádiz (€2.65, one hour) and Seville (€8.84, two hours), less on weekends.

Autocares Valenzuela (☏956 18 10 96; www.grupovalenzuela.com) has hourly buses to/from Jerez de la Frontera (€1.90, 40 minutes), fewer on weekends.

Jerez de la Frontera

POP 190,600

Stand down all other claimants. Jerez, as most savvy Hispanophiles know, *is* Andalucía. It just doesn't broadcast it in the way that Seville and Granada do. Jerez is the capital of Andalucian horse culture, stop one on the famed sherry triangle and – cue the protestations from Cádiz and Seville – the cradle of Spanish flamenco. The *bulería,* Jerez' jokey, tongue-in-cheek antidote to Seville's tragic *soleá,* was first concocted in the legendary Roma *barrios* of Santiago and San Miguel. But Jerez is also a vibrant, chic modern Andalucian city, where fashion brands live in old palaces and stylishly outfitted businesspeople sit down to distinctly contemporary cuisine. If you really want to unveil the eternal riddle that is Andalucía, start here.

◉ Sights

Scattered across town, often tucked behind other buildings, Jerez' understated sights creep up on you. It can take a day or two to bond with the city. But once you're bitten, it's like *duende* (flamenco spirit) – there's no turning back.

Jerez (the word even *means* 'sherry') has around 20 sherry bodegas. Most require bookings for visits, but a few offer tours where you can just turn up. The tourist office (p626) has details.

★ Alcázar   FORTRESS
(☏956 14 99 55; Alameda Vieja; excl/incl camera obscura €5/7; ☉9.30am-7.30pm Mon-Fri Jul–mid-Sep, 9.30am-5.30pm Mon-Fri mid-Sep–Oct & Mar-Jun, 9.30am-2.30pm Nov-Feb & Sat & Sun year-round) Jerez' muscular yet elegant 11th- or 12th-century fortress is one of Andalucía's best-preserved Almohad-era (1140–1212) relics. It's noted for its octagonal tower, a classic example of Almohad defensive forts and a fabulous spot for city views.

You enter the Alcázar via the **Patio de Armas**. On the left is the beautiful *mezquita* (mosque), transformed into a chapel by Alfonso X in 1264. On the right, the 18th-century **Palacio Villavicencio**, built over the ruins of the old Almohad palace, displays artwork but is best known for its bird's-eye views of Jerez; the camera obscura inside its tower provides a picturesque panorama of the city.

Beyond the Patio de Armas, the peaceful gardens re-create the ambience of Islamic times with geometric flower beds and tinkling fountains. The well-preserved, domed Baños Árabes (Arabic Baths), with their shafts of light, are particularly worth a look.

★ Catedral de San Salvador   CATHEDRAL
(Plaza de la Encarnación; €5; ☉10am-6.30pm Mon-Sat) Echoes of Seville colour Jerez' dramatic cathedral, a surprisingly harmonious mix of baroque, neoclassical and Gothic styles. Standout features are its broad flying buttresses and intricately decorated stone ceilings. Behind the main altar, a series of rooms and chapels shows off the cathedral's collection of art (including works by Zurbarán and Pacheco), religious garments and silverware.

★ Bodegas Tradición   SHERRY BODEGA
(☏956 16 86 28; www.bodegastradicion.com; Plaza Cordobeses 3; tours €20; ☉8am-3pm Mon-Fri Jul-Aug, 10am-6pm Mon-Fri & 10am-2pm Sat Sep-Jun, closed Sat Dec-Feb) An intriguing bodega, not only for its extra-aged sherries (at least 20 years old), but also because it houses the Colección Joaquín Rivera, a private Spanish art collection that includes important works by Goya, Velázquez and Zurbarán. Tours (in English, Spanish and German) require prior booking.

Bodegas González Byass   SHERRY BODEGA
(Bodegas Tío Pepe; ☏956 35 70 16; www.bodegastiopepe.com; Calle Manuel María González 12; tours €13; ☉tours hourly noon-5pm Mon-Sat, noon-2pm

Jerez de la Frontera

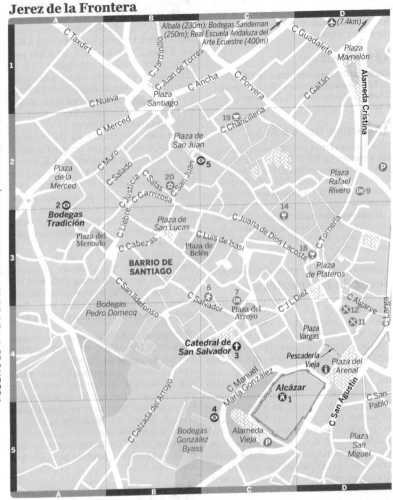

Albalá (230m); Bodegas Sandeman (250m); Real Escuela Andaluza del Arte Ecuestre (400m)

(7.4km)

C Taxdirt

C Jardinillo

C Juan de Torres

C Ancha

C Porvera

C Guadalete

C Gaitán

Plaza Mamelón

Alameda Cristina

C Nueva

Plaza Santiago

C Merced

C Chancillería

19

Plaza de San Juan

5

Plaza de la Merced

C Muro

C Salado

C Justicia

C Salas

C Carrizosa

20

San Juan

Plaza Rafael Rivero

9

2

Bodegas Tradición

C Liebre

Plaza del Mercado

C Cabezas

Plaza de San Lucas

C Luis de Isasi

Plaza de Belén

14

C Juana de Dios Lacoste

C Tornería

18

Plaza de Plateros

BARRIO DE SANTIAGO

C San Ildefonso

Bodegas Pedro Domecq

6

C Salvador

7

Plaza del Arroyo

C J L Díez

Plaza Vargas

C Algarve

12

11

C Larga

Catedral de San Salvador 3

Pescadería Vieja

Plaza del Arenal

C Manuel María González

Alcázar 1

C Calzada del Arroyo

4

Bodegas González Byass

Alameda Vieja

C San Agustín

C San Pablo

Plaza San Miguel

Sun) Home to the famous Tío Pepe brand, González Byass is one of Jerez' biggest sherry houses, handily located just west of the Alcázar. Five or six daily tours run in English and Spanish, and a couple in German. You can book online, but it isn't essential.

Bodegas Sandeman   SHERRY BODEGA
(☑ 675 647177; www.sandeman.com; Calle Pizarro 10; tours €7.50; ☺ tours 11am-2.30pm Mon, Wed & Fri, 10.15am-2pm Tue & Thu) Three or four daily tours (no bookings needed) each in English, Spanish and German, and one in French, all including tastings; the website has up-to-

date schedules. In honour of their Scottish creator, Sandeman sherries carry the black-caped 'Don' logo.

Centro Andaluz de Flamenco   ARTS CENTRE
(Andalucian Flamenco Centre; ☑ 956 90 21 34; www.centroandaluzdeflamenco.es; Plaza de San Juan 1; ☺ 9am-2pm Mon-Fri) FREE At once architecturally intriguing – note the entrance's original 15th-century Mudéjar *artesonado* and the intricate Andalucian baroque courtyard – and a fantastic flamenco resource, this unique centre holds thousands of print and musical works. Flamenco videos are

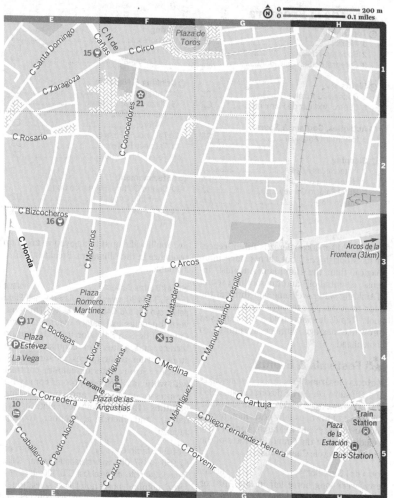

screened at 10am, 11am, noon and 1pm. Staff can provide a list of 17 local *peñas* (small private clubs), plus information on classes in flamenco dance and singing, and upcoming performances.

🏃 Activities

★ Real Escuela Andaluza del Arte Ecuestre
EQUESTRIAN SHOW

(☎ 956 31 80 08; www.realescuela.org; Avenida Duque de Abrantes; training sessions adult/child €11/6.50, exhibiciones adult/child €21/13; ☺ training sessions 10am-1pm Mon, Wed & Fri, exhibiciones noon Tue & Thu) The famous Royal Andalucian School of Equestrian Art trains horses and riders. You can watch them going through their paces in training sessions and visit the **Museo del Enganche** (Horse Carriage Museum; adult/child €4.50/2.50; ☺ 10am-2pm Mon-Fri), which includes an 18th-century Binder hunting break (carriage). The big highlight is the official *exhibición* (show), in which the handsome horses show off their tricks to classical music. Book tickets online.

Hammam Andalusí
HAMMAM

(☎ 956 34 90 66; www.hammamandalusi.com; Calle Salvador 6; baths €24, with 15/30min massage

Jerez de la Frontera

€34/53; ⊙10am-10pm) Jerez is full of echoes of its Moorish past, but there's none more magical than the Hammam Andalusí. Incense, essential oils and the soothing sound of tinkling water welcome you through the door, then you pass through three turquoise pools (tepid, hot and cold). You can even throw in a massage. Numbers are limited, so book ahead.

⭐ Festivals & Events

Motorcycle Grand Prix   MOTORCYCLES
The Circuito de Jerez (Racing Circuit; ☑956 15 11 00; www.circuitodejerez.com), on the A382 10km east of town, usually hosts motorcycle- and car-racing events in March, April or May, including one of the Grand Prix races of the World Motorcycle Championship.

Feria del Caballo   HORSES
Jerez' week-long horse fair in late April or early May is one of Andalucía's grandest festivals, with music and dance, and equestrian competitions and parades.

Festival de Jerez   FLAMENCO
(www.facebook.com/FestivalDeJerez) Jerez' biggest flamenco celebration is held in late February or early March.

🛏 Sleeping

Nuevo Hotel   HOTEL €
(☑956 33 16 00; www.nuevohotel.com; Calle Caballeros 23; s/d/tr €30/42/57; ❄🖥) One of the sweetest family-run hotels in Andalucía, the Nuevo's comfortable rooms are complemented by spectacular room 208, replete with Islamic-style stucco work and *azule-*

jos. You'll wake up thinking you've taken up residence in the Alhambra. Breakfast (€5) is available.

Hotel Bellas Artes   HOTEL €
(☑956 34 84 30; www.hotelbellasartes.net; Plaza del Arroyo 45; s/d €48/55; ❄@🖥) This converted neoclassical palace overlooks Jerez' Catedral de San Salvador from its rooftop terrace and suites. An exquisite carved stone corner pillar graces its sand-toned exterior. Strong interior colours contrast with white marble floors, rooms come with Nespresso machines and free-standing bathtubs (though some feel slightly too dated), and there's a summer rooftop Jacuzzi.

Hotel Palacio Garvey   HOTEL €€
(☑956 32 67 00; www.sferahoteles.com; Calle Tornería 24; r/ste incl breakfast €70/100; 🅿❄🖥) Jerez' nominal posh hotel is a sensational 19th-century neoclassical palace conversion, with part of the ancient city wall visible from the lift. The public areas sport leopard prints, African-themed paintings and low-slung tables, while subtle colours, luxurious leather furniture, tiled bathrooms and mirrored Moroccan-inspired bowls feature in the 16 individually decorated rooms.

Hotel Casa Grande   HOTEL €€
(☑956 34 50 70; www.hotelcasagrande.eu; Plaza de las Angustias 3; r/ste €100/165; 🅿❄🖥) This brilliant hotel occupies a beautifully restored 1920s mansion. Rooms are set over three floors around a light-flooded patio, or beside the fantastic roof terrace with views across Jerez' rooftops. All is overseen by the

congenial Monika Schroeder, a mine of information about Jerez.

✖ Eating

Jerez gastronomy combines Moorish heritage and maritime influences with international touches. Sherry, of course, flavours many traditional dishes such as *riñones al jerez* (sherry-braised kidneys) and *rabo de toro* (oxtail), and there's been a notable turn towards creative contemporary cuisine.

Cruz Blanca   TAPAS €
(www.restaurantelacruzblanca.com; Calle Consistorio 16; tapas €2.50-4; ⊙8am-midnight Mon-Fri, 9am-midnight Sat, 1pm-midnight Sun) The Cruz whips up good seafood, *revueltos* (scrambled-egg dishes), meat and salads, served at outdoor tables on a quiet little plaza or inside surrounded by smart, modern design. The marinated *salsa verde* (pesto and parsley) fish and wild tuna with soy sauce are specialities.

★ Albores   CONTEMPORARY ANDALUCIAN €€
(✆956 32 02 66; Calle Consistorio 12; tapas €2.40-5, mains €10-16; ⊙9am-midnight Mon-Sat, 11am-midnight Sun) Pitching itself among age-old city-centre favourites, Albores brings a sophisticated, contemporary edge to local flavours with its original tapas and mains combos. If there's one overall highlight it's probably the fish, particularly the monkfish, asparagus and bacon puff pastry, though the beautifully presented goats' cheese *tosta* (open sandwich on toasted bread) is just as fantastic. One of Jerez' top breakfast spots.

Albalá   CONTEMPORARY ANDALUCIAN €€
(✆956 34 64 88; www.restaurantealbala.com; cnr Calle Divina Pastora & Avenida Duque de Abrantes; tapas €2-4, mains €8-15; ⊙noon-4pm & 8.30pm-midnight) Slide into light-wood booths amid minimalist oriental decor for chef Israel Ramos' beautifully creative modern meat, fish and veg dishes infused with typical Andalucian ingredients. House specials include *rabo de toro* croquettes and king prawn burgers with ginger noodles, plus deliciously crispy chunky asparagus tempura. It's 1km north of Plaza del Arenal.

La Carboná   ANDALUCIAN €€
(✆956 34 74 75; www.lacarbona.com; Calle San Francisco de Paula 2; mains €13-20; ⊙1-4pm & 8pm-midnight Wed-Mon) This popular, cavernous restaurant with an imaginative menu occupies an old bodega with a hanging fireplace that's oh-so-cosy in winter. Delicately presented specialities include grilled meats, fresh fish and the quirky mini wild-boar burger with mango and yoghurt sauce, plus a good local wines list. If you can't decide, try the sherry pairing menu (€32).

DON'T MISS

THE GREAT TABANCO REVIVAL

Sprinkled across the city centre, Jerez' famous old *tabancos* are basic, bubbly taverns serving sherry from the barrel. Most date from the early 20th century and, although *tabanco* comes from the fusion of *tabaco* (tobacco) and *estanco* (tobacco shop), the focus is indisputably the local plonk (ie sherry). In danger of dying out just a few years ago, Jerez' *tabancos* have suddenly sprung back to life as fashionable modern-day hangouts, frequented by crowds of stylish young *jerezanos* as much as old-timers. Several stage regular flamenco, but you're just as likely to catch an impromptu performance. All are fantastic, cheap, down-to-earth places to capture that old Jerez atmosphere – sherry in hand.

The tourist office (p626) has information on the official Ruta de los Tabancos de Jerez (www.facebook.com/rutadelostabancosdejerez).

Tabanco El Pasaje (✆956 33 33 59; www.tabancoelpasaje.com; Calle Santa María 8; ⊙11am-3pm & 7-11pm, shows 8.30pm Thu-Sun & 2.30pm Fri & Sat) Born back in 1925, Jerez' oldest *tabanco* serves up its sherry with suitably raw flamenco.

Tabanco El Guitarrón de San Pedro (www.facebook.com/guitarrondesanpedro; Calle Bizcocheros 16; ⊙noon-midnight, shows 10pm Thu & Fri, 3pm Sat, 8pm Sun) Regular flamenco and occasional jazz. Sunday flamenco sessions are spontaneous – and open to all!

Tabanco Plateros (www.tabancoplateros.com; Calle Francos 1; ⊙noon-3.30pm & 7.30pm-1am) Join the crowd spilling out from this lively drinking house for sherry, beer, wine, and simple meat and cheese tapas.

DON'T MISS

JEREZ' FERTILE FLAMENCO SCENE

Jerez' moniker as the 'cradle of flamenco' is regularly challenged by aficionados in Cádiz and Seville, but the claim has merit. This surprisingly untouristed city harbours not just one but *two* Roma quarters, Santiago and San Miguel, which have produced a glut of renowned artists including Roma singers Manuel Torre and Antonio Chacón. Like its rival cities, Jerez has also concocted its own flamenco *palo* (musical form), the intensely popular *bulería*, a fast rhythmic musical style with the same *compás* (accented beat) as the *soleá*.

Begin your explorations at the **Centro Andaluz de Flamenco** (p622), Spain's only bona fide flamenco library, where you can pick up information on clubs, performances, and singing, dance and guitar lessons. From here, stroll down Calle Francos past a couple of legendary flamenco bars where singers and dancers still congregate. North of the Centro Andaluz de Flamenco, in the Santiago quarter, you'll find dozens of *peñas* (small private clubs) known for their accessibility and intimacy; entry is normally free if you buy a drink. The *peña* scene is particularly lively during the February flamenco festival (p624). Jerez' newly revitalised tabancos (p625), taverns that serve sherry from the barrel, are great for spur-of-the-moment flamenco.

Centro Cultural Flamenco Don Antonio Chacón (☎956 34 74 72; www.facebook.com/pages/D-Antonio-Chacón-Centro-Cultural-Flamenco; Calle Salas 2) One of the best *peñas* in town (and hence Andalucía), the Chacón, named for the great Jerez-born flamenco singer, is run by the jovial Tota twins, who often host top-notch flamenco performers. Happenings are usually impromptu, especially during the February flamenco festival. Call to find out about upcoming events, or contact the Centro Andaluz de Flamenco (p622).

Puro Arte (☎647 743832; www.puroarteflamencojerez.com; Calle Conocedores 28; €25, with dinner €42) Jerez' brand-new *tablao* (choreographed flamenco show) stages popular local-artist performances at 10pm daily. Advance bookings essential.

Damajuana (www.facebook.com/damajuanajerez; Calle Francos 18; ⌚8pm-3.30am Tue-Thu, 4pm-4am Fri-Sun) One of two historic bars on Calle Francos where flamenco singers and dancers have long met and drunk, with varied live music and a fun *movida flamenca* (flamenco scene).

Drinking & Nightlife

Tucked away on the narrow streets north of Plaza del Arenal are a few bars catering mostly to the under-30s. Northeast of the centre, **Plaza de Canterbury** (cnr Calles Zaragoza & N de Cañas; ⌚8.15am-2.30am Mon-Wed, 8.15am-4am Thu-Sat, 4pm-4am Sun) has a couple of pubs popular with a 20s crowd, while the late-night *bares de copas* (drinks bars) northeast along Avenida de Méjico attract a younger clientele. Jerez' tabancos (p625) are busy drinking spots.

Tetería La Jaima TEAHOUSE
(Calle Chancillería 10; dishes €9-14; ⌚4-11.30pm Tue-Thu, to 2am Fri & Sat, to 9pm Mon & Sun; 📶) You'll feel like a Moorish sultan reclining with a fruity, aromatic brew in this atmospherically dark tearoom, decked out with the best in Moroccan trinkets. If you're hungry, try some couscous or a tagine.

Information

Oficina de Turismo (☎956 33 88 74; www.turismojerez.com; Plaza del Arenal; ⌚9am-3pm & 5-6.30pm Mon-Fri, 9.30am-2.30pm Sat & Sun)

Getting There & Away

AIR

Jerez airport (☎956 15 00 00; www.aena.es), the only one serving Cádiz province, is 7km northeast of town on the A4. Taxis to/from the airport cost €15. Eight to 10 daily trains run between the airport and Jerez (€1.80, 10 minutes), El Puerto de Santa María (€2, 15 minutes) and Cádiz (€4.05, 45 minutes). Local airport buses run twice/once on weekdays/weekends, continuing from Jerez (€1.30, 30 minutes) to El Puerto de Santa María (€1.60, 50 minutes) and Cádiz (€3.75, 1½ hours).

Air Berlin (www.airberlin.com) To/from Mallorca, Frankfurt, Berlin and Düsseldorf (via Madrid).

Iberia (www.iberia.com) Daily to/from Madrid.

Ryanair (www.ryanair.com) To/from Barcelona, London Stansted and Frankfurt (seasonal).

Vueling (www.vueling.com) To/from Barcelona.

BUS

The **bus station** (956 14 99 90; Plaza de la Estación) is 1.3km southeast of the centre.

DESTINATION	FARE	DURATION	FREQUENCY
Arcos de la Frontera	€1.90	30min	1-4 daily
Cádiz	€3.75	1hr	3-9 daily
El Puerto de Santa María	€1.60	20min	3-10 daily
Ronda	€13	2¼hr	1-2 daily
Sanlúcar de Barrameda	€1.90	35min	7-13 daily
Seville	€8.90	1¼hr	5-7 daily

TRAIN

Jerez' train station is beside the bus station.

DESTINATION	FARE	DURATION	FREQUENCY
Cádiz	€4.05	45min	16 daily
Córdoba	€24	2½hr	13 daily
El Puerto de Santa María	€2	10min	half hourly
Seville	€11	1¼hr	15 daily

Arcos de la Frontera

POP 22,450

Everything you've ever dreamed a *pueblo blanco* (white town) to be miraculously materialises in Arcos de la Frontera (33km east of Jerez): a thrilling strategic clifftop location, a soporific old town full of winding streets and mystery, a swanky *parador,* and a volatile frontier history. The odd tour bus and foreign-owned guesthouse do little to dampen the drama.

For a brief period during the 11th century, Arcos was an independent Berber-ruled *taifa* (small kingdom). In 1255 it was claimed by Christian King Alfonso X El Sabio for Seville and it remained literally 'de la Frontera' (on the frontier) until the fall of Granada in 1492.

◉ Sights

★ Basílica Menor de Santa María de la Asunción
CHURCH

(Plaza del Cabildo; €2; ⊙10am-1pm & 4-6.30pm Mon-Fri, 10am-2pm Sat Mar-Dec) This Gothic-cum-baroque creation is one of Andalucía's more beautiful and intriguing small churches, built over several centuries on the site of a mosque. Check out the ornate gold-leaf altarpiece (a miniature of the one in Seville cathedral) carved between 1580 and 1608, a striking painting of San Cristóbal (St Christopher), a 14th-century mural uncovered in the 1970s, an ornate wood-carved choir and the lovely Isabelline ceiling tracery.

★ Plaza del Cabildo
SQUARE

Lined with fine ancient buildings, Plaza del Cabildo is the centre of the old town, its vertiginous mirador (Lookout) affording exquisite vistas over the Río Guadalete. The 11th-century, Moorish-built Castillo de los Duques (Plaza del Cabildo) is closed to the public, but its outer walls frame classic Arcos views. On the square's eastern side, the Parador de Arcos de la Frontera (p628) is a reconstruction of a 16th-century magistrate's house.

Iglesia de San Pedro
CHURCH

(Calle San Pedro 4; €1; ⊙9.30am-1.30pm & 3.30-6.30pm Mon-Fri, 9.30am-1.30pm Sat) A Gothic-baroque confection, sporting what is perhaps one of Andalucía's most magnificent small-church interiors.

☞ Tours

The tourist office (p628) organises daily guided old-town walking tours (per person €5, 1½ hours) at 11am and 5pm (6pm June to September); book ahead.

★ Festivals & Events

Semana Santa
HOLY WEEK

Dramatic Semana Santa processions see hooded penitents inching through Arcos' narrow streets. On Easter Sunday, a hair-raising running of the bulls takes over.

Feria de San Miguel
FAIR

Arcos celebrates its patron saint with a colourful four- or five-day fair in late September.

⊨ Sleeping

Casa Campana
GUESTHOUSE €

(600 284928; www.casacampana.com; Calle Núñez de Prado 4; r/apt €50/80; ❄@🛜) One of

several charming guesthouses in old Arcos, Casa Campana has two simple doubles and a massive five-person apartment with kitchenette that's filled with character. The flowery patio with sun loungers is a lovely private spot and the rooftop terrace is flooded with views. It's run by very knowledgeable owners, who hand out an excellent old-town walking tour brochure.

★ La Casa Grande
HISTORIC HOTEL €€

(📞 956 70 39 30; www.lacasagrande.net; Calle Maldonado 10; r €79-105, ste €94-105; ❋ @ 🛜) This gorgeous, rambling, cliffside mansion dating back to 1729 once belonged to the great flamenco dancer Antonio Ruiz Soler. With each of the seven rooms done in different but wonderfully tasteful design (all with divine views), it feels more like a home-cum-artists-retreat than a hotel. Great breakfasts, a well-stocked library, a fabulous rooftop terrace, and massage and yoga top off the perfect package.

It closes for two weeks in mid- or late January.

Parador de Arcos de la Frontera
HISTORIC HOTEL €€€

(📞 956 70 05 00; www.parador.es; Plaza del Cabildo; r €100-170; ❋ @ 🛜) A rebuilt 16th-century magistrate's residence that combines typical *parador* luxury with a magnificent cliffside setting and the best views in town. Eight of the 24 rooms have balconies opening out to sweeping clifftop panoramas; most others look out on pretty Plaza del Cabildo. The classically smart restaurant (📞 956 70 05 00; www.parador.es; mains €10-21; ⊘8-11am, noon-4pm & 8.30-11pm) offers a short but select local menu. Good discounts online.

✖ Eating

Taberna Jóvenes Flamencos
ANDALUCIAN, TAPAS €

(📞 657 133552; www.tabernajovenesflamencos. blogspot.com; Calle Deán Espinosa 11; tapas €2-3, raciones €6-10; ⊘noon-midnight Thu-Tue; 🍴) You've got to hand it to this popular place, which successfully opened up midrecession in 2012. Along with wonderful flamenco/bullfighting decor and brilliantly red tables, it has an easy-to-navigate menu of meat, fish, vegetarian and scramble dishes – including a delicious chunky courgette-and-Parmesan omelette. Service is impeccable and music and dance break out regularly.

Babel
MOROCCAN, FUSION €€

(www.restaurantebabel.es; Calle Corredera 11; dishes €7-12; ⊘1-4pm & 7.30-11.30pm Mon-Sat; 🍴) Arcos' Moorish fusion spot has some tasteful decor (the ornate stools were shipped in from Casablanca) and some equally tasty dishes: choose from tagines, couscous and hummus, or the full Arabic tea treatment with silver pots and sweet pastries.

ℹ Information

Tourist Office (📞 956 70 22 64; www. turismoarcos.es; Calle Cuesta de Belén 5; ⊘9.30am-2pm & 3-7.30pm Mon-Sat, 10am-2pm Sun) Doubles up as a Centro de Interpretación with history exhibits and a model of present-day Arcos.

ℹ Getting There & Away

Buses from Arcos' **bus station** (Calle Los Alcaldes) in the new town down to the west of the old town, off Avenida Miguel Mancheño, are operated by **Los Amarillos** (p621), **Comes** (www.tgcomes.es) and/or the **Consorcio de Transportes Bahía de Cádiz** (www.cmtbc.es). Frequency is reduced at weekends.

DESTINATION	FARE	DURATION	FREQUENCY
Cádiz	€7.25	1hr	12 daily
Jerez de la Frontera	€1.90	40min	23 daily
Málaga	€19	3¾hr	2 daily
Olvera	€7.83	1½hr	1 daily
Ronda	€9.56	2hr	2 daily
Seville	€8.97	2hr	2 daily

Parque Natural Sierra de Grazalema & Around

The rugged pillar-like peaks of the Parque Natural Sierra de Grazalema rise abruptly from the plains northeast of Cádiz, revealing sheer gorges, rare firs, wild orchids and the province's highest summits against a beautifully green backdrop. This is the wettest part of Spain – stand aside Galicia and Cantabria, Grazalema village logs an average 2000mm annually. It's gorgeous walking country (best in May, June, September and October). For the more intrepid, adventure activities abound.

The 534-sq-km park, named Spain's first Unesco Biosphere Reserve in 1977, extends into Málaga province, where it includes the Cueva de la Pileta caves.

DON'T MISS

PARQUE NATURAL SIERRA DE GRAZALEMA ACTIVITIES

Hiking, caving, canyoning, kayaking, rock climbing, cycling, birdwatching, paragliding – this gorgeous protected area crams it all in. For the more technical stuff, go with a guide; **Zahara Catur** (☑ 657 926394; www.zaharacatur.com; Plaza del Rey 3) and Grazalema-based **Horizon** (☑ 956 13 23 63; www.horizonaventura.com; Calle Las Piedras 1; ⊙ 10am-2pm & 5-8pm Mon-Sat) are respected adventure-activity outfits.

The Sierra de Grazalema is criss-crossed by beautiful marked trails. Four of the best – the **Garganta Verde**, **El Pinsapar**, **Llanos del Rabel** and **El Torreón** (⊙ Nov-May) paths – enter restricted areas and require free permits from the **Centro de Visitantes El Bosque** (☑ 956 70 97 33; cv_elbosque@agenciamedioambienteyagua.es; Calle Federico García Lorca 1; ⊙ 9.30am-2pm Sun-Tue, 9.30am-2pm & 4-6pm Wed-Sat). Ideally, book a month or two ahead. The Centro will email permits on request, usually in Spanish only. Additional (leftover) permits are sometimes available on the day; you can ask ahead by phone or email, but you'll have to collect them at the Centro on the day. Some trails are off-limits June to October due to fire risk.

The Centro de Visitantes El Bosque, the Punto de Información Zahara de la Sierra (p631) and the Grazalema tourist office have decent maps outlining the main walking possibilities. There's downloadable Spanish- and English-language hiking information with maps online at www.ventanadelvisitante.es.

Grazalema

POP 1650 / ELEV 825M

Few white towns are as generically perfect as Grazalema, with its spotless whitewashed houses sporting rust-tiled roofs and wrought-iron window bars, sprinkled on the steep rocky slopes of its eponymous mountain range. With hikes fanning out in all directions, Grazalema is the most popular base for adventures into the Parque Natural Sierra de Grazalema. It's also an age-old producer of blankets, honey, cheese, meat-filled stews and an adrenalin-filled bullrunning festival, and has its own special mountain charm.

🛏 Sleeping & Eating

Casa de las Piedras　　　　HOTEL €
(☑ 956 13 20 14; www.casadelaspiedras.net; Calle Las Piedras 32; s/d €35/48, with shared bathroom €15/25; ❈ ☞) Mountain air and a homey feel go together like Isabel and Fernando at this rustic-design hotel with a snug downstairs lounge and masses of park activities information. The simple cosy rooms, in various shapes and sizes, are decorated with Grazalema-made blankets. It's 100m west of Plaza de España.

Restaurante El Torreón　　ANDALUCIAN €€
(☑ 956 13 23 13; www.restauranteeltorreon grazalema.com; Calle Agua 44; mains €7-15; ⊙ 1-3.30pm & 7.30-11.30pm Thu-Tue) This cosy, friendly restaurant with a log fire specialises

in traditional mountain cuisine, from local chorizo and cheese platters to *tagarnina* (thistle) scrambles (a Cádiz delicacy), sirloin in green-pepper sauce, and a tasty spinach blended with pine nuts. Tables spill out on to the street when it's sunny.

ⓘ Information

Tourist Office (www.grazalema.es; Plaza de Asomaderos; ⊙ 10am-2pm & 4-7pm Mon-Sat) Parque Natural Sierra de Grazalema walking information.

ⓘ Getting There & Away

Los Amarillos (www.losamarillos.es) runs two daily buses to/from Ronda (€2.87, one hour); three daily to/from Ubrique (€2.34, 30 minutes) via Benaocaz (€1.62, 20 minutes); and one daily Monday to Friday to El Bosque (€1.45, 30 minutes), where you can change for Arcos de la Frontera.

Zahara de la Sierra

POP 1320 / ELEV 550M

Rugged Zahara, strung around a vertiginous crag at the foot of the Grazalema mountains, overlooking the turquoise Embalse de Zahara, hums with Moorish mystery. For over 150 years in the 14th and 15th centuries, it stood off against Christian Olvera, clearly visible in the distance. These days Zahara ticks all the classic white-town boxes and is a great base for hiking the Garganta Verde, so it's

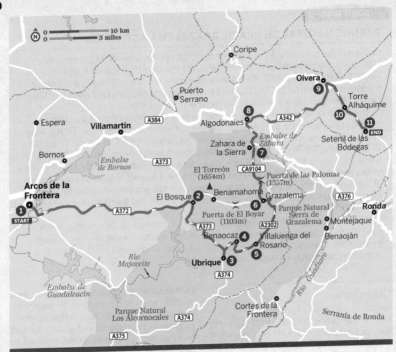

🚶 Driving Tour
White Towns

START ARCOS DE LA FRONTERA
END SETENIL DE LAS BODEGAS
LENGTH 130KM; TWO DAYS

Rev up in dramatic **1 Arcos de la Frontera** (p627), a Roman-turned-Moorish-turned-Christian citadel perched atop a sheer-sided sandstone ridge. Head 32km east along the A372 to **2 El Bosque** (p629), the western gateway to Cádiz province's Parque Natural Sierra de Grazalema and location of the park's main information centre. The A373 takes you 13km round to leather-making **3 Ubrique**, close to the borders of the Grazalema and Alcornocales natural parks. Mountains rise quickly as you drive 7km up the A2302 to tiny **4 Benaocaz**, where several Grazalema park hikes start/finish, and another 7km on to equally diminutive **5 Villaluenga del Rosario** with its artisanal cheese museum. Plying the craggy eastern face of the sierra then taking the A372 west brings you to **6 Grazalema** (p629), a red-roofed park-activity nexus also famous for its blanket-making and honey; it's the perfect overnight stop. Count the

switchbacks on the steep CA9104 as you climb up to the view-splayed Puerto de las Palomas and, beyond, quintessential white town **7 Zahara de la Sierra** (p629), with its huddle of houses spread around the skirts of a rocky crag above a glassy reservoir at the foot of the Grazalema mountains. The A2300 threads north to **8 Algodonales**, a white town on the edge of the natural park known for its guitar-making workshop and hang-gliding/paragliding obsession. Take the A384 east from here past the Peñón de Zaframagón (an important refuge for griffon vultures) to reach **9 Olvera** (p631), visible for miles around thanks to its Arabic castle but also known for its high-quality olive oil and **Vía Verde** (p633) cycling/hiking path. Following the CA9106 you'll pass the little-known white town of **10 Torre Alháquime**. From here, the CA9120 winds south towards the border with Málaga province and **11 Setenil de las Bodegas** (632), a village instantly recognisable for its cave houses. Once used for storing wine, today they offer a shady antidote to the summer heat plus some good tapas bars.

popular. Come during the afternoon siesta, however, and you can still hear a pin drop.

The precipitous CA9104 road over the ultra-steep 1331m Puerto de las Palomas (Doves' Pass) links Zahara with Grazalema (17km) and is a spectacular drive full of white-knuckle switchbacks.

◎ Sights

With vistas framed by tall palms and hot-pink bougainvillea, Zahara's streets invite exploration. The village centres on Calle San Juan; towards its eastern end stands the 18th-century baroque Iglesia de Santa María de Mesa (⊘hours vary). To climb to the 12th-century castle keep (⊘24hr) FREE, a hike of about 10 to 15 minutes, take the path almost opposite the Hotel Arco de la Villa. The castle's recapture from the Christians by Abu al-Hasan of Granada, in a 1481 night raid, provoked the Reyes Católicos (Catholic Monarchs) to launch the last phase of the Reconquista, which ended with the fall of Granada.

⏟ Sleeping

Los Tadeos   RURAL HOTEL €€
(☑956 12 30 86; www.alojamientoruralcadiz. com; Paseo de la Fuente; s/d/ste €45/63/100; P❀🛜🛋) On the western edge of Zahara, Los Tadeos has been glammed up from a family-run *pensión* (small budget hotel) to a comfy, well-equipped *hotel rural* and restaurant. The 17 rooms are tastefully done in modern-rustic style, many with big balconies and three with private Jacuzzis. The highlight is the beautiful infinity pool for drinking in the countryside and village views.

ⓘ Information

Punto de Información Zahara de la Sierra (☑956 12 31 14; Plaza del Rey 3; ⊘9am-2.30pm & 4-6pm Tue-Fri, 11am-3pm & 4-6pm Sat & Sun) Official Parque Natural Sierra de Grazalema information.

ⓘ Getting There & Away

Comes (www.tgcomes.es) runs two daily buses to/from Ronda (€4.47, one hour).

Olvera

POP 8180 / ELEV 643M

Dramatically topped by an Arabic castle, Olvera (27km northeast of Zahara de la Sierra) beckons from miles away across olive-cov-

ered country. A bandit refuge until the mid-19th century, the town now supports more family-run farming cooperatives than anywhere else in Spain. Most come to Olvera for the Vía Verde de la Sierra (p633), but as a white town par excellence, it's renowned for its olive oil, striking neoclassical church and roller-coaster history, which probably started with the Romans.

◎ Sights

Castillo Árabe   CASTLE
(Plaza de la Iglesia; adult/child €2/1; ⊘10.30am-2pm & 4-7pm Tue-Sun) Perched on a crag high atop town is Olvera's late-12th-century Arabic castle, which later formed part of Nasrid Granada's defensive systems.

Iglesia Parroquial Nuestra Señora de la Encarnación   CHURCH
(Plaza de la Iglesia; €2; ⊘11am-1pm Tue-Sun) Built over a Gothic-Mudéjar predecessor, Olvera's neoclassical top-of-town church was commissioned by the Dukes of Osuna and completed in 1843.

⏟ Sleeping & Eating

Hotel/Restaurante Estación Verde   HOTEL €
(☑661 463207; Calle Pasadera 4; s/d/tr €25/40/60) The unique Hotel/Restaurante Estación Verde just outside Olvera is the official start of the Vía Verde de la Sierra (p633), the finest of Spain's *vías verdes* (greenways which have transformed old railway lines into traffic-free thoroughfares for bikers, hikers and horse-riders). You can hire all kinds of bikes here, including tandems, kids' bikes and chariots.

Taberna Juanito Gómez   TAPAS €
(Calle Bellavista; tapas €2-3; ⊘1.30-4.30pm & 8.30-11.30pm Mon-Sat) A simple little place that does tasty, decent-value tapas and *montaditos* (bite-sized filled rolls) taking in all your usual faves: garlic prawns, grilled mushrooms, Manchego cheese and Iberian ham.

ⓘ Information

Tourist Office (☑956 12 08 16; www.turism olvera.es; Plaza de la Iglesia; ⊘10.30am-2pm & 4-7pm Tue-Sun)

ⓘ Getting There & Away

Los Amarillos (p621) runs one or two daily buses to/from Jerez de la Frontera (€9.18, two hours) and Málaga (€12, three hours), and one

WORTH A TRIP

SETENIL DE LAS BODEGAS

While most white towns sought protective status atop lofty crags, the people of Setenil did the opposite and burrowed into the dark caves beneath the steep cliffs of the River Trejo. The strategy clearly worked. It took the Christian armies a 15-day siege to dislodge the Moors from their well-defended positions in 1484. Many of the original cave-houses remain and some have been converted into bars and restaurants. In the valley below, off the CA9118 to Olvera, you can hike along the 6km (return) Ruta de los Molinos, past ancient mills to the next village of Alcalá del Valle. Ask directions locally.

The **tourist office** (Calle Villa; ⊙ 10am-4pm Tue-Sun) is near the top of the town in the 16th-century Casa Consistorial, which exhibits a rare wooden Mudéjar ceiling. A little higher up is the century **castle** (check opening hours at the tourist office), captured by the Christians just eight years before the fall of Granada.

Setenil has some great tapas bars that make an ideal pit-stop while you study its unique urban framework. Start with **Restaurante Palmero** (Plaza de Andalucía; raciones & mains €7-12; ⊙ 8am-6pm & 8pm-midnight Fri-Wed) and work your way down.

daily Monday to Friday to/from Ronda (€5.44, 1½ hours). **Comes** (www.tgcomes.es) has one daily bus Monday to Friday to/from Cádiz (€15, three hours).

Southern Costa de la Luz

Arriving on the Costa de la Luz from the Costa del Sol is like opening the window in a crowded room and gasping in the early morning sunlight. Bereft of tacky resorts and unplanned development, suddenly you can breathe again. More to the point, you're unequivocally back in Spain – a world of flat-capped farmers and clacking dominoes, grazing cows and Sunday Mass followed by a furtive slug of dry sherry. Don't ask why these wide yellow sandy beaches and spectacularly located white towns are so deserted. Just get out and enjoy them while you still can.

Vejer de la Frontera

POP 9280

Vejer – the jaw drops, the eyes blink, the eloquent adjectives dry up. Looming moodily atop a rocky hill above the busy N340, 50km south of Cádiz, this serene, compact white town is something very special. Yes, there's a labyrinth of twisting old-town streets plus some serendipitous viewpoints, a ruined castle, a surprisingly elaborate culinary scene and a tangible Moorish influence. But Vejer has something else – an air of magic and mystery, an imperceptible touch of *duende* (spirit).

⊙ Sights

Plaza de España   SQUARE

With its elaborate 20th-century, Seville-tiled fountain and perfectly white town hall, Vejer's palm-studded Plaza de España is a favourite hang-out. There's a small lookout above its western side (accessible from Calle de Sancho IV El Bravo).

Walls   WALLS

Enclosing the 40,000-sq-metre old town, Vejer's imposing 15th-century walls are particularly visible between the Arco de la Puerta Cerrada and the Arco de la Segur, two of the four original gateways to survive. The Arco de la Segur area was, in the 15th century, the *judería* (the Jewish quarter).

Castillo   CASTLE

(Calle del Castillo; tours per person €4-6; ⊙ 10am-2pm & 4pm-8pm) Vejer's much-reworked castle, once home of the Duques de Medina Sidonia, dates from the 10th or 11th century. Its small, erratically open **museum** preserves one of the black cloaks that Vejer women wore until just a couple of decades ago (covering everything but the eyes).

Currently, the only way to visit the castle is by private guided tour; check with the tourist office (p634).

⮞ Courses

★ **Annie B's**
Spanish Kitchen   COOKING COURSE
(✆ 620 560649; www.anniebspain.com; Calle Viñas 11; 1-day course €135) This is your chance to master the fine art of Andalucian cooking with top-notch local expertise. Annie's pop-

ular day classes (Andalucian-, Moroccan- or seafood-focused) end with lunch by the pool or on the fabulous roof terrace at her gorgeous old-town house. She also does a great selection of full-board six-day courses, including 'Low-Carb Deliciousness' and 'Spanish Culinary Classics'.

La Janda LANGUAGE COURSE

(📞 956 44 70 60; www.lajanda.org; Calle José Castrillón 22; per 20hr week €180) Who wouldn't want to study Spanish in Vejer, with its winding streets, authentic bars and mysterious feel? La Janda's courses emphasise cultural immersion, integrating everything from flamenco, yoga and cooking classes to Almodóvar movie nights in a lovely 18th-century village mansion.

🛏 Sleeping

⭐ **La Casa del Califa** BOUTIQUE HOTEL €€

(📞 956 44 77 30; www.lacasadelcalifa.com; Plaza de España 16; incl breakfast s €88-123, d €99-148, ste €169-220; ⊘ mid-Feb–mid-Dec; 🅿 ❋ 🛜) Rambling over several floors of maze-like corridors, this gorgeous old hotel oozes character. All rooms are peaceful, chic and wonderfully comfortable, with Moroccan-style decor. The top-floor 'Africa' suite is particularly beautiful. Special 'emir' service (€45) bags you fresh flowers, chocolates and champagne. Breakfast is a wonderful spread and, down-

stairs, there's a fabulous Moroccan/Middle Eastern restaurant (p634).

⭐ **V...** BOUTIQUE HOTEL €€€

(📞 956 45 17 57; www.hotelv-vejer.com; Calle Rosario 11-13; d €218-328; ❋ @ 🛜) V... (that's V for Vejer, and, yes, the three dots are part of the name) is one of Andalucía's most exquisite creations. It's a brilliantly run, 12-room, old-world boutique hotel where trendy, modern design features (luxurious open-plan bathrooms with huge tubs and giant mirrors) mix with antique artefacts (pre-Columbus doors).

Communal areas include a massage room in the ancient *aljibe* (cistern) and a waterfall – wait for it – on a vista-laden roof terrace next to a bubbling Jacuzzi.

🍴 Eating

Vejer has quietly morphed into a gastronomic highlight of Andalucía, where you can just as happily tuck into traditional, age-old recipes as Moroccan fusion dishes.

 Mercado de Abastos ANDALUCIAN, INTERNATIONAL €

(Calle San Francisco; dishes €2-8; ⊘ 11am-4.30pm & 7pm-1am) Freshly glammed up with cool, modern gastrobar design, Vejer's Mercado de San Francisco has been transformed into a foodie hot spot. Grab a *vino* and choose between classic favourites and contempo-

---

DON'T MISS

VIA VERDE DE LA SIERRA

Regularly touted as the finest of Spain's *vías verdes* (greenways which have transformed old railway lines into traffic-free thoroughfares for bikers, hikers and horse-riders), the Vía Verde de la Sierra (www.fundacionviaverdedelasierra.com) between Olvera and Puerto Serrano is one of 23 such schemes in Andalucía. Aside from the wild, rugged scenery, the 36km-route is notable for four spectacular viaducts, 30 tunnels (with sensor-activated lighting) and three old stations-turned-hotel/restaurants. Ironically, the train line itself was never actually completed. It was constructed in the 1920s as part of the abortive Jerez to Almargen railway, but the Spanish Civil War put a stop to construction works. The line was restored in the early 2000s.

The Hotel/Restaurante Estación Verde (p631) just outside Olvera is the official starting point. Here you can hire bikes, including tandems, kids' bikes and chariots, from €12 per day, and check out the Centro de Interpretación Vía Verde de la Sierra (adult/child €2/1; ⊘ 9.30am-5.30pm Thu-Mon). Bike hire is also available at Coripe and Puerto Serrano stations. Other services include the Patrulla Verde (📞 638 280184; ⊘ 9am-5pm Sat & Sun), a staff of bike experts who help with info and mechanical issues.

A highlight of the Vía Verde is the Peñón de Zaframagón, a distinctive crag that's a prime breeding ground for griffon vultures. The Centro de Interpretación y Observatorio Ornitológico (📞 956 13 63 72; adult/child €2/1; ⊘ 11am-4pm Sat & Sun), in the former Zaframagón station building 16km west of Olvera, allows close-up observations activated directly from a high-definition camera placed up on the crag.

rary creations at the wonderfully varied tapas stalls: ham *raciones, tortilla de patatas*, fried fish in paper cups, even sushi.

⭐ **El Jardín del Califa** MOROCCAN, FUSION €€
(☎956 44 77 30; www.jardin.lacasadelcalifa.com; Plaza de España 16; mains €12-18; ☺1-4pm & 8-11.30pm mid-Feb–mid-Dec; 🖉) The sizzling atmosphere matches the food at this exotically beautiful restaurant – also a hotel (p633) and *tetería* (teahouse). It's buried away in a cavernous house where even finding the toilets is a full-on adventure. The menu is Moroccan/Middle Eastern – tagines, couscous, hummus, falafel – and, while the presentation is fantastic, it's the Maghreb flavours (saffron, figs, almonds) that linger the longest. Book ahead.

Valvatida ANDALUCIAN, FUSION €€
(☎622 468594; Calle Juan Relinque 3; dishes €7-12; ☺noon-4pm & 8-11.30pm; 🖉) Creative cookery meets market-fresh Andalucian ingredients at this cute modern-rustic spot with fold-out chairs, dangling fishing nets and posters in the window. The short seasonal menu plays with contemporary twists on local fish and meats (fancy pigs' cheeks fajitas?), but also features delicious vegie-friendly pastas, salads and stir-fries. Your *café* is served on a tiny wooden tray.

☆ Entertainment

Peña Cultural Flamenca 'Aguilar de Vejer' FLAMENCO
(Calle Rosario 29) Part of Vejer's magic is its genuine small-town flamenco scene, best observed in this atmospheric old-town bar/performance space. Free shows usually happen on Saturdays at 9.30pm; ask at the tourist office.

ℹ Information

Oficina Municipal de Turismo (☎956 45 17 36; www.turismovejer.es; Avenida Los Remedios 2; ☺8am-3pm Mon-Fri) About 500m below the town centre, beside a big free car park.

ℹ Getting There & Away

From Avenida Los Remedios, **Comes** (www.tgcomes.es) runs services to Cádiz, Barbate, Jerez de la Frontera and Seville. More buses stop at La Barca de Vejer, on the N340 at the bottom of the hill. From here, it's a steep 20-minute walk or €6 taxi ride up to town.

DESTINATION	FARE	DURATION	FREQUENCY
Algeciras	€7.17	1¼hr	8 daily
Barbate	€1.35	15min	6 daily
Cádiz	€5.68	1½hr	5 daily
Jerez de la Frontera	€7.79	1½hr	1 daily Mon-Fri
La Línea (for Gibraltar)	€9.05	1¾hr	5 daily
Málaga	€22	3¼hr	2 daily
Seville	€15	2hr	4 daily
Seville (from Avenida Los Remedios)	€16	2hr	1 daily Mon-Fri
Tarifa	€4.52	45min	8 daily

Los Caños de Meca

POP 170

Little laid-back Los Caños de Meca, 15km southwest of Vejer, straggles along a series of spectacular open white-sand beaches that will leave you wondering why Marbella even exists. Once a hippie haven, Caños

---

WORTH A TRIP

BAELO CLAUDIA

The ruined town of Baelo Claudia (☎956 10 67 96; www.museosdeandalucia.es; €1.50, EU citizens free; ☺9am-5.30pm Tue-Sat Jan-Mar & mid-Sep–Dec, to 7.30pm Apr–mid-Jun, to 3.30pm mid-Jun–mid-Sep & Sun year-round) is one of Andalucía's most important Roman archaeological sites. These majestic beachside ruins – with fine views across to Africa – include the substantial remains of a theatre, a paved forum, thermal baths, the market, the marble statue and columns of the basilica, and the workshops that turned out the products that made Baelo Claudia famous in the Roman world: salted fish and *garum* (spicy seasoning made from leftover fish parts). There's a good museum.

Baelo Claudia particularly flourished during the reign of Emperor Claudius (AD 41–54), but declined after an earthquake in the 2nd century.

Live musical performances sometimes happen on July and August evenings.

still attracts beach lovers of all kinds and nations – especially in summer – with its alternative, hedonistic scene and nudist beaches, as well as kitesurfing, windsurfing and board-surfing opportunities.

⊙ Sights

Cabo de Trafalgar CAPE

At the western end of Los Caños de Meca, a side road (often half-covered in sand) leads out to a lighthouse (set to become a hotel) on a low spit of land. This is the famous Cabo de Trafalgar, off which Spanish naval power was swiftly terminated by a British fleet under Admiral Nelson in 1805.

🏃 Activities

Caños' main beach is straight in front of Avenida de Trafalgar's junction with the A2233 to Barbate. Nudists head to its eastern end where there are more-isolated coves, including Playa de las Cortinas, and to Playa del Faro beside Cabo de Trafalgar.

Sleepy El Palmar, 5km northwest of Caños, has Andalucía's best board-surfing waves from October to May.

★ **Parque Natural de la Breña y Marismas del Barbate** HIKING

This 50-sq-km coastal park protects important marshes and pine forest from Costa del Sol–type development. Its main entry point is the 7.2km Sendero del Acantilado between Los Caños de Meca and Barbate, along clifftops that rival Cabo de Gata in their beauty.

Escuela de Surf 9 Pies SURFING

(☑620 104241; www.escueladesurf9pies.com; Avenida de la Playa, El Palmar; board & wetsuit rental per 2/4hr €13/20, classes €28) Recommended surf school offering board hire and year-round, classes for all levels, towards the north end of El Palmar beach.

🛏 Sleeping & Eating

Casas Karen HOTEL €€

(☑649 780834, 956 43 70 67; www.casaskaren. com; Camino del Monte 6; d €85-125, q €155-190; P🐕) This eccentric, laid-back Dutch-owned hideaway has characterful rustic rooms and apartments across a flower-covered plot. Options range from a converted farmhouse to thatched *chozas* (traditional huts) and two recently remodelled split-level 'studios'. Decor is casual Andalucian-Moroccan, full

of throws, hammocks and colour. It's 1km east of the Cabo de Trafalgar turn-off.

Las Dunas CAFE €

(www.barlasdunas.es; Ctra del Faro de Trafalgar; dishes €6-11; ⊙10.30am-11.30pm Sep-Jun, to 3am Jul & Aug; 🐕) Say *hola* to the ultimate relaxation spot, where kitesurfers kick back between white-knuckle sorties launched from the beach outside. Bob Marley tunes, great *bocadillos* (filled rolls), a warming winter fire, and a laid-back, beach-shack feel.

ℹ Getting There & Away

Comes (www.tgcomes.es) has two daily weekday buses from Los Caños de Meca (€1.25, 15 minutes) to Cádiz (€6.25, 1½ hours) via El Palmar (€2.02, 30 minutes). Additional summer services may run to Cádiz and Seville.

RONDA

POP 37,000 / ELEV 744M

Perched on an inland plateau riven by the 100m fissure of El Tajo gorge, Ronda is Málaga province's most spectacular town. It has a superbly dramatic location, and owes its name ('surrounded' by mountains), to the encircling Serranía de Ronda.

Established in the 9th century BC, Ronda is also one of Spain's oldest towns. Its existing old town, La Ciudad (the City), largely dates to Islamic times, when it was an important cultural centre filled with mosques and palaces. Its wealth as a trading depot made it an attractive prospect for bandits and profiteers, and the town has a colourful and romantic past in Spanish folklore.

Ronda was a favourite with the Romantics of the late 19th century, and has attracted an array of international artists and writers, such as David Wilkie, Alexandre Dumas, Rainer Maria Rilke, Ernest Hemingway and Orson Welles.

⊙ Sights

La Ciudad, the historic old town on the southern side of El Tajo gorge, is an atmospheric area for a stroll with its evocative, still-tangible history, Renaissance mansions and wealth of museums. But don't forget the newer town, which has its distinctive charms and is home to the emblematic bullring, plenty of good tapas bars and restaurants, and the leafy Alameda del Tajo gardens. Three bridges crossing the gorge connect the old town with the new.

Ronda

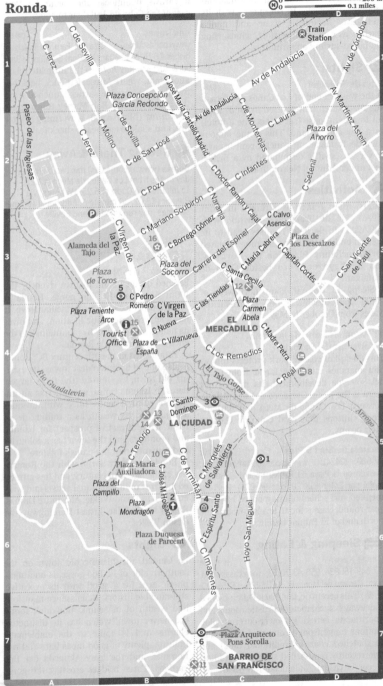

N 0
0

200 m
0.1 miles

Train Station

C. Jerez
C. de Sevilla
C. de Sevilla
Paseo de las Inglesas
C. Jerez
C. Molino
C. de San José
C de Sevilla
C. José María Castelló Madrid
Plaza Concepción García Redondo
Av de Andalucía
C de Andalucía
Av de Andalucía
Av de Córdoba
Av Martínez Astein
C de Monterejas
C Lauria
Plaza del Ahorro
C Pozo
C Doctor Ramón y Cajal
C Infantes
C Setenil
C Mariano Soubirón
C Naranja
C Borrego Gómez
C Calvo Asensio
Plaza de los Descalzos
C San Vicente de Paul
Alameda del Tajo
C Virgen de la Paz
16
Carrera del Espinel
C María Cabrera
C Capitán Cortés
Plaza del Socorro
C Santa Cecilia
Plaza de Toros
C Pedro Romero
5
C Virgen de la Paz
C las Tiendas
12
Plaza Carmen Abela
EL MERCADILLO
C Madre Petra
Plaza Teniente Arce
15
C Nueva
Tourist Office
Plaza de España
C Villanueva
C Los Remedios
7
C Real
8
Río Guadalevín
El Tajo Gorge
Arroyo
C Santo Domingo
3
LA CIUDAD
9
13
14
C Tenorio
10
C José M Holgado
C de Armiñán
1
Plaza María Auxiliadora
Plaza del Campillo
2
C Marqués de Salvatierra
Plaza Mondragón
4
C Espíritu Santo
Plaza Duquesa de Parcent
C Imágenes
Hoyo San Miguel
Plaza Arquitecto Pons Sorolla
6
11
BARRIO DE SAN FRANCISCO

Ronda

Puerta de Almocábar   GATE

The Old Town is surrounded by massive fortress walls pierced by two ancient gates: the Islamic Puerta de Almocábar, which in the 13th century was the main gateway to the castle; and the 16th-century Puerta de Carlos V. Inside, the Islamic layout remains intact, and its maze of narrow streets now takes its character from the Renaissance mansions of powerful families whose predecessors accompanied Fernando el Católico in the taking of the city in 1485.

Iglesia de Santa María La Mayor   CHURCH

(Calle José M Holgado; adult/child €4/1.50; ⏱10am-8pm) The city's original mosque metamorphosed into this elegant church. Just inside the entrance is an arch covered with Arabic inscriptions, which was part of the mosque's mihrab (prayer niche indicating the direction of Mecca). The church has been declared a national monument, and its interior is an orgy of decorative styles and ornamentation. A huge central, cedar choir stall divides the church into two sections: aristocrats to the front, everyone else at the back.

La Mina   HISTORIC SITE

This Islamic stairway comprises more than 300 steps which are cut into the rock all the way down to the river at the bottom of the gorge. These steps enabled Ronda to maintain water supplies when it was under attack.

Plaza de Toros   BULLRING

(Calle Virgen de la Paz; €7, incl audioguide €8.50; ⏱10am-8pm) Ronda's Plaza de Toros is a mecca for bullfighting aficionados. In existence for more than 200 years, it is one of the oldest and most revered bullrings in Spain and has been the site of some of the most important events in bullfighting history.

The on-site Museo Taurino is crammed with memorabilia such as blood-spattered costumes worn by 1990s star Jesulín de Ubrique. It also includes artwork by Picasso and photos of famous fans such as Orson Welles and Ernest Hemingway.

Baños Arabes   HISTORIC SITE

(Arab Baths; Hoyo San Miguel; €3, free Mon; ⏱10am-7pm Mon-Fri, to 3pm Sat & Sun) Enjoy the pleasant walk here from the centre of town. Backing on to Ronda's river, these 13th- and 14th-century Arab baths are in good condition, with horseshoe arches, columns and clearly designated divisions between the hot and cold thermal baths. They're some of the best-preserved Arab baths in Andalucía.

Museo del Bandolero   MUSEUM

(www.museobandolero.com; Calle de Armiñán 65; adult/child €3.75/free; ⏱10.30am-8pm) This small museum is dedicated to the banditry for which central Andalucía was once renowned. Old prints reflect that when the youthful *bandoleros* (bandits) were not being shot, hanged or garrotted by the authorities, they were stabbing each other in the back, literally as much as figuratively. You can pick up your fake pistol or catapult at the gift shop.

⚘ Festivals & Events

Feria de Pedro Romero   BULLFIGHTS

An orgy of partying including the important flamenco event, Festival de Cante Grande, culminates in the Corridas Goyesca (bullfights in honour of legendary bullfighter Pedro Romero). Held in the first half of September.

🛏 Sleeping

★ El Molino del Santo   HOTEL €€

(☎ 952 16 71 51; www.molinodelsanto.com; Estación de Benaoján, Benaoján; s/d incl breakfast €89/127; ⊗ Feb-Nov; P❄☷) Located near the well-signposted Benaoján train station, this British-owned hotel has a stunning setting next to a rushing stream; the main building was a former olive mill. The rooms are set amid the pretty gardens and most have private terraces or balconies. The hotel restaurant is popular with local residents and serves contemporary international cuisine.

★ Hotel San Gabriel   HOTEL €€

(☎ 952 19 03 92; www.hotelsangabriel.com; Calle José M Holgado 19; s/d incl breakfast €72/100; ❄☷) This charming hotel is filled with antiques and photographs that offer an insight into Ronda's history – bullfighting, celebrities and all. Ferns hang down the huge mahogany staircase and there is a billiard room, a cosy living room stacked with books, as well as a DVD-screening room with 10 velvet-covered seats rescued from Ronda's theatre.

Aire de Ronda   BOUTIQUE HOTEL €€

(☎ 952 16 12 74; www.airederonda.com; Calle Real 25; r from €85; P☷) Located near the Arab Baths in a particularly tranquil part of town, this hotel has smart minimalist rooms in punchy black and white, plus fabulous bathrooms with shimmering silver- or gold-coloured mosaic tiles, walk-in showers and, in one romantic couples' room, a glass partition separating the shower from the bedroom.

Hotel Ronda   BOUTIQUE HOTEL €€

(☎ 952 87 22 32; www.hotelronda.net; Ruedo Doña Elvira; s/d €53/70; ❄☷) With its geranium filled window boxes and whitewashed *pueblo* exterior, this cute-as-a-button small hotel has surprisingly contemporary rooms painted in vivid colours and accentuated by punchy original abstracts. Several overlook the beautiful Mina gardens across the way.

Enfrente Arte   HOTEL €€

(☎ 952 87 90 88; www.enfrentearte.com; Calle Real 40; r incl breakfast €80-90; ❄@☷) On an old cobblestone street, Belgian-owned Enfrente offers a huge range of facilities and funky modern-cum-oriental decor. It has a bar, pool, sauna, recreation room, flowery patio with black bamboo, film room and fantastic views out to the Sierra de las Nieves. What's more, the room price includes all drinks, to which you help yourself, and a sumptuous buffet breakfast.

🍴 Eating

Typical Ronda food is hearty mountain fare, with an emphasis on stews (called *cocido, estofado* or *cazuela*), *trucha* (trout), *rabo de toro* (oxtail stew) and game such as *conejo* (rabbit), *perdiz* (partridge) and *codorniz* (quail).

Casa María   ANDALUCIAN €

(☎ 951 083 663; Plaza Ruedo Alameda 27; menú €20; ⊗ noon-3.30pm & 7.30-10.30pm Thu-Tue; ☝) This no-frills restaurant has a kitchen run by a passionate cook who prepares dishes strictly according to what is fresh in the market. There is no menu. The selection is not huge but most diners opt for the five-course *poco de todo* (a bit of everything) tasting *menú* reflecting Maria's delicious homestyle cooking.

La Casa del Dulce   BAKERY €

(Calle Tenorio 11; cakes €0.80; ☝) Stop by La Casa del Dulce and ogle the trays of freshly baked *mantecada* biscuits; a delicious crumbly speciality based on almonds and topped with icing sugar. Don't worry, they can't be all that sinful – they're made by nuns.

Faustino   ANDALUCIAN €

(Calle Santa Cecilía; tapas €1.50, raciones €6-8; ⊗ 11.30am-midnight Tue-Sun) This is the real deal, a lively atmospheric tapas bar with plenty of seating in the open traditional atrium decorated with plants, feria posters, and bullfighting and religious pictures. Tapas and *raciones* are generous. Go with the recommendations like *champiñones a la plancha* (grilled mushrooms with lashings of garlic). The only downside is the uncomfortable, if pretty, rustic-style painted chairs. Ouch!

Restaurante Albacara   INTERNATIONAL €€€

(☎ 952 16 11 84; www.hotelmontelirio.com; Calle Tenorio 8; mains €15-22) One of Ronda's best restaurants, the Albacara is in the old stables of the Montelirio palace and teeters on the edge of the gorge. It serves up delicious meals – try the beef stroganoff or classic magret of duck. Be sure to check out the extensive wine list. Reserve your table in advance.

Restaurante
Tragabuches
MODERN SPANISH €€€

(⚹ 952 19 02 91; Calle José Aparício 1; menús €59-87; ⊙ 1.30-3.30pm & 8-10.30pm Tue-Sat) Ronda's most famous restaurant is a 180-degree turn away from the ubiquitous 'rustic' look and cuisine. Tragabuches is modern and sleek with an innovative menu to match. Choose from three set menus. People flock here from miles away to taste the food prepared by its creative chef.

☆ Entertainment

Círculo de Artistas
FLAMENCO

(Plaza del Socorro; €15; ⊙ Wed-Mon May-Sep) Stages flamenco shows in a sumptuous historical building on the square from 10pm, as well as other song and dance performances.

❶ Information

Tourist Office (www.turismoderonda.es; Paseo de Blas Infante; ⊙ 10am-7pm Mon-Fri, to 5pm Sat, to 2pm Sun) Helpful staff with a wealth of information on the town and region.

❶ Getting There & Away

BUS

The bus station is at Plaza Concepción García Redondo 2. **Comes** (www.tgcomes.es) has buses to Arcos de la Frontera (€9.56, two hours, one to two daily), Jerez de la Frontera (€13, three hours, one to three daily) and Cádiz (€18, two hours, one to three daily). **Los Amarillos** (www.losamarillos.es) goes to Seville via Algodonales and Grazalema, and to Málaga via Ardales.

TRAIN

Ronda's **train station** (⚹ 952 87 16 73; www. renfe.es; Avenida de Andalucía) is on the line between Bobadilla and Algeciras. Trains run to Algeciras via Gaucín and Jimena de la Frontera. This train ride is incredibly scenic and worth taking just for the views. Other trains depart for Málaga, Córdoba, Madrid, and Granada via Antequera. For Seville change at Bobadilla or Antequera. It's less than 1km from the train station to most accommodation. A taxi will cost around €7.

CÓRDOBA PROVINCE

Ascending over the Sierra Morena from La Mancha, the window into northern Andalucía is Córdoba province, a largely rural area renowned for its olive oil, wine and historic

Roman-founded city that, at its zenith, was the capital of Al-Andalus and home to the glittering court of Abd ar-Rahman III (889-961).

Córdoba

POP 296,000 / ELEV 110M

One building alone is enough to put Córdoba high on any traveller's itinerary: the mesmerising multiarched Mezquita. One of the world's greatest Islamic buildings, it's a symbol of the worldly and sophisticated Islamic culture that flourished here more than a millennium ago when Córdoba was the capital of Islamic Spain, and Western Europe's biggest and most cultured city. Once here, you'll find there's much more to this city: Córdoba is a great place for exploring on foot or by bicycle, staying and eating well in old buildings centred on verdant patios, diving into old wine bars, and feeling millennia of history at every turn. The narrow streets of the old *judería* (Jewish quarter) and Muslim quarter stretch out from the great mosque like capillaries (to the northwest and northeast respectively), some clogged with tourist bric-a-brac, others delightfully peaceful. The life of the modern city focuses a little further north, around Plaza de las Tendillas, where you'll find a more boisterous vibe with some excellent bars and restaurants. Andalucía's major river, the Guadalquivir, flows just below the Mezquita, and the riverfront streets are home to a growing band of lively restaurants and bars making the most of the view.

Córdoba bursts into life from mid-April to mid-June, when it stages most of its major fiestas. At this time of year the skies are blue, the temperatures are perfect and the city's many trees, gardens and courtyards drip with foliage and blooms. September and October are also excellent weatherwise, but July and August can sizzle.

History

The Roman colony of Corduba was established in 152 BC as a strategic provisioning point for Roman troops. In the 1st century AD, Emperor Augustus made the city capital of Baetica, one of the three Roman provinces on the Iberian Peninsula, ushering in an era of prosperity and cultural ascendancy that brought the writers Seneca and Lucan to the world. The Roman bridge over the Guadalquivir and the temple on Calle Claudio Marcelo are just the most visible remains of this important Roman city,

Córdoba

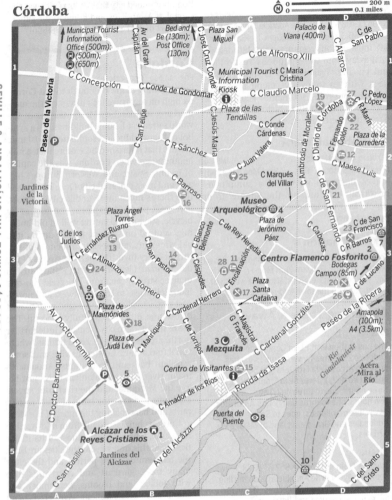

whose traces now lie a metre or two beneath the modern city. By the 3rd century, when Christianity reached Córdoba, the Roman city was already in decline. Córdoba fell to Islamic invaders in AD 711.

The city took centre stage in 756 when Abd ar-Rahman I set himself up here as the emir of Al-Andalus (the Muslim-controlled parts of the Iberian Peninsula), founding the Umayyad dynasty, which more or less unified Al-Andalus for two and a half centuries. Abd ar-Rahman I founded the great Mezquita in 785. The city's, and Al-Andalus', heyday came under Abd ar-Rahman III (r.

912–61). He named himself caliph (the title of the Muslim successors of Mohammed) in 929, ushering in the era of the Córdoba caliphate.

Córdoba was by now the biggest city in Western Europe, with a flourishing economy based on agriculture and skilled artisan products, and a population somewhere around 250,000. The city shone with hundreds of dazzling mosques, public baths, patios, gardens and fountains. This was the famed 'city of the three cultures', where Muslims, Jews and Christians coexisted peaceably and Abd ar-Rahman III's court

Córdoba

SEVILLE & ANDALUCIA'S HILL TOWNS CÓRDOBA

was frequented by scholars from all three communities. Córdoba's university, library and observatories made it a centre of learning whose influence was still being felt in Christian Europe many centuries later.

Towards the end of the 10th century, Al-Mansur (Almanzor), a ruthless general whose northward raids terrified Christian Spain, took the reins of power from the caliphs. But after the death of Al-Mansur's son Abd al-Malik in 1008, the caliphate descended into anarchy. Berber troops terrorised and looted the city and, in 1031, Umayyad rule ended. Córdoba became a minor part of the Seville *taifa* (small kingdom) in 1069, and has been overshadowed by Seville ever since.

Twelfth-century Córdoba did nevertheless produce the two most celebrated scholars of Al-Andalus – the Muslim Averroës (1126–98) and the Jewish Maimonides (1135–1204), men of multifarious talents most remembered for their efforts to reconcile religious faith with Aristotelian reason. After Córdoba was taken by Castilla's Fernando III in 1236, it declined into a provincial city and its fortunes only looked up with the arrival of industry in the late 19th century. Christian Córdoba did, however, give birth to one of the greatest Spanish poets, Luis de Góngora (1561–1627), still much remembered in the city.

⊙ Sights

★ **Mezquita**   MOSQUE, CATHEDRAL
(Mosque; ☎ 957 47 05 12; www.catedraldecordoba. es; Calle Cardenal Herrero; adult/child €8/4, 8.30-9.30am Mon-Sat free; ⊙ 8.30-9.30am & 10am-7pm Mon-Sat, 8.30-11.30am & 3-7pm Sun Mar-Oct, to 6pm daily Nov-Feb) It's impossible to overemphasise the beauty of Córdoba's great mosque, with its remarkably serene (despite tourist crowds) and spacious interior. One of the world's greatest works of Islamic architecture, the Mezquita hints, with all its lustrous decoration, at a refined age when Muslims, Jews and Christians lived side by side and enriched their city with a heady interaction of diverse, vibrant cultures.

Arab chronicles recount how Abd ar-Rahman I purchased half of the Hispano-Roman church of San Vicente for the Muslim community's Friday prayers, and then, in AD 784, bought the other half on which to erect a new mosque. Three later extensions nearly quintupled the size of Abd ar-Rahman I's mosque and brought it to the form you see today – with one major alteration: a 16th-century cathedral plonked right in the middle (hence the often-used description 'Mezquita-Catedral').

Mass is celebrated in the central cathedral at 9.30am Monday to Saturday, and at noon and 1.30pm Sundays.

Mezquita

TIMELINE

600 Foundation of a Christian church, the Basilica of San Vicente, on the site of the present Mezquita.

785 Salvaging Visigothic and Roman ruins, Emir Abd ar-Rahman I replaces the church with a *mezquita* (mosque).

833–56 Mosque enlarged by Abd ar-Rahman II.

951–2 A new minaret is built by Abd ar-Rahman III.

962–71 Mosque enlarged, and superb new **mihrab ❶** added, by Al-Hakim II.

978–9 Mosque enlarged for the last time by Al-Mansur, who also enlarged the courtyard (now the **Patio de los Naranjos ❷**), bringing the whole complex to its current dimensions.

1236 Mosque converted into a Christian church after Córdoba is recaptured by Fernando III of Castilla.

1271 Instead of destroying the mosque, the Christians modify it, creating the **Capilla de Villaviciosa ❸** and **Capilla Real ❹**.

1523 Work on a Gothic/Renaissance-style cathedral inside the Mezquita begins, with permission of Carlos I.

1593–1664 The 10th-century minaret is reinforced and rebuilt as a Renaissance-baroque **belltower ❺**.

2004 Spanish Muslims petition to be able to worship in the Mezquita again. The Vatican doesn't consent.

TOP TIPS

» **Among the oranges** The Patio de los Naranjos can be enjoyed free of charge at any time.

» **Early birds** Entry to the rest of the Mezquita is offered free every morning, except Sunday, between 8.30am and 9.30am.

» **Quiet time** Group visits are prohibited before 10am, meaning the building is quieter and more atmospheric in the early morning.

The mihrab
Everything leads to the mosque's greatest treasure – the beautiful prayer niche, in the wall facing Mecca, that was added in the 10th century. Cast your eyes over the gold mosaic cubes crafted by sculptors imported from Byzantium.

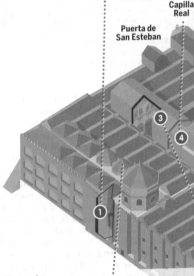

The *maksura*
Guiding you towards the mihrab, the *maksura* is a former royal enclosure where the caliphs and their retinues prayed. Its lavish, elaborate arches were designed to draw the eye of worshippers towards the mihrab and Mecca.

The cathedral choir

Few ignore the impressive *coro* (choir), built in the 16th and 17th centuries. Once you've admired the skilfully carved mahogany choir stalls depicting scenes from the Bible, look up at the impressive baroque ceiling.

❺

Belltower

Reopened to visitors in 2014 after a 24-year restoration, the 54m-tall belltower has the best views in the city. It was built in the 17th century around and above the remains of the Mezquita's 10th-century minaret.

The Mezquita arches

No, you're not hallucinating. The Mezquita's most defining characteristic is its unique terracotta-and-white striped arches that are supported by 856 pillars salvaged from Roman and other ruins. Glimpsed through the dull light they're at once spooky and striking.

Puerta del Perdón

❷

Patio de los Naranjos

Abandon architectural preconceptions all ye who enter here. The ablutions area of the former mosque is a shady courtyard embellished with orange trees that acts as the Mezquita's main entry point.

Capilla Mayor

A Christian monument inside an Islamic mosque sounds beautifully ironic, yet here it is: a Gothic high chapel sanctioned by Carlos I in the 16th century and planted in the middle of the world's third-largest mosque.

Capilla de Villaviciosa

Sift through the building's numerous chapels till you find this gem, an early Christian modification which fused existing Moorish features with Gothic arches and pillars. It served as the Capilla Mayor until the 1520s.

➡ Patio de los Naranjos

This lovely courtyard, with its orange, palm and cypress trees and fountains, forms the entrance to the Mezquita. It was formerly the site of ritual ablutions before prayer in the mosque. Its most impressive entrance is the Puerta del Perdón, a 14th-century Mudéjar archway in the base of the bell tower. The ticket office is just inside here.

➡ Torre del Alminar

The 54m-high bell tower reopened to visitors in 2014 after 24 years of intermittent restoration work, and you can climb up to its bells for fine panoramas. Originally built by Abd ar-Rahman III in 951–52 as the Mezquita's minaret, it was encased in a strengthened outer shell, and heightened, by the Christians in the 16th and 17th centuries. You can still see caliphal vaults and arches inside.

The original minaret would have looked something like the Giralda in Seville, which was practically a copy. Córdoba's minaret influenced all minarets built thereafter throughout the western Islamic world.

➡ The Mezquita's Interior

The Mezquita's architectural uniqueness and importance lies in the fact that, structurally speaking, it was a revolutionary building for its time. Earlier major Islamic buildings such as the Dome of the Rock in Jerusalem and the Great Mosque in Damascus placed an emphasis on verticality, but the Mezquita was intended as a democratically horizontal and simple space, where the spirit could be free to roam and communicate easily with God – a kind of glorious refinement of the original simple Islamic prayer space (usually the open yard of a desert home).

Men prayed side by side on the *argamasa*, a floor made of compact, reddish slaked lime and sand. A flat roof, decorated with gold and multicoloured motifs, was supported by striped arches suggestive of a forest of date palms. The arches rested on, eventually, 1293 columns (of which 856 remain today). The Patio de los Naranjos, where the ablution fountains gurgled with water, was the oasis.

Abd ar-Rahman I's initial mosque was a square split into two rectangular halves: a covered prayer hall and an open ablutions courtyard. His prayer hall – the area immediately inside the door by which visitors enter today – was divided into 11 'naves' by lines of arches striped in red brick and white stone. The columns of these arches were a mishmash of material collected from the earlier church on the site, Córdoba's Roman buildings and places as far away as Constantinople. To raise the ceiling high enough to create a sense of openness, inventive builders came up with the idea of a two-tier construction, using taller columns as a base and planting shorter ones on top.

Later enlargements of the mosque, southward by Abd ar-Rahman II in the 9th century and Al-Hakim II in the 960s, and eastward by Al-Mansur in the 970s, extended it to an area of nearly 14,400 sq metres, making it one of the biggest mosques in the world. The arcades' simplicity and number give a sense of endlessness to the Mezquita.

The final Mezquita had 19 doors along its north side, filling it with light and yielding a sense of openness. Nowadays, only one door sheds light into the dim interior, dampening the vibrant effect of the red-and-white double arches. Christian additions to the building, such as the solid mass of the cathedral in the centre and the 50 or so chapels around the fringes, further enclose and impose on the airy space.

➡ Mihrab & Maksura

Like Abd ar-Rahman II a century earlier, Al-Hakim II in the 960s lengthened the naves of the prayer hall, creating a new qiblah wall (indicating the direction of Mecca) and mihrab (prayer niche) at the south end. The bay immediately in front of the mihrab and the bays to each side form the *maksura*, the area where the caliphs and courtiers would have prayed. The mihrab and *maksura* are the most beautifully and intricately decorated parts of the whole mosque.

The greatest glory of Al-Hakim II's extension was the portal of the mihrab – a crescent arch with a rectangular surround known as an *alfiz*. For the portal's decoration, Al-Hakim asked the emperor of Byzantium, Nicephoras II Phocas, to send him a mosaicist capable of imitating the superb mosaics of the Great Mosque of Damascus, one of the great 8th-century Syrian Omayyad buildings. The Christian emperor sent the Muslim caliph not only a mosaicist but also a gift of 1600kg of gold mosaic cubes. Shaped into flower motifs and inscriptions from the Quran, this gold is what gives the mihrab portal its magical glitter. Inside the mihrab, a single block of white marble sculpted into the shape of a scallop shell, a symbol of the Quran, forms the dome that amplified the voice of the imam (the person who leads Islamic worship services) throughout the mosque.

The arches of the *maksura* are the mosque's most intricate and sophisticated, forming a forest of interwoven, lavishly decorated horseshoe shapes. Equally attractive are the *maksura*'s skylit domes, decorated with star-patterned stone vaulting. Each dome was held up by four interlocking pairs of parallel ribs, a highly advanced technique in 10th-century Europe.

➡ **Cathedral**

Following the Christian conquest of Córdoba in 1236, the Mezquita was used as a cathedral but remained largely unaltered for nearly three centuries. But in the 16th century King Carlos I gave the cathedral authorities permission to rip out the centre of the Mezquita in order to construct the Capilla Mayor (the main altar area) and *coro* (choir).

Legend has it that when the king saw the result he was horrified, exclaiming that they had destroyed something that was unique in the world. The cathedral took nearly 250 years to complete (1523–1766) and thus exhibits a range of architectural fashions, from plateresque and late Renaissance to extravagant Spanish baroque. Among the later features are the Capilla Mayor's rich 17th-century jasper and red-marble retable (altar-screen), and the fine mahogany stalls in the choir, carved in the 18th century by Pedro Duque Cornejo.

⭐ **Alcázar de los Reyes Cristianos** FORTRESS, GARDENS

(Fortress of the Christian Monarchs; www.alcazardelosreyescristianos.cordoba.es; Campo Santo de Los Mártires; admission 8.30am-2.30pm €4.50, other times incl water, light & sound show adult/child €7/free; ⊙ 8.30am-8.45pm Tue-Fri, to 4.30pm Sat, to 2.30pm Sun Sep-Jun, to 3pm Tue-Sun Jul-Aug; ⊞) Built under Castilian rule in the 13th and 14th centuries on the remains of a Moorish predecessor, this fort-cum-palace hosted both Fernando and Isabel, who made their first acquaintance with Columbus here in 1486. One hall displays some remarkable Roman mosaics, dug up from the Plaza de la Corredera in the 1950s. The Alcázar's terraced gardens – full of fish ponds, fountains, orange trees and flowers – are a delight to stroll around.

While you're here it's also interesting to visit the nearby **Baños del Alcázar Califal** (Campo Santo de los Mártires; €2.50; ⊙ 8.30am-8.45pm Tue-Fri, to 4.30pm Sat, to 2.30pm Sun mid-Sep–mid-Jun, to 3pm Tue-Sat, to 2.30pm Sun mid-Jun–mid-Sep), the impressive 10th-century bathhouse of the Moorish Alcázar.

⭐ **Centro Flamenco Fosforito** MUSEUM

(☑957 47 68 29; www.centroflamencofosforito.cordoba.es; Plaza del Potro; €2; ⊙ 8.30am-7.30pm Tue-Fri, 8.30am-2.30pm Sat, 9.30am-2.30pm Sun) Possibly the best flamenco museum in Andalucía, the Fosforito centre has exhibits, film and information panels in English and Spanish telling you the history of the guitar and all the flamenco greats. Touch-screen videos demonstrate the important techniques of flamenco song, guitar, dance and percussion – you can test your skill at beating out the *compás* (rhythm) of different *palos* (song forms). Regular live flamenco performances are held here, too.

The museum benefits from a fantastic location inside the Posada del Potro, a legendary inn that played a part in *Don Quijote,* where Cervantes described it as a 'den of thieves'. The famous square it stands on, once a horse market, features a lovely 16th-century stone fountain topped by a rearing *potro* (colt).

⭐ **Museo Arqueológico** MUSEUM

(Plaza de Jerónimo Páez 7; EU citizen/other free/€1.50; ⊙ 9am-7.30pm Tue-Sat, to 3.30pm Sun mid-Sep–mid-Jun, 9am-3.30pm Tue-Sun mid-Jun–mid-Sep) The excellent Archaeological Museum traces Córdoba's many changes in size, appearance and lifestyle from pre-Roman to early Reconquista times, with some fine sculpture, an impressive coin collection, and interesting exhibits on domestic life and religion. In the basement you can walk through the excavated remains of the city's Roman theatre.

Palacio de Viana MUSEUM

(www.palaciodeviana.com; Plaza de Don Gome 2; whole house/patios €8/5; ⊙ 10am-7pm Tue-Sat, to 3pm Sun Sep-Jun, 9am-3pm Tue-Sun Jul & Aug) A stunning Renaissance palace set around 12 beautiful patios, the Viana Palace is a particular delight to visit in spring. Occupied by the aristocratic Marqueses de Viana until 1980, the large building is packed with art and antiques. The whole-house charge covers a one-hour guided tour of the rooms and access to the patios and garden. It's an 800m walk northeast from Plaza de las Tendillas.

Puente Romano BRIDGE

Spanning the Río Guadalquivir just below the Mezquita, the handsome, 16-arched

DON'T MISS

CÓRDOBA'S JEWISH QUARTER

The *judería* (old Jewish quarter) west and north of the Mezquita is a labyrinth of narrow streets and small squares, whitewashed buildings and wrought-iron gates allowing glimpses of plant-filled patios. Some streets are now choked with gaudy souvenir shops and tourist-oriented restaurants, but others remain quiet and unblemished. The importance of the medieval Jewish community is illustrated by the Judería's proximity to the Mezquita and the city's centres of power. Spain had one of Europe's biggest Jewish communities, recorded from as early as the 2nd century AD. Persecuted by the Visigoths, they allied themselves with the Muslims following the Arab conquests. By the 10th century they were established among the most dynamic members of society, holding posts as administrators, doctors, jurists, philosophers and poets. One of the greatest Jewish theologians, Maimonides, was born in Córdoba in 1135, though he left with his family at an early age to escape Almohad persecution, eventually settling in Egypt. His magnum opus, the *Mishne Torah,* summarised the teachings of Judaism and systematised all Jewish law.

Casa de Sefarad (www.casadesefarad.es; Cnr Calles de los Judíos & Averroes; €4; ⊙10am-6pm Mon-Sat, 11am-6pm Sun) In the heart of the Judería, and once connected by tunnel to the Sinagoga (p646), the Casa de Sefarad is an interesting museum is devoted to the Sephardic (Iberian Peninsula Jewish) tradition. Different rooms cover food, domestic crafts, ritual, music, prominent Jews of Córdoba and the Inquisition. There's also a section on women intellectuals (poets, artists and thinkers) of Al-Andalus.

Sinagoga (Calle de los Judíos 20; EU citizen/other free/€0.30; ⊙9am-3.30pm Tue-Sun mid-Jun–mid-Sep, to 7.30pm Tue-Sat mid-Sep–mid-Jun) Constructed in 1315, this small, probably private or family synagogue is one of the few testaments to the Jewish presence in medieval Andalucía, though it hasn't been used as a place of worship since the expulsion of Jews in 1492. Decorated with extravagant stuccowork that includes Hebrew inscriptions and intricate Mudéjar star and plant patterns, it has an upper gallery reserved for women.

Roman bridge formed part of the ancient Via Augusta, which ran from Girona in Catalonia to Cádiz. Rebuilt several times down the centuries, it's now traffic free and makes for a lovely stroll.

Torre de la Calahorra　MUSEUM
(☑957 29 39 29; www.torrecalahorra.com; Puente Romano; adult/child incl audioguide €4.50/3; ⊙10am-7pm Oct-Apr, to 8.30pm May-Sep) At the south end of the Puente Romano stands the squat tower, erected under Islamic rule. It now houses the Museo Vivo de Al-Andalus, a museum highlighting the cultural achievements of Al-Andalus. You need the audioguide to make the most of it.

Museo Julio Romero de Torres　GALLERY
(Plaza del Potro 1; €4.50; ⊙8.30am-8.45pm Tue-Fri, to 4.30pm Sat, to 2.30pm Sun) A former hospital houses what is, surprisingly enough, Córdoba's most visited museum, devoted to much-loved local painter Julio Romero de Torres (1874–1930), who is famed for his paintings expressing his sense of Andalucian female beauty. He was

also much inspired by flamenco and bullfighting.

🎊 Festivals & Events

Fiesta de los Patios de Córdoba　PATIOS
(www.patios.cordoba.es) This 'best patio' competition sees many of Córdoba's beautiful private courtyards open for public viewing till 10pm nightly. A concurrent cultural program stages flamenco and other concerts in some of the city's grandest patios and plazas. The festival runs for two weeks, starting in early May.

Festival de la Guitarra de Córdoba　MUSIC
(www.guitarracordoba.org) A two-week celebration of the guitar in the first half of July. Live performances of classical, flamenco, rock, blues and more by top Spanish and international names in Córdoba's theatres.

🛏 Sleeping

Córdoba's many accommodation options span the spectrum from economy to deluxe. Even some of the lower-end places offer elegantly styled and spacious rooms, while others are laden with antiques and history. Booking ahead during the main festivals is essential. We quote prices for the main tourist seasons of approximately April, May, September and October. Expect to pay more during Semana Santa and the May festivals and on some weekends, but less in July, August and the depths of winter.

★ Bed and Be
HOSTEL €

(☑ 661 42 07 33; www.bedandbe.com; Calle Cruz Conde 22; dm €17-20, d with shared bathroom €50-80; ❄ 🛜) 🍃 An exceptionally good hostel option a bit north of Plaza de las Tendillas. Staff are clued up about what's on and what's new in Córdoba, and they offer a social event every evening – anything from a bike tour to a sushi dinner. The assortment of double and dorm rooms are all super-clean and as gleaming white as a *pueblo blanco*.

Extra value is added by the great roof terrace, bicycle rental (€6/10 per three/six hours) and communal kitchen and lounge area.

The new, contemporary-design **Option Be Hostel** (www.bedandbe.com; Calle Leiva Aguilar 1; dm €15-25, d €20-40; ❄ 🛜), run by the same people along similar lines but with mostly private bathrooms, should be open in the historic centre by the time you get there.

Hospedería Alma Andalusí
HOTEL €

(☑ 957 76 08 88; www.almaandalusi.com; Calle Fernández Ruano 5; r €50-60; ❄ 🛜) This guesthouse in a quiet section of the Judería (the old Jewish quarter) has been brilliantly converted from an ancient structure into a stylish, modern establishment, while rates have been kept down. There's an appealing floral theme throughout. Thoughtfully chosen furnishings, polished wood floors and blue-and-white colour schemes make for a comfortable base.

Hospedería del Atalia
BOUTIQUE HOTEL €€

(☑ 957 49 66 59; www.hospederiadelatalia.com; Calle Buen Pastor 19; r €70-160, ste €170-260; ❄ 🛜) Entered from a quiet patio in the Judería, the Atalia sports elegant, contemporary, owner-designed rooms in burgundies, russets and olive greens. Good breakfasts with a wide choice are €6, and there's a super sunny roof terrace with chairs, tables and a Mezquita view.

Hotel Hacienda Posada de Vallina
HOTEL €€

(☑ 957 49 87 50; www.hhposadadevallina.es; Calle Corregidor Luís de la Cerda 83; r €70-100;

🅿 ❄ @ 🛜) In an enviable nook on the quiet side of the Mezquita, this cleverly renovated hotel uses portraits and period furniture to enhance a plush and modern interior. There are two levels overlooking a salubrious patio, and the rooms make you feel comfortable but in-period (ie medieval Córdoba). Those upstairs are a bit airier. Columbus allegedly stayed here.

Casa de los Azulejos
HOTEL €€

(☑ 957 47 00 00; www.casadelosazulejos.com; Calle Fernando Colón 5; incl breakfast s €78, d €89-134; ❄ @ 🛜 ♨) Mexican and Andalucian styles converge in this stylish nine-room hotel, where the patio is all banana trees, ferns and potted palms bathed in sunlight. Colonial-style rooms feature tall antique doors, big beds, walls in lilac and sky blue, and floors adorned with the beautiful old *azulejos* that give the place its name.

★ Balcón de Córdoba
BOUTIQUE HOTEL €€€

(☑ 957 49 84 78; www.balcondecordoba.com; Calle Encarnación 8; r incl breakfast €120-200; ❄ 🛜) Offering top-end boutique luxury, the 10-room Balcón is a riveting place with a charming *cordobés* patio, slick rooms, antique doorways, and ancient stone relics dotted around as if it were a wing of the nearby archaeological museum. Service doesn't miss a beat and the rooms have tasteful, soothing, contemporary decor with a little art but no clutter.

The roof terrace affords great views across the rooftops to the Mezquita, and the classy restaurant does a carefully prepared selection of Cordoban-cum-global dishes.

🍴 Eating

Córdoba's signature dish is *salmorejo*, a delicious, thick, chilled soup of blended tomatoes, garlic, bread, lemon, vinegar and olive oil, sprinkled with hard-boiled egg and strips of ham. Along with *rabo de toro* (oxtail stew), it appears on every menu. There's traditional meaty and fishy Andalucian fare aplenty here – but also a good sprinkling of creative contemporary eateries putting successful fresh twists on Spanish and Mediterranean ingredients. Don't miss the wine from nearby Montilla and Moriles.

Taberna Salinas
ANDALUCIAN €

(www.tabernasalinas.com; Calle Tundidores 3; raciones €7-8; ⏱ 12.30-4pm & 8-11.30pm Mon-Sat, closed Aug) A historic bar-restaurant (since 1879), with a patio and several rooms,

Salinas is adorned in classic Córdoba fashion with tiles, wine barrels, art and photos of bullfighter Manolete. It's popular with tourists (and offers a five-language menu), but it retains a traditional atmosphere and the waiters are very helpful. Not least, the food is very good, from the orange-and-cod salad to the pork loin in hazelnut sauce.

Taberna Sociedad de Plateros   ANDALUCIAN €

(📞957 47 00 42; Calle de San Francisco 6; tapas €2-2.25, raciones €5-10; ⊙noon-4pm & 8pm-midnight Tue-Sat, noon-4pm Sun) Run by the silversmiths' guild, this well-loved traditional bar-cum-restaurant serves a selection of generous tapas and *raciones* in its light, glass-roofed patio. The seafood selection is particularly good, highlighted by such items as *bacalao rebozado* (breaded cod) and *salpicón de mariscos* (shellfish salad).

Bar Santos   TAPAS €

(Calle Magistral González Francés 3; tortilla €2; ⊙10am-midnight) Most restaurants close to the Mezquita are geared to an undiscriminating tourist market. But this legendary little bar serves the best *tortilla de patata* in town – and don't the *cordobeses* know it. Thick wedges are deftly cut from giant wheels of the stuff and customarily served with plastic forks on paper plates to eat outside under the Mezquita's walls. Don't miss it.

★ Garum 2.1   CONTEMPORARY ANDALUCIAN €€

(Calle San Fernando 122; tapas €3-7, raciones €7-17; ⊙noon-4pm & 8pm-midnight, to 2am Fri & Sat) Garum serves up traditional meaty, fishy and vegie ingredients in all sorts of creative, tasty new concoctions. We recommend the *presa ibérica con herencia del maestro* (Iberian pork with potatoes, fried eggs and ham). Service is helpful and friendly.

★ La Boca   FUSION €€

(📞957 47 61 40; www.restaurantelaboca.com; Calle San Fernando 39; mains €10-15; ⊙noon-midnight Wed-Sun, to 5pm Mon) Trendy for a reason, this cutting-edge eatery whips up exciting global variations from traditional ingredients, then presents them in eye-catching ways: Iberian pork cheeks with red curry and basmati? Battered cod chunks with almonds and garlic? It's very well done, though portions are not for giant appetites. Reservations advisable at weekends.

★ El Astronauta   MEDITERRANEAN €€

(📞957 49 11 23; www.elastronauta.es; Calle Diario de Córdoba 18; medias raciones €5.50-8.50,

raciones €9-17; ⊙1.30-5pm & 8pm-late Mon-Thu, 1.30pm-late Fri & Sat; 🖉) The Astronauta produces a galaxy of Mediterranean dishes with an emphasis on fresh, healthy ingredients: zesty salads, mezes, lamb moussaka, vegetarian burgers and much more. The decor is cosmic, the vibe alternative and the local clientele loyal.

★ Bodegas Campos   ANDALUCIAN €€

(📞957 49 75 00; www.bodegascampos.com; Calle de Lineros 32; mains & raciones €11-23; ⊙1.30-4.30pm daily, 8-11.30pm Mon-Sat) This atmospheric warren of rooms and patios is popular with smartly dressed *cordobeses*. The restaurant and more informal *taberna* (tavern) serve up delicious dishes, putting a slight creative twist on traditional Andalucian fare – the likes of cod-and-cuttlefish ravioli or pork sirloin in grape sauce. Bodegas Campos also produces its own house Montilla.

Casa Mazal   JEWISH, ANDALUCIAN €€

(📞957 94 18 88; www.casamazal.com; Calle Tomás Conde 3; mains €9-20; ⊙12.30-4pm & 7.30-11pm; 🖉) A meal here makes a fine complement to the nearby Casa de Sefarad museum, as it brings the Sephardic tradition to the table, along with some *andalusí* (Moorish) dishes. Sephardic cuisine has diverse roots in Al-Andalus, Turkey, Italy and North Africa, with such varied items as Syrian lentil-and-rice salad, an array of couscous options, and *seniyeh* lamb pie on the menu.

There are regular recitals of Sephardic, *andalusí* and early Spanish music too.

🍷 Drinking & Nightlife

★ La Bicicleta   BAR

(📞666 544690; Calle Cardenal González 1; ⊙10am-late Mon-Fri, noon-late Sat & Sun) 🚲 This friendly, informal bar welcomes cyclists (and anyone else who's thirsty) with an array of drinks, tasty snacks (light dishes €4–€9) and – best of all – long, cool, multifruit juices. There's 20% off some drinks if you come by bike!

★ Bodega Guzmán   WINE BAR

(Calle de los Judíos 7; ⊙noon-4pm & 8.15-11.45pm Fri-Wed) This atmospheric Judería drinking spot bedecked with bullfighting memorabilia is frequented by both locals and tourists. Montilla wine is dispensed from three giant barrels behind the bar: don't leave without trying some *amargoso* (bitter).

Califa

PUB

(www.cervezascalifa.com; Calle Juan Valera 3; ⊙noon-4pm & 7pm-midnight Mon-Thu, noon-late Fri & Sat, noon-4pm Sun) These enterprising Córdoba lads have opened one of the region's first craft beer pubs, challenging the hegemony of the Cruzcampos and San Miguels. In fact, it's more accurately described as a brewpub, as they concoct the ale on the premises. Try their Rubia, More-na, IPA or Sultana stout varieties – or select from two dozen other craft ales from around Spain.

Amapola

MUSIC BAR

(www.facebook.com/amapolacordoba; Paseo de la Ribera 9; ⊙5pm-3am Mon-Thu, noon-4am Fri-Sun) The artiest bar in the riverside area, with a semigrunge feel, elaborate cocktails and a great terrace looking down to the river.

WORTH A TRIP

MADINAT AL-ZAHRA

Eight kilometres west of Córdoba stands what's left of **Madinat al-Zahra** (Medina Azahara; ☑957 10 49 33; www.museosdeandalucia.es; Carretera Palma del Río Km 5.5; EU citizen/other free/€1.50; ⊙9am-7.30pm Tue-Sat Apr–mid-Jun, to 3.30pm mid-Jun–mid-Sep, to 5.30pm mid-Sep–Mar, 9am-3.30pm Sun year-round; 🅿), the sumptuous palace-city built by Caliph Abd ar-Rahman III in the 10th century. The complex spills down a hillside with the caliph's palace (the area you visit today) on the highest levels overlooking what were gardens and open fields. The residential areas (still unexcavated) were set away to each side. A fascinating modern museum has been installed below the site.

Legend has it that Abd ar-Rahman III built Madinat al-Zahra for his favourite wife, Az-Zahra. Dismayed by her homesickness and yearnings for the snowy mountains of Syria, he surrounded his new city with almond and cherry trees, replacing snowflakes with fluffy white blossoms. More realistically, it was probably Abd ar-Rahman's rivalry with the Fatimid dynasty in North Africa that drove him to declare his caliphate in 929 and construct, as caliphs were wont to do, a new capital. Building started in 940 and chroniclers record some staggering construction statistics: 10,000 labourers set 6000 stone blocks a day, with outer walls stretching 1518m east to west and 745m north to south.

It is almost inconceivable to think that such a city, built over 35 years, was to last only a few more before the usurper Al-Mansur transferred government to a new palace complex of his own in 981. Then, between 1010 and 1013, Madinat al-Zahra was wrecked by Berber soldiers. During succeeding centuries its ruins were plundered repeatedly for building materials.

The visitors' route takes you down through the city's original northern gate. Highlights of the visitable area are the grand arched Edificio Basilical Superior, which housed the main state admin offices, and the Casa de Yafar, believed to have been residence of the caliph's prime minister. The crown jewel of the site, the royal reception hall known as the Salón de Abd ar-Rahman III, was closed for restoration at the time of writing. This hall has exquisitely carved stuccowork and is said to have been decorated with gold and silver tiles, arches of ivory and ebony, and walls of multicoloured marble.

The museum, 2km downhill by road from the site entrance, takes you through the history of Madinat al-Zahra, with sections on its origins, planning and construction, its inhabitants and its eventual downfall. The sections are illustrated with beautifully displayed pieces from the site and some excellent interactive displays, and complemented by flawless English translations.

Drivers should leave Córdoba westward along Avenida de Medina Azahara. This feeds into the A431 road, with the turn-off to Madinat al-Zahra signposted after 6km. You must park at the museum and get tickets there for the site and the shuttle bus (*lanzadera*; €2.10 return) which takes you 2km up to the site.

A bus to Madinat al-Zahra leaves from a stop near Córdoba's Puerta de Almodóvar at 10.15am and 11am daily, 4.15pm Tuesday to Saturday and 11.45am Sunday (€8.50 return including the shuttle from museum to site and back). Tickets for the bus must be bought in advance at the Centro de Visitantes (p650) or at the tourist offices at the train station (p650) or Plaza de las Tendillas (p650).

☆ Entertainment

If you're searching for authentic flamenco, the Centro Flamenco Fosforito (p645) stages regular events and is a good place to ask about what else is coming up.

Jazz Café LIVE MUSIC
(www.facebook.com/joseluis.cabello1; Calle Rodríguez Marín; ⊙from 9pm; ⊛) An enticing music den decked with musical paraphernalia, Jazz Café stages blues jams on Thursdays and jazz jams on Tuesdays (both from 10pm), plus other live acts as and when. It rocks on until the wee hours; on Fridays and Saturdays you may find DJs spinning soul or funk.

🛍 Shopping

Córdoba's time-honoured craft specialities are colourful embossed leather *(cuero repujado)*, silver jewellery and some attractive pottery. The embossed leather is also known as *guadamecí* (sheepskin) or *cordobán* (goatskin). Calles Cardenal González and Manríquez have some of the classier craft shops.

Meryan HANDICRAFTS
(☑957 47 59 02; Calleja de las Flores 2; ⊙9am-8pm Mon-Fri, to 2pm Sat) Has a particularly good range of embossed-leather goods: wallets, bags, boxes, notebooks, even copies of Picasso paintings.

ℹ Information

Centro de Visitantes (Visitors Centre; ☑957 35 51 79; www.andalucia.org; Plaza del Triunfo; ⊙9am-7.30pm Mon-Fri, 9.30am-3pm Sat & Sun) The main tourist-information centre, with an exhibit on Córdoba's history, and some Roman and Visigothic remains downstairs.
Córdoba (www.cordobaturismo.es) Tourist information for the province.
Municipal Tourist Information Kiosk (☑902 20 17 74; www.turismodecordoba.org; Plaza de las Tendillas; ⊙9am-2pm & 5-7.30pm)
Municipal Tourist Information Office (☑902 20 17 74; www.turismodecordoba.org; train station; ⊙9am-2pm & 4.30-7pm) In the station's main entry hall.

ℹ Getting There & Away

BUS

The **bus station** (☑957 40 40 40; www.estacionautobusescordoba.es; Avenida Vía Augusta) is located behind the train station, 1.3km northwest of Plaza de las Tendillas.

Alsa (☑902 42 22 42; www.alsa.es)
Autocares Carrera (☑957 50 16 32; www.autocarescarrera.es)
Autocares San Sebastián (☑957 42 90 30; www.autocaressansebastian.es)
Socibus (☑902 22 92 92; www.socibus.es)
Transportes Ureña (☑957 40 45 58; http://urena-sa.com)

DESTINATION	FARE	DURATION	FREQUENCY
Almodóvar del Río	€1	30min	up to 10 daily
Baena	€5.50	1hr	8 daily
Baeza	€12	2½hr	2 daily
Granada	€15	2¾hr	8 daily
Hornachuelos	€2.20	1hr	2-5 daily except Sun
Jaén	€10	2hr	4-6 daily
Madrid	€17	5hr	6 daily
Málaga	€12	3hr	4 daily
Montilla	€3.80	45min	12 daily
Priego de Córdoba	€9.20	2hr	7 daily
Seville	€12	2hr	7 daily
Úbeda	€12	2¾hr	4 daily
Zuheros	€6.50	1¾hr	4 daily

TRAIN

Córdoba's modern **train station** (www.renfe.com; Glorieta de las Tres Culturas), 1.2km northwest of Plaza de las Tendillas, is served both by fast AVE services and by some slower regional trains.

DESTINATION	FARE	DURATION	FREQUENCY
Andújar	€10-16	50min	5 daily
Antequera	€19-33	30-40min	17 daily
Granada	€38	2¾hr	6 daily
Jaén	€15	1¾hr	4 daily
Madrid	€38-71	1¾-2hr	30 daily
Málaga	€27-41	1hr	17 daily
Seville	€14-30	45-80min	35 daily

ℹ Getting Around

BUS

Bus 3 (€1.30, every 12 to 20 minutes), from the west end of Avenida Vía Augusta (the street between the train and bus stations), runs down Calle Diario de Córdoba and Calle de San Fernando, east of the Mezquita. For the return trip, catch it on Ronda de Isasa near the Puente Romano, or from Avenida Doctor Fleming or Paseo de la Victoria.

CAR

The one-way system is nightmarish, and cars are banned from the historic centre unless they are going to park, unload or load at hotels, most of which are reasonably well signposted as you approach. There is free, unmetered parking south of the river across the Puente de Miraflores, and a mixture of free and metered parking on Paseo de la Victoria, Avenida Doctor Fleming and streets to their west. Metered zones (with blue lines along the street) are free of charge from 2pm to 5pm and 9pm to 9am, and on Saturday afternoons and all day Sunday.

Parque Natural Sierras Subbéticas

This 320-sq-km park in the southeast of the province encompasses a set of craggy, emerald-green limestone hills pocked with caves, springs and streams, with some charmingly appealing old villages and small towns set round its periphery. It makes for some lovely exploring among valleys, canyons and high peaks (the highest is 1570m La Tiñosa). Most visitors base themselves in or near picturesque Zuheros or Priego de Córdoba.

The park's visitors center, **Centro de Visitantes Santa Rita** (📞957 50 69 86; Ctra A339, Km 11.2; ⊗9am-2pm Wed-Fri, 9am-2pm & 6-8pm Sat & Sun May-Jun, 8am-2pm Fri-Sun Jul-Sep, 9am-

2pm Wed-Fri, 9am-2pm & 4-6pm Sat-Sun Oct-Apr), is 15km west of Priego. An excellent walking guide is *Walking in the Subbética Natural Park Córdoba* by local resident Clive Jarman; Zuheros' Hotel Zuhayra (p652) sells the guide for €14 and individual walks sheets for €2.50. The local tourism website, www.turismodelasubbetica.es, is a useful source on the area.

Zuheros & Around

POP 700 / ELEV 625M

Rising above the olive-tree-strewn countryside on the park's northern edge, Zuheros sits in a supremely picturesque location, its tangle of white streets and crag-top castle crouching in the lee of towering hills. Approached by twisting roads up from the A318, the village has a delightfully relaxed atmosphere.

◉ Sights

Castillo de Zuheros   CASTLE

(Plaza de la Paz; admission or tours €2; ⊗10am-2pm & 5-7pm Tue-Fri, tours 11am, 12.30pm, 2pm, 5.30pm & 6.30pm Sat, Sun & holidays, all afternoon times 1hr earlier Oct-Mar) Set on a panoramic pinnacle, Zuheros' castle is of 9th-century Moorish origin, with remains of a later Renaissance palace attached. Weekend visits are guided, and it's worth booking for these; other days visits are unguided. The ticket also includes the little **Museo Arqueológico** (Archaeological Museum; 📞957 69 45 45; Plaza de la Paz), just across the square, which doubles as Zuheros' tourist office.

VÍA VERDE DE LA SUBBÉTICA

The area's easiest and best marked path is the **Vía Verde de la Subbética** (greenway; www.viasverdes.com; 🚲), a disused railway converted to a cycling and walking track, which you can see snaking through the countryside below Zuheros. It runs 65km across southern Córdoba province from Camporreal near Puente Genil to the Río Guadajoz on the Jaén border, skirting the western and northern fringes of the natural park.

With gentle gradients and utilising old bridges, tunnels and viaducts, the greenway makes for a fun outing for travellers of all ages. There are cafes and bike-hire outlets in old station buildings along the route, and informative map-boards – it's impossible to get lost! At the Río Guadajoz it connects with the **Vía Verde del Aceite** (Olive Oil Greenway; www.viasverdes.com), which continues a further 55km to Jaén city.

Subbética Bike's Friends (📞672 605088; www.subbeticabikesfriends.com; bikes per hr/half-day/day €3.50/9.50/14.50, child seats €2; ⊗10am-6pm Sat & Sun; 🚲) at Doña Mencía station, 4km west down the hill from Zuheros, rents a range of different bikes, including children's, and can normally provide them any day of the week if you call ahead.

WORTH A TRIP

CASA OLEA

Set in its own little olive grove by a small river, British-owned country house **Casa Olea** (696 748209; www.casaolea.com; Ctra CO7204, near El Cañuelo; s/d incl breakfast €105/118;), 12km north of Priego, has a beautifully spacious and relaxed feel. It makes a great rural retreat and base for exploring the region. There are good walks in its immediate area as well as further afield in the Sierras Subbéticas, plus mountain bikes to rent (€15 per day) and a lovely pool.

Excellent dinners (two/three courses €20/25) are available five nights a week. No children under seven.

Cueva de los Murciélagos   CAVE

(Cave of the Bats; 957 69 45 45; www.cuevadelos-murcielagos.es; adult/child €6/5; guided tours 12.30pm & 5.30pm Tue-Fri, 11am, 12.30pm, 2pm, 5pm & 6.30pm Sat & Sun, afternoon tours 1hr earlier Oct-Mar;) Carved out of the limestone massif 4km above Zuheros is this extraordinary cave. From the vast hall at the start of the tour, it's a 430m loop walk through a series of corridors filled with fantastic rock formations. Traces of Neolithic rock paintings showing abstract figures of goats can be admired along the way.

Visits are by guided tour only and should be reserved by phoning Turismo Zuheros between 10am and 1.30pm Tuesday to Friday, or by emailing them.

The drive up to the cave is exhilarating, as the road twists and turns through the looming mountains, with vertiginous views from various lookout points.

🍽 Sleeping & Eating

⭐ **Hotel Zuhayra**   HOTEL €

(957 69 46 93; www.zercahoteles.com; Calle Mirador 10; s/d €48/60;) A short distance below Zuheros' castle, this hotel has breathtaking views of the countryside from every room. It makes an excellent base for exploring the area. The friendly proprietors, the Ábalos brothers (who speak English), offer masses of information about walks and other things to see and do, and can set you up with a local guide. There is also a good restaurant.

Los Balanchares   CHEESE €

(957 69 47 14; www.losbalanchares.com; Ctra A318, Km 68; 9am-2pm & 4-7pm Mon-Fri, 10am-4pm Sat & Sun) Zuheros is renowned for its cheeses and you can see and buy a top selection at this wonderful organic goat- and sheep-cheese maker, on the Doña Mencía–Baena road below Zuheros.

Mesón Atalaya   ANDALUCIAN €€

(957 69 46 97; Calle Santo 58; mains €7-20; 1-4pm & 9-11pm Tue-Sun) This family-run establishment at the east end of the village does good local fare, with plenty of lamb, pork, ham, *potajes* and *cazuelas* (types of stew), local cheese and homemade desserts. There are two nice, plant-filled patios inside.

ℹ Information

Turismo Zuheros (957 69 45 45; www.turismodezuheros.es; Plaza de la Paz 1; 10am-2pm Tue-Sun year-round, 5-7pm Tue-Fri Apr-Sep, 4-6pm Tue-Fri Oct-Mar)

ℹ Getting There & Away

Buses depart from Mesón Atalaya.

Autocares Carrera (p650) Two to four daily buses to/from Córdoba (€6.50, 1¾ hours).

Autocares Valenzuela (Seville 954 82 02 89; www.grupovalenzuela.com) Three or more daily buses to/from Doña Mencía (€1.15, 20 minutes) and two or more to/from Seville (€17, 3¾ hours).

Granada & South Coast Andalucía

Best Places to Eat

➡ La Fábula Restaurante (p672)

➡ Cantina de la Estación (p713)

➡ Casa Antonio (p709)

➡ La Consula (p693)

➡ Taberna Restaurante La Tapa (p681)

Best Places to Sleep

➡ Los Arcos (p680)

➡ Hotel Hospes Palacio de los Patos (p670)

➡ Carmen de la Alcubilla del Caracol (p668)

➡ Hotel Real de Poqueira (p681)

➡ Hotel Misiana (p702)

Why Go?

From sprawling coastal condo complexes where Spanish is the second or third language, to mountain villages barely changed since Federico Lorca penned his rural trilogy, eastern and southern Andalucía harbour microcosms of Spain, both antediluvian and super-modern. There's the Afro-European cross-fertilisation of Moorish Granada, the fiercely traditional port city of Málaga, sun-kissed tomato-growing Almería, and the shamelessly unsubtle resorts of the Costa del Sol. Incorporating the four provinces of Málaga, Granada, Jaén and Almería, this region leaves no one uncatered for. Golf fanatics: pack your clubs. Nightclub-loving beach bums: commandeer the sun lounger. Solitude-seeking outdoor types: pack a day bag and find a natural park to get lost in. Attracting all types, half of this part of Andalucía is worryingly overdeveloped; the other half remains innately Spanish and largely ignored by unknowing outsiders. Weave carefully between the two and find your own Spanish spirit.

When to Go
Granada

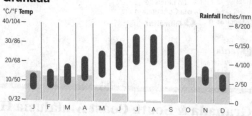

Mar–Apr A time of festivals and processions, but prices go up. Book ahead.

May–Jun The weather's bearable; there are plenty of activities if you don't mind the crowds.

Nov–Feb Mild winter weather. Accommodation prices fall. Go skiing in the Sierra Nevada.

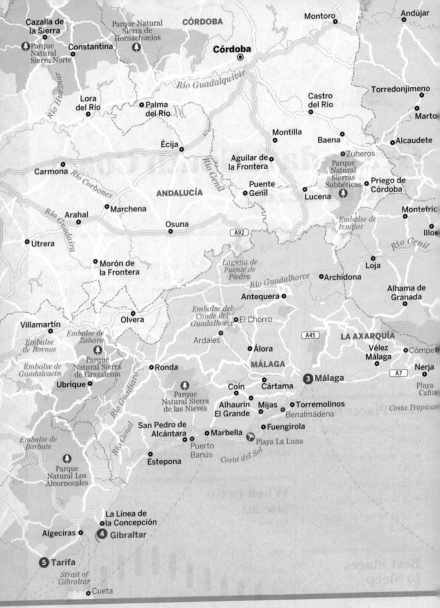

Granada & South Coast Andalucía Highlights

❶ Alhambra (p657)
Following the masses and making a pilgrimage to the Alhambra in Granada, then joining 300 others in the Plaza Bib-Rambla for churros dipped in hot chocolate.

❷ Cabo de Gata (p722)
Going long-distance hiking along Andalucía's most beautiful stretch of coast.

❸ Málaga (p684) Sifting through the fine array of art galleries and museums in this vibrant southern city.

❹ Gibraltar (p703)
Climbing the Mediterranean Steps in Gibraltar and gazing out at Africa, the jaws of the

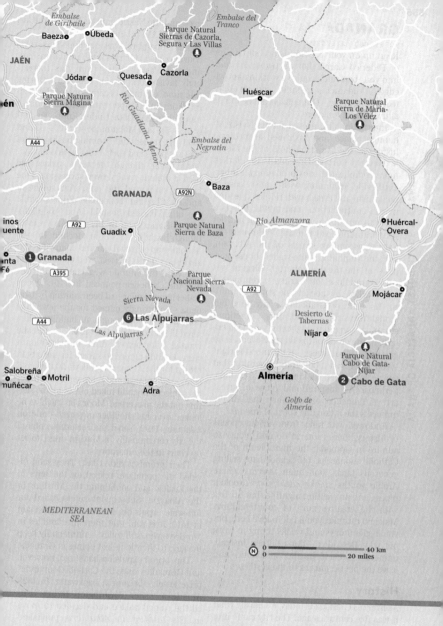

Embalse
de Giribaile

Baeza • **Úbeda**

JAÉN

**Parque Natural
Sierras de Cazorla,
Segura y Las Villas**

Embalse del
Tranco

Jódar • **Quesada** • **Cazorla**

én **Parque Natural
Sierra Mágina**

Huéscar

**Parque Natural
Sierra de María-
Los Vélez**

A44

Río Guadiana Menor

Embalse del
Negratín

GRANADA

A92N **Baza**

**Parque Natural
Sierra de Baza**

Río Almanzora

**Huércal-
Overa**

inos
uente

A92 **Guadix**

nta
Fé **1 Granada**

ALMERÍA

Mojácar

A395

**Parque
Nacional Sierra
Nevada**

A92

Sierra Nevada

Desierto de
Tabernas

A44 **6 Las Alpujarras**

Las Alpujarras

Níjar

**Parque Natural
Cabo de Gata-
Níjar**

Salobreña • **Motril**

Almería

2 Cabo de Gata

uñécar

Adra

Golfo de
Almería

MEDITERRANEAN
SEA

N

0 ———— 40 km
0 ———— 20 miles

Mediterranean and huge
flocks of gliding seabirds.

5 Tarifa (p700) Trying
your hand windsurfing,
diving, whale-watching or
horse-riding.

6 Las Alpujarras (p679)
Going shopping for local
handicrafts in the lofty
villages of the Sierra Nevada.

GRANADA

POP 258,000 / ELEV 738M

Read up on your Nasrid history, slip a copy of Federico García Lorca's *Gypsy Ballads* into your bag, and acquire a working knowledge of Andalucía's splendid Moorish architectural heritage – Granada is calling and its allure is hard to ignore.

Internationally revered for its lavish Alhambra palace, and enshrined in medieval history as the last stronghold of the Moors in Western Europe, Granada is the darker, more complicated cousin of sunny, exuberant Seville. Humming with a feisty cosmopolitanism and awash with riddles, question marks, contradictions and myths, this is a place to put down your guidebook and let your intuition lead the way – through the narrow ascending streets of the Albayzín, and the tumbling white-walled house gardens of the Realejo quarter. Elegant yet edgy, grandiose but gritty, monumental but marked by pockets of stirring graffiti, 21st-century Granada is anything but straightforward. Instead, this sometimes stunning, sometimes ugly city set spectacularly in the crook of the Sierra Nevada is an enigmatic place where – if the mood is right – you sense you might find something that you've long been looking for. A free tapa, perhaps? An inspirational piece of street art? A flamenco performance that finally unmasks the intangible spirit of *duende*?

Endowed with relics from various epochs of history, there's lots to do and plenty to admire in Granada: the mausoleum of the Catholic monarchs, old-school bars selling generous tapas, bohemian *teterías* where Arabic youths smoke *cachimbas* (hookah pipes), and an exciting nightlife that bristles with the creative aura of counterculture. Make no mistake, you'll fall in love here, but you'll spend days and weeks trying to work out why. Best idea – don't bother. Instead, immerse yourself in the splendour, and leave the poetic stanzas to the aesthetes.

History

As lively as Granada is today, it's hardly what it was five centuries ago. The city came into its own late in Spain's Islamic era. As Córdoba and Seville fell to the Catholics in the mid 13th century, a minor potentate called Muhammad ibn Yusuf ibn Nasr established an independent state based in Granada. The town was soon flooded with Muslim refu-

gees, and the Nasrid emirate became the last bastion of Al-Andalus.

The Alhambra was developed as royal court, palace, fortress and miniature city, and the Nasrids ruled from this increasingly lavish complex for 250 years. During this time, Granada became one of the richest cities in Europe, with a population of more than 350,000. Under Emirs Yusuf I (r 1333–54) and Mohammed V (r 1354–59 and 1362–91), traders did booming business, and artisans perfected such crafts as wood inlay.

As usual, though, decadent palace life bred a violent rivalry over succession. One faction supported the emir Abu al-Hasan and his Christian concubine, Zoraya, while the other backed Boabdil (Abu Abdullah), Abu al-Hasan's son by his wife Aixa – even though Boabdil was still just a child. In 1482 Boabdil started a civil war and, following Abu al-Hasan's death in 1485, won control of the city. With the emirate weakened by infighting, the Catholics pounced in 1491. Queen Isabel in particular had been smitten by Granada – so fittingly named for the jewel-like pomegranate, she thought, its buildings clustered like seeds along the hillsides – and she wanted it for herself. After an eight-month siege, Boabdil agreed to surrender the city in return for the Alpujarras valleys, 30,000 gold coins, and political and religious freedom for his subjects. Boabdil hiked out of town – letting out the proverbial 'Moor's last sigh' as he looked over his shoulder in regret – and on 2 January 1492, Isabel and Fernando entered the city ceremonially in Muslim dress, to set up court in the Alhambra.

Their promises didn't last. They soon divided the populace, relegating the Jews to the Realejo and containing the Muslims in the Albayzín. Subsequent rulers called for full-scale expulsion, first in 1570 and again in 1610. It is said that there are families in Morocco who, still today, sentimentally keep the keys to their long-lost homes in Granada.

This brutal expulsion backfired, however, and Granada – once the Catholic Monarchs' prize jewel – became a backwater. In 1828 American writer Washington Irving visited the ruined palace and decided to move in. His *Tales of the Alhambra,* published in 1832, brought tourists from all over the world to marvel at the city's Islamic heritage; they helped give the city a little push into the modern age. Now Granada thrives on a culture that mixes Spanish, Moroccan, *gitano* (Roma) and student, plus tourist, life.

⊙ Sights

Most major sights are an easy walk within the city centre, and there are buses for when the hills wear you out. Rectangular Plaza Nueva is Granada's main nexus. The Albayzín sits on a hill immediately to the north and is roughly demarcated by Gran Vía de Colón and the Río Darro. The Alhambra lies on a separate hill on the opposite side of the Darro. Granada's former Jewish quarter, the Realejo, occupies the southwestern slope of the Alhambra hill and some of the flat land beyond. Central Granada is laid out in a grid on the flat land west of the Albayzín and northwest of the Realejo. Its main square is Plaza Bib-Rambla.

⊙ Alhambra & Realejo

★ **Alhambra**   PALACE

(☑902 44 12 21; www.alhambra-tickets.es; adult/under 12yr €14/free, Generalife only €7; ⊙8.30am-8pm mid-Mar–mid-Oct, to 6pm mid-Oct–mid-Mar, night visits 10-11.30pm Tue-Sat mid-Mar–mid-Oct, 8-9.30pm Fri & Sat mid-Oct–mid-Mar) The Alhambra is Granada's – and Europe's – love letter to Moorish culture, a place where fountains trickle, leaves rustle, and ancient spirits seem to mysteriously linger. Part palace, part fort, part World Heritage site, part lesson in medieval architecture, the Alhambra has long enchanted a never-ending line of expectant visitors. As a historic monument, it is unlikely it will ever be surpassed – at least not in the lifetime of anyone reading this.

For most tourists, the Alhambra is an essential pilgrimage and, as a result, predictably crowded. At the height of summer, some 6000 visitors tramp through daily, making it difficult to pause to inspect a pretty detail, much less mentally transport yourself to the 14th century. Schedule a visit in quieter months, if possible; if not, then book in advance for the very earliest or latest time slots.

The Alhambra takes its name from the Arabic *al-qala'a al-hamra* (the Red Castle). The first palace on the site was built by Samuel Ha-Nagid, the Jewish grand vizier of one of Granada's 11th-century Zirid sultans. In the 13th and 14th centuries, the Nasrid emirs turned the area into a fortress-palace complex, adjoined by a village of which only ruins remain. After the Reconquista (Christian reconquest), the Alhambra's mosque was replaced with a church, and the Convento de San Francisco (now the Parador de Granada) was built. Carlos I (also known as the Habsburg emperor Charles V), grandson of the Catholic Monarchs, had a wing of the palaces destroyed to make space for his huge Renaissance work, the Palacio de Carlos V. During the Napoleonic occupation, the

---

ⓘ ALHAMBRA PRACTICALITIES

Some areas of the Alhambra can be visited at any time free of charge, but the highlight areas (the Palacios Nazaríes) can be entered only with a ticket at a pre-allocated time slot. Up to 6600 tickets are available each day. About one third of these are sold at the ticket office on the day, but they sell out early, especially in high season (March to October), when you need to start queuing by 7am to be reasonably sure of getting one.

Fortunately, it's also possible to buy tickets up to three months ahead online or by phone from **Alhambra Advance Booking** (☑902 88 80 01, for international calls +34 958 92 60 31; www.alhambra-tickets.es). Advance tickets can also be purchased (or prepaid tickets picked up) at the bookshop, **Tienda Librería de la Alhambra** (p676), just off Plaza Nueva, which has less manic queues than the complex itself. All advance tickets incur a 13% surcharge, meaning most visitors end up paying €15.40 for a standard entry ticket.

When full-access tickets are sold out, you can still buy a ticket to the Generalife and gardens (€7). The Palacios Nazaríes are also open for **night visits** (€8; ⊙10-11.30pm Tue-Sat Mar-Oct, 8-9.30pm Fri & Sat Nov-Feb), good for atmosphere rather than detail.

There is no explanatory signage in the complex, but a reasonable audioguide is available for €6.50. No outside food is allowed, but there is a slightly pricey cafeteria at the **Parador de Granada** (p671), plus vending machines by the ticket office and the Alcazaba.

The best access on foot is to walk up the Cuesta de Gomérez from Plaza Nueva through the *bosque* (woods) to the **Puerta de la Justicia**. Enter here if you already have your ticket, otherwise proceed further along to the ticket office. Buses C3 and C4 run up to the ticket office from Plaza Isabel la Católica.

Alhambra

TIMELINE

900 The first reference to *al-qala'a al-hamra* (Red Castle) atop Granada's Sabika Hill.

1237 Founder of the Nasrid dynasty, Mohammed I, moves his court to Granada. Threatened by belligerent Christian armies he builds a new defensive fort, the **Alcazaba ❶**.

1302–09 Designed as a summer palace-cum-country estate for Granada's foppish rulers, the bucolic **Generalife ❷** is begun by Mohammed III.

1333–54 Yusuf I initiates the construction of the **Palacio Nazaríes ❸**, still considered the highpoint of Islamic culture in Europe.

1350–60 Up goes the **Palacio de Comares ❹**, taking Nasrid lavishness to a whole new level.

1362–91 The second coming of Mohammed V ushers in even greater architectural brilliance, exemplified by the construction of the **Patio de los Leones ❺**.

1527 The Christians add the **Palacio de Carlos V ❻**. Inspired Renaissance palace or incongruous crime against Moorish art? You decide.

1829 The languishing, half-forgotten Alhambra is 'rediscovered' by American writer Washington Irving during a protracted sleep-over.

1954 The Generalife gardens are extended southwards to accommodate an outdoor theatre.

TOP TIPS

» **Queue-dodger** Reserve tickets in advance online at www.alhambra-tickets.es

» **Money-saver** You can visit the general areas of the palace free of charge any time by entering through the Puerta de Justicia.

» **Stay over** Two fine hotels are housed on the grounds: Parador de Granada (expensive) and Hotel América (more economical).

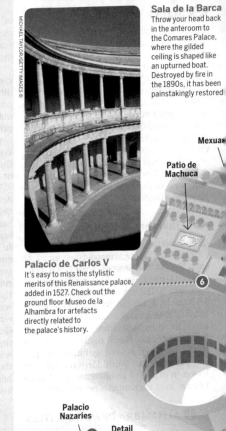

Sala de la Barca
Throw your head back in the anteroom to the Comares Palace, where the gilded ceiling is shaped like an upturned boat. Destroyed by fire in the 1890s, it has been painstakingly restored

Mexuar

Patio de Machuca

Palacio de Carlos V
It's easy to miss the stylistic merits of this Renaissance palace, added in 1527. Check out the ground floor Museo de la Alhambra for artefacts directly related to the palace's history.

Palacio Nazaríes

Detail

Puerta de Justicia

Alcazaba
Find time to explore the towers of the original citadel, the most important of which – the Torre de la Vela – takes you, via a winding staircase, to the Alhambra's best viewpoint.

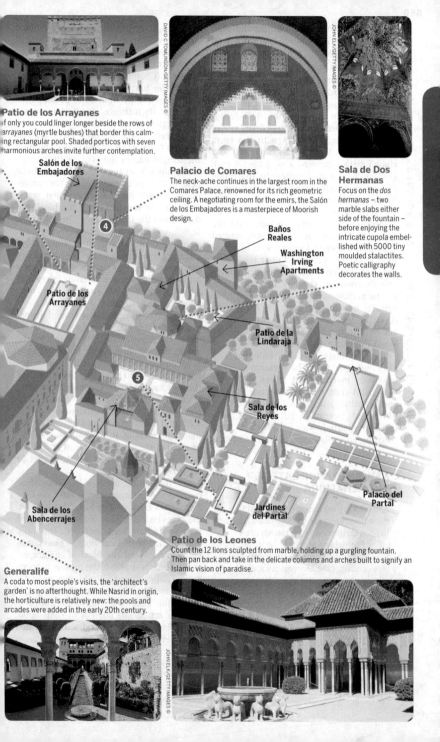

Patio de los Arrayanes
If only you could linger longer beside the rows of *arrayanes* (myrtle bushes) that border this calming rectangular pool. Shaded porticos with seven harmonious arches invite further contemplation.

Palacio de Comares
The neck-ache continues in the largest room in the Comares Palace, renowned for its rich geometric ceiling. A negotiating room for the emirs, the Salón de los Embajadores is a masterpiece of Moorish design.

Sala de Dos Hermanas
Focus on the *dos hermanas* – two marble slabs either side of the fountain – before enjoying the intricate cupola embellished with 5000 tiny moulded stalactites. Poetic calligraphy decorates the walls.

Salón de los Embajadores

Baños Reales

Washington Irving Apartments

Patio de los Arrayanes

Patio de la Lindaraja

Sala de los Reyes

Sala de los Abencerrajes

Jardines del Partal

Palacio del Partal

Patio de los Leones
Count the 12 lions sculpted from marble, holding up a gurgling fountain. Then pan back and take in the delicate columns and arches built to signify an Islamic vision of paradise.

Generalife
A coda to most people's visits, the 'architect's garden' is no afterthought. While Nasrid in origin, the horticulture is relatively new: the pools and arcades were added in the early 20th century.

Alhambra was used as a barracks and nearly blown up. What you see today has been heavily but respectfully restored.

→ **Palacios Nazaríes**

The central **palace complex** (☎ 902 44 12 21; Calle de Real de Alhama) is the pinnacle of the Alhambra's design.

Entrance is through the 14th-century **Mexuar**, perhaps an antechamber for those awaiting audiences with the emir. Two centuries later, it was converted to a chapel, with a prayer room at the far end. Look up here and elsewhere to appreciate the geometrically carved wood ceilings. From the Mexuar, you pass into the **Patio del Cuarto Dorado**. It appears to be a forecourt to the main palace, with the symmetrical doorways to the right, framed with glazed tiles and stucco, setting a cunning trap: the right-hand door leads only out, but the left passes through a dogleg hall (a common strategy in Islamic domestic architecture to keep interior rooms private) into the **Patio de los Arrayanes** (Court of the Myrtles), the centre of a palace built in the mid 14th century as Emir Yusuf I's private residence.

Rooms (likely used for lounging and sleeping) look onto the rectangular pool edged in myrtles, and traces of cobalt blue paint cling to the *muqarnas* (honeycomb vaulting) in the side niches on the north end. Originally, all the walls were lavishly coloured; with paint on the stucco-trimmed walls in the adjacent **Sala de la Barca**, the effect would have resembled flocked wallpaper. Yusuf I's visitors would have passed through this annex room to meet him in the **Salón de los Embajadores** (Chamber of the Ambassadors), where the marvellous domed marquetry ceiling uses more than 8000 cedar pieces to create its intricate star pattern representing the seven heavens.

Adjacent is the restored **Patio de los Leones** (Courtyard of the Lions), built in the second half of the 14th century under Mohammed V, at the political and artistic peak of Granada's emirate. But the centrepiece, a fountain that channelled water through the mouths of 12 marble lions, dates from the 11th century. The courtyard layout, using the proportions of the golden ratio, demonstrates the complexity of Islamic geometric design – the varied columns are placed in such a way that they are symmetrical on numerous axes. The stucco work, too, hits its apex here, with almost lacelike detail.

Walking counterclockwise around the patio, you first pass the **Sala de los Abencerrajes**. The Abencerraje family supported the young Boabdil in a palace power struggle between him and his own father, the reigning sultan. Legend has it that the sultan had the traitors killed in this room, and the rusty stains in the fountain are the victims' indelible blood. But the multicoloured tiles on the walls and the great octagonal ceiling are far more eye-catching. In the **Sala de los Reyes** (Hall of the Kings) at the east end of the patio, the painted leather ceilings depict 10 Nasrid emirs.

On the patio's north side, doors once covered the entrance to the **Sala de Dos Hermanas** (Hall of Two Sisters) – look for the holes on either side of the frame where they would have been anchored. The walls are adorned with local flora – pine cones and acorns – and the band of calligraphy at eye level, just above the tiles, is a poem praising Mohammed V for his victory in Algeciras in 1369, a rare triumph this late in the Islamic game. The dizzying ceiling is a fantastic *muqarnas* dome with some 5000 tiny cells. The carved wood screens in the upper level enabled women (and perhaps others involved in palace intrigue) to peer down from hallways without being seen. At the far end, the tile-trimmed **Mirador de Lindaraja** (Lindaraja lookout) was a lovely place for palace denizens to look onto

ℹ️ GRANADA'S BONO TURÍSTICO

Valid for five days, the Bono Turístico Granada (€32) is a card that gives admission to the city's major sights, plus 10 rides on city buses, use of the sightseeing bus for a day and discounts on the Cicerone Cultura y Ocio walking tour and a city audioguide. When you add it all up, the savings are significant only if you visit virtually all of the sights.

You can buy the Bono at this.is:granada, an orange kiosk opposite Plaza Nueva, where the bus to the Albayzín stops. For a €2.50 surcharge, you can pre-order by phone from the Bono information line (📞 958 244 500) or on the internet (www.caja-granada. es, in Spanish), then pick it up at the CajaGranada (Plaza Isabel La Católica 6; ⏰ 8.30am-2.15pm Mon-Fri) bank. Buying in advance gives you the advantage of choosing your Alhambra entrance time, rather than being assigned one.

the garden below. Traces of paint still cling to the window frames, and a few panels of coloured glass set in the wood ceiling cast a warm glow.

From the Sala de Dos Hermanas, a passageway leads past the domed roofs of the baths on the level below and into rooms built for Carlos I in the 1520s, and later used by Washington Irving. From here you descend to the pretty Patio de la Lindaraja. In the southwest corner is the bathhouse – you can't enter, but you can peer in at the rooms lit by the star-shaped skylights.

You emerge into an area of terraced gardens created in the early 20th century. The reflecting pool in front of the small Palacio del Partal, the oldest surviving palace in the Alhambra, with the Albayzín glimering in the background, is from the time of Mohammed III (r 1302–09). You can leave the gardens by a gate facing the Palacio de Carlos V or continue along a path to the Generalife.

➡ **Alcazaba, Christian Buildings & Museums**

The west end of the Alhambra grounds are the remnants of the Alcazaba, chiefly its ramparts and several towers. The Torre de la Vela (Watchtower), with a narrow staircase leading to the top terrace, is where the cross and banners of the Reconquista were raised in January 1492.

By the Palacios Nazaríes, the hulking Palacio de Carlos V clashes spectacularly with its surroundings. In a different setting its merits might be more readily appreciated – it is the only example in Spain of the Renaissance-era circle-in-a-square ground plan. Begun in 1527 by Pedro Machuca, a Toledo architect who studied under Michelangelo, it was financed, perversely,

from taxes on Granada's *morisco* (converted Muslim) population but never finished because funds dried up after the *morisco* rebellion.

Inside, the Museo de la Alhambra (⏰ 8.30am-8pm Wed-Sat, to 2.30pm Tue & Sun) FREE has a collection of Alhambra artefacts, including the door from the Sala de Dos Hermanas, while the Museo de Bellas Artes (Fine Arts Museum; non-EU/EU citizen €1.50/free; ⏰ 2.30-8pm Tue, 9am-8pm Wed-Sat, to 2.30pm Sun) displays paintings and sculptures from Granada's Christian history.

Further along, the 16th-century Iglesia de Santa María de la Alhambra sits on the site of the palace mosque, and at the crest of the hill the Convento de San Francisco, now the Parador de Granada hotel, is where Isabel and Fernando were laid to rest while their tombs in the Capilla Real were being built.

➡ **Generalife**

From the Arabic *jinan al-'arif* (the overseer's gardens), the Generalife is a soothing arrangement of pathways, patios, pools, fountains, tall trees and, in season, flowers of every imaginable hue. To reach the complex you must pass through the Alhambra walls on the east side, then head back northwest. You approach through topiary gardens on the south end, which were once grazing land for the royal herds. At the north end is the emirs' summer palace, a whitewashed structure on the hillside facing the Alhambra. The courtyards here are particularly graceful; in the second courtyard, the trunk of a 700-year-old cypress tree suggests what delicate shade once graced the patio. Climb the steps outside the courtyard to the Escalera del Agua, a delightful bit of garden engineering, where water flows along a shaded staircase.

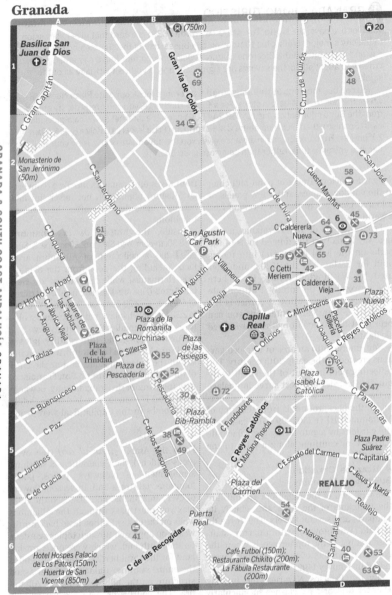

Museo Sefardí MUSEUM

(☎ 958 22 05 78; www.museosefardidegranada.es; Placeta Berrocal 5; €5; ☉ 10am-2pm, 5-9pm) Since being expelled en masse in 1492, there are very few Sephardic Jews left living in Granada today. But this didn't stop one enter-

prising couple from opening up a museum to their memory in 2013, the year that the Spanish government began offering Spanish citizenship to any Sephardic Jew who could prove their Iberian ancestry. The museum is tiny, but the selected artefacts make excellent

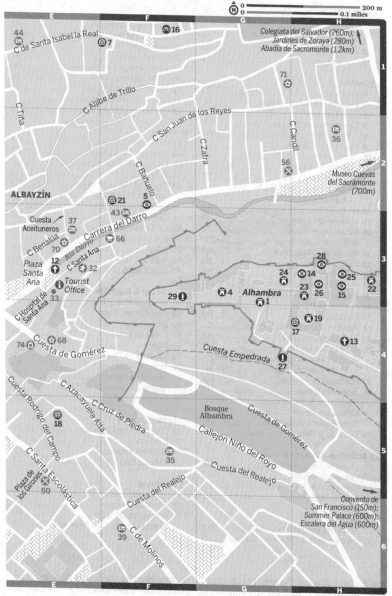

Colegiata del Salvador (260m);
Jardines de Zoraya (280m);
Abadía de Sacromonte (1.2km)

Museo Cuevas
del Sacromonte
(700m)

ALBAYZÍN

Cuesta
Aceituneros

Río Darro

Plaza
Santa
Ana

Tourist
Office

Alhambra

Bosque
Alhambra

Convento de
San Francisco (150m);
Summer Palace (600m);
Escalera del Agua (600m)

props to the passionate and fascinating historical portrayal related by the owners.

Casa-Museo Manuel de Falla   MUSEUM
(📞958 22 21 88; www.museomanueldefalla.com;
Paseo de los Mártires; adult/reduced €3/1; ☺9am-

2.30pm & 3.30-7pm Tue-Fri, to 2.30pm Sat & Sun)
Arguably Spain's greatest classical composer
and an artistic friend of Lorca, Manuel de
Falla (1876–1946) was born in Cádiz, but
spent the key years of his life in Granada
until the Civil War forced him into exile. You

Granada

can find out all about the man at this attractive *cármen* where he lived and composed, and which has been preserved pretty much as he left it. Tours are guided and intimate.

◉ Near Plaza Nueva

Iglesia de Santa Ana CHURCH
(Plaza Santa Ana) Extending from the northeast corner of Plaza Nueva, Plaza Santa Ana is dominated by the Iglesia de Santa Ana, a church which incorporates a mosque's minaret in its belltower.

Baños Árabes El Bañuelo BATHHOUSE
(Carrera del Darro 31; ⏰10am-5pm Tue-Sat) FREE
Located along narrow Carrera del Darro is this simple, yet well-preserved, 11th-century Islamic bathhouse.

⊙ Albayzín

On the hill facing the Alhambra across the Darro valley, Granada's old Muslim quarter (the Albayzín) is a place for aimless wandering; you'll get lost regularly whatever map you're using. The cobblestone streets are lined with signature only-in-Granada *cármenes* (large mansions with walled gardens, from the Arabic *karm* for garden). The Albayzín survived as the Muslim quarter for several decades after the Christian conquest in 1492.

Bus C1 runs circular routes from Plaza Nueva around the Albayzín about every seven to nine minutes, from 7.30am to 11pm.

Palacio de Dar-al-Horra   PALACE
(Callejón de las Monjas) Close to the Placeta de San Miguel Bajo, off Callejón del Gallo and down a short lane, is the 15th-century Palacio de Dar-al-Horra, a romantically dishevelled mini-Alhambra that was home to the mother of Boabdil, Granada's last Muslim ruler. It's not open to the public, but is viewable from the outside.

Calle Calderería Nueva   STREET
Linking the upper and lower parts of the Albayzín, Calle Calderería Nueva is a narrow street famous for its *teterías,* but also a good place to shop for slippers, hookahs, jewellery and North African pottery from an eclectic cache of shops redolent of a Moroccan souk.

Colegiata del Salvador   CHURCH
(Plaza del Salvador; €0.75; ◷10am-1pm & 4.30-6.30pm) Plaza del Salvador, near the top of the Albayzín, is dominated by the Colegiata del Salvador, a 16th-century church on the site of the Albayzín's former main mosque, the patio of which still survives at the church's western end.

Mirador San Nicolás   VIEWPOINT
(Callejón de San Cecilio) Callejón de San Cecilio leads to the Mirador San Nicolás, a lookout with unbeatable views of the Alhambra and Sierra Nevada. Come back here for sunset (you can't miss the trail then!). At any time of day take care: skilful, well-organised wallet-lifters and bag-snatchers operate here. Don't be put off – it is still a terrific atmosphere, with buskers and local students intermingling with camera-toting tourists.

Palacio de los Olvidados   MUSEUM
(☑655 55 33 40; www.palaciodelosolvidados.com; Cuesta de Santa Inés 6; €5; ◷10am-7pm) Lest we forget, Jews played a vital role in the glorious Nasrid Emirate of Granada that reigned from the 1200s to 1492, built on peaceful Christian, Muslim and Jewish coexistence. The aptly named 'palace of the forgotten', which opened in 2014 in the Albayzín, revisits this oft-ignored Jewish legacy. It's the second and best of Granada's new Jewish-related museums, with seven rooms filled with attractively displayed relics (scrolls, costumes and ceremonial artefacts) amassed from around Spain.

Carmen Museo Max Moreau   MUSEUM
(☑958 29 33 10; Camino Nuevo de San Nicolás 12; ◷10.30am-1.30pm & 4-6pm Tue-Sat) **FREE** Most of the Albayzín's *cármenes* are true to their original concept – quiet, private houses

---

GRANADA'S SACRED MOUNTAIN

Sacromonte, the primarily *gitano* (Roma) neighbourhood northeast of the Albayzín, is renowned for its flamenco traditions, drawing tourists to nightclubs and aficionados to music schools. But it still feels like the fringes of the city, literally and figuratively, as the homes dug out of the hillside alternate between flashy and highly extemporaneous, despite some of the caves having been established since the 14th century.

The area is good for an idle stroll, yielding great views (especially from an ad hoc cafe on Vereda de Enmedio). For some insight into the area, the **Museo Cuevas del Sacromonte** (www.sacromontegranada.com; Barranco de los Negros; €5; ◷10am-6pm) provides an excellent display of local folk art. This wide-ranging ethnographic and environmental museum and arts centre is set in large herb gardens and hosts art exhibitions, as well as flamenco and films (10pm on Wednesday and Friday from June to September). The diligent can press on to the **Abadía de Sacromonte** (admission €4; ◷10am-1pm & 4-6pm Tue-Sat, 11am-1pm & 4-6pm Sun), at the very top of the hill, where you can squeeze into underground cave chapels.

Note that it is not considered safe for lone women to wander around the uninhabited parts of Granada's Sacromonte area, day or night.

with high walls that hide beautiful terraced gardens. But you can get a rare (and free) glimpse of one of these secret domains at the former home of Belgium-born portrait painter and composer Max Moreau. His attractive house has been made into a museum displaying his former living quarters and work space, along with a gallery that showcases his best portraits.

There are fine Alhambra views.

◉ Plaza Bib-Rambla & Around

Catedral de Granada   CATHEDRAL
(☎958 22 29 59; www.catedraldegranada.com; Gran Vía de Colón 5; €4; ⊙10:45am-7.45pm Mon-Sat, 4-7pm Sun) Too boxed in by other buildings to manifest its full glory to observers at ground level, Granada's cavernous cathedral is, nonetheless, a hulking classic that sprang from the fertile imagination of the 17th-century painter-cum-sculptor-cum-architect Alonso Cano. Although commissioned by the Catholic Monarchs in the early 1500s, construction began only after Isabella's death, and didn't finish until 1704.

The result is a mishmash of styles: baroque outside, courtesy of Cano, and Renaissance inside, where the Spanish pioneer in this style, Diego de Siloé, directed operations to construct huge piers, white as meringue, a black-and-white tile floor and the gilded and painted chapel. Even more odd, the roof vaults are distinctly Gothic.

★Capilla Real   HISTORIC BUILDING
(www.capillarealgranada.com; Calle Oficios; €4; ⊙10.15am-1.30pm & 3.30-6.30pm Mon-Sat, 11am-1.30pm & 2.30-5.30pm Sun) Here they lie, Spain's notorious Catholic Monarchs, entombed in a chapel adjoining Granada's cathedral; far more peaceful in death than their tumultuous lives would have suggested. Isabella and Ferdinand commissioned the elaborate Isabelline-Gothic-style mausoleum that was to house them, but it was not completed until 1521, hence their temporary interment in the Alhambra's Convento de San Francisco.

The monarchs lie in simple lead coffins in the crypt beneath their marble monuments in the chancel, enclosed by a stunning gilded wrought-iron screen created in 1520 by Bartolomé de Jaén. Also here are the coffins of Isabella and Ferdinand's unfortunate

---

LORCA'S LEGACY

It is debatable whether you can truly understand modern Andalucía without at least an inkling of knowledge about Spain's greatest poet and playwright, Federico García Lorca (1898–1936). Lorca epitomised many of Andalucía's potent hallmarks – passion, ambiguity, exuberance and innovation – and brought them skilfully to life in a multitude of precocious works. Early popularity was found with *El romancero gitano* (Gypsy Ballads), a 1928 collection of verses on Roma themes, full of startling metaphors yet crafted with the simplicity of flamenco song. Between 1933 and 1936 he wrote the three tragic plays for which he is best known: *Bodas de sangre* (Blood Wedding), *Yerma* (Barren) and *La casa de Bernarda Alba* (The House of Bernarda Alba) – brooding and dark, dramatic works dealing with themes of entrapment and liberation. Lorca was assassinated at the start of the Civil War in August 1936. Although the whereabouts of his remains have proven elusive, recent research reaffirms the longstanding notion that he was executed by military authorities loyal to Franco, due to his perceived left-leaning political views and his homosexuality.

Lorca's summer house, **Huerta de San Vicente**, is a museum in a tidy park, a 15-minute walk from Puerta Real (head 700m down Calle de las Recogidas). In 2015 it was joined by the much delayed **Centro Lorca** (Plaza de la Romanilla), the new home of the Lorca foundation that will host a library, 424-seat theatre, and expo space in a super-modern building.

In Lorca's birthplace, the village of Fuente Vaqueros, 17km west of Granada, the **Museo Casa Natal Federico García Lorca** (☎958 51 64 53; www.patronatogarcialorca.org; Calle Poeta Federico García Lorca 4; admission €1.80; ⊙guided visits hourly 10am-2pm & 5-7pm Tue-Sat) displays photos, posters and costumes for the writer's plays. Buses (€2, 20 minutes) operated by **Ureña** (☎958 45 41 54) leave from Avenida de Andaluces in front of Granada train station (roughly hourly between 7am and 9pm weekdays, and every two hours from 9am on weekends).

GRAFFITI ART

While the UK has Banksy, Granada has El Niño de las Pinturas (real name Raúl Ruíz), a street artist whose creative graffiti has become a defining symbol of a city where the grandiose and the gritty often sit side by side. Larger-than-life, lucid and thought-provoking, El Niño's giant murals, the majority of which adorn the Realejo neighbourhood, juxtapose vivid close-ups of the human countenance with short poetic stanzas written in highly stylised lettering. Over the last two decades, El Niño has become a famous underground personality in Granada and has sometimes been known to give live painting demonstrations at the university. Although he risks criticism and occasional fines for his work, most Granadinos agree that his street art brings creative splashes of colour to their ancient city, ensuring it remains forward-thinking and edgy.

Pancho Tours (📞664 64 29 04; www.panchotours.com) FREE do a street-art tour, which takes in some of these works of public art.

daughter, Juana the Mad, and her husband, Philip of Flanders.

The sacristy contains a small but impressive museum, with Ferdinand's sword and Isabella's sceptre, silver crown and personal art collection, which is mainly Flemish but also includes Botticelli's *Prayer in the Garden of Olives*. Felipe de Vigarni's two fine early-16th-century statues of the Catholic Monarchs at prayer are also here.

Corral del Carbón   HISTORIC SITE
(Calle Mariana Pineda; ⊙10am-8pm) Tucked away just to the east of Calle Reyes Católicos is this Nasrid-era corn exchange framed by an elaborate horseshoe arch, which began life as a 14th-century inn for merchants. It has since been used as an inn for coal dealers (hence its modern name, Coal Yard) and later a theatre. It was closed for renovations at last visit, but can still be viewed from the outside.

Centro José Guerrero   GALLERY
(📞958 22 51 85; www.centroguerrero.org; Calle Oficios 8; ⊙10.30am-2pm & 4.30-9pm Tue-Sat, to 2pm Sun) FREE An art gallery named for the Granada-born abstract painter (1914–91) who went to live in the US. Exhibitions are temporary and with a modernist bent, though the gallery keeps half a dozen of Guerrero's characteristically vibrant works in a permanent collection.

⊙ Outside the Centre

Monasterio de San Jerónimo   MONASTERY
(Calle Rector López Argüeta 9; €4; ⊙10am-1.30pm & 4-8pm Mon-Fri, to 2.30pm & 4-7.30pm Sat & Sun) Another of Granada's stunning Catholic buildings is a little out of the centre. At the 16th-century Monasterio de San Jerónimo,

where nuns still sing vespers, every surface of the church has been painted – the stained glass literally pales in comparison.

★Basílica San Juan de Díos   CHURCH
(Calle San Juan de Díos; €4; ⊙10am-1pm & 4-7pm) Bored of baroque churches? Seen every gilded altarpiece you want to see? Come to the Basilica of St John of God. If Seville cathedral is the world's most voluminous church, this basilica is surely one of the most opulently decorated. Barely a square inch of the interior lacks embellishment, most of it rich and glittering.

Huerta de San Vicente   MUSEUM
(📞958 25 84 66; Calle Virgen Blanca; admission only by guided tour in Spanish €3, Wed free; ⊙9.15am-1.30pm & 5-7.30pm Tue-Sun) This house where Federico García Lorca spent summers and wrote some of his best-known works is only 1.5km south of the city centre, but still retains the evocative aura of an early-20th-century country villa. Today the modern but handsome **Parque Federico García Lorca** separates it from whizzing traffic.

To get there, head 700m down Calle de las Recogidas from Puerta Real, turn right along Calle del Arabial, then take the first left into Calle Virgen Blanca.

☞ Tours

Play Granada   CULTURAL TOUR
(www.playgranada.com; Calle Santa Ana 2; Segway tour €30) 🖉 The make or break of a good tour is the tour guide, and Play Granada's are truly fantastic. Even if you don't do a tour, you'll see the congenial guides buzzing around Plaza Nueva on their Segways, stopping to chat with anyone and everyone.

Cicerone Cultura y Ocio
WALKING TOUR

(☎ 958 56 18 10; www.ciceronegranada.com; tour €15) Informative walking tours of central Granada and the Albayzín leave daily from Plaza Bib-Rambla at 10.30am and 5pm (10am & 4pm in winter) Wednesday to Sunday.

🎓 Courses

Escuela Delengua
LANGUAGE COURSE

(☎ 958 20 45 35; www.delengua.es; Calderería Vieja 20; 2-week course €260) With a massive student population, Granada is an ideal place to learn Spanish. This school in the heart of the Albayzín starts courses every Monday and offers loads of extra-curricular activities, including free cooking demonstrations.

🎉 Festivals & Events

Semana Santa
HOLY WEEK

The two most striking events in Granada's Easter week are Los Gitanos (Wednesday), when the *fraternidad* (brotherhood) toils to the Abadía de Sacromonte, lit by bonfires, and El Silencio (Thursday), when the street-lights are turned off for a silent candlelit march.

Festival Internacional de Música y Danza
MUSIC

(www.granadafestival.org) For three weeks in June and July, first-class classical and modern performance takes over the Alhambra and other historic sites.

Feria del Corpus Cristi
RELIGIOUS

(Corpus Christi Fair) The big annual fair, which starts 60 days after Easter Sunday, is a week of bullfights, dancing and street puppets; most of the action is at fairgrounds by the bus station.

🛏 Sleeping

Central Granada – the level ground from the Realejo across to Plaza de la Trinidad – is very compact, so hotel location doesn't matter much. The prettiest lodgings are the Albayzín courtyard houses, though these call for some hill-walking, and many aren't accessible by taxi. The handful of hotels up by the Alhambra are scenic but a hassle for sightseeing further afield. Rates are highest in spring and fall, spiking over Easter. Parking, where offered, costs €15 to €20 per day, and is usually at a municipal parking lot, not on the hotel grounds.

🛏 Alhambra & Realejo

⭐ Carmen de la Alcubilla del Caracol
HISTORIC HOTEL €€

(☎ 958 21 55 51; www.alcubilladelcaracol.com; Calle del Aire Alta 12; s/d €100/120; 🅿 @ 🤶) This much-sought-after small hotel inhabits a traditional *carmen* on the slopes of the Alhambra. It feels more like a B&B than a hotel thanks to the attentiveness of its Granada-loving host, Manuel. The seven rooms are washed in pale pastel colours and furnished luxuriously, but not ostentatiously.

The highlight? The fabulous views from the spectacular terraced garden and the sounds of Granadian life wafting up from the streets below.

Hotel Molinos
HOTEL €€

(☎ 958 22 73 67; www.hotelmolinos.es; Calle Molinos 12; s/d/tr €53/85/115; 🅿 🤶) Don't let the 'narrowest hotel in the world' moniker put you off (and yes, it actually is – with the certificate from the *Guinness Book of Records* to prove it), there's plenty of breathing space in Molinos' nine recently

---

HAMMAMS

Granada has several *baños árabes* (Arab-style baths), though none is historic – nor much like a Middle Eastern *hammam*. Here the emphasis is on lazy lounging in pools, rather than getting scrubbed clean. But the dim, tiled rooms are suitably sybaritic and relaxing. All offer pool access in two-hour sessions, with the option of a 15-minute or 30-minute massage for a bit more; reservations are required. Swimwear is obligatory (you can rent it), a towel is provided and all sessions are mixed.

With three pools of different temperatures, plus a steam room and the option of a proper skin-scrubbing massage, Hammam de Al Andalus (☎ 902 33 33 34; www.granada.hammamalandalus.com; Calle Santa Ana 16; bath/bath & massage €24/36; ⏱ 10am-midnight) is the best of Granada's three Arab-style baths. Sessions are booked for two-hour sessions (reserve ahead).

boutique-ised rooms, and warm hospitality in its information-stacked lobby. Situated at the foot of the Realejo, it's an economical central option.

Hotel Palacio de Los Navas HISTORIC HOTEL €€
(☑958 21 57 60; www.palaciodelosnavas.com; Calle Navas 1; r from €120; ❄ 🛜) This Don Quijote–era 16th-century building has individually furnished rooms with lots of cool creams and whites, original columns and doors, terracotta-tiled floors and desks. The rooms surround a traditional columned patio. The hotel's location is convenient for nightlife – Calle Navas, one of Granada's quintessential tapa-crawling streets, is just outside the door.

Parador de Granada HISTORIC HOTEL €€€
(☑958 22 14 40; www.parador.es; Calle Real de la Alhambra; r €335; 🅿 ❄ @ 🛜) This is the most luxurious and highly priced of Spain's *paradores*. Head here if you are looking for romance and want to recline on a divan like Boabdil, the last emir, or, perhaps, Washington Irving (it's encased in a converted 15th-century convent located in the Alhambra grounds). Book ahead; it's megapopular – obviously.

🛏 Near Plaza Nueva

Hotel Posada del Toro HOTEL €
(☑958 22 73 33; www.posadadeltoro.com; Calle de Elvira 25; d from €50; ❄ 🛜) A lovely small hotel with rooms set around a tranquil central patio. Walls are coloured like Italian gelato in pistachio, peach and cream flavours. The rooms are similarly tasteful with parquet floors, Alhambra-style stucco, rustic-style furniture and small but perfectly equipped bathrooms with double sinks and hydromassage showers. A bargain – especially considering its central location.

Hotel Zaguán del Darro HISTORIC HOTEL €€
(☑958 21 57 30; www.hotelzaguan.com; Carrera del Darro 23; s/d €55/70; ❄ @ 🛜) This place offers excellent value for the Albayzín. The 16th-century house has been tastefully restored, with sparing use of antiques. Its 13 rooms are all different; some look out over the Río Darro below. There's a good bar-restaurant below, and the main street in front means easy taxi access – but also a bit of evening noise.

🛏 Albayzín

Hotel Casa del Capitel Nazarí HISTORIC HOTEL €€
(☑958 21 52 60; www.hotelcasacapitel.com; Cuesta Aceituneros 6; s/d €68/85; ❄ @ 🛜) Another slice of Albayzín magic in a 1503 Renaissance palace that's as much architectural history lesson as midrange hotel. Rooms have Moroccan inflections and the courtyard hosts art exhibits. It's just off Plaza Nueva, too.

Santa Isabel La Real BOUTIQUE HOTEL €€
(☑958 29 46 58; www.hotelsantaisabellareal.com; Calle de Santa Isabel La Real 19; r €105; ❄ @ 🛜) Ideally situated between the Plaza San Miguel Bajo and Mirador San Nicolás (Plaza de San Nicolás), this gorgeous 16th-century building has been tastefully restored into an exquisite small hotel. Many of the original architectural features endure, including the marble columns. Rooms are set around a central patio and are individually decorated with lacy bedspreads, embroidered pictures and hand-woven rugs.

Go for room 11 if you can, for its Alhambra view.

Casa Morisca Hotel HISTORIC HOTEL €€€
(☑958 22 11 00; www.hotelcasamorisca.com; Cuesta de la Victoria 9; d/ste €167/220; ❄ @ 🛜) You can recline like a Nasrid emir in this late-15th-century mansion, which perfectly captures the spirit of the Albayzín and nearby Alhambra. Atmosphere and history are laid on thick without sacrificing home comforts, and beautiful architectural details abound from the silver candelabras to the tiled ornamental pool.

🛏 Plaza Bib-Rambla & Around

Hotel Los Tilos HOTEL €€
(☑958 26 67 12; www.hotellostilos.com; Plaza Bib-Rambla 4; s/d €45/75; ❄) The Tilos' spacious (for downtown) rooms are simple but regularly renovated and overlook Plaza Bib-Rambla. Double-glazed windows keep out the shouts of late-night bar crawlers crawling home at 5am. Bonus: there's a small but panoramic rooftop terrace if you don't get your own Alhambra view from your room.

Hotel Párraga Siete HOTEL €€
(☑958 26 42 27; www.hotelparragasiete.com; Calle Párraga 7; s/d €65/85; ❄ 🛜) Seemingly furnished out of an Ikea-inspired style guide,

the Párraga Seven has small modern rooms that feel as new as a freshly starched shirt. Aside from the high standard of cleaning, bonuses include an afternoon bottle of water delivered to your room and a sleek downstairs bar/restaurant called Vitola Gastrobar – ideal for breakfast or tapas.

⭐**Hotel Hospes Palacio de Los Patos** LUXURY HOTEL €€€

(📞958 53 57 90; www.hospes.com; Solarillo de Gracia 1; r/ste €200/400; 🅿️❄️@🛜🏊) Put simply, the best hotel in Granada – if you can afford it – offering lucky guests sharp modernity and never-miss-a-beat service in a palatial Unesco-protected building. You could write a novella about its many memorable features: the grand staircase, the post-modern chandeliers, the Arabian garden, the Roman Emperor spa or the carnations they leave on your bed in the afternoon.

Expensive, but worth every penny.

AC Palacio de Santa Paula LUXURY HOTEL €€€

(📞902 29 22 93; www.palaciodesantapaula.com; Gran Vía de Colón 31; r from €200; 🅿️❄️@🏊) There's a surfeit of five stars in Granada including this luxury operation, which occupies a former 16th-century convent, some 14th-century houses with patios and wooden balconies, and a 19th-century aristocratic house, all with a contemporary overlay. The rooms sport every top-end luxury you might desire, and the hotel also has a fitness centre, sauna and Turkish bath.

🍴 Eating

Granada's a place where gastronomy remains reassuringly down to earth – and cheap. What it lacks in flashy *alta cocina* (haute cuisine) it makes up for in generous portions of Andalucian standards. The city has a wealth of places serving decent tapas and *raciones* (large tapas servings). It also excels in Moroccan cuisine.

🍴 Alhambra & Realejo

Café Fútbol CAFE €

(www.cafefutbol.com; Plaza de Mariana Pineda 6; churros €2; ⏰6am-1am; 👶) More about chocolate and ice cream than football, this three-storey cafe with its butter-coloured walls and gaudy chandeliers dates from 1910 and is generally packed with coiffured señoras, foreign students and families. Elderly, white-shirted waiters attend to the Sunday afternoon rush, when everyone in Granada seemingly turns up for hot chocolate and churros.

Hicuri Art Restaurant VEGAN €

(Plaza de los Girones 3; mains €7-12; ⏰10am-10pm Mon-Sat; 🌱) Granada's leading graffiti artist, El Niño de las Pinturas, has been let loose on the inner and outer walls of Hicuri, and the results are positively psychedelic. The food used to be vegetarian with a few dishes for diehard carnivores, but it recently went full-on vegan.

La Botillería TAPAS €€

(📞958 22 49 28; Calle Varela 10; mains €13-20; ⏰1pm-1am Wed-Sun, 1-8pm Mon) Establishing a good reputation for nouveau tapas, La Botillería is just around the corner from the legeandary La Tana bar, to which it has family connections. It's a more streamlined modern place than its cousin, where you can *tapear* (eat tapas) at the bar or sit down for the full monty Andalucian-style. The *solomillo* (pork tenderloin) comes in a rich, wine-laden sauce.

⭐**Carmela Restaurante** TAPAS €€

(📞958 22 57 94; www.restaurantecarmela.com; Calle Colcha 13; tapas €5-10; ⏰12.30pm-midnight) Long a bastion of traditional tapas, Granada has taken a leaf out of Seville's book and come up with something a little more out-of-the-box at this new streamlined restaurant, guarded by the statue of Jewish philosopher Yehuba ibn Tibon at the jaws of the Realejo quarter. The best of Carmela's creative offerings is the made-to-order tortilla and cured-ham croquettes the size of tennis balls.

Los Diamantes SEAFOOD €€

(www.barlosdiamantes.com; Calle Navas 26; raciones €8-10; ⏰noon-6pm & 8pm-2am Mon-Fri, 11am-1am Sat & Sun) Granada's great tapas institution has two central outlets. This old-school scruffy joint in tapa bar–lined Calle Navas, and a newer hipper Ikea-esque version in Plaza Nueva. What doesn't change is the tapa speciality – fish, which you'll smell sizzling in the fryer as soon as you open the door.

Restaurante Chikito ANDALUCIAN €€€

(📞958 22 33 64; www.restaurantechikito.com; Plaza Campillo Bajo 9; mains €16-22; ⏰12.30-3.30pm & 7.30-11.30pm Thu-Tue) Occupying the site of the legendary Café Alameda, the Chikito is perennially popular with the smart local set; its walls are plastered with Andaluz celeb pics, while its front bar contains a re-

LOCAL KNOWLEDGE

FREE TAPAS

Granada – bless its generous heart – is one of the last bastions of that fantastic practice of free tapas with every drink. Place your drink order at the bar and, hey presto, a plate will magically appear with a generous portion of something delicious-looking on it. Order another drink and another plate will materialise. The process is repeated with every round you buy – and each time the tapa gets better. As Spanish bars serve only small glasses of beer (cañas measure just 250ml) it is perfectly easy to fill up on free tapas over an enjoyable evening without getting totally inebriated. Indeed, some people 'crawl' from bar to bar getting a drink and free tapa in each place. Packed shoulder-to-shoulder with tapas institutions, Calle de Elvira and Calle Navas are good places for bar crawls. If you're hungry you can always order an extra plate or two to soak up the *cervezas*.

The free tapa practice is carried on throughout most of Granada and Jaén provinces, and also extends into Almería, where bars will even allow you to choose the tapas you wish to try.

cently imported statue of Federico García Lorca, who once convened here with other intellectuals.

The tapas bar speciality is snails. The adjacent restaurant concentrates on hearty dishes like oxtail stew and pork medallions, which it has spent many years getting just right.

Parador de Granada
INTERNATIONAL €€€

(☑ 958 22 14 40; Calle Real de la Alhambra; mains €19-22; ⊙1-4pm & 8.30-11pm) On one side, the Parador de Granada is a hushed, swanky dinner experience, with a Moroccan-Spanish-French menu that also features local goat and venison. On the other, it's a stylish little canteen for sightseers, where even your *bocadillo de jamón* tastes special – and it ought to, considering its €12 price tag. Overall, a bit inflated, but a lovely treat for the location.

✖ Near Plaza Nueva

La Bella y La Bestia
ANDALUCIAN, TAPAS €

(☑ 958 22 51 87; www.bodegaslabellaylabestia.com; Calle Carcel Baja 14; tapas €2-3; ⊙noon-midnight) Lots of beauty, but no real beast – this place wins the prize for Granada's most generous free tapas: a huge plate of bagels, chips and pasta arrives with your first drink. There are four branches, though this one is particularly well-placed, just off Calle de Elvira.

Bodegas Castañeda
TAPAS €

(Calle Almireceros; tapas €2-3; raciones €6-8; ⊙11.30am-4.30pm & 7.30pm-1.30am) A relic much loved by locals and tourists alike, the buzzing Castañeda is the Granada tapas bar to trump all others. Don't expect any fancy

new stuff here, but do expect lightning-fast service, booze from big casks mounted on the walls, and eating as a contact sport.

Ruta del Azafrán
FUSION €€

(☑ 958 22 68 82; www.rutadelazafran.es; Paseo del Padre Manjón 1; mains €13-20; ⊙1-4pm & 8-11pm) One of the few high-concept restaurants in Granada, this sleek spot with its steely-modern interior has an eclectic menu which ranges from Asian-inspired tempuras to broccoli-based pesto, lamb couscous and roasted pork. The terrace outside on the Río Darro is a great place for a snack, but you'll get better service inside.

✖ Albayzín

Arrayanes
MOROCCAN €€

(☑ 958 22 84 01; www.rest-arrayanes.com; Cuesta Marañas 4; mains €15; ⊙1.30-4.30pm & 7.30-11.30pm Sun-Fri, to 4:30pm Sat; ✐) The best Moroccan food in a city that is well known for its Moorish throwbacks? Recline on lavish patterned seating, try the rich, fruity tagine casseroles and make your decision. Note that Arrayanes does not serve alcohol.

El Ají
MODERN SPANISH €€

(☑ 958 29 29 30; Plaza San Miguel Bajo 9; mains €12-20; ⊙1-11pm; ✐) Up in the Albayzín, this chic but cosy neighbourhood restaurant is no bigger than a shoebox, but serves from breakfast right through to the evening. Chatty staff at the tiny marble bar can point out some of the highlights of the creative menu (such as prawns with tequila and honey). It's a good place to get out of the sun and rest up, especially if you are hiking up from Plaza Nueva.

✕ Plaza Bib-Rambla & Around

★ Gran Café Bib-Rambla   CAFE €

(Plaza Bib-Rambla 3; chocolate & churros €4; ⊗8am-11pm; 🚻) It's 5pm, you've just traipsed around five vaguely interesting churches and hypoglycemia is rapidly setting in. Time to hit Plaza Bib-Rambla, where Granada's best churros are served in a no-nonsense 1907-vintage cafe. Check their freshness by watching Mr Churro-maker lower them into the fryer behind the bar, and then enjoy them dipped in cups of ultra-thick hot chocolate.

★ La Bicicleta   BISTRO €€

(☑958 25 86 36; Plaza Pescadería 4; raciones €8-15; ⊗11am-11:30pm Thu-Tue) For something new and a bit different, head to this lovely bistro, which adds a touch of Parisian panache to Granada – truly the best of both worlds. It's small and intimate, and good for many things, including an excellent *huevos a la flamenca* (tomato sauce and eggs). Placed strategically by the door, the cake tray is crying out for a *merienda* (afternoon snack).

Siloé Café & Grill   INTERNATIONAL €€

(☑958 22 07 52; Plaza de Diego Siloé; mains €12-17; ⊗9am-midnight) Contrasting with the old-school Café Gran Via de Colón next door, the new-in-2014 Siloé is one of those adaptable restaurants that fits many budgets and meal configurations. Its sleek cafe-booth interior is good for late breakfasts, afternoon *meriendas*, wine and tapas, or full-blown lunch or dinner. Tasty and a bit different are the tapa-sized burgers, which are satisfying without being too over-indulgent.

Oliver   SEAFOOD €€

(☑958 26 22 00; www.restauranteoliver.com; Calle Pescadería 12; mains €12-18; ⊗1-4pm & 8pm-midnight Mon-Sat) The seafood bars on this square are a Granada institution, and Oliver is one of the best for food and unflappable service in the midst of the lunch rush. Sleek business types pack in alongside street-sweepers to devour *raciones* of garlicky fried treats at the mobbed bar, which can be ankle deep in crumpled napkins and shrimp shells come 4pm.

★ La Fábula

Restaurante   MODERN EUROPEAN €€€

(☑958 25 01 50; www.restaurantelafabula.com; Calle San Antón 28; mains €22-28; ⊗1.30-4.30pm, 8.30-11pm Tue-Sat) In Fábula it's hard to avoid the pun – the place is pretty fabulous. Hidden in the highly refined confines of the Hotel Villa Oniria, the setting matches the food, which is presented like art and tastes equally good. Stand-outs are the venison with chestnuts and quince, or the baby eels with basil in venere rice.

🍷 Drinking & Nightlife

The best street for drinking is the rather scruffy Calle de Elvira, but other chilled bars line Río Darro at the base of the Albayzín and Calle Navas. Just north of Plaza de Trinidad are a bunch of cool hipster-ish bars.

Old stalwarts on the drinking/tapas scene are Los Diamantes (two branches), La Bella y La Bestia (four branches including one in Calle de Elvira) and the eternal classic Bodegas Castañeda.

★ Taberna La Tana   BAR

(Calle Rosario; ⊗12.30-4pm & 8.30pm-midnight) Possibly the friendliest family-run bar in Granada, La Tana specialises in Spanish wines and backs it up with some beautifully paired tapas. You can't go wrong with the *surtido* plate of Spanish hams. Ask the bartender about the 'wines of the month' and state your preference – a *suave* (smooth) red, or a *fuerte* (strong).

El Bar de Eric   BAR

(Calle Escuelas 8; ⊗8:30am-2am Sun-Thu, to 3am Fri & Sat) Imagine Keith Moon reincarnated as a punk rocker and put in charge of a modern tapas restaurant. Eric's is the brainchild of Spanish rock'n'roll drummer Eric Jiménez, of Los Planetas – but in this new bastion of rock chic, things aren't as chaotic as you might think.

Mundra   BAR

(Plaza de la Trinidad; platters €10; ⊗8.30pm-2am Mon-Thu, to 3am Fri & Sat) Overlooking the leafy square, Mundra has a global-chic feel with its black barrel tables, Buddha statues and chill-out soundtracks. There are platters to share for the peckish, including fresh prawns, which come from Motril, and provolone cheese, which doesn't.

Botánico   BAR

(www.botanicocafe.es; Calle Málaga 3; ⊗10am-1am Mon-Fri, noon-1am Sat & Sun) A haven for cool dudes with designer beards, students finishing off their Lorca dissertations, and anyone else with arty inclinations, Botánico is a casual snack restaurant by day, a cafe at *merienda* time (5-7pm), and a bar and club

GRANADA'S BEST TETERÍAS

Granada's *teterías* (teahouses) have proliferated in recent years, but there's still something exotic and dandyish about their dark atmospheric interiors, stuffed with lace veils, stucco, low cushioned seats and an invariably bohemian clientele. Most offer a long list of aromatic teas along with sticky Arabic sweets. Some serve up music and more substantial snacks. Many still permit their customers to indulge in the *chachima* (shisha pipe). Narrow Calle Calderería Nueva is Granada's best 'tetería street'. Cafe hours are roughly noon to midnight.

Tetería Nazari (Calle Calderería Nueva 13) Snuggle down on the misshapen pouffes with the flamenco singers, the earnest art students and the winner of last year's Che Guevara look-alike contest.

Tetería La Cueva de Ali Baba (Puente de Epinosa 15) Slightly more refined *tetería*, where you can sip wine and pick at tapas, overlooking the Río Darro.

Tetería Dar Ziryab (📞655 446775; Calle Calderería Nueva 11) A warm stove and regular live music provide two reasons to duck into the *Arabian Nights* interior of Dar Ziryab, where amorous undergraduates share *chicambas* (hookah pipes with water filters). Then there's the 40+ teas, sweet milk shakes and lovely white-chocolate tarts.

Tetería Kasbah (Calle Calderería Nueva 4; mains €8-12) Savoury food, ample student-watching potential and amazing stucco make up for the sometimes slow service in Calle Calderería Nuevo's biggest and busiest *tetería*.

Albayzín Abaco Te (📞958 22 19 35; Calle Álamo de Marqués 5; 📞) Hidden high up in the Albayzín maze, Abaco's Arabian minimalist interior allows you to enjoy Alhambra views from a comfy-ish floor mat. Health freaks hog the carrot juice; sweet tooths bag the excellent cakes.

come dusk, with DJs or live music emphasising jazz and blues.

Boom Boom Room CLUB
(📞646 81 96 00; Calle Carcel Baja 11; ⊙3pm-6am Sun-Thu, to 7am Fri & Sat) A glittery converted cinema is now Granada's top club for the glam crowd, who recline on the gold sofas and get hip-swivelling to cheesy Spanish pop tunes.

☆ Entertainment

Do not miss the nightly shows (8pm; €30) in the Palacio de los Olvidados (p665), which combine Lorca's plays with some magnificent self-penned flamenco. Best night out in Granada. No contest!

Jardines de Zoraya FLAMENCO
(📞958 20 60 66; www.jardinesdezoraya.com; Calle Panaderos 32; tickets with drink/dinner €20/45; ⊙shows 8pm & 10.30pm) A little larger than some of Andalucía's new flamenco cultural centres, and hosted in a restaurant that serves food and drink, the Jardines de Zoraya appears, on first impression, to be a touristy *tablao* (choreographed flamenco show). But reasonable entry prices, top-

notch performers and a highly atmospheric patio make the Abayzín venue a worthwhile stop for any aficionado.

Casa del Arte Flamenco FLAMENCO
(📞958 56 57 67; www.casadelarteflamenco.com; Cuesta de Gomérez 11; tickets €18; ⊙shows 7.30pm & 9pm) A small new-ish flamenco venue that is neither *tablao* nor *peña* (private club), but something in between. The performers are invariably top-notch, while the atmosphere depends largely on the tourist-local make-up of the audience.

Le Chien Andalou FLAMENCO
(www.lechienandalou.com; Carrera del Darro 7; tickets €6-10; ⊙shows 9.30pm & 11.30pm) Small cavernous bar that was once a cistern, but now hosts two nightly flamenco shows for half the price of the bigger places. Performances can be hit or miss, but at this price, it's probably worth the gamble.

Peña La Platería FLAMENCO
(www.laplateria.org.es; Placeta de Toqueros 7) Buried in the Albayzín warren, Peña La Platería claims to be the oldest flamenco aficionados' club in Spain, founded in 1949. Unlike other more private clubs, it regularly opens it

Legacy of the Moors

Between 711 and 1492, Andalucía spent nearly eight centuries under North African influence and reminders flicker on every street, from the palatial Alhambra to the tearooms and bathhouses of Córdoba and Málaga.

Teterías

Andalucía's caffeine lovers hang around in exotic *teterías*, Moorish-style tearooms that carry a whiff of Marrakech or even Cairo in their ornate interiors. Calle Calderería Nueva in Granada's Albayzín is where the best stash are hidden, but they have proliferated in recent years; now even Torremolinos has one! Look out for dimly lit, cushion-filled, fit-for-a-sultan cafes where pots of herbal tea accompanied by plates of Arabic sweets arrive at your table on a silver salver.

Andalucian Bathhouses

Sitting somewhere between a Western spa and a Moroccan hammam, Andalucía's bathhouses retain enough old-fashioned elegance to satisfy a latter-day emir with a penchant for Moorish-era opulence. You can recline in candlelit subterranean bliss sipping mint tea, and experience the same kind of bathing ritual – successive immersions in cold, tepid and hot bathwater – as the Moors did. Seville, Granada, Almería, Córdoba and Málaga all have excellent Arabic-style bathhouses, with massages also available.

Architecture

The Alhambra was undoubtedly the pinnacle of Moorish architectural achievement in Andalucía, but there are many other buildings in the region that draw inspiration from the rulers of

1. Arch detail, Alhambra (p657)
2. Arabic sweets in a *tetería* **3.** Andalucian bathhouse, Málaga (p684)

Al-Andalus. Sometimes the influences are obvious. At others, hybrid buildings constructed in Mudéjar or neo-Moorish styles hint at former Nasrid glories: an ornate wooden ceiling, geometric tile patterns, or an eruption of stucco. Granada is the first stop for Moorish relics, closely followed by Málaga, Córdoba, Almería, Seville and Las Alpujarras.

Cuisine

Andalucía's and Spain's cuisine draws heavily upon the food of North Africa where sweet spicy meat and starchy couscous are melded with Mediterranean ingredients. The Moors introduced many key ingredients into Spanish cooking: saffron, used in paella; almonds, used in Spanish desserts; and aubergines, present in the popular Andalucian tapa, *berenjenas con miel de caña* (aubergines

with molasses). If you'd prefer the real thing, there are plenty of pure Moroccan restaurants in Andalucía, especially in Granada and Tarifa.

MOORISH HIGHLIGHTS

Granada Alhambra (p657), Albayzín (p665)

Córdoba Mezquita (p641), Madinat al-Zahra (p649)

Seville Giralda (p575), Torre del Oro (p588)

Málaga Alcazaba (p685), Castillo de Gibralfaro (p687)

Almería Alcazaba (p717)

Las Alpujarras Berber-style houses in the village of Capileira (p681)

doors to nonmembers for performances on Thursday nights (and sometimes Saturdays) at 10.30pm.

Eshavira   LIVE MUSIC
(Postigo de la Cuna 2; ⊘ from 10pm) Just off Calle Azacayas, duck down the spooky alley, cross the small patio and battle with the hefty door to slip into one of the best jazz and flamenco haunts in the city, with local musicians coming down from Sacromonte to jam. But the party doesn't get rolling till at least 1am, and that's on weeknights. There's a good formal show (earlier) on Sunday nights, if you can't stick it out till the wee hours.

🛍 Shopping

Granada's craft specialities include *taracea* (marquetry) – the best work has shell, silver or mother-of-pearl inlay, applied to boxes, tables, chess sets and more.

Alcaicería   SOUVENIRS
(Calle Alcaicería) Formerly a grand Moorish bazaar where silk was made and sold, the stalls are now taken up with souvenir shops. The setting is still very reminiscent of the past, however, especially in the early morning before the coach tours descend. You can still see where the gates once stood at the entrances, there to guard against looting and closed at night. Opening hours vary, depending on the individual shops.

Alquímia Pervane   PERFUME
(Calderería Nueva) A fragrant hole in the wall near the top of this Moroccan-themed street, with its teashops and hookah pipes, selling a wide choice of wonderful oils in pretty bottles, plus rose water and similar.

Tienda Librería de la Alhambra   SOUVENIRS
(📋 958 22 78 46; Calle Reyes Católicos 40; ⊘ 9.30am-8.30pm) This is a fabulous shop for Alhambra aficionados, with a tasteful selection of quality gifts, including excellent coffee table–style tomes, children's art books, hand-painted fans, arty stationery and stunning photographic prints, which you select from a vast digital library (from €14 for A4 size).

Artesanías González   ARTS & CRAFTS
(Cuesta de Gomérez 12; ⊘ 11am-8pm) Specialises in exceptionally fine examples of marquetry, ranging from small easy-to-pack

boxes to larger pay-the-overweight-allowance chess sets.

🛈 Information

Provincial Tourist Office (📋 958 24 71 28; www.turismodegranada.org; Plaza de Mariana Pineda 10; ⊘ 9am-8pm Mon-Fri, 10am-7pm Sat, 10am-3pm Sun) Information on all of Granada province.

Tourist Office (📋 958 22 10 22; Calle Santa Ana 1; ⊘ 9am-7.30pm Mon-Sat, 9.30am-3pm Sun) Close to Plaza Nueva.

🛈 Getting There & Away

AIR
Aeropuerto Federico García Lorca (www.aena.es) is 17km west of the city, near the A92. **Autocares J González** (www.autocaresjose-gonzalez.com) runs buses (one way €3) to Gran Vía de Colón opposite the cathedral. Links to destinations outside Spain are limited to British Airways (www.ba.com), who run thrice weekly flights to London City Airport.

BUS
Granada's **bus station** (Carretera de Jaén) is 3km northwest of the city centre. Take city bus SN2 to Cruz del Sur and change onto the LAC bus for the Gran Vía de Colón in the city centre. Taxis cost around €7-9. **Alsa** (www.alsa.es) handles buses in the province and across the region, plus a night bus direct to Madrid's Barajas airport (€25, six hours). Destinations served by Alsa buses include the following:

DESTINATION	FARE	DURATION	FREQUENCY
Almuñécar	€8.36	1¼hr	9 daily
Córdoba	€15	2¾hr	8 daily
Guadix	€5.50	1hr	15 daily
Jaén	€8.89	1¼hr	16 daily
Lanjarón	€4.28	1hr	9 daily
Málaga	€12	1½hr	22 daily
Seville	€23	3hr	9 daily

CAR
Granada is at the junction of the A44 and the A92. The Alhambra has easy car access from the A395 spur.

TRAIN
The **train station** (📋 958 24 02 02; Avenida de Andaluces) is 1.5km northwest of the centre, off Avenida de la Constitución. For the centre, walk straight ahead to Avenida de la Constitución and turn right to pick up the LAC bus to Gran Vía de Colón; taxis cost about €5.

ℹ️ Getting Around

BUS
Individual tickets are €1.20. Pay with notes or coins to the bus driver. The most useful lines are C1, which departs from Plaza Nueva and does a full circuit of the Albayzín; C2, which runs from Plaza Nueva up to Sacromonte; and C3, which goes from Plaza Isabel II up through the Realejo quarter to the Alhambra.

CAR & MOTORCYCLE
Driving in central Granada – in common with most large Andalucian cities – can be frustrating and should be avoided if possible. Park your car on the outskirts and use public transport; there are plenty of options. If you have to drive, there are several central car parks: **Alhambra Parking** (Avenida Los Alixares; per hr/day €2.50/17), **Parking San Agustín** (Calle San Agustín; per hr/day €1.75/20) and **Parking Plaza Puerta Real** (Acera del Darro; per hr/day €1.45/17).

METRO
Stalled by the economic crisis, Granada's long-awaited new metro (scheduled initially to be completed by 2012) was still not operational at the time of writing this guide, although the lines have been built.

TAXI
Taxis congregate in Plaza Nueva and at the train and bus stations.

GRANADA PROVINCE

The last citadel of the Moors in Europe is a tempestuous place where Andalucía's complex history is laid out in ornate detail. The starting point for 99% of visitors is the Alhambra, the Nasrid emirs' enduring gift to architecture, a building whose eerie beauty is better seen than described. Below it nestles a city where brilliance and shabbiness sit side by side in bohemian bars, shadowy *teterías* (teahouses), winding lanes studded with stately *cármenes* (large houses with walled gardens), and backstreets splattered with street art.

The province's alternative muse hides in the snow-capped mountains that rise behind the Alhambra. The Sierra Nevada guard the highest peaks in mainland Spain and the country's largest ski resort. The southern side of the range shelters Las Alpujarras, which are characterised by their massive canyons where white villages replete with traditional flat-roofed Berber houses practise old-fashioned craft-making.

SKIING THE SIERRA NEVADA
The ski station **Sierra Nevada Ski** (☎ 902 70 80 90; www.sierranevada.es; one-day ski pass €33-45) has its base at the resort 'village' of Pradollano, 33km from Granada on the A395. It is popular with day-skiers and hence supremely busy at weekends in season. A few of the 121 marked runs start almost at the top of 3395m-high Veleta. There are cross-country routes, too, and a dedicated snowboard area (with Spain's longest half-pipe), a new family slope and kids' snow park, plus night-skiing on Thursday and Saturday.

In summer, the station becomes a mountain bike park, keeping three of its 22 lifts open and offering 30km of trails.

For more curiosities, head north to the troglodyte city of Guadix, where cave-living never went out of fashion.

Sierra Nevada
Granada's dramatic alpine backdrop is the Sierra Nevada range, which extends about 75km from west to east and into Almería province. Its wild snow-capped peaks include the highest point in mainland Spain, while the lower reaches of the range, known as Las Alpujarras (sometimes just La Alpujarra), are dotted with tiny scenic villages. From July to early September, the higher elevations offer wonderful multiday trekking and day hikes. Outside of this period, there's risk of seriously inclement weather, but the lower Alpujarras are always welcoming, with most snow melting away by May.

The 862-sq-km Parque Nacional Sierra Nevada, Spain's largest national park, is home to 2100 of Spain's 7000 plant species, among them unique types of crocus, narcissus, thistle, clover, poppy and gentian. Andalucía's largest ibex population (about 5000) is here, too, frolicking above 2800m. Surrounding the national park at lower altitudes is the Parque Natural Sierra Nevada, with a lesser degree of protection.

ℹ️ Getting There & Away

BUS
Alsa (www.alsa.es) operates local buses. From Granada, it runs on two routes: one twice daily

Western Sierra Nevada & Las Alpujarras

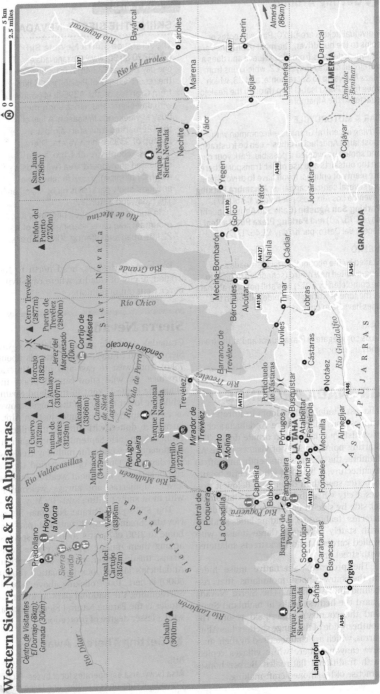

on the low road through Cádiar and Válor; the other three times daily to the higher villages and ending in Trevélez or Bérchules. Return buses start before 6am and mid-afternoon. There is a Málaga–Órgiva bus (€12, three hours, daily except Sunday), and a bus from Almería to Válor (€7.60, three hours) on Monday, Wednesday and Friday.

CAR

To reach the higher elevations of the Sierra Nevada, and the ski area, take the A395 from the eastern edge of Granada. The main road into Las Alpujarras from the west is the A348, which leaves the A44 about 34km south of Granada to pass through the relative lowlands. Just west of Órgiva, the A4132 turns off to the north to wind along the mountain slopes and pass through many of the higher villages; it merges with the A4130 and then rejoins the A348 a few kilometres north of Cádiar, via the A4127.

Mulhacén & Veleta

The Sierra Nevada's two highest peaks are Mulhacén (3479m) and Veleta (3395m). Two of three known as Los Tresmiles, because they rise above 3000m, they're on the western end of the range, close to Granada. From the ski station on the mountains' north flank, a road climbs up and over to Capileira, the highest village in the Barranco de Poqueira in the Alpujarras on the south side, but it's closed to motor vehicles on the highest stretch. From late June to the end of October (depending on snow cover), the national park operates a shuttle bus to give walkers access to the upper reaches of the range – or just a scenic guided drive.

The bus runs up from 3km above the ski station, starting at the national park information post at **Hoya de la Mora** (☑671 564407; ☉8.30am-2.30pm & 3.30-7.30pm Jun-Oct). Tickets are €5 one way or €9 return. It's best to phone ahead to check availability and reserve a place.

From the end of the bus route on the north side, it's about 4km up Veleta, an ascent of about 370m with 1½ hours' walking (plus stops); or 14km to the top of Mulhacén, with four to five hours' walking. To tackle Mulhacén from the south side, base yourself in Capileira in Las Alpujarras. From here a national park summer shuttle runs up to the Mirador de Trevélez, from where it's around three hours to the top of Mulhacén (6km, 800m ascent).

To make the trip into an overnight loop, you can bunk down at the 84-bed **Refugio**

Poqueira (☑958 34 33 49; www.refugiopoqueira.com; per person €17, breakfast €5, dinner €14), which sits at 2500m below the southwestern face of Mulhacén. The loop to Mulhacén from Mirador de Trevélez incorporating the *refugio* takes six to seven hours. Book in advance.

The **Centro de Visitantes El Dornajo** (☑958 34 06 25; ☉10am-5pm), about 23km from Granada, on the A395 towards the ski station, has plenty of information on the Sierra Nevada.

Las Alpujarras

Below the southern flank of the Sierra Nevada lies the 70km-long jumble of valleys known as Las Alpujarras. Arid hillsides split by deep ravines alternate with oasis-like white villages set beside rapid streams and surrounded by gardens, orchards and woodlands. Las Alpujarras was the last part of Spain to retain a strong Muslim population. After the fall of Granada in 1492, Moors who refused to convert took to these hills where they held out until the failed Morisco Rebellion of 1568. Many good walking routes link valley villages and head up into the Sierra Nevada: the best times to visit are between April and mid-June, and mid-September and early November. A recent surge in tourism and New Age and foreign (mainly British) settlers have given the area a new dimension.

Lanjarón

The closest of Las Alpujarras villages to Granada, leafy Lanjarón often bustles with tourists. Second only to Trevélez in ham production, it's also packed with shops selling the stuff. And that bottled water you've been drinking? It's from here as well. The therapeutic waters have been harnessed at the large **Balneario de Lanjarón** (☑958 77 01 37; www.balneariodelanjaron.com; Avenida de la Constitución; 1hr bath €30), a spa on the west edge of town, just opposite the tourist office. Promoting more active pursuits is the excellent **Caballo Blanco Trekking Centre** (☑627 794891; www.caballoblancotrekking.com; two-/four-hour treks €40/70), offering horse-riding lessons and treks into the surrounding hills and mountains. English and German are spoken. Book in advance. Top-notch birdwatching tours, both around Lanjarón and further afield, are also available via **Alpujarras Birdwatching & Nature** (www.alpujarrasbirdwatching.com).

For snacks, wander down the main street to the middle of town, to Arca de Noé (Jamones Gustavo Rubio; Avenida de la Alpujarra 38; ⏰10am-9pm), one of the better ham shops, where you can stock up on supplies or order a tasting tray and have a swig of sherry out the back. On the same street Cafetería Denebola (📞958 77 22 78; Avenida de Andalucía 38; snacks €2-3; ⏰8.30am-9pm) does fantastic coffee confections and decent breakfasts.

Órgiva

The main town of the western Alpujarras, Órgiva is a bit scruffier and considerably larger than neighbouring villages, although it shares the moniker 'Gateway to Las Alpujarras' with Lanjarón. A hippie scene has long been fertile here – the alternative lifestyle tipi village of 'Benéfico' is nearby and its inhabitants regularly come into town to sell their wares or busk at Órgiva's Thursday market. British visitors might recognise the town from Chris Stewart's best-selling book, *Driving Over Lemons*.

🛏 Sleeping & Eating

Casa Rural Jazmín   GUESTHOUSE €€
(📞958 78 47 95; www.casaruraljazmin.com; Calle Ladera de la Ermita; r €53-70; 🅿❄🐾) A sanctuary in the upper town, Casa Jazmín is a French-run house with four rooms, each decorated in a different style (Asian and Alpujarran rooms are smaller; French and African, larger). There's a communal terrace and a pool set in a dense garden. On a cul-de-sac, it has space for parking, once you make it up the winding street.

Tetería Baraka   INTERNATIONAL €€
(www.teteria-baraka.com; Calle Estación 12; mains €10-13; ⏰noon-10.30pm Sat-Wed, 9am-4.30pm Thu) This place has a laid-back vibe and an eclectic menu that includes Moroccan dishes, tofu burgers, *shwarmas*, delicious brownies and natural juices. There are also preserves, spices and teas for sale, plus bakery items to take away. Located beside the municipal car park in the upper part of town.

🛍 Shopping

Ángel Vera   CERAMICS
(Ctra Órgiva–Pampaneira) Situated 4km out of Órgiva, this workshop displays the exquisite ceramics and woodwork of Ángel Vera, with vases, tables, lamps and ornamental plates included in the display. Ceramic workshops also available.

Válor

Válor, 5km northeast of Yegen, was the birthplace of Aben Humeya, a *morisco* (converted Muslim) who led a 1568 rebellion against Felipe II's policies banning Arabic names, dress and language. The two years of guerrilla war throughout the mountains ended only after Don Juan of Austria, Felipe's half-brother, was brought in to quash the insurrection and Aben Humeya was assassinated by his cousin Aben Aboo. To re-create the historical clash, Válor musters a large Moros y Cristianos (Moors and Christians) festival on 14 and 15 September, with colourfully costumed 'armies' battling it out.

The village is known for its olive oil, goats' cheese and partridge, all of which you can sample at the notable Restaurante Aben Humeya (📞958 85 18 10; Calle Los Bolos; mains €8-12; ⏰1.30-3.30pm & 8-11pm Tue-Sun), downhill off the main road. Its menu features seasonal treats, such as local mushrooms, along with standards like baby kid in a garlic-spiked sauce and delicate *croquetas* (croquettes). For dessert, there's the deadly rich *tocino del cielo* (egg-yolk custard), or soft cheese with honey, washed down with *vino rosado* (rosé) from Albuñol.

Reason alone to visit the Alpujarra village of Válor, Los Arcos (📞958 85 17 71; www.losarcosholidays.com; Plaza de la Iglesia 3; s/d €40/60; 🅿📶) is a spacious, welcoming, down-to-earth place to convene, relax and meet the locals/owners – actually a British couple called Jill and David Drummie. Surrounded by easily accessible mountain splendour, it's the kind of B&B you'll wish you lived in yourself. The breakfasts are deliciously large – just the ticket if you're off hiking on the GR7 – and there's an expansive terrace with a complimentary-drinks bar.

La Taha

In the next valley east from Poqueira, life gets substantially more tourist-free. Still known by the Arabic term for the administrative districts into which the Islamic caliphate divided the Alpujarras, La Taha consists of the town of Pitres and its six outlying villages – Mecina Fondales, Capilerilla, Mecinilla, Ferreirola and Atalbéitar – in the valley just below, all of Roman origin. Day-trippers are few, and the expat residents have nearly blended in with the scenery.

Ancient paths between the seven hamlets (marked with signposts labelled 'Sendero

THE THREE VILLAGES OF THE BARRANCO DE POQUEIRA

When seen from the bottom of the Poqueira gorge, the three villages of Pampaneira, Bubión and Capileira, 14km to 20km northeast of Órgiva, look like splatters of white paint flicked Jackson Pollock–style against the grey stone behind. They're the most beautiful villages of the Alpujarras, and the most visited. The Poqueira is famous for its multitude of artisan crafts; leather, weaving and tilework are all practised using age-old methods. Then there is the unique cusine made using locally produced ham, jam, cheese, honey, mushrooms and grapes. Arrive with a shopping bag and fill up. Equally alluring are the hiking trails that link the villages, many of them perfectly doable in a day. The best-stocked tourist office is in Pampaneira. The bus to and from Granada stops in all three villages.

Bubión

Teide (Carretera de Sierra Nevada; mains €7-9; ⊙10am-10.30pm Wed-Mon) A good restaurant on the main road frequented by a local clientele of characters who stop by for hearty *raciones* of *jamón* and wine. The dishes are mainly Alpujarran, with a few international additions like onion soup and spaghetti with pesto.

Estación 4 (Calle Estación 4; mains €7-12; ⊙6-11pm Tue-Fri, 1-4pm & 6.30-11pm Sat & Sun; 🖉) Wind your way down below the main road to find this superb and elegant restaurant, with its minimalist dining room and varied menu, including international bites like *hummus* and vegetarian croquettes, plus some wonderful innovative salads and more traditional local fare.

Nade Taller del Telar (www.tallerdeltelar.com; Calle Trinidad 11; h11am-2.30pm & 5-8.30pm) For a glimpse of the past, visit the French-owned weaving workshop, with its historic enormous looms that come from the Albayzín in Granada. Nade only uses natural fabrics in her weaving, like alpaca wool, silk and mohair. The shawls are beautiful, starting at around €65, and well worth the investment.

Capileira

Hotel Real de Poqueira (☏958 76 39 02; www.hotelpoqueira.com; Doctor Castillas 11; s/d €50/70; 🗲🗺) Located in an old house next to Capileira's lily-white church, this place is one of several in the village all run by the same family. However, with its expansive lobby, flop-down couches and smart, boutique-like rooms, this one has the edge. It's not what you expect in a small Alpujarra village, which makes it all the more epiphanic.

⭐**Taberna Restaurante La Tapa** (☏618 30 70 30; Calle Cubo 6; mains €9-12; hnoon-4pm & 8pm-midnight; 🖉) Las Alpujarras is a culinary micro-region with its own distinct flavours and, at La Tapa, they're skilfully melded with the area's Moorish past, creating dishes such as wild boar casserole and couscous in earthenware dishes. The place is tiny but textbook Alpujarran.

Bar El Tilo (Plaza Calvario; raciones €8; ⊙11.30am-11pm) Capileira's village tavern enjoys prime position on a lovely whitewashed square with a terrace. *Raciones* such as *albóndigas* (meatballs in tomato sauce) are enormous. There are also cakes and pies made daily.

Pampaneira

Estrella de las Nieves (☏958 76 39 81; www.estrelladelasnieves.com; Calle Huerto 21; s/d €54/70; 🅿🗺) Opened in 2010, this dazzling white complex just above the town has airy, light and modern rooms with terraces overlooking the rooftops and mountains. It also has pleasant gardens and the definite perks of a car park and pool. The hotel is located just outside the village on the A4132, towards Lanjarón.

Bodega El Lagar (Calle Silencio; raciones €6-8) Located on one of the prettiest winding sidestreets, this tiny place sells local products, including preserves, and some funky clothing, plus has an attractive tucked-away terrace for trying *raciones* like chicken and garlic. It doubles as a bodega too, so ask to taste the wine – it costs less than €3 a litre and is surprisingly fruity and palatable.

L'ATELIER

Sitting ironically in the middle of a region where the main local dish, *plato alpujarreño*, is a carnivorous mélange of sausages, cured meats, fried eggs and potatoes, L'Atelier (☑ 958 85 75 01; www.atelier-mecina.com; Calle Alberca 21; mains €8-12; ◷1-4pm & 7.30-10pm; ☑) is a curious anomaly - and a welcome one if you don't eat meat.

Set in a traditional house in the hamlet of Mecina Fondales in La Taha, this snug, candlelit restaurant presents globetrotting vegetarian and vegan dishes (tabbouleh, Moroccan tagine, Miso soup included) and the results are exceptional. L'Atelier's reputation was cemented by French chef Jean-Claude Juston in the 1990s, and, despite a recent change in ownership, has lost none of its shine. L'Atelier also rents out several rooms.

Local Pitres-Ferreirola') wend their way through woods and orchards, while the tinkle of running water provides the soundtrack. About 15 minutes' walk below Fondales, an old Moorish-era bridge spans the deep gorge of the Río Trevélez. Park at the top of the town and follow signs saying 'Camino de Órgiva' and 'Camino del Campuzano'.

If you're walking in on the GR7, you'll be deposited in Pitres' Plaza La Alpujarra, where you can procure refreshments in **Bar La Taha** (Plaza La Alpujarra 5; ◷noon-11pm). Across the square a signboard displays a quote and photo of Federico García Lorca, who visited in 1928.

A good accommodation option, situated in Ferreirola, is **Sierra y Mar** (☑958 76 61 71; www.sierraymar.com; Calle Albaicín, Ferreirola; s/d incl breakfast €42/65; ⓟ🛜).

Trevélez

To gastronomes, Trevélez equals ham – or *jamón serrano* to be more precise – one of Spain's finest cured hams that matures perfectly in the village's rarified mountain air. To hikers it means a cobweb of high mountain trails including easy access to Mulhacén, mainland Spain's highest peak. To statisticians it is the second highest village in Spain after Valdelinares in Aragón.

The village, sited at 1486m on the almost treeless slopes of the Barranco de Trevélez, is divided into *alto* (high) and *bajo* (low) sections. The Alpujarra bus generally stops in both. The *alto* section is older and more labyrinthine, while *bajo* has the bulk of the tourist facilities.

Hotel La Fragua   HOTEL €

(☑958 85 86 26; www.hotellafragua.com; Calle San Antonio 4; s/d €38/50; ⓟ🛜) The rooms at La Fragua are typical mountain-village style: pine-furnished, simple and clean. Some have balconies, and there's a large rooftop deck. Early-rising walking groups can be noisy, though. The hotel is at the top of town, a 200m walk (signposted) from the highest plaza. A second, more modern property nearby (doubles for €55) has a pool and great views.

La Fragua is closed early January to early February.

Mesón Joaquín   ANDALUCIAN €

(Carretera Laujar, Órgiva Km 22; mains €8-12; ◷noon-4.30pm) Welcome to ham city! White-coated technicians slice up transparent sheets of the local product, and the trout comes from the wholesaler just behind – wrapped in ham, of course. Vegetarians be warned: scores of cured hams hang within head-butting distance from the restaurant's roof.

Jamones González   FOOD

(www.jamonescanogonzalez.com; Calle Nueva; ◷10am-1.30pm & 5-8pm Mon-Fri, to 1.30pm Sat) The place to come if you fancy buying some of the famed Trevélez cured ham to take home. Also sells other local gourmet products.

Costa Tropical

Granada's cliff-lined, 80km-long coast has a hint of Italy's Amalfi about it, although it is definitively Spanish when you get down to the nitty-gritty – Moorish relics, old-school tapas joints and some damn fine churros. Its warm climate – there's no real winter to speak of – lends it the name Costa Tropical. A sprinkling of attractive beach towns less colonised by expats than those on the Costa del Sol is linked by several daily buses to Granada, Málaga and Almería.

Almuñécar & La Herradura

POP 27,195

Dedicated to beach fun, Almuñécar is not too expensive, a little rough around the edges and very relaxed. Many of the tourists on its pebbly beaches are Spanish, and its old city centre is a scenic maze below a 16th-century castle, albeit surrounded by dreary high-rises. The next-door village of La Herradura handles some of the overflow, but maintains a more castaway feel as it caters to a younger crowd of windsurfers. The N340 runs across the northern part of both towns.

Sights

Almuñécar's beachfront is divided by a rocky outcrop, the Peñón del Santo, with **Playa de San Cristóbal** – the best beach (grey sand and small pebbles) – stretching to its west, and **Playa Puerta del Mar** to the east, backed by a strip of cool cafes.

Castillo de San Miguel   CASTLE
(Santa Adela Explanada; adult/child €2.35/1.60; ⏲10am-1.30pm & 4-6.30pm Tue-Sat, 10.30am-1pm Sun) At the top of a hill overlooking the sea, the Castillo de San Miguel was built by the conquering Christians over Islamic and Roman fortifications. The hot, circuitous climb up to the entrance rewards with excellent views and an informative little **museum**. Don't forget to peer into the dungeon at the skeleton: a reproduction of human remains discovered here.

Festivals & Events

Jazz en la Costa   MUSIC
(www.jazzgranada.es) Annual jazz festival in Almuñécar jazz festival, held in the Parque Botánico El Majuelo in mid-July.

Sleeping & Eating

Hotel Casablanca   HOTEL €
(☎958 63 55 75; www.hotelcasablancaalmunecar.com; Plaza de San Cristóbal 4; s/d €40/48) Materialising close to the beach in the town of Almuñécar, the distinctive terracotta arches of the Hotel Casablanca really could have sprung from Casablanca. The place is furnished in distinctive Al-Andalus style, with sea views from some rooms. There's a ground-floor restaurant.

★La Italiana Cafe   CAFE €
(☎958 88 23 12; www.laitaliancafe.com; Hurtado de Mendoza 5; pizza & pasta €8-9; ⏲8am-10pm; 🛜) Weirdly, considering its name and pizza/pasta menu, La Italiana is *the* place to go for local Almuñécar pastries such as *torta de al-hajú* and *cazuela mohina*. Enjoy them with a cappuccino, surrounded by ceiling frescoes and elaborately gilded pillars and mirrors.

La Ventura   ANDALUCIAN €€
(☎958 88 23 78; Calle Alta del Mar 18; mains €12-20; ⏲1-4pm & 8-11.30pm) A bit of a flamenco secret in Almuñécar and all the better for it, Ventura is best visited on Thursday and Sunday evenings when music and dance accompanies solid gold food that never veers far from local tradition: think fish salads and

GRANADA & SOUTH COAST ANDALUCÍA COSTA TROPICAL

WORTH A TRIP

WATERSPORTS IN LA HERRADURA

If you're craving a more remote beach scene than Almuñécar, or more activity, consider heading 7km west to the small, horseshoe-shaped bay at La Herradura, where a younger demographic of windsurfers and paragliders congregate. **Windsurf La Herradura** (☎958 64 01 43; www.windsurflaherradura.com; Paseo Andrés Segovia 34) is one good operator for these, as well as less extreme water sports, including kayaking.

While the western Mediterranean, with its shallow, sandy coastal waters, is of limited interest for aspiring divers, the eastern Med, more specifically the Costa Tropical around La Herradura, is a different kettle of fish. Here you'll find a varied seabed of sea grass, sand and rock flecked with caves, crevices and passages. Local dive operator **Buceo La Herradura** (☎958 82 70 83; www.buceolaherradura.com; Puerto Marina del Este; immersion with equipment €47) keep a boat moored at the marina, from where it's a five- to 10-minute journey out to various dive sites.

When you return, you can enjoy the seafood in one of the many *chiringuitos* (beach bars) on La Herradura's shore.

WHAT'S COOKING IN GRANADA & SOUTH COAST ANDALUCÍA?

Ajoblanco A cold white soup that's similar to gazpacho, but uses almonds rather than tomatoes. *Ajoblanco* is a classic dish in Andalucía's eastern provinces. Try it in Málaga's Gorki (p690), where it's served topped with grapes.

Berenjenas con miel de caña For an alternative to meat that isn't tortilla, try lightly fried aubergines covered in molasses. This sweet-savoury vegetarian delight is served all over Andalucía, but it's especially good in Málaga in El Piyayo (p690).

Paté de Perdiz Game is a popular product in Jaén province. Partridge pâté highlights many menus in the town of Úbeda, where it is served at Restaurante Antique (953 75 76 18; www.restauranteantique.com; Calle Real 25, Úbeda; mains €12-26, raciones €9-18; 1-4pm & 8-11.30pm) doused in the local olive oil.

Plato Alpujarreño A hearty mountain dish of blood sausage, fried potatoes, peppers, fried egg and the best Trevélez *jamón serrano*, Plato Alpujarreño is best enjoyed in – where else? – Las Alpujarras. Bar El Tilo (p681) in the village of Capileira does an outstanding version.

meat stews. A five-course meal is offered to coincide with the shows (9pm) for a reasonable €25.

ℹ Information

Information Kiosk (Paseo del Altillo; 10am-1.30pm & 6.30-9pm) Just north of the bus station near the N340 roundabout.

Main Tourist Office (www.almunecar.info; Avenida Europa; 10am-2pm & 6-9pm) A few blocks back from Playa de San Cristóbal on the east side, in a pink neo-Moorish mansion.

ℹ Getting There & Away

The **Almuñécar bus station** (958 63 01 40; Avenida Juan Carlos I 1) is just south of the N340. Buses go to Almería (€11.83, 3½ hours, at least five daily), Málaga (€7.44, 1¾ hours, 10 daily), Granada (€8.36, 1½ hours, nine daily), La Herradura (€1.17, 10 minutes, 16 daily), Nerja (€2.92, 30 minutes, 16 daily) and Salobreña (€1.33, 15 minutes, 16 daily). A bus goes to Órgiva (€4.69, 1¼ hours, one daily) at 4.45pm Monday to Saturday.

MÁLAGA PROVINCE

Málaga is the hip revitalised Andalucian city everyone is talking about after decades of being pointedly ignored, particularly by tourists to the coastal resorts. The city's 30-odd museums and edgy urban art scene are well matched by the contemporary chic dining choices, spanking new metro line and a shopping street voted as one of the most stylish (and expensive) in Spain. And

besides Málaga, each region of the province has equally fascinating diversity, ranging from the breathtaking mountains of La Axarquía to the tourist-driven razzle dazzle of the Costa del Sol.

Inland are the *pueblos blancos* (white towns). Or the underappreciated, elegant old town of Antequera with its nearby archaeological site and fabulous *porra antequerana* (a thick and delicious garlicky soup, similar to gazpacho).

Málaga

POP 568,479

Málaga is a world apart from the adjoining Costa del Sol: a historic and culturally rich provincial capital which has long lived in the shadow of the iconic Andalucian cities of Granada, Córdoba and Seville. Yet, it has rapidly emerged as the province's city of culture with its so-called 'mile of art' being compared to Madrid, and its dynamism and fine dining to Barcelona.

The tastefully restored historic centre is a delight: its Gothic cathedral is surrounded by narrow pedestrian streets flanked by traditional and modern bars, and shops that range from idiosyncratic and family owned, to urban-chic and contemporary. Cast your eyes up to enjoy a skyline that reflects the city's eclectic character; church spires jostle for space with russet-red tiled roofs and lofty apartment buildings while, like a grand old dame, the 11th-century Gibralfaro castle sits grandly aloft and provides the best view of all.

The former rundown port has also been grandly rebuilt and cruise-line passengers are now boosting the city's coffers and contributing to the overall increase in tourism to the city.

◎ Sights

Málaga's major sights are clustered in or near the charming old town, which is situated beneath the Alcazaba and the Castillo de Gibralfaro. A good place to start your exploring is the landmark cathedral, which towers above the surrounding streets and is thus reassuringly easy to find. The port area is home to a further three museums.

★ Catedral de Málaga CATHEDRAL
(🖉952 21 59 17; Calle Molina Lario; cathedral & museum €5, tower €6; ⊙10am-6pm Mon-Sat) Málaga's cathedral was started in the 16th century on the site of the former mosque. Of the mosque, only the Patio de los Naranjos survives, a small courtyard of fragrant orange trees.

Inside, the fabulous domed ceiling soars 40m into the air, while the vast colonnaded nave houses an enormous cedar-wood choir. Aisles give access to 15 chapels with gorgeous 18th-century retables and religious art. Climb the tower (200 steps) to enjoy stunning panoramic views of the city skyline and coast.

Building the cathedral was an epic project that took some 200 years. Such was the project's cost that by 1782 it was decided that work would stop. One of the two bell towers was left incomplete, hence the cathedral's well-worn nickname, La Manquita (the one-armed lady). The cathedral's museum displays a collection of religious items covering a period of 500 years.

★ Museo Picasso Málaga MUSEUM
(🖉902 44 33 77; www.museopicassomalaga.org; Calle San Agustín 8; €7, incl temporary exhibition €10; ⊙10am-8pm Tue-Thu & Sun, to 9pm Fri & Sat) The Museo Picasso has an enviable collection of 204 works, 155 donated and 49 loaned to the museum by Christine Ruiz-Picasso (wife of Paul, Picasso's eldest son) and Bernard Ruiz-Picasso (his grandson), and includes some wonderful paintings of the family, including the heartfelt Paulo con gorro blanco (Paulo with a white cap), a portrait of Picasso's eldest son painted in the 1920s.

Don't miss the Phoenician, Roman, Islamic and Renaissance archaeological remains in the museum's basement, discovered during construction works.

★ Centre Pompidou Málaga MUSEUM
(🖉951 92 62 00; www.centrepompidou.es; Pasaje Doctor Carrillo Casaux, Muelle Uno; €7, incl temporary exhibition €9; ⊙9.30am-8pm Wed-Mon) Opened in 2015 in the port, this offshoot of the Paris Pompidou Centre is housed in a low-slung modern building crowned by a playful multicoloured cube. The permanent exhibition includes the extraordinary Ghost, by Kader Attia, depicting rows of Muslim women bowed in prayer and created from domestic aluminum foil, plus works by such contemporary masters as Frida Kahlo, Francis Bacon and Antoni Tàpies. There are also audiovisual installations, talking 'heads' and temporary exhibitions.

★ Alcazaba CASTLE
(Calle Alcazabilla; €2.20, incl Castillo de Gibralfaro €3.40; ⊙9.30am-8pm Tue-Sun) No time to visit Granada's Alhambra? Then Málaga's Alcazaba can provide a taster. The entrance is next to the Roman amphitheatre, from where a meandering path climbs amid lush greenery: crimson bougainvillea, lofty palms, fragrant jasmine bushes and rows of orange trees. Extensively restored, this palace-fortress dates from the 11th-century Moorish period; the caliphal horseshoe arches, courtyards and bubbling fountains are evocative of this influential period in Málaga's history.

Museo de Arte Flamenco MUSEUM
(🖉952 22 13 80; www.museoflamencojuanbreva.com; Calle Franquelo 4; suggested donation €1; ⊙10am-2pm Tue-Sun) Fabulously laidout over two floors in the HQ of Málaga's oldest and most prestigious peña (private flamenco club), this collection of fans, costumes, posters and other flamenco paraphernalia is testimony to the city's illustrious flamenco scene.

Roman Amphitheatre LANDMARK, MUSEUM
(🖉951 50 11 15; Calle Alcazabilla 8) Uncovered in 1951, this Roman theatre slap-bang in the city centre had lain hidden for many

ℹ FREE ENTRY TO MUSEUMS

The Museo Picasso and the Centre Pompidou Málaga (offer free admission on Sunday afternoons from 6pm and 4pm, respectively, until closure time.

Málaga

0 200 m
0 0.1 miles

C Ollerías

C Dos Aceras

C de Coberizo de Conde

C Peña

C Frailes

C Hinestrosa

C Ramos Marín

11

C Gómez Pallete

C Puerta Buenaventura

Plaza Jerónimo Cuervo

16

21

C Madre de Dios

C Carretería

C Álamos

C Tejón y Rodríguez

C Beatas

10

Plaza de la Merced

C Mosquera

C Casapalma

C Andrés Pérez

C Comedias

C Méndez Núñez

C Juan de Padilla

27

C Marqués de Guadairo

C Franquelo

4

29

C Victoria

3

7

Plaza Mártires

C Convalecientes

20

Plaza de Uncibay

C Tomás de Cózar

9

Plaza Mitjana

C Denis Belgrano

C Niño de Guevara

OLD TOWN

C Granada

25

24

13

Parador Málaga Gibralfaro (500m); Castillo de Gibralfaro (500m)

Kelipe (150m)

3

C Luis de Velázquez

C Calderería

C Granada

17

26

Museo 2 Picasso Málaga

C Alcazabilla

C Sánchez Pastor

19

C Molina Lario

C San Agustín

6

Plaza de la Constitución

Pasaje de Chinitas

C Santa María

C Císter

30

22

Plaza de la Aduana

15

Regional Tourist Office

C Moreno Monroy

Plaza del Obispo

1

Catedral de Málaga

C Cañón

28

5

Alcazaba (180m)

Plaza de las Flores

C Salinas

C Marqués de Larios

Plaza de la Marina

18

C Strachan

C Molinalario

C Bolsa

Av de Cervantes

C Nueva

12

C Cortina del Muelle

Paseo del Parque

14

C Mesón de Vélez

C Sancha de Lara

Paseo de España

Mercado Atarazanas (80m)

23

C San Juan de Dios

Plaza de la Marina

Paseo de los Curas

Museo Alborania (120m); Centre Pompidou Málaga (250m); Muelle Uno (450m)

8

Municipal Tourist Office

Alameda Principal

C Córdoba

C Trinidad Grund

C Vendeja

Feel Málaga Hostel (200m)

Al Yamal (200m); MUES (250m); Óleo (550m); Centro de Arte Contemporáneo (550m)

Puerto

(800m)

(800m)

Málaga

hundreds of years. It was built in the time of Augustus (1st century AD) and remains relatively well preserved. An adjacent interpretive centre has touch screens and some artefacts dug up from the site. The theatre is particularly evocative at night with the Alcazaba illuminated behind it.

Museo de Málaga MUSEUM
(Palacio de la Aduana; ☑951 29 40 51; Plaza de la Aduana; ☺10am-7pm Tue-Sun) **FREE** The Museum of Málaga opened in 2015. It includes an archaeological-history section with reproductions of wall paintings found in Nerja caves and a magnificent 1.7m sculpture of a Roman soldier dating to the 2nd century AD. A further gallery concentrates on the Moorish period with a large model of Málaga's one-time medina-like market and several Nasrid ceramics. The museum also contains a fine-arts section of 19th- and 20th-century Spanish paintings.

MUES AREA
(Málaga Arte Urbano en el Soho) The antithesis of Málaga's prestigious world-class art museums is refreshingly down-to-earth MUES (Málaga Arte Urbano en el Soho) a grassroots movement originally born from an influx of street artists to the area. The result is a total transformation of the formerly rundown district between the city centre and the port (now called Soho), with edgy contemporary murals, several stories high,

as well as arty cafes, ethnic restaurants and street markets.

Muelle Uno PORT
(P) The city's long beleaguered port area underwent a radical rethink in 2013 and was redesigned to cater to the increase in cruise passengers to the city. Wide quayside walkways now embellish Muelle 1 and Muelle 2, which are lined by palm trees and backed by shops, restaurants, bars and a small aquarium, the **Museo Alborania** (☑951 60 01 08; www.museoalborania.com; Palmeral de las Sopresas, Muelle 2; adult/child €7/5; ☺11am-2pm & 5pm-midnight Jul–15 Sep, 10.30am-2.30pm & 4.30-6:30pm 15 Sep–Jun; ☝).

Museo Carmen Thyssen MUSEUM
(www.carmenthyssenmalaga.org; Calle Compañía 10; €4.50, incl temporary exhibition €9; ☺10am-7.30pm Tue-Sun) Located in an aesthetically renovated 16th-century palace in the heart of the city's former Moorish quarter, the extensive collection concentrates on 19th-century Spanish and Andalucian art and includes paintings by some of the country's most exceptional painters, including Joaquín Sorolla y Bastida, Ignacio Zuloaga and Francisco de Zurbarán. Temporary exhibitions similarly focus on 19th-century art.

Castillo de Gibralfaro CASTLE
(€2.20, incl Alcazaba €3.40; ☺9am-9pm Apr-Sep) One remnant of Málaga's Islamic past is the

craggy ramparts of the Castillo de Gibral-faro, spectacularly located high on the hill overlooking the city. Built by Abd ar-Rahman I, the 8th-century Cordoban emir, and later rebuilt in the 14th century when Málaga was the main port for the emirate of Granada, the castle originally acted as a lighthouse and military barracks.

Nothing much is original in the castle's interior, but the airy walkway around the ramparts affords the best views over Málaga.

Centro de Arte Contemporáneo   MUSEUM

(Contemporary Art Museum; www.cacmalaga.org; Calle Alemania; ⊙10am-8pm Tue-Sun) **FREE** The contemporary art museum is housed in a skilfully converted 1930s wholesale market on the river estuary. The bizarre triangular floor plan of the building has been retained, with its cubist lines and shapes brilliantly displaying the modern art. Painted entirely white, windows and all, the museum exhibits its works from well-known contemporary artists such as Tracey Emin and Damien Hirst.

Activities

Hammam Al-Andalus   HAMMAM

(☑952 21 50 18; www.hammamalandalus.com; Plaza de los Mártires 5; €30; ⊙10am-midnight) These Moorish-style baths provide *malagueños* with a luxury marble-clad setting to enjoy the same relaxation benefits as those offered by similar facilities in Granada and Córdoba. Massages are also available.

Tours

Málaga Bike Tours   BICYCLE TOUR

(☑606 978513; www.malagabiketours.eu; Calle Trinidad Grund 1; tours €25) Bike tours are an excellent way to see the sights and you can't do better than Málaga Bike Tours, which runs daily tours leaving from outside the municipal tourist office in Plaza de la Marina at 10am. Reservations are required. Book at least 24 hours ahead.

Alternatively, you can rent your own bike for €10 a day.

Festivals & Events

Feria de Málaga   FAIR

Málaga's nine-day feria (fair) in mid-August, launched by a huge fireworks display, is the most ebullient of Andalucía's summer ferias. It resembles an exuberant Rio-style street party with plenty of flamenco and *fino* (dry

and straw-coloured sherry); head for the city centre to be in the thick of it.

Semana Santa   HOLY WEEK

Each night from Palm Sunday to Good Friday, six or seven *cofradías* (brotherhoods) bear holy images for several hours through the city, watched by large crowds.

Sleeping

★ Dulces Dreams   HOSTEL €

(☑951 35 78 69; www.dulcesdreamshostel.com; Plaza de los Mártires 6; r incl breakfast €45-60; ❄ 🛜) Run by an enthusiastic young team, the rooms at Dulces (sweet) Dreams are appropriately named after desserts; 'Cupcake' is a good choice with its terrace overlooking the imposing red-brick church across the way. This is an older building so there's no lift and the rooms vary in size, but they are bright and whimsically decorated using recycled materials as far as possible.

Feel Málaga Hostel   HOSTEL €

(☑952 22 28 32; www.feelmalagahostel.com; Calle Vendeja 25; d €45, without bathroom €35, shared rooms per person from €16; @ 🛜) Located within a suitcase trundle of the city-centre train station, the accommodation here is clean and well-equipped with a choice of doubles and shared rooms. The downstairs communal area has a colourful seaside look with stripey deckchairs and minifootball, bathrooms sport classy mosaic tiles and the top-floor kitchen has all the essentials necessary to whip up a decent meal.

★ Molina Lario   HOTEL €€

(☑952 06 20 02; www.hotelmolinalario.com; Calle Molina Lario 20-22; r €116-130; ❄ 🛜 🖃) Perfect for romancing couples, this hotel has a sophisticated contemporary feel with spacious rooms decorated in a cool palette of earthy colours. There are crisp white linens, marshmallow-soft pillows and tasteful paintings, plus a fabulous rooftop terrace and pool with views to the sea. Situated within confessional distance of the cathedral.

El Hotel del Pintor   BOUTIQUE HOTEL €€

(☑952 06 09 81; www.hoteldelpintor.com; Calle Álamos 27; s/d €59/70; ❄ @ 🛜) The red, black and white colour scheme of this friendly, small hotel echoes the abstract artwork of *malagueño* artist Pepe Bornov, whose paintings are on permanent display throughout the public areas and rooms. Although convenient for most of the city's main sights, pack your earplugs: the rooms in the front can be noisy, especially on a Saturday night.

El Riad Andaluz
GUESTHOUSE €€

(☑952 21 36 40; www.elriadandaluz.com; Calle Hinestrosa 24; s/d/tr €62/89/119; ✴◉🖤) This French-run guesthouse, in the historic part of town, has eight rooms set around the kind of atmospheric patio that's known as a *riad* in Morocco. The decoration is Moroccan but each room is different, including colourful tiled bathrooms. Breakfast is available.

Parador Málaga Gibralfaro
HISTORIC HOTEL €€€

(☑952 22 19 02; www.parador.es; Castillo de Gibralfaro; r incl breakfast €130-155; P✴🖤🖤) With an unbeatable location perched on the pine-forested Gibralfaro, Málaga's stone-built *parador* (luxurious state-owned hotel) is a popular choice, although the rooms are fairly standard. Most have spectacular views from their terraces, however, and you can dine at the excellent terrace restaurant, even if you are not a guest at the hotel.

🍴 Eating

Málaga has a staggering number of tapas bars and restaurants, particularly around the historic centre (over 400 at last count), so finding a place to eat poses no problem. A gourmet food market, Mercado de La Merced is also slated to open in the historic centre, just off Plaza de la Merced, offering an eclectic choice of international and local cuisine to sample or take away.

Tapeo de Cervantes
TAPAS €

(www.eltapeodecervantes.com; Calle Cárcer 8; tapas €4-6; ⊙Tue-Sun) This place has caught on big time which, given its squeeze-in space, can mean a wait. Choose from traditional or more innovative tapas and *raciones* with delicious combinations and stylish presentation. Think polenta with oyster mushrooms, chorizo and melted cheese or the more conventional *tortilla de patatas* (potato omelette), spiked with a veg or two. Portions are generous.

Casa Aranda
CAFE €

(www.casa-aranda.net; Calle Herrería del Rey; churro €0.45; ⊙8am-3pm Mon-Sat; 🏍) Casa Aranda is in a narrow alleyway next to the market and, since 1932, has been *the* place in town to enjoy chocolate and churros. The cafe has taken over the whole street with several outlets all overseen by a team of mainly elderly white-shirted waiters who welcome everyone like an old friend (and most are).

★ Óleo
FUSION €€

(☑952 21 90 62; www.oleorestaurante.es; Edificio CAC, Calle Alemania; mains €12-16; ⊙10am-midnight Mon-Sat; 🖤) Located at the city's contemporary art museum with white-on-white minimalist decor, Óleo provides diners with the unusual choice of Mediterranean or Asian food with some subtle combinations such as duck breast with a side of seaweed with hoisin, as well as more purist Asian and gourmet palate-ticklers such as candied, roasted piglet.

★ El Mesón de Cervantes
TAPAS, ARGENTINIAN €€

(☑952 21 62 74; www.elmesondecervantes.com; Calle Álamos 11; mains €13-16; ⊙7pm-midnight Wed-Mon) Cervantes started as a humble tapas bar run by expat Argentinian Gabriel Spatz (the original bar is still operating around the corner), but has expanded into plush spacious digs with an open kitchen, fantastic family-style service and incredible meat dishes.

Batik
MODERN SPANISH €€

(☑952 22 10 45; www.batikmalaga.com; Calle Alcazabilla 12; mains €12-20; ⊙10am-midnight; 🖤) Located on the top floor of a hostel, views don't get much better than this: an outdoor terrace overlooking the Alcazaba across the way. The cuisine combines art-on-a-plate good looks with innovative culinary flair in the style of grilled beef with juniper-scented chocolate jus. Reservations recommended.

Al Yamal
MOROCCAN €€

(Calle Blasco de Garay 7; mains €9-12; ⊙noon-3pm & 7-11pm Mon-Sat) In the heart of the buzzing Soho *barrio* (district), this family-run restaurant serves delicious authentic Moroccan cuisine, including tagines, couscous, hummus and *kefta* (meatballs). The dining room has just six tables and is decorated with warm Moroccan colours and fabrics; finish off your meal with a mint tea delicately spiced with the essence of orange blossom.

El Balneario de los Baños del Carmen
SEAFOOD €€

(www.elbalneariomalaga.com; Calle Bolivia 40, La Malagueta; mains €8-15; ⊙11am-9pm Sun-Wed, to 2am Thu-Sat; P🖤) A wonderful place to sit outside on a warm balmy evening and share a plate of prawns or grilled sardines, along with some long, cold beverages. It

LOCAL KNOWLEDGE

TAPAS TRAIL

The pleasures of Málaga are essentially undemanding, easy to arrange and cheap. One of the best is a slow crawl around the city's numerous tapas bars and old bodegas (cellars).

El Piyayo (📞952 22 90 57; www.entreplatos.es; Calle Granada 36; raciones €6-10; ⊙12.30pm-midnight) A popular, traditionally tiled bar and restaurant, famed for its *pescaitos fritos* (fried fish) and typical local tapas, including wedges of crumbly Manchego cheese, the ideal accompaniment to a glass of hearty Rioja wine.

Uvedoble Taberna (www.uvedobletaberna.com; Calle Císter 15; tapas €2.70; ⊙12.30-4pm & 8pm-midnight Mon-Sat; 🛜) If you are seeking something a little more contemporary, head to this popular spot with its innovative take on traditional tapas.

La Rebaná (www.larebana.com; Calle Molina Lario 5; raciones €7-12; ⊙12.30-5pm & 7.30pm-midnight Mon-Fri, 12.30pm-1am Sat & Sun) A great, noisy and central tapas bar. The dark wood-clad interior (with its wrought-iron gallery) creates an inviting ambience. Goats' cheese with cherries, foie gras and cured meats are among the offerings.

Pepa y Pepe (📞615 656984; www.barpepaypepe.com; Calle Calderería 9; tapas €1.50-2, raciones €3.60-5.50; ⊙12.30-4.30pm & 7.30pm-12.30am) A snug tapas bar that brims with young diners enjoying tapas such as *calamares fritos* (battered squid) and fried green peppers.

Gorki (www.grupogorki.com; Calle Strachan 6; mains €9-12; ⊙12.30pm-midnight) A tastefully decorated tapas bar for enjoying sophisticated small bites such as miniburgers and sweetbreads encased in light flaky pastry.

was built in 1918 to cater to Málaga's bourgeoisie and is rekindling its past as one of the city's most celebrated venues for socialising.

El Chinitas
ANDALUCIAN €€€

(📞952 21 09 72; Calle Moreno Monroy; mains €16-25; ⊙noon-midnight) This longstanding popular restaurant offers a menu of solidly traditional Andalucian cuisine with an emphasis on meat and fish dishes; the oxtail is a speciality. The atmosphere is elegant old world with sumptuous tile-work, twinkling chandeliers, and superb service and attention to detail.

🍷 Drinking & Nightlife

The best bar hop areas are from Plaza de la Merced in the northeast to Calle Carretería in the northwest, plus Plaza Mitjana and Plaza de Uncibay.

Los Patios de Beatas
WINE BAR

(Calle Beatas 43; ⊙1-5pm & 8pm-midnight Mon-Sat, 1-6pm Sun; 🛜) Two 18th-century mansions have metaphorphised into this sumptuous space where you can sample fine wines from a selection reputed to be the most extensive in town. Stained-glass windows and beautiful resin tables inset with mosaics and shells add to the overall art-infused atmosphere. Innovative tapas and *raciones* are also served.

La Tetería
TEAHOUSE

(www.la-teteria.com; Calle San Agustín 9; speciality teas €2.50; ⊙9am-midnight Mon-Sat) Serves heaps of aromatic and classic teas, herbal infusions, coffees and juices, with teas ranging from peppermint to '*antidepresivo*'. Sit outside and marvel at the beautiful church opposite or stay inside to enjoy the wafting incense and background music.

Casa Lola
BAR

(Calle Granada 46; ⊙11am-4pm & 7pm-midnight) Fronted by traditional blue-and-white tiles, this sophisticated spot specialises in vermouth on tap, served ice cold and costing just a couple of euros. Grab a pew on one of the tall stools and peruse the arty decor and clientele.

Antigua Casa de Guardia
BAR

(www.antiguacasadeguardia.net; Alameda Principal 18; ⊙11am-midnight) This atmospheric old tavern dates to 1840 and is the oldest bar in Málaga. The peeling custard-coloured paintwork, black-and-white photographs of local boy Picasso and elderly bar staff look fittingly antique. Try the dark brown, sherry-like *seco* (dry) Málaga wine or the romantically named *lágrima tranañejo* (very old tear).

Bodegas El Pimpi
BAR

(www.bodegabarelpimpi.com; Calle Granada 62; ⊙ 11am-2am; 🕾) This rambling bar is an institution in this town. The interior encompasses a warren of rooms with a courtyard and open terrace overlooking the Roman amphitheatre. Walls are decorated with historic feria posters and photos of visitors, while the enormous barrels are signed by more well-known folk, including Tony Blair and Antonio Banderas. Tapas and meals are also available.

☆ Entertainment

Clarence Jazz Club
LIVE MUSIC

(📞 951 91 80 87; www.clarencejazzclub.com; Calle Cañón 5; €5; ⊙ 8pm-2am Wed & Thu, 4pm-4am Fri & Sat) Enjoy quality jazz gigs at this intimate club across from the cathedral. It's advisable to reserve a table at weekends.

Peña Juan Breva
FLAMENCO

(Calle Juan Franquelo 4) You'll feel like a gate-crasher at someone else's party at this private *peña*, but persevere; the flamenco is *muy puro*. Watch guitarists who play like they've got 24 fingers and listen to singers who bellow forth as if their heart had been broken the previous night. There's no set schedule. Ask about dates when/if you visit the onsite Museo de Arte Flamenco (p685).

Kelipe
FLAMENCO

(📞 692 829885; www.kelipe.net; Muro de Puerta Nueva 10; €24-35; ⊙ 9pm show Thu-Sat) Málaga's substantial flamenco heritage has its nexus to the northwest of Plaza de la Merced. This flamenco centre puts on authentic performances Thursday to Saturday at 9.30pm; €24 entry includes two drinks – reserve ahead.

🛍 Shopping

The chic marble-clad Calle Marqués de Larios is increasingly home to designer stores and boutiques. In the surrounding streets are family-owned small shops in handsomely restored old buildings, selling everything from flamenco dresses to local sweet Málaga wine. Don't miss the fabulous daily market **Mercado Atarazanas** (Calle Atarazanas; ℗).

Alfajar
ARTS & CRAFTS

(www.alfajar.es; Calle Císter 3; ⊙ 10am-2pm & 5-8pm Mon-Fri, to 2pm Sat) Perfect for hand-crafted Andalucian ceramics produced by local artisans. You can find traditional designs and glazes, as well as more modern, arty and individualistic pieces.

ℹ Information

Municipal Tourist Office (Plaza de la Marina; ⊙ 9am-8pm Mar-Sep, to 6pm Oct-Feb) Offers a range of city maps and booklets. It also operates information kiosks at the Alcazaba entrance (Calle Alcazabilla), at the main train station (Explanada de la Estación), on Plaza de la Merced and on the eastern beaches (El Palo and La Malagueta).

Regional Tourist Office (www.andalucia.org; Plaza de la Constitución 7; ⊙ 9.30am-7.30pm Mon-Fri, 10am-7pm Sat, 10am-2pm Sun) Located in a stunning 18th-century former Jesuit college with year-round art exhibitions, this small tourist office carries a range of information, including maps of the regional cities.

ℹ Getting There & Away

BUS

The **bus station** (📞 952 35 00 61; www.estabus. emtsam.es; Paseo de los Tilos) is 1km southwest of the city centre, with links to all major cities in Spain.

Destinations include the following, note that the prices listed are the minimum quoted for the route.

DESTINATION	FARE	DURATION	FREQUENCY
Almería	€19	4¾hr	8 daily
Cádiz	€27	4hr	3 daily
Córdoba	€12	3-4hr	4 daily
Granada	€12	2hr	18 daily
Jaén	€20	3¼hr	4 daily
Madrid airport	€45	10hr	5 daily
Seville	€19	2¾hr	6 daily

TRAIN

The **Maria Zambrano (Málaga-Renfe) train station** (www.renfe.es) is near the bus station. Destinations include Córdoba (€26, 2½ hours, 18 daily), Seville (€24, 2¾ hours, 11 daily) and Madrid (€80, 2½ hours, 10 daily). Note that for Córdoba and Seville the daily schedule includes faster trains at roughly double the cost.

ℹ Getting Around

TO/FROM THE AIRPORT

Málaga's **airport** (AGP; 📞 952 04 88 38; www. aena.es), the main international gateway to Andalucía, is 9km southwest of the city centre. It is a major hub in southern Spain, serving top global carriers as well as budget airlines.

Bus 75 to the city centre (€1.50, 20 minutes) leaves from outside the arrivals hall every 20 minutes, from 7am to midnight. The bus to the airport leaves from the western end of Paseo del Parque, and from outside the bus and train stations, about every half-hour from 6.30am to 11.30pm.

Trains run every 20 minutes from 6.50am to 11.54pm to the **María Zambrano station** (www.renfe.es; Explanada de la Estación) and the Málaga-Centro station beside the Río Guadalmedina. Departures from the city to the airport are every 20 minutes from 5.30am to 11.30pm.

A taxi from the airport to the city centre costs around €20.

BUS

Useful buses around town (€1.35 for all trips around the centre) include bus 11 to El Palo, bus 34 to El Pedregalejo and El Palo, and bus 35 to Castillo de Gibralfaro, all departing from Avenida de Cervantes. Destinations further afield include Antequera (€7.45, one hour, nine daily) and Ronda (€12.75, 2½ hours, nine daily).

METRO

Metro Málaga (www.metrodemalaga.info) opened in 2015 with two lines linking the suburbs to the east with Málaga University (single, €1.35), which formerly suffered from serious traffic congestion. More lines are being added, including one that will run to the city centre; check the website for updates.

Costa del Sol

While the Costa del Sol has long attracted both foreign residents and tourists to its shores, it has also attracted a fair amount of negative press over the years, mainly related to mass development and the spiralling cost of a pint. The truth is that, while there has been unsightly overbuilding here, there are still places that are genuinely picturesque and traditional, and a world away from the soulless urbanisations and Sid-and-Dot-style pubs.

In the resorts of the Costa del Sol, you'll find an abundance of hotels with an international flavour and bilingual staff. These will include some of the more well-known chains. Torremolinos alone sports more than 75 accommodation options.

Torremolinos & Benalmádena

POP 128,340

Torremolinos was developed in the 1950s and, while many of the not-so-modern blocks are Stalin-era in their grimness, there remain attractive quarters, such as the La Carihuela. Torremolinos has been known as the Costa del Sol's gay capital since its first gay bar opened in 1962. The highest concentration of gay bars and clubs lies just west of Plaza La Nogalera in the centre.

The adjacent resort of Benalmádena comprises a fairly bland built-up coastal stretch with the highlights being the **Puerto Deportivo** (leisure port), and the relatively unspoiled **Benalmádena Pueblo** (village) inland. Another resort, **Arroyo de la Miel**, also falls under the Benalmádena banner and is best known as being home to the Tivoli theme park.

Sights

La Carihuela   AREA

La Carihuela, flanking the beach, was formerly the fishing district of Torremolinos and is one of the few parts of town that has not suffered from rampant overdevelopment. The beachside promenade is lined with lowrise shops, bars and restaurants, and is one of the most popular destinations for *malagueños* to enjoy fresh seafood at weekends.

Buddhist Stupa   MUSEUM, MONUMENT

(Benalmádena Pueblo; ⊙10am-2pm & 3.30-6.30pm Tue-Sat, 10am-7.30pm Sun; P) FREE

The largest Buddhist stupa in Europe is in Benalmádena Pueblo. It rises up, majestically out of place, on the outskirts of the village, surrounded by new housing and with sweeping coastal views. The lofty interior is lined with exquisitely executed devotional paintings.

Activities

Tivoli World   AMUSEMENT PARK

(www.tivolicostadelsol.com; Arroyo de la Miel; €8, Supertivolino ticket €15; ⊙4pm-midnight Apr-Sep)

The oldest and largest amusement park in Málaga province, with various rides and slides, as well as daily dance, flamenco and children's events. Consider the good-value 'Supertivolino', which covers admission and unlimited access to some 35 rides.

Sleeping & Eating

Hostal Guadalupe   HOSTAL €€

(☑952 38 19 37; www.hostalguadalupe.com; Calle del Peligro, Torremolinos; s €35-70, d €45-80, apt €55-90; 🖤) A superb choice across from the beach; rooms are plain but comfortable and several have terraces overlooking the sea. The apartment has kitchen facilities that are great for longer stays. The staff are extremely attentive; they will park your car for you if you can't find a spot and advise on what's going on in town. There is no lift.

Rincón de la Paquita SEAFOOD €
(Calle del Cauce, Arroyo de la Miel, Benalmádena; mains €8-9, raciones €5-6; ☺noon-11pm) This place looks like it belongs in a fishing village on the beach rather than a tourist-driven resort. Squeezed into a narrow pedestrian street, with plastic tables, football on the telly and a blackboard of specials, locals rate this place as having the best seafood in town; order a selection of *raciones* to share.

★**La Consula** MODERN SPANISH €€€
(☑952 436 026; www.laconsula.com; Finca Consula Churriana; set menu €27.50; ☺1-4pm Mon-Fri Jul-Sep) This is one of the coast's top professional culinary schools. Located around 6km northwest of Torremolinos in Churriana, the daily menu reflects an innovative twist on traditional Spanish dishes with beautifully crafted plates and faultlessly delicious flavours.

ℹ Information

Tourist Office (www.pmdt.es; Plaza de la Independencia, Torremolinos; ☺9.30am-1.30pm Mon-Fri) There are additional tourist kiosks at Playamar and La Carihuela.

ℹ Getting There & Away

BUS
Avanza (www.avanzabus.com) runs services from Málaga (€2.50, 25 minutes, 14 daily) and from Marbella (€5.50, 1¼ hours, 24 daily).

TRAIN
Trains (www.renfe.es) run to Torremolinos and Arroyo de la Miel-Benalmádena every 20 minutes from Málaga (€2.35, 20 minutes) from 5.30am to 10.30pm, continuing on to the final stop, Fuengirola.

Fuengirola

POP 78,000
Fuengirola is a genuine Spanish working town, as well as being firmly on the tourist circuit. It attracts mainly northern European visitors and also has a large foreign-resident population, many of whom arrived here in the '60s – and stayed (yes, there are a few grey ponytails around). The beach stretches

for a mighty 7km, encompassing the former fishing quarter of Los Boliches.

◎ Sights

Biopark ZOO
(☑952 66 63 01; www.bioparcfuengirola.es; Avenida Camilo José Cela; adult/child €18/13; ☺10am-sunset; P) This is a zoo that treats its animals very well with spacious enclosures, conservation and breeding programs, plus educational activities. There is also a bat cave, reptile enclosure, cafes for refreshments and a large gift shop.

✕ Eating

La Cepa SEAFOOD €
(Plaza Yate 21; tapas €3, mains €7-10; ☺noon-4pm & 7-11pm Mon-Sat, to 3.30pm Sun) Hidden away on an attractive bar-and-restaurant-lined square, the menu concentrates on seafood, including such tentacle ticklers as fried squid, and prawns wrapped in bacon.

ℹ Information

Tourist Office (www.visitfuengirola.com; Paseo Jesús Santos Rein; ☺9.30am-1.30pm Mon-Fri; ☎) Has a wealth of information on the town.

ℹ Getting There & Away

BUS
Avanza (www.avanzabus.com) runs bus services including to Fuengirola from Málaga (€4.20, 40 minutes, 15 daily) and from Estepona (€8.75, 1¾ hours, 11 daily).

CAR
A toll road (AP7) connects Fuengirola with Estepona (€14), providing a (costly) alternative to the hazardous N340 coast road.

TRAIN
Trains (www.renfe.es) run every 20 minutes to Málaga from 6.20am to 12.40am, with stops including the airport and Torremolinos.

Marbella

POP 136.322
Marbella is the Costa del Sol's classiest (and most expensive) resort. This wealth glitters most brightly along the Golden Mile, a tiara of star-studded clubs, restaurants and hotels stretching from Marbella to Puerto Banús, the flashiest marina on the Costa del Sol, where black-tinted Mercs slide along a quayside of luxury yachts. Marbella has a magnificent natural setting, sheltered by the beautiful Sierra Blanca mountains, as well

as a surprisingly attractive *casco antiguo* (old town) replete with narrow lanes and well-tended flower boxes.

Marbella has a long history and has been home to Phoenicians, Visigoths and Romans, as well as being the most important town on the coast during Moorish times. Arab kings still own homes here, as do plenty of rich and famous people, such as native *malagueño* Antonio Banderas.

◎ Sights

Plaza de los Naranjos PLAZA
At the heart of Marbella's *casco antiguo* is pretty Plaza de los Naranjos, dating back to 1485, with its tropical plants, palms, orange trees and, inevitably, overpriced bars.

Museo Ralli MUSEUM
(www.therallimuseums.com; Urbanización Coral Beach; ⊙10am-2pm Tue-Sat) FREE This superb private art museum exhibits paintings by primarily Latin American and European artists in bright well-lit galleries. Part of a nonprofit foundation, its exhibits include sculptures by Henry Moore and Salvador Dalí, vibrant contemporary paintings by Argentinian surrealist Alicia Carletti and Cuban Wilfredo Lam, plus works by Joan Miró, Chagall and Chirico.

Museo del Grabado Español MUSEUM
(Calle Hospital Bazán; €3; ⊙10am-2pm & 5.30-8.30pm) This small art museum in the old town includes works by some of the great masters, including Picasso, Joan Miró and Salvador Dalí, among other, primarily Spanish painters.

⌂ Sleeping & Eating

★ Hotel Linda Marbella HOTEL €€
(☑952 85 71 71; www.lindamarbella.com; Calle Ancha 21; s €25-38, d €40-82; ☼) Look for the bright-blue shutters and crimson bougainvillea; this perfectly placed small hotel is in the centre of the old town and offers very comfortable rooms (albeit with very little storage space), set around a small central patio festooned with ivy. Bag one with a terrace overlooking the picturesque pedestrian street.

Claude BOUTIQUE HOTEL €€€
(☑952 90 08 40; www.hotelclaudemarbella.com; Calle San Francisco 5; d/ste €280/330; ❉☼) Situated in the quieter upper part of town, this sumptuous hotel is housed in a 17th-century mansion of some historical significance

– it was the former summer home of Napoleon's third wife. The decor successfully marries contemporary flourishes with the original architecture, while claw-foot tubs and crystal chandeliers add to the classic historical feel.

El Estrecho TAPAS €
(Calle San Lázaro; tapas €2.50-3.50; ⊙noon-midnight) It's always crammed, so elbow your way to a space in the small back dining room and order from a massive menu that includes tapas such as *salmorejo* (Córdoba-style thick gazpacho) and seafood salad.

★ Casanis BISTRO €€€
(☑952 90 04 50; www.casanis-restaurante-marbella.es; Calle Ancha 8; mains €20-25; ⊙10.30am-4pm & 7.30-11pm Mon-Sat) Situated on one of the prettiest streets in town, step into the dining room and be transported to a Tintin fantasy world, with walls covered in cartoon-style murals, and interspersed with (real) leafy ferns and plants. The cuisine spans the seas with dishes such as Bourgogne snails, beef Wellington and bluefin tuna from Barbate on the Cadíz coast: all prepared with culinary flair.

◖ Drinking & Nightlife

For the most spirited bars and nightlife, head to Puerto Banús, 6km west of Marbella. In town, the best area is around the small Puerto Deportivo. There are also some beach clubs open only in summer.

❶ Information

Tourist Office (www.marbellaexclusive.com; Plaza de los Naranjos; ⊙9am-8pm Mon-Fri, 10am-2pm Sat) Has plenty of leaflets and a good town map.

❶ Getting There & Away

Buses to Fuengirola (€3.75, one hour), Puerto Banús (€2.10, 20 minutes) and Estepona (€3.30, one hour) leave about every 30 minutes from Avenida Ricardo Soriano.

Estepona

POP 67,100
Estepona was one of the first resorts to attract foreign residents and tourists some 45 years ago and, despite the surrounding development, the centre of the town still has a cosy old-fashioned feel – for good reason: the town's roots date back to the 4th century. Centuries later during the Moorish era,

Estepona was an important and prosperous town due to its strategic proximity to the Straits of Gibraltar.

Estepona is steadily extending its promenade to Marbella; at its heart is the pleasant Playa de la Rada beach. The Puerto Deportivo is the centre of the nightlife, especially at weekends, and is also excellent for water sports, as well as bars and restaurants.

🛏 Sleeping & Eating

Hostal El Pilar   HOSTAL €
(☑ 952 80 00 18; www.hostalelpilar.es; Plaza de las Flores 10, Estepona; s/d €35/50; ❋) This is a charming old-fashioned *hostal* with original tile-work and a central courtyard. Wedding photos, plants and antiques contribute to the homey feel. The position is ideal, right on the town's most historic square.

La Esquina del Arte   TAPAS €
(Calle Villa; tapas €2-3; ⊙ noon-midnight Mon-Sat; 🕾) This place may be in the centre of the historic centre but there is nothing old fashioned about the creative tapas and *pintxos* (Basque tapas) here. Expect tasty bites such as prawns wrapped in flaky pastry, pâté with fig jam, and peppers stuffed with salt cod. It has excellent wines by the glass.

La Escollera   SEAFOOD €
(Puerto Pesquero, Puerto Deportivo; mains €7-10; ⊙ 1-4.30pm & 8-11.30pm Tue-Sat, 1-4.30pm Sun) Locals in the know arrive in shoals to dine on arguably the freshest and best seafood in town. Located in the port, the atmosphere is no-frills basic with plastic tables and paper cloths. When the fish tastes this good and the beer is this cold – who cares?

Venta Garcia   MODERN EUROPEAN €€
(☑ 952 89 41 91; Carretera de Casares Km 7; mains €12-18; ℗) Venta Garcia specialises in superbly presented and conceived dishes using local produce. There is an emphasis on game and venison; rabbit and quail are cooked to perfection and served with simple sides like wild asparagus with fresh lemon. The countryside views are similarly sublime, but the word is out, so be sure to reserve – especially on weekends.

It's on the road to Casares, around 7km from the centre of town.

ℹ Information

Tourist Office (www.estepona.es; Plaza de las Flores; ⊙ 9am-8pm Mon-Fri) Located on an

PICASSO IN MIJAS

The **Centro de Arte Contemporáneo de Mijas** (CAC; www.cacmijas.info; Calle Málaga 28; €3; ⊙ 10am-7pm Tue-Sun) art museum houses an extraordinary exhibition of Picasso ceramics (the second-largest collection in the world), plus some exquisite Dalí bronze figurines, glassware and bas-relief. There are also temporary exhibitions. Note that, despite the name, this museum is not affiliated with Málaga's CAC museum.

historical square, it has brochures and a decent map of town.

ℹ Getting There & Away

There are regular buses to Marbella (€3.30, one hour), and Málaga (€8, two hours).

Ardales & El Chorro

Fifty kilometres northwest of Málaga, the Río Guadalhorce carves its way through the awesome **Garganta del Chorro** (El Chorro gorge). Also called the Desfiladero de los Gaitanes, the gorge is about 4km long, as much as 400m deep and sometimes just 10m wide. Its sheer walls, and other rock faces nearby, are a major magnet for rock climbers, with hundreds of bolted climbs snaking their way up the limestone cliffs.

The pleasant, quiet town of Ardales (population 2700) is the main centre and a good base for exploring further afield. The picturesque **Embalse del Conde del Guadalhorce** is 6km from here – a huge reservoir that dominates the landscape and is noted for its carp fishing. However, most people aim for the hiking and climbing mecca of El Chorro, a small village in the midst of a spectacular and surreal landscape of soaring limestone crags. There are also a couple of easy circular hikes that start from the reservoir, including the 5km **Sendero del Guaitenejo**.

Caminito del Rey   HIKING
(www.caminitodelrey.info; €6; ⊙ 10am-6pm) El Chorro gorge is particularly famous for the Caminito del Rey (King's Path) so named because Alfonso XIII walked along it when he opened the Guadalhorce hydroelectric dam in 1921. The path had fallen into severe

disrepair by the late 1990s and became famously known as the most dangerous pathway in the world. After extensive restoration and a €5.5 million tab, it reopened in March 2015 and is now reputedly entirely safe and open to anyone with a reasonable head for heights.

Antequera

POP 42,000 / ELEV 577M

Antequera is a fascinating town, both architecturally and historically, yet it has somehow avoided being on the coach-tour circuit – which only adds to its charms. The three major influences in the region, Roman, Moorish and Spanish, have left the town with a rich tapestry of architectural gems. The highlight is the opulent Spanish-baroque style that gives the town its character and which the civic authorities have worked hard to restore and maintain. There is also an astonishing number of churches here – more than 30, many with wonderfully ornate interiors. Little wonder that the town is often referred to as the 'Florence of Andalucía'.

And there's more! Some of Europe's largest and oldest dolmens (burial chambers built with huge slabs of rock), from around 2500 BC to 1800 BC, can be found just outside the town's centre.

The flip side to all this antiquity is a vibrant city centre with some of the best tapas bars this side of Granada.

◎ Sights

★ Alcazaba   FORTRESS
(adult/child incl Colegiata de Santa María la Mayor €6/3; ◷ 10am-7pm Mon-Sat, 10.30am-3pm Sun) Favoured by the Granada emirs of Islamic times, Antequera's hilltop Moorish fortress has a fascinating history and covers a massive 62,000 sq metres. The main approach to the hilltop is from Plaza de San Sebastián, up the stepped Cuesta de San Judas and then through an impressive archway, the Arco de los Gigantes, built in 1585 and formerly bearing huge sculptures of Hercules. All that is left today are the Roman inscriptions on the stones.

Museo Conventual de las
Descalzas   MUSEUM
(Plaza de las Descalzas; compulsory guided tour €3.30; ◷ 10.30am-2pm & 5-8pm Tue-Sat, 10am-1.30pm Sun) This museum, in the 17th-century convent of the Carmelitas Descalzas (barefoot Carmelites), approximately 150m east of town's Museo Municipal, displays highlights of Antequera's rich religious-art heritage. Outstanding works include a painting by Lucas Giordano of St Teresa of Ávila (the 16th-century founder of the Carmelitas Descalzas), a bust of the Dolorosa by Pedro de Mena and a *Virgen de Belén* sculpture by La Roldana.

Dolmens   ARCHAEOLOGICAL SITE
(Cerro Romeral; ◷ 9am-7.30pm Tue-Sat, to 3.30pm Sun) FREE The Dolmen de Menga and Dolmen de Viera, both dating from around 2500 BC, are 1km from the town centre in a small, wooded park beside the road that leads northeast to the A45. Head down Calle Encarnación from the central Plaza de San Sebastián and follow the signs.

A third chamber, the Dolmen del Romeral (Cerro Romeral; ◷ 9am-6pm Tue-Sat, 9.30am-2.30pm Sun) FREE, is 5km further out of town. It is of later construction (around 1800 BC) and features the use of small stones for its walls.

Iglesia del Carmen   CHURCH
(Plaza del Carmen; €2; ◷ 11am-1.30pm & 4.30-5.45pm Tue-Fri, 11am-2pm Sat & Sun) Only the most jaded would fail to be impressed by the Iglesia del Carmen and its marvellous 18th-century Churrigueresque retable. Magnificently carved in red pine by Antequera's own Antonio Primo, it's spangled with statues of angels by Diego Márquez y Vega, and saints, popes and bishops by José de Medina. While the main altar is unpainted, the rest of the interior is a dazzle of colour and design, painted to resemble traditional tilework.

Colegiata de
Santa María la Mayor   CHURCH
(Plaza Santa María; adult/child incl Alcazaba €6/3; ◷ 10am-7pm Mon-Fri, 10.30am-3pm Sun) Just below the Alcazaba is the large 16th-century Colegiata de Santa María la Mayor. This church-cum-college played an important part in Andalucía's 16th-century humanist movement, and boasts a beautiful Renaissance facade, some lovely fluted stone columns inside and a Mudéjar *artesonado* (a ceiling of interlaced beams with decorative insertions). It also plays host to some excellent musical events and exhibitions.

✦ Festivals & Events

Semana Santa
HOLY WEEK

One of the most traditional celebrations in Andalucía; items from the town's treasure trove are actually used in the religious processions.

🛏 Sleeping & Eating

Local specialities you'll encounter on almost every Antequera menu include *porra antequerana* (a thick and delicious garlicky soup, similar to gazpacho); *bienmesabe* (literally 'tastes good to me'; a sponge dessert); and *angelorum* (a dessert incorporating meringue, sponge and egg yolk). Antequera also does a fine breakfast *mollete* (soft bread roll), served with a choice of fillings.

Hotel Coso Viejo
HOTEL €

(☑ 952 70 50 45; www.hotelcosoviejo.es; Calle Encarnación 9; s/d incl breakfast €44/54; P ✳ 🛜) This converted 17th-century neoclassical palace is right in the heart of Antequera, opposite Plaza Coso Viejo and the town museum. The simply furnished rooms are set around a handsome patio with a fountain, and there's an excellent tapas bar and restaurant. No TVs.

Parador de Antequera
HISTORIC HOTEL €€€

(☑ 952 84 02 61; www.parador.es; Paseo García del Olmo; s/d incl breakfast €125/150; P ✳ 🛜 🏊) This *parador* is in a quiet area of parkland north of the bullring and near the bus station. It's comfortably furnished and set in pleasant gardens with wonderful views, especially at sunset.

Rincón de Lola
TAPAS €

(www.rincondelola.net; Calle Encarnación 7; tapas €2, raciones €7; ⊙ noon-11.30pm Tue-Sun) A great place for inexpensive, varied tapas that can give you a taster of local dishes such as *cochinillo* (suckling pig), or *porra antequerana*. There are also piled high *tostas* (open sandwiches on toasted bread) and *raciones* such as tomatoes filled with cheese, salmon, wild mushrooms and prawns.

★ Arte de Cozina
ANDALUCIAN €€

(www.artedecozina.com; Calle Calzada 27-29; mains €12-15, tapas €2; ⊙ 1-11pm) The *simpática* (friendly) owner of this hotel-restaurant has her own garden that provides fresh ingredients for her dishes. Traditional dishes are re-interpreted, like gazpacho made with green asparagus or *porra* with oranges, plus meat, fish, and Antequeran specialities. On Thursday and Friday evenings classical musicians provide entertainment.

ℹ Information

Municipal Tourist Office (☑ 952 70 25 05; www.antequera.es; Plaza de San Sebastián 7; ⊙ 11am-2pm & 5-8pm Mon-Sat, to 2pm Sun) A helpful tourist office with information about the town and region.

ℹ Getting There & Away

BUS

The **bus station** (Paseo Garcí de Olmo) is 1km north of the centre. **Alsa** (www.alsa.es) runs buses to Seville (€14, 2½ hours, five daily), Granada (€9, 1½ hours, five daily), Córdoba (€11, two hours 40 minutes, one daily), Almería (€23,

---

WORTH A TRIP

PARAJE NATURAL TORCAL DE ANTEQUERA

South of Antequera are the weird and wonderful rock formations of the Paraje Natural Torcal de Antequera. A 12-sq-km area of gnarled, serrated and pillared limestone, it formed as a sea bed 150 million years ago and now rises to 1336m (El Torcal). It's otherworldly out here and the air is pure and fresh. There is an **information centre** (☑ 952 24 33 24; www.visitasfuentepiedra.es; ⊙ 10am-9pm) that provides details on walks, and flora and fauna.

Two marked walking trails, the 1.5km Ruta Verde (green route) and the 3km Ruta Amarilla (yellow route) start and end near the information centre. More dramatic views are along the restricted Ruta Rojo (red route), for which guided tours are organised; contact the Antequera tourist office for details. Wear shoes with good tread as the trails are rocky.

To get to El Torcal you will need your own car or a taxi. By car, leave central Antequera along Calle Picadero, which soon joins the Zalea road. After 1km or so you'll see signs on the left to Villanueva de la Concepción. Take this road and, after about 11km, a turn uphill to the right leads to the information centre after 4km.

six hours, one daily) and Málaga (€6, 1½ hours, two daily).

Buses run between Antequera and Fuente de Piedra village (€2.45, 25 minutes, three daily).

TRAIN

The **train station** (www.renfe.es; Avenida de la Estación) is 1.5km north of the centre. Six trains a day run to/from Granada (€11, 1½ hours), and there are four daily to Seville (€18, 1½ hours). Another three run to Málaga or Córdoba, but you'll need to change at Bobadilla.

East of Málaga

The coast east of Málaga, sometimes described as the Costa del Sol Oriental, is less developed than the coast to the west. The suburban sprawl of Málaga extends east into a series of unmemorable and unremarkable seaside towns – Rincón de la Victoria, Torre del Mar, Torrox Costa – which pass in a concrete high-rise blur, before culminating in more attractive Nerja, which has a large population of Brits and Scandinavians.

The area's main redeeming feature is the rugged region of La Axarquía, which is just as stunning as Granada's Las Alpujarras yet, as well as being even more difficult to pronounce (think of taking a chopper to one of those infuriating Scandinavian flatpack stores: 'axe-ikea'), is hardly known. The area is full of great walks, which are less well-known than those in the northwest of the province around Ronda. A 406-sq-km area of these mountains was declared the Parque Natural Sierras de Tejeda, Almijara y Alhama in 1999.

Nerja

POP 20,700

Nerja, 56km east of Málaga with the Sierra Almijara rising behind it, has succeeded in rebuffing developers, allowing its centre to retain a low-rise village charm, despite the proliferation of souvenir shops and day-trippers. At its heart is the perennially beautiful Balcón de Europa, a palm-lined promontory built on the foundations of an old fort, with panoramic views of the cobalt-blue sea flanked by honey-coloured coves.

The town is increasingly popular with package holidaymakers and 'residential tourists', which has pushed it far beyond its old confines. There is significant urbanisation, especially to the east. The holiday atmosphere, and seawater contamination, can be overwhelming from July to September, but the place is more *tranquilo* and the water cleaner the rest of the year.

◎ Sights

★ **Cueva de Nerja**   CAVE
(www.cuevadenerja.es; adult/child €9/5; ⊙ unguided visit 10am-1pm & 4-5.30pm Sep-Jun, 10am-6pm Jul & Aug; guided visit 1-2pm & 5.30-6.30pm Sep-Jun, 11am-noon & 6.30-7.30pm Jul & Aug) The Cueva de Nerja is the big tourist attraction in Nerja, just off the N340, 3km east of town on the slopes of the Sierra Almijara. The enormous 4km-long cave complex, hollowed out by water around five million years ago and once inhabited by Stone Age hunters, is a theatrical wonderland of extraordinary rock formations, subtle shifting colours, and stalactites and stalagmites. Large-scale performances including ballet and flamenco are staged here throughout summer.

Playa Burriana   BEACH
(P) This is Nerja's longest and best beach with plenty of towel space on the sand. You can walk here via picturesque Calle Carabeo, continuing down the steps to the beach and along to Burriana.

Balcón de Europa   VIEWPOINT
The fabulous *balcón* is located at the heart of town, a perennially beautiful sweeping terrace with panoramic views of the sea.

✸ Festivals & Events

Virgen del Carmen   RELIGIOUS
The fishermen's feast day on July 16 is marked with a procession that carries the Virgin in fishing boats.

⌷ Sleeping & Eating

★ **Hotel Carabeo**   HOTEL €€
(☑ 952 52 54 44; www.hotelcarabeo.com; Calle Carabeo 34, Nerja; d/ste incl breakfast from €85/180; ⊙ Apr-Oct; ✱@🔊🏊) Full of stylish antiques and wonderful paintings, this small, family-run seafront hotel is set above manicured terraced gardens. There's also a good restaurant and the pool is on a terrace overlooking the sea. The building is an old school house and is located on one of the prettiest pedestrian streets in town, festooned with colourful bougainvillea.

Hotel Balcón de Europa   HOTEL €€
(☑ 952 52 08 00; www.hotelbalconeuropa.com; Paseo Balcón de Europa 1; s/d €82/115; 🏊) Stealing the position of best digs in town, this

terraced hotel with private room balconies overlooks a snug section of beach lapped by the translucent Mediterranean. A pool, sauna, piano bar and restaurant with a view, all add value.

La Piqueta TAPAS €
(Calle Pintada 8; tapas €2, raciones €4.50-6; ⊙10am-midnight Mon-Sat) There are two very good reasons why this is the most popular tapas bar in town: first, the house wine is excellent, second, you get a free *tapa* with every drink (generally a miniburger; vegetarians can request cheese). On the menu are sturdy classics such as tripe and *huevos estrellados* (literally, smashed eggs) prepared with ham, garlic, potatoes and peppers.

Merendero Ayo SEAFOOD €€
(www.ayonerja.com; Playa Burriana; mains €9-13; ⊙9am-midnight; P 🔹) At this open-air place you can enjoy paella cooked in sizzling pans over an open fire – and even go back for a free second helping. It's run by Ayo, a delightful local character famed for the discovery of the Cueva de Nerja complex. He throws the rice on the *paellera* (paella dish) in a spectacular fashion, amusing all his guests.

ℹ Information

Tourist Office (www.nerja.org; Calle Carmen; ⊙10am-2pm & 6-10pm) Has plenty of useful leaflets.

ℹ Getting There & Away

Alsa (📞 952 52 15 04; www.alsa.es) runs regular buses to/from Málaga (€5.75, 1¾ hours, 23 daily), Marbella (€9.50, 1¼ hours, one daily) and Antequera (€9, 2¼ hours, two daily). There are also buses to Almería and Granada.

Cómpeta
POP 3459

This picturesque village with its panoramic views, steep winding streets and central bar-lined plaza, overlooking the 16th-century church, has long attracted a large mixed foreign population. Not only has this contributed to an active cultural scene, but Cómpeta is also home to one or two above-*pueblo*-average restaurants serving contemporary cuisine. It also has a couple of charity shops (rare in Spain) and a foreign-language bookshop. The village is a good base for hiking and other similar adrenalin-fuelled activities.

ℹ Getting There & Away

Three buses travel daily from Málaga to Cómpeta (€4.60, 1½ hours), stopping via Torre del Mar.

La Axarquía

The Axarquía region is riven by deep valleys lined with terraces and irrigation channels that date to Islamic times – nearly all the villages dotted around the olive-, almond- and vine-planted hillsides date from this era. The wild inaccessible landscapes, especially around the Sierra de Tejeda, made it a stronghold of *bandoleros* who roamed the mountains without fear or favour. Nowadays, its chief attractions include fantastic scenery; pretty white villages; strong, sweet, local wine made from sun-dried grapes; and good walking in spring and autumn.

The 'capital' of La Axarquía, **Vélez Málaga**, 4km north of Torre del Mar, is a busy but unspectacular town, although its restored hilltop castle is worth a look. From Vélez the A335 heads north past the turquoise Embalse de la Viñuela reservoir and up through the **Boquete de Zafarraya** (a dramatic cleft in the mountains) towards Granada. One bus a day makes its way over this road between Torre del Mar and Granada.

Some of the most dramatic La Axarquía scenery is up around the highest villages of **Alfarnate** (925m) and **Alfarnatejo** (858m), with towering, rugged crags such as Tajo de Gomer and Tajo de Doña Ana rising to their south.

You can pick up information on La Axarquía at the tourist offices in Málaga, Nerja, Torre del Mar or Cómpeta. Prospective walkers should ask for the leaflet on walks in the Parque Natural Sierras de Tejeda, Almijara y Alhama. Good maps for walkers are *Mapa Topográfico de Sierra Tejeda* and *Mapa Topográfico de Sierra Almijara* by Miguel Ángel Torres Delgado, both at 1:25,000. You can also follow the links at www.axarquia.es for walks in the region.

SOUTHERN CÁDIZ PROVINCE & GIBRALTAR

The southern tip of Cádiz province is called the Campo de Gibraltar and is the southernmost part of Europe. Stretching from Tarifa in the west to San Roque in the east, it's famous for its wind farms and as a desembarkation point for Morocco, clearly visible across the Strait of Gibraltar.

Tarifa

POP 13,500

Tarifa's tip-of-Spain location, where the Mediterranean and the Atlantic meet, gives it a different climate and character to the rest of Andalucía. Stiff Atlantic winds draw in surfers, windsurfers and kitesurfers who, in turn, lend this ancient yet deceptively small settlement a refreshingly laid-back international vibe. Tarifa is the last stop in Spain before Morocco, and it's also a taste of things to come. With its winding whitewashed streets and tangible North African feel, the walled windswept old town could easily pass for Chefchaouen or Essaouira. It's no secret, however, and, in August especially, the town is packed – that's half the fun.

Tarifa may be as old as Phoenician Cádiz and was definitely a Roman settlement. It takes its name from Tarif ibn Malik, who led a Muslim raid in AD 710, the year before the main Islamic invasion of the peninsula.

Sights

Tarifa's narrow old-town streets, mostly of Islamic origin, hint at Morocco. Pass through the Mudéjar Puerta de Jerez, built after the Reconquista, then pop into the action-packed Mercado de Abastos (Calle Colón; ☺8.30am-2pm Tue-Sat) before winding your way to the mainly 16th-century Iglesia de San Mateo (Calle Sancho IV El Bravo; ☺8.45am-1pm Mon, 8.45am-1pm & 6-8pm Tue-Sat, 10am-1pm & 7-8.30pm Sun). Head south of the church along Calle Coronel Moscardó then up Calle Aljaranda; the Miramar (atop part of the castle walls) has spectacular views across to Africa.

★Castillo de Guzmán   CASTLE
(Calle Guzmán El Bueno; adult/child €2/0.60; ☺11am-2.30pm & 4-9pm May–mid-Sep, to 6.30pm mid-Sep–Apr) Though built in 960 on the orders of Cordoban caliph Abd ar-Rahman III, this restored fortress is named after Reconquista hero Guzmán El Bueno. In 1294, when threatened with the death of his captured son unless he surrendered the castle to Merenid attackers from Morocco, El Bueno threw down his own dagger for his son's execution. Guzmán's descendants later became the Duques de Medina Sidonia, one of Spain's most powerful families.

 Activities

Diving

Aventura Marina   DIVING
(☑956 68 19 32; www.aventuramarina.org; Recinto Portuario) Diving in Tarifa is usually done from boats around Isla de las Palomas, where shipwrecks, corals, dolphins and octopuses await. Port-based Aventura Marina offers three-hour 'baptisms' (€75) and equipment rental (€50).

Horse Riding

There's nothing quite like contemplating Tarifa's wind-lashed coastline (or heading off into the hilly hinterland) on horseback. A one-hour beach ride along Playa de los Lances costs €30, a two-hour beach-and-mountain ride costs €50, while three-/five-hour rides start at €70/80. One recommended place, with excellent English-speaking guides, is Aventura Ecuestre (☑956 23 66 32; www.aventuraecuestre.com; Hotel Dos Mares, Ctra N340 Km 79.5), which also has private lessons (one hour €30), pony rides for kids (half-/one hour €15/30) and five-hour rides into the Parque Natural Los Alcornocales. Molino El Mastral (☑679 193503; www.mastral.com; Ctra Santuario Virgen de la Luz; per hr €30), 5km northwest of Tarifa, is also excellent.

Whale-Watching

The waters off Tarifa are one of the best places in Europe to see whales and dolphins as they swim between the Atlantic and the Mediterranean from April to October; sightings of some kind are almost guaranteed during these months. In addition to striped and bottlenose dolphins, long-finned pilot whales, orcas (killer whales) and sperm whales, you may also spot endangered fin whales and common dolphins. Sperm whales swim the Strait of Gibraltar from April to August; the best months for orcas are July and August. Find out more at Tarifa's brand-new Centro de Interpretación de Cetáceos (Avenida Fuerzas Armadas 17; ☺11am-3pm Tue-Sun Mar-Oct) FREE.

FIRMM   WHALE-WATCHING
(☑956 62 70 08; www.firmm.org; Calle Pedro Cortés 4; adult/child €30/20; ☺Apr-Oct) Of Tarifa's dozens of whale-watching outfits, not-for-profit FIRMM is a good choice. Its primary purpose is to study the whales, record data and encourage environmentally sensitive tours.

TARIFA: BEACH BLISS

Jazzed up by the colourful kites and sails of kitesurfers and windsurfers whizzing across turquoise waves, the exquisite bleach-blonde beaches that stretch northwest from Tarifa along the N340 are some of Andalucía's most beautiful. In summer they fill up with sun-kissed beach lovers and chill-out bars, though the relentless winds can be a hassle. If you tire of lazing on the sand, kitesurfing, windsurfing and horse riding await.

Playa Chica On the isthmus leading out to Isla de las Palomas at the southernmost tip of Tarifa town, tiny Playa Chica is more sheltered than other local beaches.

Playa de los Lances This spectacular, broad sweep of sand stretches for 7km northwest from Tarifa. The low dunes behind it are a *paraje natural* (protected natural area); you can hike across them on the 1.5km **Sendero de los Lances**, signposted towards the northwest end of Calle Batalla del Salado.

Playa de Valdevaqueros Sprawling between 7km and 10km northwest of Tarifa, to the great white dune at Punta Paloma, Valdevaqueros is one of Tarifa's most popular kitesurfing spots.

Punta Paloma Punta Paloma, 10km northwest of Tarifa, is famous for its huge sand dune. At its far western end, you can lather yourself up in a natural mud bath.

Kitesurfing & Windsurfing

Tarifa's legendary winds have turned the town into one of Europe's premier windsurfing and kitesurfing destinations. The most popular strip is along the coast between Tarifa and Punta Paloma, 10km northwest. Over 30 places offer equipment hire and classes, from beginner to expert level. The best months are May, June and September, but bear in mind that the choppy seas aren't always beginner's territory.

ION Club   KITESURFING, WINDSURFING
(☑ 619 340913; www.ion-club.net/en; Playa de Valdevaqueros; ☺ Mar-Dec) Recommended daily group/private windsurfing and kitesurfing classes at beginner, intermediate or advanced level, along with paddle-boarding (per hour €25). Windsurfing is usually from their other centre at the Hurricane Hotel.

Gisela Pulido Pro Center   KITESURFING
(☑ 608 577711; www.giselapulidoprocenter.com; Calle Mar Adriático 22; 3hr group courses per person €70) World champion Gisela Pulido's highly rated kitesurfing school offers year-round group/private courses, including six-hour 'baptisms' (€140) and nine-hour 'complete' courses (€210), in Spanish, French, English and German.

Hot Stick Kite School   KITESURFING, SURFING
(☑ 647 155516; www.hotsticktarifa.com; Calle Batalla del Salado 41; 1-day courses €70-80, kit rental per day €60; ☺ Mar–mid-Nov) Daily three- to four-hour kitesurfing classes, plus two- to five-day courses (Spanish, English, French and German). Also two-hour surfing and paddle-boarding sessions (€50).

Club Mistral   WINDSURFING, KITESURFING
(☑ 619 340913; www.club-mistral.com; Hurricane Hotel, Ctra N340 Km 78; equipment rental per day €90; ☺ Mar-Dec) Recommended group/private windsurfing and kitesurfing classes (beginner, intermediate or advanced level), and paddle-boarding (€25 per hour), 7km northwest of Tarifa. Three-hour group windsurfing classes are €80 per person, kitesurfing €110. Spanish, English, French and German spoken. Also at Valdevaqueros, 9km northwest of town.

Spin Out   WINDSURFING
(☑ 956 23 63 52; www.tarifaspinout.com; Playa de Valdevaqueros, Ctra N340 Km 75.5; 90-min class per person €59, board & sail rental per hour €29; ☺ Apr-Oct) Daily classes and five-day courses for beginners, kids and experts, northwest of town.

⭐ Festivals & Events

Feria de la Virgen de la Luz   FAIR
In the first week of September, Tarifa's town fair, honouring its patron, mixes religious processions, horses and typical Spanish fiesta.

🛏 Sleeping

⭐ **Hostal África**   HOSTAL €
(☑ 956 68 02 20; www.hostalafrica.com; Calle María Antonia Toledo 12; s/d €50/65, with shared

bathroom €35/50; ⊙ Mar-Nov; 🛜) This revamped 19th-century house just southwest of the Puerta de Jerez is one of the Costa de la Luz' best *hostales* (budget hotels). Full of plant pots and sky-blue-and-white arches, it's run by hospitable owners, and the 13 all-different rooms sparkle with bright colours. Enjoy the lovely, big roof terrace, with exotic cabana and views of Africa.

Hotel Misiana   BOUTIQUE HOTEL €€

(📋 956 62 70 83; www.misiana.com; Calle Sancho IV El Bravo 16; d/ste €95/200; ❋🛜) Thanks to its exquisite penthouse suite with private roof terrace and Morocco views, super-central Misiana is the best place to stay in Tarifa if you've got the money. But the doubles are pretty lovely too, with their stylish whiteness, pale greys and driftwood decor. This is real Tarifa chic and it's predictably popular; book well ahead.

Hotel Convento Tarifa   HOTEL €€

(📋 956 68 33 75; www.hotelconventotarifa.es; Calle de la Batalla del Salado 14; s/d incl breakfast €100/150; ❋🛜) White and bright are the themes in this efficient hotel built around the ruined walls of an ancient convent, just outside the old town. You can count on power showers, huge mirrors, flat-screen TVs, and vases of flowers in the rooms.

Posada La Sacristía   BOUTIQUE HOTEL €€

(📋 956 68 17 59; www.lasacristia.net; Calle San Donato 8; r €135; ❋🛜) Tucked inside a beautifully renovated 17th-century townhouse is Tarifa's most elegant boutique accommodation. Attention to detail is impeccable with 10 smart doubles that ooze style, tasteful colour schemes, big comfy beds, a sumptuous lounge, and rooms spread over two floors around a central courtyard. Buffet breakfast costs €6; a good Mediterranean fusion **restaurant** (📋 956 68 17 59; Calle San Donato 8; mains €10-18) opens in the summer.

Hotel Dos Mares   HOTEL €€€

(📋 956 68 40 35; www.dosmareshotel.com; Ctra N340 Km 79.5; r incl breakfast €195-225; ❋🛜🏊) Tarifa is all about the beach, and inviting accommodation options line the coast to its northwest. Opening on to the sand, 5km northwest of town, Moroccan-flavoured Dos Mares has comfy, bright, tile-floored rooms and bungalows in yellows, blues and burnt oranges, some with sea-facing balconies. Other perks: a sleepy cafe, a gym, a pool, and an on-site horse-riding school (p700).

Eating

Tarifa is full of good food with a strong international flavour, Italian in particular. It's also one of Andalucía's top breakfast spots – time to break out of the *tostada*-and-coffee monotony! Other treats to look for are smoothies, ethnic fusion food, organic ingredients and wonderful vegetarian meals.

★ Café Azul   BREAKFAST €

(www.facebook.com/cafeazultarifa; Calle Batalla del Salado 8; breakfasts €3.50-7.50; ⊙ 9am-3pm) This eccentric Italian-run place with eye-catching blue-and-white Moroccan-inspired decor whips up the best breakfasts in town, if not Andalucía. You'll want to eat everything. It does a wonderfully fresh fruit salad topped with muesli and yoghurt, plus good coffee, smoothies, juices, *bocadillos* (filled rolls) and cooked breakfasts. The fruit-and-yoghurt-stuffed crêpe is a work of art.

La Oca da Sergio   ITALIAN €€

(📋 615 686571; Calle General Copons 6; mains €10-20; ⊙ 1-4pm & 8pm-midnight daily Jun-Oct, 8pm-midnight Mon & Wed-Fri, 1-4pm & 8pm-midnight Sat & Sun Dec-May) Italians rule the Tarifa food scene. Amiable Sergio roams the tables Italian-style, armed with loaded plates and amusing stories, and resides over genuine home-country cooking at this popular restaurant tucked away behind the Iglesia de San Mateo. Look forward to homemade pasta, wood-oven thin-crust pizzas, cappuccinos and postdinner *limoncello*.

Bar-Restaurante Morilla   TAPAS €€

(📋 956 68 17 57; Calle Sancho IV El Bravo 2; mains €10-15; ⊙ 8.30am-11.30pm) One of numerous eateries lying in wait along Calle Sancho IV El Bravo in the heart of the old town, busy no-frills Morilla attracts more *tarifeños* than others. They pop in for the quality tapas, seafood *raciones* and lamb dishes, and for the excellent *cazuela de pescado y marisco* (fish-and-seafood stew).

Mandrágora   MOROCCAN, ANDALUCIAN €€

(📋 956 68 12 91; www.mandragoratarifa.com; Calle Independencia 3; mains €12-18; ⊙ 6.30pm-midnight Mon-Sat Mar-Jan) On a quiet street behind the Iglesia de San Mateo, this intimate palm-dotted spot serves Andalucian-Arabic food and does so terrifically well. It's hard to know where to start, but tempting choices include lamb with plums and almonds, Moroccan vegetable couscous, chicken tagine, and monkfish in a wild-mushroom-and-sea-urchin sauce.

Drinking & Nightlife

With all the surfers, kitesurfers and beach-goers breezing through, Tarifa has a busy bar scene (especially in summer), plus a few lively late-night clubs thrown into the mix. Lots of the after-dark fun centres on narrow Calles Cervantes, San Francisco and Santísima Trinidad, just east of the Alameda. Don't even bother going out before 11pm. A few *chiringuitos* get going with music and *copas* (drinks) on Playa de los Lances and the beaches northwest of town.

★ Bien*Star   BEACH BAR
(www.bienstartarifa.com; Playa de los Lances; ⊙12.30pm-1am Sat-Thu, to 3am Fri Jul & Aug, 12.30-9pm Sun-Thu, to 3am Fri Oct-Jun) Perched on perfectly white sands, this shabby-chic wind-battered beach bar is what Tarifa is all about – cool drinks, a kitesurfing crowd and a contagiously laid-back vibe. Live music happens on Fridays around 10pm. It's one of the few *chiringuitos* to stay open virtually year-round.

Almedina   BAR
(☑956 68 04 74; www.almedinacafe.net; Calle Almedina 3; ⊙8.30pm-midnight; ☎) Built into the old city walls, cavernous Almedina squeezes a flamenco ensemble into its clamorous confines on Thursdays at 10.30pm.

Café Central   CAFE
(Calle Sancho IV El Bravo 8; ⊙8.30am-midnight) Anyone for a 1-litre margarita? The town's best people-watching spot has glammed itself up a bit with cool cocktails and juices, plus some creative contemporary dishes.

ℹ Information

Tourist Office (☑956 68 09 93; Paseo de la Alameda; ⊙10am-1.30pm & 4-6pm Mon-Fri, 10am-1.30pm Sat & Sun)

ℹ Getting There & Away

BOAT

FRS (☑956 68 18 30; www.frs.es; Avenida de Andalucía 16) runs 35-minute ferries up to eight times daily between Tarifa and Tangier (Morocco; adult/child/car/motorcycle one-way €37/20/102/30). All passengers need a passport. **Inter Shipping** (☑956 68 47 29; www.intershipping.es; Recinto Portuario, Local 4) offers similar schedules to Tangier (€37/19/100/60).

BUS

Comes (www.tgcomes.es) operates from the bus station beside the petrol station at the northwestern end of Calle Batalla del Salado. In July and August, **Horizonte Sur** (www.horizontesur.es) has several daily buses from here to Punta Paloma via Tarifa's beaches.

DESTINATION	FARE	DURATION	FREQUENCY
Cádiz	€9.91	1½hr	5 daily
Jerez de la Frontera	€11	2½hr	1 daily
La Barca de Vejer (for Vejer de la Frontera)	€4.52	40min	6 daily
La Línea (for Gibraltar)	€4.49	1hr	6 daily
Málaga	€17	2¾hr	3 daily
Seville	€20	3hr	4 daily

Gibraltar

POP 32,700

Red pillar boxes, fish-and-chip shops and creaky 1970s seaside hotels: Gibraltar – as British writer Laurie Lee once commented – is a piece of Portsmouth sliced off and towed 500 miles south. As with many colonial outposts, 'the Rock' overstates its Britishness, a bonus for pub-grub and afternoon-tea lovers, but a confusing double-take for modern Brits who thought their country had moved on since the days of Lord Nelson memorabilia. Poised strategically at the jaws of Europe and Africa, Gibraltar, with its Palladian architecture and camera-hogging Barbary macaques, makes for an interesting break from Cádiz province's white towns and tapas. Playing an admirable supporting role in swashbuckling local history; lest we forget, the Rock has been British longer than the United States has been American.

This towering 5km-long limestone ridge rises to 426m, with dramatic cliffs on its northern and eastern sides. Gibraltarians speak English, Spanish, and a curiously accented, sing-song mix of the two, swapping back and forth midsentence. Signs are in English.

History

Both the Phoenicians and the ancient Greeks left traces here, but Gibraltar really entered the history books in AD 711 when Tariq ibn Ziyad, the Muslim governor of

Gibraltar

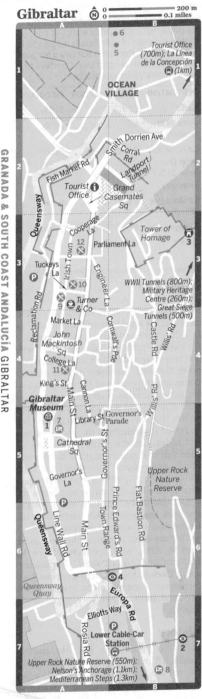

Gibraltar

◎ Top Sights
1 Gibraltar Museum.............................A5

◎ Sights
2 Apes' Den...B7
3 Moorish Castle..................................B3
4 Trafalgar Cemetery..........................B6

☉ Activities, Courses & Tours
5 Dolphin Adventure............................B1
6 Dolphin Safari...................................B1

🛏 Sleeping
7 Hotel Bristol.....................................A5
8 Rock Hotel..B7

⊗ Eating
9 Clipper..A3
10 House of Sacarello..........................A3
11 Royal Calpe.....................................A4
12 Star Bar...A3

Tangier, made it the initial bridgehead for the Islamic invasion of the Iberian Peninsula, landing with an army of 10,000 men. The name Gibraltar derives from Jebel Tariq (Tariq's Mountain).

The Almohad Muslims founded a town here in 1159 and were usurped by the Castilians in 1462. In 1704 an Anglo-Dutch fleet captured Gibraltar during the War of the Spanish Succession. Spain ceded the Rock to Britain by the 1713 Treaty of Utrecht, but didn't give up military attempts to regain it until the failure of the Great Siege of 1779–83; Spain has wanted it back ever since.

In 1969, Francisco Franco (infuriated by a referendum in which Gibraltarians voted by 12,138 to 44 to remain under British sovereignty) closed the Spain–Gibraltar border. The same year a new constitution committed Britain to respecting Gibraltarians' wishes over sovereignty, and gave Gibraltar domestic self-government and its own parliament, the House of Assembly. In 1985, just before Spain joined the European Community (now the EU), the border was reopened after 16 long years.

In a 2002 vote, Gibraltarians resoundingly rejected the idea of joint British-Spanish sovereignty. Today, the thorny issue of Gibraltar's long-term future still raises its head from time to time, with recent debates sparked by conflict over who controls the waters off the Rock. Gibraltarians believe in their right to self-determination, and the big-picture problems remain unresolved.

◉ Sights

Most Gibraltar sojourns start in Grand Casemates Sq, accessible through Landport Tunnel (at one time the only land entry through Gibraltar's walls), then continue along Main St, a slice of the British high street under the Mediterranean sun.

★ Upper Rock
Nature Reserve   NATURE RESERVE

(adult/child incl attractions £10/5, vehicle £2, pedestrian excl attractions £0.50; ⊘ 9am-6.15pm, last entry 5.45pm) The Rock is one of the most dramatic landforms in southern Europe. Most of its upper sections (but not the main lookouts) fall within the Upper Rock Nature Reserve. Entry tickets include admission to St Michael's Cave, the Apes' Den, the Great Siege Tunnels, the Moorish Castle, the Military Heritage Centre and the 100-tonne gun. The upper Rock is home to 600 plant species and is the perfect vantage point for watching bird migration between Europe and Africa.

The Rock's most famous inhabitants are the tailless Barbary macaques. Many of the 200 apes hang around the top cable-car station, the Apes' Den (near the middle cable-car station) and the Great Siege Tunnels. Legend has it that when the apes (possibly introduced from North Africa in the 18th century) disappear from Gibraltar, so will the British. Summer is best for seeing newborn apes, but keep a safe distance to avoid run-ins with protective parents. Several visitors have been attacked by apes in recent years, which led to some apes being 'exported' in 2014.

About 1km (15 minutes' walk) south down St Michael's Rd from the top cable-car station, O'Hara's Rd leads left up to O'Hara's Battery (adult/child £3/2; ⊘ 10am-5pm Mon-Fri), an emplacement of big guns on the Rock's summit (not included in your nature-reserve ticket). Slightly further down is the extraordinary St Michael's Cave (St Michael's Rd; ⊘ 9am-5.45pm, to 6.15pm Apr-Oct), a spectacular natural grotto full of stalagmites and stalactites. People once thought the cave was a possible subterranean link with Africa. Today, apart from attracting tourists in droves, it's used for concerts, plays and even fashion shows. For a more extensive look, the Lower St Michael's Cave Tour (tours per person £10) is a three-hour guided adventure into the lower cave system. The tourist office (p707) can rec-

ommend guides. Children must be over 10; wear appropriate footwear.

A 1.5km (30-minute) walk north (downhill) from the top cable-car station is Princess Caroline's Battery, housing the Military Heritage Centre (⊘ 9-5.45pm, to 6.15pm Apr-Oct). From here one road leads down to Princess Royal Battery – more gun emplacements – while another heads 300m up to the Great Siege Tunnels (⊘ 9.30am-6.15pm), a complex defence system hewn out of the Rock by the British during the siege of 1779–83 to provide gun emplacements. The WWII tunnels (adult/child £8/4; ⊘ 10am-4pm Mon-Sat), where the Allied invasion of North Africa was planned, can also be visited; these aren't included in your nature-reserve ticket, but you must have a nature-reserve ticket to visit them. Even combined, these tunnels constitute only a tiny proportion of the Rock's more than 50km of tunnels and galleries, most off-limits to the public.

On Willis' Rd, the way down to town from Princess Caroline's Battery, you'll find Gibraltar's Moorish Castle (Tower of Homage; ⊘ 9.30am-6.45pm Apr-Sep, 9am-5.45pm Oct-Mar), rebuilt in 1333 after being won back from the Spanish.

★ Gibraltar Museum   MUSEUM

(www.gibmuseum.gi; 18-20 Bomb House Lane; adult/child £2/1; ⊘ 10am-6pm Mon-Fri, to 2pm Sat) Gibraltar's swashbuckling history quickly unfolds in this fine museum, which comprises a labyrinth of rooms ranging from prehistoric and Phoenician Gibraltar to the infamous Great Siege (1779–83). Don't miss

GRANADA & SOUTH COAST ANDALUCÍA GIBRALTAR

---

❶ CABLE CAR–NATURE RESERVE COMBO

The best way to explore the Rock is to whizz up on the cable car (Lower Cable-Car Station; Red Sands Rd; adult one-way/return £8.50/11, child one-way/return £4.50/5; ⊘ 9.30am-7.45pm Apr-Oct, to 5.15pm Nov-Mar), weather permitting, then stop off at all the nature reserve sights on your way down. You can get special cable car–nature reserve one-way combo tickets for this (adult/child £20/12). Note that the lower cable-car station stops selling these about two hours before the reserve closes. For the Apes' Den, hop out at the middle station.

the well-preserved 14th-century Islamic baths, and an intricately painted 7th-century BC Egyptian mummy found in the bay in the 1800s.

Nelson's Anchorage
LANDMARK

(Rosia Rd; £1; ⊗9am-6.15pm) At the southwest end of town, Nelson's Anchorage pinpoints the site where Nelson's body was brought ashore from the HMS *Victory* – preserved in a rum barrel, so legend says. A 100-tonne British-made Victorian supergun (1870) commemorates the spot.

🏃 Activities

★ Mediterranean Steps
HIKING

Not the most well-known attraction in Gibraltar, but surely the most spectacular, this narrow, ancient path with steep steps – many hewn into the limestone – starts at the nature reserve's entrance at Jews' Gate and traverses the south end of Gibraltar before steeply climbing the crag on the eastern escarpment. It comes out on the ridge; it's best to take the road down.

The views along the way are stupendous; ornithologists won't know where to look with birds soaring above, below and around you. The 1.5km trail is mildly exposed. Allow 45 minutes to an hour.

🛏 Sleeping

Hotel Bristol
HOTEL €€

(☑20076800; www.bristolhotel.gi; 10 Cathedral Sq; s/d/tr £69/86/99; 🅿❄🛜🏊) Where else can you stay in a retro 1970s hotel that isn't even trying to be retro? The dated but de-

---

DOLPHIN-WATCHING

The Bahía de Algeciras has a sizeable year-round population of dolphins and a Gibraltar highlight is spotting them. **Dolphin Adventure** (☑20050650; www.dolphin.gi; 9 The Square, Marina Bay; adult/child £25/13) and **Dolphin Safari** (☑20071914; www.dolphinsafari.gi; 6 The Square, Marina Bay; adult/child £25/15; ⊗Feb-Nov) run excellent dolphin-watching trips of one to 1½ hours. Most of the year they usually make three daily excursions; from about April to September there may be extra trips. Dolphin Adventure also does occasional whale-watching trips (adult/child £40/25). Advance bookings essential.

---

cent Bristol has creaking floorboards, red patterned carpets, an attractive walled garden and a small swimming pool, though staff aren't particularly helpful. It's in a prime location just off Main St.

Rock Hotel
HOTEL €€€

(☑20073000; www.rockhotelgibraltar.com; 3 Europa Rd; incl breakfast s £150-174, d £160-184; 🅿❄🛜🏊) As famous as the local monkeys, Gibraltar's grand old dame is looking fab and fresh after a massive makeover. The 86 smart but cosy, creamy, wood-floored rooms with fresh flowers and sea views still smelt of paint when we visited. Tick off gym, pool, welcome drink, writing desks, bathrobes, a sparkling cafe-bar and Sunday roasts (£25).

🍴 Eating

Goodbye tapas, hello fish and chips. Gibraltar's food is unashamedly British – and pretty pricey by Andalucian standards. The staples are pub grub, beer, sandwiches, chips and stodgy desserts, though a few international flavours can be found at Queensway Quay, Marina Bay and Ocean Village.

Royal Calpe
BRITISH, PUB €

(☑20075890; 176 Main St; mains £6-8; ⊗8am-9pm; 🛜) If halfway through your quintessential Gibraltar tour, you get an unstoppable urge for heavily crusted meat pies, club sandwiches, fish and chips, and a pint of Caffrey's, look no further than the Royal Calpe, one of the Rock's more understated boozers. Head out the back to enjoy that bastion of British middle-class luxury - the conservatory.

Star Bar
PUB, INTERNATIONAL €€

(www.starbargibraltar.com; 12 Parliament Lane; mains £7-11; ⊗8am-11pm Mon-Sat, 10am-9pm Sun) The Rock's oldest bar (if house advertising is to be believed) has been revamped with contemporary flair and a Mediterranean-influenced pub menu that even features tapas. Squeeze inside for wraps, burgers, salads, ribeye steak, spinach-and-goat's-cheese pasta and, of course, fish and chips.

House of Sacarello
INTERNATIONAL €€

(www.sacarellosgibraltar.com; 57 Irish Town; mains £8-11; ⊗8.30am-7.30pm Mon-Fri, 9am-3pm Sat; 🛜🍴) A jack of all trades and master of... well...some, Sacarello's offers a great range of vegetarian options (pastas, quiches) alongside pub-style dishes in an old multi-level coffee warehouse. There's a good long coffee list, plus lots of cakes, a salad bar and daily specials. From 3.30pm to 7.30pm, you can linger over afternoon tea (£5.90).

Clipper
BRITISH, PUB €€

(78B Irish Town; mains £5-9; ⊘9am-10pm Mon-Fri, 10am-4pm Sat, 10am-10pm Sun; 🔊) Ask five…10…20 people in Gibraltar for their favourite pub and, chances are, they'll choose the Clipper. Looking sparklingly modern after a refurb that cleared out some of the dated naval decor, the Clipper does real pub grub in traditionally large portions. British faves include jacket potatoes, chicken tikka masala, Sunday roasts and that essential all-day breakfast (£5.95).

ⓘ Information

Tourist Office (www.visitgibraltar.gi; Grand Casemates Sq; ⊘9am-5.30pm Mon-Fri, 10am-3pm Sat, 10am-1pm Sun)

ⓘ Getting There & Away

AIR

British Airways (www.britishairways.com) Flies daily to/from London Heathrow.

EasyJet (www.easyjet.com) Flies daily to/from London Gatwick and three times weekly to/from Bristol.

Monarch (www.monarch.co.uk) Flies five times weekly to/from London Luton, four to/from Manchester and three to/from Birmingham.

BOAT

One weekly **FRS** (www.frs.es) ferry sails from Gibraltar to Tangier Med (Morocco; adult/child one-way £38/25, one hour) on Friday at 7pm. Book tickets at **Turner & Co** (☎20078305; 67 Irish Town; ⊘9am-1pm & 2-5pm Mon-Fri).

BUS

No buses go directly to Gibraltar, but the bus station in La Línea de la Concepción (Spain) is only 400m from the border. From here, there are regular buses to/from Algeciras, Cádiz, Málaga, Seville and Tarifa.

CAR & MOTORCYCLE

Long vehicle queues at the border and congested streets in Gibraltar make it far less time-consuming to park in La Línea and walk across the frontier (1.5km to Casemates Sq). To take a car into Gibraltar (free) you need an insurance certificate, registration document, nationality plate and driving licence. Gibraltar drives on the right.

In Gibraltar, there are car parks on Line Wall Rd, Reclamation Rd and Devil's Tower Rd. Street parking in La Línea costs €1.25 per hour, but it's easier/safer to use the underground car parks just north of Avenida Príncipe de Asturias.

ⓘ Getting Around

Bus 5 runs between town and the border every 10 to 20 minutes. Bus 2 serves Europa Point, bus 3 the southern town; bus 4 and bus 8 go to Catalan Bay. All these buses stops at Market Pl, immediately northwest of Grand Casemates Sq. Tickets cost £1.50, or £2.25 for a day pass.

JAÉN PROVINCE

For anyone who loves culture, nature, history or good food, this relatively little-visited province turns out to be one magical combination. Endless lines of pale-green olive trees – producing one-sixth of all the world's olive oil – carpet much of the landscape. Castle-crowned hills are a reminder that this was once a frontier zone between Christians and Muslims, while the gorgeous Renaissance architecture of Unesco World Heritage sites Úbeda and Baeza displays the wealth amassed by the Reconquista nobility.

Beyond the towns and olive groves, Jaén has wonderful mountain country. The Parque Natural Sierras de Cazorla, Segura y las Villas is a highlight of Andalucía for nature lovers, with rugged mountains, deep green valleys, prolific wildlife, plus good hotels, roads and trails to help you make the most of it.

Products of the forests and hills such as venison, partridge and wild mushrooms feature strongly in Jaén cuisine, and in the recipes of a surprising number of wonderfully creative chefs, especially in Úbeda.

Jaén

POP 112,000 / ELEV 575M

Set amid vast olive groves, upon which its precarious economy depends, Jaén is somewhat overshadowed by the beauty of nearby Úbeda and Baeza, and is often passed over by visitors to the province. But once you make it into town you will discover a charming, if mildly dilapidated, historic centre with hidden neighbourhoods, excellent tapas bars and a grandiose cathedral.

Muslim Yayyan was a significant city before its conquest by Castilla in 1246. Christian Jaén remained important thanks to its strategic location near the border with Nasrid Granada. After the Muslims were finally driven out of Granada in 1492, Jaén sank into a decline with many of its people emigrating to the Spanish colonies – hence

WORTH A TRIP

FORTALEZA DE LA MOTA

From a distance the Fortaleza de la Mota (www.tuhistoria.org; Alcalá la Real; adult/child €6/3; ⊙10.30am-7.30pm Apr–mid-Oct, to 5.30pm mid-Oct–Mar; [P]) looks more like a city than a mere fort, with its high church tower and doughty castle keep rising above the surrounding walls. And in a sense that's what it was, for back in the Middle Ages this fortified hill now looming over the town of Alcalá la Real *was* Alcalá la Real. It's a marvellous stop if you're heading along the Granada–Córdoba road across southwestern Jaén province, and well worth a detour even if you're not.

the existence of other Jaéns in Peru and the Philippines.

⊙ Sights

★ **Catedral de la Asunción**   CATHEDRAL
(Plaza de Santa María; adult/child incl audio guide €5/1.50; ⊙10am-2pm & 4-8pm Mon-Fri, 10am-2pm & 4-7pm Sat, 10am-noon & 4-7pm Sun) The size and opulence of Jaén's cathedral still dwarf the rest of the city, especially when seen from the hilltop eyrie of Cerro de Santa Catalina. Andrés de Vandelvira, the master architect of Úbeda and Baeza, was commissioned to create this huge house of God in the 16th century, replacing a crumbling Gothic cathedral which itself had been built on the site of a mosque.

The facade on Plaza de Santa María was not completed until the 18th century, and owes more to the baroque tradition than to the Renaissance, thanks to its host of statuary by Seville's Pedro Roldán. But the cathedral's predominant aesthetic is Renaissance – particularly evident in its huge, round arches and clusters of Corinthian columns that lend it great visual strength. Inside, a great circular dome rises over the crossing before the main altar. Check out the beautiful carving on the stone ceilings of the nave and aisles, and on the wooden seats in the choir.

★ **Castillo de Santa Catalina**   CASTLE
(Cerro de Santa Catalina; adult/child €3/1.50; ⊙10am-2pm & 3.30-7.30pm Tue-Sat, to 3pm Sun; [P]) High above the city, atop cliff-girt Cerro de Santa Catalina, this fortress' near-im-

pregnable position is what made Jaén important during the Muslim and early Reconquista centuries. At the end of the ridge stands a large cross, on the spot where Fernando III had a cross planted after Jaén finally surrendered to him in 1246; the views are magnificent.

**Palacio
de Villardompardo**   BATHHOUSE, MUSEUM
(Centro Cultural Baños Árabes; Plaza de Santa Luisa de Marillac; ⊙9am-10pm Tue-Sat, to 3pm Sun) **FREE** This Renaissance palace houses three excellent attractions: the beautiful 11th-century **Baños Árabes** (Arab Baths), one of the largest surviving Islamic-era bathhouses in Spain; the **Museo de Artes y Costumbres Populares** (Museum of People's Art & Customs), devoted to the rural life of pre-industrial Jaén province; and the **Museo Internacional de Arte Naïf** (International Museum of Naïve Art) with a large collection of colourful and witty Naïve art.

🛏 Sleeping

Hotel Xauen   HOTEL €€
(📞953 24 07 89; www.hotelxauenjaen.com; Plaza del Deán Mazas; s/d incl breakfast €55/65; [P][❋][🛜]) The Xauen has a superb location in the centre of town. Communal areas are decorated with large photos of colourful local scenes, while the rooms are a study in brown and moderately sized, but comfy and well cared-for. The rooftop sun terrace has stunning cathedral views. Parking nearby is €12.

★ **Parador Castillo
de Santa Catalina**   LUXURY HOTEL €€€
(📞953 23 00 00; www.parador.es; Cerro de Santa Catalina; r €169; [P][❋][@][🛜][🏊]) Next to the castle on the Cerro de Santa Catalina, Jaén's *parador* has an incomparable setting and theatrically vaulted halls. Rooms are luxuriously dignified with plush furnishings, some with four-poster beds. There is also an excellent restaurant and a bar with panoramic terrace seating.

🍴 Eating

There aren't many fancy restaurants in Jaén, but some of Andalucía's quirkiest tapas bars are here, and the *jiennenses* (people of Jaén) cherish and preserve them. For the highest concentration, head for the little zone of wafer-thin streets northwest of the cathedral. Here, and throughout Jaén province, bars will give you a free tapa with every drink. You only pay for any extra tapas you order.

El Pato Rojo
SEAFOOD €

(Calle de Bernabé Soriano 12; medias raciones €8-10; ⊙1-5pm & 8pm-midnight) No-frills but always packed to the gills, the 'Red Duck' concentrates on one thing – perfect seafood tapas. Unless you've grabbed one of the few tables out on the narrow pavement, it's a matter of squeezing up to the bar and ordering a beer or *fino* (straw-coloured sherry); a tapa will come free with each drink.

Taberna La Manchega
ANDALUCIAN €

(www.facebook.com/tabernalamanchega.jaen; Calle Bernardo López 12; platos combinados €6, raciones €3-10; ⊙10am-5pm & 8pm-1am Wed-Mon) La Manchega has been in action since the 1880s; while enjoying the great, traditional tapas and *raciones,* such as venison chorizo and goat kid in garlic *(choto al ajillo),* you can watch the characterful local clientele.

★Casa Antonio
SPANISH €€€

(☑953 27 02 62; www.casantonio.es; Calle Fermín Palma 3; mains €19-23; ⊙1-4pm & 8.30-11.30pm Mon-Sat, 1-4pm Sun, closed Aug) This elegant little restaurant, in an unpromising street off Parque de la Victoria, prepares top-class Spanish fare rooted in local favourites, such as the partridge pâté or Segura lamb. There's also some excellent seafood. Nothing too complicated, just top ingredients expertly prepared. Service is polished and attentive.

❶ Information

Oficina de Turismo (☑953 19 04 55; www.andalucia.org; Calle Maestra 8; ⊙9am-7.30pm Mon-Fri, 9.30am-3pm Sat & Sun) Combined city and regional tourist office with helpful multilingual staff.

❶ Getting There & Away

BUS

Alsa (☑902 42 22 42; www.alsa.es) and **Transportes Ureña** (☑953 22 01 16; www.urena-sa.com) run buses from the **bus station** (☑953 23 23 00; www.epassa.es/autobus; Plaza de la Libertad).

DESTINATION	FARE	DURATION	FREQUENCY
Baeza	€4.50	1hr	11 daily
Cazorla	€9.25	2½hr	3 daily
Córdoba	€10	2hr	4-7 daily
Granada	€8.90	1¼hr	12 daily
Málaga	€20	3½hr	4 daily
Seville	€23	4½hr	1 daily
Úbeda	€5.40	1¼hr	12 daily

TRAIN

Jaén's **train station** (www.renfe.com; Paseo de la Estación) has four trains a day to Córdoba (€15, 1¾ hours), Seville (€28, three hours) and Madrid (€35, four hours).

Baeza
POP 15,500 / ELEV 790M

The twin towns of Baeza (ba-*eh*-thah) and Úbeda, 9km apart, put paid to any notion that there is little of architectural interest in Andalucía apart from Moorish buildings. Far from any of Andalucía's more famed cultural centres, these two country towns guard a treasure trove of superb Christian Renaissance buildings from a time when a few local families managed to amass huge fortunes and spent large parts of them beautifying their home towns. Baeza, the smaller of the two, can be visited in a day trip from Úbeda, though it has some good accommodation of its own. Here a handful of wealthy, fractious families, rich from grain-growing and cloth and leather production, left a marvellous catalogue of perfectly preserved Renaissance churches and civic buildings.

Baeza was one of the first Andalucian towns to fall to the Christians (in 1227), and little is left of the Muslim town of Bayyasa after so many centuries of Castilian influence.

◉ Sights

Baeza's main sights mostly cluster in the narrow streets south of the central Plaza de España and the broad Paseo de la Constitución (once Baeza's marketplace and bullring).

★Catedral de Baeza
CATHEDRAL

(Plaza de Santa María; incl audio guide €5; ⊙10.30am-2pm & 4-7pm Mon-Fri, 10am-7pm Sat, 10am-6pm Sun) As was the case in much of Andalucía, the Reconquista destroyed Baeza's mosque and in its place built a cathedral. This was the first step towards the town's transformation into a Castilian gem. The cathedral is a stylistic melange, though the predominant style is 16th-century Renaissance, visible in the facade on Plaza de Santa María and in the basic design of the three-nave interior (by Andrés de Vandelvira).

★Oleícola San Francisco
OLIVE OIL

(☑953 76 34 15; www.oleoturismojaen.com; Calle Pedro Pérez, Begíjar; 1½hr tours €5; ⊙tours 11am

& 5pm) 🎧 These fascinating tours of a working oil mill near Baeza will teach you all you could want to know about the process of turning olives into oil, how the best oil is made and what distinguishes extra virgin from the rest. At the end you get to taste a few varieties, and you'll probably emerge laden with a bottle or two of San Francisco's high-quality product.

★ Palacio de Jabalquinto   PALACE

(Plaza de Santa Cruz; ⊙9am-2pm Mon-Fri) **FREE** Baeza's most flamboyant palace was probably built in the late 15th century for a member of the noble Benavides clan. Its chief glory is the spectacular facade in the decorative Isabelline Gothic style, with a strange array of naked humans clambering along the moulding over the doorway; at the top is a line of shields capped off with helmets topped by mythical birds and beasts.

Antigua Universidad   HISTORIC BUILDING

(Old University; Calle del Beato Juan de Ávila; ⊙10am-2pm & 4-7pm) **FREE** Baeza's historic university was founded in 1538. It became a fount of progressive ideas that generally conflicted with Baeza's conservative dominant families, often causing scuffles between the highbrow intellectuals and the well-heeled. Since 1875 the building has housed a secondary school. The main patio, with its elegant Renaissance arches, is open to visitors, as is the early-20th-century classroom of the famed poet Antonio Machado, who taught French here from 1912 to 1919.

Plaza del Pópulo   SQUARE

(Plaza de los Leones) This handsome square is surrounded by elegant 16th-century buildings. The central **Fuente de los Leones** (Fountain of the Lions)is made of carvings from the Ibero-Roman village of Cástulo and is topped by a statue reputed to represent Imilce, a local princess who became one of the wives of the famous Carthaginian general Hannibal.

🎊 Festivals & Events

Feria   FAIR

The summer fair in mid-August starts with a big Carnaval-style procession of *gigantones* (papier-mâché giants) and other colourful figures, and continues with five days of fireworks, a huge funfair, concerts and bullfights.

Semana Santa   HOLY WEEK

(www.semanasantabaeza.es) Baeza's Easter processions are solemn, grand and rooted very deep in the town's traditions. Evenings from Palm Sunday to Good Friday.

🛏 Sleeping

★ Hostal Aznaitín   HOSTAL €

(📞953 74 07 88; www.hostalaznaitin.com; Calle Cabreros 2; s/d incl breakfast Sun-Thu €38/46, Fri & Sat €52/59; 🅰🛜🏊) 🎧 Welcoming, bright and modern Aznaitín is a far cry from the dreary *hostales* of old. Rooms are stylish and well-sized, with good mattresses and large, appealing photos of Baeza sights. Reception has masses of information and ideas on things to see and do in and around Baeza.

Hotel Puerta de la Luna   HERITAGE HOTEL €€

(📞953 74 70 19; www.hotelpuertadelaluna.com; Calle Canónigo Melgares Raya 7; s €70-99, d €70-111, buffet breakfast €15; 🅿🅰@🛜🏊) There is no doubt where Baeza's Renaissance-era nobility would stay if they were to return today. This luxurious hotel in a 17th-century mansion sports orange trees and a pool in its elegant patio, and beautifully furnished salons with welcoming fireplaces. The spacious rooms are enhanced by classical furnishings and art, and good big bathrooms.

🍴 Eating

Paseo de la Constitución and Plaza de España are lined with bar-cafe-restaurants that are great for watching local life, but the best finds are tucked away in the narrow old-town streets.

Bar Paco's   TAPAS €

(Calle de Santa Catalina; tapas €3.50-6; ⊙1.30-4pm & 8.30pm-midnight Fri-Sun, 2-4pm & 8.30pm-midnight Mon-Thu) Permanently thronged with locals and visitors (get here early if you want to sit down), Paco's prepares a big array of tasty, well-presented, creative tapas. The crêpes (with fillings like smoked salmon, avocado and potato) are particularly good, and portions are bigger than your average tapa.

El Nanchoas   ANDALUCIAN €€

(www.elnanchoas.com; Calle Comendadores 6; mains €7-15; ⊙11.30am-4.30pm & 8pm-1am Mon & Wed-Sat, to 4.30pm Sun) Relaxed and friendly Nanchoas serves up well-prepared home-style Jaén favourites in a sunny little courtyard and stone-walled dining room. Try the tasty *lomo de orza* (pork loin slow-fried with spices then conserved in a clay vessel called an *orza*) with garlicky eggs, or some sheep's cheese with honey and raisins.

Drinking & Nightlife

★ **Café Teatro Central**   BAR
(www.cafeteatrocentral.com; Calle Obispo Narváez 19; ⊕4pm-4am Tue-Sun, 9pm-4am Mon) Well worth a visit, except possibly on Wednesday – karaoke night. Owner Rafael has put tons of love into creating a fascinatingly eclectic environment with his display of historic instruments, coloured lighting, and decorations ranging from giant stone Buddhas to a miniature Big Ben. There's live music at about 11.30pm every Thursday, Friday and Saturday (anything but heavy metal!).

Shopping

La Casa del Aceite   FOOD
(www.casadelaceite.com; Paseo de la Constitución 9; ⊕10am-2pm & 5-8.30pm Mon-Sat, to 2pm Sun) Sells a big range of quality olive oil, plus other local products such as wild-boar pâté, olives, cosmetics and ceramics.

Information

Tourist Office (☑953 77 99 82; www.andalucia.org; Plaza del Pópulo; ⊕9am-7.30pm Mon-Fri, 9.30am-3pm Sat & Sun)

Getting There & Away

BUS

Alsa (p709) runs services from the **bus station** (☑953 74 04 68; Avenida Alcalde Puche Pardo), 900m northeast of Plaza de España.

DESTINATION	FARE	DURATION	FREQUENCY
Cazorla	€4.90	1¾hr	3 daily
Córdoba	€12	2½hr	2 daily
Granada	€13	1½-2½hr	7 daily
Jaén	€4.50	1hr	8 daily
Úbeda	€1.20	15min	14 daily

TRAIN

The nearest train station is **Linares–Baeza** (www.renfe.com), 13km northwest of town. One Alsa bus runs from Baeza bus station to the train station, at 5.30pm (€2.70, one hour); two come back, at 7.10am and 3.45pm. A taxi costs €23.

DESTINATION	FARE	DURATION	FREQUENCY
Almería	€28	3¼hr	3 daily
Córdoba	€20	1½hr	1 daily
Granada	from €9	3hr	1 daily
Jaén	€6	45min	3 daily
Madrid	33	3-4hr	5-6 daily
Seville	29	3hr	1 daily

Úbeda

POP 33,900 / ELEV 760M

Úbeda (*oo-be-dah*) is a slightly more sophisticated proposition than its little sister Baeza. Aside from the splendour of its architecture, the town has some top-class tapas bars and restaurants, and an age-old ceramics tradition that is still turning out some very appealing wares.

The city became a Castilian bulwark on the Christian march south. Úbeda's aristocratic lions – despite a quarrelsome tendency that led Isabel la Católica to have most of the town's fortifications knocked down in 1506 – jockeyed successfully for influence at the Habsburg court in the 16th century. Francisco de los Cobos y Molina rose to be state secretary to King Carlos I, and his nephew Juan Vázquez de Molina succeeded him in the job and kept it under Carlos' successor Felipe II.

High office exposed these men to the Renaissance aesthetic just then reaching Spain from Italy. Much of the wealth that the Molinas and flourishing local agriculture brought to Úbeda was invested in what are now considered to be some of the purest examples of Renaissance architecture in Spain. As a result, Úbeda (along with neighbouring Baeza) is one of the few places in Andalucía boasting stunning architecture that was *not* built by the Moors.

Sights

★ **Sinagoga del Agua**   MUSEUM
(www.sinagogadelagua.com; Calle Roque Rojas 2; 45min tours in Spanish adult/child €4/3; ⊕10.30am-2pm & 4.45-7.30pm) The medieval Sinagoga del Agua was discovered in 2006 by a refreshingly ethical property developer who intended to build apartments here, only to discover that every swing of the pickaxe revealed some tantalising piece of an archaeological puzzle. The result is this sensitive re-creation of a centuries-old

synagogue and rabbi's house, using original masonry whenever possible. Features include the women's gallery, a bodega with giant storage vessels, and a *miqvé* ritual bath.

★ **Sacra Capilla de El Salvador** CHAPEL
(Sacred Chapel of the Saviour; www.fundacionmedinaceli.org; Plaza Vázquez de Molina; adult/child incl audio guide €5/2.50; ⊘9.30am-2pm & 5-7pm Mon-Sat, 11.30am-2pm & 5-8pm Sun Jun-Sep, afternoon hours 30min earlier Apr-May, 1hr earlier Oct-Mar) The purity of Renaissance lines is best expressed in this famous chapel, built between 1536 and 1559. The first of many works executed in Úbeda by Andrés de Vandelvira, it was commissioned by Francisco de los Cobos y Molina as his family's funerary chapel. Its main facade is a preeminent example of plateresque style, with an orgy of classical sculpture depicting Greek gods on the underside of the arch – a Renaissance touch that would have been inconceivable a few decades earlier.

★ **Casa Museo Arte Andalusí** MUSEUM
(☑953 75 40 14; Calle Narváez 11; €2; ⊘11am-2pm & 5.30-8pm) This fascinating private museum comprises a 16th-century house that was inhabited by *conversos* (Jews who converted to Christianity) and a huge, diverse collection of antiques assembled by owner Paco Castro. The informal guided tours make it all come alive. The first hint that this is somewhere special is the original 16th-century heavy carved door. Ring the bell if it is closed.

★ **Palacio de Vázquez de Molina** MANSION
(Plaza Vázquez de Molina; ⊘8am-2.30pm Mon-Fri) FREE Lucky Úbeda functionaries – the building where they push their pens has to be the most beautiful *ayuntamiento* (town hall) in Spain. It was built by Vandelvira in about 1562 as a mansion for Juan Vázquez de Molina, whose coat of arms surmounts the doorway.

Centro de Interpretación
Olivar y Aceite INTERPRETATION CENTRE
(www.centrodeolivaryaceitelaloma.com; Corredera de San Francisco 32; adult/child €3.50/free; ⊘10am-1pm & 6-9pm Tue-Sat, 10am-1pm Sun Jun-Sep, 11am-2pm & 5-8pm Tue-Sat, 11am-2pm Sun Oct-May) Úbeda's olive-oil interpretation centre explains all about the area's olive-oil history, and how the oil gets from the tree to your table, with the help of models, mill equipment and videos in English and Spanish. You get the chance to taste different oils, and to buy from a broad selection.

Hospital de Santiago ARCHITECTURE
(Calle Obispo Cobos; ⊘10am-2pm & 5-9pm, closed Sun Jul, closed Sat & Sun Aug) FREE Andrés de Vandelvira's last architectural project, completed in 1575, has been dubbed the Escorial of Andalucía in reference to the famous monastery outside Madrid, built in a similarly grand, sober late-Renaissance style. The finely proportioned building, which stands outside the old town, 500m west of Plaza de Andalucía, has a broad, two-level, marble-columned patio, and a wide staircase with colourful original frescoes.

🛏 Sleeping

Hotel El Postigo HOTEL €
(☑953 75 00 00; www.hotelelpostigo.com; Calle Postigo 5; s/d Sun-Thu €46/51, Fri & Sat €70/75; ❄@⚹⚛) A small, appealing, modern hotel on a quiet street, El Postigo provides spacious, comfy rooms in red, black and white. Staff are welcoming, and there's a pleasant courtyard as well as a large sitting room with a log fire in winter.

★ **Afán de Rivera** HERITAGE HOTEL €€
(☑953 79 19 87; www.hotelafanderivera.com; Calle Afán de Rivera 4; r €70-85; ❄⚛) This incredible small hotel lies inside one of Úbeda's oldest buildings, predating the Renaissance. Expertly run by the amiable Jorge, it has beautifully historic common areas, and comfortable rooms that offer far more than is usual at this price: shaving kits, fancy shampoos and tastefully eclectic decor combining the traditional and the contemporary.

ⓘ BONO TURÍSTICO

If you plan on visiting the monuments in Baeza and Úbeda, you may want to consider investing in a €19.90 ticket that covers not only more than nine sights, but also includes a guided tour of each town and provides discounts on the tourist trains that chug through town. The only downside is that the guided tours are only provided twice daily at 11am and 5pm. Tickets can be purchased at the sights and tourist offices.

Palacio de la Rambla HISTORIC HOTEL €€

(☎953 75 01 96; www.palaciodelarambla.com; Plaza del Marqués de la Rambla 1; incl breakfast s €70-96, d €100-130; ⊗closed Jul-Aug; ❋🛜) The lovely Palacio de la Rambla gives you the full aristocratic mansion experience. The ivy-clad patio is wonderfully romantic, there's a beautiful salon opening on to a garden-patio, and each room is clad in precious antiques, so that it feels like you're staying with aristocratic friends rather than in a hotel.

Parador Condestable
Dávalos HISTORIC HOTEL €€€

(☎953 75 03 45; www.parador.es; Plaza Vázquez de Molina; r €188; ℗❋🛜) One of Spain's original *paradores* (opened in 1930) and an inspiration for many that were to follow, this plush hotel occupies a historic monument, the **Palacio del Deán Ortega**, on the wonderful Plaza Vázquez Molina. It has, of course, been comfortably modernised in period style and is appropriately luxurious.

🍴 Eating

Úbeda is the culinary hotspot of Jaén province; its talented chefs are one of the reasons why Spaniards flock here for weekend breaks.

⭐Cantina
de la Estación CONTEMPORARY ANDALUCIAN €€

(☎687 777230; www.cantinalaestacion.com; Cuesta Corredera 1; mains €15-19; ⊗1.30-4pm & 8.15pm-midnight Thu-Sun, to 4pm Mon-Tue) The charming originality here starts with the design – three rooms with railway themes (the main dining room being the deluxe carriage). It continues with the seasonal array of inspired fusion dishes based on locally available ingredients, such as wild boar in red-wine sauce on vegetable couscous, or millefeuille of smoked salmon, Parmesan and béchamel.

⭐Misa de 12 ANDALUCÍAN €€

(www.misade12.com; Plaza 1° de Mayo 7; raciones €9-20; ⊗noon-midnight Wed-Sun) From the tiny cooking station in this little corner bar, a succession of truly succulent platters magically emerges – slices of *presa ibérica* (a tender cut of Iberian pork) grilled to perfection, juicy fillets of *bacalao* (cod), or *revuelto de pulpo y gambas* (eggs scrambled with octopus and shrimp).

Zeitúm CONTEMPORARY SPANISH €€

(www.zeitum.com; Calle San Juan de la Cruz 10; mains €12-16; ⊗1-4pm & 8.30-11.30pm Tue-Sun) Zeitúm is housed in a headily historic 14th-century building, where staff will happily show you the original well, and the stonework and beams bearing Jewish symbols. Olive-oil tastings (a selection of oils to soak bread in) are a feature here, along with the top-class preparation of diverse dishes such as organic egg with raclette and whitebait, or pork sirloin with goats' cheese.

La Tintorera CONTEMPORARY ANDALUCIAN €€

(www.latintorera.es; Calle Real 27; raciones €8-15; ⊗noon-4pm & 8-11.45pm Tue-Sat, to 4pm Sun; 🛜) With a warm, intimate atmosphere enjoyed by couples and small groups of friends, La Tintorera turns out inventive preparations of classic ingredients – try the timbale of aubergines, ham and cheese (a stack of the said ingredients baked juicily together), or *lomo de orza* with potatoes, fried egg and paprika oil. Everything except the silver-framed mirror is in black and white, including the staff's outfits.

La Taberna ANDALUCIAN €€

(Calle Real 7; mains €10-20; ⊗noon-3.30pm & 7.30pm-midnight; 🪑) Simple menu, quick service, tasty food and a wide variety of clientele – La Taberna is an oasis of solid reliability in a town where food can sometimes be a little on the expensive side.

🛍 Shopping

The main high-street-style shopping streets are Calles Mesones and Obispo Cobos, between Plaza de Andalucía and the Hospital de Santiago, with everything from international chains to independent local shops.

Artesur ARTS & CRAFTS

(Plaza del Marqués de la Rambla 2; ⊗10am-9pm) A rambling shop with a big choice of ceramics, coloured-glass lights, esparto, and brass and wrought-iron decorative items – all handcrafted locally.

Alfarería Tito CERAMICS

(Plaza del Ayuntamiento 12; ⊗9am-2pm & 4-8pm) Juan Tito's distinctive style veers away from the classic green glaze, with intricate patterns and bright colours, especially blue. His large old-town showroom/workshop displays and sells a big range of very covetable wares. You're looking at around €20 for a decorative plate; the dazzling designs and artisanship are well worth it.

ℹ Information

Oficina de Turismo (☎ 953 77 92 04; www.andalucia.org; Calle Baja del Marqués 4; ⊘9am-3.30pm Sat-Tue, to 7.30pm Wed-Fri)

ℹ Getting There & Away

BUS

Alsa (p709) runs services from the **bus station** (☎ 953 75 21 57; Calle San José 6), which is in the new part of town, 700m west of Plaza de Andalucía.

DESTINATION	FARE	DURATION	FREQUENCY
Baeza	€1.15	15min	12 daily
Cazorla	€4.05	1hr	4 daily
Córdoba	€12	2½hr	4 daily
Granada	€12	2½hr	7 daily
Jaén	€5.20	1¼hr	10 daily

TRAIN

The nearest station is **Linares–Baeza** (www.renfe.com), 21km northwest, which you can reach on Linares-bound buses (€1.95, 30 minutes, four daily). Daily trains head to Madrid, Jaén, Almería, Granada, Córdoba and Seville.

Cazorla

POP 7340 / ELEV 836M

This picturesque, bustling white town sits beneath towering crags, just where the Sierra de Cazorla rises up from a rolling sea of olive trees, 45km east of Úbeda. It makes the perfect launching pad for exploring the beautiful Parque Natural Sierras de Cazorla, Segura y las Villas, which begins dramatically among the cliffs of Peña de los Halcones (Falcon Crag) directly above the town.

⦿ Sights

The heart of town is **Plaza de la Corredera**, with busy bars and the elegant *ayuntamiento* and clock tower looking down from the southeast corner. Canyonlike streets lead south to the **Balcón de Zabaleta**. This little mirador is like a sudden window in a blank wall, with stunning views up to the Castillo de la Yedra and beyond. From here another narrow street leads down to Cazorla's most picturesque square, **Plaza de Santa María**.

★ **Castillo de la Yedra**   CASTLE
(Museo del Alto Guadalquivir; EU citizen/other free/€1.50; ⊘9am-7.30pm Tue-Sat, to 3.30pm Sun & daily mid-Jun–mid-Sep) Cazorla's dramatic Castle of the Ivy, a 700m walk above Plaza de Santa María, has great views and is home to the interesting Museum of the Upper Guadalquivir, whose diverse collections include traditional agricultural tools and kitchen utensils, religious art, models of an old olive mill, and a small chapel featuring a life-size Romanesque-Byzantine crucifixion sculpture.

🏃 Activities

There are some great walks straight out of Cazorla town – all uphill to start with, but your reward is beautiful forest paths and fabulous panoramas of cliffs, crags, circling vultures and lonely monasteries. Good maps and information in anything except Spanish are hard to come by, but the main routes are signposted and waymarked. Cazorla's tourist office has maps with descriptions in Spanish. Editorial Alpina's *Sierra de Cazorla* map is useful and sold in some shops in Cazorla.

☞ Tours

Turisnat   DRIVING TOUR
(☎ 953 72 13 51; www.turisnat.es; Avenida del Parque Natural 2; ½-day tours per person €30-39, full day €45-49) An amalgamation of seven experienced local agencies, Turisnat is a reliable option for wildlife-spotting 4WD trips along the forest tracks of the *parque natural*.

🛌 Sleeping

Casa Rural Plaza
de Santa María   CASA RURAL €
(☎ 953 72 20 87; www.plazadesantamaria.com; Callejón Plaza Santa María 5; incl breakfast s €35, d €48-58; ❉☎) This multilevel house is set round a lovely garden-patio with a fish pond. Its terraces and a couple of the rooms enjoy superb views over Plaza de Santa María, Cazorla's castle and the mountains beyond. The attractive rooms are all different, in yellows, oranges and blues, with a variety of folksy styles.

Hotel Guadalquivir   HOTEL €
(☎ 953 72 02 68; www.hguadalquivir.com; Calle Nueva 6; s/d incl breakfast €42/56; ❉☎) Welcoming, family-run Guadalquivir has well-kept, comfy, ample rooms with pine furniture, though no memorable views. It's well run, centrally located, and serves up a decent breakfast. It all equals straightforward, no-fuss, good value for money.

✕ Eating

Bar Las Vegas
TAPAS €

(Plaza de la Corredera 17; tapas €1-2, raciones €10-12; ☺10am-midnight) It might be tiny, but it's the best of Cazorla's central bars, with barrel tables outside (and packed tables inside when the weather's poor). They do great tapas including one called *gloria bendita* (blessed glory), which turns out to be scrambled eggs with prawns and capsicum, as well as *raciones* of local favourites such as cheese, ham, venison and *lomo de orza*.

★ Mesón Leandro
CONTEMPORARY SPANISH €€

(www.mesonleandro.com; Calle Hoz 3; mains €9-20; ☺1.30-4pm & 8.30-11pm Wed-Mon) Just behind the Iglesia de Santa María, Leandro brings a touch of sophistication to Cazorla dining – professional, friendly service in a bright, attractive dining room with lazy music, and just one token set of antlers on the wall. The broad menu of nicely presented dishes encompasses the likes of *fettuccine a la marinera,* as well as partridge-and-pheasant pâté and a terrific *solomillo de ciervo* (venison sirloin).

La Cueva de Juan Pedro
ANDALUCIAN €€

(Plaza de Santa María; raciones & mains €8-20, menú €10-13; ☺noon-10pm) An ancient, wood-beamed place with hams and drying peppers dangling from the bar ceiling, and boar and mouflon (wild sheep) heads protruding from the walls. Taste the traditional Cazorla *conejo* (rabbit), *trucha* (trout), *rin-rán* (a mix of salted cod, potato and dried red peppers), *jabalí* (wild boar) or *ciervo* (red-deer venison).

ℹ Information

Oficina Municipal de Turismo (☏953 71 01 02; www.cazorla.es; Plaza de Santa María; ☺10am-1pm & 4-8pm, to 7pm Oct-Mar) Inside the remains of Santa María church, with useful information on the natural park as well as the town.

ℹ Getting There & Away

Alsa (www.alsa.es) runs three to five daily buses to Úbeda (€4, one hour), Baeza (€4.80, 1¼ hours), Jaén (€9.25, two to 2½ hours) and Granada (€18, 3¾ hours). The bus stop is on Calle Hilario Marco, 500m north of Plaza de la Corredera via Plaza de la Constitución.

Parque Natural Sierras de Cazorla, Segura y Las Villas

One of the biggest drawcards in Jaén province – and, for nature lovers, in all of Andalucía – is the mountainous, lushly wooded Parque Natural Sierras de Cazorla, Segura y las Villas. This is the largest protected area in Spain – 2099 sq km of craggy mountain ranges, deep, green river valleys, canyons, waterfalls, remote hilltop castles and abundant wildlife, with a snaking, 20km-long reservoir, the Embalse del Tranco, in its midst. The abrupt geography, with altitudes varying between 460m at the lowest point up to 2107m at the summit of Cerro Empanadas, makes for dramatic changes in the landscape. The Río Guadalquivir, Andalucía's longest river, begins in the south of the park, and flows northwards into the reservoir, before heading west across Andalucía to the Atlantic Ocean.

The best times to visit the park are spring and autumn, when the vegetation is at its most colourful and temperatures pleasant. The park is hugely popular with Spanish tourists and attracts several hundred thousand visitors each year. The peak periods are Semana Santa, July, August, and weekends from April to October.

Exploring the park is a lot easier if you have a vehicle, and there are plenty of places to stay within the park as well as in Cazorla town. The network of paved and unpaved roads and footpaths reaches some pretty remote areas and offers plenty of scope for panoramic day walks or drives. If you don't have a vehicle, you have the option of guided walks, 4WD excursions and wildlife-spotting trips, which will get you out into the wild areas.

Hornos
POP 410 / ELEV 867M

Like better-known Segura de la Sierra, little Hornos is fabulously located – atop a crag backed by a sweep of mountains, with marvellous views over the shimmering Embalse del Tranco and the lush, green countryside, richly patterned with olive, pine and almond trees and the occasional tossed dice of a farmhouse.

Hornos dates back to the Bronze Age when there was a settlement here; the castle on the crag was built by Christians in the

GRANADA & SOUTH COAST ANDALUCÍA PARQUE NATURAL SIERRAS DE CAZORLA, SEGURA Y LAS VILLAS

DON'T MISS

RÍO BOROSA WALK

The most popular walk in the Parque Natural Sierras de Cazorla, Segura y las Villas follows the Río Borosa upstream through scenery that progresses from the pretty to the majestic, via a gorge and two tunnels to two beautiful mountain lakes – an ascent of 500m. The walk is 12km each way and takes about seven hours there and back.

To reach the start, turn east off the A319 at the 'Sendero Río Borosa' sign opposite the **Centro de Visitantes Torre del Vinagre** (☑ 953 72 13 51; Ctra A319 Km 48; ☉ 10am-2pm & 4-7pm, afternoons 3-8pm Jul-Sep, 4-6pm Oct-Mar, closed Mon Sep-Jun), and go 1.7km. The first section of the walk criss-crosses the tumbling river on a couple of bridges. After just over 3km, where the track starts climbing to the left, take a path forking right. This leads through a beautiful 1.5km section where the valley narrows to a gorge, the **Cerrada de Elías**, and the path changes to a wooden walkway. You re-emerge on the dirt road and continue for 4km to the **Central Eléctrica**, a small hydroelectric station.

Past the power station, the path crosses a footbridge, where a 'Nacimiento de Aguas Negras, Laguna de Valdeazores' sign directs you ahead. About 1.5km from the station, the path turns left and zigzags up into a tunnel cut into the cliff for water flowing to the power station. It takes about five minutes to walk the narrow path through the tunnel, then there's a short section in the open air before a second tunnel, which takes about one minute to get through. You emerge just below the dam of the **Laguna de Aguas Negras**, a picturesque little reservoir surrounded by hills and trees. Cross the dam then walk about 1km south to a similar-sized natural lake, the **Laguna de Valdeazores**, the end-point of the walk.

Due to its popularity, it's preferable to do this walk on a weekday! Do carry a water bottle: there are good trackside springs but the last is at the Central Eléctrica. A torch is comforting, if not essential, for the tunnels.

---

mid-13th century, probably on the site of an earlier Muslim fortification. Don't expect colour-coordinated geraniums, souvenir shops or a tourist office: Hornos' charms lie in exploring the narrow, winding streets and wondering at the view from several strategically placed miradors. Seek out the early-16th-century **Iglesia de la Asunción**, which has the oldest, albeit crumbling, plateresque portal in the province, plus a vibrant 1589 *retablo* (altarpiece) with nine painted panels.

There are a couple of restaurants and basic lodgings should you want to stay. If you want to stride out, a plaque at the village entrance shows local trails including two of about 4km each to tiny outlying villages – the PRA152 south down to Hornos El Viejo and the PRA148 east up to La Capellanía.

To get to Hornos, take the A319 12km north of the Tranco dam to a T-junction; from here the A317 winds 4km up to Hornos village.

Segura de la Sierra

POP 250 / ELEV 1145M

One of Andalucía's most picturesque villages, Segura de la Sierra perches on a 1200m-high hill crowned by a Reconquista castle, 21km north of Hornos. The village takes some of its character from its five Moorish centuries before the Knights of Santiago captured it in 1214, after which it became part of the Christian front line against the Almohads and then the Granada emirate.

As you drive up into the village, the Puerta Nueva, one of four gates of Islamic Saqura, marks the entrance to the old part of Segura. Signs to the Castillo lead you round to a junction on the northern side by the little walled bullring. Turn left here to head up to the castle itself.

◉ Sights

★**Castillo de Segura** CASTLE

(☑ 953 48 21 73; www.castillodesegura.com; adult/child incl audio guide €4/3; ☉ daily Jul-Aug, closed Jan-Feb, refer to website for hours; ♿) This lofty castle dates from Moorish times but was rebuilt after the Christian conquest in the 13th century. Abandoned in the 17th century, it was restored in the 1960s and has now become a 'frontier territory ' interpretation centre. The ticket office is also Segura's tourist information office.

Baños Árabes BATHHOUSE

(Calle Baño Moro; ⊗ hours variable) FREE
Built around 1150, probably for the local
ruler Ibn ben Hamusk, these Arab baths
at the foot of the village have the usual
three rooms (for cold, temperate and hot
temperatures), with pretty red-and-white
horseshoe arches and barrel vaults studded with skylights. You can expect them to
be open during daylight hours. You'll have
to ask directions to find them, as signage
is hopeless.

🛏 Sleeping & Eating

La Mesa Segureña APARTMENT €

(📋 953 48 21 01; https://es-la.facebook.com/lame-
sadesegura; Calle Cruz de Montoria, Segura de la Sierra; 2-person apt €60-75; 🛜) Cosy apartments
just below Segura castle, with great views, a
touch of bright art, fireplaces and minikitch-
ens. Good discounts are often available from
the quoted rates.

Mirador de Peñalta ANDALUCIAN €

(Calle San Vicente 29; mains €4-17; ⊗ 1.30-4pm
& 8-10pm Tue-Sun) On the street entering
Segura from below, this place caters to
hungry travellers with a meaty menu that
includes steaks, lamb chops and pork, as
well as some sierra specialities such as *ajo
atao* (a belly-filling fry-up of potatoes, garlic and eggs).

ALMERÍA PROVINCE

One of Almería's main draws is the weather: 3000 hours of sunshine a year. It is also
famous for being the greenhouse of Europe,
a top growing area for fruit and vegetables
sold throughout the EU. The downside of
this agriculture-driven prosperity is a blight
of plastic greenhouses in parts of the province but, turning a blind eye to them, Almería has plenty of appeal. Topping the list are
the stunning coastline, beaches and volcanic, desert-like landscape of the Parque Natural de Cabo de Gata-Níjar. Up the eastern
coast, the good-time resort of Mojácar has a
great summer beach scene. Inland, you can
visit the spectacular Sorbas caves and the
Wild West film sets in the Desierto de Tabernas, and venture up to the green, mountainous Los Vélez region. But definitely don't
skip Almería city, a vivacious Mediterrane-
an-side capital with impressive monuments,
excellent museums and superb tapas bars.

Almería

POP 165,000

Almería has come a long way. What was a
couple of decades ago basically a tough port
city, with its glory days buried firmly in the
past, is today the increasingly polished,
energetic and visitor-friendly capital of Andalucía's second-wealthiest province. Its cultural attractions are ever-growing and the
tapas-bar scene in its spruced-up old centre
rivals the best.

◉ Sights

Almería's main sights are the Alcazaba and
the cathedral, both of which can be explored
in a morning, but there are plenty of interesting additional distractions in the city's
meandering streets.

★**Catedral de la Encarnación** CATHEDRAL

(Plaza de la Catedral; €5, free Mon morning;
⊗ 10am-1.30pm & 4-5pm Mon-Fri, to 1.30pm Sat)
Cathedral or fortress? Almería's unusually
weighty, six-towered cathedral, begun in
1525, was conceived both as a place of worship and as a refuge for the population from
frequent pirate raids from North Africa.
Basically a Gothic/Renaissance building, it
had baroque and neoclassical features added in the 18th century. You enter from Calle
Velázquez via a fine cloister carved from
pale stone. The vast, impressive interior has
a beautiful ceiling with sinuous Gothic rib-
bing and is trimmed in jasper, marble and
carved walnut.

★**Alcazaba** FORTRESS

(Calle Almanzor; ⊗ 9am-7.30pm Tue-Sat Apr–
mid-Jun, to 3.30pm Tue-Sat mid-Jun–mid-Sep,
to 5.30pm Tue-Sat mid-Sep–Mar, to 3.30pm Sun
all year) FREE A looming fortification with
great curtain-like walls rising from the cliffs,
the Alcazaba was founded in the mid-10th
century and was one of the most powerful
Moorish fortresses in Spain. It lacks the intricate decoration of Granada's Alhambra,
but is nonetheless a compelling monument.
Allow about 1½ hours to see everything.
Pick up a guide leaflet in one of several languages at the kiosk, just inside the four-arch
entrance gate.

The Alcazaba is divided into three *recin-
tos* (compounds). The lowest, the **Primer Recinto**, was residential, with houses, streets,
wells, baths and other necessities – now replaced by lush gardens and water channels.
From the battlements you can see the **Mu-**

WORTH A TRIP

PARQUE NATURAL SIERRA DE ANDÚJAR

This large (748 sq km) natural park north of Andújar town has the largest expanses of natural vegetation in the Sierra Morena as well as plenty of bull-breeding ranches. Among the many varieties of wildlife are five emblematic endangered species – Iberian lynx, wolf, black vulture, black stork and Spanish imperial eagle – which attract a good number of bird- and animal-watchers to the park. The Iberian lynx population here, around 120, is the largest in the world. Staff at the park visitors centre, the **Centro de Visitantes Viñas de Peñallana** (953 54 96 28; Ctra A6177 Km 13; 10am-2pm & 4-6pm Thu-Sun, hours may vary), 13km north of Andújar town, can tell you the best areas for lynx-spotting, though chances of sightings are always slim. The best months are December and January, the mating season. Local firms offering guided wildlife and bird-watching trips **Turismo Verde** (629 518345; www.lasierradeandujar.com) and **IberianLynxLand** (636 984515; www.iberianlynxland.com).

On a hilltop in the heart of the park stands the **Santuario de la Virgen de la Cabeza** (Ctra A6177 Km 31, Cerro del Cabezo; P), a chapel that is the focus of one of Spain's biggest and most emotive religious events, the **Romería de la Virgen de la Cabeza**, on the last weekend in April. Hundreds of thousands of people converge in a huge, festive tent city to witness a small statue of the Virgin Mary, known as La Morenita, being carried around the hill for several hours on the Sunday.

A great base for wildlife watchers, rural hotel **La Caracola** (633 515679; www.lacaracolahotelrural.com; Ctra A6177 Km 13.8; d incl breakfast €60; P 🛜 ☒) sits among woodlands and offers bright, contemporary rooms, comfortable common areas and good meals – they'll serve breakfast as early as you like. It's 1.4km off the A6177, less than a kilometre north of the Andújar park visitors centre.

Andújar town is served by several daily trains and buses from Jaén and Córdoba, and by buses from Baeza and Úbeda. There are buses to the sanctuary on Saturday and Sunday.

---

ralla de Jayrán, a fortified wall built in the 11th century to defend the outlying northern and eastern parts of the city, as well as stunning city and coastal views.

In the **Segundo Recinto** you'll find the ruins of the Muslim rulers' palace, built by the *taifa* ruler Almotacín (r 1051–91), under whom medieval Almería reached its peak, plus a chapel, the **Ermita de San Juan**, that was originally a mosque. The highest section, the **Tercer Recinto**, is a citadel added by the Catholic Monarchs.

Museo de la Guitarra   MUSEUM
(950 27 43 58; Ronda del Beato Diego Ventaja; €3; 10.30am-1.30pm Tue-Sun, 6-9pm Fri & Sat Jun-Sep, 10am-1pm Tue-Sun, 5-8pm Fri & Sat Oct-May) It's worth establishing two important facts before you enter this absorbing, recently opened interactive museum. First: the word 'guitar' is derived from the Andalucian-Arabic word *qitara,* hinting at its Spanish roots. Second: all modern acoustic guitars owe a huge debt to Almerían guitar-maker Antonio de Torres (1817–92), to whom this museum is dedicated. The museum itself is a minor masterpiece that

details the history of the guitar and pays homage to Torres' part in it.

Refugios de la Guerra Civil   HISTORIC SITE
(Civil War Shelters; reservations 950 26 86 96; Plaza de Manuel Pérez García; tour €3; guided tours 10.30am & noon Tue-Sun, 6pm & 7.30pm Fri & Sat Jun-Sep, 10am & 11.30am Tue-Sun, 5pm & 6.30pm Fri & Sat Oct-May) During the civil war, Almería was the Republicans' last holdout province in Andalucía, and was repeatedly and mercilessly bombed. The attacks prompted a group of engineers to design and build the Refugios, a 4.5km-long network of concrete shelters under the city. Visits – by 1¼-hour guided tour, available in English as well as Spanish – take you through 1km of the tunnels including the re-created operating theatre and storerooms. Advance reservations essential.

🏃 Activities

Hammam Almeraya   BATHHOUSE
(www.almeraya.info; Calle Perea 9; 1½hr session incl aromatherapy €16; 4-10pm Wed-Mon) Almería's smaller *hammam* has hot and cold baths, a 'Turkish' steam bath, and

beautiful marble-and-tiled surroundings. It also offers massages, as well as a relaxing *tetería*.

Hammam Aire de Almería
BATHHOUSE

(www.airedealmeria.com; Plaza de la Constitución 5; 1½hr session incl 15min aromatherapy €23; ⏱10am-10pm) Housed in a suitably historic building, this luxurious and spacious *hammam* exudes a feeling of tranquillity throughout its marble and warm-brick interior. It offers three baths: the frigidarium (16°C), the tepidarium (36°C) and the caldarium (40°C), as well as a range of aromatherapy and other massages. Reservations are advisable.

🛌 Sleeping

Hotel Nuevo Torreluz
HOTEL €

(☏950 23 43 99; www.torreluz.com; Plaza de las Flores 10; r €50-63; ❄@🛜) An updated four-star hotel enjoying a superb location on a small square in the historic centre. Rooms are on the small side but well equipped and comfortable, with elegant grey-and-silver colour schemes and high-pressure showers. The hotel runs a trio of cafes and restaurants around the square.

⭐Plaza Vieja Hotel & Lounge
BOUTIQUE HOTEL €€

(☏950 28 20 96; www.plazaviejahl.com; Plaza de la Constitución 4; s €71-89, d €87-109; ❄@🛜) This stylish spot is perfectly situated on beautiful Plaza de la Constitución, just a few steps from some of the city's top tapas bars. Part of the plush Hammam Aire de Almería set-up, the rooms here are spacious and modern with high ceilings, soft natural colour schemes and vast photo-walls of local sights such as the Cabo de Gata.

Hotel Catedral
BOUTIQUE HOTEL €€

(☏950 27 81 78; www.hotelcatedral.net; Plaza de la Catedral 8; r €76-150; ❄@🛜) Cosied up to the cathedral and built with the same warm honey-coloured stone, the hotel building dates from 1850. It has been sensitively restored, combining clean contemporary lines with Gothic arches and an *artesonado* ceiling in the restaurant. Rooms are large, with luxury touches, and the roof terrace, with Jacuzzi, has heady cathedral views.

🍴 Eating

⭐Casa Joaquín
SEAFOOD €€

(☏950 26 43 59; Calle Real 111; raciones €10-21; ⏱1.30-3.30pm & 8.30-11pm Mon-Fri, to 4.30pm Sat, closed Sep) Reserve one of the few tables if you're really serious about your seafood. If you don't mind standing, you can jostle at the bar of this nearly century-old bodega famous for the freshness of its ingredients and their perfect, simple, traditional preparation.

Lamarca
ANDALUCIAN, DELI €€

(Calle Doctor Gregorio Marañón 33; raciones €7-14; ⏱1.30-4pm & 8pm-midnight Mon-Sat, to 4pm Sun) What started as a humble ham shop has morphed into a funky deli-cum-restaurant group with several branches around Almería. Head to the back dining room to sample ham, sausages, cheeses and wines from

---

DON'T MISS

THE OLD MEDINA

It's intriguing to wander round the maze-like Almedina neighbourhood between the Alcazaba and the sea. This was the area occupied by the original Almería – a walled medina (city), bounded by the Alcazaba on the north, the sea on the south, and what are now Calle de la Reina and Avenida del Mar on the east and west. At its heart was the city's main mosque – whose *mihrab* (niche indicating the direction of Mecca) survives inside the **Iglesia de San Juan** (Calle San Juan; ⏱open for mass 8pm Apr-Sep, 7pm Oct-Mar, except Tue & Fri) – with the commercial area of markets and warehouses spread around it. Calle de la Almedina still traces the line of the old main street running diagonally across the medina. Some of the small houses along the medina's narrow streets are in ruins, while others are recently restored as efforts are made to revive this inner-city area. An excellent place to stop is **Tetería Almedina** (p720) teahouse. Also worth seeking out is the **Plaza de Pavía market** (⏱9am-2pm Mon-Sat), at its liveliest on Saturdays, with a rowdy mix of produce, cheap shoes and churros (delicious, fat, tubular doughnuts).

all over Spain, in tapas sizes or *raciones* to share, under a ceiling of hanging hams. There are salads and egg dishes too, for the less carnivorous.

Tetería Almedina
MOROCCAN €€

(http://teteriaalmedina.com; Calle Paz 2, off Calle de la Almedina; pot tea €2-7, mains €10-15; ⊙noon-11pm or later Tue-Sun; ▯) This lovely little cafe, in the oldest part of the city below the Alcazaba, serves tasty tagines, couscous dishes, soups, salads and other Moroccan favourites, plus a fascinating range of teas, infusions and sweets, in an atmosphere redolent of a Moroccan teahouse.

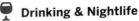

Drinking & Nightlife

New Georgia
MUSIC BAR

(Calle Padre Luque 17; ⊙4pm-3am) A successful recent reincarnation of a classic Almería jazz venue, New Georgia plays jazz, soul, blues and rock'n'roll, with live bands at midnight every Saturday.

Tetería Almeraya
TEAHOUSE

(pot of tea €2.50-9.50; ⊙9am-2pm & 4pm-midnight, closed Tue evening & Sat & Sun morning) All warm burgundies, olive greens and Moorish friezes, inviting Tetería Almeraya has an intimate vibe and plays gentle mood music to keep the romancing couples content. Along with all the teas you could possibly think of (including tea spiked with Baileys), it serves cocktails.

LOCAL KNOWLEDGE

TAPAS TOUR

The streets between Paseo de Almería and Plaza de la Constitución are packed with busy and atmospheric tapas bars. Like Granada, Almería maintains the tradition of free tapas with a drink. But it does its neighbour one better: here, all tapas are *a elegir*, meaning you choose what you want from a list. Portions are generous, and for the hungry – or to share between more than one person – almost everywhere offers *raciones* and *medias raciones* (full- and half-sized plates of tapas items).

Casa Puga (www.barcasapuga.es; Calle Jovellanos 7; wine & tapa €2.80; ⊙noon-4pm & 8pm-midnight Mon-Sat, closed Wed evening) The undisputed tapas champ (since it opened in 1870) is Casa Puga; make it an early stop, as it fills up fast. Shelves of ancient wine bottles, and walls plastered with everything from lottery tickets to ancient maps, are the backdrop for a tiny cooking station that churns out saucers of tasty stews and griddled meats, fish, mushrooms and shrimps.

Nuestra Tierra (Calle Jovellanos 16; wine & tapa €2.80; ⊙7.30am-noon Mon, 7.30am-4pm & 8pm-midnight Wed-Fri, noon-4pm & 8pm-midnight Sat, noon-4pm Sun) This tiny spot, with just five tables and a teensy bar, prepares really tasty little platters from local Almería ingredients. It's well worth getting their grilled octopus, or the ham, egg and spring onion in a bread roll, or a dozen other treats.

El Quinto Toro (Calle Juan Leal 6; drink & tapa €2.50; ⊙noon-4pm & 8pm-midnight Mon-Sat) The 'Fifth Bull' rivals Casa Puga in traditional atmosphere, with the obligatory bull's head over the bar. Treats include anchovies with Roquefort cheese and rich *albóndigas* (meatballs) in a wine sauce.

La Mala (Calle Real 69; beer & tapa €2.50, tortillas €8-12; ⊙noon-5pm & 8.30pm-1am Mon-Sat) Rock music and great *tortillas* (omelettes) are the successful recipe at this gaudily painted street-corner bar, where the crowd regularly spills into the street. Now's your chance to try an octopus or gorgonzola-and-mushroom omelette.

Entrefinos (Calle Padre Alfonso Torres 9; tapa & drink €3-5; ⊙1-4pm & 8pm-midnight) Lively Entrefinos re-creates a traditional bodega ambience with its high wood-beam ceiling, tall wooden tables and blackboard menus. The tapas, such as Angus-beef sirloin or crisp-fried John Dory, are a cut above the ordinary.

Taberna Postigo (Calle Guzmán; drink & tapa €2.20-3; ⊙11am-5pm & 7pm-1am Tue-Thu & Sun, to 3pm Fri & Sat) A major appeal of this friendly tavern is that the sprawl of tables is shaded by rows of leafy trees. Tapas *a la brasa* (grilled over hot coals) are favourites, as is the bacon with *pimientos* (peppers).

☆ Entertainment

Clasijazz
JAZZ

(http://clasijazz.com; Calle Maestro Serrano 9; admission nonmembers €2-25) Thriving music club Clasijazz has an excellent program of four or five events weekly ranging from jazz to classical to jam sessions, in a strikingly designed contemporary space.

Peña El Morato
FLAMENCO

(☑675 525460; www.elmorato.com; Calle Morato) Scooped out of a cave on the edge of town, this bar–club is about as local as it gets flamenco-wise. Live shows are most Fridays at 10.30pm. Slip in for a performance over tapas and wine and you'll soon feel like one of the family.

Peña El Taranto
FLAMENCO

(☑950 23 50 57; www.eltaranto.com; Calle Tenor Iribarne) This is Almería's top flamenco club, where local guitar star Tomatito has been known to stroke the strings. There's usually live music, song and dance at about 10pm Thursday to Saturday. Visitors are welcome if there is space (admission is free, with drinks and tapas available).

ℹ Information

Oficina Municipal de Turismo (☑950 21 05 38; www.turismodeandalucia.org; Plaza de la Constitución; ⊙10am-3pm Mon-Fri, to 2pm Sat & Sun)

Regional Tourist Office (☑950 17 52 20; www.andalucia.org; Parque de Nicolás Salmerón; ⊙9am-7.30pm Mon-Fri, 9.30am-3pm Sat & Sun)

ℹ Getting There & Away

AIR

Almería's small **airport** (☑902 40 47 04; www.aena.es) is 10km east of the city centre. **EasyJet** (www.easyjet.com), **Ryanair** (www.ryanair.com), **Monarch Airlines** (www.monarch.co.uk) and **Thomas Cook Airlines** (www.thomascookairlines.com) fly direct from various English airports (Ryanair also flies from Dublin and Brussels); **Iberia** (www.iberia.com) and **Vueling** (www.vueling.com) serve Spanish destinations.

BOAT

Acciona Trasmediterránea (☑902 45 46 45; www.trasmediterranea.es) sails from the **passenger port** (Ctra de Málaga) to Nador (Morocco; six hours) and Melilla (Morocco; 8½ hours) at least once daily, and Ghazaouet (Algeria; nine hours) at least once weekly. One-way passenger fares are €45, €38 and €92 respectively, and for two adults with a car €215, €181 and €560.

BUS

Buses and trains share the **Estación Intermodal** (☑950 26 20 98; Plaza de la Estación) just east of the centre. **Alsa** (☑902 42 22 42; www.alsa.es) provides most of the intercity bus services.

DESTINATION	FARE	DURATION	FREQUENCY
Córdoba	€29	5hr	1 daily
Granada	€14-18	2-4hr	7 daily
Guadix	€17	2¼hr	2 daily
Jaén	€20	3-5hr	2 daily
Madrid	€29	7hr	5 daily
Málaga	€19-22	3-4½hr	7 daily
Murcia	€20	3-4½hr	5 daily
Seville	€37-45	5½-9hr	3 daily

TRAIN

Trains operated by **Renfe** (www.renfe.com) run from the **Estación Intermodal**, including direct to Granada (€20, 2½ hours, four daily), Seville (€41, 5½ hours, four daily) and Madrid (€46, 6½ hours, two daily).

Desierto de Tabernas

North of the city is a stretch of barren landscape that looks as if it has been transplanted from the Mojave desert – dun-coloured hills scattered with tufts of tussocky scrub. In the 1960s Clint Eastwood, Lee Van Cleef, Claudia Cardinale and other stars strode these badlands on location for the many 'spaghetti westerns' (so called because of their Italian producers and/or directors) that were filmed here – notably Sergio Leone's 'Dollars Trilogy' (*A Fistful of Dollars*, 1964; *For a Few Dollars More*, 1965; and *The Good, the Bad and the Ugly*, 1966) and *Once Upon a Time in the West* (1968). 'Western town' film sets here have since been turned into Wild West theme parks as well as continuing to be used for film-making. They make a fun day out, especially with kids.

◉ Sights

Oasys Mini Hollywood
AMUSEMENT PARK

(☑902 53 35 32; www.oasysparquetematico.com; Ctra N340A Km 464.5; adult/child €22/13; ⊙10am-7.30pm Jun & Sep, to 9pm Jul & Aug, to 6pm Oct-May, closed Mon-Fri Nov-Mar; 🅿🚌)

This is the best-known and most expensive of the Wild West parks and provides some good family entertainment. The set itself is in decent condition, and the well-kept zoo has grown to a considerable size with some 800 animals at last count, including lions, giraffes, tigers and hippos. Children usually enjoy the 20-minute shoot-outs (resulting in an unceremonious hanging), while adults may prefer the clichéd can-can show (or at least the beer) in the saloon.

Fort Bravo
AMUSEMENT PARK

(Texas Hollywood; ☑902 07 08 14; www.fortbravo.es; Ctra N340A Km 468.5; adult/child €18/10; ⏰9am-8pm Apr-Oct, to 7pm Nov-Mar; 🅿) This place has a certain dusty charm. It stages daily Wild West and can-can shows, and has a summer pool and a saloon where David Beckham and other football stars once shot a Pepsi ad. Buggy rides, horse treks and overnight stays in log cabins are also available. Fort Bravo is 1km off the N340A, signposted 31km from Almería.

Cabo de Gata-Níjar

Some of Spain's most flawless and least crowded sandy beaches are strung like pearls between the dramatic cliffs of the Cabo de Gata promontory, southeast of Almería. With less than 200mm of rain in an average year, this is the driest place in Europe, yet more than 1000 varieties of animal and plant thrive in the arid, salty environment. A 340-sq-km area of coast and hinterland, plus a mile-wide strip of sea, are protected as the Parque Natural de Cabo de Gata-Níjar. The stark terrain, a product of volcanic activity more than 7 million years ago, is studded with agave plants and other desert succulents, and has only a few small settlements of whitewashed, flat-roofed houses and a scattering of abandoned or renovated farmsteads. The largest village is San José, a second home for many Almería city folk. The park is also a bonanza of bizarre rock formations, with an intriguing mining history, and is part of the European Geoparks (www.europeangeoparks.org) network.

There is plenty to do on Cabo de Gata besides just enjoying the beaches and walking. Diving, snorkelling, kayaking, sailing, cycling, horse riding, and 4WD and boat tours are all popular. A host of operators offers these activities from the coastal villages during Easter and from July to September, though only a few carry on year-round.

The Cabo de Gata stands at the southwest point of the promontory: its name (from

Cabo de Gata

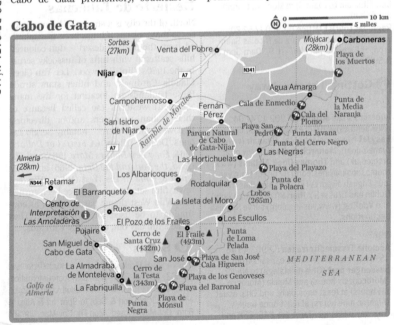

WALKING THE CABO DE GATA COAST

A network of roads and trails leads about 50km right around the coast from San Miguel de Cabo de Gata to Agua Amarga. The full hike requires three days and should be attempted only in spring or, better, autumn (when the sea is warm), as the summer heat is fierce and there is no shade. But you can embark on sections of the walk for a day or afternoon, and some of the beaches you'll pass are otherwise inaccessible.

From San José it's a fine 9km walk of about 2½ hours, passing some of the best beaches, southwest to the Torre Vigía Vela Blanca, an old lookout tower with superb panoramas. Northeast from San José to the tiny beach settlement of Los Escullos, it's a fairly level 8km walk with some good views, skirting the ancient volcano El Fraile, partly on old mining roads.

Another good stretch is from Rodalquilar along the valley to Playa del Playazo, then up the coast along scenic cliff edges to Las Negras (6km from Rodalquilar). It's another 3km to the real prize: Playa San Pedro, inaccessible by road, with its abandoned village that supports a small crew of boho-travellers. You can also drive to Las Negras, then walk to Playa San Pedro from there.

ágata, the Spanish for agate) may also refer to the entire promontory, from Retamar in the west to Agua Amarga in the east, or to the village of San Miguel de Cabo de Gata on the west coast.

Sights

★ **Gold Mines** RUIN

There is something very evocative about the old gold mines, which were at their peak of activity in the mid-20th century; a fascinating bit of industrial wreckage in a barren red-rock landscape. Stop first at La Casa de los Volcanes (☉10am-2pm Thu-Sat; ℗) FREE at the top of the village, a museum with excellent displays on the mines and the geology of Cabo de Gata. Behind the museum you can walk up among the abandoned crushing towers and decantation tanks from the 1950s.

The gravel road continues through the hills behind, pocked with abandoned mines and the ruined miners' hamlet of San Diego. It's dangerous to enter any of these, but the Sendero Cerro del Cinto walking trail, starting just below the Casa de los Volcanes, is an 11km circuit through this dramatic post-industrial landscape.

Faro de Cabo de Gata LIGHTHOUSE

(℗) At the southwest point of the promontory, this lighthouse overlooks the jagged volcanic reefs of the Arrecife de las Sirenas (Reef of the Mermaids), named after the monk seals that used to lounge here. The view into the water is fantastically clear. A side road runs 3km up to the Torre Vigía Vela Blanca, an 18th-century watchtower with wonderful views in both directions along the coast.

Torre Vigía Vela Blanca TOWER

Three kilometres east of the Faro de Cabo de Gata, this 18th-century watchtower offers wonderful views in both directions along the coast.

Salinas de Cabo de Gata SALT FLATS

(℗) Southeast of drab San Miguel de Cabo de Gata village, some of Spain's last surviving sea-salt-extraction lagoons draw flocks of migrating flamingos and other water birds from spring to autumn: by late August there can be 1000 flamingos here. Birdwatching hides are placed at a few strategic points.

Activities

El Cabo a Fondo BOAT TOUR

(☏637 449170; www.elcaboafondo.com; 1hr tour adult/child €20/15; ♠) Some of the most spectacular views of the Cabo de Gata coast are from the sea, and you'll get this perspective on Cabo a Fondo's outings starting from La Isleta del Moro, Las Negras or La Fabriquilla. Trips run up to eight times daily and are offered year-round, weather permitting (minimum numbers may be required in low seasons). Reserving ahead is essential.

Sleeping

★ El Jardín de los Sueños BOUTIQUE HOTEL €€

(☏669 184118, 950 38 98 43; www.eljardindelos suenos.es; Calle Los Gorriones; incl breakfast d €98,

DON'T MISS

CABO DE GATA BEACHES

Playa San Pedro This sandy beach, 250m long, sits 3km northeast of Las Negras, between dramatic headlands. San Pedro hamlet is inhabited by a small floating population of travellers and others hanging out in tents, abandoned buildings and the odd cave. It's only accessible on foot or by inflatable boat from Las Negras. The boats cost €10 return and their frequencies depend on demand and weather.

Playa del Playazo (P) A 400m broad, sandy strip between two headlands, one of which is topped by a small 18th-century fort (now a private home): it's 3.5km east of Rodalquilar, the last 2km along a drivable track from the main road.

Cala de Enmedio The pretty and secluded little beach of Cala de Enmedio is enclosed between striking eroded rocks. Get here via a waymarked walk of about 1.5km over a small hill southwest from Agua Amarga.

Calas del Barronal Four gorgeous, isolated, little beaches east of **Playa del Barronal**. Tides permitting (they usually do) you can walk round the foot of the cliffs from one to the next.

Playa de los Genoveses (P) The first beach you reach southwest from San José is Playa de los Genoveses, a 1km-long stretch where the Genoese navy landed in 1147 to aid in the Christian attack on Almería.

Playa de Mónsul (P) Popular Playa de Mónsul (where you may recognise the rock overhang from *Indiana Jones and the Last Crusade*) is 2.5km along the road from the **Playa de los Genoveses** turn-off.

ste €118-140; (P❄🛜⛶) Just off the highway opposite Rodalquilar, this expanded old farmhouse is surrounded by a beautiful garden of dry-climate plants and fruit trees – some of which contribute to the substantial breakfasts. It's full of character and charm, very comfortable, and open all year. Bright colours, original art, tea/coffee equipment, private terraces, the occasional chandelier and the absence of TVs distinguish the rooms.

★**MC San José**   HOTEL €€€
(📋 950 61 11 11; www.hotelesmcsanjose.com; Calle El Faro 2; incl breakfast s €129-142, d €154-215; ⊙ closed early Nov-Feb; ❄@🛜⛶) The MC offers the best of both hotel worlds: it has a chic contemporary design in gleaming whites and greys, and plenty of stylish details, but it also has the kind of hospitality that only comes from being run by a local family.

MiKasa   BOUTIQUE HOTEL €€€
(📋 950 13 80 73; www.mikasasuites.com; Carretera Carboneras 20; d incl breakfast €150-220; P❄🛜⛶) MiKasa is the luxurious romantic-getaway option, and a delight with stunning pink Galician marble and lovely rooms. All rooms differ: one has a large circular bath, another a view of the sea, another a large private terrace. The hotel has two pools, a fancy spa and a beach bar, and the top-class Restaurante La Villa (p725) is next door.

✖ Eating

★**4 Nudos**   SEAFOOD €€
(📋 620 938160; www.cuatronudossanjose.com; Puerto Deportivo; mains €12-20; ⊙ 9am-midnight Apr-Oct, 11am-8pm Tue-Fri, 9am-5pm & 7pm-midnight Sat & Sun Nov-Mar, closed 2nd half Jan) A cut above your average San José eatery, the 'Four Knots' is serious about its food but not too serious to be enjoyable. Friendly service complements terrific fresh fish and seafood – with exotica such as swordfish ceviche or tuna tataki alongside more classical preparations – and good Spanish wines.

La Gallineta   CONTEMPORARY SPANISH €€
(📋 950 38 05 01; El Pozo de los Frailes; mains €10-26; ⊙ 1.30-3.30pm & 8.30-11pm Apr–mid-Oct, closed Mon except Jul & Aug) A small elegant restaurant in a former village shop 4km north of San José, La Gallineta is where urban escapees come for inventive, freshly made dishes with local ingredients and an international twist. Try a seafood dish or one of the speciality rice dishes (which must

be ordered ahead if you want them in the evening).

You should book two or three days ahead at Easter or in July and August.

Casa Café de la Loma

MEDITERRANEAN, BASQUE **€€**

(📞950 38 98 31; www.casacafelaloma.com; La Isleta del Moro; mains €10-30; ⊙7pm-1am early Jul–end Aug; 🅿) A Mediterranean heaven with great sea views, this old *cortijo* (farmstead) runs a summer-only restaurant. The menu covers fresh fish and local meats but also plenty of creative salads and other vegetarian dishes, and there are regular jazz and flamenco concerts in the garden, by candlelight. Look for the turn-off from the main road just north of La Isleta del Moro.

★Restaurante La Villa

MEDITERRANEAN FUSION **€€€**

(📞950 13 80 90; Carretera Carboneras 18, Agua Amarga; mains €19-24; ⊙8.30pm-last customer Jul & Aug, 8pm-last customer Wed-Sun Mar-Jun & Sep-Jan, 2-5pm Sat & Sun Mar-May & Sep-Jan) Next door to Agua Amarga's top hotel, La Villa is a sophisticated restaurant with a romantically lit dining room and pretty outside terrace. The dishes try just hard enough to be original, but stop short of being slaves to drizzle and tower-building. Reservations advised.

❶ Information

Centro de Información (www.cabodegata-nijar.com; Avenida San José 27, San José; ⊙10am-2pm & 5-8pm Apr-Oct, to 2pm Nov-Mar) Park information centre and local-products shop.

Centro de Interpretación Las Amoladeras (Ctra Retamar-Pujaire Km 7; ⊙10am-3pm Thu-Sun) The park's main visitor centre, on the main road from Almería 2km west of Ruescas.

❶ Getting There & Away

Alsa (p721) Runs six daily buses from Almería to San Miguel de Cabo de Gata (€2.90, one hour), and one (except Sunday) to Las Negras (€2.90, 1¼ hours) and Rodalquilar (€2.90, 1½ hours).

Autocares Bernardo (📞950 25 04 22; www.autocaresbernardo.com) Runs buses between Almería and San José (€2.90, 1¼ hours, three Monday to Saturday, two on Sunday).

Autocares Frahermar (📞950 26 64 11; www.frahermar.com) Runs between Almería and Agua Amarga (€5.50, 1¼ hours) once daily except Tuesday and Thursday; service increases to once or twice every day in July and August.

Mojácar

POP 6337

There are two Mojácars: old Mojácar Pueblo, a jumble of white cube houses daubed over a hilltop 2km inland and dating back to at least Moorish times, and young Mojácar Playa, a low-rise modern resort spread out 7km along a broad sandy beach. As recently as the 1960s, the *pueblo* (village) was decaying and almost abandoned. A savvy mayor, Jacinto Alarcón, lured artists and others with bargain property offers, which set a distinct bohemian tone that is still palpable, despite an overlay of more generic tourism. In the picturesque *pueblo's* winding streets, there are mellow bars, galleries and intriguing small shops.

⊙ Sights

The main sight is the very pretty *pueblo*, dotted with cute little plazas, bars and cafes. To reach the *pueblo* from Mojácar Playa, turn inland at the roundabout by the Parque Comercial, a large shopping centre towards the north end of the *playa* (beach); regular buses connect the two.

El Mirador del Castillo

VIEWPOINT

A byproduct of Mojácar's revival as an arts colony, the villa called El Mirador del Castillo occupies the very top of the hill. Today it's a hotel and cafe-bar (both open Easter to October), and a mirador (lookout) to end all miradors, with panoramas stretching from the sea to a landscape studded with volcanic cones just like the one Mojácar occupies.

Iglesia de Santa María

CHURCH

(Calle Iglesia) The fortress-style Iglesia de Santa María dates from 1560 and may have once been a mosque.

Fuente Pública

FOUNTAIN

(Public Fountain, Moorish Fountain; Calle La Fuente) Near the foot of Mojácar Pueblo, this pretty public fountain is a village landmark. Locals and visitors still fill containers with the water that tumbles out of 13 spouts into marble troughs and tinkles along a courtyard below colourful plants. A plaque tells us that in 1488 this was where the Catholic Monarchs' envoy met Mojácar's last Moorish mayor, Alavez, to negotiate the village's surrender.

🛏 Sleeping & Eating

Hostal El Olívar

HOSTAL **€**

(📞950 47 20 02; www.hostalelolivar.es; Calle Estación Nueva 11, Mojácar Pueblo; s/d incl breakfast €38/59; 🛏 @ 🛜) A stylish and welcoming addition to the Mojácar Pueblo options, the Olívar has contemporary, pretty rooms with up-to-date bathrooms and tea/coffee sets. Some overlook a plaza, others the countryside. Breakfast is generous and you can take it on a panoramic terrace, when the weather is decent.

El Mirador del Castillo   RURAL HOTEL €€

(☑ 694 454768; www.elmiradordelcastillo.com; Plaza Mirador del Castillo; r €69-120, ste €136; ⊙ Easter-Oct; 🛏 🛜 🏊) Up at the tip-top of Mojácar's hill, this delightful small hotel, formerly a private villa, offers colourful, characterful rooms with superb views and rustic-style dark-wood furniture. Private terraces lead into the central garden and pool.

La Taberna   ANDALUCIAN €

(Plaza del Caño, Mojácar Pueblo; raciones €6-12; ⊙ noon-midnight, closed Wed Sep-Jun; 🍴) A big choice of both typical and original platters – meaty, fishy or veggie – gets everyone cramming into this thriving little restaurant inside a warren of intimate rooms, full of chatter and belly-full diners. It's beside an evocative old Moorish archway, the Puerta de la Ciudad.

★Tito's   INTERNATIONAL FUSION €€

(☑ 950 61 50 30; Paseo del Mediterráneo 2, Playa de las Ventanicas; mains €10-15; ⊙ 10am-9pm Apr–Oct, to midnight late Jun–Aug; 🛜) Warm-hearted ex-Californian Tito creates the perfect laid-back atmosphere at this popular, cane-canopied hang-out on the southern beach promenade. It does terrific cocktails with fresh fruit and, from 1pm to 4.30pm (and 7pm to midnight from late June to August), some of the best food in town – carefully composed treats such as brie-and-almond salad with honey-mustard sauce or Galician mussels in white wine.

ℹ️ Information

Oficina Municipal de Turismo (☑ 902 57 51 30; www.mojacar.es; Plaza Frontón, Mojácar Pueblo; ⊙ 10am-2pm & 5-8pm Mon-Sat, to 2pm Sun)

ℹ️ Getting There & Away

Buses to other towns and cities stop at various spots around the Parque Comercial roundabout. **Alsa** (☑ 902 42 22 42; www.alsa.es) runs two to four buses daily to/from Cuevas del Almanzora (€1.59, 35 minutes), Almería (€7.69, 1¼ hours, none on Sunday), Granada (€21, 4½ hours) and Murcia (€12, 2½ to three hours). For Granada and Murcia, it's necessary to buy tickets beforehand at **Hotel Simón** (☑ 950 47 87 69; Calle La Fuente 38, Mojácar Pueblo; 🛜) or at **Mojácar Tour** (☑ 950 47 57 57; Centro Comercial Montemar, Avenida de Andalucía), 200m from the Parque Comercial roundabout.

A local bus (€1.20) runs a circuit from Mojácar Pueblo down along the full length of the beach and back again, roughly every half-hour from 9am to 11.30pm, June to September, till 9pm October to May.

Valencia & Murcia

Best Places to Eat

➡ Quique Dacosta (p755)

➡ El Poblet (p743)

➡ Navarro (p743)

➡ Daluan (p753)

➡ Cervecería Sento (p760)

➡ El Granaino (p765)

Best Places to Sleep

➡ Caro Hotel (p741)

➡ Cases Noves (p763)

➡ Hotel Chamarel (p754)

➡ Villa Venecia (p757)

➡ Mont Sant (p762)

Why Go?

Principal settlement in the region and an utterly addictive city, Valencia exudes confidence. Its sophisticated cultural scene, kicking nightlife, quality museums, great restaurants, understated beach and stunning Modernista and contemporary architecture make it one of the peninsula's real jewels. Throughout this sun-bathed coastal pleasure-ground, a wealth of festivals awaits you, whether you fancy top-notch rock music at Benicàssim, hooded processions and friendly rivalry at Lorca's Semana Santa, re-enactments of Reconquista battles in the numerous Moros y Cristianos festivals or one of the world's biggest food fights at La Tomatina. While some of the coastal resorts – hello Benidorm! – are notoriously overdeveloped, there are plenty of places to explore that aren't. The ancient port of Cartagena has a magnificent array of Roman and Carthaginian ruins, while Murcia is a buzzy regional capital where there's not a fried breakfast in sight.

When to Go
Valencia City

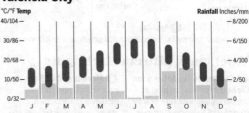

Mar Las Fallas, Valencia's wild spring festival, brings some two million visitors to town.

Aug Paint the town red at Buñol's tomato fight, then hit the coast's lively nightlife scene.

Oct The sea's still just about swimmable, there's decent weather but far fewer people.

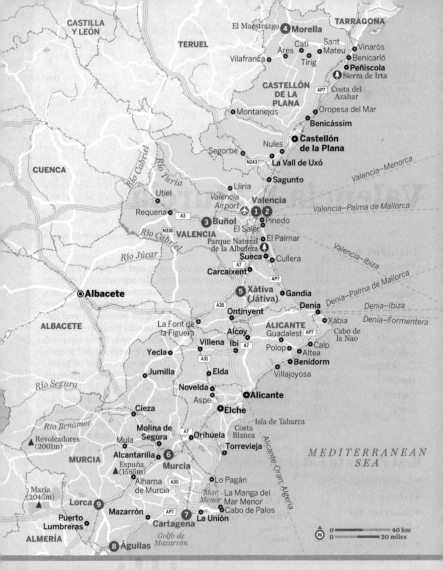

Valencia & Murcia Highlights

1 **Ciudad de las Artes y las Ciencias** (p730) Gasping at the daring architecture of this complex of Valencia buildings.

2 **Russafa** (p744) Living it up in this popular *barrio's* tapas, cafe and bar scene.

3 **La Tomatina** (p748) Painting the town red at this famous Buñol tomato fight.

4 **Morella** (p752) Savouring your first glimpse of this medieval fortress town.

5 **Castillo de Xàtiva** (p761) Trudging up to this magnificent hilltop castle and chowing down on a picnic at the top.

6 **Murcia** (p766) Strolling the centre of this underrated city, stopping at the casino and cathedral for a dose of history.

7 **Cartagena** (p770) Exploring Cartagena's fascinating Roman and Carthaginian sites.

8 **Cuatro Calas** (p772) Plunging into the warm sea at these coves west of **Águilas**.

9 **Semana Santa** (p773) Taking in the atmosphere, processions and rivalry at **Lorca's** Holy Week.

VALENCIA

POP 786,200

Spain's third-largest city is a magnificent place, content for Madrid and Barcelona to grab the headlines while it gets on with being a wonderfully liveable city with thriving cultural, eating and nightlife scenes. Never afraid to innovate, Valencia diverted its flood-prone river to the outskirts of town and converted the former riverbed into a superb green ribbon of park winding right through the city. On it are the strikingly futuristic buildings of the Ciudad de las Artes y las Ciencias, designed by local boy Santiago Calatrava. Other brilliant contemporary buildings grace the city, which also has a fistful of fabulous Modernista architecture, great museums and a large, characterful old quarter. Valencia, surrounded by its *huerta*, a fertile fruit-and-veg farmland, is famous as the home of rice dishes such as paella, but its buzzy dining scene offers plenty more besides.

History

Pensioned-off Roman legionaries founded 'Valentia' on the banks of Río Turia in 138 BC, but the first city was destroyed by Pompey in 75 BC due to the Sertorian War.

The Moors made Valencia an agricultural and industrial centre, establishing ceramics, paper, silk and leather industries and extending the network of irrigation canals in the rich agricultural hinterland.

Muslim rule was briefly interrupted in AD 1094 by the triumphant rampage of the legendary Castilian knight El Cid. Much later, the Christian forces of Jaime I definitively retook the city in 1238 after a siege. The city finally surrendered and tens of thousands of Muslims were displaced.

Valencia's golden age was the 15th and early 16th centuries, when the city was one of the Mediterranean's strongest trading centres. New World discoveries led to a Spanish pivot towards the Atlantic and began the pre-eminence of Seville as a trading city and the decline of Valencia. Economic hardship led to the Germanías revolt of 1519–22 of the guilds against the crown and aristocracy. The lean centuries were relieved in the 19th century by industrialisation and the development of a lucrative citrus trade to northern Europe.

Valencia was the capital of republican Spain during most of the Spanish Civil War after the government abandoned Madrid, fearing it was about to fall to the Nationalists. In the traumatic final days of the war, the city surrendered and a period of repression ensued.

Severe floods in 1949 and 1957 led to the Río Turia being diverted away from the centre of the city. The dry riverbed was eventually converted into a park.

◉ Sights

◉ North Ciutat Vella

The heart of historic Valencia, this area contains several of the city's key sights and is many visitors' first port of call when exploring town. The cathedral's treasures include the Holy Grail, while the magnificent Lonja is one of the great Gothic civil buildings. Other remnants of the city's storied past are scattered throughout the area, while the vibrant Mercado Central is one of Spain's most striking and best market halls.

VALENCIA & MURCIA VALENCIA

★ **Catedral**   CATHEDRAL
(Map p736; ☑963 91 81 27; www.catedraldevalencia.es; Plaza de la Virgen; adult/child incl audio guide €5/3.50; ⏱10am-5.30pm or 6.30pm Mon-Sat, 2-5.30pm Sun, closed Sun Nov-Feb) Valencia's cathedral was built over the mosque after the 1238 reconquest. Its low, wide, brick-vaulted triple nave is mostly Gothic, with neoclassical side chapels. Highlights are rich Italianate frescoes above the altarpiece, a pair of Goyas in the Capilla de San Francisco de Borja, and...ta-dah...in the flamboyant Gothic Capilla del Santo Cáliz, what's claimed to be the Holy Grail from which Christ sipped during the Last Supper. It's a Roman-era agate cup, later modified, so at least the date is right.

ⓘ VALENCIA TOURIST CARD

This **Valencia Tourist Card** (☑900 70 18 18; www.valenciatouristcard.com; 24/48/72 hr €15/20/25) has numerous options but all give free public transport and free or discounted entry to attractions. You'd normally need lots of sightseeing to make it worthwhile. The card can be bought at any tourist office or metro customer service point, as well as at many hotels and news-stands. There's a vending machine selling them at the airport too.

★ **Mercado Central**   MARKET
(Map p736; www.mercadocentralvalencia.es; Plaza del Mercado; ☉7.30am-3pm Mon-Sat) Valencia's vast Modernista covered market, constructed in 1928, is a swirl of smells, movement and colour. Spectacular seafood counters display cephalopods galore and numerous fish species, while the fruit and vegetables, many produced locally in Valencia's *huerta* (area of market gardens), are of special quality. A tapas bar lets you sip a wine and enjoy the atmosphere.

★ **La Lonja**   HISTORIC BUILDING
(Map p736; ☎962 08 41 53; www.valencia.es; Calle de la Lonja; adult/child €2/1, Sun free; ☉9.30am-7pm Mon-Sat, 9.30am-3pm Sun) This splendid building, a Unesco World Heritage site, was originally Valencia's silk and commodity exchange, built in the late 15th century when Valencia was booming. It's one of Spain's finest examples of a civil Gothic building. Two main structures flank a citrus-studded courtyard: the magnificent Sala de Contratación, a cathedral of commerce with soaring twisted pillars, and the Consulado del Mar, where a maritime tribunal sat. The top floor boasts a stunning coffered ceiling brought here from another building.

Plaza de la Virgen   SQUARE
(Map p736) Busy Plaza de la Virgen, ringed by cafes and imposing public buildings, was once the forum of Roman Valencia. The reclining figure in its central fountain represents Río Turia, while the eight maidens with their gushing pots symbolise the main irrigation canals flowing from it.

DON'T MISS

CIUDAD DE LAS ARTES Y LAS CIENCIAS

The aesthetically stunning Ciudad de las Artes y las Ciencias (City of Arts & Sciences; Map p732; ☎902 100031; www.cac.es; ♿) occupies a massive 350,000-sq-metre swath of the old Turia riverbed. It's mostly the work of world-famous, locally born architect Santiago Calatrava. He's a controversial figure for many Valencians, who complain about the expense, and various design flaws that have necessitated major repairs here. Nevertheless, if your taxes weren't involved, it's awe-inspiring stuff, and pleasingly family-oriented.

Museo de las Ciencias Príncipe Felipe (☎902 10 00 31; www.cac.es; adult/child €8/6.20, with Hemisfèric €12.60/9.60; ☉10am-6pm, 7pm or 9pm; ♿) This interactive science museum, stretching like a giant whale skeleton within the City of Arts & Sciences, has plenty of touchy-feely things for children, and machines and displays for all ages. It really has some excellent sections, with that elusive concept of learning for fun never closer. Each section has a pamphlet in English summarising its contents.

Oceanogràfic (☎902 10 00 31; www.cac.es/oceanografic; Camino de las Moreras; adult/child €28.50/21.50, audioguide €3.70, combined ticket with Hemisfèric & Museo de las Ciencias €36.90/28; ☉10am-5pm Sun-Fri, 10am-7pm Sat, 10am-midnight Jul & Aug; ♿) Spain's most famous aquarium is the southernmost building of the City of Arts & Sciences. It's an impressive display; the complex is divided into a series of climate zones, reached overground or underground from the central hub building. The sharks, complete with tunnel, are an obvious favourite, while a series of beautiful tanks present species from temperate, Mediterranean, Red Sea and tropical waters. Less happily, the aquarium also keeps captive dolphins and belugas: research suggests that this is detrimental to their welfare.

Palau de les Arts Reina Sofía (www.lesarts.com; Avenida del Professor López Piñero 1; guided visit adult/child €8/4; ☉guided visits 11.30am & 1pm Mon-Fri) Brooding over the riverbed like a giant beetle, its shell shimmering with translucent mosaic tiles – the cause of quite a few problems – this ultramodern arts complex, grafted onto the City of Arts & Sciences, has four auditoriums and enticing levels of plants poking out from under the ceramic exoskeleton. Outside of performance times, you can't enter except by guided visits. These run twice daily weekdays in Spanish, but there's usually some English summarising provided.

La Almoina
RUIN

(Map p736; ☑963 08 41 73; www.valencia.
es; Plaza Décimo Junio Bruto; adult/child €2/1,
Sun free; ⊙9.30am-7pm Mon-Sat, 9.30am-3pm
Sun) Beneath the square just to the east
of Valencia's cathedral, the archaeological
remains of the kernel of Roman, Visigoth
and Islamic Valencia shimmer through a
water-covered glass canopy. Head downstairs for an impressively excavated, atmospheric melange of Roman baths, forum
buildings and a factory, as well as bits of the
Moorish *alcázar* (fortress) and a royal cemetery. Later remains come from the building
erected on this square as a hospital for the
poor. Get the audioguide: it's tough to inter-
pret otherwise.

Baños del Almirante
HISTORIC BUILDING

(Map p736; Calle Baños del Almirante 3-5;
adult/child €2/1, Sun free; ⊙11am-2pm Tue-Sun)
FREE These Arab-style baths, constructed
in 1313, functioned continuously as public bathing facilities until 1959. It's worth
dropping in if you're passing by. Strategically placed buckets and piped sounds of
water add a little atmosphere, but it could
do with more information. Going upstairs
to see the roof, caked with pigeon drop-
pings and cigarette ends, takes away from
the romance.

⊙ Barrio del Carmen

The northwest corner of the old town is Valencia's oldest quarter, offering bohemian
local character and several good museums.
El Carme, as it is known in Valenciano, is
fertile ground for eating and drinking, with
a profusion of little bars and restaurants to
track down in its narrow, confusing medieval street plan.

★ Torres de Quart
GATE

(Map p736; Calle de Guillem de Castro; adult/
child €2/1, Sun free; ⊙10am-6pm or 7pm Tue-
Sat, 10am-3pm Sun) Spain's most magnificent city gate is quite a sight from the
new town. You can clamber to the top of
the 15th-century structure, which faces towards Madrid and the setting sun.
Up high, notice the pockmarks caused
by French cannonballs during the 19th-
century Napoleonic invasion.

Instituto Valenciano
de Arte Moderno
GALLERY

(IVAM; Map p736; www.ivam.es; Calle de Guillem de Castro 118; adult/child €2/1, Sun free;

⊙11am-7.30pm Tue-Sun Sep-May, noon-8.30pm
Tue-Sun Jun-Aug) This impressive gallery
hosts excellent temporary exhibitions and
owns a small but impressive collection of
20th-century Spanish art. The most reliably
permanent exhibition on display is the Julio
González collection. This Catalan sculptor
(1876–1942) lived in Paris and produced
exquisite work with iron that influenced
later artists like David Smith and Eduardo
Chillida.

Torres de Serranos
GATE

(Map p736; Plaza de los Fueros; adult/child
€2/1, Sun free; ⊙9.30am-7pm Mon-Sat, 9.30am-
3pm Sun) Once the main exit to Barcelona
and the north, the imposing 14th-century
Torres de Serranos overlooks the former
bed of the Río Turia. Together with the
Torres de Quart, they are all that remain of
Valencia's old city walls. Climb to the top
for a great overview of the Barrio del Carmen and riverbed.

⊙ Northern & Eastern Valencia

This large swath of the city beyond the Turia riverbed park includes the two principal
universities, which means it's a zone well-
stocked with bars, restaurants and nightclubs. The Turia itself, a 9km ribbon of park,
is a strollable highlight. The main city art
gallery and Valencia football team are two
pillars of local culture, while the suburb of
Benimaclet is lively with alternative and
community happenings.

★ Museo de Bellas Artes
GALLERY

(San Pío V; Map p732; www.museobellasartes-
valencia.gva.es; Calle de San Pío V 9; ⊙10am-
8pm Tue-Sun) **FREE** Bright and spacious, this
gallery ranks among Spain's best. Highlights include a collection of magnificent
late-medieval altarpieces, and works by
several Spanish masters, including some
great Goya portraits, a haunting Velázquez
selfie, an El Greco *John the Baptist*,

Valencia City

C Dr Nicasio Benlloch
Av de las Cortes Valencianas
Av de Burjassot
Garbi
Benicalap
Beniferri
C La Safor
Future Valencia CF Football Stadium
Av Juan XXIII
Av Dr. Peset Aleixandre
Trànsits
C de San Pancracio
Marxalenes
Parque de Marxalenes
Reus
C Reus
Av Constitución
Av General Aviles
Av Maestro Rodrigo
Campanar-La Fe
Av Campanar
Av de Pío XII
C Joaquín Ballester
C Padre Ferris
Av Burjassot
C de Llano de Zaidía
Puente de San José
Puente de las Artes
C de Blanquerías
C Valle de la Ballestera
Bus Station
Av Menéndez Pidal
See Valencia City Central Map (p736)
Bioparc
Av de Pío Baroja
Av de Tirso de Molina
Puente Ademuz
Paseo de la Pechina
Turia
28
C del Turia
Puente de Campanar
12
C de Quart
C de Lepanto
Parque de Cabecera
Puente 9 de Octubre
C de Valencia
C Castan Tobenas
Av Perez Galdos
C de Juan Llorens
C de Gabriel Miró
Ángel Guimerà
C Brasil
C de Calixto III
C Ángel Guimerà
C de Buen Orden
Plaza de España
Av del Cid
C Linares
C San José de Calasanz
C Santa Cruz de Tenerife
C Enguera
C Musico Ayllón
C Tres Forques
Av Salavert
C Cuenca
C de Jesús
C Albacete
17
Estación Joaquin Sorolla
C José María Mortes Lerma
C Archiduque Carlos
C Fontanares
C Beato Nicolás Factor
Av Giorgeta
Jesús
C San Vicente Mártir
Av Tres Cruces
Patraix
C Venezuela
Av Tres Cruces
Hospital

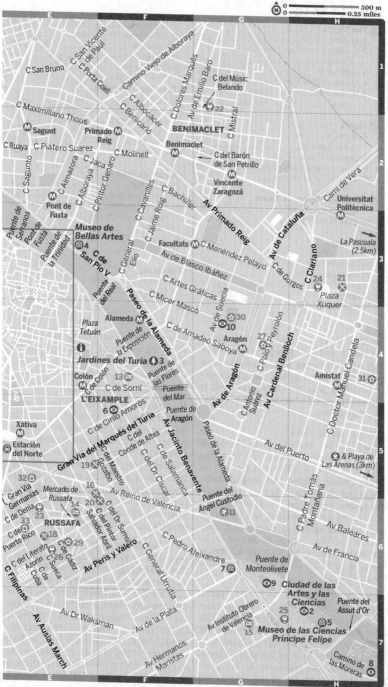

N 0 ____ 500 m
0 ____ 0.25 miles

E

C San Vicente de Paul
C San Bruno
C Porta Coeli
Camino Viejo de Alboraya
C Maximiliano Thous
Ⓜ Sagunt
C Ruaya
C Piatero Suarez
Primado Reig Ⓜ
C Sagunto
C Almazora
C Molinell
C Alboraya
C Jaca
Ⓜ Pont de Fusta
C Pintor Genaro
Puente de Serranos
Pont de Fusta
Puente de Fusta
Puente de la Trinidad
Museo de Bellas Artes 4 ⓜ
C de San Pío V
C General Elío
Puente del Real
Paseo de la Alameda
Alameda
Plaza Tetuán
Puente de la Exposición
🅘
Jardines del Turia 3
Colón Ⓜ 13 ⓞ
C de Colón
L'EIXAMPLE
6 ⓞ
C de Cirilo Amorós
Xàtiva Ⓜ
Estación del Norte
Gran Via del Marqués del Turia

F

C Albocácer
C Benicarló
C del Músic Belando
C Dolores Marqués
Av de Emilio Baro
C Mistral
22
BENIMACLET
Benimaclet Ⓜ
C del Barón de San Petrillo
C Caravilles
C Bachiller
Vincente Zaragozá
C Jaime Roig
Av Primado Reig
Facultats Ⓜ C Menéndez Pelayo
Av de Blasco Ibáñez
C Artes Gráficas
C Micer Mascó
C de Amadeo Saboya
Av de Sueca
Aragón Ⓜ
Puente de las Flores
Puente del Mar
Puente de Aragón
Av de Jacinto Benavente
C del Conde de Altea
C del Maestro Gozalbo
C del Dr Císcar
C de Salamanca
19
16
C del Pintor Salvador Abril
20
14
Av Reino de Valencia
Mercado de Russafa
32 ⓐ
C Gran Via Germanias
C de Denia
23
33
C de Puerto Rico
18
RUSSAFA
29 ⓐ
26 ⓐ
C del Literato Azorín
C de Cadiz
C de Sueca
C de Cuba
C Filipinas
Av Peris y Valero
C Pedro Aleixandre
C General Urrutia
Av Ausias March
Av Dr Waksman
Av de la Plata
Av Hermanos Maristas

G

C San Vicente de Paul
BENIMACLET
Av de Cataluña
C Gorgos
Av Primado Reig
C de Sueca
30 ⓞ
10
27
C Poly Peyrolón
Av de Aragón
C Antonio Suárez
Paseo de la Alameda
Av del Puerto
Puente del Ángel Custodio
11
7 ⓐ
9 ⓞ
Ciudad de las Artes y las Ciencias
25
2 ⓞ
15
Av Instituto Obrero de Valencia

H

1
Universitat Politècnica Ⓜ
Cami de Vera
La Pascuala (2.5km)
C Clariano
24
21
Plaza Xúquer
3
Av Cardenal Benlloch
C Doctor Manuel Candela
Amistat Ⓜ
31
4
& Playa de Las Arenas (3km)
5
C Padre Tomás Montañana
Av Baleares
Av de Francia
6
Puente de Monteolivete
Puente del Assut d'Or
5 ⓐ
Museo de las Ciencias Príncipe Felipe
8 ⓞ
Camino de las Moreras
7

Valencia City

Murillos, Riberas and works by the Ribaltas, father and son. Downstairs, an excellent series of rooms focuses on the great, versatile Valencian painter Joaquín Sorolla (1863–1923), who, at his best, seemed to capture the spirit of an age through sensitive portraiture.

★ Jardines del Turia   PARK
(Map p732; ♿) Stretching the length of Río Turia's former course, this 9km-long lung of green is a fabulous mix of playing fields, cycling, jogging and walking paths, lawns and playgrounds. As it curves around the eastern part of the city, it's also a pleasant way of getting around. See Lilliputian kids scrambling over a magnificent, everpatient **Gulliver** (Map p732; Jardines del Turia; ☉10am-8pm Sep-Jun, 10am-2pm & 5-9pm Jul & Aug; ♿; ☐19, 95) **FREE** south of the Palau de la Música.

Valencia CF Stadium   STADIUM
(Map p732; ☎963 37 26 26; www.valenciacf. com; Avenida de Suecia; adult/child €10.20/7.80; ☉10.30am-2.30pm & 3.30-6.30pm Mon-Sat, 10.30am-2.30pm Sun, last tour 1hr before closing) The guided visit to Valencia's famous Mestalla stadium takes you to the press room, the changing rooms and out onto the

hallowed turf. Hours change by season and according to fixtures, so check the website in advance.

◉ South Ciutat Vella

The southern part of the old town, centred around the sizeable town hall square, Plaza del Ayuntamiento, is a busier, more commercial area than its northern counterpart, into which it blends seamlessly. Valencia seems a big city here, with imposing buildings, a metropolitan bustle and public institutions. The area bristles with impressive Modernista buildings, shopping is first class, and lots of accommodation choices make this many people's Valencia address.

★ Museo Nacional de Cerámica   MUSEUM
(Map p736; ☎963 08 54 29; www.mecd.gob.es; Calle del Poeta Querol 2; adult/child €3/free, Sat afternoon & Sun free; ☉10am-2pm & 4-8pm Tue-Sat, 10am-2pm Sun) Inside a striking palace, this ceramics museum celebrates an important Valencia-region industry. Downstairs (if you can take your eyes off a decadent hand-painted 1753 carriage) you can learn about the history of ceramics from baroque to modern, with great information that's albeit sometimes a little difficult to relate to

the pottery on display. Upstairs, historical ceramics are cleverly dotted with modern works, but the sumptuous, over-the-top interiors, all ornate stucco, chinoiserie, damask panels and elaborate upholstery, pull plenty of focus. It's an outrageous rococo extravaganza.

★ **Museo del Patriarca**　　　　　GALLERY
(Colegio de San Juan; Map p736; Calle de la Nave 1; €2; ☺11am-1.30pm daily, also often 5-7pm Mon-Fri) This seminary was founded in the late 16th-century by San Juan de Ribera, a towering Counter-Reformation figure who wielded enormous spiritual and temporal power in Spain and beyond. With an impressive if austere Renaissance courtyard-cloister, its main attraction is a small but excellent religious-art museum. Caravaggio, El Greco and local boys José de Ribera and Juan de Juanes are all represented. Most surprising is the manuscript that Thomas More was writing while awaiting his execution in the Tower of London.

◉ L'Eixample & Southern Valencia

L'Eixample, or El Ensanche, means the 'expansion', and was developed once Valencia got too big for its old walled town. Laid out in the 19th century, it's a zone of elegant streets and wide avenues, replete with upmarket shopping and eating options. In the south of this zone, in the dry Turia riverbed, are the otherworldly buildings of the fabulous Ciudad de las Artes y las Ciencias, one of Valencia's major highlights.

Mercado de Colón　　　　　MARKET
(Map p732; www.mercadocolon.es; Calle de Cirilo Amorós; ☺7am-1.30am) This magnificent building, now colonised by cafes and boutique food outlets, was formerly a market, built in 1916 to serve the rising bourgeoisie of the new suburb of L'Eixample. Its handsome metal skeleton is garnished with Modernista flourishes to create a stunning ensemble. It's a good place to try *horchata* (a sugary drink made from tiger nuts) and a nice place to spend a Sunday, with free noon concerts.

Museo Fallero　　　　　MUSEUM
(Map p732; ☎963 52 54 78; www.valencia.es; Plaza Monteolivete 4; adult/child €2/free, Sun free; ☺9.30am-7pm Mon-Sat, 9.30am-3pm Sun) Each Fallas festival (p739), only one of the thousands of *ninots*, the figurines that pose at the base of each *falla* (huge statues of papier mâché and polystyrene), is saved from the flames by popular vote. Those reprieved over the years are displayed here. It's fascinating to see their evolution over time, and to see these comical, grotesque, sometimes moving figures up close.

◉ Western Valencia

Spanning a broad swath of suburbs west of the old town, this neighbourhood has varied attractions. At the western end of the Turia riverbed, the Bioparc zoo presents African animals in innovative ways, while the history museum gives an overview of the city's past. Various park spaces across the area give the chance for a pleasant time-out from urban life.

★ **Bioparc**　　　　　ZOO
(Map p732; www.bioparcvalencia.es; Avenida Pío Baroja 3; adult/child €24/18; ☺10am-dusk; ⊕) ✐ This zoo devoted solely to African animals has an educational and conservationist remit and an unusual approach. Though, as always, the confinement in limited spaces of creatures like gorillas raises mixed feelings, the innovative landscaping is certainly a thrill. The absence of obvious fences makes it seem that animals roam free as you wander from savannah to equatorial landscapes. Aardvarks, leopards and hippos draw crowds but most magical is Madagascar, where large-eyed lemurs gambol around your feet among waterfalls and grass.

WORTH A TRIP

RICE MUSEUM

The restored rice mill **Museo de Arroz** (☎963 67 62 91; www.museoarrozvalencia. com; Calle del Rosario 3; adult/child €2/1, Sun free; ☺9.30am-2pm & 3-7pm Tue-Sat, 9.30am-3pm Sun) gives good background on the importance to the city of the grain, grown in the nearby Albufera, with a video (English subtitles). A guide then talks you through the processing plant, where generators whirr, wheels creak, cogs turn and drive belts slap on three floors. Cereal museums don't always set the heart racing, but this is surprisingly good.

Valencia City Central

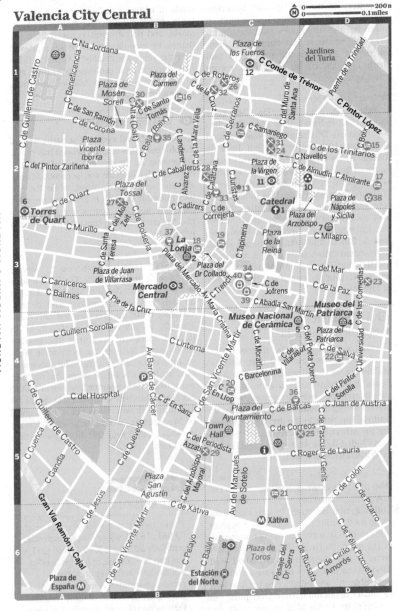

VALENCIA & MURCIA VALENCIA

👉 Tours

Liber Tours   WALKING TOUR
(Map p736; ☎978 11 88 88; www.libertours.com; Plaza de la Virgen; adult/child €17/8; ⏱10.30am Mon-Sat) Recommended 2¼-hour walking tours of the centre leaving from Plaza de la Virgen.

Separate English, Italian (4.30pm) and Spanish tours (other languages are bookable).

Valencia Guías   BICYCLE TOUR
(Map p732; ☎963 85 17 40; www.valenciaguias.com; Paseo de la Pechina 32; ⏱9.30am-2.30pm

Valencia City Central

& 3-6pm) This well-established set-up runs daily three-hour guided bicycle tours in various languages, with guaranteed departures (€25 including rental and snack). It's only an extra €5 to rent the bike for the rest of the day.

 Courses

**Escuela de Arroces
y Paella Valenciana** COOKING COURSE
(Map p736; ☑963 15 38 56; www.escuelade-arrocesypaellas.com; Calle Juristas 12; €50-55) Once you know how, cooking paella isn't nearly as intimidating as you might think. So this course might be just the thing. Start with a visit to the market, then learn to make a typical rice dish in a restaurant kitchen. Then sit down to eat it, of course. Social and fun. Book online or at the La Valenciana restaurant.

The restaurant itself is bright and friendly but – yes, we see the irony – you can eat better rice dishes elsewhere.

Mediterranean Surf School SURFING
(☑960 72 67 60; www.mediterraneansurfschool.com; Av Mare Nostrum 1; 2hr class from €28; ☺10am-8pm Mon-Fri, 9am-8pm Sat, 9am-6pm Sun; ⊕) Don't expect huge waves in Valencia, but the often-gentle swell and great weather make it a fine place to learn how to surf or paddleboard. This is a well-run set-up that will happily cater to kids, too.

Festivals & Events

**Gran Premio
de la Comunitat Valenciana** SPORTS
(www.motogp.com; A3, salida 334, Cheste) MotoGP is huge in Spain, which hosts several annual races. The Valencian version, held at a circuit at Cheste, 20km west of the centre, usually in November, has in recent years been the season's final race. The city packs out for it.

Feria de Julio FIESTA
(www.feriadejulio.com) Performing arts, brass-band competitions, fireworks and a 'battle of the flowers' in the second half of July.

DON'T MISS

VALENCIA'S BEACHES

Valencia's town beaches are 3km from the centre. Playa de las Arenas runs north into Playa de la Malvarrosa and Playa de la Patacona, forming a wide strip of sand some 4km long. It's bordered by the Paseo Marítimo promenade and a string of restaurants and cafes. The port area, refurbished for the 2007 Americas Cup, is south of here and backed by the intriguing fishermen's district of El Cabanyal, which makes for excellent exploration.

Playa de las Arenas Backed by hotels and rice restaurants, this is the classic stretch of Valencia beach, and the closest to town.

Playa de la Patacona The northern stretch of Valencia's main beach, backed by trendy, enticing eateries.

Playa de la Malvarrosa This is the middle stretch of Valencia's main beach.

**Fiesta de
San Vicente Ferrer** RELIGIOUS, THEATRE
Colourful parades and miracle plays performed around town on the Sunday and Monday the week after Easter.

Semana Santa Marinera RELIGIOUS
(www.semanasantamarinera.org) Valencia's elaborate Easter week processions have a maritime flavour, and take place in the seaside districts around the fishing *barrio* of Cabanyal.

🛏 Sleeping

Valencia has a good range of hotels, though not quite the quantity of quirky boutique options that you might expect in a city of this size. There's a huge quantity, though, of quality central apartments, which make excellent bases for an urban stay.

Lots of hostels cluster around the centre of town.

Since Valencia is a business centre, big hotels struggle to fill rooms outside the working week. Most offer fat weekend and high-summer discounts.

★**Russafa Youth Hostel** HOSTEL €
(Map p732; ☎963 28 94 60; www.russafay-outhhostel.com; Calle Padre Perera 5; dm/d incl breakfast €20/44; @⊛) You'll feel instantly at home in this super-welcoming, cute hostel set over various floors of a venerable building in the heart of vibrant Russafa. It's all beds, rather than bunks, and with a maximum of three to a room, there's no crowding. Sweet rooms and spotless bathrooms make for a mighty easy stay.

Home Youth Hostel HOSTEL €
(Map p736; ☎963 91 62 29; www.homehostels valencia.com; Calle de la Lonja 4; dm €24-27, tw €60; ⊛@⊛) Offering location, facilities and plenty more, this hostel sits right opposite the Lonja, a few steps from the central market. The rooms have happy retro decor and proper beds with decent sheets, and minimum room-mates. Kitchen, film library and cheery staff make this a top budget spot. Dorms are substantially cheaper outside high season.

Ad Hoc Carmen HOTEL €
(Map p736; ☎960 45 45 45; www.adhochotel es.com; Calle Samaniego 20; s/d/q €49/59/99; @⊛) Strategically placed for sorties to both the centre's historic buildings or the bars and restaurants of Barrio del Carmen, this hotel offers a variety of handsome modern rooms with clean lines and whitewashed wood. Many chambers are duplexes, offering good sleeping solutions for families, groups or squabbling couples. No breakfast or parking available. Good value.

Pensión París HOTEL €
(Map p736; ☎963 52 67 66; www.pensionparis. com; Calle de Salvà 12; s €26, d €34-46; ⊛) Welcoming, with spotless rooms – most with shared bathrooms, some with private facilities – is this family-run option on a quiet street. It's the antithesis of the crowded, pack-'em-in hostel. The best of the rooms have balconies and the original features of this stately old building.

★**Hostal Antigua Morellana** HOSTAL €€
(Map p736; ☎963 91 57 73; www.hostalam. com; Calle En Bou 2; s/d €55/65; ⊛⊛) This friendly, family-run, 18-room spot occupies a renovated 18th-century *posada* (where wealthier merchants bringing their produce to the nearby food market would spend the night), and has cosy, good-sized rooms, most with balconies. It's kept ex-

tremely shipshape by the rightly house-proud owners and there are loads of great features including memory-foam mattresses and hairdryers. Higher floors have more natural light. Good value.

Ad Hoc Monumental
HOTEL €€

(Map p736; ☑963 91 91 40; www.adhochoteles.com; Calle Boix 4; s/d €111/138; ✱ ⬧) Friendly Ad Hoc offers comfort and charm deep within the old quarter and also runs a splendid little restaurant. The late-19th-century building has been restored to its former splendour with great sensitivity, revealing original ceilings, mellow brickwork and solid wooden beams. Superior rooms on the top floor have a great private balcony terrace, which you can breakfast on. Rates are often substantially discounted off-season.

Hotel Sorolla Centro
HOTEL €€

(Map p736; ☑963 52 33 92; www.hotelsorollacentro.com; Calle Convento Santa Clara 5; s/d €66/88; ✱ ⬧) Neat and contemporary but without any flashy design gimmicks, this hotel offers very solid value for comfortable, well-thought-out modern rooms with powerful showers and plenty of facilities. Staff are extremely helpful and the location, on a pedestrian street so close to the main square, is fab.

Valenciaflats Rooms
HOSTAL €€

(Map p732; ☑963 35 67 93; www.roomsdeluxe.com; Avenida Instituto Obrero de Valencia 20; d/q €79/120; P ✱ ⬧) A mosaic tile's throw from the Ciudad de las Artes y las Ciencias, this spot is well equipped and modern. The private rooms all have en suites and are thematically decorated with great style and flair. Check low-season prices; they can be excellent.

Hostal Venecia
HOSTAL €€

(Map p736; ☑963 52 42 67; www.hotelvenecia.com; Plaza del Ayuntamiento 3; s/d €75/80; ✱ @ ⬧) Right on the city's main square, this sumptuous building's functional interior doesn't give many hints of the noble exterior, but it offers compact modern rooms, many with small balcony, at a sharp price. Despite the *hostal* name, facilities are those of a midrange hotel. Excellent value, its strong points are exceptionally friendly service and its prime location.

Bed & Bike Valencia
APARTMENT €€

(Map p736; ☑963 56 86 16; www.bedandbikevalencia.com; Calle del Pintor Fillol 4; apt €65-115; ✱ ⬧) Modern styling and an appealing Barrio del Carmen location make this apartment complex an ideal Valencia base, particularly for families. That means that you should be booking it quite some time ahead for summer months. Most apartments have a double room and a fold-out bed in the living area, plus a decent kitchen. Despite the name, renting a bike costs extra.

LAS FALLAS

The exuberant, anarchic swirl of **Las Fallas de San José** (www.fallas.com) – fireworks, music, festive bonfires and all-night partying – is a must if you're visiting Spain in mid-March. The *fallas* themselves are huge sculptures of papier mâché on wood built by teams of local artists.

Each neighbourhood sponsors its own *falla*, and when the town wakes after the *plantà* (overnight construction of the *fallas*) on the morning of 16 March, more than 350 have sprung up. Reaching up to 15m in height, with the most expensive costing hundreds of thousands of euros, these grotesque, colourful effigies satirise celebrities, current affairs and local customs. They range from comical to moving. It's a custom that grew through the 19th and 20th centuries.

Around-the-clock festivities include street parties, paella-cooking competitions, parades, open-air concerts, bullfights and free fireworks displays. Valencia considers itself the pyrotechnic capital of the world and each day at 2pm from 1 to 19 March, a *mascletà* (over five minutes of deafening thumps and explosions) shakes the window panes of Plaza del Ayuntamiento.

After midnight on the final day, each *falla* goes up in flames – backed by yet more fireworks. A popular vote spares the most-cherished figure, which gets housed for posterity in the Museo Fallero (p735).

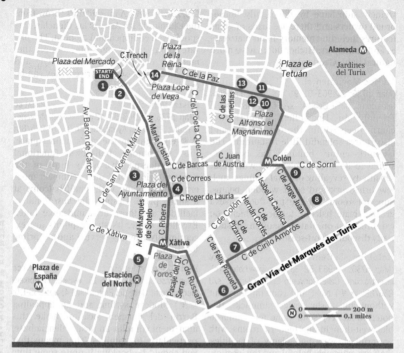

🏃 City Walk
Modernisme Meander

START MERCADO CENTRAL
END MERCADO CENTRAL
LENGTH 3.25KM; 1½ HOURS

This walk takes in Valencia's main Modernista buildings. After sniffing around ❶ **Mercado Central** (p730) take in the elaborate stucco facade – with neo-Gothic pilasters above allegories of Valencia's fertility – of ❷ **Calle Ramilletes 1**. Follow Avenida María Cristina to Plaza del Ayuntamiento, site of the ❸ **town hall** and resplendent ❹ **central post office**, a lighter neoclassical affair with 1920s flourishes. Drop in and look up to savour its leaded-glass dome. Valencia's biggest concentration of flower stalls fringes the square.

At the end of Calle Ribera, detour to ❺ **Estación del Norte** (p747), with its cute original Modernista booking area of dark wood, and adjacent hall with elaborate tilework. Take Calle de Russafa, then turn left for ❻ **Casa Ortega** (Gran Vía 9), with its ornate floral decoration and balcony, supported by a pair of handsome caryatids. Go left along Calle de Félix Pizcueta, then take the first right onto

Calle de Cirilo Amorós. From here onwards, lift your gaze above the ground-floor shops to appreciate each building's original structure. Pause by ❼ **Casa Ferrer** (No 29), garlanded with stucco roses and ceramic tiling. Continue northwards to the ❽ **Mercado de Colón** (p735), a chic spot for a drink stop, then head northwest to ❾ **Casa del Dragón** (Calle de Jorge Juan 3), named for its dragon motifs.

Cross Calle de Colón, turn right along Calle Poeta Quintana and pass the mounted statue of a haughty King Jaime I to join Calle de la Paz. Back in the 19th century, ❿ **Hotel Vincci Palace** was known as the Palace Hotel, in its time Valencia's finest. Both it and ⓫ **No 31**, opposite, have elaborate *miradors* (corner balconies), while ⓬ **Red Nest Hostel** (No 36) has delicate, leafy iron railings. Opposite, on the corner of Calle de las Comedias, ⓭ **No 21 & 23** has magnificent window and balcony work, and a columned *mirador*.

At the end of Calle de la Paz, continue straight – maybe calling in for an *horchata* at ⓮ **Horchatería de Santa Catalina** (p745). Then, at Plaza Lope de Vega, turn left into Calle Trench to return to the Mercado Central.

★ **Caro Hotel** HOTEL €€€

(Map p736; ☎ 963 05 90 00; www.carohotel.com; Calle Almirante 14; r €176-243; P ❋ ☎) Housed in a sumptuous 19th-century mansion, this hotel sits atop two millennia of Valencian history, with restoration revealing a hefty hunk of the Arab wall, Roman column bases and Gothic arches. Each room is furnished in soothing dark shades, and has a great king-sized bed and varnished cement floors. Bathrooms are tops. For special occasions, reserve the 1st-floor grand suite, once the ballroom.

Hospes Palau de la Mar HOTEL €€€

(Map p732; ☎ 963 16 28 84; www.hospes.com; Avenida Navarro Reverter 14; r €170-255; P ❋ @ ☎ ⛱) Created by the merging of two elegant 19th-century mansions (plus 18 very similar modern rooms surrounding a tranquil internal garden), this boutique hotel, all black, white, soft fuscous and beige, is cool and contemporary. There's a sauna, Jacuzzi – and a pool scarcely bigger than your bathtub.

✕ Eating

Valencia is surrounded by its *huerta,* a fertile coastal agricultural plain that supplies the city with delightfully fresh fruit and vegetables. The number of restaurants has to be seen to be believed: you're seriously spoilt for choice.

✕ North Ciutat Vella

La Pilareta TAPAS €

(Bar Pilar; Map p736; ☎ 963 91 04 97; www.barlapilareta.es; Calle del Moro Zeit 13; mussels €6.95; ☉ noon-midnight) Earthy, century-old and barely changed La Pilareta is great for hearty tapas and *clóchinas* (small, juicy local mussels), available between May and August. For the rest of the year it serves *mejillones* (mussels), altogether fatter if less tasty. A platterful comes in a spicy broth that you scoop up with a spare shell. It's got atmosphere in spades.

★ **Delicat** TAPAS €€

(Map p736; ☎ 963 92 33 57; Calle Conde Almodóvar 4; mains €10-15; ☉ 1.45-3.30pm & 8.45pm-12.30am Tue-Sat, 1.45-3.30pm Sun; ☎) At this particularly friendly, intimate option, Catina, up front, and her partner, Paco, on full view in the kitchen, offer an unbeatable-value, five-course menu of samplers for lunch and a range of truly

innovative tapas plates, designed for sharing, anytime. There's a range of influences at play; the decor isn't lavish but the food is memorable.

La Salvaora SPANISH €€

(Map p736; ☎ 963 92 14 84; www.lasalvaora.com; Calle de Calatrava 19; mains €13-19; ☉ 1.30-3.30pm & 8.30-11.30pm Thu-Mon, 1.30-3.30pm Tue & Wed) Refined, elegant but not expensive, this intimate spot is decorated with black-and-white portraits of flamenco stars. At first glance, the menu of Spanish favourites – think beef cheek, bull tail, ham, croquettes – looks familiar, but modern presentation and exquisite quality soon prove that this is no ordinary *tasca*. Exceptional value for this standard; the tapas degustation menu (€24) is a steal.

Cinnamon FUSION €€

(Map p736; ☎ 963 15 48 90; Calle de las Comedias 5; dishes €7-18; ☉ 1.30-4.30pm & 8-11.30pm Tue-Fri, 8-11.30pm Sat, 1-3.30pm Mon; ☎ ✐) This intimate space is so tiny that you wonder how they prepare anything more elaborate than a fried egg. But wonders emerge from the open kitchen, bursting with taste and freshness. Creative plates include the wild boar and green apple crunchy house salad, and there are good options for vegetarians. A very worthwhile eating experience, if there's room.

Seu Xerea FUSION €€€

(Map p736; ☎ 963 92 40 00; www.seuxerea.com; Calle Conde Almodóvar 4; mains €18-26; ☉ 1.30-3.30pm & 8.30-11.30pm Tue-Sat) Two soberly handsome dining areas and attentive service make this a fine destination for inventive, high-quality fusion food that combines some classic, deep-rooted Spanish dishes with touches sourced from Southeast Asia and beyond. The creative, regularly changing, rock-reliable, à la carte menu is

LOCAL KNOWLEDGE

WHAT'S COOKING IN VALENCIA? RICE!

Joan Francesc Peris García, Green party spokesperson, teacher and judge of *paella-fideuà* competitions, gives us the low down on Valencia's rice.

Valencian Rice Dishes

Rice is a whole world! Paella is a dry rice, the liquid evaporates. There are *caldoso* (soupy) or *meloso* rices, with broth. There are winter rices and rices made with summer produce. Rices with meat, with fish, with vegetables, with almost anything!

Best Rice Dishes to Try

Paellas are typical of the Valencian coast. Meat paellas normally have chicken and rabbit and then we'd add green beans and other vegetables in summer, or fava beans and artichokes in winter.

That's the most typical of Valencia, but then you've got fish ones, soupy with calamari or cuttlefish for the flavour and prawns or langoustines for decoration. You can also add prawns to a meat paella to make a *paella mixta*. Another one on the coast is *arroz negro* (black rice) that's made with squid ink and fish stock. There are other great winter ones too: what about one with cauliflower and salt cod? Delicious!

In the interior, they make heavier rices. In Alcoy and Xàtiva, rices are baked in the oven and might have pork, sausage, beans and black pudding. In Alicante's interior they do a tasty one with snails, rabbit and chickpeas, while around Orihuela it's *arroz con costra* (crusty rice), made in the oven with a crust of beaten egg on top. There are so many!

The Secret of Good Fideuà

Fideuà is similar to paella, but made with fine pasta. The secret is a good fish stock with fresh rockfish. Noodles cook quicker than rice so it's ready faster.

Where Locals Go for Great Rice

Mostly to houses of friends or family. The best paella is always grandma's! That's because it's a question of experience, when you've made so many you know how to judge the perfect quantity of rice to add. My mother-in-law let me make rice in her kitchen. That's a real achievement!

---

complemented by an accessible, varied wine list and degustation and tapas menus for trying lots of morsels.

✗ Barrio del Carmen

★**Refugio**　　　　　　　　　　FUSION €€
(Map p736; ☑ 690 61 70 18; www.refugiorestau-rante.com; Calle Alta 42; mains €14-22, set menu €12-15; ⊗ 2-4pm & 9pm-midnight; 🗟) Named for the civil-war hideout opposite and simply decorated in whitewashed brick, Refugio preserves some of the Carmen *barrio's* former revolutionary spirit. Excellent Med-fusion cuisine is presented in lunchtime menus of surprising quality: there are some stellar plates on show, though the vegie options aren't always quite as flavoursome. Evening dining is high quality and innovative.

Yuso　　　　　　　　　　VALENCIAN €€
(Map p736; ☑ 963 15 39 67; www.restaurante yuso.es; Calle de la Cruz 4; mains €10-15; ⊗ 1-5pm & 8.30pm-1am Fri & Sat, 1-5pm Sun; 🗟) Offering fantastic value for delicious, home-style Valencian cooking, this place tucked away in the Barrio del Carmen has a regular coterie of customers who stop by every weekend. The various set menus are cheap and delicious, and dry and wet rice dishes and *fideuàs* are succulent.

El Tap　　　　　　　TAPAS, VALENCIAN €€
(Map p736; ☑ 963 91 26 27; www.restaurante valenciaeltap.es; Calle de Roteros 9; mains €10-18; ⊗ 1.30-4pm & 7.30-11.30pm Tue-Sat, 1.30-4pm Sun; 🗟) Tap is one of Barrio del Carmen's rich selection of small, characterful restaurants. Tapas are original and delightfully prepared, and there's a carefully chosen list of both wines and boutique beers. Excellent value.

✗ Northern & Eastern Valencia

Tanto Monta TAPAS €

(Map p732; Calle del Poeta Artola 19; dishes €1.70-6.85; ☾7pm-1am Mon-Sat; 🛜) Legendary, tasty and cheap, this place absolutely packs out with students, academics and all comers jostling for a place to enjoy their delicious *montaditos*. Grab a table outside – if you can – and carefully select a mixed plate. No fighting over who eats what: they're all tops. There are toasts and salads on offer, too.

✗ South Ciutat Vella

★Navarro VALENCIAN €€

(Map p736; ☑963 52 96 23; www.restaurante navarro.com; Calle del Arzobispo Mayoral 5; rices €11-18, set menu €22; ☾1.30-4pm daily, plus 8.30-11pm Sat; 🛜) A byword in the city for decades for their quality rice dishes, Navarro is run by the grandkids of the original founders and it offers plenty of choice, outdoor seating and a set menu, including one of the rices as a main.

Vuelve Carolina MEDITERRANEAN €€

(Map p736; ☑963 21 86 86; www.vuelvecar olina.com; Calle de Correos 8; dishes €7-19; ☾1.30-4.30pm & 8.30-11.30pm Mon-Sat; 🛜) Overseen from a distance by noted chef Quique Dacosta, this upbeat bar-restaurant offers style – although those clothes-horse bar stools could be more comfy – and an inspiring selection of tapas and fuller plates. These range from exquisite Japanese-influenced creations to tacos, rices and more. Service is solicitous, and watching the open kitchen under the benevolent gaze of cardboard deer heads is always entertaining.

★El Poblet GASTRONOMY €€€

(Map p736; ☑961 11 11 06; www.elpobletres taurante.com; Calle de Correos 8; menus €35-68; ☾1.30-3.30pm Tue, 1.30-3.30pm & 8.30-10.30pm Wed-Sat & Mon; 🛜) Run by noted chef Quique Dacosta, this upstairs restaurant offers elegance and fine gastronomic dining at prices that are very competitive for this quality. Modern French and Spanish influences combine to create sumptuous degustation menus. Some of the imaginative presentation has to be seen to be believed, and staff are genuinely welcoming and helpful.

✗ L'Eixample & Southern Valencia

★La Gallineta SPANISH €€

(Map p732; ☑963 36 36 64; www.lagallineta.es; Calle del Conde de Altea 7; mains €13-19; ☾1.30-4pm Mon & Tue, 1.30-4pm & 8.30-11.30pm Wed-Sun) Driven by the markets, but thankfully by the food kind, not the stock exchange, this minimalist modern place has a short, quality menu of dishes inspired by what's fresh and good at the moment. It's intimate and luminous, and the large portrait of the fish from which it takes its name holds centre stage. The lunchtime menu for €19.50 is a steal.

✗ Western Valencia

El Pederniz SPANISH €€

(Map p732; ☑963 32 41 06; http://elpederniz.es; Pasaje de Ventura Feliú 20; mains €11-22; ☾1.30-5pm & 8.30-11.30pm Mon-Sat; 🛜) A warm, genuine welcome and lots of enthusiasm give a great first impression at this comfortably decorated restaurant a short hop from the fast-train station. Delicious seafood, game dishes and fine cuts of meat make for a reliably excellent experience here. It's a good one for a leisurely lunch before catching a train, but worth seeking out in any case.

✗ Valencia's Beaches

La Pascuala TAPAS €

(☑963 71 38 14; Calle de Eugenia Viñes 177; rolls €5-6; ☾9am-3.30pm Mon-Sat) A block back from the beach, this neighbourhood bar has barely changed since the '20s and is legendary for its huge *bocadillos* (filled rolls) that come absolutely stuffed with fillings. Half of Valencia seems to be in here around 11am for a mid-morning bite. It couldn't be more authentic. Try the super horse burger.

★Bodega Casa Montaña TAPAS €€

(☑963 67 23 14; www.emilianobodega.com; Calle de José Benlliure 69; tapas €4-14; ☾1-4pm & 8-11.30pm Mon-Fri, 12.30-4pm & 8-11.30pm Sat, 12.30-4pm Sun) One of Valencia's most characterful spots, with venerable barrels and an other-era atmosphere, this place has been around since 1836. There's a superb, changing selection of wines and a long list of exquisite tapas, including many seafood conserves. We fell in love with the smoked eel here, but it's all great. Eat in the bar or pass through it to the small rear restaurant.

Russafa

Russafa is Valencia's best place for an evening meal, with a staggering variety of options in a small area. Most lean towards modern, fusion cuisine or international specialities. It gets very busy at weekends, when the buzz is intoxicating.

Canalla Bistro FUSION €€
(Map p732; www.canallabistro.com; Calle del Maestro José Serrano 5; dishes €4-16; ⊘1.30-3.30pm & 8.30-11pm; 🐾) Chic but commodious, with an interior featuring packing crates, cartoon chickens and other decorative quirks, this is where top Valencian chef Ricard Camarena can be a little more light-hearted. Sensationally presented dishes draw their inspiration from street food from around the world. Creative, fun and delicious.

El Rodamón de Russafa FUSION, TAPAS €€
(Map p732; ☑963 21 80 14; www.elrodamon.com; Calle Sueca 47; tapas €3-11; ⊘8.30-11.30pm Mon & Tue, 2-4pm & 8.30-11.30pm Wed-Sun; 🐾) The deal here is that they've picked their favourite dishes encountered around the world and made a Valencian tapas dish out of them, so you can pick from tacos, curry, Italian porchetta, ceviche, tagine and numerous other eclectic dishes. It's modern and buzzy, with excellent staff, and the quality is all very high. There are several dozen wines available by the glass.

Ricard Camarena GASTRONOMY €€€
(Map p732; ☑963 35 54 18; www.ricardcam arenarestaurant.com; Calle de Doctor Sumsi 4; degustation menu €75-105; ⊘1.30-3.30pm & 8.30-10.30pm Tue-Sat; 🐾) Valencia's most highly rated current chef showcases the range of his abilities here, in a minimalist restaurant behind an unobtrusive facade. A range of tasting menus focuses on the Valencian ideal of fresh market produce, presented here in innovative ways that bring out exceptional and subtle flavours.

Drinking & Nightlife

Russafa has the best bar scene, with a huge range of everything from family-friendly cultural cafes to quirky bars, and also a couple of big clubs. The Barrio del Carmen is also famous nightlife territory: on weekends, Calle de Caballeros, the main street,

seethes with punters. The university area, especially around Avenidas de Aragón and Blasco Ibáñez, has enough bars and *discotecas* to keep you busy all night. In summer the port area and Malvarrosa beach leap to life.

North Ciutat Vella

⭐**Café Negrito** BAR
(Map p736; Plaza del Negrito; ⊘4pm-3am; 🐾) Something of a local legend, El Negrito has had a bit of a facelift in recent years and boasts a rather handsome interior. It hasn't changed its character though, with an intellectual, socially aware, left-wing clientele dominating and art exhibitions often focused on sustainable development or NGOs. The large terrace is a top spot to while away an evening.

Tyris on Tap MICROBREWERY
(Map p736; ☑961 13 28 73; www.cervezatyris. com; Calle Taula de Canvis 6; ⊘6pm-1am or 1.30am Tue-Sun; 🐾) White-painted industrial brick, long-drop pendant lights and no-frills decor lend an air of warehouse chic to this bar. It's an outlet for a local microbrewery, and 10 taps issue some pretty tasty craft beers (half-pint/pint €3/5). There's one of our favourite central terraces out front to enjoy it too, and some bar food to soak it up.

Barrio del Carmen

Jimmy Glass BAR
(Map p736; www.jimmyglassjazz.net; Calle Baja 28; ⊘8pm-2.30am Mon-Thu, 9pm-3.30am Fri & Sat; 🐾) Playing jazz from the owner's vast CD collection, Jimmy Glass also sometimes has live performances. It's just what a jazz bar should be – dim and serving jumbo measures of high-octane cocktails.

Northern & Eastern Valencia

⭐**Chico Ostra** BAR
(Map p732; ☑960 71 99 44; www.chicoostra. com; Calle del Músico Belando 15; ⊘6pm-midnight Sun-Thu, 6pm-1.30am Fri & Sat; 🐾) This lovable cafe-bar in Benimaclet is our favourite in the *barrio*. With a grotto-like entrance giving way to a cool white interior, it does a range of tasty snacks (€2 to €9), peddles secondhand clothes and books and has a great series of cultural happenings.

La Salamandra
BAR

(Map p732; Plaza Xúquer 6; ⊙4pm-1.30am; 🐀) Small, atmospheric and intimate, this pub is one of the classics of this lively evening square near the university. It's a favourite haunt of academics who appreciate a well-poured gin and tonic and who appreciate listening to music that was recorded years before their students were even born, but its terrace is also frequented by the young for evening beers.

🍸 South Ciutat Vella

Lotelito
COCKTAIL BAR

(Map p736; www.lotelitovalencia.com; Calle de Barcas 13; ⊙8am-1.30am; 🐀) The smooth industrial decor, moody lighting and motivated staff make this a fine venue for a pre-dancefloor or post-dinner drink. A range of spirits in a wire cage towers high over the bar: mixed drinks are well prepared, with plenty of floating seeds in your gin and tonic if you don't object, though it's best to check the prices first.

🍸 L'Eixample & Southern Valencia

L'Umbracle Terraza/Mya
BAR, CLUB

(Map p732; www.umbracleterraza.com; Avenida del Professor López Piñero 5; ⊙midnight-7.30am Thu-Sat) At the southern end of the Umbracle walkway within the Ciudad de las Artes y las Ciencias, this is a cool, sophisticated spot to spend a hot summer night. Catch the evening breeze under the stars on the terrace (from 6pm Thursday to Sunday May to October), then drop below to Mya, a top-of-the-line club with an awesome sound system. Admission covers both venues.

🍸 Russafa

La Fustería
BAR

(Map p732; www.lafusteriaruzafa.com; Calle de Cádiz 28; ⊙7-11pm Mon-Thu, 7pm-2.30am Fri & Sat; 🐀) This former carpentry workshop is now a likeably jumbled bar with mismatched furniture and bicycles bolted to the walls – they sell and repair them. It's a great venue for an after-dinner drink, with a amiable mix of folk, and regular events – flamenco when we were last there – out the back.

Ubik Café
BAR, CAFE

(Map p732; 963 74 12 55; http://ubikcafe. blogspot.com; Calle del Literato Azorín 13; ⊙5pm-

12.30am Mon & Tue, noon-12.30am Wed-Sun; 🐀🍴) This child-friendly Russafa cafe, bar and bookshop is a comfy place to lounge and browse. It has a short, well-selected list of wines and serves cheese and cold-meat platters, salads and plenty of Italian specialities. *'Como en casa'*, as they say in Spanish, meaning it's welcoming and homey. They offer language-exchange sessions too.

☆ Entertainment

Valencia has rich cultural offerings with lots of live music, theatre, sports and decent cinemas. Various magazines available at tourist offices and newspaper kiosks are handy for checking upcoming events. These include *Hello* and *Cartelera Turia*.

Live Music & Flamenco

Black Note
LIVE MUSIC

(Map p732; www.blacknoteclub.com; Calle Polo y Peyrolón 15; ⊙9pm-3.30am Mon-Sat) Valencia's most active venue for jazz, boogaloo, funk and soul, Black Note has live music around midnight most nights and good canned sounds. It's a well-established, reliable place; admission, including first drink, ranges from free to €15, depending on who's grooving.

Wah Wah
LIVE MUSIC

(Map p732; www.wahwahclub.es; Calle Campoamor 52; ⊙10.30pm-3am Thu-Sat; 🐀) For many, Wah Wah remains Valencia's hottest venue for live music, especially for underground and international indie, though classic Spanish garage and rock also get a good airing. Check the website; tickets are sometimes cheaper if they're purchased in advance.

Café del Duende
FLAMENCO

(Map p732; http://cafedelduende.com; Calle del Turia 62; entry incl drink €10; ☺ shows 11pm Thu-Sat, 8pm Sun; ☏) This intimate spot has decent-quality, reasonably authentic flamenco performances four nights a week. It's quite small, so it's worth queuing up before the show starts to avoid disappointment.

Theatre, Dance & Opera

★ **Microteatre València**
THEATRE

(Map p732; ☎963 32 56 48; http://microteatrevalencia.com; Calle de Cádiz 59; tickets €3.50; ☺7-11pm Tue, 7pm-12.30am Wed, 7pm-1.30am Thu, 7pm-2.30am Fri, 5pm-2.30am Sat, 11.30am-2.30pm & 7pm-midnight Sun; ☏) Plays in under 15 minutes, for less than 15 people, in less than 15 sq metres. That's the recipe at this innovative Russafa icon. Plays are on constant rotation in four rooms, so roll up, buy a ticket, and have a drink at the bar while you await your turn. Even if the language escapes you, it's quite an experience.

Palau de les Arts Reina Sofía
OPERA

(Map p732; ☎902 20 23 83; www.lesarts.com; Avenida del Professor López Piñero 1) A spectacular arts venue, part of the Ciudad de las Artes y las Ciencias, that offers mostly opera, but also concerts and recitals.

Espacio Inestable
DANCE

(Map p736; ☎963 91 95 50; www.espacioinestable.com; Calle de Aparisi y Guijarro 7; tickets €10; ☺8pm Thu-Sun) This edgy space presents innovative movement and dance of sometimes spectacular quality. It's a notable reference point of Valencia's alternative cultural scene. Check their website for upcoming shows, which normally run over a weekend, including Thursday and Sunday nights.

Football

★ **Valencia Club de Fútbol**
FOOTBALL

(Estadio de Mestalla; Map p732; ☎963 37 26 26; www.valenciacf.com; Avenida de Aragón) The city's principal team, and a major player in Spanish football, with famously demanding fans. A move to a new ground in the city's northwest has been stalled for several years, so for now they are still at Mestalla, an atmospheric, steeply tiered ground close to the centre. You can buy tickets a few weeks in advance via the website.

 Shopping

As befits its big-city status, Valencia has a wealth of shopping opportunities. There are lots of large shopping centres where you can find your favourite Spanish chain clothing stores such as Zara. The main area for smaller boutiques is the southern part of the Ciutat Vella and the nearby streets of L'Eixample. Russafa is the place to go for quirky and vintage purchases.

Madame Mim
VINTAGE, CLOTHING

(Map p732; ☎963 25 59 41; www.facebook.com/madame.mim.shop; Calle de Puerto Rico 30; ☺11am-2.30pm & 5.30-9.30pm Tue, Thu & Fri, 11am-2.30pm & 6-10pm Sat) Many Valencians would say that this is the city's best vintage shop, and we're always intrigued by what they've got in stock. As well as the clothes, there's a quirky line of interesting objects that's always worth a peek.

Abanicos Carbonell
HANDICRAFTS, ACCESSORIES

(Map p732; ☎963 41 53 95; www.abanicos-carbonell.com; Calle de Castellón 21; ☺9.30am-1.30pm & 4-8pm Mon-Fri) This historic fan maker, in business since 1810, offers hand-painted manual cooling units ranging from a very reasonable €10 for the basic but pretty ones to works by famous fan painters that run to thousands of euros. It's been run by the same family for five generations.

Las Ollas de Hierro
CRAFTS

(Map p736; Calle de los Derechos 4; ☺9.30am-1.30pm & 4.30-8pm Mon-Fri, 10am-2pm & 5-8pm Sat, closed Sat afternoon May-Oct) Valencia's oldest shop dates from the late 18th century, and has an intriguing history and loads of character. Its souvenir cards, Las Fallas accessories and religious items are eclipsed by its wonderful range of figures and landscapes for Christmas Nativity scenes.

Plaza Redonda
HANDICRAFTS

(Map p736; ☺hours vary) This circular 19th-century space in the heart of town – once the abattoir of Valencia's Mercado Central – is ringed by stalls. Though it feels a little over-touristy after an elaborate makeover, there are a couple of very worthwhile shops selling traditional ceramics.

ℹ Information

Joaquín Sorolla Station Tourist (Map p732; ☑ 963 80 32 63; www.turisvalencia.es; Estación Joaquín Sorolla; ☉10am-6pm Mon-Fri, 10am-3pm Sat & Sun) Office At the main long-distance train station.

Regional Tourist Office (Map p732; ☑ 963 98 64 22; www.comunitatvalenciana.com; Calle de la Paz 48; ☉10am-6pm Mon-Fri, 10am-2pm Sat & Sun) Helpful with information about the whole coastline.

Tourist Kiosk (Map p736; ☑ 963 52 49 08; www.turisvalencia.es; Plaza del Ayuntamiento; ☉9am-7pm Mon-Sat, 10am-2pm Sun) The main central city tourist office.

There's also an office at the airport. The best of several online guides to the city is www.lovevalencia.com.

ℹ Getting There & Away

AIR

Valencia's **airport** (VLC; ☑ 902 40 47 04; www.aena.es) is 10km west of the city centre along the A3, towards Madrid. Budget flights serve major European destinations including London, Paris and Berlin.

BUS

Valencia's **bus station** (Map p732; ☑ 963 46 62 66; Avenida Menéndez Pidal) is beside the riverbed. Bus 8 connects it to Plaza del Ayuntamiento.

Avanza (www.avanzabus.com) operates hourly bus services to/from Madrid (€29.75, four hours).

ALSA (www.alsa.es) has up to 10 daily buses to/from Barcelona (€29 to €35, four to five hours) and more than 10 to Alicante (€21, 2½ to 5¾ hours), most via Benidorm.

TRAIN

All fast trains now use the Valencia Joaquín Sorolla station, 800m south of the old town. It's meant to be temporary, but looks like sticking around for a long time.

It's linked with nearby **Estación del Norte** (Map p736; Calle de Xàtiva; ☉5.30am-midnight), 500m away, by free shuttle bus. Estación del Norte has slow trains to Gandia, Alicante and Madrid, as well as local *cercanía* lines.

Though there are some departures from Estación del Norte, *cercanía* lines to the west leave from Valencia San Isidro/Sant Isidre in the west of the city.

Major destinations include the following:

DESTINATION	FARE	DURATION	FREQUENCY
Alicante	€17-30	1½-2hrs	11 daily
Barcelona	€23-43	3¼-5hrs	14-18 daily
Madrid	€21-71	1¾-7hrs	13-20 daily

ℹ Getting Around

Valencia has an integrated bus, tram and metro network. Tourist offices sell the **Valencia Tourist Card** (p729), entitling you to free urban travel and various other discounts and freebies.

BICYCLE

Cycling is a great way to get around: the riverbed park gives you easy access to most of the city and there are several other bike lanes. There are numerous hire places, and most accommodation can organise it. **Valenbisi** (www.valenbisi.es) is the city-bike scheme – sign up for a short-term contract (€13) at machines at the bike racks.

PUBLIC TRANSPORT

Most buses run until about 10pm, with various night services continuing until around 1am. Buy a Bonobús Plus (€8 for 10 journeys) at major metro stations, most tobacconists and some newspaper kiosks, or pay as you get on (€1.50). One-/two-/three-day travel cards valid for the bus, metro and tram cost €4/6.70/9.70.

The tram is a pleasant way to get to the beach and port. Pick it up at Pont de Fusta or where it intersects with the metro at Benimaclet.

Metro (www.metrovalencia.es) lines cross town and serve the outer suburbs. The closest stations to the city centre are Ángel Guimerá, Xàtiva, Colón and Pont de Fusta.

AROUND VALENCIA CITY

La Albufera

About 15km south of Valencia, La Albufera is a huge freshwater lagoon separated from the sea by a narrow strip of pine-forested sand dunes. It's legendary for the rice that is grown here. It's also an important dune and wetland ecosystem and much of the area is covered by the Parque Natural de la Albufera (www.parquealbufera.com) FREE. The zone is great for birdwatching.

The most interesting Albufera communities are El Palmar, right on the lagoon, and El Saler, which has both a beach backed by piney dunes and a lagoon side. Pinedo, just across the rivermouth from Valencia, is another popular destination for its beach and rice dishes.

Sunsets can be spectacular here. You can take a boat trip from El Palmar or El Saler out on the lagoon, joining the local fisherfolk, who use flat-bottomed boats and nets to harvest fish and eels from the shallow waters.

★ **Mirador El Pujol** VIEWPOINT

(CV-500, Km 9.5) FREE Though no secret, this viewpoint – a boat dock with jetties extending into the principal lagoon of the Albufera – is still a magical place. It's a handy bird-watching spot, but comes into its own at sunset, when it's gloriously romantic, with herons slowly flapping against the reddening sky. You can take boat trips from here. Bus 25 to El Palmar stops right here.

✗ Eating

Surrounded by rice fields, La Albufera was the birthplace of paella. Every second house in the villages hereabouts is a rice restaurant. It's worth booking ahead at weekend lunchtimes, as Valencians descend in numbers to grab a bellyful of it.

El Sequer de Tonica VALENCIAN €€

(☑961 62 02 24; www.elsequerdetonica.com; Calle Redolins 85, El Palmar; rices per person €8-13; ☺10am-7pm Sun, Mon, Wed & Thu, 10am-11pm Fri & Sat; ☏) At the end of the main street in El Palmar, the luminous dining room at El Sequer de Tonica is highly esteemed by Valencians for its rice dishes, which includes one with duck (the ducks are hunted on the water-filled rice paddies in winter). Various lobster rices cost a little more.

❶ Getting There & Away

Bus 25 runs from central Valencia to El Saler and El Palmar every 20 minutes or so. Buses 14 and 15 serve Pinedo; these services are all part of the urban Valencia system. Bike lanes run from Valencia as far as El Saler and a little beyond.

Requena

POP 20,600 / ELEV 692M

Requena, 65km west of Valencia, grew rich from silk; today it's primarily wine and livestock country, producing robust reds (try the local Bobal grape), *cavas* (sparkling wines), rich sausages and spicy meats. From its heart rears La Villa, the medieval nucleus, with its twisting streets and blind alleys. It's great to explore, atmospheric without being dolled up for tourism. Check out the 15th-century guard tower at its entrance, the lovely Gothic facades, and the narrow lanes of the one-time Jewish quarter.

◉ Sights

Museo del Vino MUSEUM

(☑962 30 32 81; Carrer Somera 13; adult/child €2/1.50; ☺noon-2pm Wed & Thu, 10.30am-2pm & 5-7pm Sat & Sun) A venue for wine lovers is Museo del Vino, a wine museum within the handsome, sturdy 15th-century Palacio del Cid.

Cuevas de la Villa CAVE

(Plaza Albornoz 6; adult/child €4/3; ☺noon-2pm & 5-7pm Tue, Wed & Fri, 10.30am-2pm & 4-7pm Thu, 10.30am-2pm Sat, 4-7pm Sun) Within the intestines of Plaza Albornoz is a network of interlinked cellars, once used as storerooms, winemaking bodegas and, during strife, hideouts. They date back to Moorish times. These guided visits take you down to this intriguing subterranean world.

LA TOMATINA

The last or penultimate Wednesday in August (dates vary) marks Spain's messiest festival, La Tomatina (www.latomatina.info; tickets €10). Held in Buñol, 40km west of Valencia, La Tomatina is a tomato-throwing orgy attracting more than 20,000 visitors to a town of just 9000 inhabitants.

At 11am, more than 100 tonnes of squishy tomatoes are tipped from trucks to the waiting crowd. For one hour, everyone joins in a cheerful, anarchic tomato battle. After being pounded with pulp, expect to be sluiced down with hoses by the local fire brigade.

Participation costs €10; if you want to be pouring them off the truck you'll have to fork out €750. Don't forget a set of fresh clothes and perhaps a pair of goggles to protect your eyes. Visit the website for more background.

While most visitors just come in from Valencia for the event, it can be worthwhile staying over the night before and after. It's the locals' main fiesta and there's plenty of atmosphere, as well as concerts.

ℹ Information

Tourist Office (☎ 962 30 38 51; www.requena. es; Calle García Montés 1; ◷ 10am-2pm & 4-7pm Tue-Sat, 10am-2pm Sun) Below the main entrance to the old town. Ask for the English version of its helpful guide to La Villa.

ℹ Getting There & Away

Requena is right beside the Valencia–Madrid motorway. There are regular buses (€5.47, one hour), and *cercanías* (€5.80, 1½ hours) to/from Valencia. Most *cercanía* departures are from the Valencia San Isidro/Sant Isidre station. Note that there are also fast AVE/Avant trains that take only 25 minutes but are significantly pricier, and arrive at a different station (Requena Utiel), 6km from town.

Sagunto

POP 65,000

The port town of Sagunto (Valenciano: Sagunt), 25km north of Valencia, primarily offers spectacular panoramas of the coast, Balearics and sea of orange groves from its vast but ruinous hilltop castle complex. It's an easy half-day excursion from Valencia.

◉ Sights

★**Castillo de Sagunto**   CASTLE
(◷ 10am-6pm or 8pm Tue-Sat, 10am-2pm Sun) FREE Sagunto's castle is majestically located, with stone walls girdling a twin hilltop for almost a kilometre. Mostly in ruins, its seven rambling sections each speak of a different period in Sagunto's history. In truth, the fortress could do with a bit of care and is currently best for a stroll among the ruins and appreciating the magnificent vistas right along the coast, rather than gaining a detailed understanding of its long, long history. Don't expect interpretative panels or audioguides.

ℹ Information

Tourist Office (☎ 962 65 58 59; www. aytosagunto.es; Plaza Cronista Chabret; ◷ 9am-2.30pm & 4-7.30pm Mon-Fri, 9am-2pm & 4-6.30pm Sat, 10am-2pm Sun) The tourist office is a 15-minute walk from the train station.

ℹ Getting There & Away

The best option from Valencia to Sagunto is taking the *cercanía* trains on lines C5 and C6 (one way €3.70, 30 minutes, regular departures).

COSTA DEL AZAHAR & EL MAESTRAZGO

All along the Costa del Azahar (Blossom Coast) spread citrus groves, from whose headily scented flowers the region takes its name. The busy, developed – not always harmoniously – seaside resorts are enticing if you're after sun and sand. By contrast, the high hinterland, especially the wild, sparsely populated lands of the Maestrazgo, offer great walking solitude and hearty mountain cooking.

Benicàssim

POP 18,100

Benicàssim, scarcely a couple of blocks wide, stretches for 6km along the coast. It has been a popular resort since the 19th century, when wealthy Valencian families built their summer residences here. It's now also famous for its huge summer music festival.

◉ Sights & Activities

Desierto de les Palmes   NATURE RESERVE
The twisting, climbing CV147 leads, after about 6km, to this inland range – cooler than the coast, on occasion misty – with a Carmelite monastery and first-class restaurant at its heart. Nowadays it's a nature reserve and far from being a desert (for the monks it meant a place for mystic withdrawal), it's a green, outdoor activities area. From **Monte Bartolo** (728m), its highest point, there are staggering views. The tourist office hands out an excellent booklet listing a range of different hill walks.

✦ Festivals & Events

**Festival Internacional
de Benicàssim**   MUSIC
(FIB; www.fiberfib.com) Fans gather by the tens of thousands in mid-July for this annual four-day bash, one of Europe's major outdoor music festivals. Top acts in recent years have included some classic names but the majority are up-to-the-minute acts popular with the predominantly 20-something crowd. Late-afternoon starts mean you can spend the day on the beach.

🛏 Sleeping & Eating

Benicàssim's five camping grounds are all within walking distance of the beaches.

Rooms Boutique Benicàssim
HOSTAL €

(☑ 674 29 88 67; www.roomsboutiquebenicassim.com; Calle San Antonio 13; s/d €49/64; 🖥) Full of summertime colour and flair, this is a stylish budget option on the edge of the town centre. Rooms are comfortable and the decor upbeat; expect to be left to your own devices. Minimum stays apply in summer.

Hotel Voramar
HOTEL €€

(☑ 964 30 01 50; www.voramar.net; Paseo Pilar Coloma 1; s/d incl breakfast €95/120, with sea view €125/150; 🅿 ❄ 🖥) Venerable (in the same family for four generations) and blooded in battle (it was a hospital in the Spanish Civil War), this place has character and is spectacularly located right at the beach's northern end. Rooms – much cheaper outside high summer – will be thoroughly touched up in the winter of 2016–17. Those with balcony (and hammock) have utterly magnificent sea views and sounds.

Restaurante Desierto de las Palmas
VALENCIAN, SEAFOOD €€

(☑ 964 30 09 47; www.restaurantedesierto.com; CV147, Km 9; mains €13-21; ⊙ 9.30am-5.30pm Wed-Mon Mar-Dec, to midnight Jun-early Sep) Families flock from miles around to this popular venue, famed for its rice and seafood dishes, in the hills behind Benicàssim. Lively, noisy and very Spanish, it sits on a spur close to the Carmelite monastery and offers heart-stopping views from its broad windows.

❶ Information

Tourist Office (☑ 964 30 01 02; www.turismobenicassim.com; Calle Santo Tomás 74; ⊙ 9am-2pm & 4-7pm Mon-Fri, 10.30am-1.30pm & 4-7pm Sat, 10.30am-1.30pm Sun Oct-May, 9am-2pm & 5-8pm Mon-Fri, 10.30am-1.30pm & 5-8pm Sat & Sun Jun-Sep) In the centre of town.

❶ Getting There & Away

There are nine daily trains from Benicàssim to Valencia (€7.15 to €18.50, one to 1½ hours), and services north to Tortosa, Tarragona and Barcelona. Buses run every quarter-hour to the provincial capital Castellón de la Plana, from where there are more connections.

Peñíscola

POP 7,400

Peñíscola's old town, all cobbled streets and whitewashed houses, huddles within stone walls that protect the rocky promontory jutting into the sea. It's pretty as a postcard, and just as commercial, with ranks of souvenir and ceramics shops (one prominent item: a pot with – oh dear – a penis for a spout, a tourist-oriented pun on the town name). By contrast, the high-rises sprouting northwards along the coast are mostly leaden and charmless. But the **Paseo Marítimo** promenade makes pleasant walking, and the beach, which extends as far as neighbouring Benicarló, is superb, sandy and over 5km long. Peñíscola is quiet in low season but there's enough on to not make it spooky – and you'll have the old town to yourself.

◉ Sights

Sierra de Irta
PARK

To escape the summer crowds, seek solitude in the Sierra de Irta. Running south from Peñíscola, it's both nature park and protected marine reserve, best explored on foot or by mountain bike. You can attack the full 26km of the circular PR V194 trail or slip in one or more shorter loops. Ask at the tourist office for a trail map.

Castillo de Peñíscola
CASTLE

(☑ 964 48 00 21; www.dipcas.es; Calle Castillo; adult/child under 10 €5/free; ⊙ 10.30am-5.30pm mid-Oct-Easter, 9.30am-9.30pm Easter–mid-Oct) The rambling 14th-century castle was built by the Knights Templar on Arab foundations and later became home to Pedro de Luna ('Papa Luna', the deposed Pope Benedict XIII). There are various exhibits relating to the history of the castle and town, as well as a former cannon outpost converted into a garden with special views.

🛏 Sleeping & Eating

Pensión Chiki
PENSIÓN €

(☑ 964 48 02 84; www.restaurantechiki.es; Calle Mayor 3-5; d €55-65; 🖥) Right in the old town, this place has seven spotless, modern rooms with views and a genuine welcome. The nearby church chimes tinnily from 8am. It's homey, cosy and the price is right. From March to October, it runs an attractive restaurant (mains from €9; closed Tuesday) with a great-value three-course *menú*. The owner isn't always here, so ring ahead.

Rojo Picota
TAPAS €€

(☑ 964 48 92 60; www.rojopicota.es; Avenida Papa Luna 1; mains €9-22; ⊙ noon-4pm & 7pm-1.30am, kitchen until 11.30pm; 🖥) Open year-round (later hours in summer) and a favourite with locals as well as visitors, this place, on the waterfront road, offers a range of excellent wines by the glass, and wallet-friendly Basque-style *pintxos* (tapas) at the bar. A range of tasty plates prepared in the open kitchen, home-macerated vermouth and well-mixed gin and tonics make it an all-round star.

ℹ Information

Main Tourist Office (☑964 48 02 08; www.peniscola.es; Paseo Marítimo; ⏰9.30am-8pm mid-Jun–mid-Sep, 9.30am-5.30pm Mon-Sat, 10am-2pm Sun mid-Sep–mid-Jun) At the southern end of Paseo Marítimo. Pick up or download info on the town.

ℹ Getting There & Away

Buses run at least half-hourly between Peñíscola, Benicarló and Vinaròs, from where you can connect to Valencia or Castellón. From July to mid-September there's an hourly run to Peñíscola/Benicarló train station, 7km from town.

El Maestrazgo

Straddling northwestern Valencia and southeast Aragón, El Maestrazgo (Valenciano: El Maestrat) is a mountainous land, a world away from the coastal strip. Here spectacular ancient *pueblos* (villages) huddle on rocky outcrops and ridges. The Maestrazgo is great, wild, on-your-own trekking territory.

Sant Mateu

POP 2000 / ELEV 325M

Not as picturesque from a distance as the hilltop villages further into the region, Sant Mateu, once capital of the Maestrazgo, is an appealing spot nonetheless, whose solid

mansions and elaborate facades recall the town's more illustrious past and former wool-based wealth.

◉ Sights & Activities

Ermita de la Mare de Déu dels Àngels CHURCH
(☑605 38 29 35; ⏰11am-7pm Sat & Sun) FREE
Follow signs from the Plaza Mayor to this chapel perched on a rocky hillside, a 2.5km drive or somewhat shorter walk away. It was a monastery until the Spanish Civil War and preserves a cherub-infested baroque chapel. The views are great, and there's an excellent restaurant. It sometimes opens on weekdays too. You can phone to arrange a visit.

🛏 Sleeping & Eating

L'hostal de Cabrit HOTEL €€
(☑964 41 66 21; www.hostaldecabrit.com; Plaza Mare de Deu de la Font 19; s/d/ste incl breakfast €40/70/115; ❄☎) Decent value is to be had at this good-looking spot on a central plaza. Rooms vary in size but are cute, equipped with safe and fridge, and commodious. The suite has a king-sized bed and an in-room shower. Prices drop substantially midweek and in winter. The stone-faced cafe-restaurant does a nice line in rices and other plates (mains from €12 to €15).

Farga VALENCIAN €€
(☑663 90 95 86; www.fargarestaurant.com; Ermita de la Mare de Déu dels Àngels; set menus €30-35; ⏰noon-4pm Sun & Tue-Thu, noon-11pm Fri & Sat) This quality restaurant at a former monastery perched on a hill 2.5km from town offers incomparable views of the surrounding plain. Delicious seasonal produce is presented via degustation menus. In the winter months it's closed Tuesday and Wednesday.

OFF THE BEATEN TRACK

MAESTRAZGO VILLAGES

Blazing your own trails across the Maestrazgo on foot, bike or by car is most appealing. There are numerous lonely landscapes and lovely villages to discover. **Ares**, 30km south of Morella, is one of the most spectacular, hanging over a cliff. Around 13km from here, **Vilafranca** (del Cid) has a museum that explores its dry-stone wall tradition, the excellent **Museo de la Pedra en Sec** (☑964 44 14 32; www.ajuntamentdevilafranca.es; Calle de la Iglesia, Villafranca del Cid; adult/child €2/1.50; ⏰10am-1.30pm & 4-7pm Fri & Sat, 10.30am-1.30pm Sun). If there's no one there, ask in the tourist office opposite. And don't miss the stunning spots over the border in Teruel province!

PREHISTORIC PAINTINGS

The **Museo de Valltorta** (☏ 964 33 60 10; www.cult.gva.es; Tirig; ⏱ 10am-2pm & 4-7pm or 5-8pm Tue-Sun) is an informative museum, 2km from Tirig, itself 10km southwest of Sant Mateu. It presents a detailed overview of prehistoric art and El Maestrazgo's World Heritage ensemble of rock paintings (info in various languages available). There's a reproduction of the most interesting piece, a hunting scene. From here, free guided walks to the painting sites leave a few times daily.

ⓘ Information

Tourist Office (☏ 964 41 66 58; http://turismosantmateu.es; Carrer Historiador Betí 13; ⏱ 10am-2pm & 4-6pm Tue-Sat, 10am-2pm Sun) Very helpful. Just off the main square in a sturdy palace.

ⓘ Getting There & Away

Autos Mediterráneo (☏ 964 22 00 54; www.autosmediterraneo.com) buses link Sant Mateu with the following destinations:

DESTINATION	FARE	DURATION	FREQUENCY
Castellón	€5.20	1½hr	3 Mon-Fri, 1 Sat
Morella	€3.40	45mins	2 Mon-Fri, 1 Sat
Vinaròs	€2.70	1hr	4 Mon-Fri

Morella

POP 2600 / ELEV 984M

Bitingly cold in winter and refreshingly cool in summer, striking Morella is the Valencian Maestrazgo's principal town. This outstanding example of a medieval fortress town, breathtaking at first glimpse, is perched on a hilltop, crowned by a castle and girdled by an intact rampart wall more than 2km long. It's the ancient capital of Els Ports, the 'Mountain Passes', a rugged region offering some outstanding scenic drives and strenuous cycling excursions, plus excellent possibilities for walkers.

◉ Sights

Morella is a compact jumble of narrow streets, alleys and steep steps. Its main street, running between city gateways Puerta San Miguel and Puerta de los Estudios, is bordered by shops selling mountain honey, perfumes, cheeses, pickles, pâtés, sausages and fat hams.

On the outskirts of town, near the Puerta San Miguel, stretch the arches of a handsome 13th-century **aqueduct**. You can also get a guard's-eye view of the town by climbing up onto the **city walls**.

Combined entrance tickets can save you euros here.

Castle   CASTLE
(adult/child €3.50/2.50; ⏱ 11am-6pm Oct-Apr, to 7pm May-Sep) Though badly knocked about, Morella's castle well merits the long wiggly ascent to savour breathtaking views of the town and surrounding countryside. Built by the Moors, it was regularly remodelled and saw action in the Napoleonic and Carlist wars of the 19th century. Carlists took it in 1838 by climbing up through the long-drop toilet. At its base is the bare church and cloister of the **Convento de San Francisco**. Last entry is one hour before closing.

Basílica de Santa María la Mayor   CHURCH
(Plaza Arciprestal; ⏱ 10.30am-2pm & 3-6pm or 7pm Mon-Sat, 10.30-11.30am & 1-4pm or 5pm Sun) FREE This imposing Gothic basilica has two elaborately sculpted doorways on its southern facade. A richly carved polychrome stone staircase leads to the elaborate overhead choir, while cherubs clamber and peek all over the gilded altarpiece. Its ecclesiastical treasure is kept within the **Museo Arciprestal** (admission €1.50).

🛏 Sleeping & Eating

Hotel Cardenal Ram   HOTEL €€
(☏ 964 16 00 46; www.hotelcardenalram.com; Cuesta Suñer 1; s/d €60/80; ⓟ ❀ ☏) Bang in the heart of old Morella, this noble Renaissance palace has been completely refurbished and offers a tantalising blend of historical feel and modern amenities. Half the rooms have splendid views (and cost a little more); those without are generally very spacious. There's also a handsome restaurant and midweek discounts.

Hotel del Pastor   HOTEL €€
(☏ 964 16 10 16; www.hoteldelpastor.com; Carrer San Julián 12; s/d incl breakfast €56/74; ⓟ ❀ ☏) This central hotel is an excellent deal, with slightly old-fashioned rooms – some with

vistas – spread over four floors (there's no lift but that's the only downside of this option). Rooms are traditionally furnished and come in warm ochre colours with plenty of polished wood. Bathrooms have marble washstands, bathtubs and large mirrors.

★ **Daluan** FUSION €€
(☑ 964 16 00 71; www.daluan.es; Carreró de la Presó 6; mains €14-20, degustation menu €40; ☺ 1-3.30pm Thu-Tue plus 9-10.30pm Fri & Sat, closed Jan) Daluan is run by Avelino Ramón, a cookery teacher by trade, and his wife, Jovita. Its small interior is satisfyingly contemporary and its terrace, beside a quiet alley, is equally relaxing. Expect friendly service and a hugely creative menu that changes regularly with the seasons. A backstreet gem and very well priced for this standard.

Mesón del Pastor SPANISH €€
(☑ 964 16 02 49; www.mesondelpastor.com; Cuesta Jovaní 5; mains €8-16, set menus €18-28; ☺ 1-4pm Thu-Tue plus 9-11pm Sat) Within the dining room, bedecked with the restaurant's trophies and diplomas, this place is all about robust mountain cuisine: thick stews in winter, rabbit, juicy sausages, partridge, wild boar and goat. It's located a short walk from the hotel of the same name. In August, it opens for dinner every day bar Wednesday.

❶ Information

Tourist Office (☑ 964 17 30 32; www.morella-turistica.com; Plaza San Miguel 3; ☺ 10am-2pm & 4-6pm or 7pm Mon-Sat, 10am-2pm Sun, closed Mon Nov-Mar) The tourist office is just inside the imposing San Miguel towers and entrance gate to the old town.

❶ Getting There & Away

Morella is best reached via Castellón, which has good train connections.

Two daily weekday buses (€9.70, 2¼ hours) and one Saturday service with Autos Mediterráneo run to/from Castellón's train station. There are also weekday buses to Vinaròs on the coast and Alcañiz in Teruel province.

COSTA BLANCA

The long stripe of the Costa Blanca (White Coast) is one of Europe's most heavily visited areas. If you're after a secluded midsummer strand, stay away – or head inland to enjoy traditional villages and towns. Then again, if you're looking for a lively social scene, good beaches and a suntan...

It isn't all concrete and package deals. Although the original fishing villages have long been engulfed by the sprawl of resorts, a few old-town kernels, such as those of Xàbia (Jávea) and Altea, still survive. Alicante itself has plenty more to offer besides legendary nightlife, while Denia is an interesting blend of traditional fishing town, beach resort and enticing gastronomic destination.

Gandia

POP 75,500
Gandia's main town, once home to a branch of the Borja dynasty (more familiar as the infamous Borgias), is a prosperous commercial centre with a lively atmosphere. The other side of the coin is the fun-in-the-sun beach town and port, 6km away.

◉ Sights

★ **Palacio Ducal de los Borja** PALACE
(☑ 962 87 14 65; www.palauducal.com; Calle Duc Alfons el Vell 1; adult/child €6/5; ☺ 10am-2pm & 3-7pm Mon-Sat, 10am-1pm Sun Nov-Mar, 10am-1.30pm & 4-7.30pm Mon-Sat, 10am-1pm Sun Apr-Oct) Gandia's magnificent palace was the 15th-century home of Duque Francisco de Borja. Highlights include its finely carved *artesonado* ceilings and rich ceramic work – look out for the vivid *mapa universal* floor composition. Guided tours (in Spanish, with an English leaflet) leave regularly and cost a euro more.

⊨ Sleeping & Eating

Hostal El Nido HOSTAL €€
(☑ 962 84 46 40; Calle Alcoy 22; s/d €55/75; ☜) This homey place is the mirror opposite of all the giant resort hotels that line the beach, and the rooms are as cheerful as the owners. It's a block back from the beach. Between June and September it also runs a small bar for guests.

Hotel RH Riviera HOTEL €€€
(☑ 962 84 50 42; www.hotelrhriviera.com; Paseo Neptuno 28; s/d incl breakfast €111/185; ☺ Mar-Oct; ❂❅◎☎❄) This is one of Gandia's oldest seaside hotels, but rooms are modern, up-to-date and luxurious in a way that is unexpected for a three-star hotel. Prices

are much lower in low season. The same chain has three other options in the beach zone.

Antic Mercat
TAPAS €€

(☑962 95 10 67; Plaza Mayor 4; tapas €3-12; ☺noon-3.30pm & 8-11.30pm Wed-Sun; ☞) On the main square opposite the church and near the ducal palace in the heart of Gandia, this sweet spot is a fine destination for a delightful selection of carefully prepared little plates. A few *cocas* (Catalan 'pizzas') and little stews of things like octopus are all wholesome and delicious, served in an elegant modern ambience.

ℹ️ Information

Playa de Gandia Tourist Office (☑962 84 24 07; www.gandiaturismo.com; Paseo de Neptuno; ☺9.30am-2pm & 3.30-6.30pm Mon-Fri, 9.30am-1.30pm Sat & Sun mid-Sep–Jun, 9.30am-8.30pm Mon-Sat, 9.30am-1.30pm Sun Jul–mid-Sep) At the beach.

Town Tourist Office (☑962 87 77 88; www.gandiaturismo.com; Av Marqués de Campo; ☺9.30am-1.30pm & 3.30-7.30pm Mon-Fri, 9.30am-1.30pm Sat mid-Sep–Jun, 9.30am-2.30pm & 4-8pm Mon-Fri, 9.30am-1.30pm Sat Jul–mid-Sep) Opposite the bus and train station.

ℹ️ Getting There & Away

Cercanía trains run between Gandia and Valencia (€5.80, one hour) every 30 minutes (hourly on weekends). The combined bus and train station is opposite the town tourist office; there's also a stop near the beach. Stopping beside the office, La Marina Gandiense buses for Playa de Gandia run every 20 minutes.

ALSA runs regular buses to Denia (€3.60, 30 minutes) and other coastal towns.

Denia

POP 41,600

A major passenger port for the fairly nearby Balearic Islands, Denia is a cheery place that lives for more than just tourism. The old town snuggles up against a small hill mounted by a tumbledown castle and the town's streets buzz with life. The beaches of La Marina, to its northwest, are good and sandy, while southeastwards the fretted coastline of Les Rotes and beyond offers less-frequented rocky coves. With its excellent selection of hotels and restaurants, and mix of local and tourist life, Denia is perhaps the Costa Blanca's most appealing base.

◉ Sights & Activities

Castillo de Denia
CASTLE

(☑966 42 06 56; Calle San Francisco; adult/child €3/1; ☺10am-1.30pm & 5-8.30pm) From Plaza de la Constitución, steps lead up to the ruins of Denia's castle, from where there's a great overview of the town and coast. The castle grounds contain the **Museo Arqueològic de Denia**; a collection of potsherds illustrating the town's long history. Outside high summer, the castle opens earlier in the afternoon and closes around dusk.

🛏️ Sleeping

Hostal L'Anfora
HOSTAL €

(☑966 43 01 01; www.hostallanfora.com; Esplanada de Cervantes 8; s/d €50/69; ❄☞) The genial boss here is rightly proud of this top *hostal* on the waterfront strip. Rooms are compact but new in feel, with colourful bedcovers, faultless bathrooms and not a speck of dust or dirt. Outside of high summer, prices are very fair: a budget gem. Rooms with a sea view cost a few euros more.

★ Hotel Chamarel
BOUTIQUE HOTEL €€

(☑966 43 50 07; www.hotelchamarel.com; Calle Cavallers 13; d/ste incl breakfast €85/130; P❄☞) This delightful hotel, tastefully furnished in period style, occupies a lovably attractive, 19th-century bourgeois mansion. The rooms surround a tranquil patio and are all different, with space and lots of character; bathrooms artfully combine modern fittings with venerable floor tiles. The internal salon with marble-topped bar is equally relaxing. The whole place is a capacious gallery for the paintings of the artist owner.

Hotel Nou Roma
BOUTIQUE HOTEL €€

(☑966 43 28 43; www.hotelnouroma.com; Calle Nou 28; r incl breakfast €90; P❄☞) ✿ Perfectly located for excursions to the Calle Loreto eating strip, this is on a quietish backstreet but very central. Staff are really excellent, and the spacious rooms with their bright-tiled bathrooms are a delight. The on-site restaurant is worthwhile and the overall package very impressive. Lots of thoughtful details add that extra something to your stay.

El Raset
HOTEL €€€

(☑965 78 65 64; www.hotelelraset.com; Calle Bellavista 1; s/d incl breakfast €120/145; P❄@☞) This modern designer hotel overlooks the port with spotlit rooms, colourful bedspreads and art on the walls. There's a buzzy vibe and very friendly service. A row of house restaurants alongside gives you doorstep eating options.

Eating

Barbus
SEAFOOD €

(965 78 11 37; Plaza del Archiduque Carlos 4; dishes €4-10; noon-10pm;) Bars by bus stations aren't normally recommended for their culinary qualities, but this vivacious corner spot breaks the mould. As well as being where people drop a quick coffee before jumping on the 12.10, it's also a place to try simple, quality seafood selected daily from the market. Oysters, cuttlefish and other delights are reliably excellent.

El Baret de Miquel Ruiz
TAPAS €€

(673 74 05 95; Carrer Historiador Palau 1; tapas €4-14; 1.30-3.30pm & 8-10.30pm Wed-Sat, 1.30-3.30pm Sun & Mon) This is a real find for gastronauts. The chef had a Michelin-starred restaurant but chose to reject the pretension of that world in favour of a more normal existence. Delicious, exquisitely presented morsels of traditionally influenced dishes using market produce are taste sensations in the simple, retro-casual vibe of the front room of an old house. Book months ahead.

★ Quique Dacosta
MODERN SPANISH €€€

(965 78 41 79; www.quiquedacosta.es; Carretera Las Marinas, Km 3, El Poblet; degustation €190, wine flight €79-99; 1.30-3pm & 8.30-10.30pm Wed-Sun Feb-Jun & Sep-Nov, daily Jul & Aug) In sleek, white, minimalist premises near the beach 3km west of Denia, this coolly handsome place is one of the peninsula's temples to modern gastronomy. The eponymous chef employs molecular and other contemporary techniques to create a constantly surprising cornucopia of flavours and textures.

❶ Information

Tourist Office (966 42 23 67; www.denia. net; Plaza Oculista Buigues 9; 9.30am-1.45pm & 4-7pm Mon-Sat, 9.30am-1.45pm Sun) Near the waterfront and ferry and also close to the tram/light-rail station.

❶ Getting There & Away

Hourly light-rail services follow the scenic route southwards via Calp and Altea to Benidorm, connecting with the tram for Alicante.

ALSA (www.alsa.es) buses run around a dozen times daily to Valencia (€11.05, 1½ to two hours) and Alicante (€11.40, 1½ to three hours); there are also services to Benidorm and other Costa Blanca towns.

Xàbia
POP 27,700

With a large expat resident population, Xàbia (Spanish: Jávea) is a gentle, family-oriented place that has largely resisted the high-rise tourist developments that blight so much of the Costa Blanca. Pleasant, relaxed and picturesque, it comes in three flavours: the small old town 2km inland; El Puerto (the port), directly east of the old town; and the beach zone of El Arenal, a couple of kilometres south.

🏃 Activities

In addition to El Arenal's broad beach, the old town, with quiet plazas and boutique shops, well merits a wander. Tourist offices sell *Red Espacios Naturales Xàbia* (€1), available in various languages, with five waymarked routes in the area described, including an ascent of Montgó. This is a climb best started in the morning or evening as it's fairly exposed.

Xàbia's Bike
BICYCLE RENTAL

(966 46 11 50; www.xabiasbike.com; Avenida Lepanto 5; per day/week from €10/49; 9.30am-1.30pm & 4.30-8.30pm Mon-Fri, 9.30am-1.30pm Sat) You can rent a cycle at Xàbia's Bike in the port area. They also do guided bike tours.

🛏 Sleeping & Eating

Hotel Triskel
BOUTIQUE HOTEL €€

(966 46 21 91; www.hotel-triskel.com; Calle Sor María Gallard 3; d €100;) By the market in the old town, this cordially run place is a standout. The five lovely rooms are subtly and beautifully decorated according to themes, with thoughtful details, objets d'art and pleasing handmade wooden furniture. Everything is done with a warm personal touch and the cosy bar downstairs does a cracking G'n'T. Pets welcome and prices nearly halve in low season.

Hotel Miramar
HOTEL €€

(965 79 01 00; www.hotelmiramar.com.es; Plaza Presidente Adolfo Suárez 12; s/d €45/75;) You'll be that close to the sea that you might

want to sleep in your swimwear in this faded but comfy enough, year-round hotel right beside the port. Rooms overlooking the bay carry a €14 supplement. There's a bar and restaurant, too.

★ **La Renda**   VALENCIAN €€

(☑ 965 79 37 63; www.larenda.es; Calle Cristo del Mar 12; mains €11-22; ☺ 1-4pm & 7-11pm Tue-Sat, 1-4pm Sun) There's more than you think to a paella, and this well-priced but classy, welcoming place at the port has numerous different rice dishes, including a delicious *meloso* (with broth) rice with lobster. For most dishes a minimum of two people is required, but there's a set menu with a rice option always available.

Embruix   TAPAS, CAFE €€

(☑ 966 46 20 73; www.embruix.es; Calle Mayor 17; tapas €4-9, mains €12-18; ☺ 8.30am-11pm Wed-Mon; ☜) In the heart of the old town, this convivial spot has a popular terrace, a striking stone-vaulted interior, fine coffee and a range of delicious cakes. It also stands out for its handsomely presented tapas portions, particularly of seafood. They are bursting with flavour and backed up by some decent à la carte meat dishes.

ℹ️ Information

Arenal Tourist Office (☑ 966 46 06 05; www.xabia.org; Avenida del Pla; ☺ 9am-1.30pm Mon-Fri mid-Sep–Jun, 10am-2pm & 5-9pm daily Jul–mid-Sep) Moves to the beachfront promenade in summer.

Old Town Tourist Office (☑ 965 79 43 56; www.xabia.org; Plaza de la Iglesia; ☺ 9am-1.30pm & 4-7.30pm Mon-Fri, 10am-1.30pm Sat plus 4.30-8pm Jun-Sep)

Port Tourist Office (☑ 965 79 07 36; www.xabia.org; Plaza Presidente Adolfo Suárez 11; ☺ 9am-1.30pm & 4-7.30pm Mon-Fri, 10am-1.30pm & 4-7.30pm Sat, 10am-1.30pm Sun plus 4.30-8pm Jun-Sep)

ℹ️ Getting There & Away

ALSA (www.alsa.es) run at least six buses daily to both Valencia (€12, two to three hours) and Alicante (€10.20, 2¼ to 2¾ hours). There are also services to Denia, Madrid, Benidorm, Gandia and Calp, as well as direct buses to both Valencia and Alicante airports, the latter run by **Beniconnect** (☑ 965 85 07 90; www.beniconnect.com).

Calp

POP 21,500

The striking Gibraltaresque Peñon de Ifach, a giant limestone molar protruding from the sea, rears up from the seaside resort of Calp.

Two large bays sprawl either side of the Peñon: Playa Arenal on the southern side is backed by the old town, while Playa Levante (La Fossa), to the north, is pretty much wall-to-wall supersized tourist developments with little to offer independent travellers (except the beach, which is glorious).

From the Peñon's **Aula de Naturaleza** (Nature Centre), a fairly strenuous walking trail – allow 2½ hours for the round trip – heads through a tunnel and then climbs towards the 332m-high summit, offering great seascapes from its end point. In July and August, walkers depart every 15 minutes in batches of 20, so you may have a short wait.

🛏️ Sleeping & Eating

There are plenty of restaurants and bars around Plaza de la Constitución and along main Avenida de Gabriel Miró, plus a cluster of good fish places down by the port as well as numerous mediocre tourist restaurants.

Hostal Terra de Mar   BOUTIQUE HOTEL €€

(☑ 629 66 51 24; www.hostalterrademar.com; Calle Justicia 31; s/d €89/119; ❄☜) At this artistic and highly original hotel, a range of influences combine to exquisite effect. Each floor has its own style (via the stairs you can travel from Japan to Morocco to Africa and Paris). Some rooms have mini-balconies looking over the old-town street. There are numerous details such as intricately folded towels and a personal tea box. There's some noise between rooms.

La Llar de Bárbara   TAPAS €€

(☑ 965 83 01 60; www.facebook.com/lallarbarbara; Calle Mayor 10; tapas €3-12; ☺ 6-11pm Thu-Mon) Evening-only hours is the first sign of a made-for-foreigners spot in coastal Spain, but nevertheless La Llar de Bárbara produces some enticing tapas dishes off a short menu: dates with bacon, beetroot gazpacho and curried chicken, for example. It's a welcoming old-town place, on a plant-bedecked section of the street.

ℹ️ Information

Main Tourist Office (☑ 965 83 85 32; www.calpe.es; Plaza del Mosquit; ☺ 9am-5pm or

6pm Mon-Fri, 9am-2pm Sat) In the old town. There's another branch in the beach zone. This square doesn't appear on some maps; it's at the corner of Calles Purísima and Ermita.

ℹ Getting There & Away

Buses connect Calp with both Alicante (€7.25, 1½ hours, six to 10 daily) and Valencia (€13.55, 2¾ to 3¾ hours, six or seven daily). There are also regular services to other nearby coastal destinations including Benidorm and Altea. The **bus station** (Avenida de la Generalitat Valenciana) is just off the ring road.

Trams travel daily northwards to Denia (€2.50, 40 minutes) and south to Benidorm (€2.50, 30 minutes), connecting with trams for Alicante.

Benidorm

POP 69,000

Brash Benidorm is an infamous focus for mass tourism along its two wide sandy beaches and the high-rise development that backs them. Bingo, karaoke, fish 'n' chips, all-day fry-ups: it's here, and the profusion of expat bars where not a word of Spanish is spoken give it an atmosphere of its own.

Benidorm's nice side is the old town, set on a hill between the two beaches. From the platform where once a castle stood, the evening light and sunsets can be incredible.

Benidorm is also popular with families for its excellent theme parks.

🏃 Activities

Aqualandia　　　　　　　WATER PARK
(🖉965 86 01 00; www.aqualandia.net; adult/child €36/28; ⏰10am-dusk mid-May–mid-Oct; 🖐) Aqualandia is Europe's largest water park and can easily entertain for a full day.

Terra Mítica　　　　AMUSEMENT PARK
(🖉902 02 02 20; www.terramiticapark.com; adult/child €38/28, 2nd day free; ⏰10.30am-8pm or midnight Easter & mid-May–mid-Sep, Sat & Sun Oct; 🖐) Everything is bigger and brasher in Benidorm, so it should come as no surprise to learn that this is Spain's biggest theme park. A fun day out, especially if you're with children, it's Mediterranean (well, kind of) in theme, with plenty of scary rides, street entertainment, and areas devoted to ancient Egypt, Greece, Rome, Iberia and the islands.

🛏 Sleeping & Eating

Almost everyone's on a package deal in Benidorm, so accommodation can be ex-

pensive for the independent traveller. Book online for significant discounts.

Hostal Irati　　　　　　　HOSTAL €€
(🖉966 81 31 20; www.hostalirati.com; Calle Condestable Zaragoza 5; r with breakfast €75; ❋🖥) In the old town, this place has comfortable, neat rooms with excellent tiled bathrooms above a friendly bar. It's an excellent deal.

⭐**Villa Venecia**　　　BOUTIQUE HOTEL €€€
(🖉965 85 54 66; www.hotelvillavenecia.com; Plaza San Jaime 1; s €180-257, d €300-467; 🅿❋@🖥⛱) Up high opposite the old town's church and lording it over the seething beach crowds below, this plush five-star hotel has it all. Each room has sweeping sea views and ultramodern bathrooms. As you lounge beside its diminutive rooftop pool after a spa session, you could be nautical miles away from Benidorm. Its bar and excellent restaurant are open to all comers.

La Cava Aragonesa　　　　　TAPAS €€
(🖉966 80 12 06; www.lacavaaragonesa.es; Plaza de la Constitución; set menus €10-13, mains €10-18; ⏰1-4pm & 7.30pm-12.30am Sep-May, 1pm-12.30am Jun-Aug) What a magnificent selection of tapas, fat canapés and plates of cold cuts, all arrayed before you at the bar and labelled. Next door is its sit-down restaurant, with different wooden platters of mixed foods – and more than 600 varieties of wine. It's located in a zone with lots of nearby tapas options so you can make a satisfying crawl of it.

ℹ Information

Old Town Tourist Office (🖉965 85 13 11; www.benidorm.org; Plaza de Canalejas; ⏰9am-9pm Mon-Fri, 10am-5pm Sat, 10am-2pm Sun) There are also kiosks at the bus station, on Avenida de Europa and in Rincòn de Loix.

ℹ Getting There & Away

From Benidorm's bus station (served by local bus 41 and 47), ALSA (www.alsa.es) runs to the following destinations:

Alicante (€4 to €6, 45 minutes to one hour, frequent)

Alicante Airport (€9.45, 40 to 50 minutes, hourly)

Valencia (€16.55 to €16.90, 1¾ hours to 3¾ hours, frequent)

The tram/light-rail runs to Alicante (€3.75, 1¼ hours, every 30 minutes) and in the other direction to Altea, Calp and Denia.

Altea

POP 22,400

Altea, separated from Benidorm only by the thick wedge of the Sierra Helada, is altogether quieter, with beaches mostly of pebbles. The modern part is a bog-standard coastal resort. By contrast, the whitewashed old town, perched on a hilltop overlooking the sea, is a delightfully pretty *pueblo*.

ℹ Information

Tourist Office (☎965 84 41 14; altea@touristinfo.net; Pl José María Planelles 1; ⊗8.30am-2.30pm Mon-Fri) In the town-hall building a couple of streets back from the waterfront. The Garganes tram stop is alongside.

ℹ Getting There & Away

Altea is on the Alicante–Benidorm–Calp–Denia tram/light-rail line.

Bus 10 runs regularly between Altea and central Benidorm (€1.50, 30 minutes).

Alicante

POP 328,600

Of all Spain's mainland provincial capitals, Alicante is the most influenced by tourism, thanks to the nearby airport and resorts. Nevertheless this is a dynamic, attractive Spanish city with a castle, old quarter and long waterfront. The eating scene is exciting and the nightlife is absolutely legendary, whether you're chugging pints with the stag parties at 7pm or twirling on the dance floor with the locals seven hours later. On a weekend night it's impossibly busy and buzzy year-round.

◉ Sights

★ **Museo de Arte Contemporáneo de Alicante** GALLERY
(MACA; www.maca-alicante.es; Plaza Santa María 3; ⊗10am-8pm Tue-Sat, to 2pm Sun) FREE This splendid museum, inside the 17th-century Casa de la Asegurada, has an excellent collection of 20th-century Spanish art, including works by Dalí, Miró, Chillida, Sempere, Tàpies and Picasso.

★ **Museo Arqueológico Provincial** MUSEUM
(MARQ; ☎965 14 90 00; www.marqalicante.com; Plaza Dr Gómez Ulla; adult/child €3/1.50; ⊗10am-7pm Tue-Fri, 10am-8.30pm Sat, 10am-2pm Sun Sep-Jun, 10am-2pm & 6-10pm Tue-Sat, 10am-2pm Sun Jul-Oct) This museum has a strong collection of ceramics and Iberian art. Exhibits are displayed to give the visitor a very visual, high-tech experience, and it's all beautifully presented. The only drawback is the lack of information in English.

Castillo de Santa Bárbara CASTLE
(☎965 92 77 15; www.castillodesantabarbara.com; Calle Vázquez de Mella; ⊗10am-10pm Apr-Sep, to 8pm Oct-Mar) FREE There are sweeping views over the city from this large 16th-century castle, which houses a **museum** (MUSA; ⊗10am-2.30pm & 4-8pm) FREE recounting the history of the city and containing a couple of chambers with temporary exhibitions. It's a sweaty walk up the hill to the castle, but there's a **lift** (return €2.70; ⊗10am-7.40pm, last lift up 7.20pm) that rises through the bowels of the mountain to the summit. To return, it's a pleasant stroll downhill through **Parque de la Ereta**.

Museu de Fogueres MUSEUM
(Museo de las Hogueras; ☎965 14 68 28; Rambla de Méndez Núñez 29; ⊗10am-2pm & 5-8pm or 6-9pm Tue-Sat, 10am-2pm Sun) FREE In addition to a wealth of photographs, costumes and *ninots* (small effigies saved from the flames), this museum has a great audiovisual presentation of what the Fiesta de Sant Joan, all fire and partying, means to *alicantinos*.

✦ Festivals & Events

Hogueras de San Juan FIESTA
(Fiesta de Sant Joan; www.hogueras.org) Alicante's major festival is on the night of 23 June, when midsummer bonfires are lit. In a celebration reminiscent of Valencia's Las Fallas (p739), satirical effigies *(ninots)* go up in smoke all over town. This act, known as the *cremà*, is the culmination of several days of parades and partying, which begins when the effigies appear overnight on the 20th.

⊨ Sleeping

Guest House HOSTAL €
(☎650 71 83 53; www.guesthousealicante.com; Calle Segura 20; s/d/apt €40/50/90; P❋❐) Here's a magnificent budget choice. Each of the eight large, tastefully decorated rooms differs: some have exposed stone walls and others are painted in pale green, daffodil yellow or deep-sea blue. All come with a safe, full-sized fridge and free beverage-making facilities. There are also a couple of well-equipped apartments. Ring ahead in low season.

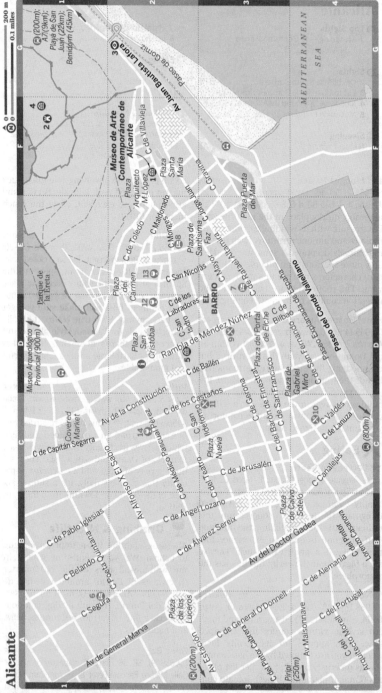

Alicante

MEDITERRANEAN SEA

0 200 m
0 0.1 miles

Ⓐ(200m): A7 (9km);
Playa de San
Juan (22km);
Benidorm (45km)

Museo de Arte
Contemporáneo de
Alicante

Museo Arqueológico
Provincial (900m)

Parque de
la Ereta

Paseo de Gomiz
Av Juan Bautista Lafora

Plaza
Santa
María

Plaza
Arquitecto
M. López

C de Villavieja
C de Toledo
C de Maldonado
C Monges
Plaza de
Santísima
Faz
C San Nicolás
C Mayor
C de Rafael Altamira
C de José Juan
C Gravina
Plaza Puerta
del Mar

Plaza
del
Carmen

EL
BARRIO

C de los
Labradores
C San
Isidro

Rambla de Méndez Núñez
C de Bailén

Plaza
San
Cristóbal

C de
Bilbao
Plaza del Portal
de Elche

Plaza de Finestrat

C de Gerona
C de San Francisco
C del Barón de Finestrat

C de San Fernando
Paseo del Conde Vallellano
Paseo de España

Plaza Puerta
del Mar

Plaza de
Gabriel
Miró

C Valdés
C de Lanuza

Av de la Constitución
C de Médico Pascual Pérez
C de los Castaños
C San Ildefonso
Plaza
Nueva
C del Teatro

Ⓜ(800m)

C de Capitán Segarra
Covered
Market

Av Alfonso X El Sabio

C de Pablo Iglesias

C de Poeta Quintana

C Belando Quintana

C de Jerusalén

C de Ángel Lozano

C de Álvarez Sereix

Plaza
de Calvo
Sotelo

C Canalejas

Av del Doctor Gadea

C de Alemania

C Segura

Plaza
de los
Luceros

Ⓜ(200m)
Av Estación

Av de General Marva

C del Pintor Cabrera

Av Maisonnave

C de General O'Donnell

Piripi
(250m)

C del Portugal

C del Moreli

C del Pintor Lorenzo Casanova

Arquitecto

Alicante

Les Monges Palace
HOTEL €€

(☑965 21 50 46; www.lesmonges.es; Calle San Agustín 4; s €45-80, d €58-95; ⓟ❋@🛜) This agreeably quirky place in the nightlife zone is a treasure with its winding corridors, tiles, mosaics and antique furniture. Each room is individually decorated – some are considerably more spacious than others – with plenty of character; some are in a more modern wing. The rooftop terrace bar is great and reception couldn't be more welcoming.

Hotel Hospes Amérigo
HOTEL €€€

(☑965 14 65 70; www.hospes.es; Calle de Rafael Altamira 7; r €160-240; ⓟ❋@🛜⊠) Within an old Dominican convent, this overpriced but commodious five-star choice harmoniously blends the traditional and ultramodern. Enjoy the views from the small rooftop pool, or build up a sweat in the fitness area – if you can tear yourself away from the comfort of your smartly designed room.

🍴 Eating

★ Cervecería Sento
TAPAS €

(Calle Teniente Coronel Chápuli 1; tapas €2.40-8; ⊙10am-5pm & 8pm-midnight Mon-Sat) Superb, quality *montaditos* (little rolls) and grilled things are the reason to squeeze into this brilliant little bar. Watching the nonstop staff in action is quite an experience too: they make it a great experience. They've got a bigger branch nearby, but this has the atmosphere.

Velvet
FUSION €€

(☑968 17 41 48; Calle de los Castaños 19; dishes €6-14; ⊙noon-1am; 🛜) Fusing retro and modern styling, with a comfortable L-shaped space, this appeals for its quality food, whether you are tempted by the bar-counter snacks on crusty bread or a fuller list of *cocas* (Catalan pizza-like dishes), tomato con-

coctions or plates involving foie gras, duck magret or pulled pork knuckle. Service and atmosphere are excellent, as is the lunch menu for €10.50.

OneOne
BISTRO €€

(☑965 20 63 99; Calle Valdés 9; mains €12-20; ⊙1-4pm & 9pm-midnight Tue-Sat, closed mid-Aug–mid-Sep) It's easier if you speak a little Spanish at this wonderfully eccentric place with its faithful following of regulars, but your ebullient host will make sure you get the best anyway. It's a true bistro, the walls scarcely visible for Parisian-style photos and posters, and there's no menu. Just listen carefully as Bartolomé intones. Characterful and memorable.

Piripi
VALENCIAN €€

(☑965 22 79 40; www.noumanolin.com; Avenida Oscar Esplá 30; mains €12-26; ⊙1-4pm & 8.15pm-midnight; 🛜) This highly regarded restaurant is strong on rice, seafood and fish, which arrives fresh daily from the wholesale markets of Denia and Santa Pola. There's a huge variety of tapas and a *valenciano* speciality that changes daily. It's a short walk west of the centre or downhill from the train station.

🍷 Drinking & Nightlife

Alicante's nightlife is an impressive thing to behold. Wet your night-time whistle in the wall-to-wall bars of the old quarter (known as El Barrio) around Catedral de San Nicolás. Alternatively, head for the sea. Paseo del Puerto, tranquil by day, is a double-decker line of casino, restaurants, bars, and nightclubs.

Söda Bar
BAR

(☑639 91 88 36; http://sodabar.wix.com/soda; Calle Médico Pascual Pérez 8; ⊙7pm-2am Thu & Fri, 5pm-2.30am Sat; 🛜) For quality drinks in a welcoming, relaxed but stylish atmosphere, head out of the mayhem of the Barrio to this place, with a friendly local crowd and its hipster tendencies. Regular events include DJs, literary readings and dance classes.

Baccus
BAR

(Plaza Quijano 6; ⊙10pm-late Thu-Sat) One of the busiest and best established of the Barrio bar-clubs, this place has two floors of drinks specials, a young crowd, top-40 Latin and international hits, and zero subtlety.

Marearock Rock-bar
BAR

(www.marearock.com; Calle Virgen de Belén 21; ⊙11pm-4am Thu & Fri, 7pm-4am Sat) One of the Barrio's most reliable spots for a decent drink, with a friendly, bohemian atmosphere and good rock and metal sounds. They also run a live-music venue and nightclub on the port.

❶ Information

Municipal Tourist Office (☑965 20 00 00; www.alicanteturismo.com; Rambla de Méndez Núñez 41; ⊙10am-6pm Mon-Fri, 10am-2pm Sat) There are also branches at the **train station** (☑965 12 56 33; www.alicanteturismo. com; Avenida de Salamanca; ⊙9.30am-2pm & 4.30-7pm Mon-Fri, 10am-2pm Sat) and airport.

❶ Getting There & Away

AIR

Alicante's El Altet airport, gateway to the Costa Blanca, is around 12km southwest of the city centre. It's served by budget airlines, charters and scheduled flights from all over Europe.

BUS

From the **bus station** (Avenida de Salamanca) destinations include the following:

DESTINATION	FARE	DURATION	FREQUENCY
Murcia	€6.19	1-2hr	11-17 daily
Valencia	€21	2½-5¾hr	18-21 daily

TRAIN

Mainline destinations from the principal train station include the following. For Murcia, there are also very regular cercanía trains (€5.75, 1¼ hours) via Elche and Orihuela.

DESTINATION	FARE	DURATION	FREQUENCY
Barcelona	€52	5-6hrs	8 daily
Madrid	€65	from 2¼hrs	9 daily
Murcia	€18	1¼hrs	5 daily
Valencia	€17-30	1½-2hrs	11 daily

TRAM

The coastal tram/light-rail service is a handy option: see the **TRAM** (www.tramalicante.es) website. Scenic Line 1 heads to Benidorm with a connection on to Denia. Catch it from beside the covered market.

❶ Getting Around

Bus C-6 (www.aerobusalicante.es; €3.85, 30 minutes, every 20 minutes) runs between Plaza Puerta del Mar and the airport, passing by the north side of the bus station, the tram station and the train station. Special 'resort buses' also run direct from the airport to resort towns up and down the coast. There are numerous car-rental offices at the airport.

INLAND FROM THE COSTA BLANCA

The borderline between the holiday *costa* and the interior is, perhaps appropriately, a motorway. Venture away from the Med, west of the AP7, to find yourself in a different, truly Spanish world. A succession of interesting towns dots the region.

Xàtiva

POP 29,300

Xàtiva (Spanish: Játiva) makes an easy and rewarding 50km day trip from Valencia or a stop on the way north or south. It has a small historic quarter and a mighty castle strung along the crest of the Serra Vernissa, at whose base the town snuggles.

The Muslims established Europe's first paper-manufacturing plant in Xàtiva, which is also famous as the birthplace of the Borgia Popes Calixtus III and Alexander VI as well as the painter José de Ribera. The glory days ended in 1707 when Felipe V's troops torched most of the town.

◉ Sights

★ Castillo de Xàtiva
CASTLE

(adult/child €2.40/1.20; ⊙10am-6pm Tue-Sun Nov-Mar, 10am-7pm Tue-Sun Apr-Oct) Xàtiva's castle, which clasps to the summit of a double-peaked hill overlooking the old town, is arguably the most evocative and interesting in all the Valencia region. Today, behind its crumbling battlements you'll find flower gardens (bring a picnic), tumbledown turrets, towers and other buildings (some used in the 20th century and hence much changed), such as dungeons and a pretty Gothic chapel. The walk up to the castle is a long one, but the views are sensational.

🛏 Sleeping & Eating

⭐ Mont Sant
HOTEL €€

(☑962 27 50 81; www.mont-sant.com; Subida al Castillo; with breakfast s €97-128, d €104-135; ☺Feb-Dec; 🅿❄🛜🏊) Enthusiastic management makes for a wonderful stay at this enchanting place, set amid city walls, the ruins of a convent and palm and citrus gardens between the old town and castle. It feels way out in the countryside rather than just a few minutes' walk from town. Stay in the beautifully adapted main building or in one of the spacious, modern, wood-faced cabins.

Picaeta de Carmeta
TAPAS €€

(☑619 51 19 71; Plaça de Mercat 19; dishes €6-16; ☺1.30-6pm Tue-Thu & Sun, 1.30-6pm & 8.30pm-1.30am Fri & Sat) At one end of this attractive old-town square, a promising destination for drinks and tapas, this is perhaps the best of the bunch, with solid barrels-and-wine decor, along with exposed brick and well-selected art. Dishes are modern creations based on solid rural fare like *mollejas* and meaty rices. It's all delicious, and there are some fine wines to accompany your meal.

Casa la Abuela
VALENCIAN €€

(☑962 27 05 25; www.casalaabuelaxativa.es; Calle de la Reina 17; mains €12-23; ☺1.30-4pm & 8.30-11pm Mon, Tue & Thu-Sat, 1.30-4pm Sun) On the main drag through town, 'Grandma's House' has an old-style front bar – unchanged in 50 years – and a more modern, formal dining room. Highlights here include *arroz con costra*, an Alicante-style rice dish finished off in the oven, and quality meat options. Prices are a little above typical grandmotherly economics.

ℹ Information

Tourist Office (☑962 27 33 46; www.xativa-turismo.com; Alameda Jaime I 50; ☺10am-2pm Tue-Fri, 10.15am-1.30pm Sat & Sun) On the Alameda, Xàtiva's shady main avenue. Hours extend in summer. Scan the QT code at the door with your mobile to download a free multilingual guide to the sights.

ℹ Getting There & Away

Frequent *cercanía* trains on line C2 connect Xàtiva with Valencia (€4.35, 40 minutes, half-hourly), and most Valencia–Madrid trains stop here too, though these are more expensive. You can also reach Alicante (€13 to €17, 1¼ hours, seven daily) from here.

Villena
POP 34,800

Villena, between Alicante and Albacete, is the most attractive of the towns along the corridor of the Val de Vinalopó. Plaza de Santiago is at the heart of its old quarter, which is topped by a castle. The town's archaeological museum is particularly notable.

◉ Sights

⭐ Museo Arqueológico
MUSEUM

(www.museovillena.com; Plaza de Santiago 1; adult/child €2/1; ☺10am-2pm Tue-Fri, 11am-2pm Sat & Sun) Plaza de Santiago is at the heart of Villena's old quarter. Within the imposing 16th-century Palacio Municipal, seat of the

---

MOROS Y CRISTIANOS

More than 80 towns and villages in the south of Valencia hold their own **Fiesta de Moros y Cristianos** (Moors and Christians festival) to celebrate the Reconquista, the region's liberation from Muslim rule.

The biggest and best known is in the town of **Alcoy** on April 22 to 24, when hundreds of locals dress up in elaborate traditional costumes representing different 'factions' – Muslim and Christian soldiers, slaves, guild groups, town criers, heralds, bands – and march through the streets in colourful processions with mock battles.

Processions converge upon Alcoy's main square and its huge, temporary wooden fortress. It's an exhilarating spectacle of sights and sounds.

Each town has its own variation on the format, steeped in traditions that allude to the events of the Reconquista. So, for example, Villena's festival (5 to 9 September) features midnight parades, while La Vila Joiosa (24 to 31 July), near Benidorm, re-enacts the landing of Muslim ships on the beaches. Some are as early as February, so you've a good chance of coinciding with one whenever it is that you visit the region.

town council, is this archaeological museum. There are some magnificent pieces in the normal collection, even before you get to the stunning late Bronze Age treasure hoards, with a series of bowls, bracelets and brooches made from solid gold. It's the most impressive sight in town.

Castillo de Atalaya CASTLE
(www.turismovillena.com; Calle Libertad; adult/child €3/1.50; ☉ guided tours 11am, noon, 1pm, 4pm, 5pm Tue-Sat, 11am, noon, 1pm Sun) Perched above the old town, this 12th-century castle has been handsomely restored and is splendidly lit at night. Entrance is by guided visit, in Spanish with English asides. Tickets can be bought at the town's tourist office or at the visitor centre near the castle's base. A double wall encloses the central *patio de armas* courtyard, overlooked by a high square keep.

🛏 Sleeping & Eating

La Casa de los Aromas B&B €
(☎ 666 47 56 12; www.casadelosaromas.es; Calle Arco 1; s/d €35/55; ✴ 🕾) In the heart of the old centre, this place offers a very genuine welcome and five sweet rooms, all with an individual aroma scheme. It's got lots of charm, and they can arrange winery visits and other activities. You get access to a fridge and microwave as well as an appealing common room with a vinyl collection to play.

La Despensa VALENCIAN, SPANISH €€
(☎ 965 80 83 37; www.mesonladespensa.com; Calle Cervantes 27; mains €12-20; ☉ 9am-midnight; 🕾) Near the station, La Despensa offers handsome traditional decor and excellent Valencian cuisine. They do some great rices, including a very tasty one with rabbit and snails, as well as some impressive slabs of meat on the grill. For tapas, try the house special with ham, quail's egg and *sobrasada* (Mallorcan pork and paprika spread).

ℹ Information

Tourist Office (☎ 966 150 236; www.turismovillena.com; Plaza de Santiago 5; ☉ 9am-2pm Mon-Fri, 11am-2pm Sat & Sun) Villena's tourist office is on the main square opposite the town hall.

Visitor Centre (☎ 965 80 38 93; www.turismovillena.com; Calle de General Prim 2; ☉ 10am-2pm & 4-6pm Tue-Sat, 10am-2pm Sun) Below the castle.

ℹ Getting There & Away

Nine trains run daily between Alicante and Villena (€5.50 to €12, 35 to 50 minutes); there are also Valencia services. Buses serve both these cities too. Note that the Villena AV station, served by fast trains, isn't anywhere near the town.

Guadalest
POP 200 / ELEV 595M

You'll be far from the first to discover the village of (El Castell de) Guadalest; coaches, heading up from the Costa Blanca resorts, disgorge millions of visitors yearly. But get here early, or stay around after the last bus has pulled out, and the place will be almost your own.

Crowds come because Guadalest, reached by a natural tunnel and overlooked by the Castillo de San José (adult/child €4/2; ☉ 10am-6pm, to 9pm Aug), is indeed very pretty, with stunning views down the valley to the sea, and over a turquoise reservoir below.

There are half a dozen or so other novelty museums, including the completely bonkers **Museo de Saleros y Pimenteros** (www.museodesalerosypimenteros.es; Avenida de Alicante 2; adult/child €3/1; ☉ 10am-6pm, to 9pm in summer), which is a museum of salt and pepper pots: more than 20,000 of them.

🛏 Sleeping

★ Cases Noves B&B €€
(☎ 965 88 53 09; www.casesnoves.es; Calle Achova 1; s/d/superior incl breakfast €84/94/114; ✴ @ 🕾) An option that is worth travelling a very long way for. Run by local lass Sofia and her husband, Toni, this is B&B taken to a whole new level. The thoughtfully designed bedrooms come with fresh flowers; in winter, toast your toes by the open fireplace; in summer, savour the gorgeous

OFF THE BEATEN TRACK

EXPLORE THE VALLEYS

Lovely though Guadalest is, it's very touristy. But the parallel valleys to the north of here are much less visited. Head on past Guadalest and follow your nose into the Vall del Pop or the Vall de Ebo. There's some wild country, picturesque villages, and solid game-based mountain food to be had.

terrace with views of the distant sea and the floodlit village.

ℹ️ Information

Tourist Office (📞 965 88 52 98; www.guadalest.es; Avenida de Alicante; ⏰10am-2pm & 3-5pm Nov-Feb, to 6pm Mar-Jun & late Oct, to 7pm Jul–mid-Oct) In the main village car park.

ℹ️ Getting There & Away

Llorente company buses run from Benidorm to Guadalest via Altea on Mondays to Fridays in the morning (two hours), with a day trip possible. In July and August they also run on Saturdays and Sundays. If you drive you'll be charged €2 to park.

Elche

POP 227,300

Precisely 23km southwest of Alicante, Elche (Valenciano: Elx) is, thanks to Moorish irrigation, an important fruit producer and also a Unesco World Heritage site twice over: for the *Misteri d'Elx,* its annual medieval play, and for its marvellous, extensive palm groves, Europe's largest, originally planted by the Phoenicians. The palms, the mosque-like churches, and the historic buildings in desert-coloured stone give it a North African feel.

⊙ Sights

Around 200,000 palm trees, each with a lifespan of some 250 years, make the heart of this busy industrial town a veritable oasis. A signed 2.5km walking trail (ask at the tourist office for the leaflet) leads from the Museu del Palmerar (📞965 42 22 40; Porta de la Morera 12; adult/child €1/0.50, Sun free; ⏰10am-2pm & 3-6pm Tue-Sat, 10am-2pm Sun) through the groves.

★ **Huerto del Cura**   GARDENS

(📞965 45 19 36; http://jardin.huertodelcura.com; Porta de la Morera 49; adult/child €5/2.50, audio guide €2; ⏰10am-sunset Mon-Sat, 10am-3pm or 6pm Sun) In the Islamic world, a garden is considered a form of Paradise. Elche's past and culture couldn't therefore be any more obvious than in these privately owned gardens, where humanity and nature have joined forces to produce something that truly approaches that ideal. The highlights are the water features and the cactus gardens.

L'Alcúdia   RUIN, MUSEUM

(📞966 61 15 06; www.laalcudia.ua.es; Ctra de Dolors, Km 1.7; adult/child €5/2; ⏰10am-8pm Tue-Sun) This well-documented site is 3.5km south of the town centre. The *Dama de Elche* was unearthed here, a masterpiece of Iberian art that's now in Madrid. Entry includes the excellent archaeological museum, displaying rich findings from a settlement occupied continuously from Neolithic

---

DON'T MISS

MISTERI D'ELX

The Misteri d'Elx (www.misteridelx.com), a two-act lyric drama dating from the Middle Ages, is performed annually in Elche's Basílica de Santa María.

One distant day, according to legend, a casket was washed up on Elche's Mediterranean shore. Inside were a statue of the Virgin and the *Consueta,* the music and libretto of a mystery play describing Our Lady's death, assumption into Heaven and coronation.

The story tells how the Virgin, realising that death is near, asks God to allow her to see the Apostles one last time. They arrive one by one from distant lands and, in their company, she dies at peace. Once received into paradise, she is crowned Queen of Heaven and Earth to swelling music, the ringing of bells, cheers all round and spectacular fireworks.

The mystery's two acts, *La Vespra* (the eve of her death) and *La Festa* (the celebration of her assumption and coronation), are performed in Valenciano by the people of Elche on 14 and 15 August respectively (with public rehearsals on the three previous days).

You can see a multimedia presentation – complete with virtual Apostle – in the Museu de la Festa (📞965 45 34 64; Carrer Major de la Vila 25; adult/child €3/1; ⏰10am-2pm & 3-6pm Tue-Sat, 10am-2pm Sun), about a block west of the basilica. The show lasts 35 minutes and is repeated several times daily, with optional English commentary.

to late-Visigoth times. The museum shuts at 6pm, which is last entry time for the site too.

Museo Arqueológico y de Historia de Elche
MUSEUM

(MAHE; ☑ 966 65 82 03; Calle Diagonal del Palau 7; adult/child €3/1, free Sun; ☺ 10am-6pm Mon-Sat, 10am-3pm Sun) This museum is a superb introduction to the town's long and eventful history. Everything is particularly well displayed and labelled, and it occupies both a purpose-built building and the town's castle.

Basílica de Santa María
CHURCH

(☑ 965 45 15 40; Pl de Santa María 2; tower adult/child €2/1; ☺ 7am-1pm & 5.30-9pm, tower 11am-7pm Jun-Sep, 10.30am-3pm Oct-May) FREE This vast baroque church is used for performances of the *Misteri d'Elx*. Climb up its tower for a sweeping, pigeon's-eye view over the palms.

🛏 Sleeping & Eating

★ Hotel Huerto del Cura
BOUTIQUE HOTEL €€

(☑ 966 61 00 11; www.hotelhuertodelcura.com; Porta de la Morera 14; r €90-165; 🅿 ✳ @ 🛜 🏊) This is a sublime hotel, with stylish white rooms and antique wooden furnishings. The accommodation is in trim bungalows within lush, palm-shaded gardens. It's a family-friendly place with a playground, large pool and babysitting service. Complete the cosseting at Elche's longest-standing luxury hotel by dining in Els Capellans, its renowned restaurant. If you aren't so mobile, request a room close to reception.

Hotel Jardín Milenio
HOTEL €€

(☑ 966 61 20 33; www.hotelmilenio.com; Calle Curtidores 17; r €78; 🅿 ✳ @ 🛜 🏊) With a lovely location right among the palms, this creeper-swathed hotel has commodious if slightly bland rooms, helpful professional service and a decent on-site restaurant. Facillities are excellent, and it's got a peaceful rural feel despite being just a few minutes' walk from the centre of the city.

★ El Granaino
SPANISH €€

(☑ 966 66 40 80; www.mesongranaino.com; Carrer Josep María Buck 40; mains €14-22; ☺ 9.30am-4pm & 8pm-midnight Mon-Sat; 🛜) Across the river from the centre, El Granaino, where the bar is lined with people scarfing down a quick, quality lunch, is worth the 10-minute walk to get here. Top seafood, delicious stews and a fine range of tapas showcase a classic, quintessentially Spanish cuisine. Fuller meals can be enjoyed outside or in the adjacent dining room. Excellent service and quality.

Mibarra
VALENCIAN €€

(☑ 965 45 14 83; www.mibarra.es; Pl de la Constitución 3; mains €8-19; ☺ 9am-5pm & 8-11pm Tue-Fri, 11am-6pm & 8pm-midnight Sat, 11am-6pm Sun) With big windows and a long bar, this modern bar-restaurant is a comfortable space and the service is notably cordial. Though the house speciality is rice, there's plenty more to choose from on the menu. Portions are generous, prices fair and the quality is all pretty good. There are some very tasty wines by the glass available too: a good all-rounder.

ℹ Information

Tourist Office (☑ 966 65 81 96; www.visit elche.com; Plaza Parque 3; ☺ 9am-6pm or 7pm Mon-Fri, 10am-6pm or 7pm Sat, also 10am-2pm Sun May-Oct) By the palm grove that is the Parque Municipal.

ℹ Getting There & Away

Elche is on the Alicante–Murcia *cercanía* train line. About 20 trains daily rattle through, bound for Alicante (€2.70) or Murcia (€3.70) via Orihuela (€2.70). Train and bus stations are beside each other on Avenida de la Libertad (Avenida del Ferrocarril).

From the bus station, destinations include the following:

DESTINATION	FARE	DURATION	FREQUENCY
Alicante	€2.25	35min	every 30min
Murcia	€4.55	45min-2hr	12-13 daily
Valencia	€13.35	2½-4hr	9-10 daily

Orihuela
POP 91,300

Beside the Río Segura and flush with the base of a barren mountain of rock, the historical heart of Orihuela, with superb Gothic, Renaissance and, especially, baroque buildings, well merits a detour. The old town is strung out between the river and a mountain topped by a ruined castle. The main sights are dotted along it, more or less in a line, and are well signposted throughout.

Orihuela has a vibrant **Moros y Cristianos festival** (http://morosycristianosorihue la.es) in mid-July, and reprises the atmosphere with an enormous medieval market at the end of January.

👁 Sights

★ **Catedral de San Salvador** CATHEDRAL
(Calle Doctor Sarget; adult/child €2/1; ⊙ 10.30am-2pm & 4-6.30pm Tue-Fri, 10.30am-2pm Sat) Low slung but achieving an understated majesty nonetheless, this cathedral is built of light-coloured stone in the centre of the old town and features three finely carved portals. Unusually, the altar is enclosed by an ornate Renaissance *reja* (filigree screen); another closes off the choir, while an earlier Gothic one, alive with vegetal motifs, screens a chapel behind the altar. The highlight, though, is the tiny exquisite two-level Renaissance cloister on the street.

🛏 Sleeping & Eating

Palacio de Tudemir HOTEL €€
(☑ 966 73 80 10; www.hotelpalaciotudemir.com; Calle Alfonxo XIII 1; s/d €86/96; P 🅿 ❄ @ 🛜) A few steps from the cathedral and tourist office, this weighty 18th-century palace offers a prime location. Staff are friendly and rooms are attractive enough – some are significantly more spacious than others – though the overall package just seems to fall short. Weddings can make Saturday stays here very noisy.

Bar Manolo TAPAS €
(☑ 965 30 20 93; Calle del Río 36; dishes €4-15, set menu €9.80; ⊙ 8am-9pm Mon-Thu, 8am-12.30am Fri, noon-12.30am Sat; 🛜) Though it doesn't look much from outside (or inside come to think of it), Bar Manolo has outdoor seating next to the river (without much of a view, however). But it's the warm personal service and cheap but scrumptious food that make this a fine tapas or meal stop. There's a set menu available lunchtimes and evenings for under a tenner.

ℹ Information

Tourist Office (☑ 965 30 46 45; www.orihue laturistica.es; Plaza de la Soledad; ⊙ 8am-2pm or 3pm Mon, 8am-2pm or 3pm & 4-7pm or 5-8pm Tue-Fri, 10am-2pm & 4-7pm or 5-8pm Sat, 10am-2pm Sun) Helpful, switched on and well furnished with information about what to see around town.

ℹ Getting There & Away

Orihuela is on *cercanía* train line C1 between Murcia (€2, 20 minutes) and Alicante (€4.20, one hour, hourly). The train and bus stations are 1km south of the old centre.

MURCIA

POP 439,900

Officially twinned with Miami, Murcia is the antithesis of the city of vice; it's a laid-back provincial capital that comes alive during the weekend *paseo* (stroll). Bypassed by most tourists and treated as a country cousin by many Spaniards, the city nevertheless more than merits a visit. The city is blessed with many excellent restaurants that use local market produce.

👁 Sights

★ **Real Casino de Murcia** HISTORIC BUILDING
(www.casinodemurcia.com; Calle de la Trapería 18; adult/child €5/3; ⊙ 10.30am-7pm) Murcia's resplendent casino first opened as a gentlemen's club in 1847. Painstakingly restored to its original glory, the building is a fabulous combination of historical design and opulence, providing an evocative glimpse of bygone aristocratic grandeur. Beyond the decorative facade are a dazzling Moorish-style patio; a classic English-style library with 20,000 books; a magnificent ballroom with glittering chandeliers; and a compelling *tocador* (ladies' powder room) with a ceiling fresco of cherubs, angels and an alarming winged woman in flames.

Catedral de Santa María CATHEDRAL
(☑ 968 35 87 49; Plaza del Cardenal Belluga; ⊙ 7am-1pm & 5-8pm Sep-Jun, 7am-1pm & 6.30-8pm Jul & Aug) 🆓 Murcia's cathedral was built in 1394 on the site of a mosque. The initial Gothic architecture was given a playful baroque facelift in 1748, with a stunning facade facing on to the plaza. The 15th-century **Capilla de los Vélez** is a highlight; the chapel's flutes and curls resemble icing. The **Museo Catedralicio** (Plaza de la Cruz 1; adult/child €3/2; ⊙ 10am-5pm Tue-Sat, 10am-1pm Sun Jul-Sep, 10am-1pm & 4-7pm Tue-Sat, 10am-1pm Sun Oct-Jun) displays religious artefacts, but is most noteworthy for the excavations on display.

Museo de Bellas Artes GALLERY
(☑ 968 23 93 46; www.museosdemurcia.com; Calle del Obispo Frutos 12; ⊙ 10am-2pm & 5-8pm Tue-Fri, 11am-2pm & 5-8pm Sat, 11am-2pm Sun, mornings only Jul & Aug) 🆓 An inviting, light gallery devoted to Spanish artists. Much is mediocre, but the 2nd-floor Siglo de Oro gallery has two fabulous Murillos – a *Crucifixion* and an *Ecce Homo* – and a powerful chiaroscuro *San Jerónimo* by Ribera. Look out for

Murcia City

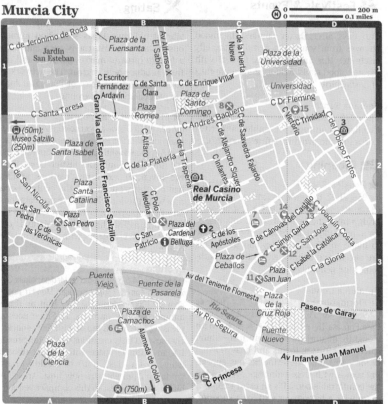

Murcia City

◎ Top Sights
1 Real Casino de Murcia...........................C2

◎ Sights
2 Catedral de Santa María............................C3
   Museo Catedralicio.........................(see 2)
3 Museo de Bellas Artes............................D2

🛏 Sleeping
4 Arco de San Juan....................................C3
5 Catalonia Conde de
   Floridablanca.....................................C4
6 Pensión Segura.......................................B4

7 Tryp Rincón de Pepe...............................C3

🍴 Eating
8 Alborada...C1
9 El Pasaje de Zabalburu............................A3
10 El Sitico...B3
11 La Pequeña Taberna...............................C3
12 Pura Cepa..C3
13 Salzillo..D2

🍷 Drinking & Nightlife
14 La Ronería y La Gintonería......................C3
15 Sala Revolver...D1

the faintest shadow of his tame lion. The 3rd floor holds temporary exhibitions.

Museo Salzillo   MUSEUM
(www.museosalzillo.es; Plaza de San Agustín 1-3; adult/child €5/free; ⊙10am-2pm Mon-Fri mid-Jun–mid-Sep, 10am-5pm Mon-Sat, 11am-2pm Sun mid-Sep–mid-Jun) Located in the baroque chapel of Ermita de Jesús, this well-laid-out space is devoted to Murcian sculptor Francisco Salzillo (1707–83). Highlights are his exquisite *pasos* (figures carried in Semana Santa processions) and nativity figurines.

VALENCIA & MURCIA MURCIA

🎊 Festivals & Events

Bando de la Huerta
FIESTA

Two days after Easter Sunday, the mood changes from sombre to joyful as the city celebrates this annual spring festival with parades, food stalls, folklore and carafe-fulls of fiesta spirit.

Semana Santa
RELIGIOUS

The city's Easter processions feature some excellent sculptural ensembles and rival Lorca's as the province's finest parades.

🛏 Sleeping

★ Pensión Segura
HOSTAL €

(☑968 21 12 81; www.pensionsegura.es; Plaza de Camachos 14; r €35-45; ❄ 🤶) Just across a bridge from the heart of town, this makes for a fine budget base. Staff go the extra mile to make you feel welcome, and the rooms are decent and shining clean, though bathrooms are generally tiny.

Catalonia Conde de Floridablanca
HOTEL €€

(☑968 21 46 26; www.hoteles-catalonia.com; Calle Princesa 18; r €80-100; 🅿 ❄ @ 🤶) With a slightly lugubrious old-Spain feel – think shields of Murcian towns and heavy formal decor – this hotel nevertheless has appealing rooms with large paintings overlooking the comfortable beds. It's an extra €25 for a room with a balcony, or €30 for a superior, which adds space, robes and slippers.

Tryp Rincón de Pepe
HOTEL €€

(☑968 21 22 39; www.melia.com; Calle de los Apóstoles 34; r €75-110; 🅿 ❄ @ 🤶) Acres of marble lobby greet guests at this corporate-style hotel. Rooms are spacious, with large luxurious bathrooms, and have been recently renovated. Facilities and location are both pleasing; there's a small casino here as well.

Arco de San Juan
HOTEL €€

(☑968 21 04 55; www.arcosanjuan.com; Plaza de Ceballos 10; d €60-80; 🅿 ❄ @ 🤶) In a former 18th-century palace, this hotel hints at its past with a massive 5m-high original door and some hefty repro columns. The rooms are classic and comfortable, with hardwood details and classy fabrics, and the low prices and top location – for both central sights and the best eating zone – are a big plus. Service is professional and welcoming.

🍴 Eating

Murcia has some excellent eating, with a vibrant old-town tapas scene and numerous restaurants. Murcia is surrounded by a *huerta* (area of market gardens) and the fresh produce here is great. The network of streets on and northeast of Plaza San Juan are particularly fertile ground.

★ El Pasaje de Zabalburu
TAPAS €

(☑622 62 21 67; www.facebook.com/elpasajedezabalburu; Plaza San Pedro 3; tapas €4-10; ☺noon-5pm & 8pm-midnight Mon-Sat, noon-5pm Sun; 🤶) It's difficult to imagine tastier tapas than the inventive, exquisite creations at this bar on the west side of the centre. Grab a pew at the long bar and enjoy fabulous fare that's playfully, joyfully presented with great originality. The house speciality is *pelochos* – ham croquettes with a spiky noodle coating...yum.

El Sitico
TAPAS €

(☑603 83 04 57; Calle Polo de Medina; tapas €3-7; ☺9am-4pm & 7.30pm-midnight Mon-Fri, noon-4pm & 7.30pm-midnight Sat; 🤶) Run by three animated young partners, El Sitico does a pleasing line in deli tapas, with fishy snacks, cheeses and tasty creations on toasted bread. It's an intimate space with several decent wines by the glass; don't be afraid to seek guidance from your friendly host. Art exhibitions add interest to this compact venue.

★ La Pequeña Taberna
SPANISH €€

(☑968 21 98 40; www.lapequenataberna.com; Plaza San Juan 7; mains €10-21; ☺1-5pm & 8pm-midnight Mon-Sat, 1-5pm Sun) Look for the cascade of market vegetables outside the door when locating this quality restaurant, which isn't quite as small as it claims. Excellent service furnishes its tables, divided by boxes of tomatoes, melons and the like, with dishes like fish carpaccio, *huevas de mújol* (fish roe), *codillo* (pork knuckle), and quality salad and vegetable platters. Delicious, as are the wines.

Pura Cepa
TAPAS €€

(☑968 21 73 97; www.purovinoclub.es; Plaza Cristo del Rescate 8; dishes €6-15; ☺1-4pm & 8pm-midnight Tue-Sat, 1-4pm Sun; 🤶) Though the menu is full of typical Spanish ingredients, there's always an innovative kick to the dishes here, which shine out for their quality. Artichokes, octopus and other local, delicious ingredients appear in everything from stir-fries to salads to exquisite appetisers. Eat outside on the heated terrace, at high tables in the bar area, or in the smart dining room.

Alborada
MODERN SPANISH €€

(☑968 23 23 23; www.alboradarestaurante.com; Calle Andrés Baquero 15; mains €15-22; ☺1-4.30pm & 9-11.30pm Mon-Sat, 1-4.30pm Sun) Not particularly noteworthy from outside, this high-ceilinged minimalist dining space offers reliably excellent cuisine using carefully selected natural products. Presentation is modern without being avant-garde, and the flavour combinations are all pleasing. During the week you can eat in the bright bar area out front for just €12. Expect regular doses of air freshener.

Salzillo
SPANISH €€€

(☑968 22 01 94; www.restaurantesalzillo.com; Calle de Cánovas del Castillo 28; mains €18-24; ☺1-5.30pm & 9pm-midnight Mon-Sat, 1-5.30pm Sun) Favoured by well-heeled conservative Murcians, this elegant but comfortable spot has a lively bar and truly excellent eating in its split-level restaurant area. Starters run to elaborate creations with local artichokes, and the quality of the meaty mains is sky-high: order *a la brasa* for the flavoursome barbecue aromas.

🍷 Drinking & Nightlife

Most through-the-night life buzzes around the university, with lots of bars in the streets around the eastern side of the old town. Start your explorations around Calle Dr Fleming.

★La Ronería y La Gintonería
BAR

(☑968 90 00 05; www.la-roneria-y-la-gintonería.com; Calle de Cánovas del Castillo 17; ☺3pm-3am Tue-Sat, 3pm-2am Sun & Mon) A quite incredible selection of rums greets you on entering this excellent bar. There are nearly a thousand available, with Caribbean travel videos playing to get you in the mood. Once you've tried them all, stagger up the stairs and start on the G'n'Ts. Hundreds of gins, dozens of tonics. And you.

Sala Revolver
BAR

(☑868 12 49 17; www.facebook.com/salarevolver.murcia; Calle Victorio 36; ☺3.30pm-3.30am; 🛜) The interior of this bar in the heart of the university-driven nightlife zone is a rock 'n' roll classic with red-vinyl booth seating, curios and photos on the walls and regular live

TAPAS IN MURCIA

Murcia is excellent for tapas, with plenty of variety, generous portions and a considerable vegetarian choice for non-carnivorous folk. Most of the restaurants we recommend are fronted by tapas bars or serve *raciones* (large/full-plate tapas servings), which are great for sharing. Overall, Murciano tapas are more inventive than the norm and reflect the province's comprehensive agriculture with their use of fresh seasonal ingredients.

music. It's very atmospheric with real rock-bar cred.

ⓘ Information

Floridablanca Tourist Kiosk (www.turismodemurcia.es; Jardín Floridablanca; ☺4.30-8.30pm Mon-Fri, 10am-2pm & 4.30-8.30pm Sat, 10am-2pm Sun)

Tourist Office (☑968 35 87 49; www.murciaturistica.es; Plaza del Cardenal Belluga; ☺10am-7pm Mon-Sat, 10am-2pm Sun; 🛜)

ⓘ Getting There & Away

Murcia-San Javier Airport is situated beside the Mar Menor, closer to Cartagena than Murcia. There are budget connections to the UK and other European nations, and direct Iberia flights from Madrid.

At least 10 buses run daily to both Cartagena (€4.75, 45 minutes to 1¼ hours) and Lorca (€5.75, 1½ hours).

Up to six trains travel daily to/from Madrid (€47, 4¼ hours). *Cercanía* trains run to Alicante (€5.75, 1¼ hours) and Lorca (€5.75, 50 minutes).

MURCIA PROVINCE

The Murcia region offers a tantalising choice of landscapes and sights, ranging from the chill-out beaches of the Costa Cálida to the medieval magic of its towns. The ancient port of Cartagena has a magnificent array of Roman and Carthaginian ruins, while Murcia is a buzzy regional capital with pleasant parks and a cracking eating scene. To appreciate fully the unspoiled hinterland, you will need your own wheels.

Cartagena

POP 217,600

Cartagena's fabulous natural harbour has been used for thousands of years. Stand on the battlements of the castle that overlook this city and you can literally see layer upon layer of history spread below you: the wharf where Phoenician traders docked their ships; the street where Roman legionaries marched; the plaza that once housed a mosque where Islamic Spain prayed to Allah; the hills over which came the armies of the Christian Reconquista; the factories of the industrial age; the Modernista buildings; and the contemporary warships of what is still an important naval base.

As archaeologists continue to reveal a long-buried – and fascinating – Roman and Carthaginian heritage, the city is finally starting to get the recognition it deserves as one of Spain's most historically fascinating places. Its extensive network of pedestrian streets and lovely waterfront make it eminently strollable.

History

In 223 BC, Hasdrubal marched his invading army into what had been the Iberian settlement of Mastia, refounding it as Qart Hadasht. The town prospered as Carthago Nova during Roman occupation and, under Muslim rule, became the independent emirate of Cartajana, finally reconquered by the Christians in 1242. Though badly bombed in the civil war – it was the principal Republican naval harbour – industry and the population flourished during the 1950s and '60s.

◉ Sights

Cartagena is rich in Modernista buildings. Particularly magnificent are the Palacio Consistorial (town hall; ☎968 12 88 00; Plaza del Ayuntamiento; ⊙10.30am-1.30pm & 5-7pm Tue-Fri, 10.30am-1.30pm & 5-8pm Sat, 10.30am-1.30pm Sun) FREE; Casa Cervantes (Calle Mayor 11); Casa Llagostera (Calle Mayor 25); the zinc-domed Gran Hotel (cnr Calles del Aire & Jara); the strawberries-and-cream confection of Casa Clares (Calle del Aire 4); and the splendid Palacio Aguirre (Plaza de la Merced), now an exhibition space for modern art (known as Muram).

The central Molinete hill has archaeological remains from everything from Phoenicians to Republicans in the civil war. Strolling over and around it reveals much,

including limited remains of the Roman forum on Calle Balcones Azules.

★ **Museo del Teatro Romano** MUSEUM, RUIN
(www.teatroromanocartagena.org; Plaza del Ayuntamiento 9; adult/child €6/5; ⊙10am-6pm Tue-Sat, 10am-2pm Sun Oct-Apr, 10am-8pm Tue-Sat, 10am-2pm Sun May-Sep) This super museum was designed by top Spanish architect Rafael Moneo. The tour transports visitors from the initial museum on Plaza del Ayuntamiento, via escalators and an underground passage beneath the ruined cathedral, to the magnificent, recently restored Roman theatre dating from the 1st century BC. The tour and layout of the museum are designed to reflect Cartagena's fascinating layers of urban history and include Roman statues and artefacts as well as the cathedral's crypt and remains of an original Moorish dwelling.

★ **Museo Nacional de Arqueología Subacuática** MUSEUM
(ARQUA; ☎968 12 11 66; http://museoarqua.mcu.es; Paseo de Alfonso XII 22; adult/child €3/free; ⊙10am-8pm or 9pm Tue-Sat, 10am-3pm Sun) This excellent, attractive space delves into the depths of the fascinating world of underwater archaeology. It starts off by explaining the work of those delvers in the deep and then sails on into the maritime history and culture of the Mediterranean. There's lots of old pots, flashy lights, buttons to press, films to watch and a replica Phoenician trading ship to marvel over. Free entry on Saturday afternoon and all day Sunday.

Barrio del Foro Romano RUIN
(www.cartagenapuertodeculturas.com; Calle Honda; adult/child €5/4; ⊙10am-5.30pm Tue-Sun Nov-Mar, 10am-7pm Tue-Sun Apr-Jun & mid-Sep–Oct, 10am-9pm daily Jul–mid-Sep) Set alongside the Molinete hill are the evocative remains of a whole town block and street linking the port with the forum, dating from the 1st century BC and including an arcade and thermal baths. One of the houses preserves a courtyard and important fragments of wall paintings.

Casa de la Fortuna RUIN
(Plaza Risueño; adult/child €2.50/2; ⊙10.30am-3.30pm Tue-Sun, closed Tue-Fri Dec-Mar) The Casa de la Fortuna consists of the fascinating remains of an aristocratic Roman villa dating back to the 1st century BC, complete with some well-preserved murals and mosaics, and part of an excavated road. Access it down some steps on the plaza.

Castillo de la Concepción `CASTLE`
(www.cartagenapuertodeculturas.com; adult/child €3.75/2.75; ☉10am-5.30pm Tue-Sun Nov-Mar, 10am-7pm Tue-Sun Apr-Jun & mid-Sep–Oct, 10am-8pm daily Jul–mid-Sep) For a sweeping panoramic view, stride up to Castillo de la Concepción, or hop on the lift (Calle de Gisbert; adult/child €2/1, with Castillo de la Concepción €4.25/3.75; ☉10am-5.30pm Tue-Sun Nov-Mar, 10am-7pm Tue-Sun Apr-Jun & mid-Sep–Oct, 10am-8pm daily Jul–mid-Sep). Within the castle's gardens, decorated by strutting peacocks, the Centro de Interpretación de la Historia de Cartagena offers a potted history of Cartagena through the centuries via audio screens and a 10-minute film (English and Spanish).

Muralla Púnica `RUIN`
(www.cartagenapuertodeculturas.com; Calle San Diego 25; adult/child €3.50/2.50; ☉10am-5.30pm Tue-Sun Nov-Mar, 10am-7pm Tue-Sun Apr-Jun & mid-Sep–Oct, 10am-8pm daily Jul–mid-Sep) The Muralla Púnica, built around a section of the old Punic wall, concentrates on the town's Carthaginian and Roman legacy. It also contains the tumbledown walls of a 16th-century hermitage complete with tombs filled with human bones.

Museo Arqueológico Municipal `MUSEUM`
(☑968 12 89 68; www.museoarqueologicocartagena.es; Calle Ramón y Cajal 45; ☉10am-2pm & 5-8pm Tue-Fri, 11am-2pm Sat & Sun) `FREE` Built above a late-Roman cemetery with a rich display of Carthaginian, Roman, Visigoth and Islamic artefacts. To get here, head northwest of the city centre, via Calle La Palma.

★彡 Festivals & Events

Semana Santa `RELIGIOUS`
(http://semanasanta.cartagena.es) During Easter week, Cartagena's haunting, elaborate processions are quite a sight.

Carthagineses y Romanos `HISTORICAL`
(www.cartaginesesyromanos.es) For 10 days during September, locals play war games in a colourful fiesta that re-enacts the battles between rival Carthaginian and Roman occupiers during the Second Punic War.

🛏 Sleeping & Eating

Pensión Balcones Azules `HOSTAL €`
(☑968 50 00 42; www.pensionbalconesazules.com; Calle Balcones Azules 12; s/d €36/55; ❉ 🗣) On a quiet central street overlooking the ruins of the forum, this modern, spotless option offers plenty of comfort for the price.

There are several types of rooms, with slightly varying rates. They are comfortable and well equipped; in many ways, this place is really a small hotel.

NH Cartagena `HOTEL €€`
(☑968 12 09 08; www.nh-hotels.com; Calle Real 2; d/superior d €77/92; 🅿 ❉ @ 🗣) The location of this business hotel can't be bettered, steps from the waterfront and the Roman theatre and just behind the town hall. Rooms are spacious, and superior chambers come with balcony or a sizeable terrace. As usual with this chain, free wi-fi is frustratingly slow and to speed it up costs a fortune. The overpriced breakfast is best avoided.

Techos Bajos `SEAFOOD €`
(www.techosbajos.com; Calle Joaquín Madrid; dishes €6-13; ☉9am-5pm Tue-Sun, 7.30am-midnight Fri & Sat) Locals absolutely flood this large, no-frills kind of place at lunchtime for its well-priced portions of fresh fish and fried seafood served on classic blue-and-white gingham paper tablecloths. You'll find it down the hill from the bus station, right opposite the fishing port.

Magoga `SPANISH €€€`
(☑968 50 96 78; www.restaurantemagoga.com; Plaza Doctor Vicente García Marcos; mains €16-24; ☉1.30-4pm & 8.30-11.30pm Tue-Sun; 🗣) A long, upbeat bar for tapas portions and an open kitchen dignify this white-exteriored local in a rather undistinguished location on a pedestrian boulevard off Calle Carlos III. The food is far above most of Cartagena's culinary offerings, with good-value rices and stews taking their place alongside superbly prepared and presented mains such as pigeon or dentex fish.

ℹ CARTAGENA DISCOUNT CARDS
Visiting all the different archaeological sites and museums in Cartagena can work out to be quite expensive. Fortunately help is at hand in the form of a variety of passes that provide cheaper admission (entry to four/five/six museums adult €12/15/18, child €9/11.25/13.50). Passes are available from the tourist office or the sites themselves. The Museo del Teatro Romano counts as two museum entries. Other options include a tourist boat and/or bus trip.

ⓘ Information

Ayuntamiento Tourist Office (☑968 12 89 55; www.cartagenaturismo.es; Plaza del Ayuntamiento 1; ☉10am-2pm & 4-6pm or 5-7pm Mon-Fri, 10am-1.30pm & 4-6pm or 5-7pm Sat, 10.30am-1.30pm Sun) Near the waterfront in the heart of town.

Muralla Púnica Tourist Office (☑968 50 64 83; www.cartagenaturismo.es; Calle San Diego 25; ☉10am-5.30pm Tue-Sun Nov-Mar, 10am-7pm Tue-Sun Apr-Jun & mid-Sep-Oct, 10am-8pm daily Jul-mid-Sep) Plenty of excellent information. In the Muralla Púnica complex.

ⓘ Getting There & Away

Buses run six to seven times daily to Alicante (€9, 2¾ hours), and roughly hourly to Murcia (€4.75, 45 minutes to 1¼ hours).

For Renfe train destinations, change in Murcia (from €5.45, 50 minutes, eight to 11 daily). Beware: take the local train as the slightly faster Altaria/Talgo trains cost a hefty full-fare €16.80.

A taxi to or from Murcia-San Javier Airport costs approximately €50.

Costa Cálida

Stretching westwards to the border with Andalucía, the Costa Cálida (Warm Coast) is aptly named. It offers a hot, dry climate with more than 300 days of annual sunshine. While the resort of La Manga is best avoided, quieter seaside towns offer a more appealing experience.

Águilas

POP 34,600

Nearing the border with Andalucía, and 30km further along the coast from Mazarrón, you'll reach low-key Águilas, with a slowish vibe and older expat population. The waterfront in town is beautiful, and still shelters a small fishing fleet; back from here is lovely Plaza de España, with dignified trees. Town beaches are divided from each other by a low headland topped by an 18th-century fortress. The real interest, though, is in the Cuatro Calas a few kilometres south of town.

⊙ Sights

★Cuatro Calas   BEACH
The real interest in the Águilas area is in the Cuatro Calas a few kilometres south of town. These four coves are largely unmolested by tourist development (though they get very busy in summer) and have shimmering waters that merge into desert rock: about as perfect as you'll find on the Spanish Med coast.

⚑ Festivals & Events

★Carnaval de Águilas   CARNIVAL
(www.carnavaldeaguilas.org) One of Spain's most interesting Carnavals (February or March), featuring four characters who represent various aspects of humanity, virtues and vices. There are parades from the Friday through to Shrove Tuesday, as well as the following weekend.

⊨ Sleeping & Eating

Hotel Mayarì   HOTEL €€
(☑964 41 97 48; www.hotel-mayari.com; Calle Río de Janeiro 14, Calabardina; s/d incl breakfast €65/98; ℙ❋☎) In the seaside settlement of Calabardina, 7km from Águilas, this villa offers exceptional hospitality among dry hillscapes. Rooms are all themed differently, with cool, fresh decor. Some have sea views, and there are brilliant home-cooked dinners available, as well as helpful hillwalking advice.

El Tiburón   SEAFOOD €€
(☑968 44 71 28; www.restaurantetiburon.es; Calle Iberia 8; mains €7-15; ☉12.30-4pm & 7-11pm Tue-Sat, 1-4pm Sun; ☎) A cheerful bar-restaurant with more of a local feel than most and a luminous dining room, this is in the southwestern part of the centre, across a bridge on the main road through town and just back from the beach. They do tasty fish tapas, a wide range of meat and seafood, good rices, and have an excellent-value €15 nighttime set menu.

ⓘ Information

Tourist Office (☑968 49 32 85; www.aguilas.es; Plaza Antonio Cortijos; ☉10am-2pm & 5-7pm Mon-Sat, 10am-2pm Sun) Near the water in the heart of town.

ⓘ Getting There & Away

Buses go to Lorca (€3, 30 minutes, three to seven daily) and Murcia (€8.90, 1½ hours, two to four daily) as well as Almería.

Cercanía trains on the C2 line run from Murcia (€7.95, 1¾ hours) via Lorca three times daily.

Lorca

POP 91,800

The market town of Lorca has long been known for its pretty old town crowned by a 13th-century castle and for hosting one of Spain's most flamboyant Semana Santa (Holy Week) celebrations. In 2011 an earthquake struck here, leaving nine people dead, and many injured and homeless. It caused significant damage to the town; with the old town affected particularly badly. Things are on the up again though, and it's well worth dropping by.

◎ Sights

★ La Fortaleza del Sol
CASTLE

(Castillo de Lorca; ☎ 968 47 90 03; www.lorcatallerdeltiempo.com; Carretera de la Parroquia; adult/child €5/4; ◷ 10.30am-dusk; ⊞) The town's castle, high over town, is an impressive place, a huge medieval complex characterised by two towers. The basic entry includes an audioguide and access to the Torre del Espolón, reconstructed after the earthquake, and plenty of dioramas and interactive gadgetry. They make a big effort for kids. The Torre Alfonsina and the reconstructed synagogue plus ruins of the Jewish quarter can be visited thrice or more daily by guided tour (€4). A combined €10 entrance fee includes both tours.

★ Plaza de España
SQUARE

The highlight of the old town is a group of baroque buildings around Plaza de España, including the Pósito, a 16th-century former granary; the 18th-century Casa del Corregidor; and the town hall. Lording over the square is the golden limestone Colegiata de San Patricio, a church with a handsome baroque facade and predominantly Renaissance interior. It suffered earthquake damage and is currently closed to the public. Repairs have revealed unsuspected paintings, which are being restored. It's due to open by 2017.

Museo de Bordados del Paso Blanco
MUSEUM

(muBBla; ☎ 650 27 20 04; www.mubbla.org; Calle Santo Domingo 8; adult/child €2.50/free; ◷ 10.30am-2pm & 4.30-7pm Mon-Sat, 10.30am-2pm Sun) Attached to the church of Santo Domingo, this is the museum of the Blanco (White) brotherhood. Here you can see a collection of the beautifully elaborate robes worn by them during the passionately sup-ported Holy Week processions and see the chapel of the Virgen del Rosario.

Museo de Bordados del Paso Azul
MUSEUM

(☎ 968 47 20 77; www.pasoazul.com; Calle Cuesta de San Francisco; adult/child €2.50/free; ◷ 10am-1.30pm & 5-7.30pm Mon-Fri, 10.30am-1pm Sat) Attached to the San Francisco monastery, this is the modern museum of the Azul (Blue) Holy Week brotherhood, and exhibits the magnificent Semana Santa costumes. Some cloaks are up to 5m in length and all are elaborately hand-embroidered in silk, depicting colourful religious and historical scenes.

★✶ Festivals & Events

Semana Santa
RELIGIOUS

(http://semanasantalorca.com) If you're from Lorca, you're passionately Blanco (White) or Azul (Blue), the colours of the two major brotherhoods that have competed every year since 1855 to see who can stage the most lavish Semana Santa display. Lorca's Easter parades are very distinct from the sombre processions elsewhere. While still deeply reverential, they're full of colour and vitality, mixing Old Testament tales with the Passion story.

Each brotherhood has a statue of the Virgin (one draped in a blue mantle, the other in white, naturally), a banner and a spectacular museum. The result of this intense and mostly genial year-round rivalry is just about the most dramatic Semana Santa you'll see anywhere in Spain.

🛏 Sleeping & Eating

Hotel Félix
HOTEL €

(☎ 968 46 76 54; www.hotelfelix.es; Avenida de las Fuerzas Armadas 14; s €33-38, d €44-49; ❋ 🖙) Compact modern rooms with just OK bathrooms and friendly staff make this Lorca's best budget hotel.

Parador de Lorca
PARADOR €€

(☎ 968 40 60 47; www.parador.es; Castillo de Lorca; s/d €80/90; 🅿 ❋ @ 🖙 🏊) Memorably situated in the castle complex way above town is this modern, spick-and-span *parador* (*paradores* are luxurious state-run hotels, often set in historic buildings). Rooms are tip-top, there's an indoor pool and spa and the views are just stunning. Various archaeological fragments are integrated into the hotel, including the ruins of a synagogue accessed via the car park.

Bar Plaza de España
TAPAS €

(Cafe Bar España; ☑ 646 89 25 30; www.facebook.com/barplazaespagnalorca; Calle Alamo 2; tapas €1.50-2.50; ⏱ 8am-11pm) Right on Plaza de España, this is an old-time Spanish bar that does decent *tostas* and tapas for a pittance. If you think the geriatric Spanish male is a gentlemanly type, you should get in here to watch a dominoes game.

Taberna El Camino
SPANISH €€

(☑ 968 46 69 07; Calle Santo Domingo 13; dishes €8-18; ⏱ 11am-4pm & 7-11pm Tue-Sat, noon-4pm Sun) Set in a 400-year-old building, this place has a marvellous brick-vaulted dining area hung with memorabilia. Its flowerpots outside and paraphernalia of the Rocío pilgrimage suggest an Andalucian tavern, and the cuisine reveals the owners' Cordoban roots, with *salmorejo* (thick, cold tomato soup) featuring, as well as delicious local dishes such as artichokes with foie gras. Pleasant outdoor tables are also available.

🛍 Shopping

⭐ Centro para la Artesanía
HANDICRAFTS

(☑ 968 46 39 12; www.carm.es; Calle Lope Gisbert; ⏱ 10am-2pm & 5-8.30pm Mon-Fri, 11am-1.30pm Sat) 🌱 It's quite a surprise to go through the door here, and gradually descend into an enormous concrete structure replete with all kinds of handicrafts, from colourful rugs to wine and marvellous ceramics. A government initiative, it's a great place to browse and buy. No street number; it's opposite number 7.

ℹ Information

The friendly folk at Lorca's **tourist office** (☑ 968 44 19 14; www.lorcaturismo.es; Puerto de San Ginés; ⏱ 10am-2pm & 4-6.30pm Mon-Fri, 10am-2pm & 4.30-6.30pm Sat, 10am-2pm Sun, to 7pm or 7.30pm in summer) were evicted from their original home by an earthquake and are currently housed in the **Centro de Visitantes** (☑ 968 47 74 37; www.lorcatallerdeltiempo.com; Puerto de San Ginés; ⏱ 10am-2pm & 4-6.30pm Mon-Fri, 10am-2pm & 4.30-6.30pm Sat, 10am-2pm Sun, to 7pm or 7.30pm in summer), though at time of research restorations there had shifted them into a nearby concrete bunker.

ℹ Getting There & Away

Hourly buses (€5.95, 1½ hours) and C2-line *cercanía* trains (€5.75, 50 minutes) run between Lorca and Murcia. Various bus services run into Almería province and beyond.

Parque Regional de Sierra Espuña

The Sierra Espuña, a 40-minute drive southwest of Murcia towards Lorca, is an island of pine forest rising high into the sky above an ocean of heat and dust down below. Sitting just north of the N340, the natural park that protects this fragile and beautiful environment has more than 250 sq km of unspoilt highlands covered with trails and is popular with walkers and climbers. Limestone formations tower above the sprawling forests. In the northwest of the park are many *pozos de la nieve* (ice houses) where, until the arrival of industrial refrigeration, snow was compressed into ice, then taken to nearby towns in summer.

◉ Sights

Access to the park is best via **Alhama de Murcia**. The informative **Centro de Visitantes Ricardo Codorniu** (☑ 968 43 14 30; www.sierraespuna.com; ⏱ 9am-2pm & 3-5.30pm Tue-Sun Oct-May, 8.30am-3.30pm Tue-Sun Jun-Sep) is located in the heart of the park. A few walking trails leave from this visitor centre, and it can provide good maps for these and several other picturesque hikes.

The village of **El Berro** makes for a great base for the sierra. It has a couple of restaurants and the friendly **Camping Sierra Espuña** (☑ 968 66 80 38; www.campingsierraespuna.com; site per person/tent/car €5/5/5, 2-/6-person bungalows €55-106; 🅿 🛜 ⋓). For something altogether more luxurious, you can't beat the **Bajo el Cejo** (☑ 968 66 80 32; www.bajoelcejo.com; r €105-145; 🅿 ❄ 🛜 ⋓).

Another base for the sierra, and for northern Murcia in general, is the town of **Mula**. The town is a web of old streets squashed up against a pinnacle of dry rock topped by the very battered remnants of a **castle**. From a distance, the town actually looks like it's dropped straight out of a Middle Eastern fairy tale. Excellent accommodation is available at **El Molino de Felipe** (☑ 968 66 20 13; www.hospederiaruralmolinodefelipe.es; Carretera Ribera de los Molinos 321; d €48, apt €70-135; 🅿 ❄ 🛜 ⋓), about 4km from town.

ℹ Getting There & Away

The park is best accessed by car. The town of Alhama de Murcia is easily reached by bus from Murcia, but it's 19km from here to the visitor centre in the heart of the park. Mula is also accessible by bus from Murcia.

Understand Spain

Spain Today

Spain has turned a corner. Unemployment may remain stubbornly high, Catalonia still wants to secede and the scars of a long, deep and profoundly damaging economic crisis may still be evident. But there is light at the end of the tunnel – the economy is making baby steps towards recovery, a new kind of politics is emerging and there is a widespread feeling that the worst may finally be over.

Best on Film

Jamón, jamón (1992) Dark comedy that brought Penélope Cruz and Javier Bardem to prominence.

Todo sobre mi madre (1999) Classic Pedro Almodóvar romp through sex and death.

Mar adentro (2004) Alejandro Amenabar's study of a Galician quadriplegic.

Volver (2006) Almodóvar's lush and offbeat portrait of a Spanish family in crisis.

Alatriste (2006) War and betrayal pursue a Spanish musketeer in this 17th-century epic.

Best in Print

A Late Dinner: Discovering the Food of Spain (Paul Richardson) Erudite journey through Spain's fascinating culinary culture.

A Handbook for Travellers (Richard Ford) This 1845 classic is witty, informative and downright rude.

The Train in Spain (Christopher Howse) Amusing yet insightful reflections from a veteran Spain-watcher.

The New Spaniards (John Hooper) A journey through three decades (until 2006) of democratic Spain.

Don Quijote (Miguel de Cervantes) Spain's best-known novel remains a classic journey through inland Spain.

Economic Crisis

Spain's economy went into free fall in late 2008. Unemployment, which had dropped as low as 6% as Spain enjoyed 16 consecutive years of growth, rose above 26%, which equated to six million people, with catastrophic youth unemployment rates nudging 60%. Suicide rates were on the rise, Spain's young professionals fled the country in unprecedented numbers and Oxfam recently predicted that a staggering 18 million Spaniards – 40% of the population – were at risk of social marginalisation. Finally, in 2014, the tide began to turn. That was the first year in seven in which the country enjoyed the first full year of positive economic growth, and unemployment dipped below 25%. That this growth was largely fuelled by private consumption – by the increased spending of Spaniards – led many to hope that things were very much improving for ordinary Spaniards. Spain remains a country in dire economic straits, and many Spaniards are still doing it tough. But these days it's difficult to find anyone in Spain who doesn't think that the next decade will be better than the last.

A New Politics

Spain's political spoils have, for decades, been divided up between the left (the Socialist Workers Party, or PSOE) and the right (the conservative Popular Party, or PP). Not any more. A radical shift in the way that Spain does politics began in Madrid on 15 May 2011, when the *indignados* (those who are indignant) took over the iconic Plaza de la Puerta del Sol in the city centre with a peaceful sit-in protest. Maintaining popularity through social-media networks, they stayed for months in what was the forerunner to numerous similar movements around the world, including Occupy Wall Street and its offshoots. These community-based networks spoke for the widespread dissatisfaction that ordinary Spaniards felt for the prevailing political class. In 2015, that groundswell of community activism took on the form of a revolution when left-leaning Podemos and the centrist Ciudadanos won scores of seats across the country, first in municipal and regional elections, and then nationally. Madrid, for example, elected a new mayor, a retired former judge who catches the Metro to work, while Podemos came within two percentage points of pushing the Socialists into third place at a national level.

Catalan Independence?

More than any other country in continental Europe, Spain often seems at risk of falling apart, and for decades it was the Basque Country that seemed most likely to break off and go its own way. Then came Spain's economic crisis and the sense of economic injustice in the northeastern region of Catalonia became overwhelming – Catalonia is one of Spain's most prosperous regions, and it puts far more into the national coffers than it receives in return. In November 2014, a referendum organised by the Catalan regional government (but not recognised by Spain's national government or Spain's Constitutional Court) saw 80% vote in favour of independence; opinion polls suggest that any official referendum would be much closer. Catalonia's regional parliament promises to secede by mid-2017, though major political parties the PP and PSOE are threatening to block any such moves. Podemos, the left-wing party that won 20% of the national vote in 2015, is promising to let an official referendum proceed. Watch this space.

Uncertain Times

If there is a downside to Spain's bold new political future, it is the uncertainty that many Spaniards feel at a time when many of them need stability the most. Elections on 20 December 2015 produced no clear winners and negotiations for forming a new government dragged on well into February 2016. The Popular Party (PP) may have won the most seats, but largely found itself with neither allies nor willing coalition partners as a result of the election. Two months after the polls closed, the PP acknowledged as much and the baton passed to the Socialists, who similarly struggled to build a viable coalition. If they prove unable to do so, new elections must be called. Exciting as it may be to see new voices emerging in the national debate, this political instability – which may well be the way of the future – has economists worried at a time when a steady hand is needed to help guide the Spanish economy towards prosperity.

POPULATION: **48.15 MILLION**

AREA: **505,370 SQ KM**

GDP PER CAPITA: **US$33,800**

INFLATION: **−0.2%**

UNEMPLOYMENT: **24.5%**

if Spain were 100 people

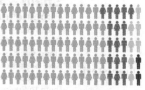

74 would speak Castilian Spanish
17 would speak Catalan
7 would speak Galician
2 would speak Basque

belief systems
(% of population)

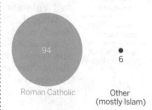

94 Roman Catholic

6 Other (mostly Islam)

population per sq km

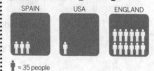

SPAIN   USA   ENGLAND

≈ 35 people

History

Spain's story is one of Europe's grand epics. It is a story shaped by ancient and not-so-ancient civilisations sweeping down through the Iberian Peninsula, and by the great ideological battles between Muslims and Christians of the Middle Ages. Later it became the tale of an empire upon which the sun never set and of near endemic conflict over the spoils. And the 20th century was a match for anything that went before with the Civil War, dictatorship and a stunning return to democracy.

Spain & the Ancient Civilisations

Phoenicians & Greeks

The Phoenician Empire (1500–300 BC) was the first of the grand civilisations of the Ancient World to set their sights on Spain. From their base along what is now the southern Lebanese coast, the Phoenicians may have been the world's first rulers of the sea. They were essentially traders rather than conquerors, and it was indeed commerce that first brought them to Spain around 1000 BC. They arrived on Spanish shores bearing perfumes, ivory, jewellery, oil, wine and textiles, which they exchanged for Spanish silver and bronze.

Conquest may not have been the Phoenicians' aim, but as their reach expanded, so too did their need for safe ports around the Mediterranean rim. One of these was Carthage in modern-day Tunisia, founded in 814 BC; in Iberia they established coastal trading colonies at Almuñécar (which they called Ex or Sex), Huelva (Onuba) and Cádiz (Gadir). Cádiz, that breezy and thoroughly Andalucian city in Spain's deep south, can as a result make a pretty strong claim to be the oldest continuously inhabited settlement in Europe.

While the Phoenicians were busy establishing themselves around Spain's southern coastline, groups of Ancient Greek traders began to arrive further north along the coast. In the 7th century BC, the Greeks founded a series of trading settlements mainly along the Mediterranean coast – the biggest was Emporion (present day Empúries) at L'Escala in Catalonia.

Top Prehistoric Sites

Cueva de Altamira, near Santillana del Mar

Atapuerca, near Burgos

Cueva de Tito Bustillo, Ribadesella

Dolmens, Antequera

Cueva de la Pileta, near Ronda

Siega Verde, near Ciudad Rodrigo

TIMELINE	c 1.2 million BC	c 15,000–10,000 BC	6th century BC
	Europe's earliest-known humans leave their fossilised remains in the Sima del Elefante at Atapuerca, near the northern city of Burgos.	Palaeolithic (Old Stone Age) hunters of the Magdalenian culture paint beautiful, sophisticated animal images in caves at Altamira and other sites along Spain's northern coastal strip.	Carthage, a former Phoenician colony in North Africa, supplants the Phoenicians and Greeks as the major trading power in the western Mediterranean.

The most important gifts of the Phoenicians and Greeks to Spain were not cities, only fragments of which remain today, but rather what they brought with them. Iron and other metals, along with several things now considered quintessentially Spanish – the olive tree, the grapevine and the donkey – arrived with the Phoenicians and Greeks, along with other useful skills and items such as writing, coins, the potter's wheel and poultry.

The Romans

They might have been here first, but the hold of the Phoenicians and Greeks over their Spanish 'territories' was always rather tenuous and never destined to last.

From about the 6th century BC, the Phoenicians and Greeks were pushed out of the western Mediterranean by newly independent Carthage, a former Phoenician colony that established a flourishing settlement on Ibiza. For a brief period during the 3rd century BC, during the so-called Punic Wars in which Rome and Carthage battled for control over the Mediterranean, Carthage conquered southern Spain. The Second Punic War (218–201 BC) saw Carthaginian general Hannibal march his elephants on from here and over the Alps to threaten Rome, but Rome's victory at Ilipa, near Seville, in 206 BC, ultimately gave it control over the Iberian Peninsula. The first Roman town in Spain, Itálica, was founded near the battlefield soon afterwards.

The Romans held sway on the Iberian Peninsula for 600 years. It took them 200 years to subdue the fiercest of local tribes, but by AD 50 most of Hispania (as the Romans called the peninsula) had adopted the Roman way of life.

Rome's legacy to Spain was incalculable, giving Hispania a road system, aqueducts, temples, theatres, amphitheatres and bathhouses, along with the religion that still predominates today – Christianity – and a Jewish population who were to play a big part in Spanish life for more than 1000 years. The main languages still spoken on the Iberian Peninsula – Castilian Spanish, Catalan, Galician and Portuguese – are all versions of the colloquial Latin spoken by Roman legionaries and colonists, filtered through 2000 years of linguistic mutation; the Basques, though defeated, were never Romanised like the rest and hence their language never came within the Latin orbit.

It was also the Romans who first began to cut (for timber, fuel and weapons) the extensive forests that in their time covered half the *meseta*. In return, Hispania gave Rome gold, silver, grain, wine, fish, soldiers, emperors (Trajan, Hadrian, Theodosius) and the literature of Seneca, Martial, Quintilian and Lucan.

Top Roman Remains

Mérida

Segovia

Itálica

Tarragona

Baelo Claudia, Bolonia

Lugo

Villa Romana La Olmeda

Villa Romana La Dehesa

HISTORY SPAIN & THE ANCIENT CIVILISATIONS

218 BC	1st to 3rd centuries AD	4th to 7th centuries AD	711
Roman legions arrive in Spain during the Second Punic War against Carthage, initiating the 600-year Roman occupation of the Iberian Peninsula; it takes two centuries to subdue all local resistance.	Pax Romana (Roman Peace), a period of stability and prosperity. The Iberian Peninsula is divided into three provinces: Baetica (capital: Córdoba); Lusitania (Mérida) and Tarraconensis (Tarragona).	Germanic tribes enter the Iberian Peninsula, ending the Pax Romana. The Visigoths establish control and bring 200 years of relative stability in which Hispano-Roman culture survives.	Muslims invade Iberia from North Africa, overrunning it within a few years, becoming the dominant force on the peninsula for nearly four centuries, and then a potent one for four centuries more.

Richard Fletcher's *Moorish Spain* is an excellent short history of Al-Andalus (the Muslim-ruled areas of the peninsula) and assumes little or no prior knowledge of the subject.

The Roman centuries were something of a golden age for Spain, but the Pax Romana (Roman Peace; the long, prosperous period of stability under the Romans) in Spain began to crumble in the 3rd and 4th centuries AD when Germanic tribes began to sweep down across the Pyrenees. The Visigoths, another Germanic people, sacked Rome itself in 410, but later became Roman allies. When the Germanic Franks pushed the Visigoths out of Gaul in the 6th century, they settled in the Iberian Peninsula, making Toledo their capital.

Throughout their rule, the roughly 200,000 Visigoths maintained a precarious hold over the millions of more-sophisticated Hispano-Romans, to the extent that the Visigoths tended to ape Roman ways. Nonetheless, the Roman era had come to an end.

Moorish Spain & La Reconquista

The Moorish Arrival

The death of the Prophet Mohammed in far-off Arabia in 632 sent shockwaves across the known world and Spain, too, would soon feel the effects. Under Mohammed's successors, known as caliphs (from the Arabic word for 'follower'), the new religion spread with extraordinary speed. Much of the Middle East was theirs by 656 and by 682 Islam had reached the shores of the Atlantic in Morocco. Spain, and with it Europe, now lay within sight and within reach.

For a modern take on Spain's Moorish history, see Jason Webster's *Andalus: Unlocking the Secrets of Moorish Spain*. Other titles include *Homage to al-Andalus: The Rise and Fall of Islamic Spain* by Michael B. Barry, and *The Ornament of the World* by Maria Rosa Menocal.

They had chosen a good moment to arrive: with the disintegration of the Visigothic kingdom through famine, disease and strife and infighting among the aristocracy, the Iberian Peninsula was in disarray and ripe for invasion.

For all its significance, there is an element of farce to what happened next. If you believe the myth, the Muslims were ushered into Spain by the sexual misadventures of the last Visigoth king, Roderic, who reputedly seduced Florinda, the daughter of the governor of Ceuta on the Moroccan coast. The governor, Julian, sought revenge by approaching the Muslims with a plan to invade Spain, and in 711 Tariq ibn Ziyad, the Muslim governor of Tangier, landed at Gibraltar with around 10,000 men, mostly Berbers (indigenous North Africans).

Roderic's army was decimated, probably near Río Guadalete or Río Barbate in western Andalucía, and he is thought to have drowned while fleeing the scene. Visigothic survivors fled north and within a few years the Muslims had conquered the whole Iberian Peninsula, except for small areas behind the mountains of the Cordillera Cantábrica in the north. Their advance into Europe was only checked by the Franks at the Battle of Poitiers in 732.

718	756	854	929
Christian nobleman Pelayo establishes the Kingdom of Asturias in northern Spain. With his victory over a Muslim force at the Battle of Covadonga around 722, the Reconquista begins.	Abd ar-Rahman I establishes himself in Córdoba as the emir of Al-Andalus (the Islamic areas of the peninsula) and launches nearly three centuries of Cordoban supremacy.	Mohammed I, emir of Córdoba, establishes the fortress of Mayrit (Magerit), one of many across the so-called MiddleMarch, a frontierland connecting Al-Andalus with the Christian kingdoms of the north. Madrid is born.	Abd ar-Rahman III inaugurates the Córdoba Caliphate, under which Al-Andalus reaches its zenith and Córdoba, with up to half a million people, becomes Europe's biggest and most cultured city.

THE MOORISH LEGACY

Muslim rule left an indelible imprint upon the country. Great architectural monuments such as the **Alhambra** in Granada and the **Mezquita** in Córdoba are the stars of the Moorish legacy, but thousands of other buildings large and small are Moorish in origin (including the many churches that began life as mosques). The tangled, narrow street plans of many a Spanish town and village, especially in the south, date back to Moorish times, and the Muslims also developed the Hispano-Roman agricultural base by improving irrigation and introducing new fruits and crops, many of which are still widely grown today. The Spanish language contains many common words of Arabic origin, including the names of some of those new crops – *naranja* (orange), *azúcar* (sugar) and *arroz* (rice). Flamenco, though brought to its modern form by Roma people in post-Moorish times, has clear Moorish roots. It was also through Al-Andalus that much of the learning of Ancient Greece and Rome – picked up by the Arabs in the eastern Mediterranean – was transmitted to Christian Europe, where it would exert a profound influence on the Renaissance.

Al-Andalus: The Early Years

The enlightened Islamic civilisation that would rule much of the Iberian Peninsula for centuries would be called Al-Andalus.

Initially Al-Andalus was part of the Caliphate of Damascus, which ruled the Islamic world. Once again, as it had been in ancient times, Spain had become a distant outpost of someone else's empire. In 750, however, the Umayyads were overthrown in Damascus by a rival clan, the Abbasids, who shifted the caliphate to Baghdad. One aristocratic Umayyad survivor made his way to Spain and established himself in Córdoba in 756 as the independent emir of Al-Andalus, Abd ar-Rahman I. It was he who began construction of Córdoba's Mezquita, one of the world's greatest Islamic buildings. Just as importantly, Córdoba was the capital of an empire that relied on no foreign powers. For almost the first time in Spanish history, Spain (in this case, Al-Andalus) was both powerful and answerable only to itself.

Córdoba's Golden Age

From the middle of the 8th century to the mid-11th century, the frontier between Muslim and Christian territory lay across the north of the peninsula, roughly from southern Catalonia to northern Portugal, with a protrusion up to the central Pyrenees. South of this line, Islamic cities such as Córdoba, Seville and Granada boasted beautiful palaces, mosques and gardens, universities, public baths and bustling *zocos* (markets). Al-Andalus' rulers allowed freedom of worship to Jews and

Almohad rule saw a cultural revival in Seville, and the great Cordoban philosopher Averroës (1126–98) exerted a major influence on medieval Christian thought with his commentaries on Aristotle, trying to reconcile science with religion.

1031	1035	1085	1091
The Córdoba Caliphate disintegrates into dozens of *taifas* (small kingdoms) after a devastating civil war. The most powerful *taifas* include Seville, Granada, Toledo and Zaragoza.	Castilla, a county of the northern Christian kingdom of León (successor to the kingdom of Asturias), becomes an independent kingdom and goes on to become the leading force of the Reconquista.	Castilla captures the major Muslim city of Toledo in central Spain after infighting among the *taifas* leaves them vulnerable to attack.	North African Muslim Almoravids invade the peninsula, unifying Al-Andalus, ruling it from Marrakesh and halting Christian expansion. Almoravid rule crumbles in the 1140s; Al-Andalus splits into *taifas*.

Best Moorish Monuments

Alhambra, Granada

Mezquita, Córdoba

Albayzín, Granada

Alcázar, Seville

Giralda, Seville

Aljafería, Zaragoza

Alcazaba, Málaga

Christians (known as mozárabes and Mozarabs respectively). Jews mostly flourished, but Christians had to pay a special tax, so most either converted to Islam (to be known as *muladíes* or *muwallad*) or left for the Christian north.

In 929, the ruler Abd ar-Rahman III gave himself the title caliph, launching the Caliphate of Córdoba (929–1031), during which Al-Andalus reached its peak of power and lustre. Córdoba in this period was the biggest and most dazzling city in Western Europe. Astronomy, medicine, mathematics and botany flourished and one of the great Muslim libraries was established in the city.

Later in the 10th century, the fearsome Cordoban general Al-Mansour (or Almanzor) terrorised the Christian north with 50-odd forays into the territory in 20 years. He destroyed the cathedral at Santiago de Compostela in northwestern Spain in 997 and forced Christian slaves to carry its doors and bells to Córdoba, where they were incorporated into the building of the great mosque. There was, it seemed, no limit to Córdoba's powers.

Al-Andalus: The Later Years

Just when it seemed that Córdoba's golden age would last forever, Al-Andalus turned the corner into a long, slow decline.

After Al-Mansour's death the caliphate collapsed into a politically devastating civil war, ending Umayyad rule. Córdoba remained powerful, but in 1031 the emirate finally broke up into dozens of *taifas* (small kingdoms).

Political unity was restored to Al-Andalus by the invasion of a strict Muslim sect of Saharan or Berber nomads, the Almoravids, in 1091. The Almoravids had conquered North Africa and were initially invited to the Iberian Peninsula to support Seville, one of the strongest *taifas,* against the growing Christian threat from the north.

Sixty years later a second Berber sect, the Almohads, invaded the peninsula after overthrowing the Almoravids in Morocco. Both sects convincingly defeated the Christian armies they encountered in Spain, and maintained a strong Muslim hold over the southern half of the peninsula.

Reconquista Castles on the Web

www.castillosnet.org

www.castlesof spain.co.uk

The near-constant infighting of Muslim versus Muslim was, however, starting to take its toll. While the Almohad's successors, the Nasrids, retreated to Granada and contributed to the architectural splendours of the Alhambra, the Christian armies of the Reconquista were starting to close in.

1160–73	1195	1212	1229–38
The Almohads, another strict Muslim sect from North Africa, conquer Al-Andalus. They make Seville their capital and revive arts and learning.	The Almohads inflict a devastating defeat on Alfonso VIII of Castilla at the Battle of Alarcos, near Ciudad Real – the last major Christian reverse of the Reconquista.	Combined armies of the northern Christian kingdoms defeat the Almohads at Las Navas de Tolosa in Andalucía, and the momentum of the Christian–Muslim struggle swings decisively in favour of the Christians.	Catalonia enjoys its golden age under King Jaume I of Aragón, who takes the Balearic Islands and Valencia from the Muslims and makes Catalonia the major power in the western Mediterranean.

The Reconquista

The Christian Reconquest of the Iberian Peninsula began in about 722 at Covadonga, Asturias, and ended with the fall of Granada in 1492. In between these two dates lay almost eight centuries of misadventures, stirring victories and missed opportunities.

An essential ingredient in the Reconquista was the cult of Santiago (St James), one of the 12 Apostles. In 813, the saint's supposed tomb was discovered in Galicia. The city of Santiago de Compostela grew around the site, to become the third-most-popular medieval Christian pilgrimage goal after Rome and Jerusalem. Christian generals experienced visions of Santiago before forays against the Muslims, and Santiago became the inspiration and special protector of soldiers in the Reconquista, earning the sobriquet *Matamoros* (Moor-slayer). Today he is the patron saint of Spain.

Castilla Rises

Covadonga lies in the Picos de Europa mountains, where some Visigothic nobles took refuge after the Muslim conquest. Christian versions of the 722 battle there tell of a small band of fighters under their leader, Pelayo, defeating an enormous force of Muslims; Muslim accounts make it a rather less important skirmish. Whatever the facts of Covadonga, by 757 Christians had clawed back nearly a quarter of the Iberian Peninsula.

The Asturian kingdom eventually moved its capital south to León and became the Kingdom of León, which spearheaded the Reconquista until the Christians were set on the defensive by Al-Mansour in the 10th century. Castilla, initially a small principality within León, developed into the dominant Reconquista force as hardy adventurers set up towns in the no-man's-land of the Duero basin. The capture of Toledo in 1085, by Alfonso VI of Castilla, led the Seville Muslims to call in the Almoravids from North Africa.

In 1212 the combined armies of the Christian kingdoms routed a large Almohad force at Las Navas de Tolosa in Andalucía. This was the beginning of the end for Al-Andalus: León took key towns in Extremadura in 1229 and 1230; Aragón took Valencia in the 1230s; Castilla's Fernando III El Santo (Ferdinand the Saint) took Córdoba in 1236 and Seville in 1248; and Portugal expelled the Muslims in 1249. The sole surviving Muslim state on the peninsula was now the Emirate of Granada.

Aragón was one of the most powerful kingdoms in medieval Spain, a crown created in 1137 when Ramón Berenguer IV of Catalonia married Petronilla, heiress of Aragón, to create a formidable new Christian power block in the northeast, with Barcelona as its power centre.

1248	1469	1478	January 1492
Having captured Córdoba 12 years earlier, Castilla's Fernando III takes Seville after a two-year siege, making the Nasrid Emirate of Granada the last surviving Muslim state on the peninsula.	Isabel, the 18-year-old heir to Castilla, marries Fernando, heir to Aragón and one year her junior, uniting Spain's two most powerful Christian states.	Isabel and Fernando, the Reyes Católicos (Catholic Monarchs), stir up religious bigotry and establish the Spanish Inquisition that will see thousands killed between now and its abolition in 1834.	Isabel and Fernando capture Granada, completing the Reconquista. Boabdil, the last Muslim ruler, is scorned by his mother for weeping 'like a woman for what you could not defend like a man'.

THE CATHOLIC MONARCHS

Few individuals in any time or place have had such an impact on their country's history as Spain's Reyes Católicos, Isabel of Castilla and Fernando of Aragón. Indeed, Spain owes its very existence to their marriage in 1469 (which effectively united the Iberian Peninsula's two biggest Christian kingdoms) and to their conquest of Granada (1492) and annexation of Navarra (1512).

Isabel, by all accounts, was pious, honest, virtuous and very determined, while Fernando was an astute political operator – a formidable team. Isabel resisted her family's efforts to marry her off to half a dozen other European royals before her semi-clandestine wedding to Fernando at Valladolid – the first time the pair had set eyes on each other. They were second cousins; she was 18 and he 17. Isabel succeeded to the Castilian throne in 1474, and Fernando to Aragón's in 1479. By the time Isabel died in 1504, the pair had:

➡ set up the Spanish Inquisition (1478)

➡ completed the Reconquista by conquering Granada (1492)

➡ expelled all Jews (1492) and Muslims (1500) who refused to convert to Christianity

➡ helped to fund Columbus' voyage to the Americas (1492), opening the door to a vast overseas empire for Spain

➡ crushed the power of Castilla's rebellious nobility

Today Isabel and Fernando lie side by side in the beautiful Gothic church they commissioned as their own mausoleum, Granada's Capilla Real (p666).

Granada Falls

In 1476 Emir Abu al-Hasan of Granada refused to pay any more tribute to Castilla, spurring Isabel (queen of Castilla) and Fernando (king of Aragón) to launch the Reconquista's final crusade, against Granada, with an army largely funded by Jewish loans and the Catholic Church. The Christians took full advantage of a civil war within the Granada emirate, and on 2 January 1492 Isabel and Fernando entered the city of Granada at the beginning of what turned out to be the most momentous year in Spanish history.

The surrender terms were fairly generous to Boabdil, the last emir, who got the Alpujarras valleys south of Granada and 30,000 gold coins. History has been less kind. Whether true or not, it is often recounted how Boabdil turned for one last tearful look at his beloved Granada as he headed into exile, whereupon his mother scolded him by saying: 'Do not weep like a woman for that which you were unable to defend like a

Giles Tremlett's *Catherine of Aragón: The Spanish Queen of Henry VIII* brings to life all the scheming and intrigue of royal Europe in the 16th century through the story of Isabel and Fernando's daughter.

April 1492	October 1492	1494	1512
Isabel and Fernando expel Jews who refuse Christian baptism. Some 200,000 leave, establishing Jewish communities around the Mediterranean; Spain's economy suffers from the loss of their knowledge.	Christopher Columbus, funded by Isabel and Fernando, lands in the Bahamas, opening up the Americas to Spanish colonisation. The bulk of Spanish maritime trade shifts from Mediterranean to Atlantic ports.	The Treaty of Tordesillas (near Valladolid) divides recently discovered lands west of Europe between Spain and Portugal, giving the Spanish the right to claim vast territories in the Americas.	Fernando, ruling as regent after Isabel's death in 1504, annexes Navarra, bringing all of Spain under one rule for the first time since Roman days.

man!' The remaining Muslims were promised respect for their religion, culture and property, but this didn't last long.

Eight centuries after it began, Al-Andalus was no more.

The Spanish Inquisition

Spain's new Catholic rulers made it clear from the beginning that Islam's enlightened policies of religious coexistence would be a thing of the past.

Not content with territorial conquest, the Catholic monarchs' Christian zeal led to the founding of the Spanish Inquisition to root out those believed to be threatening the Catholic Church. The Inquisition's leading figure was Grand Inquisitor Tomás de Torquemada, who was appointed Queen Isabel's personal confessor in 1479. He was, centuries later, immortalised by Dostoevsky as the articulate Grand Inquisitor who puts Jesus himself on trial in *The Brothers Karamazov,* and satirised by Monty Python in the *Flying Circus.*

The Inquisition focused first on *conversos* (Jews converted to Christianity), accusing many of continuing to practise Judaism in secret; in an interesting footnote to history, Torquemada was himself born to *converso* parents.

During the Inquisition, the 'lucky' sinners had their property confiscated, which had, prior to the fall of Granada, served as a convenient fund-raiser for the war of Reconquista against the Muslims. The condemned were then paraded through towns wearing the *sambenito,* a yellow shirt emblazoned with crosses that was short enough to expose their genitals, then marched to the doors of the local church and flogged.

If you were unlucky, you underwent unimaginable tortures before going through an *auto-da-fé,* a public burning at the stake. Those that recanted and kissed the cross were garrotted before the fire was set, while those that recanted only were burnt quickly with dry wood. If you stayed firm and didn't recant, the wood used for the fire was green and slow-burning.

In the 15 years Torquemada was Inquisitor General of the Castilian Inquisition, he ran some 100,000 trials and sent about 2000 people to burn at the stake. On 31 March 1492, Fernando and Isabel, on Torquemada's insistence, issued their Edict of Expulsion, as a result of which all Jews who refused Christian baptism were forced to leave Spain within two months on pain of death. Up to 100,000 converted, but some 200,000 – the first Sephardic Jews – left Spain for other Mediterranean destinations. The bankrupt monarchy seized all unsold Jewish property. A talented middle class was gone.

Echoes of the Middle Ages

....

Sos del Rey Católico, Aragón

....

Albarracín, Aragón

....

Santiago de Compostela

....

Morella, Valencia

....

La Tahá, Las Alpujarras

....

Santo Domingo de la Calzada, La Rioja

....

Ávila

....

Albayzín, Granada

HISTORY THE SPANISH INQUISITION

1517–56	1521	1533	1556–98
Reign of Carlos I, Spain's first Habsburg monarch, who comes to rule more of Europe than anyone since the 9th century, plus rapidly expanding areas of South and Central America.	Hernán Cortés, from Medellín, Extremadura, conquers the Aztec empire in present-day Mexico and Guatemala with a small band of conquistadors, in the name of the Spanish crown.	Francisco Pizarro, from Trujillo, Extremadura, conquers the Inca empire in South America with a small band of conquistadors, in the name of the Spanish crown.	Reign of Felipe II, the zenith of Spanish power. The American territories expand into the modern United States and enormous wealth arriving from the colonies is used for grandiose architectural projects.

Cardinal Cisneros, Torquemada's successor as overseer of the Inquisition, tried to eradicate Muslim culture too. In the former Granada emirate he carried out forced mass baptisms, burnt Islamic books and banned the Arabic language. After a revolt in Andalucía in 1500, Muslims were ordered to convert to Christianity or leave. Most (around 300,000) underwent baptism and stayed, becoming known as *moriscos* (converted Muslims), but their conversion was barely skin deep and they never assimilated. The *moriscos* were finally expelled a century later, between 1609 and 1614.

Spain's Empires

Conquering a New World

In April 1492 the Catholic monarchs granted the appeal of Genoese sailor Christopher Columbus (Cristobel Colón in Spanish), and provided funds for his voyage across the Atlantic in search of a new trade route to the Orient.

Columbus sailed from the Andalucian port of Palos de la Frontera on 3 August 1492, with three small ships and 120 men. After a near mutiny as the crew despaired of sighting land, they finally arrived on the island of Guanahaní, in the Bahamas, and went on to find Cuba and Hispaniola. Columbus returned to a hero's reception from the Catholic monarchs in Barcelona, eight months after his departure. Columbus made three more voyages, founding the city of Santo Domingo on Hispaniola, finding Jamaica, Trinidad and other Caribbean islands, and reaching the mouth of the Orinoco and the coast of Central America. But he died impoverished in Valladolid in 1506, still believing he had reached Asia.

Brilliant but ruthless conquistadors such as Hernán Cortés and Francisco Pizarro followed Columbus' trail, seizing vast tracts of the American mainland for Spain. By 1600 Spain controlled Florida, all the biggest Caribbean islands, nearly all of present-day Mexico and Central America, and a large strip of South America. The new colonies sent huge cargoes of silver, gold and other riches back to Spain, where the crown was entitled to one-fifth of the bullion (the *quintoreal,* or royal fifth). Seville enjoyed a monopoly on this trade and grew into one of Europe's richest cities.

Entangled in the Old World

It wasn't just the Americas that the monarchs thought should be theirs. Ever scheming, Isabel and Fernando embroiled Spain in European affairs by marrying their five children into the royal families of Portugal, the Holy Roman Empire and England. After Isabel's death

1571	c 1600–1660	1609–14	1676
The Holy League fleet, led by Spain and Venice and commanded by Felipe II's half-brother Don Juan de Austria, defeats the Ottoman fleet at Lepanto, ending Ottoman expansion into Europe.	Spain enjoys a cultural golden age with the literature of Cervantes and the paintings of Velázquez, Zurbarán and El Greco scaling new heights of artistic excellence as the empire declines.	The *moriscos* (converted Muslims) are expelled from Spain in a final purge of non-Christians that undermines an already faltering economy.	The devastation caused by the third great plague to hit Spain in a century is compounded by poor harvests. In all, more than 1.25 million Spaniards die through plague and starvation during the 17th century.

in 1504 and Fernando's in 1516, their thrones passed to their grandson Carlos I (Charles I), who arrived in Spain from Flanders in 1517, aged 17. In 1519 Carlos also succeeded to the Habsburg lands in Austria and was elected Holy Roman Emperor (as Charles V) – meaning he now ruled all of Spain, the Low Countries, Austria, several Italian states, parts of France and Germany, and the expanding Spanish colonies in the Americas.

For all Spain's apparent power and wealth, European conflicts soaked up a great deal of the monarchy's new American income, and a war-weary Carlos abdicated shortly before his death in 1556, retiring to the Monasterio de Yuste in Extremadura and dividing his many territories between his son Felipe II (Philip II; r 1556–98) and his brother Fernando.

Felipe got the lion's share, including Spain, the Low Countries and the American possessions, and presided over the zenith of Spanish power, though his reign is a study in contradictions. He enlarged the American empire and claimed Portugal on its king's death in 1580, but lost Holland after a long drawn-out rebellion. His navy defeated the Ottoman Turks at Lepanto in 1571, but the Spanish Armada of 1588 was routed by England. He was a fanatical Catholic, who spurred the Inquisition to new persecutions, yet readily allied Spain with Protestant England against Catholic France. He received greater flows of silver than ever from the Americas, but went bankrupt.

Felipe too died in a monastery – the immense monastery at San Lorenzo de El Escorial, which he himself had commissioned, and which stands as a sombre monument to his reign and to the follies of Spain's colonial era.

A Country Divided

Out of Step with Europe

At one level, a flourishing arts scene in 17th-century Spain created the illusion of a thriving, modern European nation. It was at this time that Spain was immortalised on canvas by great artists such as Velázquez, El Greco, Zurbarán and Murillo, and in print by the likes of Miguel de Cervantes (creator of the beloved Don Quijote) and the prolific playwright Lope de Vega.

And yet weak, backward-looking monarchs, a highly conservative Church and an idle nobility allowed the economy to stagnate, leading to food shortages in a country where there were gross inequalities between the haves and the have-nots. Spain lost Portugal and faced revolts in Catalonia, Sicily and Naples. Silver shipments from the Americas shrank disastrously. And the sickly Carlos II (Charles II;

Echoes of Spain's American Colonies

Trujillo, Extremadura

Lugares Colombinos, near Huelva

Casa-Museo de Colón, Valladolid

Columbus' Tomb, Seville Cathedral

Tordesillas, near Valladolid

Palacio de Sobrellano, Comillas

Museo de América, Madrid

1700	1702–13	1793	1805
Felipe V, first of the Bourbon dynasty, takes the throne after the Habsburg line dies out with Carlos II. Felipe is second in line to the French throne, which causes concern across Europe.	Rival European powers support Charles of Austria against Felipe V in the War of the Spanish Succession: Felipe survives as king but Spain loses Gibraltar and the Low Countries.	Spain declares war on France after Louis XVI is beheaded, but within a couple of years the country is supporting the French in their struggles against the British.	A combined Spanish–French fleet is defeated by British ships under Nelson at the Battle of Trafalgar. Spanish sea power is effectively destroyed, and discontent against the king's pro-French policies grows.

**Echoes
of the
Napoleonic
Wars**

....

*Cabo de Trafalgar,
Los Caños de Meca*

....

*Trafalgar Cemetery,
Gibraltar*

....

*Museo de las
Cortes de Cádiz,
Cádiz*

....

*Xardín de San
Carlos, A Coruña*

....

*Cementerio de la
Florida, Madrid*

....

*Plaza de Dos de
Mayo, Madrid*

r 1665–1700), known as El Hechizado (the Bewitched), failed to produce children, a situation that eventually led to the War of the Spanish Succession (1702–13).

During the war, things got even worse – Spain lost its last possessions in the Low Countries to Austria, and Gibraltar and Menorca to Britain. Felipe V (Philip V; r 1700–46), to whom Carlos II had bequeathed the Spanish throne, renounced his right to the French throne but held on to Spain. He was the first of the Bourbon dynasty, still in place today.

This was Europe's Age of Enlightenment, but Spain's powerful Church and Inquisition were at odds with the rationalism that trickled in from France. Two-thirds of the land was in the hands of the nobility and Church, and inequality and unrest were rife.

France Invades

When France's Louis XVI, cousin to Spain's Carlos IV (Charles IV; r 1788–1808), was guillotined in 1793 in the aftermath of the French Revolution of 1789, Spain declared war on France. The war was short-lived: Spain made peace with the French Republic just two years later. In 1805 a combined Spanish–French navy was beaten by the British fleet, under Admiral Nelson, off the Cabo de Trafalgar, putting an end to any Spanish sea power.

In 1807, French forces poured into Spain, supposedly on the way to Portugal, but by 1808 this had become a French occupation of Spain, and Carlos IV was forced to abdicate in favour of Napoleon's brother Joseph Bonaparte (José I).

In Madrid crowds revolted, as immortalised by Goya in his paintings *El dos de mayo* and *el tres de mayo,* which now hang in Madrid's Museo del Prado. Across the country Spaniards took up arms guerilla-style, reinforced by British and Portuguese forces led by the Duke of Wellington. A national Cortes (Parliament) meeting at Cádiz in 1812 drew up a new liberal constitution, incorporating many of the principles of the American and French prototypes. The French were finally driven out after their defeat at Vitoria in 1813.

Spain's Decline

Although momentarily united to see off the French, Spain was deeply divided, not to mention increasingly backward and insular. For much of the 19th century, internal conflicts raged between liberal groups (who wanted vaguely democratic reforms) and the conservatives (the Church, the nobility and others who preferred the earlier status quo).

1808–13	1809–24	1814	1881
French forces occupy Spain; Carlos IV abdicates in favour of Napoleon's brother, José I. The ensuing Peninsular War sees British forces helping the Spanish defeat the French.	Most of Spain's American colonies win independence as Spain is beset by problems at home. By 1824 only Cuba, Puerto Rico, Guam and the Philippines are under Spanish rule.	Fernando VII becomes king and revokes the 1812 Cádiz Constitution (an attempt by Spanish liberals to introduce constitutional reforms) just weeks after agreeing to uphold its principles.	The Partido Socialista Obrero Español (PSOE; Spanish Socialist Workers' Party) is founded in a backroom of Casa Labra, still one of Madrid's most prestigious tapas bars.

Uncertainties over royal succession resulted in the First Carlist War (1833–39). During the war, violent anticlericalism emerged, religious orders were closed and, in the Disentailment of 1836, church property and lands were seized and auctioned off by the government. It was the army alone that emerged victorious from the fighting. Another Carlist War (1872–76) followed, again between different claimants to the throne.

In 1873 the liberal-dominated Cortes proclaimed the country a federal republic. But it was too late; this First Republic had lost control of the regions and in 1874 the army put Isabel II's son Alfonso on the throne as Alfonso XII (r 1874–85), in a coalition with the Church and landowners.

Barely able to hold itself together, Spain had little chance of maintaining its few remaining colonies. In 1898, Spain lost Cuba, the Philippines, Guam and Puerto Rico.

For a country that had ruled one of the greatest empires of the age, this sealed an ignominious fall from grace.

Bourbon Baubles

Palacio Real, Madrid

Palacio Real, Aranjuez

La Granja de San Ildefonso, near Segovia

HISTORY THE SPANISH CIVIL WAR

The Spanish Civil War

Seeds of War

Spain was by the early years of the 20th century locked in an unending power struggle between liberal and conservative forces, with neither able to maintain the upper hand for long.

For a time, the left seemed ascendant. In the 1890s and the 1900s, anarchists bombed Barcelona's Liceu opera house, assassinated two prime ministers and killed 24 people with a bomb at King Alfonso XIII's wedding to Victoria Eugenie of Battenberg in May 1906. Along with the rise of the left came the growth of Basque and Catalan separatism. In the Basque country, nationalism emerged in the 1890s in response to a flood of Castilian workers into Basque industries: some Basques considered these migrants a threat to their identity. In 1909 a contingent of Spanish troops was wiped out by Berbers in Spanish Morocco. The government's decision to call up Catalan reservists sparked the so-called Semana Trágica (Tragic Week) in Barcelona, which began with a general strike and turned into a frenzy of violence. The government responded by executing many workers.

Spain stayed neutral during WWI, but it remained a deeply troubled nation. In 1921, 10,000 Spanish soldiers were killed by Berbers at Anual in Morocco, and two years later General Miguel Primo de Rivera, an eccentric Andalucian aristocrat, established his own mild dictatorship in Spain.

During the First Republic some Spanish cities declared themselves independent states, and some, such as Seville and nearby Utrera, even declared war on each other.

1898	1909	1923–30	1931
Spain loses Cuba, Puerto Rico, Guam and the Philippines, its last remaining colonies, after being defeated in the Spanish–American War by the US, which declared war in support of Cuban independence.	The Semana Trágica (Tragic Week) in Barcelona begins after Catalan reservists are called up to fight in Morocco; a general strike becomes a violent riot and dozens of civilians are killed.	General Miguel Primo de Rivera launches an army uprising in support of King Alfonso XIII and then establishes himself as dictator. He retires and dies in 1930.	Alfonso XIII goes into exile after Republicans score sweeping gains in local elections. Spain's Second Republic is launched, left-wing parties win a national election, and a new constitution enfranchises women.

Pre-Civil War Books

As I Walked out One Midsummer Morning by Laurie Lee

South from Granada by Gerald Brenan

The Spanish Labyrinth by Gerald Brenan

Modern Spain, 1875–1980 by Raymond Carr

Sketches of Spain: Impressions and Landscapes by Federic García Lorca

National elections in 1931 brought in a government composed of socialists, republicans and centrists. A new constitution gave women the vote, granted autonomy-minded Catalonia its own parliament, legalised divorce, stripped Catholicism of its status as official religion, and banned priests from teaching. But only two years later, in the 1933 elections, Spain lurched back to the right. One new force on the right was the fascist Falange, led by José Antonio Primo de Rivera, son of the 1920s dictator.

By 1934, violence was spiralling out of control. Catalonia declared itself independent (within a putative federal Spanish republic), and workers' committees took over the northern mining region of Asturias. A violent campaign against the Asturian workers by the Spanish Legion (set up to fight Moroccan tribes in the 1920s), led by generals Francisco Franco and José Millán Astray, split the country firmly into left and right.

In the February 1936 elections, the right-wing National Front was narrowly defeated by the left-wing Popular Front, with communists at the fore.

Something had to give.

The Civil War Begins

On 17 July 1936, the Spanish army garrison in Melilla, North Africa, rose up against the Popular Front government, followed the next day by garrisons on the mainland. The leaders of the plot were five generals, among them Francisco Franco. The civil war had begun.

The civil war split communities, families and friends, killed an estimated 350,000 Spaniards (some writers and historians say 500,000), and caused untold damage and misery. Both sides committed atrocious massacres and reprisals. The rebels, who called themselves Nationalists because they believed they were fighting for Spain, shot or hanged tens of thousands of supporters of the Republic. Republicans did likewise to Nationalist sympathisers, including some 7000 priests, monks and nuns.

At the start of the war many of the military and the Guardia Civil police force went over to the Nationalists, whose campaign quickly took on overtones of a crusade against the enemies of God. In Republican areas, anarchists, communists or socialists ended up running many towns and cities, and social revolution followed.

Nationalist Advance

Most cities with military garrisons fell immediately into Nationalist hands – this meant almost everywhere north of Madrid except Catalonia and the north coast, as well as parts of Andalucía. Franco's force

1933–35	1936	1936–39	1938
Right-wing parties win a new election; political violence spirals and a ruthless army operation against workers in Asturias irrevocably polarises Spain into left- and right-wing camps.	The left-wing National Front wins a national election. Right-wing 'Nationalist' rebels led by General Francisco Franco rise up against it, starting the Spanish Civil War.	The Spanish Civil War: the Nationalist rebels, under Franco, supported by Nazi Germany and Fascist Italy, defeat the USSR-supported Republicans. About 350,000 people die in fighting and atrocities.	The Nationalists defeat the Republicans' last major offensive, in the Ebro Valley, with 20,000 killed. The Soviet Union ends its support for the Republican side.

of legionnaires and Moroccan mercenaries were airlifted to Seville by German warplanes in August. Essential to the success of the revolt, they moved northward through Extremadura towards Madrid, wiping out fierce resistance in some cities. At Salamanca in October, Franco pulled all the Nationalists into line behind him.

Madrid, reinforced by the first battalions of the International Brigades (armed foreign idealists and adventurers organised by the communists), repulsed Franco's first assault in November and then endured, under communist inspiration, over two years' siege. But the International Brigades never numbered more than 20,000 and couldn't turn the tide against the better armed and organised Nationalist forces.

Nazi Germany and Fascist Italy supported the Nationalists with planes, weapons and men (75,000 from Italy, 17,000 from Germany), turning the war into a testing ground for what was to come during WWII. The Republicans had some Soviet planes, tanks, artillery and advisers, but other countries refused to become involved (although some 25,000 French fought on the Republican side).

Republican Quarrels

With Madrid besieged, the Republican government moved to Valencia in late 1936 to preside over the quarrelsome factions on its side, which encompassed anarchists, communists, moderate democrats and regional separatists.

In April 1937 German planes bombed the Basque town of Guernica (Gernika), causing terrible casualties; this became the subject of Picasso's famous pacifist painting, which now hangs in Madrid's Centro de Arte Reina Sofía. All the north coast fell to the Nationalists that year, while Republican counter-attacks near Madrid and in Aragón failed. Meanwhile divisions among the Republicans erupted into fierce street fighting in Barcelona, with the Soviet-influenced communists completely crushing the anarchists and Trotskyites, who had run the city for almost a year. The Republican government moved to Barcelona in autumn 1937.

Nationalist Victory

In early 1938, Franco repulsed a Republican offensive at Teruel in Aragón, then swept eastward with 100,000 troops, 1000 planes and 150 tanks, isolating Barcelona from Valencia. In July the Republicans launched a last offensive in the Ebro Valley. This bloody encounter, won by the Nationalists, cost 20,000 lives. The USSR withdrew from the war in September 1938, and in January 1939 the Nationalists took Barcelona unopposed. The Republican government and hundreds of

---

HISTORY THE SPANISH CIVIL WAR

Civil War Reads

For Whom the Bell Tolls by Ernest Hemingway

Homage to Catalonia by George Orwell

Blood of Spain by Ronald Fraser

The Spanish Civil War by Hugh Thomas

The Battle for Spain by Antony Beevor

Paul Preston's searing *The Spanish Holocaust: Inquisition and Extermination in Twentieth-Century Spain* lays bare the brutality of Spain's civil war (neither side comes out well) and the oppression by victorious Franco forces after the war.

1939	1939–50	1955–65	1959
The Nationalists take Barcelona in January. The Republican government flees to France, and the Nationalists enter Madrid on 28 March. Franco declares the war over on 1 April.	Franco establishes a right-wing dictatorship, imprisoning hundreds of thousands. Spain stays out of WWII but is later excluded from NATO and the UN and suffers a damaging international trade boycott.	Spain is admitted to the UN after agreeing to host US bases. The economy is boosted by US aid and mass tourism on the Costa Brava and Costa del Sol.	Euskadi Ta Askatasuna (ETA; Basque Homeland and Freedom) is founded with the aim of gaining Basque independence. The terrorist group will murder more than 800 people,.

thousands of thier supporters fled to France. Although the Republicans still held Valencia and Madrid, and had 500,000 people under arms, in the end their army simply evaporated. The Nationalists entered Madrid on 28 March 1939 and Franco declared the war over on 1 April.

Franco's Dictatorship

The Early Franco Years

An estimated 100,000 people were killed or died in prison in the years immediately following the war. The hundreds of thousands imprisoned included many intellectuals and teachers; others fled abroad, depriving Spain of a generation of scientists, artists, writers, educators and more.

Despite Franco's overtures to Hitler, Spain remained on the sidelines of WWII. In 1944 Spanish leftists launched a failed attack on Franco's Spain from France; small leftist guerrilla units continued a hopeless struggle in parts of the north, Extremadura and Andalucía until the 1950s.

After WWII Franco's Spain was excluded from the UN and NATO, and suffered a UN-sponsored trade boycott that helped turn the late 1940s into Spain's *años de hambre* (years of hunger). But the onset of the Cold War saved Franco: the US wanted bases in Spain, and Franco agreed to the establishment of four, in return for large sums of aid. In 1955 Spain was admitted to the UN.

Franco's Spain

By the late 1950s, the essential elements of Franco's rule were in place. Regional autonomy aspirations were simply not tolerated. The army provided many government ministers and enjoyed a most generous budget. And Catholic supremacy was fully restored.

In 1959 a new breed of technocrats in government, linked to the Catholic group Opus Dei, engineered a Stabilisation Plan, which brought an economic upswing. Spanish industry boomed, modern machinery, technology and marketing were introduced, transport was modernised and new dams provided irrigation and hydropower.

The recovery was funded in part by US aid and remittances from more than a million Spaniards who had gone to work abroad, but above all by the tourism industry, which was developed initially along Andalucía's Costa del Sol and Catalonia's Costa Brava. By 1965 the number of tourists arriving in Spain had risen to 14 million a year. These were the so-called *años de desarollo* (years of development). Industry took off, foreign investment poured in and the services and

1960s	1973	1975	1976
After two decades of economic hardship, the decade becomes known as the *años de desarollo* (years of development) with investment and rural immigrants flooding into Madrid and other cities.	Admiral Carrero Blanco, Franco's prime minister and designated successor, is assassinated by ETA in a car-bomb attack in Madrid's Salamanca district after he leaves Mass.	Franco dies and is succeeded by King Juan Carlos I. The monarch had been schooled by Franco to continue his policies but soon demonstrates his desire for change.	The king appoints Adolfo Suárez as prime minister. Suárez engineers a return to democracy. Left-wing parties are legalised, despite military opposition, and the country holds free elections in 1977.

banking sectors blossomed. In 1960 fewer than 70,000 cars were on the road in Madrid. Ten years later, more than half a million clogged the capital's streets.

Although Spaniards' standard of living was improving, the jails were full of political prisoners and large garrisons were still maintained outside every major city. From 1965 opposition to Franco's regime became steadily more vocal. The universities were repeatedly the scene of confrontation, and clandestine trade unions also began to make themselves heard again. The waves of protest were not restricted to Madrid. In the Basque Country the terrorist group Euskadi Ta Askatasuna (ETA; Basque Homeland and Freedom) began to fight for Basque independence. Their first important action outside the Basque Country was in 1973, the assassination of Admiral Carrero Blanco, Franco's prime minister and designated successor, in Madrid in a car-bomb attack.

In what seemed like a safe bet, Franco chose as his new successor Prince Juan Carlos, the Spanish-educated grandson of Alfonso XIII. In 1969 Juan Carlos swore loyalty to Franco and the Movimiento Nacional. He allowed cautious reforms by Franco's last prime minister, Carlos Arias Navarro, which provoked violent opposition from right-wing extremists.

Franco finally died on 20 November 1975.

Democratic Spain

The Transition

Juan Carlos I, aged 37, took the throne two days after Franco died. The new king's links with the dictator inspired little confidence in a Spain now clamouring for democracy, but Juan Carlos had kept his cards close to his chest. In July 1976 he appointed Adolfo Suárez, a 43-year-old former Franco apparatchik with film-star looks, as prime minister. To general surprise, Suárez got the Cortes to approve a new, two-chamber parliamentary system, and in 1977 political parties, trade unions and strikes were all legalised. Franco's Movimiento Nacional was abolished.

Suárez's centrist party, the Unión de Centro Democrático (UCD; Central Democratic Union), won nearly half the seats in the new Cortes in 1977. A new constitution in 1978 made Spain a parliamentary monarchy with no official religion. In response to the fever for local autonomy, by 1983 the country was divided into 17 'autonomous communities' with their own regional governments controlling a range of policy areas. Personal and social life enjoyed a rapid liberation after Franco. Contraceptives, homosexuality and divorce were legalised, and the Madrid

Paul Preston's *Franco* is the big biography of one of history's little dictators – and it has very little to say in the man's favour. Conspiracy theorists will love Peter Day's *Franco's Friends: How British Intelligence Helped Bring Franco to Power in Spain.*

1978	1981	1982–96	1986
A new constitution, overwhelmingly approved by referendum, establishes Spain as a parliamentary democracy with no official religion and the monarch as official head of state.	On 23 February a group of armed Guardia Civil led by Antonio Tejero attempt a coup by occupying the parliament building. The king denounces them on national TV; the coup collapses.	Spain is governed by the centre-left Partido Socialista Obrero Español (PSOE; Spanish Socialist Workers' Party). The country experiences an economic boom but the government becomes associated with scandals and corruption.	Spain joins the European Community (now the EU). Along with its membership of NATO since 1982, this is a turning point in the country's post-Franco international acceptance.

LA MOVIDA

After the long, dark years of dictatorship and conservative Catholicism, Spaniards, especially those in Madrid, emerged onto the streets with all the zeal of ex-convent schoolgirls. Nothing was taboo in a phenomenon known as '*la movida*' (the scene) or '*la movida madrileña*' (the Madrid scene) as young *madrileños* discovered the '60s, '70s and early '80s all at once. Drinking, drugs and sex suddenly were OK. All-night partying was the norm, drug taking in public was not a criminal offence (that changed in Madrid in 1992) and Madrid in particular howled. All across Madrid and other major cities, summer terraces roared to the chattering, drinking, carousing crowds and young people from all over Europe (not to mention cultural icons such as Andy Warhol) flocked here to take part in the revelry.

What was remarkable about *la movida* in Madrid is that it was presided over by Enrique Tierno Galván, an ageing former university professor who had been a leading opposition figure under Franco and was affectionately known throughout Spain as 'the old teacher'. A socialist, he became mayor in 1979 and, for many, launched *la movida* by telling a public gathering '*a colocarse y ponerse al loro*', which loosely translates as 'get stoned and do what's cool'. Unsurprisingly he was Madrid's most popular mayor ever and when he died in 1986, a million *madrileños* turned out for his funeral.

But *la movida* was not just about rediscovering the Spanish art of *salir de copas* (going out for a drink). It was also accompanied by an explosion of creativity among the country's musicians, designers and film-makers keen to shake off the shackles of the repressive Franco years.The most famous of these was film director Pedro Almodóvar. Still one of Europe's most creative directors, his riotously colourful films captured the spirit of *la movida*, featuring larger-than-life characters who pushed the limits of sex and drugs. Although his later films became internationally renowned, his first films, *Pepi, Luci, Bom y Otras Chicas del Montón* (Pepi, Luci, Bom and the Other Girls; 1980) and *Laberinto de Pasiones* (Labyrinth of Passion; 1982) are where the spirit of the movement really comes alive. When he wasn't making films, Almodóvar immersed himself in the spirit of *la movida*, doing drag acts in smoky bars that people-in-the-know would frequent.

Other important cultural figures to emerge from *la movida* include actor Antonio Banderas, fashion designer Agatha Ruiz de la Prada, and film director Fernando Trueba.

party and arts scene known as *la movida madrileña* formed the epicentre of a newly unleashed hedonism that still reverberates through Spanish life.

The Suárez government granted a general amnesty for deeds committed in the civil war and under the Franco dictatorship. There were no truth commissions or trials for the perpetrators of atrocities. For the next three decades, Spain cast barely a backward glance.

1992	1996	11 March 2004	14 March 2004
Barcelona holds the Olympic Games, putting Spain in the spotlight and highlighting the country's progress since 1975. Madrid is European Capital of Culture and Seville hosts a world expo.	Disaffection with PSOE sleaze gives the centre-right Partido Popular (PP), led by José María Aznar, a general election victory at the start of a decade of sustained economic growth.	A terrorist bombing kills 191 people on 10 Madrid commuter trains. The following day, an estimated 11 million people take to the streets across Spain.	The PSOE led by José Luis Rodríguez Zapatero sweeps to power and ushers in eight years of Socialist rule, characterised by sweeping changes to social legislation.

A Maturing Democracy

The main left-of-centre party, the Partido Socialista Obrero Español (PSOE; Spanish Socialist Workers' Party), led by a charismatic young lawyer from Seville, Felipe González, came second in the 1977 election and then won power with a big majority in 1982. González was to be prime minister for 14 years. The PSOE's young and educated leadership came from the generation that had opened the cracks in the Franco regime in the late 1960s and early 1970s. Unemployment rose from 16% to 22% by 1986. But that same year, Spain joined the European Community (now the EU), bringing on a five-year economic boom. The middle class grew ever bigger, the PSOE established a national health system and improved public education, and Spain's women streamed into higher education and jobs.

Spaniards got the fright of their lives in February 1981 when a pistol-brandishing, low-ranking Guardia Civil (Civil Guard) officer, Antonio Tejero Molina, marched into the Cortes in Madrid with an armed detachment and held parliament captive for 24 hours. Throughout a day of high drama the country held its breath. With the nation glued to their TV sets, King Juan Carlos I made a live broadcast denouncing Tejero and calling on the soldiers to return to their barracks. The coup fizzled out.

In 1992 – the 500th anniversary of the fall of Granada and Columbus' first voyage to the Americas – Spain celebrated its arrival in the modern world by staging the Barcelona Olympics and the Expo 92 world fair in Seville. But the economy was in a slump and the PSOE was mired in scandals. It came as no surprise when the PSOE lost the 1996 general election.

The party that won the 1996 election was the centre-right Partido Popular (PP; People's Party), led by José María Aznar, a former tax inspector from Castilla y León. Aznar promised to make politics dull, and he did, but he presided over eight years of solid economic progress, winning the 2000 election as well. The PP cut public investment and sold off state enterprises and liberalised sectors, such as telecommunications; during the Aznar years Spain's economy grew a lot faster than the EU average, while unemployment fell dramatically.

Perhaps just as importantly, Spain's changes of government were orderly, electoral affairs, the economic graphs moved in a general upward direction and the improvement in ordinary people's lives was steady.

Troubled Times

On 11 March 2004, Madrid was rocked by 10 bombs on four rush-hour commuter trains heading into the capital's Atocha station. When the dust cleared, 191 people had died and 1755 were wounded, many of

October 2008	November 2011	2012	September 2013
Spain's unemployment rate soars from less than 6% to 12.3% in a single month. Spain's finance minister admits that Spain has entered 'its deepest recession in half a century'.	The conservative Partido Popular, led by Mariano Rajoy (who had been defeated in 2004 and 2008), sweeps to power in national elections, ending eight years of Socialist Party rule.	Spain's deep economic crisis continues with unemployment rising above 25% of the workforce, with more than 50% of young Spaniards out of work.	The Spanish economy officially climbs out of recession but unemployment remains stubbornly high.

them seriously. It was the biggest such terror attack in the nation's history.

In a stunning reversal of pre-poll predictions, the PP, who insisted that ETA was responsible despite overwhelming evidence to the contrary, was defeated by the PSOE in elections three days after the attack.

Modern Spain Reading

....

Ghosts of Spain by Giles Tremlett

....

The New Spaniards by John Hooper

....

Juan Carlos: Steering Spain from Dictatorship to Democracy by Paul Preston

....

Roads to Santiago: Detours & Riddles in the Land and History of Spain by Cees Nooteboom

....

Driving over Lemons by Chris Stewart

The new socialist government of José Luis Rodríguez Zapatero gave Spain a makeover by introducing a raft of liberalising social reforms. Gay marriage was legalised, Spain's arcane divorce laws were overhauled, almost a million illegal immigrants were granted residence, and a law seeking to apportion blame for the crimes of the Civil War and Franco dictatorship entered the statute books. Although Spain's powerful Catholic Church cried foul over many of the reforms, the changes played well with most Spaniards. Spain's economy was booming, the envy of Europe.

And then it all fell apart.

Spain's economy went into freefall in late 2008 and remains in desperate straits. Zapatero's government waited painfully long to recognise that a crisis was looming and was replaced, in November 2011, with a right-of-centre one promoting a deep austerity drive that threatens the generous welfare state on which Spaniards have come to depend. The conservative government also turned back the liberalising reforms of the socialists, introducing some of Europe's strictest anti-abortion laws and restoring the role of the Catholic Church in education.

That the country remains firmly democratic, however, suggests that modern Spaniards have, for the first time in Spain's tumultuous history, found means other than war for resolving the many differences that divide them. And perhaps that is the strongest sign of just how far Spain has come.

June 2014 〉	November 2014 〉	May 2015 〉	November 2015 〉
After a series of scandals that envelop the Spanish royal family, King Juan Carlos, who had reigned since 1975, abdicates and his son begins his reign as Felipe VI.	A referendum not recognised by the Spanish state or Spain's Constitutional Court votes in favour of independence for the restive region of Catalonia.	A political earthquake sweeps the country as new parties Podemos, Ciudadanos and others make significant gains in regional and municipal elections.	The ruling Partido Popular government loses its majority in regional elections, with strong gains for the left-wing Podemos party and centrist Ciudadanos. A new coalition government is formed.

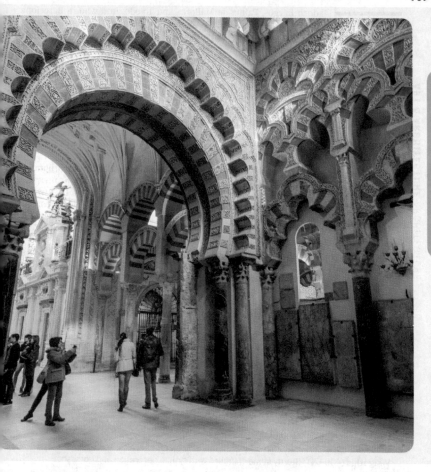

Art & Architecture

Spain's artistic and architectural landscapes are some of the richest of their kind in Europe. A rich heritage of painters – think Goya and Velázquez, Picasso and Dalí – down through the ages is an enduring hallmark of Spain's cultural scene, while the country's architecture tells a beguiling story that takes in the cinematic sweep of its history, from glorious Moorish creations in Andalucía and the singular imagination of Gaudí to soaring cathedrals and temples to contemporary creativity.

Architecture

You can almost see centurions marching beneath the great Roman aqueduct in Segovia, while the Alhambra similarly conjures up Spain's Islamic era. Elsewhere, the Middle Ages comes alive amid the Monasterio de Santo Domingo de Silos' Romanesque cloisters, castles dot the countryside from Catalonia to Castilla, and great Gothic cathedrals

Above Mezquita (p641), Córdoba

Only one unruly part of northern Spain, in what is now Asturias, was never conquered by the Muslims. During the 9th century a unique building style emerged there, exaggerating Visigothic styles. Oviedo's Palacio de Santa María del Naranco, for instance, has dramatically elongated proportions, delicate relief carvings and tall, thin arches.

adorn Burgos, Palma de Mallorca and Toledo. And who in Barcelona isn't carried away by Gaudí's Modernista fantasies? Welcome to Spain, one of Europe's most intriguing architectural stories.

The Introduction of Islam

In 784, with Córdoba well established as the new capital of the western end of the Umayyad Empire, Syrian architects set to work on the grand Mezquita (p641), conjuring up their homeland with details that echo the Umayyad Mosque in Damascus, such as delicate horseshoe arches and exquisite decorative tiles with floral motifs. But the building's most distinctive feature – more than 500 columns that crowd the interior of the mosque – was repurposed from Roman and Visigothic ruins.

In the centuries that followed, Moorish architecture incorporated trends from all over the Islamic empire. The technique of intricately carved stucco detailing was developed in 9th-century Iraq, while *muqarnas* (honeycomb) vaulting arrived via Egypt in the 10th century. Square minarets, such as the Giralda (p575) in Seville (now a church tower), came with the Almohad invasion from Morocco in the 12th century.

The finest remnants of the Islamic era are in Andalucía, although the Aljafería (p365) in Zaragoza is a beautiful exception. Perhaps the most magnificent creation is the core of Granada's Alhambra (p657), the Palacios Nazaríes (Nasrid Palaces). From the 13th to the 15th century, architects reached new heights of elegance, creating a study in balance between inside and outside, light and shade, spareness and intricate decoration. Eschewing innovation, the Alhambra refined welltried forms, as if in an attempt to freeze time and halt the collapse of Moorish power, which, at the time, was steadily eroding across the peninsula.

SPANISH ARCHITECTURE: THE BASICS

Roman (210 BC – AD 409) Bridges, waterworks, walls, whole cities that inspired later traditions.

Visigothic (409–711) Sturdy stone churches with simple decoration and horseshoe arches.

Moorish (711–1492) Horseshoe arches, square minarets, intricate geometric design.

Mudéjar (1100–1700) Post-Reconquista work by Muslims adapting the Moorish tradition of decoration to more common materials.

Romanesque (1100–1300) Spare decoration and proportions based on Byzantine churches.

Gothic (1200–1600) Flying buttresses enable ceilings to soar, and arches become pointy to match.

Plateresque (1400–1600) A dazzling ornate style of relief carving on facades.

Churrigueresque (1650–1750) Spain's special twist on baroque with spiral columns and gold-leaf everything.

Modernisme (1888–1911) The Spanish version of art nouveau took a brilliant turn in Barcelona.

Contemporary (1975–present) Previously unimaginable directions since the death of Franco.

Albarracín (p396), Aragón

Romanesque & Gothic

As the tide turned against the Muslims, the Romanesque style was sweeping medieval Europe, taking root in Spain in part because it was the aesthetic opposite of Islamic fashions – architect and art historian Josep Puig i Cadafalch posited that each Romanesque detail was a systematic riposte to an Islamic one. These buildings were spare, angular and heavy, inspired by the proportions of classical structures. Many of these Romanesque structures were not-so-subtle statements about the success of the Reconquista.

Romanesque structures had perfectly semicircular arches – none of the stylised horseshoe look that had come before. In churches, this was expressed in a semicylindrical apse (or, in many cases, triple apse), a shape previously found in Byzantine churches. The round arch also graced doorways, windows, cloisters and naves. Entrances supported stacks of concentric arches – all the more eye-catching because they were often the only really decorative detail. Some great, lesser-known examples include the Iglesia de San Martín (p176) in Frómista, and Sant Climent de Taüll (p340), one of many fine examples in the Catalan Pyrenees. Later, during the 12th century, Spanish architects began to modify these semicircles, edging towards the Gothic style, as they added pointed arches and ribbed vaults. The Monasterio de la Oliva in Navarra was among the first to show such features, and cathedrals in Ávila (p142), Sigüenza (p228) and Tarragona (p355) all display at least some transitional elements.

The trend elsewhere in Europe towards towering cathedrals made possible by the newfangled flying buttresses caught on in Spain by the 13th century, when the cathedrals at Burgos (p186), León (p178) and

The Camino de Santiago is also an architecture pilgrimage route, for such Romanesque beauties as the Monasterio de Santo Domingo de Silos, the smaller cloister in the Monasterio de las Huelgas in Burgos, the restored Iglesia de San Martín in Frómista and the cathedral itself in Santiago de Compostela.

Catedral, Toledo (p205)

Toledo (p205) were built. Some changes were subtle, such as placing choir stalls in the centre of the nave, but one was unmissable: the towering, decorative *retablo* (altarpiece) that graced the new churches. Spanish Gothic architects also devised the star vault, a method of distributing weight with ribbed vaults projecting out from a central point.

Many great buildings were begun aret the height of Romanesque fashion but not completed until long after the Gothic style had gained the upper hand. The cathedral in Burgos, for instance, was begun in 1221 as a relatively sober construction, but its 15th-century spires are a product of German-inspired late-Gothic imagination. Mudéjar influences also made themselves felt. Toledo boasts many gloriously original buildings with a Gothic-Mudéjar flair, as does part of Aragón, where the fanciful brick structures have been declared a Unesco World Heritage site.

The Catalan approach to the Gothic was more sober, bereft of pinnacles. Architects developed incredibly broad, unsupported vaults without the use of flying buttresses. In contrast, the Isabelline Gothic look, inspired by the Catholic queen, reflects her fondness of Islamic exotica and heraldic imagery. It's on display in Toledo's San Juan de los Reyes (p207) and the Capilla Real (p666) in Granada, where she and Fernando are buried.

Most of the innumerable castles scattered across the country also went up in Gothic times – an extraordinary example is the sumptuous castle at Coca (p164), not far from Segovia. In Barcelona, some marvellous civil Gothic architecture can be admired, including the once-mighty shipyards that are now home to the Museu Marítim (p249).

The Gothic fascination lasted into the 16th century, when there was a revival of pure Gothic, perhaps best exemplified in the new cathedral in Salamanca (p147), although the Segovia cathedral was about the last, and possibly most pure, Gothic structure raised in Spain.

Modernisme & Art Deco

At the end of the 19th century, Barcelona's prosperity unleashed one of the most imaginative periods in Spanish architecture. The architects at work here, who drew on prevailing art-nouveau trends as well as earlier Spanish styles, came to be called the Modernistas. Chief among them, Antoni Gaudí sprinkled Barcelona with jewels of his singular imagination. They range from his immense, unfinished Sagrada Família (p251) to the simply weird Casa Batlló (p256) and the only slightly more sober La Pedrera (p258). Gaudí's structural approach owed much to the austere era of Catalan Gothic, which inspired his own inventive work with parabolic arches. The works of two other Catalan architects, Lluís Domènech i Montaner and Josep Puig i Cadafalch, are also Barcelona landmarks.

While Barcelona went all wavy, Madrid embraced the rigid glamour of art deco. This global style arrived in Spain just as Madrid's Gran Vía (p86) was laid out in the 1920s. One of the more overwhelming caprices from that era is the Palacio de Comunicaciones on Plaza de la Cibeles (p95).

The 1936–39 Civil War and more than three decades of dictatorship brought such frivolities to an abrupt end.

Art

Spain has an artistic legacy that rivals anything found elsewhere in Europe. In centuries past, this impressive portfolio (dominated by Goya and Velázquez in particular) owed much to the patronage of Spanish kings who lavished money upon the great painters of the day. In the 20th century, however, it was the relentless creativity of artists such as Pablo Picasso, Salvador Dalí and Joan Miró, all of whom thumbed their noses at artistic convention, who became the true masters.

The Golden Century – Velázquez & Friends

The star of the 17th-century art scene, which became known as Spain's artistic Golden Age, was the genius court painter, Diego Rodríguez de Silva Velázquez (1599–1660). Born in Seville, Velázquez later moved to Madrid as court painter and composed scenes (landscapes, royal portraits, religious subjects, snapshots of everyday life) that owe their vitality not only to his photographic eye for light, contrast and the details of royal finery, but also to a compulsive interest in the humanity of his subjects so that they seem to breathe on the canvas. With Velázquez, any trace of the idealised stiffness that characterised the previous century's spiritless mannerism fell by the wayside. His masterpieces include *Las meninas* (Maids of Honour) and *La rendición de Breda* (Surrender of Breda), both in the Museo del Prado (p87).

Francisco de Zurbarán (1598–1664), a friend and contemporary of Velázquez, ended his life in poverty in Madrid and it was only after his death that he received the acclaim that his masterpieces deserved. He is best remembered for the startling clarity and light in his portraits of monks, a series of which hangs in the Real Academia de Bellas Artes de San Fernando (p83), with other works in the Museo del Prado (p87).

Other masters of the era whose works hang in the Museo del Prado include José (Jusepe) de Ribera (1591–1652), who was influenced by

ART & ARCHITECTURE   **ART**

Best Baroque

Monasterio de Nuestra Señora de la Asunción (Monasterio de la Cartuja), Granada

Plaza Mayor, Salamanca

Cathedral facade, Santiago de Compostela

Catedral de Santa María, Murcia

Real Academia de Bellas Artes de San Fernando, Madrid

Altarpiece, Catedral de Toledo

Robert Hughes' *Barcelona* is a thorough, erudite history of the city, with an emphasis on architecture. The Gaudí chapters provide special insight into the designer's surprisingly conservative outlook.

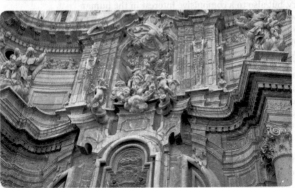

Above Puente Romano (p645) and Mezquita (p641), Córdoba

Left Catedral de Santa María (p766), Murcia

INJUS/SHUTTERSTOCK ©

Plaza Mayor (p147), Salamanca

Caravaggio and produced fine chiaroscuro works, and Bartolomé Esteban Murillo (1618–82).

Goya & the 19th Century

There was nothing in the provincial upbringing of Francisco José de Goya y Lucientes (1746–1828), who was born in a tiny village in Aragón, to suggest that he would become one of the towering figures of European art. Goya began his career as a cartoonist in the Real Fábrica de Tapices (Royal Tapestry Workshop) in Madrid. Illness in 1792 left him deaf; many critics speculate that his condition was largely responsible for his wild, often merciless style that would become increasingly unshackled from convention. By 1799 Goya was appointed Carlos IV's court painter.

Several distinct series and individual paintings mark his progress. In the last years of the 18th century he painted enigmatic masterpieces, such as *La maja vestida* (The Young Lady Dressed) and *La maja desnuda* (The Young Lady Undressed), identical portraits but for the lack of clothes in the latter. The Inquisition was not amused by the artworks, which it covered up. Nowadays all is bared in Madrid's Museo del Prado.

The arrival of the French and the war in 1808 had a profound impact on Goya. Unforgiving portrayals of the brutality of war are *El dos de mayo* (The Second of May) and, more dramatically, *El tres de mayo* (The Third of May). The latter depicts the execution of Madrid rebels by French troops.

Goya spent the last years of his life in voluntary exile in France, where he continued to paint until his death.

Velázquez so much wanted to be made a Knight of Santiago that in *Las Meninas* he cheekily portrayed himself with the cross of Santiago on his vest, long before his wish was finally fulfilled.

WHERE TO SEE GOYA

Reach into the tortured mind of one of Spain's greatest artists with the help of Robert Hughes' riveting work *Goya*. And to see what all of the fuss is about, Madrid's **Museo del Prado** (p87) has the richest collection of Goyas, but the city's **Real Academia de Bellas Artes de San Fernando** (p83) is also good, while the **Ermita de San Antonio de la Florida** (p100) has fabulous ceiling frescoes painted by Goya. Beyond Madrid, Zaragoza's **Museo Goya – Colección Ibercaja** (p365) has an outstanding collection of Goya etchings, while Fuendetodos, the Aragonese village south of Zaragoza where Goya was born, has the **Casa Natal de Goya** (p370) and the **Museo del Grabado de Goya** (p371).

Goya saved his most confronting paintings for the end. After he retired to the Quinta del Sordo (Deaf Man's House) in Madrid, he created his nightmarish Pinturas negras (Black Paintings), which now hang in Madrid's Museo del Prado (p87). *The Saturno devorando a su hijo* (Saturn Devouring His Son) captures the essence of Goya's genius, and *La romería de San Isidro* (The Pilgrimage to San Isidro) and *El akelarre* (*El gran cabrón*; The Great He-Goat) are profoundly unsettling. The former evokes a writhing mass of tortured humanity, while the latter two are dominated by the compelling individual faces of the condemned souls of Goya's creation.

Picasso, Dalí & Miró

In the early years of the 20th century, the genius of the mischievous *malagueño* (Málaga native), Pablo Ruiz Picasso (1881–1973), came like a thunderclap. A child when he moved with his family to Barcelona, Picasso was formed in an atmosphere laden with the avant-garde freedom of Modernisme.

Picasso must have been one of the most restless artists of all time. His work underwent repeated revolutions as he passed from one creative phase to another. From his gloomy Blue Period, through the brighter Pink Period and on to cubism – in which he was accompanied by Madrid's Juan Gris (1887–1927) – Picasso was nothing if not surprising. Cubism, his best-known form, was inspired by Picasso's fascination with primitivism, primarily African masks and early Iberian sculpture. This highly complex form reached its high point in *Guernica*, which hangs in Madrid's Centro de Arte Reina Sofía (p92). Picasso consistently cranked out paintings, sculptures, ceramics and etchings until the day he died. A good selection of his early work can be viewed in Barcelona's Museu Picasso (p249), while the Museo Picasso Málaga (p685) has more than 200 Picasso works. The remaining works are scattered around different galleries.

Check out www. arteespana.com, an interesting website that covers broad swaths of Spanish art history. You can buy art books or even models of Spanish monuments.

Separated from Picasso by barely a generation, two other artists reinforced the Catalan contingent in the vanguard of 20th-century art: Dalí and Miró. Although he started off dabbling in cubism, Salvador Dalí (1904–89) became more readily identified with the surrealists. This complex character's 'hand-painted dream photographs', as he called them, are virtuoso executions brimming with fine detail and nightmare images dragged up from a feverish and Freud-fed imagination. Preoccupied with Picasso's fame, Dalí built himself a reputation as an outrageous showman and shameless self-promoter. The single best display of his work can be seen at the Teatre-Museu Dalí (p322) in Figueres, but you'll also find important works in the Museu

Centro de Arte Reina Sofía (p92), Madrid

de Cadaqués (p320) in Cadaqués, the Casa Museu Dalí (p320) in Portlligat and Madrid's Centro de Arte Reina Sofía (p92).

Slower to find his feet, Barcelona-born Joan Miró (1893–1983) developed a joyous and almost childlike style that earned him the epithet 'the most surrealist of us all' from the French writer André Breton. His later period is his best known, characterised by the simple use of bright colours and forms in combinations of symbols that represented women, birds (the link between earth and the heavens) and stars (the unattainable heavenly world, source of imagination). The Fundació Joan Miró (p265) in Barcelona and the Fundació Pilar i Joan Miró in Palma de Mallorca are the pick of the places to see his work, with some further examples in Madrid's Centro de Arte Reina Sofía.

People & Culture

The iconic forms of entertainment and public expressions of culture Spanish-style capture the powerful, soul-stirring passions of a nation. Flamenco is one of the world's most recognisable musical forms, an uplifting combination of sorrow and joy given extraordinary musical form, while the controversial and quintessentially Spanish realm of bullfighting may leave you angry or spellbound, but never indifferent. And then there's football, that near-universal obsession of the country's people. Put them all together and you'll find yourself looking through a window into the Spanish soul.

Flamenco

El Mundo Flamenco (www.elmundoflamenco.co.uk) is an online shop that stocks everything and anything flamenco-based.

Flamenco's passion is clear to anyone who has heard its melancholic strains in the background of a crowded Spanish bar or during an uplifting live performance. And yet, flamenco can at times seem like an impenetrable world. If you're lucky, you'll experience that single uplifting moment when flamenco's raw passion suddenly transports you to another place (known as *duende*), where joy and sorrow threaten to overwhelm you. If you do, you'll quickly become one of flamenco's lifelong devotees.

The Birth of Flamenco

Flamenco's origins have been lost to time. Some have suggested that it derives from Byzantine chants used in Visigothic churches. But most musical historians agree that it probably dates back to a fusion of songs brought to Spain by the Roma people, with music and verses from North Africa crossing into medieval Muslim Andalucía.

Flamenco as we now know it first took recognisable form in the 18th and early 19th centuries among Roma people in the lower Guadalquivir valley in western Andalucía. The Seville, Jerez de la Frontera and Cádiz axis is still considered flamenco's heartland and it's here, purists believe, that you'll encounter the most authentic flamenco experience.

Flamenco – The Essential Elements

Seville's Museo del Baile Flamenco (p587) trawls through flamencos past and present and, with its frequent flamenco classes, gives you the chance to perfect your *sevillana*. Also excellent is the Centro Andaluz de Flamenco (p622) in Jerez de la Frontera.

A flamenco singer is known as a *cantaor* (male) or *cantaora* (female); a dancer is a *bailaor* or *bailaora*. Most of the songs and dances are performed to a rush of guitar from the *tocaor* or *tocaora*. Percussion is provided by tapping feet, clapping hands, and sometimes castanets.

Flamenco *coplas* (songs) come in many different types, from the anguished *soleá* or the intensely despairing *siguiriya* to the livelier *alegría* or the upbeat *bulería*. The first flamenco was *cante jondo* (deep song), an anguished instrument of expression for a group on the margins of society. *Jondura* (depth) is still the essence of pure flamenco.

The traditional flamenco costume – shawl, fan and long, frilly *bata de cola* (tail gown) for women, and flat Cordoban hats and tight black trousers for men – dates from Andalucían fashions in the late 19th century.

Flamenco Legends

The great singers of the 19th and early 20th centuries were Silverio Franconetti and La Niña de los Peines, from Seville, and Antonio Chacón and

FLAMENCO RESOURCES

Flama (www.guiaflama.com) Good for upcoming live concerts and background information.

De Flamenco (www.deflamenco.com) Everything from flamenco venues and courses to flamenco products for sale.

Duende: A Journey into the Heart of Flamenco (Jason Webster) The author's gripping journey through the underbelly of flamenco.

Camarón (2005) A terrific biopic of El Camarón de la Isla, directed by Jaime Chávarri.

Bodas de sangre (Blood Wedding; 1981) and **Flamenco** (1995) These two Carlos Saura films are flamenco classics; the former is a film version of Federico García Lorca's dramatic play of the same name.

Centro Andaluz de Flamenco (www.juntadeandalucia.es/cultura/centroandaluz flamenco) The website of the Andalucían Centre for Flamenco in Jerez de la Frontera.

Manuel Torre, from Jerez de la Frontera. Torre's singing, legend has it, could drive people to rip their shirts open and upturn tables. The dynamic dancing and wild lifestyle of Carmen Amaya (1913–63), from Barcelona, made her the Roma dance legend of all time. Her long-time partner Sabicas was the father of the modern solo flamenco guitar, inventing a host of now-indispensable techniques.

After a trough in the mid-20th century, when it seemed that the *tablaos* (touristy flamenco shows emphasising the sexy and the jolly) were in danger of taking over, *flamenco puro* got a new lease of life in the 1970s through singers such as Terremoto, La Paquera, Enrique Morente, Chano Lobato and, above all, El Camarón de la Isla (whose real name was José Monge Cruz) from San Fernando near Cádiz.

Some say that Madrid-born Diego El Cigala (b 1968) is El Camarón's successor. This powerful singer launched onto the big stage with the extraordinary *Lágrimas negras* (2003), a wonderful collaboration with Cuban virtuoso Bebo Valdés that mixes flamenco with Cuban influences, and its follow-up, *Dos Lagrimas* (2008). Other fine Diego El Cigala albums include *Picasso en mis Ojos* (2005), *Cigala&Tango* (2010) and *Romance de la Luna Tucumana* (2013).

Another singer whose fame endures is Enrique Morente (1942–2010), referred to by one Madrid paper as 'the last bohemian'. While careful not to alienate flamenco purists, Morente, through his numerous collaborations across genres, helped lay the foundations for Nuevo Flamenco and Fusion. His untimely death in 2010 was mourned by a generation of flamenco aficionados.

Paco de Lucía (1947–2014), from Algeciras, was the doyen of flamenco guitarists. So gifted was he that by the time he was 14, his teachers admitted that they had nothing left to teach him, and for many in the flamenco world, he is the personification of *duende*, that indefinable capacity to transmit the power and passion of flamenco. From 1964 Paco de Lucía teamed up with *madrileño* guitarist Ricardo Modrego, but began, in 1968, flamenco's most exciting partnership with his friend El Camarón de la Isla (1950–92); together they recorded nine classic albums. De Lucía would go on to transform the flamenco guitar into an instrument of solo expression with new techniques, scales, melodies and harmonies that have gone far beyond traditional limits. Dozens of albums – including anthologies and live performances – showcase the work of this peerless maestro.

Although existing somewhat in Paco de Lucía's shadow, other guitar maestros include Tomatito (b 1958), who also accompanied El Camarón

Flamenco Playlist

Pata Negra, Blues de la frontera (1987)

El Camarón de la Isla, Una leyenda flamenca (1992)

Paco de Lucía, Antología (1995)

Chambao, Flamenco chill (2002)

Diego El Cigala & Bebo Valdés, Lágrimas Negras (2003)

Paco de Lucía, Cositas Buenas (2004)

Enrique Morente, Sueña la Alhambra (2005)

Diego El Cigala, Romance de la luna tucumana (2013)

de la Isla, and members of the Montoya family (some of whom are better known by the sobriquet of Los Habichuela), especially Juan (b 1933) and Pepe (b 1944).

Many of the most talented flamenco stars have spent time in prison, and each year Spain's penitentiary system holds *El Concurso de Cante Flamenco del Sistema Penitenciario* (The Prison Flamenco Competition).

Flamenco Today

Rarely has flamenco been as popular as it is today, and never so innovative.

Universally acclaimed is José Mercé, from Jerez, Estrella Morente from Granada (Enrique Morente's daughter and internationally best known for being the 'voice' behind the 2006 film *Volver)* and Miguel Poveda from Barcelona. La Tana from Seville are young singers steadily carving out niches in the first rank of performers.

Dance, always the readiest of flamenco arts to cross boundaries, has reached its most adventurous in the person of Joaquin Cortés, born in Córdoba in 1969. Cortés fuses flamenco with contemporary dance, ballet and jazz in spectacular shows with music at rock-concert amplification.

Among guitarists, listen out for Manolo Sanlúcar from Cádiz and Tomatito from Almería, as well as Vicente Amigo from Córdoba and Moraíto Chico from Jerez, who both accompany today's top singers.

Seeing Flamenco

The intensity and spontaneity of flamenco have never translated well onto CDs or studio recordings. Instead, to ignite the goosebumps and inspire the powerful emotional spirit known to aficionados as '*duende*', you have to be there.

Flamenco is easiest to catch in Seville, Jerez de la Frontera, Granada and Madrid. Seeing flamenco can be expensive – at the *tablaos* (restaurants where flamenco is performed) expect to pay €25 to €35 just to see the show. The admission price usually includes your first drink, but you pay extra for meals (up to €50 per person) that aren't always worth the money. For that reason, we often suggest you eat elsewhere and simply pay for the show (after having bought tickets in advance), albeit on the understanding that you won't have a front-row seat. The other important thing to remember is that most of these shows are geared towards tourists. That's not to say that the quality isn't often top-notch – on the contrary, often it's magnificent, spine-tingling stuff – it's just that they sometimes lack the genuine, raw emotion of real flamenco.

The best places for live performances are *peñas* (clubs where flamenco fans band together). The atmosphere in such places is authentic and at times very intimate, proof that flamenco feeds off an audience that knows its flamenco. Most Andalucían towns have dozens of *peñas*, and

THE SHRIMP FROM THE ISLAND

Possibly the most important flamenco singer of all time, José Monge Cruz (aka El Camarón de la Isla; Shrimp of the Island) did more to popularise flamenco in the last half of the 20th century than anyone else. Born to Roma parents, Camarón started his career at a young age by singing in local bars. Eventually he met that great of flamenco, guitarist Paco de Lucía, with whom he recorded nine much-praised albums between 1969 and 1977. Later in his career Camarón worked with one of Paco's students, Tomatito.

Camarón was an intense introvert and hated publicity, but so extraordinary was his talent that publicity was to hound him everywhere he went and, so many say, it was eventually to lead him to an early grave in the best live-fast, die-young rock-star fashion. He was idolised for his voice by flamenco fans across the world, and it was his fellow Roma who really elevated him almost to the status of a god.

He died of lung cancer in 1992 at the age of just 42. It's estimated that more than 100,000 people attended his funeral. The Shrimp's best recordings include *La leyenda del tiempo, Soy gitano* and *Una leyenda flamenca*.

FLAMENCO FESTIVALS

Flamenco festivals attract the best artists in the genre. The following are some of the best flamenco festivals:

Festival de Jerez (p624), Jerez de la Frontera

Suma Flamenca (p102), Madrid

Festival de la Guitarra de Córdoba (p646), Córdoba

Bienal de Flamenco (p592), Seville

many tourist offices – especially those in Seville, Jerez de la Frontera and Cádiz – have lists of those that are open to visitors.

Festivals are another place to see fabulous live flamenco.

Football

National Team

Spanish football fans had almost given up on their team ever winning anything. All of that changed when Spain's national team won the European Championships against Germany in 2008, having last won in 1964. Two years later, the national team won their first World Cup, against the Netherlands in 2010.

When La Selección successfully defended their European Championship title in 2012, Spain confirmed its reputation as the best team in the world. But the clock was ticking on the finest generation of footballers the country had ever produced: at the 2014 World Cup in Brazil, Spain was thrashed 5-1 by the Netherlands and were knocked out in the first round.

Even so, they qualified with ease for the 2016 European Championships in France and occupied a highly respectable third place in FIFA's World Rankings at the beginning of 2016.

La Liga

Spain's La Liga is one of the world's best football leagues. Unlike in the UK and elsewhere, Spanish football stadiums are extraordinarily one-sided places, with very few travelling fans, but the atmosphere can be electric.

Real Madrid and FC Barcelona have something approaching a monopoly on the silverware: between them they have carried off the league title 55 times – Real Madrid has won 32 times, Barcelona 23. In recent times Barca has been very much on top, winning La Liga in 2009, 2010, 2011, 2013 and 2015.

Real Madrid remains the most successful club in European history, having won the European Cup (which later became the UEFA Champions League) a record 10 times, including most recently in 2014. Barcelona has won the title five times.

Bullfighting

An epic drama of blood and sand or a cruel blood 'sport' that has no place in modern Europe? This most enduring and controversial of Spanish traditions is all this and more: for some, an ancient ritual and compelling theatre; for others, a violent, gory spectacle that sees 40,000 bulls killed in around 17,000 fights every year in Spain. Ernest Hemingway – a bullfighting fan – described it as a 'wonderful nightmare'.

Whether or not you watch a bullfight is very much a personal decision. Aficionados say the bull is better off dying at the hands of a matador than in the *matadero* (abattoir), but detractors say the whole thing is little short of torturing the animal to death. Those who do attend a bullfight

Books about Football

Spain: The Inside Story of La Roja's Historic Treble (2013) by Graham Hunter

White Storm: The Story of Real Madrid (2003) by Phil Ball

Morbo: The Story of Spanish Football (2011) by Phil Ball

Barca: A People's Passion (2016 edition) by Jimmy Burns

Fear and Loathing in La Liga: Barcelona vs Real Madrid (2014) by Sid Lowe

PEOPLE & CULTURE BULLFIGHTING

might glean some insight into the traditions and thinking behind this most controversial of events, but many travellers will weigh the arguments for and against and opt not to witness the spectacle at all.

The Basics

The matador (more often called the *torero* in Spanish) is the star of the team. Adorned in his glittering *traje de luces* (suit of lights), it is his fancy footwork, skill and bravery before the bull that has the crowd in raptures or in rage, depending on his (or very occasionally her) performance. A complex series of events takes place in each clash, which can last from about 20 to 30 minutes (there are usually six fights in a program). *Peones* (the matador's 'footmen', whose job it is to test the strength of the bull) dart about with grand capes in front of the bull; horseback *picadores* (horsemen) drive lances into the bull's withers; and *banderilleros* (flagmen) charge headlong at the bull in an attempt to stab its neck. Finally, the matador kills the bull, unless the bull has managed to put him out of action, as sometimes happens.

If you do plan to attend a bullfight, it's important to understand what you're about to witness. The bull's back and neck are repeatedly pierced by the lances, resulting in quite a lot of blood, as well as considerable pain and distress. The bull gradually becomes weakened through blood loss before the *torero* delivers the final sword thrust. If done properly, the bull dies instantly from this final thrust, albeit after bleeding for some time from its other wounds. If the coup de grace is not delivered well, the animal dies a slow death. When this happens, the scene can be extremely disturbing.

The Bullfighting Debate

While bullfighting remains strong in some parts of the country, notably Andalucía, in other areas such as Galicia, Cantabria and other northern regions it's never really been a part of local culture. A recent poll found that just 17% of Spaniards under 25 had any interest in bullfighting, compared with 41% of those aged over 64. Similar polls suggest that 75% of Spaniards have no interest in the sport.

A lack of interest is one thing, but many believe that bullfighting is cruel and immoral and there is a growing anti-bullfighting movement in Spain. The socialist government banned children under 14 from attending bullfights in 2006 and forbade state-run TV from broadcasting live coverage of bullfights (some private broadcasters continued to televise). This latter decision was later overturned by the newly elected Popular Party government, and live broadcasts of bullfighting (at 6pm) resumed on the state-run channel. The bullfighting world was nonetheless given a blow when the Catalan government's ban on bullfighting officially became law on 1 January 2012. On the flip side, bullfighting does still have some fans in high places. Juan Carlos I, Spain's king until 2014, is on record as saying: 'The day the EU bans bullfighting is the day Spain leaves the EU'.

That this is a debate at all in Spain owes a little to bullfighting's waning popularity and arguably more to the country's growing integration with the rest of Europe since Spain's return to democracy in the late 1970s. The fall in bullfighting's popularity has fostered some anti-bullfighting organisations, but the greatest impetus still comes from groups beyond Spanish shores.

Bullfights are vehemently opposed by numerous animal-welfare organisations, among them PETA (www.peta.org.uk), the World Society for the Protection of Animals (www.worldanimalprotection.org.uk) and the League Against Cruel Sports (www.league.org.uk). Two Spanish animal-rights, anti-bullfighting NGOs are ADDA (www.addaong.org) and Igualdad Animal (www.igualdadanimal.org). For information on creative protests against bullfighting, see www.runningofthenudes.com.

Survival Guide

Directory A–Z

Accommodation

Spain's accommodation is generally of a high standard, from small, family-run *hostales* (budget hotels) to the old-world opulence of *paradores* (state-owned hotels).

Officially, places to stay are classified into *hoteles* (hotels; one to five stars), *hostales* (one to three stars) and *pensiones* (basically small private *hostales*, often family businesses in rambling apartments; one or two stars). These are the categories used by the annual *Guía Oficial de Hoteles*, sold in bookshops, which lists almost every such establishment in Spain (except for one-star *pensiones)*, with approximate prices. Tourist offices and their websites also have lists of local accommodation options.

Checkout time in most establishments is noon.

Reservations

Reserving a room is always recommended in the high season. Finding a place to stay without booking ahead in July and August along the coast can be difficult

and many places require a minimum stay of at least two nights during high season. Always check out hotel websites for discounts.

Although there's usually no need to book ahead for a room in the low or shoulder seasons (Barcelona is a notable exception), booking ahead is usually a good idea, if for no other reason than to avoid a wearisome search for a room. Most places will ask for a credit-card number or will hold the room for you until 6pm unless you have provided credit card details as security or you have let them know that you'll be arriving later.

Online booking services like Airbnb (www.airbnb.com) offer a range of accommodation types, from apartments and houses to private rooms in somebody's house.

Seasons

What constitutes low or high season depends on where and when you're looking. Most of the year is high season in Barcelona or Madrid, especially during trade fairs that you're unlikely to know about. August can be dead in cities, but high season along the

coast. Winter is high season in the ski resorts of the Pyrenees and low season along the coast (many coastal towns seem to shut down between November and Easter).

Weekends are high season for boutique hotels and *casas rurales* (rural homes), but low season for business hotels (which often offer generous specials) in Madrid and Barcelona.

Prices

Accommodation in Spain can be outrageously good value by European standards.

At the lower end of the budget category there are dorm beds (from around €20 per person) in youth hostels or private rooms with shared bathrooms in the corridor. If you're willing to pay a few euros more, there are many budget places, usually *hostales*, with good, comfortable rooms and private bathrooms. In relatively untouristed or rural areas, the prices of some boutique or other hotels can sometimes drop into the budget category, especially during low season.

Spain's midrange hotels are generally excellent; you should always have your own private bathroom, and breakfast is sometimes included in the room price. Boutique hotels, including many that occupy artistically converted historical buildings, largely fall into this category and are almost always excellent choices.

BOOK YOUR STAY ONLINE

For more accommodations reviews by Lonely Planet authors, check out http://lonelyplanet.com/hotels/. You'll find independent reviews, as well as recommendations on the best places to stay. Best of all, you can book online.

Top-end hotels range from stunning, character-filled temples to good taste to reliably luxurious international chains.

And a final word about terminology. A *habitación doble* (double room) is frequently just that: a room with two beds (which you can often shove together). If you want to be sure of a double bed *(cama matrimonial)*, ask for it!

Accommodation Types

APARTMENTS, VILLAS & CASAS RURALES

Throughout Spain you can rent self-catering apartments and houses from one night upwards. Villas and houses are widely available on the main holiday coasts and in popular country areas.

A simple one-bedroom apartment in a coastal resort for two or three people might cost as little as €40 per night, although more often you'll be looking at nearly twice that much, and prices jump even further in high season. More luxurious options with a swimming pool might come in at anything between €200 and €400 for four people.

Rural tourism has become immensely popular, with accommodation available in many new and often charming *casas rurales*. These are usually comfortably renovated village houses or farmhouses with a handful of rooms – check whether you're renting a room or the whole house (which is more common) for *casas rurales*. They often go by other names, such as *cases de pagès* in Catalonia, *casas de aldea* in Asturias, *posadas* and *casonas* in Cantabria and so on. Some just provide rooms, while others offer meals or self-catering accommodation. Lower-end prices typically hover around €30/50 for a single/double per night, but classy boutique establishments can

easily charge €100 or more for a double. Many are rented out by the week.

Agencies include:

Apartments-Spain (www.apartments-spain.com)

Associació Agroturisme Balear (www.rusticbooking.com)

Atlas Rural (www.atlasrural.com)

Casas Cantabricas (www.casas.co.uk)

Cases Rurals de Catalunya (www.casesrurals.com)

Escapada Rural (www.escapadarural.com)

Fincas 4 You (www.fincas4you.com)

Owners Direct (www.ownersdirect.co.uk)

Ruralka (www.ruralka.com)

Rustic Rent (www.rusticrent.com)

Rusticae (www.rusticae.es)

Secret Places (www.secretplaces.com)

Top Rural (www.toprural.com)

Traum Ferienwohnungen (www.traum-ferienwohnungen.de)

Villas 4 You (www.villas4you.co.uk)

Vintage (vintagetravel.co.uk)

CAMPING & CARAVAN PARKS

Spain has around 1000 officially graded *campings* (camping grounds). Some of these are well located in woodland or near beaches or rivers, but others are on the outskirts of towns or along highways. Few of them are near city centres, and camping isn't particularly convenient if you're relying on public transport. Tourist offices can always direct you to the nearest camping ground. Camping grounds are officially rated as 1st class (1ªC), 2nd class (2ªC) or 3rd class (3ªC). There are also some that are not officially graded, usually equivalent to 3rd class. Facilities generally range from reasonable to very good, although any camping ground

can be crowded and noisy at busy times (especially July and August). Even a 3rd-class camping ground is likely to have hot showers, electrical hook-ups and a cafe. The best ones have heated swimming pools, supermarkets, restaurants, laundry service, children's playgrounds and tennis courts.

Camping grounds usually charge per person, per tent and per vehicle – typically €4.50 to €10 for each. Children usually pay less than adults. Many camping grounds close from around October to Easter. You occasionally come across a *zona de acampada* or *área de acampada*, a country camping ground with minimal facilities (maybe just tap water or a couple of barbecues), little or no supervision and little or no charge. If it's in an environmentally protected area, you may need to obtain permission from the local environmental authority to camp there. With certain exceptions – such as many beaches and environmentally protected areas and a few municipalities that ban it – it is legal to camp outside camping grounds (but not within 1km of official ones!). Signs usually indicate wild camping is not allowed. If in doubt, you can always check with tourist offices. You'll need permission to camp on private land.

Useful websites:

Campinguía (www.campinguia.com) Comments (mostly in Spanish) and links.

Campings Online (www.campingsonline.com/espana) Booking service.

Guía Camping (www.guiacampingfecc.com) Online version of the annual *Guía Camping* (€14), which is available in bookshops around the country.

CAMAS, FONDAS & HOSPEDAJES

At the budget end of the market, places listing

SLEEPING PRICE RANGES

Accommodation listings are grouped according to price bracket. Establishments within each bracket are then listed in order of author preference. Each place to stay is accompanied by one of the following symbols (the price refers to a double room with private bathroom):

€ less than €65

€€ from €65 to €140

€€€ more than €140

The price ranges for Madrid and Barcelona are inevitably higher:

€ less than €75

€€ from €75 to €200

€€€ more than €200

accommodation use all sorts of overlapping names to describe themselves. In broad terms, the cheapest are usually places just advertising *camas* (beds), *fondas* (a basic eatery and inn combined, though one of these functions is now often missing) and *casas de huéspedes* or *hospedajes* (guesthouses). Most such places will be bare and basic. Bathrooms are likely to be shared, although if you're lucky you may get an in-room *lavabo* (washbasin). In winter you may need to ask for extra blankets.

PENSIONES

A *pensión* is usually a small step up from the *camas*, *fondas* and *hospedajes* in standard and price. Some cheap establishments forget to provide soap, toilet paper or towels. Don't hesitate to ask for these. On the other hand, many are charming, family-run places with clean rooms and willing service.

HOSTALES

Hostales are a step up from *pensiones* and operate as simple, small hotels – you'll find them everywhere across the country and the better ones can be bright and spotless, with rooms boasting full en-suite bathrooms – *baño privado*, most often with a *ducha* (shower) rather than bathtub, and usually a

TV, air-conditioning and/or heating.

HOTELS

Spain's *hoteles* run the gamut of quality, from straightforward roadside places, bland but clean, through to charming boutique gems and on to super-luxurious hotels. Even in the cheapest hotels, rooms are likely to have an attached bathroom and there will probably be a restaurant or, at the very least, a breakfast room.

Among the more tempting hotels for those with a little fiscal room to manoeuvre are the 90 or so **paradores** (☎in Spain 902 54 79 79; www. parador.es), a state-funded chain of hotels in often stunning locations, among them towering castles and former medieval convents. Similarly, you can find beautiful hotels in restored country homes and old city mansions, and these are not always particularly expensive.

A raft of cutting-edge, hip design hotels with cool staff and a New York feel can be found in the big cities and major resort areas. At the top end you may pay more for a room with a view – especially sea views or with a *balcón* (balcony) – and will often have the option of a suite.

Many places have rooms for three, four or more people where the per-person cost is lower than in a single or

double, which is good news for families.

Many of the agencies listed under Apartments, Villas & Casas Rurales (p813) also have a full portfolio of hotels.

MONASTERIES

An offbeat possibility is staying in a monastery. In spite of the expropriations of the 19th century and a sometimes rough run in the 20th, numerous monastic orders have survived across the country. Some offer rooms to outsiders – often fairly austere monks' or nuns' cells.

Monastery accommodation is generally a single-sex arrangement, and the idea in quite a few is to seek refuge from the outside world and indulge in quiet contemplation and meditation. On occasion, where the religious order continues ancient tradition by working on farmland, orchards and/or vineyards, you may have the opportunity (or there may be the expectation) to work too.

Useful resources include the following:

Alojamientos en Monasterios (www.alojamientomonasterios. com)

Alojamientos Monásticos de España A guidebook to Spain's monasteries by Javier de Sagastizabal and José Antonio Egaña, although it's in desperate need of an update (the latest edition dates to 2003).

REFUGIOS

Refugios (hostels) for walkers and climbers are liberally scattered around most of the popular mountain areas (especially the Pyrenees), except in Andalucía, which has only a handful. They're mostly run by mountaineering and walking organisations. Accommodation, usually bunks squeezed into a dorm, is often on a first-come, first-served basis, although for some *refugios* you can book ahead. In busy seasons (July and August in most areas) they can fill up quickly, and you should try to book in advance or arrive by mid-afternoon to be sure of a place. Prices per person range from nothing to €15 or more a night. Many *refugios* have a bar and offer meals (dinner typically costs €8 to €12), as well as a cooking area (but no cooking equipment). Blankets are usually provided, but you'll have to bring any other bedding yourself (or rent it at the *refugio*). Bring a torch too.

The Aragonese Pyrenees are particularly well served with *refugios;* check out the following:

Albergues & Refugios de Aragón (www.alberguesyref ugiosdearagon.com) To make reservations in *refugios* and *albergues*.

Federación Aragonesa de Montañismo (www.fam.es) The FAM in Zaragoza can provide information, and a card will get you substantial discounts on *refugio* stays.

La Central de Refugis (www. lacentralderefugis.com) Refugios in the Pyrenees of Catalonia.

YOUTH HOSTELS

Spain has 250 or so youth hostels – *albergues juveniles*, not be confused with *hostales* (budget hotels) – as well as hundreds of backpackers' hostels around the country. These are often the cheapest places for lone travellers, but two people can usually get a better double room elsewhere for a similar price.

The hostel experience in Spain varies widely. Some hostels are only moderate value, lacking in privacy, often heavily booked by school groups, and with night-time curfews and no cooking facilities (although if there's nowhere to cook there's usually a cafeteria). Others, however, are conveniently located, open 24 hours and composed mainly of small dorms, often with a private bathroom. An increasing number have rooms adapted for people with disabilities. Some even occupy fine historic buildings.

Most Spanish youth hostels are members of the **Red Española de Albergues Juveniles** (www.reaj.com), the Spanish representative of Hostelling International.

Most of the REAJ member hostels are also members of the youth hostel association of their region (Andalucía, Catalonia, Valencia etc). Each region usually sets its own price structure and has a central booking service where you can make reservations for most of its hostels. You can also book directly with hostels themselves.

Prices at youth hostels often depend on the season, and vary from about €15 to €21 for those under 26 (the lower rate is usually applied to people with ISIC cards too) and between €18 and €28 for those 26 and over. In some hostels the price includes breakfast. A few hostels require you to rent sheets (around €2 to €5 for your stay) if you don't have your own or a sleeping bag.

For youth hostels, most require you to have an HI card or a membership card from your home country's youth hostel association. You can obtain an HI card in Spain at most hostels.

A growing number of hostel-style places not connected with HI or REAJ often have individual rooms as well the more typical dormitory options. Prices can vary

PRACTICALITIES

Currency

Euro (€)

Electric Current

230V, 50Hz

Smoking

Banned in all enclosed public spaces.

Weights & Measures

The metric system is used.

Media

Newspapers The three main newspapers are the centre-left *El País* (www.elpais.com), centre-right *El Mundo* (www.elmundo.es) and right-wing *ABC* (www. abc.es); the widely available *International New York Times* includes an eight-page supplement of articles from *El País* translated into English, or check out www. elpais.com/elpais/inenglish.html.

Radio Nacional de España (RNE) has Radio 1, with general interest and current-affairs programs; Radio 5, with sport and entertainment; and Radio 3 (Radio d'Espop). Stations covering current affairs include the left-leaning Cadena Ser, or the right-wing COPE. The most popular commercial pop and rock stations are 40 Principales, Kiss FM, Cadena 100 and Onda Cero.

TV Spain's state-run Televisión Española (TVE1 and La 2) or the independent commercial stations (Antena 3, Tele 5, Cuatro and La Sexta). Regional governments run local stations, such as Madrid's Telemadrid, Catalonia's TV-3 and Canal 33 (both in Catalan), Galicia's TVG, the Basque Country's ETB-1 and ETB-2, Valencia's Canal 9 and Andalucía's Canal Sur.

greatly as, not being affiliated to any organisation, they are not subject to any pricing system. A good resource for seeking out hostels, affiliated or otherwise, is **Hostel World** (www.hostelworld.com).

Finally, you will sometimes find independent *albergues* offering basic dormitory accommodation for around €10 to €18, usually in villages in areas that attract plenty of Spanish walkers and climbers. These are not specifically youth hostels – although the clientele tends to be under 35. They're a kind of halfway house between a youth hostel and a *refugio*. Some will rent you sheets for a couple of euros, if you need them.

Customs Regulations

Duty-free allowances for travellers entering Spain from outside the EU include 2L of wine (or 1L of wine and 1L of spirits), and 200 cigarettes or 50 cigars or 250g of tobacco.

There are no restrictions on the import of duty-paid items into Spain from other EU countries for personal use. You *can* buy VAT-free articles at airport shops when travelling between EU countries.

Discount Cards

At museums, never hesitate to ask if there are discounts for students, young people, children, families or seniors.

➡ **Senior cards** Reduced prices for people over 60, 63 or 65 (depending on the place) at various museums and attractions (sometimes restricted to EU citizens) and occasionally on transport.

➡ **Student cards** Discounts (usually half the normal fee) for students. You will need some kind of identification (eg an International Student Identity Card; www.isic.org) to prove student status. Not accepted everywhere.

➡ **Youth cards** Travel, sights and youth-hostel discounts with the European Youth Card (www.eyca.org), known as Carnet Joven in Spain.

Electricity

In Gibraltar, the two-pin continental plugs used in Spain and the three-square-pin plugs from the UK are both used, though the latter is more common.

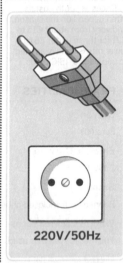

220V/50Hz

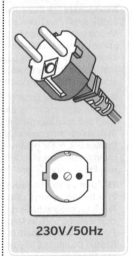

230V/50Hz

Embassies & Consulates

The embassies are located in Madrid. Some countries also maintain consulates in major cities, particularly in Barcelona.

Australian Embassy (☑91 353 66 00; www.spain.embassy.gov. au; 24th fl, Paseo de la Castellana 259D, Madrid)

Canadian Embassy (☑91 382 84 00; www.canadainterna tional.gc.ca/spain-espagne/; Torre Espacio, Paseo de la Castellana 259D; ⓜVelázquez)

Canadian Consulate (Barcelona) (☑93 270 36 14; 1st fl, Plaça de Catalunya 9; ⓢ9am-12.30pm Mon-Fri; ⓜCatalunya)

Canadian Consulate (Málaga) (☑95 222 33 46; Plaza de la Malagueta 2)

Dutch Embassy (☑91 353 75 00; http://espana.nlembajada. org; Torre Espacio, Paseo de la Castellana 259D)

French Embassy (☑91 423 89 00; www.ambafrance-es.org; Calle de Salustiano Olózaga 9)

French Consulate (☑93 270 30 00; www.consulfrance-bar celone.org; Ronda de la Universitat 22bis; ⓜUniversitat, Catalunya) Further consulates in Bilbao and Seville.

German Embassy (☑91 557 90 00; www.spanien.diplo.de; Calle de Fortuny 8)

German Consulate (☑93 292 10 00; www.barcelona.diplo.de; Torre Mapfre, Calle de Marina 16-18, 30A.) Further consulates in Málaga and Palma de Mallorca.

Irish Embassy (☑91 436 40 93; www.embassyofireland.es; Paseo de la Castellana 46)

Japanese Embassy (☑91 590 76 00; www.es.emb-japan.go.jp; Calle de Serrano 109; ⓜGregorio Marañon)

Moroccan Embassy (☑91 563 10 90; www.embajada-marrue cos.es; Calle de Serrano 179; ⓜSanto Domingo)

Moroccan Consulate (🖉93 289 25 30; Carrer de la Diputació 68; MRocafort) Further consulates-general in Algeciras, Almería, Bilbao, Seville, Tarragona and Valencia.

New Zealand Embassy (🖉91 523 02 26; www.mfat.govt.nz/en/embassies; 3rd fl, Calle de Pinar 7, Madrid)

UK Embassy (🖉91 714 63 00; www.gov.uk/government/world/spain; Paseo de la Castellana 259D, Torre Espacio, Madrid)

UK Consulate (🖉93 366 62 00; Avinguda Diagonal 477; MHospital Clínic) Further consulates in Alicante, Bilbao, Ibiza, Palma de Mallorca and Málaga.

US Embassy (🖉91 587 22 00; http://madrid.usembassy.gov; Calle de Serrano 75, Madrid)

US Consulate (🖉93 280 22 27; http://barcelona.usconsulate.gov; Passeig de la Reina Elisenda de Montcada 23-25; ☉9am-1pm Mon-Fri; 🚇FGC Reina Elisenda) Consular agencies in A Coruña, Fuengirola, Palma de Mallorca, Seville and Valencia.

GLBTI Travellers

Spain has become perhaps the most gay-friendly country in southern Europe. Homosexuality is legal and the age of consent is 13, as it is for heterosexuals. In 2005 the Socialist president, José Luis Rodríguez Zapatero, gave the country's conservative Catholic foundations a shake with the legalisation of same-sex marriages in Spain.

Lesbians and gay men generally keep a fairly low profile, but are quite open in the cities. Madrid, Barcelona, Sitges, Torremolinos and Ibiza have particularly lively scenes. Sitges is a major destination on the international gay party circuit; gays take a leading role in the wild **Carnaval** (www.carnavaldesitges.com; ☉Feb/Mar) there in February/March. There are also

gay parades, marches and events in several cities on and around the last Saturday in June, when Madrid's **gay and lesbian pride march** (www.orgullogay.org) takes place.

Madrid also hosts the annual **Les Gai Cine Mad** (🖉915 930 540; www.lesgaicinemad.com; ☉late Oct or early Nov) festival, a celebration of lesbian, gay and transsexual films.

Resources

In addition to the following resources, Barcelona's tourist board publishes *Barcelona: The Official Gay and Lesbian Tourist Guide* biannually, while Madrid's tourist office has a useful information on its website (www.esmadrid.com/lgtb-madrid).

Chueca (www.chueca.com) Useful gay portal with extensive links.

GayBarcelona (www.gaybarcelona.com) News and views and an extensive listings section covering bars, saunas, shops and more in Barcelona and Sitges.

Gay Iberia (www.gayiberia.com) Gay guides to Barcelona, Madrid, Sitges and 26 other Spanish cities.

Gay Madrid 4 U (www.gaymadrid4u.com) A good overview of Madrid's gay bars and nightclubs.

Night Tours.com (www.nighttours.com) A reasonably good guide to gay nightlife and other attractions in Madrid, Barcelona and 18 other Spanish locations.

Orgullo Gay (www.orgullogay.org) Website for Madrid's gay and lesbian pride march and links to gay organisations across the country. In need of an update.

Shangay (www.shangay.com) For news, upcoming events, reviews and contacts. It also publishes Shanguide, a Madrid-centric biweekly magazine jammed with listings (including saunas and hard-core clubs) and contact ads. Its companion publication Shangay Express is better for articles with a handful of listings

and ads. They're available in gay bookshops and gay and gay-friendly bars.

Universo Gay (guia.universogay.com) A little bit of everything.

Organisations

Casal Lambda (🖉93 319 55 50; www.lambda.cat; Carrer de Verdaguer i Callís 10; ☉7-9pm Mon-Sat; MUrquinaona) A gay and lesbian social, cultural and information centre in Barcelona's La Ribera.

Colectivo de Gais y Lesbianas de Madrid (Cogam; 🖉91 523 00 70, 91 522 45 17; www.cogam.es; Calle de la Puebla 9; ☉10am-2pm & 5-9pm Mon-Fri; MCallao, Gran Vía) Offers activities and has an information office and social centre.

Coordinadora Gai-Lesbiana Barcelona (🖉93 298 00 29; Carrer de Violant d'Hongria 156; MPlaça del Centre) Barcelona's main coordinating body for gay and lesbian groups.

Federación Estatal de Lesbianas, Gays, Transexuales & Bisexuales (🖉91 360 46 05; www.felgtb.org; 4th fl, Calle de las Infantas 40; ☉8am-8pm Mon-Thu, 8am-3.30pm Fri; MGran Vía) A national advocacy group, based in Madrid, that played a leading role in lobbying for the legalisation of gay marriages.

Fundación Triángulo (🖉91 593 05 40; www.fundaciontriangulo.org; 1st fl, Calle de Meléndez Valdés 52; ☉10am-2pm & 4-8pm Mon-Fri; MArgüelles) One of several sources of information on gay issues in Madrid.

Health

Spain has an excellent health-care system.

Availability & Cost of Health Care

If you need an ambulance, call 🖉061. For emergency treatment, go straight to the *urgencias* (casualty) section of the nearest hospital.

Farmacias offer valuable advice and sell over-the-counter medication. In Spain, a system of *farmacias de guardia* (duty pharmacies) operates so that each district has one open all the time. When a pharmacy is closed, it posts the name of the nearest open one on the door.

Medical costs are lower in Spain than many other European countries, but can still mount quickly if you are uninsured. Costs if you attend casualty range from nothing (in some regions) to around €80.

Altitude Sickness

➡ If you're hiking at altitude, altitude sickness may be a risk. Lack of oxygen at high altitudes (over 2500m) affects most people to some extent.

➡ Symptoms of Acute Mountain Sickness (AMS) usually develop during the first 24 hours at altitude but may be delayed by up to three weeks.

➡ Mild symptoms include headache, lethargy, dizziness, difficulty sleeping and loss of appetite.

➡ AMS may become more severe without warning and can be fatal.

➡ Severe symptoms include breathlessness, a dry, irritative cough (which may progress to the production of pink, frothy sputum), severe headache, lack of coordination and balance, confusion, irrational behaviour, vomiting, drowsiness and unconsciousness.

➡ Treat mild symptoms by resting at the same altitude until recovery, usually for a day or two.

➡ Paracetamol or aspirin can be taken for headaches.

➡ If symptoms persist or become worse, immediate descent is necessary; even 500m can help.

➡ Drug treatments should never be used to avoid descent or to enable further ascent.

Hypothermia

➡ The weather in Spain's mountains can be extremely changeable at any time of year.

➡ Proper preparation will reduce the risks of getting hypothermia: always carry waterproof garments and warm layers, and inform others of your route.

➡ Hypothermia starts with shivering, loss of judgment and clumsiness; unless rewarming occurs, the sufferer deteriorates into apathy, confusion and coma.

➡ Prevent further heat loss by seeking shelter, wearing warm dry clothing, drinking hot sweet drinks and sharing body warmth.

Bites & Stings

➡ Be wary of the hairy reddish-brown caterpillars of the pine processionary moth – touching the hairs sets off a severely irritating allergic skin reaction.

➡ Some Spanish centipedes have a very nasty but non-fatal sting.

➡ Jellyfish, which have stinging tentacles, are an increasing problem at beaches along the Mediterranean coastline.

➡ Lataste's viper is the only venomous snake that is even relatively common in Spain. It has a triangular-shaped head, grows up to 75cm long, and is grey with a zigzag pattern. It lives in dry, rocky areas, away from humans. Its bite can be fatal and needs to be treated with a serum, which state clinics in major towns keep in stock.

Tap Water

Tap water is generally safe to drink in Spain. If you are in any doubt, ask, *¿Es potable el agua (de grifo)?* (Is the (tap) water drinkable?). Do not drink water from rivers or lakes as it may contain bacteria or viruses that can cause diarrhoea or vomiting.

Insurance

A travel-insurance policy to cover theft, loss, medical problems and cancellation or delays to your travel arrangements is a good idea. Paying for your ticket with a credit card can often provide limited travel-accident insurance and you may be able to reclaim the payment if the operator doesn't deliver. Worldwide travel insurance is available at lonelyplanet.com/bookings. You can buy, extend and claim online anytime – even if you're on the road.

Internet Access

Wi-fi is almost universally available at hotels, as well as in some cafes, restaurants and airports; generally (but not always) it's free. Connection speed often varies from room to room in hotels (and coverage is sometimes restricted to the hotel lobby), so always ask when you check in or make your reservation. Some tourist offices may have a list of wi-fi hot spots in their area.

Legal Matters

If you're arrested, you will be allotted the free services of an *abogado de oficio* (duty solicitor), who may speak only Spanish. You're also entitled to make a phone call. If you use this to contact your embassy or consulate, the staff will probably be able to do no more than refer you to a lawyer who speaks your language. If you end up in court, the authorities are obliged to provide a translator.

In theory, you are supposed to have your national ID card or passport with you at all times. If asked for it by the police, you are supposed to be able to produce it on the spot. In practice it is rarely an issue and many people choose to leave passports in hotel safes.

The Policía Local or Policía Municipal operates at a local level and deals with such issues as traffic infringements and minor crime. The Policía Nacional (☏091) is the state police force, dealing with major crime and operating primarily in the cities. The military-linked Guardia Civil (created in the 19th century to deal with banditry) is largely responsible for highway patrols, borders, security, major crime and terrorism. Several regions have their own police forces, such as the Mossos d'Esquadra in Catalonia and the Ertaintxa in the Basque Country.

Cannabis is legal but only for personal use and in very small quantities. Public consumption of any illicit drug is illegal. Travellers entering Spain from Morocco should be prepared for drug searches, especially if you have a vehicle.

Maps

Spain has some excellent maps if you're driving around the country – many are available from petrol stations. Topographical and hiking maps are available from specialist stores.

Small-Scale Maps

Some of the best maps for travellers are by Michelin, which produces the 1:1,000,000 *Spain Portugal* map and six 1:400,000 regional maps covering the whole country. These are all pretty accurate and are updated regularly, even down to the state of minor country roads. Also good are the GeoCenter maps published by Germany's RV Verlag.

Probably the best physical map of Spain is *Península Ibérica, Baleares y Canarias* published by the **Centro Nacional de Información Geográfica** (www.cnig. es), the publishing arm of

the **Instituto Geográfico Nacional** (IGN; www.ign.es; Calle General de Ibáñez de Ibero 3, Madrid). Ask for it in good bookshops.

Walking Maps

Useful for hiking and exploring some areas (particularly in the Pyrenees) are Editorial Alpina's *Guía Cartográfica* and *Guía Excursionista y Turística* series. The series combines information booklets in Spanish (and sometimes Catalan) with detailed maps at scales ranging from 1:25,000 to 1:50,000. They are an indispensable tool for hikers (and some come in English and German), but they have their inaccuracies.

The Institut Cartogràfic de Catalunya puts out some decent maps for hiking in the Catalan Pyrenees that are often better than their Editorial Alpina counterparts. Remember that for hiking only, maps scaled at 1:25,000 are seriously useful. The CNIG also covers most of the country in 1:25,000 sheets.

You can often pick up Editorial Alpina publications and CNIG maps at bookshops near trekking areas, and at specialist bookshops such as the following:

Altaïr (Map p256; ☏93 342 71 71; www.altair.es; Gran Via de les Corts Catalanes 616; ⊙10am-8.30pm Mon-Sat; ☎; Ⓜ Catalunya) In Barcelona.

De Viaje (Map p98; ☏91 577 98 99; www.deviaje.com; Calle de Serrano 41; ⊙10am-8.30pm Mon-Fri, 10.30am-2.30pm & 5-8pm Sat; Ⓜ Serrano) In Madrid.

La Tienda Verde (☏91 535 38 10; www.tiendaverde.es; Calle de Maudes 23; ⊙10am-2pm & 5-8pm Mon-Fri, 10am-2pm Sat) In Madrid.

Librería Desnivel (Map p84; ☏91 429 12 81; www.libreria-desnivel.com; Plaza de Matute 6; ⊙10am-8.30pm Mon-Fri, 11am-8pm Sat; Ⓜ Antón Martín) In Madrid.

Money

The most convenient way to bring your money is in the form of a debit or credit card, with some extra cash in case of an emergency.

Many credit and debit cards can be used for withdrawing money from *cajeros automáticos* (ATMs) that display the relevant symbols such as Visa, MasterCard, Cirrus etc. There is usually a charge (around 1.5% to 2%) on ATM cash withdrawals abroad.

Cash

Most banks and building societies will exchange major foreign currencies and offer the best rates. Ask about commissions and take your passport.

Credit & Debit Cards

These can be used to pay for most purchases. You'll often be asked to show your passport or some other form of identification. Among the most widely accepted are Visa, MasterCard, American Express (Amex), Cirrus, Maestro, Plus and JCB. Diners Club is less widely accepted. If your card is lost,

---

EATING PRICE RANGES

In our reviews, restaurants are grouped according to price range (€ to €€€). The order within each of those ranges follows the author's preference. The following price brackets refer to a standard main dish:

€ less than €10

€€ from €10 to €20

€€€ more than €20

stolen or swallowed by an ATM, you can call the following telephone numbers to have an immediate stop put on its use: **Amex** (☑902 814 500), **Diners Club** (☑900 801 331, 91 211 43 00), **MasterCard** (☑900 971 231) and **Visa** (☑900 991 124).

Moneychangers

You can exchange both cash and travellers cheques at *cambio* (exchange) offices. Generally they offer longer opening hours and quicker service than banks, but worse exchange rates and higher commissions.

Taxes & Refunds

➡ In Spain, value-added tax (VAT) is known as IVA (eeba; *impuesto sobre el valor añadido*).

➡ Hotel rooms and restaurant meals attract an additional 10% (usually included in the quoted price but always ask); most other items have 21% added.

➡ Visitors are entitled to a refund of the 21% IVA on purchases costing more than €90.16 from any shop, if they are taking them out of the EU within three months. Ask the shop for a cash-back (or similar) refund form showing the price and IVA paid for each item, and identifying the vendor and purchaser.

➡ Present your IVA refund form to the customs booth for refunds at the airport, port or border when you leave the EU.

Tipping

Tipping is almost always optional.

Restaurants Many Spaniards leave small change, others up to 5%, which is considered generous.

Taxis Optional, but most locals round up to the nearest euro.

Bars It's rare to leave a tip in bars (even if the bartender gives you your change on a small dish).

Travellers Cheques

Travellers cheques can be changed at most banks and building societies, often with a commission. Visa, Amex and Travelex are widely accepted brands with (usually) efficient replacement policies. It's vital to keep your initial receipt, and a record of your cheque numbers and the ones you have used, separate from the cheques themselves.

Opening Hours

Standard opening hours are for high season only and tend to be shorter outside that time.

Banks 8.30am to 2pm Monday to Friday; some also open 4pm to 7pm Thursday and 9am to 1pm Saturday

Central post offices 8.30am to 9.30pm Monday to Friday, 8.30am to 2pm Saturday (most other branches 8.30am to 8.30pm Monday to Friday, 9.30am to 1pm Saturday)

Nightclubs Midnight or 1am to 5am or 6am

Restaurants Lunch 1pm to 4pm, dinner 8.30pm to 11pm or midnight

Shops 10am to 2pm and 4.30pm to 7.30pm or 5pm to 8pm; big supermarkets and department stores generally open 10am to 10pm Monday to Saturday

Post

Correos (☑902 197 197; www.correos.es), the Spanish postal system, is generally reliable, if a little slow at times.

Postal Rates & Services

➡ *Sellos* (stamps) are sold at most *estancos* (tobacconists; look for 'Tabacos' in yellow letters on a maroon background), as well as at post offices.

➡ A postcard or letter weighing up to 20g costs

€1.15 from Spain to other European countries, and €1.30 to the rest of the world.

➡ For a full list of prices for *certificado* (certified) and *urgente* (express post), go to www.correos.es and click on 'Calculador de Tarifas.'

Sending Mail

Delivery times are erratic but ordinary mail to other Western European countries can take up to a week (although often as little as three days); to North America up to 10 days; and to Australia or New Zealand between 10 days and three weeks.

Public Holidays

The two main periods when Spaniards go on holiday are Semana Santa (the week leading up to Easter Sunday) and July and August. At these times accommodation in resorts can be scarce and transport heavily booked, but other places are often half-empty.

There are at least 14 official holidays a year – some observed nationwide, some locally. When a holiday falls close to a weekend, Spaniards like to make a *puente* (bridge), meaning they take the intervening day off too. Occasionally when some holidays fall close, they make an *acueducto* (aqueduct)! Here are the national holidays:

Año Nuevo (New Year's Day) 1 January

Viernes Santo (Good Friday) March/April

Fiesta del Trabajo (Labour Day) 1 May

La Asunción (Feast of the Assumption) 15 August

Fiesta Nacional de España (National Day) 12 October

La Inmaculada Concepción (Feast of the Immaculate Conception) 8 December

Navidad (Christmas) 25 December

Regional governments set five holidays and local councils two more. Common dates include the following:

Epifanía (Epiphany) or **Día de los Reyes Magos** (Three Kings' Day) 6 January

Jueves Santo (Good Thursday) March/April; not observed in Catalonia and Valencia.

Corpus Christi June. This is the Thursday after the eighth Sunday after Easter Sunday.

Día de Santiago Apóstol (Feast of St James the Apostle) 25 July

Día de Todos los Santos (All Saints Day) 1 November

Día de la Constitución (Constitution Day) 6 December

Safe Travel

Most visitors to Spain never feel remotely threatened, but a sufficient number have unpleasant experiences to warrant some care. The main thing to be wary of is petty theft (which may of course not seem so petty if your passport, cash, travellers cheques, credit card and camera go missing).

Scams

There must be 50 ways to lose your wallet. As a rule, talented petty thieves work in groups and capitalise on distraction. Tricks usually involve a team of two or more (sometimes one of them an attractive woman to distract male victims). While one attracts your attention, the other empties your pockets. More imaginative strikes include someone dropping a milk mixture onto the victim from a balcony. Immediately a concerned citizen comes up to help you brush off what you assume to be pigeon poo, and thus suitably occupied, you don't notice the contents of your pockets slipping away.

Beware: not all thieves look like thieves. Watch out for an old classic: the ladies offering flowers for good luck. We don't know how they do it, but if you get too involved in a friendly chat with these people, your pockets almost always wind up empty.

On some highways, especially the AP7 from the French border to Barcelona, bands of thieves occasionally operate. Beware of men trying to distract you in rest areas, and don't stop along the highway if people driving alongside indicate you have a problem with the car. While one inspects the rear of the car with you, his pals will empty your vehicle. Another gag has them puncturing tyres of cars stopped in rest areas, then following and 'helping' the victim when they stop to change the wheel. Hire cars and those with foreign plates are especially targeted. When you do call in at highway rest stops, try to park close to the buildings and leave nothing of value in view. If you do stop to change a tyre and find yourself getting unsolicited aid, make sure doors are all locked and don't allow yourself to be distracted.

Even parking your car can be fraught. In some towns fairly dodgy self-appointed parking attendants operate in central areas where you may want to park. They will direct you frantically to a spot. If possible, ignore them and find your own. If unavoidable, you may well want to pay them some token not to scratch or otherwise damage your vehicle after you've walked away. You definitely don't want to leave anything visible in the car (or open the boot – trunk – if you intend to leave luggage or anything else in it) under these circumstances.

Theft

Theft is mostly a risk in tourist resorts, big cities and when you first arrive in a new city and may be off your guard. You are at your most vulnerable when dragging around luggage to or from your hotel. Barcelona, Madrid and Seville have the worst reputations for theft and, on very rare occasions, muggings.

Anything left lying on the beach can disappear in a flash when your back is turned. At night avoid dingy, empty city alleys and backstreets, or anywhere that just doesn't feel 100% safe.

Report thefts to the national police – visit www.policia.es for a full list of *comisarías* (police stations) around the country. You are unlikely to recover your goods but you need to make this formal *denuncia* for insurance purposes. To avoid endless queues at the *comisaría*, you can make the report by phone (☎902 102 112) in various languages or online at www.policia.es (click on 'Denuncias por Internet') although the instructions are in Spanish only. The following day you go to the station of your choice to pick up and sign the report, without queuing.

Telephone

The once-widespread, but now fast-disappearing, blue payphones are easy to use for international and domestic calls. They accept coins, *tarjetas telefónicas* (phonecards) issued by the national phone company Telefónica and, in some cases, various credit cards. Calling from your smartphone, tablet or computer using an internet-based service such as Skype is generally the cheapest and easiest option.

Collect Calls

Placing *una llamada a cobro revertido* (an international collect call) is simple. Dial ☎99 00 followed by the code for the country you're calling (numbers starting with ☎900 are national toll-free numbers):

Mobile Phones

Spain uses GSM 900/1800, which is compatible with the rest of Europe and Australia but not with the North American system unless you have a GSM/GPRS-compatible phone (some AT&T and T-Mobile cell phones may work), or the system used in Japan. From those countries, you will need to travel with a tri-band or quadric-band phone.

You can buy SIM cards and prepaid time in Spain for your mobile phone, provided you own a GSM, dual- or tri-band cellular phone. This only

works if your national phone hasn't been code-blocked; check before leaving home.

All the Spanish mobile-phone companies (Telefónica's MoviStar, Orange and Vodafone) offer *prepagado* (prepaid) accounts for mobiles. The SIM card costs from €10, to which you add some prepaid phone time. Phone outlets are scattered across the country. You can then top up in their shops or by buying cards in outlets, such as *estancos* (tobacconists) and newspaper kiosks. **Pepephone** (www.pepephone.com) is another option.

If you plan on using your own phone while in Spain, check with your mobile provider for information on roaming charges, especially if you're using a phone from outside the EU.

Area Codes

Mobile (cell) phone numbers start with ☎6. Numbers starting with ☎900 are national toll-free numbers, while those starting ☎901 to 905 come with varying costs. A common one is ☎902, which is a national standard rate number, but which can only be dialled from within Spain. In a similar category are numbers starting with ☎800, 803, 806 and 807.

International access code 00

Spain country code 34

Local area codes None

Phonecards

Cut-rate prepaid phonecards can be good value for international calls. They can be bought from *estancos*, small grocery stores, *locutorios* (private call centres) and newspaper kiosks in the main cities and tourist resorts. If possible, try to compare rates. Many of the private operators offer better deals than those offered by Telefónica. *Locutorios* that specialise in cut-rate overseas calls have popped up all over the place in bigger cities.

Useful Phone Numbers

Emergencies ☎112

English-speaking Spanish international operator ☎1008 (for calls within Europe) or ☎1005 (rest of the world)

International directory enquiries ☎11825 (calls to this number cost €2)

National directory enquiries ☎11818

Operator for calls within Spain ☎1009 – including for domestic reverse-charge (collect) calls

Time

Time zone Same as most of Western Europe (GMT/UTC plus one hour during winter and GMT/UTC plus two hours during the daylight-saving period).

Daylight saving From the last Sunday in March to the last Sunday in October.

UK, Ireland, Portugal & Canary Islands One hour behind mainland Spain.

Morocco Morocco is on GMT/UTC year-round. From the last Sunday in March to the last Sunday in October, subtract two hours from Spanish time to get Moroccan time; the rest of the year, subtract one hour.

USA Spanish time is USA Eastern Time plus six hours and USA Pacific Time plus nine hours.

Australia During the Australian winter (Spanish summer), subtract eight hours from Australian Eastern Standard Time to get Spanish time; during the Australian summer, subtract 10 hours.

12- and 24-hour clock Although the 24-hour clock is used in most official situations, you'll find people generally use the 12-hour clock in everyday conversation.

Toilets

Public toilets are rare to nonexistent in Spain and it's not really the done thing to go into a bar or cafe solely to use the toilet; ordering a quick coffee is a small price to pay for relieving the problem. Otherwise you can usually get away with it in a larger, crowded place where they can't really keep track of who's coming and going. Another option in some larger cities is the department stores of El Corte Inglés.

Tourist Information

All cities and many smaller towns have an *oficina de turismo* or *oficina de información turística*. In the country's provincial capitals you will sometimes find more than one tourist office – one specialising in information on the city alone, the other carrying mostly provincial or regional information. National and natural parks also often have their own visitor centres offering useful information.

Turespaña (www.spain. info) is the country's national tourism body, and it operates branches around the world. Check the website for office locations.

Travellers with Disabilities

Spain is not overly accommodating for travellers with disabilities, but some things are slowly changing. For example, disabled access to some museums, official buildings and hotels represents a change in local thinking. In major cities more is slowly being done to facilitate disabled access to public transport and taxis; in some cities, wheelchair-adapted taxis are called 'Eurotaxis'. Newly constructed hotels in most areas of Spain are required to have wheelchair-adapted rooms. With older places, you need to be a little wary of hotels who advertise themselves as being disabled-friendly, as this can mean as little as wide doors to rooms and bathrooms, or other token efforts.

Some tourist offices – notably those in Madrid and Barcelona – offer guided tours of the city for travellers with disabilities.

Inout Hostel (☏ 93 280 09 85; www.inouthostel.com; Major del Rectoret 2; dm €22; @🛜🏊; 🚆 FGC Baixador de Vallvidrera) 🕮 Worthy of a special mention is Barcelona's Inout Hostel, which is completely accessible for those with disabilities, and nearly all the staff that work there have disabilities of one kind or another. The facilities and service are first-class.

Museo Tiflológico (Museum for the Blind; ☏ 91 589 42 19; http://museo.once.es; Calle de la Coruña 18; ⊙ 10am-2pm & 5-8pm Tue-Fri, 10am-2pm Sat 1st half of Aug, closed 2nd half of Aug; Ⓜ Estrecho) 🆓 This attraction is specifically for people who are visually impaired. Run by the National Organisation for the Blind (ONCE), its exhibits (all of which may be touched) include paintings, sculptures and tapestries, as well as more than 40 scale models of world monuments, including Madrid's Palacio Real and Cibeles fountain, as well as La Alhambra in Granada and the aqueduct in Segovia. It also provides leaflets in Braille and audioguides to the museum.

Organisations

Madrid Accesible (www.esma drid.com/madrid-accesible) Your first stop for more information on accessibility for travellers in Madrid should be the tourist office website section known as Madrid Accesible, where you can download a PDF of their excellent *Guia de Turismo Accesible* in English or Spanish. It has an exhaustive list of the city's attractions and transport and a detailed assessment of their accessibility, as well as a list of accessible restaurants.

Accessible Travel & Leisure (☏ 01452-729739; www.accessibletravel.co.uk) Claims to be the biggest UK travel agent dealing with travel for people with a disability, and encourages independent travel.

Barcelona Turisme (☏ 93 285 38 34; www.barcelona-access. com) Website devoted to making Barcelona accessible for visitors with a disability.

ONCE (Organización Nacional de Ciegos Españoles; Map p104; ☏ 91 577 37 56, 91 532 50 00; www.once.es; Calle de Prim 3; Ⓜ Chueca, Colón) The Spanish association for those who are blind. You may be able to get hold of guides in Braille to Madrid, although they're not published every year.

Society for Accessible Travel & Hospitality (www.sath.org) A good resource, which gives advice on how to travel with a wheelchair, kidney disease, sight impairment or deafness.

Transport

When it comes to transport, metro or tram lines, or stations built (or upgraded) since the late 1990s generally have elevators for wheelchair access, but the older lines can be ill equipped (including many of Madrid's lines; check the map at www.metromad rid.es). Even in stations with wheelchair access, remember that not all platforms will necessarily have functioning escalators or elevators.

The single-deck *piso bajo* (low floor) buses are now commonplace in most Spanish cities, have no steps inside and in some cases have ramps that can be used by people in wheelchairs.

If you call any taxi company and ask for a 'eurotaxi' you should be sent one adapted for wheelchair users.

Visas

Spain is one of 26 member countries of the Schengen Convention, under which 22 EU countries (all but Bulgaria, Cyprus, Ireland, Romania and the UK) plus Iceland, Norway, Liechtenstein and Switzerland have abolished checks at common borders.

The visa situation for entering Spain is as follows:

➡ **Citizens or residents of EU & Schengen countries** No visa required.

➡ **Citizens or residents of Australia, Canada, Israel, Japan, New Zealand & the USA** No visa required for tourist visits of up to 90 days out of every 180 days.

➡ **Other countries** Check with an embassy or consulate.

➡ **To work or study in Spain** A special visa may be required – contact a Spanish embassy or consulate before travel.

Extensions & Residence

Schengen visas cannot be extended. You can apply for no more than two visas in any 12-month period and they are not renewable once you are in Spain. Nationals of EU countries, Iceland, Norway, Liechtenstein and Switzerland can enter and leave Spain at will without a *tarjeta de residencia* (residence card), although they are meant to apply for residence papers.

People of other nationalities who want to stay in Spain longer than 90 days have to get a residence card, and for them it can be a drawn-out process, starting with an appropriate visa issued by a Spanish consulate in their country of residence. Start the process well in advance.

Volunteering

Volunteering possibilities in Spain:

Earthwatch Institute (www. earthwatch.org) Occasionally Spanish conservation projects appear on its program.

Go Abroad (www.goabroad.com) At last count it had links to 66 different volunteering opportunities in Spain.

Sunseed Desert Technology (✆950 52 57 70; www.sunseed. org.uk) This UK-run project, developing sustainable ways to live in semi-arid environments, is based in the hamlet of Los Molinos del Río Agua in Almería.

Transitions Abroad (www.transitionsabroad.com) A good website to start your research.

Women Travellers

Travelling in Spain as a woman is as easy as travelling anywhere in the Western world. That said, you should be choosy about your accommodation. Bottom-end fleapits with all-male staff can be insalubrious locations to bed down for the night. Lone women should also take care in city streets at night – stick with the crowds. Hitching for solo women travellers, while feasible, is risky.

Spanish men under about 40, who've grown up in the liberated post-Franco era, conform far less to old-fashioned sexual stereotypes, although you might notice that sexual stereotyping becomes a little more pronounced as you move from north to south, and from city to country.

Work

Nationals of EU countries, Switzerland, Liechtenstein, Norway and Iceland may freely work in Spain. If you are offered a contract, your employer will normally steer you through any bureaucracy.

Virtually everyone else is supposed to obtain a work permit from a Spanish consulate in their country of residence, and if they plan to stay more than 90 days, a residence visa. These procedures are well-nigh impossible unless you have a job contract lined up before you begin.

You could look for casual work in fruit picking, harvesting or construction, but this is generally done with imported labour from Morocco and Eastern Europe, with pay and conditions that can often best be described as dire.

Translating and interpreting could be an option if you are fluent in Spanish and have a language in demand.

Language Teaching

Language-teaching qualifications are a big help when trying to find work as a teacher, and the more reputable places will require TEFL qualifications. Sources of information on possible teaching work – in a school or as a private tutor – include foreign cultural centres such as the British Council and Alliance Française, foreign-language bookshops, universities and language schools. Many have noticeboards where you may find work opportunities or can advertise your own services.

Tourist Resorts

Summer work on the Mediterranean coasts is a possibility, especially if you arrive early in the season and are prepared to stay a while. Check any local press in foreign languages, such as the Costa del Sol's *Sur in English* (www.surinenglish.com), which lists ads for waiters, nannies, chefs, babysitters, cleaners and the like.

Yacht Crewing

It is possible to stumble upon work as crew on yachts and cruisers. The best ports include (in descending order) Palma de Mallorca, Gibraltar and Puerto Banús.

In summer the voyages tend to be restricted to the Mediterranean, but from about November to January, many boats head for the Caribbean. Such work is usually unpaid and about the only way to find it is to ask around on the docks.

Transport

GETTING THERE & AWAY

Spain is one of Europe's top holiday destinations and is well linked to other European countries by air, rail and road. Regular car ferries and hydrofoils run to and from Morocco, and there are ferry links to the UK, Italy, the Canary Islands and Algeria.

Flights, tours and rail tickets can be booked online at lonelyplanet.com/bookings.

Entering the Country

Immigration and customs checks (which usually only take place if you're arriving from outside the EU) normally involve a minimum of fuss, although there are exceptions.

Your vehicle could be searched on arrival from Andorra. The tiny principality of Andorra is not in the European Union (EU), so border controls remain in place. Spanish customs look out for contraband duty-free products destined for illegal resale in Spain. The same may apply to travellers arriving from Morocco or the Spanish North African enclaves of Ceuta and Melilla. In this case the search is for controlled substances. Expect long delays at these borders, especially in summer.

Passports

Citizens of other EU member states as well those from Norway, Iceland, Liechtenstein and Switzerland can travel to Spain with their national identity card alone. If such countries do not issue ID cards – as in the UK – travellers must carry a valid passport. All other nationalities must have a valid passport.

By law you are supposed to carry your passport or ID card with you in Spain at all times.

Air

There are direct flights to Spain from most European countries, as well as North America, South America, Africa, the Middle East and Asia. Those coming from Australasia will usually have to make at least one change of flight.

High season in Spain generally means Christmas, New Year, Easter and roughly June to September. The applicability of seasonal fares varies depending on the specific destination. You may find reasonably priced flights to Madrid from elsewhere in Europe in August, for example, because it is stinking hot and everyone else has fled to the mountains or the sea. As a general rule, November to March (aside from Christmas and New Year) is when airfares

CLIMATE CHANGE & TRAVEL

Every form of transport that relies on carbon-based fuel generates CO_2, the main cause of human-induced climate change. Modern travel is dependent on aeroplanes, which might use less fuel per kilometre per person than most cars but travel much greater distances. The altitude at which aircraft emit gases (including CO_2) and particles also contributes to their climate change impact. Many websites offer 'carbon calculators' that allow people to estimate the carbon emissions generated by their journey and, for those who wish to do so, to offset the impact of the greenhouse gases emitted with contributions to portfolios of climate-friendly initiatives throughout the world. Lonely Planet offsets the carbon footprint of all staff and author travel.

to Spain are likely to be at their lowest, and the intervening months can be considered shoulder periods.

Airports & Airlines

All of Spain's airports share the user-friendly website and flight information telephone number of **Aena** (☎91 321 10 00, 902 404 704; www.aena.es), the national airports authority. To find more information on each airport, choose 'English' and click 'Airports' then 'Airport Network'. Each airport's page has details on practical information (including parking and public transport) and a full list of (and links to) airlines using that airport. It also has current flight information.

Iberia (www.iberia.com) is Spain's national carrier and it has an extensive international network of flights and a good safety record.

Madrid's **Adolfo Suárez Madrid-Barajas Airport** (☎902 404704; www.aena. es; Ⓜ Aeropuerto T1, T2 & T3, Aeropuerto T4) is Spain's busiest (and Europe's sixth-busiest) airport, while Barcelona's **Aeroport del Prat** (☎902 404704; www. aena.es) comes in 10th. Other major airports include Málaga, Alicante, Girona, Valencia, Seville, Vigo and Bilbao.

Land

Spain shares land borders with France, Portugal and Andorra.

Apart from shorter cross-border services, **Eurolines** (www.eurolines.com) are the main operators of international bus services to Spain from most of Western Europe and Morocco.

In addition to the rail services connecting Spain with France and Portugal, there are direct trains between Zurich and Barcelona (via Bern, Geneva, Perpignan and Girona), and between Milan and Barcelona (via Turin, Perpignan and Girona). For these and other services, visit the 'Internacional' section of the **Renfe** (www.renfe.com) website, the Spanish national railway company.

Andorra

Regular buses connect Andorra with Barcelona (including winter ski buses and direct services to the airport) and other destinations in Spain (including Madrid) and France. Regular buses run between Andorra and Barcelona's Estació d'Autobusos de Sants (€29.50, three hours) or Barcelona's Aeroport del Prat (€33.50, 3½ hours).

France

BUS

Eurolines (☎ in France 08 92 89 90 91; www.eurolines.com) heads to Spain from Paris and more than 20 other French cities and towns. It connects with Madrid (17¾ hours), Barcelona (14¾ hours) and many other destinations. There's at least one departure per day for main destinations.

CAR & MOTORCYCLE

The main road crossing into Spain from France is the highway that links up with Spain's AP7 tollway, which runs down to Barcelona and follows the Spanish coast south (with a branch, the AP2, going to Madrid via Zaragoza). A series of links cuts across the Pyrenees from France and Andorra into Spain, as does a coastal route that runs from Biarritz in France into the Spanish Basque Country.

TRAIN

The principal rail crossings into Spain pierce the Franco-Spanish frontier along the Mediterranean coast and via the Basque Country. Another rail route runs inland across the Pyrenees from Latour-de-Carol to Barcelona.

In addition to the options listed below, two or three TGV (high-speed) trains leave from Paris-Montparnasse for Irún, where you change to a normal train for the Basque Country and on towards Madrid. Up to three TGVs also put you on track to Barcelona (leaving from Paris Gare de Lyon), with a change of train at Montpellier or Narbonne. For more information on French rail services, check out the **SNCF** (www.voyages-sncf. com) website.

There are plans for a high-speed rail link between Madrid and Paris. In the meantime, high-speed services travel via Barcelona. These

BUS PASSES

Travellers planning broader European tours that include Spain could find one of the following passes useful.

Busabout (☎ in the UK 084 5026 7514; www.busabout.com) A UK-based hop-on/hop-off bus service aimed at younger travellers. Its network includes more than 30 cities in nine countries, and the main passes are of interest only to those travelling a lot beyond Spain, where there are five stops: Barcelona, Madrid, Valencia, San Sebastián and Pamplona.

Eurolines (www.eurolines.com) Offers a high-season pass valid for 15 days (adult/under 26 years €320/270) or 30 days (€425/350). This pass allows unlimited travel between 51 European cities, including a handful of Spanish ones.

RAIL PASSES

InterRail Passes

InterRail (www.interrailnet.eu) passes are available to people who have lived in Europe for six months or more. They can be bought at most major stations, student travel outlets and online.

Youth passes are for people aged 12 to 25, and adult passes are for those 26 and over. Children aged 11 and under travel for free if travelling on a family pass.

Global Pass Encompasses 30 countries that comes in seven versions, ranging from five days' travel in 15 days to a full month's travel. Check out the website for a full list of prices.

One-country Pass Can be used for three, four, six or eight days within one month in Spain. For the eight-day pass you pay €395/252/186 for adult 1st class/adult 2nd class/youth 2nd class.

Eurail Passes

Eurail (www.eurail.com) passes are for those who've lived in Europe for less than six months. They are supposed to be bought outside Europe, either online or from leading travel agencies.

Be sure you will be covering a lot of ground to make your Eurail pass worthwhile. To be certain, check the **Renfe** (www.renfe.com) website for sample prices in euros for the places in which you intend to travel.

For most of the following passes, children aged between four and 11 pay half-price for the 1st-class passes, while those aged under 26 can get a cheaper 2nd-class pass. The Eurail website has a full list of prices, including special family rates and other discounts.

Eurail Global Passes Good for travel in 28 European countries; forget it if you intend to travel mainly in Spain. There are nine different passes, from five days within one month to three months' continuous travel.

Eurail Select Pass Provides between five and 10 days of unlimited travel within a two-month period in two to four bordering countries (eg Spain, France, Italy and Switzerland).

Spain Pass With the one-country Spain Pass you can choose from three to eight days' train travel in a one-month period for any of these passes. The eight-day Spain Pass costs €406/325/265 for adult 1st class/adult 2nd class/youth 2nd class.

---

are the major cross-border services:

Paris to Madrid (€118 to €187, 9¾ to 12½ hours, eight daily) The slow route runs via Les Aubrais, Blois, Poitiers, Irún, Vitoria, Burgos and Valladolid. The quicker route goes via the high-speed AVE train to Barcelona and change from there.

Paris to Barcelona (from €100, 6½ hours, two daily) A recently inaugurated high-speed service runs via Valence, Nimes, Montpellier, Beziers, Narbonne, Perpignan, Figueres and Girona. Also high-speed services run from Lyon (from €96, five hours) and Toulouse (from €66, three to four hours)

Portugal

BUS

Avanza (☏902 020 999; www.avanzabus.com) runs three daily buses between Lisbon and Madrid (€43.30, 7½ hours, two daily).

Other bus services run north via Porto to Tui, Santiago de Compostela and A Coruña in Galicia, while local buses cross the border from towns such as Huelva in Andalucía, Badajoz in Extremadura and Ourense in Galicia.

CAR & MOTORCYCLE

The A5 freeway linking Madrid with Badajoz crosses the Portuguese frontier and continues on to Lisbon. There are many other road connections up and down the length of the Spain–Portugal border.

TRAIN

From Portugal, the main line runs from Lisbon across Extremadura to Madrid.

Lisbon to Madrid (chair/sleeper class from €60.50/84, 10½ hours, one daily)

Lisbon to Irún (chair/sleeper class €69/94, 13½ hours, one daily)

Sea

A useful website for comparing routes and finding links to the relevant ferry companies is www.ferrylines.com.

Algeria

Trasmediterránea (☑902 454645; www.trasmediterranea.es) Runs year-round ferries between Almería and Ghazaouet (twice weekly) and Oran (weekly).

Algérie Ferries (www.algerieferries.com) Operates year-round services from Alicante to Oran (11 hours, one to three weekly) as well as summer services from Alicante to Algiers and Mostaganem.

Italy

Most Italian routes are operated by **Grimaldi Lines** (www.grimaldi-lines.com) or **Grand Navi Veloci** (www.gnv.it).

Civitavecchia (near Rome) to Barcelona (20 hours, six weekly)

Genoa to Barcelona (19 hours, once or twice weekly)

Livorno (Tuscany) to Barcelona (21 hours, weekly)

Porto Torres (Sardinia) to Barcelona (12 hours, five weekly)

Savona (near Genoa) to Barcelona (18 hours, three weekly)

Morocco

Ferries run to Morocco from mainland Spain. Most services are run by the Spanish national ferry company, **Trasmediterránea** (☑902 454645; www.trasmediterranea.es). You can take vehicles on most routes. Other companies that connect Spain with Morocco include the following:

Baleària (www.baleria.com)

FRS Iberia (www.frs.es)

Grand Navi Veloci (www.gnv.it)

Grimaldi Lines (www.grimaldi-lines.com)

Naviera Armas (www.navieraarmas.com)

Services between Spain and Morocco include the following:

Al-Hoceima to Motril (3½ hours, weekly)

Nador to Almería (six hours, daily)

Nador to Motril (3½ hours, three weekly)

Tangier to Algeciras (one to two hours, up to eight daily) Buses from several Moroccan cities converge on Tangier to make the ferry crossing to Algeciras, then fan out to the main Spanish centres.

Tangier to Tarifa (35 to 40 minutes, up to eight daily)

Tangier to Barcelona (32 to 35 hours, one to two weekly)

Tangier to Motril (eight hours, daily)

UK

Brittany Ferries (☑0871 244 0744; www.brittany-ferries.co.uk) runs the following services:

Plymouth to Santander (20½ hours, weekly) Mid-March to November only.

Portsmouth to Santander (24 hours, two weekly)

Portsmouth to Bilbao (24 hours, two to three weekly)

GETTING AROUND

Spain's network of train and bus services is one of the best in Europe and there aren't many places that can't be reached using one or the other. The tentacles of Spain's high-speed train network are expanding rapidly, while domestic air services are plentiful over longer distances and on routes that are more complicated by land.

Air

Spain has an extensive network of internal flights. These are operated by both Spanish airlines and a handful of low-

cost international airlines, which include the following:

Air Europa (www.aireuropa.com) Madrid to A Coruña, Vigo, Bilbao, and Barcelona, as well as other routes between Spanish cities.

Iberia (www.iberia.com) Spain's national airline and its subsidiary, Iberia Regional-Air Nostrum, have an extensive domestic network.

Ryanair (www.ryanair.com) Some domestic Spanish routes include Madrid to Santiago de Compostela or Seville to Barcelona.

Volotea (www.volotea.com) Budget airline that flies domestically and internationally. Domestic routes take in Málaga, Seville, Valencia, Vigo, Bilbao, Zaragoza, Oviedo and the Balearics (but not Madrid or Barcelona).

Vueling (www.vueling.com) Spanish low-cost company with loads of domestic flights within Spain, especially from Barcelona.

Bicycle

Years of highway improvement programs across the country have made cycling a much easier prospect than it once was, although there are few designated bike lanes. Cycling on *autopistas* (tollways) is forbidden. Driver attitudes on open roads is generally good, less so in the cities where cycling is not for the faint-hearted.

If you get tired of pedalling, it is often possible to take your bike on the train. All regional trains have space for bikes (usually marked by a bicycle logo on the carriage), where you can simply load the bike. Bikes are also permitted on most *cercanías* (local-area trains around big cities such as Madrid and Barcelona). On long-distance trains there are more restrictions. As a rule, you have to be travelling overnight in a sleeper or couchette to have the (dismantled) bike accepted as normal luggage. Otherwise, it can only be sent separately as a parcel. It's often possible to take your bike on a bus – usually you'll just be asked to remove the front wheel.

Hire & Bike Sharing Schemes

Bicycle rental is not as widespread as in some European countries, though it's becoming more so, especially in the case of *bici todo terreno* (mountain bikes) and in Andalucía, Barcelona and popular coastal towns. Costs vary considerably, but expect to pay around €8 to €10 per hour, €15 to €20 per day, or €50 to €60 per week.

A number of cities have introduced public bicycle systems with dozens of automated pick-up and drop-off points. These schemes involve paying a small subscription fee, which then allows you to pick up a bicycle at one location and drop it off at another.

Madrid (☑010, 91 529 82 10; www.bicimad.com; 1/2hr €2/6; ☺24hr)

Seville (☑902 011032; www. sevici.es; ☺7am-9pm)

Zaragoza (☑902 319 931; www.bizizaragoza.com; 3-day card €5)

Boat

Ferries and hydrofoils link the mainland (La Península) – or more specifically, Barcelona, Valencia and Denia – with Palma de Mallorca. There are also services to Spain's North African enclaves of Ceuta and Melilla.

Baleària (www.baleria.com) Runs between the mainland and Palma de Mallorca. On overnight services between the mainland and Palma de Mallorca, you can opt for seating or sleeping accommodation in a cabin.

Trasmediterránea (☑902 454645; www.trasmediterranea.es) The main national ferry company runs a combination of slower car ferries and modern, high-speed, passenger-only fast ferries and hydrofoils.

Bus

There are few places in Spain where buses don't go. Numerous companies provide bus links, from local routes between villages to fast inter-city connections. It is often cheaper to travel by bus than by train, particularly on long-haul runs, but also less comfortable.

Local services can get you just about anywhere, but most buses connecting villages and provincial towns are not geared to tourist needs. Frequent weekday services drop off to a trickle, if they operate at all, on Saturday and Sunday. Often just one bus runs daily between smaller places during the week, and none operate on Sunday. It's usually unnecessary to make reservations; just arrive early enough to get a seat.

On many regular runs – say, from Madrid to Toledo – the ticket you buy is for the next bus due to leave and *cannot* be used on a later bus. Advance purchase in such cases is generally not possible. For longer trips (such as Madrid to Seville or to the coast), and certainly in peak holiday season, you can (and should) buy your ticket in advance. On some routes you have the choice between express and stopping-all-stations services.

In most larger towns and cities, buses leave from a single *estación de autobuses* (bus station). In smaller places, buses tend to operate from a set street or plaza, often unmarked. Locals will know where to go and where to buy tickets.

Bus travel within Spain is not overly costly. The trip from Madrid to Barcelona starts from around €32 one way. From Barcelona to Seville, which is one of the longest trips (15 to 16 hours), you can pay at least €100 one way.

People under 26 should inquire about discounts on long-distance trips.

Among the hundreds of bus companies operating in Spain, the following have the largest range of services:

ALSA (☑902 422 242; www. alsa.es) The biggest player, this company has routes all over the country in association with various other companies.

Avanza (☑902 020 999; www. avanzabus.com) Operates buses from Madrid to Extremadura, western Castilla y León and Valencia via eastern Castilla-La Mancha (eg Cuenca), often in association with other companies.

Socibus (☑902 229292; www. socibus.es) Operates services between Madrid, western Andalucía and the Basque Country.

Car & Motorcycle

Every vehicle should display a nationality plate of its country of registration and you must always carry proof of ownership of a private vehicle. Third-party motor

---

BEATING PARKING FINES

If you've parked in a street parking spot and return to find that a parking inspector has left you a parking ticket, don't despair. If you arrive back within a reasonable time after the ticket was issued (what constitutes a reasonable time varies from place to place, but it is rarely more than a couple of hours), don't go looking for the inspector, but instead head for the nearest parking machine. Most machines in most cities allow you to pay a small penalty (usually around €5) to cancel the fine (keep both pieces of paper just in case). If you're unable to work out what to do, ask a local for help.

insurance is required throughout Europe. A warning triangle and a reflective jacket (to be used in case of breakdown) are compulsory.

Automobile Association

The **Real Automóvil Club de España** (RACE; ☎900 100 992; www.race.es; Calle de Eloy Gonzalo 32, Madrid) is the national automobile club. They may well come to assist you in case of breakdown, but in any event you should obtain an emergency telephone number for Spain from your own insurer or car-rental company.

Driving Licences

All EU member states' driving licences are fully recognised throughout Europe. Those with a non-EU licence are supposed to obtain a 12-month International Driving Permit (IDP) to accompany their national licence, which your national automobile association can issue. In practice, however, car-rental companies and police rarely ask for one. People who have held residency in Spain for one year or more should apply for a Spanish driving licence.

Fuel

➡ *Gasolina* (petrol) is pricey in Spain, but generally slightly cheaper than in its major EU neighbours (including France, Germany, Italy and the UK); *gasoleo* is diesel fuel.

➡ Petrol is about 10% cheaper in Gibraltar than in Spain and 15% cheaper in Andorra.

➡ You can pay with major credit cards at most service stations.

Hire

To rent a car in Spain you have to have a licence, be aged 21 or over and, for the major companies at least, have a credit or debit card. Smaller firms in areas where car hire is particularly com-

mon sometimes waiver this last requirement. Although those with a non-EU licence should also have an IDP, you will find that national licences from countries such as Australia, Canada, New Zealand and the US are usually accepted without question.

With some of the low-cost companies, beware of 'extras' that aren't quoted in initial prices.

Avis (☎902 180854; www.avis.es)

Enterprise Rent-a-Car (☎902 100 101; www.enterprise.es)

Europcar (☎902 105 030; www.europcar.es)

Firefly (www.fireflycarrental.com)

Hertz (☎91 749 77 78; www.hertz.es)

Pepecar (☎807 414243; www.pepecar.com)

SixT (☎902 491616; www.sixt.es)

Other possibilities include the following:

Auto Europe (www.autoeurope.com) US-based clearing house for deals with major car-rental agencies.

BlaBlaCar (www.blablacar.com) Car-sharing site which can be really useful for outlying towns, and if your Spanish is up to it, you get to meet people too.

Holiday Autos (☎900 838 014; www.holidayautos.com) A clearing house for major international companies.

Ideamerge (www.ideamerge.com) Car-leasing plans, motor-home rentals and much more.

Insurance

Third-party motor insurance is a minimum requirement in Spain and throughout Europe. Ask your insurer for a European Accident Statement form, which can simplify matters in the event of an accident. A European breakdown-assistance policy such as the AA Five Star Service or RAC Eurocover Motoring Assistance is a good investment.

Car-hire companies also provide this minimum insurance, but be careful to understand what your liabilities and excess are, and what waivers you are entitled to in case of accident or damage to the hire vehicle.

Road Rules

Blood-alcohol limit 0.05%. Breath tests are common, and if found to be over the limit, you can be judged, condemned, fined and deprived of your licence within 24 hours. Fines range up to around €600 for serious offences. Nonresident foreigners may be required to pay up on the spot (at 30% off the full fine). Pleading linguistic ignorance will not help – the police officer will produce a list of infringements and fines in as many languages as you like.

Legal driving age (cars) 18 years.

Legal driving age (motorcycles & scooters) 16 (80cc and over) or 14 (50cc and under) years. A licence is required.

Motorcyclists Must use headlights at all times and wear a helmet if riding a bike of 125cc or more.

Overtaking Spanish truck drivers often have the courtesy to turn on their right indicator to show that the way ahead of them is clear for overtaking (and the left one if it is not and you are attempting this manoeuvre). Make sure, however, that they're not just turning right!

Roundabouts (traffic circles) Vehicles already in the circle have the right of way.

Side of the road Drive on the right.

Speed limits In built-up areas, 50km/h (and in some cases, such as inner-city Barcelona, 30km/h), which increases to 100km/h on major roads and up to 120km/h on *autovías* and *autopistas* (toll-free and tolled dual-lane highways, respectively). Cars towing caravans are restricted to a maximum speed of 80km/h.

Hitching

Hitching is never entirely safe, and we don't recommend it. Travellers who hitch should understand that they are taking a small but potentially serious risk. People who do choose to hitch will be safer if they travel in pairs and let someone know where they are planning to go.

Hitching is illegal on *autopistas* and *autovías*, and difficult on other major highways. Choose a spot where cars can safely stop before highway slipways, or use minor roads. The going can be slow on the latter, as the traffic is often light.

Local Transport

Most of the major cities have excellent local transport. Madrid and Barcelona have extensive bus and metro systems, and other major cities also benefit from generally efficient public transport. By European standards, prices are relatively cheap.

Bus

Cities and provincial capitals all have reasonable bus networks. You can buy single tickets (usually between €1 and €2) on the buses or at *estancos* (tobacconists), but in cities such as Madrid and Barcelona, you are better off buying combined 10-trip tickets that allow the use of a combination of bus and metro, and which work out cheaper per ride. These can be purchased in any metro station and from some tobacconists and newspaper kiosks.

Regular buses run from about 6am to shortly before midnight and even as late as 2am. In the big cities, a night bus service generally kicks in on a limited number of lines in the wee hours. In Madrid they are known as *búhos* (owls) and in Barcelona more prosaically as *nitbusos* (night buses).

Metro

Madrid has the country's most extensive metro network. Barcelona has a reasonable system. Valencia, Zaragoza, Bilbao and Seville have limited but nonetheless useful metro (or light rail) systems.

➡ Tickets must be bought in metro stations (from counters or vending machines), or sometimes from *estancos* (tobacconists) or newspaper kiosks.

➡ Single tickets cost the same as for buses (around €1.50).

➡ Visitors wanting to move around the major cities over a few days are best off getting 10-trip tickets, known in Madrid as Metrobús (€12.20) and in Barcelona as T-10 (€10.30).

➡ Monthly and seasonal passes are also available.

Taxi

You can find taxi ranks at train and bus stations, or you can telephone for radio taxis. In larger cities, taxi ranks are also scattered about the centre, and taxis will stop if you hail them in the street – look for the green light and/or the *libre* sign on the passenger side of the windscreen. The bigger cities are well populated with taxis, although you might have to wait a bit longer on a Friday or Saturday night. No more than four people are allowed in a taxi.

➡ Daytime flagfall (generally to 10pm) is, for example, €2.40 in Madrid, and up to €2.90 after 9pm to 7am, and on weekends and holidays.

MEMORABLE TRAIN JOURNEYS

The romantically inclined could opt for an opulent and slow-moving, old-time rail adventure with numerous options across the peninsula. The trains don't travel at night, making sleeping aboard easy and providing the opportunity to stay out at night.

Transcantábrico (☎902 555 902; www.renfe.com/trenesturisticos) For a journey on a picturesque narrow-gauge rail route, from Santiago de Compostela (by bus as far as O Ferrol) via Oviedo, Santander and Bilbao along the coast, and then a long inland stretch to finish in León. The eight-day trip costs from €3150 per person in high season. The trip can also be done in reverse or in smaller chunks. There are 11 departures from April to October. Check if your package includes various visits along the way, including the Museo Guggenheim Bilbao, the Museo de Altamira, Santillana del Mar, and the Covadonga lakes in the Picos de Europa. The food is exceptional, with some meals being eaten on board but most in various locations.

Al-Andalus (☎902 555 902; www.renfe.com/trenesturisticos) Despite the name, this line covers a significant proportion of the peninsula, from loops through Andalucía to slower routes between Madrid and Sevilla, Madrid and Zaragoza, Zaragoza to León, and León to Santiago de Compostela. Options vary from three to five nights. Prices for the seven-day/six-night itineraries start at €3500 per person in high season.

Train Routes

You then pay €1.05 to €1.20 per kilometre depending on the time of day.

➡ There are airport and (sometimes) luggage surcharges.

➡ A cross-town ride in a major city will cost about €10 – absurdly cheap by European standards – while a taxi between the city centre and airport in either Madrid or Barcelona will cost €30 with luggage.

Tram

Trams were stripped out of Spanish cities decades ago, but they're making a minor comeback in some. Barcelona has a couple of new suburban tram services in addition to its tourist Tramvia Blau run to Tibidabo.

Valencia has some useful trams to the beach, while various limited lines also run in Seville, Bilbao, Murcia and, most recently, Zaragoza.

Train

Renfe (☎902 243 402; www. renfe.com) is the excellent national train system that runs most of the services in Spain. A handful of small private railway lines also operate.

You'll find *consignas* (left-luggage facilities) at all main train stations. They are usually open from about 6am to midnight and charge from €4 to €6 per day per piece of luggage.

Spain has several types of trains, and *largo recorrido* or *Grandes Líneas* (long-dis-

tance trains) in particular have a variety of names.

Alaris, Altaria, Alvia, Arco & Avant Long-distance intermediate-speed services.

Cercanías (*rodalies* in Catalonia) For short hops and services to outlying suburbs and satellite towns in Madrid, Barcelona and 11 other cities.

Euromed Similar to the Tren de Alta Velocidad Española (AVE) trains, they connect Barcelona with Valencia and Alicante.

FEVE (Ferrocarriles de Vía Estrecha) Narrow-gauge network along Spain's north coast between Bilbao and Ferrol (Galicia), with a branch down to León.

Regionales Trains operating within one region, usually stopping all stations.

Talgo & intercity Slower long-distance trains.

Tren de Alta Velocidad Española (AVE) High-speed trains that link Madrid with Albacete, Barcelona, Burgos, Cádiz, Córdoba, Cuenca, Huesca, León, Lerida, Málaga, Palencia, Salamanca, Santiago de Compostela, Seville, Valencia, Valladolid, Zamora and Zaragoza. There are also Barcelona–Seville, Barcelona–Málaga and Valencia–Seville services. In coming years, Madrid–Bilbao should also come on line, and travel times to Galicia should fall.

Trenhotel Overnight trains with sleeper berths.

Classes & Costs

All long-distance trains have 2nd and 1st classes, known as *turista* and *preferente*, respectively. The latter is 20% to 40% more expensive.

Fares vary enormously depending on the service (faster trains cost considerably more) and, in the case of some high-speed services such as the AVE, on the time and day of travel. Tickets for AVE trains are by far the most expensive. A one-way trip in 2nd class from Madrid to Barcelona (on which route only AVE trains run) could cost as much as €107 (it could work

CHEAPER TRAIN TICKETS

Train travel can be expensive in Spain but there is one trick worth knowing. Return tickets cost considerably less than two one-way tickets. If you're certain that you'll be returning on the same route sometime over the coming months (three months is usually the limit), buy a return ticket and you can later change the return date, which works out a lot cheaper than buying two one-way tickets.

out significantly cheaper if you book well in advance).

Children aged between four and 12 years are entitled to a 40% discount; those aged under four travel for free (except on high-speed trains, for which they pay the same as those aged four to 12). Buying a return ticket often gives you a 10% to 20% discount on the return trip. Students and people up to 25 years of age with a Euro<26 Card (Carnet Joven in Spain) are entitled to 20% to 25% off most ticket prices.

If you're travelling as a family, ask for one of a group of four seats with a table when making your reservation.

On overnight trips within Spain on *trenhoteles*, it's worth paying extra for a *litera* (couchette; a sleeping berth in a six- or four-bed

compartment) or, if available, single or double cabins in *preferente* or *gran clase* class. The cost depends on the class of accommodation, type of train and length of journey. The lines covered are Madrid–A Coruña, Barcelona–Granada, Barcelona–A Coruña-Vigo and Madrid–Lisbon, as well as international services to France.

Reservations

Reservations are recommended for long-distance trips, and you can make them in train stations, **Renfe** (✆902 243 402; www.renfe. com) offices and travel agencies, as well as online. In a growing number of stations, you can pick up prebooked tickets from machines scattered about the station concourse.

Language

Spanish (*español*) – or Castilian (*castellano*), as it is also called – is spoken throughout Spain, but there are also three co-official, regional languages: Catalan (*català*), spoken in Catalonia, the Balearic Islands and Valencia; Galician (*galego*), spoken in Galicia; and Basque (*euskara*), which is spoken in the Basque Country and Navarra.

The pronunciation of most Spanish sounds is very similar to that of their English counterparts. If you read our coloured pronunciation guides as if they were English, you'll be understood. Note that kh is a throaty sound (like the 'ch' in the Scottish *loch*), r is strongly rolled, ly is pronounced as the 'lli' in 'million' and ny as the 'ni' in 'onion'. You may also notice that the 'lisped' th sound is pronounced as s in Andalucia. In our pronunciation guides, the stressed syllables are in italics.

Where necessary in this chapter, masculine and feminine forms are marked with 'm/f', while polite and informal options are indicated by the abbreviations 'pol' and 'inf'.

BASICS

Hello.	Hola.	o·la
Goodbye.	Adiós.	a·*dyos*
Yes./No.	Sí./No.	see/no
Excuse me.	Perdón.	per·*don*
Sorry.	Lo siento.	lo *syen*·to
Please.	Por favor.	por fa·*vor*

WANT MORE?

For in-depth language information and handy phrases, check out Lonely Planet's *Spanish Phrasebook*. You'll find it at **shop.lonelyplanet.com**, or you can buy Lonely Planet's iPhone phrasebooks at the Apple App Store.

QUESTION WORDS

How?	¿Cómo?	*ko*·mo
What?	¿Qué?	ke
When?	¿Cuándo?	*kwan*·do
Where?	¿Dónde?	*don*·de
Who?	¿Quién?	kyen
Why?	¿Por qué?	por ke

Thank you.	Gracias.	*gra*·thyas
You're welcome.	De nada.	de *na*·da
How are you?	¿Qué tal?	ke tal
Fine, thanks.	Bien, gracias.	byen *gra*·thyas

What's your name?
¿Cómo se llama Usted?	*ko*·mo se *lya*·ma oo·*ste* (pol)
¿Cómo te llamas?	*ko*·mo te *lya*·mas (inf)

My name is ...
Me llamo ...	me *lya*·mo ...

Do you speak English?
¿Habla inglés?	a·bla een·*gles* (pol)
¿Hablas inglés?	a·blas een·*gles* (inf)

I don't understand.
No entiendo.	no en·*tyen*·do

ACCOMMODATION

hotel	hotel	o·tel
guesthouse	pensión	pen·*syon*
youth hostel	albergue juvenil	al·*ber*·ge khoo·ve·*neel*

I'd like a ... room.	Quisiera una habitación ...	kee·*sye*·ra oo·na a·bee·ta·*thyon* ...
single	individual	een·dee·vee·*dwal*
double	doble	*do*·ble

air-con	aire acondicionado	*ai*·re a·kon·dee·thyo·*na*·do

bathroom	*baño*	*ba*·nyo
window	*ventana*	ven·*ta*·na

NUMBERS

1	*uno*	*oo*·no
2	*dos*	dos
3	*tres*	tres
4	*cuatro*	*kwa*·tro
5	*cinco*	*theen*·ko
6	*seis*	seys
7	*siete*	*sye*·te
8	*ocho*	*o*·cho
9	*nueve*	*nwe*·ve
10	*diez*	dyeth
20	*veinte*	*veyn*·te
30	*treinta*	*treyn*·ta
40	*cuarenta*	kwa·*ren*·ta
50	*cincuenta*	theen·*kwen*·ta
60	*sesenta*	se·*sen*·ta
70	*setenta*	se·*ten*·ta
80	*ochenta*	o·*chen*·ta
90	*noventa*	no·*ven*·ta
100	*cien*	thyen
1000	*mil*	meel

How much is it per night/person?
¿Cuánto cuesta por kwan·to kwes·ta por
noche/persona? no·che/per·so·na

Does it include breakfast?
¿Incluye el desayuno? een·*kloo*·ye el de·sa·*yoo*·no

DIRECTIONS

Where's ...?
¿Dónde está ...? *don*·de es·*ta* ...

What's the address?
¿Cuál es la dirección? kwal es la dee·rek·*thyon*

Can you please write it down?
¿Puede escribirlo, *pwe*·de es·kree·*beer*·lo
por favor? por fa·*vor*

Can you show me (on the map)?
¿Me lo puede indicar me lo *pwe*·de een·dee·*kar*
(en el mapa)? (en el *ma*·pa)

at the corner	*en la esquina*	en la es·*kee*·na
at the traffic lights	*en el semáforo*	en el se·*ma*·fo·ro
behind ...	*detrás de ...*	de·*tras* de ...
in front of ...	*enfrente de ...*	en·*fren*·te de ...
left	*izquierda*	eeth·*kyer*·da
next to ...	*al lado de ...*	al *la*·do de ...
opposite ...	*frente a ...*	*fren*·te a ...
right	*derecha*	de·*re*·cha
straight ahead	*todo recto*	*to*·do *rek*·to

EATING & DRINKING

What would you recommend?
¿Qué recomienda? ke re·ko·*myen*·da

What's in that dish?
¿Que lleva ese plato? ke *lye*·va e·se *pla*·to

I don't eat ...
No como ... no *ko*·mo ...

Cheers!
¡Salud! sa·*loo*

That was delicious!
¡Estaba buenísimo! es·*ta*·ba bwe·*nee*·see·mo

Please bring us the bill.
Por favor, nos trae por fa·*vor* nos *tra*·e
la cuenta. la *kwen*·ta

I'd like to book a table for ...	*Quisiera reservar una mesa para ...*	kee·*sye*·ra re·ser·*var* oo·na *me*·sa pa·ra ...
(eight) o'clock	*las (ocho)*	las (*o*·cho)
(two) people	*(dos) personas*	(dos) per·so·nas

Key Words

bottle	*botella*	bo·*te*·lya
breakfast	*desayuno*	de·sa·*yoo*·no
(too) cold	*(muy) frío*	(mooy) *free*·o
dinner	*cena*	*the*·na
food	*comida*	ko·*mee*·da
fork	*tenedor*	te·ne·*dor*
glass	*vaso*	*va*·so
highchair	*trona*	*tro*·na
hot (warm)	*caliente*	ka·*lyen*·te
knife	*cuchillo*	koo·*chee*·lyo
lunch	*comida*	ko·*mee*·da
market	*mercado*	mer·*ka*·do
(children's) menu	*menú (infantil)*	me·*noo* (een·fan·*teel*)
plate	*plato*	*pla*·to
restaurant	*restaurante*	res·tow·*ran*·te
spoon	*cuchara*	koo·*cha*·ra
vegetarian food	*comida vegetariana*	ko·*mee*·da ve·khe·ta·*rya*·na

CATALAN

The recognition of Catalan as an official language in Spain is the end result of a regional government campaign that began when the province gained autonomy at the end of the 1970s. Until the Battle of Muret in 1213, Catalan territory extended across southern France, taking in Roussillon and reaching into the Provence. Catalan was spoken, or at least understood, throughout these territories and in what is now Catalonia and Andorra. In the couple of hundred years that followed, the Catalans spread their language south into Valencia, west into Aragón and east to the Balearic Islands. It also reached Sicily and Naples, and the Sardinian town of Alghero is still a partly Catalan-speaking outpost today. Catalan is spoken by up to 10 million people in Spain.

In Barcelona you'll hear as much Spanish as Catalan. Your chances of coming across English speakers are also good. Elsewhere in the province, don't be surprised if you get replies in Catalan to your questions in Spanish. However, you'll find that most Catalans will happily speak to you in Spanish, especially once they realise you're a foreigner. This said, the following Catalan phrases might win you a few smiles and perhaps help you make some new friends.

Hello.	Hola.	Monday	dilluns
Goodbye.	Adéu.	Tuesday	dimarts
Yes.	Sí.	Wednesday	dimecres
No.	No.	Thursday	dijous
Please.	Sisplau./Si us plau.	Friday	divendres
Thank you (very much).	(Moltes) gràcies.	Saturday	dissabte
You're welcome.	De res.	Sunday	diumenge
Excuse me.	Perdoni.		
May I?/Do you mind?	Puc?/Em permet?	1	un/una (m/f)
I'm sorry.	Ho sento./Perdoni.	2	dos/dues (m/f)
		3	tres
What's your name?	Com et dius? (inf)	4	quatre
	Com es diu? (pol)	5	cinc
My name is ...	Em dic ...	6	sis
Where are you from?	D'on ets?	7	set
Do you speak English?	Parla anglès?	8	vuit
I understand.	Ho entenc.	9	nou
I don't understand.	No ho entenc.	10	deu
Could you speak in	Pot parlar castellà	11	onze
Castilian, please?	sisplau?	12	dotze
How do you say ... in	Com es diu ... en	13	tretze
Catalan?	català?	14	catorze
		15	quinze
I'm looking for ...	Estic buscant ...	16	setze
How do I get to ...?	Com puc arribar a ...?	17	disset
Turn left.	Giri a mà esquerra.	18	divuit
Turn right.	Giri a mà dreta.	19	dinou
near	a prop de	20	vint
far	a lluny de	100	cent

Meat & Fish

beef	carne de vaca	kar·ne de va·ka
chicken	pollo	po·lyo
duck	pato	pa·to
lamb	cordero	kor·de·ro
lobster	langosta	lan·gos·ta
pork	cerdo	ther·do
prawns	camarones	ka·ma·ro·nes
tuna	atún	a·toon
turkey	pavo	pa·vo
veal	ternera	ter·ne·ra

Fruit & Vegetables

apple	manzana	man·tha·na
apricot	albaricoque	al·ba·ree·ko·ke
banana	plátano	pla·ta·no
beans	judías	khoo·dee·as
cabbage	col	kol
capsicum	pimiento	pee·myen·to
carrot	zanahoria	tha·na·o·rya
cherry	cereza	the·re·tha
corn	maíz	ma·eeth
cucumber	pepino	pe·pee·no
fruit	fruta	froo·ta
grape	uvas	oo·vas
lemon	limón	lee·mon
lettuce	lechuga	le·choo·ga
mushroom	champiñón	cham·pee·nyon
nuts	nueces	nwe·thes
onion	cebolla	the·bo·lya
orange	naranja	na·ran·kha
peach	melocotón	me·lo·ko·ton
peas	guisantes	gee·san·tes
pineapple	piña	pee·nya
plum	ciruela	theer·we·la
potato	patata	pa·ta·ta
spinach	espinacas	es·pee·na·kas
strawberry	fresa	fre·sa
tomato	tomate	to·ma·te
vegetable	verdura	ver·doo·ra
watermelon	sandía	san·dee·a

Other

bread	pan	pan
cheese	queso	ke·so

GALICIAN

Galician is the official language of the Autonomous Community of Galicia and is also widely understood in the neighbouring regions of Asturias and Castilla y Léon. It's very similar to Portuguese. Galicians are likely to revert to Spanish when addressing a stranger, especially a foreigner, but making a small effort to communicate in Galician will always be welcomed.

Hello.	Ola.
Good day.	Bon dia.
Goodbye.	Adeus./Até logo.
Many thanks.	Moitas grácias.
Do you speak English?	Fala inglés?
I don't understand.	Non entendo.
Could you speak in Castilian, please?	Pode falar en español, por favor?
What's this called in Galician?	Como se chama iso en galego?

egg	huevo	we·vo
honey	miel	myel
jam	mermelada	mer·me·la·da
rice	arroz	a·roth
salt	sal	sal
sugar	azúcar	a·thoo·kar

Drinks

beer	cerveza	ther·ve·tha
coffee	café	ka·fe
(orange) juice	zumo (de naranja)	thoo·mo (de na·ran·kha)
milk	leche	le·che
red wine	vino tinto	vee·no teen·to
tea	té	te
(mineral) water	agua (mineral)	a·gwa (mee·ne·ral)
white wine	vino blanco	vee·no blan·ko

EMERGENCIES

Help!	¡Socorro!	so·ko·ro
Go away!	¡Vete!	ve·te
Call ...!	¡Llame a ...!	lya·me a ...
a doctor	un médico	oon me·dee·ko
the police	la policía	la po·lee·thee·a

I'm lost.
Estoy perdido/a.   es·toy per·dee·do/a (m/f)

I'm ill.
Estoy enfermo/a.   es·toy en·fer·mo/a (m/f)

It hurts here.
Me duele aquí.   me dwe·le a·kee

I'm allergic to (antibiotics).
Soy alérgico/a a   soy a·ler·khee·ko/a a
(los antibióticos).   (los an·tee·byo·tee·kos) (m/f)

Where are the toilets?
¿Dónde están los   don·de es·tan los
servicios?   ser·vee·thyos

SHOPPING & SERVICES

I'd like to buy ...
Quisiera comprar ...   kee·sye·ra kom·prar ...

I'm just looking.
Sólo estoy mirando.   so·lo es·toy mee·ran·do

Can I look at it?
¿Puedo verlo?   pwe·do ver·lo

I don't like it.
No me gusta.   no me goos·ta

How much is it?
¿Cuánto cuesta?   kwan·to kwes·ta

That's too expensive.
Es muy caro.   es mooy ka·ro

Can you lower the price?
¿Podría bajar un   po·dree·a ba·khar oon
poco el precio?   po·ko el pre·thyo

BASQUE

Basque is spoken at the western end of the Pyrenees and along the Bay of Biscay – from Bayonne in France to Bilbao in Spain, and inland, almost to Pamplona. No one quite knows its origin, but the most likely theory is that Basque is the lone survivor of a language family that once extended across Europe, and was wiped out by the languages of the Celts, Germanic tribes and Romans.

Hello.	*Kaixo.*
Goodbye.	*Agur.*
How are you?	*Zer moduz?*
Fine, thank you.	*Ongi, eskerrik asko.*
Excuse me.	*Barkatu.*
Please.	*Mesedez.*
Thank you.	*Eskerrik asko.*
You're welcome.	*Ez horregatik.*
Do you speak English?	*Ingelesez ba al dakizu?*
I don't understand.	*Ez dut ulertzen.*

There's a mistake in the bill.
Hay un error en   ai oon e·ror en
la cuenta.   la kwen·ta

ATM	*cajero*	ka·khe·ro
	automático	ow·to·ma·tee·ko
internet cafe	*cibercafé*	thee·ber·ka·fe
post office	*correos*	ko·re·os
tourist office	*oficina*	o·fee·thee·na
	de turismo	de too·rees·mo

TIME & DATES

What time is it?	*¿Qué hora es?*	ke o·ra es
It's (10) o'clock.	*Son (las diez).*	son (las dyeth)
Half past (one).	*Es (la una)*	es (la oo·na)
	y media.	ee me·dya
At what time?	*¿A qué hora?*	a ke o·ra
At ...	*A la(s) ...*	a la(s) ...

morning	*mañana*	ma·nya·na
afternoon	*tarde*	tar·de
evening	*noche*	no·che

yesterday	*ayer*	a·yer
today	*hoy*	oy
tomorrow	*mañana*	ma·nya·na
Monday	*lunes*	loo·nes
Tuesday	*martes*	mar·tes
Wednesday	*miércoles*	myer·ko·les
Thursday	*jueves*	khwe·bes
Friday	*viernes*	vyer·nes
Saturday	*sábado*	sa·ba·do
Sunday	*domingo*	do·meen·go

TRANSPORT

Public Transport

boat	*barco*	bar·ko
bus	*autobús*	ow·to·boos
plane	*avión*	a·vyon
train	*tren*	tren

first	*primer*	pree·mer
last	*último*	ool·tee·mo
next	*próximo*	prok·see·mo

| **a ... ticket** | *un billete de ...* | oon bee·lye·te de ... |

1st-class	primera clase	pree·me·ra kla·se
2nd-class	segunda clase	se·goon·da kla·se
one-way	ida	ee·da
return	ida y vuelta	ee·da ee vwel·ta

aisle seat	asiento de pasillo	a·syen·to de pa·see·lyo
station	estación	es·ta·thyon
ticket office	taquilla	ta·kee·lya
timetable	horario	o·ra·ryo
window seat	asiento junto a la ventana	a·syen·to khoon·to a la ven·ta·na

I want to go to ...
Quisiera ir a ...　　kee·sye·ra eer a ...

At what time does it arrive/leave?
¿A qué hora llega/sale?　a ke o·ra lye·ga/sa·le

Does it stop at (Madrid)?
¿Para en (Madrid)?　pa·ra en (ma·dree)

Which stop is this?
¿Cuál es esta parada?　kwal es es·ta pa·ra·da

Please tell me when we get to (Seville).
¿Puede avisarme　pwe·de a·vee·sar·me
cuando lleguemos　kwan·do lye·ge·mos
a (Sevilla)?　a (se·vee·lya)

I want to get off here.
Quiero bajarme aquí.　kye·ro ba·khar·me a·kee

Driving and Cycling

I'd like to hire a ...	Quisiera alquilar ...	kee·sye·ra al·kee·lar ...
4WD	un todoterreno	oon to·do·te·re·no
bicycle	una bicicleta	oo·na bee·thee·kle·ta
car	un coche	oon ko·che
motorcycle	una moto	oo·na mo·to
child seat	asiento de seguridad para niños	a·syen·to de se·goo·ree·da pa·ra nee·nyos
helmet	casco	kas·ko
mechanic	mecánico	me·ka·nee·ko
petrol	gasolina	ga·so·lee·na
service station	gasolinera	ga·so·lee·ne·ra

How much is it per day/hour?
¿Cuánto cuesta por　kwan·to kwes·ta por
día/hora?　dee·a/o·ra

Is this the road to (Barcelona)?
¿Se va a (Barcelona)　se va a (bar·the·lo·na)
por esta carretera?　por es·ta ka·re·te·ra

(How long) Can I park here?
¿(Por cuánto tiempo)　(por kwan·to tyem·po)
Puedo aparcar aquí?　pwe·do a·par·kar a·kee

The car has broken down (at Valencia).
El coche se ha averiado　el ko·che se a a·ve·rya·do
(en Valencia).　(en va·len·thya)

I have a flat tyre.
Tengo un pinchazo.　ten·go oon peen·cha·tho

I've run out of petrol.
Me he quedado sin　me e ke·da·do seen
gasolina.　ga·so·lee·na

GLOSSARY

Unless otherwise indicated, the following terms are from Castilian Spanish. The masculine and feminine forms are indicated with the abbreviations 'm/f'.

ajuntament – Catalan for *ayuntamiento*
alameda – tree-lined avenue
albergue – refuge
albergue juvenil – youth hostel
alcázar – Muslim-era fortress
aljibe – cistern
artesonado – wooden Mudéjar ceiling with interlaced beams leaving a pattern of spaces for decoration
autopista – tollway
autovía – toll-free highway
AVE – Tren de Alta Velocidad Española; high-speed train
ayuntamiento – city or town hall

bailaor/bailaora – m/f flamenco dancer
baile – dance in a flamenco context
balneario – spa
barrio – district/quarter (of a town or city)
biblioteca – library
bici todo terreno (BTT) – mountain bike
bodega – cellar (especially wine cellar); also a winery or a traditional wine bar likely to serve wine from the barrel
búhos – night-bus routes

cabrito – kid
cala – cove
calle – street
callejón – lane
cama – bed
cambio – change; also currency exchange
caña – small glass of beer
cantaor/cantaora – m/f flamenco singer
capilla – chapel
capilla mayor – chapel containing the high altar of a church
carmen – walled villa with gardens, in Granada

Carnaval – traditional festive period that precedes the start of Lent; carnival
carretera – highway
carta – menu
casa de huéspedes – guesthouse; see also *hospedaje*
casa de pagès – *casa rural* in Catalonia
casa rural – village, country house or farmstead with rooms to let
casco – literally 'helmet'; often used to refer to the old part of a city; more correctly, *casco antiguo/histórico/viejo*
castellano/a (m/f) – Castilian; used in preference to *español* to describe the national language
castellers – Catalan human-castle builders
castillo – castle
castro – Celtic fortified village
català – Catalan language; a native of Catalonia
catedral – cathedral
cercanías – local train network
cervecería – beer bar
churrigueresco – ornate style of baroque architecture named after the brothers Alberto and José Churriguera
ciudad – city
claustro – cloister
CNIG – Centro Nacional de Información Geográfica; producers of good-quality maps
cofradía – see *hermandad*
colegiata – collegiate church
coll – Catalan for *collado*
collado – mountain pass
comarca – district; grouping of *municipios*
comedor – dining room
comunidad – fixed charge for maintenance of rental accommodation (sometimes included in rent); community
conquistador – conqueror
copa – drink; literally 'glass'
cordillera – mountain range
coro – choir: part of a church, usually the middle
correos – post office
Cortes – national parliament

costa – coast
cruceiro – standing crucifix found at many crossroads in Galicia
cuesta – lane, usually on a hill
custodia – monstrance

dolmen – prehistoric megalithic tomb

embalse – reservoir
encierro – running of the bulls Pamplona-style; also happens in many other places around Spain
entrada – entrance
ermita – hermitage or chapel
església – Catalan for *iglesia*
estació – Catalan for *estación*
estación – station
estación de autobuses – bus station
estación de esquí – ski station or resort
estación marítima – ferry terminal
estany – Catalan for *lago*
Euskadi Ta Askatasuna (ETA) – the name stands for Basque Homeland & Freedom
extremeño/a (m/f) – Extremaduran; a native of Extremadura

fallas – huge sculptures of papier mâché (or nowadays more often polystyrene) on wood used in Las Fallas festival of Valencia
farmacia – pharmacy
faro – lighthouse
feria – fair; can refer to trade fairs as well as to city, town or village fairs that are basically several days of merrymaking; can also mean a bullfight or festival stretching over days or weeks
ferrocarril – railway
festa – Catalan for *fiesta*
FEVE – Ferrocarriles de Vía Estrecha; a private train company in northern Spain
fiesta – festival, public holiday or party
fútbol – football (soccer)

gaditano/a (m/f) – person from Cádiz

gaita – Galician version of the bagpipes

gallego/a (m/f) – Galician; a native of Galicia

gitanos – Roma people

glorieta – big roundabout (traffic circle)

Gran Vía – main thoroughfare

GRs – *(senderos de) Gran Recorrido;* long-distance hiking paths

guardia civil – military police

hermandad – brotherhood (including men and women), in particular one that takes part in religious processions

hórreo – Galician or Asturian grain store

hospedaje – guesthouse

hostal – cheap hotel

huerta – market garden; orchard

iglesia – church

infanta/infante – princess/ prince

IVA – *impuesto sobre el valor añadido,* or value-added tax

jamón – cured ham

jardín – garden

judería – Jewish *barrio* in medieval Spain

lago – lake

librería – bookshop

lidia – the art of bullfighting

locutorio – private telephone centre

madrileño/a (m/f) – person from Madrid

malagueño/a (m/f) – person from Málaga

manchego/a (m/f) – La Manchan; a person from La Mancha

marcha – action, life, 'the scene'

marismas – wetlands

marisquería – seafood eatery

medina – narrow, maze-like old section of an Arab or North African town

mercado – market

mercat – Catalan for *mercado*

meseta – plateau; the high tableland of central Spain

mihrab – prayer niche in a mosque indicating the direction of Mecca

mirador – lookout point

Modernista – an exponent of Modernisme, the architectural and artistic style influenced by art nouveau and sometimes known as Catalan Modernism, whose leading practitioner was Antoni Gaudí

monasterio – monastery

morería – former Islamic quarter in a town

movida – similar to *marcha;* a *zona de movida* is an area of a town where lively bars and discos are clustered

mozárabe – Mozarab (Christian living under Muslim rule in early medieval Spain)

Mozarabic – style of architecture developed by Mozarabs, adopting elements of classic Islamic construction to Christian architecture

Mudéjar – Muslims who remained behind in territory reconquered by Christians; also refers to a decorative style of architecture using elements of Islamic building style applied to buildings constructed in Christian Spain

muelle – wharf or pier

municipio – municipality, Spain's basic local administrative unit

muralla – city wall

murgas – costumed groups

museo – museum

museu – Catalan for *museo*

nitbus – Catalan for 'night bus'

oficina de turismo – tourist office; also *oficina de información turística*

parador – luxurious state-owned hotels, many of them in historic buildings

parque nacional – national park; strictly controlled protected area

parque natural – natural park; protected environmental area

paseo – promenade or boulevard; to stroll

paso – mountain pass

pasos – figures carried in *Semana Santa* parades

pelota vasca – Basque form of handball, also known simply as *pelota,* or *jai-alai* in Basque

peña – a club, usually of flamenco aficionados or Real Madrid or Barcelona football fans; sometimes a dining club

pensión – small private hotel

pinchos – tapas

pintxos – Basque tapas

piscina – swimming pool

plaça – Catalan for *plaza*

plateresque – early phase of Renaissance architecture noted for its intricately decorated facades

platja – Catalan for *playa*

playa – beach

plaza – square

plaza de toros – bullring

port – Catalan for *puerto*

PP – Partido Popular (People's Party)

PRs – *(senderos de) Pequeño Recorrido;* short-distance hiking paths

PSOE – Partido Socialista Obrero Español (Spanish Socialist Workers Party)

pueblo – village

puente – bridge; also means the extra day or two off that many people take when a holiday falls close to a weekend

puerta – gate or door

puerto – port or mountain pass

punta – point or promontory

ración/raciones – large/full-plate-size tapas serving; literally 'rations'

rambla – avenue or riverbed

rastro – flea market; car-boot sale

REAJ – Red Española de Albergues Juveniles; the Spanish HI youth hostel network

real – royal

Reconquista – Christian reconquest of the Iberian Peninsula from the Muslims (8th to 15th centuries)

refugi – Catalan for *refugio*

refugio – mountain shelter, hut or refuge

Renfe – Red Nacional de los Ferrocarriles Españoles; the national rail network

retablo – altarpiece

Reyes Católicos – Catholic monarchs; Isabel and Fernando

ría – estuary

río – river

riu – Catalan for *río*

rodalies – Catalan for *cercanías*

romería – festive pilgrimage or procession

ronda – ring road

sacristía – sacristy; the part of a church in which vestments, sacred objects and other valuables are kept

sagrario – sanctuary

sala capitular – chapter house

salinas – salt-extraction lagoons

santuario – shrine or sanctuary

Semana Santa – Holy Week; the week leading up to Easter Sunday

Sephardic Jews – Jews of Spanish origin

seu – cathedral (Catalan)

sidra – cider

sidrería – cider bar

sierra – mountain range

tablao – tourist-oriented flamenco performances

taifa – small Muslim kingdom in medieval Spain

tasca – tapas bar

techumbre – roof

teleférico – cable car; also called *funicular aéreo*

terraza – terrace; pavement cafe

terrazas de verano – open-air late-night bars

tetería – teahouse, usually in Middle Eastern style, with low seats around low tables

torero – bullfighter

torre – tower

trascoro – screen behind the *coro*

turismo – means both tourism and saloon car; *el turismo* can also mean 'tourist office'

urgencia – emergency

vall – Catalan for *valle*

valle – valley

villa – small town

VO – abbreviation of *versión original;* a foreign-language film subtitled in Spanish

zarzuela – Spanish mix of theatre, music and dance

Behind the Scenes

SEND US YOUR FEEDBACK

We love to hear from travellers – your comments keep us on our toes and help make our books better. Our well-travelled team reads every word on what you loved or loathed about this book. Although we cannot reply individually to your submissions, we always guarantee that your feedback goes straight to the appropriate authors, in time for the next edition. Each person who sends us information is thanked in the next edition – the most useful submissions are rewarded with a selection of digital PDF chapters.

Visit **lonelyplanet.com/contact** to submit your updates and suggestions or to ask for help. Our award-winning website also features inspirational travel stories, news and discussions.

Note: We may edit, reproduce and incorporate your comments in Lonely Planet products such as guidebooks, websites and digital products, so let us know if you don't want your comments reproduced or your name acknowledged. For a copy of our privacy policy visit lonelyplanet.com/privacy.

OUR READERS

Many thanks to the travellers who used the last edition and wrote to us with helpful hints, useful advice and interesting anecdotes:

Amanda McGough, Anaëlle Gourlet, Anne Hodges, Brett Crawford, David Allan, Erik Kamman, Greg Kroll, Jean Simon, Joël Graf, Johanna Akkerman, John Havercroft, John Peckham, Jose Bezares, Juhani Myllynen, Jurek Romaniec, Karine Hallé, Karla Bohn, Katia Moretti, Lee Blumner, Maresha Hoddenbach, Nick de Ruiter, Sabita Soneji, Sally Norris, Sarah Grief, Selwyn Allen, Stefanie von Zeschau, Stephen Barber, Stuart Cook, Timothy Coates, Tone Earwaker, Tony Furse, Zohra Naciri

AUTHOR THANKS

Anthony Ham

Special thanks once again to Itziar Herrán, and to the many locals (in tourist offices and elsewhere) who sent me off in new and enticing directions, especially Lucia (Medinaceli), Roberto (Astorga), Fernando (El Burgo de Osma), Ana (Zamora) and Josefina (Guijuelo). Thanks also to Lorna Parkes, Cliff Wilkinson, Darren O'Connell and all the wonderful Spain authors. And to Marina, Carlota and Valentina – you are everything that is good about this wonderful country.

Sally Davies

Thanks chiefly go to my Barcelona support team, especially Mary-Ann Gallagher and Matthew Wrigley,

but also Sarah Davison, Aurélie Herrou, Jane Darroch and John O'Donovan. Thanks to Regis St Louis for fielding questions and sharing intel, and hat tip to foodies Buster Turner, Paul Richardson and Llibert Figueras for some excellent lunches. Extra special thanks to Tess, for putting up with it all.

Bridget Gleeson

Thank you to my Spanish friends in Madrid, Pamplona, and Mallorca for the warm welcome they've shown me in their country over the years – and on this trip, especially Carlota. Thanks to the sisters at Pensión Lorea in San Sebastián for their practical advice and insights into Basque Country. As ever, I'm grateful to all the travellers and Lonely Planet readers I met on the road – your perspective and enthusiasm for Spain inspired me.

Anita Isalska

Warmest thanks to everyone who enlivened my research trip with humour and local tips. Thank you in particular to Tony Capanna for the hiking expertise; Maxim and Laura, for cultural insights and undercover Sitges; the Catalan Tourist Board team for information galore; and Normal Matt for his endless good cheer and mountain driving skills.

Isabella Noble

Gracias to everyone who helped out on the road, whether knowingly or not. Cheers to Karissa in Extremadura; Sonia, Manuela, Nacho, Eneida and Eneida in Santander; and Emma in Asturias. Thanks to my hardworking co-authors, to Jacky and Sarah

BEHIND THE SCENES

for support, and to Andrew for keeping me out late in Santande. Extra special thanks to Papi, my favourite wine- and tapas-tasting companion.

John Noble

Special thanks to Jesús and Rosa on the Costa da Morte and to fellow author Izzy for help and constant chatter!

Josephine Quintaro

Josephine would like to extend a mighty grand *gracias* to the numerous staff at the various tourist offices. She would also like to thank Robin Chapman for joining her in all that dining and wining research, as well as Jorge Guzman, a valuable contact in Málaga along with all her Spanish *malagueño* friends who provided endless advice and tips. Finally she would like to thank Lorna Parkes and everyone else involved in the title at Lonely Planet.

Brendan Sainsbury

Thanks to all the untold bus drivers, chefs, hotel receptionists, tour guides, and innocent bystanders who helped me during this research. Special thanks to my wife Liz and ten-year-old son Kieran for their company on the road. Thanks also to Miguel de Cervantes for writing a very funny book.

Regis St Louis

I'm grateful to the many friends and acquaintances who provided guidance and tips along the way. Biggest thanks go to co-author Sal Davies for all her assistance, including the temporary crash pad, and to kind hosts Xabi and Lucia in El Born. Thanks also to Cristiano Nogueira for making the detour from France. Finally, big hugs to my family for all their support.

Andy Symington

I owe thanks to numerous people along the way who provided me with information and company. I am lucky enough to have a group of wonderful and generous friends in Valencia who helped with every facet of research and provided brilliant hospitality. I'm grateful to all, but especially to Rosa Martínez Sala, Delfina Soria Bonet, Dolors Roca Ferrerfabrega, Enrique Lapuente Ojeda, Adrián Lapuente Roca and Laura Martínez Rudilla, who went out of their way to assist me. Thanks to Richard Wheatley for a great weekend of hardcore tapas research; thanks also to Eduardo Cuadrado Diago, Richard Prowse, Joan Francesc Peris García, to the Lonely Planet team, Anthony Ham, my co-authors and to my family for their constant support.

ACKNOWLEDGEMENTS

Climate map data adapted from Peel MC, Finlayson BL & McMahon TA (2007) 'Updated World Map of the Köppen-Geiger Climate Classification', Hydrology and Earth System Sciences, 11, 163344.

Barcelona metro map © Ferrocarril Metropolità de Barcelona, SA 2011.

Illustrations pp90-1, 242-3, 252-3, 268-9, 580-81, 642-3 and 658-9 by Javier Zarracina

Cover photograph: Mezquita, Córdoba, Matteo Colombo/AWL.

THIS BOOK

This 11th edition of Lonely Planet's *Spain* guidebook was curated by Anthony Ham and researched and written by Anthony Ham, Sally Davies, Bridget Gleeson, Anita Isalska, Isabella Noble, John Noble, Josephine Quintaro, Brendan Sainsbury, Regis St Louis and Andy Symington. This guidebook was commissioned in Lonely Planet's London office, and produced by the following:

Destination Editors Lorna Parkes, Clifton Wilkinson

Product Editors Kirsten Rawlings, Vicky Smith, Luna Soo

Senior Cartographer Anthony Phelan

Book Designers Mazzy Prinsep, Wendy Wright

Assisting Editors Helen Koehne, Victoria Harrison, Jodie Martire, Charlotte Orr, Jeanette Wall

Assisting Cartographers Julie Dodkins, David Kemp

Assisting Book Designer Wibowo Rusli

Cover Researcher Naomi Parker

Thanks to Carolyn Boicos, Joel Cotterell, Kate James, Anne Mason, Kathryn Rowan, Ross Taylor, Angela Tinson, Tony Wheeler, Amanda Williamson

Index

Map Pages **000**
Photo Pages **000**

Map Legend

Sights
- Beach
- Bird Sanctuary
- Buddhist
- Castle/Palace
- Christian
- Confucian
- Hindu
- Islamic
- Jain
- Jewish
- Monument
- Museum/Gallery/Historic Building
- Ruin
- Shinto
- Sikh
- Taoist
- Winery/Vineyard
- Zoo/Wildlife Sanctuary
- Other Sight

Activities, Courses & Tours
- Bodysurfing
- Diving
- Canoeing/Kayaking
- Course/Tour
- Sento Hot Baths/Onsen
- Skiing
- Snorkelling
- Surfing
- Swimming/Pool
- Walking
- Windsurfing
- Other Activity

Sleeping
- Sleeping
- Camping

Eating
- Eating

Drinking & Nightlife
- Drinking & Nightlife
- Cafe

Entertainment
- Entertainment

Shopping
- Shopping

Information
- Bank
- Embassy/Consulate
- Hospital/Medical
- Internet
- Police
- Post Office
- Telephone
- Toilet
- Tourist Information
- Other Information

Geographic
- Beach
- Gate
- Hut/Shelter
- Lighthouse
- Lookout
- Mountain/Volcano
- Oasis
- Park
- Pass
- Picnic Area
- Waterfall

Population
- Capital (National)
- Capital (State/Province)
- City/Large Town
- Town/Village

Transport
- Airport
- Border crossing
- Bus
- Cable car/Funicular
- Cycling
- Ferry
- Metro station
- Monorail
- Parking
- Petrol station
- S-Bahn/Subway station
- Taxi
- T-bane/Tunnelbana station
- Train station/Railway
- Tram
- Tube station
- U-Bahn/Underground station
- Other Transport

Routes
- Tollway
- Freeway
- Primary
- Secondary
- Tertiary
- Lane
- Unsealed road
- Road under construction
- Plaza/Mall
- Steps
- Tunnel
- Pedestrian overpass
- Walking Tour
- Walking Tour detour
- Path/Walking Trail

Boundaries
- International
- State/Province
- Disputed
- Regional/Suburb
- Marine Park
- Cliff
- Wall

Hydrography
- River, Creek
- Intermittent River
- Canal
- Water
- Dry/Salt/Intermittent Lake
- Reef

Areas
- Airport/Runway
- Beach/Desert
- Cemetery (Christian)
- Cemetery (Other)
- Glacier
- Mudflat
- Park/Forest
- Sight (Building)
- Sportsground
- Swamp/Mangrove

Note: Not all symbols displayed above appear on the maps in this book

OUR STORY

A beat-up old car, a few dollars in the pocket and a sense of adventure. In 1972 that's all Tony and Maureen Wheeler needed for the trip of a lifetime – across Europe and Asia overland to Australia. It took several months, and at the end – broke but inspired – they sat at their kitchen table writing and stapling together their first travel guide, *Across Asia on the Cheap*. Within a week they'd sold 1500 copies. Lonely Planet was born.

Today, Lonely Planet has offices in Franklin, London, Melbourne, Oakland, Beijing and Delhi, with more than 600 staff and writers. We share Tony's belief that 'a great guidebook should do three things: inform, educate and amuse'.

OUR WRITERS

Anthony Ham

Madrid, Castilla y León In 2001 Anthony fell in love with Madrid on his first visit to the city. Less than a year later, he arrived on a one-way ticket, with not a word of Spanish and not knowing a single person. After ten years living in the city, he recently returned to Australia with his Spanish-born family, but he still adores his adopted country as much as he did on the first day he arrived and returns often. When he's not writing for Lonely Planet, Anthony writes about Spain, Australia and Africa for newspapers and magazines around the world (www.anthonyham.com).

Sally Davies

Barcelona Sally landed in Seville in 1992 with a handful of pesetas and five words of Spanish and, despite a complete inability to communicate, promptly snared a lucrative number handing out leaflets at Expo '92. In 2001 she settled in Barcelona, where she is still incredulous that her daily grind involves researching fine restaurants, wandering about museums and finding ways to convey the beauty of this spectacular city.

Bridget Gleeson

Basque Country, La Rioja, Navarra Based in Buenos Aires, Bridget is a travel writer and occasional photographer. Before her years in South America, she lived in Italy and travelled extensively in Spain; along the way, thanks to her *madrileño* friends, she's learned how to use *vosotros* and *tío*, how to make a proper tortilla, and how to stay out all night.

Anita Isalska

Catalonia Formerly Lonely Planet's digital editor, Anita surprised no one when she swapped office life for travelling the world with her trusty laptop. Spain has long been an obsession, from hikes in the rugged north via Madrid all-nighters to the full quota of Costas, but it's Catalonia that keeps luring her back. Anita is a freelance copywriter and journalist for a host of international publications, specialising in budget travel, offbeat adventures and food. Check out some of her work on www.anitaisalska.com.

Read more about Anita at:
lonelyplanet.com/members/anitatravels

OVER PAGE MORE WRITERS

Published by Lonely Planet Publications Pty Ltd
ABN 36 005 607 983
11th edition – Nov 2016
ISBN 978 1 78657 211 0
© Lonely Planet 2016   Photographs © as indicated 2016
10 9 8 7 6 5 4 3 2 1
Printed in China

Although the authors and Lonely Planet have taken all reasonable care in preparing this book, we make no warranty about the accuracy or completeness of its content and, to the maximum extent permitted, disclaim all liability arising from its use.

Isabella Noble

Andalucía, Cantabria & Asturias, Extremadura English-Australian-Spanish, Isabella has lived and travelled in Spain since 1994. Her in-depth investigations of distant northern regions far from her Andalucian home began at the age of 12. Now based in London, Isabella writes on Spain, India, Southeast Asia and beyond for Lonely Planet, Telegraph Travel (where she's the Northern Spain expert) and others. Highlights this trip: tapas-touring in Cáceres, rediscovering Cantabria's prehistoric cave paintings and 'researching' Galician wines. Find Isabella on Twitter and Instagram (@isabellamnoble).

Read more about Isabella at:
lonelyplanet.com/members/isabellanoble

John Noble

Andalucía, Galicia John, originally from England's Ribble Valley, has lived in an Andalucian mountain village since 1995. He has travelled lengthily all over Andalucía and most of the rest of the Spain and helped write every edition of Lonely Planet's *Spain* and *Andalucía* guides. The diversity of Spain's many distinct regions is endlessly fascinating and John loves returning to the green pastures, spectacular coastlines, old stone architecture, warm hospitality and distinctive culture of the far northwest, Galicia – in many ways, almost a different country from the rest of Spain, where the food and wine seem to be getting better and better with every trip!

Read more about John at:
lonelyplanet.com/members/ewoodrover

Josephine Quintero

Málaga Province Josephine has lived in a small village just outside Málaga since 1992. As well as continually 'discovering' the Costa capital, Josephine loves strolling along the beachside promenades throughout the coastal resorts. A highlight this trip was discovering a Roman sulphur spring that has escaped being commercialised and enjoying inspirational art during an open studio weekend in the picturesque mountainside village of Gaucín.

Brendan Sainsbury

Seville, Granada Province, Aragón, Castilla La Mancha Originally from Hampshire, England, Brendan first went to Spain on an Inter-rail ticket in the 1980s. He went back as a travel guide several years later and met his wife-to-be in a small village in rural Andalucia in 2003. He has been writing books for Lonely Planet for over a decade, including three previous editions of the *Spain* guide. For this trip, Brendan loved going underground in Zaragoza, reading *Don Quijote* in La Mancha, and walking (and running) ridiculous distances when he ran out of buses.

Regis St Louis

Barcelona Regis fell in love with Barcelona a decade ago, after arriving in the city and being awestruck by its wild architecture, culinary creativity and warm-hearted people. Since then he has returned frequently, learning Spanish and a smattering of Catalan, and delving into the endless layers of Barcelona's deep cultural heritage. Favourite memories from his most recent trip include fêting the arrival of three bearded kings during Día de los Reyes, catching a surreal circus arts show in a seaside suburb, and exploring far-flung corners of Montjuïc at sunrise. Regis authored three editions of *Barcelona*, and he has contributed to *Spain, Portugal* and dozens of other Lonely Planet titles. When not on the road, he lives in New Orleans.

Andy Symington

Valencia, Murcia Andy hails from Australia but has been living in Spain for fifteen years, where, to shatter a couple of stereotypes of the country, he can frequently be found huddled in sub-zero temperatures watching the tragically poor local football team. He has authored and co-authored many Lonely Planet guidebooks and other publications on Spain and elsewhere; in his spare time he walks in the mountains, embarks on epic tapas trails, and co-bosses a rock bar.